LSAT® PREMIER 2015

KAPLAN

PUBLISHING

New York

Special thanks to those who made this book possible:

Matthew Belinkie, Kim Bowers, Jack Chase, Jesse Evans, John Fritschie, Christopher George, Joseph Gordon, Joanna Graham, Craig Harman, Richard Hillary, Gar Hong, Rebecca Houck, Kevin Hupy, Michael Kermmoade, Matthew Levy, Terrence McGovern, Walt Neidner, Christine Novello, Rachel Pearsall, Larry Rudman, Amjed Saffarini, Adele Shapiro, Jessica Smith, Ethan Sterling, Glen Stohr, Sascha Strelka, Jay Thomas

LSAT® is a registered trademark of the Law School Admission Council, which neither sponsors nor endorses this product.

This publication is designed to provide accurate and authoritative information in regard to the subject matter covered. It is sold with the understanding that the publisher is not engaged in rendering legal, accounting, or other professional service. If legal advice or other expert assistance is required, the services of a competent professional should be sought.

Published by Kaplan Publishing, a division of Kaplan, Inc.
395 Hudson Street
New York, NY 10014

Printed in the United States of America

10 9 8 7 6 5 4 3 2 1

ISBN: 978-1-61865-638-4

TABLE OF CONTENTS

PART FIVE: COUNTDOWN TO TEST DAY

PART SIX: PRACTICE TESTS

About Your Kaplan Resources

Welcome to Kaplan's *LSAT Premier* book! Your Kaplan LSAT resources will be all you need to prepare for the LSAT. Included with the book is your Online Center and a DVD—more on those in a bit. Let's start with how you should use this book.

HOW TO USE THIS BOOK

First—Get Acquainted with the LSAT

Start by reading the "Introduction to the LSAT" chapter, which will introduce you to the details about the test, including structure, scoring, registration info, and how best to study.

Second—Start Becoming an LSAT Warrior

In the subsequent chapters, you'll work on the skills needed for LSAT success. We've broken down each of the skills into discrete **Learning Objectives**. Each section of the book will inform you of the Learning Objectives you're about to master, and you'll be provided with an opportunity to practice them thoroughly. This may involve full LSAT questions or it may simply involve drills that will prepare you to tackle full LSAT questions. All the full questions presented in this book are from real LSATs. Each year, there are four major dates on which the LSAT is given, and three of those exams are *released* by the Law School Admission Council. This means that all of the questions that were on the scored portion of that exam are available to use as study material.

Each released exam contains four scored sections and is called a **PrepTest**. This book contains every question from PrepTests 46, 48, 50, 52, 54, 56, 58, 60, and 62—this is all recent material that came out between 2005 and 2010, over 900 questions! Beneath each LSAT-released question in this book you'll see a Source ID (e.g., PrepTest 62, Sec 2, Q 2, which means that question appears in the released LSAT from PrepTest 62 in December 2010, in Section 2, as the 2nd question).

Throughout this book, you'll see how LSAT experts—Kaplan teachers who have scored in the 99th percentile—analyze questions, games, and passages from recent LSAT exams. Study these "worked examples" carefully; they provide a chance for you to think along with an LSAT expert as he or she attacks the LSAT efficiently and accurately. Expert analysis is always laid out with the test material in the left-hand column and the expert's thinking immediately to the right or beneath. Where the LSAT expert demonstrates a multistep method, we've included the steps to help you train to take the most effective route through the question.

Here are a few things to be aware of whenever you study expert analyses:

This column contains test material; always read it first, so you know what the expert is analyzing.

In this column, you'll see the LSAT expert's analysis of each part of the test question—here's your coach "thinking out loud" for your benefit.

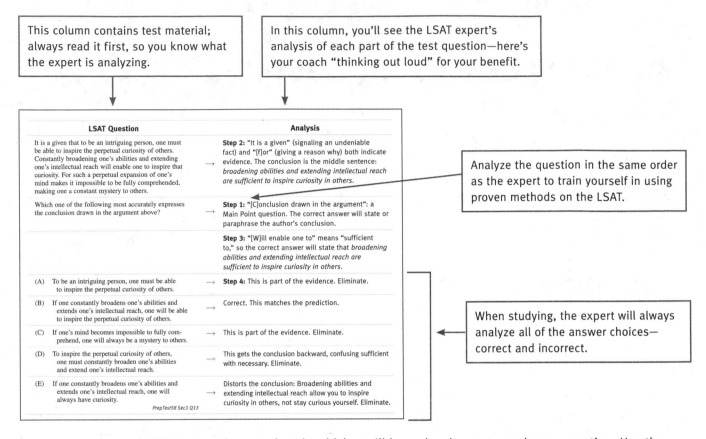

Analyze the question in the same order as the expert to train yourself in using proven methods on the LSAT.

When studying, the expert will always analyze all of the answer choices—correct and incorrect.

From time to time, you'll have practice exercises in which you'll have the chance to analyze a question. Use the spaces in the right-hand column to record your own analysis. On the following pages, we'll always provide expert analysis so that you can compare your thinking to that of an LSAT expert.

LSAT Question	My Analysis
11. Certain companies require their managers to rank workers in the groups they supervise from best to worst, giving each worker a unique ranking based on job performance. The top 10 percent of the workers in each group are rewarded and the bottom 10 percent are penalized or fired. But this system is unfair to workers. Good workers could receive low rankings merely because they belong to groups of exceptionally good workers. Furthermore, managers often give the highest rankings to workers who share the manager's interests outside of work.	Step 2:
Which one of the following most accurately expresses the conclusion drawn in the argument?	Step 1:
	Step 3:
(A) Some companies require their managers to give unique rankings to the workers they supervise.	Step 4:
(B) Under the ranking system, the top 10 percent of the workers in each group are rewarded and the bottom 10 percent are penalized or fired.	
(C) The ranking system is not a fair way to determine penalties or rewards for workers.	
(D) Workers in exceptionally strong work groups are unfairly penalized under the ranking system.	
(E) Managers often give the highest rankings to workers who share the manager's outside interests.	

PrepTest52 Sec1 Q1

The format of our expert analysis is the result of work by leading academics in learning science. Merely doing LSAT questions and checking to see when you got the right answer is good for you, but studies indicate that practicing questions by studying expert thinking alongside actual test material produces better results and is a more effective (and faster) way to master LSAT skills. As you complete the questions, don't just check to see if you got them right or wrong. If you use each question as an opportunity to better understand the patterns of the test as well as your own strengths and weaknesses, you will see improved performance. The Explanations for questions not completely covered within the chapter are located at the end of each chapter. The easiest way to find them is to look at the top of the page for a navigational direction on how to get to the Explanation for that question.

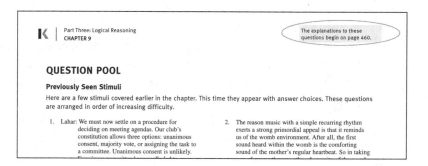

The Explanations break each question down step-by-step and provide detailed reasons why the one credited answer is correct and each of the others is wrong. The Explanations also include information about the relative difficulty of the question you just attempted. That way, you can see how you're performing on easy vs. difficult content. Each question is rated on a star system: one-star questions are the easiest, four-star questions are the hardest. These star rankings have come from thousands of Kaplan students who have used our products and studied for the LSAT just as you are about to do.

sequencing sketch and therefore has a large amount of freedom.

47. (B) CANNOT/Must Be False ★★★☆

This question asks for a seminar that cannot be the second seminar on day two. The Limited Options show only Telemarketing as a seminar that could definitely be the second seminar on the second day (Option I), but Telemarketing isn't even listed as a possible answer. Anyone who skips this question though and completes the last question of the set before this one will be rewarded with a sketch that shows Humor, Objections, and Goals as possible second seminars for the second day. That would eliminate choices **(A)**, **(C)**, and **(E)**, leaving only choices **(B)** and **(D)** for testing.

To test **(B)**, put Persuasion as the second seminar of the second day. This is only possible in Option II. However, in that case, there would be no room for Negotiating after Persuasion because the third day is filled. That would violate Rule 3. Therefore, choice **(B)** cannot be true, making it the correct answer.

For practice, test answer choice **(D)**. If Negotiating is the second spot on the second day, you must still be in Option II. Persuasion could then go on the morning of the second day, while Humor and either Objections or Goals could fill the spots in the first day. This would be an acceptable sketch, so **(D)** is incorrect.

48. (D) "If"/Could Be True ★★★☆

Humor could only be scheduled for the second day in the Option II. That would leave Negotiating as the long seminar for the first day. Because Persuasion has to come before Negotiating, it must be the first seminar. That leaves either Goals or Objectives as the short seminar for the second day. The order for the second day doesn't matter.

1		2	3
P	N	H o/g	g/o T

Or

1		2	3
P	N	o/g H	g/o T

With that, only choice **(D)** is possible.

Answer choices **(A)** and **(C)** both contradict Option II by putting Telemarketing on a day other than the third day. The "If" in this question puts Humor, a long seminar, on the second day, so **(B)** cannot be true because Negotiating is also a long seminar, and Rule 1 requires only one long seminar per day. Answer choice **(E)** also contradicts Option II by putting Persuasion on the already full third day.

Third—Test Out Your LSAT Skills

In the back of the book, there are four full-length tests, along with four testing grids. You've got several options for best using these tests. Some future test takers like to take a test as the first thing they do to get a baseline idea of what their performance is before they've started their practice. Other people will want to dive in to the material, learn what they can, and then try their hand at a test. Either way is acceptable, but it is recommended that you save two of the tests to take in the last couple of weeks before your actual test as a dry run and final rehearsal. You can use the other two as a couple of midterms or as a baseline and midterm depending on your preference. Although the answer key and scoring scale are contained at the back of each test, we recommend entering your answers into Smart Reports® (see Online Center info in the next section).

Do I Have to Go through This Whole Book?

You may have already noticed that there's a lot of material in this book, and that's great for those who have the time and determination to maximize their preparation. However, other people may want just some targeted practice before the exam, or they may not have the opportunity to finish up everything. Here's a quick rundown on which chapters may be considered prerequisites for the others.

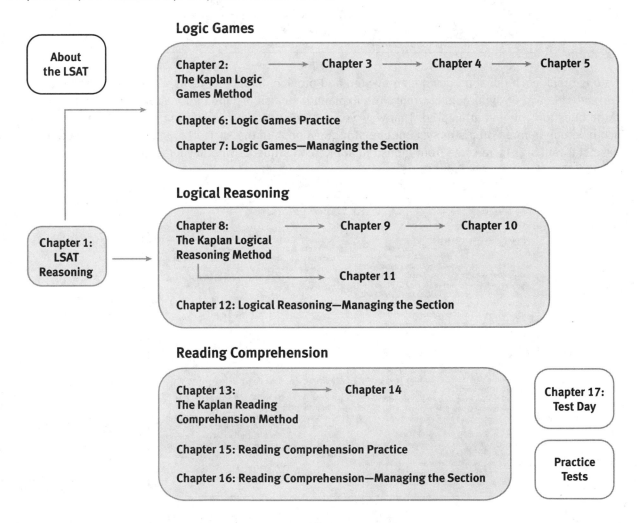

Also, if there's anything you want to approach without instruction, the question pools contained in Chapters 6 and 15, and at the end of Chapters 9, 10, and 11, serve as quick access to individual question practice material. The four tests serve as full-length or full-section practice material.

HOW TO USE THE ONLINE RESOURCES

First—Register for Your Online Center

The Online Center gives you access to even more test prep, including two four-section practice tests, several instructional videos, Smart Reports® (our data analysis of your performance), and more!

Register for your Online Center using these simple steps:

1. Go to http://kaptest.com/lsatpremier2015

2. Enter the password as directed. Instructions for the password are given in the registration form.

3. Click on "Register Now" and follow the on-screen instruction.

4. Once registered, click on the "Go to your Student Homepage" link to access your online companion materials.

Please have a copy of your book with you because you will need information from the book to access your account.

Access to the Online Center is limited to the original owner of this book and is nontransferable. Kaplan is not responsible for providing access to the Online Center for customers who purchase or borrow used copies of this book. Access to the Online Center expires one year after you register.

Second—Study Plans

This is a big book, and you might not have the time to approach everything in it. That's where our online study plans come in. In your Online Center, you'll find several study plans to review that provide you guidance on how best to use the resources depending on the hours/days/weeks/months you have available to study.

Third—Online Videos

As you're studying, if you need a bit more help in a certain area, check out our online library of LSAT videos. None of these is necessary for your preparation, but you may find it helpful to get a little extra guidance as you go. Some videos deal with LSAT content, whereas others provide you with information from the latest on law school applications and admissions.

Fourth—Scoring Your Tests in Smart Reports®

For each full-length test taken from the back of the book, you can see how you scored by section and by individual question/passage/game type where applicable. You can also review your responses and the Kaplan explanations to each question. In Smart Reports®, you can view your performance on an individual test or section, or look at your overall performance as you progress through the four tests.

Fifth—Two Additional PrepTests Online

With nine PrepTests fully used in this book, that's a lot of material, but you may want even more! In your Online Center, you'll find two additional PrepTests that you can print out and use for even more practice. Many students will opt to use these for Timing practice—more about that in the Study Skills section of the "Introduction to the LSAT" chapter.

HOW TO USE THE DVD

The DVD contains several videos, such as our Understanding Formal Logic Master Class and How to Review a Full-Length Test tutorial. You will also find access to some LSAT and law school admissions content. Note that all of the videos on the DVD are also available via the Online Center, but they are reproduced for you on the DVD in the event that you would like to access them without an Internet connection.

LOOKING FOR MORE?

At Kaplan, we're thrilled you've chosen us to help you on your journey to law school. Beyond this book, there's a wealth of additional resources accessible to you that we invite you to check out to aid you with your LSAT preparation and your law school application.

- ▪ – Our blog, the180.com, featuring several articles a week on the nuances of LSAT preparation and applying to law school, authored by Kaplan instructors and admissions experts.

- ▪ THE 180 LIVE – "The 180–Live" is our monthly talk show exclusively for pre-law students. Free to attend, The 180–Live is the perfect place to meet and interact with law school admissions officers, law students, attorneys, and LSAT experts. Join us for a new and unique show each and every month. Show information and highlights from past episodes are available at the180.com.

- ▪ f ▾ You Tube – Facebook, Twitter, YouTube—Kaplan is wherever you are. Like us. Follow us. Subscribe to us. Get regular tips all throughout the course of your study.

- ▪ Kaplanlsat.com – Of course, we'd be remiss if we did not mention the world's most popular LSAT preparation courses. Visit our website to learn about our comprehensive prep options. Choose from Classroom On Site, Classroom Anywhere™ (Live Online), On Demand (Recording Online) and Private Tutoring options depending on your needs and learning style.

As you can plainly see, you have so much you can do. Ready to get started? Let's do this!

About the LSAT

WHY THE LSAT

You're reading this book because you want to be a law student. Well, your legal education starts now.

Every year, Kaplan surveys the admissions officers from law schools all around the country, and every year, the majority of them tells us that the LSAT is the most important factor in your law school application. In fact, in the 2012 survey, 63 percent indicated the LSAT was the top consideration—more important than GPA, the personal statement, letters of recommendation, and other application requirements. You may already know how important the LSAT is, but what you may not know is why. The reasons relate to the nature and design of the exam. Think about it. It's the one factor common to all applications. It levels the playing field for candidates regardless of background. The LSAT doesn't care what you majored in or where you went to school.

The LSAT is probably unlike any other test you've taken in your academic career. Most tests you've encountered in high school and college have been content based—that is, they required you to recall a certain body of facts, formulas, theorems, or other acquired knowledge. But the LSAT is a skills-based test. It doesn't ask you to repeat memorized facts or to apply learned formulas to specific problems. You will be rewarded for familiarity with patterns that make the LSAT repeatable, and ultimately all you'll be asked to do on the LSAT is think—thoroughly, quickly, and strategically. There's no required content to study! Sound too good to be true? Well, before you get the idea that you can skate into the most important test of your life without preparing, let's clarify the skills that you'll need to build to be prepared. Admissions officers care about your score because the LSAT tests the skills you'll use on a daily basis in law school. It's the best predictor law schools have of the likelihood of your success at their institution.

WHAT THE LSAT TESTS

Now you may be thinking, "What does the Logic Games section have to do with torts? How can Logical Reasoning predict my success in Civil Procedure?" In this book, you are going to be taught a series of Learning Objectives, which are bundled around four key skills—key because they're what the LSAT rewards, key because they're what law school demands. We'll call them the Core Skills:

Reading Strategically

Reading for structure and staying ahead of the author (anticipating) is what Strategic Reading is all about. Both your law professors and the LSAT want you to cut through the jargon and explain what the case or passage says. Reading strategically helps you zero in on exactly what opinions are present and how that knowledge will be rewarded in the question set.

Analyzing Arguments

The essence of Logical Reasoning and the essence of lawyering is Analyzing Arguments. To analyze an argument in the LSAT sense, distinguish the argument's conclusion from its evidence. Then, determine what the person making the argument is taking for granted. The assumptions the author makes are what allow you to strengthen or challenge arguments on the LSAT. Likewise, in a courtroom, for example, attorneys will need to understand, analyze, evaluate, manipulate, and draw conclusions from the arguments of their opponent, their own clients, and the judge.

Understanding Formal Logic

Conditional, or If/Then statements, are incredibly important in rules of law. "If/Thens" tell you what must, can, or can't be true in a given situation or when a particular rule is or isn't applicable. The very first chapter will train you to seek out the Formal Logic embedded in LSAT questions and logic games and to manage the implications flawlessly. For a lot of students, this is the most intimidating of the Core Skills, but facing up to it is incredibly valuable. It brings a rigor to your reasoning that will allow you to answer questions—on the LSAT and in law school—with precision.

Making Deductions

Making Deductions is rewarded in every section of the test, but it is key in Logic Games. In that section, you're given a set of conditions and rules and then asked to apply them to various hypothetical cases: "If J goes on Wednesday, what must be true . . ." "If the van has more miles than the sedan, and the sedan has more miles than the motorcycle, what could be false . . . ." That's just what law school exams demand. In law school, the rules and restrictions come from the dozens (potentially hundreds) of cases and statutes you will read during a semester. Just as you'll learn to do with Logic Games rules, judges synthesize rules in order to determine the outcome of a case.

STRUCTURE OF THE LSAT

The LSAT consists of five multiple-choice sections: two Logical Reasoning sections, one Logic Games section, one Reading Comprehension section, and one unscored "experimental" section that will look exactly like one of the other multiple-choice sections. With the exception of the Writing Sample, which will always be last, the five multiple-choice sections can appear in any order on Test Day. A 10- or 15-minute break will come between the third and fourth sections of the test.

Section	→	Number of Questions	→	Minutes
Logical Reasoning		24–26		35
Logical Reasoning		24–26		35
Reading Comprehension		26–28		35
Logic Games		22–24		35
"Experimental"		22–28		35
Writing Sample		n/a		35

Familiarize yourself with the structure of each section.

Logical Reasoning

Each of the two Logical Reasoning sections consists of 24–26 questions based on short passages, which we'll call *stimuli*, which are typically two to five sentences each. Each stimulus may be a short argument or a series of statements of fact. Each stimulus will also have one corresponding question that tests your ability to do such things as spot the structure of arguments, identify assumptions and flaws, strengthen or weaken arguments, or find inferences. Together, the two Logical Reasoning sections comprise the most important part of the test, counting for approximately half of your overall score.

Reading Comprehension

This section consists of three passages, typically made up of two to five paragraphs—about 55–65 lines of text (i.e., about 500 words apiece)—and one set of paired passages, together about the same length as each of the three longer passages. Each passage is accompanied by anywhere from five to eight questions. A Reading Comprehension section will have 26–28 questions but has had 27 questions on every released test since 2007. Reading Comprehension on the LSAT is an exercise in reading for structure and for multiple points of view. You'll learn to trace the outline of the passage as you read and to distinguish the author's viewpoint from the viewpoints of others mentioned in the passage, as well as to stay a step ahead of where the author is going by reading predictively.

Analytical Reasoning (Logic Games)

Analytical Reasoning, otherwise known popularly and in this book as Logic Games, consists of four game scenarios along with accompanying rules. Each game is accompanied by 5–7 questions. A Logic Games section will have 22–24 questions but has had 23 questions on every released test since 2007. With only 23 questions, it is the least valuable of the scored sections. Logic Games may nevertheless be the section you fear the most—many students do. Others, however, immediately take to the puzzle aspect of the section. Logic Games tests your ability to apply, combine, and manipulate rules and to deduce what can and cannot happen as a result. While the games may look daunting at first, they can be mastered with a systematic technique and proper use of scratchwork.

Experimental

The experimental section is an additional, unscored section of Logical Reasoning, Reading Comprehension, or Logic Games. You will not know what type of section you will get, and it can show up anywhere, including after the break. You'll have to bring your A-game for the entire test, as there is no reliable way to determine which section is experimental while you're taking the test.

The Writing Sample

After you complete the five multiple-choice sections of the test, you'll write a short essay in which you choose between courses of action and explain your choice. While unscored, your Writing Sample is submitted to all law schools to which you apply, and law schools use it as part of the evaluation process.

LSAT Scored Sections

Logic Games

One section with four games and 22–24 questions

Logic Games reward you for sequencing, matching, distributing, or selecting entities on the basis of rules that combine to limit the acceptable arrangements.

Logical Reasoning

Two sections with 24–26 questions each

Logical Reasoning rewards you for analyzing arguments to strengthen or weaken them or to identify their assumptions and flaws. Other LR questions require you to draw valid inferences from a set of facts.

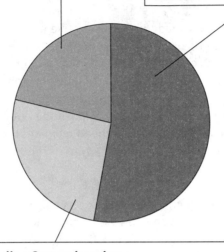

Reading Comprehension

One section with four passages and 26–28 questions

Reading Comp questions reward you for identifying the author's purpose and main idea, drawing valid inferences from the passage, and determining how and why the author uses certain details.

There is no wrong-answer penalty on the LSAT. Mark every answer even if you have to guess!

HOW THE LSAT IS SCORED

Here's how the LSAT is scored. Below you see what looks like three different scoring scales: your raw score (# correct), your scaled score, and your percentile.

Percentile (Scaled score)	10th (139)	20th (143)	30th (146)	40th (149)	50th (151)	60th (154)	70th (156)	80th (160)	90th (164)	95th (167)	99th (172)
# Correct	38	45	50	55	58	64	67	72	80	85	91

Source – PrepTest 68 (December 2012)

LSAT Score Breakdown

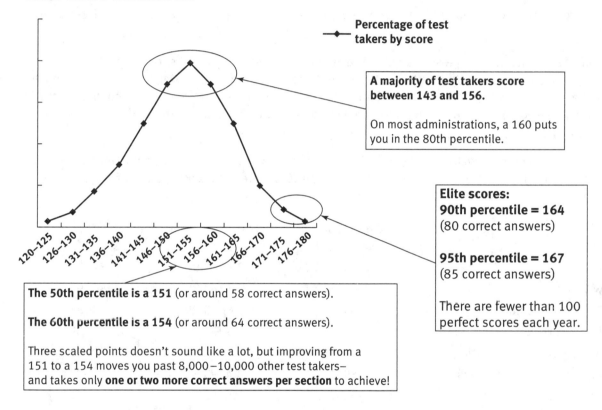

Percentage of test takers by score

A majority of test takers score between 143 and 156.

On most administrations, a 160 puts you in the 80th percentile.

Elite scores:
90th percentile = 164
(80 correct answers)

95th percentile = 167
(85 correct answers)

There are fewer than 100 perfect scores each year.

The 50th percentile is a 151 (or around 58 correct answers).

The 60th percentile is a 154 (or around 64 correct answers).

Three scaled points doesn't sound like a lot, but improving from a 151 to a 154 moves you past 8,000–10,000 other test takers— and takes only **one or two more correct answers per section** to achieve!

Your raw score is simply the number of questions you answered correctly.

Your scaled score, the 120–180 number you may be familiar with, is just a conversion of your raw score. Here, a raw score of 67—that is, 67 correct answers—converts to a scaled score of 156. A raw score of 58—meaning 58 correct answers—converts to a scaled score of 151. On a different test, a raw score of 58 might convert to a 150 or a 152. To account for differences in overall difficulty, each test has a slightly different raw score–to–scaled score conversion table.

However, the conversion from scaled score to percentile remains largely unchanged, with only minor variation over the years. A 151 is approximately a 50th percentile score. Note the difference between a 154 (raw score of 64) and a 156 (raw score of 67 or 68): 3 or 4 right answers and a 10 percentile difference. In any given testing year, that can translate to nearly 8,000–10,000 other test takers and applicants to law school. A small score improvement means a tremendous advantage in the admissions process.

That's all interesting information. But, how do you use it? Two ways:

- First, the number of right answers determines your score. That's it. So, there's no guessing penalty. Never leave a question blank on the LSAT.
- Second, every question is worth the same, regardless of how hard it is. That's why it's so important to learn how to spot difficult questions and leave them for the end of each section. Find the easy questions and rack up points. If you're going to run out of time or need to blindly guess, you want to do so on the tough stuff.

And as you've seen, sometimes even one additional correct answer can leapfrog you ahead of thousands of other test takers, your competition. How's that for inspiration?

What's a Good LSAT Score?

What you consider a good LSAT score depends on your own expectations and goals, but here are a few interesting statistics.

If you got about half of all of the scored questions right (a raw score of roughly 50), you'd earn a scaled score of roughly 146 or 147, putting you in about the 30th percentile—not a great performance. However, as you saw above, a little improvement goes a long way. Getting only 1 additional question right every 10 minutes (throughout the scored sections) would give you a raw score of 64, pushing you up to 154, which is about the 60th percentile—a huge improvement.

So you don't have to be perfect to do well. On a typical LSAT, you can still get 25 wrong and end up in the 160s— or about 20 wrong and get a 164, a 90th percentile score. Even a perfect score of 180 often allows for a question or two to be missed.

Rank*	School	25th–75th %ile LSAT* (Scaled)	25th–75th %ile UGPA*	25th–75th %ile LSAT** (Raw)
1	Yale University	170–176	3.82–3.97	89–95
6	New York University	168–172	3.57–3.85	86–91
9	University of California—Berkeley	163–169	3.66–3.89	79–88
10	Duke University	165–170	3.59–3.84	82–89
15	University of Texas—Austin	163–168	3.43–3.82	79–86
20	George Washington University	159–167	3.42–3.82	72–85
27	Boston University	161–166	3.44–3.77	76–84
31	University of Wisconsin—Madison	156–163	3.21–3.70	67–79
46	Tulane University	156–162	3.12–3.60	67–77
49	University of Utah	155–161	3.31–3.68	65–76
61	University of Miami (FL)	155–160	3.16–3.60	65–74
87	Seattle University	153–158	3.03–3.55	62–70
93	St. Louis University	151–158	3.15–3.66	58–70

* U.S. News & World Report, 2015 Law School Rankings
** LSAT PrepTest 68, December 2012 Exam

REGISTRATION FOR AND ADMINISTRATION OF THE LSAT

At this point, we've told you what will be on the test, how it's scored, and what constitutes a good score. Still on board? Excellent. In a bit, we'll talk about the right way to study for the test, but right now you might be wondering how to sign up and when to take the test!

The LSAT is administered by the Law School Admission Council (LSAC) (www.lsac.org) four times each year.

LSAT FACTS

Each year, the LSAT is administered four times:

- a Saturday morning in February
- a Monday afternoon in June
- a Saturday morning in late September or early October
- a Saturday morning in December

There are some exceptions to these four typical administrations. For example, Saturday Sabbath observers have the option to take the test on a specified weekday following a typical Saturday administration. Also, if you're taking the test outside the United States, Canada, and the Caribbean, check the LSAC website to verify exact dates and locations as the timing may differ by a couple of weeks from when the test is administered in the United States, Canada, and the Caribbean.

You can register for the LSAT online at www.lsac.org. Because your preferred test administration may fill up quickly, you should register as soon as possible. Please consult the LSAC website to ensure that you get your registration in on time. Registration is typically due about five weeks before Test Day, with an additional week of registration allowed subject to a "Late Registration" fee. Test dates and locations can also be changed via the LSAC website by paying the applicable fee. Once again, please check the LSAC for full details on the procedures, deadlines, and fee schedules. Also, check the application deadlines for the law schools you wish to apply to. While some schools require the LSAT be taken by December for admission the following fall, other schools will still accept a February LSAT score. Taking the test earlier is better—those who take the test in June or September/October maximize their chances of getting admitted based on rolling admissions; also, by taking the test earlier, test takers have the opportunity to repeat the test if they want to seek out a higher score.

Upon registering for the LSAT, you can also sign up for the Credential Assembly Service (CAS). The CAS is a service that every ABA-approved law school requires as part of the application process. Once CAS receives your school transcripts, letters of recommendation, and evaluations, it will then distribute that information to each of the law schools that you apply to, along with a report that summarizes your undergraduate work. Please check the LSAC website for full details on the fees, sign-up procedures, and aspects covered by the CAS.

Repeating the LSAT

The LSAT can be taken up to three times in a two-year period (it is possible, but difficult, to be granted an exception to this policy from the LSAC). This limit includes tests that have been canceled. More on that in Chapter 17: Test Day.

Any test taker who wishes to take the test a second time will need to re-register for the test. How law schools view multiple administrations varies from school to school. Although a few schools average the scores, all scores from a five-year period are considered when the law school makes its admissions decisions. Applicants cannot pick and choose which scores to send as part of their application. If a test taker intends to repeat the test, there should be a good reason for the repeat. Good reasons include unforeseen circumstances that hindered performance or now having additional time and effort to put into raising the test taker's skill set. You can get more information on repeating the test directly from the LSAC website. Ultimately, the best strategy is to fully prepare for the test, take it once, and use that score.

Accommodations

If you have a disability, you may be able to receive testing accommodations for the LSAT. Accommodations are granted for physical, learning, and cognitive impairments severe enough to qualify as a disability relevant to test taking. A wide variety of accommodations are available. You must be registered for a test date before you can request accommodations, however, so register early. Your application for accommodations will require you to submit a full evaluation by a qualified professional who specializes in your particular disability as well as score reports from previous standardized admissions tests (SAT, GRE, etc.) and any accommodations records from your undergraduate institution(s). All of these things can take time to prepare and must be submitted several weeks before your test date, so start your process as early as possible. If for any reason you move test dates, you will be required to resubmit your application, so be sure to hold on to copies of your records just in case.

Be aware that qualifying for accommodations for the LSAT is generally harder than it is for undergraduate accommodations. Prior accommodations from schools or even other standardized admissions tests do not guarantee that you will be similarly accommodated for the LSAT. Keep in mind that LSAC grants accommodations only when documentation clearly demonstrates disability in an area directly related to test taking. If you are denied accommodations and feel the denial was in error, you can submit an appeal with additional documentation provided that there is enough time for the LSAC to process the appeal before Test Day.

As this book goes to press, if you are granted accommodations from LSAC, your score will be flagged as accommodated on your official score report and no percentile rank will be given. However, most law schools have official policies stating that they do not look upon accommodated scores any differently than standard scores.

If you believe you have a disability that requires testing accommodations, start by reviewing the accommodations page on the LSAC website to get the most updated information on deadlines and required forms. Remember that this process is subject to change by LSAC at any time, so it is crucial that you get the most recent information directly from LSAC.

LSAT STUDY SKILLS

Imagine you want to lose a few pounds, so you get yourself a gym membership. Will the gym membership be sufficient for you to shed the weight? Of course not. You actually have to use the gym. And, once you get started, you'll need to use proper technique to maximize your results. If you're not sure how to get started, if you're overwhelmed by all the machines you find, or if you try to take shortcuts and don't put in the appropriate time and effort, you may not see the results you were hoping for.

You see where this is going. Kaplan is your gym. We're your mental workout. You've already committed to using our materials. But just as showing up at the gym is not enough for you to lose weight, picking up this book is not enough to raise your score either. You need to work out. You've been provided with a suite of assets, both print and online. But it's up to you to use them. And here's the best part: you have the support of personal trainers—the work of dozens of Kaplan teachers, researchers, and testing experts has gone into creating not only the expert analysis in this book but also the Smart Reports analytics, online material, and study plans that accompany it.

The LSAT is entirely a skills-based test. It is coachable. It is practicable. And there are lots of ways to practice. Some methods are great; others not so much. Expect us to show you the best ways to practice. We'll show you the patterns of the test and how to tackle every question type. Expect us to show you how to manage every section.

To reach your full potential on the LSAT, you're going to need to work—hard. Like learning how to play any new sport or musical instrument, mastering the test takes lots of practice. We will show you precisely what you need to do, but ultimately it's up to you to do it.

LSAT Strategy and the Three Levels of Practice

On Test Day, you'll be asked to deal with stringent testing policies and procedures, answer approximately 125 multiple-choice questions (of which typically 101 will count toward your score), and write a short essay. It's a grueling and intense four hours. And, depending on how efficient your test proctors are, that four-hour process may end up lasting five or more hours.

For those sections that count toward your score, taking control means increasing your speed only to the extent you can do so without sacrificing accuracy. Objectively, you just want to get as many questions right as possible. Your goal is not to attempt as many questions as possible; your goal is to get as many questions right as possible.

For many people, the single biggest challenge of the LSAT is time. If you had unlimited time to take this test, you'd likely perform quite well. But you don't. You have a strict 35 minutes to complete each section, and many students are not able to tackle every question in the time allotted. For you, this means three things:

- It's important that you learn not only how to answer the questions effectively but also how to answer them efficiently.
- It's important to approach each section strategically, knowing which questions to attack first and which questions to save for last.
- It's important that you prepare for the rigors of 3 1/2 hours of testing. You'll want to maintain your focus in the final section as well as you did in the first.

Achieving these goals won't happen overnight. Obviously you need to put in the work to get better. Specifically, though, you need to work on your foundational knowledge first, then improve on moving through the test more quickly and efficiently. That's why to achieve your goals, you'll want to work on three key levels: Mastery, Timing, and Endurance.

Mastery is about learning the patterns of the exam and how to identify them in new questions. You'll gain command of new efficient, effective techniques that you will repeatedly practice on specific drills as well as on individual question types. You'll study the answers and explanations to learn how the testmaker builds questions and answer choices. You'll identify why right answers are right and why wrong answers are wrong. What traps do you consistently fall into? How do you avoid them? That's precisely what Mastery practice is for.

Once you've learned the skills individually, it's time to try full-length section practice, or *Timing*. At 3 1/2 hours, the LSAT can seem like a marathon, but it's really a series of sprints—five 35-minute tests, plus a writing sample. Learning section management—how to recognize and apply the patterns you've learned efficiently to maximize the number of questions you get correct—is what Timing practice teaches you to do.

And finally, there's *Endurance*. Can you maintain your ability to identify and apply these patterns efficiently throughout the whole exam? Some students discover that they are great at focusing for two hours, then struggle through the last two sections of the test. Taking practice tests will help you build your stamina. But a word of warning: the single biggest trap students fall into as they prepare for the LSAT is taking test after test after test. Think about it like learning a musical instrument. If you're trying to learn the piano, do you schedule a piano recital every other day? No, of course not. It's the piano *practice* that allows you to improve. You'll have plenty of opportunities to take tests, but repeated full-length test taking is not the recommended way to raise your score. While practice tests are important, they should be spaced out and taken only when you're sure you've made some improvement through your Mastery and Timing practice.

By approaching your preparation this way—starting with Mastery and then layering in Timing first and then Endurance—you'll be fully and properly prepared by Test Day.

Keeping Time on the LSAT

One of the most common concerns heard about the LSAT is "If I only had more time, I would be able to get through all the Games/Reading Comp passages/Logical Reasoning questions." Though it may seem unfortunate that you only have 35 minutes for each section, keep in mind that this timing constraint is deliberate. You are not alone in thinking that it's difficult to get through the sections in the given time. But the timing constraint isn't necessarily a hindrance to success; precisely *because* concerns about timing are so universal, you can get a big leg up on your competition by understanding how to maximize your performance in those 35 minutes. Timing is a key skill for LSAT success.

Initially, your goal when working on Mastery questions is to understand and use Kaplan Methods while becoming more familiar with question types and gaining greater competency. Once a degree of mastery has been attained, it is time to turn your attention to completing a section within the 35-minute time period.

On Test Day, you can expect to see a clock in the testing room. The proctors may put the start and stop time of each section on the board and will occasionally note the time; a verbal five-minute warning will be given toward the end of the section. However, it is ultimately your responsibility to keep track of the time. While it is rare, proctors have been known to forget to give five-minute warnings, and in some facilities, clocks don't keep accurate time. As you begin your LSAT prep, invest in the purchase of a watch—one with a large face and easy-to-read numbers. Remember, LSAC does not allow the use of digital watches, stopwatches, or timers; you are allowed to use only a good, old-fashioned watch with hands, known as an analog watch.

Get used to using your watch. During timing practice, use your watch to read and roadmap a passage or set up a game in four minutes. Keep track of how long it is taking to work through Logical Reasoning questions.

Here is a quick tip for efficiency on Test Day: as you begin every section, set your watch back to 12:00. At a glance, you will be able to tell how much time you have used and how much time is left until 12:35, when the section will end. This way, you won't need to waste precious time calculating the minutes left.

LSAT Attitude

In the succeeding chapters, we will arm you with the tools you need to do well on the LSAT—both content and strategy. But you must wield this LSAT arsenal with the right spirit. This involves taking a certain stance toward the entire test.

Those who approach the LSAT as an obstacle and rail against the necessity of taking it don't fare as well as those who see the LSAT as an opportunity. Think about it: this is your chance to show law schools your proficiency in the Core Skills. A great LSAT score will distinguish your application from those of your competition.

- Look at the LSAT as a challenge but try not to obsess over it; you certainly don't want to psych yourself out of the game.
- Remember that the LSAT is important, but this one test will not single-handedly determine the outcome of your life.
- Try to have fun with the test. Learning how to unlock the patterns of the test and approach the content in the way the testmaker has crafted the exam can be very satisfying, and the skills you'll acquire will benefit you in law school and your career.

Confidence

Confidence in your ability leads to quick, sure answers and a sense of well-being that translates into more points. Confidence feeds on itself; unfortunately, so does self-doubt. If you lack confidence you end up reading sentences and answer choices two, three, or four times, until you confuse yourself and get off track. This leads to timing difficulties that perpetuate a downward spiral of anxiety, rushing, and poor performance.

If you subscribe to the proper LSAT mindset, however, you'll gear all of your practice toward taking control of the test. When you've achieved that goal—armed with the principles, techniques, strategies, and methods Kaplan has to offer—you'll be ready to face the LSAT with confidence.

Stamina

The LSAT is a grueling experience, and some test takers simply run out of gas before it's over. To avoid this, take full-length practice tests in the weeks before the test. That way, five sections plus a writing sample will seem like a breeze (well, maybe not a breeze, but at least not a hurricane). On the other hand, don't just rush from one practice test right into another. Learn what you can from your review of each test, then work on your weaknesses and build your strengths before tackling another full-length test. You should plan on spending just as much time to review your practice tests as you did to take them.

Managing Stress

Take Control. Research shows that if you don't have a sense of control over what's happening in your life, you can easily end up feeling helpless and hopeless. Try to identify the sources of the stress you feel. Which of these can you do something about?

Set Realistic Goals. Facing your problem areas gives you some distinct advantages. What do you want to accomplish in the time remaining? Make a list of realistic goals. You can't help but feel more confident when you know you're actively improving your chances of earning a higher test score.

Focus on Your Strengths. Make a list of your strengths that will help you do well on the test. Many students are experts at listing which aspects of the test they struggle with. But a student who also has knowledge of her ever-expanding list of strengths will have more confidence and a better perspective on what to target to improve.

Exercise and Nutrition. Whether it is jogging, biking, yoga, or a pickup basketball game, physical exercise stimulates your mind and body and improves your ability to think and concentrate. Likewise, good nutrition helps you focus and think clearly. A surprising number of students fall out of good habits in these areas, ironically because they're spending so much time preparing for exams.

Keep Breathing. Conscious attention to breathing is an excellent way to manage stress. Most of the people who get into trouble during tests take shallow breaths. They breathe using only their upper chests and shoulder muscles and may even hold their breath for long periods of time. Breathe deeply in a slow, relaxed manner.

Stretch. If you find yourself getting spaced out or burned out as you're studying for or taking the test, stop for a brief moment and stretch. Stretching will help to refresh you and refocus your thoughts.

Imagine Yourself Succeeding. If you are continually filled with self-doubt about the test, it will be difficult to overcome those feelings and perform well on the test. Although preparing for the test can take many weeks or months of extensive practice, you must be able to visualize that you will achieve a level of confidence and control of the test. Confidence gained through preparation will lead to better performance. Do not wait for it to occur the other way around.

The Dirty Dozen

This list shows the most common mistakes students make when preparing for the LSAT. Read them now, but expect them to become even more meaningful as you progress through your practice and encounter more and more of the situations discussed here. If you want to spend your prep time wisely, avoid these misguided actions. Revisit this list as you prep to make sure you are not falling into any of these unfavorable practices.

#12 Doing the same thing as everybody else

While you may be an ace at logic games, your study buddy may struggle to make Formal Logic deductions. Each of you needs a distinct study plan; while your buddy should work on improving in logic games, you may need to spend more time working on arguments. Each LSAT test taker has his or her own unique strengths and weaknesses. Determine what yours are early on, then use that knowledge to help you study effectively.

#11 Letting stress get in the way

A little bit of stress can be a good thing; it's what propels you to study and work hard. But becoming consumed and overwhelmed by stress can lead to disastrous outcomes. One of the best ways to manage test anxiety is to become familiar with the LSAT and to develop action steps for each section and each question on the test. Focus on what you can control; anything that doesn't get you closer to right answers should not be a consideration.

#10 Timing yourself in the beginning

Being able to work through problems *quickly* on the LSAT does you no good if you're not also able to work through them *correctly*. Success on the LSAT starts with Mastery. You must first learn how the test's arguments, games, and passages fundamentally operate. Once you have that knowledge, then you can begin to time yourself and push yourself to get through questions more quickly.

#9 Overly focusing on difficulty levels

Every correct answer on the LSAT is worth the same—unlike your eighth-grade history exam, no bonus points are awarded for difficulty level. That means there's no benefit to trying to find and correctly answer the most difficult questions on practice tests or during your studies. In fact, one particularly bad habit some students fall into is they immediately seek out the toughest problems to do in practice. This is because, they imagine, if they can do the hard ones, then they can also do the easy ones. This is a recipe for frustration and failure. If you were learning the piano, you wouldn't start with Rachmaninoff's Piano Sonata No. 2; you'd start with "Chopsticks." It's the same here. Start with the basics and develop your Mastery with one-star games/passages/arguments. Once you have that foundational understanding, move up to harder questions.

#8 Testing under non-test-like conditions

If you were trying to become certified to be a pilot, you wouldn't practice by driving a car. Instead, you'd find every opportunity to log actual practice hours in the air. The LSAT is the same. It doesn't do you much good to get really proficient at taking practice LSATs in your pajamas, late at night, in your bedroom because you're not going to take the LSAT in your pajamas, late at night, in your bedroom. Whenever you take a practice LSAT, try to replicate the experience of Test Day as much as possible. Find a library or academic building and take the test in the morning, starting around 8:30 A.M. (or 12:00 P.M. for June test takers). And, though this should go without saying, remember to always strictly time yourself when taking practice tests.

#7 Not committing to your study schedule

Lawyers are professionals who need to complete projects in a set amount of time. Imagine the LSAT as a case that you're working on. You wouldn't put it off and then roll into court unprepared. Give the LSAT the attention it requires by formulating a study schedule and sticking to it in the months prior to the test.

#6 Reading now/practicing later

As you prepare for the exam, be sure you are always putting into practice the various strategies, methods, and approaches that you are learning. It's not enough to say, "Okay, so in an Assumption question, you need to find the gap between the evidence and the conclusion. Got it. What next?" The LSAT is just not that easy. It's a test that evaluates skills, not content, and becoming proficient in those skills requires time, practice, and reflection.

#5 Only studying the right answers/only reviewing questions you got wrong

Because the LSAT is a test of repeatable patterns, it's invaluable to understand the underlying structure and logic of every question you face, as well as every answer choice you see. When you answer a question correctly, look at the explanations to see if your thinking lined up with the thinking of a Kaplan expert. Did you just get lucky, or did you approach the question methodically and with purpose? Additionally, check out the way the testmaker phrases incorrect answer choices and learn why those answer choices are incorrect. This is a skill that will help you tackle future questions.

#4 Ignoring your strengths

When law schools review your application, they'll see your LSAT score, but they won't see how well you did in each individual section. So if your target score is, say, a 165, and you're currently only scoring around 60 percent in Logic Games but 80% in Reading Comp and Logical Reasoning, you have a choice to make. Do you sink all of your efforts into bringing up that Logic Games score, or do you balance your time and continue to work to improve in Reading Comp and Logical Reasoning as well? The student who sinks all of his or her time into Logic Games is flirting with disaster: not only is there no guarantee that that section will increase, there's also no guarantee that the other sections won't see a score drop. If you are particularly strong in a section, keep devoting time to it to maintain that high level and possibly even push it higher. Don't forget about your strengths just to work on your weaknesses.

#3 Forgoing explanations and resenting mistakes

Making mistakes as you practice for the LSAT isn't a bad thing—it only becomes a bad thing if you end up making those same mistakes on Test Day. As you practice and review, embrace your mistakes. It's by tackling a question incorrectly that you are able to recognize an error in your thinking and then fix it. That's why it's so important to always read the explanations of every question you face in practice. Make sure you're approaching the questions correctly.

#2 Making it about the number, not the process

As we mentioned before, LSAT Mastery starts with the fundamentals. First, understand the structure and logic of the test; then worry about improving your score. If you are trying to adopt a new way of thinking, and if you are truly working on developing new skills, then it's entirely possible that the score on your second (or even third) practice test will stay the same or even go down a bit. But that's absolutely okay. Because at the end of the day, nobody cares about what you got on an LSAT practice test. The only thing that matters is your score on Test Day. Always focus on continuing to develop your skills and use your test results to determine where your thinking was in error and how you can improve. Students who have this mindset early often see big gains later.

#1 Taking test after test after test after test

Because the LSAT is a skills-based test, you must develop your skills before you see score improvement. In many ways, improving on the LSAT is like learning a musical instrument. And if you were trying to become proficient at the piano, as mentioned earlier in the chapter, you wouldn't schedule a practice recital every other day. It's the piano *practice* that allows you to improve. It's the same with the LSAT. Taking practice tests will help you determine your present skill level, and it will help you build your endurance, but it won't help you figure out the test any better. Instead, always fully review your results and continue to practice for Mastery. A good standard is to never take another practice test until you have seen significant improvement in your Mastery and Timing practice.

APPLYING THE CORE SKILLS

Now that you've learned about the test, it's time to get better at it. As you turn to the chapter on LSAT Reasoning and the subsequent chapters on the various sections and question types, keep in mind the skills-based nature of the exam. While you're learning the specific methods and strategies that will help you master the test, reflect on how each of them is helping you to apply the Core Skills. The refinement and rigor you'll learn to bring to the LSAT is going to benefit you not only on Test Day, but even later, as you matriculate at law school.

CHAPTER 1

LSAT Reasoning

Welcome to your LSAT studies! By the time you get to the end of this book, you'll have learned all of the skills and strategies necessary to master the LSAT. You'll begin that process, however, by building foundational skills. In this chapter, you'll build important critical thinking and reasoning skills and thereby lay the groundwork for all that is to come. In fact, it's likely that you'll want to come back to this chapter several times as you encounter the skills introduced here applied to LSAT questions in the various sections of the test.

By the way, if you haven't read the front section titled "How to Use This Book," you'll want to do that now, before proceeding. There, you'll learn how the chapters and sections are organized, what to study first, and the most efficient ways to practice with the material.

You need very little "content" knowledge for the LSAT. There's no math, science, or history you're supposed to know. The LSAT is largely a test of skills—skills you'll use in law school and in legal practice. By working with dozens of expert LSAT test takers, psychometricians (those who measure mental processes), and learning scientists, we've identified the most important of these skills and devised methods and strategies that you can apply successfully to the test. There is little doubt that you'll think, read, and analyze information differently (and more skillfully) when you've mastered the LSAT.

LEVELS OF TRUTH

Throughout the test, you'll be asked to assess the truth or validity of certain statements. You'll be asked to apply these analyses to the complex rules of logic games; the short, dense statements and arguments in Logical Reasoning questions; and the dry, academic prose of the Reading Comprehension passages. In each case, your ability to distinguish what could be true from what must be false in a given scenario will make the difference between right and wrong answers. This may sound somewhat complicated (and for many unprepared test takers, it turns out to be harder than it sounds), but LSAT experts recognize that it breaks down into a handful of patterns they'll use again and again.

LEARNING OBJECTIVES

In this section, you'll learn to:

- Characterize the levels of truth in statements (and thus of the correct and incorrect answers in various LSAT question stems).
- Determine what must be true, what could be true or false, and what must be false given a set of statements.

Characterizing Levels of Truth

As a first step, it's important to understand that LSAT thinking and deductions are deeply rooted in recognizing that every statement displays what we'll call a "level of truth." There are three such levels of truth in the universe: true, false, and possible. Statements that are true are true at all times without question. Statements that are false are false at all times without question. Statements that are possible could be true or could be false—we just don't know without being given more information. To complete our understanding of these, let's look at the opposites of true and false:

If a statement is not true, then it is either false or possible.

If a statement is not false, then it is either true or possible.

Now, "possible" can be expressed as "could be true" and also as "could be false"—possible statements could be either true or false, so those two phrases describe the same thing. However, it's useful for us to get used to those two phrases because the LSAT often includes them in its question stems. Teasing out "possible" into those two alternatives gives us two more pairs of opposites:

If a statement does not qualify as "could be true," then it must be false.

If a statement does not qualify as "could be false," then it must be true.

Understanding all those pairs of opposites is very useful in thinking through what LSAT question stems are asking for. Consider how an LSAT expert views a very common LSAT question:

Question Stem	Analysis
Which one of the following must be true? →	The right answer must be true.
	Therefore, the four wrong answers must be false, or are merely possible (i.e., could be false).

So you can think of your job on this question in two different ways: identify the statement that must be true, or eliminate all of the statements that are false or merely possible. Notice that the test taker above took a moment to make clear not only which level of truth the correct answer would display but also which categories of truth she should eliminate as denoting wrong answers.

Consider another common LSAT question stem:

Question Stem	Analysis
Each of the following must be true EXCEPT: →	We're looking for the one thing that is NOT a "must be true." In other words, the right answer will be a false statement or else a statement that's merely possible (could be false).
	All of the wrong answers must be true.

A couple of useful pointers here: First, as you may have already guessed, it's critical that you separate in your mind the concepts of "right answers" and "wrong answers" from the concepts of "true statements" and "false statements" and "could be true/could be false statements." The example we just saw demonstrates that sometimes on the LSAT, *false statements* are *right answers*. And *true statements* could be *wrong answers* while the *right answer* is a merely *possible statement*, and so forth.

Second, notice what the word *EXCEPT* (which the LSAT will put in all caps to help you notice it) does to the question stem: you're looking for the one statement that does not fit the description right before the "EXCEPT." Thus, you can remember that the phrase before the "EXCEPT" always describes the wrong answers. Suppose, to use a silly and unrealistic example, that an LSAT question said, "Each of the following is a purple spotted lizard EXCEPT": You'd know automatically to cross off all of the purple spotted lizards and circle the one thing that isn't a purple spotted lizard.

Let's establish one more thing before we go any further:

LSAT STRATEGY

The LSAT always gives you exactly one right answer, so there's only ever one answer that falls into the level of truth targeted by the question stem.

There will never be a true answer and another somehow "truer" answer to fool you. There's only *one* answer that does the job, and the other four will always be objectively, demonstrably wrong. "One right, four wrong" will become your mantra. Remember that throughout your LSAT studies.

Now, if you're wondering how you'll know which answer choices are true, which are false, and which are possible, that's what the rest of this book is about. But first you need to develop the mental habit of classifying all statements as being true, false, or possible. You also need to get very good at determining which level of truth you're being asked for.

Practice

Now get some practice with this. For each of the following, make a note of which level or levels of truth the correct answer choice must display. Then make a note of which level or levels of truth the wrong answer choices will display. At any time, you can compare your analysis to the expert thinking immediately following these question stems.

Question Stem	My Analysis
1. Which of the following could be true?	
2. Which of the following could be false?	

Question Stem	My Analysis
3. Which of the following must be false?	
4. Each of the following must be false EXCEPT:	
5. If James chooses the peach, then Suzy can choose the	
6. Bob's schedule on Monday could include all of the following EXCEPT:	
7. Based on the statements above, it is possible that which of the following is true of honeybees?	
8. Which of the following is an acceptable assignment of players to seats?	
9. Each of the following could be true EXCEPT:	
10. Which of the following paddles can never be assigned?	

Question Stem	My Analysis
11. The schedule of performances CANNOT include:	
12. Each of the following could be false EXCEPT:	
13. If Larissa is assigned the second shift, then the third shift must go to	
14. The basketball player could wear the	
15. Entrée selections must include all of the following EXCEPT:	

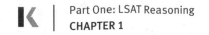

Here's how an LSAT expert analyzed each of those question stems.

Question Stem		Analysis
1. Which of the following could be true?	→	Correct answer could be true. In this question, a "must be true" answer could also fill the bill.
		Wrong answers choices will all be "must be false" statements.
2. Which of the following could be false?	→	Correct answer could be false. So a correct answer could be either false or merely possible.
		Wrong answer choices will all be "must be true" statements.
3. Which of the following must be false?	→	Correct answer must be false.
		Wrong answer choices will be true or possible statements.
4. Each of the following must be false EXCEPT:	→	Correct answer will be true or possible.
		Incorrect answer choices will all be "must be false" statements.
5. If James chooses the peach, then Suzy can choose the	→	"Can" signals "possible." Correct answer will be what Suzy does choose or could choose. In other words, correct answer will be true or possible.
		Wrong answer choices will all be things Suzy can't choose—that is, they all must be false.
6. Bob's schedule on Monday could include all of the following EXCEPT:	→	Correct answer is one thing that isn't possible: correct answer must be false.
		Incorrect answers are things Bob's schedule could or does include. They'll be "must be true" or possible statements.
7. Based on the statements above, it is possible that which of the following is true of honeybees?	→	"[P]ossible" is the key word here. Correct answer will be a statement that could be true.
		Incorrect choices will be "must be false" statements.
8. Which of the following is an acceptable assignment of players to seats?	→	"An acceptable assignment" is one that can work, so this is equivalent to a "could be true." Correct answer is true or possible.
		Incorrect choices will all be impossible—that is, they must be false.

Question Stem	Analysis
9. Each of the following could be true EXCEPT:	$\longrightarrow$ Correct answer is a "must be false" statement. Incorrect answer choices all "could be true"—they'll be either true or possible statements.
10. Which of the following paddles can never be assigned?	$\longrightarrow$ "[C]an never" signals that the right answer must be false. Incorrect answer choices are possible or true.
11. The schedule of performances CANNOT include:	$\longrightarrow$ Correct answer must be false. Incorrect answer choices are things that are or could be included in the schedule—that is, they're true or possible statements.
12. Each of the following could be false EXCEPT:	$\longrightarrow$ Correct answer must be true. Incorrect answer choices all "could be false." A "must be false" statement would also qualify as an incorrect answer here.
13. If Larissa is assigned the second shift, then the third shift must go to	$\longrightarrow$ "Must go" signals that the correct answer must be true. Incorrect answer choices are possible or false.
14. The basketball player could wear the	$\longrightarrow$ "Could" indicates that the correct answer is something the ball player *could* wear or *does* wear: true or possible. Incorrect answers are all things she cannot wear—that is, they're all "must be false" statements.
15. Entrée selections must include all of the following EXCEPT:	$\longrightarrow$ Correct answer is an entrée that is definitely or possibly not included. Incorrect answer choices are entrées that must be included.

Reflection

Every time you do practice problems in this book, you'll be invited to pause afterward and look over your practice to learn more. Don't speed through this step. Carefully reviewing your practice can hugely enrich your understanding of

- why a right answer is right—maybe you got a question right for the wrong reasons, and you need to clarify your understanding.
- why the wrong answers are wrong—maybe your intuition told you an answer was wrong, but you couldn't explain or replicate your thinking.
- which of your LSAT skills are already strong and what you need to work on.
- what patterns LSAT questions display—the best thing you can do on the LSAT is to learn to spot its patterns, and it's frequently in the review stage that students begin to do so.

In this case, look back at your practice and think about these questions:

- Where was it easier for me to correctly identify the level of truth I was being asked for?
- Once I had identified the level of truth the correct answer would display, did I always take a moment to think about what level or levels of truth would be displayed by the wrong answers?
- What did I find challenging about this exercise?

Determining What Must Be True, What Must Be False, and What Could Be True or False from a Set of Statements

Gaining facility with levels of truth is the groundwork for thinking logically. Despite the fact that the LSAT has dozens of different types of questions, they really all test the same thing: your ability to think logically.

What is logical thinking? It's not synonymous with thinking in general because lots of mental activities can be described as thinking. Rather, logic is one type of thinking—specifically, a way of thinking in which you are given premises and you make deductions (that is, you conclude what else must be true) on the basis of them. A premise is a statement you can accept as true. Premises serve to provide support for deductions or conclusions. The LSAT is often said to involve "Formal Logic" because the test asks you to ignore whether given premises are true in real life and to focus instead on how to draw logical deductions (removed from real-world knowledge).

The ability to make valid deductions is at the heart of the LSAT because law schools understand how important this skill is to your success in the practice of law. The LSAT tests deductions in a number of ways. Sometimes, the test will give you premises and ask you to make a valid deduction. In other cases, the LSAT gives you somebody's premises and conclusion and asks you why his conclusion does not follow validly from his premises. In yet other question types (very important ones given the number of LSAT points they represent), the LSAT testmaker gives you a conclusion and a premise or premises purported to support it and asks you to supply a missing premise that would make the reasoning valid or complete. In all of these cases, the exam is really testing the same reasoning skill, just in different ways.

Let's start making deductions. For example, if you are given the premises . . .

> Navel oranges never have seeds.
> This orange is a navel orange.

. . . then you could make a correct deduction:

> This orange does not have seeds.

Given the first two statements, the third statement must be true. You just engaged in a piece of logical thinking.

If that example were an LSAT question, the correct deduction would be one of five answer choices. Your task in that case would be to sort out the correct deduction—the "must be true"—from among four other statements—each a false or "could be false" statement. For example:

> Navel oranges never have seeds.
> This orange is a navel orange.

Based on the statements above, which of the following must be true?

- This orange is delicious.
- This orange has seeds.
- This orange doesn't have seeds.
- There is not enough evidence to deduce whether this orange has seeds or not.
- The next orange will not have seeds.

How would an expert LSAT test taker look at a question like that? Here's her thinking laid out piece by piece:

Logic Example	Analysis
Navel oranges never have seeds. This orange is a navel orange. Based on the statements above, which of the following must be true?	→ Determine which statement *must be true*; it will be helpful to classify the other statements as either false or possible (could be true/could be false).
This orange is delicious.	→ Could be true/could be false: we don't have any information about whether this orange is delicious or not.
This orange has seeds.	→ Must be false: based on the premises, the orange can't have seeds.
This orange doesn't have seeds.	→ Must be true: this is correct.
There is not enough evidence to deduce whether this orange has seeds or not.	→ Must be false: we do have enough evidence to determine that this orange does not have seeds.
The next orange will not have seeds.	→ Could be true/could be false: we have no information about other oranges.

Notice that the first and fifth statements are merely possible—not *necessarily* false. An answer choice isn't false just because it isn't supported by the premises. Only if an answer choice *contradicts* the premises is it false. Given the same premises, other *possible* statements could be these:

> Some oranges have seeds.
>
> Many oranges don't have seeds.
>
> Maria's orange has seeds.
>
> Blood oranges have seeds.

Some Seville oranges are navel oranges.

There are no snakes in Ireland.

Joe will win the tennis tournament.

All of these statements could be true or could be false: none are supported by the premises, but none contradict the premises, either.

(By the way, have you ever eaten a freakish navel orange that had seeds? Maybe you have. It doesn't matter. As we mentioned earlier, the LSAT doesn't test your knowledge of the real world or ask you to apply it to the test questions. The LSAT uses carefully worded language—"Which one of the following, *if true*" or "*If* the above statements are *true*, then . . ."—to remind you to work with premises as though they were true. Don't argue with the rules in logic games or with the evidence used to support arguments in the Logical Reasoning or Reading Comprehension sections.)

Practice

Here are some opportunities for you to engage in logical thinking skills.

In the exercise below, you are given a set of premises and a set of statements that may or may not be valid deductions given those premises. Note whether each would-be deduction is true (that is, a valid deduction), false, or merely possible (could be true/could be false). After each, you can check the expert thinking on the next page.

Premises and Possible Deductions	My Analysis
April showers always bring May flowers. However, when it doesn't rain in April, then May flowers do not bloom. This year, there was no rain during the month of April.	
Based solely on the statements above, characterize each of the following statements as must be true, must be false, or merely possible.	
16. If it rained in April last year, then May flowers bloomed last year.	
17. A lack of April rain is the only reason May flowers do not bloom.	
18. It is unlikely that May flowers will bloom next year.	
19. No May flowers bloomed this year.	
20. May flowers are the most beautiful flowers of the year.	
21. Even if it rains next April, there may be no May flowers next year.	

Here's how an LSAT expert would analyze the example you just worked with.

Premises and Possible Deductions	Analysis
April showers always bring May flowers. However, when it doesn't rain in April, then May flowers do not bloom. This year, there was no rain during the month of April. Based solely on the statements above, characterize each of the following statements as must be true, must be false, or merely possible.	
16. If it rained in April last year, then May flowers bloomed last year.	Must be true according to the first statement.
17. A lack of April rain is the only reason May flowers do not bloom.	Merely possible (could be true or false). Nothing in the statements indicates that a lack of rain is the *only* reason May flowers will not bloom, just that it is one reason.
18. It is unlikely that May flowers will bloom next year.	Merely possible (could be true or false). Nothing in the statements makes any prediction about next year.
19. No May flowers bloomed this year.	Must be true. The second and third premises, taken together, establish that no flowers bloomed in May of this year.
20. May flowers are the most beautiful flowers of the year.	Merely possible (could be true or false). None of the statements tell us how to rate the beauty of flowers.
21. Even if it rains next April, there may be no May flowers next year.	Must be false. This contradicts the first statement.

Reflection

Look back over your practice:

- Did you keep the task clearly in mind and stay focused on identifying what was true, false, and possible?
- Did you find yourself getting confused between true and possible statements or between false and possible statements?

This kind of analysis is something you can do all the time. You hear or read arguments that purport to draw conclusions from one or more premises every time you listen to a political commentator, read an editorial, or even watch a television commercial. Pay attention to the deductions you hear or see other people making and try to evaluate their validity based on the premises in the those arguments.

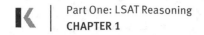
FORMAL LOGIC: CONDITIONAL STATEMENTS

Now that you have some practice with logical thinking, you're ready to expand those skills. Frequently on the LSAT, the premises from which you make deductions are conditional statements—that is, they're statements that can be expressed in "if . . . then" form (though not all conditional statements contain those exact words). Before we address the statement in parentheses, take a closer look at what an "if . . . then" statement is and what it means.

LEARNING OBJECTIVES

In this section, you'll learn to:

- Identify what is and is not a conditional statement (that is, understand what it means for a statement to be a conditional statement).
- Understand conditional statements that include *and* or *or*.
- Translate a sentence that expresses a conditional relationship into If/Then format.
- Make deductions on the basis of conditional statements.

Identifying Conditional Statements

Consider this conditional statement:

> If you are in New York, then you are in the United States.

What does that statement mean? It expresses a relationship of *logical necessity:* being in New York logically necessitates—that is, requires—that you be in the United States. On the other hand, "if . . . then" language does not necessarily express a causal relationship: being in New York doesn't *cause* you to be in the United States. (Consider the case of someone who flies from Atlanta to New York: she was in the United States the whole time.) And the word "then" doesn't express a chronological relationship: you aren't in New York *before* you're in the United States.

Every conditional statement has two parts: the "sufficient term" and the "necessary term":

- The *sufficient term* is the part that immediately follows "if." "Sufficient" means "enough," and this part of a conditional statement is sufficient—it's enough—to require the other part. You don't need any additional information to know that the other part is true. Being in New York is enough to know that you are in the United States. In this book, we may also sometimes call this sufficient term the *trigger* because it precipitates the occurrence or truth of something else, logically speaking.
- The *necessary term* is the part that immediately follows the "then." "Necessary" means "required," and this part of a conditional statement is required whenever the sufficient term is present. Being in the United States is required—it's necessary—whenever you're in New York. If you're not in the United States, you simply cannot be in New York. We may also call this term the *result* because it's the logical consequence of the "trigger" in the sufficient term. Whenever you have the trigger, you've got to have the result.

Let's focus a little more on what a conditional statement does and doesn't mean. In the example above, you absolutely cannot be in New York without being in the United States (because being in the United States is necessary to being in New York). But can you be in the United States without being in New York? Sure—you could be in California, South Dakota, or Texas. So, the necessary term doesn't serve as a logical trigger.

Let's look at another real-world example in order to clarify this further. Consider this statement: If you're driving your car, then your car has an engine.

You driving your car logically necessitates that it have an engine. And you driving it is sufficient—that is, it's all we need to know—in order to determine that your car has an engine. But can it have an engine without you driving it? Obviously! At times when your car is sitting in the garage, cold and unused, it still most likely has an engine.

Do you find yourself nevertheless tempted to tease out the logical possibilities by beginning a sentence like this?

"So if your car has an engine, then . . . "

. . . resist that temptation! There's no way, given only the original statement above, to complete that sentence. There's no logical result of your car having an engine other than, well, your car having an engine.

The fact that the necessary term by itself doesn't logically trigger anything is a tremendously important concept to remember on the LSAT. Unless the LSAT argument or game explicitly tells you otherwise, always assume that it's possible to have the necessary term without having the sufficient term. Moreover, the LSAT uses many examples that involve fictional people or ambiguous terms, which means that you can't rely on real-world knowledge to sort out what triggers something else or what is necessary for the trigger as you could with the examples above. Let's demonstrate how to think about this using a rule from an LSAT logic game. Here's how an expert test taker would understand a conditional statement in a logic game:

Conditional Statement	Analysis
If Rochelle volunteers, then so does Masatomo. *PrepTest58 Sec3 Qs7–12*	If Rochelle volunteers, that's sufficient to know that Masatomo must volunteer.
$\longrightarrow$	Or, to put that another way, if Rochelle volunteers, it is necessary that Masatomo volunteers also. So Rochelle cannot be the only person who volunteers.
	But Masatomo could volunteer without Rochelle volunteering. Given only this rule, Masatomo could volunteer alone.

We identify and understand conditional statements all the time in the real world. Each of the following expresses a relationship of sufficiency and necessity:

No shirt, no shoes, no service.

You can't legally drink unless you're 21 or older.

You must be over 48 inches tall to ride the roller coaster.

Most likely, you intuitively understand statements like this in real life. They're simply relationships in which one thing is needed for another to happen, and that's the essence of a conditional relationship. However, you'll notice that none of them contain the words *if* or *then*. And just as in real life, many conditional statements on the LSAT are phrased in ways that don't involve the specific words *if* and *then*. On the test, it's important for you to spot conditional relationships when they appear, regardless of how they're phrased.

Consider whether each of the following statements contains a trigger-and-result ("if" . . . "then") relationship. Keep in mind there are a couple of ways to think about spotting these: if one thing is sufficient—is enough—to make the other happen, then they have a trigger-and-result relationship. Similarly, if one thing is necessary—is required—whenever something else happens, that also signals a trigger-and-result relationship. In the Analysis here, the LSAT expert categorizes the statements "Yes, it contains a sufficient-necessary relationship" or "No, it does not."

Statement		Analysis
Drivers must pay a toll in order to cross the bridge.	→	Yes. Paying a toll is *necessary* for anyone wishing to cross the bridge.
The company ought to adopt the consultant's proposal.	→	No. This is a recommendation. It doesn't contain a condition necessary for another condition to occur.
How many tomatoes did you buy?	→	No. Like recommendations, questions do not express a Formal Logic relationship.
The state of California requires that all passengers wear a seatbelt when riding in a moving vehicle.	→	Yes. The word *requires* indicates wearing a seatbelt is *necessary* for passengers riding in a moving vehicle in California.
Any student in the halls after the bell rings will get a detention slip.	→	Yes. Regardless of the student's status or reason for being in the hallway, the fact that he is there after the bell rings is *sufficient* to tell us that he will receive a detention slip.
The LSAT is a prerequisite for getting into law school.	→	Yes. The word *prerequisite* indicates that the LSAT is *required* for getting into law school.
You can't make an omelet without breaking a few eggs.	→	Yes. *Without* is the word to pay attention to here. In order to make an omelet, it is *necessary* to break a few eggs.
Let them have cake.	→	No. This is simply a declarative statement with neither a necessary nor a sufficient condition.
Cheaters never prosper.	→	Yes. The knowledge that someone is a cheater is *sufficient* to know that she will never prosper.
Sara cannot go to the movies unless she cleans her room.	→	Yes. The word *unless* makes a clean room a *necessary* condition that must be met in order for Sara to go to the movies.

Each of the statements that received a "yes" answer above—that is, every conditional statement above—can be expressed in If/Then format. A bit later in this chapter, we'll devote a section to learning how to make those translations. For now, though, it's critical to hone your ability to spot trigger-and-result relationships in prose.

Practice

Here's your chance to practice this. Take a look at each of the following statements and note to yourself whether it expresses a relationship of sufficiency and necessity and how you know whether it does or not. After each one, you can look ahead to see the expert thinking.

Statement	My Analysis
22. There's a strong possibility the election will oust the incumbent senator.	
23. The car cannot run without gasoline.	
24. Each of the apples in the basket has been rinsed off.	
25. Make it so.	
26. It may be the case that germs cause your headaches.	
27. Everything on the menu is vegan-friendly.	
28. Mammals don't have gills.	

Statement	My Analysis
29. Only members of the book club receive that discount.	
30. Did you pick up milk on your way home?	
31. Unless they beat the Eagles, the Lions won't make it to the playoffs.	
32. The car needs an oil change before your trip.	
33. Some wildcats are striped.	

Here's how an LSAT expert would evaluate the statements on the basis of whether each is an example of a conditional Formal Logic statement.

Statement		Analysis
22. There's a strong possibility the election will oust the incumbent senator.	→	No. This is a possibility and contains no condition sufficient or necessary for another to occur. No Formal Logic here.
23. The car cannot run without gasoline.	→	Yes. Gasoline is *necessary* for the car to run. The car running is *sufficient* to tell you it has gas.
24. Each of the apples in the basket has been rinsed off.	→	Yes. Telling me an apple is in that basket is enough, or *sufficient*, for me to know that it has been rinsed off. If it's in the basket, it's required for it to have been rinsed off.
25. Make it so.	→	No. This is just a command.
26. It may be the case that germs cause your headaches.	→	No. Because it only "may" be the case, you can't say that either term is sufficient for or requires the other.
27. Everything on the menu is vegan-friendly.	→	Yes. Knowing that an item appears on this menu is *sufficient* to tell you that it's vegan-friendly. "Vegan-friendly" is a status *required* of any item that is on the menu.
28. Mammals don't have gills.	→	Yes. Knowledge that an animal is a mammal is *sufficient* to know that it does not have gills. Likewise, it's a *necessary* requirement for mammals to lack gills. (Having gills would be a sure sign that an animal is not a mammal.)
29. Only members of the book club receive that discount.	→	Yes. Being a member of the book club is *necessary* in order to receive this discount, and if a person is getting the discount, that's enough (*sufficient*) to guarantee that the person is in the book club.
30. Did you pick up milk on your way home?	→	No. Questions do not express conditional statements.
31. Unless they beat the Eagles, the Lions won't make it to the playoffs.	→	Yes. Beating the Eagles is a *necessary* condition for the Lions to make it to the playoffs. If the Lions do make it to the playoffs, that's *sufficient* to tell us that they must have beaten the Eagles.
32. The car needs an oil change before your trip.	→	Yes. An oil change is *necessary* if this car goes on a trip. If you're driving this car on your trip, that's enough to guarantee that this car had an oil change.*
33. Some wildcats are striped.	→	No. It is not necessary for a wildcat to be striped because only some of them are.

*Note that in day-to-day experience we often use *need* very loosely in place of *ought* or *should*. On the LSAT, you must treat a word such as *need* very strictly.

Again, each one of the exercises that is a conditional statement can be expressed in If/Then format, and later in this chapter, you'll get lots of practice with making those translations.

Reflection

Look back over your practice.

- Did you accurately identify which statements were conditional statements and which weren't?
- What words were helpful to you in identifying that relationship of logical necessity?
- Did you notice all of the different ways in which sufficient-and-necessary relationships can be phrased?

Practice identifying conditional, Formal Logic statements in everyday life. Even simple interactions often reveal our understanding of necessary-sufficient relationships. Have you ever responded to someone who told you some electrical device wasn't working by asking, "Are you sure it's plugged in?" Your response is based on the fact that you know that a power source is necessary for the electrical device to operate. In no time, you'll treat all sorts of statements—"I can't serve you unless I see an ID," "Registration required," etc.—as indicative of Formal Logic.

A Note About Cause-and-Effect Relationships

We're going to steadily build on our understanding of conditional statements because you're going to see multiple instances of them on every section of the LSAT. Before we proceed, however, take a moment for an important caveat about conditional statements and cause-and-effect relationships. In a causal relationship, one thing is the reason *why* another happens. Examples of statements indicating cause-and-effect relationships include these:

Mike gets good grades because he studies every night.

Low pressure systems can cause headaches.

Many house fires are the result of faulty wiring.

The cause is the reason why the effect occurred, and the effect is what the cause brought about.

It's tempting to assume that causal relationships can be expressed in If/Then terms. Indeed, *sometimes* they can. For example, imagine a scientific experiment in which every time, without exception, pressing a button causes a bell to ring. In that case, you could say:

If you press the button, then the bell will ring.

The cause here (pressing the button) becomes the sufficient term, and the effect (the bell ringing) becomes the necessary term.

At other times, however, it is inappropriate to express causal relationships using conditional If/Then terms. Consider another example:

Colds are caused by exposure to germs.

Germs are the cause, and colds are the effect. Can we validly say the following?

If someone is exposed to germs, then he gets a cold.

The If/Then terminology doesn't fit here because the statement isn't true in all cases. We're exposed to cold germs all the time without necessarily getting colds; we only get colds a small percentage of the time. However, it is the case that every single person who has a cold has been exposed to cold germs, so we can say:

If you have a cold, then you have been exposed to germs.

Notice that in this case, the cause becomes the necessary term, and the effect becomes the sufficient term—very different from the example about the button and bell.

Take another example:

> Throwing a brick at the window may cause the window to break.

Can we put that into If/Then format, like this?

> If you throw a brick, then the window will break.

No, because of that word *may*. It's possible that in some circumstances the window doesn't break when someone throws a brick at it. So it isn't always a true statement. (Now, it would be legitimate to say, "If you throw a brick at the window, then the window *may* break." But If/Then statements with *maybe* in them usually aren't terribly useful and, thus, are not very common on the LSAT.)

If you're confused at this point, don't worry about it. The takeaway here is merely that *you must not automatically conflate cause-and-effect relationships with sufficient-necessary relationships*. Remember that throughout your LSAT studies.

Understanding Conditional Statements with "And" or "Or"

Let's look at a variation some conditional statements can display. So far, we've seen conditional statements of the form "If *x*, then *y*," but sometimes a conditional statement can involve more than two items, linked with *and* or *or*. It's important to understand what those simple conjunctions mean in logical statements:

LSAT STRATEGY

In Formal Logic

- *And* means you need both terms for the conditional to be relevant or fulfilled.
- *Or* means you need at least one of the terms (the first or the second or both) for the conditional to be relevant or fulfilled. *Or* does not express a mutually exclusive relationship unless you're explicitly told otherwise.

Let's explain a little further about *and*. *And* might appear in the trigger:

> If X and Y, then Z.

In that case, both X and Y must be true in order to apply the conditional statement. X by itself doesn't ensure that Z will happen; neither does Y by itself. So the conditional statement simply isn't relevant unless we have *both* X and Y.

And could also appear in the result:

> If A, then B and C.

Here, whenever we have A, we have to have *both* B and C. Once we have A, it's just not possible that we could have B without C, or C without B. Given A, the statement can't be fulfilled without both B and C.

What about *or*? *Or* could appear in the trigger:

> If G or H, then J.

Either G or H by itself is sufficient to ensure that you've got to have J. And if you have both G and H, this conditional still applies: You still have to have J.

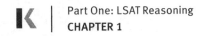

Or could also appear in the result:

> If M, then N or P.

Given M, then we have to have at least one of either N or P. If we have M, we don't *have* to have both N and P, but we do have to have one of them. And we *might* have both: M, N, and P all happening doesn't violate this rule.

Notice that in the last two examples, the word *or* doesn't preclude the possibility of having both of the terms linked by *or*. In other words, *or* doesn't express a relationship of mutual exclusivity. If the LSAT wants you to know that two items joined by *or* do have a relationship of mutual exclusivity, it will make this explicit as follows:

> If S, then T or V *but not both*.

Here, if we have S, we have to have either T or V. But, given S, we *can't* have both T and V. Whenever you *do not* see language that explicitly expresses *but not both*, however, you should assume that the two things joined by *or* could go together.

Let's see how an expert test taker would think through some conditional statements containing *and* or *or*.

Conditional Statement		Analysis
If Miranda goes to the store, then she will buy apples or bananas.		Miranda going to the store logically necessitates that she buy either apples, or bananas, or *both* apples and bananas. This statement allows her to buy both, but she doesn't have to.
	$\longrightarrow$	Say that Miranda went to the store and that she didn't buy apples. In that case, she definitely did buy bananas.
		No logical deductions stem from a statement beginning "If Miranda buys apples or bananas or both," because those are necessary but not sufficient conditions for Miranda's going to the store.
If the league doesn't approve the new contract, then the players will go on strike and the city will lose valuable revenue.		The league's failure to approve the contract would necessitate both a strike by the players and the loss of revenue by the city.
	$\longrightarrow$	Suppose the players were on strike and the city had lost valuable revenue. No deduction about whether the league had approved or denied the new contract would follow from that. (And if the league actually did approve a new contract, the players could still strike or the city could still lose revenue for other reasons.)

Conditional Statement	Analysis
If Fatima does the grocery shopping and Pablo cleans the house, then the chores will be done before noon.	Fatima's grocery shopping and Pablo's house cleaning logically guarantee that the chores will be done before noon.
	→ If Fatima does the grocery shopping but Pablo doesn't clean the house, this statement simply doesn't apply. It's impossible to deduce whether the chores will get done before noon or not. (For example, someone else might clean the house.)
	Likewise, if the chores are finished before noon, it's not certain that Pablo cleaned house or that Fatima went grocery shopping. Those two activities are sufficient to know that the chores are done before noon but not necessary to the completion of the chores by that time. (So, if the chores are done by noon, perhaps a third person pitched in to help or Pablo did everything himself. Who knows?)
If the chicken is soaked in buttermilk or brine, then it will stay moist while cooking.	A soak in either buttermilk or brine will ensure that the chicken stays moist while cooking. Do either one and the chicken will be moist.
	→ What would happen if the chicken was soaked in BOTH buttermilk and brine? Again, the chicken would be moist, guaranteed! (Although it might not taste that good.) The "or" here is not exclusive; it doesn't have to be just one or the other.

You'll notice, both on the LSAT and in life, that *and* and *or* relationships can be expressed in a variety of ways. In particular, when those terms are negated, you might see them joined by *neither . . . nor*. Just make a mental note now that *neither x nor y* means *not x and not y*. Like this:

Conditional Statement	Analysis
If it neither rains nor snows, then we'll go on our trip tomorrow.	→ If it does not rain and it does not snow, then we'll go on our trip tomorrow.
Neither Jane nor Thomas will go to the dinner if it starts later than 8 P.M.	→ If the dinner starts later than 8 P.M., then Jane will not go and Thomas will not go.

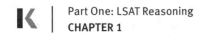
What if a conditional statement includes a phrase like *but not both*? We have to work that into our understanding of the statement, and the easiest way to do that is to think of it as being two statements.

Conditional Statement		Analysis
If the sous chef makes the soup, she will also make either the salad or the dessert but not both.	→	(1) The sous chef making the soup is sufficient to tell us that she must also make the salad or the dessert.
		(2) The sous chef making the soup also requires that she NOT make both salad and dessert.

Practice

Check your understanding of each of the following conditional statements.

Conditional Statement	My Analysis
34. If Meagan buys a juicer, then she buys kale or mangos. What do we know if Meagan buys a juicer? What do we know if Meagan buys kale? What do we know if Meagan buys mangos? What do we know if Meagan buys neither mangos nor kale?	
35. If Ian draws a spaceship, he gives it lasers or a tractor beam, but not both. What do we know if we are told Ian is drawing a spaceship? What do we know if Ian is drawing lasers? What do we know if Ian is drawing a tractor beam? What do we know if Ian is drawing both lasers and a tractor beam?	
36. If Patricia makes nachos, then she'll also make salsa and bean dip. What do we know if we are told that Patricia makes nachos? What do we know if we are told that Patricia doesn't make salsa? What do we know if we are told that Patricia makes salsa and bean dip?	

Here's how an LSAT expert would analyze the conditional statements you just analyzed.

Conditional Statement		Analysis
34. If Meagan buys a juicer, then she buys kale or mangos.		
What do we know if Meagan buys a juicer?	$\longrightarrow$	She buys kale or mangos or both.
What do we know if Meagan buys kale?	$\longrightarrow$	Nothing additional
What do we know if Meagan buys mangos?	$\longrightarrow$	Nothing additional
What do we know if Meagan buys neither mangos nor kale?	$\longrightarrow$	Then she can't have bought a juicer.
35. If Ian draws a spaceship, he gives it lasers or a tractor beam, but not both.		
What do we know if we are told Ian is drawing a spaceship?	$\longrightarrow$	He gives his spaceship either lasers or a tractor beam, but he absolutely won't give it both lasers and a tractor beam.
What do we know if Ian is drawing lasers?	$\longrightarrow$	Nothing additional
What do we know if Ian is drawing a tractor beam?	$\longrightarrow$	Nothing additional
What do we know if Ian is drawing both lasers and a tractor beam?	$\longrightarrow$	Then he can't have drawn a spaceship.
36. If Patricia makes nachos, then she'll also make salsa and bean dip.		
What do we know if we are told that Patricia makes nachos?	$\longrightarrow$	Then she'll make both salsa and bean dip. She can't make just one of those—she has to make both.
What do we know if we are told that Patricia doesn't make salsa?	$\longrightarrow$	Then she can't have made nachos.
What do we know if we are told that Patricia makes salsa and bean dip?	$\longrightarrow$	Nothing additional

Translating Conditional Statements into If/Then Format

It's helpful at this point to develop a simple system of notation for conditional statements. (The value of a uniform notation will become very clear when you start working with real LSAT problems.) Whenever you see a conditional statement on the LSAT, translate it into something that looks like this:

If Trigger (sufficient) → Result (necessary)

Write the sufficient term on the left, the necessary term on the right, and an arrow in the middle pointing from left to right (to indicate which direction the logical trigger-and-result relationship flows). If the statement includes a negative (*not* or *no*), there are a couple of ways to handle this. Some people write out the word *not*, others use a tilde symbol to mean *not*, and still others strike through a negated term. So you might write the statement "If A then not B," in shorthand in any of these ways:

If A → NOT B

If A → ~B

If A → B̸

Symbolize negated terms however you like, but be consistent about it and make sure the entire term is legible. We'll alternate between using the word *not* and using the tilde in this book and in our online materials.

Armed with that simple notation, you're ready to learn how to distill conditional relationships from sometimes complicated prose into clear, brief shorthand notes. You've already learned that conditional statements can be phrased in lots of different ways; you'll see that some of those are more common than others on the LSAT, but they all appear from time to time. This section will give a library of ways that the testmaker phrases conditional statements so that you can quickly and easily translate them into If/Then form.

Think of If/Then statements as generalizations (or rules) that do not admit any exceptions. In the example we started with, every single time anybody is in New York, she has to be in the United States. The test could express this "rule" in a number of ways:

All people in New York are in the United States.

Everyone who is in New York is in the United States.

When (or whenever) someone is in New York, he is in the United States.

A person is in the United States every time he is in New York.

In these sentences, the word that tells you you're looking at a generalization (*all*, *any*, *every*, etc.) also serves to denote the sufficient term. Let's make a short catalog:

LSAT STRATEGY

Words that denote that one thing is sufficient for another to happen:

- *All*
- *Any* (*anytime, anyplace, anybody*, etc.)
- *Every* (*every time, everybody*, etc.)
- *Whenever*
- *Each*

Negatives

The same is true for the opposites of those words: words like *none* or *no one* or *never* also signal a generalization without exceptions—that is, they also signal a sufficient-and-necessary relationship. These deserve special discussion, however, because sentences containing these negative words frequently employ a word order that can be confusing if you aren't familiar with how to parse it. Consider an example:

No one who is in New York is in Europe.

It may be tempting, if you just glance at the word order, to start your If/Then translation with "If not New York . . . ." But think about the statement's subject: the sentence isn't about people who are not in New York. Rather, it's about people who *are* in New York, and it's saying that those people are *not* in Europe.

> If in New York → NOT in Europe

Be very careful about the way sentences are worded. A good practice is to always ask yourself: Who or what is this sentence *about*? That will point you to the sufficient term.

Only

Just as there are words and phrases that signal that one thing is sufficient for another to happen, there are words and phrases that signal conditional relationships by denoting the necessary term, and a common one on the LSAT is the word *only*. To return to our original example:

> Only people in the United States can be in New York.

Whom is this sentence about? It's about people in New York. Thus, "[o]nly" signals the necessary term. You can translate *only* to *then*:

> If in New York → in United States

Consider a similar example:

> A person can be in New York only if she is in the United States.

Who is the subject of this sentence? The sentence is about people in New York. Don't let the word "if" throw you off there; when "if" follows "only" to make "only if," it always signals a necessary term:

> If in New York → in United States.

Treat this as another rule to memorize: "only if" equals *only* equals *then*.

There is one use of the word *only*, however, that produces a different interpretation. Preceded by the definite article, "the only" signals the sufficient term in a conditional relationship:

> The only people who are in New York are people who are in the United States.

Again, whom is this sentence about? People in New York, so that's the sufficient term. The translation now looks familiar:

> If in New York → in United States.

Note: The meaning of the statement remains the same throughout all three examples. (Of course it does, as it is a statement we know to be true from real life in this case.) The part of the conditional logic signaled by the word *only*, however, was different: "Only" (by itself) and "only if" indicated necessity, whereas "the only" indicates sufficiency.

LSAT STRATEGY

The word *only* in Formal Logic

· *Only* signals the necessary term.
· *Only if* signals the necessary term.
· *The only* signals the sufficient term.

(By the way, notice that, in the prose examples above, the sufficient and necessary terms appear in either order; the sufficient term doesn't always appear first in the plain-language English sentence. Nevertheless, in every Formal Logic "translation," the order was identical: If sufficient → necessary.)

Unless/Without

Take a look at another way of expressing the same sufficient-necessary relationship we've been illustrating throughout this section:

> No one can be in New York unless he's in the United States.

Once again, this translates to our familiar If/Then statement:

> If in New York → in United States.

This one needs some unpacking, but close examination will show you that it conforms to the way you use *unless* all the time in day-to-day conversation. *Unless* signals a requirement—that is, it signals the necessary term—so you can think, "*unless* equals *then*." But notice what "unless" does to the phraseology in the sufficient clause—we've had to add the negation "no one." The original statement ("If a person is in New York, then he is in the United States") didn't have a *no* in it. Do you see why? The word "unless" indicates that were the necessary condition to be absent, the sufficient condition would have to be absent as well. That means that to fit the sufficient condition into a sentence containing *unless*, you must negate the sufficient term.

If this seems tricky, just put it into an easily understandable real-life situation. Most people don't want to eat dry cereal without milk. For them, "I will not eat cereal unless I have milk," is an easy rule to articulate. Now, just think through what that means in Formal Logic terms. Because the person won't eat cereal unless she has milk, "milk" is *necessary* for her to eat cereal. Thus, the rule could just as easily be expressed in If/Then terms: If eat cereal → have milk.

What does a sentence containing *unless* mean if the sufficient term is not negated? Again, apply a real-world example and work it out. Imagine you hear a friend say, "I will go to the mall unless it rains." (Notice that this time, the term at the beginning of the sentence is positive—"I *will* go to the mall"—as opposed to the "I will *not* eat cereal" in the example above.) Treat your friend's statement as a rule; he means precisely what he says. His statement means "I will go to the mall in every case except one: rain." So, you can translate your friend's rule into "If I do *not* go to the mall, then it is raining."

As the following Strategy Box illustrates, you can translate any Formal Logic statement with *unless* by negating the sufficient statement and substituting *then* for the word *unless*.

LSAT STRATEGY

The word *unless* in Formal Logic

- "No X unless Y" translates to "If X then Y."
- "A unless B" translates to "If not A then B."

Note: The word *without* functions exactly the same way as *unless* in conditional Formal Logic statements. For example, "I will not eat cereal without having milk" has the same meaning as "I will not eat cereal unless I have milk."

If, But Only If

One other Formal Logic structure you'll occasionally see on the LSAT is *if, but only if*. Here's an example:

Piper goes to the beach if, but only if Kinsley goes to the beach

This means that Piper's going to the beach is sufficient *and* necessary for Kinsley's going. (Notice that the term "Kinsley goes to the beach" is preceded in the sentence by "if" [sufficient] and by "only if" [necessary].) It can be broken down into two statements:

If Piper goes to the beach → Kinsley goes to the beach

If Kinsley goes to the beach → Piper goes to the beach

Ultimately, the impact is this: either they both go or neither of them does.

The expert LSAT test taker automatically (either mentally or in simple shorthand) translates all conditional statements into If/Then format. Follow the expert's lead by practicing these skills until they are second nature. Here are a number of conditional statements along with the expert's translations:

Conditional Statement		Analysis
All visitors must check in at the front desk.	→	"All" is modifying "visitors," which makes that term sufficient: If visitor → check in at the front desk
Each of the contestants has been given one hour to prepare a dish.	→	"Each" indicates that being a contestant is sufficient: If contestant → one hour to prepare a dish
Every building on this street was built before the turn of the century.	→	"Every" is a modifier for the entire phrase "building on this street" and indicates sufficiency: If building on this street → built before the turn of the century
Anyone not on the list will be asked to leave.	→	"Anyone" is categorical language pertaining to all people not on the list; it indicates sufficiency: If NOT on the list → asked to leave
In order to start the car, the key must be in the ignition.	→	The phrase "in order to" and the word "must" combine to indicate that the key is required (necessary) for the car to start: If start the car → key in the ignition
The children in Ms. Hatcher's class all speak French.	→	The word order of this sentence is a little tricky. Whom is this sentence about? It's about students who are in Ms. Hatcher's class. Accordingly, "all" (which indicates sufficiency) is modifying the children in Ms. Hatcher's class: If in Ms. Hatcher's class → speaks French

Conditional Statement		Analysis
No one in Ms. Hatcher's class speaks German.	→	Whom is this sentence about? The kids in Ms. Hatcher's class. "No one" indicates that being in that class is sufficient to know a student does not speak German: If in Ms. Hatcher's class → NOT speak German
The only people allowed on the field at this time are members of the press.	→	"The only," because it has the definite article, indicates sufficiency: If allowed on the field → member of the press at this time
Everyone in the audience will get a copy of my new book.	→	"Everyone" indicates that being a person in the audience is sufficient to receive a copy of the new book: If in the audience → book
In order for us to make a diagnosis, we need an accurate patient history.	→	The phrase "in order to" and the word "need" combine to indicate that an accurate patient history is necessary for a diagnosis: If diagnosis → accurate patient history
They will name the baby Maya if, but only if, it's a girl.	→	"If but only if" indicates that a statement is both sufficient and necessary for the other and vice versa. If baby named Maya → girl If girl → baby named Maya

Practice

Using the previous pages as a glossary, translate each of the following statements, each of which expresses a sufficient-and-necessary relationship, into If/Then format. Note them down in simple shorthand relationships using arrows.

Conditional Statement	My Analysis
37. All employees are required to attend the meeting.	
38. I'll skip the party only if I'm sick.	
39. Malinda will not win the race unless she trains hard and avoids injuries.	
40. All of those in the path of the tornado are being evacuated.	
41. Everyone in the cinema must turn their cell phones off now.	
42. Only if you have proper identification and a ticket will you be allowed to board the plane.	
43. All of those in attendance this evening are asked to give generously to the scholarship fund.	

Conditional Statement	My Analysis
44. Anyone over the age of fifty can remember disco music.	
45. Every city in the tristate region is currently suffering through the worst flu epidemic in twenty years.	
46. Candace will sign up for softball this year only if Jarvis or Tempest signs up as well.	
47. School is not canceled for bad weather unless there is snow accumulation in excess of three feet.	
48. A lake has experienced an infestation of Frankenfish if, but only if, it's in Travis County.	
49. Any fruit we received in the last shipment is bound to be spoiled by now.	
50. The only rooms big enough to accommodate the wedding party are booked for that weekend.	
51. Only when spring arrives and warmer weather returns do the swallows return to Capistrano.	

Here's how an LSAT expert would notate each of the examples you just worked on. In every case, the shorthand employs the format "If [sufficient] → [necessary]."

Conditional Statement		Analysis
37. All employees are required to attend the meeting.	→	If employee → attend
38. I'll skip the party only if I'm sick.	→	If skip party → sick
39. Malinda will not win the race unless she trains hard and avoids injuries.	→	If Malinda wins → trained hard AND avoided injuries
40. All of those in the path of the tornado are being evacuated.	→	If path of tornado → evacuated
41. Everyone in the cinema must turn their cell phones off now.	→	If in cinema → turn cell phone off
42. Only if you have proper identification and a ticket will you be allowed to board the plane.	→	If allowed to board the plane → proper ID AND a ticket
43. All of those in attendance this evening are asked to give generously to the scholarship fund.	→	If in attendance → asked to give to scholarship
44. Anyone over the age of fifty can remember disco music.	→	If over 50 → remember disco
45. Every city in the tristate region is currently suffering through the worst flu epidemic in twenty years.	→	If city in tristate region → suffering flu epidemic
46. Candace will sign up for softball this year only if Jarvis or Tempest signs up as well.	→	If Candace signs up → Jarvis signs up OR Tempest signs up
47. School is not canceled for bad weather unless there is snow accumulation in excess of three feet.	→	If school canceled → more than 3 feet of snow
48. A lake has experienced an infestation of Frankenfish if, but only if, it's in Travis County.	→	If lake in Travis County → infested with Frankenfish If infested with Frankenfish → lake in Travis County
49. Any fruit we received in the last shipment is bound to be spoiled by now.	→	If fruit from last shipment → spoiled
50. The only rooms big enough to accommodate the wedding party are booked for that weekend.	→	If big enough to hold the party → booked
51. Only when spring arrives and warmer weather returns do the swallows return to Capistrano.	→	If swallows return → spring arrives AND warmer weather returns

Reflection

Review your practice. Consider these questions:

- How well did you spot the sufficient and necessary terms? What words or phrases tended to mislead you?
- When noting the statements down in shorthand, did you always keep the sufficient term on the left and the necessary term on the right, with an arrow pointing to the necessary term?
- If you were able to spot which thing is needed for another in some of the examples, did you remember what that means about which one is necessary and which one is sufficient?

Translating conditional, Formal Logic statements is something you can practice every day. When you hear friends, coworkers, or others use words like *all*, *every*, *none*, *never*, *if*, *only if*, *unless*, and so on, treat their statements as rules and determine how the statements they've made would translate into If/Then statements.

Making Valid Deductions from Conditional Statements

Now that you understand conditional relationships and know how to spot them when you come across them in prose, you're ready to think about how to combine them to make deductions. You saw a small example of this in our demonstration about navel oranges above, and you'll see a great deal of it in the course of learning how to do Logic Games and Logical Reasoning questions on the LSAT.

The idea is simple: you can combine conditional statements when the same term appears in more than one statement. Where the sufficient terms are the same, they can be combined like this:

> If A, then B.
>
> If A, then C.
>
> Deduction: If A, then both B and C.

If the same term appears in the necessary parts of two conditional statements, you can combine them like this:

> If T, then V.
>
> If W, then V.
>
> Deduction: If either T or W (or both), then V.

Finally, by far the most useful opportunity to combine conditional statements occurs when the same term appears in the necessary part of one conditional statement and in the sufficient part of another. In that case, those two statements allow you to deduce an altogether new idea:

> If X, then Y.
>
> If Y, then Z.
>
> Deduction: If X, then Z.

(That pattern of three statements is called a syllogism, by the way. You certainly won't have to know that word on the LSAT, but the test will definitely reward your ability to accurately combine statements in this way.)

More than two premises with shared terms can produce multiple deductions:

> If D, then E.
>
> If E, then F.
>
> If F, then G.
>
> If G, then H.

Deductions:

> If D, then E and F and G and H.
>
> If E, then F and G and H.
>
> If F, then G and H.

By the way, what can you deduce if you know that you have H? Answer: Not a thing. Remember, the necessary term of an If/Then doesn't trigger any results.

Take a look at how an LSAT expert might draw deductions from a set of conditional statements:

Conditional Statements		Analysis
If Jane goes to the movies, she'll also go to the beach.	→	If movies → beach
If Jane goes to the beach, she won't go to the museum.	→	If beach → ~museum
If Jane goes to the beach, she'll go to the amusement park.	→	If beach → amusement park
If Jane goes to the amusement park, she will buy a funnel cake.	→	If amusement park → buy funnel cake

If we know that Jane...	then we also know that she...
goes to the movies	—goes to the beach —does not go to the museum —goes to the amusement park —buys a funnel cake
goes to the beach	—does not go to the museum —goes to the amusement park —buys a funnel cake We don't know whether she goes to the movies or not.
doesn't go to the museum	We can't deduce anything.
buys a funnel cake	We can't deduce anything.

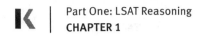

Practice

In the following exercise, first translate the given conditional statements so that you can use them to create a chain of logic. Then, answer questions about what we must know, given our new chain. The expert analysis is found on the next page.

Conditional Statements	My Analysis
52. If John doesn't bake a pie, he doesn't buy apples.	
If John bakes chocolate chip cookies, he does not bake a pie.	
If John doesn't buy apples, he doesn't have applesauce or doesn't have jelly.	
If John buys bananas, then he bakes chocolate chip cookies.	
If John goes to the store, then he buys bananas.	

If we know that John...	then we also know that John...
bought bananas	
bakes chocolate chip cookies	
does not bake a pie	
doesn't have applesauce or jelly	

Here's how the LSAT expert translated the logic and the valid deductions she drew from it.

Conditional Statements		Analysis
52.	If John doesn't bake a pie, he doesn't buy apples.	→	If NOT bake pie → NOT buy apples
	If John bakes chocolate chip cookies, he does not bake a pie.	→	If bake c/c cookies → NOT bake pie
	If John doesn't buy apples, he doesn't have applesauce or doesn't have jelly.	→	If NOT buy apples → NOT have applesauce OR NOT have jelly
	If John buys bananas, then he bakes chocolate chip cookies.	→	If buy bananas → bakes c/c cookies
	If John goes to the store, then he buys bananas.	→	If goes to store → buy bananas

If we know that John...		then we also know that John...
bought bananas	→	baked chocolate chip cookies, did not bake a pie, didn't buy apples, and doesn't have applesauce or doesn't have jelly
bakes chocolate chip cookies	→	does not bake a pie, didn't buy apples, and doesn't have applesauce or doesn't have jelly
does not bake a pie	→	didn't buy apples and doesn't have applesauce or doesn't have jelly
doesn't have applesauce or jelly	→	We can't deduce anything.

FORMAL LOGIC: CONTRAPOSITIVES

You've seen that despite the many ways to express a conditional statement in prose, the logic underlying such statements is remarkably consistent. You're about to learn one more feature of these statements: the contrapositive. The contrapositive is simply another way to express any If/Then statement, but your ability to quickly and accurately form a statement's contrapositive is an incredibly important tool for you to have in your LSAT toolkit.

LEARNING OBJECTIVES

In this section, you'll learn to:

- Translate a conditional statement into its contrapositive.
- Make valid deductions from the contrapositive of a conditional statement.
- Analyze correctly the implications of conditional statements containing *and* and *or*.
- Analyze correctly the implications of conditional statements containing an "exclusive or."

While a conditional statement and its contrapositive express exactly the same logical premise, forming contrapositives explicitly is valuable to the LSAT test taker because the contrapositive provides another logical trigger to work with.

Translating If/Then Statements into Contrapositives

Let's return to our very first example to start thinking about contrapositives.

> If you're in New York, then you are in the United States.

Every single time you are in New York, then you absolutely have to be in the United States. Being in the United States is necessary for a person to be in New York. So, if someone is not in the United States, there's no way he can be in New York. Put another way, negating the necessary term means negating the sufficient term. Contrapositives are built on this insight, and forming the contrapositive is pretty straightforward:

- Reverse the terms—put the term on the left of the arrow on the right and vice versa.
- Negate the terms—where a negation word (like *not*, *no*, or *never*) appears, take it out; where such a word does not appear, put it in.

Like this:

> Original statement: If in New York → in the United States

- Reverse: If in the United States → in New York, *and*
- Negate: If NOT in the United States → NOT in New York

That's the contrapositive: If NOT in the United States → NOT in New York. If you're not in the United States, then you're not in New York.

Note: You must always reverse *and* negate simultaneously. Doing just one of those two actions distorts the meaning of the original statement:

- Reversing without negating produces "If you're in the United States, then you're in New York." Well, we know that to be wrong in real life, and it's a logical fallacy to do this to any conditional statement. The resulting sentence doesn't mean the same thing as the original. In fact, it confuses the necessary term for the sufficient one.
- Negating without reversing gives "If you're not in New York, then you're not in the United States." Again, we know that sentence is incorrect in real life as well as being a distortion of the original.

The test will include numerous wrong answers—in Logic Games and Logical Reasoning especially—that reflect both of those mistakes. Learning to avoid those wrong answers can be just as important as learning to spot correct answers that translate Formal Logic statements correctly.

It's very important to fully absorb that you can never negate without reversing or reverse without negating. This is easy to remember when you're dealing with a real-life example but easy to forget when you're in the heat of a logic game, arranging abstract doo-dads, or plowing through a Logical Reasoning argument with unfamiliar scientific terms. Make sure you wrap your head around this principle now so it doesn't trip you up later.

We said earlier that a conditional statement and its contrapositive express exactly the same idea. As proof, notice that the contrapositive can be contraposed into the original statement:

> If NOT in United States → NOT in New York
> Reverse and negate: If in New York → in United States

Before you practice this, there's one more consideration for forming valid contrapositives: along with reversing and negating, you must whenever relevant also change *and* to *or* and *or* to *and*. To see why, and to discern when this is the case, consider an example. Treat the following statement as a rule:

> If it doesn't rain, then we will go to the park or we will go to the beach.

In other words, a lack of rain is sufficient to know that we will go to either the park or the beach (or maybe both, if we have time). Now, translate into simple shorthand:

> If NOT rain → park OR beach

Do the first two operations needed to form the contrapositive:

- Reverse: If park OR beach → NOT rain, *and*
- Negate: If NOT park OR NOT beach → rain

But that's mistaken. What would the statement mean if we left it like that? Not going to the park would be enough to absolutely require that it rain. But that's not consistent with the original statement. According to the original statement, if it doesn't rain, we might choose to go to the beach and not to the park. Preserving the *or* in the contrapositive has warped the meaning of the original statement. But watch how the meaning of the original is preserved if we change *or* to *and* in the contrapositive:

> If NOT park AND NOT beach → rain

If we're neither at the park nor at the beach, it's raining. Now we have a statement that is logically equivalent to the original.

Our example involved an *or* in the necessary term, but you must change *and* to *or* and vice versa regardless of whether those terms appear in the sufficient or necessary term.

Another important note here: When you're dealing with multiple terms in a conditional statement, negate *each one* to avoid confusion. If we formed our contrapositive by saying "if not beach and park → rain," that could have gotten very confusing.

LSAT STRATEGY

To form the contrapositive of an If/Then statement

- · Reverse the terms.
- · Negate *each* term.
- · Change *and* to *or* and change *or* to *and* (whenever applicable).

Study the LSAT expert's work as she translates the following If/Then statements and forms the correct contrapositive for each. Note that, in every case, it would not matter whether the expert translated the original statement in negative or positive terms because, having formed the contrapositive, both the negative and positive equivalent statements would be clear.

Conditional Statement		Analysis
If the skies stay clear and the wind remains calm, we set sail tomorrow.	→	If skies clear AND winds calm → we sail tomorrow If NOT sail tomorrow → skies NOT clear OR winds NOT calm
There are no vacancies at the hotel unless we have a cancellation.	→	If vacancies → cancellation If NO cancellation → NO vacancies
If Joan is late for dinner, then either traffic is bad or she's lost her way.	→	If Joan is late → bad traffic OR lost If NOT bad traffic AND NOT lost → Joan is NOT late
Only the best players were invited to the tournament.	→	If invited → one of the best players If NOT one of the best players → NOT invited
If this substance is properly classified as a mineral, then it is neither animal nor vegetable.	→	If mineral → NOT animal AND NOT vegetable If animal OR vegetable → NOT mineral*

*NOTE: Remember that *neither x nor y* translates to *not x AND not y*.

Now, you're ready to pull together all of the thinking that an LSAT expert does whenever she encounters a statement indicating a sufficient-necessary relationship. She recognizes the presence of Formal Logic, translates it into If/Then format, and forms the contrapositive explicitly. When you're able to do these things accurately and quickly—in other words, when these processes become second nature—you'll be well on your way to getting a number of LSAT points that may have eluded you before (and will continue to elude your less well-trained competition).

Practice

Translate each of the following statements into simple shorthand and form the contrapositives. After each one, you can turn the page to see the work of an LSAT expert with these same statements.

Conditional Statement	My Analysis
53. Each of the boys is wearing blue and yellow.	

Conditional Statement	My Analysis
54. When it rains, it pours.	
55. If we have turkey for dinner, we won't have ham.	
56. Any bowl that doesn't contain goldfish contains bettas.	
57. Arianna drives to Rochester only if she visits Syracuse.	
58. If the exhibition comes to the city zoo, then it will feature elephants but not pandas.	
59. If the talent show does not have a magician, then it will have either a dance number or a comedian.	
60. All triathlon participants must undergo a physical and sign a waiver.	
61. All the horses in the stable are either roan or palomino.	

Conditional Statement	My Analysis
62. If the train is late, then Bret won't make it to Chicago today.	
63. None of the coffee in this room is decaf.	
64. All sodas in the cupboard are either diet or cherry.	
65. We visit the Colosseum today only if we also visit the Pantheon but not the Roman Forum.	
66. Pre-med students must take organic chemistry and biology.	
67. Unless it rains, we will go to either the beach or the park.	
68. If she injured her anterior cruciate ligament or her medial collateral ligament, then she won't be able to play for the remainder of the season.	
69. Greg can join neither the swim team nor the debate team unless he brings up his grades.	

Conditional Statement	My Analysis
70. If Matt wins the lottery, then he will buy a boat and sail around the world.	
71. Only faculty and staff are allowed in the lounge.	

Here's how the LSAT expert translated and contraposed each of the statements you just worked with.

Conditional Statement	Analysis
53. Each of the boys is wearing blue and yellow.	If boy → wearing blue AND wearing yellow → If NOT wearing blue OR NOT wearing yellow → NOT boy
54. When it rains, it pours.	→ If rains → pours If NOT pour → NOT rain
55. If we have turkey for dinner, we won't have ham.	→ If turkey → NOT ham If ham → NOT turkey
56. Any bowl that doesn't contain goldfish contains bettas.	→ If NOT goldfish → bettas If NOT bettas → goldfish
57. Arianna drives to Rochester only if she visits Syracuse.	If Arianna drives to Rochester → visits Syracuse → If NOT visit Syracuse → Arianna NOT drive to Rochester
58. If the exhibition comes to the city zoo, then it will feature elephants but not pandas.*	If city zoo → elephants AND NOT pandas → If NOT elephants → NOT city zoo** OR if pandas
59. If the talent show does not have a magician, then it will have either a dance number or a comedian.	If NOT magician → dance number OR comedian → If NOT dance number → magician AND NOT comedian
60. All triathlon participants must undergo a physical and sign a waiver.	If triathlon participant → undergo physical AND sign waiver → If NOT sign waiver OR NOT undergo physical → NOT triathlon participant
61. All the horses in the stable are either roan or palomino.	If horse in stable → roan OR palomino → If NOT roan AND NOT palomino → NOT horse in stable

Conditional Statement		Analysis
62.	If the train is late, then Bret won't make it to Chicago today.	→	If train late → Bret NOT make it to Chicago If Bret makes → train NOT late it to Chicago
63.	None of the coffee in this room is decaf.	→	If coffee in this room → NOT decaf If decaf → NOT coffee in this room
64.	All sodas in the cupboard are either diet or cherry.	→	If soda in the cupboard → diet OR cherry If NOT diet AND → NOT soda in the cupboard NOT cherry
65.	We visit the Colosseum today only if we also visit the Pantheon but not the Roman Forum.*	→	If Colosseum → Pantheon AND NOT Roman Forum If NOT Pantheon OR → NOT Colosseum if Roman Forum
66.	Pre-med students must take organic chemistry and biology.	→	If pre-med student → take organic chemistry AND take biology If NOT take organic → NOT pre-med student chemistry OR NOT take biology
67.	Unless it rains, we will go to either the beach or the park.	→	If NOT beach AND NOT park → rain If NOT rain → beach OR park
68.	If she injured her anterior cruciate ligament or her medial collateral ligament, then she won't be able to play for the remainder of the season.	→	If ACL OR MCL → NOT play rest of season If plays (at all → NOT ACL AND NOT MCL*** during the) rest of season
69.	Greg can join neither the swim team nor the debate team unless he brings up his grades.	→	If swim team OR debate team → brings up grades If NOT bring up grades → NOT swim team AND NOT debate team
70.	If Matt wins the lottery, then he will buy a boat and sail around the world.	→	If Matt wins lottery → buy boat AND sail around the world If NOT buy boat OR NOT → Matt NOT win lottery sail around the world
71.	Only faculty and staff are allowed in the lounge.	→	If allowed in the lounge → faculty OR staff If NOT faculty AND → NOT allowed in the lounge NOT staff

*The word *but*, though rhetorically different from *and*, actually functions the same as *and* in Formal Logic translations.

**Be careful with statements like this one. In the contrapositive here, the expert has jotted down "If NOT elephants or if pandas. . . ." The "if" before pandas there helps to avoid the mistaken interpretation that would result from the prose clause "If not elephants or pandas," which makes it sound as if both terms are negated. In this contrapositive, elephants are not present, but pandas *are*.

***Note that the expert has included the idea of playing at any point during the rest of the season. This makes clear, in the contrapositive, that if the athlete plays at all during the rest of the season, you can be certain she didn't injure her ACL or MCL.

Reflection

Review your practice.

- Were you careful to translate each sentence into shorthand before forming the contrapositive?
- What did you find challenging about forming the contrapositives?
- In cases involving *and* or *or*, did you convert them correctly? And did you negate each term?

In the coming days, use every opportunity you encounter to spot conditional reasoning in day-to-day life. The next time you see a sign such as "No Shirt, No Shoes, No Service," for example, translate it into If/Then terms. "If a person is not wearing shoes or is not wearing a shirt, then the person will not be served." Treat that as a rule without exceptions and practice forming the contrapositive: "If a person is being served, then he is wearing shoes and is wearing a shirt." You'll find it remarkable how often you engage in Formal Logic reasoning without even noticing it. You'll be noticing it a lot between now and Test Day.

Making Valid Deductions from the Contrapositive of a Conditional Statement

As you've seen (and practiced), a conditional statement and its contrapositive express exactly the same idea, but the contrapositive has a different trigger. Therefore, it's useful to write out the contrapositive for reference as you're thinking through how you can combine conditional statements to reveal further deductions. To start with, notice how a conditional statement and its contrapositive nicely define the field of what you do and don't know. Take a simple (and likely fictional) example:

> If a creature is a cat, then that creature has nine lives.

Start by translating that into simple shorthand and then making the contrapositive:

> If cat → nine lives
> If NOT nine lives → NOT cat

You've already learned that you can have the result without the trigger (that is to say, the necessary term without the sufficient term), so a creature could have nine lives without being a cat. In fact, you don't know about any creature other than a cat. If someone asked you whether a unicorn has nine lives, you'd have to respond—based solely on the statement above—"I don't know." It can be useful mental shorthand on the LSAT to remember that the necessary terms of an If/Then statement and its contrapositive are not mutually exclusive. In the example above, a creature that's not a cat may or may not have nine lives.

The contrapositive (and its implications) broadens your ability to make deductions from a set of conditional statements. Look again at the exercise about Jane and her entertainment choices and see how an expert LSAT test taker looks at the statements and their contrapositives:

Conditional Statements		Analysis

If Jane goes to the movies, she'll also go to the beach.

$\longrightarrow$

If movies $\longrightarrow$ beach
If NOT beach $\longrightarrow$ NOT movies

If Jane goes to the beach, she won't go to the museum.

$\longrightarrow$

If beach $\longrightarrow$ NOT museum
If museum $\longrightarrow$ NOT beach

If Jane goes to the beach, she'll go to the amusement park.

$\longrightarrow$

If beach $\longrightarrow$ amusement park
If NOT amusement park $\longrightarrow$ NOT beach

If Jane goes to the amusement park, she will buy a funnel cake.

$\longrightarrow$

If amusement park $\longrightarrow$ funnel cake
If NOT funnel cake $\longrightarrow$ NOT amusement park*

$\longrightarrow$ All the deductions made earlier are still valid, but by including the contrapositives, the following deductions are also now clear:

If Jane doesn't buy a funnel cake, then she doesn't go to the amusement park, she doesn't go to the beach, *and* she doesn't go to the movies.

It's possible for Jane to choose none of these activities: movies, beach, museum, amusement park. The negated version of each (for example, "not movies") appears in the "results" column, but none of those negated versions is a trigger that forces her to do another of the activities.

Suppose that Jane chooses none of the activities: that is, she doesn't to go the movies, beach, museum, or amusement park. In that case, does she buy a funnel cake? She may or may not.

*Notice that our expert LSAT test taker has kept all of the arrows all aligned. That really makes it easier for her to run her eye down the list of triggers to search for additional deductions. You'll want to get into that habit whenever you are working with a set of related conditional statements.

Practice

It's time to get some practice using contrapositives to make all the possible deductions from a set of conditional statements. For each statement below, turn it into shorthand, form the contrapositive, and then make notes about how each one can be combined with other conditional statements in the same set to make deductions. At any time, you can turn the page to see the expert test taker's approach.

Conditional Statements	My Analysis
72. If it is Tuesday, Mary is playing tennis.	
If Mary plays tennis, she is playing with John.	
If Mary does not play tennis, then she buys golf shoes.	
If Mary does not buy golf shoes, then she is in Hawaii.	

Here's the LSAT expert's thorough analysis of the example you just practiced. Compare your work to his by making sure you translated all of the rules and formed all of the contrapositives correctly. Then, compare your list of deductions to those made by the expert.

Conditional Statements	Analysis
72. If it is Tuesday, Mary is playing tennis.	→ If Tuesday → tennis If NOT tennis → NOT Tuesday
If Mary plays tennis, she is playing with John.	→ If tennis → plays with John If NOT play with John → NOT tennis
If Mary does not play tennis, then she buys golf shoes.	→ If NOT tennis → golf shoes If NOT golf shoes → tennis
If Mary does not buy golf shoes, then she is in Hawaii.	→ If NOT golf shoes → in Hawaii If NOT in Hawaii → golf shoes

If we know that...	then we also know that...
If it is Tuesday	Mary plays tennis and John plays tennis with her
Mary plays tennis	John plays tennis with her
John plays tennis	Nothing
John is not playing tennis	It is not Tuesday, Mary is not playing tennis, Mary buys golf shoes
Mary does not play tennis	It is not Tuesday and Mary buys golf shoes
Mary does not buy golf shoes	Mary plays tennis, John plays tennis with her, Mary is in Hawaii
Mary buys golf shoes	Nothing
Mary is in Hawaii	Nothing

Reflection

Look back over your practice.

- Did you carefully note each If/Then statement in shorthand?
- Did you carefully and correctly make all the contrapositives before trying to combine statements?
- Did you remember that a result doesn't trigger anything?
- Did you miss logical deductions that were available?

Start to pay attention to "chains" of logic that you encounter in the real world. You'll hear them in business meetings at work: "If we are able to cut shipping costs, we'll have additional capital. With additional capital, we can hire another developer. With another developer, the new product line can reach the market before our competitor's product." You might encounter something like this watching a news channel: "Without reductions in spending, programs for education will fail. Without adequate education, our nation's students won't obtain crucial skills for the global marketplace. If we lack talent for companies trying to compete globally, we will need to reform immigration laws." The more you pay attention to this kind of reasoning wherever you might see or hear it, the better you'll be at spotting mistakes and gaps in the logic. These are exactly the skills the LSAT rewards on Test Day.

Making Valid Deductions from Conditional Statements Containing "And" and "Or"

We saw previously in this chapter that the inclusion of *and* or *or* in a conditional statement adds a layer of complexity. We also saw that you have to be careful, when forming the contrapositive of a statement containing *and* or *or*, to exchange those conjunctions consistently and in the right way. This warrants additional practice. In this section, we'll look at how a test taker can make deductions by combining conditional statements that contain conjunctions and get some more practice translating these statements in the bargain.

As a reminder, to make the contrapositive of a conditional statement, do the following:

- Reverse the terms.
- Negate the terms.
- Change *and* to *or* and change *or* to *and* (whenever applicable).

Now, when we first discussed conditional statements with the word *or*, we noted that the word *or* does not express a relationship of mutual exclusivity unless the LSAT explicitly tells you otherwise. As another reminder, here's how to think about these statements in terms of Formal Logic:

Given the statement:

If *x*, then *y* or *z*

we understand it to mean:

If we have *x*, then we have to have at least *y* or *z*, and we might also have both.

Given the statement:

If *a* or *b*, then *c*

we understand it to mean:

Whenever we have *a*, then we have *c*.
Whenever we have *b*, then we have *c*.
Whenever we have both *a* and *b*, then we have *c*.

That's an important point to remember when you're employing conditional statements with *or* to draw further deductions. That's your next task: making logical deductions from sets of conditional statements in which some of the statements contain *and* or *or*. Review the LSAT expert's thorough analysis of the following set of statements:

Conditional Statements		Analysis	
Thomas can take a road trip only if he fills up his car with gas and gets the oil changed.	→	If road trip If NOT gas OR NOT oil change	→ gas AND oil change → NOT road trip
If Thomas's friend comes to town, the two will take a road trip to Big Sur.	→	If friend in town If NOT road trip	→ road trip → NOT friend in town
If Thomas fills up his car with gas, he will also get a car wash or buy snacks.	→	If gas If NOT car wash AND NOT snacks	→ car wash OR snacks → NOT gas
Thomas cannot get an oil change unless he schedules an appointment to do so.	→	If oil change If NOT appointment	→ appointment → NOT oil change

If we know that...	then we also know that...
Thomas's friend comes to town	Thomas goes on road trip, changes oil in car, gets gas for car, makes appointment to change oil, and gets a car wash or snacks or both
Thomas does not make an appointment for an oil change	Thomas doesn't get oil change and does not go on road trip. His friend does not come to town. (We don't know whether he gets gas or not.)
Thomas does not get an oil change OR does not fill his car up with gas or both	does not go on a road trip, and friend not in town
Thomas does not get his car washed	no deductions
Thomas does not buy any snacks	no deductions
Thomas does not get a car wash and also does not get snacks	doesn't get gas, doesn't go on a road trip, and his friend doesn't come to town

Practice

Now, get some practice translating and contraposing conditional statements containing *and* or *or*.

For each of the following statements, translate it into simple shorthand in the format: If sufficient → necessary. Then, form the contrapositives and take a moment to absorb what each one means. You can turn the page at any time to compare your work to the expert thinking.

Conditional Statements	My Analysis
73. If a white knight slays the green dragon or the purple ogre, he will save the princess.	
74. If Barry drinks his juice, he will become strong and mean.	
75. Jack will not have a lot of friends unless Jill or Jenny dates him.	
76. The flight will depart later than scheduled if the pilot and co-pilot fall asleep.	

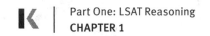

Here's how the LSAT expert interpreted the If/Then statements, formed their contrapositive, and drew valid deductions about what was certain, possible, and/or impossible given each one.

Conditional Statements	Analysis
73. If a white knight slays the green dragon or the purple ogre, he will save the princess.	If slays green dragon OR slays purple ogre → saves the princess If NOT save the princess → NOT slays green dragon AND NOT slays the purple ogre So if he slays just one of the two, he will save the princess. If he slays both, the princess will also be saved. If he doesn't save the princess, neither the dragon nor the ogre will be slain.
74. If Barry drinks his juice, he will become strong and mean.	If juice → strong AND mean If NOT strong OR NOT mean → NOT juice So if Barry drinks his juice, he becomes both strong and mean. We also know that if Barry become neither strong nor mean, he did not drink his juice.
75. Jack will not have a lot of friends unless Jill or Jenny dates him.	If has a lot of friends → dates Jill OR dates Jenny If NOT date Jill AND NOT date Jenny → NOT a lot of friends So if Jack has a lot of friends, either Jill or Jenny dates him, and possibly both. If neither Jill nor Jenny dates Jack, Jack does not have a lot of friends.
76. The flight will depart later than scheduled if the pilot and co-pilot fall asleep.	If pilot sleeps AND co-pilot sleeps → flight late If flight NOT late → pilot does NOT sleep OR copilot does NOT sleep So if both the pilot and co-pilot fall asleep, the flight will depart late. If the flight departs on time or even early, at least one of the pilot and copilot did not fall asleep.

Reflection

Look back over your practice:

- Did you carefully make shorthand translations of each statement and contrapositives for each?
- Did you remain clear in your mind about the meaning of *or* in each one?
- Were there logical deductions you missed?

Spot conditional statements in day-to-day life and work through their implications. If you hear someone say something along the lines of "If I forget to call my mom on her birthday, I'll have to send flowers or take her out to dinner next weekend," what does he mean? Treat the statement as a rule. If he's forgetful, could he do both? Sure.

If you know this fellow didn't send flowers and didn't take his mother out for dinner, what could you validly deduce? In that case, you'd know that he didn't forget to call.

Making Valid Deductions from Conditional Statements Containing an "Exclusive Or" Provision

So far we've emphasized the fact that *or*, by itself, does not denote a relationship of mutual exclusivity. Put simply, you can have both of the things connected by an *or* unless the LSAT explicitly tells you otherwise, as in the following example from earlier in the chapter:

Conditional Statement	Analysis
If the sous chef makes the soup, she will also make either the salad or the dessert but not both. →	(1) The sous chef making the soup is sufficient to tell us that she must also make the salad *or* the dessert.
	(2) The sous chef making the soup also requires that she NOT make both the salad *and* the dessert.

When we first showed this example, we discussed the fact that it's most easily understood when broken into two statements, as the LSAT expert did in the previous example. But now that you've expanded your Formal Logic skills to the point that you're habitually making contrapositives for all conditional statements, it's time to get some practice with contraposing this type of "exclusive or" statement. The simplest way: Break it out into two statements, translate them both into simple shorthand, and contrapose both, like this:

Conditional Statement	Analysis	
If the sous chef makes the soup, she will also make either the salad or the dessert but not both. →	If soup	→ salad OR dessert
	If NOT salad AND NOT dessert	→ NOT soup
	If soup	→ NOT [salad/dessert combo]
	If [salad/dessert combo]	→ NOT soup

Notice how the expert test taker, when turning the second part of this statement into shorthand, found a way to express that the *combination* of salad and dessert (rather than salad or dessert separately) was the necessary term. If he'd noted it down like this . . .

> If soup → not salad and dessert

then his automatic contrapositive-making habits might have kicked in, and he might have been tempted to make the contrapositive like this:

> If salad or not dessert → not soup

. . . which is not at all correct. Thus, decide for yourself on a shorthand you'll use whenever a term in a conditional statement is a combination of two things so that you won't get confused and start treating them separately. That shorthand will usually only be necessary in statements like this that have an "exclusive or" clause—that is, with the phrase "but not both" appended to a clause containing *or*. You won't see many of these on the LSAT, but when you do, you'll want to know that you have the logical implications of the statement worked out perfectly.

Clear notation will be your best friend when it comes to combining conditional statements, some of which contain "exclusive or" clauses. Consider the following demonstration of an LSAT expert's work with a set of If/Thens:

Conditional Statements		Analysis	

If today is a holiday, then Marisol does not work.

→

If holiday → NOT work

If work → NOT holiday

If post office is closed, then today is a holiday.

→

If post office closed → holiday

If NOT holiday → post office open

If the post office is open, then Marisol collects her mail.

→

If post office open → collects mail

If NOT collect mail → post office closed

If it is not the weekend, Marisol goes to bed early.

→

If NOT weekend → bed early

If NOT bed early → weekend

If NOT holiday → weekend OR post office open

If today is not a holiday, then it is the weekend or the post office is open, but not both.

→

If NOT weekend AND post office closed → holiday

If NOT holiday → NOT [both weekend and post office open]

If [both weekend and post office open] → holiday

→ The final statement contains an "exclusive or." When it is not a holiday, two mutually exclusive possibilities are offered: either it is the weekend or the post office is open, but both together cannot be true. [Remember: These "but not both" statements can be broken down into two separate statements, with contrapositives being formed for both statements.]

Translating these statements and forming the contrapositives allows for further deductions.

For instance, if Marisol does not collect her mail, then the post office is closed. And when the post office is closed, it must be a holiday, and when it's a holiday, Marisol does not work.

What would happen if Marisol were at work? First, it is not a holiday. And when it's not a holiday, the post office is open. But "not a holiday" appears in more than one of our conditional statements. It also triggers the "exclusive or." When it's not a holiday, either it is the weekend or the post office is open, but not both. Because the post office is open, it can't be the weekend. And when it's not the weekend, Marisol goes to bed early.

Here's an opportunity to practice forming contrapositives and making deductions with conditional statements, some of which contain "exclusive or" clauses.

Practice

Record each of the following statements in If/Then shorthand and form their contrapositives.
You can turn the page at any time to check your work.

Conditional Statements	My Analysis
77. When we go to the amusement park, we always ride either the teacups or the Himalayan, but we never ride both.	
78. I've noticed something about life: if you ask, you get what you asked for—but it'll be either at the right time or in the right place but never both at once!	
79. In Professor Smith's class, you'll get an A if you write an extra paper or if you do a presentation in class. Oddly enough, though, if you both write an extra paper and do a presentation, then Smith will think you're just trying to curry favor, and in that case you definitely won't get an A!	
80. If Maria is selected for the team, then Kevin or Charles will be selected but not both. Unless Vivian is selected, Kevin will not be selected. David is not selected for the team if Charles is selected. If Kevin and Charles are both selected for the team, Angela will also be selected.	

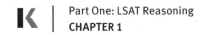
Here's how the LSAT expert looked at those two exercises. Compare your work recording the If/Then statements and forming the contrapositives. Check to see if you made all of the available deductions.

	Conditional Statements	Analysis
77.	When we go to the amusement park, we always ride either the teacups or the Himalayan, but we never ride both.	If amusement park → teacups OR Himalayan If NOT teacups AND → NOT amusement park NOT Himalayan If amusement park → NOT [teacups and Himalayan combo] If [teacups and → NOT amusement park Himalayan combo] [So, if we are somewhere and we have just ridden both a teacups and a Himalayan, then we're somewhere other than the amusement park—the county fair, perhaps?]
78.	I've noticed something about life: if you ask, you get what you asked for—but it'll be either at the right time or in the right place but never both at once!	If ask → right time OR right place If NOT right time AND → NOT ask NOT right place If ask → NOT [right time and right place combo] If [right time and → NOT ask right place combo] [So, if you get what you want in the right place and at the right time, you must not have asked for it (paradoxically enough).]
79.	In Professor Smith's class, you'll get an A if you write an extra paper or if you do a presentation in class. Oddly enough, though, if you both write an extra paper and do a presentation, then Smith will think you're just trying to curry favor, and in that case you definitely won't get an A!	If extra paper OR → A presentation If NOT A → NOT extra paper AND NOT presentation If [extra paper and → NOT A presentation combo] If A → NOT [extra paper and presentation combo]

Conditional Statements	Analysis
80. If Maria is selected for the team, then Kevin or Charles will be selected but not both.	If Maria → Kevin OR Charles If NOT Kevin AND → NOT Maria NOT Charles If Maria → NOT [Kevin and Charles combo] If [Kevin and → NOT Maria Charles combo]
Unless Vivian is selected, Kevin will not be selected.	If Kevin → Vivian If NOT Vivian → NOT Kevin
David is not selected for the team if Charles is selected.	If Charles → NOT David If David → NOT Charles
If Kevin and Charles are both selected for the team, Angela will also be selected.	If Kevin AND → Angela Charles If NOT Angela → NOT Kevin OR NOT Charles

If we know that...	then we also know that...
Kevin is selected	Vivian is selected. We don't know anything else.
Charles is not selected	No deductions.
Maria is selected	Kevin or Charles is selected and the other one is not. Because we don't know which one, no further deductions.
David is selected	Charles is not selected. No other deductions.
Angela is selected	No deductions: Angela being selected is never a trigger.
Kevin and Charles are selected	Maria and David are not selected. Angela and Vivian are selected.

FORMAL LOGIC: NUMERICAL DEDUCTIONS FROM CONDITIONAL STATEMENTS

LEARNING OBJECTIVES

In this section, you'll learn to:

· Determine the valid deductions from a Conditional Statement with the "If X → ~ Y" Structure.
· Determine the valid deductions from a Conditional Statement with the "If ~ X → Y" Structure.

You've already gotten some practice in making deductions from conditional statements. Now, we're going to devote a section of this chapter to two particular types of deductions because both are very common on the LSAT. You'll find it immensely helpful to be able to think through them quickly and accurately.

Determining the Valid Deduction from a Conditional Statement with the "If X → ~ Y" Structure

This type of conditional is very common on the LSAT:

If Charlene acts in the play, then Daisy will not act in the play.

The trigger involves something that *does* happen, and the result is that something else *cannot* happen.

In dealing with this, let's put the statement into our standard shorthand and make the contrapositive, just as we always will when we encounter conditional statements:

If C → ~ D
If D → ~ C

Now, if you don't push your understanding of the rule beyond that point, you'll still be able to get through the game or Logical Reasoning stimulus . . . slowly. But you can distill the logic further, and doing so will save you from having to write it all out. Take another look at the statement and its contrapositive together. Every time you have either one of these entities acting in the play, you can't have the other one. In other words, you can't ever include both of them in the play. Be very clear, however, that it's possible for neither one to act in the play. They can't be together in the play, but they could both sit in the audience. So, there are three possible outcomes from this statement:

• C in, D out
• D in, C out
• Both C and D out

Thus, if you prefer, instead of writing out the statement and its contrapositive, you could simply note the one result that cannot happen:

Never C and D in together

Already you've saved yourself some time. But there's another deduction to be drawn here. Before you were given this rule, it may have been possible that all actors available to be in the play are, in fact, *in* the play. This rule, however, has made that impossible. The maximum number of actors who can be in the play is now at least one less than the total pool of actors. This type of rule reduces the acceptable maximum number, which is (always in logic games, sometimes in Logical Reasoning questions) an invaluable deduction.

You'll get to practice making this type of deduction after we cover the other type of rule that commonly affects numbers on the LSAT.

Determining the Valid Deduction from a Conditional Statement with "If ~ X → Y" Structure

We just got to know a common format for a rule in which two things can't go together or can't both happen. That rule always reduces the maximum number of things that can happen. There's a sort of corollary rule that also affects numbers, and it has this structure:

> If Edith doesn't act in the play, then Frank will.

The trigger is something *not* happening, and the result is that something *does* happen.

In dealing with this, let's once again put the statement into standard shorthand and make the contrapositive, just as we always will with conditional statements:

> If ~E → F
> If ~F → E

As before, if you don't push your understanding of this rule beyond that point, you'll still be able to get through the game or Logical Reasoning stimulus. But you can become more efficient in your treatment of this type of rule by noticing something about it right now: the absence of one of the entities requires the presence of the other one—every single time. Thus, one or the other of them must always be included. If either one is left out, then the other one must be in as a consequence. And can they both be in the play? Of course, because you can have the logical results without the triggers.

So we could have . . .

- E out, F in
- F out, E in
- Both E and F in

Thus, if you find it easier, you could skip the Formal Logic translation and note the rule in shorthand with something like this:

> At least one of E or F in the play (maybe both)

Think for a moment about what this rule does to the numbers. Prior to this rule, it may have been possible that we were dealing with an avant garde play in which no one appears on stage and the audience is treated to five minutes of darkness and the sound of rain. Can that happen now? No. This rule establishes a minimum: this play has at least one actor, if not more, who appears. And knowledge of the minimum acceptable number, just like knowledge of the maximum, is priceless when reasoning through LSAT questions.

Practice

Here's an opportunity to practice working with conditional statements that affect maxima and minima, as well as everything else you've learned in this chapter.

For each of the following, translate any conditional statements into simple shorthand. You can do this by forming the If/Then and its contrapositive, or you can cut straight to one of the simpler shorthand notes described above, if appropriate. Not all of the statements will fit the two patterns discussed in this section, but part of the object here is to recognize a minimum-increaser or a maximum-reducer when you see it. If there's more than one statement, note down any logical deductions that can be made by combining them. It is possible that some of these statements might not be conditional Formal Logic statements at all. If that's the case, note that no If/Then translation is possible. Expert thinking follows on the page immediately after your practice.

Conditional Statement	My Analysis
81. If Bob gets Gouda at the store, he won't also get Emmenthaler.	
82. Wherever mosquitoes are not prevalent, rates of malaria drop significantly.	
83. If your sophomore students aren't assigned the time-consuming *War and Peace*, they will be assigned both *Anna Karenina* and *Resurrection*.	
84. If I don't get my taxes done by a professional, I will at least use tax-preparation software.	
85. Sheila can't go to the event if her husband doesn't stay home with the kids.	
86. If you can't say something nice, then just nod and smile.	
87. Paul won't eat anything that has mushrooms or mayonnaise.	
88. No one who really cares would ever just give to a charity without understanding how the charity operates.	

Conditional Statement	My Analysis
89. If Bob can't find Gouda at the store, then he'll get Edam instead. If he can't get Gouda and can't get Edam, then he will yell at the guy at the cheese counter.	
90. Soup that doesn't taste spicy needs a lot of salt.	
91. We can reopen the unused factory unless it's either sitting on a fault line or is contaminated with mercury.	
92. We ought to go to the memorial service.	
93. Whenever I think about Paris, I think about lights reflected in the Seine—and about not being able to get a decent taco!	
94. Mary does a great improvised barbeque, but she can cook indoors only if you give her a very specific recipe.	
95. No one who wants to be a doctor should set a bad example by smoking.	
96. Don't bother getting eggs at the store unless you also get butter in which to cook them. Don't get margarine unless they're out of butter or the butter is more than $4.	
97. The X organization won't support a bill if the Y organization is backing it. The Y organization refuses to support anything backed by the Z organization.	
98. I never believe what I read in the *Menda City Daily News*.	
99. I will make the phone call if, but only if, I can find my cell phone.	

Here's how an LSAT expert would diagram each of the statements you just worked with. In some cases, the expert has added an additional comment to remind you of easily overlooked exceptions to or implications of these statements.

Conditional Statement	Analysis
81. If Bob gets Gouda at the store, he won't also get Emmenthaler.	If G → NOT E If E → NOT G → OR Never both G and E
82. Wherever mosquitoes are not prevalent, rates of malaria drop significantly.	If mosquitoes NOT prevalent → malaria rates drop If malaria rates NOT drop → mosquitoes prevalent → OR [always] either malaria rates drop or mosquitoes are prevalent, or both
83. If your sophomore students aren't assigned the time-consuming *War and Peace*, they will be assigned both *Anna Karenina* and *Resurrection*.	If NOT WP → AK AND R If NOT AK OR NOT R → WP OR [always] Either WP or [AK and R combo] Note: Students could be assigned *War and Peace* and one of the other two books, or they could be assigned all three. The triggers in the original statement and its contrapositive are all negative statements, so there's no way to determine what happens if they *are* assigned one or more of these books. Another helpful way to translate this statement would be to break it down into smaller pieces: If ~WP → AK If ~AK → WP If ~WP → R If ~R → WP Notice how that translation covers all of the triggers and results in the statement.

Conditional Statement	**Analysis**
84. If I don't get my taxes done by a professional, I will at least use tax-preparation software.	If NOT pro → software If NOT software → pro OR [I will use] Either a professional or software or both
85. Sheila can't go to the event if her husband doesn't stay home with the kids.	If husband NOT home → Sheila NOT at event If Sheila at event → husband home [Remember: It is possible for Sheila's husband to stay home and for her not to go to the event.]
86. If you can't say something nice, then just nod and smile.	If NOT say something nice → nod AND smile If NOT nod OR NOT smile → say something nice [always] Either say something nice or [nod and smile combo] Note: A person could say something nice and do one of the other two gestures, or they could do all three. The triggers in the original statement and its contrapositive are all negative statements, so there's no way to determine what happens if they *do* say something nice or if they *do* nod or smile. Another helpful way to translate this statement would be to break it down into smaller pieces: If ~say something nice → nod If ~nod → say something nice If ~say something nice → smile If ~smile → say something nice Notice how that translation covers all of the triggers and results in the statement.
87. Paul won't eat anything that has mushrooms or mayonnaise.	If mushrooms OR mayo → Paul NOT eat If Paul eat → NOT mushrooms AND NOT mayo
88. No one who really cares would ever just give to a charity without understanding how the charity operates.	If really cares → does NOT give without understanding If gives without understanding → does NOT really care [Remember: You can't have "really cares" and "gives without understanding" at the same time (that is, in the same individual).]

Conditional Statement		Analysis
89. If Bob can't find Gouda at the store, then he'll get Edam instead. If he can't get Gouda and can't get Edam, then he will yell at the guy at the cheese counter.	→	If NOT G → E If NOT E → G [that is:] Either E or G or both at all times If NOT G AND NOT E → yell If NOT yell → G OR E [If the first rule is obeyed, the second one will never be triggered. Note that it's possible for Bob to buy Gouda or Edam or both and still yell at the guy at the cheese counter without violating these rules.]
90. Soup that doesn't taste spicy needs a lot of salt.	→	If NOT spicy → salt If NOT salt → spicy [Soup must always be either salty or spicy *or both* by the conditions of this rule.]
91. We can reopen the unused factory unless it's either sitting on a fault line or is contaminated with mercury.	→	If can NOT reopen → fault line OR mercury If NOT fault line AND → can reopen NOT mercury [Either we can reopen the factory, or it is sitting on a fault line, or it has mercury. Remember, though, that it is possible for the factory to sit on a fault line and be contaminated with mercury and still be reopened. "Can reopen" is not a trigger in this rule. Sitting on a fault line or mercury contamination are necessary to the factory's remaining closed. Their absence is not required for its reopening.]
92. We ought to go to the memorial service.	→	Not a conditional; no translation. This is a statement of opinion.
93. Whenever I think about Paris, I think about lights reflected in the Seine—and about not being able to get a decent taco!	→	If think about Paris → think about lights AND think about can't-get-taco If NOT think about lights → NOT think about Paris OR NOT think about can't-get-taco
94. Mary does a great improvised barbeque, but she can cook indoors only if you give her a very specific recipe.	→	[First clause is not a conditional. Second clause translates:] If NOT give specific recipe → can NOT cook indoors If can cook indoors → give specific recipe
95. No one who wants to be a doctor should set a bad example by smoking.	→	If want to be doctor → should NOT smoke If smoke → NOT want to be doctor

Conditional Statement	Analysis
96. Don't bother getting eggs at the store unless you also get butter in which to cook them. Don't get margarine unless they're out of butter or the butter is more than $4.	If eggs → butter If NOT butter → NOT eggs If margarine → NOT butter OR butter = $4+ If butter AND NOT butter = $4+ → NOT margarine → That is, if the store has butter *and* it's not $4 or more, then don't get margarine. [Consider the following: —If I get eggs at the store, then I bought butter. Did I also buy margarine? If I paid $4 or less for the butter, then I did not buy margarine. If I paid more than $4 for the butter, then maybe I did buy margarine, but I don't know for sure. —If they have butter for $3, I could buy it, but I don't know that I do. I also don't know whether I buy eggs, though I do know I don't buy margarine.]
97. The X organization won't support a bill if the Y organization is backing it. The Y organization refuses to support anything backed by the Z organization.	If Y supports → X NOT support If X supports → Y NOT support That is, X and Y never support the same bill. If Z supports → Y NOT support If Y supports → Z NOT support That is, Y and Z never support the same bill. → [Deductions: • If Y supports a bill, both X and Z will refuse to support it. • If Z supports a bill, Y will not support it, but we don't know about X. • If X supports a bill, Y will not also support it, but we don't know about Z. • At any time, all three could oppose the same bill.]

Conditional Statement	Analysis
98. I never believe what I read in the *Menda City Daily News*.	If read in MCDN → NOT believe If believe → NOT read in MCDN → OR An item can never be both printed in MCDN and believed by me
99. I will make the phone call if, but only if, I can find my cell phone.	If make the phone call → can find my cell phone If can NOT find my cell phone → will NOT make the phone call → If can find my cell phone → make the phone call If NOT make the phone call → can NOT find my cell phone [Deduction: Either both events will happen or neither will.]

Reflection

Look back over your practice:

- Did you take the time to understand each conditional statement before noting it down in shorthand?
- If you couldn't immediately see how to write it down in one sentence, did you make the If/Then and its contrapositive? (If so, that's great!)
- Did you tend to get confused about the side of the arrow on which *not* should appear?
- Did you remember that you can have the result without the trigger in each case?

Now, take a moment to look back over all of Chapter 1. You may not have even been thinking about it, but you've successfully employed a great many essential LSAT skills, skills you'll continue to use in law school and in the practice of law. Now that you've built this foundation, you're ready to tackle a range of LSAT material. Chapters 2–7 will take you through the Method and strategies for the Logic Games section. Chapters 8–12 cover the Method and strategies for the Logical Reasoning sections. Finally, Chapters 13–16 outline what you need to know to master Reading Comprehension. You may be tackling any of those sections in the next part of your practice. Regardless, we strongly encourage you to return to Chapter 1 whenever you feel you need a refresher about these critical thinking and Formal Logic fundamentals that form the heart of LSAT reasoning.

CHAPTER 2

The Kaplan Logic Games Method

Every administration of the LSAT features one scored Logic Games section. There are always four games with a total of 22–24 questions. If you've taken an LSAT, you may well have considered Logic Games to be the hardest or most confusing section on the test, as do a majority of test takers the first time they see the exam. Each game has a number of "moving parts" that can, in theory, be arranged in dozens or even hundreds of ways. While that may seem daunting, the method and strategies you'll learn in this chapter will allow you to treat games as concrete, solvable puzzles. In fact, once you have internalized the strategies introduced here, you may find yourself making a greater improvement in Logic Games than in any other section of the test. By Test Day, it's not uncommon for students to describe games and the thinking they entail as fun, or for students to identify this as their favorite LSAT section.

If you've done the work in Chapter 1, "LSAT Reasoning," then much of what the Logic Games section rewards will already be familiar. Take a look at a typical LSAT Logic Games question.

---

6. If M was begun in a later year than L, then which one of the following could be true?

    (A)   F was begun in 603.
    (B)   G was begun in 602.
    (C)   H was begun in 605.
    (D)   L was begun in 603.
    (E)   S was begun in 604.

PrepTest58 Sec3 Q6

We'll give you the context you need to answer this question in a moment. First, though, notice the question stem. It starts by providing a condition, just like the opening clause of a Formal Logic statement. The stem then proceeds to ask you about your level of certainty, in this case, about what "could be true." You can see that logic games target the LSAT's core reasoning skills, asking you to take a set of conditions—rules, restrictions, limitations—and deduce what must be true, what is impossible, and what is undetermined.

Now take a look at the game and its questions on the next page. There's question 6 in context as part of a set of questions related to the short scenario at the beginning of the game. For the LSAT expert, the questions are simply applications of the limitations, rules, and restrictions described in the opening scenario. An important and encouraging note to remember is that the opening setup—even when it seems complex and abstract—always gives you everything you need to answer all of the questions.

Analysis: This paragraph sets out the task. It defines the players or entities to account for, tells what to do with them—put the entities in order, group them, select some and reject others, or assign them certain attributes— and provides the rules and restrictions on how the entities can be arranged. This "setup" always contains all of the information needed to answer every question.

Questions 1–6

Historical records show that over the course of five consecutive years—601, 602, 603, 604, and 605—a certain emperor began construction of six monuments: F, G, H, L, M, and S. A historian is trying to determine the years in which the individual monuments were begun. The following facts have been established:

L was begun in a later year than G, but in an earlier year than F.

H was begun no earlier than 604.

M was begun earlier than 604.

Two of the monuments were begun in 601, and no other monument was begun in the same year as any of the other monuments.

1. Which one of the following could be an accurate matching of monuments to the years in which they were begun?

    (A) 601: G; 602: L, S; 603: M; 604: H; 605: F
    (B) 601: G, M; 602: L; 603: H; 604: S; 605: F
    (C) 601: G, M; 602: S; 603: F; 604: L; 605: H
    (D) 601: G, S; 602: L; 603: F; 604: M; 605: H
    (E) 601: G, S; 602: L; 603: M; 604: H; 605: F

2. What is the latest year in which L could have been begun?

    (A) 601
    (B) 602
    (C) 603
    (D) 604
    (E) 605

3. The years in which each of the monuments were begun can be completely determined if which one of the following is discovered to be true?

    (A) F was begun in 603.
    (B) G was begun in 602.
    (C) H was begun in 605.
    (D) M was begun in 602.
    (E) S was begun in 604.

4. Which one of the following must be true?

    (A) F was begun in a later year than M.
    (B) F was begun in a later year than S.
    (C) H was begun in a later year than F.
    (D) H was begun in a later year than S.
    (E) M was begun in a later year than G.

5. L must be the monument that was begun in 602 if which one of the following is true?

    (A) F was begun in 605.
    (B) G was begun in 601.
    (C) H was begun in 604.
    (D) M was begun in 601.
    (E) S was begun in 603.

6. If M was begun in a later year than L, then which one of the following could be true?

    (A) F was begun in 603.
    (B) G was begun in 602.
    (C) H was begun in 605.
    (D) L was begun in 603.
    (E) S was begun in 604.

PrepTest58 Sec3 Qs1–6

Analysis: In one way or another, all of the questions reward an understanding of what is and is not possible given the game's action and restrictions—the differences between what must be true and what could be false, or between what must be false and what could be true. One question here—Q 6—has an additional condition that applies only to that specific question. Another—Q 3—asks for a condition that will determine the placement of all the entities. Still others—Qs 1, 2, 4, and 5—can be answered from the information in the opening paragraph.

Try out this game on your own. The remainder of the chapter will use it to illustrate the Kaplan Method for Logic Games. As you work through the chapter, you'll learn how an LSAT expert uses the method to manage all logic games.

THE KAPLAN METHOD FOR LOGIC GAMES

Let's not be shy about saying that logic games are challenging and some are downright hard. On Test Day, you have about 8½ minutes to process a game's task, sketch it out and account for all of its rules and restrictions, and then answer anywhere from five to seven questions. This chapter will lay out an efficient method for approaching any game you encounter on the LSAT. Learning and practicing this method will make you efficient with your time as you manage all of the game's information and effective at applying it to correctly answer the questions.

THE KAPLAN LOGIC GAMES METHOD

Step 1: Overview

Step 2: Sketch

Step 3: Rules

Step 4: Deductions

Step 5: Questions

In subsequent chapters, we'll go into more detail on these steps and the skills associated with them. For now, let's see how an LSAT expert would apply this method to the game about the ancient emperor's monuments. As we go along, you'll learn what each step of the method entails and how this will allow you to approach games of varying types and difficulty levels in the same consistent, repeatable way.

Step 1: Overview

Before you can accomplish anything in an LSAT logic game, you have to understand your task. Fortunately, the testmaker describes game scenarios as small, well-defined, real-world jobs; you may have to make a schedule of appointments, assign athletes to teams, match different costume elements to different actors in a play, or choose some items from a catering menu while rejecting others. In any event, you need to invest the first few seconds of tackling any logic game in clearly understanding your task. Doing so will allow you to make a useful, accurate sketch in which to record the specific details of the rules and restrictions set out.

LSAT Question	Analysis
Historical records show that over the course of five consecutive years—601, 602, 603, 604, and 605—a certain emperor began construction of six monuments: F, G, H, L, M, and S. A historian is trying to determine the years in which the individual monuments were begun. The following facts have been established: *PrepTest58 Sec3 Qs1–6*	Task: Figure out the year in which each of six monuments—F, G, H, L, M, S—was begun. This is a Sequencing action, figuring out the order in which construction began. The fact that six monuments were begun over a five-year period means that at least one year saw more than one monument started.

Asking four questions as you conduct your overview of the game's first paragraph will ensure that you always extract the relevant information. We'll refer to them as the SEAL questions.

STEP 1: OVERVIEW—THE SEAL QUESTIONS

Situation—What is the real-world scenario being described? What is the deliverable information—an ordered list, a calendar, a chart showing what's matched up?

Entities—Who or what are the "moving parts," the people or things I'm distributing, selecting, sequencing, or matching?

Action—What is the specific action—distribution, selection, sequencing, matching, or a combination of those—that I'm performing on the entities?

Limitations—Does the game state parameters (e.g., select four of seven, sequence the entities one per day, etc.) that restrict how I'll set up and sketch the game?

Asking those questions of the game's opening paragraph should give you a clear mental picture of your task. Notice that, in the Monuments game, the LSAT expert even spotted the fact that she would be sequencing six entities over the course of five years, meaning that at least one of the years would see multiple monuments begun. In the next chapter, you'll see games representing all of the common LSAT logic games actions, and you'll refine your skill at spotting the features that help you account for what is similar and what is unique among various examples of those game types.

Step 2: Sketch

Just as important as your internal visualization of a game's task is the actual physical picture of the game you draw on the page: your sketch. Logic games are almost impossible if you try to keep all of the information in your head. By depicting the game's setup and rules, an LSAT expert is able to quickly and confidently understand a game's parameters. The ideal sketch provides a framework that captures the scenario in a clear, simple way and provides spaces in which you can record the more specific and detailed rules of the game.

LSAT Question	Analysis
Historical records show that over the course of five consecutive years—601, 602, 603, 604, and 605—a certain emperor began construction of six monuments: F, G, H, L, M, and S. A historian is trying to determine the years in which the individual monuments were begun. The following facts have been established: *PrepTest58 Sec3 Qs1–6*	F G H L M S → 601 | 602 | 603 | 604 | 605

Here you see how the LSAT expert has turned her understanding of the Monument game's Sequencing task into a simple, effective sketch. As she determines when monuments were begun, she can record the monuments under the appropriate year. It is always a good idea to list out the entities above your sketch framework so that you can catalog which entities are or aren't restricted without having to go back and read the opening paragraph again and again. In the next chapter, you'll be turning your overviews of several games into effective sketches. You'll soon see that certain actions produce similar sketches time after time, resulting in some time-saving patterns. Don't ever become complacent about sketching, however. A useful sketch must reflect the game's task, and sometimes you'll need to render unique twists or variations on standard sketch patterns.

Step 3: Rules

Once you have the basic framework for your sketch, you're ready to record the game's rules. The rules are always listed under the game's opening paragraph, and they're indented in the test booklet so that they're easy to distinguish from the overall setup.

Whenever possible, build a rule directly into the framework of your sketch. When a rule is not specific enough to designate the precise spaces or boxes in which to place the entities, write the rule in shorthand just below or to the side of the sketch. Try to make your shorthand clear and comprehensible, using the same vocabulary of symbols you used to create the sketch framework.

LSAT Question	Analysis

Historical records show that over the course of five consecutive years—601, 602, 603, 604, and 605—a certain emperor began construction of six monuments: F, G, H, L, M, and S. A historian is trying to determine the years in which the individual monuments were begun. The following facts have been established:

    L was begun in a later year than G, but in an earlier year than F.

    H was begun no earlier than 604.

    M was begun earlier than 604.

    Two of the monuments were begun in 601, and no other monument was begun in the same year as any of the other monuments.

PrepTest58 Sec3 Qs1–6

F G H L M S

601	602	603	604	605

$\rightarrow$

~H   ~H   ~H   ~M   ~M

G . . . L . . . F

As you depict the rules, pay careful attention to what each rule determines and what it leaves open. Note how the LSAT expert drew Rule 1 in the monument game, using ellipses to show that G-L-F must conform to the defined sequence but leaving open the possibility that the construction of G may have begun one, two, or three years before that of L. Note too that the LSAT expert found it more concrete to draw the negative implications of Rules 2 and 3 than to write out their affirmative possibilities. It's not clear, for example, whether M was begun in 601, 602, or 603, but it is absolutely certain that you won't place M in 604 or 605. Finally, note that Rule 4 affected the sketch framework rather than any of the entities. Rule 4 is wordy, but its impact on the game is quite clear: two monuments were begun in 601, and one monument was begun in each of the subsequent years.

LSAT STRATEGY

Don't make assumptions in logic games. Any restrictions must be *stated*.

The last rule in the Monuments game is actually very important because it rules out the possibility that there were some years in which no monuments were begun. When they first read the game's opening setup, many test takers assume that every year will see the construction of a new monument. An LSAT expert, on the other hand, realizes that the setup puts no restrictions on the number of monuments that the emperor began in a given year. It is not until the game's final rule that this limitation is determined.

In Chapter 4, you'll have the opportunity to sketch out the rules from games representing each of the common LSAT game types. You'll also have the chance to do drills for further practice.

Step 4: Deductions

This is the step that the majority of untrained or poorly trained LSAT test takers miss. Even students who instinctively appreciate the value of creating a sketch and of symbolizing the rules often don't take the time to determine what must be true or must be false beyond what the rules explicitly state. In most games, however, it is possible to combine the rules with each other or to combine rules with the game's overall limitations in a way that produces a lot more certainty when you go to tackle the questions. It is always highly advantageous—in terms of both speed and accuracy—to make all of the available deductions before moving on to the questions.

In Chapter 4, you'll learn to spot the rules that produce the greatest restrictions within the game. It is not uncommon for a game's initial setup to allow for hundreds (or even thousands) of permutations. After you apply all of the rules, however, there are sometimes only a dozen (or even fewer) permutations that remain acceptable. The more of those restrictions you can see, the easier the game will be for you to work out. By starting from the most concrete rules and seeing how those interact with other rules to further limit the acceptable arrangements within the game, you can produce a final sketch that reveals everything that is determined in the game and shows just how much or how little remains to be locked down.

LSAT Question	Analysis

Historical records show that over the course of five consecutive years—601, 602, 603, 604, and 605—a certain emperor began construction of six monuments: F, G, H, L, M, and S. A historian is trying to determine the years in which the individual monuments were begun. The following facts have been established:

  L was begun in a later year than G, but in an earlier year than F.

  H was begun no earlier than 604.

  M was begun earlier than 604.

  Two of the monuments were begun in 601, and no other monument was begun in the same year as any of the other monuments.

PrepTest58 Sec3 Qs1–6

FGHLMS

601	602	603	604	605
___	___	___	___	___
~H	~H	~H	~M	~M

G . . . L . . . F

Deductions

Rule 1 affects three entities. Its negative implications limit the entities that can go in the earliest and latest years.

Rule 4 makes 601 a crucial year. It takes two of the entities but cannot have H, L, or F.

FGHLMS

GM
GS
MS

601	602	603	604	605
___	___	___	___	___
~H	~H	~H	~M	~M
~F	~F		~G	~G
~L				~L

G . . . L . . . F

Deductions (cont.)

At the other end, since H has to be in 604 or 605 (Rule 2), there's no way to have the G-L-F string in years 603-604-605. That means G cannot have begun in 603 and L cannot have begun in 604. Additionally, the only entity not mentioned in the rules is S. That means that S can float to any available spot. S is marked in the roster of entities above the sketch with an asterisk to indicate that it is a Floater.

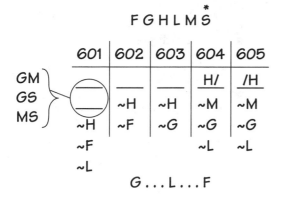

Making all of the available deductions in a game without spending time chasing down dead ends or making unwarranted speculations is a subtle, but enormously important, skill to master. It takes time and practice to perfect, but once you do, you'll be well on your way to mastery of Logic Games.

Fortunately, just five kinds of restrictions produce the lion's share of available deductions in logic games. They're easy to remember with the mnemonic BLEND.

STEP 4: DEDUCTIONS

Blocks of Entities—two or more players who are always grouped together

Limited Options—rules or restrictions that limit the overall setup to one of two acceptable arrangements

Established Entities—a player locked into a specific space or group

Number Restrictions—rules or limitations that provide guidance about the number of entities assigned to a group or space

Duplications—entities that appear in two or more rules and allow the rules to be combined

---

You'll focus on Deductions in Chapter 4, but it's important to note that BLEND is a checklist, not a series of steps. You don't look for Blocks of Entities first necessarily, and not every game will have all of these types of rules or restrictions. Think of it as a way to make sure no available deductions slip through your fingers. The end result of Step 4 is a Master Sketch containing all of the rules, restrictions, and deductions.

Step 5: Questions

The purpose of the first four steps is to answer the game's questions quickly and accurately. You'll have about 8½ minutes per game on Test Day. To get to all of the questions in that short amount of time, the LSAT expert leverages her Master Sketch to save time. Don't be surprised if you spend three or four minutes setting up the game. You'll find that answering the questions can be a quick and confident exercise once you have an adequate Master Sketch.

Here's how the LSAT expert manages the questions from the Monuments game.

LSAT Question	**Analysis**

Historical records show that over the course of five consecutive years—601, 602, 603, 604, and 605—a certain emperor began construction of six monuments: F, G, H, L, M, and S. A historian is trying to determine the years in which the individual monuments were begun. The following facts have been established:
    L was begun in a later year than G, but in an earlier year than F.
    H was begun no earlier than 604.
    M was begun earlier than 604.
    Two of the monuments were begun in 601, and no other monument was begun in the same year as any of the other monuments.	

1. Which one of the following could be an accurate matching of monuments to the years in which they were begun?	→ The right answer is acceptable; each wrong answer violates a rule.
(A) 601: G; 602: L, S; 603: M; 604: H; 605: F	→ Violates Rule 4 by having two monuments begun in 602. Eliminate.
(B) 601: G, M; 602: L; 603: H; 604: S; 605: F	→ Violates Rule 2 by having H begun in 603. Eliminate.
(C) 601: G, M; 602: S; 603: F; 604: L; 605: H	→ Violates Rule 1 by having L begun later than F was. Eliminate.
(D) 601: G, S; 602: L; 603: F; 604: M; 605: H	→ Violates Rule 3 by having M begun in 604. Eliminate.
(E) 601: G, S; 602: L; 603: M; 604: H; 605: F	→ Correct. This one abides by all of the rules.

PrepTest58 Sec3 Q1

Almost every logic game has one of these Acceptability questions, asking for an answer choice that could be an accurate placement of all the entities. The LSAT expert simply checks each rule against the answer choices. This question exhibits a very common pattern: each of the four rules eliminates one of the wrong answer choices. You'll become fast and confident in dealing with Acceptability questions by using the rules to eliminate violators.

LSAT Question	**Analysis**
2. What is the latest year in which L could have been begun?	According to our deductions, construction of L cannot have started later than 603. Rule 1 says F always follows L, and Rule 2 says that H always takes 604 or 605.

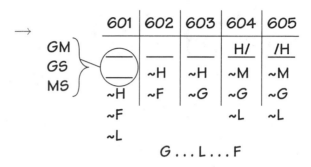

	(A)	601	
	(B)	602	
	(C)	603	→ Correct.
	(D)	604	
	(E)	605	

PrepTest58 Sec3 Q2

Most games offer one or two questions that directly reward you for making the available deductions. Seeing how Rules 1 and 2 combine to restrict L to 602 or 603 makes this one a snap. Always remember that rules and restrictions are your greatest allies in logic games; after all, the test wants to know what must, cannot, or could be true.

LSAT Question	Analysis
3. The years in which each of the monuments were begun can be completely determined if which one of the following is discovered to be true? →	The correct answer will determine each monument's starting date. Information about S will help. S is the one monument not mentioned in the rules, the one that needs pinning down.
(A) F was begun in 603.	This doesn't tell us whether H was begun in 604 and S in 605 or vice versa. Eliminate.

→

601	602	603	604	605
G	L	F	H/S	S/H
M				

(B) G was begun in 602.	This doesn't tell us whether H was begun in 604 and F in 605 or vice versa. Eliminate.

→

601	602	603	604	605
S	G	L	H/F	F/H
M				

(C) H was begun in 605.	This leaves a number of possibilities open. Eliminate.

F G H L M S

→

601	602	603	604	605
				H

G . . . L . . . F

S – ? ? ?

(D) M was begun in 602.	This doesn't tell us whether H was begun in 604 and F in 605 or vice versa. Eliminate.

→

601	602	603	604	605
S	M	L	H/F	F/H
G				

(E) S was begun in 604.	Correct. There's only one way to sequence all six monuments here.

→

601	602	603	604	605
G	L	F	S	H
M				

PrepTest58 Sec3 Q3

You'll likely see only one "completely determine" question on Test Day (and maybe none at all). When you do, keep in mind that the correct answer must add a lot of concreteness to the arrangement. The expert analysis here anticipated that information about S would restrict the pattern enormously. Zeroing in on "likely suspects" will improve your speed and confidence.

LSAT Question	**Analysis**
4. Which one of the following must be true?	The correct answer must be true. That means the four wrong answers could be false. The Master Sketch will reveal which choice must be true.

$$\overset{*}{F\ G\ H\ L\ M\ S}$$

	601	602	603	604	605
GM	⎰ ⎱	—	—	H/	/H
GS	⎬ ⎯⎯	~H	~H	~M	~M
MS	⎱ ~H	~F	~G	~G	~G
	~F			~L	~L
	~L				

$$G \ldots L \ldots F$$

(A) F was begun in a later year than M.	→	Correct. The earliest year for F is 603, and M can never be in 604 or 605.
(B) F was begun in a later year than S.	→	S could take any year, even 605, so F could begin before S. Eliminate.
(C) H was begun in a later year than F.	→	F could take 605, while H could take 604. Eliminate.
(D) H was begun in a later year than S.	→	S could take any year, even 605, while H could take 604. Eliminate.
(E) M was begun in a later year than G.	→	M and G could both take 601, or M could be with S in 601 while G takes 602. Eliminate.

PrepTest58 Sec3 Q4

This question should remind you of the critical thinking practice you did in Chapter 1, "LSAT Reasoning." When you encounter a question like this one on Test Day, remember to characterize the answer choices before you evaluate them. When the right answer must be true, all four wrong answers could be false.

LSAT Question	**Analysis**
5. L must be the monument that was begun in 602 if which one of the following is true?	The correct answer is a statement that forces L into the year 602. L's only options are 602 and 603, so any answer that places a monument other than L in 603 will be correct.

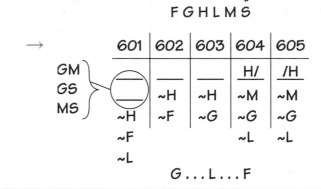

(A) F was begun in 605.

(B) G was begun in 601.

(C) H was begun in 604.

(D) M was begun in 601.

(E) S was begun in 603.   → Correct.

PrepTest58 Sec3 Q5

An LSAT expert never evaluates the choices until she's certain of what the correct choice must contain. Here, the correct answer is a condition that will result in L taking year 602. That question was easy for the expert analyst because she had a fully realized Master Sketch. Imagine how much more time consuming this would have been if we hadn't made all of the deductions up front. Remember this as you're learning to set up games in Chapters 3 and 4. The payoff in quick, easy points comes only from learning to do strong critical reasoning up front.

LSAT Question		**Analysis**

6. If M was begun in a later year than L, then which one of the following could be true?

A new "If" condition needs a new sketch. M can't take 604 or 605, so M after L means that M takes 603, L takes 602, and G and S are pushed up into 601.

→

601	602	603	604	605
G	L	M	H/F	F/H
S				

The only unknown is whether F takes 604 with H in 605 or vice versa.

(A) F was begun in 603. → Must be false—F takes 604 or 605 here. Eliminate.

(B) G was begun in 602. → Must be false—G takes 601 here. Eliminate.

(C) H was begun in 605. → Correct. This could be true.

(D) L was begun in 603. → Must be false—L takes 602 here. Eliminate.

(E) S was begun in 604. → Must be false—S takes 601 here. Eliminate.

PrepTest58 Sec3 Q6

Think of a new "if" condition in a question stem as a rule that applies only to that question. The LSAT expert instinctively responds to new "if" conditions in a question stem by drawing out the basics of the Master Sketch and adding the new restriction. Then, she makes all of the available deductions within this new scenario. It's like a brief repeat of steps 2 through 4 of the Method. Don't try to handle all of this information in your head. It takes a few seconds to copy out the new sketch, but the certainty it provides as you evaluate the answer choices makes it a very good investment of time.

Now that you've seen the Logic Games Method and learned what each step entails, it's time to apply it to the different game types you're most likely to see on Test Day. In Chapter 3, you'll work on Steps 1 and 2, determining what games are asking you to do and setting up solid sketches. In Chapter 4, you'll focus on rules and deductions using the same games found in Chapter 2. Then, in Chapter 5, you'll get the payoff, tackling the questions from those games and learning all of the various question types the LSAT uses. Once you've completed those chapters, Chapter 6 contains a number of full games for you to practice, with complete explanations at the end of the chapter. Chapter 7 finishes off the Logic Games part of this book with a discussion of how best to manage your time in the Logic Games section.

CHAPTER 3

Logic Games: Overviews, Sketches, and Game Types

In the last chapter, you saw a demonstration of how an expert LSAT test taker tackles an entire logic game. But before you're ready to do the same, you need to learn more about each step of the Logic Games Method. Your approach to games should be methodical, consistent, and carefully analytical. As you observed the LSAT expert doing in the last chapter, you'll tackle each piece of information in the game individually before bringing them together into a coherent picture complete with all possible deductions.

LEARNING OBJECTIVES

In this chapter, you'll learn to:

- Characterize a game's action and limitations given various game setups.
- Create a valid sketch based on a game's action and limitations.

These two learning objectives correspond to Steps 1 and 2 of the Kaplan Method for Logic Games. This chapter will define and demonstrate those two steps. But this chapter serves another function as well: because a game can be usefully identified as being one of a certain *type* based on information you glean from the game in Step 1, and because different *types* of games are best served by different types of sketches, we'll teach you how to catalog the various types of games. (Don't worry—there are only a few!)

Thus, this chapter has four components:

First, we'll learn more about Step 1 of the Kaplan Method for Logic Games, and we'll see it applied to a real LSAT game.

Second, we'll discuss Step 2 and its application to the same logic game.

Third, we'll demonstrate the various types of logic games, discuss how to identify them, and apply Steps 1 and 2 of the Logic Games Method to all those game types using examples from real LSATs.

Fourth, you'll get some practice working through Steps 1 and 2 in several drills.

STEP 1 OF THE LOGIC GAMES METHOD: WORKING WITH GAME OVERVIEWS

You saw in the last chapter that a well-developed logic game sketch shows what must be true, must be false, and could be true in the game. You also saw that those determinations of what is true, false, and possible translate directly into points. But before you can make a useful sketch, you have to digest some crucial information in the paragraph that opens the game. Without this important step, your sketch may be incomplete or inaccurate.

We'll call that opening paragraph the "overview," and we mean just this part:

> Individual hour-long auditions will be scheduled for each of six saxophonists—Fujimura, Gabrieli, Herman, Jackson, King, and Lauder. The auditions will all take place on the same day. Each audition will begin on the hour, with the first beginning at 1 P.M. and the last at 6 P.M. The schedule of auditions must conform to the following conditions:

Jackson auditions earlier than Herman does.
Gabrieli auditions earlier than King does.
Gabrieli auditions either immediately before or immediately after Lauder does.
Exactly one audition separates the auditions of Jackson and Lauder.

PrepTest56 Sec1 Qs1–6

(We'll discuss working with the indented statements, or "rules," in depth in the next chapter.)

The SEAL Questions

As you learned in the last chapter, you'll ask four questions when dealing with the overview, and those four questions can be represented with the acronym SEAL:

Situation—What is the real-world scenario being described? What is the deliverable information—an ordered list, a calendar, a chart showing what's matched up?

Entities—Who or what are the "moving parts,"—the people or things I'm distributing, selecting, sequencing, or matching?

Action—What is the specific action—distribution, selection, sequencing, matching, or a combination of those—that I'm performing with the entities?

Limitations—Are there overall limitations (e.g., select four of seven, sequence the entities one per day, etc.) that control how I'll set up the game?

Situation and Entities

Identifying the game's *situation* is important to develop a mental picture of the game and to understand the sketch you ultimately create. Imagine that a logic game asks you to put items in a store in order from highest priced to lowest priced. Some test takers may picture the items on a shelf, running from left to right. Other test takers may picture a list of the items with the most expensive at the top of the list. Whatever your mental picture may be, you're likely to tend to revert to it as you're working through the game, so it makes sense to set it up that way to begin with.

Identifying the game's *entities* is also an important first step. The Overview usually lists these for you. At the outset of each game, make a list composed of the first initials of each entity—like a roster of players in this logic game. Doing so will help you keep them all in mind as you're sketching and making deductions.

LSAT Overview	Analysis
Individual hour-long auditions will be scheduled for each of six saxophonists—Fujimura, Gabrieli, Herman, Jackson, King, and Lauder. The auditions will all take place on the same day. Each audition will begin on the hour, with the first beginning at 1 P.M. and the last at 6 P.M. The schedule of auditions must conform to the following conditions: *PrepTest56 Sec1 Qs1–6*	*Situation:* Some people are auditioning at different times; perhaps it looks like a page from a day-planner with times listed and names by the time slots.* *Entities:* The six saxophonists F, G, H, J, K, L

*It doesn't matter whether you picture the list of time slots going from top to bottom or left to right. Use whichever orientation is most intuitive for you—just be consistent about it throughout a given game.

Actions

Now that you've developed a mental picture of the game and a roster of entities, you're ready to figure out the task. Every game asks you to *do* something, such as to put entities into a sequential order or to sort them into groups. Your task is the game's *action*. There are almost always words and phrases in the overview that signal the action; sometimes those words are verbs, and sometimes they're hints about what the worked-out game will ultimately look like. Consider the following example from a real LSAT:

LSAT Overview	Analysis
Individual hour-long auditions will be scheduled for each of six saxophonists—Fujimura, Gabrieli, Herman, Jackson, King, and Lauder. The auditions will all take place on the same day. Each audition will begin on the hour, with the first beginning at 1 P.M. and the last at 6 P.M. The schedule of auditions must conform to the following conditions: *PrepTest56 Sec1 Qs1–6*	"[W]ill be scheduled" and "schedule"—a sequence of events from earliest to latest Time frames—"first [audition] at 1 P.M." to the final one at 6 P.M.—more evidence of a sequence of events *Action:* Put the saxophonists in sequence from the 1 P.M. audition to the 6 P.M. audition.

Notice how the expert test taker found several clues in the game's overview that helped her identify the action: there was the verb "will be scheduled," a noun describing the final outcome ("[t]he schedule of auditions" in the last sentence), and references to several hours on a single day. We'll learn, when we come to discussing the various types of games, that each one has some characteristic markers (this, for example, is a Sequencing game, and Sequencing games often involve arranging events in chronological order). But keep an eye out for *any* clues that point you toward identifying your task.

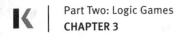
Practice

Imagine that the following statements appeared in logic game overviews. What words or phrases help define your task—the game's action? Circle or underline them. Look both for verbs and for phrases that describe the finished product. Then go to the next page to see the expert test taker's thinking.

Overview Statement	My Analysis
1. Teams of three players each will be chosen from among nine participants in a trivia game.	
2. While shopping, Maria will select four shirts from a rack that contains seven shirts.	
3. Each of four boats docked in a harbor is painted blue, green, or red and no other color.	
4. Each of three friends shopping at a supermarket will choose exactly two of the following items: apples, bananas, carrots, donuts, éclairs, and flour.	

Overview Statement		Analysis
1. Teams of three players each will be chosen from among nine participants in a trivia game.	$\longrightarrow$	Clues: "will be chosen" "Teams of three players each" Task: Sort players into groups of three each.
2. While shopping, Maria will select four shirts from a rack that contains seven shirts.	$\longrightarrow$	Clues: "will select" "four shirts from . . . seven shirts" Task: Figure out which shirts Maria buys and which she doesn't.
3. Each of four boats docked in a harbor is painted blue, green, or red and no other color.	$\longrightarrow$	Clues: "is painted blue, green, or red" Task: Match colors to boats.
4. Each of three friends shopping at a supermarket will choose exactly two of the following items: apples, bananas, carrots, donuts, éclairs, and flour.	$\longrightarrow$	Clues: "Each of three friends . . . will choose" "choose exactly two" Task: Match each person to the products they buy.

Limitations

Some less-than-well-prepared LSAT test takers may be satisfied with pulling only that much information (situation, entities, and action) out of the game's overview. However, there's usually more guidance about how the game works to be gleaned from the overview. We'll call these additional pieces of information *limitations*. Limitations are useful to formulate those point-getting statements about what's true, false, and possible in a game. Think of them as the instructions that come with a board game: without absorbing those, you don't always know the various ways to get points in the game.

Limitations come in two kinds. On the one hand, the overview often gives you some specific instructions about working the game, as in these examples:

- Use one entity per slot (or two or three, etc.).
- Select a specific number of entities out of the original group.
- There are no ties in a ranking of entities.
- Use each entity exactly once (or twice, etc.).

On the other hand, an overview often leaves some gaps in information about how the game works. If the game overview does *not* tell you to use a specific number of the entities, it's important to realize that you don't know how many of them to use (at least until the game's rules narrow down the possibilities). If the game overview does *not* specify that there are no ties in a ranking of entities, then it's important to remember that there might be ties in the game. If you aren't told to put an entity in every slot, then keep in mind you may have open slots. And so on.

In particular, pay attention to numerical limitations as you're examining a game's overview—and pay attention to the way numbers interact with the other instructions (or lack thereof). If you have, for example, five entities and five slots, then you *may* have a one-to-one matchup between entities and slots, but you can't take that for granted unless the overview tells you to use one entity per slot. In the absence of that specification, you may put more than one entity in some slots and leave others blank. Imagine another game in which you are given seven entities and four slots. The careless test taker might assume that some slots will take more than one entity. But you can't assume that unless and until you're told to use all the entities.

You'll get a lot more practice teasing out all varieties of logic game limitations. For starters, consider how the expert LSAT test taker thinks through the Saxophonists game:

LSAT Overview	Analysis
Individual hour-long auditions will be scheduled for each of six saxophonists—Fujimura, Gabrieli, Herman, Jackson, King, and Lauder. The auditions will all take place on the same day. Each audition will begin on the hour, with the first beginning at 1 P.M. and the last at 6 P.M. The schedule of auditions must conform to the following conditions: *PrepTest56 Sec1 Qs1–6*	Specific instructions: "Individual": No two auditioners go in the same slot. "each of six saxophonists": Use all six of the entities. "The auditions will all take place on the same day": Nobody will fall outside this 1 P.M.–6 P.M. time frame. → "Each audition will begin on the hour": No auditions begin at, say, 2:30; in other words, there are exactly six slots. Given six slots and no two entities in the same slot, and given that all entities audition, there's a one-to-one matchup between entities and slots. Gaps in information: Don't know what order the saxophonists go in (after all, that's what the whole game is about), but that's the only unknown.

This game had a fair number of specific instructions and few gaps in information. Not all games work that way. Contrast this game with the one covered in Chapter 2:

LSAT Overview	Analysis
Historical records show that over the course of five consecutive years—601, 602, 603, 604, and 605—a certain emperor began construction of six monuments: F, G, H, L, M, and S. A historian is trying to determine the years in which the individual monuments were begun. The following facts have been established: *PrepTest58 Sec3 Qs1–6*	Task: Figure out the year in which each of six monuments—F, G, H, L, M, S—was begun. This is a Sequencing action, figuring out the order in which construction began. The fact that six monuments were begun over a five-year period means that at least one year saw more than one monument started.

These two games have several characteristics in common: sequential numbered slots, only one kind of entity, and the same type of action (namely Sequencing, putting things in chronological order). But notice the difference in limitations: the Saxophonists game gives us specific instructions that we have a one-to-one match-up between saxophonists and time slots, while the Monuments game gives us more entities than slots and (at least initially) allows us to double up entities or leave years blank. (You may remember that the final rule in the Monuments game closes this loophole, but the testmaker could have chosen not to include that rule and to let the numbers remain less defined. Defining the boundaries of what you do and don't know at the outset is a critical step.)

In summary, the very first thing you should do when you encounter an LSAT logic game is to carefully digest the overview paragraph. Identify the game's situation, entities, action, and limitations. With practice, all of that will take you only a few seconds. Once you've examined the overview, you're ready to make a sketch.

STEP 2 OF THE LOGIC GAMES METHOD: MAKING A SKETCH

You've seen that there's much more to Step 1 of the Kaplan Method for Logic Games than *reading* the overview of a game. You've learned to ask the SEAL questions before moving on from the initial paragraph. Once you're done with the overview, you're going to put those insights to use by making a sketch.

What's the value of a sketch? Keep in mind the ultimate goal of logic games: to answer questions asking for what must be true, could be true, and must be false in the game. After working through the rules of any given logic game, you'll make deductions about what is true, false, and possible. A sketch is an efficient way to record and retrieve those deductions; in fact, it's a schema of everything true, false, and possible in the game. A well-defined sketch, complete with deductions, will make the process of answering questions faster and easier.

You may be wondering: Why make a sketch at this point, rather than after you've read the rules? After all, you'll have lots more information about how the game works after you've read all the rules. The reason is that as you work through those rules, you're going to want to interpret them in relation to an underlying framework, and that framework is your sketch. You'll often build information from the rules directly into your sketch, and when you can't, you'll note the rules in a shorthand that makes sense in light of the game's framework. Think of the sketch as being like a skeleton and the rules as muscles; the rules (muscles) need to attach to the sketch (skeleton) in order to work.

The next step is learning how to make a sketch. You'll learn that each of the different types of games works best with a particular type of sketch, and you'll develop a mental library of those sketch types. But first, note the principles of good sketches.

A sketch must be (1) easy to read, (2) quick to replicate, and (3) able to accommodate some ambiguity (for cases in which the game's framework contains uncertainties). Your sketch needs to be easy to read because you will be referring to it repeatedly as you're answering questions. Your sketch should also be built so that you can replicate it quickly because you're going to make a new sketch for some questions (those that give you additional restrictions; you'll learn about these in Chapter 5). Finally, your sketch needs to be able to accommodate some ambiguity because you're never going to determine the placement of all the entities in your initial sketch. You may deduce, for example, that entity A will go in either slot 3 or slot 5, but not in both.

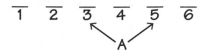

Or you may find that a certain group contains four *or* five members.

Team Red	Team Blue
— —	— —
— —	— —
(—)	

Or you may find that a group may have more than two members, but you don't know how many more.

	≥2	
Team A	Team B	Team C
—	—	—
—	—	—
—	(—)	—
—	(—)	

You'll want some way to capture those areas of uncertainty in your sketch.

LSAT STRATEGY

A Few Notes on Logic Game Sketches:

- Make sure your sketch is (1) easy to read, (2) quick to replicate, and (3) able to accommodate some ambiguity.
- Throughout this book, you'll see a library of sketch types and a standard notation for turning rules into shorthand. You don't have to use Kaplan's notation or sketches, but the explanations will use this notation, and you'll use the explanations to analyze practice problems.
- The Kaplan notation is pretty intuitive: even if you don't use it yourself, you will likely be able to read and understand it in a logic games explanation.
- Try to keep your shorthand and your sketches clear, consistent, and easy to read—*for you*. Check to see that you can return to a game you've worked on and understand the limitations and restrictions based on your shorthand rules and sketches. Use the same type of sketches for games of the same type and similar notation for similar rules.
- Position your Master Sketch on the page so that it is large enough to be readable but not so large that you don't have any room to write down rules underneath or off to the side.
- Here's some good news: Recently, the LSAT began printing each logic game on two pages instead of one. This new format leaves much more room underneath the game overview for sketching. Because the change is so recent, though, most of the practice LSAT games you'll encounter will still be all on one page. Just be aware that you'll likely have more space on the page on Test Day.

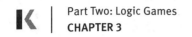

Let's begin our study of sketches by using the same game we have been working with so far. Here, to refresh your memory, is our expert test taker's work on Step 1 of the Logic Games Method:

LSAT Overview	Analysis
Individual hour-long auditions will be scheduled for each of six saxophonists—Fujimura, Gabrieli, Herman, Jackson, King, and Lauder. The auditions will all take place on the same day. Each audition will begin on the hour, with the first beginning at 1 P.M. and the last at 6 P.M. The schedule of auditions must conform to the following conditions: *PrepTest56 Sec1 Qs1–6* $\longrightarrow$	**Step 1:** *Situation:* people auditioning at different times; picture times listed and names by the time slots *Entities:* F, G, H, J, K, L *Action:* Put the saxophonists in sequence from the 1 P.M. audition to the 6 P.M. audition. *Limitations:* "Individual": No two auditioners go in the same slot.
	"[E]ach of six saxophonists": Use all six of the entities. "The auditions will all take place on the same day": Nobody will fall outside this 1 P.M.–6 P.M. time frame. "Each audition will begin on the hour": No auditions begin at, say, 2:30; in other words, we only have six slots. Given six slots and no two entities in the same slot, and given that all entities audition, there is a one-to-one matchup between entities and slots.

The first step in making *any* sketch is to create a roster of entities. Next, consider what the framework should look like. Our mental picture is one of time slots into which we'll pencil the saxophonists (once we figure out who goes where), and our limitations tell us that we have a one-to-one match-up between slots and entities. Thus, it makes perfect sense to simply draw out those slots and put the times under or next to them:

LSAT Overview	Analysis
Individual hour-long auditions will be scheduled for each of six saxophonists—Fujimura, Gabrieli, Herman, Jackson, King, and Lauder. The auditions will all take place on the same day. Each audition will begin on the hour, with the first beginning at 1 P.M. and the last at 6 P.M. The schedule of auditions must conform to the following conditions: *PrepTest56 Sec1 Qs1–6*	**Step 2:** F G H J K L 1 2 3 4 5 6

You could also draw the slots in order vertically. Whichever orientation makes the most intuitive sense to you is fine. Just be consistent about it throughout the game.

Now, measure this sketch against the criteria for good sketches. First, it's easy to read. If we determine when some or all of the saxophonists audition, we can easily slot them in. Second, given its simplicity, it will be quick to replicate. Third, it can accommodate ambiguity. If we learned, for example, that either J or K auditions at 2 P.M., we can write something like "J/K" above slot 2. Take another example: if we learned that F auditions at either 3 P.M. or 5 P.M., our sketch gives us room to incorporate that (perhaps by putting F above or below our sketch, with arrows pointing to those two times).

You'll get to see the rest of this game worked out from start to finish, including its questions and answers, in Chapters 4 and 5. But before you tackle rules and deductions, it will be helpful for you to get familiar with the various types of games and see Steps 1 and 2 of the Logic Games Method applied to all those types of games. You'll have an opportunity for practice throughout the following sections and at the end of this chapter.

GAME TYPES

When we say there are a limited number of game types, we really mean there are a limited number of *actions* in logic games. Game types are defined by actions because once you have identified a game's action, you have a good sense of the limitations you should look out for, and you also have a pretty good idea of what your sketch will look like.

Sequencing Games

The Saxophonists game, as well as the Monuments game you saw in Chapter 2, are *Sequencing* games. Sequencing games are the most common type of LSAT game: over 50 percent of logic games on the LSAT in the last five years have been Sequencing games, and you're highly likely to see one or more on your LSAT on Test Day.

> ## LSAT STRATEGY
>
> Sequencing games ask you to put things in order
>
> - Chronologically (either using units of time—such as years, days, weeks, or the hours in the example above—or else simply using the ideas of "earlier" and "later")
> - Spatially (either vertically or horizontally; imagine runners about to run a race taking their places in numbered lanes or, on the other hand, a tall cake with different layers, one on top of another)
> - By rank (similar to a top ten list)
> - By size or amount (imagine a list of prices from cheapest to most expensive)

So, in general, the clues buried in the overview that point you toward identifying a game as a Sequencing game will suggest one of those types of ordering. There are lots of possible clues, but consider how the following clues hint at Sequencing:

  Amount-related hints: greater, less, cheaper

Your sketch for a Sequencing game will usually be slots with numbers (arranged either vertically or horizontally), just like our sketches for the Monuments game in Chapter 2 and for the Saxophonists game above.

Similarly, the limitations to look out for in Sequencing games are usually related to how many entities can go into each of the slots: sometimes you'll have a one-to-one match-up, and sometimes the numbers will be less well defined.

A Note About Loose Sequencing

There's one type of Sequencing game in which your sketch will look different from those we've been making so far, and that's a *Loose Sequencing* game. (By the way, we'll refer to Sequencing games that aren't "loose" as *Strict*

Sequencing games.) Before we address the question of how Loose Sequencing games differ from Strict Sequencing games, let's first clarify how they're similar:

In other words, the ultimate task is very much the same.

However, here's the difference: in Strict Sequencing games, the rules (remember, those are the indented statements beneath the overview paragraph) will affirmatively relate the entities to the underlying framework in some way. Here are some examples of this type of rule:

Each of those rules involves not just the order of the entities but also the number of slots between them or the specific slots they must fill or avoid. A game that gives you at least some rules of this type is a *Strict Sequencing* game.

Some rules, however, involve only entities and relate those entities only to each other. Consider these examples:

Notice that none of these rules relate the entities to the underlying framework of numbered slots. That means it would be very hard to work them into a sketch based on numbered slots. Some LSAT logic games give you *only* rules of this type, and those games are *Loose Sequencing* games. (Note: You may, in Loose Sequencing, see a rule that relates entities to spaces negatively—for example, "W is not seventh"—but you won't see rules that affirmatively tie entities to particular spaces or that dictate a set number of spaces to appear between entities.) When you meet a Loose Sequencing game, you'll end up with a sketch that relates the entities to each other without relating them to numbered slots. The Loose Sequencing sketch will come out of the rules, rather than the overview. Take a look at the following example:

LSAT Overview	Analysis
Workers at a water treatment plant open eight valves—G, H, I, K, L, N, O, and P—to flush out a system of pipes that needs emergency repairs. To maximize safety and efficiency, each valve is opened exactly once, and no two valves are opened at the same time. The valves are opened in accordance with the following conditions: *PrepTest52 Sec2 Qs1–7*	**Step 1:** *Situation:* Opening valves at a plant: perhaps the mental picture is one of a worker's to-do list. *Entities:* Valves G, H, I, K, L, N, O, P *Action:* "[N]o two valves are opened at the same time": chronology is important; a Sequencing game *Limitations:* Specific instructions: "each valve is opened exactly once": No reuse of any entity "no two valves are opened at the same time": No slots with more than one entity in them; in other words, a one-to-one matchup between slots and entities Gaps in information: The instructions of the game are well defined.

So far, this is a Sequencing game quite similar to the Saxophonists game. And we could make a sketch with numbered slots for it. But suppose that the expert test taker quickly runs her eye down the list of rules and notices that they're all of the Loose Sequencing variety—that is, they give only the relative order among entities, with no mention of specific spaces or the number of spaces between any two entities. In that case, she may choose to draw a sketch that simply relates the entities to each other. Here is the game complete with rules, and here is the sketch our expert test taker draws based on them:

LSAT Overview	Analysis

LSAT Overview

Workers at a water treatment plant open eight valves—G, H, I, K, L, N, O, and P—to flush out a system of pipes that needs emergency repairs. To maximize safety and efficiency, each valve is opened exactly once, and no two valves are opened at the same time. The valves are opened in accordance with the following conditions:

    Both K and P are opened before H.
    O is opened before L but after H.
    L is opened after G.
    N is opened before H.
    I is opened after K.

PrepTest52 Sec2 Qs1–7

Analysis

Step 2: All rules relate entities to each other, with no mention of slots or the number of spaces between entities.

Rule 1:

Rule 2: Note that H is already in the sketch.

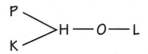

Rule 3: Note that L is already in the sketch.

→
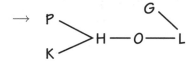

Rule 4: Note that H is already in the sketch.

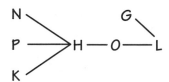

Rule 5: Note that K is already in the sketch.

N
                    G
P ——→ H — O —→ L
K
      I

LSAT Overview	Analysis

You could also draw the diagram like this:

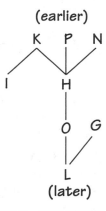

Notice how the expert test taker built each Loose Sequencing rule onto the ones that came before that. In other games, it may be best to digest each rule individually. You'll learn more about the skills of combining rules, and get some practice on it, in Chapter 4. For now, simply note that the finished sketch displays relationships among all of the entities without putting them into slots. The expert test taker has used straight lines to indicate that an entity must come after another. (Note: As always, you could make this sketch vertical or horizontal. Use the orientation that's more intuitive for you and be consistent about it throughout the game.)

Many LSAT games blend both strict and loose elements. Sometimes, you'll make an initial sketch with numbered slots, work some of the entities directly into that sketch, and also create a mini-tree relating two or three entities to each other until you can place them into the line of numbered slots.

It takes a glance at the rules to know whether a Sequencing game is Strict or Loose. As you practice additional games, it will become second nature to quickly check whether the rules mention specific slots and numbers of spaces (Strict), or whether they designate *only* the relative positions among the entities (Loose). Don't sweat it if you jot down a Strict sketch only to discover that a Loose arrangement will work better for the game you're solving. Additionally, you will find that some Loose Sequencing questions give strict "If" conditions that require you to make a new sketch with slots for that question only. You'll cover questions like that in Chapter 5. For now, just remember that the LSAT expert will distinguish between Strict and Loose Sequencing and use the appropriate sketch in each case.

Because the distinction between Strict and Loose Sequencing is driven by the nature of the rules you're given, we'll talk more about it in Chapter 4. In the meantime, assume that the games you meet below in the practice section are all Strict Sequencing and make sketches accordingly.

Practice

In each of the following examples, apply Steps 1 and 2 of the Logic Games Method. That is, identify the situation, entities, action, and limitations and make a simple sketch, complete with a roster of entities up at the top. Pay particular attention to the clues that tell you that you're dealing with a Sequencing game. You can check the next page at any time to see the expert analysis.

Overview	My Analysis
5. A newspaper editor will rank the top five college football teams (A, B, C, D, and E) from first to fifth, and there are no ties.	
6. A teacher is assigning the front row of seats in her class according to the age of six students (A, B, C, D, E, and F). There are six seats in the front row. The youngest student will sit on the far left and the oldest student will sit on the far right.	

Here's how the expert test taker approaches the setups you just saw:

Overview	Analysis
5. A newspaper editor will rank the top five college football teams (A, B, C, D, and E) from first to fifth, and there are no ties.	**Step 1:** *Situation:* An editor is ranking teams. *Entities:* The five college football teams (A, B, C, D, E) *Action:* There are five teams, and the editor is going to "rank" them from first to fifth. Because order matters, this is a *Sequencing* game. → *Limitations:* "[T]here are no ties," so the editor will place each of the five teams in a separate spot. **Step 2:** Write out dashes for each of the five possible ranking spots; then place the entities above the sketch.

$$\begin{array}{ccccc} A & B & C & D & E \\ \overline{} & \overline{} & \overline{} & \overline{} & \overline{} \\ 1 & 2 & 3 & 4 & 5 \end{array}$$

Overview	Analysis
6. A teacher is assigning the front row of seats in her class according to the age of six students (A, B, C, D, E, and F). There are six seats in the front row. The youngest student will sit on the far left and the oldest student will sit on the far right.	**Step 1:** *Situation:* A classroom with a row of seats *Entities:* The six students (A, B, C, D, E, F) *Action:* The teacher is putting students "in the front row," and some students are younger and some are older. Because the task here is to order the students according to their age, this is a *Sequencing* game. → *Limitations:* Students won't sit on top of each other, so each seat will be assigned one student. **Step 2:** In addition to setting up a standard Sequencing sketch, it will be important to signify which end of the row is the youngest and which is the oldest.

$$\text{(Youngest)}\quad\begin{array}{cccccc} A & B & C & D & E & F \\ \overline{} & \overline{} & \overline{} & \overline{} & \overline{} & \overline{} \\ 1 & 2 & 3 & 4 & 5 & 6 \end{array}\quad\text{(Oldest)}$$

Reflection

Take a look back at your practice. Did you answer the SEAL questions for each game prior to setting up a sketch for it? Did you set up each sketch based on your knowledge of the game's central action? Were your sketches easy to read, quick to replicate, and able to accommodate ambiguity? What have you learned from this exercise?

Over the coming days, take note of real-life Sequencing tasks—scheduling, ranking, prioritizing. Try to envision how the testmaker could create logic games and the types of rules and restrictions the LSAT would need to impose.

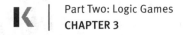

Selection Games

We've mentioned that Sequencing games are the most common type of LSAT game. Another game type that has been fairly common in recent years (though its frequency pales in comparison to that of Sequencing) is *Selection*: 10 percent of games on LSATs over the last five years have been of this type. A Selection game gives you a group of entities and asks you to choose some of those entities to make a smaller group. Let's see that process in action in this example from a real LSAT by applying Step 1 of the Method to this game:

LSAT Overview	Analysis
A company organizing on-site day care consults with a group of parents composed exclusively of volunteers from among the seven employees—Felicia, Leah, Masatomo, Rochelle, Salman, Terry, and Veena—who have become parents this year. The composition of the volunteer group must be consistent with the following: *PrepTest58 Sec3 Q7–12*	**Step 1**: *Situation:* Formation of a group of volunteers *Entities*: F, L, M, R, S, T, V *Action:* Clues about the action: "The composition of the volunteer group": Figure out who is in the volunteer group. "[A] group . . . from among the seven": The group will come from the larger group we're given in this overview. Task: Select some people from those seven to be the volunteers. *Limitations:* Specific instructions: "[C]omposed exclusively of volunteers": No entities other than these will be used.* Gaps in information: How many volunteers to select? At this point, we could select all or none or anywhere in between.

*By the way, with this limitation, the LSAT is merely making sure you're clear about the fact that you can't bring in entities from the outside. In other words, you can't invent volunteers named Wanda, Joe, and Nala. However, you can't ever do that in a logic game; you'll always work with only the entities you're given.

You can spot the action in Selection games by looking for verbs that suggest it, such as *select*, *choose*, or *pick*. Those words may or may not be present, but Selection can also be signaled by any clues that suggest that some entities are *in* and some are *out*. Consider the following situations:

In all of these situations, some entities are in and some are out. That's the hallmark of a Selection game.

Since Selection games involve choosing a smaller group from a larger group, you can probably imagine why numbers are important in these games. Key limitations to look out for involve the number of entities to select, but keep in mind that there are often gaps in information. When you are not given a minimum or maximum number in the overview, expect the game's questions to ask about those numbers.

Selection sketches can be very simple, and, like all logic games sketches, they should be informed by your own mental picture formed when you first identified the situation. When you imagined yourself picking volunteers in the example above, what did you see? Did you imagine creating a list of who is chosen? Or simply writing down all the entities and circling some? Did you imagine creating two lists: one for "in" and one for "out"? Any of those approaches works. However, our recommendation is to keep it as simple as possible: write out your roster of entities, circle the ones you deduce are selected, and cross out the ones you deduce are excluded. We'll be using that type of sketch throughout our Selection games examples in this book, like this:

LSAT Overview	Analysis
A company organizing on-site day care consults with a group of parents composed exclusively of volunteers from among the seven employees—Felicia, Leah, Masatomo, Rochelle, Salman, Terry, and Veena—who have become parents this year. The composition of the volunteer group must be consistent with the following: *PrepTest58 Sec3 Q7–12*	**Step 2:** → F L M R S T V

Practice

In each of the following examples, apply Steps 1 and 2 of the Logic Games Method. Pay particular attention to the clues that tell you that these are Selection games. You can check the following page at any time to see the expert thinking.

Overview	My Analysis
7. Each of the seven members of a fraternity—A, B, C, D, E, F, and G—is deciding whether or not to go to the football game this weekend.	
8. A chef is making soup using exactly five ingredients. She chooses from among four types of spices (A, B, C, and D), three types of meat (e, f, and g), and three vegetables (H, I, and J).	

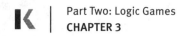
Here's how the expert test taker approaches the setups you just saw:

Overview	Analysis
7. Each of the seven members of a fraternity—A, B, C, D, E, F, and G—is deciding whether or not to go to the football game this weekend.	**Step 1:** *Situation:* A group of people deciding whether or not to attend an event *Entities:* The seven fraternity members (A, B, C, D, E, F, G) *Action:* The only action is to figure out who is going to the game and who is not, so this must be a *Selection* game. *Limitations:* Right now, anywhere from zero to seven fraternity members could go to the game. The rules will add restrictions. **Step 2:** The sketch for a Selection game is simply the list of entities. A B C D E F G
8. A chef is making soup using exactly five ingredients. She chooses from among four types of spices (A, B, C, and D), three types of meat (e, f, and g), and three vegetables (H, I, and J).	**Step 1:** *Situation:* A chef in a kitchen, picking ingredients for a soup *Entities:* The various ingredients—four types of spices (A, B, C, D), three types of meat (e, f, g), and three types of vegetables (H, I, J). *Action:* Selection—pick 5 out of 10 possible ingredients. *Limitations:* No limits on the number of spices, meats, or vegetables the chef must use. Expect the rules to add restrictions along these lines. **Step 2:** This is a Selection game, so the sketch can be a list of the entities. However, because the entities are sorted into groups, differentiate those groups in the sketch.

(pick 5 of 10)

spices	meats	veggies
A B C D	e f g	H I J

Reflection

Take a look back at your practice. Did you answer the SEAL questions for each game prior to setting up a sketch for it? Did you set up each sketch based on your knowledge of the game's central action? Were your sketches easy to read, quick to replicate, and able to accommodate ambiguity? What have you learned from this exercise?

Over the coming days, spot the Selection tasks you encounter in everyday life—choosing what to serve for dinner or whom to invite for a get-together, for example. How would the testmaker turn each of them into a logic game? What sort of rules or restrictions would apply?

Matching Games

So now we've seen Sequencing and Selection games, and all of the examples we've seen so far for both of those game types involved just one type of entity (e.g. saxophonists or volunteers). However, some LSAT games present you with two types of entities and ask you to match them to each other. *Matching* games represent about 12 percent of games on LSATs over the last five years. Take a look at the following example from a recent LSAT:

LSAT Overview	Analysis
An artisan has been hired to create three stained glass windows. The artisan will use exactly five colors of glass: green, orange, purple, rose, and yellow. Each color of glass will be used at least once, and each window will contain at least two different colors of glass. The windows must also conform to the following conditions: *PrepTest62 Sec3 Qs7–13*	**Step 1:** *Situation:* Making stained glass windows; the mental picture could be of the artisan sorting piles of glass for use in each window. *Entities:* Two types of entities: the windows (which aren't given names, so call them 1, 2, 3) and the colors G, O, P, R, Y *Action:* First, look for clues: "[E]ach window will contain at least two different colors of glass": A small set of things (the windows) take on attributes (the colors). Task: Figure out which colors each of the windows has. → *Limitations:* Buried rules: "The artisan will use exactly five colors of glass": He'll use all five colors and no fewer. "Each color of glass will be used at least once": All the colors will be used. "[E]ach window will contain at least two different colors of glass": Establishes a minimum number of colors for each window. Gaps in information: No maximum number of colors to use in each window, so each window can have between two and five colors. No cap on how many times we can use each color. Expect rules to add restrictions on these questions.

Notice how the expert test taker spotted that this was a Matching game: the fact that there is more than one type of entity is one good clue, and the fact that we're linking them in some way is another. Often in Matching games, one of the types of entities will be attributes that the other type of entity takes on. Here, the windows take on colors. Frequently, members of one entity type can be used more than once, as in this game, where the overview gives us no indication that any one color could be "used up."

Limitations to watch out for in Matching games frequently relate to numbers—or the lack thereof. In this game, we were given a minimum number of colors to use in each window but no maximum. Also, it was important for our expert test taker to remain aware that she may be able to use each color multiple times. Pay close attention, in each Matching game you encounter, to limitations related to repeating entities and numbers.

Now let's consider a sketch. What did you see in your mind while asking yourself the SEAL questions? As with most types of logic games, there's more than one way to make a workable Matching sketch. Once again, the best course is to keep your sketch as simple and flexible as possible. In this case, create three columns—one for each of the windows. That allows you to list colors beneath each column header as you deduce the matches. Don't forget to begin with a roster of entities across the top of your sketch.

LSAT Overview	**Analysis**
An artisan has been hired to create three stained glass windows. The artisan will use exactly five colors of glass: green, orange, purple, rose, and yellow. Each color of glass will be used at least once, and each window will contain at least two different colors of glass. The windows must also conform to the following conditions: *PrepTest62 Sec3 Qs7–13*	**Step 2:** G O P R Y (at least once each) 1 | 2 | 3 ——— | ——— | ——— ——— | ——— | ———

Notice that the sketch is easy to read and replicate, thanks to its simplicity. It's also capable of expressing ambiguity: if you were to deduce, for example, that green and rose are found together in either one or two of the windows, this sketch gives room to express that in any one of a number of ways. You may be wondering how the expert decided to put the windows across the top rather than the colors. A sketch will be much easier to work with if it is anchored by the most concrete entity. This game has exactly three windows but unknown numbers of greens, oranges, roses, etc. Hence, it makes the most sense to keep the windows at the top of the columns in our sketch and write in deductions and uncertainties regarding the colors.

Alternatively, some students find grids intuitive for Matching games. Here's how we'd set up the same game using a grid:

LSAT Overview	**Analysis**

An artisan has been hired to create three stained glass windows. The artisan will use exactly five colors of glass: green, orange, purple, rose, and yellow. Each color of glass will be used at least once, and each window will contain at least two different colors of glass. The windows must also conform to the following conditions:

PrepTest62 Sec3 Qs7–13

Step 2:

→

1	2	3	
			G
			O
			P
			R
			Y

(use each at least once)

That sketch is also easy to read. It would take slightly longer to replicate, but that's a trade-off you may choose to make if you find it more intuitive. Just be sure that you have a way to notate ambiguity, since this type of sketch makes it somewhat more difficult to build in ambiguous deductions. For example, if you deduce that green and rose go together in one or two of the windows, note that off to the side in very clear shorthand.

Practice

Apply Steps 1 and 2 of the Logic Games Method to the following examples. Pay particular attention to the words and phrases that indicate that each game is a Matching game. You can turn the page at any time to see the expert thinking.

Overview	**My Analysis**

9. Four friends—A, B, C, and D—meet for dinner at a restaurant. There are five items on the menu—e, f, g, h, and i—and each person will order either 2 or 3 items.

10. Three buildings (A, B, and C) sit next to each other on a city block, and each building has three floors. On each floor, the lights are either on or off.

Here's how the expert test taker approaches the examples you just worked with:

Overview	Analysis
9. Four friends—A, B, C, and D—meet for dinner at a restaurant. There are five items on the menu—e, f, g, h, and i—and each person will order either 2 or 3 items.	**Step 1:** *Situation:* Friends at a restaurant, ordering items off a menu *Entities:* The four friends (A, B, C, D) and the five menu items (e, f, g, h, i) *Action:* Because we're matching menu items to the people at the restaurant and because menu items are not "used up" if they get selected, this must be a Matching game. *Limitations:* Each person is going to select a minimum of 2 and a maximum of 3 menu items, and the items are not exhaustible (multiple friends can select the same menu item).

→ *Limitations:* Each person is going to select a minimum of 2 and a maximum of 3 menu items, and the items are not exhaustible (multiple friends can select the same menu item).

Step 2: Matching games can be set up either as a table or as a grid.

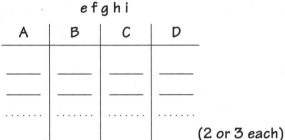

e f g h i

A	B	C	D
—	—	—	—
—	—	—	—
...	...	...	...

(2 or 3 each)

Or

	A	B	C	D
e				
f				
g				
h				
i				

Overview	Analysis
10. Three buildings (A, B, and C) sit next to each other on a city block, and each building has three floors. On each floor, the lights are either on or off.	**Step 1:** *Situation:* Buildings on a street, and some of the floors have their lights on. Envision standing on the opposite side of the street, looking at the building and noting which floors have lights on or off.

Entities: The three buildings (A, B, C) and the three floors of each building

Action: The positions of the buildings and floors are set—no Sequencing element. Rather, assign each floor a designation of "lights on" or "lights off"— this is a Matching game.

Limitations: Each floor will either have its lights on or off—there is no in-between designation, such as "partially on" or "mostly on."

→ **Step 2:** Set up this Matching game in a grid because each building has exactly three floors. In the box for each individual floor, write "on" or "off" (or "✓" or "✗").

	A	B	C
3			
2			
1			

Reflection

Take a look back at your practice. Did you answer the SEAL questions for each game prior to setting up a sketch for it? Did you set up each sketch based on your knowledge of the game's central action? Were your sketches easy to read, quick to replicate, and able to accommodate ambiguity? What have you learned from this exercise?

In the coming days, take note of real-life Matching tasks. What kinds of restrictions apply ("Ushers will wear black and groomsmen wear green," for example)? How would the LSAT turn these into logic games? What sorts of restrictions would the testmaker need to articulate?

Distribution Games

There are four actions the LSAT might task you with on Test Day, and we've now met three of them: Sequencing, Selection, and Matching. The only remaining single-action game type is *Distribution*. In recent years, Distribution has been rare, representing less than 10 percent of logic games over the past five years. Distribution games give you a larger group of entities and ask you to sort them into more than one smaller group (most often, two or three subgroups). Consider the following example from a real LSAT:

LSAT Overview	Analysis
On a field trip to the Museum of Natural History, each of six children—Juana, Kyle, Lucita, Salim, Thanh, and Veronica—is accompanied by one of three adults—Ms. Margoles, Mr. O'Connell, and Ms. Podorski. Each adult accompanies exactly two of the children, consistent with the following conditions: *PrepTest52 Sec2 Qs8–12*	**Step 1:** *Situation:* A field trip: perhaps the mental picture is one of little groups forming in the lobby of the museum. *Entities:* Six children: J, K, L, S, T, V *Action:* Look for clues: "[E]ach of six children . . . is accompanied by one" adult: children grouped by chaperone. "Each adult accompanies exactly two of the children": Results in three groups of one adult and two children. *Task:* Distribute the children evenly into those three groups. *Limitations:* Specific instructions: "[E]ach of six children": No unaccompanied children "[A]ccompanied by one of three adults": No child will be accompanied by more than one adult. "Each adult accompanies exactly two of the children": Gives us a firm number for our groups. The numerical restrictions tell us that we'll use each child once and sort them into three groups of two each. *Gaps in information:* The numbers and rules of the game are very well defined here.

$\longrightarrow$

Notice how the LSAT expert discerned that this was a Distribution game: she homed in on the verb "accompanies" and the overview's description of three groups of two. Other examples of Distribution tasks might include the following:

The formation of groups is the key task in each of these.

This task is different from that in a Selection game, where you are given a larger group and asked to choose a single, smaller group. In Distribution games, you are asked to sort the entities into two or more smaller groups (and to use all of them in doing so). In most Distribution games, each entity is placed only one time—if Kyle is chaperoned by Ms. Podorski, that's that; he's not chaperoned by Mr. O'Connell too. Notice how that distinguishes Distribution from Matching—in the Stained-Glass Windows game, rose might be used in Windows 1 and 3, or purple might be used in all three windows.

Key limitations to watch out for in Distribution games relate to numbers: How large will the groups be? (You may or may not be told.) Is each group required to have members? (It could be that some groups are empty.) Are groups required to contain certain types of individuals? (This might happen if the entities are divided to represent people of two different professions, for example, with a restriction such as "each committee will be assigned at least one physician").

Now that we have answered the SEAL questions for the Museum Chaperone game, it's time to make a sketch. Given that we're simply making groups, each one anchored by one of the adults in the game, let's make short columns headed by the adults. Because we know that each group contains two children, we can draw in two slots for each group (something we wouldn't do if we didn't know how many members each group had).

LSAT Overview	Analysis
On a field trip to the Museum of Natural History, each of six children—Juana, Kyle, Lucita, Salim, Thanh, and Veronica—is accompanied by one of three adults—Ms. Margoles, Mr. O'Connell, and Ms. Podorski. Each adult accompanies exactly two of the children, consistent with the following conditions: *PrepTest52 Sec2 Qs8–12*	**Step 2:** J K L S T V Mar | O'Con | Pod ___ | ___ | ___ ___ | ___ | ___

This is our recommended sketch for Distribution games: a set of columns headed by the name of each group or team—easy to read, quick to replicate, and able to accommodate ambiguity.

Now, you may have noticed that the sketch for our Distribution game looks very similar to our sketch for the Matching game we saw a few pages ago. That's true: The recommended sketches look the same. And you may also have noticed the similarity in the task: as you're working each game, you create a list of entities under each column heading. The key difference is conceptual: think of a Distribution game as similar to putting individuals on teams, while a Matching game is more like assigning attributes to individuals. However, whether you mentally label a game as Matching or Distribution is relatively unimportant, provided you understand the game, your task, and the limitations you're given in the overview and provided that your sketch is clear and accurate.

Practice

In each of the following examples, apply Steps 1 and 2 of the Logic Games Method to each. Pay particular attention to the clues that signal that you're looking at a Distribution game. You can check the following pages at any time to see the expert analysis.

Overview	**My Analysis**

11. Each of the seven members of a sorority—A, B, C, D, E, F, and G—is deciding whether to attend tonight's basketball game or tonight's volleyball game. Each member will attend exactly one of the games.

12. Each of exactly eight movies—H, I, J, K, L, M, N, and O—will be shown in only one of three theaters. Each theater must show at least two of the movies.

Here's how the expert test taker discerns the action in those game setups you just saw:

Overview	Analysis
11. Each of the seven members of a sorority—A, B, C, D, E, F, and G—is deciding whether to attend tonight's basketball game or tonight's volleyball game. Each member will attend exactly one of the games.	**Step 1:** *Situation:* Individual sorority members are deciding which game to go to. *Entities:* The seven members of the sorority (A, B, C, D, E, F, G) *Action:* Separate the women into two groups: those going to the basketball game and those going to the volleyball game; because a woman cannot go to both games at the same time, this is a *Distribution* game, not a *Matching* game. *Limitations:* No limitations on the number of women going to either the volleyball game or the basketball game; it's possible they all go to one of the games together, or they could split up with some going to the volleyball game and others going to the basketball game. (Expect the rules to provide further restrictions here.) **Step 2:** Sketch: Columns representing the two different games; underneath each column, add the women going to that game.

$$A\ B\ C\ D\ E\ F\ G$$

Volley	Basket

Overview	Analysis
12. Each of exactly eight movies—H, I, J, K, L, M, N, and O—will be shown in only one of three theaters. Each theater must show at least two of the movies.	**Step 1:** *Situation:* Figuring out which movies are playing in which theaters *Entities:* The eight movies (H, I, J, K, L, M, N, O). *Action:* Assign the movies to the different theaters. Because each movie will be shown in only one theater, this is a *Distribution* game, not a Matching game. *Limitations:* Eight movies and three theaters, with each theater showing at least two movies; that must mean at least one and possibly two theaters show more than two movies. $\longrightarrow$ **Step 2:** There are three "groups" in which to place entities, with a minimum number restriction on each group.

$$\text{H I J K L M N O}$$

Theat 1	Theat 2	Theat 3
___	___	___
___	___	___
....	....	....
....	....	....

Reflection

Take a look back at your practice. Did you answer the SEAL questions for each game prior to setting up a sketch for it? Did you set up each sketch based on your knowledge of the game's central action? Were your sketches easy to read, quick to replicate, and able to accommodate ambiguity? What have you learned from this exercise?

Over the coming days, take note of real-life Distribution tasks. What sorts of restrictions do you notice (e.g., "Each team has the same number of players," "Each committee must have at least one person from the finance division and one from the marketing team")? How would the LSAT testmaker turn these into logic games? What additional rules or limitations would the testmaker have to add?

Hybrid Games

You've now seen examples of each of the actions you might see in LSAT games. There's one more way the LSAT can construct a game's central task—by combining in a single game two (or sometimes three) of the actions discussed above. There is usually one Hybrid game on any given LSAT (though some tests have had zero or two). And combining two or more actions is frequently (but not always) how the LSAT creates its most difficult game. Consider the following example:

LSAT Overview	Analysis
Five executives—Quinn, Rodriguez, Sasada, Taylor, and Vandercar—are being scheduled to make site visits to three of their company's manufacturing plants—Farmington, Homestead, and Morningside. Each site will be visited by at least one of the executives and each executive will visit just one site. Each of the three site visits will take place on a different day. The schedule of site visits must conform to the following requirements: *PrepTest56 Sec1 Qs17–23*	**Step 1:** *Situation:* Executives visiting manufacturing plants on three different days: Perhaps the mental picture is a spreadsheet where this program is being planned.

Step 1: *Situation:* Executives visiting manufacturing plants on three different days: Perhaps the mental picture is a spreadsheet where this program is being planned.

Entities: Executives: Q, R, S, T, V

Plants/sites: Farm, Home, Morn

Action: Look for clues:

"[S]cheduled" and "Each of the three site visits will take place on a different day" suggest Sequencing.

"Each site will be visited by at least one of the executives"—group sites and executives together.

This game has two actions: part of our job is Sequencing—putting the site visits in order—and part of our job is Distribution—sorting out which executives visit which sites.

→ *Limitations:* Specific instructions:

"Five executives" visit "three of their company's manufacturing plants": Tells us we have more executives than plants, so at least one plant will have more than one executive visiting it.

"Each site will be visited by at least one of the executives": Tells us that no plants will be left blank.

"[E]ach executive will visit just one site": Tells us that we won't use any of the executives twice.

"Each of the three site visits will take place on a different day": We know that we're going to use three days—one for each site visit.

Gaps in information:

We know that we have more executives than sites, but we don't know how those numbers are distributed over the three sites.

The expert test taker knew that this was a Hybrid game because she kept her eyes open for clues and she spotted both Sequencing and Distribution clues. That's how to spot Hybrid games: watch for the kinds of clues you're already familiar with from your practice on the single-action games above. (So, from this point forward, don't stop looking for clues that point you toward an action in a logic game just because you've already identified one action in the overview. There might be another action; be on the lookout for it.)

Theoretically, the LSAT could combine any two of the four actions in a Hybrid game, and you should be prepared for that. However, in recent years some combinations have been more common than others. In particular, Sequencing-Distribution and Sequencing-Matching together represent over 60% of Hybrid games on recent exams. Every once in a while, the LSAT will combine more than two actions.

Similarly, the limitations to watch out for are indicated by the actions involved. But in Hybrid games, take an extra moment to make sure you're clear about which limitations apply to which action. For example, notice that one action in this game has a tight numerical restriction (there's a one-to-one alignment between sites and days) but the other action has looser numerical restrictions (we don't know the exact numbers of executives who visit each site).

It's difficult to generalize about sketches for Hybrid games because different combinations of actions call for different sketches. But we can outline a couple of principles:

In this case, let's assume that we don't immediately see a way to combine the two actions into one sketch. We know that we have a Sequencing action and a Distribution action, so let's draw two initial sketches representing those two actions:

LSAT Overview	Analysis
Five executives—Quinn, Rodriguez, Sasada, Taylor, and Vandercar—are being scheduled to make site visits to three of their company's manufacturing plants—Farmington, Homestead, and Morningside. Each site will be visited by at least one of the executives and each executive will visit just one site. Each of the three site visits will take place on a different day. The schedule of site visits must conform to the following requirements: *PrepTest56 Sec1 Qs17–23*	**Step 2:** Farm, Home, Morn Q R S T V __ __ __ Farm | Home | Morn 1 2 3

(Notice that we didn't fill in slots for our Distribution sketch since we don't yet know how many executives visit each site.)

Those two sketches together would allow you to make all available deductions as you work through the rules. But in this case, it's worth consolidating the sketches. Sequencing-Distribution Hybrid games are relatively common on the LSAT, and thus this consolidated sketch is of a type you'll likely be able to reuse in the future. Anchor the sketch with the Sequencing action because that's definite in nature, and you can fill in the slots below with the initials of manufacturing plants. It makes sense, then, to let those slots also be column headers so that you can eventually write the names of executives below them.

LSAT Overview

Five executives—Quinn, Rodriguez, Sasada, Taylor, and Vandercar—are being scheduled to make site visits to three of their company's manufacturing plants—Farmington, Homestead, and Morningside. Each site will be visited by at least one of the executives and each executive will visit just one site. Each of the three site visits will take place on a different day. The schedule of site visits must conform to the following requirements:

PrepTest56 Sec1 Qs17–23

Analysis

Step 2:

$\longrightarrow$

	1	2	3
Farm Home Morn	___	___	___
QRSTV	___	___	___

(+ _ _ more execs)

Of course, there may still be information that you'll need to note off to the side. Imagine, for example, that you learn that Quinn visits Homestead, but you don't yet know on which day. You can't place that information in a specific day yet, but the sketch allows you to accommodate deductions that relate to *both* Sequencing and Distribution in one place, and that will make life easier. This type of sketch is, in fact, recommended for both Sequencing-Distribution and Sequencing-Matching Hybrid games.

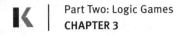
Practice

In each of the following examples, apply Steps 1 and 2 of the Logic Games Method to these Hybrid games. Take your time identifying actions and limitations and pay attention to the clues that indicate each action. You can check the following pages at any time to see the expert thinking.

Overview	My Analysis
13. Five drivers—A, B, C, D, and E—are waiting to get their cars washed. The cars are in a line, first to last, and each car is exactly one of three different colors—f, g, or h.	
14. Six friends—A, B, C, D, E, and F—are going canoeing through a state park. The friends will rent exactly two canoes, and each canoe has a front, middle, and rear position. All six friends seat themselves in the canoes, one person per position.	

Here's how the expert test taker approaches those game overviews and sketches:

Overview	Analysis
13. Five drivers—A, B, C, D, and E—are waiting to get their cars washed. The cars are in a line, first to last, and each car is exactly one of three different colors—f, g, or h.	**Step 1:** *Situation:* A line of cars outside a car wash *Entities:* The drivers of cars (A, B, C, D, E) and the colors (f, g, h). *Action:* Because the cars are in a line "first to last," positional arrangement must matter; this is a *Sequencing* game. And once the cars are in order, we'll also need to *match* the car of each driver to a specific color. This must be a *Sequencing-Matching Hybrid* game. *Limitations:* The five drivers definitely have to be used up, so we'll use all of them, but we're not sure about the colors. There are no restrictions telling us how many colors we must use. Therefore, it's possible that all three colors are used; alternatively, it's possible that all five cars are the same color. **Step 2:** It is easy to envision this *Matching-Sequencing Hybrid* game as just two Sequencing games layered on top of each other. We can place the drivers on one layer and match the color of their cars to the other layer. 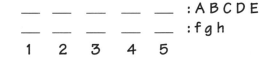

Overview	Analysis

14. Six friends—A, B, C, D, E, and F—are going canoeing through a state park. The friends will rent exactly two canoes, and each canoe has a front, middle, and rear position. All six friends seat themselves in the canoes, one person per position.

Step 1: *Situation:* Friends at a park, trying to figure out who sits where and in which canoe

Entities: The friends (A, B, C, D, E, F) and the positions (front, middle, rear)

Action: A pretty straightforward Distribution game—divide a group of friends into two smaller subgroups. Positioning also matters—"front, middle, and rear" signifies that friends sit *in front of* or *behind* others. This is a *Distribution-Sequencing Hybrid* game.

Limitations: Straightforward, with no uncommon limitations. Six people and six spots in which to put them.

Step 2: Each entity is placed only once in the sketch (Distribution), and order matters (Sequencing). List the entities above the grid and add them to the sketch when you know their spot.

A B C D E F

	Canoe 1	Canoe 2
front		
mid		
rear		

Or

A B C D E F

	front	mid	rear
Canoe 1			
Canoe 2			

Reflection

Take a look back at your practice. Did you answer the SEAL questions for each game prior to setting up a sketch for it? Did you tease out all the actions that were present in each game? Did you make clear, simple sketches (regardless of whether you made one or two for each game)? Were you clear about which limitations applied to which action? Were there any limitations you missed?

In the coming days, take note of Hybrid tasks in real life: Do you have to select some of your employees and put them on teams? Will you choose whom to invite to a wedding and decide which table they're assigned to at the reception? How would the testmaker turn these into logic games? What restrictions and rules would you need to make the final arrangements?

Summary: Game Types and Sketches

... of the Logic Games Method in action. You've learned a great deal about ... 've also met the full catalog of game types:

... the opportunity not only to apply Steps 1 and 2 to each overview, as ... practice with discerning which type of game each one represents. Be ... and feel free to refer to your work earlier in this chapter to review which ... you encounter.

... for Logic Games to each of the following game overviews. Determine the ... described. Then make a simple sketch, complete with a roster of entities. ... taker's approach.

My Analysis

... d F—graduated
... ent annual

... out some books
... books she really
... d H. She will
... . The library
... oks at a time.

The receipt (overlaying left column) reads:

```
            Chapters

Store# 00770 Chapters Dalhousie
   5005 Dalhousie Drive, N.W.
      Calgary,AB T3A 5R8
      Phone: (403) 202-4600

Tell us about your visit today
and enter to win a $500 giftcard!
    Complete our survey at:
     www.indigofeedback.com
 See survey site for contest details.

Store# 00770 Term# 003 Trans# 583882
Operator: 914CLL   07/03/2014 16:05
          IREWARDS SALE
            ****3534
************************************
KAPLAN LSAT PREMIER 2015 WIT    $61.19G
9781618656384
Original Price          $67.99
IRewards Discount       $-6.80
************************************
Items: 1
          Subtotal:           $61.19
          GST:    5.0%         $3.06
          Total:              $64.25
          VISA:               $64.25
************************************

Your Total Savings: $6.80
   Promotions: $0.00
     irewards: $6.80

************************************

Store# 00770 Term# 003 Trans# 583882
  GST Registration # R897152666

       *0077000305838821*

TYPE: PURCHASE

ACCT: VISA           $     64.25

CARD NUMBER:     ***********8732
DATE/TIME:       14/07/03 16:06:24
REFERENCE #:     66144733 0014610800 C
AUTHOR. #:       087311
INVOICE NUMBER:  30032981

VISA CREDIT
A0000000031010
0080008000  F800

   01/027  APPROVED - THANK YOU

      -- IMPORTANT --
Retain This Copy For Your Records

    *** CUSTOMER COPY ***
```

Overview	My Analysis

17. A young boy is organizing seven baseball cards—A, B, C, D, E, F and G—into three categories, numbered 1, 2, and 3. Each card will be placed into exactly one of the three categories.

18. A four-story building houses five businesses— Shops A, B, C, D, and E—and each floor has at least one business on it. Shop B needs to be on a higher floor than Shop E.

19. Six bicycles numbered 1 through 6 are lined up in a store window. Each bicycle is colored either A or B, is made by company c or d, and has handlebars of type E or F.

Overview	My Analysis
20. Eight students—A, B, C, D, E, F, G and H—hope to meet with a piano teacher this week. The piano teacher has one opening in the morning and one in the afternoon on each of Monday, Tuesday, and Wednesday. The piano teacher will schedule one lesson for each opening on her schedule, and she can only see one student at a time.	
21. Two high school teachers—teacher 1 and teacher 2—will choose students to be on a debate team that will be composed of exactly five students. Each teacher will choose from among students in her own class, and each class is made up of five students—A, B, C, D, and E in teacher 1's class and F, G, H, I, and J in teacher 2's class. The final team must have at least two students from each teacher's class.	
22. While preparing for a trip to Europe, each of three friends—A, B, and C—will research at least one and up to four countries. The friends have narrowed down the list of countries that they want to visit to five—d, e, f, g, and h.	

Overview	My Analysis

23. A child is going to choose five books, all with different titles, to take to her grandmother's house. She has seven books to choose from—A, B, C, D, E, F, and G—and each book is written by exactly one of four different authors—h, j, k, and m.

24. Exactly three juniors—A, B, and C—and five seniors—d, e, f, g, and h—are working on a recycling project. In order to be more effective, they are going to create two 4-person teams. Each team needs to have at least one junior.

Here's how the expert test taker analyzed the overview and created the initial sketch for each of the games you just saw:

Overview	Analysis
15. Each of six people—A, B, C, D, E, and F—graduated from Big City High School in a different annual class, from the years 1999 to 2004.	**Step 1:** *Situation:* Figure out who graduated in what year.
	Entities: The graduates (A, B, C, D, E, F) and the years (1999 through 2004)
	Action: Because there are six people, and each graduated in a different class (no overlap), this is a *Sequencing* game. Each student needs to be assigned to exactly one of the six years.
	Limitations: Six people, six spots, no ties
	Step 2:

$$A\ B\ C\ D\ E\ F$$

—	—	—	—	—	—
99	00	01	02	03	04

Overview	Analysis
16. A woman goes to the library to check out some books for a long trip. She has a list of eight books she really wants to read—A, B, C, D, E, F, G, and H. She will select at least two books for her trip. The library only allows her to check out five books at a time.	**Step 1:** *Situation:* A woman at the library is trying to figure out which books to check out.
	Entities: The books (A, B, C, D, E, F, G, H)
	Action: Because the woman is going to "check out" or *select* only some books out of a larger total number of books, this is a *Selection* game.
	Limitations: The woman is going to check out at least two books, but she can't check out more than five. So this Selection game has minimum and maximum restrictions.
	Step 2: A Selection game sketch is no more than the list of entities. Note, however, the minimum and maximum number restrictions.
	(pick 2–5 out of 8) A B C D E F G H

Overview	**Analysis**
17. A young boy is organizing seven baseball cards—A, B, C, D, E, F and G—into three categories, numbered 1, 2, and 3. Each card will be placed into exactly one of the three categories.	**Step 1:** *Situation:* A young boy is trying to decide how to organize his baseball cards.

Entities: Baseball cards (A, B, C, D, E, F, G) and the different groups into which the boy will place them (1, 2, 3)

Action: Separating cards into categories—because each card can only go into one category, or group—makes this a *Distribution* game.

Limitations: No stated minimum or maximum number of cards placed in each category. The rules will give more restrictions.

→ **Step 2:** Typical Distribution sketch—the groups positioned at the top of a table, with columns for the cards once we know where they go

A B C D E F G

Group 1	Group 2	Group 3

---

18. A four-story building houses five businesses—Shops A, B, C, D, and E—and each floor has at least one business on it. Shop B needs to be on a higher floor than Shop E.

Step 1: *Situation:* A building with four floors and five businesses

Entities: The shops (A, B, C, D, E)

→ **Action:** Because Shop B needs to be on a higher floor than Shop E, positional arrangement matters. This is a *Sequencing* game.

Limitations: Because there are five businesses and four floors, and because each floor must hold at least one business, exactly one floor holds two businesses and the other four floors hold one business apiece.

Step 2: Buildings are vertical, so it makes "real-word" sense to draw this sketch vertically.

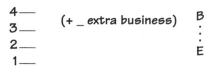

A B C D E

4 ——
3 ——   (+ _ extra business)
2 ——
1 ——

B
:
:
E

Overview	Analysis

19. Six bicycles numbered 1 through 6 are lined up in a store window. Each bicycle is colored either A or B, is made by company c or d, and has handlebars of type E or F.

Step 1: *Situation:* Bikes in a shop window, each one possessing a variety of features

Entities: There are the bikes (1 through 6), each bike's color (either A or B), the company that makes each bike (c or d), and the type of handlebars for each bike (E or F)

Action: The bicycles are in fixed positions, so there's no Sequencing action. The task is to match features to the bikes. Determining the attributes of fixed entities makes this a *Matching* game.

Limitations: Each bicycle is matched to exactly one of each type of attribute (color, manufacturer, and

→ handlebar type).

Step 2: Create a grid—each of the six bikes will have exactly three characteristics. On one row of the grid, enter A or B, for color. On the next row, add c or d for brand. On the last row, place E or F for handlebar type.

1	2	3	4	5	6	
						A or B
						c or d
						E or F

| Overview | Analysis |

20. Eight students—A, B, C, D, E, F, G and H— hope to meet with a piano teacher this week. The piano teacher has one opening in the morning and one in the afternoon on each of Monday, Tuesday, and Wednesday. The piano teacher will schedule one lesson for each opening on her schedule, and she can only see one student at a time.

Step 1: *Situation:* A piano teacher is trying to schedule piano lessons for the week.

Entities: The eight students (A, B, C, D, E, F, G, H), the three days of the week (Mon, Tue, Wed), and the time of day of each appointment (morning or afternoon)

Action: Eight students but only six openings— one task is to *select* the six students getting appointments. Days of the week and times of the day indicate sequential ordering—a second task is to determine the *order* in which the students are scheduled to meet with the teacher. This is a *Selection-Sequencing Hybrid* game.

$\longrightarrow$ *Limitations:* The teacher can only see one student at a time—no "double" appointments. The teacher picks six students, so two students are out. Knowing which students *are not* selected is as helpful as knowing who is selected.

Step 2: The intuitive sketch here mimics a calendar. Circle or cross-out entities to keep track of students who are definitively selected or rejected for appointment times.

A B C D E F G H

	Mon	Tues	Wed
A.M.			
P.M.			

Overview	Analysis
21. Two high school teachers—teacher 1 and teacher 2—will choose students to be on a debate team that will be composed of exactly five students. Each teacher will choose from among students in her own class, and each class is made up of five students—A, B, C, D, and E in teacher 1's class and F, G, H, I, and J in teacher 2's class. The final team must have at least two students from each teacher's class.	**Step 1:** *Situation:* Deciding whom to pick for a high school debate team

Step 1: *Situation:* Deciding whom to pick for a high school debate team

Entities: The teachers' classes (1 and 2) and the students (A, B, C, D, E, F, G, H, I, J)

Action: Five students will be chosen out of 10 students, so this is selection game.

Limitations: Five-person team with at least two from each class—either teacher 1 = two students and teacher 2 = three students or vice versa.

Step 2: Use a Selection sketch, but signify the two classes with a table.

(pick 5 out of 10)

(2 – 3) class 1	(2 – 3) class 2
A B C D E	F G H I J

---

22. While preparing for a trip to Europe, each of three friends—A, B, and C—will research at least one and up to four countries. The friends have narrowed down the list of countries that they want to visit to five—d, e, f, g, and h.

Step 1: *Situation:* Friends researching different countries before a trip

Entities: The friends (A, B, C) and the countries (d, e, f, g, h).

Action: The task is to determine the country or countries each friend researches—this is a *Matching* game.

Limitations: Each friend must research at least one country, but no friend can research all five. Countries can be assigned to more than one friend.

Step 2: Use a table or grid for Matching games. Set up the table to indicate that the number of countries each friend researches is unknown. Indicate number limitations above.

d e f g h

(1 – 4) A	(1 – 4) B	(1 – 4) C

Overview	Analysis
23. A child is going to choose five books, all with different titles, to take to her grandmother's house. She has seven books to choose from—A, B, C, D, E, F, and G—and each book is written by exactly one of four different authors—h, j, k, and m.	**Step 1:** *Situation:* A child picking some books to take with her on a trip *Entities:* The seven books (A, B, C, D, E, F, G) and the different authors (h, j, k, m) *Action:* Choose five of seven books—a *Selection* action. Additionally, each book has an author. Because the authors are not "used up," this also has a *Matching* action. This is a *Selection-Matching Hybrid* game. *Limitations:* No mention of the number of authors that must be selected in this game. With five books and four authors, however, at least one author must be chosen twice. **Step 2:** Make a sketch linking the Selection and Matching tasks. Circle the selected books and cross out the rejected ones. Beneath each book, put a slot for the matching author.

$$\text{A} \quad \text{B} \quad \text{C} \quad \text{D} \quad \text{E} \quad \text{F} \quad \text{G} \quad \text{(5 of 7)}$$
$$\underline{\quad} \; \underline{\quad} \; \underline{\quad} \; \underline{\quad} \; \underline{\quad} \; \underline{\quad} \; \underline{\quad} \quad : \text{h j k m}$$

24. Exactly three juniors—A, B, and C—and five seniors—d, e, f, g, and h—are working on a recycling project. In order to be more effective, they are going to create two 4-person teams. Each team needs to have at least one junior.	**Step 1:** *Situation:* Creating teams for a recycling project *Entities:* The juniors (A, B, C) and the seniors (d, e, f, g, h) *Action:* Eight total students divided into two groups of four. This is a *Distribution* game. *Limitations:* Each group must have exactly four students. Because each team must have at least one junior, and because there are only three juniors, one team will have one junior and three seniors, while the other has two juniors and two seniors. **Step 2:** Set up a table with the teams on top and four dashes in each column to represent the students.

jun: A B C   Team 1 | Team 2
sen: d e f g h

Team 1	Team 2	
——	——	jun
——	——	jun/sen
——	——	sen
——	——	sen

Reflection

Take a look back at your practice. Did you answer the SEAL questions for each game prior to setting up a sketch for it? Did you spot the textual clues that pointed you toward the appropriate game actions? Were there valuable clues you missed? Did you set up each sketch based on your knowledge of the game's central action? Were your sketches easy to read, quick to replicate, and able to accommodate ambiguity? What have you learned from this exercise?

Did you make some mistakes? You probably did, and you should be grateful for them and put them to good use! Each and every mistake you make in your practice tells you something valuable about what mistakes you'd be likely to make if you took the LSAT today. Use that information to help you understand what you most need to work on before Test Day.

Summary

All of the work you've done in this chapter involved logic games' overviews—just their opening paragraphs—and yet you've learned so much about how each game will proceed. From the overview, you're able to discern the game's situation, entities, action, and limitations, and you're able to make a sketch that will accommodate all of the game's restrictions. Now that you have some solid practice in all of those skills, you're ready to start building information into that sketch—in other words, you're ready to tackle the *rules*.

CHAPTER 4

Logic Games: Rules and Deductions

Most LSAT experts would agree that the skills you'll learn in this chapter are the most important tools you can add to your logic games repertoire. Here, you'll learn to analyze and draw a game's rules and then—and this is what sets real Logic Games masters apart from the crowd—to combine the game's rules and limitations to determine everything that can be deduced about what must, can, and cannot be true about the arrangement of entities. Gaining mastery of the skills in this chapter is your ticket to handling the questions quickly and accurately on a consistent basis.

To this point, you've seen how LSAT experts conduct the Overview and Sketch steps of the Logic Games Method. They analyze the Situation, Entities, Action, and overall Limitations to form a clear mental picture of their task. Then, they translate that mental picture into a diagram that will hold all of the relevant restrictions. In Chapter 3, we avoided displaying the rules to focus your practice on clearly analyzing a game's big picture. Now, we'll add in the rules and use the next two steps of the Logic Games Method to produce a comprehensive Master Sketch for each game we see. Along the way, you'll have plenty of opportunities to practice analyzing and sketching rules and then combining them to make all available deductions.

STEP 3 OF THE LOGIC GAMES METHOD: ANALYZE AND DRAW THE RULES

Individual hour-long auditions will be scheduled for each of six saxophonists—Fujimura, Gabrieli, Herman, Jackson, King, and Lauder. The auditions will all take place on the same day. Each audition will begin on the hour, with the first beginning at 1 P.M. and the last at 6 P.M. The schedule of auditions must conform to the following conditions:

Jackson auditions earlier than Herman does.
Gabrieli auditions earlier than King does.
Gabrieli auditions either immediately before or
    immediately after Lauder does.
Exactly one audition separates the auditions of Jackson
    and Lauder.

PrepTest56 Sec1 Qs1–6

Here's a game you saw in Chapter 3, but now we've displayed the rules below the setup paragraph, just as they would appear on the LSAT. Try drawing them into the sketch. How would you do it? Do the rules combine to create additional restrictions that you can deduce? Later in the chapter, we'll show you how an LSAT expert would handle the rules and create a Master Sketch allowing her to answer all of the game's questions quickly and accurately. (You'll learn to answer all of the Logic Games question types in Chapter 5, by the way.)

When an LSAT expert draws out a game's rules, she depicts them clearly, in a way that matches and fits into the framework of her sketch and accounts for what the rule does and does not mean. In the first part of this chapter, you'll see how the LSAT expert is able to do that within each of the common game types using the typical sketches introduced in Chapter 3.

LEARNING OBJECTIVES

In this section, you'll learn to:

- Determine accurately what a rule restricts and what it leaves undetermined.
- Determine whether to draw a rule into the Sketch framework or display it off to the side.
- Analyze and sketch rules.
- Decide whether a rule is more helpful drawn in positive or negative terms.

Because you have to apply these objectives to every rule, you can think of them as part of one overarching component of LSAT mastery: Analyze and Draw the Rules. As you practice with the examples and drills below, we'll remind you of the questions you need to ask in order to manage every rule effectively. We'll introduce the rules by game type so that you can see them within the context in which they're most likely to appear on Test Day.

Rules in Sequencing Games

From previous chapters, you know that Sequencing is by far the most common game type on recent LSATs. It's not uncommon for two of the four games in a Logic Games section to be Sequencing games or for one to be a Sequencing game and another to be a Hybrid game with a Sequencing action. It's unlikely that you need more motivation for taking Sequencing rules seriously than the knowledge that half or more of your Logic Games score will likely depend on mastering this game type. Think for a moment about what you've already learned about Sequencing games. In these games, you're always tasked with determining the order of a number of entities. That should help you anticipate the types of rules you're going to encounter here.

LSAT STRATEGY

Sequencing rules basically tell you one or more of the following things:

- The order in which two or more entities are placed
- The number of spaces between two or more entities
- The slot(s) in which a given entity can or cannot be placed

As you read through the LSAT expert's analyses of the rules in Sequencing games, think back to that list and ask in what way each rule is restricting or defining the arrangement of entities.

In Chapter 2, you saw how an LSAT expert analyzed and drew the rules for the Monuments game, a game you'll now quickly recognize as a Strict Sequencing game. Reflect on that example with each rule broken out individually.

LSAT Question	Analysis
Historical records show that over the course of five consecutive years—601, 602, 603, 604, and 605—a certain emperor began construction of six monuments: F, G, H, L, M, and S. A historian is trying to determine the years in which the individual monuments were begun. The following facts have been established:	**Steps 1 and 2:** F G H L M S 601 | 602 | 603 | 604 | 605
L was begun in a later year than G, but in an earlier year than F.	**Step 3:** G . . . L . . . F
H was begun no earlier than 604.	601 | 602 | 603 | 604 | 605 ~H ~H ~H
M was begun earlier than 604.	601 | 602 | 603 | 604 | 605 ~M ~M
Two of the monuments were begun in 601, and no other monument was begun in the same year as any of the other monuments. *PrepTest58 Sec3 Qs1–6*	601 | 602 | 603 | 604 | 605

Take note of how the LSAT expert drew out each rule and see what that tells you about her thinking. **Rule 1:** This rule tells us the order of three entities but not the number of spaces between any two of them. **Rule 2:** This rule doesn't tell us exactly when H was begun, but it rules out three years—the negative restrictions are clear. **Rule 3:** This rule doesn't tell us exactly when M was begun, but it rules out two years—again, the negative implications are unequivocal. **Rule 4:** This rule affects the framework of the sketch—we now know that one year (601) has exactly two monuments and the others all have one each.

In that game, Rule 1 restricted the order of three entities but told you nothing about the number of spaces between them. Rules 2 and 3 both ruled out certain spaces for two different entities. Rule 4 is somewhat rare among Sequencing rules because most Sequencing games contain the limitation of one entity per space. For the LSAT expert (who would notice immediately that six monuments need to be spaced over five years), this rule is invaluable for understanding the parameters of the game.

Now, take a look at the first Sequencing game you saw illustrated in Chapter 3. This time, we've added the LSAT expert's analysis and drawing for each rule. As you review the expert's thinking, take note of any ways in which he's made sure to note what the rule does and does not prescribe. (NOTE: If at any time in this chapter you have trouble remembering how the LSAT expert arrived at a particular sketch, flip back to Chapter 3 for a moment and review the Step 1 and Step 2 analysis there.)

LSAT Question	Analysis
Individual hour-long auditions will be scheduled for each of six saxophonists—Fujimura, Gabrieli, Herman, Jackson, King, and Lauder. The auditions will all take place on the same day. Each audition will begin on the hour, with the first beginning at 1 P.M. and the last at 6 P.M. The schedule of auditions must conform to the following conditions:	**Steps 1 and 2:** F G H J K L $\overline{1}$ $\overline{2}$ $\overline{3}$ $\overline{4}$ $\overline{5}$ $\overline{6}$
Jackson auditions earlier than Herman does.	**Step 3:** J . . . H
Gabrieli auditions earlier than King does.	G . . . K
Gabrieli auditions either immediately before or immediately after Lauder does.	$\underline{G}\ \underline{L}$ or $\underline{L}\ \underline{G}$ Or $\underline{G/L}\ \underline{L/G}$
Exactly one audition separates the auditions of Jackson and Lauder. *PrepTest56 Sec1 Qs1–6*	$\underline{J}\ \_\_\ \underline{L}$ or $\underline{L}\ \_\_\ \underline{J}$ Or $\underline{J/L}\ \_\_\ \underline{L/J}$

The rules in the Saxophonists game break down evenly. Rules 1 and 2 dictate the order of, but not distance between, pairs of entities. Rules 3 and 4 dictate the distance between pairs of entities but say nothing about the order in which the entities in those pairs appear. By using an ellipsis between the entities in Rules 1 and 2, the LSAT expert has made the entities' order clear without giving any hint that he knows how close together or far apart they may wind up. By showing both possible orders in his drawing for Rules 3 and 4 (and note that there are two different ways in which you might depict this), the LSAT expert has made sure to avoid the mistake of assuming that G comes right before L in Rule 3 or that J comes two spaces before L in Rule 4. L may be the earlier or later entity in either of those rules.

We'll return to that game in the next section and make all of the deductions provided for by these rules. Before you leave the Saxophonists game, though, take a moment and realize what you already know from the first two rules. Because those rules dictate the order between two pairs of entities, you can be certain that neither Jackson nor

Gabrieli will have an audition at 6 P.M. Likewise, neither Herman nor King can take the first slot at 1 P.M. Always keep in mind that the negative implications of a rule may be as strong as or stronger than the affirmative restrictions it calls for.

Loose Sequencing Rules

From Chapter 3, you'll remember the description and example of Loose Sequencing, the less common variant among Sequencing games. The distinguishing characteristic of Loose Sequencing is that all of the rules are relative; they tell you only about the order among the entities and include no information about how far apart the entities are spaced. The nature of Loose Sequencing rules often allows you to combine the rules as you're interpreting them. Every time an entity is shared between two or more rules, stitching the rules together allows you to see the full impact of their restrictions.

In the following analysis, we'll show you the expert's thinking about the rule, and we'll show you how she combines the rules as she goes along. While this may not apply to every Loose Sequencing game you encounter, expect to be able to combine at least some of the rules as you analyze them.

LSAT Question	Analysis
Workers at a water treatment plant open eight valves—G, H, I, K, L, N, O, and P—to flush out a system of pipes that needs emergency repairs. To maximize safety and efficiency, each valve is opened exactly once, and no two valves are opened at the same time. The valves are opened in accordance with the following conditions:	**Steps 1 and 2:** A glance at the rules—they're all relative—tells us this is a Loose Sequencing game. A roster of entities will suffice to start with. G H I K L N O P
Both K and P are opened before H.	**Step 3:** K P \\ / V H
O is opened before L but after H.	H | O | L Because Rule 1 and Rule 2 both mention H, they combine. K P \\ / H | O | L

LSAT Question	Analysis
L is opened after G.	G | L

	Because Rule 2 and Rule 3 both mention L, this rule can be added to the overall sketch.
	
	→ K P
	    \\ /
	    H
	    |
	    O
	    | G
	    L

N is opened before H.	N | H

	Because Rule 1 and Rule 4 both mention H, this rule can be added to the overall sketch.
	
	→ K P N
	    \\\|/
	    H
	    |
	    O
	    | G
	    L

I is opened after K. *PrepTest52 Sec2 Qs1–7*	K | I

	Because Rule 1 and Rule 5 both mention K, this rule can be added to the overall sketch.
	
	→ K P N
	   / \\\|/
	  I H
	      |
	      O
	      | G
	      L

Let's be clear. There is nothing wrong with jotting down all of the rules individually and then taking a few seconds in Step 4, the Deductions step, to combine them into a comprehensive Master Sketch. The LSAT expert's analysis showed her combining as she went to illustrate how that may be done. As you practice Loose Sequencing, try both ways and use the approach that works better for you. In either case, you'll need to read the rules very carefully (did you notice that the testmaker kept changing between "before" and "after" to reward the test taker who was paying attention?) and combine the rules that share entities before tackling the questions.

One other note on Loose Sequencing sketches: Make sure you don't make unwarranted assumptions based on the picture you draw. In the final sketch above, for example, all you know about G is that it is before L. From the rules, you have no idea of its position in the order beyond that. Valve G might be the first one turned on. Similarly, you don't know anything about Valve I other than it must follow K; Valve I cannot be first, but it could be turned on at any point from second to eighth. Valve H, on the other hand, is quite restricted. You know it must follow Valves K, P, and N, so the earliest it could be turned on is fourth. Likewise, it must be turned on earlier than Valves O and L, so the latest it could be is sixth. We'll go even deeper in our analysis of this game in the next section of the chapter. For now, reflect for a few moments on what you know and don't know about each entity and start learning to avoid the unwarranted visual assumptions that poor test takers make in Loose Sequencing games.

Practice

Now, you'll have the chance to practice reading, analyzing, and drawing some common Sequencing rules. In this exercise, we won't include full games, so don't worry about the overall sketch unless some indication of it is provided. Rather, focus on the kind of detail-oriented, critical analysis that an LSAT expert does with each individual rule in logic games. Here are the questions you should ask about each rule.

LSAT STRATEGY

When analyzing and drawing a rule, always ask:

- What does the rule restrict?
- What does the rule leave undetermined?
- Is the rule stated in affirmative or negative terms?
- If stated affirmatively, can I learn something concrete from its negative implications (or vice versa)?
- Can I place the rule directly into the sketch framework?
- If not, how can I best draw the rule to account for what it does and does not restrict?

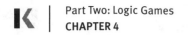

Here are a couple of examples of an LSAT expert putting those questions to work.

Rule	Analysis
A and B are placed in adjacent seats.	The rule says that A and B sit next to one another. It does not determine whether A or B comes first. → The rule is in affirmative terms. The negative implication is that there are never any spaces between A and B. The rule doesn't assign specific seats, so this can't be placed directly into the framework. Sketch: A/B B/A *Or* A B or B A
There are at least two days after D's appointment but before C's appointment.	The rule tells us the order—D before C—and gives some restriction about the distance between the two. The rule does not say exactly how many days separate the two entities' appointments. → The rule is stated affirmatively. The negative implication is that D and C never have appointments one or two days apart. Also, C's appointment is never earlier than the fourth day and D's appointment is never later than the fourth day from the end. The rule doesn't assign specific days, so it cannot be built into the calendar. Sketch: D __ __ ... C

The following is a list of other rules associated with Sequencing games (and Hybrid games with a Sequencing action).

Rule	Analysis
A appears on some day before B.	$\longrightarrow$ A . . . B
A appears on some day before B and also on some day before C.	A . . . B and A . . . C Or $\longrightarrow$ A ∧ B C
A appears the day immediately before the day on which B appears.	$\longrightarrow$ AB
Appointments V and W have exactly one appointment separating them.	$\underline{\quad V \quad}$ __ $\underline{\quad W \quad}$ or $\underline{\quad W \quad}$ __ $\underline{\quad V \quad}$ $\longrightarrow$ Or $\underline{\text{V/W}}$ __ $\underline{\text{W/V}}$
Appointments V and W have at least one appointment separating them.	$\underline{\quad V \quad}$ __ . . . $\underline{\quad W \quad}$ or $\underline{\quad W \quad}$ __ . . . $\underline{\quad V \quad}$ $\longrightarrow$ Or $\underline{\text{V/W}}$ __ . . . $\underline{\text{W/V}}$
In a game disallowing ties: R never appears before S.	$\longrightarrow$ S...R
In a game allowing ties: R never appears before S	$\longrightarrow$ $\boxed{\begin{array}{c} R \\ \hline S \end{array}}$ or S . . . R NOT R . . . S
C occurs on the third day after D.	$\longrightarrow$ $\underline{\quad D \quad}$ __ __ $\underline{\quad C \quad}$
In a game in which every entity is used exactly once and there are 8 entities: If R is not on day 3, then R must be on day 5.	If ~R3 → R5 If ~R5 → R3 Or $\longrightarrow$ $\underline{1}$ $\underline{2}$ $\underline{3}$ $\underline{4}$ $\underline{5}$ $\underline{6}$ $\underline{7}$ $\underline{8}$ $\quad\quad$↖ ↗ $\quad\quad$ R
D must appear before B but after H.	$\longrightarrow$ H . . . D . . . B
B appears before (but not immediately before) C.	$\longrightarrow$ $\underline{\quad B \quad}$ . . . __ $\underline{\quad C \quad}$
In a game disallowing ties: B appears before C, or B appears before D, but not both.	$\longrightarrow$ D . . . B . . . C or C . . . B . . . D

Rule	Analysis
In a game disallowing ties: B appears before C, or D appears before B, but not both.	$(B \ldots C \text{ and } B \ldots D)$ *or* $(D \ldots B \text{ and } C \ldots B)$ *Or* $\underset{C \quad D}{\overset{B}{\wedge}}$ *or* $\underset{B}{\overset{D \quad C}{\vee}}$
There are exactly three appointments between M and R.	$\underline{\ M\ } \ __ \ __ \ __ \ \underline{\ R\ } \ $ *or* $ \ \underline{\ R\ } \ __ \ __ \ __ \ \underline{\ M\ }$ *Or* $\underline{M/R} \ \_\_ \ \_\_ \ \_\_ \ \underline{R/M}$
In a game disallowing ties: Whenever A precedes B, C is fifth.	If A . . . B → C5 If ~C5 → B . . . A

Now, try it out yourself. Examine each of the rules below. Ask the analysis questions just outlined and make your best effort at drawing the rule. You can compare your work to an LSAT expert's analysis that follows.

Rule	My Analysis
1. P is the fourth data packet received after R.	
2. P cannot be received until M, Q, and R have been received.	
3. S must be screened before L but after N.	
4. Of F, G, and H, G is the most productive.	
5. Of F, G, and H, G is the least productive.	
6. M is photographed either immediately before or immediately after N.	

Rule	My Analysis
7. In a game with seven train stops: The train line's second or third stop is P.	
8. In a game with seven train stops: The fifth stop is either S or T.	
9. In a game lining up six cars at a gas station: The red car is behind, but not immediately behind, the gray car.	
10. There is at most one car between the blue car and the yellow car.	
11. In a game disallowing ties: If S is served before J, then A is served before S.	
12. If R gets out at the fourth bus stop, then M does not get out at the first bus stop.	
13. In a game disallowing ties: F never precedes H unless A is third.	
14. In a game having people stand in line: G stands immediately ahead of J unless J is third in line.	

Here's how an LSAT expert would draw the rules you just saw. Don't worry if you didn't use exactly the same symbols in your pencil work, but make sure that you didn't over- or underdetermine the restriction called for by each rule.

Rule		**Analysis**
1.	P is the fourth data packet received after R.	$\longrightarrow$ R _ _ _ P
2.	P cannot be received until M, Q, and R have been received.	$\longrightarrow$ M ⋮ Q ⋯ P Or M Q R ＼│／ R ⋰ P
3.	S must be screened before L but after N.	$\longrightarrow$ N . . . S . . . L Or N │ S │ L
4.	Of F, G, and H, G is the most productive.	$\longrightarrow$ G ⋰ F ⋱ H Or G ／＼ F H
5.	Of F, G, and H, G is the least productive.	$\longrightarrow$ F ⋱ G ⋰ H Or F H ＼／ G
6.	M is photographed either immediately before or immediately after N.	$\longrightarrow$ MN or NM Or M/N N/M
7.	In a game with seven train stops: The train line's second or third stop is P.	$\longrightarrow$ $\overline{1}$ $\overline{2}$ $\overline{3}$ $\overline{4}$ $\overline{5}$ $\overline{6}$ $\overline{7}$ ↖↗ P
8.	In a game with seven train stops: The fifth stop is either S or T.	$\longrightarrow$ $\overline{1}$ $\overline{2}$ $\overline{3}$ $\overline{4}$ $\overset{S/T}{\overline{5}}$ $\overline{6}$ $\overline{7}$
9.	In a game lining up six cars at a gas station: The red car is behind, but not immediately behind, the gray car.	$\longrightarrow$ G . . . __ R
10.	There is at most one car between the blue car and the yellow car.	$\longrightarrow$ B __ Y or Y __ B Or BY or YB Or B/Y __ Y/B Or B/Y Y/B

Rule		Analysis
11.	In a game disallowing ties: If S is served before J, then A is served before S.	If S . . . J → A . . . S (so A . . . S . . . J) If S . . . A → J . . . S (so J . . . S . . . A) There are exactly two possibilities: A . . . S . . . J or J . . . S . . . A
12.	If R gets out at the fourth bus stop, then M does not get out at the first bus stop.	If R4 → ~M1 If M1 → ~R4 **Never R4 and M1** *Or* NOT $\left[\begin{array}{cc} M & R \\ \hline 1 & 4 \end{array}\right]$
13.	In a game disallowing ties: F never precedes H unless A is third.	If F . . . H → A3 If ~A3 → H . . . F
14.	In a game having people stand in line: G stands immediately ahead of J unless J is third in line.	If ~J3 → GJ If ~GJ → J3

As you continue your practice with the games in Chapter 6 and with full-length LSATs, you'll have ample opportunity to analyze and sketch Sequencing rules. The wording will change slightly, but the test will use the same types of restrictions you've just seen.

Reflection

Over the coming days, pay attention to "sequencing" tasks you encounter in everyday life. Anytime you have to schedule a series of appointments or even put things in alphabetical order, you're sequencing. Notice how the real-life restrictions you face determine the way you handle your task. Alphabetizing, for example, determines the order in which you'll put two things, but not the number of spaces between them (at least not until you have a complete list of whatever you're alphabetizing). Some scheduling tasks, on the other hand, may offer different types of rules. You may need to meet with one person before you can meet with another, or you might need to take care of two different errands on the same day. The more you can demystify logic games and see that they mirror much of the same thinking and reasoning you do every day, the less intimidating and unfamiliar they'll seem on Test Day.

Rules in Selection Games

Selection games are less common than Sequencing games and do not appear on every test. Because these games always involve choosing some entities and rejecting others, almost all Selection rules involve conditional Formal Logic statements—choosing one entity may require you to reject another, for example. If you are strong at Formal Logic, you'll likely embrace Selection games and perform well on them. If not, you may want to revisit Chapter 1: LSAT Reasoning and brush up on the basics of Formal Logic before you work in depth with Selection rules.

LSAT STRATEGY

Selection rules tell you one or more of the following things:

- That at least one of two entities must be rejected
- That at least one of two entities must be selected
- That two entities must be selected or rejected as a pair (one cannot be selected or rejected without the other)

Think back to what you learned about Selection games in Chapter 3. Do you recall that the suggested sketches for Selection games are nothing more than a list or roster of the entities? That is because, to handle the Selection task, you need do no more than circle the entities you know are chosen and cross out those you know are rejected. When you need to re-create the sketch for another question, you just write out the list of entities and start circling or crossing out again. That simple sketch combined with the conditional nature of nearly all Selection rules means that you have no need to build the rules into the sketch in Selection games. The best approach for recording Selection rules is to keep a neat list of the rules (often, but not always, in "If — → —" format) right beneath your roster of entities. Whenever you jot down a Formal Logic rule in a Selection game, determine and record its contrapositive as well. Selection games will nearly always reward you for being able to see each rule in both affirmative and negative terms.

Take a look at how the LSAT expert recorded the rules associated with the Day Care Volunteers game you first saw in Chapter 3.

LSAT Question	Analysis
A company organizing on-site day care consults with a group of parents composed exclusively of volunteers from among the seven employees—Felicia, Leah, Masatomo, Rochelle, Salman, Terry, and Veena—who have become parents this year. The composition of the volunteer group must be consistent with the following:	**Steps 1 and 2:** → F L M R S T V
If Rochelle volunteers, then so does Masatomo.	**Step 3:** → If Ⓡ →Ⓜ If ~M → ~R
If Masatomo volunteers, then so does Terry.	→ IfⓂ→Ⓣ If ~T → ~M
If Salman does not volunteer, then Veena volunteers.	If ~S →Ⓥ If ~V →Ⓢ → *Or* At least one of Ⓢ and Ⓥ *(maybe both)*
If Rochelle does not volunteer, then Leah volunteers.	If ~R →Ⓛ If ~L →Ⓡ → *Or* At least one of Ⓛ and Ⓡ *(maybe both)*

LSAT Question	Analysis
If Terry volunteers, then neither Felicia nor Veena volunteers. *PrepTest58 Sec3 Qs7–12* $\longrightarrow$	If Ⓣ $\longrightarrow$ ~F and ~V If Ⓕ or Ⓥ $\longrightarrow$ ~T *Or* Never Ⓣ Ⓕ Never Ⓣ Ⓥ

Note, as the LSAT expert did, the implications of each rule. Rules 1 and 2 are the least definite. In both cases, the selection of one entity—Rochelle and Masatomo, respectively—requires the selection of another—Masatomo and Terry, respectively. But, don't overstate the rules. Selecting Masatomo does not require the selection of Rochelle; neither does the selection of Terry require the selection of Masatomo. As the contrapositives make clear, however, rejecting Terry means rejecting Masatomo, and rejecting Masatomo means rejecting Rochelle.

Rules 3 and 4 need careful analysis. In each, rejecting an entity—Salman and Rochelle, respectively—requires selecting another—Veena and Leah, respectively. As you can see from the contrapositives, both rules wind up telling you that at least one of the two entities in each rule must be selected. Be careful to remember that these rules allow for the selection of both entities: Salman and Veena can both be volunteers, as can both Rochelle and Leah. What is unacceptable is a selection of volunteers that rejects both Salman and Veena or one that rejects both Rochelle and Leah. Many expert test takers will jot down "at least one of S and V" instead of writing out the Formal Logic. As we'll explore in greater detail when we turn to the Deductions step on this game, Rules 3 and 4 tell you that the volunteer group includes a minimum of two parents (one of Salman and Veena and one of Rochelle and Leah).

Finally, Rule 5 reduces the maximum number of parents who can be included. If Terry volunteers, Felicia and Veena are both out. So, when Terry is in, the group has a maximum of five volunteers. Likewise, if either Felicia or Veena volunteers, the group maximum is six volunteers because Terry must bow out in this case. Note the alternative notation in the expert's analysis. Use whichever symbols work best for you.

Of course, this game doesn't include all of the variations on Formal Logic that appear in Selection games. Below, you'll see other common Selection rules and work though an exercise that will give you practice with a more exhaustive list.

Practice

Now, you'll have the chance to practice reading, analyzing, and drawing some common Selection rules. In this exercise, we won't include full games, so don't worry about the overall sketch unless some indication of it is provided. Rather, focus on the kind of detail-oriented, critical analysis that an LSAT expert does with each individual rule in logic games. Following are the questions you should ask about each rule. Keep in mind that you're unlikely to draw Selection rules directly into the sketch because you'll just use a roster of entities, circling or crossing out to show each entity's selection status.

LSAT STRATEGY

When analyzing and drawing a rule, always ask:

- What does the rule restrict?
- What does the rule leave undetermined?
- Is the rule stated in affirmative or negative terms?
- If stated affirmatively, can I learn something concrete from its negative implications (or vice versa)?
- How can I best draw the rule to account for what it does and does not restrict?

The following is a list of other rules commonly associated with Selection games.

Rule		Analysis
R is selected only if S is selected.	→	If Ⓡ → Ⓢ If ~S → ~R
If G is selected and H is selected then J is not selected.	→	If Ⓖ and Ⓗ → ~J If Ⓙ → ~G or ~H
B is not selected unless C is selected.	→	If Ⓑ → Ⓒ If ~C → ~B
M is not selected unless Y and Z are also selected.	→	If Ⓜ → Ⓨ and Ⓩ If ~Y or ~Z → ~M Or If Ⓜ → Ⓨ If ~Y → ~M If Ⓜ → Ⓩ If ~Z → ~M
A and B cannot both be selected.	→	If Ⓐ → ~B If Ⓑ → ~A Or Never AB
At least one of P and Q must always be selected.	→	If ~P → Ⓠ If ~Q → Ⓟ Or At least one of Ⓟ and Ⓠ (maybe both)
Exactly one of P and Q must be selected.	→	Ⓟ or Ⓠ (not both)

Rule	Analysis
F is selected if and only if G is selected.	If Ⓕ → Ⓖ If ~G → ~F If Ⓖ → Ⓕ If ~F → ~G *Or* *FG—both or neither*
Any arrangement that includes N includes neither R nor S.	IfⓃ → ~R and ~S IfⓇorⓈ→ ~N *Or* IfⓃ → ~R IfⓇ → ~N IfⓃ → ~S IfⓈ → ~N *Or* *Never*ⓃⓇ *Never*ⓃⓈ
T may not be included in any arrangement that includes V.	IfⓋ → ~T IfⓉ → ~V *Or* *Never*ⓉⓋ
W will be included if Y is included.	IfⓎ → Ⓦ If ~W → ~Y
In a game concerning a restaurant that could potentially serve three types of waffles (A, B, C) and three types of pancakes (d, e, f): The restaurant serves exactly two types of waffles and two types of pancakes.	*Exactly 2 of A B C; exactly 2 of d e f* *Or* Waf pan A B C d e f __ __ __ __
If A is selected, then either B or C is also selected but not both.	IfⒶ → Ⓑ or Ⓒ IfⒶ → *not [B and C combo]* If ~B and ~C → ~A If [Ⓑ and Ⓒ] → ~A

Now, try it out yourself. Examine each of the rules below. Ask the analysis questions previously outlined and make your best effort at drawing the rule. You can compare your work to an LSAT expert's analysis on the following pages.

Rule	My Analysis
15. Given that T is chosen, so is X.	
16. A is not selected if B is selected.	
17. C is included in the bag of jellybeans only if D is not.	
18. H is selected unless G is selected.	
19. In a game selecting a team of 5 specialists from a group of 4 archaeologists (A, B, C, D), 4 anthropologists (s, t, v, u), and 4 linguists (w, x, y, z): If the team includes more than 2 archaeologists, then it may include at most one anthropologist.	
20. If M is included, then neither O nor P is included.	
21. R is a member of any group of which P is a member.	
22. S is a member of any group of which Q is not a member.	
23. V is not a member of any group of which Z is a member.	
24. A is selected if but only if B is not selected.	
25. In a game that asks you to select an unspecified number of employees to be promoted from a group of 8: Only those employees with superb connections can be promoted.	
26. H cannot be chosen without L and K.	

Here's how an LSAT expert would draw the rules you just saw. Don't worry if you didn't use exactly the same symbols in your pencil work, but make sure that you didn't over- or underdetermine the restriction called for by each rule.

Rule		Analysis
15. Given that T is chosen, so is X.	→	If Ⓣ →Ⓧ If ~X → ~ T
16. A is not selected if B is selected.	→	If Ⓑ → ~A If Ⓐ → ~B *Or* Never Ⓐ Ⓑ
17. C is included in the bag of jellybeans only if D is not.	→	If Ⓒ → ~D If Ⓓ → ~C *Or* Never Ⓒ Ⓓ
18. H is selected unless G is selected.	→	If ~G →Ⓗ If ~H →Ⓖ *Or* Must have Ⓗ or Ⓖ or both.
19. In a game selecting a team of 5 specialists from a group of 4 archaeologists (A, B, C, D), 4 anthropologists (s, t, v, u), and 4 linguists (w, x, y, z): If the team includes more than 2 archaeologists, then it may include at most one anthropologist.	→	If 3 or 4 of A, B, C, D → 0 or 1 of s, t, v, u If 2, 3, or 4 of s, t, v, u → 0, 1, or 2 of A, B, C, D
20. If M is included, then neither O nor P is included.	→	If Ⓜ → ~O and ~P If Ⓞ or Ⓟ → ~M *Or* Never Ⓜ Ⓞ Never Ⓜ Ⓟ *Or* If Ⓜ → ~O If Ⓞ → ~M If Ⓜ → ~P If Ⓟ → ~M
21. R is a member of any group of which P is a member.	→	If Ⓟ →Ⓡ If ~R → ~P

Rule	Analysis
22. S is a member of any group of which Q is not a member.	$\longrightarrow$ If ~Q → Ⓢ If ~S → Ⓠ *Or* Must have Ⓠ or Ⓢ or both.
23. V is not a member of any group of which Z is a member.	$\longrightarrow$ If Ⓩ → ~V If Ⓥ → ~Z *Or* Never Ⓥ Ⓩ
24. A is selected if but only if B is not selected.	$\longrightarrow$ If Ⓐ → ~B AND If ~B → Ⓐ If Ⓑ → ~A If ~A → Ⓑ Both parts of the rule must be observed, so A or B, but not both, must always be selected. Ⓐ or Ⓑ (not both)
25. In a game that asks you to select an unspecified number of employees to be promoted from a group of 8: Only those employees with superb connections can be promoted.	$\longrightarrow$ If promoted → superb connections If ~superb connections → ~promoted
26. H cannot be chosen without L and K.	$\longrightarrow$ If Ⓗ → Ⓛ and Ⓚ If ~L or ~K → ~H

As you continue your practice with the games in Chapter 6 and with full-length LSATs, you'll have the opportunity to analyze and sketch additional Selection rules. More than any other game type, Selection games will test your Formal Logic skills. If you find that you need further practice, don't hesitate to return to the drills and examples in Chapter 1: LSAT Reasoning where we introduced the skills associated with identifying and translating Formal Logic statements, formulating contrapositives, and making valid deductions from multiple conditional statements.

Reflection

Over the coming days, pay attention to Selection tasks you encounter in everyday life. Anytime you have to choose certain people or items from a larger group, you're selecting. Notice how the real-life restrictions you face determine the way you handle your task. Even something as simple as a prix fixe restaurant menu may give rise to Selection rules: pick one of three appetizers and pick one of three desserts. If you choose the chicken, you may not have the prime rib. Another real-world Selection example would be a coach's task of selecting a starting lineup of 5 basketball players from a roster of 12. There, the coach faces rules along the lines of "Choose 1 center, 2 forwards, and 2 guards." The more you can demystify logic games and see that they mirror much of the same thinking and reasoning you do every day, the less intimidating and unfamiliar they'll seem on Test Day.

Rules in Matching and Distribution Games

Like Selection games, Matching and Distribution games are also less common than Sequencing and do not appear on every test. Matching and Distribution tasks are often included in Hybrid games, however, so your work on these game types is likely to be rewarded by at least one game on a typical test. Because both game types call for you to group entities under a number of headings, Matching and Distribution games often have very similar rules. The primary distinction to keep in mind is that Matching games usually allow you to "reuse" entities (e.g., matching a red jacket to one person doesn't prevent you from matching it to another), whereas Distribution typically requires you to place each entity just one time and into just one group.

In both of these game types, the Number Restrictions are central. Knowing exactly how many entities must be assigned to each group (Distribution) or how many attributes must be assigned to each entity (Matching) will be the most helpful information you can have. As you review the expert analysis and do your own practice with Matching and Distribution rules, focus on how the rules help to establish constraints on the numbers involved in the game.

LSAT STRATEGY

Distribution rules tell you one or more of the following things:

- Entities that must or cannot be assigned to the same group
- The number of entities that must, can, or cannot be assigned to a group or the relative sizes among groups (e.g., The Blue Group must have more members than the Green Group.)
- Conditions triggering the assignment of an entity to a particular group (e.g., If Rachel joins the marketing team, then Gar joins the service team.)

Matching rules tell you one or more of the following things:

- Attributes that must or cannot be matched to the same entity
- The number of attributes that must, can, or cannot be assigned to an entity or the relative numbers among entities (e.g., Sascha will be assigned more of the tasks than Craig will be assigned.)
- Conditions triggering the assignment of an attribute to a particular entity (e.g., If Rebecca is assigned copyediting, then Jesse is assigned layout.)

As you saw in Chapter 3, Matching and Distribution games use similar, if not identical, sketches. In both, columns under which you can record the assignment of an entity or attribute to a particular group or individual serve well to organize the restrictions and deductions. Whenever possible, record what you know about the number of entities you must, can, or cannot place in each column. Use slots to remind you that Group 1 will have four entities and Group 2 will have five, for example. Because the rules often include information about both the entities and the groups, drawing Matching and Distribution rules can be a little complicated at times. As you review the following expert analysis of the games and rules, pay special attention to how the LSAT expert accounts for all of the information in a rule without drawing it in a way that suggests the rule means more than it says.

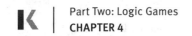
Take a look at how the LSAT expert recorded the rules associated with the Stained Glass Windows Matching game you first saw in Chapter 3.

LSAT Question	Analysis
An artisan has been hired to create three stained glass windows. The artisan will use exactly five colors of glass: green, orange, purple, rose, and yellow. Each color of glass will be used at least once, and each window will contain at least two different colors of glass. The windows must also conform to the following conditions:	**Steps 1 and 2:** G O P R Y 1st | 2nd | 3rd ___ ___ ___ ___ ___ ___
Exactly one of the windows contains both green glass and purple glass.	**Step 3:** $\frac{G}{P}$ 1x
Exactly two of the windows contain rose glass.	R = 2x
If a window contains yellow glass, then that window contains neither green glass nor orange glass.	If Y ⟶ ~G and ~O If O or G ⟶ ~Y Or Never YG Never YO
If a window does not contain purple glass, then that window contains orange glass. *PrepTest62 Sec3 Qs7–13*	If ~P ⟶ O P or O (maybe both) If ~O ⟶ P in every window

You'll recall this as an example of a Matching game because the colors can be reused (indeed, as the rules make clear, some of the colors must be assigned to more than one window). This is a game that will allow for numerous deductions as the rules are combined, but for now, examine what the LSAT expert has noted with his drawing of each rule. Rule 1 tells us that green and purple will appear *together* exactly one time. Don't overstate this rule. It does not say that the window with green and purple can have no other color, and it does not prevent green or purple from appearing in other windows so long as they are not together there. Rule 2 gives a precise number restriction to the color rose. Rule 3 creates two impossible pairings; no window may have both yellow and green, and no window may have both yellow and orange. Finally, Rule 4 tells us that every window must have either purple or orange. Be careful with Rule 4, however, as it allows for purple and orange to appear together in a window. Rule 4 is triggered when purple (or orange) glass does *not* appear; when purple (or orange) glass does appear, Rule 4 is not in play.

In the Deductions Step, we'll be able to reach additional conclusions about the Number Restrictions within the game. We'll know with certainty, for example, that purple glass must be used in at least two of the windows (maybe all three) and that green and orange glass will appear in at most two of the windows (never all three). If you don't see these deductions yet, don't worry; we'll cover all this shortly. But take a moment to reflect on the game again now that the rules are in place. The LSAT expert is always interested in what the rules for Matching and Distribution games tell him about the acceptable numbers for groups, entities, and attributes.

Now, take a look at the Museum Field Trip game with its rules interpreted by an LSAT expert. Take note of similarities you see between the rules here and in the Stained Glass Windows game. Keep in mind, however, that the Museum Field Trip game is a Distribution game. Each student will be assigned one time to one chaperone. No "reuse" is allowed here.

LSAT Question	Analysis
On a field trip to the Museum of Natural History, each of six children—Juana, Kyle, Lucita, Salim, Thanh, and Veronica—is accompanied by one of three adults—Ms. Margoles, Mr. O'Connell, and Ms. Podorski. Each adult accompanies exactly two of the children, consistent with the following conditions:	**Steps 1 and 2:** J K L S T V → Mar | O'Con | Pod ___ ___ ___ ___ ___ ___
If Ms. Margoles accompanies Juana, then Ms. Podorski accompanies Lucita.	**Step 3:** → If $\frac{Mar}{J} \longrightarrow \frac{Pod}{L}$ If $\frac{Pod}{\sim L} \longrightarrow \frac{Mar}{\sim J}$
If Kyle is not accompanied by Ms. Margoles, then Veronica is accompanied by Mr. O'Connell.	If $\frac{Mar}{\sim K} \longrightarrow \frac{O'Con}{V}$ → If $\frac{O'Con}{\sim V} \longrightarrow \frac{Mar}{K}$
Either Ms. Margoles or Mr. O'Connell accompanies Thanh.	Mar | O'Con | Pod → ___ ___ ___ ___ ___ ___ ~T ↖ T ↗
Juana is not accompanied by the same adult as Kyle; nor is Lucita accompanied by the same adult as Salim; nor is Thanh accompanied by the same adult as Veronica. *PrepTest52 Sec2 Qs8–12*	**Never JK** → **Never LS** **Never TV**

The Number Restrictions in this Distribution game are completely defined by the opening setup paragraph—three chaperones, six students, two students per chaperone—so the rules aren't able to add any further clarification in that regard here. In many Distribution games, however, you'll find that rules preventing entities from being grouped together (such as Rule 4 here) will help you understand the possible numbers within each group.

In any case, notice how similar the rules for this game are to those for the Stained Glass Windows game above. Here, Rules 1 and 2 are both written as Formal Logic. In Rule 1, the assignment of a student to a chaperone (Juana to Ms. Margoles) triggers the assignment of a different student (Lucita to Ms. Podorski). Rule 2 is a little different, so keep on your toes. Here, the trigger is a failure to assign a student to a given chaperone: "If Kyle is not accompanied by Ms. Margoles"—that's the same as saying "If Kyle is accompanied by Mr. O'Connell or by Ms. Podorski." Many poorly trained test takers will make the simple mistake of missing the word *not* in this rule and, as a result, will miss points they could have had.

Rule 3 is affirmatively worded. Thanh has two choices. The negative implication of this rule is even stronger: Thanh never goes with Ms. Podorski. You can note that certainty right in the sketch by placing "~T" under Ms. Podorski's column.

Rule 4 creates three impossible pairings. These rules are best recorded just to the side of your sketch so that you can quickly consult them as you tackle the questions. By the way, the testmaker could just as easily have written the three restrictions in Rule 4 as Formal Logic statements. Do you see how? "Juana is not accompanied by the same adult as Kyle" is precisely equivalent to the statement "If a given adult accompanies Juana, then that same adult cannot accompany Kyle." Don't let "If/Then" wording intimidate you; the practical impact of Formal Logic on the game is often simple and always concrete.

Practice

Now, you'll have the chance to practice reading, analyzing, and drawing some common Matching and Distribution rules. In this exercise, we won't include full games, so don't worry about the overall sketch unless some indication of it is provided. Rather, focus on the kind of detail-oriented, critical analysis that an LSAT expert does with each individual rule in logic games. Here are the questions you should ask about each rule.

LSAT STRATEGY

When analyzing and drawing a rule, always ask:

- What does the rule restrict?
- What does the rule leave undetermined?
- Is the rule stated in affirmative or negative terms?
- If it's stated affirmatively, can I learn something concrete from its negative implications (or vice versa)?
- Can I place the rule directly into the sketch framework?
- How can I best draw the rule to account for what it does and does not restrict?

The following is a list of other rules commonly associated with Matching and Distribution games. (Remember to keep in mind that in Distribution games, all entities are used exactly once; that is, each entity is placed into exactly one subgroup.)

Rule		**Analysis**
In a game matching lamps to 2–3 shades each: Any lamp matched to a shade of type C may not be matched to a shade of type G.	$\longrightarrow$	If $C \rightarrow \sim G$ If $G \rightarrow \sim C$ Never CG
In a game matching pencils to one or more colored erasers: Any pencil matched to a red eraser may not be matched to an orange eraser but must be matched to a green eraser.	$\longrightarrow$	If R $\rightarrow$ G and $\sim$O If O or $\sim$G $\rightarrow$ $\sim$R Or If R $\rightarrow$ $\sim$O If O $\rightarrow$ $\sim$R Never OR If R $\rightarrow$ G If $\sim$G $\rightarrow$ $\sim$R
In a game matching 3 flower beds to some combination of flowers (P, Q, R, S, T) planted in them: Bed #1 contains exactly 3 flower varieties.	$\longrightarrow$	
Exactly two beds must contain flower types P and R.	$\longrightarrow$	$\dfrac{P}{R}$ 2x
At least two beds must contain flower types S and T.	$\longrightarrow$	$\dfrac{S}{T}$ 2 – 3x
In a game distributing 8 colored marbles into bags A and B: Bag A contains either 3 or 5 marbles; the remaining marbles go into bag B.	$\longrightarrow$	

Rule	Analysis
In a game matching styles of ringtone to cell phones: The pink phone always plays jazz.	$\rightarrow$ If $\dfrac{\text{Pink}}{} \rightarrow \dfrac{\text{Pink}}{\text{J}}$ (Note, that does not mean all phones that play jazz are pink)
In a game matching each of 5 students, F, G, H, J, and K, to the 2 or 3 textbooks each one purchases: Students J and K purchase exactly the same textbooks as each other.	$\rightarrow$ J = K
In a Distribution game distributing errands onto Thursday, Friday, and Saturday: Errand R and Errand S must be on different days.	**Never RS** Or $\rightarrow$ Never $\boxed{\begin{array}{c} R \\ \hline S \end{array}}$
In a game distributing entities onto Thursday and Friday: If R is on Thursday, then S is on Friday.	If $R_{\text{Thurs}} \rightarrow S_{\text{Fri}}$ If $S_{\text{Thurs}} \rightarrow R_{\text{Fri}}$ $\rightarrow$ (Note that the contrapositive is affirmative because the entities are being distributed between exactly two days. Note, too, that R and S could both be on Friday.)
In a game distributing entities onto Thursday and Friday: If P is on Thursday, then M is on Thursday.	If $P_{\text{Thurs}} \rightarrow M_{\text{Thurs}}$ If $M_{\text{Fri}} \rightarrow P_{\text{Fri}}$ $\rightarrow$ (Note that P and M need not be on the same day. M could be on Thursday and P on Friday.)

Now, try it out yourself. Examine each of the rules below. Ask the analysis questions outlined previously in the "LSAT Strategy" box and make your best effort at drawing the rule. You can compare your work to an LSAT expert's analysis on the following pages.

Rule	My Analysis
27. In a Distribution game: C is in a group with exactly two others.	
28. In a Distribution game: E and F are never in the same group.	

Rule	My Analysis
29. In a Distribution game: G and H are always in the same group.	
30. In a game distributing 6 people into 2 groups: Exactly twice as many people are in group 1 as in group 2.	
31. In a game matching 3 children's birthday parties to a maximum of 5 games played at each one: A minimum of 3 and a maximum of 4 games are played at party #3.	
32. In a game distributing 7 types of jellyfish (M, N, O, P, Q, R, S) into 3 tanks at a research aquarium: M is in tank 2 only if N is in tank 1.	
33. In a game distributing 7 types of jellyfish (M, N, O, P, Q, R, S) into 2 tanks at a research aquarium: M is in tank 2 only if N is in tank 1.	
34. In a game distributing 7 types of jellyfish (M, N, O, P, Q, R, S) into 2 tanks at a research aquarium: Any tank that contains O cannot contain P and cannot contain S.	
35. In a game distributing 7 types of jellyfish (M, N, O, P, Q, R, S) into 2 tanks at a research aquarium: Any tank that contains O must also contain M.	
36. In a game matching each of 5 tables (P, Q, R, S, T) to the 1–3 types of wood used to manufacture them: Table P uses more types of wood than table T.	
37. In a game matching each of 5 tables (P, Q, R, S, T) to the 1–3 types of wood used to manufacture them: Table R must have exactly one type of wood in common with table S.	

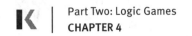

Here's how an LSAT expert would draw the rules you just saw. Don't worry if you didn't use exactly the same symbols in your pencil work, but make sure that you didn't over- or underdetermine the restriction called for by each rule.

Rule	**Analysis**
27. In a Distribution game: C is in a group with exactly two others.	$\rightarrow$ $\boxed{\begin{array}{c} C \\ \hline \underline{} \\ \hline \underline{} \end{array}}$
28. In a Distribution game: E and F are never in the same group.	$\rightarrow$ Never $\boxed{\dfrac{E}{F}}$
29. In a Distribution game: G and H are always in the same group.	$\rightarrow$ $\boxed{\dfrac{G}{H}}$
30. In a game distributing 6 people into 2 groups: Exactly twice as many people are in group 1 as in group 2.	$\rightarrow$ $\begin{array}{c c} \underline{} & \underline{} \\ \underline{} \ \underline{} & \underline{} \ \underline{} \\ \underline{} \ \underline{} & \end{array}$ with columns 1 and 2

31. In a game matching 3 children's birthday parties to a maximum of 5 games played at each one:
A minimum of 3 and a maximum of 4 games are played at party #3.

$$\begin{array}{c|c|c} 1 & 2 & 3 \\ \hline & & \underline{} \ \underline{} \\ & & \underline{} \ (\underline{}) \end{array}$$

Or

$\rightarrow$

(I)
$$\begin{array}{c|c|c} 1 & 2 & 3 \\ \hline & & \underline{} \ \underline{} \\ & & \underline{} \end{array}$$

(II)
$$\begin{array}{c|c|c} 1 & 2 & 3 \\ \hline & & \underline{} \ \underline{} \\ & & \underline{} \ \underline{} \end{array}$$

32. In a game distributing 7 types of jellyfish (M, N, O, P, Q, R, S) into 3 tanks at a research aquarium: M is in tank 2 only if N is in tank 1.	$\rightarrow$ If $M_2 \rightarrow N_1$ If $\sim N_1 \rightarrow \sim M_2$
33. In a game distributing 7 types of jellyfish (M, N, O, P, Q, R, S) into 2 tanks at a research aquarium: M is in tank 2 only if N is in tank 1.	$\rightarrow$ If $M_2 \rightarrow N_1$ If $N_2 \rightarrow M_1$ (M and N can both be in tank 1.)

Rule	Analysis
34. In a game distributing 7 types of jellyfish (M, N, O, P, Q, R, S) into 2 tanks at a research aquarium: Any tank that contains O cannot contain P and cannot contain S.	If O → ~P and ~S If P or S → ~O *Or* If O → ~P If P → ~O Never OP If O → ~S If S → ~O Never OS
35. In a game distributing 7 types of jellyfish (M, N, O, P, Q, R, S) into 2 tanks at a research aquarium: Any tank that contains O must also contain M.	If O → M If ~M → ~O
36. In a game matching each of 5 tables (P, Q, R, S, T) to the 1–3 types of wood used to manufacture them: Table P uses more types of wood than table T.	P > T P = 2 or 3 T = 1 or 2
37. In a game matching each of 5 tables (P, Q, R, S, T) to the 1–3 types of wood used to manufacture them: Table R must have exactly one type of wood in common with table S.	 or R-S exactly 1 in common

As you continue your practice with the games in Chapter 6 and with full-length LSATs, you'll have the opportunity to analyze and sketch additional Matching and Distribution rules. In these games, you'll find the greatest emphasis on Number Restrictions. Throughout your practice, focus on how knowing the entities and attributes that must, can, or cannot be assigned together helps you to determine the acceptable arrangements within the games.

Reflection

Over the coming days, pay attention to "matching" and "distribution" tasks you encounter in everyday life. Maybe something along these lines will sound familiar: you're in charge of producing a newsletter or maintaining a website for a charity organization. You have a small team that helps you manage the tasks involved. You might assign one of your volunteers the job of taking photographs, editing articles, and bringing the donuts for the group meeting. You might need another volunteer to take photographs, too. In addition, this second person might also have the job of drafting one of the articles you'll post this month. This scenario describes a Matching game perfectly. Similarly, imagine assigning nine coworkers to three different committees for upcoming presentations. Everyone is too busy to be on more than one committee. Also, you have some coworkers whom you know cannot be assigned together (maybe their expertise is too similar, or maybe you know they'll just goof off if they are on the same team—the reason doesn't really matter). This is a Distribution game. We actually encounter little "logic games" almost every day. The more you can demystify logic games and see that they mirror much of the same thinking and reasoning you do every day, the less intimidating and unfamiliar they'll seem on Test Day.

Rules in Hybrid Games

The term *Hybrid games rules* is a bit misleading. Because Hybrid games combine two or three of the common games tasks, most of the rules you find in Hybrid games are exactly like those you see in single-action games. Usually, only one or two of the rules affect both actions. For example, in a Sequencing-Matching Hybrid game about a company's semiannual presentations, two rules might cover the relative order of pairs of entities (e.g., "Carla presents before Lionel"), two might affect attributes that can be matched to entities (e.g., "Paola does not present on marketing"), and one might combine the two actions (e.g., "If Joe is the third presenter, he presents financials").

The other thing to remember about Hybrid games is that the two actions, considered separately, are typically quite simple. Continuing with our imaginary Sequencing-Matching Hybrid game, it's likely the testmaker will ask you to Sequence five or six presenters and to match each of them to a single presentation. So, don't let Hybrid games intimidate you. In the previous chapter, you learned how to create sketches that integrate the two actions. Now, as you analyze the rules, you'll determine which of them you can draw inside the sketch framework and which you'll record beneath or off to the side of the framework, just as you do with all other games.

LSAT STRATEGY

Hybrid rules tell you one of the following things:

- How the first of the actions is restricted
- How the second of the actions is restricted
- How the two actions are restricted simultaneously

Take a look at the Sequencing-Distribution Hybrid game you encountered in Chapter 3, the one in which executives visit manufacturing plants. We'll start with the integrated sketch you learned to produce, but now we'll add the LSAT expert's analysis and drawing for each rule as well. As you go over the expert's work, recall the tasks involved: you must sequence the three site visits and determine which one of those site visits each of five executives participates in.

LSAT Question	Analysis

Five executives—Quinn, Rodriguez, Sasada, Taylor, and Vandercar—are being scheduled to make site visits to three of their company's manufacturing plants—Farmington, Homestead, and Morningside. Each site will be visited by at least one of the executives and each executive will visit just one site. Each of the three site visits will take place on a different day. The schedule of site visits must conform to the following requirements:

→

Steps 1 and 2:

Farm, Home, Morn :

QRSTV :

The Farmington visit must take place before the Homestead visit.

→

Steps 3:

(I)

Farm	Home/Morn	Morn/Home
__	__	__

(II)

Morn	Farm	Home
__	__	__

The Farmington visit will include only one of the executives.

→

(I)

Farm	Home/Morn	Morn/Home
═	__	__

(II)

Morn	Farm	Home
__	═	__

The site visit that includes Quinn must take place before any site visit that includes either Rodriguez or Taylor.

→

Q ⋰ R
  ⋱ T

The site visit that includes Sasada cannot take place after any site visit that includes Vandercar.

PrepTest56 Sec1 Qs17–23

→

S
V

or S . . . V

Did you distinguish the rules relating to the Sequencing action from those relating to the Distribution action? And did you see how the Hybrid nature of the game made you start to think about the sequence among the executives as well as the sequence among the sites? The rules begin by referring only to the sites. Rule 1 is a typical Sequencing rule. At this point in the book, you've seen several rules similar to this one. Rule 2 is a typical Distribution rule: this entity—Farmington—gets exactly one slot, so close off the Farmington column by placing a double line beneath Farmington's one slot in each sketch. Rules 3 and 4 affect the sequence *of the executives*—as you distribute the executives to the sites, you'll have to keep these relative orderings in mind.

Even with the rules in place, you have quite a bit of ambiguity left in this game, so expect a couple of big breakthroughs in the Deductions step. We'll rejoin this game in the next section of this chapter. For now, take a moment to reflect on which of the actions—Sequencing the sites or Distributing the executives to them—is more restricted. Because there are only three sites, it will make sense to start your deductions with them. How does Rule 1 affect the potential order of the sites? How does Rule 2 affect the number of executives that may be distributed to each site? Once you answer those two questions, you'll have this game pretty well under control.

Practice

Now, you'll have the chance to practice reading, analyzing, and drawing some Hybrid games. In this exercise, we won't include full games, so don't worry about the overall sketch unless some indication of it is provided. Rather, focus on the kind of detail-oriented, critical analysis that an LSAT expert does with each individual rule in logic games. Here are the questions you should ask about each rule.

LSAT STRATEGY

When analyzing and drawing a rule, always ask:

- Does the rule affect one or both of the actions in the Hybrid? If only one, which one?
- What does the rule restrict?
- What does the rule leave undetermined?
- Is the rule stated in affirmative or negative terms?
- If it's stated affirmatively, can I learn something concrete from its negative implications (or vice versa)?
- Can I place the rule directly into the sketch framework?
- How can I best draw the rule to account for what it does and does not restrict?

The following is a list of rules that could be associated with Hybrid games. Given that the nature of the rules will be determined by the actions the testmaker has included in the Hybrid game, it's impossible to give an exhaustive list. Use these examples to practice thinking about Hybrid games and the ways in which the LSAT can create restrictions on two actions at once.

Rule	Analysis
In a Sequencing-Matching game that sequences N, O, P, Q, and R and matches each to a, b, or c: P is not matched to a unless N is first. $\longrightarrow$	If $P_a \longrightarrow \dfrac{N}{1}$ If $\dfrac{\sim N}{1} \longrightarrow P_{\sim a}$

Rule	Analysis
In a Distribution-Sequencing game disallowing ties that distributes music students A, B, C, D, E, and F into piano or violin classes and then orders them by age: If B plays piano, then A also plays piano, and A is older than B.	If $B_P \rightarrow A_P$ If $B_P \rightarrow A \dots B$ Contrapositive: If $A_V \rightarrow B_V$ If $B \dots A \rightarrow B_V$
In a Sequencing-Matching game that sequences the towns a train passes through and also matches the towns to their respective industries: The train passes L at some time before it passes M but at some time after it passes the shoe factory.	$\underline{\quad} \dots \dfrac{L}{\text{Shoe}} \dots \underline{M}$
In a Sequencing-Matching game that sequences 8 fire trucks in order of their arrival at the station and also matches them to their respective colors (red vs. chartreuse): Truck G, which arrives 3rd, is the first red truck to arrive.	$\begin{array}{cccccccc} & & G \\ \overline{1} & \overline{2} & \overline{3} & \overline{4} & \overline{5} & \overline{6} & \overline{7} & \overline{8} \\ \underline{C} & \underline{C} & \underline{R} & \underline{\;} & \underline{\;} & \underline{\;} & \underline{\;} & \underline{\;} \end{array}$
In a Selection-Sequencing game that selects 6 paintings from a group of 9 and then arranges the chosen paintings in a straight line on a wall: P is chosen for display only if R is displayed in the second position.	If ⓟ $\rightarrow R_2$ If $\sim R_2 \rightarrow \sim P$
In a Selection-Matching game that selects 3 rubber balls from a group of 7 and also matches the 3 balls chosen to their respective colors: L is not chosen unless it is red.	Ⓛ $\rightarrow \dfrac{L}{\text{Red}}$
In a Distribution-Selection game that selects 6 of 8 entities and then distributes the 6 selected entities onto Thursday and Friday: If R is on Thursday, then S is on Friday.	If $R_T \rightarrow S_F$ If $\sim S_F \rightarrow \sim R_T$ Because we do not know whether R and S will both be selected, the opposite of "S on Friday" is "S on Thursday or S left out." It follows that we cannot write the contrapositive as "If $S_T \rightarrow R_F$" as for the similar distribution rule treated earlier.
In a Distribution-Selection game that selects 6 of 8 entities and then distributes the 6 selected entities onto Thursday and Friday: If R is on Thursday, then S is on Thursday.	If $R_T \rightarrow S_T$ If $\sim S_T \rightarrow \sim R_T$ Again, the opposite of "on Thursday" is "on Friday or left out," so we cannot write the contrapositive of this rule as "If $S_F \rightarrow R_F$." Be sure to think very carefully about the opposites of the sufficient and necessary conditions when writing contrapositives.

Rule	Analysis
In a Selection-Sequencing game that selects 5 of 7 entities and then sequences the chosen entities: If A appears before B, then C is fifth.	If A . . . B → C_5 If $\sim C_5$ → $\sim$(A . . . B) → Here, the opposite of "A before B" is not necessarily "B before A" because A or B or both could be left out. So just write the opposite of "A before B" as "A not before B."
In a Selection-Matching game that selects 3–4 yarn colors for a scarf from 6 yarn colors (A, B, D, C, E, F) and then matches the 3–4 chosen colors to the 4 stripes of the scarf: Exactly one of the last two colors is color A.	→ 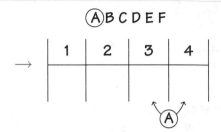

Now, try it out yourself. Examine each of the following rules. Ask the analysis questions outlined above in the "LSAT Strategy" box and make your best effort at drawing the rule. You can compare your work to an LSAT expert's analysis that follows.

Rule	My Analysis
38. In a Selection-Matching game that selects an unknown number of employees who carpool together and determines which of two cars the selected employees ride in: K rides in whatever car J rides in.	
39. In the same game: Unless L is left out of the carpool, M rides in car 1.	
40. In a Selection-Sequencing game that selects 5 pies from a group of 7 (H, J, K, L, M, P, Q) and then arranges them on a banquet table: Q is not chosen unless M is 3rd or 5th.	
41. In a Sequencing-Distribution game that sequences the 6 cabs at a taxi stand by driver and matches each driver to one or more passengers: R, who drives the 4th cab, picks up two passengers, one of whom is y.	

Rule	**My Analysis**
42. In a Distribution-Sequencing-Selection game that constructs a lineup for two 4-person relay swim teams from a group of 9 available swimmers: X is in the first position on team 1 only if W is in the third position on team 2.	
43. In a Sequencing-Matching game that sequences 7 old airplanes arriving at a hangar in preparation for an airshow and also determines whether each plane that arrives is a monoplane or a biplane: Q, the 6th plane to arrive, is also the last monoplane to arrive.	
44. In a Sequencing-Matching game that sequences 5 lectures and matches them to the experts delivering them: The first and fourth lectures must be delivered by the same expert.	
45. In the same game: The second lecture is delivered by E if and only if the third lecture is delivered by H.	
46. In a Sequencing-Matching game with a no-ties limitation: A is 2nd only if F is matched to c.	
47. In a Selection-Matching-Sequencing game that selects 5 of 6 pieces of furniture (P, Q, R, S, T, U) and matches those that are chosen to types of wood (c, d, e, f, g, h), and then sequences those pieces of furniture: Exactly two of the first three pieces of furniture are of type d wood.	

Here's how an LSAT expert would draw the rules you just saw. Don't worry if you didn't use exactly the same symbols in your pencil work but make sure that you didn't over- or underdetermine the restriction called for by each rule.

Rule	Analysis
38. In a Selection-Matching game that selects an unknown number of employees who carpool together and determines which of two cars the selected employees ride in: K rides in whatever car J rides in.	If (J) → (K) If ~K → ~J
39. In the same game: Unless L is left out of the carpool, M rides in car 1.	If (L) → (M1) If ~M1 → L out
40. In a Selection-Sequencing game that selects 5 pies from a group of 7 (H, J, K, L, M, P, Q) and then arranges them on a banquet table: Q is not chosen unless M is 3rd or 5th.	If (Q) → (M3) or (M5) If ~M3 and ~M5 → ~Q
41. In a Sequencing-Distribution game that sequences the 6 cabs at a taxi stand by driver and matches each driver to one or more passengers: R, who drives the 4th cab, picks up two passengers, one of whom is y.	$\dfrac{R}{4}$ layout: positions 1 2 3, then position 4 = R over y (two passengers), 5 6
42. In a Distribution-Sequencing-Selection game that constructs a lineup for two 4-person relay swim teams from a group of 9 available swimmers: X is in the first position on team 1 only if W is in the third position on team 2.	If (X1$_{first}$) → (W2$_{third}$) If ~W2$_{third}$ → ~X1$_{first}$
43. In a Sequencing-Matching game that sequences 7 old airplanes arriving at a hangar in preparation for an airshow and also determines whether each plane that arrives is a monoplane or a biplane: Q, the 6th plane to arrive, is also the last monoplane to arrive.	1 2 3 4 5 6 7 position 6 = Q (m), position 7 = b
44. In a Sequencing-Matching game that sequences 5 lectures and matches them to the experts delivering them: The first and fourth lectures must be delivered by the same expert.	1 2 3 4 5 positions 1 and 4 — Same expert

Rule	Analysis
45. In the same game: The second lecture is delivered by E if and only if the third lecture is delivered by H. $\longrightarrow$	If $E_2 \rightarrow H_3$ If $\sim H_3 \rightarrow \sim E_2$ If $H_3 \rightarrow E_2$ If $\sim E_2 \rightarrow \sim H_3$ Both E_2 and H_3 or neither
46. In a Sequencing-Matching game with a no-ties limitation: A is 2nd only if F is matched to c. $\longrightarrow$	If $\dfrac{A}{2} \longrightarrow F_c$ If $\sim F_c \longrightarrow \dfrac{A}{\sim 2}$
47. In a Selection-Matching-Sequencing game that selects 5 of 6 pieces of furniture (P, Q, R, S, T, U) and matches those that are chosen to types of wood (c, d, e, f, g, h), and then sequences those pieces of furniture: Exactly two of the first three pieces of furniture are of type d wood. $\longrightarrow$	P,Q,R,S,T,U $\underline{\ \ }$ $\underline{\ \ }$ $\underline{\ \ }$ $\underline{\ \ }$ $\underline{\ \ }$ c,d,e,f,g,h $\ \ \ 1\ \ \ 2\ \ \ 3\ \ \ 4\ \ \ 5$ $\underbrace{\hspace{3cm}}$ *d exactly twice*

As you continue your practice with the games in Chapter 6 and with full-length LSATs, you'll have ample opportunity to analyze and sketch additional Hybrid game rules. Taken as a group, Hybrid games are the second most popular game type behind Sequencing games. Remember, though, that most Hybrid games contain a Sequencing action, so your Sequencing and Hybrid practice will reinforce many of the same skills. In any Hybrid game, identify the actions as you conduct the Overview step and try to build an integrated sketch to manage the restrictions. As you turn to the rules, ask which of the actions each rule restricts. As always, pay attention to what the rule leaves undetermined as well. Whenever possible, draw the rule within the sketch framework but, failing that, record it in shorthand beneath or to the side of the framework you've set up.

Reflection

Over the coming days, pay attention to "hybrid" tasks you encounter in everyday life. Indeed, most of the real-life logic puzzles we solve involve multiple tasks. You may have to choose bridesmaids and groomsmen for a wedding (Selection), but you're also going to determine the order in which they stand at the altar (Sequencing) and even whom they're paired with as they walk down the aisle (Matching). Or imagine you manage a clothing store. You might have to choose which outfits to put on display in a window (Selection) and, once you have the items, decide which will be placed on each of three mannequins (Matching). The varieties may seem endless, but if you focus on tasks combining the four standard LSAT logic game actions—Sequencing, Matching, Selection, and Distribution—you'll soon start to see patterns emerge. Demystify logic games by seeing how common the LSAT actions are in our lives.

STEP 4 OF THE LOGIC GAMES METHOD: COMBINE THE RULES AND RESTRICTIONS TO MAKE DEDUCTIONS

Now that you've learned to analyze and draw the rules, you're ready for Step 4 of the Logic Games Method—Deductions. In this section, you'll learn to catalog the restrictions and rules limiting the possible arrangements within a game and to combine them to establish what must and cannot be true in all cases. More than any of the other steps, this is the one that separates the LSAT expert from other test takers. Making all of the available deductions within a game will put you in control of the questions to a degree others cannot match.

LEARNING OBJECTIVES

In this section, you'll learn to:

· Identify the points of greatest restriction within a logic game.
· Use the BLEND checklist to make all available deductions with a logic game.
· Identify *Floaters* (unrestricted entities) after making all available deductions.
· Know when all available deductions have been made (and it is time to move on to answering questions).

Although making deductions stands as a distinct step within the Logic Games Method, you've actually had a bit of a head start on the thinking and analysis you'll do here. You were already making deductions when you noted, for example, that a rule like "Jody is scheduled for an earlier day of the week than Enrique is scheduled," means that Enrique will not take the first day of appointments and Jody will not take the last day. Deductions of this sort just make explicit the implications of a rule. A similar example stems from a rule such as "Kelly and Andre will not be drafted by the same team." In a Distribution game with exactly two teams, you can deduce that each team drafts at least one player.

The work you'll do in this section takes making deductions a step further. Here, instead of making the implications of a single rule explicit, you'll learn to combine two or more rules and bring the implications of that combination to light. To see a simple example, imagine that a Sequencing game with six positions has the following rules: (1) "Barney may not occupy the first position," and (2) "Joanna will be assigned a higher-numbered position than Barney's position."

```
 1    2    3    4    5    6
~B   ~J                  ~B
~J
          B . . . J
```

From Rule 1 alone, you can exclude Barney from Position 1. From the second rule alone, you know Joanna may not take Position 1 and Barney may not take Position 6. By combining these two rules, you can deduce that the earliest position Joanna may occupy is Position 3 and exclude her from Position 2 as well. Deductions like this may not seem earth-shattering, but knowing with certainty (and noting in your Master Sketch) that an entity cannot occupy a particular position will help you answer one or more of the questions. The testmaker may reward you directly with a correct answer that mirrors the deduction or indirectly by including wrong answers suggesting that an arrangement you've determined is impossible is actually acceptable.

When they first approach Step 4, the Deductions step, some students feel that something mysterious or almost magical is happening as so much of the game takes shape. The LSAT expert, however, knows that nothing could be further from the truth. The step of making deductions is thoroughly practical and methodical. You work from what is most certain and concrete in the game and check for anything else that information allows you to determine. Moreover, the LSAT expert knows that deductions stem from combinations of five types of rules, easily memorized with the BLEND checklist you first saw in Chapter 2.

LSAT STRATEGY

Blocks of Entities—two or more players who are always grouped together

Limited Options—rules or restrictions that limit the overall setup to one of two acceptable arrangements

Established Entities—a player locked into a specific space or group

Number Restrictions—rules or limitations that provide guidance about the number of entities assigned to a group or space

Duplications—entities that appear in two or more rules, thus allowing the rules to be combined

Remember, BLEND is not a series of steps, and not all games contain all five types of rules and restrictions. As you note down a game's limitations and rules, learn to ask which of the five BLEND elements they represent. That way, you'll head into Step 4 anticipating the likely deductions you'll make.

From here, we'll revisit the games you've already seen the LSAT expert working on. Once again, we'll organize these by game type so that you can begin to discern the patterns the testmaker uses. After we demonstrate the LSAT expert's analysis of the Deductions step, you'll have the chance to practice with some additional examples. Here, we'll start with Steps 1, 2, and 3 already completed. If you want to refresh your memory about how we arrived at the work in those steps, just glance back at the expert analysis earlier in this chapter. After you work through the remainder of this chapter and learn the logic games question types in Chapter 5, you can practice the complete Logic Games Method on full logic games in Chapter 6.

Deductions in Sequencing Games

Sequencing games involve putting entities in order. It stands to reason, then, that the most concrete restrictions within Sequencing games come from rules that place an entity precisely (Established Entities) or those involving the relative positions of two or more entities (Blocks of Entities). Keep in mind, though, that a rule such as "Thomas is placed exactly one position after Marianne is placed," is much more restrictive than one saying "Thomas is placed in some position after the position in which Marianne is placed." The first of those creates a Block of Entities that must occupy two consecutive positions. Given the other rules in the game, there may be only one or two places within the game's framework where you can find two open positions together.

Here, once again, is the Monuments game first shown in Chapter 2. While we went over the Deductions step for this game there, it's worth revisiting it now that you've had so much more practice with Steps 1–3. As you review the game now, pay attention to how the LSAT expert spots the entities and positions that are most restricted, and how she uses these to determine what must or cannot be true of any acceptable arrangement.

LSAT Question	**Analysis**

Historical records show that over the course of five consecutive years—601, 602, 603, 604, and 605—a certain emperor began construction of six monuments: F, G, H, L, M, and S. A historian is trying to determine the years in which the individual monuments were begun. The following facts have been established:

> L was begun in a later year than G, but in an earlier year than F.
> H was begun no earlier than 604.
> M was begun earlier than 604.
> Two of the monuments were begun in 601, and no other monument was begun in the same year as any of the other monuments.

PrepTest58 Sec3 Qs1–6

Steps 1–3:

F G H L M S

601	602	603	604	605
___	___	___	___	___
	~H	~H	~M	~M
~H				

→

G . . . L . . . F

Rule 4 is crucial. It lays out the exact number of monuments that were begun in each year.

Deductions

Step 4:

Rule 1 is highly restrictive; it affects *three* entities. Its negative implications limit the entities that can go in the earliest and latest years. G cannot go in 604 or 605, L cannot go in 601 or 605, and F cannot go in 601 or 602.

F G H L M S

601	602	603	604	605
___	___	___	___	___
~H	~H	~H	~M	~M
~F	~F		~G	~G
~L				~L

G . . . L . . . F

The year 601 is the most restricted year. It takes two of the entities but cannot have H, L, or F. That means it has GM, GS, or MS.

F G H L M S

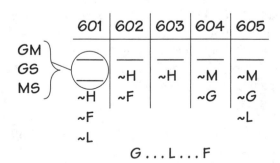

GM
GS
MS

601	602	603	604	605
___	___	___	___	___
~H	~H	~H	~M	~M
~F	~F		~G	~G
~L				~L

G . . . L . . . F

LSAT Question	**Analysis**

Deductions (cont.)

Now, at the other end, because H has to be in 604 or 605 (Rule 2), there's no way to have the G-L-F string in years 603-604-605. That means G cannot have begun in 603 and L cannot have begun in 604. There are no rules about S, so S is the Floater and is therefore marked with a star.

With that Master Sketch (the final sketch containing the framework, the rules, and all available deductions), the LSAT expert should have enormous confidence that she can tackle the question set.

You may be asking, "Why not go further? Why don't we draw out what happens when G is in 601 and then what happens when it's in 602? Couldn't we even, with enough speculation, figure out all of the acceptable permutations?" The answer to that last question is actually "Yes, in theory we could," but the time it would take would probably make it impossible to complete the game's questions within the 8–9 minutes you have for each game. The LSAT expert chose to stop where she did for two reasons: (1) she had exhausted the BLEND checklist—there are no more Established Entities, Duplications, or Blocks of Entities to find; and (2) she is at the point where making deductions—rigorously determining what must and what cannot be true—would turn into speculation—a seemingly endless series of "Well, what if . . ." questions that would eat up her time. Knowing when to end the Deductions step and move on to the question set takes practice, but asking the questions that correspond to the criteria identified with the LSAT expert—Have I noted all rules in this game from the BLEND checklist? Have I moved beyond deduction into mere speculation?—will help you get a feel for when you've learned all that's helpful from Step 4.

Next, take a look at the LSAT expert's deductions in the Saxophonists game. Again, focus on how he focuses on Blocks and Established Entities to spot the entities and spaces most likely to give additional clarity within the game.

LSAT Question	**Analysis**

Individual hour-long auditions will be scheduled for each of six saxophonists—Fujimura, Gabrieli, Herman, Jackson, King, and Lauder. The auditions will all take place on the same day. Each audition will begin on the hour, with the first beginning at 1 P.M. and the last at 6 P.M. The schedule of auditions must conform to the following conditions:

    Jackson auditions earlier than Herman does.

    Gabrieli auditions earlier than King does.

    Gabrieli auditions either immediately before or immediately after Lauder does.

    Exactly one audition separates the auditions of Jackson and Lauder.

PrepTest56 Sec1 Qs1–6

Steps 1–3:

F G H J K L

$\overline{1}$ $\overline{2}$ $\overline{3}$ $\overline{4}$ $\overline{5}$ $\overline{6}$

~H   ~J

~K   ~G

J . . . H

G . . . K

$\underline{G}$ $\underline{L}$ or $\underline{L}$ $\underline{G}$

$\underline{J/L}$ __ $\underline{L/J}$

Deductions

Step 4:

All four rules affect two entities apiece. There are no Established Entities, and the Number Restrictions are already as simple as can be—one audition per hour. Rules 3 and 4, which identify specific numbers of spaces between the entities, are stronger; they're the right ones to start with.

Rule 3 duplicates Gabrieli with Rule 2. Combined, they produce this:

$\underline{G}$ $\underline{L}$ . . . K   or $\underline{L}$ $\underline{G}$ . . . K

It's worth noting that the earliest King can audition is 3 P.M. because the G-L block has to come earlier in the day.

Rule 4 duplicates Jackson with Rule 1. Combined, they produce this:

      . . H

$\underline{J/L}$ __ $\underline{L/J}$

           . . H

From here, there are many ways to combine the entities, so no need to start speculating. Note Fujimura as an unrestricted Floater (F can audition at any hour) by putting a star above it. Final Master Sketch:

   *
F G H J K L

$\overline{1}$ $\overline{2}$ $\overline{3}$ $\overline{4}$ $\overline{5}$ $\overline{6}$

     $\underline{G}$ $\underline{L}$ . . . K   or $\underline{L}$ $\underline{G}$ . . . K

      . . H

    $\underline{J/L}$ ___ $\underline{L/J}$ . . .

             H

That game is an excellent illustration of the LSAT expert knowing how far to push the Deductions step. Take a moment to consider Jackson, an entity restricted by two rules. Jackson could take any audition slot from 1 P.M. to 5 P.M. You can draw the same conclusion about Gabrieli. Your time is too valuable to try to sketch out all of those permutations. Trust, as the LSAT expert does (and as you'll see in the question set), that the LSAT has provided all the information you'll need to answer the questions.

Before turning to practice, take a few minutes to review the work of the LSAT expert on the Loose Sequencing example with which you've been working, the Water Valves game. Recall that the LSAT expert demonstrated that, in Loose Sequencing, you may combine the rules even as you're analyzing and drawing them out. Indeed, that's the approach you'll likely use on Test Day. For now, though, we'll start with the rules listed individually and demonstrate one more time how to combine them. In Loose Sequencing games, almost all of the deductions will spring from Duplications, the "D" of BLEND. That's because, in most cases, at least two rules share each entity. The rules thus "snap together" to create the Master Sketch.

LSAT Question	Analysis

Workers at a water treatment plant open eight valves—G, H, I, K, L, N, O, and P—to flush out a system of pipes that needs emergency repairs. To maximize safety and efficiency, each valve is opened exactly once, and no two valves are opened at the same time. The valves are opened in accordance with the following conditions:

    Both K and P are opened before H.
    O is opened before L but after H.
    L is opened after G.
    N is opened before H.
    I is opened after K.

PrepTest52 Sec2 Qs1–7

Steps 1–3:

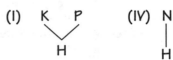

(I) 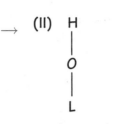   (IV) N
                        |
                        H

(II) H   (V) K
    | |
    O   I
    |
    L

(III) G
     |
     L

Deductions

Step 4:

Rules 1 and 2 share H.

Rules 2 and 3 share G.

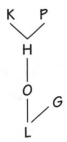

LSAT Question	Analysis

Deductions (cont.)

Rules 1, 2, and 4 share H.

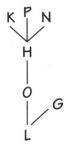

Rules 1 and 5 share K.

This is the Master Sketch.

From this sketch, the following possibilities are clear:

G takes a position from 1 to 7 (only L need come later than G).

H takes a position from 4 to 6 (K, N, and P must come earlier than H, and O and L must come later than H).

I takes a position from 2 to 8 (only K must come earlier than I).

K takes a position from 1 to 4 (H, I, O, and L must all come after K).

L takes either position 7 or 8 (only I could come later than L).

N takes a position from 1 to 5 (H, L, and O must come later than N).

O takes a position from 5 to 7 (H, K, N, and P must come earlier than O, and only L need come later).

P takes a position from 1 to 5 (H, L, and O must come later than P).

On Test Day, the LSAT expert probably will not take the time to list out the possible positions for each entity as you see above, but she will be able to determine any of those possibilities in seconds. She understands that the sketch represents the sum total of restrictions and can use them to determine what must, can, and cannot be true at a glance. At the same time, she avoids unwarranted assumptions. From the sketch, it may appear that I and H are opened at roughly the same time. The lack of any restriction after I's position, however, is a clear indication to the LSAT expert that I could come as late as eighth in the sequence.

Practice

Now, try your hand at the Deductions step. Use the following brief examples to practice identifying the elements of the BLEND checklist you see represented. Look for the points of greatest restriction in the game setup. Starting from these restrictions, combine the rules and limitations to determine what else must or cannot be true.

Take five minutes for each of the following examples. Review the expert's work on Steps 1–3 of the Logic Games Method. Analyze and draw the rules if the expert has not done so. Then, use the BLEND checklist to make all available deductions. Once you're finished, check your work against the LSAT expert's analysis on the following pages.

Game	My Analysis

48. A four-story building houses five businesses—Shops A, B, C, D, and E—and each floor has at least one business on it. Shop B needs to be on a higher floor than Shop E.
    Shop A is on a higher floor than Shop B.
    Shop D is on a floor by itself.
	Step 1: *Situation:* Building with 4 floors and 5 shops
	
	Entities: The shops (A, B, C, D, E)
	
	Action: Positional arrangement matters, so this is a Sequencing game.
	
	Limitations: One floor will hold two shops, and Shop B is on a higher floor than Shop E.

$\longrightarrow$ **Step 2:**

A B C D E

```
4—
3—      (+ ___ extra business)
2—
1—
```

Step 3: (Transcribe the rules here.)

Deductions

Step 4: (Make your deductions and Master Sketch here)

Game	**My Analysis**
49. A teacher is assigning the front row of seats in her class according to the age of six students (A, B, C, D, E, and F). There are six seats in the front row. The youngest student will sit on the far left, and the oldest student will sit on the far right.	**Step 1:** *Situation:* A classroom with a row of seats

49. A teacher is assigning the front row of seats in her class according to the age of six students (A, B, C, D, E, and F). There are six seats in the front row. The youngest student will sit on the far left, and the oldest student will sit on the far right.

   Student B is either the 4th or 6th youngest student in class.

   Students A and D are separated by exactly one seat.

   The youngest student is either C or E.

   Students A and F cannot sit next to each other.

Step 1: *Situation:* A classroom with a row of seats

Entities: The six students (A, B, C, D, E, F)

Action: Sequence the students according to age.

Limitations: Each seat will be assigned one student.

Step 2:

$\longrightarrow$

A B C D E F

___ ___ ___ ___ ___ ___
(Youngest) 1   2   3   4   5   6 (Oldest)

Step 3: (Transcribe rules here.)

Deductions

Step 4: (Make your Deductions and Master Sketch here.)

Now, compare your deductions and Master Sketch on the examples you just tried to those of the LSAT expert.

Game	Analysis

48. A four-story building houses five businesses—Shops A, B, C, D, and E—and each floor has at least one business on it. Shop B needs to be on a higher floor than Shop E.

    Shop A is on a higher floor than Shop B.
    Shop D is on a floor by itself.

Step 1: *Situation:* Building with 4 floors and 5 shops

Entities: The shops (A, B, C, D, E)

Action: Positional arrangement matters, so this is a Sequencing game.

Limitations: One floor will hold two shops, and Shop B is on a higher floor than Shop E.

Step 2:

A B C D E

4 —
3 —   (+ __ extra business)
2 —
1 —

→ **Step 3:** (Limitation):

B
·
·
E

Rule 1:

A
·
·
B

Rule 2:

D alone

None of these rules can, on its own, be directly added to the sketch.

Game	Analysis

Deductions

Step 4:

Both the limitation in the overview and the first rule discuss Shop B. This is a duplicate entity and, by combining both rules, we get this:

A
.
.
B
.
.
E

Combining those rules creates a larger Block of Entities. In Sequencing games, Blocks of Entities (even Blocks connected together by Loose Sequencing rules) are crucially important. In some cases, those Blocks lead to Limited Options (arrangements in which only two alternatives are acceptable). Here, three shops are connected together vertically, but there are only four floors onto which those shops can be placed. Looking at the Block of Entities, it's clear that Shop A must be on the highest floor of the three shops. And because two floors below A are filled up with B and E, A can only go on Floor 4 or Floor 3. Placing Shop A on Floor 4 doesn't lead to any more concrete deductions, but placing Shop A on Floor 3 forces Shops B and E into specific locations on the sketch. Create a Limited Options sketch.

Opt. 1   *Opt. 2*

4 A   4 ___
3 ___ B   3 A
2 ___   E   2 B
1 ___   1 E

The last rule says that Shop D is on a floor by itself. The Limited Option sketches show that in Option 2, Shop D must go on Floor 4 because every other floor is occupied. In Option 1, which is much more open, D can end up on any of the bottom three floors. In that case, there's no point adding that information to the sketch.

Shop C, a Floater, is not constrained to any particular floor or restricted by any other business. Because A, B, and E are all separated from each other, and because D is on a floor by itself, C *must* be one of the shops that shares a floor. Each rule has now been evaluated and combined with other rules. No more deductions can be made, so move on to the questions.

Opt. 1   *Opt. 2*

4 A   4 D
3 ___ B   3 A   C shares a floor
2 ___   E   2 B
1 ___   1 E

Game	Analysis
49. A teacher is assigning the front row of seats in her class according to the age of six students (A, B, C, D, E, and F). There are six seats in the front row. The youngest student will sit on the far left, and the oldest student will sit on the far right.	**Step 1:** *Situation:* A classroom with a row of seats

49. A teacher is assigning the front row of seats in her class according to the age of six students (A, B, C, D, E, and F). There are six seats in the front row. The youngest student will sit on the far left, and the oldest student will sit on the far right.

    Student B is either the 4th or 6th youngest student in class.

    Students A and D are separated by exactly one seat.

    The youngest student is either C or E.

    Students A and F cannot sit next to each other.

Step 1: *Situation:* A classroom with a row of seats

Entities: The six students (A, B, C, D, E, F)

Action: Sequence the students according to age.

Limitations: Each seat will be assigned one student.

Step 2:

$$A\ B\ C\ D\ E\ F$$

youngest 1 2 3 4 5 6 oldest

Step 3: Rule 1: (add directly to sketch)
Rule 2: A/D __ D/A
Rule 3: (add directly to sketch)
Rule 4: Never AF or FA

youngest $\frac{C/E}{1}$ $\frac{}{2}$ $\frac{}{3}$ $\frac{}{4}$ $\frac{}{5}$ $\frac{}{6}$ oldest (B over 4→6)

A/D __ D/A

never [AF] or [FA]

Deductions

Step 4:

    <u>Opt. 1</u>

youngest $\frac{C/E}{1}$ $\frac{A/D}{2}$ $\frac{}{3}$ $\frac{D/A}{4}$ $\frac{}{5}$ $\frac{}{6}$ oldest

    <u>Opt. 2</u>

youngest $\frac{C/E}{1}$ $\frac{}{2}$ $\frac{A/D}{3}$ $\frac{}{4}$ $\frac{D/A}{5}$ $\frac{}{6}$ oldest

In Strict Sequencing games, Blocks of Entities often lead to deductions. Here, students A and D are blocked together in either order with a mystery student in between. Where can the A-D block go? It can't start in seat 1, which takes either C or E. What about starting in seat 2? That would put entities A and D in seats 2 and 4 (in either order, with the mystery entity in seat 3). That works. What about the A-D in seats 3 and 5? That works, too. But trying to place the A-D block in seats 4 and 6 causes a problem: Student B must go in one of those two seats. Because the A-D block has only two options, create the Limited Options sketch shown above.

Game	Analysis

Deductions (cont.)

Now, consider Rule 1. It says that B is either the fourth or sixth youngest. In Option 1, seat 4 is occupied by either A or D, so B must take seat 6. Add that information directly the sketch. In Option 2, both 4 and 6 are still open, so B gets drawn below the sketch, with arrows indicating it can go to either 4 or 6.

Opt. 1

youngest $\frac{C/E}{1}$ $\frac{A/D}{2}$ $\frac{}{3}$ $\frac{D/A}{4}$ $\frac{}{5}$ $\frac{B}{6}$ oldest

Opt. 2

youngest $\frac{C/E}{1}$ $\frac{}{2}$ $\frac{A/D}{3}$ $\frac{}{4}$ $\frac{D/A}{5}$ $\frac{}{6}$ oldest

B (arrows to 4 or 6)

Rule 3 has been added to the sketch, but what about Rule 4? That rule says that A and F can never sit side by side. Option 1 shows that A will sit in seat 2 or seat 4; either way, F will never be able to sit in seat 3. Because the only other open spot is seat 5, F must take seat 5. That, in turn, forces A into seat 2, which forces D into seat 4. At this point, the only open seat is seat 3, which must be filled by either C or E.

Check Option 2. Rule 4 says that A and F can never sit together. Because A will sit in either 3 or 5, student F cannot take seat 4.

Opt. 1

youngest $\frac{C/E}{1}$ $\frac{A}{2}$ $\frac{C/E}{3}$ $\frac{D}{4}$ $\frac{F}{5}$ $\frac{B}{6}$ oldest

Opt. 2

youngest $\frac{C/E}{1}$ $\frac{}{2}$ $\frac{A/D}{3}$ $\frac{}{4}$ $\frac{D/A}{5}$ $\frac{}{6}$ oldest

~F B (arrows to 4 or 6)

Can more deductions be made? At this point, every rule has been combined with other rules and added directly to the sketch. The effect that each rule has on the Master Sketch, and on other rules, has been evaluated. There aren't any more deductions to be made, so it's time to move on to the questions.

Reflection

Congratulations. You've now tackled the most important steps for gaining mastery over the most important type of logic games, Sequencing games. Take a moment to summarize what you've learned about the Deductions step in Sequencing games.

LSAT STRATEGY

In Sequencing games, deductions are likely to stem from:

- **Blocks of Entities**—two or more entities that are linked together; when one is placed, the other's movement is determined or restricted.
- **Duplications**—entities shared by two or more rules; duplicators are almost always at the heart of Loose Sequencing games.
- **Established Entities**—entities placed into a specific space; even if no rule directly provides for an Established Entity, you may be able to determine an entity's exact position by combining other rules.

In Sequencing games, deductions may involve:

- **Limited Options**—the situation that arises when a Block of Entities or a *key player* (an entity affecting the positions of other entities) can take either of two positions; when this occurs, create dual Limited Options sketches.
- **Numbers Restrictions**—limitations or rules affecting the number of entities that can be placed in a given position; this is rare in Sequencing games—typically, the limitation is one per space.

You'll see these same deductions resurface when you turn your attention to Hybrid games because many of those involve a Sequencing action. In Chapter 5, you'll have a chance to see how the LSAT expert applied the deductions in the LSAT games covered previously when we turn to Step 5 of the Logic Games Method and answer the questions.

Deductions in Selection Games

In Selection games, your task is to choose a small number of entities out of a larger group. The test offers two standard variations on Selection games. In the first, the number of entities you are to choose is left open. In these cases, pay special attention to deductions involving the minimum or maximum number of entities you're able to select. In the second variation, the testmaker tells you how many entities must be selected (four out of seven or five out of nine, for example). In these games, the testmaker often categorizes the entities—in a game asking you to select a menu, for example, you might encounter three appetizers, two main courses, and three desserts. Numbers Restrictions are equally important in this variation of Selection, especially rules or limitations that set limits on how many entities from a specific category you can or must select.

Review the Day Care Volunteers game that you've seen the LSAT expert working. We'll start with the expert's work on Steps 1–3 of the Logic Games Method and then show how he analyzed and combined the rules to make additional deductions. As you're going through this example, pay special attention to the expert's notes regarding the number of volunteers who can or must be chosen.

LSAT Question	Analysis

A company organizing on-site day care consults with a group of parents composed exclusively of volunteers from among the seven employees—Felicia, Leah, Masatomo, Rochelle, Salman, Terry, and Veena—who have become parents this year. The composition of the volunteer group must be consistent with the following:
 	
    If Rochelle volunteers, then so does Masatomo.
    If Masatomo volunteers, then so does Terry.
    If Salman does not volunteer, then Veena volunteers.
    If Rochelle does not volunteer, then Leah volunteers.
    If Terry volunteers, then neither Felicia nor Veena volunteers.
 	
PrepTest58 Sec3 Qs7–12 →
	Steps 1–3:
	
	F L M R S T V
	
	If (R) ⟶ (M)
	If ~M ⟶ ~R
	
	If (M) ⟶ (T)
	If ~T ⟶ ~M
	
	If ~S ⟶ (V)
	If ~V ⟶ (S)
	(At least one of S, V—maybe both)
	
	If ~R ⟶ (L)
	If ~L ⟶ (R)
	(At least one of R, L—maybe both)
	
	If (T) ⟶ ~F and ~V
	If (F) or (V) ⟶ ~T
	(NOT TF and NOT TV)

Deductions

Step 4:

The Overview does not specify a minimum or maximum to be chosen. Rules 3 and 4, however, make clear that at least two volunteers must be chosen—at least one of S and V and at least one of R and L. R duplicates in Rule 1. If R is in, then so is M. M, in turn, duplicates in Rule 2. If M is in, so is T. Thus,

Minimum = 2 (SL or VL)

Minimum with R selected = 4 (R, M, T, and S)

The only rule that decreases the maximum is Rule 5. If T is in, then two entities are out, F and V. If either F or V is in, then T must be out. But, T is duplicated in Rule 2. If T is out, so is M. And M, in turn, is duplicated in Rule 1. When M is out, so is R. Thus,

Maximum with T selected = 5 (L, M, R, S, and T)

Maximum with F or V selected = 4 (F, L, S, and V)

In Selection games, the majority of rules are Formal Logic statements. It's very important to be able to see the impact of those rules on the number of entities you can choose. Here, the LSAT expert recognized that both Rule 3 and Rule 4 require at least one of two entities to be selected, but these rules don't prevent both of the entities in the pair from being selected. (The volunteer group could, for example, include both Salman and Veena or both Rochelle and Leah).

Part and parcel of the deductions the LSAT expert made were "chains" of Formal Logic. In Chapter 1: LSAT Reasoning, you learned that anytime the result ("then" clause) of one Formal Logic statement matches the trigger ("if" clause) of another, those two statements can be combined. In the Day Care Volunteers game, Rules 1, 2, and 5 chain up very clearly. If Rochelle volunteers, then so does Masatomo. If Masatomo volunteers, then so does Terry. If Terry volunteers, then Felicia and Veena do not. Some LSAT experts will write out the chains of Formal Logic as part of their Master Sketch; others are content to spot the conditions that trigger all or part of the chain. Use whichever approach works best for you. Whether or not they write out the chains of logic, all LSAT experts will record the contrapositives next to or beneath each Formal Logic rule. This allows them to see that the chain works in reverse as well. If either Felicia or Veena volunteers, then Terry does not. When Terry does not volunteer, then neither does Masatomo. And when Masatomo does not volunteer, then neither does Rochelle.

Selection Deductions Practice

Now, try your hand at the Deductions step. Use the following brief examples to practice identifying the elements of the BLEND checklist you see represented. Look for the points of greatest restriction in the game setup. Starting from these restrictions, combine the rules and limitations to determine what else must or cannot be true.

Take five minutes for each of the following examples. Review the expert's work on Steps 1–3 of the Logic Games Method. Analyze and draw the rules if the expert has not done so. Then, use the BLEND checklist to make all available deductions. Once you're finished, check your work against the LSAT expert's analysis on the following pages.

Game	**My Analysis**
50. Each of the seven members of a fraternity (A, B, C, D, E, F, and G) is deciding whether or not to go to the football game this weekend.	**Step 1:** *Situation:* Members of a group each deciding whether or not to go somewhere
If A goes to the game, then so does C.	*Entities:* The fraternity members (A, B, C, D, E, F, G)
C won't go to the game unless B does.	
Either G or F will go to the game, but not both.	*Action:* Select from a larger group
If G goes to the game, then B will not go.	*Limitations:* We have no information about a minimum or maximum number to select.
	Step 2:
	$\rightarrow$ A B C D E F G
	Step 3: (Transcribe rules here.)

Game	**My Analysis**

Deductions

Step 4: (Make your Deductions and Master Sketch here.)

Game	**My Analysis**

51. A chef is going to make a soup using exactly
five ingredients. She is choosing from
among four types of spices (A, B, C, and D),
three types of meat (e, f, and g), and three
vegetables (H, I, and J).

    The chef will choose at least one of each type
of ingredient.

    If she chooses spice A, she will also choose
spice B.

    She will choose meat f only if she chooses
vegetable J.

    Anytime the chef selects exactly two types of
meat, she will also select exactly two types of
vegetables, and anytime she selects exactly
two types of vegetables, she will also select
exactly two types of meat.

    The chef will select at most two types of spices.

$\longrightarrow$

Step 1: *Situation:* A chef picking ingredients for a
soup

Entities: 4 types of spices (A, B, C, D), 3 types of
meat (e, f, g), 3 types of vegetables (H, I, J)

Action: Select 5 of the 10 ingredients.

Limitations: Must pick 5 of 10, but there are no
limitations within each subcategory.

Step 2:

pick 5 of 10

spices	meats	vegetables
A B C D	e f g	H I J

Step 3: (Transcribe rules here.)

Deductions

Step 4: (Make your Deductions and Master Sketch here.)

Now, compare your deductions and Master Sketch to those of the LSAT expert on the examples you just tried.

Game	Analysis
50. Each of the seven members of a fraternity (A, B, C, D, E, F, and G) is deciding whether or not to go to the football game this weekend. If A goes to the game, then so does C. C won't go to the game unless B does. Either G or F will go to the game, but not both. If G goes to the game, then B will not go.	**Step 1:** *Situation:* Members of a group each deciding whether or not to go somewhere *Entities:* The fraternity members (A, B, C, D, E, F, G) *Action:* Select from a larger group *Limitations:* We have no information about a minimum or maximum number to select.

Step 2:

A B C D E F G

Step 3: Selection game rules that are expressed in Formal Logic should be immediately transcribed, along with the contrapositive.

Rule 1:   If Ⓐ ⟶ Ⓒ
          If ~C ⟶ ~A

⟶

Rule 2:   If Ⓒ ⟶ Ⓑ
          If ~B ⟶ ~C

Rule 3:   If Ⓖ ⟶ ~F
          If Ⓕ ⟶ ~G (never GF)
          If ~G ⟶ Ⓕ
          If ~F ⟶ Ⓖ (at least F or G)

This rule can also be expressed without Formal Logic translation:

This indicates "exactly one of these must be chosen."

Rule 4: If Ⓖ → ~B
        If Ⓑ → ~G (never GB)

Game	Analysis

Deductions

Step 4:

In a Selection game, the conditional rules can rarely be built into the sketch framework. The best deductions will come from combining rules that share a common entity (Duplications, the "D" in BLEND). For example, combining Rules 1 and 2 (if A goes to the game, then C goes to the game, and if C goes, then B goes) creates the following deduction: if A goes, then B goes. Moreover, B also shows up in Rule 4. Combine Rules 1, 2, and 4: if G goes, then B doesn't go, which means C doesn't go, and then neither does A.

Minimums and Maximums: At least one member goes to the game—either F or G (per Rule 3).

Two rules—Rules 3 and 4—reduce the maximum number of members who can attend. If F attends, G is out, but everyone else could go, so the maximum with F selected is 6. If G attends, however, F is knocked out (per Rule 3) and B is knocked out (per Rule 4). Knocking out B sets off the chain involving Rules 1 and 2. With B out, C is out, too. And with C out, so is A. The maximum if G attends is 3 (D, E, and G). In this game, members D and E are Floaters, and are each marked with an asterisk.

[Some experts will note the following: Rule 3 can be depicted in a Limited Options sketch. Make one option with F selected and G out. Make another with G selected and F out. The one with G selected triggers the chain involving Rules 1, 2, and 4, as well.]

Opt. 1

A̶ B̶ C̶ Ḋ* Ė* F̶ (G)

Opt. 2

A B C Ḋ* Ė* (F) G̶

Game	Analysis
51. A chef is going to make a soup using exactly five ingredients. She is choosing from among four types of spices (A, B, C, and D), three types of meat (e, f, and g), and three vegetables (H, I, and J).	**Step 1:** *Situation:* A chef picking ingredients for a soup

Game

51. A chef is going to make a soup using exactly five ingredients. She is choosing from among four types of spices (A, B, C, and D), three types of meat (e, f, and g), and three vegetables (H, I, and J).

  The chef will choose at least one of each type of ingredient.

  If she chooses spice A, she will also choose spice B.

  She will choose meat f only if she chooses vegetable J.

  Anytime the chef selects exactly two types of meat, she will also select exactly two types of vegetables, and anytime she selects exactly two types of vegetables, she will also select exactly two types of meat.

  The chef will select at most two types of spices.

Analysis

Step 1: *Situation:* A chef picking ingredients for a soup

Entities: 4 types of spices (A, B, C, D), 3 types of meat (e, f, g), 3 types of vegetables (H, i, j)

Action: Select 5 of the 10 ingredients.

Limitations: Must pick 5 of 10, but there are no limitations within each subcategory.

Step 2:

pick 5 of 10

spices	meats	vegetables
A B C D	e f g	H I J

Step 3:

→ Rule 1: **At least one of each type** (can add directly to the sketch, with a designation above each subcategory)

Rule 2: If Ⓐ ⟶ Ⓑ
  If ~B ⟶ ~A

Rule 3: If Ⓕ ⟶ Ⓙ
  If ~J ⟶ ~f

Rule 4: If 2 meats ⟶ 2 vegetables
  If ~2 vegetables ⟶ ~2 meats
  If 2 vegetables ⟶ 2 meats
  If ~2 meats ⟶ ~2 vegetables

Rule 5: **At most two types of spices** (can indicate in the sketch)

pick 5 of 10

(1–2) spices	(1–3) meats	(1–3) vegetables
A B C D	e f g	H I J

Game	Analysis

Deductions

Step 4:

Most Selection games rely primarily on Duplications (the D in BLEND), but this game requires other BLEND deductions. Most readily apparent in this game are the Numbers Restrictions (the N in BLEND). These are (1) the Overview limitation—5 out of 10 ingredients must be selected; (2) Rule 1—at least one of each ingredient type is selected; (3) Rule 5—at most two types of spices will be selected; and (4) the complex Rule 4—if the chef selects either two types of meat or two types of vegetables, she must also select two types of vegetables and two types of meat.

Evaluate Rule 4 closely. Affirmatively, the rule says:

If 2 meat → 2 vegetable

And

If 2 vegetable → 2 meat

Either way, if the chef has 2 meats and 2 veggies, she can only have 1 spice (because of the Overview limitation that says choose 5 ingredients out of 10).

The contrapositives of the rule state:

If ~2 meat → ~2 vegetable

And

If ~2 vegetable → ~ 2 meat

But Rule 1 says the chef must have at least one of each ingredient type. So, if the chef doesn't have 2 meats, she could have 1 or 3. If she has 1 or 3 meats, she must not have 2 vegetables. Again, this could be 1 or 3. This limits the chef to three acceptable number arrangements for the ingredient types:

Scenario 1: 1 spice, 2 meats, 2 veggies

Scenario 2: 1 spice, 3 meats, 1 veggie (and the veggie will have to be J because meat f is selected)

Scenario 3: 1 spice, 1 meat, 3 veggies

Game	Analysis

Deductions (cont.)

No scenario with two spices is acceptable, because that would require the chef to choose three ingredients from among meats and veggies. If she chooses two of either meats or veggies, she must choose two of the other ingredient type as well. That would make for a total of six (violating the Overview limitation—choose 5 of 10). Because the chef cannot select two spices, she can never select Spice A because Rule 2 would require her to select Spice B as well. Cross Spice A off the list once and for all.

Choosing three or four spices is forbidden by Rule 5.

pick 5 of 10

①	(1–3)	(1–3)
spices	meats	vegetables
ᴀB C D	e f g	H I J

number limitations:

    1 meat, 3 veg, and 1 spice
    2 meat, 2 veg, and 1 spice
    3 meat, 1 veg, and 1 spice

Reflection

Because of their focus on Formal Logic, Selection games can seem very different from other game types. Make no mistake. To master Selection games, you must sharpen your Formal Logic skill set. But don't lose sight of the crucial role that numbers play in these games as well. When the game does not specify the number of entities to be selected, at least one or two questions will usually reward you for being able to figure out the minimum or maximum number of selections that are acceptable. When the test tells you an exact number of entities to select, it will often set up a situation in which you have to choose from among different categories, and it will typically make you account for the numbers from each of those categories.

LSAT STRATEGY

In Selection games, deductions are likely to stem from:

· **Duplications**—entities shared by two or more rules; Selection games often feature "chains" of Formal Logic linked by shared entities.

· **Numbers Restrictions**—limitations on the number of entities to be selected or determinations of the minimum and maximum numbers that can be selected given the game's rules.

In Selection games, deductions may involve:

· **Limited Options**—the situation that arises when a rule specifies that only one of two selection patterns is acceptable (e.g., G is selected and F is not selected, or F is selected and G is not selected).

· **Blocks of Entities**—two or more entities that must be selected or rejected as a pair.

· **Established Entities**—entities that must be selected or rejected; this is very rare in Selection games where all or most rules are conditional; occasionally, the Numbers Restrictions will allow you to determine that a specific entity may never be selected.

You'll have additional opportunities to practice Selection deductions in some Hybrid games involving a Selection action and in Chapter 6 and in the full-length tests at the back of this book. In Chapter 5, you'll have a chance to see how the LSAT expert applied the deductions in the Day Care Volunteers game when we turn to Step 5 of the Logic Games Method and answer the questions.

Deductions in Matching Games

To get a feel for Matching games deductions, imagine a real-world scenario. You're equipping a team of six archaeologists who will hike in to a relatively remote site to do an initial excavation. If everyone's backpacks will have exactly the same thing—one laptop, one bag of food, one set of tools, etc.—you don't have much of a logic game. If you instead imagine the six people lined up on one side of a room and a big stack of supplies of various types on the other, you start to get the picture. Maybe the group needs three boxes of foodstuffs. Maybe the group only needs two sets of tools. Four people, on the other hand, will need to carry water. And so on. Now, you can start to put together the rules for your task. Food and tools are heavy, so the same person cannot carry both. Anyone taking tools will also carry water. Some members of the team are physically capable of taking more than others can. In an LSAT Matching game, the reasons for the restrictions and rules may not be as practical or explicit, but the result will be the same. You'll have to figure out the number and types of items each entity can be matched with, so keep your eyes on rules involving Numbers Restrictions and Duplications. (Note: Order does not matter in Matching games. There will be no rules that stipulate Archaeologist A is provisioned before Archaeologist B, for example. Adding rules of that kind would transform the game into a Sequencing-Matching Hybrid game.)

With that background in mind, take another look at the Stained Glass Windows game. Pay special attention to what the LSAT expert discerns about the number of colors each window must, can, or cannot contain and how she deals with rules that mention the same color(s). Remember that the order of the windows does not affect this Matching game. The Sketch will label the windows "1st," "2nd," and "3rd" for convenience, but there are no rules stating that one color must be used earlier or later than another.

LSAT Question	Analysis

An artisan has been hired to create three stained glass windows. The artisan will use exactly five colors of glass: green, orange, purple, rose, and yellow. Each color of glass will be used at least once, and each window will contain at least two different colors of glass. The windows must also conform to the following conditions:

    Exactly one of the windows contains both green glass and purple glass.

    Exactly two of the windows contain rose glass.

    If a window contains yellow glass, then that window contains neither green glass nor orange glass.

    If a window does not contain purple glass, then that window contains orange glass.

PrepTest62 Sec3 Qs7–13

$\longrightarrow$

Steps 1–3:

GOPRY

1st	2nd	3rd

$\dfrac{G}{P}$ 1x

R=2x

Never $\dfrac{Y}{G}$

Never $\dfrac{Y}{O}$

P or O or both in every window

Deductions

Step 4:

Rule 1 says that exactly one window has green *and* purple. The windows aren't numbered, so just let the "first" window (on the left) take G and P.

1st	2nd	3rd
G		
P		

Because that window contains green, it cannot contain yellow (Rule 3). Green is duplicated in Rules 1 and 3.

1st	2nd	3rd
G		
P		
~Y		

Every color of glass must be used (Overview limitation), so give the "second" (middle) window yellow. Because of Rule 3, that means the second (middle) window cannot have green and cannot have orange.

LSAT Question	Analysis

Deductions (cont.)

1st	2nd	3rd
<u>G</u>	<u>Y</u>	
<u>P</u>		
~Y	~G	
	~O	

Any window without orange glass must have purple (Rule 4), so give the second (middle) window purple, too.

1st	2nd	3rd
<u>G</u>	<u>Y</u>	
<u>P</u>	<u>P</u>	
~Y	~G	
	~O	

Rule 4 also makes it clear that the "third" (right) window must have orange or purple or both. Because it's unclear whether it has orange, there's nothing else for certain that can be determined except that it cannot have both purple and green (a combination that must be used only once—Rule 1).

1st	2nd	3rd
<u>G</u>	<u>Y</u>	<u>P/O</u> (Maybe both)
<u>P</u>	<u>P</u>	
~Y	~G	
	~O	

That is the Master Sketch. The artist will have to use rose two times, but rose can go along with any other color.

(Here's an alternative Master Sketch that some LSAT experts might employ. Use the approach that works best for you.)

1st	2nd	3rd	
Ⓖ	G̶	G	
O	O̶	O	At least 1
Ⓟ	Ⓟ	P	
R	R	R	Exactly 2
Y̶	Ⓨ	Y	

Because Matching games have two sets of entities (or a set of entities and a set of attributes to match to those entities, if you prefer to think of it that way), making them visual is key to keeping track of all the information. The LSAT expert has sketched a triptych of windows (with the understanding that the three panels may come in any order), making it easy to depict the restrictions she encounters. The Numbers Restrictions cut across both the windows (at least two colors each) and the colors (all of them must be used; rose will be used twice; green and purple will appear together exactly once). The other rules restrict various combinations (yellow can't appear with green or with orange, and either orange or purple must always appear). By the time the LSAT expert has assembled these rules and limitations, some things have become clear: for example, purple is the only color that can be used in all three windows, and at least one window will have three or more colors (because the "first" and "second" windows already have two colors and one or both of them must include rose glass as well). The test is likely to reward you for these kinds of insights, as you'll see when we answer the questions to this game in Chapter 5.

Practice

Now, try your hand at the Deductions step. Use the following brief examples to practice identifying the elements of the BLEND checklist you see represented. Look for the points of greatest restriction in the game setup. Starting from these restrictions, combine the rules and limitations to determine what else must or cannot be true.

Take five minutes for each of the following examples. Review the expert's work on Steps 1–3 of the Logic Games Method. Analyze and draw the rules if the expert has not done so. Then, use the BLEND checklist to make all available deductions. Once you're finished, check your work against the LSAT expert's analysis on the following pages.

Game	**My Analysis**

52. Three buildings (A, B, and C) sit next to each other on a city block, and each building has three floors. On each floor, the lights are either on or off.

    Building B has more floors with lights on than does Building C.

    The first floor of Building C has its lights on.

    Exactly two buildings have their second-floor lights on.

    The lights on the second floor of Building B are off if the lights on the third floor of Building A are off.

$\longrightarrow$

Step 1: *Situation:* Buildings on a street; different floors have lights on or off.

Entities: The three buildings (A, B, C) and the three floors of each building

Action: Assign each floor a designation of "lights on" or "lights off." "On" and "off" are attributes the floors are taking on, so this is a Matching game.

Limitations: Based on the information in the Overview, we can use "on" and "off" any number of times. It's also possible, based on the Overview, for all the lights to be either on or off.

Step 2:

	A	B	C
3			
2			
1			

Step 3: (Transcribe the rules here.)

Deductions

Step 4: (Make your Deductions and Master Sketch here.)

Game	My Analysis
53. Four friends (A, B, C, and D) meet for dinner at a restaurant. There are five items on the menu (e, f, g, h, and i), and each person will order either 2 or 3 items. Exactly three friends order g. A orders more menu items than D. Each person will order either e or h, but no person orders both. Any menu item D orders, C also orders. B orders i, but A does not.	**Step 1:** *Situation:* Friends ordering items off a menu *Entities:* 4 friends (A, B, C, D) and 5 menu items (e, f, g, h, i) *Action:* Matching menu items to the people at the restaurant *Limitations:* Minimum of 2 and a maximum of 3 menu items per person. We aren't told to use all the menu items; some may remain unused. **Step 2:** 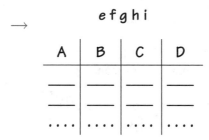 **Step 3:** (Transcribe the rules here.)

Deductions

Step 4: (Make your Deductions and Master Sketch here.)

Now, compare your deductions and Master Sketches for the examples you just tried to those of the LSAT expert.

Game	Analysis

52. Three buildings (A, B, and C) sit next to each other on a city block, and each building has three floors. On each floor, the lights are either on or off.

   Building B has more floors with lights on than does Building C.

   The first floor of Building C has its lights on.

   Exactly two buildings have their second-floor lights on.

   The lights on the second floor of Building B are off if the lights on the third floor of Building A are off.

Step 1: *Situation:* Buildings on a street; different floors have lights on or off.

Entities: The three buildings (A, B, C) and the three floors of each building

Action: Assign each floor a designation of "lights on" or "lights off." "On" and "off" are attributes the floors are taking on, so this is a Matching game.

Limitations: Based on the information in the Overview, we can use "on" and "off" any number of times. It's also possible, based on the Overview, for all the lights to be either on or off.

→ **Step 2:**

	A	B	C
3			
2			
1			

Step 3:

Rule 1: B > C

Rule 2: (can add directly to the sketch)

Rule 3: *exactly 2 buildings: second floor "on"*

Rule 4: If A3 off → B2 off
       If B2 on → A3 on

Game	Analysis

Deductions

Step 4:

Rule 2 creates an Established Entity: C1 = on. This, in turn, triggers the Numbers Restriction in Rule 1. Building B must have at least two lighted floors. If another floor of Building C is lit, Building B must have all three floors lighted.

Rule 3 says that *exactly* two buildings have their second floors lit. If Building C has its second floor light on, then it would have two total floors lit. Based on the deduction from Rules 1 and 2, Building B would have all its floors lit in this case, and Building A would have its second floor unlit. If, on the other hand, Building C had its second floor light off, then the "exactly two buildings" with lighted second floors would be Buildings A and B. Display the two "second floor" scenarios as Limited Options:

Opt. 1

	A	B	C
3		ON	OFF
2	OFF	ON	ON
1		ON	ON

Opt. 2   (2–3) (1–2)

	A	B	C
3			
2	ON	ON	OFF
1			ON

Because Building B's second floor is always lit, the contrapositive of Rule 4 makes clear that the third story of Building A must always be lit.

In Option 1, Building C cannot have its third floor lit (Rule 1). The only question in Option 1 is whether Building A's first floor is lit or unlit.

In Option 2, Building B must have at least one more floor lit (Rule 1); if Building C has its third floor lit Building B must have all its floors lit.

Opt. 1

	A	B	C
3	ON	ON	OFF
2	OFF	ON	ON
1		ON	ON

Opt. 2   (2–3) (1–2)

	A	B	C
3	ON		
2	ON	ON	OFF
1			ON

Game	**Analysis**
53. Four friends (A, B, C, and D) meet for dinner at a restaurant. There are five items on the menu (e, f, g, h, and i), and each person will order either 2 or 3 items.	**Step 1:** *Situation:* Friends ordering items off a menu

53. Four friends (A, B, C, and D) meet for dinner at a restaurant. There are five items on the menu (e, f, g, h, and i), and each person will order either 2 or 3 items.

   Exactly three friends order g.

   A orders more menu items than D.

   Each person will order one of either e or h, but no person orders both.

   Any menu item D orders, C also orders.

   B orders i, but A does not.

Step 1: *Situation:* Friends ordering items off a menu

Entities: 4 friends (A, B, C, D) and 5 menu items (e, f, g, h, i)

Action: Matching menu items to the people at the restaurant

Limitations: Minimum of 2 and a maximum of 3 menu items per person. We aren't told to use all the menu items; some may remain unused.

Step 2:

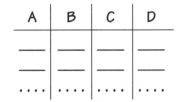

Step 3: Rule 1: Exactly 3 order g

Rule 2: A will order three items and D will order two. (Add directly to the sketch by adding/removing lines in appropriate columns or by writing "2" and "3" above the columns.)

Rule 3: (Add directly to the sketch by filling in one slot for each person with "e/h." Also note to the side "Never eh.")

Rule 4: If D orders → C orders
      If ~C orders → ~D orders

| **Game (cont.)** | **Analysis (cont.)** |

Rule 5: (can add directly to sketch)

$\rightarrow$

(3)	(2–3)	(2–3)	(2)
A	B	C	D
e/h	e/h	e/h	e/h
	i		
	. . . .	. . . .	
~i			

Exactly 3g
Never eh
D orders $\longrightarrow$ C orders
~C orders $\longrightarrow$ ~D orders

Deductions

Step 4:

The sketch already has a good deal of information from the rules and their implications, but there are further deductions. Friend A is restricted directly by Rules 2 and 5 and implicitly by Rule 3, which applies to all of the friends. That means that A orders three items (more than D orders, and everyone orders two or three according to the Overview), A doesn't order item i, and A orders exactly one of items e and h. Thus, A will order both item g and item f. Place that information directly in the sketch.

Rule 1 says that three friends will order item g (and the previous deduction shows that one of these is A). This triggers the contrapositive of Rule 4. Friend C must also order item g, for if she does not, then D won't either. In that case, only Friends A and B could order item g, violating Rule 1. Match item g to Friend C. The third order of item g could go to either B or D.

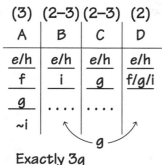

(3)	(2–3)	(2–3)	(2)
A	B	C	D
e/h	e/h	e/h	e/h
f	i	g	f/g/i
g	. . . .	. . . .	
~i			

Exactly 3g
Never eh
D orders $\longrightarrow$ C orders
~C orders $\longrightarrow$ ~D orders

Reflection

By asking you to match a set of attributes to a set of entities, Matching games lend themselves to sketches that resemble grids or tables. Almost always, the rules will create restrictions on both "axes." That is, some will limit the number of attributes you can assign to one or two of the entities, while others limit the number of entities to whom an attribute can be assigned. Setting out your sketch in a way that allows you to see the interactions among both types of restrictions is essential. In each of the examples above, deductions sprang from the combination of rules about the entities (each window must feature at least two colors; Building B must have more floors lit than Building C; each friend orders two or three dishes) and restrictions about the attributes (rose glass must be used twice; two of the second floors are lit; Dish g is ordered by three of the friends). Expect similar interactions on nearly every Matching game you encounter.

LSAT STRATEGY

In Matching games, deductions are likely to stem from:

- **Duplications**—entities shared by two or more rules; one rule might assign a certain attribute to entity X, and another might tell you that entity Y has more attributes matched to it than X does.
- **Numbers Restrictions**—limitations on the number of attributes that can be assigned to a given entity or limitations on the number of entities to which an attribute can be matched.
- **Established Entities**—matches between entities and attributes that must be maintained throughout the game (e.g., Entity X wears the red jacket); Established Entities are quite common in Matching games.

In Matching games, deductions may involve:

- **Blocks of Entities**—two or more entities that must both be assigned a given attribute or two or more attributes that must be assigned to the same entity or entities; Blocks are somewhat rare in Matching games.
- **Limited Options**—the situation that arises when a rule or combination of rules makes all acceptable arrangements fall into one of two patterns; Limited Options is a rare deduction to find in Matching games.

You'll have additional opportunities to practice Matching deductions in Hybrid games (Sequencing-Matching is the most common Hybrid pattern), among the Chapter 6 practice games, and in the full-length tests at the back of this book. In Chapter 5, you'll have a chance to see how the LSAT expert applied the deductions in the Stained Glass Windows game when we turn to Step 5 of the Logic Games Method and answer the questions.

Deductions in Distribution Games

Distribution games are distinguished from Matching games because instead of featuring attributes that can be "reused" and assigned to multiple entities, Distribution games ask you to dole out entities among a number of groups. In Distribution games, once you've distributed an entity (assigned it to a group), the entity is "done," and you cannot assign it to a second group. This difference in task makes for a slight difference in where the LSAT expert expects to spot the game's deductions. In all Distribution games, Numbers Restrictions are paramount. If a game's Overview establishes the number of entities per group up front (e.g., three boats with three seats each), then the key deductions will involve entities that must stay together (Blocks of Entities) or must be assigned to different groups. When the game doesn't establish the number of entities per group up front, the LSAT expert focuses on rules that help establish or limit the possibilities. For example, if the game has two teams and you're told that X and Y must be assigned to different teams and that P and Q must be assigned to different teams, you now know that each team has at least two entities.

Take another look at the Field Trip Chaperones game you've seen the LSAT expert analyze up through Step 3. It's a game in which the number of entities assigned to each group is predetermined, so focus on how the LSAT expert uses the restrictions on who can and cannot be grouped together to make additional deductions.

LSAT Question	Analysis

On a field trip to the Museum of Natural History, each of six children—Juana, Kyle, Lucita, Salim, Thanh, and Veronica—is accompanied by one of three adults—Ms. Margoles, Mr. O'Connell, and Ms. Podorski. Each adult accompanies exactly two of the children, consistent with the following conditions:

    If Ms. Margoles accompanies Juana, then Ms. Podorski accompanies Lucita.
    If Kyle is not accompanied by Ms. Margoles, then Veronica is accompanied by Mr. O'Connell.
    Either Ms. Margoles or Mr. O'Connell accompanies Thanh.
    Juana is not accompanied by the same adult as Kyle; nor is Lucita accompanied by the same adult as Salim; nor is Thanh accompanied by the same adult as Veronica.

PrepTest52 Sec2 Qs8–12

$\rightarrow$

Steps 1–3:

J K L S T V

Mar	O'Con	Pod	
—	—	—	Never JK
—	—	—	Never LS
		~T	Never TV

T

If $\dfrac{Mar}{J} \longrightarrow \dfrac{Pod}{L}$

If $\dfrac{Pod}{\sim L} \longrightarrow \dfrac{Mar}{\sim J}$

If $\dfrac{Mar}{\sim K} \longrightarrow \dfrac{O'Con}{V}$

If $\dfrac{O'Con}{\sim V} \longrightarrow \dfrac{Mar}{K}$

Deductions

Step 4:

Two things about this game suggest that there will be few solid deductions to add to the rules: (1) the numbers are predefined—two students per chaperone with no wiggle room, and (2) all of the rules are conditional or present options. Running through the BLEND checklist: the rules contain no Blocks of Entities, nothing to suggest Limited Options, no Established Entities, no Numbers Restrictions, and no Duplications that yield additional certainties.

Rule 3 is the most concrete rule, but it does not lead to additional deductions. Its negative implication is that Thanh is never accompanied by Ms. Podorski. Note that in the Master Sketch and move on to the questions.

Some games simply produce fewer deductions. In these cases, expect the question set to offer a number of new-"If" questions or others that test the applicability of the conditional rules. As you'll see when we cover the questions associated with this game, the Master Sketch above (thin as it is) contains everything you need to answer the questions effectively. Learning to trust that you've checked for available deductions and found none is important to time management in the Logic Games section. Poorly trained test takers often stare at rules and sketches, fruitlessly searching for additional information that simply isn't there. The BLEND checklist is helpful not only for finding deductions but also for being certain that there are no more to find.

As you continue to practice Distribution games, don't expect them all to be like the Field Trip Chaperones game. In some Distribution games, you'll be able to make a number of Deductions. In fact, when Numbers Restrictions provide for it, this is a game type where you're likely to find Limited Options. Imagine a scenario in which you must distribute nine students between two vans, with either four in Van 1 and five in Van 2 or vice versa. Anytime you encounter a scenario like this, build dual Limited Options sketches. They are almost guaranteed to lead to additional certainty in one or both of the sketches as you work through the rest of the rules.

Practice

Now, try your hand at the Deductions step. Use the following brief examples to practice identifying the elements of the BLEND checklist you see represented. Look for the points of greatest restriction in the game setup. Starting from these restrictions, combine the rules and limitations to determine what else must or cannot be true.

Take five minutes for each of the following examples. Review the expert's work on Steps 1–3 of the Logic Games Method. Analyze and draw the rules if the expert has not done so. Then, use the BLEND checklist to make all available deductions. Once you're finished, check your work against the LSAT expert's analysis on the following pages.

Game	My Analysis
54. Each of the seven members of a sorority (A, B, C, D, E, F, and G) is deciding whether to attend tonight's basketball game or to attend tonight's volleyball game. Each member will attend exactly one of the games.	**Step 1:** *Situation:* The individual members of a sorority are deciding which game to attend.

54. Each of the seven members of a sorority (A, B, C, D, E, F, and G) is deciding whether to attend tonight's basketball game or to attend tonight's volleyball game. Each member will attend exactly one of the games.

    No sorority member attends either event alone.

    A attends the volleyball game if C attends the basketball game.

    B and F do not attend the same event.

    D attends the basketball game if and only if G attends the basketball game.

    D does not attend the basketball game unless E attends the volleyball game.

Step 1: *Situation:* The individual members of a sorority are deciding which game to attend.

Entities: The seven members of the sorority (A, B, C, D, E, F, G) and two groups into which they will be subdivided: volleyball and basketball

Action: Separate the sorority members into two groups: basketball and volleyball. Because no one can go to both games at the same time, this is a Distribution game, not a Matching game.

$\longrightarrow$

Limitations: Each sorority member attends one and only one game. At this point, it is entirely possible that they all go to one of the games and no one goes to the other.

Step 2:

Basketball | Volleyball
‾‾‾‾‾‾‾‾‾‾‾‾‾‾‾‾‾‾‾‾‾‾‾‾‾‾

Step 3: (Transcribe the rules here.)

Deductions

Step 4: (Make your Deductions and Master Sketch here.)

Game	My Analysis
55. A young boy is organizing seven baseball cards (A, B, C, D, E, F, and G) into three categories (1, 2, and 3). Each card will be placed into exactly one of the three categories.	**Step 1:** *Situation:* A young boy is trying to decide how to organize his baseball cards.

55. A young boy is organizing seven baseball cards (A, B, C, D, E, F, and G) into three categories (1, 2, and 3). Each card will be placed into exactly one of the three categories.

    The number of cards in category 3 is one greater than the number of cards in categories 1 and 2 combined.

    B and E cannot be placed into the same category.

    C and F cannot be placed into the same category.

    A is placed into the same category as D, G, and one other card.

    If there are no cards in category 1 then there must be exactly 2 cards in category 2, and if there are no cards in category 2 then there must be exactly 2 cards in category 1.

$\longrightarrow$

Step 1: *Situation:* A young boy is trying to decide how to organize his baseball cards.

Entities: There are two sets: the baseball cards (A, B, C, D, E, F, G) and the different groups into which he'll place them (1, 2, 3).

Action: The boy is separating his cards into categories, and because each card can only go into one category, this is a Distribution game.

Limitations: The overview does not posit any minimum or maximum restrictions on the number of cards being placed into each category. So far, it is not clear whether all categories have to be used, or how many cards will wind up in each one.

Step 2:

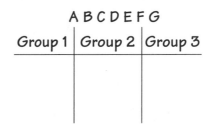

Step 3: (Transcribe the rules here.)

Deductions

Step 4: (Make your Deductions and Master Sketch here.)

Now, compare your deductions and Master Sketches to those of the LSAT expert for the examples you just tried.

Game	Analysis

54. Each of the seven members of a sorority (A, B, C, D, E, F, and G) is deciding whether to attend tonight's basketball game or to attend tonight's volleyball game. Each member will attend exactly one of the games.
 	
    No sorority member attends either event alone.
    A attends the volleyball game if C attends the basketball game.
    B and F do not attend the same event.
    D attends the basketball game if and only if G attends the basketball game.
    D does not attend the basketball game unless E attends the volleyball game.
	Step 1: *Situation:* The individual members of a sorority are deciding which game to attend.
	
	Entities: The seven members of the sorority (A, B, C, D, E, F, G) and two groups into which they will be subdivided: volleyball and basketball
	
	Action: Separate the sorority members into two groups: basketball and volleyball. Because no one can go to both games at the same time, this is a Distribution game, not a Matching game.
	
	Limitations: Each sorority member attends one and only one game. There don't appear to be any limitations on the number of sorority members going to either the volleyball game or the basketball game, so at this point, it is entirely possible that they all go to one of the games and no one goes to the other.

Step 2:

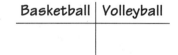

Step 3:

Rule 1: **Never 1 person at the basketball game**
Never 1 person at the volleyball game

Rule 2: **If C basketball → A volleyball**
    If A basketball → C volleyball

(Note that A and C can attend the volleyball game together.)

Rule 3: **Never BF**

Rule 4: **If D basketball → G basketball**
    If G volleyball → D volleyball
    If G basketball → D basketball
    If D volleyball → G volleyball

(In other words, DG always go together, either to volleyball or to basketball.)

Game	Analysis
$\longrightarrow$	Rule 5: If D *basketball* → E *volleyball* If E *basketball* → D *volleyball* (Note that D and E can attend the volleyball game together.)

Deductions

Step 4:

Rule 1 states that no one attends either event alone. Rule 3, placing B and F at different events, forces at least one person to attend each event. Combining those rules, it's clear that at least two of the sorority members attend each game.

Basketball	Volleyball
B/F	F/B

This further narrows the numerical possibilities: there will be groups of 2 and 5 or else of 3 and 4. No other numerical combinations are possible, and keep in mind that D and G form a Block of Entities who see a game together (Rule 4).

According to Rule 5, it is possible to put E and D together at the volleyball game, and according to Rule 2, it is possible to put A and C together at the volleyball game. But, given the Numbers Restrictions on the game, there is not enough room for A, C, D, and E all to attend the volleyball game. D will always take Block partner G (Rule 4), and one of B or F will also attend the volleyball game. If all of these entities attended volleyball, the one of B and F attending the basketball game would be there alone (violating Rule 1). Add this deduction beside the sketch framework:

Never ACDE all in volleyball

The takeaway is that D and E must split up, or A and C must split up, or both pairs of entities must split up.

Game	**Analysis**
55. A young boy is organizing seven baseball cards (A, B, C, D, E, F, and G) into three categories (1, 2, and 3). Each card will be placed into exactly one of the three categories.	**Step 1:** *Situation:* A young boy is trying to decide how to organize his baseball cards.

The number of cards in category 3 is one greater than the number of cards in categories 1 and 2 combined.

B and E cannot be placed into the same category.

C and F cannot be placed into the same category.

A is placed into the same category as D, G, and one other card.

If there are no cards in category 1, then there must be exactly 2 cards in category 2, and if there are no cards in category 2, then there must be exactly 2 cards in category 1.

Entities: There are two sets: the baseball cards (A, B, C, D, E, F, G) and the different groups into which he'll place them (1, 2, 3).

Action: The boy is separating his cards into categories, and because each card can only go into one category, this is a Distribution game.

Limitations: The overview does not posit any minimum or maximum restrictions on the number of cards being placed into each category. So far, it is not clear that all categories have to be used or how many cards will wind up in each one.

Step 2:

A B C D E F G

$\rightarrow$

Step 3: Rule 1: 7 cards total, and one more in the third category than in the first two categories combined, so there must be 4 cards in the third category and 3 cards in the first two categories combined.

Rule 2: **Never BE**

Rule 3: **Never CF**

Rule 4:

A

D

G

———

Rule 5:

If 1 empty	→ exactly two cards in 2
If ~exactly two cards in 2	→ 1 not empty
If 2 empty	→ exactly two cards in 1
If ~exactly two cards in 1	→ 2 not empty

Game	Analysis

Deductions

Step 4:

Numbers Restrictions (the N in BLEND) are central in Distribution games. Rule 1 means that there are four cards in the third category and three cards in the first two categories combined. Rule 5 says that if category 1 or 2 is empty, the other of those categories must contain exactly two cards. But this is incompatible with Rule 1, which stipulates that categories 1 and 2 contain a total of three cards. It follows that neither category 1 nor category 2 can ever be empty. So there are really only two numerical possibilities: 1:2:4 or 2:1:4. A Limited Options sketch is in order:

I.

1	2	3
__	__	__
	__	__
		__

II.

1	2	3
__	__	__
__		__
		__

Dealing with the numbers first makes it clear that the A-D-G block must go into category 3:

I.

1	2	3
__	__	A
	__	D
		G
		__

II.

1	2	3
__	__	A
__		D
		G
		__

Game	Analysis

Deductions (cont.)

Now, add Rules 2 and 3—"Never BE" and "Never CF." In each sketch, there are exactly 4 slots left open that must be filled by B, C, E, and F. Start with Option I. B and E cannot both go into category 2, but if B and E are placed into categories 1 and 3, then C and F must go together into category 2, which is also impermissible. A similar problem arises when C and F are put into categories 1 and 3; that forces B and E together in category 2, which is impermissible. The only way to split up both pairs of entities is to place ONE of B/E and ONE of C/F into category 2:

```
I.    1 | 2   | 3
    ___ | B/E | A
        | C/F | D
        |     | G
        |     | ___
```

The same applies in Option II:

```
II.   1   | 2 | 3
    B/E   |___| A
    C/F   |   | D
          |   | G
          |   | ___
```

It is not possible to determine which of B, C, E, and F fill the remaining two slots in either Option. No more deductions can be made, so move on to the questions.

Reflection

Numbers Restrictions dominate Distribution actions. It stands to reason. If your boss or teacher asked you to form two teams from a roster of coworkers or classmates, the first questions you'd likely ask are "How many per team? Do the teams need to have equal numbers?" and the like. Only after that would you dig into other questions, such as "Are there any people you definitely want working together or that you think should be kept apart?" When the game specifies the number of entities to be assigned to each group, focus on rules that create Blocks of Entities and those that prevent entities from being placed together. When the game gives you exactly two options for the number of entities per group, draw out both possibilities in a dual Limited Options sketch and fill in the subsequent deductions under both patterns. When the game tells you nothing up front about the number of entities per group, use the Blocks of Entities and/or rules preventing entities from being placed together to establish as much certainty as possible about the number of entities per group.

LSAT STRATEGY

In Distribution games, deductions are likely to stem from:

- **Numbers Restrictions**—limitations on the number of entities per group or determinations of the minimum and maximum numbers of entities per group; in Distribution games, rules preventing entities from being assigned to the same group may act as de facto Numbers Restrictions (e.g., B and F must see different events; ergo, each event has at least one attendee).
- **Blocks of Entities**—two or more entities that must be placed in the same group.
- **Limited Options**—the situation that arises when the game specifies only two possible patterns for the number of entities per group (e.g., Group A contains four students and Group B contains five students, or Group A contains five students and Group B contains four students); in Distribution games, you can sometimes determine a Limited Options numbers scenario by applying other rules to the game's overall framework.
- **Duplications**—entities shared by two or more rules; a common occurrence in Distribution games is one rule that says A and B will be in the same group and another rule that says A and C cannot be in the same group—from this, you can deduce that B and C cannot be in the same group.

In Distribution games, deductions may involve

- **Established Entities**—entities that are assigned to one group for the entire game; this is not too common in Distribution games.

You'll have additional opportunities to practice Distribution deductions in some Hybrid games involving a Distribution action and in Chapter 6 and in the full-length tests at the back of this book. In Chapter 5, you'll have a chance to see how the LSAT expert applied the deductions in the Field Trip Chaperones game when we turn to Step 5 of the Logic Games Method and answer the questions.

Deductions in Hybrid Games

Just as we said earlier about Hybrid rules, the notion of Hybrid deductions is a bit of a misnomer. Because Hybrid games combine the actions of two (or occasionally three) of the standard logic games actions, the deductions you're likely to encounter correspond to the actions the testmaker has chosen to create the game. Thus, if you have a Selection-Sequencing Hybrid game, expect to see Numbers Restrictions informing the Selection action and Blocks of Entities driving the Sequencing action. In Sequencing-Matching Hybrids (the most common Hybrid actions), Blocks of Entities are likely to form the basis for Sequencing deductions and Duplications and/or Numbers Restrictions will give you further certainty for the Matching component. The one type of deduction unique to Hybrid games comes from rules and restrictions that cross over between the actions, providing deductions in one part of the game based on restrictions in the other.

The Executives Visits game provides an example of these shared Hybrid deductions. As you'll recall from your review of the LSAT expert's previous analyses in Steps 1 through 3, this game is a Sequencing-Distribution Hybrid.

You're asked to schedule visits to manufacturing plants and then determine which executives visit which of the sites. As you review the expert's work on Step 4, pay attention to how information about the order of the site visits allows you to make deductions about the executives who will attend each one and vice versa.

LSAT Question	Analysis
Five executives—Quinn, Rodriguez, Sasada, Taylor, and Vandercar—are being scheduled to make site visits to three of their company's manufacturing plants—Farmington, Homestead, and Morningside. Each site will be visited by at least one of the executives and each executive will visit just one site. Each of the three site visits will take place on a different day. The schedule of site visits must conform to the following requirements:	**Steps 1–3:**

The Farmington visit must take place before the
  Homestead visit.
The Farmington visit will include only one of the
  executives.
The site visit that includes Quinn must take place
  before any site visit that includes either Rodriguez or
  Taylor.
The site visit that includes Sasada cannot take place
  after any site visit that includes Vandercar.

PrepTest56 Sec1 Qs17–23

Farm, Home, Morn :

QRSTV

→

Farm . . . Home

Farm

$\dfrac{R}{Q\cdots T}$ Q···R / Q···T

$\dfrac{S}{V}$ or S . . . V

Deductions

Step 4:

There are three sites, and Rule 1 determines the relative order of two of them. Because Farmington cannot be the last visit, it can be either the first or second. That provides for a Limited Options framework.

QRSTV

(I)	Farm	Home/Morn	Morn/Home
	___	—	—

(II)	Morn	Farm	Home
	—	___	—

$\dfrac{R}{Q\cdots T}$ Q···R / Q···T

$\dfrac{S}{V}$ or S . . . V

LSAT Question	**Analysis**

Rules 3 and 4 are ostensibly about which executives distribute to which visits, but they're written as Sequencing rules. From Rule 3, you know that Quinn will never visit the third site and that Rodriguez and Taylor will never visit the first site. Add that to each option. Additionally, because V can never precede S, in the first option note that V cannot be in the first visit—Farmington—because it will have only one executive. S and V could be together in the first visit—Morningside—in the second option.

Q R S T V

(I)

Farm	Home/Morn	Morn/Home
═══	───	───
~R		~Q
~T		
~V		

(II)

Morn	Farm	Home
───	═══	───
~R		~Q
~T		

Beyond that, there's nothing else to determine. While Farmington gets one executive, Morningside and Homestead could host two executives each or, depending on where they appear in the order of visits, one might host one executive while the other hosts three.

The Executives Visits game provides another good reminder about Hybrid games: the individual actions are relatively easy. Here, the Sequencing action has only three entities (the manufacturing sites), and the Distribution action has you doling out only five entities. On their own, these actions would provide little challenge. Use that simplicity to your advantage by making a sketch that integrates both actions. That will allow you to see when the restrictions on one of the actions provide further certainty about what must or cannot happen in the other.

It's tough to generalize about Hybrid deductions given the various combinations of actions you may encounter. The best approach is to remember that, no matter what actions the Hybrid combines, the game's individual elements are familiar. If you practice the Logic Games section assiduously, you'll see all of the game types and the variety of rules that accompany each. Hybrid games are no exception.

Practice

Now, try your hand at the Deductions step. Use the following brief examples to practice identifying the elements of the BLEND checklist you see represented. Look for the points of greatest restriction in the game setup. Starting from these restrictions, combine the rules and limitations to determine what else must or cannot be true.

Take five minutes for each of the following examples. Review the expert's work on Steps 1–3 of the Logic Games Method. Analyze and draw the rules if the expert has not done so. Then, use the BLEND checklist to make all available deductions. Once you're finished, check your work against the LSAT expert's analysis on the following pages.

Game

56. Five drivers (A, B, C, D, and E) are waiting to get their cars washed. The cars are in a line, first to last, and each car is exactly one of three different colors (f, g, or h).

    C and E must be separated from one another by exactly two positions in line.

    A must be second or third in line.

    There is only one car of color g, and it is immediately behind A.

    The first car in line is not color f.

My Analysis

Step 1: *Situation:* A line of cars outside a car wash

Entities: The cars (A, B, C, D, E) and the colors (f, g, h)

Action: Sequence the cars from first to last and match a color to each car. This is a Sequencing-Matching Hybrid game.

Limitations: The five cars all must be used, but there is no such restriction for the colors.

Step 2: It is easy to envision this Sequencing-Matching Hybrid game as just two Sequencing games layered on top of each other. We can place the cars on one layer and match the color on the other layer.

$$\overline{}\ \ \overline{}\ \ \overline{}\ \ \overline{}\ \ \overline{}\ (f\ g\ h)$$
$$\underset{1}{\overline{}}\ \ \underset{2}{\overline{}}\ \ \underset{3}{\overline{}}\ \ \underset{4}{\overline{}}\ \ \underset{5}{\overline{}}\ (A\ B\ C\ D\ E)$$

Step 3: (Transcribe the rules here.)

Deductions

Step 4: (Make your Deductions and Master Sketch here.)

Game	My Analysis

57. Six friends (A, B, C, D, E, and F) are going canoeing through a state park. The friends rent exactly two canoes, and each canoe has a front, middle, and rear position. All six friends seat themselves in the canoes, one person per position.
 	
    B sits in Canoe 2.
    If A sits in Canoe 1, then C will sit in a middle position.
    E sits in a position closer to the front of a canoe than does C.
    C and F sit in different canoes but in the same position.
	Step 1: *Situation:* Determining who sits where in two canoes
	
	Entities: Friends (A, B, C, D, E, F), canoes (1, 2), and positions (front, middle, rear)
	
	Action: Divide a group of friends into two smaller subgroups; then, place them in front, middle, or rear positions. It's a Distribution-Sequencing Hybrid Game.
	
	Limitations: Six people and six spots
	
	Step 2:

Step 2:

A B C D E F

	Canoe 1	Canoe 2
front		
mid		
rear		

Step 3:

Deductions

Step 4: (Make your Deductions and Master Sketch here.)

Now, compare your deductions and Master Sketches for the examples you just tried to those of the LSAT expert.

Game	Analysis

56. Five drivers (A, B, C, D, and E) are waiting to get their cars washed. The cars are in a line, first to last, and each car is exactly one of three different colors (f, g, or h).
 	
   C and E must be separated from one another by exactly two positions in line.
   A must be second or third in line.
   There is only one car of color g, and it is immediately behind A.
   The first car in line is not color f.
	Step 1: *Situation:* A line of cars outside a car wash

Entities: The cars (A, B, C, D, E) and the colors (f, g, h)

Action: Sequence the cars from first to last and match a color to each car. This is a Sequencing-Matching Hybrid game.

Limitations: The five cars all must be used, but there is no such restriction for the colors.

Step 2: It is easy to envision this Sequencing-Matching Hybrid game as just two Sequencing games layered on top of each other. We can place the cars on one layer and match the color on the other layer.

$$\underline{} \quad \underline{} \quad \underline{} \quad \underline{} \quad \underline{} \text{ (f g h)}$$

$$\underset{1}{\underline{}} \quad \underset{2}{\underline{}} \quad \underset{3}{\underline{}} \quad \underset{4}{\underline{}} \quad \underset{5}{\underline{}} \text{(A B C D E)}$$

Step 3:

Rule 1:

C/E __ __ E/C

Rule 2:

$$\underline{} \quad \underline{} \quad \underline{} \quad \underline{} \quad \underline{} \text{ (f g h)}$$

$$\underline{} \quad \underset{\nwarrow A \nearrow}{\underline{}} \quad \underline{} \quad \underline{} \quad \underline{} \text{(A B C D E)}$$

Rule 3: Only 1 g

$$\underline{} \quad \underline{g}$$

$$\underline{A} \quad \underline{}$$

Rule 4: The color of the first car must be g or h:

$$\underline{g/h} \quad \underline{} \quad \underline{} \quad \underline{} \quad \underline{} \text{ (f g h)}$$

$$\underline{} \quad \underset{\nwarrow A \nearrow}{\underline{}} \quad \underline{} \quad \underline{} \quad \underline{} \text{(A B C D E)}$$

Game	Analysis

Deductions

Step 4:

The C/E _ _ E/C block (Rule 1) is a good place to start because it affects two entities and four positions. This Block can only go in positions 1 and 4 or in positions 2 and 5. Set up Limited Options, keeping in mind that A must be in position 2 or 3 (Rule 2):

```
I.   g/h  __   __   __   __
     C/E  __   __   E/C  __
            ↖A↗
```

```
II.  g/h  __   __   __   __
     __   C/E   A   __   E/C
```

Rule 3 states that the one car of color g must be immediately behind car A. That means that in Option I, car 3 or car 4 must be of color g, while in Option II, it must be car 4 that is of color g. Moreover, combine Rules 3 and 4 to deduce that because f cannot be the first car's color, and neither can g (because there is only a single g and it must be third or fourth), the only possible match for the first car is color h:

```
                ⟋g⟍
I.   h   __   __   __   __
     C/E  __   __   E/C  __
            ↖A↗
```

```
II.  h   __   __    g   __
     __   C/E   A   __   E/C
```

Cars A, C, and E have all been placed, so position 5 in Option I must be car B or car D. Similarly, in Option II, B and D must fill positions 1 and 4 (in either order). Because there is just one car of color g, also fill in all slots that cannot be g with "f/h":

```
                 ⟋g⟍
I.   h   f/h   __   __   f/h
     C/E  __   __   E/C  B/D
            ↖A↗
```

```
II.  h   f/h  f/h   g   f/h
     B/D  C/E   A   D/B  E/C
```

Game	Analysis

57. Six friends (A, B, C, D, E, and F) are going canoeing through a state park. The friends rent exactly two canoes, and each canoe has a front, middle, and rear position. All six friends seat themselves in the canoes, one person per position.
 	
    B sits in Canoe 2.
    If A sits in Canoe 1, then C will sit in a middle position.
    E sits in a position closer to the front of a canoe than does C.
    C and F sit in different canoes but in the same position.
	Step 1: *Situation:* Determining who sits where in two canoes
	
	Entities: Friends (A, B, C, D, E, F), canoes (1, 2), and positions (front, middle, rear)
	
	Action: Divide a group of friends into two smaller subgroups, then place them in front, middle, or rear positions. It's a Distribution-Sequencing Hybrid Game.
	
	Limitations: Six people and six spots

$\rightarrow$ **Step 2:**

ABCDEF

	Canoe 1	Canoe 2
front		
mid		
rear		

Game	Analysis

Analysis

Step 3: Rule 1: (can add directly to the sketch)

	Canoe 1	Canoe 2
front		
mid		
rear		
		B

$\rightarrow$

Rule 2: If A canoe 1 → C middle
If ~C middle → A canoe 2

Rule 3:

E
.
.
C

Rule 4: C=F or F=C; can also write this rule as

C/F	F/C

Deductions

Step 4:

This is a Sequencing-Distribution Hybrid game, so make deductions by finding an entity that is bound by both sets of game restrictions. C shows up in multiple rules, making it a good target. Rule 3 states that E sits closer to the front than C. Because there are only three positions in each canoe, E must therefore sit in a front or middle position, and C must sit in a middle or rear position.

The last rule also deals with C. It states that C and F sit in different canoes but in the same position. Combined with the previous deduction, F must also sit in a middle or rear position.

Rule 2 also deals with C. The contrapositive of this rule states that if C does not sit in the middle position in one of the canoes, A will sit in Canoe 2. Because C must sit in the rear position if he is not in the middle position, then this rule becomes: if C sits in the rear position, A sits in Canoe 2.

Game	Analysis

Deductions (cont.)

At this point, create a Limited Options sketch: the C/F block must go in either the middle or rear position. When placed in the rear, this block forces A and B (in whichever order) into the front and middle positions of Canoe 2. The only two entities remaining, D and E, must therefore occupy the front and middle positions (in whichever order) of Canoe 1.

Opt. I

	Canoe 1	Canoe 2
front	D/E	A/B
mid	E/D	B/A
rear	C/F	F/C

If the C/F block is placed instead in the middle positions, then E will be forced into one of the two front positions. Because B must go in Canoe 2, the only entities that can go in the rear position of Canoe 1 are A and D.

Opt. II

	Canoe 1	Canoe 2	
front			E
mid	C/F	F/C	
rear	A/D		
		B	

Reflection

In Hybrid games, use your knowledge of the standard game actions to anticipate the deductions you're likely to see. Remain on the lookout for cases in which restrictions in one action impact the arrangements acceptable in the other action.

LSAT STRATEGY

In Hybrid games, deductions are likely to stem from:

· **BLEND**—Because Hybrid games may involve any of the standard logic games actions, all five of the BLEND elements are on the table.
· **"Cross Over" rules**—Keep an eye out in Hybrid games for rules that present restrictions to both of the actions in the game.

You'll have additional opportunities to practice making deductions in Hybrid games in Chapter 6 and in the full-length tests at the back of this book. In Chapter 5, you'll have a chance to see how the LSAT expert applied the deductions in the Executives Visits game when we turn to Step 5 of the Logic Games Method and answer the questions.

Summary

All of the work you've done thus far in logic games has really been in preparation for the next chapter. Now, we'll get to answer the logic games questions and get the points. Steps 1–4 of the Method have covered two substantial chapters. On Test Day, those steps will take you about 3–4 minutes per game. But, you'll be glad that you've taken that time. The setup, sketch, and deductions you make will put you in a position to answer the questions much more quickly, confidently, and accurately than would have been possible without them. As you dive into Chapter 5 and the questions and then move on to logic games practice in Chapter 6, you'll be glad you spent the time to master the first four steps of the Method. Your practice will be much more valuable than if you had jumped into the questions without such a strong understanding of logic games mechanics.

Logic Games: The Questions

LOGIC GAMES QUESTION TYPES

This is where all of your work on Logic Games pays off. All that you've learned so far—how to conduct an Overview, build a Sketch, populate it with the Rules, and combine the rules to make Deductions—has prepared you for the skills you'll learn and practice here. If you've taken the preceding chapters seriously— if you've really conquered Steps 1 through 4 of the Logic Games Method—you may be surprised by how quickly and confidently you are able to answer Logic Games questions. Indeed, that's the reason that LSAT experts spend 3–4 minutes before tackling a game's questions by doing the setup and critical thinking steps that you've been practicing up to this point.

Nonetheless, there are still a few skills to learn in order to handle the Logic Games question sets efficiently and to avoid needless and costly mistakes. Indeed, one of the biggest components of mastery in this chapter involves identifying, quickly and accurately, what each question is calling for. Many test takers lose points in the Logic Games section because after having done strong analyses, they quite simply answer the wrong question. They might, for example, choose an answer that clearly must be true even though the question stem calls for the choice that *could be false*. Or, they pick out a scenario that could be true when the question credits only the choice that *must be true*. You first learned to assess levels of certainty and truth values back in Chapter 1: LSAT Reasoning. If you feel like you need to brush up on these concepts or if you skipped over that section initially, now is the time to revisit that chapter.

Other mistakes that poorly trained test takers make with Logic Games questions lead to wasted time and effort even when they don't lead to wrong answers. Students who try to test every choice by drawing innumerable diagrams lose time that an LSAT expert, confident in the deductions she has made in the Master Sketches, is able to preserve. Others, who are in too much of a hurry to draw even one new sketch (to account for a new condition in a question stem, let's say), become so confused trying to hold dozens of arrangements in their heads that they can't quickly or confidently eliminate wrong answers.

In this chapter, you'll learn how best to handle every Logic Games question. We'll break the questions into a handful of question types and show you effective strategies for each one.

LSAT STRATEGY

Logic Games Question Types

- Acceptability Questions
- Must Be/Could Be Questions
- New-"If" Questions
- Other Question Types
  - Complete and Accurate List Questions
  - Completely Determine Questions
  - Numerical Questions
    - » Minimum/Maximum Questions
    - » Earliest/Latest Questions
    - » "How Many" Questions
  - Rule Alteration Questions
    - » Rule Change Questions
    - » Rule Substitution Questions
  - Supply the "If" Questions

Using This Chapter Effectively

You can't practice LSAT questions without having the setup, sketch, rules, and deductions in place. So, to learn to handle LSAT questions, you'll be drawing once again on the same games you've been using in Chapters 2, 3, and 4. Where it's important, we'll present the game setup along with the Master Sketch you derived for it in Chapter 4. If you don't feel like you remember the work we did to come up with the Master Sketch, feel free to review the game in the previous chapters. For most of these games, however, taking a minute or two to review the game and study the Master Sketch will probably remind you of all the work you did in Steps 1–4, and you'll feel ready to apply the Master Sketch to the questions.

At a few key points in the chapter, you will also encounter drills to help reinforce effective analysis of Logic Games question stems.

After you've completed this chapter, there are several additional full logic games in Chapter 6. There, you can practice the Logic Games Method from start to finish and feel confident that you can handle any games you encounter on Test Day. In those games, you'll see all of the question types described here.

ACCEPTABILITY QUESTIONS

Most LSAT Logic Games feature one Acceptability question, and usually it is the first question in the set. (On rare occasions, you'll find a game with no Acceptability question and, very rarely, a game with two.) That's good news because, as you'll see, Acceptability questions can be answered in seconds if you use the LSAT expert's strategy.

LEARNING OBJECTIVES

In this section, you'll learn to:

- Answer Acceptability questions strategically.

Here's the Acceptability question from the Monuments game you first saw in Chapter 2. Try it out on your own, but don't spend too much time on it. We'll show you, step-by-step, how the LSAT expert attacks this question with ease.

Historical records show that over the course of five consecutive years—601, 602, 603, 604, and 605—a certain emperor began construction of six monuments: F, G, H, L, M, and S. A historian is trying to determine the years in which the individual monuments were begun. The following facts have been established:

L was begun in a later year than G, but in an earlier year than F.

H was begun no earlier than 604.

M was begun earlier than 604.

Two of the monuments were begun in 601, and no other monument was begun in the same year as any of the other monuments.

Which one of the following could be an accurate matching of monuments to the years in which they were begun?

(A) 601: G;   602: L, S; 603: M; 604: H; 605: F
(B) 601: G, M; 602: L;   603: H; 604: S; 605: F
(C) 601: G, M; 602: S;   603: F; 604: L; 605: H
(D) 601: G, S;   602: L;   603: F; 604: M; 605: H
(E) 601: G, S;   602: L;   603: M; 604: H; 605: F

PrepTest58 Sec3 Q1

Because the correct answer is an acceptable arrangement, each of the wrong answers is unacceptable for some reason. The LSAT expert knows that's because each of the wrong answers violates one or more rules or limitations in the game. Now, going through each choice to confirm that it's error-free can be time-consuming and confusing. It is hard to prove that nothing is wrong with a choice. There's a better way. It is easy to prove that there is something wrong with a choice. The LSAT expert checks not answer by answer but rule by rule. Observe.

LSAT Question	**Analysis**

Historical records show that over the course of five consecutive years—601, 602, 603, 604, and 605—a certain emperor began construction of six monuments: F, G, H, L, M, and S. A historian is trying to determine the years in which the individual monuments were begun. The following facts have been established:

> L was begun in a later year than G, but in an earlier year than F.
>
> H was begun no earlier than 604.
>
> M was begun earlier than 604.
>
> Two of the monuments were begun in 601, and no other monument was begun in the same year as any of the other monuments.

Which one of the following could be an accurate matching of monuments to the years in which they were begun? →	**Step 5:** The right answer is acceptable; each wrong answer violates a rule. Start with Rule 1. Does any answer choice violate it?

(A)   601: G;   602: L, S; 603: M;   604: H; 605: F

(B)   601: G, M; 602: L;   603: H;   604: S; 605: F

(C)   ~~601: G, M; 602: S;   603: F;   604: L; 605: H~~   →   Violates Rule 1 by having L begin later than F. Eliminate.

(D)   601: G, S; 602: L;   603: F;   604: M; 605: H

(E)   601: G, S; 602: L;   603: M;   604: H; 605: F ·

PrepTest58 Sec3 Q1

Notice that the LSAT expert crosses out choice (C) entirely. It's unacceptable because it violates Rule 1, so it doesn't matter if it's wrong for any other reason, and there's no reason to recheck it and waste time. The expert presses on.

LSAT Question	**Analysis**

Historical records show that over the course of five consecutive years—601, 602, 603, 604, and 605—a certain emperor began construction of six monuments: F, G, H, L, M, and S. A historian is trying to determine the years in which the individual monuments were begun. The following facts have been established:

> L was begun in a later year than G, but in an earlier year than F.
>
> H was begun no earlier than 604.
>
> M was begun earlier than 604.
>
> Two of the monuments were begun in 601, and no other monument was begun in the same year as any of the other monuments.

LSAT Question		Analysis
Which one of the following could be an accurate matching of monuments to the years in which they were begun?	→	**Step 5:** The right answer is acceptable; each wrong answer violates a rule. One down. Does any remaining answer choice violate Rule 2?
(A) 601: G; 602: L, S; 603: M; 604: H; 605: F		
(B) ~~601: G, M; 602: L; 603: H; 604: S; 605: F~~	→	Violates Rule 2 by having H begin in 603. Eliminate.
(C) ~~601: G, M; 602: S; 603: F; 604: L; 605: H~~	→	Violates Rule 1 by having L begin later than F. Eliminate.
(D) 601: G, S; 602: L; 603: F; 604: M; 605: H		
(E) 601: G, S; 602: L; 603: M; 604: H; 605: F		

PrepTest58 Sec3 Q1

Now you get the value of this approach (and maybe see the benefit to when the testmaker includes exactly four rules).

LSAT Question		Analysis
Historical records show that over the course of five consecutive years—601, 602, 603, 604, and 605—a certain emperor began construction of six monuments: F, G, H, L, M, and S. A historian is trying to determine the years in which the individual monuments were begun. The following facts have been established: 　　L was begun in a later year than G, but in an earlier year than F. 　　H was begun no earlier than 604. 　　M was begun earlier than 604. 　　Two of the monuments were begun in 601, and no other monument was begun in the same year as any of the other monuments.		
Which one of the following could be an accurate matching of monuments to the years in which they were begun?	→	**Step 5:** The right answer is acceptable; each wrong answer violates a rule. Does any remaining answer choice violate Rule 3?
(A) 601: G; 602: L, S; 603: M; 604: H; 605: F		
(B) ~~601: G, M; 602: L; 603: H; 604: S; 605: F~~	→	Violates Rule 2 by having H begin in 603. Eliminate.
(C) ~~601: G, M; 602: S; 603: F; 604: L; 605: H~~	→	Violates Rule 1 by having L begin later than F. Eliminate.
(D) ~~601: G, S; 602: L; 603: F; 604: M; 605: H~~	→	Violates Rule 3 by having M begin in 604. Eliminate.
(E) 601: G, S; 602: L; 603: M; 604: H; 605: F		

PrepTest58 Sec3 Q1

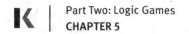

One rule left and one more wrong answer to eliminate.

LSAT Question	Analysis

Historical records show that over the course of five consecutive years—601, 602, 603, 604, and 605—a certain emperor began construction of six monuments: F, G, H, L, M, and S. A historian is trying to determine the years in which the individual monuments were begun. The following facts have been established:

> L was begun in a later year than G, but in an earlier year than F.
>
> H was begun no earlier than 604.
>
> M was begun earlier than 604.
>
> Two of the monuments were begun in 601, and no other monument was begun in the same year as any of the other monuments.

LSAT Question	Analysis
Which one of the following could be an accurate matching of monuments to the years in which they were begun? →	**Step 5:** The right answer is acceptable; each wrong answer violates a rule. Does any remaining answer choice violate Rule 4?
(A) 601: G; 602: L, S; 603: M; 604: H; 605: F →	Violates Rule 4 by having two monuments begin in 602. Eliminate.
(B) 601: G, M; 602: L; 603: H; 604: S; 605: F →	Violates Rule 2 by having H begin in 603. Eliminate.
(C) 601: G, M; 602: S; 603: F; 604: L; 605: H →	Violates Rule 1 by having L begin later than F. Eliminate.
(D) 601: G, S; 602: L; 603: F; 604: M; 605: H →	Violates Rule 3 by having M begin in 604. Eliminate.
(E) 601: G, S; 602: L; 603: M; 604: H; 605: F →	Correct. This one abides by all of the rules.

PrepTest58 Sec3 Q1

We won't reprint the questions multiple times from here on out, but you should keep this example in mind as you tackle every Acceptability question from this point forward. Use the rules to eliminate the violators. The correct answer will always be left at the end. From time to time, you'll find cases in which one rule eliminates two answer choices and cases in which a certain rule is violated by none of the answer choices. That's all right. Just remember that four of the answers are not acceptable, and work to eliminate them quickly. If you need to confirm your choice, you can check it against each of the rules and restrictions, but most of the time, the violations are so clear and demonstrable that you'll cross out four choices confidently and select the one that remains.

Take a look at the Acceptability questions from a couple of the other games you've seen in previous chapters. As you go over them, keep in mind that the LSAT expert checked the answers rule by rule, so review them using that same pattern. Start with Rule 1. Spot the choice that violates it. Then confirm that your analysis conforms to that of the expert.

First up, here's the Acceptability question from the Stained Glass Windows game. Take a minute to review the setup and rules before you study the analysis. Do you remember what type of game this is? We'll tell you after you've tried out the question.

LSAT Question	Analysis

An artisan has been hired to create three stained glass windows. The artisan will use exactly five colors of glass: green, orange, purple, rose, and yellow. Each color of glass will be used at least once, and each window will contain at least two different colors of glass. The windows must also conform to the following conditions:
    Exactly one of the windows contains both green glass and purple glass.
    Exactly two of the windows contain rose glass.
    If a window contains yellow glass, then that window contains neither green glass nor orange glass.
    If a window does not contain purple glass, then that window contains orange glass.	

Which one of the following could be the color combinations of the glass in the three windows? →	**Step 5:** An Acceptability question. Go through the rules one-by-one and use each rule to eliminate as many violators as possible.

(A)   window 1: green, purple, rose, and orange
    window 2: rose and yellow
    window 3: green and orange →
	Violates Rule 4 because window 2 has neither purple glass nor orange glass. Eliminate.

(B)   window 1: green, purple, and rose
    window 2: green, rose, and orange
    window 3: purple and yellow →
	Correct. This is an acceptable matching of glass to windows.

(C)   window 1: green, purple, and rose
    window 2: green, purple, and orange
    window 3: purple, rose, and yellow →
	Violates Rule 1 because two windows have both green glass and purple glass. Eliminate.

(D)   window 1: green, purple, and orange
    window 2: rose, orange, and yellow
    window 3: purple and rose →
	Violates Rule 3 because window 2 has yellow glass and orange glass together. Eliminate.

(E)   window 1: green, purple, and orange
    window 2: purple, rose, and yellow
    window 3: purple and orange →
	Violates Rule 2 because only one window has rose glass. Eliminate.

PrepTest62 Sec3 Q7

That game is a Matching game. Each color of glass may appear more than once. Notice, however, that the game type made little difference in your approach to the Acceptability question. There are four rules, and each one eliminated one of the wrong answers.

Take a look at the Acceptability question from yet another game type. This one involves the selection of the Day Care Volunteer group. This is a Selection game and thus features Formal Logic rules. As you look for violators, keep in mind the "If" condition of each rule. If you're checking Rule 1, for example, you only need to look for answers in which Rochelle is selected; you do not need to look for the trigger of the contrapositive.

LSAT Question	Analysis
A company organizing on-site day care consults with a group of parents composed exclusively of volunteers from among the seven employees—Felicia, Leah, Masatomo, Rochelle, Salman, Terry, and Veena—who have become parents this year. The composition of the volunteer group must be consistent with the following:	
If Rochelle volunteers, then so does Masatomo. If Masatomo volunteers, then so does Terry. If Salman does not volunteer, then Veena volunteers. If Rochelle does not volunteer, then Leah volunteers. If Terry volunteers, then neither Felicia nor Veena volunteers.	
Which one of the following could be a complete and accurate list of the volunteers? →	**Step 5:** An Acceptability question. Go through the rules one-by-one and use each rule to eliminate as many violators as possible.
(A) Felicia, Salman →	Violates Rule 4 because Rochelle does not volunteer and neither does Leah. Eliminate.
(B) Masatomo, Rochelle →	Violates Rule 2 because Masatomo is selected but Terry is not. Eliminate.
(C) Leah, Salman, Terry →	Correct. This is an acceptable selection.
(D) Salman, Rochelle, Veena →	Violates Rule 1 because Rochelle is selected but Masatomo is not. Eliminate.
(E) Leah, Salman, Terry, Veena *PrepTest58 Sec3 Q7* →	Violates Rule 5 because Terry volunteers and so does Veena. Eliminate.

Note that in this example, the game had five rules. Once the LSAT expert had eliminated choice (D) because of Rule 1 and choice (B) because of Rule 2, there were no choices remaining that violated Rule 3. Don't panic or doubt yourself in such a case. The match of rules to wrong answers is not always one-to-one. Likewise, if you've been through all the rules and you still have answers remaining, it is likely that a limitation from the game's overview will knock out the remaining wrong answer(s).

Although you'll usually complete your Master Sketch, including the deductions you've made, before answering the questions, you really don't use it to evaluate the answer choices for Acceptability questions. Keep that in mind on Test Day. If you're running very short on time for the last game you start, you may want to grab the Acceptability point quickly without completing your Master Sketch. Likewise, if you're having trouble figuring out how to get started setting up a game, try its Acceptability question to get an idea of how the testmaker pictures the arrangement of entities and the impact that the rules have.

Practice

Now, try out a few Acceptability questions on your own. In this practice set, you'll find the Acceptability questions from each of the remaining games you've seen thus far in the book. For each, take a minute to reacquaint yourself with the game's action, sketch, and rules before you tackle the questions. Once you start on the question, however, use the rule-by-rule elimination strategy and work as quickly as you can.

For each of the questions below, use the rules to evaluate the answer choices. Eliminate answer choices that violate rules and select the one choice that offers an acceptable arrangement of entities for the game. After you've selected the correct answer, check your work against that of the LSAT expert on the following pages.

LSAT Question	My Analysis

Workers at a water treatment plant open eight valves—G, H, I, K, L, N, O, and P—to flush out a system of pipes that needs emergency repairs. To maximize safety and efficiency, each valve is opened exactly once, and no two valves are opened at the same time. The valves are opened in accordance with the following conditions:

    Both K and P are opened before H.
    O is opened before L but after H.
    L is opened after G.
    N is opened before H.
    I is opened after K.

Steps 1–4:

Master Sketch

G H I K L N O P

→

1. Which one of the following could be the order, from first to last, in which the valves are opened?

   → **Step 5:**

(A) P, I, K, G, N, H, O, L

(B) P, G, K, N, L, H, O, I

(C) G, K, I, P, H, O, N, L

(D) N, K, P, H, O, I, L, G

(E) K, I, N, G, P, H, O, L

PrepTest52 Sec2 Q1

LSAT Question	My Analysis

On a field trip to the Museum of Natural History, each of six children—Juana, Kyle, Lucita, Salim, Thanh, and Veronica—is accompanied by one of three adults—Ms. Margoles, Mr. O'Connell, and Ms. Podorski. Each adult accompanies exactly two of the children, consistent with the following conditions:

> If Ms. Margoles accompanies Juana, then Ms. Podorski accompanies Lucita.
>
> If Kyle is not accompanied by Ms. Margoles, then Veronica is accompanied by Mr. O'Connell.
>
> Either Ms. Margoles or Mr. O'Connell accompanies Thanh.
>
> Juana is not accompanied by the same adult as Kyle; nor is Lucita accompanied by the same adult as Salim; nor is Thanh accompanied by the same adult as Veronica.

Steps 1–4:

Master Sketch

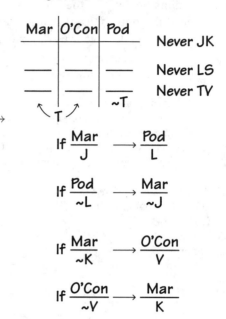

2. Which one of the following could be an accurate matching of the adults to the children they accompany?

→ **Step 5:**

(A) Ms. Margoles: Juana, Thanh; Mr. O'Connell: Lucita, Veronica; Ms. Podorski: Kyle, Salim

(B) Ms. Margoles: Kyle, Thanh; Mr. O'Connell: Juana, Salim; Ms. Podorski: Lucita, Veronica

(C) Ms. Margoles: Lucita, Thanh; Mr. O'Connell: Juana, Salim; Ms. Podorski: Kyle, Veronica

(D) Ms. Margoles: Kyle, Veronica; Mr. O'Connell: Juana, Thanh; Ms. Podorski: Lucita, Salim

(E) Ms. Margoles: Salim, Veronica; Mr. O'Connell: Kyle, Lucita; Ms. Podorski: Juana, Thanh

PrepTest52 Sec2 Q8

LSAT Question	My Analysis

Individual hour-long auditions will be scheduled for each of six saxophonists—Fujimura, Gabrieli, Herman, Jackson, King, and Lauder. The auditions will all take place on the same day. Each audition will begin on the hour, with the first beginning at 1 P.M. and the last at 6 P.M. The schedule of auditions must conform to the following conditions:

Jackson auditions earlier than Herman does.
Gabrieli auditions earlier than King does.
Gabrieli auditions either immediately before or immediately after Lauder does.
Exactly one audition separates the auditions of Jackson and Lauder.

Steps 1–4:

Master Sketch

$\overset{*}{F}$ G H J K L

$\overline{1}$ $\overline{2}$ $\overline{3}$ $\overline{4}$ $\overline{5}$ $\overline{6}$

$\cdot\cdot$H
$\underline{J}$ $\underline{}$ $\underline{L}$

or

$\underline{L}$ $\underline{}$ $\underline{J}$ ... H

$\underline{G/L}$ $\underline{L/G}$ ... K

3. Which one of the following is an acceptable schedule for the auditions, listed in order from 1 P.M. through 6 P.M.?

→ **Step 5:**

   (A) Fujimura, Gabrieli, King, Jackson, Herman, Lauder

   (B) Fujimura, King, Lauder, Gabrieli, Jackson, Herman

   (C) Fujimura, Lauder, Gabrieli, King, Jackson, Herman

   (D) Herman, Jackson, Gabrieli, Lauder, King, Fujimura

   (E) Jackson, Gabrieli, Lauder, Herman, King, Fujimura

PrepTest56 Sec1 Q1

LSAT Question	**My Analysis**

Five executives—Quinn, Rodriguez, Sasada, Taylor, and Vandercar—are being scheduled to make site visits to three of their company's manufacturing plants—Farmington, Homestead, and Morningside. Each site will be visited by at least one of the executives and each executive will visit just one site. Each of the three site visits will take place on a different day. The schedule of site visits must conform to the following requirements:

The Farmington visit must take place before the Homestead visit.

The Farmington visit will include only one of the executives.

The site visit that includes Quinn must take place before any site visit that includes either Rodriguez or Taylor.

The site visit that includes Sasada cannot take place after any site visit that includes Vandercar.

Steps 1–4:

Master Sketch

4. Which one of the following could be the executives included in each of the site visits, with the sites listed in the order in which they are visited?

Step 5:

(A) Farmington: Quinn
Homestead: Rodriguez, Sasada
Morningside: Taylor, Vandercar

(B) Farmington: Quinn
Homestead: Rodriguez, Vandercar
Morningside: Sasada, Taylor

(C) Farmington: Rodriguez
Morningside: Quinn, Taylor
Homestead: Sasada, Vandercar

(D) Homestead: Sasada
Farmington: Quinn
Morningside: Rodriguez, Taylor, Vandercar

(E) Morningside: Quinn
Farmington: Rodriguez, Sasada
Homestead: Taylor, Vandercar

PrepTest56 Sec1 Q17

Here's how the LSAT expert managed each of those Acceptability questions. As you review, ask yourself if you correctly interpreted each rule and took the shortest route to the correct answer by eliminating rule violators.

LSAT Question	Analysis

Workers at a water treatment plant open eight valves—G, H, I, K, L, N, O, and P—to flush out a system of pipes that needs emergency repairs. To maximize safety and efficiency, each valve is opened exactly once, and no two valves are opened at the same time. The valves are opened in accordance with the following conditions:

  Both K and P are opened before H.
  O is opened before L but after H.
  L is opened after G.
  N is opened before H.
  I is opened after K.

$\longrightarrow$

Steps 1–4:

Master Sketch

GHIKLNOP

1. Which one of the following could be the order, from first to last, in which the valves are opened? $\longrightarrow$	**Step 5:** An Acceptability question. Go through the rules one-by-one and use each rule to eliminate as many violators as possible.
(A) P, I, K, G, N, H, O, L $\longrightarrow$	Violates Rule 5 by having I before K. Eliminate.
(B) P, G, K, N, L, H, O, I $\longrightarrow$	Violates Rule 2 by having O after L. Eliminate.
(C) G, K, I, P, H, O, N, L $\longrightarrow$	Violates Rule 4 by having N after H. Eliminate.
(D) N, K, P, H, O, I, L, G $\longrightarrow$	Violates Rule 3 by having L before G. Eliminate.
(E) K, I, N, G, P, H, O, L $\longrightarrow$	Correct. This is an acceptable sequence.

PrepTest52 Sec2 Q1

LSAT Question	**Analysis**

On a field trip to the Museum of Natural History, each of six children—Juana, Kyle, Lucita, Salim, Thanh, and Veronica—is accompanied by one of three adults—Ms. Margoles, Mr. O'Connell, and Ms. Podorski. Each adult accompanies exactly two of the children, consistent with the following conditions:

> If Ms. Margoles accompanies Juana, then Ms. Podorski accompanies Lucita.
>
> If Kyle is not accompanied by Ms. Margoles, then Veronica is accompanied by Mr. O'Connell.
>
> Either Ms. Margoles or Mr. O'Connell accompanies Thanh.
>
> Juana is not accompanied by the same adult as Kyle; nor is Lucita accompanied by the same adult as Salim; nor is Thanh accompanied by the same adult as Veronica. $\longrightarrow$

Steps 1–4:

Master Sketch

J K L S T V

Mar	O'Con	Pod	
			Never JK
—	—	—	Never LS
—	—	~T	Never TV

If $\dfrac{\text{Mar}}{\text{J}} \longrightarrow \dfrac{\text{Pod}}{\text{L}}$

If $\dfrac{\text{Pod}}{\text{~L}} \longrightarrow \dfrac{\text{Mar}}{\text{~J}}$

If $\dfrac{\text{Mar}}{\text{~K}} \longrightarrow \dfrac{\text{O'Con}}{\text{V}}$

If $\dfrac{\text{O'Con}}{\text{~V}} \longrightarrow \dfrac{\text{Mar}}{\text{K}}$

---

2. Which one of the following could be an accurate matching of the adults to the children they accompany? $\longrightarrow$

Step 5: An Acceptability question. Check the answers against the rules and eliminate rule violators.

(A)	Ms. Margoles: Juana, Thanh; Mr. O'Connell: Lucita, Veronica; Ms. Podorski: Kyle, Salim	$\longrightarrow$	Violates Rule 1—Juana is with Margoles, but Lucita is not with Podorski. Eliminate.
(B)	Ms. Margoles: Kyle, Thanh; Mr. O'Connell: Juana, Salim; Ms. Podorski: Lucita, Veronica	$\longrightarrow$	Correct. This is an acceptable distribution.
(C)	Ms. Margoles: Lucita, Thanh; Mr. O'Connell: Juana, Salim; Ms. Podorski: Kyle, Veronica	$\longrightarrow$	Violates Rule 2—Kyle is not with Margoles, but Veronica is not with O'Connell. Eliminate.
(D)	Ms. Margoles: Kyle, Veronica; Mr. O'Connell: Juana, Thanh; Ms. Podorski: Lucita, Salim	$\longrightarrow$	Violates Rule 4—Lucita and Salim are with the same adult. Eliminate.
(E)	Ms. Margoles: Salim, Veronica; Mr. O'Connell: Kyle, Lucita; Ms. Podorski: Juana, Thanh	$\longrightarrow$	Violates Rule 3—Thanh is not with Margoles or O'Connell. Eliminate.

PrepTest52 Sec2 Q8

LSAT Question	**Analysis**
Individual hour-long auditions will be scheduled for each of six saxophonists—Fujimura, Gabrieli, Herman, Jackson, King, and Lauder. The auditions will all take place on the same day. Each audition will begin on the hour, with the first beginning at 1 P.M. and the last at 6 P.M. The schedule of auditions must conform to the following conditions: Jackson auditions earlier than Herman does. Gabrieli auditions earlier than King does. Gabrieli auditions either immediately before or immediately after Lauder does. Exactly one audition separates the auditions of Jackson and Lauder.	**Steps 1–4:** **Master Sketch** $\overset{*}{F}$ G H J K L $\overline{1}$ $\overline{2}$ $\overline{3}$ $\overline{4}$ $\overline{5}$ $\overline{6}$ 　　　.·H 　$\underline{J}$ $\underline{\ }$ $\underline{L}$ or 　$\underline{L}$ $\underline{\ }$ $\underline{J}$...H $\underline{G/L}$ $\underline{L/G}$...K

3.	Which one of the following is an acceptable schedule for the auditions, listed in order from 1 P.M. through 6 P.M?	**Step 5:** An Acceptability question. Go through the rules one-by-one and use each rule to eliminate as many violators as possible.
(A)	Fujimura, Gabrieli, King, Jackson, Herman, Lauder	Violates Rule 3 because Gabrieli and Lauder are not adjacent. Eliminate.
(B)	Fujimura, King, Lauder, Gabrieli, Jackson, Herman	Violates Rule 2 because King is earlier than Gabrieli. Eliminate.
(C)	Fujimura, Lauder, Gabrieli, King, Jackson, Herman	Violates Rule 4 because Jackson and Lauder are separated by 2 spaces, not 1. Eliminate.
(D)	Herman, Jackson, Gabrieli, Lauder, King, Fujimura	Violates Rule 1 because Herman is earlier than Jackson. Eliminate.
(E)	Jackson, Gabrieli, Lauder, Herman, King, Fujimura	Correct. This is an acceptable sequence.

PrepTest56 Sec1 Q1

LSAT Question	Analysis

Five executives—Quinn, Rodriguez, Sasada, Taylor, and Vandercar—are being scheduled to make site visits to three of their company's manufacturing plants—Farmington, Homestead, and Morningside. Each site will be visited by at least one of the executives and each executive will visit just one site. Each of the three site visits will take place on a different day. The schedule of site visits must conform to the following requirements:

The Farmington visit must take place before the Homestead visit.

The Farmington visit will include only one of the executives.

The site visit that includes Quinn must take place before any site visit that includes either Rodriguez or Taylor.

The site visit that includes Sasada cannot take place after any site visit that includes Vandercar.

Steps 1–4:

Master Sketch

QRSTV

(I)

Farm	Home/Morn	Morn/Home
___	___	___
===		
~R		~Q
~T		
~V		

Q ⟨ R / T

(II)

Morn	Farm	Home
___	___	___
	===	
~R		~Q
~T		

[S/V] or S...V

---

4. Which one of the following could be the executives included in each of the site visits, with the sites listed in the order in which they are visited?

Step 5: An Acceptability question. Go through the rules one-by-one and use each rule to eliminate as many violators as possible.

(A) Farmington: Quinn
Homestead: Rodriguez, Sasada
Morningside: Taylor, Vandercar

Correct. Both the sequence of visits and the distribution of executives to sites is acceptable here.

(B) Farmington: Quinn
Homestead: Rodriguez, Vandercar
Morningside: Sasada, Taylor

Violates Rule 4 because Sasada's visit takes place after Vandercar's. Eliminate.

(C) Farmington: Rodriguez
Morningside: Quinn, Taylor
Homestead: Sasada, Vandercar

Violates Rule 3 because Quinn's visit takes place after Rodriguez's and at the same time as Taylor's. Eliminate.

(D) Homestead: Sasada
Farmington: Quinn
Morningside: Rodriguez, Taylor, Vandercar

Violates Rule 1 because Homestead is visited before Farmington here. Eliminate.

(E) Morningside: Quinn
Farmington: Rodriguez, Sasada
Homestead: Taylor, Vandercar

Violates Rule 2 because Farmington hosts two executives. Eliminate.

PrepTest56 Sec1 Q17

Acceptability questions provide a nice entry point into the question set in almost every game, and there's little reason not to just jump in and tackle the Acceptability question as soon as you've completed your Master Sketch. The remainder of the questions, however, you may decide to handle out of order depending on how much certainty you've established in the Deductions step. For the purposes of arranging this chapter, we'll introduce you to Must Be/Could Be questions before New-"If" questions, but the two types will be mixed up together in the question set and, as you'll see, you can sometimes use information from one question to help you eliminate choices in another.

A Note on Complete and Accurate List Questions

One of the Acceptability questions you just reviewed had the following question stem:

> Which one of the following could be a complete and accurate list of the volunteers?
>
> *PrepTest58 Sec3 Q7*

That particular wording amounts to asking for an acceptable selection, and the correct answer will represent one possible "solution" to the game.

It's worth noting, however, that the testmaker will, occasionally, use the phrase "complete and accurate list" for questions that focus on a narrower part of the game. In a Sequencing game, for example, one of these questions might ask for "a complete and accurate list of the days on which Johnson's appointment may be scheduled." In a Distribution game, on the other hand, you might run across a question such as "Which of following is a complete and accurate list of all players who could play on Team B?"

For Complete and Accurate List questions such as these, the correct answer must contain *any and all* of the acceptable slots or entities called for by the question stem. In other words, each wrong answer will either be incomplete—it will not contain all of the days on which Johnson's appointment can be scheduled, or it will be missing players who are eligible for Team B—or the wrong answer will be inaccurate—it will include days on which Johnson's appointment cannot be scheduled or players ineligible for Team B. That makes sense when you think about the question. If the right answer is "complete and accurate," all four wrong answers must be incomplete or inaccurate.

Don't spend too much time trying to hunt down examples of this rare question type. (There were none among the questions for the games you've studied thus far.) You will see the following example when you tackle the games in Chapter 6.

> Which one of the following is a complete and accurate list of the talks any one of which Rivera and Spivey could attend together?
>
> *PrepTest62 Sec3 Q16*

When you do come across Complete and Accurate List questions, don't panic or change your strategic approach to logic games. These questions are too rare to be a type that makes or breaks your score. Just distinguish them from Acceptability questions and remember that the wrong answers are always inaccurate or incomplete. Once you've characterized the answer choices, you just consult the Master Sketch to eliminate the violators and find the right answer.

While we're on the subject of completeness, let's look at another rare Logic Games question type: the Completely Determine question.

COMPLETELY DETERMINE QUESTIONS

From time to time, the LSAT will pose a question asking you for a statement that would completely determine the sequence, selection, matching, or distribution of all entities in the game. Completely Determine questions are not common—among the 60 logic games (345 questions) released from 2008 through 2012, there were only 12 of these questions. It turns out, however, that one of them was in the Monuments game.

You'll recall that this game asked you to Sequence the beginning of six monuments over the course of five years. The correct answer to this question will be a statement that determines the exact order of all six monuments. That means that the four wrong answers will leave one or more of the monuments' positions undetermined. As you review the LSAT expert's analysis of this question, pay attention to the monument(s) with which he's most concerned. The less restricted a monument is initially, the more likely that locking down its position will impact the other monuments as well.

LSAT Question	Analysis

Historical records show that over the course of five consecutive years—601, 602, 603, 604, and 605—a certain emperor began construction of six monuments: F, G, H, L, M, and S. A historian is trying to determine the years in which the individual monuments were begun. The following facts have been established:

  L was begun in a later year than G, but in an earlier year than F.

  H was begun no earlier than 604.

  M was begun earlier than 604.

  Two of the monuments were begun in 601, and no other monument was begun in the same year as any of the other monuments.

→

Steps 1–4:
Master Sketch

FGHLMS*

	601	602	603	604	605
GM				H/	/H
GS	⌒	——	——	~M	~M
MS	——	~H	~H	~M	~M
	~H	~F	~G	~G	~G
	~F			~L	~L
	~L				

G . . . L . . . F

The years in which each of the monuments were begun can be completely determined if which one of the following is discovered to be true?

→

Step 5: Use the Master Sketch to evaluate the choices. The correct answer will provide certainty about each monument's starting date. Information about S will likely be helpful because it's the one monument not mentioned at all in the rules.

(A) F was begun in 603.

This doesn't tell us whether H was begun in 604 and S in 605 or vice versa. Eliminate.

→

601	602	603	604	605
G	L	F	H/S	S/H
M				

LSAT Question	Analysis
(B) G was begun in 602.	This doesn't tell us whether H was begun in 604 and F in 605 or vice versa. Eliminate.

$\longrightarrow$

601	602	603	604	605
S	G	L	H/F	F/H
M				

(C) H was begun in 605.	This leaves a number of possibilities open. S, for example, could have been started in 601, 602, 603, or 604. Eliminate.

F G H L M S

$\longrightarrow$

601	602	603	604	605
				H

G...L...F

S–???

(D) M was begun in 602.	This doesn't tell us whether H was begun in 604 and F in 605 or vice versa. Eliminate.

$\longrightarrow$

601	602	603	604	605
S	M	L	H/F	F/H
G				

(E) S was begun in 604.	Correct. There's only one way to sequence all six monuments here.

PrepTest58 Sec3 Q3

$\longrightarrow$

601	602	603	604	605
G	L	F	S	H
M				

It's not always the case that the correct answer to a Completely Determine question will involve a Floater (an unrestricted entity), but the correct answer must always impose restrictions sufficient to lock down all of the entities, including the Floater(s). It's not always necessary to test every answer choice with a sketch. Once you're sure that an answer choice leaves one or more of the entities free to change positions, you can confidently eliminate it. Indeed, the sketches in the expert analysis above are included primarily so that you can see directly which spaces and entities remain undetermined.

Practice

Now, try a Completely Determine question on your own. This one came from the Saxophonists game, another Strict Sequencing game. If you just finished the Acceptability questions above, this game is probably fresh in your mind, but we'll give you a clue for this question anyway. The Floater in this game—Fujimura—is not mentioned in any of the answer choices. All four wrong answers, however, fail to lock down Fujimura's position. Only the correct answer leaves exactly one space for the Floater and thus completely determines the order.

Try the following question. Read the question stem and characterize the one correct and four wrong answer choices. Then, evaluate the answer choices by consulting the Master Sketch. When you finish, check your work against that of the LSAT expert on the following page.

LSAT Question	My Analysis

Individual hour-long auditions will be scheduled for each of six saxophonists—Fujimura, Gabrieli, Herman, Jackson, King, and Lauder. The auditions will all take place on the same day. Each audition will begin on the hour, with the first beginning at 1 P.M. and the last at 6 P.M. The schedule of auditions must conform to the following conditions:
    Jackson auditions earlier than Herman does.
    Gabrieli auditions earlier than King does.
    Gabrieli auditions either immediately before or immediately after Lauder does.
    Exactly one audition separates the auditions of Jackson and Lauder.
	Steps 1–4:
	
	Master Sketch
	
	$\overset{*}{F}$ G H J K L
	$\overline{1}\ \ \overline{2}\ \ \overline{3}\ \ \overline{4}\ \ \overline{5}\ \ \overline{6}$
	    ·.·H
	  J __ L
	or
	  L __ J...H
	G/L L/G...K

5. The order in which the saxophonists are scheduled to audition is completely determined if which one of the following is true? → **Step 5:**

(A) Herman's audition is scheduled to begin at 4 P.M.

(B) Jackson's audition is scheduled to begin at 1 P.M.

(C) Jackson's audition is scheduled to begin at 5 P.M.

(D) Lauder's audition is scheduled to begin at 1 P.M.

(E) Lauder's audition is scheduled to begin at 2 P.M.

PrepTest56 Sec1 Q4

Here's how the LSAT expert analyzed and answered the question you just tried. Examine the sketches the expert has provided to demonstrate why each of the wrong answers fails to completely determine the order.

LSAT Question	Analysis

Individual hour-long auditions will be scheduled for each of six saxophonists—Fujimura, Gabrieli, Herman, Jackson, King, and Lauder. The auditions will all take place on the same day. Each audition will begin on the hour, with the first beginning at 1 P.M. and the last at 6 P.M. The schedule of auditions must conform to the following conditions:

Jackson auditions earlier than Herman does.
Gabrieli auditions earlier than King does.
Gabrieli auditions either immediately before or immediately after Lauder does.
Exactly one audition separates the auditions of Jackson and Lauder.

→

Steps 1–4:

Master Sketch

*
F G H J K L
_____
1 2 3 4 5 6

. . . H

J ___ L

or

L ___ J . . . H

G/L   L/G . . . K

---

5. The order in which the saxophonists are scheduled to audition is completely determined if which one of the following is true?

→ **Step 5:** A Completely Determine question—the correct answer will lock down all six audition times. The wrong answers will leave two or more spaces undetermined.

(A) Herman's audition is scheduled to begin at 4 P.M.

→ Leaves four spaces undetermined. Eliminate.

J/L   G   L/J   H   F/K   K/F
 1   2   3   4   5   6

(B) Jackson's audition is scheduled to begin at 1 P.M.

→ Leaves four spaces undetermined. Eliminate.

J   ___   L   ___   ___   ___
1   2   3   4   5   6

(C) Jackson's audition is scheduled to begin at 5 P.M.

→ Correct. The only acceptable sequence here is

F   G   L   K   J   H
1   2   3   4   5   6

(D) Lauder's audition is scheduled to begin at 1 P.M.

→ Leaves three spaces undetermined. Eliminate.

                    F/K/H
L   G   J   ⌒‾‾‾‾‾⌒
1   2   3   4   5   6

(E) Lauder's audition is scheduled to begin at 2 P.M.
PrepTest56 Sec1 Q4

→ Leaves four spaces undetermined. Eliminate.

G/F   L   ___   J   ___   ___
 1   2   3   4   5   6

Don't spend time trying to chase down additional examples of this rare question type. Your time is much better spent practicing. Must Be/Could Be and New-"If" questions. Before you move on, though, take a few minutes to practice the following drill.

Characterizing the Answer Choices in Acceptability, Complete and Accurate List, and Completely Determine Questions

Take a few minutes to study the sample question stems below. For each, you'll see the LSAT expert's analysis identifying the question type and characterizing the one correct and four incorrect answer choices. Remember, the analysis you see below is mental work the expert is doing. There is no need to write down any of this on Test Day. Once you feel comfortable identifying these question types, try the practice drill on the following pages to test your ability to characterize the choices on similar questions.

Question Stem	Analysis
Which of the following could be a complete and accurate list of the race cars crossing the finish line, in order from first to last?	This question asks for one possible, acceptable arrangement of the entities and is thus a standard Acceptability question. The correct answer could be true; the four incorrect choices must be false because they each break one or more rules. Attack Acceptability questions by going through the rules and knocking out all choices that break at least one rule. The choice that remains is the correct answer.
Which of the following could be an accurate matching of children to party hats?	Another Acceptability question. Correct answer could be true; incorrect choices must be false because they each break at least one rule.
Which of the following could be a complete and accurate list of each of the clients served by lawyer Z?	This one is a Partial Acceptability question: it doesn't ask for an acceptable arrangement of all the clients and lawyers, just a matching of lawyer Z to her clients. As in all Acceptability questions, the correct answer could be true, while incorrect choices must be false.
Which of the following is NOT an acceptable schedule of appointments, from earliest to latest?	Acceptability EXCEPT question: correct answer must be false; incorrect choices could be true. Because the incorrect choices all represent acceptable arrangements of the entities, go through the rules as in an ordinary Acceptability question—but the moment you find a choice that breaks a rule, stop. That's the correct answer.
Which of the following could be a complete and accurate list of the types of grass seeds selected?	Acceptability question. Correct answer could be true; incorrect choices must be false.
Which of the following CANNOT be a complete and accurate list of the types of grass seed selected?	Acceptability EXCEPT question. Correct answer must be false; incorrect choices could be true.

Question Stem	Analysis
Which of the following could be a complete and accurate list of the types of grass seed NOT selected?	Note the difference between this question and the last one. The preceding question asks for an *unacceptable* list of *selected* entities. This question, in contrast, asks for an *acceptable* list of entities that are *left out*. This is also an Acceptability question, but the line of attack will be different. For each answer choice, first deduce which entities *are* included. Then apply the rules as you would in an ordinary Acceptability question.
Which of the following is a complete and accurate list of all possible flowerbeds to which M could be assigned?	Note the word "is," as opposed to the "could be" phrasing common in Acceptability questions. This is a Complete and Accurate List question, asking for all the possible places M could go. The correct answer will list *all* the slots M could ever occupy; the incorrect choices will either give only partial lists of slots that M can occupy or will list slots M cannot occupy (or both).
Which of the following is a complete and accurate list of the flowers any one of which could be assigned to bed 3?	A Complete and Accurate List question, this time asking for all entities allowed in flowerbed 3. The correct answer will list *all* entities that could be placed into bed 3; the incorrect choices will give only partial lists of entities that could go in bed 3 or will list entities that cannot be placed into bed 3 (or both).
Which of the following is a complete and accurate list of those flowers that CANNOT be assigned to bed 2?	Complete and Accurate List question. Correct answer will list *all* entities that cannot be assigned to bed 2. Incorrect choices will give only partial lists of entities that cannot be assigned to bed 2 or will list entities that can be assigned to bed 2 (or both).
The roster for the spelling bee is completely determined if which of the following is true?	Completely Determine question. Correct answer provides a condition that pins down the position of every entity. Incorrect choices will each provide a condition that allows for more than one possible arrangement of entities.
There is only one acceptable group of 5 amphibians that can be selected for the school terrarium if which of the following pairs of amphibians is selected?	Completely Determine question. Correct answer provides a pair of entities that forces the selection of three additional entities so that there is only one way to select the group of five. Incorrect choices will each allow for more than one possible group of five entities.

Now, try it out on your own. The question stems below are similar, though certainly not identical, to those in the list above and the questions you've seen so far in this chapter.

Practice

For each of the following question stems, identify the question type and characterize the one correct and four incorrect answer choices. When you're done, check your work against the LSAT expert's analysis on the following pages.

Question Stem	My Analysis
6. Which of the following could be a complete and accurate ordering of the books on shelf 2, from left to right?	
7. Which of the following is a complete and accurate list of those books that CANNOT be placed on shelf 1?	
8. Which of the following is an acceptable selection of pies and punch recipes for the office meeting?	
9. The selection of pies and punch recipes for the office meeting is completely determined if which of the following is true?	
10. Each of the following could be an accurate assignment of streets to trees planted on them EXCEPT:	
11. Which of the following is a complete and accurate list of the streets on which tree R could be planted?	
12. Which of the following is a complete and accurate list of trees that CANNOT be planted on Street B?	
13. All students' grades are known if which of the following is FALSE?	
14. Which of the following CANNOT be a complete and accurate ranking of brownie mixes, from most popular to least popular?	
15. Which of the following, if true, would cause the ranking of brownie mixes from most popular to least popular to be completely determined?	
16. Which of the following could be a complete and accurate matching of horses to rider W?	
17. Which of the following is NOT an acceptable matching of glasses to tableware?	

Here's how the LSAT expert analyzed each of the question stems you just practiced. Compare your work with that of the expert. You'll see more questions of these types as you practice the games in Chapter 6 and those in the full-length tests at the end of the book.

Question Stem	Analysis
6. Which of the following could be a complete and accurate ordering of the books on shelf 2, from left to right?	Partial Acceptability question because it only asks about shelf 2, not all shelves. Correct answer could be true, and the incorrect choices must be false. Attack the same way as you would a standard Acceptability question: go through the rules and knock out choices that break one or more rules. The one choice that does not break any rules will be the correct answer.
7. Which of the following is a complete and accurate list of those books that CANNOT be placed on shelf 1?	Complete and Accurate List question. Correct answer will provide a complete list of those books that cannot be on shelf 1, while the incorrect choices will each either leave out at least one book that cannot be on shelf 1 or will list at least one book that can be on shelf 1 (or both).
8. Which of the following is an acceptable selection of pies and punch recipes for the office meeting?	Acceptability question. Correct answer could be true (because it does not break any rules). Incorrect choices must be false (because they each break at least one rule).
9. The selection of pies and punch recipes for the office meeting is completely determined if which of the following is true?	Completely Determine question. Correct answer will provide a condition that allows for only one possible selection of pies and only one possible selection of punch recipes. Incorrect choices will each provide a condition that allows for multiple selections of pies, or multiple selections of punch recipes, or both.
10. Each of the following could be an accurate assignment of streets to trees planted on them EXCEPT:	Acceptability EXCEPT question. Incorrect choices each represent an acceptable arrangement and therefore could be true. Correct answer breaks at least one rule and therefore must be false.
11. Which of the following is a complete and accurate list of the streets on which tree R could be planted?	Complete and Accurate List question. Correct answer will provide *all* the streets where R can go. Incorrect choices will either leave out at least one street where R can go, or will list streets where R cannot go, or both.
12. Which of the following is a complete and accurate list of trees that CANNOT be planted on Street B?	Complete and Accurate List question. Correct answer will provide *all* trees that cannot go on street B. Incorrect choices will either leave out at least one tree that cannot go on street B, or will list at least one tree that can go on street B, or both.

Question Stem		Analysis
13. All students' grades are known if which of the following is FALSE?	$\longrightarrow$	Completely Determine question. Correct answer will provide a condition that, if false, forces one possible matching of students to grades. Incorrect choices will each provide a condition that, if false, allows more than one possible matching of students to grades, or that results in a conflict between rules.
14. Which of the following CANNOT be a complete and accurate ranking of brownie mixes, from most popular to least popular?	$\longrightarrow$	Acceptability EXCEPT question. Incorrect choices could be true (because they do not break any rules); correct answer must be false (because it breaks at least one rule).
15. Which of the following, if true, would cause the ranking of brownie mixes from most popular to least popular to be completely determined?	$\longrightarrow$	Completely Determine question. Correct answer will provide a condition that pins down the rank of every single entity. Incorrect choices will each provide a condition that allows for more than one possible ordering.
16. Which of the following could be a complete and accurate matching of horses to rider W?	$\longrightarrow$	Partial Acceptability question. Correct answer could be true; incorrect choices must be false.
17. Which of the following is NOT an acceptable matching of glasses to tableware?	$\longrightarrow$	Acceptability EXCEPT question. Correct answer must be false; incorrect choices could be true.

Even though those question stems weren't associated with any game setup in that exercise, were you able to imagine the entities and actions those games would include? If so, you're really getting familiar with the Logic Games section and the kinds of the games the testmaker uses over and over.

You'll see two more drills like that one later in the chapter. It's very important that you're able to understand exactly what the questions are calling for and to be able to recognize right and wrong answers as you evaluate them. Keep that in mind as you move on in the chapter. The next two question types we'll discuss are, by far, the most important because they account for a large majority of points available in the Logic Games section.

MUST BE/COULD BE QUESTIONS

Combined, this section of the chapter and the next section (on New-"If" questions) account for the large majority of Logic Games questions you'll see on Test Day. Together, these two categories account for roughly 70 percent of all questions in the Logic Games section. And the two question types are related. Must Be/Could Be questions (about 24 percent of the section) ask you for an answer that states something that must be true, could be true, could be false, or must be false in the game. New-"If" questions ask largely the same things but add a new condition, unique to that question alone, and make you account for its implications before they pose the Must Be/Could Be question.

Because characterizing the correct and incorrect answer choices is so important to both of these question types, we'll start with the Must Be/Could Be questions without "If" conditions. Before you're done, though, you'll see and practice with plenty of examples of both question types, as there are numerous examples from all the games you've been working with up to this point.

Here's a Must Be True question from the Monuments game. The question stem is straightforward in defining the criteria of the correct answer. Still, the LSAT expert knows that it's important to characterize the wrong answers before evaluating the choices. It may be much more efficient to eliminate choices that could be false than to spot the one that must be true.

Which one of the following must be true?

(A) F was begun in a later year than M.
(B) F was begun in a later year than S.
(C) H was begun in a later year than F.
(D) H was begun in a later year than S.
(E) M was begun in a later year than G.

PrepTest58 Sec3 Q4

You'll see the LSAT expert's analysis of that question and several others shortly. Because there are no New-"If" conditions in the stems of these questions, you can answer them by consulting your Master Sketch. Indeed, you should anticipate that one or more of these questions will reward you directly for making the game's central deduction(s).

LEARNING OBJECTIVES

In this section, you'll learn to:

- Identify and answer Must Be/Could Be Questions.
- Characterize accurately the correct and incorrect answer choices in Must Be/Could Be questions.

Even with a perfect Master Sketch, many test takers will miss points from Must Be/Could Be Questions because they don't take the time to characterize the correct answer. They'll consult their well-made Master Sketch but forget whether they're checking for what must be true or what could be false. As mentioned earlier in this chapter, levels of certainty (must/could) and truth value (true/false) were discussed and drilled in Chapter 1. If you're hesitant about applying these concepts, revisit that chapter for a refresher.

Now, take a look at the LSAT expert's analysis of the question from the previous page.

LSAT Question	Analysis

Historical records show that over the course of five consecutive years—601, 602, 603, 604, and 605—a certain emperor began construction of six monuments: F, G, H, L, M, and S. A historian is trying to determine the years in which the individual monuments were begun. The following facts have been established:

L was begun in a later year than G, but in an earlier year than F.

H was begun no earlier than 604.

M was begun earlier than 604.

Two of the monuments were begun in 601, and no other monument was begun in the same year as any of the other monuments.

→

Steps 1–4:

Master Sketch

*
F G H L M S

	601	602	603	604	605
GM				H/	/H
GS	—	~H	~H	~M	~M
MS	~H	~F	~G	~G	~G
	~F			~L	~L
	~L				

G . . . L . . . F

Which one of the following must be true?	→	**Step 5:** Use the Master Sketch to evaluate the choices. The correct answer must be true. Four wrong answers could be false.
(A) F was begun in a later year than M.	→	Correct. The earliest year for F is 603, and M can never be in 604 or 605.
(B) F was begun in a later year than S.	→	S could take any year. Eliminate.
(C) H was begun in a later year than F.	→	F could take 605, while H could take 604. Eliminate.
(D) H was begun in a later year than S.	→	S could take any year. Eliminate.
(E) M was begun in a later year than G.	→	M and G could both take 601, or M could be with S in 601 while G takes 602. Eliminate.

PrepTest58 Sec3 Q4

On Test Day, the LSAT expert could have been absolutely certain of the answer as soon as she evaluated choice (A). In fact, the LSAT expert would stop right there, circle choice (A), and move on to the next question. That's a wonderful time-saver, but taking advantage of it requires enormous confidence. Looking at the expert's analysis on choices (B) through (E) reveals where that confidence comes from. The expert's analysis is so certain—she knows exactly what constitutes a correct and incorrect answer—that she would fly through this question regardless of the order in which the answer choices were presented.

The Monuments game presents a Strict Sequencing action, but open-ended Must Be/Could Be questions can be (and will be) associated with any game type. Take a look at a handful of other examples from the games you've been working with. In each case, pay attention to how the expert characterizes the one right and four wrong answers.

The first example is from the Saxophonists game. As you review the expert's analysis, note that the question stem is identical to the question above from the Monuments game. The following question, however, is more difficult for two reasons. First, the answer choices are more complex. Second, assuming you evaluate the answer choices in order, you won't find the correct answer until the end. The LSAT expert doesn't let this throw him. He establishes the criteria for the correct answer before assessing the choices, and he will not be satisfied until he finds the answer that must be true.

LSAT Question	Analysis

Individual hour-long auditions will be scheduled for each of six saxophonists—Fujimura, Gabrieli, Herman, Jackson, King, and Lauder. The auditions will all take place on the same day. Each audition will begin on the hour, with the first beginning at 1 P.M. and the last at 6 P.M. The schedule of auditions must conform to the following conditions:
  Jackson auditions earlier than Herman does.
  Gabrieli auditions earlier than King does.
  Gabrieli auditions either immediately before or immediately after Lauder does.
  Exactly one audition separates the auditions of Jackson and Lauder.
	Steps 1–4:
	
	Master Sketch
	
	$\overset{*}{F}$ G H J K L
	
	$\underline{1}\ \underline{2}\ \underline{3}\ \underline{4}\ \underline{5}\ \underline{6}$
	
	$\underset{.\cdot}{}$ H
	
	$\underline{J}\ \_\ \underline{L}$
	
	or $\underline{L}\ \_\ \underline{J}\ ...\ H$
	
	$\underline{G/L}\ \underline{L/G}\ ...\ K$

Which one of the following must be true?	**Step 5:** Use the Master Sketch to evaluate the choices. The correct answer must be true. The four wrong answers could be false.
(A) Gabrieli's audition is scheduled to begin before 5 P.M.	Could be false—Gabrieli at 5 P.M. is fine: $\underline{F}\ \underline{J}\ \underline{H}\ \underline{L}\ \underline{G}\ \underline{K}$ $\ 1\ \ 2\ \ 3\ \ 4\ \ 5\ \ 6$
(B) Herman's audition is scheduled to begin after 2 P.M.	Could be false—Herman at 2 P.M. is fine: $\underline{J}\ \underline{H}\ \underline{L}\ \underline{G}\ \underline{F/K}\ \underline{K/F}$ $\ 1\ \ 2\ \ 3\ \ 4\ \ \ 5\ \ \ \ 6$
(C) Herman's audition is scheduled to begin before 6 P.M.	Could be false—Herman at 6 P.M. leaves open all sorts of possibilities.
(D) King's audition is scheduled to begin before 6 P.M.	Could be false—see choices (A) and (B).
(E) Lauder's audition is scheduled to begin before 5 P.M. *PrepTest56 Sec1 Q6*	Correct. The deduction from Rules 2 and 3 shows that Lauder cannot be at 6 P.M. Try Lauder at 5 P.M. $\underline{\ }\ \underline{\ }\ \underline{J}\ \underline{G}\ \underline{L}\ \underline{K}\ \ H???$ $\ 1\ \ 2\ \ 3\ \ 4\ \ 5\ \ 6$ There is no way to obey all four Rules in this case. Because Lauder cannot audition at 5 P.M. or 6 P.M., he must audition before 5 P.M. This must be true.

So far, the questions you've seen have had simple question stems: "Which one of the following must be true?" Of course, the testmaker will also ask, "Which one of the following could be true?" or "Which one of the following must be false?" In fact, the must-be-false variety is the test's favorite, constituting just over half of the Must Be/Could Be questions on recent exams. With practice, however, you won't let these changes in wording throw you. An LSAT expert always takes a couple of seconds to characterize both the right and wrong answer choices and states to himself why each choice is right or wrong as he evaluates them. You'll have practice with all of the variations on these stems in the drill that follows the New-"If" section of this chapter.

Here's an example of a Must Be False question. Before you review the expert's analysis of the question, however, take a moment to refresh your memory of our earlier work on the Stained Glass Windows game. Specifically, take note of the fact that the windows are not named or numbered in any way. We'll talk about that again after you've reviewed the expert's work on this example.

LSAT Question		Analysis
An artisan has been hired to create three stained glass windows. The artisan will use exactly five colors of glass: green, orange, purple, rose, and yellow. Each color of glass will be used at least once, and each window will contain at least two different colors of glass. The windows must also conform to the following conditions: Exactly one of the windows contains both green glass and purple glass. Exactly two of the windows contain rose glass. If a window contains yellow glass, then that window contains neither green glass nor orange glass. If a window does not contain purple glass, then that window contains orange glass.	$\rightarrow$	**Steps 1–4:** **Master Sketch** G O P R Y <table><tr><td>"1st"</td><td>"2nd"</td><td>"3rd"</td></tr><tr><td>G</td><td>Y</td><td>P/O</td></tr><tr><td>P</td><td>P</td><td></td></tr><tr><td>~Y</td><td>~G</td><td></td></tr><tr><td></td><td>~O</td><td></td></tr></table> GP = exactly 1x R = 2x If Y ⟶ ~G and ~O If G or O ⟶ ~Y [Never YG, Never YO] If ~P ⟶ O If ~O ⟶ P [At least one of P/O in every window]
Which one of the following CANNOT be the complete color combination of the glass in one of the windows?	$\rightarrow$	**Step 5:** Use the Master Sketch to evaluate the choices. The correct answer cannot be the only colors in one of the windows. The four wrong answers all contains pairs of colors that *could* be the only colors in one of the windows.
(A) green and orange	$\rightarrow$	Could be true in the "third" window. Eliminate.
(B) green and purple	$\rightarrow$	Could be true in the "first" window. Eliminate.
(C) green and rose	$\rightarrow$	Correct. This directly violates Rule 4—every window must have purple or orange.
(D) purple and orange	$\rightarrow$	Could be true in the "third" window. Eliminate.
(E) rose and orange	$\rightarrow$	Could be true in the "third" window. Eliminate.

PrepTest62 Sec3 Q8

Because the windows aren't designated by name or number, this question is simply asking what must be false in any case. All four wrong answers could be true of one or more of the windows. The LSAT expert can use the three cases in the Master Sketch to eliminate all four wrong answers, or he could pick out choice (C) as correct as soon as he notes that it violates one of the rules.

In the next part of this section, we'll take a look at questions that ask what must or could be true or false of specific entities or spaces within the game.

Game-Specific Must Be/Could Be Questions

Many Must Be/Could Be question stems are as straightforward as those you've just reviewed. Others, however, ask questions more tailored to the specific task or arrangement of the game. They might ask what could be true of a given entity or what must be false about a certain slot in the sequence, for example. When you encounter questions like these, use the question stem to characterize the one correct and four incorrect choices just as you would with more garden-variety Must Be/Could Be stems.

On the following pages, take a look at how the LSAT expert analyzed a few of these game-specific Must Be/Could Be questions.

The first comes from the Distribution game about the Field Trip Chaperones.

LSAT Question	Analysis
On a field trip to the Museum of Natural History, each of six children—Juana, Kyle, Lucita, Salim, Thanh, and Veronica—is accompanied by one of three adults—Ms. Margoles, Mr. O'Connell, and Ms. Podorski. Each adult accompanies exactly two of the children, consistent with the following conditions: If Ms. Margoles accompanies Juana, then Ms. Podorski accompanies Lucita. If Kyle is not accompanied by Ms. Margoles, then Veronica is accompanied by Mr. O'Connell. Either Ms. Margoles or Mr. O'Connell accompanies Thanh. Juana is not accompanied by the same adult as Kyle; nor is Lucita accompanied by the same adult as Salim; nor is Thanh accompanied by the same adult as Veronica.	**Steps 1–4:** **Master Sketch** J K L S T V Mar │ O'Con │ Pod ——————————————— Never JK —— │ —— │ —— Never LS —— │ —— │ —— Never TV ↖ T ↗ ~T If $\dfrac{\text{Mar}}{\text{J}} \longrightarrow \dfrac{\text{Pod}}{\text{L}}$ If $\dfrac{\text{Pod}}{\sim\text{L}} \longrightarrow \dfrac{\text{Mar}}{\sim\text{J}}$ If $\dfrac{\text{Mar}}{\sim\text{K}} \longrightarrow \dfrac{\text{O'Con}}{\text{V}}$ If $\dfrac{\text{O'Con}}{\sim\text{V}} \longrightarrow \dfrac{\text{Mar}}{\text{K}}$
Ms. Podorski CANNOT accompany which one of the following pairs of children?	**Step 5:** Use the Master Sketch to evaluate the choices. The correct answer is a pair of children who cannot go with Podorski at the same time. The wrong answers are all pairs that would be acceptable for Podorski. (Note that because of Rule 3, Podorski cannot accompany Thanh.)
(A) Juana and Lucita	
(B) Juana and Salim	
(C) Kyle and Salim	
(D) Salim and Thanh	Correct. This directly violates Rule 3.
(E) Salim and Veronica	

PrepTest52 Sec2 Q11

That example amounts to a Must Be False question, but it asks about a specific chaperone and presents pairs of children (not individual entities) in the answer choices. Nonetheless, the LSAT expert characterizes the choices to make evaluation simple: if the right answer is a pair Podorski cannot chaperone, then all four wrong answers are pairs she *can* chaperone. Then, he immediately notes what the Master Sketch has to say about Podorski. The right answer turns out to be nothing more than the implication of one rule: if Thanh has to go with either Margoles or O'Connell, then he sure can't go with Podorski. If you charged into the answer choices for that question without knowing what to look for, you could wind up drawing several sketches, but with practice you will, as the LSAT expert does, analyze and evaluate efficiently and learn to identify the "likely suspects" among the answer choices.

Here's another example of a game-specific Must Be/Could Be stem, this time from the Water Valves Loose Sequencing game. As you review it, take the time to spell out precisely what the correct and incorrect answers' characteristics must be. Compare your analysis to the LSAT expert's and then see how she used her characterization to evaluate the answer choices.

LSAT Question		Analysis
Workers at a water treatment plant open eight valves—G, H, I, K, L, N, O, and P—to flush out a system of pipes that needs emergency repairs. To maximize safety and efficiency, each valve is opened exactly once, and no two valves are opened at the same time. The valves are opened in accordance with the following conditions: 　Both K and P are opened before H. 　O is opened before L but after H. 　L is opened after G. 　N is opened before H. 　I is opened after K.	→	**Steps 1–4:** **Master Sketch** G H I K L N O P
Each of the following could be the fifth valve opened EXCEPT:	→	**Step 5:** The correct answer CANNOT be opened fifth. It will contain an entity that either has five or more entities before it or four or more entities after it. The four wrong answers name valves that can be opened fifth.
(A)　H	→	H could be opened fourth, fifth, or sixth. Eliminate.
(B)　I	→	I could be opened second through eighth. Eliminate.
(C)　K	→	Correct. K can only be opened first through fourth. There are eight entities, and H, I, L, and O all must be opened after K.
(D)　N	→	N could be opened first through fifth. Eliminate.
(E)　O <div align="center">*PrepTest52 Sec2 Q2*</div>	→	O could be opened fifth, sixth, or seventh. Eliminate.

This question is a variation on the Must Be False question stem, but here, the test asks for what could be true *of a specific position* within the sequence. If the right answer cannot be true of that position, the LSAT expert knows that all four wrong answers could be true. By the way, did you remember that in the Deductions step for this game, we discussed how to determine the acceptable positions for any given entity? Here, you see exactly how the LSAT expert puts that analysis into action.

Take a look at another example before you do some practice. This one comes from the Selection game about the Day Care Volunteers. Study the expert's characterization of the correct and incorrect answer choices very carefully and then review the Master Sketch. This is the type of question that many test takers may get wrong simply because they don't take the time to understand what the question is asking for and to consider how much they already know about the game's deductions.

LSAT Question	Analysis
A company organizing on-site day care consults with a group of parents composed exclusively of volunteers from among the seven employees—Felicia, Leah, Masatomo, Rochelle, Salman, Terry, and Veena—who have become parents this year. The composition of the volunteer group must be consistent with the following: If Rochelle volunteers, then so does Masatomo. If Masatomo volunteers, then so does Terry. If Salman does not volunteer, then Veena volunteers. If Rochelle does not volunteer, then Leah volunteers. If Terry volunteers, then neither Felicia nor Veena volunteers.	**Steps 1–4:** **Master Sketch** F L M R S T V If ⓡ ⟶ Ⓜ If ~M ⟶ ~R If Ⓜ ⟶ Ⓣ If ~T ⟶ ~M ⟶ If ~S ⟶ Ⓥ If ~V ⟶ Ⓢ (At least one of S, V—maybe both) If ~R ⟶ Ⓛ If ~L ⟶ ⓡ (At least one of R, L—maybe both) If Ⓣ ⟶ ~F and ~V If Ⓕ or Ⓥ ⟶ ~T (NOT TF and NOT TV)
Which one of the following pairs of employees is such that at least one member of the pair volunteers?	**Step 5:** Use the Master Sketch to evaluate the choices. Each answer has a pair of volunteers. The correct answer features a pair who, if both are rejected, leave an *unacceptable* selection. In the four wrong answers, both members of the pair can be rejected and there is still an acceptable selection. Rules 3 and 4 both designate pairs one member of which must be selected. Any arrangement without Salman and without Veena is unacceptable (Rule 3). Any arrangement without Rochelle and without Leah is unacceptable (Rule 4). Look for an answer choice that would knock out both members of one of those pairs.

LSAT Question	Analysis
(A) Felicia and Terry	Rejecting Felicia doesn't trigger anything. Rejecting Terry triggers Rule 2, so reject Masatomo. That, in turn, triggers Rule 1, so reject Rochelle, too. But Leah is still available, so this allows for an acceptable selection. Eliminate.
(B) Leah and Masatomo	Correct. Rejecting Leah triggers Rule 4, meaning Rochelle needs to be included. But rejecting Masatomo triggers Rule 1, so Rochelle would have to be rejected. Getting rid of these two volunteers doesn't leave any acceptable selections.
(C) Leah and Veena	Rejecting Leah triggers Rule 4, so Rochelle must be included. Rejecting Veena triggers Rule 3, so Salman must be included. Nothing prevents Rochelle and Salman from being selected, however, so this allows for an acceptable selection. Eliminate.
(D) Rochelle and Salman	Rejecting Rochelle triggers Rule 4, so Leah must be included. Rejecting Salman triggers Rule 3, so Veena must be included. Nothing prevents Leah and Veena from being selected, however, so this allows for an acceptable selection. Eliminate.
(E) Salman and Terry *PrepTest58 Sec3 Q12*	Rejecting Salman triggers Rule 3, so Veena must be included. Rejecting Terry triggers Rule 2, so reject Masatomo. That, in turn, triggers Rule 1, so reject Rochelle, too. Rejecting Rochelle triggers Rule 4, so Leah must be included. Nothing prevents Veena and Leah from being selected, however, so this allows for an acceptable selection. Eliminate.

Response Data

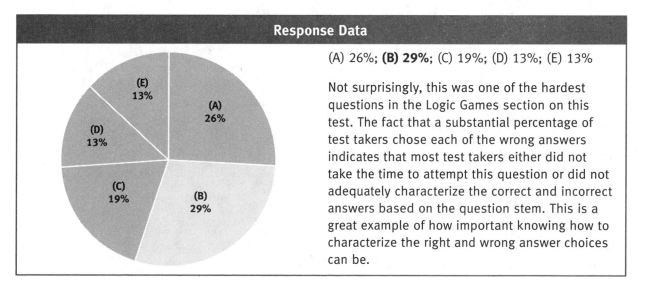

(A) 26%; **(B) 29%**; (C) 19%; (D) 13%; (E) 13%

Not surprisingly, this was one of the hardest questions in the Logic Games section on this test. The fact that a substantial percentage of test takers chose each of the wrong answers indicates that most test takers either did not take the time to attempt this question or did not adequately characterize the correct and incorrect answers based on the question stem. This is a great example of how important knowing how to characterize the right and wrong answer choices can be.

In Selection games (or any game with long chains of Formal Logic), you can expect the testmaker to ask one or more questions that reward your ability to string together the triggers and results of the conditional statements. That's one skill that you can master through diligent practice, and with your work in Chapter 1 of this book, you may already feel more comfortable with this type of reasoning. Don't miss questions that you could get because you misunderstood the question stem. The LSAT expert's characterization of the right and wrong answers here is just as central to her success on the question as her ability to handle the Formal Logic involved in the answer choices.

Practice

Now, work with a handful of Must Be/Could Be questions from the games you've been analyzing. In each case, we'll supply the game's setup and Master Sketch. As always, if you want to review how we arrived at the Master Sketch, refer to the preceding chapters.

For each of the following questions, analyze the question stem and characterize the one correct and four incorrect answer choices. Then, use the Master Sketch and the deductions it contains to select the correct answer. You can compare your work to an LSAT expert's analysis on the following pages.

LSAT Question	My Analysis

Individual hour-long auditions will be scheduled for each of six saxophonists—Fujimura, Gabrieli, Herman, Jackson, King, and Lauder. The auditions will all take place on the same day. Each audition will begin on the hour, with the first beginning at 1 P.M. and the last at 6 P.M. The schedule of auditions must conform to the following conditions:
    Jackson auditions earlier than Herman does.
    Gabrieli auditions earlier than King does.
    Gabrieli auditions either immediately before or immediately after Lauder does.
    Exactly one audition separates the auditions of Jackson and Lauder.
	Steps 1–4:
	
	Master Sketch

18.	Which one of the following must be true?	→	**Step 5:**

(A) Lauder is scheduled to audition earlier than Herman.

(B) Lauder is scheduled to audition earlier than King.

(C) Jackson's audition is scheduled to begin at either 1 P.M. or 5 P.M.

(D) Fujimura and Jackson are not scheduled to audition in consecutive hours.

(E) Gabrieli and King are not scheduled to audition in consecutive hours.

PrepTest56 Sec1 Q2

LSAT Question	My Analysis

On a field trip to the Museum of Natural History, each of six children—Juana, Kyle, Lucita, Salim, Thanh, and Veronica—is accompanied by one of three adults—Ms. Margoles, Mr. O'Connell, and Ms. Podorski. Each adult accompanies exactly two of the children, consistent with the following conditions:
    If Ms. Margoles accompanies Juana, then Ms. Podorski accompanies Lucita.
    If Kyle is not accompanied by Ms. Margoles, then Veronica is accompanied by Mr. O'Connell.
    Either Ms. Margoles or Mr. O'Connell accompanies Thanh.
    Juana is not accompanied by the same adult as Kyle; nor is Lucita accompanied by the same adult as Salim; nor is Thanh accompanied by the same adult as Veronica.
	Steps 1–4:
	
	Master Sketch
	
	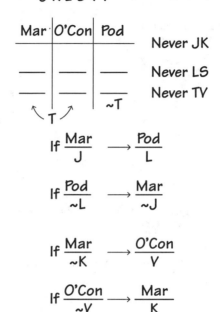

---

19. Mr. O'Connell CANNOT accompany which one of the following pairs of children?   →   **Step 5:**

    (A)   Juana and Lucita

    (B)   Juana and Veronica

    (C)   Kyle and Thanh

    (D)   Lucita and Thanh

    (E)   Salim and Veronica

    PrepTest52 Sec2 Q12

LSAT Question	My Analysis

Workers at a water treatment plant open eight valves—G, H, I, K, L, N, O, and P—to flush out a system of pipes that needs emergency repairs. To maximize safety and efficiency, each valve is opened exactly once, and no two valves are opened at the same time. The valves are opened in accordance with the following conditions:

    Both K and P are opened before H.
    O is opened before L but after H.
    L is opened after G.
    N is opened before H.
    I is opened after K.

Steps 1–4:

Master Sketch

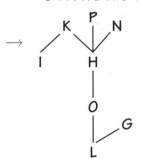

20. Which one of the following must be true? → **Step 5:**

(A) At least one valve is opened before P is opened.

(B) At least two valves are opened before G is opened.

(C) No more than two valves are opened after O is opened.

(D) No more than three valves are opened after H is opened.

(E) No more than four valves are opened before N is opened.

PrepTest52 Sec2 Q 5

LSAT Question	My Analysis

An artisan has been hired to create three stained glass windows. The artisan will use exactly five colors of glass: green, orange, purple, rose, and yellow. Each color of glass will be used at least once, and each window will contain at least two different colors of glass. The windows must also conform to the following conditions:

Exactly one of the windows contains both green glass and purple glass.

Exactly two of the windows contain rose glass.

If a window contains yellow glass, then that window contains neither green glass nor orange glass.

If a window does not contain purple glass, then that window contains orange glass.

→

Steps 1–4:

Master Sketch

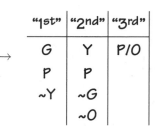

GOPRY

"1st"	"2nd"	"3rd"
G	Y	P/O
P	P	
~Y	~G	
	~O	

GP = exactly 1x
R = 2x
If Y ⟶ ~G and ~O
If G or O ⟶ ~Y
[Never YG, Never YO]
If ~P ⟶ O
If ~O ⟶ P
[At least one of P/O
in every window]

---

21. Which one of the following could be used in all three windows? → **Step 5:**

(A) green glass

(B) orange glass

(C) purple glass

(D) rose glass

(E) yellow glass

PrepTest62 Sec3 Q12

The next two questions both come from the Manufacturing Site Visits game.

LSAT Question	My Analysis

Five executives—Quinn, Rodriguez, Sasada, Taylor, and Vandercar—are being scheduled to make site visits to three of their company's manufacturing plants—Farmington, Homestead, and Morningside. Each site will be visited by at least one of the executives and each executive will visit just one site. Each of the three site visits will take place on a different day. The schedule of site visits must conform to the following requirements:

The Farmington visit must take place before the Homestead visit.

The Farmington visit will include only one of the executives.

The site visit that includes Quinn must take place before any site visit that includes either Rodriguez or Taylor.

The site visit that includes Sasada cannot take place after any site visit that includes Vandercar.

→

Steps 1–4:

Master Sketch

QRSTV

(I) | Farm | Home/Morn | Morn/Home |
___	___	~Q
___		
~R		
~T		
~V		

Q ⟨R / ~T

S / V or S...V

(II) | Morn | Farm | Home |
___	___	~Q
	___	
~R		
~T		

LSAT Question		**My Analysis**

22. The executives who visit Homestead CANNOT be $\longrightarrow$ **Step 5:**

(A) Quinn and Vandercar only

(B) Rodriguez and Taylor only

(C) Sasada and Taylor only

(D) Quinn, Sasada, and Vandercar

(E) Rodriguez, Sasada, and Taylor

PrepTest56 Sec1 Q20

LSAT Question		**My Analysis**

23. Which one of the following must be true? $\longrightarrow$ **Step 5:**

(A) The Farmington visit takes place earlier than the Morningside visit.

(B) The site visit that includes Vandercar takes place earlier than the site visit that includes Rodriguez.

(C) One of the first two site visits includes Sasada.

(D) The second of the three site visits includes at least two of the executives.

(E) At least one of the first two site visits includes only one of the executives.

PrepTest56 Sec1 Q22

Here's how an LSAT expert analyzed and answered the questions you just saw.

LSAT Question	Analysis

Individual hour-long auditions will be scheduled for each of six saxophonists—Fujimura, Gabrieli, Herman, Jackson, King, and Lauder. The auditions will all take place on the same day. Each audition will begin on the hour, with the first beginning at 1 P.M. and the last at 6 P.M. The schedule of auditions must conform to the following conditions:
 	
Jackson auditions earlier than Herman does.
Gabrieli auditions earlier than King does.
Gabrieli auditions either immediately before or immediately after Lauder does.
Exactly one audition separates the auditions of Jackson and Lauder.
	Steps 1–4:
	
	Master Sketch
	
	*
	F G H J K L
	
	1 2 3 4 5 6
	
	    .·H
	  J __ L
	or
	  L __ J...H
	
	G/L L/G...K

18.	Which one of the following must be true?	**Step 5:** Use the Master Sketch to evaluate the choices. The correct answer must be true. All four wrong answers could be false. (Expect the correct answer to reward a deduction.)
(A)	Lauder is scheduled to audition earlier than Herman.	Could be false—J-H-L is an acceptable Block. Eliminate.
(B)	Lauder is scheduled to audition earlier than King.	Correct. Lauder must be adjacent to Gabrieli (Rule 3) and Gabrieli must be earlier than King (Rule 1). L/G G/L ...K
(C)	Jackson's audition is scheduled to begin at either 1 P.M. or 5 P.M.	Could be false—Jackson could also be scheduled for 2 P.M., 3 P.M., or 4 P.M. Eliminate.
(D)	Fujimura and Jackson are not scheduled to audition in consecutive hours.	Could be false—Fujimura is the Floater and could be adjacent to Jackson. Eliminate.
(E)	Gabrieli and King are not scheduled to audition in consecutive hours. *PrepTest56 Sec1 Q2*	Could be false—so long as King is later than Gabrieli, nothing prevents them from being adjacent. Eliminate.

LSAT Question	Analysis

On a field trip to the Museum of Natural History, each of six children—Juana, Kyle, Lucita, Salim, Thanh, and Veronica—is accompanied by one of three adults—Ms. Margoles, Mr. O'Connell, and Ms. Podorski. Each adult accompanies exactly two of the children, consistent with the following conditions:

> If Ms. Margoles accompanies Juana, then Ms. Podorski accompanies Lucita.
> If Kyle is not accompanied by Ms. Margoles, then Veronica is accompanied by Mr. O'Connell.
> Either Ms. Margoles or Mr. O'Connell accompanies Thanh.
> Juana is not accompanied by the same adult as Kyle; nor is Lucita accompanied by the same adult as Salim; nor is Thanh accompanied by the same adult as Veronica.

Steps 1–4:

Master Sketch

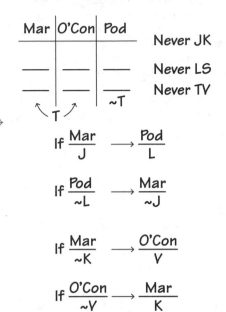

19. Mr. O'Connell CANNOT accompany which one of the following pairs of children?

Step 5: Use the Master Sketch to evaluate the choices. The correct answer is a pair of children who cannot go with O'Connell at the same time. The wrong answers are all pairs that would be acceptable for O'Connell. (Note that Rule 2 mentions O'Connell.)

(A)	Juana and Lucita	Could be true—having Juana and Lucita with O'Connell triggers the contrapositives of Rules 1 and 2, but still creates an acceptable arrangement. Eliminate.
(B)	Juana and Veronica	Could be true—nothing is triggered by having Juana and Veronica with O'Connell. Eliminate.
(C)	Kyle and Thanh	Correct. When Kyle is not with Margoles, Veronica needs to be with O'Connell (Rule 2). Kyle clearly isn't with Margoles here, and yet Veronica is not with O'Connell.
(D)	Lucita and Thanh	Could be true—having Lucita and Thanh with O'Connell triggers the contrapositives of Rules 1 and 2, but still creates an acceptable arrangement. Eliminate.
(E)	Salim and Veronica	Could be true—nothing is triggered by having Salim and Veronica with O'Connell. Eliminate.

PrepTest52 Sec2 Q12

LSAT Question	Analysis

Workers at a water treatment plant open eight valves—G, H, I, K, L, N, O, and P—to flush out a system of pipes that needs emergency repairs. To maximize safety and efficiency, each valve is opened exactly once, and no two valves are opened at the same time. The valves are opened in accordance with the following conditions:

Both K and P are opened before H.
O is opened before L but after H.
L is opened after G.
N is opened before H.
I is opened after K.

Steps 1–4:

Master Sketch

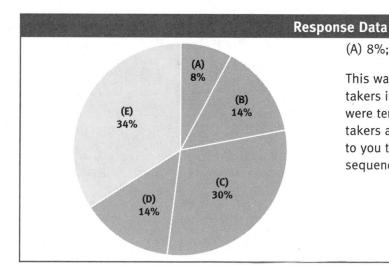

20. Which one of the following must be true?

Step 5: The correct answer must be true. The four wrong answers could be false. Evaluate the choices against the Master Sketch.

(A) At least one valve is opened before P is opened.

Could be false—P could be opened anywhere from first through fifth. Eliminate.

(B) At least two valves are opened before G is opened.

Could be false—G could be opened anywhere from first through seventh. Eliminate.

(C) No more than two valves are opened after O is opened.

Could be false—G, I, and L could be opened after O is opened. Eliminate.

(D) No more than three valves are opened after H is opened.

Could be false—G, I, L, and O could be opened after H is opened. Eliminate.

(E) No more than four valves are opened before N is opened.

Correct. The only valves that could be opened before N is opened are G, I, K, and P. Valves H, L, and O must be opened after N is opened.

PrepTest52 Sec2 Q 5

Response Data

(A) 8%; (B) 14%; (C) 30%; (D) 14%; **(E) 34%**

This was, by far, the hardest question for most test takers in an otherwise manageable game. If you were tempted by choice (C), as clearly many test takers are, check your Master Sketch. Was it clear to you that I and G could come later than O in the sequence?

LSAT Question	Analysis

An artisan has been hired to create three stained glass windows. The artisan will use exactly five colors of glass: green, orange, purple, rose, and yellow. Each color of glass will be used at least once, and each window will contain at least two different colors of glass. The windows must also conform to the following conditions:

Exactly one of the windows contains both green glass and purple glass.

Exactly two of the windows contain rose glass.

If a window contains yellow glass, then that window contains neither green glass nor orange glass.

If a window does not contain purple glass, then that window contains orange glass.

Steps 1–4:

Master Sketch

GOPRY

"1st"	"2nd"	"3rd"
G	Y	P/O
P	P	
~Y	~G	
	~O	

GP = exactly 1x
R = 2x
If Y ⟶ ~G and ~O
If G or O ⟶ ~Y
[Never YG, Never YO]
If ~P ⟶ O
If ~O ⟶ P
[At least one of P/O in every window]

---

21. Which one of the following could be used in all three windows?

Step 5: Use the Master Sketch to evaluate the choices. The correct answer is the only color that could be used in all three windows. The Master Sketch shows that to be purple. All other colors are limited to a maximum of two windows—rose by Rule 2 and yellow, green, and orange by Rule 3.

(A) green glass

(B) orange glass

(C) purple glass — Correct.

(D) rose glass

(E) yellow glass

PrepTest62 Sec3 Q12

LSAT Question	**Analysis**

Five executives—Quinn, Rodriguez, Sasada, Taylor, and Vandercar—are being scheduled to make site visits to three of their company's manufacturing plants—Farmington, Homestead, and Morningside. Each site will be visited by at least one of the executives and each executive will visit just one site. Each of the three site visits will take place on a different day. The schedule of site visits must conform to the following requirements:

The Farmington visit must take place before the Homestead visit.

The Farmington visit will include only one of the executives.

The site visit that includes Quinn must take place before any site visit that includes either Rodriguez or Taylor.

The site visit that includes Sasada cannot take place after any site visit that includes Vandercar.

Steps 1–4:

Master Sketch

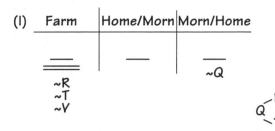

22. The executives who visit Homestead CANNOT be

Step 5: Evaluate this question using the Master Sketch. The correct answer is a pair or group of executives who cannot visit Homestead. All four wrong answers are pairs or groups who can visit Homestead.

(A)   Quinn and Vandercar only

Could be true in Option I. Eliminate.

Farm	Home	Morn
S	Q	R
	V	T

LSAT Question (cont.)	**Analysis (cont.)**
(B) Rodriguez and Taylor only	Could be true in either Option. Eliminate.

Opt. I

Farm	Morn	Home
Q	S	R
===	V	T

$\rightarrow$

Opt. II

Morn	Farm	Home
S	Q	R
V	===	T

Note, in Option I, Rodriguez and Taylor could both visit Homestead as the 2nd visit too.

(C) Sasada and Taylor only	Could be true in Option I. Eliminate.

$\rightarrow$

Farm	Home	Morn
Q	S	R
===	T	V

(D) Quinn, Sasada, and Vandercar	Correct. Homestead cannot be the first site visited (Rule 1). If Sasada and Quinn are both in the second (or third) site, no one can make the first visit.

(E) Rodriguez, Sasada, and Taylor	Could be true in Option I. Eliminate.

PrepTest56 Sec1 Q20

$\rightarrow$ Opt. I

Farm	Home	Morn
Q	R	V
===	S	
	T	

In that analysis, the sketches for each wrong answer choice are included for your benefit. The LSAT expert would not draw out sketches here provided that she could simply check answer choices against the Master Sketch and see that they were acceptable in one or both options.

LSAT Question	Analysis
23. Which one of the following must be true?	**Step 5:** Evaluate the choices using the Master Sketch. The correct must be true in both options. The four wrong answers could be false in at least one of the options.
(A) The Farmington visit takes place earlier than the Morningside visit.	Must be false in Option II. Eliminate.

(B) The site visit that includes Vandercar takes place earlier than the site visit that includes Rodriguez.

Could be false in either option. Vandercar could go the same day as Rodriguez or a day later than Rodriguez. For example:

Opt. I example:

Farm	Home/Morn	Morn/Home
Q	S	R
	T	V

Opt. II example:

Morn	Farm	Home
Q	R	T
S		V

Eliminate.

(C) One of the first two site visits includes Sasada.

Could be false. Sasada could go in the third visit in either option. For example:

Opt. I example:

Farm	Home/Morn	Morn/Home
Q	R	S
	T	V

Opt. II example:

Morn	Farm	Home
Q	R	S
		T
		V

Eliminate.

| (D) The second of the three site visits includes at least two of the executives. | Must be false in Option II, where Farmington is the second site. Eliminate. |
| (E) At least one of the first two site visits includes only one of the executives. | Correct. Farmington is always the first or second site (Rule 1), and it has exactly one executive (Rule 2). |

PrepTest56 Sec1 Q22

With practice, analyzing these question stems will become second nature, and you'll feel faster and more confident with the Must Be/Could Be questions. As you turn to the games in Chapter 6, remain diligent about characterizing the right and wrong answers before evaluating the choices. Simply by avoiding the mistake of answering the wrong question, you can improve your score and outperform other test takers.

NEW-"IF" QUESTIONS

The next question type—the New-"If" question—is by far the most important in the Logic Games section. Nearly half of all Logic Games points come from this question type. Fortunately, once you learn to handle it strategically, the additional condition or restriction in the question stem—the distinguishing characteristic of this question type—actually makes the question easier to answer.

LEARNING OBJECTIVES

In this section, you'll learn to:

- Identify and answer New-"If" questions.
- Create new sketches to account for the "If" condition in New-"If" questions and make additional deductions applicable to the question.

Take a look at one of these questions associated with the Monuments game, and we'll break down how these questions work.

If M was begun in a later year than L, then which one
of the following could be true?

(A) F was begun in 603.
(B) G was begun in 602.
(C) H was begun in 605.
(D) L was begun in 603.
(E) S was begun in 604.

PrepTest58 Sec3 Q6

Notice that you can break a question of this type into two pieces before and after the comma in the middle of the question. The first part is a condition or, if you like, an additional rule just for this question. (Don't apply the "If" to any of the questions that come later in the question set.) Because rules and restrictions add certainty to logic games, the condition in a New-"If" question reduces the number of arrangements available. Shortly, you'll see how the LSAT expert draws a quick sketch, copying the essential information from the Master Sketch and adding the new-"If" condition. From this, she draws any additional deductions applicable to this question. The expert will then use the completed sketch to evaluate the answer choices.

The part of the question after the comma reads almost exactly like a Must Be/Could Be question. To know what you're looking for in the correct answer, characterize the one right and four wrong answers just as you would in Must Be/Could Be questions without a new-"If" clause.

Now, take a look at how the LSAT expert handled the New-"If" question from the Monuments game. Take note of her thinking about the question's condition and how she turns that into a quick sketch and how she uses that sketch to evaluate the answer choices.

LSAT Question	Analysis

Historical records show that over the course of five consecutive years—601, 602, 603, 604, and 605—a certain emperor began construction of six monuments: F, G, H, L, M, and S. A historian is trying to determine the years in which the individual monuments were begun. The following facts have been established:

L was begun in a later year than G, but in an earlier year than F.

H was begun no earlier than 604.

M was begun earlier than 604.

Two of the monuments were begun in 601, and no other monument was begun in the same year as any of the other monuments.

Steps 1–4:

Master Sketch

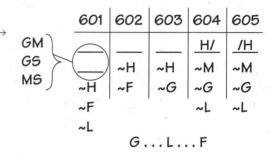

If M was begun in a later year than L, then which one of the following could be true?

Step 5: A New-"If" question. Redraw the sketch; add the stem condition and make any available deductions.

M can't take 604 or 605, so M after L means that M takes 603, L takes 602, and G and S are pushed up into 601.

601	602	603	604	605
G	L	M	H/F	F/H
S				

The only unknown is whether F takes 604 with H in 605 or vice versa. Use that sketch to evaluate the choices. The correct answer could be true. The four wrong answers must be false under this question's conditions.

(A)	F was begun in 603.	→	Must be false—F takes 604 or 605 here. Eliminate.
(B)	G was begun in 602.	→	Must be false—G takes 601 here. Eliminate.
(C)	H was begun in 605.	→	Correct. This could be true.
(D)	L was begun in 603.	→	Must be false—L takes 602 here. Eliminate.
(E)	S was begun in 604.	→	Must be false—S takes 601 here. Eliminate.

PrepTest58 Sec3 Q6

In that question, the "If" condition required additional analysis. The fact that M was after L was not concrete enough to build directly into the sketch. Rather, that condition needed to be combined with information in the Master Sketch in order to definitively slot the newly restricted entities. Contrast that question stem with New-"If"s that unequivocally tell you what to draw into a new sketch. Questions that give more concrete conditions, such as "If J is in the 4th position" or "If A is on Team Green," tend to be easier than questions that give a vaguer New-"If," such as "If J is NOT fourth," "If J is earlier than H," or "If Team Green has more members than Team Blue." If you're struggling with a game, or just being mindful to approach easier questions before difficult questions, consider approaching questions with concrete "If" conditions before tackling those with vague "If"s. As for the Monuments Game question, once the expert combined the "If" with the information from the Master Sketch, the situation became quite restrictive, and the answer choice was apparent. Adding that "rule" to the Master Sketch determined four of the six entities' positions absolutely. On any given test, you'll see a few examples that work just like that.

Other New-"If" questions, however, require further steps to derive all of the available deductions. Examine how the LSAT expert handled the following New-"If" question from the Field Trip Chaperones game. This time, the new condition is concrete and can be added immediately to a copy of the Master Sketch. Once in place, it triggers a number of the game's original rules. Follow the LSAT expert's reasoning as he applies the new-"If" condition and then uses its implications to establish more certainty.

LSAT Question	Analysis

On a field trip to the Museum of Natural History, each of six children—Juana, Kyle, Lucita, Salim, Thanh, and Veronica—is accompanied by one of three adults—Ms. Margoles, Mr. O'Connell, and Ms. Podorski. Each adult accompanies exactly two of the children, consistent with the following conditions:

> If Ms. Margoles accompanies Juana, then Ms. Podorski accompanies Lucita.
> If Kyle is not accompanied by Ms. Margoles, then Veronica is accompanied by Mr. O'Connell.
> Either Ms. Margoles or Mr. O'Connell accompanies Thanh.
> Juana is not accompanied by the same adult as Kyle; nor is Lucita accompanied by the same adult as Salim; nor is Thanh accompanied by the same adult as Veronica. →

Steps 1–4:

Master Sketch

JKLSTV

LSAT Question	Analysis
If Ms. Margoles accompanies Lucita and Thanh, then which one of the following must be true?	**Step 5:** A New-"If" question. Redraw the sketch; add the stem condition and make any available deductions. 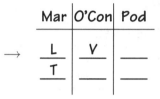 This triggers Rule 2. Kyle is not with Margoles, so Veronica must be with O'Connell. As for the rest, Juana and Kyle can't be together (Rule 4), so one goes with O'Connell and one with Podorski. That leaves a spot with Podorski for Salim. Use that sketch to evaluate the choices. The correct answer must be true. The four wrong answers could be false. (Note that everyone is locked down except Juana and Kyle.)
(A) Juana is accompanied by the same adult as Veronica.	Could be false—Juana can go with either O'Connell or Podorski here. Eliminate.
(B) Kyle is accompanied by the same adult as Salim.	Could be false—Kyle can go with either O'Connell or Podorski here. Eliminate.
(C) Juana is accompanied by Mr. O'Connell.	Could be false—Juana can go with either O'Connell or Podorski here. Eliminate.
(D) Kyle is accompanied by Ms. Podorski.	Could be false—Kyle can go with either O'Connell or Podorski here. Eliminate.
(E) Salim is accompanied by Ms. Podorski. *PrepTest52 Sec2 Q9*	Correct. This must be true, as the New-"If" sketch makes clear.

The preceding examples give you a great baseline for thinking about New-"If" questions. On any given LSAT, a number of the Logic Games questions will work more or less as those did. Because you've been working with a

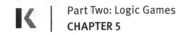
variety of games, let's use them to see a few more examples of New-"If" questions and consider how they may vary slightly in different types of games.

New-"If" Questions in Loose Sequencing

In most Loose Sequencing games, the Master Sketch consists of a "string" or "tree" showing the relative positions of the entities. There are no empty slots, so to speak, in Loose Sequencing sketches. However, when a New-"If" question adds restrictions to a Loose Sequencing game that definitively place an entity, draw a new sketch in Strict Sequencing format, and place the newly established entity or entities as stipulated in the New-"If" condition. Then map into the slots of the sketch the other deductions you can make.

Take a look at two New-"If" questions from the Water Valves game. As you review the LSAT expert's work, pay attention to how he has noted the "If" condition from each question's stem.

LSAT Question	Analysis

Workers at a water treatment plant open eight valves—G, H, I, K, L, N, O, and P—to flush out a system of pipes that needs emergency repairs. To maximize safety and efficiency, each valve is opened exactly once, and no two valves are opened at the same time. The valves are opened in accordance with the following conditions:
 	
    Both K and P are opened before H.
    O is opened before L but after H.
    L is opened after G.
    N is opened before H.
    I is opened after K.
	Steps 1–4:
	
	Master Sketch
	
	GHIKLNOP
	
	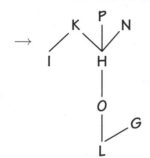

If L is the seventh valve opened, then each of the following could be the second valve opened EXCEPT:	**Step 5:** A New-"If" question. Redraw the sketch; add the stem condition and make any available deductions. 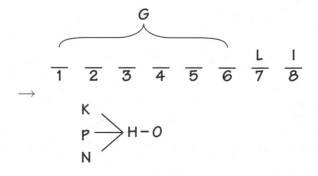 Use that sketch to evaluate the choices. The correct answer CANNOT be opened second. The four wrong answers could be opened second.

LSAT Question		Analysis
(A) G	→	G could be opened anywhere from first through sixth in this scenario. Eliminate.
(B) I	→	Correct. For L to be opened seventh (the stem condition), I must be opened eighth.
(C) K	→	K could be opened anywhere from first through fourth in this scenario. Eliminate.
(D) N	→	N could be opened anywhere from first through fourth in this scenario. Eliminate.
(E) P *PrepTest52 Sec2 Q4*	→	P could be opened anywhere from first through fourth in this scenario. Eliminate.

LSAT Question		Analysis
If K is the fourth valve opened, then which one of the following could be true?		**Step 5:** A New-"If" question. Redraw the sketch; add the stem condition and make any available deductions.

Use that sketch to evaluate the choices. The correct answer could be true. The four wrong answers must be false.

(A)	I is the second valve opened.	→	Must be false—in this scenario, the earliest I could be opened is fifth. Eliminate.
(B)	N is the third valve opened.	→	Correct. N could be opened first, second, or third under this question's stem condition.
(C)	G is the fifth valve opened.	→	Must be false—in this scenario, the latest G could be opened is third. Eliminate.
(D)	O is the fifth valve opened.	→	Must be false—in this scenario, the earliest O could be opened is sixth. Eliminate.
(E)	P is the sixth valve opened. *PrepTest52 Sec2 Q6*	→	Must be false—in this scenario, the latest P could be opened is third. Eliminate.

Be patient when you work through the question stem in Loose Sequencing New-"If" questions. Remember that all of the original relationships and restrictions continue to apply. In the new, question-specific sketch, you're just adding more certainty. Don't rush so much that you inadvertently undo any of the deductions in the Master Sketch.

New-"If" Questions in Selection Games

Selection games often use New-"If" questions to test your facility with chains of Formal Logic. The "If" condition in the question stem acts as a trigger for one of the Formal Logic rules. That, in turn, may set off a long string of deductions as additional rules are triggered. Take a look at a couple of New-"If" questions from the Day Care Volunteers game to see this in action. As you review the expert's work, keep in mind that the sketches you see are really just steps in a single, quick new sketch the expert is creating step-by-step as she notes the question's additional deductions.

LSAT Question	Analysis

A company organizing on-site day care consults with a group of parents composed exclusively of volunteers from among the seven employees—Felicia, Leah, Masatomo, Rochelle, Salman, Terry, and Veena—who have become parents this year. The composition of the volunteer group must be consistent with the following:
 	
If Rochelle volunteers, then so does Masatomo.
If Masatomo volunteers, then so does Terry.
If Salman does not volunteer, then Veena volunteers.
If Rochelle does not volunteer, then Leah volunteers.
If Terry volunteers, then neither Felicia nor Veena volunteers.
	Steps 1–4:
	
	Master Sketch
	
	F L M R S T V
	
	If (R) ⟶ (M)
	If ~M ⟶ ~R
	
	If (M) ⟶ (T)
	If ~T ⟶ ~M
	
	⟶ If ~S ⟶ (V)
	If ~V ⟶ (S)
	(At least one of S, V—maybe both)
	
	If ~R ⟶ (L)
	If ~L ⟶ (R)
	(At least one of R, L—maybe both)
	
	If (T) ⟶ ~F and ~V
	If (F) or (V) ⟶ ~T
	(NOT TF and NOT TV)

LSAT Question	Analysis
If Veena volunteers, then which one of the following could be true?	**Step 5:** A New-"If" question. Redraw the sketch; add the stem condition and make any available deductions.
	Start with the roster. Select Veena.
	F L M R S T (V)
	Selecting Veena triggers Rule 5. Reject Terry.
	F L M R S T̶ (V)
	Rejecting Terry triggers Rule 2. Reject Masatomo.
	F L M̶ R S T̶ (V)
	Rejecting Masatomo triggers Rule 1. Reject Rochelle.
	F L M̶ R̶ S T̶ (V)
	Rejecting Rochelle triggers Rule 4. Select Leah.
	F (L) M̶ R̶ S T̶ (V)
	Felicia or Salman could volunteer in this case, but they don't have to.
	Use the new sketch to evaluate the choices. The correct answer could be true. All four wrong answers must be false under this question's condition.
(A) Felicia and Rochelle also volunteer.	Must be false—Rochelle is rejected here. Eliminate.
(B) Felicia and Salman also volunteer.	Correct. Felicia and Salman are the two volunteers that cannot be determined in this question.
(C) Leah and Masatomo also volunteer.	Must be false—Masatomo is rejected here. Eliminate.
(D) Leah and Terry also volunteer.	Must be false—Terry is rejected here. Eliminate.
(E) Salman and Terry also volunteer.	Must be false—Terry is rejected here. Eliminate.

PrepTest58 Sec3 Q8

LSAT Question	Analysis
If Felicia volunteers, then which one of the following must be true?	**Step 5:** A New-"If" question. Redraw the sketch; add the stem condition and make any available deductions.
	Start with the roster of entities. Select Felicia.
	Ⓕ L M R S T V
	Selecting Felicia triggers Rule 5. Reject Terry.
	Ⓕ L M R S T̸ V
	Rejecting Terry triggers Rule 2. Reject Masatomo.
	Ⓕ L M̸ R S T̸ V
	Rejecting Masatomo triggers Rule 1. Reject Rochelle.
	Ⓕ L M̸ R̸ S T̸ V
	Rejecting Rochelle triggers Rule 4. Select Leah.
	Ⓕ Ⓛ M̸ R̸ S T̸ V
	At least one (and maybe both) of Salman and Veena must be selected (Rule 3), but it's impossible to know which one. However, since the stem calls for a choice that must be true, the correct answer is likely to follow from the final deduction in the new sketch: Leah volunteers.
	Use the new sketch to evaluate the choices. The correct answer must be true. All four wrong answers could be false under this question's condition.
(A) Leah volunteers.	Correct. Leah must volunteer when Rochelle does not.
(B) Salman volunteers.	Could be false—Salman is undetermined in this question. Eliminate.
(C) Veena does not volunteer.	Could be false—Veena is undetermined in this question. Eliminate.
(D) Exactly three of the employees volunteer.	Could be false—there could be four volunteers (F, L, S, an V) in this question. Eliminate.
(E) Exactly four of the employees volunteer. *PrepTest58 Sec3 Q11*	Could be false—there could be only three volunteers (F, L, and S or F, L, and V) in this question. Eliminate.

In each of those New-"If" questions, the expert was able to make a number of additional deductions that followed from the New-"If" condition. You can expect that kind of reasoning to be tested often in Selection games. Fortunately, the sketches—mere rosters of the entities—are so quick and easy to draw that you can work out the chains of Formal Logic efficiently on the page of the test booklet.

New-"If" Questions in Games with Limited Options Sketches

Games in which you can work out a Limited Options sketch sometimes allow for shortcuts in dealing with New-"If" questions. Indeed, on some games with Limited Options, the "If" condition in the question stem amounts to no more than telling you which of the options to consider as you evaluate the answer choices for that question. That's convenient when it occurs, and you should take full advantage of Limited Options whenever you can.

Don't think, however, that just because you could work out a game into Limited Options that you never need to draw a new sketch for a New-"If" question. Sometimes, the condition in the question stem will point you to one of the two options but still allow for additional deductions. Other times, the "If" will be a condition that you can add to both of the options. Take a look at the LSAT expert's work with two questions from the Manufacturing Site Visits game to see what we mean.

LSAT Question	Analysis

Five executives—Quinn, Rodriguez, Sasada, Taylor, and Vandercar—are being scheduled to make site visits to three of their company's manufacturing plants—Farmington, Homestead, and Morningside. Each site will be visited by at least one of the executives and each executive will visit just one site. Each of the three site visits will take place on a different day. The schedule of site visits must conform to the following requirements:

    The Farmington visit must take place before the Homestead visit.

    The Farmington visit will include only one of the executives.

    The site visit that includes Quinn must take place before any site visit that includes either Rodriguez or Taylor.

    The site visit that includes Sasada cannot take place after any site visit that includes Vandercar.

Steps 1–4:

Master Sketch

$\longrightarrow$

QRSTV

(I)

Farm	Home/Morn	Morn/Home
$\underline{\underline{}}$	$\underline{}$	$\underline{}$
~R		~Q
~T		
~V		

Q $\overset{\nearrow R}{\underset{\searrow T}{}}$

(II)

Morn	Farm	Home
$\underline{}$	$\underline{\underline{}}$	$\underline{}$
~R		~Q
~T		

$\boxed{\begin{array}{c} S \\ V \end{array}}$ or S...V

LSAT Question	**Analysis**
If the second of the three site visits includes both Rodriguez and Taylor, which one of the following must be true?	**Step 5:** A New-"If" question. Redraw the sketch; add the stem condition and make any available deductions.

Because the second visit has two executives, the second site cannot be Farmington (Rule 2). So, use Option I and place R and T under the second site.

Farm	Home/Morn	Morn/Home
═══	R T	—

Rodriguez's and Taylor's visits to the second site mean that Quinn visits the first site. Because the first site is Farmington, Quinn is the only one visiting the first site.

→

Farm	Home/Morn	Morn/Home
Q ═══	R T	—

Now, the question is about Sasada and Vandercar. Vandercar will take the third visit no matter what. Sasada could take either the second or the third.

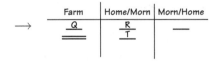

Farm	Home/Morn	Morn/Home
Q ═══	R T	V

It doesn't matter at all whether Homestead is second and Morningside third or vice versa.

The correct answer must be true. The four wrong answers could be false under this question's conditions.

(A)	The Farmington visit includes Quinn.	→	Correct. This must be true under this question's scenario.
(B)	The Homestead visit includes Vandercar.	→	Could be false—Homestead could be the second or third site. Eliminate.
(C)	The Morningside visit includes Sasada.	→	Could be false—Sasada visits Morningside or Homestead, but there's no way to figure out which. Eliminate.
(D)	The second of the three site visits includes Sasada.	→	Could be false—Sasada can take either the second or the third site. Eliminate.
(E)	The second of the three site visits includes exactly three of the executives.	→	Could be false—the second site might have two or three visitors in this scenario. Eliminate.

PrepTest56 Sec1 Q18

Remember, on Test Day, the LSAT expert would likely have stopped evaluating choices as soon as she discovered that (A) was correct.

LSAT Question	Analysis
If the Farmington visit includes Sasada, which one of the following must be true?	**Step 5:** A New-"If" question. Redraw the sketch; add the stem condition and make any available deductions.

Here, Sasada is Farmington's sole visitor. That can happen in either option:

In Option I, Quinn must make the second visit, with Rodriguez and Taylor making the third (Rule 3). → Vandercar can make either the second or third visit.

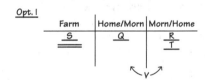

In Option II, Quinn must make the first visit, with Rodriguez and Taylor making the third visit (Rule 3). Vandercar must also make the third visit (Rule 4).

Opt. II

Morn	Farm	Home
Q	S	R
		T
		V

Use those sketches to evaluate the choices. The correct answer must be true in *both* sketches. The four wrong answers could be false in at least one of the sketches.

(A)	One of the site visits includes exactly three of the executives.	→ Could be false in Option I if Vandercar takes the second visit. Eliminate.
(B)	The last of the three site visits includes Rodriguez.	→ Correct. It must be true that Rodriguez takes the third visit in both cases.
(C)	The Homestead visit includes Quinn.	Could be false in Option I (there's no way to tell if Homestead is second or third) and must be false in Option II (where Quinn visits Morningside). Eliminate.
(D)	The Morningside visit includes Taylor.	Could be false in Option I (there's no way to tell if Homestead is second or third) and must be false in Option II (where Taylor visits Homestead). Eliminate.
(E)	The site visit that includes Vandercar also includes Quinn.	Could be false in Option I (where Vandercar might make the third visit) and must be false in Option II. Eliminate.

PrepTest56 Sec1 Q23

Did you notice how the "If" conditions affected those two questions a little differently? In the first, it was clear to the expert that only Option I applied. In the second, however, she made new sketches for both options. You'll have a chance to practice with two more questions from that game and you'll see other games that work out into Limited Options among the practice games in Chapter 6.

New-"If" Conditions Involving Numbers Restrictions

Especially in Distribution and Matching games, you will encounter New-"If" questions that add Numbers Restrictions to the game. Sometimes these are very concrete rules, such as "If team 2 has exactly three members . . . ." At other times, the rules are more relative, for example, "If team 2 has more members than team 1 . . . ." In either event, treat these conditions as new rules and expect to make deductions about the placement of entities based on them.

Take a look at an LSAT expert's work on two questions from the Stained Glass Windows game to see New-"If" questions of this type. Pay attention to how the expert thinks through the impact of the Numbers Restrictions before translating them into new question-specific sketches.

LSAT Question	Analysis
An artisan has been hired to create three stained glass windows. The artisan will use exactly five colors of glass: green, orange, purple, rose, and yellow. Each color of glass will be used at least once, and each window will contain at least two different colors of glass. The windows must also conform to the following conditions: 　Exactly one of the windows contains both green glass and purple glass. 　Exactly two of the windows contain rose glass. 　If a window contains yellow glass, then that window contains neither green glass nor orange glass. 　If a window does not contain purple glass, then that window contains orange glass.	**Steps 1–4:** **Master Sketch** 　　GOPRY

	"1st"	"2nd"	"3rd"	
$\rightarrow$	G	Y	P/O	GP = exactly 1x
	P	P		R = 2x
	~Y	~G		If Y ⟶ ~G and ~O
		~O		If G or O ⟶ ~Y
				[Never YG, Never YO]
				If ~P ⟶ O
				If ~O ⟶ P
				[At least one of P/O in every window]

LSAT Question	Analysis
If two of the windows are made with exactly two colors of glass each, then the complete color combination of the glass in one of those windows could be	**Step 5:** A New-"If" question. Redraw the sketch; add the stem condition and make any available deductions.

The "first" and "second" windows already have two colors, and at least one of them must get rose, too. So, the other window that could have exactly two colors is the "third," and it must take rose glass.

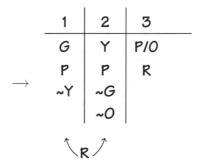

So, one of the windows here must have purple and rose or orange and rose.

Use that sketch to evaluate the choices. The correct answer contains an acceptable window. All four wrong answers contain color combinations that cannot represent a window under this question's condition.

(A)	rose and yellow	→	Unacceptable—this window has neither purple nor orange (Rule 4). Eliminate.
(B)	orange and rose	→	Correct. This matches the prediction for the "third" window.
(C)	orange and purple	→	This would have to be the "third" window, but without rose there's no way to have two windows with exactly two colors each. Eliminate.
(D)	green and rose	→	Unacceptable—this window has neither purple nor orange (Rule 4). Eliminate.
(E)	green and orange *PrepTest62 Sec3 Q9*	→	This would have to be the "third" window, but without rose there's no way to have two windows with exactly two colors each. Eliminate.

LSAT Question	Analysis
If orange glass is used in more of the windows than green glass, then the complete color combination of the glass in one of the windows could be	**Step 5:** A New-"If" question. Redraw the sketch; add the stem condition and make any available deductions. Green glass is already used one time. Orange cannot be used in the "second" window with yellow. The only way to use orange more than green is to use orange in the "first" and "third" windows and ban green from the "third" window.

$$\longrightarrow$$

1	2	3	
G	Y	O	
P	P		
O	~O	~G	2R
~Y	~G	~Y	

With orange in the "third" window, yellow is banned from that window as well (Rule 3).

Use that sketch to evaluate the choices. The correct answer represents an acceptable color combination for one of the windows. All four wrong answers are impossible color combinations under this question's condition.

(A)	orange and purple	$\longrightarrow$	Correct. This could be the complete color combination for the "third" window here.
(B)	green, purple, and rose	$\longrightarrow$	Impossible—the "first" window has the one green and purple combination (Rule 1), but it must also have orange to follow the "If" condition in the stem. Eliminate.
(C)	green and purple	$\longrightarrow$	Impossible—the "first" window has the one green and purple combination (Rule 1), but it must also have orange to follow the "If" condition in the stem. Eliminate.
(D)	green and orange	$\longrightarrow$	Impossible—the "first" window has green and orange, but it must also take purple; the "third" window has orange, but under this question's "If" condition, it can't take green. Eliminate.
(E)	green, orange, and rose *PrepTest62 Sec3 Q11*	$\longrightarrow$	Impossible—the "first" window has green and orange, and while it could take rose, it *must* also take purple; the "third" window has orange, and while it could take rose, under this question's "If" condition, it can't take green. Eliminate.

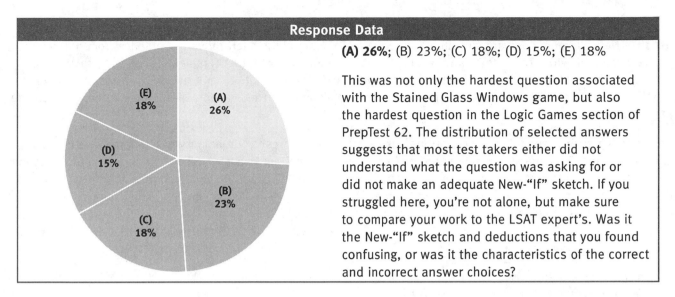

Response Data

(A) 26%; (B) 23%; (C) 18%; (D) 15%; (E) 18%

This was not only the hardest question associated with the Stained Glass Windows game, but also the hardest question in the Logic Games section of PrepTest 62. The distribution of selected answers suggests that most test takers either did not understand what the question was asking for or did not make an adequate New-"If" sketch. If you struggled here, you're not alone, but make sure to compare your work to the LSAT expert's. Was it the New-"If" sketch and deductions that you found confusing, or was it the characteristics of the correct and incorrect answer choices?

Take a moment to reflect on all of the New-"If" questions you've just seen demonstrated. In every case, the "If" condition required the expert to pause for a moment to consider how the new restriction affected the Master Sketch, to build the new question-specific sketch, and to characterize the correct and incorrect answer choices. But in all of the questions, that pause and the critical thinking it allowed provided a new sketch that made the expert's evaluation of the answer choices faster and more certain.

Practice

Because New-"If" questions are so common, there are a number of them left for you to practice from the games you've been reviewing. That's fortunate because you're now familiar with these games. So, as you practice the following questions, focus on the question stems. Analyze the new conditions and decide how to depict them in brief new sketches. Push the new sketch to certainty by making all of the available deductions. Then, characterize the right and wrong answers.

Before trying each of the following questions, take a moment to refresh your memory of the game's setup, rules, and deductions. Reacquaint yourself with the Master Sketch. Then, analyze the question stem and paraphrase the new-"If" condition it contains. Draw a new sketch containing the "If" condition and make any additional deductions that it triggers. Characterize the correct and incorrect answers and evaluate the choices. When you're done, compare your work to that of the LSAT expert on the following pages.

LSAT Question	My Analysis

Individual hour-long auditions will be scheduled for each of six saxophonists—Fujimura, Gabrieli, Herman, Jackson, King, and Lauder. The auditions will all take place on the same day. Each audition will begin on the hour, with the first beginning at 1 P.M. and the last at 6 P.M. The schedule of auditions must conform to the following conditions:

    Jackson auditions earlier than Herman does.
    Gabrieli auditions earlier than King does.
    Gabrieli auditions either immediately before or immediately after Lauder does.
    Exactly one audition separates the auditions of Jackson and Lauder.

→

Steps 1–4:

Master Sketch

$\overset{*}{F}$ G H J K L

$\overline{1}$ $\overline{2}$ $\overline{3}$ $\overline{4}$ $\overline{5}$ $\overline{6}$

    $\cdot$ H

$\underline{J}$ _ $\underline{L}$

or

$\underline{L}$ _ $\underline{J}$ ... H

$\underline{G/L}$ $\underline{L/G}$ ... K

24. If Fujimura's audition is not scheduled to begin at 1 P.M., which one of the following could be true?

→ **Step 5:**

(A) Herman's audition is scheduled to begin at 6 P.M.

(B) Gabrieli's audition is scheduled to begin at 5 P.M.

(C) Herman's audition is scheduled to begin at 3 P.M.

(D) Jackson's audition is scheduled to begin at 2 P.M.

(E) Jackson's audition is scheduled to begin at 5 P.M.

PrepTest56 Sec1 Q5

The next two questions both come from the Water Valves game.

LSAT Question	My Analysis

Workers at a water treatment plant open eight valves—G, H, I, K, L, N, O, and P—to flush out a system of pipes that needs emergency repairs. To maximize safety and efficiency, each valve is opened exactly once, and no two valves are opened at the same time. The valves are opened in accordance with the following conditions:

  Both K and P are opened before H.
  O is opened before L but after H.
  L is opened after G.
  N is opened before H.
  I is opened after K.

$\longrightarrow$

Steps 1–4:

Master Sketch

G H I K L N O P

```
        P
    K   |   N
     \  |  /
      \ | /
   I    H
        |
        O
        | \
        |  G
        L
```

25. If I is the second valve opened, then each of the following could be true EXCEPT: $\longrightarrow$ **Step 5:**

  (A) G is the third valve opened.

  (B) H is the fourth valve opened.

  (C) P is the fifth valve opened.

  (D) O is the sixth valve opened.

  (E) G is the seventh valve opened.

PrepTest52 Sec2 Q 3

26. If G is the first valve opened and I is the third valve opened, then each of the following must be true EXCEPT: $\longrightarrow$ **Step 5:**

  (A) K is the second valve opened.

  (B) N is the fourth valve opened.

  (C) H is the sixth valve opened.

  (D) O is the seventh valve opened.

  (E) L is the eighth valve opened.

PrepTest52 Sec2 Q7

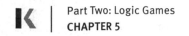
The next question comes from the Field Trip Chaperones game.

LSAT Question	**My Analysis**

On a field trip to the Museum of Natural History, each of six children—Juana, Kyle, Lucita, Salim, Thanh, and Veronica—is accompanied by one of three adults—Ms. Margoles, Mr. O'Connell, and Ms. Podorski. Each adult accompanies exactly two of the children, consistent with the following conditions:

    If Ms. Margoles accompanies Juana, then Ms. Podorski accompanies Lucita.

    If Kyle is not accompanied by Ms. Margoles, then Veronica is accompanied by Mr. O'Connell.

    Either Ms. Margoles or Mr. O'Connell accompanies Thanh.

    Juana is not accompanied by the same adult as Kyle; nor is Lucita accompanied by the same adult as Salim; nor is Thanh accompanied by the same adult as Veronica.

→

Steps 1–4:

Master Sketch

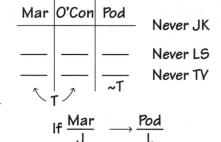

27. If Ms. Podorski accompanies Juana and Veronica, then Ms. Margoles could accompany which one of the following pairs of children? → **Step 5:**

(A) Kyle and Salim

(B) Kyle and Thanh

(C) Lucita and Salim

(D) Lucita and Thanh

(E) Salim and Thanh

PrepTest52 Sec2 Q10

The next two questions are both from the Day Care Volunteers game.

LSAT Question	My Analysis

A company organizing on-site day care consults with a group of parents composed exclusively of volunteers from among the seven employees—Felicia, Leah, Masatomo, Rochelle, Salman, Terry, and Veena—who have become parents this year. The composition of the volunteer group must be consistent with the following:

    If Rochelle volunteers, then so does Masatomo.

    If Masatomo volunteers, then so does Terry.

    If Salman does not volunteer, then Veena volunteers.

    If Rochelle does not volunteer, then Leah volunteers.

    If Terry volunteers, then neither Felicia nor Veena volunteers.

Steps 1–4:

Master Sketch

F L M R S T V

If (R) ⟶ (M)
If ~M ⟶ ~R

If (M) ⟶ (T)
If ~T ⟶ ~M

⟶ If ~S ⟶ (V)
If ~V ⟶ (S)
(At least one of S, V—maybe both)

If ~R ⟶ (L)
If ~L ⟶ (R)
(At least one of R, L—maybe both)

If (T)   ⟶ ~F and ~V
If (F) or (V) ⟶ ~T
(NOT TF and NOT TV)

28. If Terry does not volunteer, then which one of the following CANNOT be true?

  ⟶ **Step 5:**

  (A) Felicia volunteers.

  (B) Leah volunteers.

  (C) Rochelle volunteers.

  (D) Salman volunteers.

  (E) Veena volunteers.

PrepTest58 Sec3 Q9

29. If Masatomo volunteers, then which one of the following could be true?

  ⟶ **Step 5:**

  (A) Felicia volunteers.

  (B) Leah volunteers.

  (C) Veena volunteers.

  (D) Salman does not volunteer.

  (E) Terry does not volunteer.

PrepTest58 Sec3 Q10

The next two questions are both from the Stained Glass Windows game.

LSAT Question	My Analysis

An artisan has been hired to create three stained glass windows. The artisan will use exactly five colors of glass: green, orange, purple, rose, and yellow. Each color of glass will be used at least once, and each window will contain at least two different colors of glass. The windows must also conform to the following conditions:

Exactly one of the windows contains both green glass and purple glass.

Exactly two of the windows contain rose glass.

If a window contains yellow glass, then that window contains neither green glass nor orange glass.

If a window does not contain purple glass, then that window contains orange glass.

Steps 1–4:

Master Sketch

$\quad$ G O P R Y

$\longrightarrow$

"1st"	"2nd"	"3rd"
G	Y	P/O
P	P	
~Y	~G	
	~O	

GP = exactly 1x
R = 2x
If Y ⟶ ~G and ~O
If G or O ⟶ ~Y
[Never YG, Never YO]
If ~P ⟶ O
If ~O ⟶ P
[At least one of P/O
in every window]

30. If the complete color combination of the glass in one of the windows is purple, rose, and orange, then the complete color combination of the glass in one of the other windows could be

$\longrightarrow$ **Step 5:**

(A) green, orange, and rose

(B) green, orange, and purple

(C) orange and rose

(D) orange and purple

(E) green and orange

PrepTest62 Sec3 Q10

31. If none of the windows contains both rose glass and orange glass, then the complete color combination of the glass in one of the windows must be

$\longrightarrow$ **Step 5:**

(A) green and purple

(B) green, purple, and orange

(C) green and orange

(D) purple and orange

(E) purple, rose, and yellow

PrepTest62 Sec3 Q13

The next two questions both come from the Manufacturing Site Visits game.

LSAT Question	My Analysis

Five executives—Quinn, Rodriguez, Sasada, Taylor, and Vandercar—are being scheduled to make site visits to three of their company's manufacturing plants—Farmington, Homestead, and Morningside. Each site will be visited by at least one of the executives and each executive will visit just one site. Each of the three site visits will take place on a different day. The schedule of site visits must conform to the following requirements:

The Farmington visit must take place before the Homestead visit.

The Farmington visit will include only one of the executives.

The site visit that includes Quinn must take place before any site visit that includes either Rodriguez or Taylor.

The site visit that includes Sasada cannot take place after any site visit that includes Vandercar.

Steps 1–4:

Master Sketch

QRSTV

(I)

Farm	Home/Morn	Morn/Home
═══	—	—
~R ~T ~V		~Q

Q ⟨R ⟨T

(II)

Morn	Farm	Home
—	═══	—
~R ~T		~Q

[S/V] or S...V

32. If one of the site visits includes both Quinn and Sasada, which one of the following could be true?

Step 5:

(A) The Farmington visit is the first of the three site visits.

(B) The Homestead visit is the second of the three site visits.

(C) One of the site visits includes only Vandercar.

(D) The second of the three site visits includes Sasada.

(E) The second of the three site visits includes exactly two of the executives.

PrepTest56 Sec1 Q19

33. If the Morningside visit includes both Quinn and Vandercar, which one of the following could be true?

Step 5:

(A) One of the site visits includes both Rodriguez and Sasada.

(B) The second of the three site visits includes exactly three of the executives.

(C) The last of the three site visits includes exactly three of the executives.

(D) The Homestead visit takes place earlier than the Morningside visit.

(E) The Morningside visit takes place earlier than the Farmington visit.

PrepTest56 Sec1 Q21

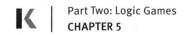

Here's how an LSAT expert approached each of the questions you just tried. As you review the expert's work, compare your new sketches. Did you accurately record the question stem's "If" condition? Did you make the deductions available for this question?

LSAT Question	Analysis
Individual hour-long auditions will be scheduled for each of six saxophonists—Fujimura, Gabrieli, Herman, Jackson, King, and Lauder. The auditions will all take place on the same day. Each audition will begin on the hour, with the first beginning at 1 P.M. and the last at 6 P.M. The schedule of auditions must conform to the following conditions: Jackson auditions earlier than Herman does. Gabrieli auditions earlier than King does. Gabrieli auditions either immediately before or immediately after Lauder does. Exactly one audition separates the auditions of Jackson and Lauder.	**Steps 1–4:** **Master Sketch** $\overset{*}{\text{F}}$ G H J K L $\overline{1}\ \overline{2}\ \overline{3}\ \overline{4}\ \overline{5}\ \overline{6}$ $\underset{\cdot\,\cdot}{\ \ }$·H J __ L or L __ J...H G/L L/G...K

24. If Fujimura's audition is not scheduled to begin at 1 P.M., which one of the following could be true?

Step 5: A New-"If" question. Redraw the sketch; add the stem condition and make any available deductions.

If Fujimura cannot take 1 P.M., who can? Only Gabrieli, Jackson, or Lauder.

$\underline{G}\ \underline{L}\ \underline{\ \ }\ \underline{J}\ \underline{\ \ }\ \underline{\ \ }$

$\underline{J}\ \underline{G/}\ \underline{L}\ \underline{/G}\ \underline{\ \ }\ \underline{\ \ }$

$\underline{L}\ \underline{G}\ \underline{J}\ \underline{\ \ }\ \underline{\ \ }\ \underline{\ \ }$

There's no way to determine the spaces of Fujimura (the Floater), Herman, or King.

Use that sketch to evaluate the choices.

(A) Herman's audition is scheduled to begin at 6 P.M. → Correct. Herman could take 6 P.M. in any of the scenarios under this question's stem condition.

(B) Gabrieli's audition is scheduled to begin at 5 P.M. → Gabrieli cannot take a time later than 4 P.M. here. Eliminate.

(C) Herman's audition is scheduled to begin at 3 P.M. → Herman cannot take a time earlier than 4 P.M. here. Eliminate.

(D) Jackson's audition is scheduled to begin at 2 P.M. → Jackson is restricted to 1 P.M., 3 P.M., or 4 P.M. under this question's condition.

(E) Jackson's audition is scheduled to begin at 5 P.M. → Under this question's conditions, the latest Jackson can audition is 4 P.M.

PrepTest56 Sec1 Q5

LSAT Question	Analysis

Workers at a water treatment plant open eight valves—G, H, I, K, L, N, O, and P—to flush out a system of pipes that needs emergency repairs. To maximize safety and efficiency, each valve is opened exactly once, and no two valves are opened at the same time. The valves are opened in accordance with the following conditions:

Both K and P are opened before H.
O is opened before L but after H.
L is opened after G.
N is opened before H.
I is opened after K.

Steps 1–4:

Master Sketch

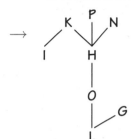

---

25. If I is the second valve opened, then each of the following could be true EXCEPT:

Step 5: A New-"If" question. Redraw the sketch; add the stem condition and make any available deductions.

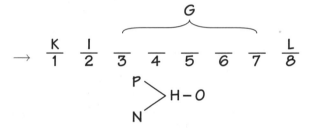

Use that sketch to evaluate the choices. The correct answer must be false. The four wrong answers could be true.

(A) G is the third valve opened.

Could be true—G could be opened anywhere from third through seventh in this scenario. Eliminate.

(B) H is the fourth valve opened.

Correct. The earliest H can be opened here is fifth—K, I, P, and N all must be opened before H under this question's condition.

(C) P is the fifth valve opened.

Could be true—P could be opened anywhere from third through fifth in this scenario. Eliminate.

(D) O is the sixth valve opened.

Could be true—O could be opened sixth or seventh in this scenario. Eliminate.

(E) G is the seventh valve opened.

PrepTest52 Sec2 Q3

Could be true—G could be opened anywhere from third through seventh in this scenario. Eliminate.

LSAT Question	**Analysis**

Workers at a water treatment plant open eight valves—G, H, I, K, L, N, O, and P—to flush out a system of pipes that needs emergency repairs. To maximize safety and efficiency, each valve is opened exactly once, and no two valves are opened at the same time. The valves are opened in accordance with the following conditions:

Both K and P are opened before H.
O is opened before L but after H.
L is opened after G.
N is opened before H.
I is opened after K.

Steps 1–4:

Master Sketch

→

G H I K L N O P

---

26. If G is the first valve opened and I is the third valve opened, then each of the following must be true EXCEPT:

Step 5: A New-"If" question. Redraw the sketch; add the stem condition and make any available deductions.

→

$\frac{G}{1}$	$\frac{K}{2}$	$\frac{I}{3}$	$\frac{P/N}{4}$	$\frac{N/P}{5}$	$\frac{H}{6}$	$\frac{O}{7}$	$\frac{L}{8}$

Use that sketch to evaluate the choices. The correct answer could be false. The four wrong answers must be true.

(A) K is the second valve opened.

→ Must be true under this question's condition. Eliminate.

(B) N is the fourth valve opened.

→ Correct. N could be fourth or fifth here—so this could be false.

(C) H is the sixth valve opened.

→ Must be true under this question's condition. Eliminate.

(D) O is the seventh valve opened.

→ Must be true under this question's condition. Eliminate.

(E) L is the eighth valve opened.

PrepTest52 Sec2 Q7

→ Must be true under this question's condition. Eliminate.

LSAT Question	**Analysis**

On a field trip to the Museum of Natural History, each of six children—Juana, Kyle, Lucita, Salim, Thanh, and Veronica—is accompanied by one of three adults—Ms. Margoles, Mr. O'Connell, and Ms. Podorski. Each adult accompanies exactly two of the children, consistent with the following conditions:

> If Ms. Margoles accompanies Juana, then Ms. Podorski accompanies Lucita.
>
> If Kyle is not accompanied by Ms. Margoles, then Veronica is accompanied by Mr. O'Connell.
>
> Either Ms. Margoles or Mr. O'Connell accompanies Thanh.
>
> Juana is not accompanied by the same adult as Kyle; nor is Lucita accompanied by the same adult as Salim; nor is Thanh accompanied by the same adult as Veronica.

Steps 1–4:

Master Sketch

J K L S T V

Mar	O'Con	Pod	
—	—	—	Never JK
—	—	—	Never LS
—	—	~T	Never TV

↖ T ↗   ~T

$$\text{If } \frac{Mar}{J} \longrightarrow \frac{Pod}{L}$$

$$\text{If } \frac{Pod}{\sim L} \longrightarrow \frac{Mar}{\sim J}$$

$$\text{If } \frac{Mar}{\sim K} \longrightarrow \frac{O'Con}{V}$$

$$\text{If } \frac{O'Con}{\sim V} \longrightarrow \frac{Mar}{K}$$

→

The question associated with this game is on the following page.

LSAT Question	**Analysis**
27. If Ms. Podorski accompanies Juana and Veronica, then Ms. Margoles could accompany which one of the following pairs of children?	**Step 5:** A New-"If" question. Redraw the sketch; add the stem condition and make any available deductions.

Mar	O'Con	Pod
—	—	J
—	—	V

This triggers Rule 2. Veronica is not with O'Connell, so Kyle must be with Margoles.

Mar	O'Con	Pod
K	—	J
—	—	V

As for the rest, Lucita and Salim can't be together (Rule 4), so one goes with Margoles and one with O'Connell. That leaves a spot with O'Connell for Thanh.

Mar	O'Con	Pod
K	T	J
L/S	S/L	V

The correct answer is a pair of children who could go with Margoles, so it will say either "Kyle and Lucita" or "Kyle and Salim." |
(A) Kyle and Salim	→ Correct.
(B) Kyle and Thanh	→ Thanh cannot go with Margoles here. Eliminate.
(C) Lucita and Salim	→ Kyle must go with Margoles here. Eliminate.
(D) Lucita and Thanh	→ Thanh cannot go with Margoles here. Eliminate.
(E) Salim and Thanh	→ Thanh cannot go with Margoles here. Eliminate.

PrepTest52 Sec2 Q10

LSAT Question	**Analysis**

LSAT Question

A company organizing on-site day care consults with a group of parents composed exclusively of volunteers from among the seven employees—Felicia, Leah, Masatomo, Rochelle, Salman, Terry, and Veena—who have become parents this year. The composition of the volunteer group must be consistent with the following:

    If Rochelle volunteers, then so does Masatomo.
    If Masatomo volunteers, then so does Terry.
    If Salman does not volunteer, then Veena volunteers.
    If Rochelle does not volunteer, then Leah volunteers.
    If Terry volunteers, then neither Felicia nor Veena volunteers.

Analysis

Steps 1–4:

Master Sketch

F L M R S T V

If (R) ⟶ (M)
If ~M ⟶ ~R

If (M) ⟶ (T)
If ~T ⟶ ~M

⟶ If ~S ⟶ (V)
If ~V ⟶ (S)
(At least one of S, V—maybe both)

If ~R ⟶ (L)
If ~L ⟶ (R)
(At least one of R, L—maybe both)

If (T)   ⟶ ~F and ~V
If (F) or (V) ⟶ ~T
(NOT TF and NOT TV)

The questions associated with this game start on the following page.

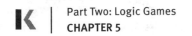

LSAT Question	Analysis
28. If Terry does not volunteer, then which one of the following CANNOT be true?	**Step 5:** A New-"If" question. Redraw the sketch; add the stem condition and make any available deductions.
	Start with the roster. Reject Terry.
	F L M R S T̸ V
	Rejecting Terry triggers Rule 2. Reject Masatomo.
	F L M̸ R S T̸ V
	Rejecting Masatomo triggers Rule 1. Reject Rochelle.
⟶	F L M̸ R̸ S T̸ V
	Rejecting Rochelle triggers Rule 4. Select Leah.
	F Ⓛ M̸ R̸ S T̸ V
	At least one (and maybe both of) of Salman and Veena must be selected (Rule 3), but it's impossible to know which one.
	Use the new sketch to evaluate the choices. The correct answer must be false. The four wrong answers could be true under this question's condition.
(A) Felicia volunteers.	⟶ Could be true—Felicia is undetermined in this question. Eliminate.
(B) Leah volunteers.	⟶ Must be true. Eliminate.
(C) Rochelle volunteers.	⟶ Correct. This must be false. If Terry does not volunteer, then Rules 1 and 2 combine to state that Rochelle does not volunteer.
(D) Salman volunteers.	⟶ Could be true—Salman is undetermined in this question. Eliminate.
(E) Veena volunteers.	⟶ Could be true—Veena is undetermined in this question. Eliminate.

PrepTest58 Sec3 Q9

LSAT Question	Analysis
29. If Masatomo volunteers, then which one of the following could be true?	**Step 5:** A New-"If" question. Redraw the sketch; add the stem condition and make any available deductions. Start with the roster of entities. Select Masatomo. F L Ⓜ R S T V Selecting Masatomo triggers Rule 2. Select Terry. F L Ⓜ R S Ⓣ V Selecting Terry triggers Rule 5. Reject Felicia and reject Veena. F̶ L Ⓜ R S Ⓣ V̶ Rejecting Veena triggers Rule 3. Select Salman. F̶ L Ⓜ R Ⓢ Ⓣ V̶ At least one of (and maybe both of) Leah and Rochelle must be selected (Rule 4), but there's no way to tell which. Use the new sketch to evaluate the choices. The correct answer could be true. The four wrong answers must be false under this question's condition.
(A) Felicia volunteers.	⟶ Must be false. Eliminate.
(B) Leah volunteers.	⟶ Correct. This could be true in this question.
(C) Veena volunteers.	⟶ Must be false. Eliminate.
(D) Salman does not volunteer.	⟶ Must be false. Eliminate.
(E) Terry does not volunteer.	⟶ Must be false. Eliminate.

PrepTest58 Sec3 Q10

LSAT Question	**Analysis**

An artisan has been hired to create three stained glass windows. The artisan will use exactly five colors of glass: green, orange, purple, rose, and yellow. Each color of glass will be used at least once, and each window will contain at least two different colors of glass. The windows must also conform to the following conditions:

Exactly one of the windows contains both green glass and purple glass.

Exactly two of the windows contain rose glass.

If a window contains yellow glass, then that window contains neither green glass nor orange glass.

If a window does not contain purple glass, then that window contains orange glass.

Steps 1–4:

Master Sketch

GOPRY

"1st"	"2nd"	"3rd"	
G	Y	P/O	GP = exactly 1x
P	P		R = 2x
~Y	~G		If Y ⟶ ~G and ~O
	~O		If G or O ⟶ ~Y
			[Never YG, Never YO]
			If ~P ⟶ O
			If ~O ⟶ P
			[At least one of P/O in every window]

30. If the complete color combination of the glass in one of the windows is purple, rose, and orange, then the complete color combination of the glass in one of the other windows could be

Step 5: A New-"If" question. Redraw the sketch; add the stem condition and make any available deductions.

The purple, rose, orange window described in the stem must be the "third" window. The other two windows already have either green or yellow in them.

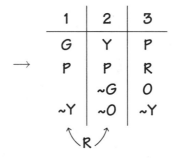

1	2	3
G	Y	P
P	P	R
	~G	O
~Y	~O	~Y

One more window is required to have rose (Rule 2).

The correct answer will be an acceptable color combination for the "first" or "second" window under this question's condition. The wrong answers will be impossible color combinations for the "first" or "second" windows here.

| (A) green, orange, and rose | Impossible—the "first" window has green and could have orange and rose, but it *must* have purple. Eliminate. |
| (B) green, orange, and purple | Correct. This would be an acceptable combination for the "first" window here. |

LSAT Question (cont.)	Analysis (cont.)
(C) orange and rose	→ Impossible—both the "first" and "second" windows already have colors other than these. Eliminate.
(D) orange and purple	→ Impossible—the "first" window could contain orange and purple, but it must also contain green. The "second" window cannot contain orange. Eliminate.
(E) green and orange *PrepTest62 Sec3 Q10*	→ Impossible—the "first" window has green and could have orange, but it *must* have purple. Eliminate.

31. If none of the windows contains both rose glass and orange glass, then the complete color combination of the glass in one of the windows must be

Step 5: A New-"If" question. Redraw the sketch; add the stem condition and make any available deductions.

Orange must be used at least once, and it can only take the "first" or "third" windows. To keep orange and rose apart and yet still have rose two times, the "second" window will need to take rose.

The correct answer is the color combination one window *must* have. The four wrong answers might not be the color combination of any windows under this question's condition.

Because it's impossible to tell whether rose goes to the "first" window and orange to the "third" or vice versa, the only window that must have a certain combination is the "second"—the correct answer will say "purple, rose, and yellow."

(A) green and purple

(B) green, purple, and orange

(C) green and orange

(D) purple and orange

(E) purple, rose, and yellow

PrepTest62 Sec3 Q13

→ Correct.

LSAT Question	**Analysis**

Five executives—Quinn, Rodriguez, Sasada, Taylor, and Vandercar—are being scheduled to make site visits to three of their company's manufacturing plants—Farmington, Homestead, and Morningside. Each site will be visited by at least one of the executives and each executive will visit just one site. Each of the three site visits will take place on a different day. The schedule of site visits must conform to the following requirements:

The Farmington visit must take place before the Homestead visit.

The Farmington visit will include only one of the executives.

The site visit that includes Quinn must take place before any site visit that includes either Rodriguez or Taylor.

The site visit that includes Sasada cannot take place after any site visit that includes Vandercar.

Steps 1–4:

Master Sketch

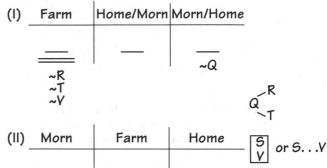

32. If one of the site visits includes both Quinn and Sasada, which one of the following could be true?

Step 5: A New-"If" question. Redraw the sketch; add the stem condition and make any available deductions.

Quinn and Sasada trigger Rules 3 and 4. If they're together, they must take the first visit. (If they were second, no one would be able to take the first visit.) Because Farmington cannot have two visits, use Option II.

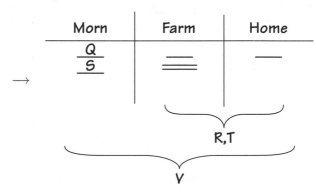

Rodriguez and Taylor must take the second or third visits, individually or together. Vandercar can take any of the three visits.

The correct answer could be true. The four wrong answers must be false under this question's condition.

LSAT Question (cont.)		Analysis (cont.)
(A)	The Farmington visit is the first of the three site visits.	→ Must be false—Farmington is the second visit in this case. Eliminate.
(B)	The Homestead visit is the second of the three site visits.	→ Must be false—Homestead is the third site in this scenario. Eliminate.
(C)	One of the site visits includes only Vandercar.	→ Correct. This could be true: Vandercar could go alone to Farmington, the second visit here. Rodriguez and Taylor would go to Homestead in that case.
(D)	The second of the three site visits includes Sasada.	→ Must be false—to stay with Quinn here, Sasada must make the first visit. Eliminate.
(E)	The second of the three site visits includes exactly two of the executives. *PrepTest56 Sec1 Q19*	→ Must be false—Farmington has to be the second visit here, and Farmington hosts only one executive (Rule 2). Eliminate.

33. If the Morningside visit includes both Quinn and Vandercar, which one of the following could be true?

Step 5: A New-"If" question. Redraw the sketch; add the stem condition and make any available deductions.

This could work in either option (provided Morningside comes earlier than Homestead in Option I, to accommodate Rule 3):

Opt. I

Farm	Morn	Home
═══	Q	
	V	

Opt. II

→

Morn	Farm	Home
Q		
V	═══	

In the Option I version, Sasada will take the first visit (Rule 4, and someone has to go first), and Rodriguez and Taylor will take the third visit (Rule 3).

Opt. I

Farm	Morn	Home
S	Q	R
═══	V	T

LSAT Question (cont.)		Analysis (cont.)

In the Option II version, Sasada will take the first visit (Rule 4), and Rodriquez and Taylor will take the second and third visits individually in either order (Rule 3).

Opt. II

→

Morn	Farm	Home
Q	R/T	T/R
V	===	
S		

Evaluate the choices against both options. The correct answer is the only one that could be true in one of the new sketches. All four wrong answers must be false in both sketches.

(A) One of the site visits includes both Rodriguez and Sasada. → False in both options here. Eliminate.

(B) The second of the three site visits includes exactly three of the executives. → False in both options here. Eliminate.

(C) The last of the three site visits includes exactly three of the executives. → False in both options here. Eliminate.

(D) The Homestead visit takes place earlier than the Morningside visit. → False in both options here. Eliminate.

(E) The Morningside visit takes place earlier than the Farmington visit. → Correct. This sequence is possible in Option II.

PrepTest56 Sec1 Q21

Response Data

(A) 12%; (B) 21%; (C) 26%; (D) 20%; **(E) 21%**

On this question, test takers outperformed a random guess by only 1 percentage point. Moreover, most probably spent an inordinate amount of time testing the answer choices. Let this question stand as an example of how powerful and efficient good sketching and Limited Options can be. A small investment of time in your sketch saves time *and* helps you avoid wrong answers.

Congratulations. You've completed your practice on the most important Logic Games question types. Let's pause briefly to talk about how you can use some questions to help you answer others in the same logic game more quickly. Then, you can practice analyzing and characterizing more Must Be/Could Be and New-"If" question stems in a drill.

Using Previous Work to Answer Logic Games Questions

Occasionally, you'll encounter a Must Be/Could Be question that just seems too complex or confusing to handle without drawing out several sketches to test each answer choice. In those cases, LSAT experts will often put off tackling that question until they've completed the New-"If" questions associated with the game. Then, they'll use the "mini sketches" they've made for the New-"If" questions to help them evaluate the answer choices in the tough Must Be/Could Be question. This can be a very effective time-saving strategy, but you must use it carefully.

Each new sketch you make for a New-"If" question represents one acceptable arrangement for the entities in the game. So too does the correct answer in the Acceptability question. Thus, these sketches and the correct Acceptability answer choice represent what *could be true* in the game. If you have an open-ended Could Be True question and you see that one of the answer choices represents something you know could be true from your New-"If" sketches or Acceptability answer, you can confidently select that choice in the Could Be True question. Likewise, if you have a Must Be False question, you can eliminate any choice that *could be true* based on your other work. Be careful not to overdetermine the level of certainty: seeing that an arrangement of entities *could be true* (in the correct answer to an Acceptability question or in the sketch for a New-"If") does *not* mean that the arrangement must be true.

Remember that the correct answer to a Must Be/Could Be question is always something that you can determine from the game's Master Sketch. But when you have sketches and other previous work to draw upon, using it judiciously can be very beneficial. Chapter 7, Logic Games: Managing the Section, will provide further discussion of how to effectively use your previous work.

Characterizing the Answer Choices in Must Be/Could Be and New-"If" Questions

Take a few minutes to study the sample question stems below. For each, you'll see the LSAT expert's analysis identifying the question type and characterizing the one correct and four incorrect answer choices. Once you feel comfortable identifying these question types, try the practice drill on the following pages to test your ability to characterize the choices on similar questions.

Question Stem	Analysis
If the cat receiving the third place ribbon is the Siamese, then which one of the following must be true?	This question provides new information, so it will require a new sketch including that information. Once the new information has been added, try to make further deductions based on the preexisting rules. The correct answer will either be something drawn into this sketch or a scenario consistent across multiple sketches. The incorrect answers will include entities that have alternative possibilities.

Question Stem		Analysis
Which of the following presenters must be scheduled for Tuesday afternoon?	$\longrightarrow$	This question provides no new information, so a new sketch won't be needed. The Master Sketch should have a presenter already marked in the Tuesday afternoon position, which will be the correct answer. If not, further revision to the Master Sketch may be necessary. When the upfront deductions in a game are particularly challenging, other questions may also provide the answer through their sketches, so long as the same presenter consistently appears in the Tuesday afternoon position.
If Janna is assigned to be Francis's lab partner, which of the following CANNOT be true?	$\longrightarrow$	This question again provides new information, requiring a new sketch and further deductions. The question asks for what cannot be true, which is logically equivalent to what must be false. The correct answer will contradict something determined in the sketch, while the incorrect answers could be true.
Which of the following must be false?	$\longrightarrow$	This question provides no new information and no clue in the stem as to what kind of answer it is looking for. Characterizing the answer choices will provide some insight into what the answer should look like, and scanning the sketch will enable a prediction. The correct answer will place an entity in an impossible position or contradict one or more rules. The wrong answers will all be allowed by the sketch. As with Must Be True questions, previous work from other questions can be helpful. The big difference is that in Must Be False questions, you eliminate wrong answers that you've already seen as possible.
If Katarina plays soccer, which of the following could be true?	$\longrightarrow$	More information with which to produce a new sketch and deductions. The correct answer will include entities that haven't yet been nailed down, while each of the wrong answers will violate the rules or contradict the sketch in some way.
Which of the following could be false?	$\longrightarrow$	With no new information, this question will only reference the Master Sketch. The correct answer could be false, while each wrong answer must be true.

Question Stem		Analysis
If the taco wagon occupies stall 4, each of the following could be true EXCEPT:	→	Use the new information to draw a new sketch. Each of the incorrect answers is something that could be true. Therefore, the correct answer must contradict the refined sketch in some way.
If Jayce is assigned to present on the day immediately after the day on which Otis is assigned to present, each of the following must be false EXCEPT:	→	The new information in this question is creating a new Block of Entities. It can be helpful to quickly sketch this new Block out before adding it into a new sketch. Because all of the incorrect answers will contradict the sketch in some way, the correct answer will be something that is still possible and may even be something that must be true.
If all of the odd numbered folders are green, then each of the following must be true EXCEPT:	→	Use the new information to draw a new sketch integrating that information with further deductions. The wrong answers will all be concretely known entities, while the correct answer will contain a statement that could be or must be false.
Each of the following could be false EXCEPT:	→	There is no new information, so the wrong answers will all be scenarios that are undetermined in the Master Sketch. The correct answer must be true.

Practice

Question Stem	My Analysis
34. If Summertide park has a fountain and a merry-go-round, then Falling Water could have each of the following EXCEPT:	
35. If Sabin is scheduled for the 3 P.M. meeting, which of the following could be true?	
36. If the west garden is planted with only begonias and cherry trees, which of the following must be true?	
37. If the last valve opened is valve H, which of the following could be false?	
38. If K is assigned to present the lecture on integration, which of the following presenters must be assigned to present the lecture on day 3?	
39. Which of the following must be false?	
40. Which of the following could be true?	

Question Stem	My Analysis
41. Which of the following items CANNOT be auctioned first?	
42. Each of the following could be true EXCEPT:	
43. Each of the following could be false EXCEPT:	

Here's how the LSAT expert analyzed each of the question stems you just practiced. Compare your work with that of the expert. You'll see more questions of these types as you practice the games in Chapter 6 and those in the full-length tests at the end of the book.

Question Stem		Analysis
34. If Summertide park has a fountain and a merry-go-round, then Falling Water could have each of the following EXCEPT:	→	This new information will need a new sketch, which allows for further deductions. The wrong answers will all be features permissible at Falling Water. The correct answer will be a feature that Falling Water cannot have.
35. If Sabin is scheduled for the 3 P.M. meeting, which of the following could be true?	→	With new information comes a new sketch. The correct answer will include an entity placed in a position that is possible, while each of the wrong answers will include entities placed in positions that are not possible.
36. If the west garden is planted with only begonias and cherry trees, which of the following must be true?	→	The new information allows for a new sketch that incorporates new deductions. The right answer will be an entity that has been concretely placed, while each of the wrong answers will have alternative possibilities.
37. If the last valve opened is valve H, which of the following could be false?	→	Place the new information in a new sketch; then, make as many deductions as possible. Each of the wrong answers will describe a placement or relationship that is now concretely determined. The correct answer will allow for an alternative possibility.
38. If K is assigned to present the lecture on integration, which of the following presenters must be assigned to present the lecture on day 3?	→	There's new information to work into the game, so a new sketch incorporating that information and new deductions is warranted. The correct answer will be the entity concretely placed on day 3, while the wrong answers will include entities that either cannot or can, but need not, be assigned to that position.

Question Stem	Analysis
39. Which of the following must be false?	This question provides no new information and no clue in the stem as to what kind of answer it is looking for. Characterizing the answer choices will provide some insight into what the answer should look like, and scanning the sketch will enable a prediction. The correct answer will place an entity in an impossible position or contradict one or more rules. The wrong answers will all be allowed by the sketch.
40. Which of the following could be true?	There's no information to add to a new sketch, so this question will rely on the Master Sketch. The correct answer will place an entity in an allowed location. Each of the wrong answers will contradict the sketch in some way. All previous work can be used to provide examples of arrangements that could be true.
41. Which of the following items CANNOT be auctioned first?	This question doesn't add anything new, so a new sketch isn't necessary. The correct answer will be an entity that can never be placed in the first position, while each of the incorrect answers will be possible in the first position. Remember, your previous sketches can be a great reference for eliminating wrong answers.
42. Each of the following could be true EXCEPT:	Without any new information, this question will rely on the original Master Sketch. Each of the wrong answers will mention an entity or scenario that the Master Sketch allows, but the correct answer will contradict the Master Sketch in some way.
43. Each of the following could be false EXCEPT:	There is no new information, so the wrong answers will all be scenarios that are possible or definitely ruled out based on the Master Sketch. The correct answer will either be an entity that has been concretely placed in the sketch, or it will be a relationship that must appear in all possible sketches.

Even though those question stems weren't associated with any game setup in that exercise, were you able to imagine the entities and actions those games would include? If so, you're really getting familiar with the Logic Games section and the kinds of the games the testmaker uses over and over.

You'll see one more drill like that one near the end of this chapter. That drill will cover the handful of rare questions you're about to learn. None of these question types is likely to make or break your score, and some will not even appear on some administrations of the LSAT. Still, it's helpful to know what you might see so that you won't be caught off guard when these questions do pop up.

OTHER LOGIC GAMES QUESTION TYPES

In this section, we'll introduce a handful of other question types that have appeared in the LSAT Logic Games section. The games you've been practicing with don't contain all of these question types, and indeed, it would be hard if not impossible to find even a single Logic Games section that contains an example of all the question types we'll discuss here. Here's a list of the question types we'll discuss.

LSAT STRATEGY

Other Logic Games Question Types

- Numerical Questions
  - Minimum/Maximum Questions
  - Earliest/Latest Questions
  - "How Many" Questions
- Rule Alteration Questions
  - Rule Change Questions
  - Rule Substitution Questions
- Supply the "If" Questions

For each of these rare types, we'll define the question and give examples of how the question stem is worded. Then, we'll outline how to characterize the correct and incorrect answer choices. Where the games we've been working with contain examples of these questions, you'll have a chance to review an LSAT expert's analysis. Finally, in the drill near the end of this chapter, you can see additional examples of these unusual questions and practice identifying them.

Numerical Questions

You've already seen several ways in which Numbers Restrictions can help you set up a game, make deductions, and answer questions. Numerical questions focus directly on number limits within a game.

Minimum/Maximum Questions

The test might, for example, ask you to determine the minimum or maximum number of entities that may be selected (in a Selection game) or placed within a certain group (in a Distribution game, for instance). In one of the games you'll practice in Chapter 6, you'll see the following question stem:

What is the maximum number of courses the student could take during the summer school session?

PrepTest58 Sec3 Q19

This question is, of course, part of the question set for a Selection game. You'll use your expertise in Formal Logic to determine the maximum number of courses the student could choose. Any rule of the type "If A → ~B" reduces the maximum number of entities that may be selected. Rules in that pattern translate to "Never AB." Because you must exclude one of the two entities, the maximum available for selection has been reduced by one. On the flip side, rules fitting the pattern "If ~C → D" establish that at least one of C and D must be selected and so increase the minimum by one. (See Chapter 1: LSAT Reasoning if you don't remember the reasoning cited here.)

The answer choices are always listed in numerical order, either lowest to highest or the other way around. The correct answer cites the precise minimum or maximum number. The wrong answers are either too high or too low. In tests released from 2008 to 2012, there were a total of six Minimum/Maximum questions.

Earliest/Latest Questions

Sequencing games (and Hybrid games with a Sequencing action) may feature a related question type: the Earliest/Latest question. In fact, you've seen one of these already, in Chapter 2. It was found in the Monuments game. Take another look at it and review the LSAT expert's analysis.

LSAT Question	Analysis

Historical records show that over the course of five consecutive years—601, 602, 603, 604, and 605—a certain emperor began construction of six monuments: F, G, H, L, M, and S. A historian is trying to determine the years in which the individual monuments were begun. The following facts have been established:

　　L was begun in a later year than G, but in an earlier year than F.

　　H was begun no earlier than 604.

　　M was begun earlier than 604.

　　Two of the monuments were begun in 601, and no other monument was begun in the same year as any of the other monuments.

→

Steps 1–4:

Master Sketch

F G H L M S̊*

	601	602	603	604	605
GM	⟨	—	—	H/	/H
GS		~H	~H	~M	~M
MS	~H	~F	~G	~G	~G
	~F			~L	~L
	~L				

G . . . L . . . F

What is the latest year in which L could have been begun?

→

Step 5: Use the Master Sketch to evaluate the choices. The correct answer is the latest year L could have been started. The other choices are either too early or too late.

According to the deductions, construction of L cannot have started later than 603. Rule 1 says F always follows L, and Rule 2 says that H always takes 604 or 605.

(A)	601	→	Too early. Eliminate.
(B)	602	→	Too early. Eliminate.
(C)	603	→	Correct.
(D)	604	→	Too late. Eliminate.
(E)	605	→	Too late. Eliminate.

PrepTest58 Sec3 Q2

From that example, you can see that Earliest/Latest questions are the Sequencing version of Minimum/Maximum questions. The correct answer gives the precise slot that represents the earliest or latest that the entity in question could appear. The incorrect answers are either too early or too late.

Practice

There was an Earliest/Latest question associated with the Saxophonists game as well. That gives you the chance to practice one of these on your own.

Try the following question. First, refresh your memory of the game's setup, rules, and deductions. Then, read and analyze the question stem. Characterize the one correct and four incorrect answers and evaluate the choices. When you're finished, you can compare your work to the LSAT expert analysis on the following pages.

LSAT Question	My Analysis
Individual hour-long auditions will be scheduled for each of six saxophonists—Fujimura, Gabrieli, Herman, Jackson, King, and Lauder. The auditions will all take place on the same day. Each audition will begin on the hour, with the first beginning at 1 P.M. and the last at 6 P.M. The schedule of auditions must conform to the following conditions: 　Jackson auditions earlier than Herman does. 　Gabrieli auditions earlier than King does. 　Gabrieli auditions either immediately before or 　　immediately after Lauder does. 　Exactly one audition separates the auditions of Jackson 　　and Lauder.	**Steps 1–4:** **Master Sketch** $\overset{*}{F}$ G H J K L $\overline{1}\ \overline{2}\ \overline{3}\ \overline{4}\ \overline{5}\ \overline{6}$ 　　.·H 　J　_　L or 　L　_　J...H G/L　L/G...K

---

44. The earliest King's audition could be scheduled to begin is

    → **Step 5:**

    (A) 5 P.M.

    (B) 4 P.M.

    (C) 3 P.M.

    (D) 2 P.M.

    (E) 1 P.M.

PrepTest56 Sec1 Q3

Here's how the LSAT expert attacked this question. Compare your work with hers, paying particular attention to how she was able to predict the correct answer before evaluating the choices.

LSAT Question	Analysis
Individual hour-long auditions will be scheduled for each of six saxophonists—Fujimura, Gabrieli, Herman, Jackson, King, and Lauder. The auditions will all take place on the same day. Each audition will begin on the hour, with the first beginning at 1 P.M. and the last at 6 P.M. The schedule of auditions must conform to the following conditions: Jackson auditions earlier than Herman does. Gabrieli auditions earlier than King does. Gabrieli auditions either immediately before or immediately after Lauder does. Exactly one audition separates the auditions of Jackson and Lauder.	**Steps 1–4:** **Master Sketch** * F G H J K L 1 2 3 4 5 6 $\cdot\cdot\text{H}$ J __ L or L __ J...H G/L L/G...K

44. The earliest King's audition could be scheduled to begin is	**Step 5:** Use the Master Sketch to evaluate the choices. The correct answer is King's earliest potential audition time. The wrong answers are either too early or too late. Deduction from Rule 1 + Rule 3: King follows Gabrieli and Lauder. So, 1 P.M. and 2 P.M. are too early. Test 3 P.M. to see if King can take that spot. $\dfrac{G}{1}\ \dfrac{L}{2}\ \dfrac{K}{3}\ \dfrac{J}{4}\ \dfrac{H/F}{5}\ \dfrac{F/H}{6}$ 3 P.M. is acceptable for King. That's what the right answer will say.
(A) 5 P.M.	Too late. Eliminate.
(B) 4 P.M.	Too late. Eliminate.
(C) 3 P.M.	Correct.
(D) 2 P.M.	Too early. Eliminate.
(E) 1 P.M.	Too early. Eliminate.

PrepTest56 Sec1 Q3

Notice that in both of the examples here, the LSAT expert was able to predict the correct answer before evaluating the choices. That should always be the case for you in Minimum/Maximum and Earliest/Latest questions.

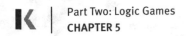
If you've set up the Sequencing game carefully and made all of the available deductions, Earliest/Latest questions should feel fairly straightforward. Too bad you're unlikely to see more of these on Test Day. Among all the tests released between 2008 and 2012, there were only two Earliest/Latest questions. It turns out you've now seen them both.

"How Many" Questions

These questions ask you about numbers that can be firmly established in the game. There's little chance you'll misinterpret one of these stems. They tend to be extremely straightforward:

How many of the workshops are there that could be the
one given on Wednesday morning?

> *PrepTest60 Sec2 Q6*

How many of the students are there any one of whom
could perform fourth?

> *PrepTest65 Sec2 Q5*

Exactly how many of the actors are there any one of
whom could appear sixth?

> *PrepTest60 Sec2 Q9*

The correct answer gives the correct number, and the four wrong answers are either too high or too low. Among the tests released between 2008 and 2012, there have been only 12 "How Many" questions. Interestingly, exactly half of them have been of the New-"If" variety. Here's an example:

If Dr. Shelby is hired by County General Hospital, for how many of the doctors is it known exactly which hospital hires them?

Should you encounter one of these questions in practice or on Test Day, simply make sure you've made all available deductions and count the relevant entities. You should always be able to predict the correct answer precisely before evaluating the choices.

Rule Alteration Questions

Some tests feature no questions from this subcategory, and historically, those that do have exactly one. That's good news because these questions tend to be difficult for most test takers, and they are time-consuming even for those who get them right.

Rule Substitution Questions

These questions didn't make their debut on the LSAT until PrepTest 57, so if you study with older materials, you'll never see one. Since that time, there has been exactly one on each released administration of the exam except for PrepTests 60, 67, and 68. You'll have a chance to practice a couple of these in Chapter 6. Take a look at the question stems for those questions, and you'll quickly get the gist of what these questions ask for.

Which one of the following, if substituted for the
restriction that if music is taken, then neither physics
nor theater can be taken, would have the same effect in
determining which courses the student can take?

PrepTest58 Sec3 Q23

Which one of the following, if substituted for the
condition that the telephone appointment cannot be
scheduled for the sixth day, would have the same effect
in determining the order of the appointments?

PrepTest62 Sec3 Q6

As you can see, the correct answer supplies a rule that would have the same impact on the game as the rule cited
in the question stem. The four wrong answers will either be too weak or too strong to substitute exactly for the rule
in the stem.

To answer Rule Substitution questions, review the rules and the Master Sketch. Summarize exactly what the rule
cited in the question stem says and its impact on other entities within the Master Sketch. Then, imagine removing
it from the Master Sketch and swapping in each answer choice. The correct answer will produce precisely the same
deductions and Master Sketch you produced at the end of Step 4 of the Logic Games Method.

The placement of Rule Substitution questions within the Logic Games section suggests that the testmaker uses
them to reward good time management. Rule Substitution questions have been at the end of the first game three
times, at the end of the second game 4 times, and at the end of the fourth game 2 times. Because these questions
can be quite time-consuming, your best strategy may be simply to guess on these questions and leave ample time
to get to any remaining games and all of the points they can contribute to your LSAT score.

Rule Change Questions

In times past, Rule Change questions were more common than they have been in recent years. In fact, between
2008 and 2012, there has been only one Rule Change question among all 60 released logic games. There's a
strong chance that you'll never encounter a question of this type either in practice or on Test Day. On the off
chance that you do, here's what you should know. Rule Change question stems tell you to ignore one of the rules
cited in the game's setup and to use another rule (described in the stem) instead. Then, based on these altered
circumstances, the stem will usually pose a Must Be/Could Be-type question.

In a sense, you can think of Rule Change questions as a cousin of the New-"If" question. The main difference
is that New-"If" questions preserve the original rules, deductions, and Master Sketch and add an additional
restriction, whereas the Rule Change question suspends one of the original rules. Still, if you happen across a Rule
Change question, your instinct should be to create a new sketch and consult it as you evaluate the answer choices.
Just make sure you actively undo the part of the Master Sketch suspended in the Rule Change question stem along
with any deductions you drew using that rule.

Supply the "If" Questions

There's one more very rare question type: the Supply the "If" question. Between 2008 and 2012, there were only
three of these questions among the 60 logic games released by the LSAC. By chance, one of them was associated
with the Monuments game, so you have the opportunity to see the question and an LSAT expert's analysis of it.

LSAT Question	**Analysis**

Historical records show that over the course of five consecutive years—601, 602, 603, 604, and 605—a certain emperor began construction of six monuments: F, G, H, L, M, and S. A historian is trying to determine the years in which the individual monuments were begun. The following facts have been established:

> L was begun in a later year than G, but in an earlier year than F.
>
> H was begun no earlier than 604.
>
> M was begun earlier than 604.
>
> Two of the monuments were begun in 601, and no other monument was begun in the same year as any of the other monuments.

→

Steps 1–4:

Master Sketch

Step 5: Use the Master Sketch to evaluate the choices. The correct answer is a statement that forces L into the year 602. L's only options are 602 and 603, so any answer that places a monument other than L in 603 will be correct.

L must be the monument that was begun in 602 if which one of the following is true?

→

(A) F was begun in 605.

(B) G was begun in 601.

(C) H was begun in 604.

(D) M was begun in 601.

(E) S was begun in 603.   → Correct.

PrepTest58 Sec3 Q5

These unusual questions are like New-"If" questions in reverse. The question stem gives you the necessary result and asks you to supply the sufficient condition. As you can see from the LSAT expert's work, the best approach is to use the Master Sketch to see the possibilities for the entity or slot in question and then use that analysis to determine the kind of additional restriction that would guarantee the desired result.

As you learned, the questions covered in this section are not common. You're best served by trying these questions when they do appear among your practice games and tests but not by spending time trying to find more examples of them in older tests. It is your facility with Acceptability, Must Be/Could Be, and New-"If" questions that will make or break your LSAT Logic Games score. You might see a single example of one or two of these question types on your official LSAT. If you do, analyze the question stem patiently, consult your Master Sketch, and remember that the testmaker always includes every piece of information you need to answer every question the test asks.

Characterizing the Answer Choices in Other Logic Games Questions

Take a few minutes to study the sample question stems below. For each, you'll see the LSAT expert's analysis identifying the question type and characterizing the one correct and four incorrect answer choices. Once you feel comfortable identifying these question types, try the practice drill on the following pages to test your ability to characterize the choices on similar questions.

Question Stem		Analysis
What is the maximum number of departments that could be located on the second floor?	→	This question is looking for a number of entities belonging to one of several floors. Because it wants the maximum, one approach is to try assigning as many as possible, keeping on the lookout for entities that will force others into other floors. The limitations of the game will likely also dictate how spread out the entities must or cannot be. Be on the lookout for Numbers deductions from your setup of the game and what the apparent maximum is from any previously worked "If" questions.
If Printing is located on the floor immediately above Shipping, what is the minimum number of floors above Bankruptcy but below Mediation?	→	With new information, further deductions will be available. The question asks for the minimum number of positions between two entities, so a good strategy is to draw a sketch that forces Bankruptcy and Mediation as close together as possible. If an answer forces the new rule to be broken, it cannot be correct.
If the shelter wants to hire as many volunteers as possible, which of the following volunteers CANNOT be hired?	→	This question tells you to look for the maximum, and then determine what can't be chosen. So, even though the "If" asks about a maximum, the answer is an entity who cannot be selected, making this a New-"If"/Must Be False question. The correct answer may be an entity whose selection forces many other entities to be deselected. If the deduction isn't obvious from the Formal Logic presented, previous work may help—look for an entity who is not present in answers that have a large number or entities.
Which of the following lists the minimum number and maximum number, respectively, of breeds that could be present at the show?	→	Even though the question asks for both minimum and maximum, it's a better strategy to look for one or the other first and narrow options accordingly. Each Not-Both rule involving a distinct pair of entities will decrease the maximum by 1, and every At-Least-One rule will increase the minimum by 1, but there may be more subtle interactions as well.
If Margaery selects both species F and H, what is the maximum number of species she does NOT select?	→	Use the new information to determine what other species have been selected or deselected. Then, if a species is optional, treat it as deselected. The answer will be the largest number of species that are simultaneously deselected.

Question Stem		Analysis
What is the maximum number of actors who can be offstage at any given time?	→	This question is looking for the maximum number of entities that aren't selected. It may help to instead think of the minimum number of entities that *are* selected because the correct answer will be the total number of entities minus that minimum number who can be onstage. Every At-Least-One rule will increase the minimum by 1.
Suppose the condition stating that Johnson's meeting with Tycho must occur before his meeting with Solari is replaced with a condition stating that Johnson's meeting with Solari must occur before his meeting with Tycho. If all other conditions remain the same, which of the following must be true?	→	This is a Rule Change question, which at the least will take a full rework of the Master Sketch. Because it is difficult to tell which deductions were dependent on T being before S, the best route is to rebuild the sketch from scratch, using the new rule. Given the time and work necessary, this question should therefore be tackled last, and in many cases it can be saved until all other games and questions have been dealt with. Once the revised sketch is complete, the question can be treated as a typical Must Be True question.
Suppose that the condition requiring Human Resources to be assigned to the 4th floor is replaced with a condition requiring Human Resources to be assigned to a higher-numbered floor than Mediation. If all other conditions remain unchanged, which of the following could be false?	→	Another Rule Change question, requiring a full rework of the Master Sketch. An Established Entity is being removed as a rule, and several deductions might have depended on it. The sketch will need to be completely rebuilt, with the new rule substituted for the old. It should therefore be tackled last, and in many cases it can be saved until all other games and questions have been dealt with. Once the sketch is complete, the question can be treated as a typical Could Be False question.
Suppose that the condition requiring that if Guevara is on the second team, Jedaris cannot be assigned to any team is removed. Which of the following conditions, if substituted in its place, would provide the same effect in the assignment of members to teams?	→	A Rule Substitution question. The correct answer will provide an identical effect as the original rule. Because this rule uses Formal Logic, the correct answer may be as simple as the contrapositive, but it may be more complicated and involve other entities as well. It's best to tackle this kind of question at the end of a section because it will often require testing answer choices.
Which of the following, if substituted for the condition that the Taco truck must be assigned to a higher numbered stall than the Pizza truck, would have the same effect in determining the order of the trucks?	→	A Rule Substitution question. The correct answer will provide an identical effect as the original rule. It's best to tackle this kind of question at the end of a section because it will often require testing answer choices.

Now, try it out on your own. The question stems below are similar, though certainly not identical, to those in the list above and the questions you've seen so far in this chapter.

Practice

For each of the following question stems, identify the question type and characterize the one correct and four incorrect answer choices. When you're done, check your work against the LSAT expert's analysis on the following pages.

Question Stem	My Analysis
45. Which of the following lists the minimum and maximum numbers, respectively, of groups marching in the parade this year?	
46. If the driver delivers to Sanzenin last, what is the maximum number of deliveries that could be scheduled between Takeshi and Rhea?	
47. What is the maximum number of students who do NOT speak French?	
48. If Steven visits the doctor's office on Tuesday, what is the minimum number of errands he must perform on Wednesday?	
49. What is the maximum number of days that can separate the visits to site L and site R?	
50. If Joffrey is assigned to do as many chores as possible, to which of the following chores must he be assigned?	
51. Suppose that instead of the host opening door M third, he opens it fifth. If all other conditions remain the same, which of the following could be true?	
52. Which one of the following is the latest day of the week on which Michael could be scheduled to work?	
53. Gretchen must occupy the third seat if which one of the following is true?	
54. Suppose that the condition requiring that if Jason joins the ski team, Katherine joins the tennis team is removed. Which of the following rules, if added in its place, would provide the same effect in determining the assignment of players to teams?	

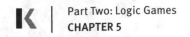
Here's how the LSAT expert analyzed each of the question stems you just practiced. Compare your work with that of the expert. You'll see further examples of these question types as you practice the games in Chapter 6 and those in the full-length tests at the end of the book.

Question Stem	Analysis
45. Which of the following lists the minimum and maximum numbers, respectively, of groups marching in the parade this year?	As this is a question asking for both minimum and maximum numbers, it's better to focus on one or the other first and narrow down the answers from there. Remember that Not-Both rules and At-Least-One rules will influence these numbers.
46. If the driver delivers to Sanzenin last, what is the maximum number of deliveries that could be scheduled between Takeshi and Rhea?	This question is looking to place as much distance between two entities as possible. Draw a new sketch including the additional rule and any deductions it provides, then try to force the two entities to opposite ends of the sketch.
47. What is the maximum number of students who do NOT speak French?	Looking for the maximum number of entities that *aren't* part of a group can also be determined by finding the minimum number of entities that *are* and subtracting that from the total number of entities. Use At-Least-One rule deductions to help find the right number, but be wary of potentially more subtle interactions.
48. If Steven visits the doctor's office on Tuesday, what is the minimum number of errands he must perform on Wednesday?	Use the new information to draw a new, refined sketch. Then try to see how many entities can be forced out of Wednesday.
49. What is the maximum number of days that can separate the visits to site L and site R?	This question is looking for the maximum distance between L and R. If the Master Sketch doesn't already place them as far apart as possible, look for rules that would prevent their placement at opposite ends of the sketch. Because the question does not dictate the order of L and R, double-check whether reversing their order opens up a greater distance.
50. If Joffrey is assigned to do as many chores as possible, to which of the following chores must he be assigned?	This is a New-"If"/Must Be True question. The stipulation to maximize the number of chores Joffrey takes on is in the "If" clause. (Distinguish this from a question in which the correct answer represents an acceptable minimum or maximum.) The goal here is to find a way of maximizing the number of chores assigned to Joffrey. Look for rules that force the selection of several entities.

Question Stem		Analysis
51.	Suppose that instead of the host opening door M third, he opens it fifth. If all other conditions remain the same, which of the following could be true?	$\rightarrow$	This is a Rule Change question, which at the least will take a full rework of the Master Sketch. Because many of the deductions made might rely on the host opening door M third, the sketch will need to be completely rebuilt with door M being opened fifth instead. Given the amount of work and the complete restructuring of the game necessary, this question should therefore be tackled last, and in many cases it can be saved until all other games and questions have been dealt with. Once the revised sketch is complete, the question can be treated as a typical Could Be True question.
52.	Which one of the following is the latest day of the week on which Michael could be scheduled to work?	$\rightarrow$	This is an Earliest/Latest question. Look for rules (or chains of deductions) that force certain entities into days later than Michael's or that force entities other than Michael to occupy days late in the week even if those entities aren't directly related to Michael in the rules.
53.	Gretchen must occupy the third seat if which one of the following is true?	$\rightarrow$	A Supply the "If" question. The correct answer will state a condition that limits Gretchen to the third position. Look for answer choices with entities that affect Gretchen's position either directly or indirectly (through a chain of deductions, for example).
54.	Suppose that the condition requiring that if Jason joins the ski team, Katherine joins the tennis team is removed. Which of the following rules, if added in its place, would provide the same effect in determining the assignment of players to teams?	$\rightarrow$	A Rule Substitution question. The correct answer will provide an identical effect as the original rule. Because this rule uses Formal Logic, the correct answer may be as simple as the contrapositive but may be more complicated and involve other entities as well. It's best to tackle this kind of question at the end of a section because it will often require testing answer choices.

Reflection

In the coming days, take note of real-life cases in which people ask you Logic Games–type questions. You'll find that people are constantly posing Must Be/Could Be– and New-"If"–type questions. "If Barbara is free this Saturday, what are you guys going to do?" "If they're out of the prawns, what will you order?" The main difference between LSAT questions and their day-to-day counterparts is that the test always provides information adequate to answer the question, whereas in everyday life, we're often merely speculating about what "must" happen or giving our opinion or preference. When you encounter these questions in everyday life, try to determine whether you are answering with adequate information and, if not, what you would need to know in order to establish a concrete answer. This reflection exercise can help make you aware of instances on the LSAT in which you are speculating rather than deducing.

If you've completed Chapters 2–5 (or at least the portions of them for which your study time allows), you're ready to practice full games. You'll find games of each type in Chapter 6, followed by complete explanations for how to set up the games and answer all of their questions.

Logic Games Practice

Now that you've mastered the steps in the Logic Games Method, it's time to apply what you've learned to full games. In the pages that follow, you'll find nine games of various types, all from recently released tests. The game types you've seen to this point are largely represented here. In fact, the games are highly representative of the frequency of the various game types that have appeared on official LSATs over the past five years. If you notice, for example, that there are more Sequencing games here than any other game type, that's because Sequencing has been the testmaker's favorite. When you try the full-length tests at the back of this book, you'll see a very similar pattern. It makes sense to practice what you're most likely to encounter on Test Day.

NOTES ON LOGIC GAMES PRACTICE

The games in this chapter are arranged by game type. You need not do all of the games in order, and if you haven't yet studied a particular game type, hold off on practicing a full game of that type until you're familiar with it. As you practice, keep the following pointers in mind.

Use the Logic Games Method Consistently
Chapters 3 through 5 were organized around the five-step Logic Games Method first introduced in Chapter 2. That's because having a consistent, strategic approach is so important in this section of the test. Be conscious of each step as you practice. If you practice without instilling the Method and its associated strategies, you're likely to repeat your old patterns, and that means continuing to be frustrated by the same aspects of Logic Games over and over again.

For your convenience, here's the Logic Games Method one more time.

THE KAPLAN LOGIC GAMES METHOD

Step 1: Overview—Ask the SEAL questions to understand your task and get a mental picture of the actions and limitations.

Step 2: Sketch—Create a simple, helpful framework in which you can record the game's rules and restrictions.

Step 3: Rules—Analyze each rule; build it into the framework or jot it down in shorthand just to the side.

Step 4: Deductions—Combine rules and restrictions to determine what must be true or false about the arrangement of entities in the game.

Step 5: Questions—Use your understanding of the game and your Master Sketch to attack the questions efficiently and confidently.

As you practice, pay special attention to your work with Steps 1 and 4 of the Method. Many test takers underestimate the importance of these steps. If you start work on the Sketch or Rules without fully understanding the game's task and limitations, there's a good chance you'll misrepresent the game. If you launch into the questions without having taken the time to combine the rules and extract solid Deductions, you're likely to waste time by testing every answer choice against an incomplete Master Sketch.

Review Your Work Thoroughly

Complete explanations for the games in this chapter follow right after the games. Take the time to study them even if you get all of the game's questions correct. Review how expert test takers set up the games—how they recorded the rules and made deductions. You may well discover that you could have been more efficient and knocked out the questions more quickly. Of course, when you miss a question, determine whether the problem came from a misunderstanding or oversight in the question itself or whether you missed a rule or deduction in the earlier steps.

Another way in which you can effectively use the explanations is to try Steps 1 through 4 of the game—answer the SEAL questions, create a sketch, jot down the rules, and make deductions. Then, review just that much of the explanation for the game before you even try the questions. This will let you know how you're doing in recognizing game types and setting them up. After you're sure that you understand the game, try the questions and review them as well. This approach is especially helpful when you find a particular game frustrating and you feel that you're making little progress in working through the questions.

Finally, each question's difficulty is ranked in the explanations—from ★★★★ for the toughest questions to ★ for the easiest. Consulting these rankings will tell you a lot about the games and questions you're practicing. You might, for example, distinguish a very hard question in an otherwise easy game. In that case, you'll focus your review on what makes that question confusing for test takers but reassure yourself that your overall approach was on target. On the other hand, you may find a game in which, say, four out of five questions rate ★★★ or ★★★★. In that case, you'll know the game was tough for everyone and spend extra time reviewing the game's setup and deductions to discover how the testmaker made it so challenging.

Practice and Timing

On Test Day, you'll have about 8 1/2 minutes per game. Naturally, that kind of time pressure can make even routine logic games feel stressful. As you're practicing individual games, work as quickly as you can, but make your focus the successful implementation of the Method. If you try to practice too quickly, you'll introduce time pressure at a point where you should really be working on consistency and accuracy. Speed will come with familiarity, practice, and (believe it or not) patience. When you take full tests or try 35-minute Logic Games sections, time yourself strictly. But don't be in such a rush to get faster that you don't gain the efficiencies that come from practicing the methodical application of good strategy to logic games. Chapter 7 will address timing in depth and will introduce you to strategies for effectively managing the 35-minute Logic Games section you'll be completing on Test Day. In the present chapter, practice logic games one by one and perfect your approach.

QUESTION POOL

Try out some practice on games that have not appeared in earlier chapters. These games are arranged by type.

Sequencing Games

Questions 1–6

A motel operator is scheduling appointments to start up services at a new motel. Appointments for six services—gas, landscaping, power, satellite, telephone, and water—will be scheduled, one appointment per day for the next six days. The schedule for the appointments is subject to the following conditions:

> The water appointment must be scheduled for an earlier day than the landscaping appointment.
> The power appointment must be scheduled for an earlier day than both the gas and satellite appointments.
> The appointments scheduled for the second and third days cannot be for either gas, satellite, or telephone.
> The telephone appointment cannot be scheduled for the sixth day.

1. Which one of the following is an acceptable schedule of appointments, listed in order from earliest to latest?

   (A) gas, water, power, telephone, landscaping, satellite
   (B) power, water, landscaping, gas, satellite, telephone
   (C) telephone, power, landscaping, gas, water, satellite
   (D) telephone, water, power, landscaping, gas, satellite
   (E) water, telephone, power, gas, satellite, landscaping

2. If neither the gas nor the satellite nor the telephone appointment is scheduled for the fourth day, which one of the following must be true?

   (A) The gas appointment is scheduled for the fifth day.
   (B) The power appointment is scheduled for the third day.
   (C) The satellite appointment is scheduled for the sixth day.
   (D) The telephone appointment is scheduled for the first day.
   (E) The water appointment is scheduled for the second day.

3. Which one of the following must be true?

   (A) The landscaping appointment is scheduled for an earlier day than the telephone appointment.
   (B) The power appointment is scheduled for an earlier day than the landscaping appointment.
   (C) The telephone appointment is scheduled for an earlier day than the gas appointment.
   (D) The telephone appointment is scheduled for an earlier day than the water appointment.
   (E) The water appointment is scheduled for an earlier day than the gas appointment.

4. Which one of the following CANNOT be the appointments scheduled for the fourth, fifth, and sixth days, listed in that order?

   (A) gas, satellite, landscaping
   (B) landscaping, satellite, gas
   (C) power, satellite, gas
   (D) telephone, satellite, gas
   (E) water, gas, landscaping

5. If neither the gas appointment nor the satellite appointment is scheduled for the sixth day, which one of the following must be true?

   (A) The gas appointment is scheduled for the fifth day.
   (B) The landscaping appointment is scheduled for the sixth day.
   (C) The power appointment is scheduled for the third day.
   (D) The telephone appointment is scheduled for the fourth day.
   (E) The water appointment is scheduled for the second day.

6. Which one of the following, if substituted for the condition that the telephone appointment cannot be scheduled for the sixth day, would have the same effect in determining the order of the appointments?

   (A) The telephone appointment must be scheduled for an earlier day than the gas appointment or the satellite appointment, or both.
   (B) The telephone appointment must be scheduled for the day immediately before either the gas appointment or the satellite appointment.
   (C) The telephone appointment must be scheduled for an earlier day than the landscaping appointment.
   (D) If the telephone appointment is not scheduled for the first day, it must be scheduled for the day immediately before the gas appointment.
   (E) Either the gas appointment or the satellite appointment must be scheduled for the sixth day.

PrepTest62 Sec3 Qs1–6

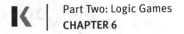

The explanations to these questions
begin on page 347.

Questions 7–11

Exactly six witnesses will testify in a trial: Mangione, Ramirez, Sanderson, Tannenbaum, Ujemori, and Wong. The witnesses will testify one by one, and each only once. The order in which the witnesses testify is subject to the following constraints:

Sanderson must testify immediately before either Tannenbaum or Ujemori.

Ujemori must testify earlier than both Ramirez and Wong.

Either Tannenbaum or Wong must testify immediately before Mangione.

7. Which one of the following lists the witnesses in an order in which they could testify?

(A) Ramirez, Sanderson, Tannenbaum, Mangione, Ujemori, Wong

(B) Sanderson, Tannenbaum, Ujemori, Ramirez, Wong, Mangione

(C) Sanderson, Ujemori, Tannenbaum, Wong, Ramirez, Mangione

(D) Tannenbaum, Mangione, Ujemori, Sanderson, Ramirez, Wong

(E) Wong, Ramirez, Sanderson, Tannenbaum, Mangione, Ujemori

8. If Tannenbaum testifies first, then which one of the following could be true?

(A) Ramirez testifies second.
(B) Wong testifies third.
(C) Sanderson testifies fourth.
(D) Ujemori testifies fifth.
(E) Mangione testifies sixth.

9. If Sanderson testifies fifth, then Ujemori must testify

(A) first
(B) second
(C) third
(D) fourth
(E) sixth

10. Which one of the following pairs of witnesses CANNOT testify third and fourth, respectively?

(A) Mangione, Tannenbaum
(B) Ramirez, Sanderson
(C) Sanderson, Ujemori
(D) Tannenbaum, Ramirez
(E) Ujemori, Wong

11. Which one of the following pairs of witnesses CANNOT testify first and second, respectively?

(A) Sanderson, Ujemori
(B) Tannenbaum, Mangione
(C) Tannenbaum, Sanderson
(D) Ujemori, Tannenbaum
(E) Ujemori, Wong

PrepTest62 Sec3 Qs19–23

Questions 12–17

A bread truck makes exactly one bread delivery to each of six restaurants in succession—Figueroa's, Ginsberg's, Harris's, Kanzaki's, Leacock's, and Malpighi's—though not necessarily in that order. The following conditions must apply:

Ginsberg's delivery is earlier than Kanzaki's but later than Figueroa's.

Harris's delivery is earlier than Ginsberg's.

If Figueroa's delivery is earlier than Malpighi's, then Leacock's delivery is earlier than Harris's.

Either Malpighi's delivery is earlier than Harris's or it is later than Kanzaki's, but not both.

12. Which one of the following accurately represents an order in which the deliveries could occur, from first to last?

(A) Harris's, Figueroa's, Leacock's, Ginsberg's, Kanzaki's, Malpighi's
(B) Leacock's, Harris's, Figueroa's, Ginsberg's, Malpighi's, Kanzaki's
(C) Malpighi's, Figueroa's, Harris's, Ginsberg's, Leacock's, Kanzaki's
(D) Malpighi's, Figueroa's, Kanzaki's, Harris's, Ginsberg's, Leacock's
(E) Malpighi's, Figueroa's, Ginsberg's, Kanzaki's, Harris's, Leacock's

13. If Figueroa's delivery is fourth, then which one of the following must be true?

(A) Ginsberg's delivery is fifth.
(B) Harris's delivery is second.
(C) Harris's delivery is third.
(D) Leacock's delivery is second.
(E) Malpighi's delivery is first.

14. If Malpighi's delivery is first and Leacock's delivery is third, then which one of the following must be true?

(A) Figueroa's delivery is second.
(B) Harris's delivery is second.
(C) Harris's delivery is fourth.
(D) Kanzaki's delivery is fifth.
(E) Kanzaki's delivery is last.

15. Which one of the following must be true?

(A) Figueroa's delivery is earlier than Leacock's.
(B) Ginsberg's delivery is earlier than Leacock's.
(C) Harris's delivery is earlier than Kanzaki's.
(D) Leacock's delivery is earlier than Ginsberg's.
(E) Malpighi's delivery is earlier than Harris's.

16. If Kanzaki's delivery is earlier than Leacock's, then which one of the following could be true?

(A) Figueroa's delivery is first.
(B) Ginsberg's delivery is third.
(C) Harris's delivery is third.
(D) Leacock's delivery is fifth.
(E) Malpighi's delivery is second.

17. Which one of the following must be false?

(A) Figueroa's delivery is first.
(B) Ginsberg's delivery is fifth.
(C) Harris's delivery is third.
(D) Leacock's delivery is second.
(E) Malpighi's delivery is fourth.

PrepTest52 Sec2 Qs18–23

The explanations to these questions
begin on page 352.

Selection Games

Questions 18–23

A student is choosing courses to take during a summer
school session. Each summer school student must take at
least three courses from among the following seven: history,
linguistics, music, physics, statistics, theater, and writing.
The summer school schedule restricts the courses a student
can take in the following ways:

> If history is taken, then neither statistics nor music can
> be taken.
> If music is taken, then neither physics nor theater can
> be taken.
> If writing is taken, then neither physics nor statistics can
> be taken.

18. The student could take which one of the following
     groups of courses during the summer school session?

     (A)   history, linguistics, and statistics
     (B)   history, music, and physics
     (C)   history, physics, and theater
     (D)   linguistics, physics, theater, and writing
     (E)   music, theater, and writing

19. What is the maximum number of courses the student
     could take during the summer school session?

     (A)   seven
     (B)   six
     (C)   five
     (D)   four
     (E)   three

20. If the student takes neither physics nor writing, then it
     could be true that the student also takes neither

     (A)   history nor linguistics
     (B)   history nor music
     (C)   history nor statistics
     (D)   linguistics nor music
     (E)   statistics nor theater

21. If the student takes music, then which one of the
     following must the student also take?

     (A)   writing
     (B)   theater
     (C)   statistics
     (D)   physics
     (E)   linguistics

22. The student must take one or the other or both of

     (A)   history or statistics
     (B)   linguistics or theater
     (C)   linguistics or writing
     (D)   music or physics
     (E)   theater or writing

23. Which one of the following, if substituted for the
     restriction that if music is taken, then neither physics
     nor theater can be taken, would have the same effect in
     determining which courses the student can take?

     (A)   If music is taken, then either statistics or writing
           must also be taken.
     (B)   The only courses that are eligible to be taken
           together with music are linguistics, statistics,
           and writing.
     (C)   The only courses that are eligible to be taken
           together with physics are history and
           linguistics.
     (D)   The only courses that are eligible to be taken
           together with theater are history, linguistics,
           and writing.
     (E)   If both physics and theater are taken, then music
           cannot be taken.

PrepTest58 Sec3 Qs18–23

Matching/Distribution Games

Questions 24–28

Four people—Grace, Heather, Josh, and Maria—will help each other move exactly three pieces of furniture—a recliner, a sofa, and a table. Each piece of furniture will be moved by exactly two of the people, and each person will help move at least one of the pieces of furniture, subject to the following constraints:

  Grace helps move the sofa if, but only if, Heather helps move the recliner.
  If Josh helps move the table, then Maria helps move the recliner.
  No piece of furniture is moved by Grace and Josh together.

24. Which one of the following could be an accurate matching of each piece of furniture to the two people who help each other move it?

  (A)   recliner: Grace and Maria; sofa: Heather and Josh; table: Grace and Heather
  (B)   recliner: Grace and Maria; sofa: Heather and Maria; table: Grace and Josh
  (C)   recliner: Heather and Josh; sofa: Grace and Heather; table: Josh and Maria
  (D)   recliner: Heather and Josh; sofa: Heather and Maria; table: Grace and Maria
  (E)   recliner: Josh and Maria; sofa: Grace and Heather; table: Grace and Maria

25. If Josh and Maria help each other move the recliner, then which one of the following must be true?

  (A)   Heather helps move the sofa.
  (B)   Josh helps move the sofa.
  (C)   Maria helps move the sofa.
  (D)   Grace helps move the table.
  (E)   Heather helps move the table.

26. If Heather helps move each of the pieces of furniture, then which one of the following could be true?

  (A)   Grace helps move the recliner.
  (B)   Maria helps move the recliner.
  (C)   Josh helps move the sofa.
  (D)   Maria helps move the sofa.
  (E)   Grace helps move the table.

27. Which one of the following could be a pair of people who help each other move both the recliner and the table?

  (A)   Grace and Josh
  (B)   Grace and Maria
  (C)   Heather and Josh
  (D)   Heather and Maria
  (E)   Josh and Maria

28. If Josh and Maria help each other move the sofa, then which one of the following could be true?

  (A)   Heather and Josh help each other move the recliner.
  (B)   Heather and Maria help each other move the recliner.
  (C)   Grace and Josh help each other move the table.
  (D)   Grace and Maria help each other move the table.
  (E)   Heather and Maria help each other move the table.

PrepTest56 Sec1 Qs7–11

Questions 29–33

A town has exactly two public parks—Graystone Park and Landing Park—which are to be planted with North American trees. There are exactly four varieties of trees available— maples, oaks, sycamores, and tamaracks. The planting of the trees must be in accord with the following:

   Each of the parks is planted with exactly three of the varieties.
   At least one of the parks is planted with both maples and sycamores.
   Any park that is planted with oaks will also be planted with tamaracks.
   Graystone Park is planted with maples.

29. Which one of the following could be a complete and accurate list of the varieties of trees planted in each of the parks?

   (A)   Graystone Park: maples, oaks, sycamores
         Landing Park: maples, oaks, sycamores
   (B)   Graystone Park: maples, oaks, tamaracks
         Landing Park: maples, oaks, tamaracks
   (C)   Graystone Park: maples, sycamores, tamaracks
         Landing Park: maples, oaks, sycamores
   (D)   Graystone Park: maples, sycamores, tamaracks
         Landing Park: maples, oaks, tamaracks
   (E)   Graystone Park: oaks, sycamores, tamaracks
         Landing Park: maples, sycamores, tamaracks

30. Which one of the following must be true?

   (A)   Graystone Park is planted with sycamores.
   (B)   Landing Park is planted with maples.
   (C)   Landing Park is planted with tamaracks.
   (D)   The number of the parks planted with maples is equal to the number of the parks planted with sycamores.
   (E)   The number of the parks planted with maples is greater than the number of parks planted with sycamores.

31. If both parks are planted with sycamores, which one of the following could be true?

   (A)   The number of the parks planted with maples is equal to the number of the parks planted with oaks.
   (B)   The number of the parks planted with maples is greater than the number of the parks planted with sycamores.
   (C)   The number of the parks planted with oaks is equal to the number of the parks planted with sycamores.
   (D)   Graystone Park is planted with both maples and oaks.
   (E)   Landing Park is planted with both maples and oaks.

32. Which one of the following must be false?

   (A)   Both parks are planted with oaks.
   (B)   Both parks are planted with sycamores.
   (C)   Both parks are planted with tamaracks.
   (D)   Exactly one of the parks is planted with maples.
   (E)   Exactly one of the parks is planted with sycamores.

33. Which one of the following could be true?

   (A)   The number of the parks planted with oaks is equal to the number of the parks planted with tamaracks.
   (B)   The number of the parks planted with oaks is greater than the number of the parks planted with sycamores.
   (C)   Exactly one of the parks is planted with tamaracks.
   (D)   Neither park is planted with tamaracks.
   (E)   Both parks contain exactly the same three varieties of trees as each other.

PrepTest56 Sec1 Qs12–16

Hybrid Games

Questions 34–38

A conference on management skills consists of exactly five talks, which are held successively in the following order: Feedback, Goal Sharing, Handling People, Information Overload, and Leadership. Exactly four employees of SoftCorp—Quigley, Rivera, Spivey, and Tran—each attend exactly two of the talks. No talk is attended by more than two of the employees, who attend the talks in accordance with the following conditions:

> Quigley attends neither Feedback nor Handling People.
> Rivera attends neither Goal Sharing nor Handling People.
> Spivey does not attend either of the talks that Tran attends.
> Quigley attends the first talk Tran attends.
> Spivey attends the first talk Rivera attends.

34. Which one of the following could be a complete and accurate matching of the talks to the SoftCorp employees who attend them?

   (A)   Feedback: Rivera, Spivey
         Goal Sharing: Quigley, Tran
         Handling People: None
         Information Overload: Quigley, Rivera
         Leadership: Spivey, Tran
   (B)   Feedback: Rivera, Spivey
         Goal Sharing: Quigley, Tran
         Handling People: Rivera, Tran
         Information Overload: Quigley
         Leadership: Spivey
   (C)   Feedback: Rivera, Spivey
         Goal Sharing: Quigley, Tran
         Handling People: Tran
         Information Overload: Quigley, Rivera
         Leadership: Spivey
   (D)   Feedback: Rivera, Spivey
         Goal Sharing: Tran
         Handling People: Tran
         Information Overload: Quigley, Rivera
         Leadership: Quigley, Spivey
   (E)   Feedback: Spivey
         Goal Sharing: Quigley, Tran
         Handling People: Spivey
         Information Overload: Quigley, Rivera
         Leadership: Rivera, Tran

35. If none of the SoftCorp employees attends Handling People, then which one of the following must be true?

   (A)   Rivera attends Feedback.
   (B)   Rivera attends Leadership.
   (C)   Spivey attends Information Overload.
   (D)   Tran attends Goal Sharing.
   (E)   Tran attends Information Overload.

36. Which one of the following is a complete and accurate list of the talks any one of which Rivera and Spivey could attend together?

   (A)   Feedback, Information Overload, Leadership
   (B)   Feedback, Goal Sharing, Information Overload
   (C)   Information Overload, Leadership
   (D)   Feedback, Leadership
   (E)   Feedback, Information Overload

37. If Quigley is the only SoftCorp employee to attend Leadership, then which one of the following could be false?

   (A)   Rivera attends Feedback.
   (B)   Rivera attends Information Overload.
   (C)   Spivey attends Feedback.
   (D)   Spivey attends Handling People.
   (E)   Tran attends Goal Sharing.

38. If Rivera is the only SoftCorp employee to attend Information Overload, then which one of the following could be false?

   (A)   Quigley attends Leadership.
   (B)   Rivera attends Feedback.
   (C)   Spivey attends Feedback.
   (D)   Tran attends Goal Sharing.
   (E)   Tran attends Handling People.

PrepTest62 Sec3 Qs14–18

The explanations to these questions
begin on page 363.

Questions 39–43

Flyhigh Airlines owns exactly two planes: P and Q.
Getaway Airlines owns exactly three planes: R, S, T. On
Sunday, each plane makes exactly one flight, according to
the following conditions:

> Only one plane departs at a time.
> Each plane makes either a domestic or an international
> flight, but not both.
> Plane P makes an international flight.
> Planes Q and R make domestic flights.
> All international flights depart before any domestic
> flight.
> Any Getaway domestic flight departs before Flyhigh's
> domestic flight.

39. Which one of the following could be the order, from
first to last, in which the five planes depart?

(A) P, Q, R, S, T
(B) P, Q, T, S, R
(C) P, S, T, Q, R
(D) P, S, T, R, Q
(E) T, S, R, P, Q

40. The plane that departs second could be any one of
exactly how many of the planes?

(A) one
(B) two
(C) three
(D) four
(E) five

41. If plane S departs sometime before plane P, then
which one of the following must be false?

(A) Plane S departs first.
(B) Plane S departs third.
(C) Plane T departs second.
(D) Plane T departs third.
(E) Plane T departs fourth.

42. Which one of the following must be true?

(A) Plane P departs first.
(B) Plane Q departs last.
(C) Plane R departs second.
(D) Plane S departs first.
(E) Plane T departs fourth.

43. If plane S departs third, then each of the following can
be true EXCEPT:

(A) Plane R departs sometime before plane S and
sometime before plane T.
(B) Plane S departs sometime before plane Q and
sometime before plane T.
(C) Plane S departs sometime before plane R and
sometime before plane T.
(D) Plane T departs sometime before plane P and
sometime before plane S.
(E) Plane T departs sometime before plane R and
sometime before plane S.

PrepTest58 Sec3 Qs13–17

Questions 44–48

Three short seminars—Goals, Objections, and Persuasion—and three long seminars—Humor, Negotiating, and Telemarketing—will be scheduled for a three-day sales training conference. On each day, two of the seminars will be given consecutively. Each seminar will be given exactly once. The schedule must conform to the following conditions:

> Exactly one short seminar and exactly one long seminar will be given each day.
> Telemarketing will not be given until both Goals and Objections have been given.
> Negotiating will not be given until Persuasion has been given.

44. Which one of the following could be an accurate schedule for the sales training conference?

   (A) first day: Persuasion followed by Negotiating
       second day: Objections followed by Telemarketing
       third day: Goals followed by Humor
   (B) first day: Objections followed by Humor
       second day: Goals followed by Telemarketing
       third day: Persuasion followed by Negotiating
   (C) first day: Objections followed by Negotiating
       second day: Persuasion followed by Humor
       third day: Goals followed by Telemarketing
   (D) first day: Objections followed by Goals
       second day: Telemarketing followed by Persuasion
       third day: Negotiating followed by Humor
   (E) first day: Goals followed by Humor
       second day: Persuasion followed by Telemarketing
       third day: Objections followed by Negotiating

45. If Goals is given on the first day of the sales training conference, then which one of the following could be true?

   (A) Negotiating is given on the first day.
   (B) Objections is given on the first day.
   (C) Persuasion is given on the first day.
   (D) Humor is given on the second day.
   (E) Telemarketing is given on the second day.

46. If Negotiating is given at some time before Objections, then which one of the following must be true?

   (A) Negotiating is given at some time before Goals.
   (B) Persuasion is given at some time before Goals.
   (C) Persuasion is given at some time before Objections.
   (D) Humor is given at some time before Objections.
   (E) Negotiating is given at some time before Humor.

47. Which one of the following CANNOT be the second seminar given on the second day of the sales training conference?

   (A) Humor
   (B) Persuasion
   (C) Objections
   (D) Negotiating
   (E) Goals

48. If Humor is given on the second day of the sales training conference, then which one of the following could be true?

   (A) Telemarketing is given on the first day.
   (B) Negotiating is given on the second day.
   (C) Telemarketing is given on the second day.
   (D) Objections is given on the third day.
   (E) Persuasion is given on the third day.

PrepTest52 Sec2 Qs13–17

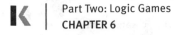

Part Two: Logic Games
CHAPTER 6

These explanations refer to questions that begin on page 335.

ANSWERS AND EXPLANATIONS

Video explanations for select Logic Games are available in your Online Center.

Sequencing Games

Motel Service Appointments

Step 1: Overview

Situation: Scheduling service appointments at a motel

Entities: The six services: G, L, P, S, T, and W

Action: Sequencing—arrange the six services in order from earliest to latest.

Limitations: The six services are spread out over six days. This limitation ensures a straightforward sequencing game with no blanks or ties.

Step 2: Sketch

Scan the rules to check whether this game is Strict or Loose. Rules 3 and 4 are concrete, so draw the basic Strict Sequencing sketch—list the entities and draw six slots.

$$\text{G L P S T W}$$

1	2	3	4	5	6

Step 3: Rules

Rule 1 is a basic Loose Sequencing rule, so pause for a moment and make sure you orient it correctly: "earlier" in this game means to the *left*. Water and landscaping can't be last and first, respectively.

$$\text{W . . . L}$$

1	2	3	4	5	6
~L					~W

Rule 2 is another Loose Sequencing rule. Since two services are scheduled after power, it can't be fifth or sixth, and neither gas nor satellite can be first.

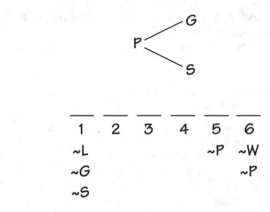

1	2	3	4	5	6
~L				~P	~W
~G					~P
~S					

Rules 3 and **4** tell you where services *can't* go, so make those notations in your Master Sketch:

$$G \neq 2,3$$
$$S \neq 2,3$$
$$T \neq 2,3,6$$

1	2	3	4	5	6
~L	~G	~G		~P	~W
~G	~S	~S			~P
~S	~T	~T			~T

Step 4: Deductions

The Big Deductions in this game rest on the critical concept of *turning negatives into positives*. In fact, you've been making those deductions as you recorded the rules. Whenever you learn that an entity can't go in a slot, ask yourself: Where *can* it go? What *does* go in that slot? In this game, there are four days from which three entities are stricken. Since there are only six entities in the game, deduce that each of those days must have one of the other three entities:

These explanations refer to questions that begin on page 335.

Part Two: Logic Games
Logic Games Practice

K

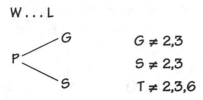

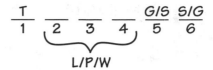

Since this is a Must Be True question, the right choice must be true *all* of the time. That means it has to match what's in your sketch, and the only thing you know for certain is that telephone is first. Scan the choices for this fact: it's in choice **(D)**, so circle it and move on. The remaining choices talk about other entities, each of which could go in multiple days.

3. (E) Must Be True ★★★☆

The correct answer to a Must Be True question is one that's *always* true in your Master Sketch. But your Master Sketch hasn't placed any entities, and the choices themselves don't offer concrete relationships. When you encounter a situation like this, don't panic—*skip the question* and do it at the end of the game. The sketches you draw for other questions may make the choices easier to eliminate.

(E) is the only choice that fits all of your sketches and confirms the Master Sketch. Since water can't be sixth and gas can't be first, second, or third, the only way to put gas earlier than water is to put gas fourth and water fifth. But doing that would force landscaping into sixth, leaving no space for satellite. Thus, no matter where water goes, it's earlier than gas.

(A) fails because landscaping is later than telephone when telephone comes first, which happens in question 2, question 5, and the acceptable list in question 1.

(B) fails in question 2, whose sketch allows landscaping to be scheduled earlier than power.

(C) is tempting because all of your main sketches feature telephone going first. However, the Master Sketch allows telephone to go as late as fifth, in which case gas could be fourth and satellite sixth.

(D) is tempting for the same reason as **(C)**—telephone always seems to end up first—but if you place telephone fourth or fifth, water would be forced to precede it.

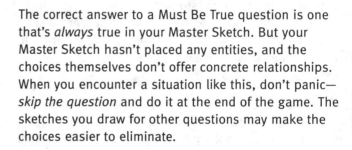

Step 5: Questions

1. (D) Acceptability ★☆☆☆

For Acceptability questions, start with the rules and apply them to the choices.

To test Rule 1, look for the choice that schedules water *later* than landscaping. That's choice **(C)**—eliminate it.

Next, eliminate choice **(A)** for violating Rule 2: gas can't be scheduled before power.

For Rule 3, look for the choice that has either gas, satellite, or telephone on the second or third day. Choice **(E)** puts telephone second, so cross it out.

Rule 4 states that telephone can't be last, quickly eliminating **(B)**. Circle **(D)** and move on.

2. (D) "If" / Must Be True ★★☆☆

The new information in this choice effectively extends Rule 3 to the fourth day. Draw a new sketch for this "If" question, then consider what you know about the entities it mentions: gas, satellite, and telephone. All of a sudden, gas and satellite are squeezed out of the first four days, forcing them to be fifth and six. That leaves just one day for the telephone appointment: the first day.

These explanations refer to questions that begin on page 335.

Here's a quick sketch that shows **(C)** and **(D)** can be false:
W L P G T S

4. (E) Must Be False ★★☆☆

First, translate the phrase "CANNOT be" so that you're clear on the task: the correct choice can *never* happen. That means if a choice can happen even once, it's incorrect.

Next, consider what you know about the fourth through sixth days. You know that the fifth and sixth days prohibit some entities, but when you scan the choices for a clear violation, you'll see there isn't one. Thus, you must think about the rest of the sketch. The most concrete piece of information at your disposal is the fact that power, landscaping, and water are your only candidates for the second and third days, Thus, if two of them appear elsewhere, you'll run out of legal entities for days 2 and 3.

Scan the choices again: choice **(E)** uses water and landscaping in the second half of the sketch, which means that an illegal entity will go in either the second or third day. Circle **(E)** and continue.

For completeness, here's an acceptable list of entities for each of the other choices:

(A): T W P G S L

(B): T W P L S G

(C): T W L P S G

(D): P W L T S G

5. (B) "If" / Must Be True ★☆☆☆

This question is very similar to question 2: draw a sketch with the new information, then pick the choice that matches what is *always* true in the sketch. The time you took to turn negatives into positives in Step 4 pays off here in a big way: if gas and satellite aren't sixth, then the only appointment that can be sixth is landscaping. Scan the choices: there's your deduction in choice **(B)**.

If you skipped question 3, it's worth your while to draw the new sketch. The fourth and fifth days are the only places gas and satellite can go, forcing the telephone appointment to again be first.

T	P/W	W/P	G/S	S/G	L
1	2	3	4	5	6

Choice **(D)** incorrectly places telephone fourth, and choices **(A)**, **(C)**, and **(E)** all make claims about entities whose exact placement is uncertain.

6. (A) Rule Substitution ★★★★

Any question that asks you to substitute a rule is a great candidate to skip on sight and revisit later. These questions can take a long time. In this scenario, if you skipped question 3, you'd go back to complete that, then move on to the next game.

When you do tackle a Rule Changer, look at your Master Sketch and identify the exact effects of the rule being changed. With Rule 4 in effect, telephone can't be sixth, which means it must be either first, fourth, or fifth. Furthermore, by striking telephone from the sixth slot, Rule 4 forces either landscaping, gas, or satellite to be sixth. Look for the rule that replicates these effects.

(A) correctly mimics the rule. If telephone comes before gas or satellite, then it can't be sixth, but it could still be first, fourth, or fifth. The only concern is that if telephone is fifth, then gas or satellite would be sixth, which seems to add a new restriction by prohibiting landscaping from going sixth. However, under the rules as written, this restriction is already in place: if telephone is fifth and landscaping is sixth, then gas and satellite run out of places to go.

(B) adds a new restriction by forcing telephone *directly* before gas or satellite. Under the rules as written, this doesn't have to happen if telephone is first.

(C) appears to work because it stops telephone from going sixth. However, the current rules allow—and in fact force—landscaping to be scheduled *before* telephone when telephone is either fourth or fifth.

(D) is also tempting because it stops telephone from going sixth. However, as in choice **(B)**, the word "immediately" adds an incorrect restriction. Under the rules as written, if telephone is fourth or fifth, it can be immediately before satellite instead of gas.

(E) is incorrect because it precludes landscaping from going sixth.

These explanations refer to questions that begin on page 336.

Part Two: Logic Games
Logic Games Practice | **K**

Testifying Witnesses

Step 1: Overview

Situation: Witnesses testify at a trial.

Entities: Six witnesses—M, R, S, T, U, and W

Action: Arrange the witnesses in the order they testify—this is a Sequencing game.

Limitations: The witnesses testify only one at a time and only once each, ensuring that this Sequencing game doesn't contain any curveballs.

Step 2: Sketch

Scan the rules to determine whether this Sequencing game is Strict or Loose. Since Rules 1 and 3 form Blocks, draw a Strict Sequencing sketch: list the six entities and draw a slot for each.

$$\text{M R S T U W}$$
$$\underline{\quad}\ \underline{\quad}\ \underline{\quad}\ \underline{\quad}\ \underline{\quad}\ \underline{\quad}$$
$$\ 1 \quad 2 \quad 3 \quad 4 \quad 5 \quad 6$$

Step 3: Rules

According to **Rule 1**, Sanderson forms a Block with either Tannenbaum or Ujemori. This rule means that Sanderson will never be sixth.

$$\boxed{\text{ST}}\ \text{or}\ \boxed{\text{SU}}$$

Rule 2 provides a Loose Sequencing relation. Before sketching it, take care to note that "earlier" in this game is to the left and "later" is to the right. Also note that no relationship is provided between Ramirez and Wong.

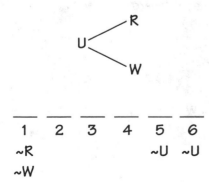

Rule 3 is worded differently than Rule 1, but it restricts the game in a similar way. This rule means Mangione will never be in the first slot.

$$\boxed{\text{TM}}\ \text{or}\ \boxed{\text{WM}}$$

Step 4: Deductions

The vagueness and small quantity of rules suggest that this is a deduction-free game, but work through BLEND just in case. Beginning with Blocks, note that Sanderson can't be last and Mangione can't be first. Rule 2 demonstrates that Ujemori can be neither fifth nor sixth, while neither Wong nor Ramirez can go first. However, since no Block is definite, you can't place anything further. No entities are Established or provide an avenue for Limited Options, and since this is a Sequencing game, there's nothing you can do with Numbers. Finally, some entities are Duplicated among the rules, but the relationships are too vague to pin anything down.

Don't worry when a game offers few deductions: as long as you know you haven't missed anything, you can be confident that the questions will give you the information you need to solve them.

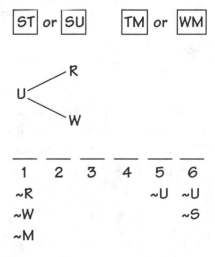

Step 5: Questions

7. (B) Acceptability ★★★★

For Acceptability questions, start with the rules and apply them to the choices.

K | Part Two: Logic Games
CHAPTER 6

These explanations refer to questions that begin on page 336.

Checking Rule 1, choice **(D)** puts Ramirez after Sanderson, which is illegal. Choices **(A)** and **(E)** put Ramirez before Ujemori, violating Rule 2. Finally, choice **(C)** violates Rule 3 by sticking Ramirez right before Wong.

Circle **(B)** and move on.

8. (E) "If" / Could Be True ★☆☆☆

The new "If" means a new sketch. Place Tannenbaum in the first spot. That triggers Rule 1: Sanderson must now follow Ujemori. Rule 3, in turn, places Ujemori earlier than both Ramirez and Wong.

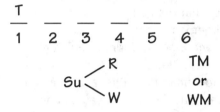

According to Rule 3, Mangione's testimony must follow immediately after either Tannenbaum's or Wong's. Either placement for Mangione is possible here, so depict both to check the possibilities.

T	M	S	u	R/W	W/R
1	2	3	4	5	6

T	S	u			
1	2	3	4	5	6

R/WM (under 4, 5, 6)

Choices **(A)** and **(B)** break the game by putting Ramirez and Wong too early in the lineup, while choices **(C)** and **(D)** don't work because they place Sanderson and Ujemori too late. Choice **(E)** is the only choice that could work—circle it and move on.

9. (A) "If" / Must Be True ★☆☆☆

Once again, it's time to redraw your sketch and make deductions from the new information. Place Sanderson fifth and look at the rules that mention him. Only Rule 1 does, which would place either Tannenbaum or Ujemori sixth. However, Ujemori can't go there without breaking Rule 2, so that means Tannenbaum must be sixth.

Now that Tannenbaum has been placed behind Sanderson, the Master Sketch shows that the only witness able to take the first position is Ujemori.

$$\frac{U}{1} \quad \frac{}{2} \quad \frac{}{3} \quad \frac{}{4} \quad \frac{S}{5} \quad \frac{T}{6}$$

~M (under 2)   ~W (under 4)

U → R
U → WM (boxed)

The only way everyone will fit is if Ujemori goes first. Circle **(A)** and move on.

10. (A) Must Be False ★★★☆

The question asks you what CANNOT work, so the correct choice is a statement that must be false. By contrast, the four wrong choices will be statements that could be true at least once.

This is a great question to skip and do later because it offers no new information on a game with sparse deductions. Specifically, your Master Sketch tells you nothing whatsoever about slots 3 and 4. Fortunately, when you do come back and start to test the choices, you can stop after choice **(A)**. If Tannenbaum comes *after* Mangione, then the only way to satisfy Rule 3 is to place Mangione after Wong. Since choice **(A)** puts Mangione third, Wong is forced to testify second, which would put Ujemori first (to satisfy Rule 2). However, that leaves no room for Sanderson to precede Tannenbaum or Ujemori, violating Rule 1. Since the question asks for the choice that breaks the game, don't bother checking the other choices. Circle **(A)** and approach the final question.

For completeness, here are acceptable lists for choices **(B)** through **(E)**:

(B): U W R S T M

(C): T M S U R W

(D): S U T R W M

(E): T S U W M R

These explanations refer to questions that begin on page 336.

Part Two: Logic Games
Logic Games Practice

K

11. (D) Must Be False ★★☆☆

This question is very similar to the previous one, except that your Master Sketch provides some information about the first slot. Once again, you'll cross out the choices that could be true and circle the one that breaks the game.

Choices **(A)**, **(B)**, **(C)**, and **(E)** don't cause the game to break. Choice **(D)**, however, makes it impossible to satisfy Rule 1. Circle it and review any questions you may have skipped in this section.

For completeness, here are acceptable lists for choices **(A)**, **(B)**, **(C)**, and **(E)**:

(A): S U T M R W

(B): T M S U R W

(C): T S U W M R

(E): U W S T M R

Bread Delivery

Step 1: Overview

Situation: A bread truck makes deliveries to six restaurants on its route.

Entities: The six restaurants: F, G, H, K, L, and M

Action: Sequencing. You must determine the order in which the truck delivers bread to the restaurants. A quick glance at the rules reveals that there are no Established Entities or Blocks of Entities, so this will be Loose Sequencing.

Limitations: Exactly one delivery to each restaurant in succession. So, all entities are sequenced, one at a time.

Step 2: Sketch

Because this is a Loose Sequencing game, simply jot down a list of entities. You'll build a Loose Sequencing tree after going through the rules.

F G H K L M

Step 3: Rules

Rule 1. This rule gives a typical Loose Sequencing relationship. G will come before K and after F:

F —— G —— K

Rule 2. This rule gives another, even simpler relationship (**H — G**). Build it onto the information so far:

Rule 3. This rule introduces some Formal Logic. Although not common in Loose Sequencing, it's still handled as any other Formal Logic rule:

If F —— M → L —— H

The basic contrapositive would normally look like this:

If Not L —— H → Not F —— M

However, when forming the contrapositive, try to turn negatives into positives. Because the truck delivers to each restaurant one at a time, another way of saying "The truck doesn't deliver to L before H," is "The truck delivers to H before L." Same goes for F and M. Having positive triggers and results will make dealing with the Formal Logic much easier. So the contrapositive would be easier to work with if it looked like this:

If H —— L → M —— F

Rule 4. This rule gives a lot of information, so it's important to analyze it piece by piece. First, start out with the two possibilities:

M —— H or K —— M

Then, the final part of the rule says that you can't have both. That means if the truck delivers to M before H, it can't deliver to K before M. In that case, the truck would deliver to M before K.

Similarly, if the truck delivers to K before M, it can't deliver to M before H. So in that case, it would have to deliver to H before M.

Finally, because one of these two scenarios must happen, you get two possible outcomes:

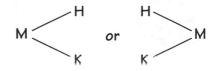

K | Part Two: Logic Games
CHAPTER 6

These explanations refer to questions that begin on page 337.

This means that the truck will deliver to M either before both H and K or after them both.

Step 4: Deductions

Because Rule 4 provides two possible outcomes that use half the entities, and some of those entities are duplicated in the other rules, this is an ideal situation for Limited Options.

Start with the two sketches set up by Rule 4. Add G to both options such that G comes after H (Rule 2) and before K (Rule 1). This will likely require some redrawing.

Opt I
M — H — G — K

Opt II
H — G — K — M

Once that's set up, add F before G (by Rule 1) in both options.

Opt I
M — H — G — K
         F

Opt II
H — G — K — M
     F

The last thing to consider is the Formal Logic of Rule 3. In the first option, the relationship between M and F is undetermined: either of them could come before the other. Therefore, L cannot be placed. However, in the second option, the truck delivers to F before M. This triggers the Formal Logic, requiring L to be delivered before H.

Final Visualization

Opt I
M — H — G — K
         F

(L is a Floater)

Opt II
L — H — G — K — M
         F

Finally, with Loose Sequencing, always take a moment to determine what could be first and what could be last.

In the first option, no restaurants need to be delivered to before M and F, so they can be first. Also, because L is a Floater in this option, it can also be first. Then, because no restaurants have to be delivered to after K, K could be last. However, so could the Floater, L.

In the second option, no restaurants need to be delivered to before L or F, so either one of those could be first. However, M is the only restaurant that doesn't have another restaurant delivery following it, so M must be sixth. Before that must come K, making K fifth. Before that comes G, making G fourth. That's where the deductions end because you don't know whether F or H comes third.

Step 5: Questions

12. (C) Acceptability   ★★☆☆

For Acceptability questions, go through the rules one at a time, eliminating answers that violate the rules.

Choice **(D)** violates Rule 1 by making Ginsberg's delivery after Kanzaki's. Choice **(E)** violates Rule 2 by making Harris's delivery after Ginsberg's. Both choices **(A)** and **(B)** have Figueroa's delivery before Malpighi's, but choice **(A)** then has Harris's delivery before Leacock's, which violates the Formal Logic of Rule 3. Finally, choice **(B)** violates Rule 4 by having Malpighi's delivery after Harris's and before Kanzaki's, satisfying neither rule's criteria. Therefore, the only answer to follow the rules is choice **(C)**.

These explanations refer to questions that begin on page 337.

Part Two: Logic Games
Logic Games Practice

13. (A) "If" / Must Be True ★★☆☆

Figueroa's delivery can only be fourth in the first option. In the second option, the latest the truck can deliver to Figueroa's is third.

So, looking using the first option, if Figueroa's delivery is fourth, there are two restaurants that must be delivered to later: Ginsberg's, then Kanzaki's. Therefore, Kanzaki's delivery is sixth, and Ginsberg's must be fifth. That makes choice **(A)** correct.

$$\underline{}\ \ \underline{}\ \ \underline{}\ \ \underline{F}\ \ \underline{G}\ \ \underline{K}$$
$$\ \ 1\ \ \ \ 2\ \ \ \ 3\ \ \ \ 4\ \ \ \ 5\ \ \ \ 6$$

Meanwhile, the first, second, and third deliveries are undetermined. Because Malpighi's must come before Harris's, the truck must deliver to Malpighi's either first or second. Harris's, then, could be second or third. Leacock's, however, could come first, second, or third. That flexibility means answer choices **(B)** through **(E)** all could be true, but none of them must be.

14. (E) "If" / Must Be True ★★★★

Because this question establishes two entities, start by drawing a Strict Sequencing sketch and placing M and L in the first and third spaces, respectively.

Malpighi's delivery can only be first in the first option. With Leacock's established, the only restaurant that can be delivered to last in that option is Kanzaki's, so Kanzaki's is sixth, and Ginsberg's is right before it at fifth. The only uncertainty is the order of Figueroa's and Harris's deliveries.

$$\underline{M}\ \ \underline{F/H}\ \ \underline{L}\ \ \underline{F/H}\ \ \underline{G}\ \ \underline{K}$$
$$\ \ 1\ \ \ \ \ 2\ \ \ \ \ 3\ \ \ \ \ 4\ \ \ \ \ 5\ \ \ \ 6$$

With that, choice **(E)** must be true. Answer choices **(A)**, **(B)**, and **(C)** all could be true because Figueroa's and Harris's order is undetermined. Choice **(D)**, however, must be false because the truck delivers to Kanzaki's last.

15. (C) Must Be True ★★☆☆

Remember that with Limited Options, a Must Be True answer has to be true in *both* options, not just one.

(C) is confirmed in both options, making this the right answer. For the record:

Because Leacock's is a Floater in the first option, its delivery doesn't have to be earlier or later than any other restaurant's. That eliminates choices **(A)**, **(B)**, and **(D)**.

(E) is definitely false in the second option.

16. (C) "If" / Could Be True ★★★★

Kanzaki's delivery can only be before Leacock's in the first option. Because these two restaurants were the only possibilities for the last delivery, that means Leacock's delivery is sixth. Working backward, Kanzaki's must be fifth, which eliminates choice **(D)**, and Ginsberg's must be fourth, which eliminates choice **(B)**.

$$\underline{}\ \ \underline{}\ \ \underline{}\ \ \underline{G}\ \ \underline{K}\ \ \underline{L}$$
$$\ \ 1\ \ \ \ 2\ \ \ \ 3\ \ \ \ 4\ \ \ \ 5\ \ \ \ 6$$

That leaves Malphigi's, Harris's, and Figueroa's deliveries to fill the first three spots, with Malphigi's delivery coming before Harris's.

With no other deductions standing out, it's time to go back to the Formal Logic. Because Leacock's delivery is last, Harris's delivery must come before it. This triggers the contrapositive of the Formal Logic in Rule 3, which means the truck must deliver to Malpighi's before Figueroa's. Now, because Malpighi's must come before both Figueroa's and Harris's, that means Malpighi's delivery is first, eliminating choices **(A)** and **(E)** and leaving choice **(C)** as the correct answer.

17. (E) Must Be False ★★★★

Again, with Limited Options, the correct answer to a "must be" question needs to be confirmed by both options.

Checking choice **(E)** in the first option, there are three restaurants that must be delivered to after Malpighi's. That's too many for Malpighi's to be the fourth delivery. In the second option, Malpighi's delivery must be last, so this answer must be false, making it the right answer. For the record:

EXPLANATIONS

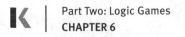

These explanations refer to questions that begin on page 338.

Choice **(A)** could be true in either option, so this is a quick elimination.

In the first option, Ginsberg's delivery only has to come before Kanzaki's. Therefore, its delivery certainly could be fifth, which eliminates choice **(B)**. (Furthermore, this is confirmed by the sketches for the second and third questions of the set.)

In the second option, only three restaurants have to be delivered to after Harris's, meaning that it can be delivered to third. That eliminates choice **(C)**.

Because Leacock's is a Floater in the first option, it can be delivered to at any time, eliminating choice **(D)**.

Selection Games

Summer School Courses

Step 1: Overview

Situation: Summer school sessions

Entities: Seven courses

Action: Select which of the seven courses the student takes.

Limitations: At least three courses must be selected, but there's no maximum.

Step 2: Sketch

Since the number of courses isn't completely determined, merely list the seven entities. As you go through the game, circle courses that are selected and cross out courses that are rejected.

H L M P S T W

Step 3: Rules

Rules 1, 2, and **3** all provide straightforward Formal Logic rules. Translate each statement and its contrapositive:

$$H \rightarrow \text{No S and No M}$$
$$S \text{ or } M \rightarrow \text{No H}$$

$$M \rightarrow \text{No P and No T}$$
$$P \text{ or } T \rightarrow \text{No M}$$

$$W \rightarrow \text{No P and No S}$$
$$P \text{ or } S \rightarrow \text{No W}$$

Rule 1 can also be interpreted to say that the student can't take history and statistics together and the student can't take history and music together.

Never HS; Never HM

Rule 2 can be interpreted to say that the student can't take music and physics together and the student can't take music and theater together.

Never MP; Never MT

Rule 3 can be interpreted to say that the student can't take writing and physics together and the student can't take writing and statistics together.

Never WP; Never WS

Step 4: Deductions

When a game is entirely dependent on Formal Logic, as this game is, there usually aren't any major deductions to be made. That's because all of the rules are conditional, which means that the rules will only be utilized under certain conditions—none of which have been provided yet.

However, it's important to keep a few things in mind for this game. First, the student must take a minimum of three courses. Since all of the rules prohibit certain courses from being offered together, you have to be careful about what courses are chosen to avoid eliminating too much from the schedule. Numbers are crucial to games such as this.

Second, linguistics is never mentioned in any of the rules. That means that linguistics can always be selected or rejected without affecting any of the other courses.

Finally, it should be noted that music is the most limiting course, since that would eliminate three courses (history by Rule 1 and physics and theater by Rule 2). That will play an important role in keeping track of the numbers.

These explanations refer to questions that begin on page 338.

Part Two: Logic Games
Logic Games Practice   **K**

Final Visualization

H L M P S T W

H → No S and No M

S or M → No H

M → No P and No T

P or T → No M

W → No P and No S

P or S → No W

Never HS; Never HM
Never MP; Never MT
Never WP; Never WS

Step 5: Questions

18. (C) Acceptability   ★☆☆☆

Rule 1 dictates that history and statistics can't be taken together, nor can history and music. That eliminates **(A)** and **(B)**. Rule 2 dictates that music and theater can't be taken together. That eliminates **(E)**. Rule 3 dictates that writing and physics can't be taken together. That eliminates **(D)**.

That leaves **(C)** as the correct answer—the only one that doesn't violate any of the rules.

19. (D) Minimum / Maximum   ★★★☆

Because of the restrictions placed on so many courses, the student certainly couldn't take all seven courses. That eliminates **(A)**.

Selecting music would eliminate three other courses, automatically dropping the number of courses to, at most, four. To maximize the number of courses, eliminate M. That leaves six courses. However, many of these courses (e.g., history and statistics) can't be together. So six courses can't be done. That eliminates **(B)**.

With music eliminated, writing and statistics become the most limiting entities. Writing would eliminate physics and statistics, leaving four courses at most. Statistics would eliminate history and writing, again leaving four courses at most. If we get rid of one, the other would still be around—reducing the course count

to a maximum of four. So, to maximize the course load, we should eliminate both. However, that *still* leaves only four courses at most.

No matter what we do—if we keep writing or statistics, or if we get rid of them both—we can't select more than four courses. That eliminates **(C)**.

The final question is: Can four courses be selected? If we do eliminate writing and statistics, we'd be left with history, linguistics, physics, and theater. That selection doesn't violate any of the rules, so it is possible to take four courses. That means **(D)** is the correct answer.

Note: Now it is clear that the student will either select three courses (the minimum) or four courses (the maximum).

20. (B) "If" / Could Be True   ★★★★

For the purposes of this particular question, the correct answer will be two courses that the student could also not take, while the four wrong answer choices will contain courses that, if selected, will violate at least one of the rules.

If the student doesn't take physics and doesn't take writing, then that leaves five courses: history, linguistics, music, statistics, and theater.

At this point, history and music are the two most limiting courses. Each one would eliminate two of the remaining courses. That would leave three courses—the minimum that must be selected. So it makes sense to start with **(B)**.

(B) works because that would get rid of the two most restrictive entities. That would leave linguistics, statistics, and theater—an acceptable trio of courses. Thus, **(B)** is the correct answer. For the record:

(A) and **(C)** don't work because both answers would leave music and theater together, which violates Rule 2.

(D) doesn't work because it would leave history and statistics together, which violates Rule 1.

(E) doesn't work because it would leave history and music together, which also violates Rule 1.

K | Part Two: Logic Games
CHAPTER 6

These explanations refer to questions that begin on page 338.

21. (E) "If" / Must Be True ★★★★

If music is taken, then that eliminates history (by Rule 1), physics (by Rule 2), and theater (also by Rule 2). That leaves linguistics, statistics, and writing. To satisfy the minimum of three courses, we need at least two of the remaining courses. However, Rule 3 prohibits statistics and writing to both be selected. So, to satisfy the minimum requirement, one of those must be selected along with linguistics.

Since linguistics has to be selected in either case, **(E)** is the correct answer.

22. (B) Must Be True ★★★★

For the purposes of this particular question, the correct answer "must be true," while the four wrong answers "could be or must be false."

Once the courses are selected, that selection must include at least one of the courses in the correct answer. In other words, it would be unacceptable to select neither course in the correct answer choice.

To test the answers, determine what would happen if both courses were removed. If you can still select the minimum of three courses, then you have your answer.

According to **(B)**, if linguistics and theater were removed from selection, that would leave history, music, physics, statistics, and writing. Taking music would eliminate history (by Rule 1) and physics (by Rule 2). That would leave writing and statistics as the remaining two courses. However, that would violate Rule 3.

If music were not taken, taking writing would eliminate physics and statistics (by Rule 3). However, that would leave only history. That wouldn't satisfy the minimum of three.

If music and writing weren't taken, that would leave history, physics, and statistics as the three courses. However, that violates Rule 1.

Therefore, in any case, it is impossible to select at least three courses when linguistics and theater are taken out of the picture. Therefore, the selection must include at least one of them, making **(B)** the correct answer.

Note: You can also use your previous sketches on this question to knock off wrong answer choices quickly.

For the record:

(A), (D) A course load of linguistics, theater, and writing shows why the selection doesn't have to include history, statistics, music, or physics. The sketch for this game's fourth question shows that these choices could be false.

(C) A course load of history, physics, and theater shows why the selection doesn't have to include linguistics, or writing. Refer to the correct answer in the Acceptability question to see that this choice could be false.

(E) A course load of history, linguistics, and physics shows why the selection doesn't have to include theater or writing. The sketch for the fourth question in the set shows that you can eliminate choice **(E)**.

23. (B) Rule Substitution ★★★★

For this question, Rule 2 is removed from the game and replaced with one of the answers. The correct answer will be the one replacement that will create the exact same scenario that Rule 2 created.

Specifically, by removing Rule 2, music can now be selected along with physics or theater. The correct answer will reestablish the limitation that music will be taken with neither physics nor theater.

The only other information we know about music is that, by Rule 1, it can't be taken with history. If, as **(B)** says, music can only be selected with linguistics, statistics, and/or writing, then that means it can't be selected with history (which we know from Rule 1), physics, or theater. That brings back the same exact restrictions dictated by Rule 2 without adding anything new. That makes **(B)** the correct answer. For the record:

(A) This adds two different restrictions to music that were never dictated by the original rules.

(C) This reinstates the condition that physics and math can't be taken together. However, it doesn't reestablish that music and theater can't be taken together. It also puts restrictions on physics (e.g., physics cannot be

These explanations refer to questions that begin on page 339.

Part Two: Logic Games
Logic Games Practice K

taken with statistics) that the original rules never suggested.

(D) This reinstates the condition that theater and math can't be taken together. However, it doesn't reestablish that music and physics can't be taken together. It also puts restrictions on theater (i.e., theater cannot be taken with physics) that the original rules never suggested.

(E) This answer takes away the possibility of having physics, theater, and math all together, which partially replaces Rule 2. However, this answer eliminates math if physics *and* theater are taken. The problem is that it doesn't eliminate math if physics or theater alone is taken. Rule 2 would not have allowed that, so this rule doesn't completely serve the exact same function.

Matching/Distribution Games

Furniture Moving

Step 1: Overview

Situation: People helping move furniture

Entities: Four people (Grace, Heather, Josh, and Maria) and three pieces of furniture (recliner, sofa, and table)

Action: Matching. Assign pairs of people to move each piece of furniture. This is a straightforward Matching game because at least one entity will repeat.

Limitations: There will be six slots to fill: two slots for each piece of furniture. Each person will be matched up at least once. So, at least one person and at most two people will be assigned more than once.

Step 2: Sketch

With the numbers so definite, this game lends itself nicely to a column sketch. The sketch should be anchored around the three pieces of furniture, which will never change in number or kind. Two slots should then be drawn under each piece of furniture for each pair of movers. The initial sketch should look like so:

REC	SOF	TAB
—	—	—
—	—	—

Step 3: Rules

Rule 1 is a Formal Logic statement that presents two rules in one. Statements with "if, but only if" (as well as "if, and only if") can be divided into two parts:

The first part requires that Grace move the sofa *if* Heather moves the recliner. Regardless of where "if" appears in a sentence, when it appears alone, it precedes a sufficient condition.

$$\frac{REC}{H} \longrightarrow \frac{SOF}{G}$$

The contrapositive prevents Heather from moving the recliner if Grace does not move the sofa. Write down this part of the rule like this:

$$\frac{\sim SOF}{G} \longrightarrow \frac{\sim REC}{H}$$

The second part of the rule requires that Grace move the sofa *only if* Heather moves the recliner. Recall that "only if" precedes the necessary result in a Formal Logic statement. The contrapositive prevents Grace from moving the sofa if Heather does not move the recliner. So, write down this part of the rule like this:

$$\frac{SOF}{G} \longrightarrow \frac{REC}{H}$$

$$\frac{\sim REC}{H} \longrightarrow \frac{\sim SOF}{G}$$

Before moving on, think about what these two rules mean in conjunction. If either Heather or Grace moves her respective piece of furniture, the other must as well. Conversely, if either one *doesn't*, the other won't either. In other words, either Heather and Grace will both move their respective pieces of furniture, or neither will.

Rule 2 is a simpler if-then Formal Logic statement. Write out the original and contrapositive statement like so:

$$\frac{TAB}{J} \longrightarrow \frac{REC}{M}$$

$$\frac{\sim REC}{M} \longrightarrow \frac{\sim TAB}{J}$$

EXPLANATIONS

These explanations refer to questions that begin on page 339.

Rule 3 prohibits Grace and Josh from being paired up to move any piece of furniture. Note this as follows:

NEVER | G
       | J

Step 4: Deductions

When a majority of the rules are conditional statements, you need to ensure that you have correctly contraposed the statements. Keep an eye out for statements that can be combined. In this game, nothing definitively places any person with any piece of furniture. So be ready to let the new information in the questions lead to key deductions.

Step 5: Questions

24. (A) Acceptability ★★★☆

As always, running through the rules one at a time helps eliminate all the wrong answers. Because of the dense Formal Logic of the first rule, it's easier to start with simpler rules (like Rule 3) and work backward.

Rule 3 states that Grace and Josh can never move furniture together, so that eliminates choice **(B)**, which has them both moving the table. Rule 2 states that whenever Josh helps move the table, Maria must move the recliner. This eliminates choice **(C)** because Josh is moving the table without Maria moving the recliner. Finally, Rule 1, with its two rules in one, will likely eliminate the remaining two wrong answer choices. Remember, either Grace moves the sofa and Heather moves the recliner, or Grace doesn't move the sofa and Heather doesn't move the recliner. Choice **(D)** can be eliminated because Heather is moving the recliner without Grace moving the sofa. Likewise, eliminate choice **(E)** because Grace is moving the sofa without Heather moving the recliner. That leaves choice **(A)** as the correct answer.

25. (D) "If" / Must Be True ★★★☆

If Josh and Maria move the recliner, the contrapositive for Rule 1 kicks in: Heather is not moving the recliner, which mandates that Grace not move the sofa. But Grace *must* move at least one piece of furniture, so she must move the table. A quick scan of the answer choices leads to choice **(D)**—a perfect match to the big deduction!

REC	SOF	TAB
J	—	G
M	—	—

(A) might be true but doesn't have to be. Heather could move the sofa, but she might only move the table. That would leave Josh and Maria to move the sofa, which is a perfectly valid sketch.

(B) might be true but doesn't have to be. Josh is already moving the recliner and doesn't have to move anything else.

(C) could be true but doesn't have to be. Maria is already moving the recliner and doesn't have to move anything else.

(E) could also be true but doesn't have to be. Heather could move the sofa instead, along with Josh or Maria. In that case, Maria would move the table with Grace.

26. (B) "If" / Could Be True ★★☆☆

For this question, Heather is a repeating furniture mover—in fact she moves everything! That means the remaining three people will each move one piece of furniture. By Rule 1, because Heather is moving the recliner, Grace must move the sofa. That leaves Josh and Maria to help with the recliner and table, in either order:

REC	SOF	TAB
H	H	H
J/M	G	M/J

That leaves choice **(B)** as the only possible answer. **(A)**, **(C)**, **(D)**, and **(E)** all must be false based on the sketch.

27. (B) Could Be True ★★★★

At first glance, it appears that trial and error is necessary. However, Rule 3 removes two answer choices immediately from consideration. Grace and Josh will never be paired up to move furniture, so choice **(A)** can be eliminated. Likewise, if Heather and Maria are paired up to move two pieces of furniture, that will force Grace and Josh to move the third piece

These explanations refer to questions that begin on page 339.

Part Two: Logic Games
Logic Games Practice

K

of furniture together. Eliminate choice **(D)**. After strategically narrowing down the answer choices, now you can try out the remaining contenders.

Incorporating choice **(B)** will force Heather and Josh to move the sofa together:

REC	SOF	TAB
G	H	G
M	J	M

This does not violate any of the rules, so choice **(B)** is the correct answer.

For the record, choice **(C)** will force Grace and Maria to move the sofa. The problem here stems from Rule 2. With Josh moving the table, Maria must move the recliner. Eliminate.

Choice **(E)** will force both Grace and Heather to move only the sofa. This violates Rule 1's requirement that Heather moves the recliner whenever Grace moves the sofa. Eliminate.

28. (E) "If" / Could Be True ★★★★

Assigning Josh and Maria to move the sofa will trigger Rule 1's contrapositive: Grace is not moving the sofa, which mandates that Heather not move the recliner. But Heather *must* move at least one piece of furniture, so she must move the table. Additionally, because Heather does not move the recliner, two of the three of Grace, Josh, and Maria must. Grace and Josh can never move furniture together, so the recliner will be moved by Maria and one of Grace or Josh:

REC	SOF	TAB
M	J	H
G/J	M	

That is as far as you can deduce. The sketch eliminates choices **(A)** and **(B)**, which both have Heather moving the recliner. Choices **(C)** and **(D)** are not possible because Heather is for sure one of the two people moving the table, not to mention in choice **(C)**, in light of Rule 3, Grace and Josh can never be paired up. That leaves only choice **(E)** as possible.

Parks and Trees
Step 1: Overview

Situation: Planting varieties of trees in two public parks

Entities: Two public parks (Graystone and Landing) and four kinds of trees (maples, oaks, sycamores, and tamaracks)

Action: Matching. You need to match each park with which of the four types of trees it has. A type of tree can be at more than one park, but doesn't *have* to be at any park.

You could also construe this as a double Selection game where you select which three of four types of tree each park has. Nonetheless, how you characterize the game is less important than being able to understand the rules and build them into a helpful Master Sketch.

Limitations: From the introduction, there are no numeric limitations. Each park can have any number of trees, and trees can appear in one park or both—or possibly neither! Don't assume all trees must be used. A quick glance at Rule 1 gives a definite assignment of the number of trees to each park, which will help in setting up the sketch. Going through the remaining rules, look for limitations on which trees can be planted in the same park together.

Step 2: Sketch

Use a standard Matching column sketch with the roster of entities above to yield the following:

M O S T

GRAY	LAND
—	—
—	—
—	—

If you had viewed the game as a double Selection game, you would set the sketch up by listing each of the two parks along with the potential roster of entities at each park. Then each type of tree would get circled or crossed out as with any typical Selection game:

Gray: M O S T
Land: M O S T

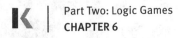

Part Two: Logic Games
CHAPTER 6

These explanations refer to questions that begin on page 340.

The remainder of the explanations will continue with just the Matching sketch.

Step 3: Rules

Rule 1 assigns *exactly* three trees per park. If you hadn't already built this into your sketch, now is the time. Also be sure to take note of how this limits the numbers. With a total of six spaces and only four types of trees, at least two tree varieties will be duplicated, meaning at least two types of trees will appear in both parks.

Rule 2 suggests the possibility of Limited Options. Note this rule in shorthand for now and come back to it in Step 4.

At least one park: MS

Rule 3 provides a conditional statement, common to Selection games. Use your Formal Logic skills to translate and contrapose this statement as follows:

$$\text{If } O \longrightarrow T$$
$$\text{If } {\sim}T \longrightarrow {\sim}O$$

Rule 4 gives a definite assignment. Place an M under Graystone Park in your master sketch.

Step 4: Deductions

Revisit Rule 2 to see what can be gleaned from that information. Because there are only two parks, there are two possibilities: Either Graystone or Landing will have both maples and sycamores. This sets up Limited Options like so:

Option 1:

GRAY	LAND
M	—
S	—
—	—

Option 2:

GRAY	LAND
M	M
—	S
—	—

Note that each option also includes the possibility that *both* parks will boast maples and sycamores.

Now, think about Rule 3. In order for oaks to be planted in a park, there must also be tamaracks. That means if oaks are planted, two slots must be available. Because each park can only have three types of trees, the park that already has both maples and sycamores will *never* have oaks. So the third tree in that park will always have to be the only remaining variety: tamaracks.

Think through this a bit more. Every park that has oaks planted in it will also have tamaracks. Any park that *doesn't* have oaks planted in it will always have the remaining three varieties of trees—including tamaracks. So, it can be deduced that, no matter what, each park *must* have tamaracks planted in it. Adding in this information results in two solid options:

Option 1:

GRAY	LAND
M	—
S	—
T	T

Option 2:

GRAY	LAND
M	M
—	S
T	T

$$\text{If } O \longrightarrow T$$
$$\text{If } {\sim}T \longrightarrow {\sim}O$$

Step 5: Questions

29. (D) Acceptability ★★★★

As with any Acceptability question, attack each of the rules eliminating any answers that violate one. Rule 1 requires that each park be planted with exactly three trees. No answer violates that rule. Rule 2 requires at least one park have both maples and sycamores. **(B)** has neither park with sycamores. Eliminate. Rule 3 requires that any park with oaks also have tamaracks. In **(A)**, Graystone and Landing have oaks but do not

These explanations refer to questions that begin on page 340.

Part Two: Logic Games
Logic Games Practice K

also have tamaracks. In **(C)**, Landing has oaks but no tamaracks. Eliminate **(A)** and **(C)**. Finally, Rule 4 indicates Graystone Park has maples. However, in choice **(E)** it does not. Eliminate. That leaves choice **(D)** as the correct answer.

30. (C) Must Be True ★★★☆

With Limited Options, remember the correct answer to a "Must Be True" question is definitely true in *both* options. Once again, keep in mind the major deduction of this game: both parks must have tamaracks. That immediately leads you to choice **(C)**. For the record:

(A) and **(B)** assign a tree variety that could be included but, according to the Limited Options sketches, doesn't need to be. On Must Be True questions, something that is merely possible is not enough.

(D) and **(E)** are numerically possible but, again, not necessarily true.

31. (A) "If" / Could Be True ★★★☆

For this question, both parks are planted with sycamores. This is possible in either option, so consider redrawing both options with the new information. Adding a sycamore to Landing in the first option leaves one more space in Landing, which could be filled by either maples or oaks. Adding a sycamore to Graystone in the second option fills the sketch completely:

Option 1:

GRAY	LAND
M	S
S	M/O
T	T

Option 2:

GRAY	LAND
M	M
S	S
T	T

The correct answer only needs to be possible in one of the options. Eliminate the answer choices that are impossible in both options. Choice **(A)** could be true in the first option, if the third variety under Landing is oaks. Then maples and oaks would each appear in exactly one park. Thus, **(A)** is possible and the correct answer.

For the record, because both parks will have sycamores in this scenario, it is impossible to have more maples than sycamores planted. This eliminates choice **(B)**. It is also impossible to have the same number of oaks as sycamores planted. If sycamores are in both parks, then oaks would need to be in both parks, which can't happen because at least one park will always have maples, sycamores, and tamaracks. This eliminates choice **(C)**. Choice **(D)** is impossible because in both options Graystone has only the tree varieties of maples, sycamores, and tamaracks. Likewise, Landing only has the option of maples *or* oaks in the first option, never both, which eliminates choice **(E)**.

32. (A) Must Be False ★★☆☆

With Limited Options, something that Must Be False has to be impossible in both options. If an answer is possible in either option, then it must be eliminated,

Looking at both options, maples, sycamores, and tamaracks will be the three trees planted in at least one of the parks. So, it is impossible for both parks to have oaks, as **(A)** says, in either option. Thus, **(A)** must be false and is the correct answer choice.

Even if you didn't get the Limited Options in the beginning, you can still use your deductive reasoning skills to answer this question quickly and efficiently by combining Rules 2 and 3. If at least one park is planted with sycamores and maples *and* any park planted with oaks must be planted with tamaracks, then it's impossible for the park planted with sycamores and maples to have oaks, too, as that would require a fourth tree: tamaracks. Thus, at least one park will never have oaks. **(A)** is impossible. **(B)**, **(D)**, and **(E)** all could be possible, according to your sketch, while **(C)** is your big deduction and must be *true*, not false.

EXPLANATIONS

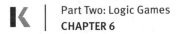

Part Two: Logic Games
CHAPTER 6

These explanations refer to questions
that begin on page 340.

33. (E) Could Be True ★★★★

With Limited Options, the correct answer to a Could Be True merely needs to be possible in either option. Only eliminate answers that cannot happen in both options. Using previous work can also sometimes help verify the correct answer.

Because one park in each option contains maples, sycamores, and tamaracks, oaks are limited to one park. There will always be two parks with tamaracks, so it is impossible to have an equal number of parks with oaks and tamaracks. This eliminates choice **(A)**. Similarly, at least one park will always have sycamores planted in it. So, it's impossible for oaks to outnumber sycamores. Eliminate choice **(B)**.

From the earlier big deduction, both parks must have tamaracks. That eliminates choices **(C)** and **(D)**. That leaves **(E)** as the only possible answer choice. This can be verified by looking at the second sketch of the third question of the set.

Hybrid Games

Management Conference

Step 1: Overview

Situation: Employees attend talks at a management skills conference.

Entities: Four employees—Q, R, S, and T—and five talks—Fb, Gs, Hp, Io, and Ls.

Action: Match the employees to the talks they attend (Matching). There is also a Sequencing element because the talks occur in order.

Limitations: Each employee attends exactly two talks, and each talk holds a maximum of two employees. Start thinking about Numbers: Either one talk goes unattended while the other four are full, or three of the talks are full while the other two get a person each. In numeric terms, the distribution is either 2-2-2-2-0 or 2-2-2-1-1 (not necessarily in that order, though!).

Step 2: Sketch

Sequencing tends to be a dominant action when it appears in Hybrid games, so let it serve as the backbone of your sketch. Arrange the talks in order and

leave space below for the employees, but don't draw any slots—as you saw in Step 1, it's possible for a talk to be empty. Don't make a notation that makes you think any of the talks *must* have an employee in them.

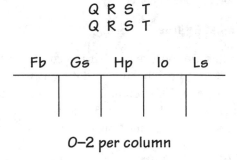

0–2 per column

Step 3: Rules

Rule 1 limits the placement of Quigley. Make a note below Feedback and Handling People that Quigley can never attend them.

$$Q \neq Fb, Hp$$

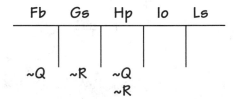

Rule 2 works the same way—mark that Rivera never attends Goal Sharing or Handling People.

$$Q \neq Fb, Hp$$

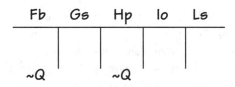

Analyze **Rule 3** and notate it in the simplest way: simply put, Spivey and Tran are never together.

~~ST~~

Rule 4 brings in the Sequencing element of the game. Make sure your notation captures that information. Since no employee can attend the same talk twice, one of

These explanations refer to questions that begin on page 341.

Part Two: Logic Games
Logic Games Practice

K

Tran's two talks must be earlier than the other one. That talk will have Quigley in attendance, forming a Block.

$$T_1Q$$

Rule 5 works identically to Rule 4. Make a Block with Rivera's first talk and one of Spivey's.

$$R_1S$$

Step 4: Deductions

Any time a game has a Block, think critically about where it can go. This simple step frequently reaps big deductions. In this game, you have a Block each from Rules 4 and 5. Tran's first talk, with Quigley in tow, must be either in Goal Sharing or Information Overload. Feedback and Handling People don't work because Quigley can't attend them, and Leadership doesn't work because Tran's first talk can't be the last talk of the conference—if she attends Leadership, that's her *second* talk, not her first. Similarly, Rivera's first talk, which she'll attend with Spivey, can only be Feedback or Information Overload.

Now another classic LSAT concept comes to light: anytime you find yourself saying, It's either this . . . or that, immediately think Limited Options. Blocks make great Limited Options because placing a Block usually fills a significant portion of the game. In this case, placing a Block of two workers accounts for fully a quarter of the game. So, Limited Options are definitely worth doing. Either Block will work, but Rivera's is slightly better because her placement is more constrained than Tran's. Draw the two possibilities, noting that if Rivera's first talk is the fourth of the conference, then her second talk must be Leadership, the only talk left.

Opt. 1

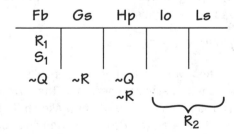

Opt. 2

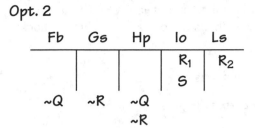

Now consider what else you can deduce in each option. Quigley and Rivera are still limited as before, which is significant in Option 2: With Information Overload full, Quigley must attend Goal Sharing and Leadership.

Opt. 2

Fb	Gs	Hp	Io	Ls
	Q_1		R_1	R_2
			S	Q_2
~Q	~R	~Q		
		~R		

Option 2 is starting to fill up, but Tran and Quigley's Block remains unaccounted for. The only way Tran can partner up with Quigley is to attend Goal Sharing. In that case, since Information Overload and Leadership are already full, Tran must attend Handling People for her second talk.

Opt. 2

Fb	Gs	Hp	Io	Ls
	T_1	T_2	R_1	R_2
	Q_1		S	Q_2
~Q	~R	~Q		
		~R		

The only thing left is Spivey's other talk. Since she can't go with Tran and everything else is full, she must attend Feedback. The entire sketch is complete!

Opt. 2

Fb	Gs	Hp	Io	Ls
S_1	T_1	T_2	R_1	R_2
	Q_1		S_2	Q_2
~Q	~R	~Q		
		~P		

K Part Two: Logic Games
CHAPTER 6

These explanations refer to questions
that begin on page 341.

Option 1 is still open, but you've solved the entire game in Option 2. That's the power of combining Blocks and Limited Options deductions.

Step 5: Questions

34. (C) Acceptability ★☆☆☆

For Acceptability questions, start with the rules and apply them to the choices.

The easiest rule to test is Rule 3: Spivey never attends a talk with Tran. Choice **(A)** violates this rule.

Rules 1 and 2 are the next easiest to test. No choice violates Rule 1, but Rivera attends Handling People in Choice **(B)**, violating Rule 2.

To test Rule 4, find Tran's first talk and make sure Quigley attends it, too. Choice **(D)** violates this rule.

Finally, to test Rule 5, find Rivera's first talk and make sure Spivey is there. Choice **(E)** breaks this rule.

Circle **(C)** and move on.

35. (A) "If" / Must Be True ★★★★

New "Ifs" in a game with Limited Options often limit you to one option or the other. Check for that first, then draw a new sketch if necessary. Handling People can only be empty in Option 1. Looking immediately for a choice that *must be true* in that option, you hit the jackpot in choice **(A)**: Rivera attending Feedback is drawn right into your sketch. Circle it and move on.

The incorrect choices are all statements that may or may not be true in Option 1. Choice **(B)** is wrong because Rivera could avoid Leadership by attending Information Overload instead. Choice **(C)** fails because Spivey could attend either Goal Sharing or Leadership for her other talk. Choices **(D)** and **(E)** don't work because Tran's Block with Quigley could be in either Goal Sharing or Information Overload but doesn't *necessarily* need to be in one or the other, and Tran's second talk can dodge both by being Leadership.

36. (A) Complete and Accurate List ★★★★

Always translate Complete and Accurate List questions into simpler phrasing. This one asks, in so many words, "Which talks could Rivera and Spivey attend together?" Your Limited Options are excellent here.

Rivera and Spivey attend Feedback together in Option 1 and Information Overload in Option 2. Any choice missing one or the other is wrong, so cross out choices **(C)** and **(D)**. The rules prohibit Rivera from attending Goal Sharing, so that eliminates **(B)**. The difference between choices **(A)** and **(E)** is Leadership, which Rivera and Spivey could attend together in Option 1. Circle **(A)** and move on.

37. (D) "If" / Could Be False ★★★☆

Always check the new "If" to see whether it limits you to one option or the other; then draw a new sketch if necessary. Quigley must attend Leadership with Rivera in Option 2, so redraw the Option 1 sketch with Quigley attending Leadership by herself. The rest of the sketch fills in nicely: if Rivera can't join Quigley in Leadership, then the only other place for her is Information Overload. Putting her there leaves Goal Sharing as the only available talk for Tran's Block with Quigley. Finally, since Spivey and Tran can't be together, they must be split across Handling People and Information Overload.

Fb	Gs	Hp	Io	Ls
R_1	T_1	S_2/T_2	R_2	Q_2
S_1	Q_1		S_2/T_2	

You've filled the whole sketch, so take a moment to characterize the answer choices to make sure you don't lose the point with a small mistake. On a Could Be False question, the correct answer could be true or false, but the incorrect answers can *never* be false. Thus, cross out the choices that *must be true*.

(A), **(B)**, **(C)**, and **(E)** directly match information in your sketch and therefore must be true. Only **(D)** could be false: Spivey could attend Information Overload instead, leaving Handling People for Tran. Circle **(D)** and go to the last question.

38. (E) "If" / Could Be False ★★★★

This question works out almost identically to the previous one. As always, check how the new "If" limits your options and draw a new sketch if needed. In Option 2, Rivera attends Information Overload with Spivey, so she can only be there by herself in Option 1. This forces Tran's Block with Quigley into Goal

These explanations refer to questions that begin on page 342.

Part Two: Logic Games
Logic Games Practice

K

Sharing, and Quigley's second session only fits in Leadership. As before, since Spivey and Tran can't be together, they must be split across the two remaining sessions: Handling People and Leadership.

Fb	Gs	Hp	Io	Ls
R_1	T_1	S_2/T_2	R_2	Q_2
S_1	Q_1			S_2/T_2

Once again, the right choice could be true or false, while the incorrect choices must be true. Choices **(A)**, **(B)**, **(C)**, and **(D)** match your sketch directly, so they must be true. Only **(E)** could be false: Tran could attend either Handling People or Leadership. Circle **(E)** and advance to the next game.

Flyhigh and Getaway Airlines

Step 1: Overview

Situation: Flights for two airlines

Entities: Five planes

Action: The overview provides little information other than the entities for the game. However, a quick glance at the first two rules provides the action: Determine the order in which the planes take off (Sequencing) and determine whether each flight is domestic or international (Matching).

Limitations: From the overview, the only limitation is that each plane will take off exactly once. The rules will provide further limitations.

Step 2: Sketch

After the overview, the best that can be done is to list the five entities, separated into their respective subgroups (Flyhigh Airlines and Getaway Airlines). Once the actions are established by the first two rules, the basic sketch for a Sequencing/Matching Hybrid game is to have two rows of five ordered spaces—one row for the five flights and one row for the type of flight:

Flyhigh: P Q Getaway: r s t	1	2	3	4	5
	—	—	—	—	—
dom/int	—	—	—	—	—

Step 3: Rules

Rule 1 establishes that the five flights will take off one at a time, confirming that the Sequencing game action will be a strict 1:1 ratio.

Rule 2 adds the Matching action to the game: Each flight must be categorized as either domestic or international—not both.

Rules 3 and **4** provide some concrete information that defines the flight categorization for P (international), Q (domestic), and r (domestic). For now, this information can be written off to the side in shorthand:

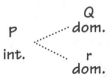

Once the categorizations are determined, **Rule 5** states that all international flights must depart first, then the domestic flights:

$$\text{All int.} \ldots \text{All dom.}$$

Rule 6 requires that any Getaway flights that are domestic must depart before any Flyhigh flight that is domestic.

$$\text{All \textit{Getaway} dom.} \ldots \text{All \textit{Flyhigh} dom.}$$

Step 4: Deductions

The rules for this game are fairly direct and concrete. Therefore, it's important to consider how all of this information can be incorporated into the Master Sketch.

Rules 3, 4, and 5 provide the most helpful information immediately. By Rules 3 and 4, there are already one international flight and two domestic flights. Since all international flights must depart before all domestic flights (by Rule 5), at least the first flight must be

K | Part Two: Logic Games
CHAPTER 6

These explanations refer to questions that begin on page 342.

international, and at least the last two flights must be domestic.

The only international flight determined so far is P, but that doesn't have to be the first flight. If any other flights are international, those could be first.

Of the two domestic flights determined (Q and r), Q must go later because of Rule 6. However, Q is the only possible domestic Flyhigh flight (since the other Flyhigh flight, P, is international). Therefore, by Rule 6, there can't be any flights after Q. So, Q must be the fifth and final flight.

r does not have to be the fourth flight, since any of the other Getaway flights could also be domestic.

Final Visualization

1	2	3	4	5
				Q
int.			dom.	dom.

Step 5: Questions

39. (D) Partial Acceptability ★☆☆☆

Using the Big Deduction made during the game setup, Q must be the fifth and final flight. This eliminates choices **(A)**, **(B)**, and **(C)**. Rule 5 dictates that international flights must depart before domestic flights. Since P is international (by Rule 3) and r is domestic (by Rule 4), that eliminates **(E)**. Thus, **(D)** is the correct answer.

If you missed the Big Deduction early on, you can still use the rules to attack the answer choices. Rule 1 is not violated by any of the answer choices. Rules 2, 3, and 4 focus on the matching aspect of the game, which is not indicated in the answer choices. However, this information will be helpful in testing the later rules.

Rule 5 dictates that international flights must depart before domestic flights. Since P is international (by Rule 3) and r is domestic (by Rule 4), that eliminates **(E)**. Rule 6 dictates that any Getaway domestic flight must depart before Flyhigh's domestic flight. The only Flyhigh domestic flight is Q (by Rule 4), and R is a

Getaway domestic flight (by Rule 4). That eliminates **(A)**, **(B)**, and **(C)**.

That leaves **(D)** as the correct answer—the only one that doesn't violate any of the rules.

40. (D) How Many ★★★★

Using the Big Deduction made during the game setup, Q must be the fifth and final flight. So that leaves four flights that could depart second. If one of Getaway's flights is international, then it could depart first, allowing P to depart second. If all of Getaway's flights are domestic, then any one of them (r, s, or t) could be second. So, with four possible planes that can depart second, **(D)** is the correct answer.

41. (B) "If" / Must Be False ★★☆☆

If s departs sometime before P (an international flight, according to Rule 3), then s must be an international flight (per Rule 5). At this point, the relative order of four of the flights can be determined. Since s and P (in that order) are international, they must depart before domestic flights r and Q (in that order, by Rule 6):

$$s...P...r...Q$$

The only plane not in the sequence is t, which could depart at any time except for fifth (since we deduced that Q is always fifth). Eliminate **(C)**, **(D)**, and **(E)**. Depending on when t takes off, the departing position of the remaining planes can be s first or second; P second or third; r third or fourth; Q fifth.

Since s can only depart first or second, **(B)** is the only answer that must be false.

42. (B) Must Be True ★★☆☆

For this particular question, the correct answer "must be true," and the four wrong answers "could be or must be false."

Based on the deductions made, Q must be the last plane to depart. That makes **(B)** the correct answer. For the record:

(A) is a clever trap, since some people may assume that P is the only international flight and therefore

These explanations refer to questions that begin on page 342.

Part Two: Logic Games
Logic Games Practice

K

must depart first. However, if any Getaway flight is also international, then that flight can depart first.

(C), **(D)**, and **(E)** can all be eliminated using previous work. The answer to the acceptability question shows that r, s, and t could all hold different departure positions than each answer choices indicates.

43. (C) "If" / Could Be True EXCEPT ★★★☆

For the purposes of this particular question, the correct answer "must be false," while the four wrong answers "could be true."

If s is the third flight to depart, there's no definite way of determining whether s is domestic or international.

If s were international, then the first three flights would have to be international (by Rule 5). With two domestic flights already determined (Getaway's r and Flyhigh's Q), the remaining planes would all be international (Flyhigh's P and Getaway's t and s). R and Q would have to depart in that order (by Rule 6), and P and T could depart in any order:

1	2	3	4	5
P/t	t/P	s	r	Q
int.	int.	int.	dom.	dom.

If s were domestic, then t could still be domestic or international, departing in any open position:

1	2	3	4	5
P	t/r	s	r/t	Q
int.	int./dom.	dom.	dom.	dom.

1	2	3	4	5
t	P	s	r	Q
int.	int.	dom.	dom.	dom.

Despite the many possibilities, **(C)** must be false since that would make r and t the two planes to depart fourth and fifth (in some order). However, Q must be the fifth plane to depart, so that cannot happen. That makes **(C)** the correct answer.

Sales Conference Seminars

Step 1: Overview

Situation: Several seminars are presented at a three-day sales training conference.

Entities: Six seminars (three long: H, N, T; three short: g, o, p) and three days

Action: Hybrid-Distribution/Sequencing. At first glance, this seems like a standard Distribution game: determine which seminars will be held each day. However, the overview states that the seminars are given consecutively, suggesting a Sequencing component, making this game a hybrid of both actions.

Limitations: Each seminar will be given exactly once with exactly two seminars each day.

Step 2: Sketch

Start by setting up a Distribution chart. Then, line up slots within each column to account for the Sequencing. When you list the entities, use lowercase and uppercase letters to differentiate between short and long seminars.

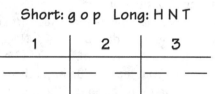

Step 3: Rules

Rule 1 states that each day must have one short and one long seminar. However, it doesn't say which one has to come first. Because of the sequencing component of this game, you can't simply label one slot "short" and one slot "long" in each column, so just write this rule in shorthand off to the side.

Rule 2 provides a sequencing element: Goals and Objections (both short) have to be given before Telemarketing. The shorthand for this rule will be just like in any other sequencing game:

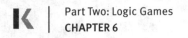

Part Two: Logic Games
CHAPTER 6

These explanations refer to questions
that begin on page 343.

Note that Goals and Objections cannot be on the same day (because of Rule 1). However, nothing in the rule prevents Goals or Objections from being on the same day as Telemarketing, as long as Telemarketing is the second seminar of the day.

Rule 3. This rule provides more sequencing.

$$p \text{ —— } N$$

Again, these two seminars do not have to be on different days. They can be given on the same day with Persuasion first and Negotiating second.

Step 4: Deductions

The first rule greatly limits the placement of Telemarketing. Because it has to be preceded by two short seminars, it can be placed only on either the second or third day of the conference. The placement of Telemarketing affects not only Goals and Objections but also the other two long seminars, Humor and Negotiating. This makes it worth drawing out Limited Options.

In Option I, if Telemarketing is on the second day, Goals and Objections must be the short seminars for days one and two, in either order. Whichever one is on the second day must precede Telemarketing that day. Furthermore, that leaves the last short seminar, Persuasion, for the third day. By Rule 3, Negotiating will also have to be on the third day, with Persuasion coming before it. That leaves Humor as the long seminar for the first day, although the order of the seminars that day cannot be determined.

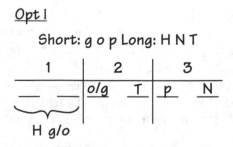

For Option II, Telemarketing goes on the third day. If Telemarketing is on the third day, that leaves Humor and Negotiating as the long seminars for the first and second days. Because Persuasion cannot come after Negotiating (by Rule 3), the short seminar for the third day must be either Goals or Objections. Whichever

one is there must precede Telemarketing on that day (by Rule 1).

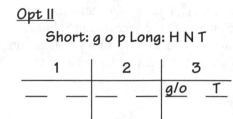

Step 5: Questions

44. (B) Acceptability ★★☆☆

For Acceptability questions, go through the rules one at a time, eliminating answers that violate the rules. Choice **(D)** puts two short seminars, Goals and Objections, on the first day, violating Rule 1. Choice **(A)** puts Goals after Telemarketing, and choice **(E)** puts Objections after Telemarketing. Both answers violate Rule 2. Choice **(C)** has Persuasion after Negotiating, violating Rule 3. That leaves choice **(B)** as the right answer.

45. (E) "If" / Could Be True ★★★★

Option I shows Goals is a possible seminar for day one. That sketch shows Telemarketing is an acceptable seminar for day two, which matches answer choice **(E)**, the correct answer.

Even without Limited Options, you could have gotten this answer. If Goals is on the first day, the other seminar that day will be a long seminar. It can't be Negotiating because that has to come after Persuasion. And it can't be Telemarketing because Telemarketing still needs Objections before it. So, the only long seminar left is Humor. Knowing that Goals and Humor are the two seminars for the first day eliminates answer choices **(A)**, **(B)**, **(C)**, and **(D)**.

46. (C) "If" / Must Be True ★★★★

Putting Negotiating before Objections allows you to combine the two Sequencing rules to create a long string:

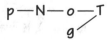

With five of the six entities lined up, the sequencing is very limited. However, based on the answer choices, you

These explanations refer to questions that begin on page 343.

Part Two: Logic Games
Logic Games Practice

don't have to worry about distributing them into the three days. All of the answers refer to the relative sequencing. A quick scan reveals choice **(C)**, which is definitely supported by the sequencing sketch. Answer choices **(A)** and **(B)** could be true based on the sketch but don't have to be true. Answer choices **(D)** and **(E)** both include Humor, which isn't included in the sequencing sketch and therefore has a large amount of freedom.

47. (B) CANNOT / Must Be False ★★★☆

This question asks for a seminar that cannot be the second seminar on day two. The Limited Options show only Telemarketing as a seminar that could definitely be the second seminar on the second day (Option I), but Telemarketing isn't even listed as a possible answer. Anyone who skips this question though and completes the last question of the set before this one will be rewarded with a sketch that shows Humor, Objections, and Goals as possible second seminars for the second day. That would eliminate choices **(A)**, **(C)**, and **(E)**, leaving only choices **(B)** and **(D)** for testing.

To test **(B)**, put Persuasion as the second seminar of the second day. This is only possible in Option II. However, in that case, there would be no room for Negotiating after Persuasion because the third day is filled. That would violate Rule 3. Therefore, choice **(B)** cannot be true, making it the correct answer.

For practice, test answer choice **(D)**. If Negotiating is the second spot on the second day, you must still be in Option II. Persuasion could then go on the morning

of the second day, while Humor and either Objections or Goals could fill the spots in the first day. This would be an acceptable sketch, so **(D)** is incorrect.

48. (D) "If" / Could Be True ★★★☆

Humor could only be scheduled for the second day in the Option II. That would leave Negotiating as the long seminar for the first day. Because Persuasion has to come before Negotiating, it must be the first seminar. That leaves either Goals or Objectives as the short seminar for the second day. The order for the second day doesn't matter.

1		2	3
p	N	H o/g	g/o T

Or

1		2	3
p	N	o/g H	g/o T

With that, only choice **(D)** is possible.

Answer choices **(A)** and **(C)** both contradict Option II by putting Telemarketing on a day other than the third day. The "If" in this question puts Humor, a long seminar, on the second day, so **(B)** cannot be true because Negotiating is also a long seminar, and Rule 1 requires only one long seminar per day. Answer choice **(E)** also contradicts Option II by putting Persuasion on the already full third day.

EXPLANATIONS

CHAPTER 7

Logic Games: Managing the Section

INTRODUCTION

Of the LSAT's four scored sections, Logic Games is worth the fewest points: there are typically 22–24 questions in this section, as opposed to 24–26 questions in each of the two Logical Reasoning sections and 26–28 questions in the Reading Comprehension section. Yet Logic Games is by far the most daunting section for many students, and the anxiety produced by this section can become a distraction that impacts performance on the other sections of the exam as well. Like it or not, though, Logic Games must be dealt with; you want as big a portion of those 22–24 points as you can get, and you certainly don't want this section, the one worth the fewest points, to become a psychological obstacle to doing well on the rest of the test. Even if you like Logic Games and feel confident while doing them, you should by no means take your performance on this section for granted. This chapter will present you with strategies to get the maximum possible points from the Logic Games section, no matter whether you love doing games or not.

LEARNING OBJECTIVES

In this chapter, you'll learn to:

- Become more efficient, and therefore faster, at attacking game setups and questions.
- Prioritize easy games and questions over difficult ones to net the maximum number of points from the Logic Games section.

As you have already learned, the Logic Games section is composed of four separate games, each of which comes with five to seven questions. Each question is worth one point, but they are not equally difficult, and neither are all games equally challenging to set up. Moreover, even games requiring complex deductions typically come with at least one easy question, while games that are comparatively simple to set up typically come with one or more difficult questions. You can see this by breaking down the Logic Games section of PrepTest 62 by difficulty:

Game 1 - Strict Sequencing	
Question	Difficulty Level
1	★
2	★★
3	★★★
4	★★
5	★
6	★★★★

Game 2 - Matching	
Question	Difficulty Level
7	★
8	★★★
9	★★★
10	★★★
11	★★★★
12	★★
13	★★★★

Game 3 - Hybrid: Sequencing-Matching	
Question	Difficulty Level
14	★
15	★★★★
16	★★★★
17	★★★
18	★★★★

Game 4 - Strict Sequencing	
Question	Difficulty Level
19	★
20	★
21	★
22	★★★
23	★★

Students who did the games and questions straight through, in the order in which they appeared in this section, might well have become bogged down by Question 6 or Game 3. Spending too much time on one difficult question costs you time that could have been spent getting easier points. An expert test taker is strategic, skipping or guessing on the most difficult questions when that means getting more of the straightforward ones right. In fact, notice that in PrepTest 62, you could have omitted all the 4-star questions in this section and still netted over 70 percent of the points.

Getting the greatest possible number of points out of the Logic Games section—and feeling confident while doing so—employs two basic skill sets: (1) facility and efficiency in setting up the game and attacking the questions and (2) the ability to discern quickly which games and questions to prioritize. We'll call these twin pillars of Logic Games competence "mastering the games" and "managing the section," respectively.

MASTERING THE GAMES

You've already learned the Logic Games Method. Now it's time to practice the Method until it becomes second nature. If you've been practicing logic games but feel frustrated, determine which of the Method's five steps are still most difficult for you and practice those steps intensively. Are you creating an appropriate sketch but failing to see the deductions? Or are you rushing past the SEAL questions and jumping into the rules before you have a workable sketch? Each step in the method builds upon the previous step: the answers to the SEAL questions tell you the game type, which in turn tells you which type of sketch you need. Then you build the rules into the sketch, and then you combine the rules to make deductions that you use to fill in more of the sketch. Finally, you use your completed Master Sketch to answer the questions. Mastery and consistent application of the Kaplan Method for Logic Games will make you more efficient, and thus faster, as well as more confident.

Overview and Sketch

You have 4 games to do in 35 minutes. That works out to an average of about 8.5 minutes per game. Some games may take you more time and others less, but in all games, if you spend too much time trying to figure out the best possible (or most aesthetically pleasing) sketch, you will waste precious time that you could use to make deductions and answer questions. The answers to the SEAL questions you ask in the Overview step tell you what type of sketch to make. It doesn't need to be pretty; the lines in your sketch don't need to be perfectly parallel, and the letters don't need to be perfectly formed, just legible. If you are a visual perfectionist, try to let go of those tendencies as far as LSAT sketches are concerned. No one other than you will see your sketches; a quick, serviceable sketch (as long as you can read it!) will earn you more points than a beautiful one that takes too long to make. Once you have thoroughly practiced game overviews and sketches, it shouldn't take you more than 60–90 seconds to read the overview paragraph and set up the sketch. There's no need to write down the answers to the SEAL questions; just hold them in your head long enough to create your sketch. Time yourself as you conduct the Overview step and make a sketch for the following game scenario:

Overview	My Analysis
Five cards are dealt from a partial deck of 8 cards (A, B, C, D, E, F, G, H). Each card is exactly one of the following suits: clubs, diamonds, hearts, or spades.	

Now, take a look at the way an LSAT expert conducted the Overview step, using the SEAL questions to focus on those elements directly relevant to creating a serviceable sketch.

Overview	Analysis
Five cards are dealt from a partial deck of 8 cards (A, B, C, D, E, F, G, H). Each card is exactly one of the following suits: clubs, diamonds, hearts, or spades. →	**Step 1:** *Situation*: Dealing out cards *Entities*: Cards (A, B, C, D, E, F, G, H) Suits (c, d, h, s) *Action*: Select 5 cards of 8. Match cards to suits. This is a Selection-Matching Hybrid. *Limitations*: Choose 5 cards. One suit per card. **Step 2:** Draw a Selection sketch with enough room above or below the cards to note the suit of each one as you deduce it: A B C D E F G H _ _ _ _ _ _ _ _ : Suit (c, d, h, s)

Though this example is a Hybrid game, the overview paragraph is very short, and the sketch is uncomplicated. If it took you more than 60 seconds to come up with answers to the SEAL questions and arrive at the sketch, keep practicing these steps.

Rules

It is important to understand that the Logic Games section is testing not only your ability to make deductions, but also your attention to detail. Indeed, the way games are presented, the testmaker has stripped away any unnecessary verbiage. In this regard, the Logic Games section is the diametrical opposite of the Reading Comprehension section, which tests your ability to assimilate the main lines of a passage and identify important details from the passage's structure without getting caught up in the minutiae. Adjust your approaches to those two different sections accordingly.

In practicing logic games, you have most likely already experienced what happens if you misinterpret a rule—or interpret it correctly in your head but write it down incorrectly. The deductions hinge on the rules, so if a rule is incorrectly recorded in your sketch, your deductions will be incorrect as well. Answer the questions based on faulty deductions and you'll lose points and, at some point, find yourself with a question that appears to have more than one right answer (or no right answer at all). The key when going through the rules is precision and accuracy; ask yourself what the rule doesn't mean, just as much as what it does mean, so you don't assume something that the testmaker didn't say. In short, *get it right the first time*. Few things are as frustrating as discovering halfway through the question set that you messed up a rule that caused you to make faulty deductions.

For example, let's say that you encounter the following rule: "C is chosen if B is chosen." If you're reading too quickly, your brain registers the word *if*, and you think, *Aha, that's Formal Logic*, and immediately start scribbling it down, with the entities in the order in which they appear in the sentence: If C → B. But that's not what the rule says. The word *if* isn't in front of the C; it's in front of the B. So B is sufficient for C, and the correct translation is If B → C. Always take the time to read the rules thoroughly. You cannot afford a single mistake here.

Deductions

You've probably noticed by now that while some games have lots of deductions for you to make, other games have very few, if any. The Logic Games Method tells you to make all possible deductions up front and then use those deductions to answer the questions. That's well and good in theory, but how can you tell if you've got them all? How long do you stare at your sketch trying to fill it in before moving on to the questions? It's a thorny issue: rush to the questions, and you may miss deductions that are vital to your efficiency in getting through the question set. Stare at the rules and Master Sketch too long, especially in a game that doesn't allow many deductions, and you'll waste time that you should spend on the questions.

Fortunately, a quick glance at the question set can settle this dilemma. Imagine a question set that consists of nothing but one Acceptability question and five new-"If" questions. You can answer the Acceptability question simply by using the rules; you don't need any deductions there. And each of the new-"If" questions will give you new information that will usually allow you to make all the deductions you need to answer the question. So in this hypothetical game, if you weren't able to make many deductions, you may still be able to answer most or all of the questions correctly. On the other hand, imagine a game that has no Acceptability question and no new-"If" questions at all. This is a rare scenario, but such a game clearly requires deductions for you to answer the questions correctly and efficiently. If you see very few new-"If" questions, and you don't have any deductions, you are most probably missing something. Nevertheless, if you have been through the BLEND acronym and you simply don't see any deductions, go on to the question set anyway. Sometimes you can get a better grasp of the game while doing the questions, and just staring at the rules costs you time.

If you generally have trouble finding all the deductions, target this skill by splitting a logic game in half: do Steps 1–4, then review those steps in the game's explanation. Don't worry about the questions yet. Analyze your work from Overview through Deductions, taking note of any deductions you did not make. (You might even keep track of missed deductions in a notebook; over time, you'll begin to recognize those types of deductions you previously missed.) When you have a solid understanding of the setup, return to the game and do the questions.

Questions

Imagine a question set that contains the following question: "Each of the following could be false EXCEPT." An inefficient test taker's mental process goes something like this: "Could A be false? Gosh, I don't know. What does that even mean? Well, could B be false? Hmm. How about C? Could that be false? I can't tell. Could D or E be false? Gosh, I'd better just guess and go to the next one . . ."

What is wrong with this approach? Note that this student is mechanically about to move on to the next question; he is simply doing the questions in the order in which they appear on the page. Also, note that he checks each answer choice even though he doesn't thoroughly understand what he is looking for.

It is considerably more difficult to think in terms of what could be false than to think in terms of what must be true. Asking yourself whether an answer choice "could be false" is asking your brain to do a task it is not particularly good at. Instead, characterize the choices: If four of them *could be false*, the correct answer *must be true*. You've just changed a daunting task into a much simpler one. You're now simply looking for the one choice that must be true. Characterizing the answer choices is absolutely essential in "must be false" and "could be false" question stems, as well as in EXCEPT questions.

Moreover, there is no need to do the questions in order! Efficient test takers know which questions are likely to be more difficult to answer than others; they prioritize the easy points and leave the tougher ones for later, or skip them entirely in favor of saving time and getting the most points possible out of another game. They also realize that they may be able to consult work from a question they've already answered by noting what was or was not true in that case. How best to prioritize certain questions (and also certain games) belongs to the topic of managing the section and will be discussed below.

Putting It All Together

Given the fact that you'll need to make it through four games in 35 minutes on Test Day, you will have an average of 8–9 minutes to do each game. Many students stumble where timing is concerned and conclude that they are simply "not fast enough." But LSAT success is more a matter of efficiency than a matter of speed, and you can improve your timing incrementally. Once your practice has you feeling solid in how to use the Logic Games Method, start timing yourself on individual games. If it takes you longer, on average, than 8–9 minutes to get through a game—and keep in mind that some games will take longer, and others less time, depending on their difficulty levels—then isolate the problem by using a stopwatch to note how long it takes you to get as far as the Deductions step and how long it takes you to do the questions. If you spend longer than 2½ minutes setting up a game that provides for no big deductions or longer than four minutes setting up a game that allows for many deductions, keep practicing steps 1–4. On the other hand, if you are on pace making deductions but lose time on the question set, then time yourself on each individual question; you may find that you spend an inordinate amount of time on one or two questions that could be skipped. The next section of this chapter discusses the relative difficulty level of different question types and how to get the most points out of each question set in the time allotted.

MANAGING THE SECTION

Clearly, if you had a bit more time to complete the Logic Games section, or if that section contained, say, only two games instead of four and fewer questions, you would almost surely answer a higher percentage of questions correctly. But the timing restriction is real, and it can affect your accuracy: Your performance on a logic game given unlimited time is probably *not* indicative of your performance on that same logic game under timed conditions. Remember that time restrictions put pressure on everyone—you and your competition alike. By learning to manage the Logic Games section, you can outperform less well-trained test takers and turn an obstacle into an advantage.

To make the best of the exam's stringent time constraint, remember that every question counts the same; every question that you answer correctly adds one point to your raw score, no matter whether it was easy or difficult, and *no matter how much time it took you to answer*. So if you spend three to four minutes on a single high-difficulty question and get it right, that's one point for your raw score—but if you had used those three to four minutes to answer four low-difficulty questions instead, that would be four points for your raw score. Every question carries with it the risk that you won't be able to answer it correctly, of course—but that risk is much lower for easy questions than for hard ones. Moreover, the potential reward for attempting easy questions is greater than the reward for attempting hard questions because you can do several easy questions in the same amount of time it takes you to do a single difficult question. Prioritizing easy questions over hard ones, then, is a no-brainer. So is developing your sense of timing: you need to know how far into the section you are, how much time you have left, and how you will use that time most wisely to get the most points.

Learning solid section management skills, however, takes practice. You'll need to learn which questions and games to skip and which ones to do first. You'll need to learn to let go of questions when it becomes clear that the correct answer is not worth investing "just another minute or so" and to let go of an entire game when it becomes clear that you don't know how to set it up, or else that you have set it up incorrectly. Remember that what you actually do on Test Day will be what you have been practicing in the preceding weeks and months. If you have not practiced good section management, then you will not make good and timely decisions about what to do and what to skip when you sit for the real exam. To maximize the effectiveness of your practice, you should set tangible goals for yourself every time you do a practice Logic Games section or take a full-length practice test, such as "I will not spend longer than one minute on any given question." Once you set your goal, be sure to hold yourself to it by recording your actions as you move through the section. For example, if your goal the next time you take a practice test is to spend one minute or less on any given question, then use a stopwatch to record exactly how long each question actually takes you, and once you finish the test, assess how close you came to achieving your goal.

Best Practices for Section Management: Game Triage

Managing the Logic Games section begins when you turn the page and see the first game. Because some games are more difficult to set up than others, it makes sense to start with the easiest one and to save the most difficult for last. There are a number of strategies that you can use; which one you choose will be personal to you, but be sure to stick to one game triage strategy during your practice so that it becomes second nature by Test Day.

The simplest triage strategy is to do the games in the order in which they are presented but to scan each game quickly before you start setting it up and to skip games that you feel will be more time-consuming than average. Your thinking might go something like this: "Okay, this first one looks like a straightforward Strict Sequencing game. I like those. I'll do this one," or "This second one is a Hybrid, and those tend to give me trouble, so I'll skip it for now." You should still plan to allocate your time so that you will have time to come back to the games you skipped, but you'll have grabbed the easier points by then—and your confidence will have received a boost as a result.

If you like to know what you're up against from the beginning, you might prefer a different triage strategy: scan all four games before you actually start any of them. Make two decisions: which game do you think will be easiest, and which do you think will be the most difficult? Start with the easiest and leave the most difficult for last. A variation of this strategy would be to start with the first game, which is nearly always one of the two easiest games for most students, and then scan the three remaining games and order them by difficulty.

It may also be efficient to do the games in the order in which they appear and simply skip the hardest questions in each one. Do be aware, though, that the games are not usually printed in precise order of increasing difficulty. (The two most common patterns, in order of increasing difficulty, are 1-2-4-3 and 2-1-3-4, with 1-2-3-4 just a little less common). And if you have trouble (even sporadically) setting up games and making deductions, then it would be more advisable to use one of the other approaches just mentioned.

So what makes a game more or less difficult? There are three criteria: (1) familiarity and preference, (2) simplicity and brevity, and (3) concreteness.

Familiarity and Preference

By the time of your official LSAT Test Day, you will feel more comfortable with certain game types than with others. You may have practiced more Sequencing games than other game types, for instance, and therefore feel confident in your mastery of them. Alternatively, you may have a preference for Selection games because you enjoy Formal Logic, or you may like Distribution games because Distribution sketches make intuitive sense to you. Different test takers display different preferences, and that's fine. Whatever your favorite game type, make a habit of prioritizing it over game types that you are less comfortable with.

As you practice, you may also develop a predilection for games that allow many deductions or, alternatively, for games that allow few deductions—and again, you should definitely prioritize whichever kind you feel more comfortable with. You can recognize a game that likely allows many deductions by the presence of two or more non-"If" Must Be True or Must Be False questions in the question set. Conversely, you can recognize a game that probably doesn't allow many deductions by the presence of many new-"If" questions.

Simplicity and Brevity

Single-action games are generally (though not always) easier than Hybrid games, so other factors being equal, it is logical to prioritize single-action games over Hybrids. Moreover, games that have a very long overview paragraph tend to be more complex than games with a short overview paragraph, and games with five or more rules are often more challenging than games with fewer rules. However, more rules frequently allow more deductions, so if you prefer games that allow more deductions, you may want to prioritize games with more rules over games with fewer.

Concreteness

Watch for words like *exactly*, *only*, *just*, *precisely*, or *always*. Games that include concrete terms like this are typically easier than games that have more unknowns. For example, imagine a game that asks you to select "exactly" five entities from seven versus a game that asks you to select "at most" five entities from seven. The latter game could have zero, one, two, three, four, or five selected entities. That produces a great many more possibilities than if the number you are asked to select is "exactly" five.

Best Practices for Section Management: Strategic Skipping of Questions

Talking about section management presents a paradox. You are studying and practicing in order to master logic games, and the ideal outcome would be to get so fast and so confident that you can roar through the section and get the majority of points without breaking a sweat. But the reality is that time will remain an issue for most students, and you may have to skip or guess on at least a few questions. The solution is to realize that you are in control of your time and you are the one that chooses which questions to tackle and the order in which to tackle them. Skipping or guessing *strategically* is not a failure but a success.

Strategic Guessing

Many students guess only when they feel defeated by a question (and that usually means after they've spent too much time with it already). In turn, bubbling in a guess worsens their sinking confidence. But when done properly, guessing is empowering and will raise your score. We noted at the very beginning of this chapter that even the most difficult games come with easy questions and that even the easiest games come with difficult questions. Now, let's say that your target on Logic Games is 18 correct. In a section that has four games, each with six questions, you could theoretically get those 18 points by doing only three games and getting every question correct—but because even easy games often come with one or more high-difficulty questions, getting every single question correct for each game is quite a challenge, at least within the allotted time. An alternate approach to getting those 18 points is to do all four games but to consciously choose to skip the most difficult one or two questions in each game. Purposely skipping the hardest questions means that you'll have more time to answer the easier ones—and you will be more likely to get them right. Strategic skipping also puts you in the driver's seat: Instead of allowing the section to control you, you are taking control of how you attack the section. Strategic guessing thus helps you to get the maximum possible points from the section, and it also boosts your confidence. It's a winning combination.

Strategic Ordering of Questions

So which questions are the ones you should do, and which should you skip? In what order should you approach those questions that you choose to do? This will be determined largely by what you know about the game after you complete Steps 1–4 of the Logic Games Method. If you've made strong, certain deductions, you can anticipate at least one or two Must Be True–type questions that will reward your analysis. If the game is still open-ended, you will look to the new-"If" questions to add concreteness. You cannot separate a strategic approach to the question set from a methodical approach to the game. That said, here are some general guidelines to manage the question set:

Acceptability Questions

Most games have one Acceptability question, and it is usually the first question in the set. Even in cases where Acceptability appears later in the set, get into the habit of doing Acceptability questions first. Done the right way— that is, by using the rules to knock out the incorrect choices (Chapter 5)—an Acceptability question should take no more than 30 seconds. If you've interpreted the rules correctly, Acceptability questions yield an easy point, and doing the Acceptability question first also reaffirms your understanding of the rules and thus of the game.

New-"If" Questions

Most new-"If" questions provide a new condition that you can build into a new mini sketch supplementing the game's original rules. More restriction means more concreteness, and that will be helpful, especially in a game that gave you few solid deductions up front. Keep in mind that the second clause of a new-"If" question stem may range from "then which of the following must be true" to "then each of the following must be false EXCEPT," tasks that vary in difficulty. However, given that the "If" clause adds certainty, you'll often find these good questions to tackle right after the Acceptability question. Moreover, keep in mind that question stems with affirmative restrictions (such as "If P is placed in space 3") add more concreteness than those with negative restrictions (such as "If P is not placed in space 5"). Because you are likely to create a mini sketch illustrating one possible solution for the game, you can sometimes use new-"If" sketches to help answer open-ended Could Be True or Must Be False questions as well.

Must Be True/Must Be False Questions

Questions that ask for what must be true or false are usually based on a game's deductions. If you have been able to make solid deductions, then do these questions immediately after the Acceptability question; it will simply be a matter of scanning the choices for what you already know to be true. As we said a moment ago, however, if you have not been able to make deductions, then postpone these questions and prioritize new-"If" questions, as the mini sketches for this latter question type often gives you a better grasp of the game. At all times, remember to characterize what a question stem calls for. An open-ended stem telling you "each of the following could be false EXCEPT" is really just a Must Be True question. Likewise, a stem that asks "Which of the following CANNOT be in space 3?" is a Must Be False question targeted to a specific slot within your framework.

Could Be True/Could Be False Questions

These questions are not always difficult, but they can be time-consuming if your approach amounts to drawing out five new sketches to test the five answer choices. In games with new-"If" questions, you are often rewarded for postponing these questions until you have some additional sketches to consult. Remember, if you've seen that a given condition could be true in one of the mini sketches, then it amounts to a correct answer for an open-ended Could Be True question (or a wrong answer for a Must Be False question, for that matter). In any event, you must characterize the one right and four wrong answer choices clearly to take full control over Could Be True/Could Be False questions. If you wind up guessing on a Could Be question, choose a Floater or largely unrestricted entity.

Complete and Accurate List Questions

These questions can be very easy in a game with a fairly complete Master Sketch, such as a Limited Options game. However, if your sketch is blank, postpone Complete and Accurate List questions until you have some previous work to help you.

Completely Determine Questions

Questions that ask you for a condition that will determine the placement of every single entity are potentially time-consuming because they may require you to check every answer choice. These questions are best postponed and are good candidates for skipping.

Rule Change and Rule Suspension Questions

These questions look like new-"If"s, but instead of adding a new rule to the ones that already exist—which does not change your original deductions—Rule Changers ask you to swap in a new rule to replace one of the original rules, while Rule Suspenders invalidate one of the original rules. Your Master Sketch is built using deductions made from the original rules, so changing or discarding one of those rules invalidates your deductions and thus your Master Sketch. Rule Changers and Rule Suspenders require a unique sketch constructed one rule at a time, just like the original Master Sketch, and are therefore time-consuming. Unless you are consistently able to get through all of the questions in the Logic Games section and to get the vast majority of them right, skip and guess on these questions.

Rule Substitution Questions

These questions ask for a rule that, if substituted for one of the original rules, would have the same effect as the original rule. They require careful analysis of the effect that the original rule has on the entire game, as well as the ability to recognize the answer choice that has precisely that same effect. These are highly challenging questions and are best skipped by all but the most expert test takers. It is worth noting that these questions almost always appear at the end of a game's question set, so they take your time precisely at the moment when you could move on to the next game and rack up its points. That makes them great reminders to never allow a single question to derail your timing for an entire Logic Games section. Fortunately, you will likely see only one question like this in a given section, if you see one at all.

Best Practices for Section Management: Time Management

Even if you are triage games brilliantly and your question-skipping strategy is perfect, you may still lose easy points if you have no sense of how much time you have used or how much remains.

If you can get through individual games in an average of 8–9 minutes and answer most of the questions correctly but still get caught short when you do an entire Logic Games section, try using a stopwatch and writing down the time at which you finish each game. Doing this will make you more aware of timing and will also present you with a record of exactly which games slowed you down.

You should also develop an appropriate bubbling strategy. Some students prefer to bubble in each answer as they arrive at it, but reaching for your grid at every question is likely to break your concentration (and thus indirectly cost you time). Moreover, if you do questions out of order (as you should!), you may make bubbling mistakes if you grid each question as you answer it. Try bubbling in the responses for each game after you finish the entire game, and talk to yourself (silently, of course) as you do so to prevent needless errors: "Question 1 is (A); 2 is (D); 3, I'm skipping for now; 4 is (B)," and so on.

Above all, be honest with yourself. If you repeatedly score 14–16 points on a Logic Games section under timed conditions, don't assume that it will be different on Test Day—and definitely don't switch to an untested strategy on Test Day in the hope that doing so will magically make you more efficient. If you want more points than you currently get out of the section, pinpoint exactly where the problem lies: Is it less-than-perfect mastery of the method? Is it an inability to triage games correctly? Is it a tendency to get stuck on a single question? Is it a poor sense of timing? We discuss some common problems below, but remember that everyone is different. Only you can ascertain exactly what is keeping you from achieving your dream performance in Logic Games.

COMMON FRUSTRATIONS—DIAGNOSING YOUR ISSUE AND WAYS TO IMPROVE

What follows is a description of four archetypal students: "The Anxious One," "The Rusher," "The Perfectionist," and "The Incomplete Sketch Malcontent." Chances are that none of these imaginary students will describe you perfectly, but do ask yourself whether any of their problems apply to you—and if they do, then try out the recommended fixes.

The Anxious One

Some test takers find logic games much easier to understand and complete when there are no timing restrictions, but the moment the clock starts ticking, anxiety kicks in and overwhelms their ability to concentrate. A student who is thinking about perceived time pressure is not really focusing on the game at hand. An unfortunate negative feedback loop can result: time pressure produces anxiety, which reduces concentration, which means a reduced grasp of the games, which in turn results in more anxiety, and so on. In extreme cases, timing anxiety can bleed from the section inducing it (in this case, Logic Games) into the remainder of the exam: "Oh no, I bombed that section, I have to make it up on this next section . . . . But I'm not really concentrating well, and that's bad, because Logical Reasoning is usually my strong suit . . . (etc.)." Timing anxiety is a grave problem that can cause a test taker to score significantly lower than he or she should.

One fix for this problem uses a two-step process: (1) mastery of the Logic Games Method and (2) incremental work on timing. Once the Method is so ingrained that it has become second nature, confidence naturally follows and anxiety decreases. Mastery of the Method automatically brings greater efficiency and, hence, greater speed. Indeed, the only way to become faster while maintaining accuracy is to become more efficient. (See "The Rusher" below.) So practice at your own pace until you do games fairly automatically. Then start to work on timing as follows. Do individual games, not entire sections. Split each game in half. The first time, get as far as the deductions step, then write down how long it took you to finish making deductions. Now proceed to the question set and write down how long that took; also note the order in which you did the questions and if there were specific questions that took longer than one minute. Next, work incrementally to become more efficient. For instance, if a game setup takes you seven minutes at first, analyze where in the process you were inefficient (e.g., overlooking a limitation or a duplicated entity) and then try to do the next one in 6½ minutes by correcting this inefficiency. Repeat this exercise and you will become more efficient, bit by bit, in your setups. Likewise, become more efficient at the question set; look for inefficiencies in your approach, such as spending two minutes on a Could Be True question that you could have answered nearly instantly had you first completed one of the new-"If" questions. Once you can set up the game in 4 minutes or less and answer the questions you choose to do in five minutes or less, you're ready to start practicing complete 35-minute timing sections.

Once you start on full sections, treat each section not as one continuous period of 35 minutes but as 4 chunks of 8–9 minutes each. Because games will take different amounts of time, it is best to try to complete the easiest game in less than eight minutes in order to bank a little time for the most difficult game. Set a goal that you think is manageable: say, one minute for triage, 6–7 minutes for the easiest game, 8½ minutes for each of the medium difficulty games, and 10–11 minutes for the most difficult game. Use a watch to note the time when each game is completed (for example, 7:19, 16:02, etc.) Writing down the time will make you more aware of where you are in the section and will also serve as a record of where in the section you became bogged down.

The Rusher

This is a student who confuses speed and efficiency. "I have to do four games in 35 minutes, so I'll have to go really, really fast! That means I don't have time to do all this rule transcribing. I'll just make a quick sketch framework, and I'll keep the rules in my head." Unfortunately, skipping steps of the Logic Games Method inevitably wastes time and reduces efficiency. Trying to keep the rules in your head, or skipping the deductions step, or failing to make a separate sketch for a new-"If" question leads to confusion, which costs both time and accuracy.

The best way to fix this problem is to shift your sense of urgency: scoring well in Logic Games is not about going faster but about using the minimum possible number of steps to arrive at correct answers. Trust the Logic Games Method you learned in previous chapters; it is constructed for maximum efficiency. Err on the side of using your pencil more, rather than less: making a separate sketch for a new-"If" question only takes a few seconds, while trying to do the question in your head may result in several false starts, as well as a higher probability of an incorrect answer.

The Perfectionist

Certain students get stuck on individual questions that they believe they should be able to answer correctly. It is essentially a matter of an ego battle with the question "How can there possibly be two correct answers to this question? I can't imagine I made a mistake somewhere. I mean, this rule is correctly transcribed, and this deduction is also right, and my previous work from this other question shows xyz to be true. I'm not making a mistake! The test must be making a mistake!" As discussed previously, there are a few questions in any given Logic Games section that are written to be exceptionally difficult. It would be a shame to spend months studying for the LSAT but to get a low score because you were tripped up by one of these high-difficulty questions and couldn't let it go.

The fix for this problem is very simple: if you've spent longer than a minute on a given question, *move on*.

The Incomplete Sketch Malcontent

The same sort of "ego battle" can take place in the deductions step. You may feel that you cannot move on to the questions until you've made every available deduction. On the other side of the coin, you may feel that you've wasted time looking for additional deductions that aren't there. When should you let go of trying to make more deductions? Quite simply, when you have looked for them in the logical places—duplicated entities, numbers limitations (in short, those elements of BLEND that apply to the game you are working on)—and you don't see any more deductions. As we discussed earlier in this chapter, the question set will give you some indication of whether or not you are likely missing deductions—but whether or not you are, *move on*. Often the question set will give you a better handle on the game. For example, imagine a Sequencing game that includes the following question: "Which of the following must be fifth?" If the fifth slot in your sketch is blank, but you have several excluded entities noted beneath it (ones that show up in the answer choices), doing this question might get you a relatively quick point and might also give you a deduction that you can use while you complete the remaining questions.

Chances are that none of these four imaginary students is exactly like you. Nevertheless, you can probably glean one or more useful suggestions to improve your Logic Games score from these accounts. Ultimately, whatever your personal obstacles to stellar Logic Games performance, it is up to you to ferret them out and do what is needed to overcome them. Be brutally honest in your assessment and attack those issues that you discover head on. Your efforts will be rewarded on Test Day.

CHAPTER 8

The Kaplan Logical Reasoning Method

The most important skills you'll learn and master for the LSAT are those pertaining to the Logical Reasoning sections. The reason is pretty clear: With two scored sections on every test, Logical Reasoning accounts for half of your LSAT score. Recent Logical Reasoning sections have had 25 or 26 questions, but unlike Logic Games and Reading Comprehension questions, each question in the Logical Reasoning section is self-contained. The questions may ask you to identify what is missing in a short argument or ask you to identify a fact that would strengthen or weaken the argument. Other Logical Reasoning questions reward you for describing an argument's logical flaw or its author's argumentative strategy. Still others contain no argument but instead ask you to draw valid deductions from a set of statements or to pinpoint which of five facts resolves a discrepancy. In Chapters 9, 10, and 11, you'll learn to identify each of the Logical Reasoning question types, and you'll practice all of the skills you need to answer them quickly and accurately. In this chapter, however, we'll focus on two features that all Logical Reasoning questions have in common: (1) their overall structure and (2) the way their incorrect answer choices are devised.

LOGICAL REASONING QUESTION FORMAT AND THE KAPLAN LOGICAL REASONING METHOD

The first and most important commonality among LSAT Logical Reasoning questions is their structure. Every Logical Reasoning question will begin with a *stimulus*, usually a paragraph-length argument or set of assertions. The stimulus is the text you need to untangle or analyze in order to understand the author's argument or his set of premises. Below the stimulus is the *question stem*, the specific question or task the LSAT is posing for you in relation to the stimulus. Finally, there are always five *answer choices*, exactly one of which is correct, while the other four are demonstrably incorrect.

The Kaplan Logical Reasoning Method leverages the consistent structure of Logical Reasoning questions to allow you to approach each one in the most efficient and effective manner possible.

THE KAPLAN LOGICAL REASONING METHOD

Step 1: Identify the Question Type

Step 2: Untangle the Stimulus

Step 3: Predict the Correct Answer

Step 4: Evaluate the Answer Choices

There is nothing abstract about this approach. In fact, take a look at the Method mapped onto a Logical Reasoning question and you'll see just how, well, logical this way of attacking the questions is.

Mayor: Local antitobacco activists are calling for expanded antismoking education programs paid for by revenue from heavily increased taxes on cigarettes sold in the city. Although the effectiveness of such education programs is debatable, there is strong evidence that <the taxes themselves would produce the sought-after reduction in smoking.> Surveys show that cigarette sales drop substantially in cities that impose stiff tax increases on cigarettes.

Which one of the following, if true, most undermines the reasoning in the argument above?

(A) A city-imposed tax on cigarettes will substantially reduce the amount of smoking in the city if the tax is burdensome to the average cigarette consumer.

(B) Consumers are more likely to continue buying a product if its price increases due to higher taxes than if its price increases for some other reason.

(C) Usually, cigarette sales will increase substantially in the areas surrounding a city after that city imposes stiff taxes on cigarettes.

(D) People who are well informed about the effects of long-term tobacco use are significantly less likely to smoke than are people who are not informed.

(E) Antismoking education programs that are funded by taxes on cigarettes will tend to lose their funding if they are successful.

PrepTest52 Sec3 Q6

Step 1: Identify the Question Type
Start here, so you know what to look for in the stimulus.

Step 2: Untangle the Stimulus
Zero in on what is relevant. Here, the entire question can be answered from just the circled and underlined text.

Step 3: Predict the Correct Answer
In your own words, state what the correct answer must say.

Step 4: Evaluate the Answer Choices
Identify the answer that matches your prediction. Eliminate those that do not.

Notice that the LSAT expert always starts with the question stem. After all, there's no reason to read through the stimulus unless you know what you're looking for. As you learn to identify the various Logical Reasoning questions used by the testmaker, you'll start to recognize words and phrases that signal your task and, in turn, you'll be able to anticipate the relevant portions of the stimulus before you untangle its sometimes dense prose.

Note, too, that the LSAT expert takes a moment to reflect on the information from the stimulus and to predict the correct answer before wading into the answer choices. If you've taken the LSAT before picking up this book, you know that tackling the answer choices unprepared can lead you to reread the stimulus over and over, double-checking what it said and comparing it to each choice. The Method you'll learn here avoids all of that unnecessary repetition. By predicting the meaning or content of the correct answer first, you can evaluate each choice by asking, "Does this match my prediction?" If not, eliminate that answer choice. If it matches your prediction, you've got the right answer.

Let's walk through a Logical Reasoning question step-by-step and see the LSAT expert's analysis as it develops using this approach.

LSAT Question	Analysis
Mayor: Local antitobacco activists are calling for expanded antismoking education programs paid for by revenue from heavily increased taxes on cigarettes sold in the city. Although the effectiveness of such education programs is debatable, there is strong evidence that the taxes themselves would produce the sought-after reduction in smoking. Surveys show that cigarette sales drop substantially in cities that impose stiff tax increases on cigarettes.	
Which one of the following, if true, most undermines the reasoning in the argument above? $\longrightarrow$	**Step 1:** The right answer will undermine the author's reasoning—a Weaken question. I need to analyze the argument in the stimulus.
(A) A city-imposed tax on cigarettes will substantially reduce the amount of smoking in the city if the tax is burdensome to the average cigarette consumer.	
(B) Consumers are more likely to continue buying a product if its price increases due to higher taxes than if its price increases for some other reason.	
(C) Usually, cigarette sales will increase substantially in the areas surrounding a city after that city imposes stiff taxes on cigarettes.	
(D) People who are well informed about the effects of long-term tobacco use are significantly less likely to smoke than are people who are not informed.	
(E) Antismoking education programs that are funded by taxes on cigarettes will tend to lose their funding if they are successful.	
PrepTest52 Sec3 Q6	

You'll learn all about Strengthen and Weaken questions in Chapter 10. For now, follow the LSAT expert as he untangles the lengthy argument in the stimulus.

LSAT Question	Analysis
Mayor: Local antitobacco activists are calling for expanded antismoking education programs paid for by revenue from heavily increased taxes on cigarettes sold in the city. Although the effectiveness of such education programs is debatable, there is strong evidence that the taxes themselves would produce the sought-after reduction in smoking. Surveys show that cigarette sales drop substantially in cities that impose stiff tax increases on cigarettes.	**Step 2:** Conclusion: Higher taxes will result in a decrease in smoking in the city. *because* → Evidence: Cigarette sales drop in cities with high cigarette taxes. The part about the taxes being spent for tobacco education is a distraction, since the author thinks the taxes themselves will reduce smoking whether the education program is effective or not.
Which one of the following, if true, most undermines the reasoning in the argument above?	**Step 1:** The right answer will undermine the author's reasoning—a Weaken question. I need to analyze the argument in the stimulus.

(A)   A city-imposed tax on cigarettes will substantially reduce the amount of smoking in the city if the tax is burdensome to the average cigarette consumer.

(B)   Consumers are more likely to continue buying a product if its price increases due to higher taxes than if its price increases for some other reason.

(C)   Usually, cigarette sales will increase substantially in the areas surrounding a city after that city imposes stiff taxes on cigarettes.

(D)   People who are well informed about the effects of long-term tobacco use are significantly less likely to smoke than are people who are not informed.

(E)   Antismoking education programs that are funded by taxes on cigarettes will tend to lose their funding if they are successful.

PrepTest52 Sec3 Q6

As you'll see in the upcoming chapters, your reading and untangling of the stimulus will vary, depending on the type of information relevant to the answer. Here, because the LSAT expert recognized this as a Weaken question, he focused on analyzing the mayor's argument. In particular, he zeroed in on the mayor's reason for believing that the new antismoking education tax will reduce smoking in the city. Now, the expert is ready to predict the correct answer.

LSAT Question	**Analysis**
Mayor: Local antitobacco activists are calling for expanded antismoking education programs paid for by revenue from heavily increased taxes on cigarettes sold in the city. Although the effectiveness of such education programs is debatable, there is strong evidence that the taxes themselves would produce the sought-after reduction in smoking. Surveys show that cigarette sales drop substantially in cities that impose stiff tax increases on cigarettes.	**Step 2:** Conclusion: Higher taxes will result in a decrease in smoking in the city. *because* Evidence: Cigarette sales drop in cities with high cigarette taxes. The part about the taxes being spent for tobacco education is a distraction, since the author thinks the taxes themselves will reduce smoking whether the education program is effective or not.
Which one of the following, if true, most undermines the reasoning in the argument above?	**Step 1:** The right answer will undermine the author's reasoning—a Weaken question. I need to analyze the argument in the stimulus.
	Step 3: Citing evidence that cigarette sales decline within cities that impose cigarette taxes, the mayor concludes that the new tax in her city will reduce smoking. The correct answer will weaken that argument by offering a fact that suggests people in the city will continue to smoke as much as ever, even if they buy fewer cigarettes in the city.

(A) A city-imposed tax on cigarettes will substantially reduce the amount of smoking in the city if the tax is burdensome to the average cigarette consumer.

(B) Consumers are more likely to continue buying a product if its price increases due to higher taxes than if its price increases for some other reason.

(C) Usually, cigarette sales will increase substantially in the areas surrounding a city after that city imposes stiff taxes on cigarettes.

(D) People who are well informed about the effects of long-term tobacco use are significantly less likely to smoke than are people who are not informed.

(E) Antismoking education programs that are funded by taxes on cigarettes will tend to lose their funding if they are successful.

PrepTest52 Sec3 Q6

After you read the expert's prediction in Step 3, look back at the question stem for a moment. The words "if true" tell you to treat each of the answer choices as a fact. The correct answer is a fact that attacks the mayor's reasoning. The expert cannot anticipate the exact fact the test will offer, but his prediction is tailored to evaluate the answer choices effectively. The correct answer will undermine the connection between a drop in cigarette *sales* within the city and a drop in *smoking* within the city. The wrong answers will either miss this connection or make it stronger. In any event, the correct answer will weaken the argument, and the four wrong answers will not.

LSAT Question	Analysis
Mayor: Local antitobacco activists are calling for expanded antismoking education programs paid for by revenue from heavily increased taxes on cigarettes sold in the city. Although the effectiveness of such education programs is debatable, there is strong evidence that the taxes themselves would produce the sought-after reduction in smoking. Surveys show that cigarette sales drop substantially in cities that impose stiff tax increases on cigarettes.	**Step 2:** Conclusion: Higher taxes will result in a decrease in smoking in the city. *because* Evidence: Sales drop in cities with high cigarette taxes. The part about the taxes being spent for tobacco education is a distraction, since the author thinks the taxes themselves will reduce smoking whether the education program is effective or not.
Which one of the following, if true, most undermines the reasoning in the argument above?	**Step 1:** The right answer will undermine the author's reasoning—a Weaken question. I need to analyze the argument in the stimulus.
	Step 3: Citing evidence that cigarette sales decline within cities that impose cigarette taxes, the mayor concludes that the new tax in her city will reduce smoking. The correct answer will weaken that argument by offering a fact that suggests people in the city will continue to smoke as much as ever, even if they buy fewer cigarettes in the city.
(A) A city-imposed tax on cigarettes will substantially reduce the amount of smoking in the city if the tax is burdensome to the average cigarette consumer.	**Step 4:** This answer makes the mayor's argument stronger. It's a 180 answer because it does the opposite of what the question stem calls for. Eliminate.
(B) Consumers are more likely to continue buying a product if its price increases due to higher taxes than if its price increases for some other reason.	This is an Irrelevant Comparison answer. The mayor's evidence establishes that higher cigarette taxes in a city result in reduced sales there. The fact that sales would go down even more if the price rose for other reasons has no impact on her argument. Eliminate.
(C) Usually, cigarette sales will increase substantially in the areas surrounding a city after that city imposes stiff taxes on cigarettes.	Correct. If the smokers in the city just go outside the city limits to buy their cigarettes, it's less likely that the new tax will result in decreased smoking.
(D) People who are well informed about the effects of long-term tobacco use are significantly less likely to smoke than are people who are not informed.	This choice is an Irrelevant Comparison. The mayor argues that the taxes themselves will cause a decrease in smoking. This choice supports antismoking education efforts, something the mayor treats as an aside. Eliminate.
(E) Antismoking education programs that are funded by taxes on cigarettes will tend to lose their funding if they are successful. *PrepTest52 Sec3 Q6*	This choice is Outside the Scope. The mayor's point is that taxes will reduce smoking. In that case, the antismoking education program would be irrelevant anyway. Eliminate.

There you see the Method in action. As you practice it on the various question types, you'll find that you'll get faster and more accurate throughout the Logical Reasoning section. For the sake of completeness, we included the analysis of all five answer choices, but the fact is, on the test, our LSAT expert would have been able to stop evaluating the answer choices as soon as he reached (C). That's the power of making a prediction in Step 3. It's a bit like making a list of features you must have in a new car before you go to the dealership. You're able to rule out any number of choices that won't fit your needs and zero in on the model that's going to make you happy. It won't happen on every Logical Reasoning question, but with practice, you'll find that, on a majority of questions, you're able to anticipate the correct answer before you assess the answer choices.

Notice, too, that the expert has mentally labeled the wrong answer choices, describing why each one does not fit what's called for by the question stem: choice (A) strengthened the argument instead of weakening it; choice (B) made a comparison about consumer behavior in two different cases, one of which didn't apply to the argument; choice (D) made an Irrelevant Comparison about the likelihood that different groups will smoke; and (E) was Outside the Scope. This brings us to the second universal feature of LSAT Logical Reasoning questions: the test uses the same kinds of wrong answers over and over again.

WRONG ANSWERS IN LOGICAL REASONING QUESTIONS

The LSAT is nothing if not consistent. Each test administration offers the same sections and question types, designs logic games from a small pool of actions, and even draws on much the same subject matter for passages and stimuli. It's no surprise, then, that the testmaker repeatedly employs the same types of wrong answers as well. Because, on the LSAT, you get points only for selecting and bubbling in the correct answer, you may wonder why it's valuable to label the wrong answers by type. It is valuable because recognizing the common wrong answer patterns will make you more confident (and thus faster) when you eliminate choices.

Many students, when they practice, will simply check to see if they got a question right. If so, they'll move on, ignoring any analysis of the wrong answers. On Test Day, that's fine—get the right answer and go. But in practice, take the time to review the wrong answers as well. By doing so, you'll internalize the patterns—even the words and phrases—that repeatedly identify incorrect choices.

Take a look at three more Logical Reasoning questions worked out with the expert analysis. Read them through in order, from Step 1 through Step 4, so that you start to get the rhythm of the method. This time, though, pay special attention to the analysis of each wrong answer. At the end of these examples, we'll distill a list of the most common wrong answer types in Logical Reasoning. As you work through subsequent chapters, you'll see these same types of distractors appear over and over again, and in no time you'll be eliminating wrong answers without having to reread and double-check the stimulus to assuage your doubts.

LSAT Question	Analysis
Beck: Our computer program estimates municipal automotive use based on weekly data. Some staff question the accuracy of the program's estimates. But because the figures it provides are remarkably consistent from week to week, we can be confident of its accuracy. $\longrightarrow$	**Step 2:** Conclusion: Our computer's estimates are accurate. *because* Evidence: Our computer's estimates are consistent.
The reasoning in Beck's argument is flawed in that it $\longrightarrow$	**Step 1:** A Flaw question: The correct answer will describe how Beck's reasoning goes off track.
	Step 3: "Consistent" is not the same thing as "accurate." The computer could be programed in a way that gives consistent but inaccurate estimates.
(A) fails to establish that consistency is a more important consideration than accuracy $\longrightarrow$	**Step 4:** Irrelevant Comparison. Beck doesn't compare the relative values of consistency and accuracy; he takes consistency to be evidence of accuracy. Eliminate.
(B) fails to consider the program's accuracy in other tasks that it may perform $\longrightarrow$	Outside the Scope. The computer's "other tasks" are not at issue here. Eliminate.
(C) takes for granted that the program's output would be consistent even if its estimates were inaccurate $\longrightarrow$	Distortion. This mischaracterizes Beck's reasoning; he thinks consistency is evidence of accuracy. Eliminate.
(D) regards accuracy as the sole criterion for judging the program's value $\longrightarrow$	Extreme. Beck doesn't say accuracy is the "sole criterion." It's just the one he's trying to prove. Eliminate.
(E) fails to consider that the program could produce consistent but inaccurate output $\longrightarrow$ *PrepTest52 Sec1 Q6*	Correct. This matches the prediction exactly and clearly states the flaw in Beck's argument.

You'll be especially happy that you made a clear, helpful prediction when the correct answer is choice (E). While the untrained test taker is rereading the stimulus as he evaluates each choice, you'll be able to see that choices (A) through (D) don't match what the correct answer must say. As you become better at identifying why choices are incorrect, you'll be able to do a question like the one above faster than your competition will.

LSAT Question	Analysis
Acme Corporation offers unskilled workers excellent opportunities for advancement. As evidence, consider the fact that the president of the company, Ms. Garon, worked as an assembly line worker, an entry-level position requiring no special skills, when she first started at Acme.	**Step 2:** Conclusion: Acme offers unskilled workers a great chance for advancement. *because* Evidence: Acme's president worked on the assembly line, doing an unskilled task, when she first started with the company.
Which one of the following statements, if true, most weakens the reasoning above?	**Step 1:** A Weaken question: The correct answer will state a fact that makes the author's conclusion less likely to follow from his evidence.
	Step 3: The author assumes two things that may or may not be true. First, he assumes that the president was unskilled (the evidence is that she worked in an unskilled position, not that she was in fact unskilled). Second, he assumes that her case is fairly representative (maybe she's the only one who ever had that experience at Acme). The right answer will undermine one, or both, of those assumptions.
(A) Acme's vice president of operations also worked as an assembly line worker when he first started at Acme.	**Step 4:** 180. This helps the author's argument by giving another, similar success story. Eliminate.
(B) Acme regularly hires top graduates of business schools and employs them briefly in each of a succession of entry-level positions before promoting them to management.	Correct. This suggests that the author's assumption that the president was unskilled when she first started is incorrect. If that's the case, her story is poor evidence for the claim that unskilled workers can advance at Acme.
(C) Acme promotes its own employees to senior management positions much more frequently than it hires senior managers from other companies.	Irrelevant Comparison. Since this comparison focuses only on people already in senior management, it is irrelevant to opportunities for the unskilled. Eliminate.
(D) Ms. Garon worked at Acme for more than 20 years before she was promoted to president.	Outside the Scope. *How long* it took the president to advance is beside the point. Eliminate.
(E) Acme pays entry-level employees slightly higher wages than most other businesses in the same industry.	Irrelevant Comparison. Starting pay is irrelevant to opportunities for advancement. Eliminate.

PrepTest56 Sec2 Q3

Notice that the LSAT expert was able to discern what the author was assuming and anticipated that the correct answer would puncture one of those assumptions. In Chapter 10, you'll learn how to deal with the entire family of assumption-based questions. It's the most important set of skills you'll acquire for the Logical Reasoning section. It's not by chance that three of the wrong answers (choices (C), (D), and (E)) missed the point of the author's argument while choice (A) actually strengthened one of the author's assumptions (which is the opposite of what you want the answer choice to do in a Weaken question).

LSAT Question	Analysis
Caldwell: The government recently demolished a former naval base. Among the complex's facilities were a gymnasium, a swimming pool, office buildings, gardens, and housing for hundreds of people. Of course the government was legally permitted to use these facilities as it wished. But clearly, using them for the good of the community would have benefited everyone, and thus the government's actions were not only inefficient but immoral.	**Step 2:** Conclusion: The government's demolition of the recreational facilities was legal, but inefficient and immoral. *because* Evidence: Community use of the facilities would have benefitted everyone.
Caldwell's argument is most vulnerable to criticism on the grounds that it	**Step 1:** A Flaw question: The correct answer will describe an error in Caldwell's reasoning, a criticism to which his argument is susceptible.
	Step 3: The author leaps from pointing out an advantage of maintaining the facilities to saying that their destruction was immoral. But, who knows? Maybe they were cleared away to build a hospital or because they were dangerous. One possible upside to keeping them doesn't mean tearing them down was wrong.
(A) fails to consider that an action may be morally permissible even if an alternative course of action is to everyone's advantage	**Step 4:** Correct. This matches the prediction and points out that Caldwell doesn't have enough evidence to conclude that razing the facilities was immoral.
(B) presumes, without providing justification, that the actual consequences of an action are irrelevant to the action's moral permissibility	180. This gets Caldwell's reasoning backward. He claims that the consequences (no community use) *are* relevant to the morality of tearing down the facilities. Eliminate.
(C) presumes, without providing justification, that the government never acts in the most efficient manner	Extreme. This overstates Caldwell's position. He doesn't say the government is *never* efficient, just that it wasn't in this case. Eliminate.
(D) presumes, without providing justification, that any action that is efficient is also moral	Distortion. Caldwell doesn't claim that tearing down the buildings was immoral *because* doing so was inefficient. He claims that because everyone could benefit from them, tearing them down is both inefficient and immoral. Eliminate.
(E) inappropriately treats two possible courses of action as if they were the only options *PrepTest52 Sec3 Q8*	Distortion. Caldwell doesn't say community use is the only alternative, it's just the one he likes. Eliminate.

The answer choices in this last question are worded in abstract, descriptive language—they don't mention the details of the argument, such as the swimming pool or gymnasium. This is fairly common on the LSAT, especially in questions that ask you to describe how an argument works or what went wrong with its reasoning. Nonetheless, the expert test taker can see how even these generic-sounding choices fit the wrong answer categories so often used by the testmaker.

The Logical Reasoning Wrong Answer Types

Not every wrong answer you see will fit neatly into one of the types you see described here. After all, sometimes when a question asks for what the author assumes, the wrong answer will just be something she doesn't assume, without clearly being a 180 or Extreme. Other wrong answers might fit more than one category. Still, it's worth your time to learn the wrong answer types in the list that follows. You'll see them referred to many times in the questions illustrated in the coming chapters.

LOGICAL REASONING: WRONG ANSWER TYPES

- **Outside the Scope**—a choice containing a statement that is too broad, too narrow, or beyond the purview of the stimulus

- **Irrelevant Comparison**—a choice that compares two items or attributes in a way not germane to the author's argument or statements

- **Extreme**—a choice containing language too emphatic to be supported by the stimulus; Extreme choices are often (though, not always) characterized by words such as *all, never, every,* or *none*

- **Distortion**—a choice that mentions details from the stimulus but mangles or misstates the relationship between them given or implied by the author

- **180**—a choice that directly contradicts what the correct answer must say (for example, a choice that strengthens the argument in a Weaken question)

- **Faulty Use of Detail**—a choice that accurately states something from the stimulus but in a manner that answers the question incorrectly; this type is rarely used in Logical Reasoning

---

Along the way, you'll see a handful of wrong answer types that apply to specific question types. In Assumption or Main Point questions, for example, it's common to see wrong answers that simply repeat the author's evidence instead of his unstated assumption or conclusion. We'll cover these wrong answers when they appear and explain why they aren't credited on the test.

It's also important to bring up Formal Logic statements here. Imagine a case in which the correct answer must say: "To vote in County Y, it is necessary to register 60 days prior to the election." A common wrong answer might say, "Anyone registered 60 days prior to the election can vote in County Y." For the purposes of our wrong answer types, that would be a Distortion. But if you think back to Chapter 1, "LSAT Reasoning," you'll recognize that the first statement, the one that matches the correct answer, holds that meeting the registration requirement is *necessary* for voting, while the wrong answer holds that the registration requirement is *sufficient* to be able to vote. Being clear with Formal Logic is just as important (arguably, *more* important) in Logical Reasoning than it is in Logic Games. Anytime you need a brush up on necessity and sufficiency, return to Chapter 1 and review the examples and drills there.

Now that you have the big picture of Logical Reasoning in order, it's time to focus on specific questions and their associated skills. The argument-based questions in Chapter 9 provide a foundation for the more numerous (and often more difficult) assumption-based questions in Chapter 10. The non-argument-based questions in Chapter 11 reward you for different skills but still conform precisely to the question format, method, and wrong answer types you've learned in this chapter.

Argument-Based Questions

In the Logical Reasoning sections of the LSAT, the majority of questions—indeed over 70 percent of questions on tests released from 2008 to 2012—reward your ability to analyze arguments. That's well over a third of all the questions on the exam. So, the skills you'll acquire in this chapter and the next have the potential to make your LSAT score skyrocket.

As we'll discuss it here, the word *argument* does not refer to a dispute between two people, though occasionally, the LSAT will present a brief dialogue in which each party presents an argument. An LSAT argument is one person's attempt to convince the reader that some assertion is true or that some action is advisable. LSAT arguments are defined by two explicit components: (1) a *conclusion*, the author's main point, and (2) one or more pieces of *evidence*, the facts or analyses he offers in support of the conclusion.

LSAT STRATEGY

Every LSAT argument contains

- a conclusion—the assertion, evaluation, or recommendation of which the author is trying to convince his readers; and
- evidence—the facts, studies, or contentions the author believes support or establish the conclusion.

The testmaker has designed several Logical Reasoning question types—Main Point, Role of a Statement, Method of Argument, Point at Issue, and Parallel Reasoning questions—to test your ability to recognize, identify, and characterize the explicit parts of arguments or to describe how the author is putting the pieces of the argument together. In this chapter, you'll learn what you need to know to answer the first four of those types (Parallel Reasoning questions will be covered in Chapter 10 after you've learned to analyze flawed arguments). Together, the questions introduced in this chapter account for 7–8 questions per test on recent LSATs.

But notice that we keep referring to the conclusion and evidence as the *explicit* parts of each LSAT argument. That's because almost every argument used in the stimulus of a Logical Reasoning question also contains an implicit *assumption*. Three more question types—the extremely important Assumption, Strengthen/Weaken, and Flaw questions, which are all covered in Chapter 10—reward you for identifying the unstated premise in the argument. Together, those questions account for around 24 questions per test. While it might be tempting to leap ahead to these popular question types, you should take the time to first study and practice the learning objectives outlined in Chapter 9. Without the skills to analyze the explicit parts of LSAT arguments, the all-important "Assumption family" questions are nearly impossible.

CONCLUSIONS AND MAIN POINT QUESTIONS

> ## LEARNING OBJECTIVES
>
> In this section, you'll learn to:
>
> · Identify the conclusion in an LSAT argument.
> · Characterize and paraphrase the conclusion.
> · Identify Main Point questions and characterize their correct and incorrect answer choices.

Here's a Main Point question. Feel free to try it now. You'll see a complete analysis later in this section. By the end of this section, you'll be able to answer questions of this type.

Dietitian: Many diet-conscious consumers are excited about new "fake fat" products designed to give food the flavor and consistency of fatty foods, yet without fat's harmful effects. Consumers who expect the new fat substitute to help them lose weight are likely to be disappointed, however. Research has shown that when people knowingly or unknowingly eat foods containing "fake fat," they tend to take in at least as many additional calories as are saved by eating "fake fat."

Which one of the following most accurately expresses the conclusion of the dietitian's argument?

(A)   People tend to take in a certain number of daily calories, no matter what types of food they eat.

(B)   Most consumers who think that foods with "fake fat" are more nutritious than fatty foods are destined to be disappointed.

(C)   "Fake fat" products are likely to contribute to obesity more than do other foods.

(D)   "Fake fat" in foods is probably not going to help consumers meet weight loss goals.

(E)   "Fake fat" in foods is indistinguishable from genuine fat by most consumers on the basis of taste alone.

PrepTest52 Sec3 Q2

Main Point questions reward you for directly locating (and sometimes for accurately paraphrasing) the author's conclusion. Since spotting the conclusion forms the basis of all argument analyses on the test, jump right in and practice this important skill.

Identify the Conclusion

Think of the conclusion as the author's point, the statement she's trying to convince you is true. In our day-to-day lives, we identify conclusions all the time, though we're seldom aware that we're doing so. When your spouse or roommate says, "I don't feel like cooking; we should order something for delivery," the second part of that sentence is his conclusion. This is because the second part of the sentence is what he's trying to convince you to do, and he offers the first part of the sentence (the evidence) as a reason why you should accept his point. Indeed, conclusions are always statements that call out for a reason; they always elicit the question "Why?"

LSAT arguments are usually (though not always) a good deal more complex than that example, but they feature multiple ways in which to identify the conclusion.

Many LSAT arguments use Keywords to introduce the conclusion.

LSAT Question	Analysis
Science journalist: Europa, a moon of Jupiter, is covered with ice. Data recently transmitted by a spacecraft strongly suggest that there are oceans of liquid water deep under the ice. Life as we know it could evolve only in the presence of liquid water. Hence, it is likely that at least primitive life has evolved on Europa. *PrepTest62 Sec4 Q10*	"Hence" signals the author's conclusion here: *Europa probably has or had some form of life.* Everything else is either background or evidence.
People want to be instantly and intuitively liked. Those persons who are perceived as forming opinions of others only after cautiously gathering and weighing the evidence are generally resented. Thus, it is imprudent to appear prudent. *PrepTest52 Sec1 Q17*	The commentator's conclusion follows the word "[t]hus": *it is imprudent to appear prudent.* The first two sentences provide the author's evidence for this odd claim.

Other conclusion Keywords or phrases include *therefore, thus, consequently, as a result, so,* and *it follows that.* When conclusion Keywords are present, they can be the quickest way to spot the author's point. Don't become overly reliant on conclusion Keywords, however; sometimes the author may use one or more subsidiary conclusions as part of the evidence. Look at this example.

LSAT Question	Analysis
The reason music with a simple recurring rhythm exerts a strong primordial appeal is that it reminds us of the womb environment. After all, the first sound heard within the womb is the comforting sound of the mother's regular heartbeat. So in taking away from us the warmth and security of the womb, birth also takes away a primal and constant source of comfort. Thus it is extremely natural that in seeking sensations of warmth and security throughout life, people would be strongly drawn toward simple recurring rhythmic sounds. *PrepTest68 Sec4 Q3*	Two conclusion Keywords: "[s]o" and "[t]hus." What follows "[s]o" is a conclusion drawn from the previous sentence: *birth takes away the comfort of our first sound, the mother's rhythmic heartbeat.* That, in turn, supports what follows "[t]hus": *losing that comfort makes it natural for us to seek out rhythmic sounds.* All of that supports the first sentence, the argument's conclusion: *we like rhythmic music because it reminds us of the womb.* The sentences following "[s]o" and "[t]hus" are both subsidiary conclusions in support of the author's ultimate point.

In other LSAT arguments, Keywords may signal the evidence. The most common examples are "because," "for," and "since."

LSAT Question		Analysis
It is a given that to be an intriguing person, one must be able to inspire the perpetual curiosity of others. Constantly broadening one's abilities and extending one's intellectual reach will enable one to inspire that curiosity. For such a perpetual expansion of one's mind makes it impossible to be fully comprehended, making one a constant mystery to others. *PrepTest58 Sec1 Q13*	→	"It is a given" (signaling an undeniable fact) and "[f]or" (giving a reason why) both indicate evidence. The conclusion is the middle sentence: *broadening abilities and extending intellectual reach are sufficient to inspire curiosity in others.*
The average length of stay for patients at Edgewater Hospital is four days, compared to six days at University Hospital. Since studies show that recovery rates at the two hospitals are similar for patients with similar illnesses, University Hospital could decrease its average length of stay without affecting quality of care. *PrepTest52 Sec3 Q16*	→	"Since" (giving a reason why) indicates evidence. The conclusion is the clause that follows the comma: *the hospital could maintain quality of care even with shorter stays for its patients.*

The toughest arguments in which to locate the conclusion are those with neither conclusion nor evidence Keywords. In these cases, you need to follow the logical flow of the argument by asking, "What is the author's point, and what is she offering to support that point?" We call this the One-Sentence Test because you're trying to strip away anything other than the one sentence or clause that constitutes the author's ultimate point. As an active reader, question the author's position and zero in on that to which she has designed the entire argument to lead.

LSAT Question		Analysis
Any museum that owns the rare stamp that features an airplane printed upside down should not display it. Ultraviolet light causes red ink to fade, and a substantial portion of the stamp is red. If the stamp is displayed, it will be damaged. It should be kept safely locked away, even though this will deny the public the chance to see it. *PrepTest52 Sec3 Q1*	→	The author's opinion—that *the rare stamp be locked away and not displayed*—is his conclusion. This opinion (indicated by "should") begs for an explanation. Why not? The fact that the stamp will fade is evidence supporting the conclusion.

One special case—often associated with Main Point questions, by the way—occurs when the author's conclusion is an assertion that another person's position is incorrect. Arguments with this structure will often begin with language such as "some believe" or "biologists contend" or "it has been proposed." The author's rejection of whatever these other parties are arguing for is then signaled by a Contrast Keyword, such as *but* or *however*, or a flat-out refutation, such as "This is incorrect."

LSAT Question		Analysis
Gardener: Researchers encourage us to allow certain kinds of weeds to grow among garden vegetables because they can repel caterpillars from the garden. While it is wise to avoid unnecessary use of insecticides, the researchers' advice is premature. For all we know, those kinds of weeds can deplete the soil of nutrients and moisture that garden crops depend on, and might even attract other kinds of damaging pests. *PrepTest56 Sec3 Q5*	→	The author concludes that the researchers have jumped the gun in recommending that gardeners allow certain weeds to grow and offers evidence after the word "[f]or." The Keyword "[w]hile" indicates that the author concedes that the researchers have a reasonable basis for their advice but thinks more research is needed.
In order to expand its mailing lists for e-mail advertising, the Outdoor Sports Company has been offering its customers financial incentives if they provide the e-mail addresses of their friends. However, offering such incentives is an unethical business practice, because it encourages people to exploit their personal relationships for profit, which risks damaging the integrity of those relationships. *PrepTest56 Sec2 Q16*	→	The author concludes that "offering such incentives is unethical" and offers evidence after the word "because." The Keyword "[h]owever" signals that the author's conclusion rejects the company's practice.

While the author's conclusion in these two arguments is the clause or sentence following the Contrast Keyword, your understanding of the author's point entails your understanding of his opponent's position as well. Imagine an argument that begins: "Members of the other party argue that we should adopt the proposed city budget. But, they are mistaken." Here, the author's conclusion is the second sentence, but the meaning of the conclusion is "we should not adopt the proposed budget." Notice, too, that the argument would continue with the author's evidence: Here's why we should not adopt the budget. You'll practice paraphrasing conclusions shortly, and you'll look more closely at authors' evidence in the next section. First, however, get in a little practice locating the conclusion in LSAT arguments.

TEST DAY TIP

Bracket the conclusion of an argument in your test booklet. Get in the habit of doing this for all Argument-based and Assumption-family questions.

Practice

Now, practice locating the conclusion in a handful of LSAT arguments.

In each of the following arguments, locate and bracket the conclusion and, in your own words, explain how you knew that the sentence or clause you selected is the author's main point. After each, check the next page to see the expert analysis and check your work.

LSAT Question	My Analysis
1. Editorialist: In a large corporation, one of the functions of the corporation's president is to promote the key interests of the shareholders. Therefore, the president has a duty to keep the corporation's profits high. *PrepTest52 Sec1 Q4*	
2. Dietitian: Many diet-conscious consumers are excited about new "fake fat" products designed to give food the flavor and consistency of fatty foods, yet without fat's harmful effects. Consumers who expect the new fat substitute to help them lose weight are likely to be disappointed, however. Research has shown that when people knowingly or unknowingly eat foods containing "fake fat," they tend to take in at least as many additional calories as are saved by eating "fake fat." *PrepTest52 Sec3 Q2*	
3. Speaker: Like many contemporary critics, Smith argues that the true meaning of an author's statements can be understood only through insight into the author's social circumstances. But this same line of analysis can be applied to Smith's own words. Thus, if she is right we should be able, at least in part, to discern from Smith's social circumstances the "true meaning" of Smith's statements. This, in turn, suggests that Smith herself is not aware of the true meaning of her own words. *PrepTest62 Sec2 Q15*	
4. This boulder is volcanic in origin and yet the rest of the rock in this area is sedimentary. Since this area was covered by southward-moving glaciers during the last ice age, this boulder was probably deposited here, hundreds of miles from its geological birthplace, by a glacier. *PrepTest56 Sec2 Q8*	

Here's how an LSAT expert looks at each of the arguments you've just examined.

LSAT Question	Analysis
1. Editorialist: In a large corporation, one of the functions of the corporation's president is to promote the key interests of the shareholders. Therefore, the president has a duty to keep the corporation's profits high. *PrepTest52 Sec1 Q4*	"Therefore" signals the author's conclusion: *a president is obligated to keep corporate profits high.* The first sentence is evidence for that claim.
2. Dietitian: Many diet-conscious consumers are excited about new "fake fat" products designed to give food the flavor and consistency of fatty foods, yet without fat's harmful effects. Consumers who expect the new fat substitute to help them lose weight are likely to be disappointed, however. Research has shown that when people knowingly or unknowingly eat foods containing "fake fat," they tend to take in at least as many additional calories as are saved by eating "fake fat." *PrepTest52 Sec3 Q2*	"[L]ikely to be disappointed" indicates the author's opinion (and begs "Why?"), while "however" shows that it contrasts with the consumers' expectations in the first sentence. The conclusion is *the new "fake fat" products won't help consumers lose weight.* The argument's final sentence is the evidence.
3. Speaker: Like many contemporary critics, Smith argues that the true meaning of an author's statements can be understood only through insight into the author's social circumstances. But this same line of analysis can be applied to Smith's own words. Thus, if she is right we should be able, at least in part, to discern from Smith's social circumstances the "true meaning" of Smith's statements. This, in turn, suggests that Smith herself is not aware of the true meaning of her own words. *PrepTest62 Sec2 Q15*	"Thus" at the beginning of the third sentence indicates a conclusion drawn upon the second sentence: *applying Smith's reasoning to her own work means her "true meaning" is determined by her social world.* However, "[t]his, in turn, suggests" at the start of the fourth sentence shows that the third sentence is a subsidiary conclusion used as evidence for the author's ultimate point: *Smith does not know the "true meaning" of her own words.*
4. This boulder is volcanic in origin and yet the rest of the rock in this area is sedimentary. Since this area was covered by southward-moving glaciers during the last ice age, this boulder was probably deposited here, hundreds of miles from its geological birthplace, by a glacier. *PrepTest56 Sec2 Q8*	There are no conclusion Keywords, but "[s]ince" (giving a reason why) indicates evidence. The conclusion is the clause following the first comma: *the boulder was likely deposited here by a glacier.*

Paraphrase and Characterize the Conclusion

Now that you can spot conclusions, you're ready to tackle the task of understanding what they actually mean. LSAT arguments don't always use the simplest or most succinct wording, and as you've seen, sometimes you'll need to combine two sentences to accurately articulate the author's main point.

Being able to put the author's conclusion into your own words is important because in some questions, the LSAT will paraphrase the author's conclusion in the correct answer. Indeed, it will directly quote another part of the argument in a wrong answer. Being able to zero in on and accurately capture the author's meaning is a skill you'll use in the Reading Comprehension section as well.

Here's how an LSAT expert sees a complex conclusion.

LSAT Question	Analysis
Educator: It has been argued that our professional organization should make decisions about important issues—such as raising dues and taking political stands—by a direct vote of all members rather than by having members vote for officers who in turn make the decisions. This would not, however, be the right way to decide these matters, for the vote of any given individual is much more likely to determine organizational policy by influencing the election of an officer than by influencing the result of a direct vote on a single issue. *PrepTest52 Sec1 Q19*	"It has been argued" indicates another person's point of view, and "however" signals the author's disagreement. The author thinks the other view is not the way to decide "these matters," the issues discussed in the first sentence. So, the educator's conclusion is *the teacher's association should not decide things like raising dues and announcing political positions by direct vote.* Or, phrased affirmatively, she concludes *we should decide these issues by electing officers and having them make the decisions.*

As you practice paraphrasing conclusions, it's valuable to know that the conclusions to every LSAT argument fall into one of six categories.

LSAT STRATEGY

Conclusions of LSAT arguments almost always match one these six types:

· Prediction (X *will* or *will not* happen in the future)

· Recommendation (we *should* or *should not* do X)

· Comparison (X is taller/shorter/more common/less common/etc. than Y)

· Assertion of Fact (X is true or X is false)

· If/Then (a conditional prediction, recommendation, or assertion; e.g., If X is true, then so is Y or If you are an M, you should do Y)

· Value Judgment (an evaluative statement; e.g., Action X is unethical or Y's recital was poorly sung)

Learning to spot the category into which a conclusion falls is valuable for many Logical Reasoning question types. When the testmaker asks you to identify the conclusion in a Main Point question, the correct answer must, naturally, match the conclusion in the stimulus. In Parallel Reasoning questions, even though the arguments in the answer choices deal with different subject matter than does the stimulus argument, the conclusion type in the correct answer must match that in the stimulus. (You'll work on Parallel Reasoning in depth in the next chapter.) Even in the all-important Assumption-family questions, noting a particular conclusion type can help reveal the pattern in the argument, making your analysis more efficient. By the way, some conclusions fall into more than one of these categories. If an author concludes, for example, "If the city's budget is not balanced next year, the council should vote to cut funding to animal shelters," his conclusion is both an If/Then and a Recommendation.

Take a look at how an LSAT expert would recognize the conclusion types in these examples.

LSAT Question	Analysis
In order to reduce traffic congestion and raise revenue for the city, the mayor plans to implement a charge of $10 per day for driving in the downtown area. Payment of this charge will be enforced using a highly sophisticated system that employs digital cameras and computerized automobile registration. This system will not be ready until the end of next year. Without this system, however, mass evasion of the charge will result. Therefore, when the mayor's plan is first implemented, payment of the charge will not be effectively enforced. *PrepTest52 Sec1 Q10*	The author's conclusion (signaled by "[t]herefore")—*that the mayor's planned charge will not be enforced*—is a prediction. Notice that the author limits her prediction to the period after the plan is first implemented.
Any museum that owns the rare stamp that features an airplane printed upside down should not display it. Ultraviolet light causes red ink to fade, and a substantial portion of the stamp is red. If the stamp is displayed, it will be damaged. It should be kept safely locked away, even though this will deny the public the chance to see it. *PrepTest52 Sec3 Q1*	The conclusion here—*that a museum should lock away and not display the rare stamp*—is a recommendation. [In this case, the author is stating both what the museum *should* (lock it safely away) and *should not* (display it) do. Typically, the author gives only a single positive or negative recommendation.]
Neural connections carrying signals from the cortex (the brain region responsible for thought) down to the amygdala (a brain region crucial for emotions) are less well developed than connections carrying signals from the amygdala up to the cortex. Thus, the amygdala exerts a greater influence on the cortex than vice versa. *PrepTest 52 Sec1 Q20*	The conclusion (signaled by "[t]hus")—*that the amygdala influences the cortex more than the cortex influences the amygdala*—is a comparison. Anytime you see "greater . . . than," you have a comparison.

LSAT Question	**Analysis**
The reason music with a simple recurring rhythm exerts a strong primordial appeal is that it reminds us of the womb environment. After all, the first sound heard within the womb is the comforting sound of the mother's regular heartbeat. So in taking away from us the warmth and security of the womb, birth also takes away a primal and constant source of comfort. Thus it is extremely natural that in seeking sensations of warmth and security throughout life, people would be strongly drawn toward simple recurring rhythmic sounds. *PrepTest58 Sec4 Q3*	$\longrightarrow$ The conclusion here—*that a similarity to the womb environment is why people are attracted to rhythmic music*—is an assertion of fact. The author is simply stating that he believes this to be true. [Note: Assertions of causality—*this is why X occurs*—are very common in LSAT arguments.]
Economist: Our economy's weakness is the direct result of consumers' continued reluctance to spend, which in turn is caused by factors such as high-priced goods and services. This reluctance is exacerbated by the fact that the average income is significantly lower than it was five years ago. Thus, even though it is not a perfect solution, if the government were to lower income taxes, the economy would improve. *PrepTest58 Sec1 Q19*	$\longrightarrow$ The conclusion here—*that, were the government to lower taxes, the economy would improve*—is an If/then conclusion. The author's prediction of improvement is conditioned upon tax cuts. [Note: The "then" part of an If/then conclusion could be a prediction, an assertion of fact, a recommendation, or even a value judgment. This conclusion type is characterized by its conditional nature.]
In order to expand its mailing lists for e-mail advertising, the Outdoor Sports Company has been offering its customers financial incentives if they provide the e-mail addresses of their friends. However, offering such incentives is an unethical business practice, because it encourages people to exploit their personal relationships for profit, which risks damaging the integrity of those relationships. *PrepTest56 Sec2 Q16*	$\longrightarrow$ The conclusion here—*that offering incentives for customers to share their friends' e-mail addresses is unethical*—is a value judgment. The author is passing judgment on the company's practice.

Now that you're familiar with the types of conclusions, practice locating and paraphrasing the conclusions in the following arguments. Make sure to note into which of the six conclusion categories each one falls.

Practice

In each of the arguments below, locate the conclusion, identify the conclusion type, and give a simple, accurate paraphrase of the author's meaning in your own words. After each, you can turn to the pages following the exercise to see the expert thinking and check your work.

LSAT Question	My Analysis
5. Anyone who believes in democracy has a high regard for the wisdom of the masses. Griley, however, is an elitist who believes that any artwork that is popular is unlikely to be good. Thus, Griley does not believe in democracy. *PrepTest58 Sec4 Q19*	
6. All etching tools are either pin-tipped or bladed. While some bladed etching tools are used for engraving, some are not. On the other hand, all pin-tipped etching tools are used for engraving. Thus, there are more etching tools that are used for engraving than there are etching tools that are not used for engraving. *PrepTest62 Sec4 Q16*	
7. University president: Our pool of applicants has been shrinking over the past few years. One possible explanation of this unwelcome phenomenon is that we charge too little for tuition and fees. Prospective students and their parents conclude that the quality of education they would receive at this institution is not as high as that offered by institutions with higher tuition. So, if we want to increase the size of our applicant pool, we need to raise our tuition and fees. *PrepTest62 Sec2 Q25*	
8. Medications with an unpleasant taste are generally produced only in tablet, capsule, or soft-gel form. The active ingredient in medication M is a waxy substance that cannot tolerate the heat used to manufacture tablets because it has a low melting point. So, since the company developing M does not have soft-gel manufacturing technology and manufactures all its medications itself, M will most likely be produced in capsule form. *PrepTest62 Sec2 Q3*	

LSAT Question	**My Analysis**
9. Gardener: Researchers encourage us to allow certain kinds of weeds to grow among garden vegetables because they can repel caterpillars from the garden. While it is wise to avoid unnecessary use of insecticides, the researchers' advice is premature. For all we know, those kinds of weeds can deplete the soil of nutrients and moisture that garden crops depend on, and might even attract other kinds of damaging pests. *PrepTest56 Sec3 Q5*	
10. Politician: We should impose a tariff on imported fruit to make it cost consumers more than domestic fruit. Otherwise, growers from other countries who can grow better fruit more cheaply will put domestic fruit growers out of business. This will result in farmland's being converted to more lucrative industrial uses and the consequent vanishing of a unique way of life. *PrepTest58 Sec1 Q23*	

Here's how an LSAT expert looks at each of the arguments you've just examined.

LSAT Question	Analysis
5. Anyone who believes in democracy has a high regard for the wisdom of the masses. Griley, however, is an elitist who believes that any artwork that is popular is unlikely to be good. Thus, Griley does not believe in democracy. *PrepTest58 Sec4 Q19*	"Thus" signals the conclusion: *Griley doesn't believe in democracy*, a strong assertion of fact.
6. All etching tools are either pin-tipped or bladed. While some bladed etching tools are used for engraving, some are not. On the other hand, all pin-tipped etching tools are used for engraving. Thus, there are more etching tools that are used for engraving than there are etching tools that are not used for engraving. *PrepTest62 Sec4 Q16*	"Thus" signals the conclusion: *more etching tools are used for engraving than not so used*, a comparison between different uses of tools.
7. University president: Our pool of applicants has been shrinking over the past few years. One possible explanation of this unwelcome phenomenon is that we charge too little for tuition and fees. Prospective students and their parents conclude that the quality of education they would receive at this institution is not as high as that offered by institutions with higher tuition. So, if we want to increase the size of our applicant pool, we need to raise our tuition and fees. *PrepTest62 Sec2 Q25*	"So" indicates the conclusion: *if the goal is more applicants, then the school has to increase tuition.* This is an If/then conclusion, where the "then" is an assertion of fact.
8. Medications with an unpleasant taste are generally produced only in tablet, capsule, or soft-gel form. The active ingredient in medication M is a waxy substance that cannot tolerate the heat used to manufacture tablets because it has a low melting point. So, since the company developing M does not have soft-gel manufacturing technology and manufactures all its medications itself, M will most likely be produced in capsule form. *PrepTest62 Sec2 Q3*	"So" signals the conclusion is coming up, but "since" indicates that evidence is inserted first. The conclusion is *M will probably come to market as a capsule.* It's a "soft" prediction—the author thinks this outcome is "likely," not certain.
9. Gardener: Researchers encourage us to allow certain kinds of weeds to grow among garden vegetables because they can repel caterpillars from the garden. While it is wise to avoid unnecessary use of insecticides, the researchers' advice is premature. For all we know, those kinds of weeds can deplete the soil of nutrients and moisture that garden crops depend on, and might even attract other kinds of damaging pests. *PrepTest56 Sec3 Q5*	The conclusion here—*that the researchers' advice is premature*—is a value judgment. The author questions the value of the recommendation without further information.

LSAT Question	Analysis
10. Politician: We should impose a tariff on imported fruit to make it cost consumers more than domestic fruit. Otherwise, growers from other countries who can grow better fruit more cheaply will put domestic fruit growers out of business. This will result in farmland's being converted to more lucrative industrial uses and the consequent vanishing of a unique way of life. *PrepTest58 Sec1 Q23*	→	The conclusion is the first sentence; "should" indicates the author's point of view, which requires support. This is a recommendation: *our country should levy a tariff to the point that imported fruit is more expensive than comparable domestic products.*

Identify and Answer Main Point Questions

Once you know how to locate and paraphrase conclusions, you're ready to answer Main Point questions. On tests released from 2008 through 2012, there were an average of 2–3 Main Point questions per test with a high count of four on two exams given in 2012. While Main Point questions do not constitute a great number of questions, keep in mind how fundamental the conclusion-based skills are. You'll be analyzing the author's conclusion on dozens of questions on Test Day.

Employing the Kaplan Method for Logical Reasoning, you begin with the question stem. Although the testmaker uses different wording from time to time, Main Point questions always call for the author's final conclusion. The correct answer either restates the conclusion or paraphrases it without changing the meaning. Incorrect answers often state a piece of the author's evidence or one of his subsidiary conclusions that serve as evidence in the argument. Other incorrect answers distort or contradict the author's conclusion. If another party's position is mentioned in the argument, the testmaker may include an incorrect answer that accurately states that party's point.

Here are a handful of Main Point question stems seen on recent exams.

LSAT Question	Analysis
Which one of the following most accurately expresses the conclusion drawn in the argument? *PrepTest52 Sec1 Q1*	→	"[C]onclusion drawn in the argument": a Main Point question. The correct answer will state or paraphrase the author's conclusion.
Which one of the following is the most accurate rendering of the political scientist's main conclusion? *PrepTest62 Sec4 Q12*	→	"[A]ccurate rendering of the . . . main conclusion": a Main Point question. The correct answer will state or paraphrase the political scientist's conclusion.

Once you've identified a Main Point question, untangle the stimulus to locate the author's conclusion. Remember that you can use conclusion Keywords, evidence Keywords, or the One-Sentence Test. Paraphrase the conclusion and use that paraphrase as your prediction of the correct answer. Evaluate the answer choices by finding the correct answer that mirrors your prediction or by eliminating choices that restate the evidence, distort or contradict the author's conclusion, or refer to another party's point of view.

Here's how an LSAT expert would view a couple of complete Main Point questions associated with arguments you've already analyzed.

LSAT Question	Analysis
Dietitian: Many diet-conscious consumers are excited about new "fake fat" products designed to give food the flavor and consistency of fatty foods, yet without fat's harmful effects. Consumers who expect the new fat substitute to help them lose weight are likely to be disappointed, however. Research has shown that when people knowingly or unknowingly eat foods containing "fake fat," they tend to take in at least as many additional calories as are saved by eating "fake fat."	**Step 2:** "[L]ikely to be disappointed" indicates the author's opinion (and begs "Why?"), while "however" shows that it contrasts with the consumers' expectations in the first sentence. The conclusion is *the new "fake fat" products won't help consumers lose weight*. The argument's final sentence is the evidence.
Which one of the following most accurately expresses the conclusion of the dietitian's argument?	**Step 1:** "[A]ccurately expresses the conclusion": a Main Point question. The correct answer will state or paraphrase the dietitian's conclusion.
	Step 3: The correct answer will say, in effect, *the new "fake fat" products won't help consumers lose weight*.
(A) People tend to take in a certain number of daily calories, no matter what types of food they eat.	**Step 4:** This relates to the author's *evidence* (that people who eat "fake fat" will then take in additional calories), not to his conclusion. Eliminate.
(B) Most consumers who think that foods with "fake fat" are more nutritious than fatty foods are destined to be disappointed.	"[M]ore nutritious" distorts the conclusion, which is about weight loss. Eliminate.
(C) "Fake fat" products are likely to contribute to obesity more than do other foods.	Distorts the author's conclusion, which is that the products won't help you lose weight, not that they'll make you more obese. Eliminate.
(D) "Fake fat" in foods is probably not going to help consumers meet weight loss goals.	Correct. This paraphrases the dietitian's conclusion and matches the prediction.
(E) "Fake fat" in foods is indistinguishable from genuine fat by most consumers on the basis of taste alone. *PrepTest52 Sec3 Q2*	"Fake fat" is designed to be like this, but this misses the author's main point about "fake fat": that it won't help dieters lose weight. Eliminate.

LSAT Question	Analysis
It is a given that to be an intriguing person, one must be able to inspire the perpetual curiosity of others. Constantly broadening one's abilities and extending one's intellectual reach will enable one to inspire that curiosity. For such a perpetual expansion of one's mind makes it impossible to be fully comprehended, making one a constant mystery to others.	**Step 2:** "It is a given" (signaling an undeniable fact) and "[f]or" (giving a reason why) both indicate evidence. The conclusion is the middle sentence: *broadening abilities and extending intellectual reach are sufficient to inspire curiosity in others.*
Which one of the following most accurately expresses the conclusion drawn in the argument above?	**Step 1:** "[C]onclusion drawn in the argument": a Main Point question. The correct answer will state or paraphrase the author's conclusion.
	Step 3: "[W]ill enable one to" means "sufficient to," so the correct answer will state that *broadening abilities and extending intellectual reach are sufficient to inspire curiosity in others.*
(A) To be an intriguing person, one must be able to inspire the perpetual curiosity of others.	**Step 4:** This is part of the evidence. Eliminate.
(B) If one constantly broadens one's abilities and extends one's intellectual reach, one will be able to inspire the perpetual curiosity of others.	Correct. This matches the prediction.
(C) If one's mind becomes impossible to fully comprehend, one will always be a mystery to others.	This is part of the evidence. Eliminate.
(D) To inspire the perpetual curiosity of others, one must constantly broaden one's abilities and extend one's intellectual reach.	This gets the conclusion backward, confusing sufficient with necessary. Eliminate.
(E) If one constantly broadens one's abilities and extends one's intellectual reach, one will always have curiosity.	Distorts the conclusion: Broadening abilities and extending intellectual reach allow you to inspire curiosity in others, not stay curious yourself. Eliminate.

PrepTest58 Sec1 Q13

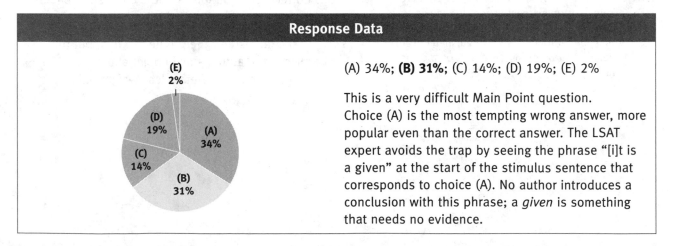

Response Data

(E) 2%
(D) 19%
(A) 34%
(C) 14%
(B) 31%

(A) 34%; **(B) 31%**; (C) 14%; (D) 19%; (E) 2%

This is a very difficult Main Point question. Choice (A) is the most tempting wrong answer, more popular even than the correct answer. The LSAT expert avoids the trap by seeing the phrase "[i]t is a given" at the start of the stimulus sentence that corresponds to choice (A). No author introduces a conclusion with this phrase; a *given* is something that needs no evidence.

Notice that the correct answers in both examples mirror the meaning, if not necessarily the wording, of the author's main point. And, just as we suspected, the wrong answers almost always do one of the following: Restate the evidence instead of the conclusion, distort the conclusion or miss its scope, or state the view of someone other than the author.

Now, try some Main Point questions yourself. Use everything you've learned about locating, characterizing, and paraphrasing the conclusion. Take your time and record your thinking for each step in the Kaplan Method.

Practice

Apply the Kaplan Method to each Logical Reasoning question. To compare your work to the thinking of an LSAT expert, turn to the pages following this exercise.

LSAT Question	My Analysis
11. Certain companies require their managers to rank workers in the groups they supervise from best to worst, giving each worker a unique ranking based on job performance. The top 10 percent of the workers in each group are rewarded and the bottom 10 percent are penalized or fired. But this system is unfair to workers. Good workers could receive low rankings merely because they belong to groups of exceptionally good workers. Furthermore, managers often give the highest rankings to workers who share the manager's interests outside of work.	**Step 2:**
Which one of the following most accurately expresses the conclusion drawn in the argument?	**Step 1:**
	Step 3:
(A) Some companies require their managers to give unique rankings to the workers they supervise.	**Step 4:**
(B) Under the ranking system, the top 10 percent of the workers in each group are rewarded and the bottom 10 percent are penalized or fired.	
(C) The ranking system is not a fair way to determine penalties or rewards for workers.	
(D) Workers in exceptionally strong work groups are unfairly penalized under the ranking system.	
(E) Managers often give the highest rankings to workers who share the manager's outside interests.	

PrepTest52 Sec1 Q1

LSAT Question	My Analysis
	Step 2:

12. Leslie: I'll show you that your quest for the treasure is irrational. Suppose you found a tablet inscribed, "Whoever touches this tablet will lose a hand, yet will possess the world." Would you touch it?

Erich: Certainly not.

Leslie: Just as I expected! It is clear from your answer that your hands are more important to you than possessing the world. But your entire body is necessarily more important to you than your hands. Yet you are ruining your health and harming your body in your quest for a treasure that is much less valuable than the whole world. I rest my case.

Which one of the following most accurately expresses the main conclusion drawn in Leslie's argument?

Step 1:

Step 3:

(A) Erich would not sacrifice one of his hands in order to possess the world.

Step 4:

(B) Erich should not risk his physical well-being regardless of the possible gains that such risks might bring.

(C) Erich is irrationally risking something that is precious to him for something that is of no value.

(D) Erich can be convinced that his quest for the treasure is irrational.

(E) Erich is engaging in irrational behavior by pursuing his quest for the treasure.

PrepTest56 Sec3 Q19

LSAT Question	My Analysis

13. Marine biologist: Scientists have long wondered why the fish that live around coral reefs exhibit such brilliant colors. One suggestion is that coral reefs are colorful and, therefore, that colorful fish are camouflaged by them. Many animal species, after all, use camouflage to avoid predators. However, as regards the populations around reefs, this suggestion is mistaken. A reef stripped of its fish is quite monochromatic. Most corals, it turns out, are relatively dull browns and greens.

Step 2:

Which one of the following most accurately expresses the main conclusion drawn in the marine biologist's argument?

Step 1:

Step 3:

(A) One hypothesis about why fish living near coral reefs exhibit such bright colors is that the fish are camouflaged by their bright colors.

Step 4:

(B) The fact that many species use camouflage to avoid predators is one reason to believe that brightly colored fish living near reefs do too.

(C) The suggestion that the fish living around coral reefs exhibit bright colors because they are camouflaged by the reefs is mistaken.

(D) A reef stripped of its fish is relatively monochromatic.

(E) It turns out that the corals in a coral reef are mostly dull hues of brown and green.

PrepTest62 Sec4 Q1

Here's how an LSAT expert would look at those three questions.

LSAT Question	Analysis
11. Certain companies require their managers to rank workers in the groups they supervise from best to worst, giving each worker a unique ranking based on job performance. The top 10 percent of the workers in each group are rewarded and the bottom 10 percent are penalized or fired. But this system is unfair to workers. Good workers could receive low rankings merely because they belong to groups of exceptionally good workers. Furthermore, managers often give the highest rankings to workers who share the manager's interests outside of work.	**Step 2:** The author's conclusion follows "[b]ut" in the third sentence: *the ranking system for performance evaluation is unfair to workers.* It's a value judgment. The first two sentences describe the ranking system, while the argument's final two sentences give the author's evidence for why the system is unfair.
Which one of the following most accurately expresses the conclusion drawn in the argument?	**Step 1:** "[C]onclusion drawn in the argument": a Main Point question. The correct answer will state or paraphrase the author's conclusion.
	Step 3: The correct answer will echo the author's judgment: *a system in which managers rank all employees is unfair to workers.*
(A) Some companies require their managers to give unique rankings to the workers they supervise.	**Step 4:** This is what some companies do, but the author's conclusion is a judgment about this. Eliminate.
(B) Under the ranking system, the top 10 percent of the workers in each group are rewarded and the bottom 10 percent are penalized or fired.	This is more of what the companies do, but it misses the author's point: *such a system is unfair.* Eliminate.
(C) The ranking system is not a fair way to determine penalties or rewards for workers.	Correct. This is precisely what the author concludes, and it matches the prediction beautifully.
(D) Workers in exceptionally strong work groups are unfairly penalized under the ranking system.	Part of the evidence—the author thinks this is *why* the system is unfair. Eliminate.
(E) Managers often give the highest rankings to workers who share the manager's outside interests.	More evidence—as in (D), this is *why* the author believes his conclusion. Eliminate.

PrepTest52 Sec1 Q1

LSAT Question	Analysis
12. Leslie: I'll show you that your quest for the treasure is irrational. Suppose you found a tablet inscribed, "Whoever touches this tablet will lose a hand, yet will possess the world." Would you touch it? Erich: Certainly not. Leslie: Just as I expected! It is clear from your answer that your hands are more important to you than possessing the world. But your entire body is necessarily more important to you than your hands. Yet you are ruining your health and harming your body in your quest for a treasure that is much less valuable than the whole world. I rest my case.	**Step 2:** "I'll show you" announces what Leslie intends to prove. Her conclusion is aimed at Erich: *your quest for the treasure is irrational*. This is a value judgment. Everything else in the dialogue is her attempt to support that point.
Which one of the following most accurately expresses the main conclusion drawn in Leslie's argument?	**Step 1:** "[A]ccurately expresses the main conclusion": a Main Point question. The correct answer will state or paraphrase Leslie's conclusion.
	Step 3: The correct answer will mean *Erich's quest for the treasure is irrational*.
(A) Erich would not sacrifice one of his hands in order to possess the world.	**Step 4:** This is part of Leslie's evidence. Eliminate.
(B) Erich should not risk his physical well-being regardless of the possible gains that such risks might bring.	Leslie's conclusion is a value judgment (irrational), not a recommendation (should). Eliminate.
(C) Erich is irrationally risking something that is precious to him for something that is of no value.	Too extreme. Leslie doesn't contend that the treasure has "no value." Eliminate.
(D) Erich can be convinced that his quest for the treasure is irrational.	Distortion. Leslie concludes that she can *show* Erich that his quest is irrational, not that he'll be convinced. Eliminate.
(E) Erich is engaging in irrational behavior by pursuing his quest for the treasure. *PrepTest56 Sec3 Q19*	Correct. This is exactly Leslie's main point, and it matches the prediction perfectly.

Response Data

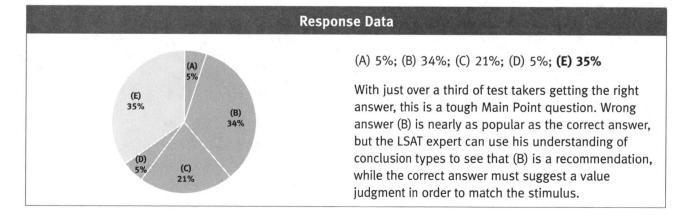

(A) 5%; (B) 34%; (C) 21%; (D) 5%; **(E) 35%**

With just over a third of test takers getting the right answer, this is a tough Main Point question. Wrong answer (B) is nearly as popular as the correct answer, but the LSAT expert can use his understanding of conclusion types to see that (B) is a recommendation, while the correct answer must suggest a value judgment in order to match the stimulus.

LSAT Question	Analysis
13. Marine biologist: Scientists have long wondered why the fish that live around coral reefs exhibit such brilliant colors. One suggestion is that coral reefs are colorful and, therefore, that colorful fish are camouflaged by them. Many animal species, after all, use camouflage to avoid predators. However, as regards the populations around reefs, this suggestion is mistaken. A reef stripped of its fish is quite monochromatic. Most corals, it turns out, are relatively dull browns and greens.	**Step 2:** The Keyword "[h]owever" and the author's opinion—"this suggestion is mistaken"—reveal the conclusion in the fourth sentence: *those who suggest that fish near coral reefs are colorful for camouflage purposes are wrong.* The two sentences after the conclusion provide evidence.
Which one of the following most accurately expresses the main conclusion drawn in the marine biologist's argument?	**Step 1:** "[A]ccurately expresses the main conclusion": a Main Point question. The correct answer will state or paraphrase the biologist's conclusion.
	Step 3: The correct answer could be worded in two ways: (1) *those who suggest camouflage as the reason coral reef fish are brightly colored are wrong,* or (2) *coral reef fish are brightly colored for some reason other than camouflage.* Be ready to spot the right answer regardless of how it is phrased.
(A) One hypothesis about why fish living near coral reefs exhibit such bright colors is that the fish are camouflaged by their bright colors.	**Step 4:** This is not the author's conclusion; in fact, this is the suggestion he concludes is mistaken. Eliminate.
(B) The fact that many species use camouflage to avoid predators is one reason to believe that brightly colored fish living near reefs do too.	The author concedes that many species do camouflage themselves, but he says this is *not* why coral reef fish are colored so brightly. Eliminate.
(C) The suggestion that the fish living around coral reefs exhibit bright colors because they are camouflaged by the reefs is mistaken.	Correct. This mirrors the author's point exactly. Camouflage is the "[o]ne suggestion" from the argument's second sentence that the author ends up rejecting as "mistaken."
(D) A reef stripped of its fish is relatively monochromatic.	This is part of the evidence. Eliminate.
(E) It turns out that the corals in a coral reef are mostly dull hues of brown and green.	This is more of the evidence. Eliminate.

PrepTest62 Sec4 Q1

FOR FURTHER PRACTICE

You'll find more Main Point questions in the Question Pool at the end of this chapter.

Keep in mind that you'll practice locating, characterizing, and paraphrasing conclusions in all of the upcoming Assumption, Strengthen/Weaken, Flaw, Parallel Reasoning, and Method of Argument questions—and many Principle, Role of a Statement, and Point at Issue questions as well.

These are skills you'll reuse and reinforce throughout your Logical Reasoning practice.

Reflection

Congratulations on developing a core set of Logical Reasoning skills and on mastering your first Logical Reasoning question type. Over the next few days, reflect on this session.

Take note of how often you or someone you're talking to makes an argument. What was his or her conclusion? What type was it? Even statements as simple and everyday as "We should go get some ice cream," or "The singing on this song is really weak," can help reinforce your mastery of LSAT conclusion types.

When you're watching TV or reading the news, keep an eye out for arguments. When you spot them, locate and characterize their conclusions. You'll be shocked by how many arguments you encounter on a daily basis.

EVIDENCE AND ARGUMENTS: ROLE OF A STATEMENT, METHOD OF ARGUMENT, AND POINT AT ISSUE QUESTIONS

Several question types besides Main Point questions reward your ability to understand argument structures and parts, and we're about to learn the skills necessary for grabbing those points. Taken together, questions we'll cover in this chapter are worth 7–8 questions on an average LSAT. In addition, the more you know about working with arguments, the better prepared you'll be to start tackling Assumptions and other key question types in Chapter 10. Remember, argument-based questions make up over 70 percent of the LR section and over one-third of the LSAT. Also, keep in mind that a strong understanding of arguments will serve you well in the Reading Comprehension section, too—not to mention in law school.

So far in this chapter, you've learned how to identify conclusions. Take a moment to look back at the questions you just practiced earlier in this chapter and notice how many different ways the authors tried to establish their main points. You're about to work in greater depth with these different ways of supporting a conclusion. In other words, you're ready to tackle *evidence*.

Evidence and Role of a Statement Questions

LEARNING OBJECTIVES

In this section, you'll learn to:

· Distinguish evidence from background information.
· Identify Role of a Statement questions and characterize the correct and incorrect answers.

You learned in the previous section that evidence is the set of facts, analyses, or other considerations that an author uses to try to persuade her reader that her conclusion is correct. Evidence can be long or short, convincing or questionable, and accurate or wildly fictitious. Don't get hung up on comparing the claims you read on the LSAT with what you know about real life. You'll never be asked whether an author's evidence, by itself, is true or believable, but you will frequently be asked about how an author's evidence interacts with her conclusion: whether her evidence does a good job supporting her conclusion, how that support could be made stronger or weaker, or what additional evidence is needed to establish the conclusion. The first step in being able to answer those questions is to identify and paraphrase an author's evidence.

(By the way, evidence is sometimes referred to on the LSAT as the author's "premises." The premises of an argument are that argument's complete set of evidence, and "a premise" is a piece of evidence.)

Just as conclusions are sometimes marked with Keywords, evidence also is sometimes marked with a Keyword. Similarly, just as conclusions can come anywhere in an argument (first sentence, last sentence, in the middle), so too can evidence. Authors use evidence Keywords to say, "Here's why I think the conclusion is true."

Chicago is a great city. After all, there's so much fun stuff to do there.

Notice that there's no conclusion Keyword, but "after all" signals that the second sentence exists to support the first one. That second sentence is the author's evidence.

We could write that same argument a different way:

Because there's so much fun stuff to do there, Chicago is a great city.

Here the conclusion and evidence appear in the same sentence. The first clause of that sentence is evidence, and the second clause is the author's overall conclusion. Don't be thrown off when wording changes on the LSAT. Stay focused on the role played by each clause in the argument and take advantage of evidence Keywords like "because." Other common Keywords indicating evidence are *since* and *for*. Remember, too, that phrases like *this shows* and *from this one can conclude* indicate a conclusion and tell you that the main evidence comes just prior to this in the argument.

Restate the argument about Chicago using each of those Keywords. (Of course, you can substitute the city of your choice if you like.) How would you construct that same argument using the various evidence Keywords in this list? Which evidence Keywords work best *after* a conclusion, and which work best *before* a conclusion?

Practice using evidence Keywords to spot an author's evidence. Take a look at this example from a real LSAT question:

LSAT Question	Analysis
The average length of stay for patients at Edgewater Hospital is four days, compared to six days at University Hospital. Since studies show that recovery rates at the two hospitals are similar for patients with similar illnesses, University Hospital could decrease its average length of stay without affecting quality of care. *PrepTest52 Sec3 Q16*	Conclusion? No conclusion Keywords, but the One-Sentence Test points to the final clause of the second sentence: *U Hospital could release patients sooner without damage to its quality of care.* What about evidence Keywords? "Since" is synonymous with "because," so the evidence is *U Hospital and E Hospital (which releases patients earlier) have similar recovery rates for patients with similar illnesses.*

(By the way, did you have trouble buying the author's reasoning here? If so, good for you! Many LSAT arguments are flawed, and the LSAT frequently rewards you for spotting argumentative flaws. We'll discuss flaws thoroughly in Chapter 10.)

Sometimes evidence isn't marked with a Keyword. In those cases, you need to ask yourself which parts of the argument answer the question "Why so?" That is, identify the author's conclusion using conclusion Keywords or the One-Sentence Test. Then imagine yourself saying to the author, "Here's your claim. Why so? What makes you believe that?" The parts of the argument that answer that question are the author's evidence. Revisit this argument, which you saw in the last section:

LSAT Question	Analysis
Dietitian: Many diet-conscious consumers are excited about new "fake fat" products designed to give food the flavor and consistency of fatty foods, yet without fat's harmful effects. Consumers who expect the new fat substitute to help them lose weight are likely to be disappointed, however. Research has shown that when people knowingly or unknowingly eat foods containing "fake fat," they tend to take in at least as many additional calories as are saved by eating "fake fat." *PrepTest52 Sec3 Q2*	Conclusion? "[H]owever" is a clue, and the One-Sentence Test homes in on the main idea: *Consumers who want to lose weight are going to be disappointed by "fake fat."* What about evidence? No words like "because," "since," or "for." So, author, why are these consumers likely to be disappointed? The author answers in the last sentence: *when consumers take in "fake fat," they still eat just as many calories or more.* That's the evidence.

Did anything strike you about the nature of the evidence in that argument? The author used research studies to back up her claim. (In fact, the phrase "[r]esearch has shown" is a subtle clue that you're looking at evidence.) It's frequently helpful on the LSAT to note what kind of evidence an author is using: Is it made up of examples? Research studies? General principles about how the universe works? Expert opinion? Something else? We'll practice characterizing an author's argumentative strategy later in this chapter. For now, get in the habit of making a mental note of the kind of evidence you're looking at.

One more thought before we embark on some practice problems: Sometimes the LSAT will show you two arguments at once by allowing one speaker to paraphrase someone else's argument. In these cases, it's important to sort out which pieces of evidence belong to which speaker.

LSAT Question	Analysis
Historian: In rebuttal of my claim that West influenced Stuart, some people point out that West's work is mentioned only once in Stuart's diaries. But Stuart's diaries mention several meetings with West, and Stuart's close friend, Abella, studied under West. Furthermore, Stuart's work often uses West's terminology which, though now commonplace, none of Stuart's contemporaries used. *PrepTest52 Sec3 Q18*	Historian's conclusion? The One-Sentence Test. Here, the historian's point is *West influenced Stuart.* But there's another point of view in this stimulus. "[S]ome people" rebut the author's position, so their main point is that West didn't influence Stuart. What they "point out" is their evidence: *West's work is mentioned only once in Stuart's diaries.* Now, Historian, why do you say West influenced Stuart? He answers in the last two sentences: *Stuart's diaries reference meetings with West, Stuart's friend studied with West, and Stuart used West's terminology.* All of that is the Historian's evidence.

By the way, did the sentence structure make locating the author's conclusion challenging here? The conclusion is buried in the first sentence as a very short clause in a longer sentence. But there is still a helpful, albeit subtle, conclusion Keyword: "my claim that . . ." Anytime the author labels a piece of the argument as being his "claim"—or *opinion, position, contention,* or *thesis*—you're likely looking at his conclusion.

TEST DAY TIP

Underline (or use a checkmark to denote) the evidence in your test booklet. This will highlight the evidence and keep it distinct from the bracketed conclusion. Get in the habit of doing this for all Argument-based and Assumption-family questions.

Practice

Now, practice identifying the evidence in a handful of LSAT arguments.

In each of the arguments below, locate the evidence the author or speaker in question uses to support her conclusion. In your own words, explain how you knew that the sentence or clause you selected is evidence for the author's conclusion. After each, you can turn to the expert thinking and check your work.

LSAT Question	My Analysis
14. Therapist: The ability to trust other people is essential to happiness, for without trust there can be no meaningful emotional connection to another human being, and without meaningful emotional connections to others we feel isolated. *PrepTest56 Sec3 Q16*	
15. A retrospective study is a scientific study that tries to determine the causes of subjects' present characteristics by looking for significant connections between the present characteristics of subjects and what happened to those subjects in the past, before the study began. Because retrospective studies of human subjects must use the subjects' reports about their own pasts, however, such studies cannot reliably determine the causes of human subjects' present characteristics. *PrepTest62 Sec2 Q9*	

In this next question, what is Mariah's evidence? What's Joanna's evidence?

LSAT Question	My Analysis
16. Mariah: Joanna has argued that Adam should not judge the essay contest because several of his classmates have entered the contest. However, the essays are not identified by author to the judge and, moreover, none of Adam's friends are classmates of his. Still, Adam has no experience in critiquing essays. Therefore, I agree with Joanna that Adam should not judge the contest. *PrepTest56 Sec3 Q3*	

Here's how an LSAT expert looks at each of the arguments you've just examined.

LSAT Question	Analysis
14. Therapist: The ability to trust other people is essential to happiness, for without trust there can be no meaningful emotional connection to another human being, and without meaningful emotional connections to others we feel isolated. *PrepTest56 Sec3 Q16*	Conclusion? One-Sentence Test points to the first clause: *an ability to trust is essential to happiness.* Evidence? A great evidence Keyword: "for." The evidence is everything that follows. A good paraphrase is *you'll feel isolated if you don't have emotional connection, and you can't have emotional connection if you don't have trust* (or *to avoid feeling isolated, you need emotional connections, and to have those you need trust*).

Did you notice the Formal Logic in this argument? You may not need to map out the conditional statements just to identify evidence, but you should use your Formal Logic skills to make sure you're paraphrasing correctly. In the argument above, notice that both pieces of evidence share the term "meaningful emotional connection." This sets up a simple chain of Formal Logic. In order not to feel isolated, you need meaningful emotional connections. To have meaningful emotional connections, you need the ability to trust others. So, the evidence here can collapse into a single statement: in order to avoid feeling isolated, you need the ability to trust others. Go back and review Formal Logic in Chapter 1 if you were uncertain about how to understand the "without" clauses in this stimulus.

LSAT Question	Analysis
15. A retrospective study is a scientific study that tries to determine the causes of subjects' present characteristics by looking for significant connections between the present characteristics of subjects and what happened to those subjects in the past, before the study began. Because retrospective studies of human subjects must use the subjects' reports about their own pasts, however, such studies cannot reliably determine the causes of human subjects' present characteristics. *PrepTest62 Sec2 Q9*	Conclusion? The contrast Keyword "however" helps, as does the One-Sentence Test: *retrospective studies can't tell us why people have the characteristics they have.* Evidence? Keyword "because," so focus on the clause following that word: *retrospective studies use peoples' own stories about their pasts.*

What purpose does the first sentence serve in this example? It's background information that we need in order to understand the author's argument, but does not, by itself, advance the author's conclusion.

LSAT Question	**Analysis**
16. Mariah: Joanna has argued that Adam should not judge the essay contest because several of his classmates have entered the contest. However, the essays are not identified by author to the judge and, moreover, none of Adam's friends are classmates of his. Still, Adam has no experience in critiquing essays. Therefore, I agree with Joanna that Adam should not judge the contest. *PrepTest56 Sec3 Q3*	Mariah's conclusion? Great Keyword in "[t]herefore." So Mariah's main point is *Adam should not judge the contest.* Mariah's evidence? She cites several facts, but the only one that really answers the question "Why?" is *Adam has no experience in critiquing essays.* That's her relevant evidence. Joanna's conclusion? She "argued that" *Adam should not judge the contest.* Her conclusion matches Mariah's. Joanna's evidence? "[B]ecause" *Adam has classmates in the contest.*

What about all those other facts Mariah cites—that the essays aren't identified by author and Adam's friends aren't his classmates? They aren't support for Mariah's claim—rather, she's using them to debunk Joanna's argument. That's helpful to note, but don't confuse it with support for Mariah's own conclusion. Although Mariah and Joanna reach the same conclusion, they do so based on entirely different evidence.

Reflection

Review your practice above: How efficiently were you able to identify the author's evidence? Did you paraphrase the evidence in your own words? Did you make a mental note of what kind of evidence the author was using? What, if anything, distracted you from homing in on the relevant evidence?

Did you make some mistakes? That's great! Mistakes are a tremendously valuable source of information for you: Every error tells you something about what you need to work on before Test Day. How did you misidentify the evidence in this practice? Do you see any patterns in your mistakes?

Identify and Answer Role of a Statement Questions

You've gotten some practice with identifying conclusions and evidence. Ready to put it to use? One LSAT question type, called Role of a Statement, rewards your ability to simply identify the various pieces of an argument—such as evidence, conclusion, opponent's argument, or background information. You know you're dealing with a Role of a Statement question if you see a question stem like this:

LSAT Question	Analysis
Which one of the following most accurately describes the role played in the philosopher's argument by the claim that at least sometimes when sleeping, people are truly happy, even though they are not doing anything? *PrepTest52 Sec3 Q17*	The stem quotes a claim or statement from the stimulus (here "at least sometimes when sleeping, people are truly happy, even though they are not doing anything"). We're asked for the "role played" by the statement. Our job will be to say whether the statement in question is conclusion, evidence, or something else.

As always when working with arguments on the LSAT, start with identifying and paraphrasing evidence and conclusion. Then formulate a prediction to use when looking at the answer choices. Your prediction on a Role of a Statement question will sound something like this: "the statement is evidence," "the statement is the author's conclusion," or "the statement is evidence cited by the author's opponents." Wrong answer choices on a Role of a Statement question will likely describe *other* parts of the author's argument or distort the argument in some way.

Let's look at this example of a full LSAT Role of a Statement question.

LSAT Question	Analysis
Farmer: In the long run, it is counterproductive for farmers to use insecticides. Because insects' resistance to insecticides increases with insecticide use, farmers have to use greater and greater amounts of costly insecticides to control insect pests.	**Step 2:** Conclusion? The One-Sentence Test points us to the first sentence. *Pesticides are counterproductive in the long run.* Evidence? Everything else: *insects become resistant, and because of this, farmers have to keep using more and more pesticides.* The second part of that evidence is a statement from the question stem. It's a subsidiary conclusion, supported by the first part of the evidence, and itself supports the ultimate conclusion.
Which one of the following most accurately describes the role played in the farmer's argument by the proposition that farmers have to use greater and greater amounts of costly insecticides to control insect pests?	**Step 1:** "[R]ole" tells us it's a Role of a Statement question. The statement we're looking out for is *farmers have to use greater and greater amounts of costly pesticides to control insect pests.*
	Step 3: The statement in question is evidence in the form of a subsidiary conclusion. It follows from one piece of evidence and, in turn, serves to support the conclusion.
(A) It is the argument's main conclusion, but not its only conclusion.	**Step 4:** The statement is not the main conclusion. Eliminate.
(B) It is a claim for which a causal explanation is provided and which itself is used as direct support for the argument's only conclusion.	Correct. (B) matches the prediction.
(C) It is the argument's only conclusion.	The argument has two conclusions. The statement in question is a subsidiary one. Eliminate.
(D) It is a claim that is used as direct support for an intermediary conclusion, which in turn is used as direct support for the argument's main conclusion.	This describes the first piece of evidence: *resistance to pesticides increases with use.* Eliminate.
(E) It identifies a phenomenon for which the argument's main conclusion offers a causal explanation. *PrepTest56 Sec2 Q25*	This distorts the author's conclusion, which is a value judgment ("counterproductive"), not a causal explanation for something. Eliminate.

On Test Day, you could stop with (B) once you've seen that it matches your prediction perfectly. As you're practicing for the LSAT, however, it's always valuable to review all four wrong answers and make sure you see why each is incorrect.

Practice

Practice solving Role of a Statement questions using the approach just illustrated.

Apply the Kaplan Logical Reasoning Method to answer each of the following questions. Here, note clues in the question stem to determine that these are Role of a Statement questions. Then, untangle the stimulus by identifying the author's conclusion and evidence. Find and underline the statement cited in the question stem and describe the role it plays in the argument. Use that as your prediction of the correct answer and evaluate the answer choices. After each question, you can turn to the expert thinking and check your work.

LSAT Question	My Analysis
17. Philosopher: Graham argues that since a person is truly happy only when doing something, the best life is a life that is full of activity. But we should not be persuaded by Graham's argument. People sleep, and at least sometimes when sleeping, they are truly happy, even though they are not doing anything.	**Step 2:**
Which one of the following most accurately describes the role played in the philosopher's argument by the claim that at least sometimes when sleeping, people are truly happy, even though they are not doing anything?	**Step 1:**
	Step 3:
(A) It is a premise of Graham's argument.	**Step 4:**
(B) It is an example intended to show that a premise of Graham's argument is false.	
(C) It is an analogy appealed to by Graham but that the philosopher rejects.	
(D) It is an example intended to disprove the conclusion of Graham's argument.	
(E) It is the main conclusion of the philosopher's argument.	

PrepTest52 Sec3 Q17

LSAT Question	My Analysis
18. Paleontologists recently excavated two corresponding sets of dinosaur tracks, one left by a large grazing dinosaur and the other by a smaller predatory dinosaur. The two sets of tracks make abrupt turns repeatedly in tandem, suggesting that the predator was following the grazing dinosaur and had matched its stride. Modern predatory mammals, such as lions, usually match the stride of prey they are chasing immediately before they strike those prey. This suggests that the predatory dinosaur was chasing the grazing dinosaur and attacked immediately afterwards.	**Step 2:**
Which one of the following most accurately describes the role played in the argument by the statement that the predatory dinosaur was following the grazing dinosaur and had matched its stride?	**Step 1:**
	Step 3:
(A) It helps establish the scientific importance of the argument's overall conclusion, but is not offered as evidence for that conclusion.	**Step 4:**
(B) It is a hypothesis that is rejected in favor of the hypothesis stated in the argument's overall conclusion.	
(C) It provides the basis for an analogy used in support of the argument's overall conclusion.	
(D) It is presented to counteract a possible objection to the argument's overall conclusion.	
(E) It is the overall conclusion of the argument.	

PrepTest62 Sec4 Q4

Here's how an LSAT expert looks at each of the arguments you've just examined.

LSAT Question	Analysis
17. Philosopher: Graham argues that since a person is truly happy only when doing something, the best life is a life that is full of activity. But we should not be persuaded by Graham's argument. People sleep, and at least sometimes when sleeping, they are truly happy, even though they are not doing anything.	**Step 2:** Conclusion: The Contrast Keyword "[b]ut" tells us that Philosopher disagrees with Graham. In other words, *the best life is not necessarily full of activity.* Evidence: *Sleeping people are sometimes happy, even though they're not doing anything.* This is the claim from the stem.
Which one of the following most accurately describes the role played in the philosopher's argument by the claim that at least sometimes when sleeping, people are truly happy, even though they are not doing anything?	**Step 1:** "[R]ole" tells us it's an ROS. Keep an eye out for *at least sometimes when sleeping, people are truly happy, even though they are not doing anything.*
	Step 3: The statement in question is the philosopher's evidence. Specifically, it attacks Graham's evidence.
(A) It is a premise of Graham's argument.	**Step 4:** Totally backward; the statement in question is evidence against Graham. Eliminate.
(B) It is an example intended to show that a premise of Graham's argument is false.	Correct. This matches the prediction and describes the role of the statement perfectly.
(C) It is an analogy appealed to by Graham but that the philosopher rejects.	The statement is not an analogy and goes against Graham. Doubly wrong. Eliminate.
(D) It is an example intended to disprove the conclusion of Graham's argument.	The statement we're evaluating contradicts Graham's evidence. Eliminate.
(E) It is the main conclusion of the philosopher's argument.	The statement in the stem is not anyone's conclusion. Eliminate.

PrepTest52 Sec3 Q17

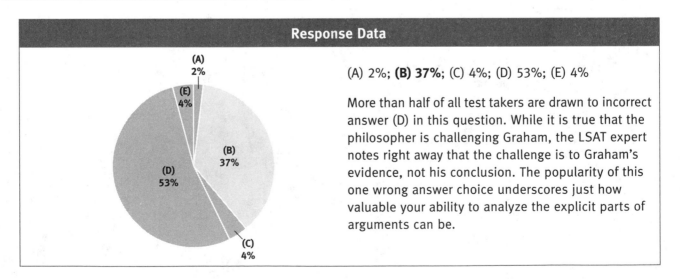

Response Data

(A) 2%; **(B) 37%**; (C) 4%; (D) 53%; (E) 4%

More than half of all test takers are drawn to incorrect answer (D) in this question. While it is true that the philosopher is challenging Graham, the LSAT expert notes right away that the challenge is to Graham's evidence, not his conclusion. The popularity of this one wrong answer choice underscores just how valuable your ability to analyze the explicit parts of arguments can be.

Let's say that you got as far as recognizing that the statement in question was the philosopher's evidence but didn't characterize it further than that. Just by realizing that it is evidence, you've knocked out answer choices (A), (C), and (E). Deciding between (B) and (D) is a matter of doing just a little more analysis on the stimulus.

LSAT Question	**Analysis**
18. Paleontologists recently excavated two corresponding sets of dinosaur tracks, one left by a large grazing dinosaur and the other by a smaller predatory dinosaur. The two sets of tracks make abrupt turns repeatedly in tandem, suggesting that the predator was following the grazing dinosaur and had matched its stride. Modern predatory mammals, such as lions, usually match the stride of prey they are chasing immediately before they strike those prey. This suggests that the predatory dinosaur was chasing the grazing dinosaur and attacked immediately afterwards.	**Step 2:** Conclusion? The phrase "[t]his suggests that" tells us that what came before is evidence. The conclusion is the last sentence: *the predatory dinosaur chased the grazing one and then immediately attacked.* Evidence? Facts about the dinosaur prints: *the predator appears to have followed and then matched the stride of the grazing dinosaur.* An analogous situation: *Modern predators do that just before attacking prey.*
Which one of the following most accurately describes the role played in the argument by the statement that the predatory dinosaur was following the grazing dinosaur and had matched its stride?	**Step 1:** "[R]ole" tells us this is a Role of a Statement question. Keep an eye out for the claim that *the predatory dinosaur was following the grazing dinosaur and had matched its stride.*
	Step 3: The statement in question supports the conclusion by suggesting that prehistoric predators acted in a manner analogous to modern predators that match their prey's stride right before attacking.
(A) It helps establish the scientific importance of the argument's overall conclusion, but is not offered as evidence for that conclusion.	**Step 4:** It is offered as support for the conclusion, and "scientific importance" is Outside the Scope. Eliminate.
(B) It is a hypothesis that is rejected in favor of the hypothesis stated in the argument's overall conclusion.	The author believes the statement is right in line with the conclusion. Indeed, given how modern predators behave, it supports the conclusion. Eliminate.
(C) It provides the basis for an analogy used in support of the argument's overall conclusion.	Correct. The author uses the modern analogy to show that the statement in question supports his conclusion.
(D) It is presented to counteract a possible objection to the argument's overall conclusion.	The argument doesn't deal with potential objections. This is Outside the Scope. Eliminate.
(E) It is the overall conclusion of the argument. *PrepTest62 Sec4 Q4*	The conclusion is that the dinosaur matched the grazer's pace and immediately attacked. The statement in question is what led the author to that conclusion. Eliminate.

Look back over your practice. Did you identify and paraphrase the author's conclusion and evidence before making a prediction about the statement quoted in the question stem? Did you keep your prediction in mind as you evaluated answer choices?

If these questions didn't go well, treat that as a blessing in disguise by using your mistakes as powerful sources of information about what you need to work on. What led you to misidentify the role played by the statement you were asked about?

Outlining Complete Arguments and Point at Issue Questions

> ### LEARNING OBJECTIVES
>
> In this section, you'll learn to:
>
> · Outline complete arguments.
> · Identify Point at Issue questions and characterize the correct and incorrect answers.

Here you see a Point at Issue question. You'll review it piece-by-piece shortly. These questions reward you for zeroing in on the particular point about which two speakers disagree. Preparing to tackle this question type provides the perfect opportunity to learn another valuable LSAT Logical Reasoning skill: outlining complete arguments.

Samuel: Because communication via computer is usually conducted privately and anonymously between people who would otherwise interact in person, it contributes to the dissolution, not the creation, of lasting communal bonds.

Tova: You assume that communication via computer replaces more intimate forms of communication and interaction, when more often it replaces asocial or even antisocial behavior.

On the basis of their statements, Samuel and Tova are committed to disagreeing about which one of the following?

(A)   A general trend of modern life is to dissolve the social bonds that formerly connected people.

(B)   All purely private behavior contributes to the dissolution of social bonds.

(C)   Face-to-face communication is more likely to contribute to the creation of social bonds than is anonymous communication.

(D)   It is desirable that new social bonds be created to replace the ones that have dissolved.

(E)   If people were not communicating via computer, they would most likely be engaged in activities that create stronger social bonds.

PrepTest52 Sec3 Q10

Outline Complete Arguments

Expert LSAT test takers are able to sum up and paraphrase the arguments in Logical Reasoning questions logically and accurately. They sort out the complex prose and sometimes indirect sentence structure in a way that makes every argument as simple as saying, "The author believes *y* (his conclusion) because of *x* (his evidence)."

Recall some of the arguments you've seen already in this chapter. At times, the evidence appeared before the conclusion, and at other times, after it. You've even seen arguments that had two pieces of evidence, one before and one after the conclusion. All of those ways can be effective ways of expressing an argument, but when you're outlining the argument—summarizing and paraphrasing it for your own understanding—you'll want to arrange the premises and conclusion logically:

[Conclusion] because [Evidence]

or

[Evidence]. Thus, [Conclusion]

Take a look at how an LSAT expert would outline this LSAT Logical Reasoning argument.

LSAT Question	Analysis
The average length of stay for patients at Edgewater Hospital is four days, compared to six days at University Hospital. Since studies show that recovery rates at the two hospitals are similar for patients with similar illnesses, University Hospital could decrease its average length of stay without affecting quality of care. *PrepTest52 Sec3 Q16*	Concl: U Hospital can maintain quality of care while decreasing length of stay *because* → Ev: E Hospital stays are two days shorter than U Hospital stays *and* Ev: E Hospital and U Hospital have equal recovery rates

That argument's author uses a very straightforward structure: Evidence 1 and Evidence 2 lead to Conclusion. LSAT authors aren't always roundabout or indirect, but keep in mind that the same argument could have been written quite differently. The author might have said, for example:

"Studies show that hospitals A and B have similar recovery rates for patients will similar conditions. This proves that hospital B could reduce its patients' stays without sacrificing quality of care, for it is also known that patient stays at hospital A are, on average, two days shorter than those at hospital B."

While the sentence and paragraph structures have changed in that example, the logic of the argument has not. An LSAT expert would outline the argument identically in both cases.

Here are a couple more examples. Notice that the arguments below aren't quite as simple as the one you just reviewed. Nonetheless, the expert thinker can simplify and rearrange them for better understanding.

LSAT Question	Analysis
Farmer: In the long run, it is counterproductive for farmers to use insecticides. Because insects' resistance to insecticides increases with insecticide use, farmers have to use greater and greater amounts of costly insecticides to control insect pests. *PrepTest56 Sec2 Q25*	Concl: Farmers' use of pesticides is counterproductive *because* Ev: Farmers have to use ever increasing amounts of pesticides *and that's because* Ev: Insects grow more resistant to pesticides
Dietitian: Many diet-conscious consumers are excited about new "fake fat" products designed to give food the flavor and consistency of fatty foods, yet without fat's harmful effects. Consumers who expect the new fat substitute to help them lose weight arc likely to be disappointed, however. Research has shown that when people knowingly or unknowingly eat foods containing "fake fat," they tend to take in at least as many additional calories as are saved by eating "fake fat." *PrepTest52 Sec3 Q2*	Concl: Diet-conscious consumers won't lose weight by eating "fake fat" foods *because* Ev: Research shows that those who eat "fake fat" foods eat as many or more additional calories as they save by eating "fake fat"
The reason music with a simple recurring rhythm exerts a strong primordial appeal is that it reminds us of the womb environment. After all, the first sound heard within the womb is the comforting sound of the mother's regular heartbeat. So in taking away from us the warmth and security of the womb, birth also takes away a primal and constant source of comfort. Thus it is extremely natural that in seeking sensations of warmth and security throughout life, people would be strongly drawn toward simple recurring rhythmic sounds. *PrepTest58 Sec4 Q3*	Concl: Rhythmic music is appealing because it reminds people of the womb *because* Ev: The first sound people hear in the womb is the mother's rhythmic heartbeat *and* Ev: Birth takes us away from the mother's rhythmic heartbeat *and so* Ev: People seeking comfort/security are drawn to rhythmic sounds

Notice how the test expert untangles the argument so that she can outline it in a way that progresses logically through the author's reasoning. You'll find that having the ability to summarize and outline LSAT arguments in this way is enormously helpful in many Logical Reasoning question types—Assumption, Strengthen/Weaken, Flaw, and Parallel Reasoning, as well as two question types still to come in this chapter, Point at Issue and Method of Argument.

Practice

Now, try untangling and outlining a handful of LSAT arguments on your own. Strive to make your summaries as clear and simple as the expert thinking you saw above.

For each of the following arguments, locate the conclusion and the relevant evidence. Then, outline the complete argument in the following format: [Conclusion] because [Evidence]. When the argument has more than one piece of evidence, make sure you can outline the logical progression of the author's reasoning. When you're done, you can check your work and review the expert thinking on the next page.

LSAT Question	My Analysis
19. The *Iliad* and the *Odyssey* were both attributed to Homer in ancient times. But these two poems differ greatly in tone and vocabulary and in certain details of the fictional world they depict. So they are almost certainly not the work of the same poet. *PrepTest52 Sec1 Q21*	
20. Sociologist: Widespread acceptance of the idea that individuals are incapable of looking after their own welfare is injurious to a democracy. So legislators who value democracy should not propose any law prohibiting behavior that is not harmful to anyone besides the person engaging in it. After all, the assumptions that appear to guide legislators will often become widely accepted. *PrepTest52 Sec1 Q25*	
21. Humanitarian considerations aside, sheer economics dictates that country X should institute, as country Y has done, a nationwide system of air and ground transportation for conveying seriously injured persons to specialized trauma centers. Timely access to the kind of medical care that only specialized centers can provide could save the lives of many people. The earnings of these people would result in a substantial increase in country X's gross national product, and the taxes paid on those earnings would substantially augment government revenues. *PrepTest52 Sec3 Q13*	

Here's how an LSAT expert would untangle the arguments you just looked at.

LSAT Question	Analysis
19. The *Iliad* and the *Odyssey* were both attributed to Homer in ancient times. But these two poems differ greatly in tone and vocabulary and in certain details of the fictional world they depict. So they are almost certainly not the work of the same poet. *PrepTest52 Sec1 Q21*	Concl: The *Iliad* and the *Odyssey* were not written by the same poet *because* Ev: The *Iliad* and the *Odyssey* differ in tone and vocabulary and depict inconsistent fictional worlds

Note that the first sentence in the argument above is just background. It may be interesting that people used to think the two epics were by the same author, but it's not part of the argument.

LSAT Question	Analysis
20. Sociologist: Widespread acceptance of the idea that individuals are incapable of looking after their own welfare is injurious to a democracy. So legislators who value democracy should not propose any law prohibiting behavior that is not harmful to anyone besides the person engaging in it. After all, the assumptions that appear to guide legislators will often become widely accepted. *PrepTest52 Sec1 Q25*	Concl: Lawmakers who value democracy should not propose laws that punish people for actions that can't harm anyone else *because* Ev: Legislators' apparent assumptions often become widely accepted *and* Widespread acceptance that people can't take care of themselves is bad for democracy
21. Humanitarian considerations aside, sheer economics dictates that country X should institute, as country Y has done, a nationwide system of air and ground transportation for conveying seriously injured persons to specialized trauma centers. Timely access to the kind of medical care that only specialized centers can provide could save the lives of many people. The earnings of these people would result in a substantial increase in country X's gross national product, and the taxes paid on those earnings would substantially augment government revenues. *PrepTest52 Sec3 Q13*	Concl: Country X should set up an air/ground emergency transport system for the seriously injured *because* Ev: Getting to emergency trauma centers could save the seriously injured *and* Those saved will contribute to GNP and pay taxes

Did the reasoning in the third argument surprise you a little bit? We don't usually support calls for medical aid by saying, "Well, it would keep more taxpayers alive." It's a good reminder not to bring in your outside presumptions and expectations. The LSAT always rewards you for dealing with the arguments exactly as written, even when they might seem odd or unconvincing.

Identify and Answer Point at Issue Questions

As you master the skill of untangling and outlining complete arguments, you're ready to tackle another LSAT Logical Reasoning question type: Point at Issue questions. Point at Issue questions are relatively rare—a typical test will likely have 1–3 of them. PrepTests 65 and 66 had a total of three Point at Issue questions, while PrepTest 56, from

December 2008 also had three, all in a single section. While you won't practice a lot of these questions, keep in mind that they benefit from and reinforce the same analysis of argument skills rewarded by a majority of Logical Reasoning questions. One interesting note about Point at Issue questions is that the testmaker often asks similar questions along with the Comparative Reading passages in the Reading Comprehension section.

Point at Issue questions always have a dialogue in the stimulus. Both speakers make arguments, and they always disagree about one particular aspect of their arguments. The correct answer states or paraphrases this point of disagreement. The wrong answers to these questions come in three flavors: (1) a point about which only one of the speakers has an opinion, (2) a point outside the scope of both speakers' arguments, or (3) a point over which the two speakers *agree*. That last wrong answer type can be tempting since it is something both speakers have expressed an opinion about.

Take a look at a couple of typical Point at Issue question stems.

LSAT Question		Analysis
On the basis of their statements, Samuel and Tova are committed to disagreeing about which one of the following? *PrepTest52 Sec3 Q10*	→	"[C]ommitted to disagreeing about"—a Point at Issue question. The correct answer will be a statement about which the speakers have diametrically opposite opinions.
The dialogue provides the most support for the claim that Glen and Sara disagree about whether *PrepTest56 Sec2 Q17*	→	"[D]isagree about"—a Point at Issue question. The correct answer is a statement about which one speaker would say "yes" and the other "no."

On very rare occasions, the testmaker will ask a Point of Agreement question, in which case the correct answer will be the one containing a statement on which the two speakers have the same point of view. You'll see one of these below. Let it serve as a reminder never to take the question stem for granted. Make sure that you always respond to the task the test has set out for you.

Once you've identified a Point at Issue question, untangle both speakers' arguments to make sure you understand their conclusions and how they're supporting them. The two parties in the dialogue won't always disagree with each other's conclusions. Here's a simple example:

Tom: Our football team will win this game because our quarterback is great.

Jenny: You're wrong. Our quarterback is pretty average. We're going to win because our defense is so strong.

Here, Tom and Jenny share the same conclusion: their team is going to win. They disagree about why that will be the case. In particular, they are directly at odds in their assessment of the quarterback.

In other cases, the two speakers may share the same evidence but reach different conclusions.

Michelle: The expansion of Superior Corporation's factory will bring workers into the area. That means a lot of new houses will be built in our town.

Sundeep: But these aren't the kind of jobs that lead to housing starts. The workers coming for jobs at Superior will be seasonal, so they'll likely seek apartments or other rental options.

Michelle and Sundeep see eye to eye on the fact that the factory expansion will bring workers into the area, but from that information, they draw opposed inferences about what this means for the town's housing market.

When you're able to spot the issue over which the two speakers are at odds, you have predicted the correct answer and can evaluate the answer choices.

> **TEST DAY TIP**
>
> A great way to evaluate the answer choices in Point at Issue questions is to apply the questions in Kaplan's Point at Issue Decision Tree.

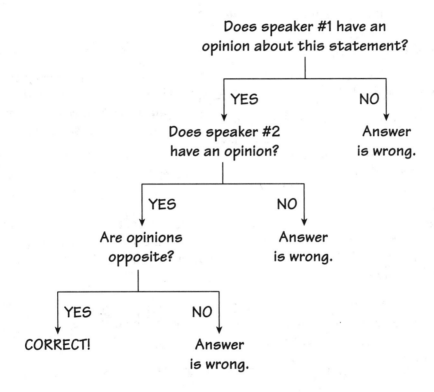

Since the correct answer must be the one statement over which the two speakers are committed to disagreeing, it will be the only choice that produces a "yes" to all three questions in the Decision Tree.

Take a look at how an LSAT expert approaches a Point at Issue question.

LSAT Question	Analysis
Samuel: Because communication via computer is usually conducted privately and anonymously between people who would otherwise interact in person, it contributes to the dissolution, not the creation, of lasting communal bonds. Tova: You assume that communication via computer replaces more intimate forms of communication and interaction, when more often it replaces asocial or even antisocial behavior.	**Step 2:** Samuel's argument: [Conclusion] Computer communication dissolves communal bonds *because* [Evidence] it replaces personal interaction with private action. Tova's argument: [Implied Conclusion] Computer communication doesn't dissolve communal bonds *because* [Evidence] the kind of interaction it replaces is antisocial.
On the basis of their statements, Samuel and Tova are committed to disagreeing about which one of the following?	**Step 1:** "[C]ommitted to disagreeing about"—a Point at Issue question. The correct answer will be a point over which the two speakers have opposite opinions.
	Step 3: Samuel thinks that the personal interaction replaced by computer time would strengthen communal bonds, while Tova thinks such interaction is often antisocial.
(A) A general trend of modern life is to dissolve the social bonds that formerly connected people.	**Step 4:** Neither speaker expresses an opinion about the "general trend of modern life." Eliminate.
(B) All purely private behavior contributes to the dissolution of social bonds.	"All" is too strong to apply to either speaker. Samuel's point is specifically about such behavior *when* it replaces personal interaction. Eliminate.
(C) Face-to-face communication is more likely to contribute to the creation of social bonds than is anonymous communication.	Tova doesn't express an opinion on this one. Eliminate.
(D) It is desirable that new social bonds be created to replace the ones that have dissolved.	Neither party addresses this comparison at all. Eliminate.
(E) If people were not communicating via computer, they would most likely be engaged in activities that create stronger social bonds. *PrepTest52 Sec3 Q10*	Correct. For Samuel to make his argument, he must agree with this statement; Tova explicitly disagrees.

By the way, choice (C) is by far the most difficult wrong answer for most students to eliminate. It's a great example of why careful reading is so important throughout the LSAT. While Tova disagrees with Samuel's contention that computer communication dissolves communal bonds, she never makes the precise comparison stated in choice (C).

Practice

Now, try a couple of Point at Issue questions on your own. Remember to outline each side's argument before you evaluate the answer choices. Use the Decision Tree to help you eliminate wrong answers and zero in on the one credited response.

Apply the Kaplan Logical Reasoning Method to answer the following questions. When you're done, check your work and review the expert thinking on the pages that follow questions 22–23.

LSAT Question	My Analysis
22. Denise: Crime will be reduced only when punishment is certain and is sufficiently severe to give anyone considering committing a crime reason to decide against doing so.	Step 2:
Reshmi: No, crime will be most effectively reduced if educational opportunities are made readily available to everyone, so that those who once viewed criminal activity as the only means of securing a comfortable lifestyle will choose a different path.	
Their dialogue provides the most support for the claim that Denise and Reshmi agree that*	Step 1:
	Step 3:
(A) people are capable of choosing whether or not to commit crimes	Step 4:
(B) crime is the most important issue facing modern society	
(C) reducing crime requires fair and consistent responses to criminal behavior	
(D) crimes are committed in response to economic need	
(E) reducing crime requires focusing on assured punishments	

PrepTest56 Sec2 Q2

*For this question, notice that the question stem asks for the point on which Denise and Reshmi *agree*.

LSAT Question	My Analysis
23. Tania: A good art critic is not fair in the ordinary sense; it is only about things that do not interest one that one can give a truly unbiased opinion. Since art is a passion, good criticism of art cannot be separated from emotion. Monique: Art is not simply a passion. The best art critics passionately engage with the artwork, but render their criticism only after shedding all of their biases and consulting general principles of aesthetics.	**Step 2:**
The dialogue most strongly supports the claim that Tania and Monique disagree about whether	**Step 1:**
	Step 3:
(A) art is not simply a passion	**Step 4:**
(B) good art criticism is sometimes unbiased	
(C) art critics should not feel emotion toward artworks	
(D) fairness generally requires minimizing the influence of bias	
(E) the passionate engagement of the art critic with the artwork is the most important aspect of art criticism *PrepTest56 Sec2 Q21*	

Here's how LSAT experts would answer the problems you just tried.

LSAT Question	Analysis
22. Denise: Crime will be reduced only when punishment is certain and is sufficiently severe to give anyone considering committing a crime reason to decide against doing so. Reshmi: No, crime will be most effectively reduced if educational opportunities are made readily available to everyone, so that those who once viewed criminal activity as the only means of securing a comfortable lifestyle will choose a different path.	**Step 2:** Denise: [Conclusion] Severe and certain punishment is needed to reduce crime *because* [Evidence] this level of punishment gives people a reason to decide against criminal actions. Reshmi: [Conclusion] Education is the most effective crime deterrent *because* [Evidence] it gives those who thought crime was the only way a chance to choose differently.
Their dialogue provides the most support for the claim that Denise and Reshmi agree that	**Step 1:** "[S]upport for the claim . . . agree"—this is a Point at Issue variant. The correct answer will be the only one on which the two speakers have the same opinion.
	Step 3: The two speakers both agree that people can choose not to engage in crime (although they have different ideas about what will persuade people to avoid it).
(A) people are capable of choosing whether or not to commit crimes	**Step 4:** Correct. Serena thinks punishment makes people decide not to commit crimes, while Reshmi thinks education allows them to choose another path.
(B) crime is the most important issue facing modern society	Neither speaker says this. Eliminate.
(C) reducing crime requires fair and consistent responses to criminal behavior	"[F]air and consistent" falls outside either speaker's argument. Reshmi doesn't talk about a "response" to crime at all. Eliminate.
(D) crimes are committed in response to economic need	Reshmi seems to agree, but Denise doesn't weigh in on this point. Eliminate.
(E) reducing crime requires focusing on assured punishments *PrepTest56 Sec2 Q2*	This is Denise's point, but Reshmi would actually disagree. If this were a regular Point at Issue question, this would be the right answer, but not here. Eliminate.

As you learned earlier, the "Point of Agreement" variation is rare in the Logical Reasoning section of the LSAT, but similar questions often appear along with Comparative Reading passages in the Reading Comprehension section.

LSAT Question	Analysis
23. Tania: A good art critic is not fair in the ordinary sense; it is only about things that do not interest one that one can give a truly unbiased opinion. Since art is a passion, good criticism of art cannot be separated from emotion. Monique: Art is not simply a passion. The best art critics passionately engage with the artwork, but render their criticism only after shedding all of their biases and consulting general principles of aesthetics.	**Step 2:** Tania's argument: [Conclusion] Good art criticism has to be biased *because* [Evidence] the only way to be unbiased is to be disinterested *and* since art is a passion, one can't be unemotional about it. Monique's argument: [Conclusion] Good art critics are emotional but then shed their bias and consult aesthetic principles *because* [Evidence] art is not simply a passion.
The dialogue most strongly supports the claim that Tania and Monique disagree about whether	**Step 1:** "[D]isagree about"—a Point at Issue question. The correct answer will be a claim over which the two speakers totally disagree.
	Step 3: The two parties differ on whether good art criticism has to be biased. Tania says "yes" and Monique, "no."
(A) art is not simply a passion	**Step 4:** Tania never says art is "simply" a passion. She may believe much more is involved in the appreciation of art. Eliminate.
(B) good art criticism is sometimes unbiased	Correct. The two speakers are squarely opposed on this claim.
(C) art critics should not feel emotion toward artworks	Both speakers would disagree with this statement, thus agreeing with one another. Eliminate.
(D) fairness generally requires minimizing the influence of bias	How to achieve fairness falls outside the scope of either speaker's argument. Eliminate.
(E) the passionate engagement of the art critic with the artwork is the most important aspect of art criticism *PrepTest56 Sec2 Q21*	Neither speaker defines the "most important" aspect of criticism. This answer is too extreme to fit the dialogue. Eliminate.

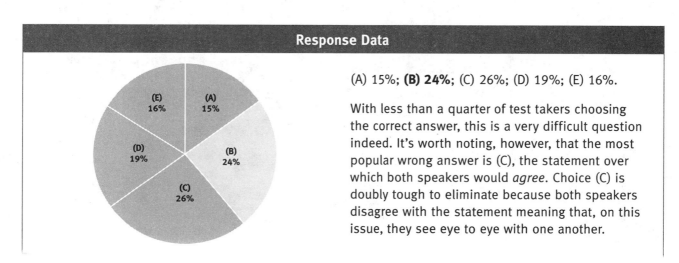

Response Data

(A) 15%; **(B) 24%**; (C) 26%; (D) 19%; (E) 16%.

With less than a quarter of test takers choosing the correct answer, this is a very difficult question indeed. It's worth noting, however, that the most popular wrong answer is (C), the statement over which both speakers would *agree*. Choice (C) is doubly tough to eliminate because both speakers disagree with the statement meaning that, on this issue, they see eye to eye with one another.

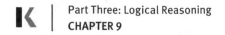
Reflection

Pay attention to some of the arguments, disputes, and disagreements you see or hear. Are the parties actually talking about the same thing? Try to pinpoint the actual issue(s) over which they disagree.

When you're listening to disagreements, try to determine whether the two speakers accept the same facts but draw different conclusions from them or see the same result but attribute it to different causes. These are like LSAT dialogues, which almost always feature a disagreement involving the reasoning, that is, a dispute about what the facts mean. Distinguish these from day-to-day arguments in which the parties simply disagree about the facts. The LSAT almost never features a dispute of that kind.

Describing Argumentative Strategy and Method of Argument Questions

> **LEARNING OBJECTIVES**
>
> In this section, you'll learn to:
>
> · Describe an author's argumentative strategy.
> · Identify Method of Argument questions and characterize the correct and incorrect answers.

Now that you've gotten some practice with describing arguments and their structures, you're ready to learn to characterize an author's argumentative strategy.

You saw as you were working with different kinds of evidence in the previous section that authors make choices about how to support their conclusions. One author might think that citing studies is really compelling, while another tries to persuade her readers by applying commonsense principles to the subject at hand. Another makes a generalization and backs it up with a handful of examples. Another author might claim that a statement must be true because Professor Thingummy, who's an expert, said so. Yet another might simply attack her opponent's position and figure that doing so will make her own position seem more compelling.

All those choices can be thought of as argumentative strategies, a phrase we'll use a great deal in this section. You've already gotten some good practice identifying *what* an author says and putting it into your own words. Now you'll learn how to describe in your own words *how* the author tries to convince the reader. Then, in a few pages, you'll meet a question type that rewards you for doing just that.

Always start by identifying and paraphrasing the author's conclusion, then the author's evidence. Then describe how the author has chosen to back up her conclusion.

LSAT Question	Analysis
Lahar: We must now settle on a procedure for deciding on meeting agendas. Our club's constitution allows three options: unanimous consent, majority vote, or assigning the task to a committee. Unanimous consent is unlikely. Forming a committee has usually led to factionalism and secret deals. Clearly, we should subject meeting agendas to majority vote. <div align="right">*PrepTest52 Sec3 Q5*</div>	Conclusion? Good Keyword in "[c]learly." Lahar's conclusion is that *we should decide meeting agendas via majority vote.* Evidence? *We have three options as to how to decide on meeting agendas, and two of those options won't work.* Argumentative strategy? Lahar lists some options and then discredits all but one of them. In other words, he supports a recommendation by eliminating alternatives.

The key here is to describe in your own words what Lahar does without getting caught up in the content of what Lahar says.

LSAT Question	Analysis
The Kiffer Forest Preserve, in the northernmost part of the Abbimac Valley, is where most of the bears in the valley reside. During the eight years that the main road through the preserve has been closed the preserve's bear population has nearly doubled. Thus, the valley's bear population will increase if the road is kept closed. *PrepTest58 Sec1 Q24* →	Conclusion? Nice Keyword in "[t]hus," and the last sentence passes the One-Sentence Test. Conclusion: *Keeping the road closed will result in an increase in the valley's bear population.* Evidence? The second sentence answers the question "Why so?" The author's evidence is that *in the past, keeping the road closed has coincided with an increase in the bear population.* Argumentative strategy? The conclusion is a prediction. The evidence describes what's happened before this point. In short, the author supports a prediction about the future using data from the past.

Again, stay focused on what the author *does*—not what the author says. This strategy could be applied in any number of arguments about any number of subjects.

Sometimes the LSAT presents you with an exchange between two different speakers. The LSAT may ask you to work with the first speaker's argument, with the second speaker's, or with the overlap or disagreement between the two. Here, imagine that we're asked to characterize Samantha's argumentative strategy:

LSAT Question	Analysis
Robert: The school board is considering adopting a year-round academic schedule that eliminates the traditional three-month summer vacation. This schedule should be adopted, since teachers need to cover more new material during the school year than they do now. Samantha: The proposed schedule will not permit teachers to cover more new material. Even though the schedule eliminates summer vacation, it adds six new two-week breaks, so the total number of school days will be about the same as before. *PrepTest52 Sec1 Q9* →	Quickly ID Robert's conclusion: *we should adopt the proposed schedule.* Samantha's conclusion? Keyword in "so," but give it the One-Sentence Test too. The main point is Samantha's rebuttal of Robert—*the proposed schedule won't let teachers cover more material.* (Turns out the "so" was marking a subsidiary conclusion.) Samantha's evidence? *The proposed schedule adds some time but takes away other time from the school year.* In other words, Robert is wrong in thinking the new schedule would result in more school days. Argumentative strategy? It's helpful here to look at what Robert's argument gives us: a description of the proposed school schedule. Samantha responds by adding some facts that Robert simply hasn't taken into consideration and using those new facts to discredit his conclusion.

There are lots of argumentative strategies in the world. However, a few common types tend to appear over and over again on the LSAT:

LSAT STRATEGY

Methods of Argument Common on the LSAT:

- Argument by analogy, in which an author draws parallels between two unrelated (but purportedly similar) situations
- Use of examples, in which an author cites specific cases in order to justify a generalization
- Use of counterexamples, in which an author seeks to discredit an opponent's argument by citing a specific case in which an opponent's conclusion appears to be invalid
- Appeal to authority, in which an author cites an expert or other authority figure as support for her conclusion
- Eliminating alternatives, in which an author lists possibilities and discredits all but one
- Ad hominem attack, in which an author attacks not her opponent's argument but rather her opponent's personal credibility
- Means/Requirement, in which the author argues that something is needed to achieve a desired result

---

There are others, but this is a helpful list of some common types. Be prepared to describe any argument's strategy in your own words on Test Day.

Practice

Practice describing argumentative strategies using the following LSAT questions.

In each of the following arguments, identify the author's conclusion and the relevant evidence. Once you've done so, describe in your own words *how* the author goes about supporting her conclusion. After each question, use the expert thinking on the next page to check your work.

LSAT Question	My Analysis
24. Acme Corporation offers unskilled workers excellent opportunities for advancement. As evidence, consider the fact that the president of the company, Ms. Garon, worked as an assembly line worker, an entry-level position requiring no special skills, when she first started at Acme. *PrepTest56 Sec2 Q3*	

In the following question, what is Lana's argumentative strategy?

LSAT Question	My Analysis
25. Chinh: Television producers should not pay attention to the preferences of the viewing public when making creative decisions. Great painters do not consider what the museum-going public wants to see. Lana: But television is expressly for the viewing public. So a producer is more like a CEO than like an artist. Just as a company would be foolhardy not to consider consumers' tastes when developing products, the TV producer must consider viewers' preferences. *PrepTest56 Sec2 Q5*	
26. One should never sacrifice one's health in order to acquire money, for without health, happiness is not obtainable. *PrepTest62 Sec2 Q17*	

Here's how an LSAT expert looks at each of the arguments you've just examined.

LSAT Question	Analysis
24. Acme Corporation offers unskilled workers excellent opportunities for advancement. As evidence, consider the fact that the president of the company, Ms. Garon, worked as an assembly line worker, an entry-level position requiring no special skills, when she first started at Acme. *PrepTest56 Sec2 Q3*	Conclusion? The One-Sentence Test points to the first sentence: *unskilled workers can advance at Acme.* Evidence? Great Keyword in "[a]s evidence." Evidence is one employee's story: *Ms. Garon started at entry level and is now president.* Argumentative strategy? The author makes a generalization about Acme and backs it up with a single example.
25. Chinh: Television producers should not pay attention to the preferences of the viewing public when making creative decisions. Great painters do not consider what the museum-going public wants to see. Lana: But television is expressly for the viewing public. So a producer is more like a CEO than like an artist. Just as a company would be foolhardy not to consider consumers' tastes when developing products, the TV producer must consider viewers' preferences. *PrepTest56 Sec2 Q5*	Quickly ID Chinh's conclusion: *TV producers shouldn't consider their viewers' preferences.* Lana's conclusion? Give it the One-Sentence Test: *TV producers should consider viewers' preferences.* Lana's evidence? Chinh thinks TV producers are like artists, but Lana says *they're more like CEOs* and *companies listen to their consumers.* Lana's argumentative strategy? Notice that Lana says a producer is "like" a CEO. She's drawing a parallel between producers and CEOs. In other words, she's employing an analogy.

By the way, did you have trouble identifying Lana's conclusion? It helps here to realize that Lana is contradicting Chinh; notice the word "[b]ut" right up front. So her conclusion is probably the opposite of Chinh's main point.

LSAT Question	Analysis
26. One should never sacrifice one's health in order to acquire money, for without health, happiness is not obtainable. *PrepTest62 Sec2 Q17*	Conclusion? The first clause: *don't sacrifice health for money.* Evidence? Good evidence Keyword in "for." *You can't have happiness without health.* That's a general statement about the world—a principle. Argumentative strategy? The author makes a recommendation and supports it with a principle.

Reflection

Look back over your practice. Did you identify and paraphrase the author's conclusion and evidence before describing the entire argument? Did you describe the argumentative strategy in your own words? Did you stay focused on what the author *does* instead of what the author *says*? Did you stay focused on the speaker you were being asked about?

Did you make some mistakes? Good! Use those mistakes as sources of insight about what you need to work on. How did you mischaracterize the author's evidence? Do you see any patterns in your mistakes?

Identify and Answer Method of Argument Questions

Your ability to fully break down and analyze arguments will be rewarded with points throughout the LR and RC sections. One question type that rewards those skills in a very direct way is the MOA question. There are typically 1–2 of these on an average LSAT. As you described argumentative strategies in the last section, you were, without knowing it perhaps, already applying the Kaplan method for Method of Argument questions.

Method of Argument questions on the LSAT reward you for describing an author's argumentative strategy. The following are examples of question stems that tell you you're looking at a Method of Argument question:

LSAT Question		Analysis
The philosopher's argument proceeds by attempting to *PrepTest58 Sec1 Q26*	$\longrightarrow$	The Keywords "proceeds by" tell us to focus on the argument's rhetorical moves rather than on the argument's content—describe *how* rather than *what*.
The argument does which one of the following? *PrepTest58 Sec1 Q6*	$\longrightarrow$	"[D]oes" is also a Keyword that tells you to focus on the author's argumentative strategy rather than on content.
In her argument, Rahima *PrepTest58 Sec4 Q12*	$\longrightarrow$	This stem has fewer clues, but notice that it's the start of a sentence. Imagine the verb clause that would follow—it will describe *how* Rahima makes her argument.

It's important to be able to predict what you're looking for in the correct answer choice. The right choice will match your description of the author's argumentative strategy. The wrong answers may describe argumentative strategies not used by the author, or they might distort the argument in some way.

Look at how an expert LSAT taker attacks a Method of Argument question:

LSAT Question	Analysis
It is virtually certain that the government contract for building the new highway will be awarded to either Phoenix Contracting or Cartwright Company. I have just learned that the government has decided not to award the contract to Cartwright Company. It is therefore almost inevitable that Phoenix Contracting will be awarded the contract.	**Step 2:** Conclusion: Keyword "therefore" and One-Sentence Test give us *Phoenix will get the contract.* Evidence: *Either Phoenix or Cartwright is likely to get the contract, and Cartwright is now out of the running.*
The argument proceeds by	**Step 1:** "[P]roceeds by" tells you it's a Method of Argument question. The job here is to describe the author's argumentative strategy.
	Step 3: The author sets out two likely alternatives and eliminates one.
(A) concluding that it is extremely likely that an event will occur by ruling out the only probable alternative	**Step 4:** Correct. This matches our prediction perfectly!
(B) inferring, from a claim that one of two possible events will occur, that the other event will not occur	Reverses the evidence and conclusion. The author doesn't support a claim that Cartwright won't get the contract by citing evidence that Phoenix will—it's the other way around. Eliminate.
(C) refuting a claim that a particular event is inevitable by establishing the possibility of an alternative event	This is a 180. The author doesn't establish the possibility of an alternative; she denies the likely alternative. Eliminate.
(D) predicting a future event on the basis of an established pattern of past events	Mischaracterizes the evidence: there's no pattern cited in the argument. Eliminate.
(E) inferring a claim about the probability of a particular event from a general statistical statement	This also mischaracterizes the evidence: no statistics appear in the argument. Eliminate.

PrepTest62 Sec4 Q21

Keep in mind: On Test Day, you don't need to read past choice (A).

We saw earlier that LSAT questions sometimes give us two speakers in dialogue. Here's another example:

LSAT Question	Analysis
Music professor: Because rap musicians can work alone in a recording studio, they need not accommodate supporting musicians' wishes. Further, learning to rap is not as formal a process as learning an instrument. Thus, rap is an extremely individualistic and nontraditional musical form. Music critic: But rap appeals to tradition by using bits of older songs. Besides, the themes and styles of rap have developed into a tradition. And successful rap musicians do not perform purely idiosyncratically but conform their work to the preferences of the public.	**Step 2:** Quickly ID the music professor's conclusion: *rap is individualistic and nontraditional.* The music critic's conclusion? The music critic just gives us a string of facts. His conclusion is implicit and is signaled by the contrast Keyword "[b]ut"—he disagrees with the professor. So the critic's main point is that *rap is not as nontraditional and individualistic as the professor claims.* The critic's evidence? *Rap references tradition, has itself formed some traditions, and tries to appeal to the public.*
The music critic's response to the music professor's argument	**Step 1:** The question stem is the start of a sentence about what the music critic *does*, so it's a Method of Argument question.
	Step 3: The music critic's argumentative strategy: He doesn't disagree with the professor's evidence. Rather, he puts forward new evidence not considered by the professor.
(A) challenges it by offering evidence against one of the stated premises on which its conclusion concerning rap music is based	**Step 4:** (A) is a miss: the critic argues against the professor's conclusion, not against his premises. Eliminate.
(B) challenges its conclusion concerning rap music by offering certain additional observations that the music professor does not take into account in his argument	Correct. "[O]ffering . . . additional observations" matches the prediction perfectly.
(C) challenges the grounds on which the music professor generalizes from the particular context of rap music to the broader context of musical tradition and individuality	This one goes wrong in two ways: The critic (1) challenges the professor's conclusion, not his evidence, and (2) doesn't generalize from rap to anything broader. Eliminate.
(D) challenges it by offering an alternative explanation of phenomena that the music professor cites as evidence for his thesis about rap music	Here again the focus is incorrectly placed on the professor's evidence. Eliminate.
(E) challenges each of a group of claims about tradition and individuality in music that the music professor gives as evidence in his argument	Like (A), this choice wrongly suggests that the critic challenges the professor's evidence. Eliminate.

PrepTest62 Sec2 Q14

The wrong answer choices all suggest that the critic responds to the professor's *evidence*. But the critic completely ignores the professor's evidence. A good prediction for the correct answer helped you see that the critic attacked *only* the professor's conclusion and did so using *different* evidence.

Practice

Let's get some practice applying this method to Method of Argument questions.

In each of the arguments below, identify the author's conclusion and the relevant evidence. Once you've done so, describe in your own words *how* the author goes about supporting her conclusion. That description is the prediction you'll use to evaluate each answer choice. Find the answer choice that matches your prediction. Keep in mind the wrong answers will describe *other* argumentative strategies or somehow distort the argument. When you're done, check your work by reviewing the expert analysis that follows.

LSAT Question	My Analysis
27. Executive: We recently ran a set of advertisements in the print version of a travel magazine and on that magazine's website. We were unable to get any direct information about consumer response to the print ads. However, we found that consumer response to the ads on the website was much more limited than is typical for website ads. We concluded that consumer response to the print ads was probably below par as well.	**Step 2:**
The executive's reasoning does which one of the following?	**Step 1:**
	Step 3:
(A) bases a prediction of the intensity of a phenomenon on information about the intensity of that phenomenon's cause	**Step 4:**
(B) uses information about the typical frequency of events of a general kind to draw a conclusion about the probability of a particular event of that kind	
(C) infers a statistical generalization from claims about a large number of specific instances	
(D) uses a case in which direct evidence is available to draw a conclusion about an analogous case in which direct evidence is unavailable	
(E) bases a prediction about future events on facts about recent comparable events	

PrepTest56 Sec3 Q6

LSAT Question	My Analysis
28. Lance: If experience teaches us nothing else, it teaches us that every general rule has at least one exception.	**Step 2:**
Frank: What you conclude is itself a general rule. If we assume that it is true, then there is at least one general rule that has no exceptions. Therefore, you must withdraw your conclusion.	
Frank's argument is an attempt to counter Lance's conclusion by	**Step 1:**
	Step 3:
(A) demonstrating that Lance assumes the very thing he sets out to prove	**Step 4:**
(B) showing that Lance's conclusion involves him in a contradiction	
(C) showing that no general rule can have exceptions	
(D) establishing that experience teaches us the opposite of what Lance concludes	
(E) showing that it has no implications for any real cases	

PrepTest56 Sec2 Q11

LSAT Question	**My Analysis**
29. Philosopher: Wolves do not tolerate an attack by one wolf on another if the latter wolf demonstrates submission by baring its throat. The same is true of foxes and domesticated dogs. So it would be erroneous to deny that animals have rights on the grounds that only human beings are capable of obeying moral rules.	**Step 2:**
The philosopher's argument proceeds by attempting to	**Step 1:**
	Step 3:
(A) provide counterexamples to refute a premise on which a particular conclusion is based	**Step 4:**
(B) establish inductively that all animals possess some form of morality	
(C) cast doubt on the principle that being capable of obeying moral rules is a necessary condition for having rights	
(D) establish a claim by showing that the denial of that claim entails a logical contradiction	
(E) provide evidence suggesting that the concept of morality is often applied too broadly	

PrepTest58 Sec1 Q26

Here's how an expert test taker works through the problems you just saw:

LSAT Question	Analysis
27. Executive: We recently ran a set of advertisements in the print version of a travel magazine and on that magazine's website. We were unable to get any direct information about consumer response to the print ads. However, we found that consumer response to the ads on the website was much more limited than is typical for website ads. We concluded that consumer response to the print ads was probably below par as well.	**Step 2:** Conclusion? Keywords "[w]e concluded that." Conclusion is *consumers didn't respond in typical numbers to the print ads.* Evidence? *They ran print and web ads. The response to web ads was not so hot.*
The executive's reasoning does which one of the following?	**Step 1:** The phrase "executive's reasoning does" tells us it's a Method of Argument question.
	Step 3: Argumentative strategy? The executive doesn't have information about the print ads but does have information about the web ads. He draws a parallel between the two and uses data from the one situation to draw a conclusion about the other situation.
(A) bases a prediction of the intensity of a phenomenon on information about the intensity of that phenomenon's cause	**Step 4:** This choice distorts the argument in two ways: (1) by calling it a "prediction" (the executive isn't making a statement about the future) and (2) by suggesting the executive draws his info from the "phenomenon's cause." Neither type of ad caused the other. Eliminate.
(B) uses information about the typical frequency of events of a general kind to draw a conclusion about the probability of a particular event of that kind	Mischaracterizes the relationship between web and print ads: one is not a particular instance of the other. Eliminate.
(C) infers a statistical generalization from claims about a large number of specific instances	Also distorts the evidence. The executive doesn't generalize from cases; he's talking about two different phenomena. Eliminate.
(D) uses a case in which direct evidence is available to draw a conclusion about an analogous case in which direct evidence is unavailable	Correct. "[A]nalogous case" matches our prediction.
(E) bases a prediction about future events on facts about recent comparable events *PrepTest56 Sec3 Q6*	(E) goes wrong by characterizing the executive's conclusion as a "prediction." Eliminate.

LSAT Question	Analysis
28. Lance: If experience teaches us nothing else, it teaches us that every general rule has at least one exception.	**Step 2:** Quickly ID Lance's conclusion: *all generalizations have exceptions.*
Frank: What you conclude is itself a general rule. If we assume that it is true, then there is at least one general rule that has no exceptions. Therefore, you must withdraw your conclusion.	Franks conclusion? Good Keyword in "[t]herefore." Frank concludes that Lance is wrong: *not all generalizations have exceptions.*
	Frank's evidence? *Lance's own conclusion is a generalization that doesn't allow for any exceptions, so if Lance is right, then Lance is also wrong.*
Frank's argument is an attempt to counter Lance's conclusion by	**Step 1:** "Frank [does something] by" tells us we're looking for *how* Frank argues rather than *what* Frank argues. It's a Method of Argument question.
	Step 3: Frank's argumentative strategy? He doesn't offer any new evidence or reinterpret any of Lance's evidence. Rather, he explains that Lance's argument has an internal contradiction.
(A) demonstrating that Lance assumes the very thing he sets out to prove	This describes a different type of argumentative flaw—circular reasoning. Eliminate.
(B) showing that Lance's conclusion involves him in a contradiction	Correct. Circle it and stop reading.
(C) showing that no general rule can have exceptions	Mischaracterizes Frank's conclusion; Frank doesn't say that no general rule can have exceptions. Eliminate.
(D) establishing that experience teaches us the opposite of what Lance concludes	Goes wrong by suggesting that Frank supports his argument by reference to experience. Lance mentions experience, but Frank doesn't. Eliminate.
(E) showing that it has no implications for any real cases *PrepTest56 Sec2 Q11*	(E) is a distortion: neither Lance nor Frank extends his arguments so far as to discuss the implications for real cases. Eliminate.

LSAT Question		Analysis
29. Philosopher: Wolves do not tolerate an attack by one wolf on another if the latter wolf demonstrates submission by baring its throat. The same is true of foxes and domesticated dogs. So it would be erroneous to deny that animals have rights on the grounds that only human beings are capable of obeying moral rules.	$\longrightarrow$	**Step 2:** Conclusion? The Keyword "[s]o" points us to the last sentence. Somebody seems to have said that animals don't have rights because animals don't obey moral rules, and the philosopher is rebutting that somebody. The punchline? *Animals are capable of obeying moral rules, so we can't deny them rights on that basis.* Evidence? *Wolves don't tolerate wolf-on-wolf violence if the attacked wolf bares its throat. Neither do dogs or foxes.*
The philosopher's argument proceeds by attempting to	$\longrightarrow$	**Step 1:** The phrase "argument proceeds by" tells us it's a Method of Argument question.
		Step 3: The philosopher's argumentative strategy involves citing counterexamples to somebody's claim.
(A) provide counterexamples to refute a premise on which a particular conclusion is based	$\longrightarrow$	Correct. This perfectly matches our prediction.
(B) establish inductively that all animals possess some form of morality	$\longrightarrow$	Too extreme. The philosopher doesn't establish that *all* animals have morality. Eliminate.
(C) cast doubt on the principle that being capable of obeying moral rules is a necessary condition for having rights	$\longrightarrow$	Distorts the philosopher's argument. She attacks somebody's claim that animals don't have morality. Eliminate.
(D) establish a claim by showing that the denial of that claim entails a logical contradiction	$\longrightarrow$	Distortion. The philosopher doesn't point out a logical contradiction in somebody's argument. Eliminate.
(E) provide evidence suggesting that the concept of morality is often applied too broadly *PrepTest58 Sec1 Q26*	$\longrightarrow$	Gets the philosopher's argument backward. She thinks somebody applies the concept of morality too narrowly—not too broadly. Eliminate.

Response Data

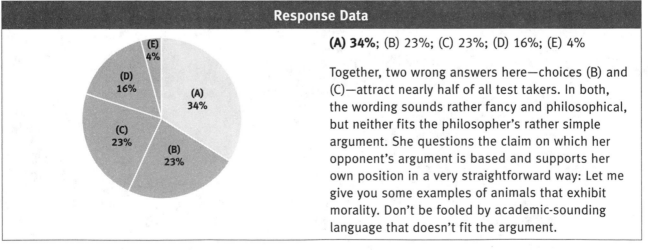

(A) 34%; (B) 23%; (C) 23%; (D) 16%; (E) 4%

Together, two wrong answers here—choices (B) and (C)—attract nearly half of all test takers. In both, the wording sounds rather fancy and philosophical, but neither fits the philosopher's rather simple argument. She questions the claim on which her opponent's argument is based and supports her own position in a very straightforward way: Let me give you some examples of animals that exhibit morality. Don't be fooled by academic-sounding language that doesn't fit the argument.

By the way, did you notice a big gap between the philosopher's evidence and the philosopher's conclusion? You may have realized that these stories about wolves and dogs and so forth don't explicitly involve morality, which is key to the philosopher's conclusion. Lots of LSAT arguments have gaps of this kind. In Chapter 10, we're going to start working in depth with those gaps, otherwise known as assumptions, and we're going to pick up a lot of points in doing so. But your work so far in this chapter—analyzing evidence and conclusions—has been necessary groundwork for getting those points. You should congratulate yourself for building a good foundation to tackle assumptions!

Reflection

Look back over your practice in this section. Did you describe the argumentative strategy in your own words? Did you formulate a prediction regarding the author's argumentative strategy before looking at answer choices? Did you efficiently eliminate answer choices that didn't match your prediction?

If you made some mistakes in this practice section, good! You now have some valuable information about where you need to work on your skills before Test Day. How did you mischaracterize the arguments? Do you see any commonalities among the wrong answer choices you were drawn to?

QUESTION POOL

Previously Seen Stimuli

Here are a few stimuli covered earlier in the chapter. This time they appear with answer choices. These questions are arranged in order of increasing difficulty.

1. Lahar: We must now settle on a procedure for deciding on meeting agendas. Our club's constitution allows three options: unanimous consent, majority vote, or assigning the task to a committee. Unanimous consent is unlikely. Forming a committee has usually led to factionalism and secret deals. Clearly, we should subject meeting agendas to majority vote.

Lahar's argument does which one of the following?

(A) rejects suggested procedures on constitutional grounds
(B) claims that one procedure is the appropriate method for reaching every decision in the club
(C) suggests a change to a constitution on the basis of practical considerations
(D) recommends a choice based on the elimination of alternative options
(E) supports one preference by arguing against those who have advocated alternatives

PrepTest52 Sec3 Q5

2. The reason music with a simple recurring rhythm exerts a strong primordial appeal is that it reminds us of the womb environment. After all, the first sound heard within the womb is the comforting sound of the mother's regular heartbeat. So in taking away from us the warmth and security of the womb, birth also takes away a primal and constant source of comfort. Thus it is extremely natural that in seeking sensations of warmth and security throughout life, people would be strongly drawn toward simple recurring rhythmic sounds.

Which one of the following most accurately expresses the main conclusion drawn in the reasoning above?

(A) The explanation of the strong primordial appeal of music with a simple recurring rhythm is that it reminds us of the womb environment.
(B) The comforting sound of the mother's regular heartbeat is the first sound that is heard inside the womb.
(C) Birth deprives us of a primal and constant source of comfort when it takes away the warmth and security of the womb.
(D) People seek sensations of warmth and security throughout life because birth takes away the warmth and security of the womb.
(E) The comforting sound of the mother's regular heartbeat is a simple recurring rhythmic sound.

PrepTest58 Sec4 Q3

3. Gardener: Researchers encourage us to allow certain
    kinds of weeds to grow among garden
    vegetables because they can repel caterpillars
    from the garden. While it is wise to avoid
    unnecessary use of insecticides, the
    researchers' advice is premature. For all we
    know, those kinds of weeds can deplete the soil
    of nutrients and moisture that garden crops
    depend on, and might even attract other kinds
    of damaging pests.

    Which one of the following most accurately expresses
    the main conclusion of the gardener's argument?

    (A)   To the extent that it is possible to do so, we
            should eliminate the use of insecticides in
            gardening.
    (B)   Allowing certain kinds of weeds to grow in
            vegetable gardens may contribute to a net
            increase in unwanted garden pests.
    (C)   Allowing the right kinds of weeds to grow in
            vegetable gardens can help toward controlling
            caterpillars without the use of insecticides.
    (D)   We should be cautious about the practice of
            allowing certain kinds of weeds to grow
            among garden vegetables.
    (E)   We should be skeptical about the extent to
            which certain kinds of weeds can reduce the
            presence of caterpillars in gardens.

    PrepTest56 Sec3 Q5

The explanations to these
questions begin on page 461.

New Questions

Try out some practice on questions that have not yet appeared. These questions are arranged in order of increasing difficulty.

4. Gigantic passenger planes currently being developed will have enough space to hold shops and lounges in addition to passenger seating. However, the additional space will more likely be used for more passenger seating. The number of passengers flying the air-traffic system is expected to triple within 20 years, and it will be impossible for airports to accommodate enough normal-sized jet planes to carry that many passengers.

Which one of the following most accurately states the conclusion drawn in the argument?

(A) Gigantic planes currently being developed will have enough space in them to hold shops and lounges as well as passenger seating.

(B) The additional space in the gigantic planes currently being developed is more likely to be filled with passenger seating than with shops and lounges.

(C) The number of passengers flying the air-traffic system is expected to triple within 20 years.

(D) In 20 years, it will be impossible for airports to accommodate enough normal-sized planes to carry the number of passengers that are expected to be flying then.

(E) In 20 years, most airline passengers will be flying in gigantic passenger planes.

PrepTest62 Sec2 Q10

5. When a nation is on the brink of financial crisis, its government does not violate free-market principles if, in order to prevent economic collapse, it limits the extent to which foreign investors and lenders can withdraw their money. After all, the right to free speech does not include the right to shout "Fire!" in a crowded theatre, and the harm done as investors and lenders rush madly to get their money out before everyone else does can be just as real as the harm resulting from a stampede in a theatre.

The argument does which one of the following?

(A) tries to show that a set of principles is limited in a specific way by using an analogy to a similar principle that is limited in a similar way

(B) infers a claim by arguing that the truth of that claim would best explain observed facts

(C) presents numerous experimental results as evidence for a general principle

(D) attempts to demonstrate that an explanation of a phenomenon is flawed by showing that it fails to explain a particular instance of that phenomenon

(E) applies an empirical generalization to reach a conclusion about a particular case

PrepTest58 Sec1 Q6

6. Political scientist: It is not uncommon for a politician to criticize his or her political opponents by claiming that their exposition of their ideas is muddled and incomprehensible. Such criticism, however, is never sincere. Political agendas promoted in a manner that cannot be understood by large numbers of people will not be realized for, as every politician knows, political mobilization requires commonality of purpose.

Which one of the following is the most accurate rendering of the political scientist's main conclusion?

(A) People who promote political agendas in an incomprehensible manner should be regarded as insincere.

(B) Sincere critics of the proponents of a political agenda should not focus their criticisms on the manner in which that agenda is promoted.

(C) The ineffectiveness of a confusingly promoted political agenda is a reason for refraining from, rather than engaging in, criticism of those who are promoting it.

(D) A politician criticizing his or her political opponents for presenting their political agendas in an incomprehensible manner is being insincere.

(E) To mobilize large numbers of people in support of a political agenda, that political agenda must be presented in such a way that it cannot be misunderstood.

PrepTest62 Sec4 Q12

7. Sahira: To make a living from their art, artists of
    great potential would have to produce work
    that would gain widespread popular acclaim,
    instead of their best work. That is why
    governments are justified in subsidizing
    artists.

    Rahima: Your argument for subsidizing art depends
    on claiming that to gain widespread popular
    acclaim, artists must produce something other
    than their best work; but this need not be true.

    In her argument, Rahima

    (A) disputes an implicit assumption of Sahira's
    (B) presents independent support for Sahira's
        argument
    (C) accepts Sahira's conclusion, but for reasons
        different from those given by Sahira
    (D) uses Sahira's premises to reach a conclusion
        different from that reached by Sahira
    (E) argues that a standard that she claims Sahira
        uses is self-contradictory

    PrepTest58 Sec4 Q12

8. Rifka: We do not need to stop and ask for directions.
    We would not need to do that unless, of
    course, we were lost.

    Craig: The fact that we are lost is precisely why we
    need to stop.

    In the exchange above, the function of Craig's
    comment is to

    (A) contradict the conclusion of Rifka's argument
        without offering any reason to reject any of
        Rifka's implicit premises
    (B) deny one of Rifka's implicit premises and
        thereby arrive at a different conclusion
    (C) imply that Rifka's argument is invalid by
        accepting the truth of its premises while
        rejecting its conclusion
    (D) provide a counterexample to Rifka's
        generalization
    (E) affirm the truth of the stated premise of Rifka's
        argument while remaining noncommittal
        about its conclusion

    PrepTest56 Sec2 Q9

9. Glen: An emphasis on law's purely procedural side
    produces a concern with personal rights
    that leads to the individual's indifference to
    society's welfare. Law's primary role should be
    to create virtuous citizens.

    Sara: But such a role would encourage government
    to decide which modes of life are truly
    virtuous; that would be more dangerous than
    government's being overprotective of
    individuals' rights.

    The dialogue provides the most support for the claim
    that Glen and Sara disagree about whether

    (A) citizens can be assumed to be capable of
        making good choices without governmental
        interference
    (B) virtuousness on the part of citizens is more
        important than the protection of citizens'
        rights
    (C) there is an inherent danger in allowing
        government to decide what constitutes
        virtuous behavior among citizens
    (D) an emphasis on law's purely procedural side
        results in government's being overprotective
        of citizens' rights
    (E) the cultivation of virtue among citizens should
        be the primary role of law

    PrepTest56 Sec2 Q17

K | Part Three: Logical Reasoning
CHAPTER 9

These explanations refer to
questions that begin on page 456.

ANSWERS AND EXPLANATIONS

1. (D) Method of Argument ★☆☆☆

Step 1: Identify the Question Type

The "argument does which of the following" language lets us know that the correct answer will describe the Method of Argument. Use Keywords to determine structure and focus on how the author makes the argument, rather than what the argument is about.

Step 2: Untangle the Stimulus

Lahar lays out three possible options for how to decide on meeting agendas, then proceeds to explain why two of them won't work. Finally, with the conclusion Keyword "[c]learly," he concludes by recommending the remaining option.

Step 3: Make a Prediction

Lahar's method is to argue for one option, not by offering evidence for it, but by instead rejecting other possibilities.

Step 4: Evaluate the Answer Choices

(D) matches nicely because Lahar's recommendation is based on eliminating the alternatives.

(A) is Outside the Scope because no constitutional grounds are offered for the options Lahar advocates rejecting; he says all three are allowed by the club's constitution.

(B) is Extreme. It partly matches the conclusion because Lahar does say one procedure is appropriate. However, Lahar recommends that procedure for one specific task: setting an agenda. This choice goes beyond Lahar's recommendation by suggesting that one procedure would work for "every" decision.

(C) is a Distortion. It misses the mark because Lahar never recommends changing the constitution; he draws on the constitution to find the three options he evaluates.

(E) is also a Distortion because Lahar doesn't introduce an ad hominem attack; he argues against alternatives, not their supporters.

2. (A) Main Point ★★☆☆

Step 1: Identify the Question Stem

This is a Main Point question, since the stem simply asks us to find the answer choice that expresses the main conclusion of the argument.

Step 2: Untangle the Stimulus

In the first sentence, the author explains why we are drawn to music with a simple recurring rhythm. Such music reminds us of being in the womb. The support for this is given throughout the rest of the argument. At birth, a baby is deprived of the comforting sound of the mother's regular heartbeat. So when a person seeks out warmth and security, it makes sense to be drawn to simple recurring sounds that mimic the mother's heartbeat.

Step 3: Make a Prediction

When predicting the answer to a Main Point question, be careful about using Keywords. Here, the obvious conclusion Keyword is "[t]hus," but this Keyword, like many conclusion Keywords in Main Point arguments, signals a subsidiary conclusion, not the main one. The author's main point isn't that it is natural for us to be strongly drawn to simple recurring rhythmic sounds. The author's main point is that we are strongly drawn to such sounds because those sounds remind us of the womb, which was the first place in which we encountered the comfort that sound could bring.

Step 4: Evaluate the Answers

(A) matches our prediction of the author's main point. None of the other answer choices discusses music at all, which was the whole reason the author introduced any evidence relating to birth, the womb, or the mother's heartbeat.

(B) is a piece of information that is found in the second sentence of the argument, a sentence beginning with "[a]fter all," which is a key phrase that generally signals evidence. Besides, the author only brings up this point in an attempt to prove that the mother's heartbeat has a recurring rhythm not unlike the musical rhythms people find most comforting.

(C) is a piece of information that is only offered as part of a larger explanation for why we seek out music that has a simple recurring rhythm—because we have a primordial desire to replicate the sense of comfort we felt inside the womb.

(D) is close, but it doesn't incorporate the appeal of music with a simple recurring rhythm, which is the whole reason the author brings up the warmth and security of the womb in the first place.

(E) is a Distortion. The comforting sound of the mother's regular heartbeat may be why we are attracted to music with a simple recurring rhythmic sound, but the author's point isn't that the heartbeat itself is a simple recurring rhythmic sound.

3. (D) Main Point ★★☆☆

Step 1: Identify the Question Type

The phrase "most accurately expresses the main conclusion" identifies this as a Main Point question. Focus on Keywords, look out for subsidiary conclusions, and expect to combine statements in the argument to paraphrase the author's main point. Also consider using the One-Sentence Test and remember that words of contrast frequently indicate the author's disagreement with previous statements and, by extension, the author's conclusion.

These explanations refer to questions that begin on page 458.

Part Three: Logical Reasoning
Argument-Based Questions

K

Step 2: Untangle the Stimulus

The gardener starts off by introducing a recommendation made by researchers: allow some weeds to grow in gardens to repel caterpillars. However, once the gardener starts the second sentence with the word "[w]hile," you get the sense that the gardener has a bone of contention with the researchers. Sure enough, the gardener calls the recommendation "premature." This surely seems like the gardener's main point. Following this claim are two other possible outcomes weeds' presence may engender: depleted soil and the attraction of other pests. In other words, they are evidence to back up the gardener's dissent.

Step 3: Make a Prediction

Simply put, the gardener's overall point is that researchers' recommendation to allow weeds to grow is premature.

Step 4: Evaluate the Answer Choices

(D) is correct and nicely summarizes the gardener's cautionary opinion.

(A) is incorrect because it summarizes the gardener's concession to the researchers, not his final conclusion. The gardener does claim that it's wise to avoid using pesticides, but this is not the primary concern at hand. The gardener is far more concerned about the recommendation to let weeds grow.

(B) is a Distortion. It incorrectly focuses on the gardener's evidence, not his conclusion. As support, he states in the last sentence that weeds may attract other kinds of damaging pests, but that doesn't mean he thinks there will necessarily be a net increase. The number of other pests may be less than the number of repelled caterpillars.

(C) is a 180. This summarizes the researchers' argument, not the gardener's. The gardener is not ready to accept this argument.

(E) is a Distortion. While the gardener *is* skeptical about the researchers' argument, his focus is not on how well growing weeds will achieve the intended effect (reducing caterpillars) but on what unconsidered, unwanted effects the weeds might cause.

4. (B) Main Point ★★★★

Step 1: Identify the Question Type

This question simply asks for the conclusion of the argument. Keywords can often help, but be ready to paraphrase.

Step 2: Untangle the Stimulus

First, the author tells us that new passenger planes will have extra space for shops and lounges in addition to passenger seating. The next sentence begins with the Keyword "[h]owever," which signals that the author is going to make a contrasting point—the space will more likely be used for

seating. The last sentence elaborates on why this might be true—the increase in passengers and the need for bigger jets.

Step 3: Make a Prediction

The conclusion, signaled by the Keyword "[h]owever," sums up the author's opinion about the first sentence—the extra space will more likely be used for passenger seating than for shops and lounges.

Step 4: Evaluate the Answer Choices

(B) fits the prediction precisely.

(A) is not the conclusion but rather a fact that the author of the argument is taking issue with. The word "[h]owever" that starts the next sentence tells us this.

(C) and **(D)** restate the facts that explain why the space will more likely be used for passengers. This is all evidence, not the conclusion.

(E) is an inference drawn from the evidence, but it is not the main conclusion. If the number of passengers will triple and the airports won't be able to accommodate enough normal-sized planes, it follows that more passengers will fly in the gigantic planes. Choice **(E)** states an implicit subsidiary conclusion that provides support for the main conclusion—that the extra space on these planes will be used for passenger seating.

5. (A) Method of Argument ★★★★

Step 1: Identify the Question Stem

Since this question is focused on what the argument does, rather than what the argument says, this is a Method of Argument question.

Step 2: Untangle the Stimulus

The author concludes that freedom of markets doesn't take away a government's right to regulate the withdrawal of money by lenders and investors in a climate of impending financial crisis. The support for this conclusion is the idea that freedom of speech doesn't take away a government's right to forbid someone from yelling "Fire!" in a crowded theater, since that could cause a dangerous stampede.

Step 3: Make a Prediction

To predict the answer to a Method of Argument question, focus not on the content of the argument (what it assumes, what would strengthen or weaken it, etc.) but on the structure, that is, *how* the author proceeds from evidence to conclusion. Here, the author supports the conclusion that free-market principles are not violated by the government's need to prevent total economic collapse by making an analogy to a similar situation in which free-speech principles are not violated by the government's need to prevent dangerous stampedes in crowded places such as theaters.

K | Part Three: Logical Reasoning
CHAPTER 9

These explanations refer to
questions that begin on page 458.

Step 4: Evaluate the Answers

(A) matches our prediction of the structure of the argument. In fact, (A) is the only choice that points out the author's use of an analogy.

(B) The author doesn't support the conclusion on the basis that the conclusion would best explain a set of observations. There is no set of observations offered in the argument.

(C) No experimental results are offered to support the author's conclusion.

(D) No explanations for phenomena are discussed, and the author doesn't cite the analogy of the crowded theater as a specific instance of a nation on the brink of financial crisis. They're two totally different events that are analogous in a key respect.

(E) The author doesn't reach the conclusion by using an empirical generalization. A specific, analogous example (that of yelling "Fire!" in a crowded theater) is used to prove the author's point.

6. (D) Main Point ★★☆☆

Step 1: Identify the Question Type

The phrase "main conclusion" signals a Main Point question. Identify the conclusion and combine multiple statements in the argument, if necessary to complete a summary of it.

Step 2: Untangle the Stimulus

The contrast Keyword "however" in the second sentence highlights the author's strong opinion: "Such criticism … is never sincere." To give context to the conclusion, search the first sentence to see what criticism the author is referring to. The opening line states that politicians often criticize their opponents for expressing their views in an unclear way.

Step 3: Make a Prediction

When a Main Point question features a conclusion with a phrase that points elsewhere in the stimulus ("such criticism"), refer to additional portions of the stimulus to paraphrase the author's main idea. The author believes it is *not* sincere to criticize your political opponents for expressing their views in a muddled way.

Step 4: Evaluate the Answer Choices

(D) is an excellent match to your prediction. Don't be thrown by the long sentence: the outlying structure "A politician criticizing . . . is being insincere" tells you that you're on the right track, and the middle three lines reiterate the first sentence of the stimulus.

(A) is a subtle Distortion. The author doesn't claim that incomprehensible people are insincere; in fact, she suggests that no politician is truly incomprehensible. The people she calls insincere are the ones who *accuse* people of being incomprehensible.

(B) is cleverly Out of Scope. The author's conclusion is about people who are *not* sincere; what it would take to establish that someone *is* sincere misses the mark of the argument.

(C) is also Out of Scope. The author criticizes a particular brand of criticism but never mentions criteria for "refraining from" or "engaging in" criticism in general.

(E) is a classic Distortion. It summarizes the last sentence of the stimulus, which is the author's evidence, not her conclusion.

7. (A) Method of Argument ★★☆☆

Step 1: Identify the Question Stem

This is about as short as Logical Reasoning question stems get. However, even from these few words (and a glance at the answer choices), we get the sense that the question is much more interested in what Rahima does to structure her argument than the particulars of what she says. That makes this a Method of Argument question.

Step 2: Untangle the Stimulus

Let's read Sahira's argument first for context. Sahira argues that governments are justified in subsidizing artists. Her justification for this is the idea that otherwise, great artists would pander to the tastes of the public instead of producing their best work simply because they'd be worried about making ends meet. Rahima responds by saying that Sahira's argument depends on the idea that artists have to produce work that isn't their best in order to capture popular acclaim. Rahima then goes on to say that this isn't necessarily true.

Step 3: Make a Prediction

Let's focus on Rahima's response to Sahira. We don't need to figure out her conclusion or evidence or assumption; we just need to determine *how* her argument works. First, Rahima points out an idea on which Sahira's argument depends, and then she challenges it. Always form your predictions in this general way and use verbs if you can; this will help you see which answer choice most closely matches your prediction.

Step 4: Evaluate the Answers

(A) is a match for our prediction.

(B) is a 180, since Rahima challenges a crucial component of Sahira's argument, which is a far cry from supporting it.

(C) is incorrect because Rahima doesn't indicate whether or not she agrees with Sahira's conclusion. If anything, by disputing Sahira's assumption, it seems more likely that Rahima doesn't accept Sahira's conclusion.

(D) doesn't make sense because Rahima doesn't reach her own conclusion and she actually challenges one of Sahira's implicit premises.

These explanations refer to questions that begin on page 459.

Part Three: Logical Reasoning
Argument-Based Questions

(E) is Outside the Scope. Rahima doesn't mention any standard used by Sahira, and she certainly doesn't accuse Sahira of being self-contradictory.

8. (B) Method of Argument ★★★★

Step 1: Identify the Question Stem

Because the question asks about the "function" of Craig's argument, the answer will focus on *how* Craig responds, rather than just *what* he says. This focus makes this a Method of Argument question. Look for the tactic Craig uses when he responds to Rifka.

Step 2: Untangle the Stimulus

Start by summarizing Rifka's argument. Rifka's conclusion is that stopping is unnecessary. Rifka's evidence includes a Formal Logic statement. The Keywords "not . . . unless" is the clue. Translate this statement: if they need to stop for directions → they are lost. Craig concludes that they do need to stop based on the evidence that they are lost.

Step 3: Make a Prediction

Craig's response suggests that he has both a different conclusion and different evidence than does Rifka. Craig flips Rifka's Formal Logic statement around: they are lost, so they need to ask for directions.

Step 4: Evaluate the Answer Choices

(B) captures how Craig rejects both Rifka's evidence and conclusion.

(A) is Half Right, Half Wrong. Craig does contradict Rifka's conclusion, but he also rejects Rifka's implicit evidence that they're not lost.

(C) similarly misses how Craig reverses Rifka's evidence. He can't, therefore, be accepting the truth of Rifka's evidence.

(D) goes Outside the Scope by suggesting that Craig has provided a counterexample. A counterexample would be a specific instance, but Craig's counterargument is no more specific than Rifka's argument.

(E) is a 180 because it wrongly suggests that Craig has no opinion about Rifka's conclusion. In actuality, Craig disagrees with Rifka's conclusion.

9. (E) Point at Issue ★★★★

Step 1: Identify the Question Type

When the question stem indicates that the right answer is a "claim" that two speakers "disagree about," it is a Point at Issue question. First, summarize each speaker's argument. Then, use the Kaplan Decision Tree to narrow down the correct answer choice. The speakers must each have an opinion on the correct answer choice, and those opinions must differ.

Step 2: Untangle the Stimulus

Glen argues the main thing law should do is make virtuous citizens. His evidence is that when the law emphasizes procedure, individuals become indifferent about society's welfare. In response, Sara argues that if the law's role were to create virtuous citizens, then the government would have to decide what is virtuous. Sara notes this would be a danger far worse than the government's overprotection of individual rights.

Step 3: Make a Prediction

Sara's rebuttal of Glen suggests that she disagrees with his main conclusion about the primary role for law. Scan for a choice that matches that prediction or use the Kaplan Point at Issue Decision Tree. To use the Decision Tree, take an answer choice and ask these three questions: Does Glen have an opinion on this matter? Does Sara have an opinion on this matter? Do they disagree on this matter? The correct answer choice will answer all three of those questions in the affirmative.

Step 4: Evaluate the Answer Choices

(E) captures Glen's main point, with which Sara disagrees.

(A) is Outside the Scope because neither Glen nor Sara speaks to citizens' ability to make good choices. Additionally, while they disagree over government's role, neither of them discusses a situation where government doesn't interfere at all.

(B) seems close, but it ignores the role of law. It's possible both Sara and Glen agree with this statement. Sara simply doesn't think government—or law—should be the body concerned with promoting virtuousness. But she still may think virtuousness in general is more important than rights.

(C) is something Sara would agree with, but Glen's opinion on this is unclear. Sara introduces the idea that government would have to decide what is virtuous; Glen may think law can primarily focus on creating virtuous citizens without *government* having to decide what is virtuous.

(D) is unsupported. Glen would agree with this statement, but so might Sara. Sara isn't attacking Glen's opinion on what occurs when law's procedural side is emphasized; rather, she is concerned with what he thinks law's primary role should be.

CHAPTER 10

Assumption Family Questions

As you learned in Chapter 9, the ability to analyze arguments is a valuable skill for LSAT mastery. A student who is able to separate evidence from conclusion in an LSAT argument will dominate Main Point, Role of a Statement, and Method of Argument questions. But this skill is useful for other, even more important question types. In this chapter, you'll face Assumption, Flaw, Strengthen, Weaken, and select Principle questions—together known as the Assumption Family questions—that also require you to quickly and effectively analyze arguments into their constituent parts. There is one big difference, though, between the types of questions you saw in Chapter 9 and the types of questions you'll see in this chapter: here, the untangling of arguments into their explicit parts (evidence and conclusion) is an important but insufficient task. That's because Assumption Family questions also depend on your ability to determine the implicit assumption, or unstated premise, of an argument. They reward test takers who are constantly skeptical of the arguments presented and, more precisely, skeptical of the shift from the author's evidence to the author's conclusion.

One thing that is consistently true about arguments on the LSAT is that too little evidence is provided in support of a conclusion that the author reaches too quickly. This jump to the conclusion means that there is an informational gap between the evidence and the conclusion. Because of this gap in the argument's reasoning, the testmaker is able to generate questions that test your ability to do a number of things: to find the assumption in an argument, to point out the error in an author's reasoning, or to strengthen or weaken an argument.

> ## LSAT STRATEGY
>
> Every Assumption Family argument contains:
>
> - A conclusion—the author's main point: an assertion, evaluation, or recommendation
> - Evidence—the facts and information the author presents in support of the conclusion
> - An assumption—the *unstated* premise that logically connects the evidence to the conclusion

Knowing the structure of these arguments is crucial to test takers. By learning and understanding the common ways in which an LSAT argument can move from evidence to conclusion and by developing strategies to identify an author's assumption (the unstated evidence in an argument), you are able to anticipate, or predict, the correct answer choices before you begin evaluating the answer choices. For the vast majority of the argument-based questions discussed in this section, predicting the correct answer will help you earn more points, and earn them more quickly, than will a process of elimination or guesswork.

In this chapter, we will focus on two big ideas: In the first half of the chapter, you'll learn to identify the common ways in which arguments on the LSAT move from evidence to conclusion. In the second half of the chapter, you'll learn to approach strategically the question types that reward the ability to analyze arguments. Understanding the structure of arguments and identifying authors' assumptions are the most valuable skills you can develop for the LSAT. In fact, more than a quarter of all questions on the LSAT test your ability to do just these things.

> ## LEARNING OBJECTIVES
>
> In this chapter, you'll learn to:
>
> · Identify Mismatched Concepts in an argument.
> · Identify Overlooked Possibilities in an argument.
> · Identify the assumption in both types of arguments.
> · Use an argument's assumption to predict a correct answer for each Assumption Family question type.

The first thing we'll do is discuss the ways in which arguments on the LSAT tend to be constructed. The jump from the evidence to the conclusion takes two basic forms: either (1) the author moves from a discussion of certain terms and concepts in the evidence to a conclusion that introduces a new, seemingly unrelated or irrelevant term or concept (what we will refer to as a "Mismatched Concepts" argument), or (2) the author uses relevant evidence to jump to a conclusion that is too extreme, without considering potential objections or alternatives to that conclusion (an "Overlooked Possibilities" argument).

MISMATCHED CONCEPTS

Consider this argument:

Chemical X is harmful because poison is harmful.

Does this argument seem completely sound to you? It probably doesn't. That's because, just like the arguments you will see on Test Day, the argument above is incomplete. There is a gap between what the evidence states and what the author concludes. Assumption Family arguments always follow this pattern—the evidence presented is never enough to completely support the argument's conclusion. Your job, then, will be to determine *why* a particular argument's evidence isn't enough. Take a moment now and describe to yourself what's wrong with the Chemical X argument. Here's the catch, though: you have to do it without using any of the following words (or synonyms): chemical X, poison, harmful, or assumes.

Having a hard time? There's a good chance you already know what's missing in this argument: the piece of evidence that should be there but isn't. But how do you know what it is? And more importantly, how will you know what the missing piece is in more complicated LSAT arguments? To learn how to spot the problem in an argument, you first need to learn what those problems are.

Take a look at this argument from a different angle. Imagine a game in which a person is given a piece of evidence, and his task is to predict a conclusion based on that evidence. If he guesses correctly, his award is a million-dollar prize. Now, imagine that the person is given this piece of evidence: "poison is harmful." How long would it take to guess that the conclusion is "Chemical X is harmful"? Frankly, that contestant is probably never going to see that million-dollar prize. The reason is simple: the concept *Chemical X is*, for all we know, completely unrelated to the concept *poison*. That's the problem with this argument: the author is using evidence that, within the context of her argument and without an additional, unstated assumption, is irrelevant to the conclusion.

Mismatched Concepts: The Basics

LSAT STRATEGY

How can you tell an argument contains mismatched concepts?

· The terms or concepts in the evidence appear unrelated to the conclusion.

· A new term or concept—not related to the evidence—appears in the conclusion.

In Assumption Family questions, the LSAT consistently tests your ability to determine when an author is using evidence that is irrelevant or unrelated to the conclusion. Think of these as Apples and Oranges arguments: the author is concluding something about apples, while the evidence deals with oranges. In these arguments, just because the author *assumes* that a relationship between the terms or concepts is apparent does not mean that the relationship is true. Our job then is to learn how to spot when the author is making this leap, then build a bridge between the mismatched concepts that completes the argument. This bridge is known as the author's assumption: the piece of evidence that isn't there but needs to be for the argument to make sense. The good news is that there is a straightforward, repeatable process you can go through to derive the assumption when you're dealing with Mismatched Concepts arguments.

Let's go back to Chemical X to illustrate the process. First, one of the most common signs of irrelevant evidence is a conclusion that brings up an entirely new concept that never appeared in the evidence. Taking a look at our argument, it's clear that the new, out-of-nowhere term in the conclusion is *Chemical X*.

Conclusion	Evidence
Chemical X is harmful	

Next, take a look at the evidence and check for any mismatched concepts there—a concept that is in the evidence but never showed up in the conclusion. In this case, that would be *poison*.

Conclusion	Evidence
Chemical X is harmful	because **poison** is harmful

Now that you have your mismatched concepts, ask whether these two things are actually related to each other. Most arguments are going to have something new in the conclusion, but your job is to figure out when that new thing is unrelated to the information in the evidence. Usually the concepts *could* be related, but they don't *have to be* related—this is what creates the gap between the evidence and the conclusion. In this instance, given that we have no idea what Chemical X is, it's safe to say that it isn't by definition related to poison. It's possible, but without more evidence (that is, without an unstated assumption on the author's part), there's no way to know for sure

If you have two unrelated, mismatched concepts, then relate them to each other in a way that fixes the argument. Ask what must the author believe to be true about *Chemical X* and *poison* to fix this argument? The answer is that the author needs Chemical X *to be* a poison. If that's true, then the argument is complete! If Chemical X is a poison, and poisons are harmful, then it must be true that Chemical X is harmful:

Chemical X is harmful because

Chemical X is a poison and **poison is harmful.**

Mismatched Concepts arguments won't always use such straightforward terminology. In fact, many arguments on the LSAT contain academic, legal, or philosophical jargon that might make it difficult to understand the argument in full. Don't get flustered. Sometimes, the abstract nature of the concepts presented in arguments makes it easier for you to spot the mismatched concepts in the evidence and conclusion. Take this argument as an example:

Dweezil is a zulzey alien. Therefore, Dweezil can perform the amazing *yeerchta* move.

These are all made-up terms, of course—we have no real-world understanding of these things. Start by looking for any mismatched concepts in the conclusion. In both the evidence and conclusion, we have Dweezil; because there is no gap between Dweezil in the evidence and Dweezil in the conclusion, we don't have to "build a bridge" between them. The conclusion mentions the amazing *yeerchta* move, which never showed up in the evidence. From there, search the evidence for signs of a mismatch—zulzey aliens are discussed there, though such things are never mentioned in the conclusion. Because these concepts are made up, there is no known relationship between them. However, based on the structure of the argument, we can relate the two concepts in a way that makes sense of the argument. In this case, the author's assumption must be that all zulzey aliens are able to do the amazing *yeerchta* move. If the author had simply bothered to mention that in the evidence, then there would be no problem with this argument. With the assumption filled in, however, the argument becomes whole, and the conclusion makes sense; it follows from the evidence.

Mismatched Concepts arguments don't always use abstract or unfamiliar terms, though. In fact, the more realistic or understandable an argument is, the more cognizant you need to be of your *own* assumptions. There are times on the LSAT when it can be all too easy for you to mentally fill in an argument's assumption without even realizing it—you read the argument and think, "Oh, right, that makes sense." Take this argument as an example:

Kim is a nice person. Therefore, it's easy for Kim to make friends.

A quick look at the conclusion shows us that it's about making friends, but the evidence is about being a nice person. The next step is to ask ourselves if these things are necessarily related to each other. It's easy to think, "Okay, sure. Kim is a nice person. People tend to like other people who are nice, so Kim should be able to make friends easily. Makes sense to me!" The problem is that the relevance of being nice to the ease of making friends has not, *within this argument*, been established. Maybe being nice does affect your ability to make friends, but then again, maybe not. The argument's assumption, then, is that people who are nice make friends easily. Indeed, if this assumption were *not* true, then the evidence would not support the conclusion.

Even when an argument seems to make all the sense in the world, evaluate the evidence and conclusion with an eye toward spotting mismatched concepts. Are the terms and concepts discussed in the conclusion relevant to those presented in the evidence? When you are a lawyer, part of your job will be to expose the weaknesses in others' arguments. Looking at every argument and saying, "Sure, that argument makes all the sense in the world to me!" is, to put it mildly, an ineffective legal skill. Finding the gap in an argument, on the other hand, will expose its weakness. Starting today, train yourself to become a skeptical thinker.

LSAT STRATEGY

When tackling an argument containing Mismatched Concepts

- Separate concepts in evidence from concepts in conclusion.
- Identify the mismatched concepts that the author assumes are somehow related.
- Find the assumption by making a sentence that logically relates the mismatched concepts—this sentence serves as a bridge to make the evidence relevant to the conclusion.

Mismatched Concepts: Sample Arguments

Here are some brief Mismatched Concepts arguments and the Assumption of each. After reviewing these examples, you'll have a chance to try some others on your own.

Argument		Analysis
Cady attended North High School. Therefore, Cady is good at sculpture.	→	The author assumes North High School students are good at sculpture.
Spending time with pets relieves stress. Therefore, spending time with pets makes people happy.	→	The author assumes relieving stress makes people happy.
Ivan is an astronaut. Therefore, Ivan doesn't like jazz.	→	The author assumes astronauts don't like jazz.
You haven't done your homework. Therefore, you can't go to the concert.	→	The author assumes you need to do your homework before going to the concert.
People who play ping pong are also good at skiing. Therefore, the wealthy are good at skiing.	→	The author assumes that the wealthy play ping pong.
The city council members are all vegan. Therefore, Grace is a vegan.	→	The author assumes Grace is a member of the city council.

Practice

Practice your ability to spot the gap between concepts in the evidence and the conclusion by analyzing the following simple arguments. In each one of these arguments, follow this simple approach:

- · Separate the evidence from the conclusion.
- · Identify a new term or concept in the conclusion that was not present in the evidence.
- · Look in the evidence for an important term or concept not in the conclusion.
- · Determine the relationship the author assumes exists between those terms.
- · Put the mismatched terms or concepts into a sentence to form the author's assumption.

After each argument, feel free to look at the expert analysis on the next two pages. If you're feeling confident, try all four and then read the expert's thinking.

Argument	My Analysis
1. Brand D teddy bears are fluffy; therefore, children like Brand D teddy bears.	
2. Because Ariel likes to have fun, he enjoys amusement parks.	
3. Gopher tortoises burrow in the desert. Therefore, gopher tortoises don't eat grubs.	
4. People who text while driving are not safe drivers because one needs to be attentive in order to be a safe driver.	

Now take a look at how an LSAT expert would analyze these arguments you've just evaluated.

Argument	Analysis
1. Brand D teddy bears are fluffy; therefore, children like Brand D teddy bears.	Conclusion: Kids like Brand D teddy bears.
	Evidence: Brand D teddy bears are fluffy.
	Analyze: What "kids like" is in conclusion but not evidence. "Fluffy" is in evidence but not conclusion. The author assumes some sort of relationship exists between these distinct concepts. Connect the terms in a sentence to form the piece of evidence that the author assumes is true:
	"Kids like things that are fluffy."
2. Because Ariel likes to have fun, he enjoys amusement parks.	Conclusion: Ariel enjoys amusement parks.
	Evidence: Ariel likes to have fun.
	Analyze: The conclusion is about "amusement parks," but there's nothing about them in the evidence. The evidence is about "having fun," but there's nothing in the conclusion about fun. The author assumes a relationship exists between these distinct concepts. Connect the terms in a sentence to form the piece of evidence that the author assumes is true:
	"Anyone who likes to have fun enjoys amusement parks."
3. Gopher tortoises burrow in the desert. Therefore, gopher tortoises don't eat grubs.	Conclusion: Gopher tortoises don't eat grubs.
	Evidence: Gopher tortoises burrow in the desert.
	Analyze: The conclusion is about "not eating grubs," but the evidence isn't about that at all. The evidence is about "burrowing in the desert," but that isn't in the conclusion. The author assumes some sort of relationship exists between these otherwise unrelated concepts. Connect the terms in a sentence to form the piece of evidence that the author assumes is true:
	"Tortoises that burrow in the desert don't eat grubs."

Argument	Analysis
4. People who text while driving are not safe drivers because one needs to be attentive in order to be a safe driver.	Conclusion: Drivers who are texting aren't safe.
	Evidence: Safe drivers must be attentive.
→	Analyze: The conclusion is about "drivers who text," but the evidence never mentions that. The evidence is about "being attentive," but that isn't in the conclusion. The author assumes some sort of relationship exists between these two concepts. Connect the terms in a sentence to form the piece of evidence that the author assumes is true:
	"Drivers who text aren't attentive."

The LSAT, of course, will present more difficult arguments than the ones shown above, but the fundamental *structure* of arguments with mismatched concepts will remain the same. Regardless of the topic being discussed in the argument—whether it be on matters philosophical, legal, or scientific—your method and objective will always remain the same. First, separate evidence from conclusion. Then, analyze the concepts discussed in both. If the author introduces a distinct or unrelated term or idea in the conclusion, find the assumption by connecting a mismatched concept in the evidence to the mismatched concept in the conclusion.

Try that now with an actual LSAT argument.

LSAT Argument	My Analysis
Theater managers will not rent a film if they do not believe it will generate enough total revenue—including food-and-beverage concession revenue—to yield a profit. Therefore, since film producers want their films to be shown as widely as possible, they tend to make films that theater managers consider attractive to younger audiences. *PrepTest58 Sec1 Q14*	

Did you see a new term or concept in the conclusion that seemed to come out of the blue? Did the evidence seem unrelated or irrelevant to the conclusion drawn by the author? Take a look at how an LSAT expert would break down this argument.

LSAT Argument	**Analysis**
Theater managers will not rent a film if they do not believe it will generate enough total revenue—including food-and-beverage concession revenue—to yield a profit. Therefore, since film producers want their films to be shown as widely as possible, they tend to make films that theater managers consider attractive to younger audiences. *PrepTest58 Sec1 Q14*	Keywords "[t]herefore" and "since" indicate evidence, followed by the conclusion. Conclusion: Movie producers make films theater managers will consider attractive to young people. *because* Evidence: Movie producers want their films to be shown as widely as possible (and theater owners only rent films they believe will be profitable). The mismatched terms are *films theater owners believe will be profitable* (in the evidence) and *films theater managers consider attractive to young people* (in the conclusion). So the author's assumption connects these distinct terms: theater owners believe that films attractive to young people will be profitable.

This argument was made a bit more difficult by the fact that the evidence came in two pieces: (1) film producers want their films to be shown as widely as possible, and (2) theater managers won't rent a film that is not profitable. Test experts are able to synthesize multiple pieces of evidence and make a deduction. Doing so allows for an easier comparison between evidence and conclusion. Here, while both the evidence and conclusion discuss film producers and theater managers, a new, possibly jarring concept appears in the conclusion that was not in the evidence: films that are "attractive to younger audiences." Nothing in the evidence is explicitly relevant to films that are attractive to younger audiences. Instead, the evidence discusses films that film producers and theater managers believe are profitable. Experts are attuned to finding gaps between concepts in the evidence and conclusion and are able to articulate authors' assumptions efficiently.

Hopefully you're starting to get the hang of evaluating arguments that introduce a new, unrelated concept in the conclusion. Let's dive in even deeper and discuss some of the most common relationships you'll see between mismatched concepts in LSAT arguments.

Going Deeper: Common Relationships Between Mismatched Concepts

By now, you've seen the benefit of skeptically looking at the relationship between the concepts in an argument's evidence and its conclusion. If the author introduces, seemingly out of nowhere, a new term or concept in an argument's conclusion, suspect a Mismatched Concepts argument. Connect those mismatched concepts in a sentence to identify the argument's assumption. Fortunately, a few relationships between the mismatched concepts will make up the bulk of the arguments you will see. Knowing what they are can make you faster and more efficient at tackling Assumption Family questions.

LSAT STRATEGY

The most commonly assumed relationships between mismatched concepts are

- The terms or concepts are alike/equivalent.
- The terms or concepts are mutually exclusive.
- One term or concept is needed for the other.
- One term or concept represents another.

For many questions, merely finding the mismatched concepts is enough to get you to the correct answer, as the correct answer will be the only choice to mention both of them. But for more challenging questions, you may be asked to choose between two or more answer choices, each one of which contains the same mismatched concepts. The difference between the answer choices will be the specific relationships between the mismatched concepts. One answer choice may say that the two concepts are mutually exclusive, while another may say that they are alike. As you go deeper into Assumption Family questions, the ability to determine the difference between an argument that assumes two things are equivalent and an argument that assumes one thing is representative of another, for example, will become increasingly important. Fortunately, the fact that most arguments make use of one of just a few relationships makes this easier than it may sound.

Consider the following statement:

> I like games because I am serious.

The conclusion is about liking games, but the evidence is about being serious. These two concepts are not automatically related to each other, so the author is making an assumption. In this case, the author is assuming that liking games and being serious are equivalent to each other—that one leads to the other. But what if we change the wording slightly:

> I don't like games because I am serious.

The statement uses all the same terms as the previous one; it's still about liking games and being serious. Now, however, there's a very different relationship between liking games and being serious. The author in this example is assuming that liking games and being serious are incompatible or mutually exclusive—you can't like games and be serious at the same time. Now let's change the wording one last time:

> I don't like games because I am not serious.

This last example again has the same mismatched concepts as the examples above, but it has a very different relationship from the previous two. In the last example, the author is assuming that being serious is a necessary condition to liking games. It's worth noting that a Mismatched Concepts argument in the form of *Not X because Not Y* will always mean that the evidence concept (Y) is necessary for the conclusion concept (X). Expect answer choices in these arguments to test you on which concept is necessary!

While the three relationships above are the most common, there is a fourth relationship that you will probably also see on the LSAT. In these arguments, the author assumes that one thing represents another. Representation arguments on the LSAT usually involve a mismatch between one group in the evidence and a different group in the conclusion. Consider the following argument:

> The oranges at my local store are all rotten. I know this because the three I just bought from that store are rotten.

Notice that the author uses information about the three oranges he bought to draw a conclusion about *all* of the oranges in the local store. The author assumes that the three oranges purchased must represent all of the oranges at the store. Be on the lookout for arguments in which the author uses a particular sample in the evidence and tries to draw an overly general conclusion from it. Though this kind of argument is most common in Flaw questions, it can show up in any of the Assumption Family questions.

The reality is that most Mismatched Concepts arguments on the LSAT are just more elaborate versions of the four arguments above. Your job isn't to find a new and unique relationship between mismatched concepts every time you see an Assumption Family argument—that would be frustrating and far too difficult. Instead, your goal is to spot the mismatched concepts, then connect the concepts in a way that matches up with other arguments like these.

Take a look at the following LSAT argument and try to match it up with one of the relationships above:

> Reducing stress lessens a person's sensitivity to pain. This is the conclusion reached by researchers who played extended audiotapes to patients before they underwent surgery and afterward while they were recovering. One tape consisted of conversation; the other consisted of music. Those who listened only to the latter tape required less anesthesia during surgery and fewer painkillers afterward than those who listened only to the former tape.
>
> *PrepTest52 Sec3 Q9*

The phrase "[t]his is the conclusion" at the beginning of the second sentence is a dead giveaway: the first sentence is the argument's conclusion, and the rest of the argument functions as evidence. The evidence is lengthy, so paraphrase it: researchers have found that people who listen to tapes of music are less sensitive to pain than those who listen to tapes of conversation. So this argument amounts to "Because listening to music lessens sensitivity to pain, reducing stress lessens sensitivity to pain." The mismatched terms are "listening to music" and "reducing stress." The next question is this: Which stock relationship does the author need these two concepts to have? If you said alike/equivalent, then you are correct. Much like the author of the very first example (liking games and being serious), this author is assuming that the mismatched concepts are equivalent in some way—that listening to music reduces stress. Even though alike/equivalent is by far the most common relationship you'll see in Mismatched Concepts arguments, the other relationships show up often enough that it's important to be prepared for them.

Now try some LSAT Mismatched Concepts arguments on your own. Your job is to match the following two arguments to one of these four examples:

- · I like games because I am serious. (alike/equivalent)
- · I don't like games because I am serious. (mutually exclusive)
- · I don't like games because I am not serious. (need evidence for conclusion)
- · The store's oranges are all rotten because the ones I bought from them are. (representation)

LSAT Argument	My Analysis
5. The odds of winning any major lottery jackpot are extremely slight. However, the very few people who do win major jackpots receive a great deal of attention from the media. Thus, since most people come to have at least some awareness of events that receive extensive media coverage, it is likely that many people greatly overestimate the odds of their winning a major jackpot. *PrepTest58 Sec4 Q21*	
6. Critic: The idealized world portrayed in romance literature is diametrically opposed to the debased world portrayed in satirical literature. Nevertheless, the major characters in both types of works have moral qualities that reflect the worlds in which they are presented. Comedy and tragedy, meanwhile, require that the moral qualities of major characters change during the course of the action. Therefore, neither tragedy nor comedy can be classified as satirical literature or romance literature. *PrepTest56 Sec2 Q10*	

Having an understanding of the specific relationship between mismatched terms will help you form the correct assumption. Do the terms have a positive relationship? Are they mutually exclusive? Check out how an LSAT expert evaluated the same arguments.

LSAT Argument	Analysis
5. The odds of winning any major lottery jackpot are extremely slight. However, the very few people who do win major jackpots receive a great deal of attention from the media. Thus, since most people come to have at least some awareness of events that receive extensive media coverage, it is likely that many people greatly overestimate the odds of their winning a major jackpot. *PrepTest58 Sec4 Q21* →	Conclusion: It's likely that many people overestimate their chances of winning the lottery. Evidence: Most people have some awareness of the few people who win lottery jackpots. The author talks in the evidence about people becoming aware of lottery winners; in the conclusion, the author shifts to a discussion of people who overestimate their chances of winning the lottery. The author assumes a connection between these very different groups: "some people who become aware of lottery winners then overestimate their chances of winning the lottery." This is just a more elaborate version of an "I like games because I am serious" equivalence argument.
6. Critic: The idealized world portrayed in romance literature is diametrically opposed to the debased world portrayed in satirical literature. Nevertheless, the major characters in both types of works have moral qualities that reflect the worlds in which they are presented. Comedy and tragedy, meanwhile, require that the moral qualities of major characters change during the course of the action. Therefore, neither tragedy nor comedy can be classified as satirical literature or romance literature. *PrepTest56 Sec2 Q10* →	Conclusion: Tragedy and comedy are not satire or romance. Evidence: Tragedy and comedy require that the moral qualities of major characters change. The mismatched concepts in the conclusion and evidence, respectively, are "not satire or romance" and "moral qualities change." This is just a more complicated version of "I don't like games because I am serious." The relationship is mutually exclusive: the author assumes that satirical and romantic literature can't involve changing the moral qualities of major characters.

For now, though, remember this: Whenever you are trying to link mismatched concepts for your prediction, keep the four common relationships in mind. The LSAT has a limited menu of relationships, and your job is to simply learn to recognize them in slightly different clothing.

Yet another tool for analyzing Mismatched Concepts arguments is in the toolbox of every LSAT expert: understanding Formal Logic.

Formal Logic in Mismatched Concepts

As you've seen in earlier chapters in this book, a fundamental understanding of Formal Logic is an enormously useful skill in mastering Logic Games. Deconstructing rules and making deductions based on conditional rules is the key to simplifying and demystifying some of that section's most difficult games. But having a firm grasp of the machinery of Formal Logic isn't helpful only in the Logic Games section of the LSAT. In fact, arguments that are composed of sufficient and necessary terms litter the Logical Reasoning section of the exam as well. Sometimes the Formal Logic relationship between terms is explicit; other times it is more subtle. In this section, we'll lay out for you some of the most basic patterns of Formal Logic found in Mismatched Concepts arguments.

A quick word of warning before we begin: though a mastery of Formal Logic is a valuable tool that will help you in this section, most Assumption Family questions don't have conditional statements at all. The most important skill you can develop in evaluating Mismatched Concepts arguments is the ability to recognize the gap between evidence and conclusion and then connect the mismatched terms or concepts. Looking at every argument as a Formal Logic puzzle that needs to be decoded will lead to frustration. Instead, think of tackling Mismatched Concepts arguments as a two-step process: start by identifying the relationships between the mismatched terms or concepts and then, if needed, use Formal Logic to determine the directionality of the concepts in the assumption.

LEARNING OBJECTIVES

In this section, you'll learn to

- Recognize common Formal Logic patterns in arguments containing Mismatched Concepts.
- Use knowledge of Formal Logic and contrapositives to determine an argument's assumption.
- Understand when directionality of terms is important.

When Mismatched Concepts arguments on the LSAT contain Formal Logic, the most basic structural pattern is as follows: "If A then B. Therefore, if A then C," where the letters A, B, and C represent unique terms.

	Sample Argument	My Analysis
evidence	If A → B	
assumption		
conclusion	If A → C	

First of all, how would you know that this argument contains mismatched concepts? The evidence discusses A and B, while the conclusion jumps to a discussion of A and C. This is about as straightforward as a Mismatched Concepts argument gets. The author must assume that B and C are in some way connected. Give it a shot: How would you fill in the assumption in this argument?

	Sample Argument	Analysis
evidence	If A → B	If A → **B**
assumption		
conclusion	If A → C	If A → **C**

If you said that the assumption must be "If B then C" (or drew If B → C), then good work.

	Sample Argument	Analysis
evidence	If A → B	If A → **B**
assumption		**If B → C**
conclusion	If A → C	If A → **C**

This assumption, combined with the evidence, produces a chain of logic: If A → B → C. It is then clear that the author can deduce that If A → C, the argument's conclusion. To see how this plays out in an argument that uses less abstract terms, consider this argument:

Dolphins are social animals that live in groups. Therefore, dolphins are intelligent.

Both the evidence and the conclusion discuss dolphins, but only the evidence mentions "social animals," while the conclusion moves to a discussion of "intelligence." Therefore, it's easy to see that this is a Mismatched Concepts argument. But how would you know that the evidence and conclusion also use Formal Logic? Words like *are*, *every*, and *any* allow the statements to be turned into conditional statements:

	Sample Argument	My Analysis
evidence	If dolphins → social animals that live in groups	
assumption		
conclusion	If dolphins → intelligent	

To make this argument work, we need to make a connection between "social animals" and "intelligent." But which direction? Is it that animals that are intelligent live in groups? Or that social animals are intelligent? The missing piece, the assumption, will not just connect the mismatched terms but connect them in the right direction:

	Sample Argument	Analysis
evidence	If dolphins → social animals that live in groups	If dolphins → **social animals that live in groups**
assumption		**If social animals that live in groups → intelligent**
conclusion	If dolphins → intelligent	If dolphins → **intelligent**

As you can see, the argument fits the original pattern of If "A → B; therefore, If A → C." That means the assumption must be If B → C in order for the conclusion to be logically inferred. Now, based on the above example, which of these would be an assumption that would allow the conclusion to be logically drawn?

(1) Social animals that live in groups are intelligent.

(2) All intelligent animals are social and live in groups.

In this case, the correct choice is (1), not (2). The assumption is that social animals living in groups must be intelligent, not that all animals that are intelligent are social animals living in groups. Although the testmaker won't always include answer choices with the same terms relating to each other in different ways, it does happen occasionally. By offering two answer choices that appear to the unprepared test taker to be nearly identical—and particularly by offering two distinct choices in which the relationship between concepts is alike/equivalent—the testmaker is able to increase the difficulty of a question. This shows up most often in Sufficient Assumption questions, which we will discuss later in the chapter. For now, just remember this: when you analyze an argument that contains Formal Logic, pay attention to which terms are sufficient and necessary.

If the above example seems to you to be too obvious to be a real LSAT question, you're right: the testmaker will most likely not evaluate your understanding of such a short, simple argument. Instead, the testmaker will present an argument with the same structural argument as the one about intelligent dolphins but dress it up with verbose language, abstract jargon, or confusing double negatives. Take the real LSAT argument below as an example:

A retrospective study is a scientific study that tries to determine the causes of subjects' present characteristics by looking for significant connections between the present characteristics of subjects and what happened to those subjects in the past, before the study began. Because retrospective studies of human subjects must use the subjects' reports about their own pasts, however, such studies cannot reliably determine the causes of human subjects' present characteristics.

PrepTest62 Sec2 Q9

Even though this argument is significantly longer and wordier than the one about dolphins, it is structurally similar. First, find and separate the evidence from the conclusion; this will go a long way in simplifying the argument. Here, the entire first sentence is simply background information that describes what a retrospective study is and what it attempts to achieve. The meat of the argument appears in the second sentence, which provides the evidence (after the Keyword "[b]ecause") and conclusion (the final clause):

Conclusion: Retrospective studies cannot reliably determine the causes of subjects' present characteristics.

Evidence: Retrospective studies of human subjects must use the subjects' reports about their own pasts.

The evidence and the conclusion state what a retrospective study must do and cannot do, respectively. But the conclusion introduces a new, seemingly unrelated idea to the argument: being able to reliably determine the causes of human subjects' present characteristics. That seems to come out of the blue. The evidence only ever talked about using subjects' reports about their own past. So, first and foremost, we're dealing with a Mismatched Concepts argument. But we should diagram this as Formal Logic and use it to help find the assumption.

	Sample Argument	My Analysis
evidence	If retrospective → use subjects' reports study about own past	
assumption		
conclusion	If retrospective → can't reliably study determine causes of subjects' present characteristics	

Note the use of the words "must" and "cannot." Such categorical language is indicative of Formal Logic in Logical Reasoning arguments. Other words that you are already familiar with—*only, unless, necessary, requires, needs*—also signify that you're dealing with an argument in which statements can be translated into Formal Logic. And once you do, you'll see that finding the assumption is a matter of connecting the mismatched terms, just as in the argument about the intelligent dolphins.

	Sample Argument	Analysis
evidence	If retrospective → use subjects' reports study about own past	If retrospective → **use subjects' reports** study **about own past**
assumption		**If use subjects'** → **can't reliably** **reports about** **determine causes** **own past** **of subjects' present** **characteristics**
conclusion	If retrospective → can't reliably study determine causes of subjects' present characteristics	If retrospective → **can't reliably** study **determine causes of** **subjects' present** **characteristics**

Written out, the assumption is if a subject reports about his or her own past, then one cannot reliably determine the cause of that person's present characteristics.

A quick note here about contrapositives in Formal Logic statements in Logical Reasoning arguments. Let's say you had translated the Formal Logic in the stimulus by contraposing both the evidence and the conclusion. Would you still be able to come up with the correct assumption? Absolutely. Even though your assumption may read a bit differently, it's still fundamentally identical: if one *can* reliably determine the cause of a human subject's present characteristics, then that person did *not* report about his or her own past. Don't get hung up on whether or not the correct answer choice matches your prediction or the contrapositive of your prediction. So long as you're comfortable with Formal Logic, you'll be able to spot either formulation as the correct answer.

Making It More Difficult: Adding an Extra Concept in the Evidence

Though the most basic Formal Logic Mismatched Concepts argument structure includes three terms (two terms in the evidence and two terms in the conclusion, with one term in the evidence identical to one term in the conclusion), many arguments contain more than just three concepts. A common pattern is for the testmaker to construct arguments with one or more extra terms in the evidence. If the terms are necessary for each other, combine them and remove the redundant term. This makes the evidence simpler and, in turn, easier to compare to the conclusion. For example, take a look at the following argument:

> All students in Dr. Peterson's class are juniors. Every junior has taken a public speaking class. Therefore, all students in Dr. Peterson's class have given a speech to a large crowd.

Notice that in the evidence, *juniors* is a term that shows up twice—it is connected both to students in Dr. P's class and to having taken a public speaking class. Connect these terms: because all of the students in Dr. P's class are juniors, and because all juniors have taken a public speaking class, the deduction can be made that all students in Dr. P's class have taken a public speaking class. By removing the redundant term *juniors*, the evidence has been simplified: all of the students in Dr. P's class have taken a public speaking class.

It's clear that we are back to the basic "If A → B; therefore, If A → C" argument structure. Putting the mismatched terms into a sentence, the assumption here can be articulated as: If the students in Dr. P's class have taken a public speaking class, then they have given a speech to a large crowd. Another way to put it: Giving a speech to a large crowd is a requirement of taking a public speaking class.

Now, let's try this out with an actual LSAT argument. Find and paraphrase the evidence and the conclusion, then compare.

Therapist: The ability to trust other people is essential to happiness, for without trust there can be no meaningful emotional connection to another human being, and without meaningful emotional connections to others we feel isolated.

PrepTest56 Sec3 Q16

The Keyword "for" in the second line indicates the separation between the conclusion (first clause) and the evidence (the rest of the sentence).

Like the argument above about Dr. P's class, this argument also contains three separate concepts in the evidence: trust, emotional connection, and isolation. Is it possible to combine the concepts in the evidence and make a deduction by eliminating a redundant term? Sure: without trust, a person won't have an emotional connection to others, and without an emotional connection to others, a person will feel isolated. Therefore, make the deduction that without trust, a person will feel isolated.

	Argument	**My Analysis**
evidence	If no trust → feel isolated	
assumption		
conclusion	If no trust → cannot be happy	

Once again, the argument has been simplified to the common "[If A → B], then [If A → C]" form. Find the assumption by connecting the mismatched terms.

	Argument	Analysis
evidence	If no trust → feel isolated	If no trust → **feel isolated**
assumption		**If feel isolated → cannot be happy**
conclusion	If no trust → cannot be happy	If no trust → **cannot be happy**

Putting the mismatched terms into a sentence, the assumption here can be articulated as: If a person feels isolated, then he or she cannot be happy. The contrapositive allows us to think of the assumption in a different way: If a person is happy, then he or she does not feel isolated. The correct answer choice could potentially show up in either form. Either way, we have an assumption whose terms are mutually exclusive: a person can't be both happy and isolated at the same time.

Same Necessary Terms

Though the most common Formal Logic arrangement in Mismatched Concepts arguments contains evidence and conclusion with the same sufficient or "trigger" term, Formal Logic–based arguments can take other structural forms, as well. One variation includes an argument in which both the evidence and the conclusion contain the same *necessary* terms. In other words, instead of an argument with the structure of "If **A** → B; therefore, If **A** → C," these arguments will say "If B → **C**; therefore, If A → **C**." Here's an example:

> Animals with big teeth are scary. Therefore, tigers are scary.

Even though this argument is similar to the arguments above, here the mismatched concepts are the sufficient, not the necessary terms. The author isn't assuming that the mismatched concept in the evidence is sufficient for the mismatched concept in the conclusion, but rather vice versa. For this argument to make sense, the author must be assuming that the tigers have big teeth.

	Argument	Analysis
evidence	If animal → scary with big teeth	**If animal with big teeth** → scary
assumption		**If tiger → animal with big teeth**
conclusion	If tiger → scary	**If tiger** → scary

Another way to evaluate an argument that includes the same necessary terms in both the evidence and the conclusion is to contrapose both. Doing this creates an argument with the same sufficient terms—in other words, the argument reverts back to the same "If A → B; therefore, If A → C" structure.

	Argument	Analysis
evidence	If not scary → not animal with big teeth	If not scary → **not animal with big teeth**
assumption		**If not animal with big teeth → not tiger**
conclusion	If not scary → not tiger	If not scary → **not tiger**

Once again, we see the benefit of being able to evaluate Formal Logic statements both as they are written and as they *can* be written according to their contrapositives. Knowing that the terms can be switched and negated is a powerful tool that will help you see certain LSAT arguments more clearly and more flexibly than other test takers.

Mismatched Concepts in the Evidence—Rare

Mismatched Concepts arguments overwhelmingly move from one concept in the evidence to a new concept in the conclusion, but it's also possible for an author to present two mismatched concepts in the evidence. Though this is rare, it does occasionally show up, so don't be surprised if you see such an argument on the exam. For example, take a look at the following argument:

> Whenever people watch a good movie, they get a happy feeling. And people always do the right thing when they feel the urge to help others. Therefore, watching a good movie makes people do the right thing.

At first blush, this argument doesn't appear to be one of mismatched concepts—after all, both of the terms in the conclusion show up in the evidence, and we've said to recognize mismatched concepts by noting a new, unrelated concept in the conclusion. An argument like this causes many test takers to get rattled or frustrated, because the argument does not conform to their understanding of how mismatched concepts work. But take a look at the evidence: the terms that show up only once in this argument are both in the evidence: "feeling happy" and "feeling the urge to help others." For this argument to make sense, the author must be assuming that a person who feels happy will feel the urge to help others.

	Argument		Analysis
evidence	If watch good movie	→ feel happy	If watch good movie → **feel happy**
assumption			**If feel happy → urge to help others**
evidence	If urge to help others	→ do the right thing	**If urge to help others** → do the right thing
conclusion	If watch good movie	→ do the right thing	If watch good movie → do the right thing

Again, an argument with mismatched concepts in the evidence is rare—in fact, you might not even see it on the LSAT you take. Just know that the testmaker *can* present an argument this way; to find the assumption, find the mismatched concepts in the evidence and connect them.

Strict Formal Logic statements tend to show up most often in Sufficient Assumption questions, which we will discuss in depth later in this chapter. In other Assumption Family questions, strict Formal Logic is less common.

The thing to keep in mind is that the underlying Formal Logic structure of "If A → B (evidence); therefore, If A → C (conclusion)" *is* common. Knowing that this pattern underlies many of the Mismatched Concepts arguments you'll see on the LSAT will help you achieve mastery in Assumption Family questions. Remember to approach Mismatched Concepts arguments in two steps: start by identifying the relationships between the mismatched terms or concepts and then, if needed, use Formal Logic to determine the directionality of the concepts in the assumption.

LSAT STRATEGY

Formal Logic in arguments containing Mismatched Concepts:

· The most common structure is: "If A → B; therefore, If A → C."
· When possible, connect multiple terms in the evidence and simplify.
· Difficult wrong answer choices may confuse necessary and sufficient terms.

Hopefully you have a more solid understanding of the common relationships and patterns you'll see in Mismatched Concepts arguments. Later in this chapter, you'll get much more practice identifying and analyzing these types of arguments in Assumption Family questions. Now, though, let's turn our attention to the other type of argument structure you'll see in Assumption Family arguments: Overlooked Possibilities.

OVERLOOKED POSSIBILITIES

Consider this evidence:

> Last night Maria parked her car in an area of town where many car thefts occur. This morning, Maria woke up and discovered that her car was no longer in its parking spot.
>
> Therefore, _____.

Now, say we're playing the same game we mentioned earlier. Your job is to figure out what the conclusion is by filling in the blank. Take a moment and think about it.

Unlike in the argument you saw earlier about poison and Chemical X, you probably *would* be able to come up with the conclusion fairly quickly: "I bet the author's going to say that Maria's car was stolen." And if you guessed something along those lines, you're making a reasonable conjecture as to the author's conclusion. Remember, though, that the LSAT doesn't present complete, reasonable arguments—it presents incomplete arguments. Here's what an LSAT argument would likely say:

> Last night Maria parked her car in an area of town where many car thefts occur. This morning, Maria woke up and discovered that her car was no longer in its parking spot. Therefore, Maria's car **must** have been stolen.

Take a moment now and try to describe to yourself what is wrong with the LSAT version of this argument without using any of the words from the stimulus.

To understand what is wrong with the argument, begin by envisioning the author's argument as a road: the author is driving from the evidence to the conclusion. As far as she's concerned, it's a clear path, but an LSAT expert is trained to see all of the roadblocks along the way that the author can't. That's exactly what went wrong with the argument above: the author starts the trip with evidence that introduces the *possibility* of the car having been stolen, and from there she tries to reach a conclusion that it *must* be the explanation for the disappearance. Unfortunately for the author, there are many possible explanations for the car's disappearance, and if even one of them is possible, the author's entire conclusion falls apart. These are the roadblocks (in other words, the possible objections) to the argument. The only way the author's argument will work is if they're all removed.

Overlooked Possibilities: The Basics

Not all LSAT arguments have a problem of relevance. The reason why you could reasonably predict the conclusion in this argument is that it does use the right *kind* of evidence: the information given helps us figure out whether or not Maria's car was stolen. Contrast that with the Chemical X example from earlier in the chapter. In that argument, the evidence about poison didn't help us figure out whether or not Chemical X was harmful. In fact, on roughly half of the LSAT arguments you'll see on Test Day, the author is using pieces of evidence that *are* in some way related and relevant to the terms and concepts in the conclusion, but the author's conclusion will be too extreme for its evidence. Instead of a jump or shift in the *types* of concepts discussed, the author's shift will be one of *degree*.

LSAT STRATEGY

How can you identify an argument containing Overlooked Possibilities?

- The terms or concepts in the evidence *are* related to the conclusion.
- The conclusion reached is too strong or extreme based on the evidence.
- The author has failed to consider possible objections to the conclusion.

Finding the assumption in these arguments is fundamentally different from our approach to Mismatched Concepts problems. Instead of linking two concepts from within the stimulus, our job is to consider the potential objections to the author's conclusion: any unconsidered information that would prove the conclusion false. Going back to Maria's vanishing car, for example, couldn't it also be true that Maria's car was towed? Or that she gave her keys to a friend, who took the car? Or that the car was impounded due to Maria's failure to make her loan payments in a timely manner? We could actually spend all day thinking of all of the various fates that could have befallen her poor car aside from being stolen, and there's often no way to know which one will be brought up in the correct answer. Overlooked Possibilities assumptions are thus best thought of as negative assumptions—they are about all of the things that **didn't** happen. In this case, the author is assuming that there are **no** other reasons for the car's disappearance—if that's true, then all potential objections have been removed from the argument. Most of the time, the questions will specifically test you on these unconsidered objections.

LSAT STRATEGY

When tackling an argument containing Overlooked Possibilities:

- Focus on the conclusion.
- Determine the possible objections to that conclusion.
- Understand the assumption in negative terms: the author assumes that the possible objections are not present, or did not happen.

Overlooked Possibilities: Sample Arguments

Here are some brief Overlooked Possibilities arguments and the Assumption of each. After reviewing these examples, you'll have a chance to try some others on your own.

Argument		Analysis
These berries taste delicious. Therefore, we should eat them!	$\rightarrow$	The author assumes that there are no other considerations when determining whether or not to eat the berries.
When I wore a tracksuit to the party, I was ignored. Therefore, the tracksuit caused people to ignore me.	$\rightarrow$	The author assumes that nothing else, besides the tracksuit, caused people to ignore him at the party.
Sad movies make my friend cry. She's crying now. Therefore, she must have watched a sad movie.	$\rightarrow$	The author assumes that there is no other possible explanation for why her friend is crying.
There's no cash in William's wallet. Therefore, he won't be able to buy any gum.	$\rightarrow$	The author assumes that there's no other possible way for William to pay for gum besides cash from William's wallet.
Our team has the best player in the game. Therefore, we will win the game.	$\rightarrow$	The author assumes that there are no other considerations to take into account when determining the winner besides which team has the best player.

Practice

Practice your ability to evaluate Overlooked Possibilities arguments by analyzing the following arguments. In each one of these arguments, follow this approach:

- · Separate the evidence from the conclusion.
- · Describe to yourself why the evidence is relevant.
- · Ask yourself what the possible objections to the conclusion are.
- · Phrase the assumption in negative terms (i.e., what didn't happen).

After each argument, feel free to turn to the next page to see the expert analysis.

Argument	My Analysis
7. Medication B has more side effects than Medication A. Therefore, we should use Medication A.	
8. The pet store down the street has only cats and dogs for sale. I'm definitely going to get a pet, but my parents won't let me get a cat. Clearly, then, I'm going to get a dog.	
9. Sally suggests driving to work on the highway, but the highway tends to have much more traffic than the side streets. So I am going to ignore Sally's advice and take the side streets instead.	

Now take a look at how an LSAT expert would look at the arguments you've just evaluated.

Argument	Analysis
7. Medication B has more side effects than Medication A. Therefore, we should use Medication A.	Conclusion: We should use Med. A (instead of Med. B).
	Evidence: Med. B has more side effects than Med. A.
	→ The author considers only the side effects of the two medications in making a decision; therefore, the author is *not* considering any other reasons why Med. B might be preferable to Med. A. What if Med. A simply isn't effective? Or if Med. A is astronomically expensive? Phrase the assumption negatively: "There are no unconsidered benefits of Med. B and no unconsidered drawbacks of Med. A."
8. The pet store down the street has only cats and dogs for sale. I'm definitely going to get a pet, but my parents won't let me get a cat. Clearly, then, I'm going to get a dog.	Conclusion: I have to get a dog.
	Evidence: The store down the street only has cats and dogs, and I can't get a cat.
	→ There's nothing new in the conclusion, but the conclusion goes too far. The unconsidered objections to this argument would be anything that says the author *doesn't* have to get a dog. Specifically, there may be other pet stores in the area that sell more than just cats and dogs. Phrase the assumption negatively: "There is no other place to get a pet aside from the pet store down the street."
9. Sally suggests driving to work on the highway, but the highway tends to have much more traffic than the side streets. So I am going to ignore Sally's advice and take the side streets instead.	Conclusion: I'm going to take the side streets to work.
	Evidence: The highway tends to have more traffic than side streets.
	→ There's nothing new in this conclusion either, but much as in the first argument, the author is not considering potential objections to the conclusion. Specifically, the author fails to rule out any additional reasons why the highway may be a good idea or additional information about potential cons of the side streets. Phrase the assumption negatively: "There are no unconsidered pros of the highway or cons of the side streets that would make the highway the better choice."

The LSAT, of course, will present more difficult arguments than the ones shown above, but the fundamental *structure* of Overlooked Possibilities arguments will remain the same. Regardless of the topic being discussed in the argument—whether it be on matters philosophical, legal, or scientific—your method and objective will always remain the same. First, separate evidence from conclusion. Then, evaluate the concepts discussed in both—if the author uses relevant information to draw a conclusion that is too strong or extreme, find the assumption by identifying the factors the author is not considering.

Try that now with an actual LSAT argument.

LSAT Argument	My Analysis
10. Area resident: Childhood lead poisoning has declined steadily since the 1970s, when leaded gasoline was phased out and lead paint was banned. But recent statistics indicate that 25 percent of this area's homes still contain lead paint that poses significant health hazards. Therefore, if we eliminate the lead paint in those homes, childhood lead poisoning in the area will finally be eradicated. *PrepTest62 Sec2 Q5*	

Did the terms and concepts in the evidence relate to the conclusion drawn? Did the author then overlook potential objections to the conclusion? Take a look at how an LSAT expert would break down this argument.

LSAT Argument	Analysis
10. Area resident: Childhood lead poisoning has declined steadily since the 1970s, when leaded gasoline was phased out and lead paint was banned. But recent statistics indicate that 25 percent of this area's homes still contain lead paint that poses significant health hazards. Therefore, if we eliminate the lead paint in those homes, childhood lead poisoning in the area will finally be eradicated. *PrepTest62 Sec2 Q5* $\longrightarrow$	Conclusion: Eliminating lead paint in homes will *eradicate* all childhood lead poisoning. Evidence: Childhood lead poisoning is declining; lead paint is one source of lead poisoning and is present in 25 percent of homes. (Leaded gasoline was another source, but it was eliminated in the 1970s.) Though the evidence does relate to lead paint and lead poisoning, the author jumps to a very extreme conclusion: Eliminating lead paint in homes will eradicate childhood lead poisoning. The possible objections the author fails to consider are other sources of lead poisoning. The author assumes that there are *no other* potential sources of lead besides leaded gasoline and paint.

Hopefully you're starting to get the hang of evaluating these types of arguments. Let's dive in even deeper and discuss some of the most common types of Overlooked Possibilities arguments you'll see on the LSAT.

Going Deeper: Common Patterns and Relationships in Arguments with Overlooked Possibilities

By now, you've seen the benefit of skeptically looking at an argument in which the author uses relevant evidence to support a conclusion that goes too far. In doing so, the author chooses to overlook alternate possibilities that would hurt his conclusion. Indeed, the author's assumption is that no potential objections to the conclusion exist. Now we'll take a look at several of the most common patterns that show up in Overlooked Possibilities arguments.

No Other Explanation, Reason, or Outcome

One of the most common patterns within the Overlooked Possibilities argument class consists of a conclusion that posits only one explanation or reason for something or only one likely outcome. Invariably, the assumption will then be that there is no other possible explanation, reason, or outcome. For example, consider the following simple argument:

> Chlorophyll A is a type of green-pigmented chlorophyll abundant in plants. Clearly, the presence of chlorophyll A must be what gives plants their green coloration.

Notice that the conclusion provides only one explanation for the green color of plants: it must be due to the presence of chlorophyll A. Yet the evidence alludes to the fact that chlorophyll A isn't the only type of chlorophyll in existence. The author is overlooking the possibility that there are other kinds of chlorophyll—or other pigments unrelated to chlorophyll—that also contribute to the green color of plants. In other words, the possible objections to this argument are other explanations for the green color of plants.

Now take a look at an LSAT stimulus built on this same pattern. You've seen this argument before, in Chapter 8. Here, see if you can spot the overlooked explanation or outcome; then compare your thinking to the expert analysis presented below.

LSAT Argument	My Analysis
11. Mayor: Local antitobacco activists are calling for expanded antismoking education programs paid for by revenue from heavily increased taxes on cigarettes sold in the city. Although the effectiveness of such education programs is debatable, there is strong evidence that the taxes themselves would produce the sought-after reduction in smoking. Surveys show that cigarette sales drop substantially in cities that impose stiff tax increases on cigarettes. *PrepTest52 Sec3 Q6*	

Does this conclusion strike you as particularly strong? "Strong evidence exists that taxes on cigarettes *will* reduce smoking." Such a confident-sounding conclusion indicates we are probably dealing with an Overlooked Possibilities argument.

LSAT Argument	Analysis
11. Mayor: Local antitobacco activists are calling for expanded antismoking education programs paid for by revenue from heavily increased taxes on cigarettes sold in the city. Although the effectiveness of such education programs is debatable, there is strong evidence that the taxes themselves would produce the sought-after reduction in smoking. Surveys show that cigarette sales drop substantially in cities that impose stiff tax increases on cigarettes. *PrepTest52 Sec3 Q6*	Conclusion: The cigarette taxes would produce a reduction in smoking. Evidence: Surveys show that cigarette sales drop substantially in cities that post stiff tax increases on cigarettes. $\rightarrow$ The author uses relevant information to draw an extreme conclusion. Though cigarette sales have dropped in the city, does that prove smoking has also decreased? Overlooked objections to the author's conclusion include anything that explains how reduced sales might not lead to lower smoking rates. The author assumes that these possible objections don't exist.

Here, the mayor is overlooking the possibility that when cigarette taxes go up locally, smokers just go somewhere else to purchase cigarettes—like, for example, the nearest town without such taxes.

Although overlooked explanations constitute one of the most common overlooked possibilities, this argument class includes a number of other variants as well. The ability to recognize the following five patterns will give you an advantage over other test takers who have to reinvent the wheel each time they see an argument type they do not recognize. Try out the examples for each pattern and watch for them while you practice.

Necessity vs. Sufficiency: Assuming That What Is Sufficient Is Actually Necessary

You've seen how Formal Logic statements can be tested in Mismatched Concepts arguments. Occasionally, though, an author will commit a Formal Logic error in an Overlooked Possibilities argument. This happens when an argument either confuses sufficient and necessary terms or incorrectly negates the terms. The result of both of these errors is that the author overlooks other potential causes for a given event. For instance, take a look at the following simple argument:

> Every time my cat jumps onto the coffee table, she knocks over the lamp. I just got home and found the lamp on the coffee table knocked over. Obviously my cat has been at it again.

This author concludes that there is only one possible cause for the lamp having been knocked over: the cat. But is that necessarily true? Just because the cat *can* cause the lamp to fall over doesn't mean that there are no other ways it could happen. Perhaps the dog is at fault, for example, or perhaps a human living in the house is responsible, or perhaps there was an earthquake. Think of it in terms of sufficiency and necessity: the fact that the cat is sufficient to cause the lamp to fall down does not mean that the cat is necessary for the lamp to fall down—there could be lots of other sufficient conditions as well.

Looking at this argument in clear Formal Logic terminology helps illuminate the error:

Evidence: If cat on table $\rightarrow$ lamp down

Conclusion: If lamp down $\rightarrow$ cat on table

As you remember from Chapter 1, you can't read the conditional statement "If cat then lamp down" backwards as "If lamp down then cat." Whenever an author switches the necessary and sufficient sides of a conditional statement without negating the terms, she automatically overlooks the fact that there could be other triggers for an event, just as the author of the cat-and-lamp argument above assumes no other factor besides the cat could have caused the lamp to be knocked over.

Try out the following LSAT argument that confuses necessary and sufficient conditions:

LSAT Argument	**My Analysis**
12. If Agnes's research proposal is approved, the fourth-floor lab must be cleaned out for her use. Immanuel's proposal, on the other hand, requires less space. So if his proposal is approved, he will continue to work in the second-floor lab. Only those proposals the director supports will be approved. So since the director will support both proposals, the fourth-floor lab must be cleaned out. *PrepTest56 Sec2 Q15*	

The use of terms *if*, *only*, and *must* indicates that this argument definitely uses Formal Logic. In such arguments, suspect either a Mismatched Concepts argument or an Overlooked Possibilities argument that confuses necessary and sufficient terms.

LSAT Argument	**Analysis**
12. If Agnes's research proposal is approved, the fourth-floor lab must be cleaned out for her use. Immanuel's proposal, on the other hand, requires less space. So if his proposal is approved, he will continue to work in the second-floor lab. Only those proposals the director supports will be approved. So since the director will support both proposals, the fourth-floor lab must be cleaned out. *PrepTest56 Sec2 Q15*	Conclusion: The fourth-floor lab must be cleaned out. Evidence: If Agnes's proposal is approved, then the fourth-floor lab must be cleaned out; only those proposals the director supports will be approved; the director will support Agnes's proposal. The author says that the director will support the proposals. But "[o]nly those proposals the director supports will be approved" means → that the director's support is *necessary*, not sufficient, for approval. In other words: If approved → director supports The director's support doesn't necessarily mean that the proposal was approved. In concluding that the fourth-floor lab must be cleaned out based on the director's support of Agnes's proposal, the author confuses necessary and sufficient terms. Stated differently, the author of this argument assumes that there are no other necessary factors besides the director's support that impact the approval of Agnes' proposal.

Assuming That There Are No Overlooked Advantages or Disadvantages That Impact a Recommendation

Consider the following:

> The deli down the street is currently offering a lunch special, so we should eat lunch there today.

Okay, so the deli's running a special. But what if it's still more expensive than the pizza place across the street from it? Or what if the deli's been cited for food safety violations repeatedly during the past month and, in fact, your friend just got sick from eating there yesterday? Or what if the deli's food doesn't taste good? If any of these disadvantages exists, should you still eat there? Perhaps not.

Whenever the author of an LSAT argument cites an advantage (or disadvantage) and makes a recommendation based upon it, the possible objections to the argument are any disadvantages (or advantages) that outweigh it. In the argument above, the author assumes that the deli offers no disadvantages that would tilt the scale in favor of eating elsewhere.

Now try to spot the author's assumption in an LSAT argument that involves a recommendation based upon advantages or disadvantages:

LSAT Argument	**My Analysis**
13. Perry: Worker-owned businesses require workers to spend time on management decision-making and investment strategy, tasks that are not directly productive. Also, such businesses have less extensive divisions of labor than do investor-owned businesses. Such inefficiencies can lead to low profitability, and thus increase the risk for lenders. Therefore, lenders seeking to reduce their risk should not make loans to worker-owned businesses.	
PrepTest52 Sec1 Q12	

Notice that the conclusion of this argument is a recommendation. If the author of the argument bases the recommendation on citing advantages or disadvantages to the proposal, suspect an Overlooked Possibilities argument. Take a look at how an LSAT expert evaluates the same argument.

LSAT Argument	**Analysis**
13. Perry: Worker-owned businesses require workers to spend time on management decision-making and investment strategy, tasks that are not directly productive. Also, such businesses have less extensive divisions of labor than do investor-owned businesses. Such inefficiencies can lead to low profitability, and thus increase the risk for lenders. Therefore, lenders seeking to reduce their risk should not make loans to worker-owned businesses. *PrepTest52 Sec1 Q12*	Conclusion: Lenders seeking to reduce their risk should not make loans to worker-owned businesses. Evidence: The inefficiencies inherent in worker-owned businesses can lead to lower profitability, which can raise the risk for lenders. The author cites a possible disadvantage to lending to worker-owned businesses, then makes a recommendation to avoid lending. The unconsidered objections here are reasons why lenders should make these loans. As usual, the author assumes that there are no advantages that would outweigh the risks of making such loans.

Assuming That Something That Could Occur, Will Occur

The fact that something might happen doesn't necessarily mean that it actually will happen. Yet, authors of LSAT arguments sometimes wrongly assume the opposite—that is, they assume that something merely possible is definitely true. Here's a simplified example to illustrate:

> Skateboarding can cause all sorts of injuries. It follows that Aaron, who just went skateboarding, must be injured.

The fact that skateboarding *can* cause injuries does not mean that it *always* causes injuries. But that's exactly what this author assumes in concluding that Aaron must be injured just because he went skateboarding. Stated differently, the author overlooks the possibility that Aaron might have managed to go skateboarding without incurring an injury.

See if you can spot the overlooked possibility in this LSAT argument:

LSAT Argument	**My Analysis**
14. To keep one's hands warm during the winter, one never needs gloves or mittens. One can always keep one's hands warm simply by putting on an extra layer of clothing, such as a thermal undershirt or a sweater. After all, keeping one's vital organs warm can keep one's hands warm as well. *PrepTest58 Sec4 Q2*	

Now take a look at the same argument, through the lens of an LSAT expert:

LSAT Argument	Analysis
14. To keep one's hands warm during the winter, one never needs gloves or mittens. One can always keep one's hands warm simply by putting on an extra layer of clothing, such as a thermal undershirt or a sweater. After all, keeping one's vital organs warm can keep one's hands warm as well. *PrepTest58 Sec4 Q2*	Conclusion: During the winter, gloves aren't needed to stay warm; an extra layer of clothing will do. Evidence: Keeping one's vital organs warm can keep one's hands warm as well. → The evidence is provisional: keeping one's vital organs warm *can* keep one's hands warm. But the conclusion uses much stronger language: one "never" needs gloves in winter; one can "always" keep the hands warm with an extra layer of clothing. This argument's author assumes that something that can be true is always true and thus overlooks the fact that there may be circumstances in which the extra layer of clothing is not enough to keep the hands warm (say, in subzero temperatures or in damp weather).

Causal Arguments: Assuming That a Correlation Proves a Causal Relationship

Thing A happens. At the same time, Thing B happens. So A caused B. This is the classic argument of causation based on evidence of a correlation. Because they come with such a wealth of overlooked possibilities, causal arguments show up most frequently in Flaw, Strengthen, and Weaken questions, as you'll see later in this chapter (though they have also, on occasion, appeared in Assumption questions). Here's a basic example of a causal argument:

> Over the past half century, worldwide sugar consumption has nearly tripled. During the same time period, there has been a marked increase in the rate of global technological advancement. It follows that the increase in global sugar consumption has caused the acceleration in technological advancement.

The evidence in this argument is a correlation between an increase in worldwide sugar consumption and an acceleration in global technological advancement. The author concludes that increased sugar consumption has caused the acceleration in technological advancement. In doing so, the author assumes that there are *no other possible relationships* between sugar consumption and technological advancement. Specifically, the three possible objections to any causal argument are these:

1. There is an **alternate cause**. Here, instead of sugar consumption causing accelerated technical advancement, perhaps something else caused the accelerated technological advancement.

2. The causation is **reversed**. Instead of sugar consumption causing technological advancement, perhaps it's the other way around: technological advances allow for easier sugar refinement, which leads to higher sugar consumption.

3. The correlation is purely **coincidental**. Perhaps there is no relationship between sugar consumption and technological advancement at all and the fact that they have occurred during the same time period is merely a coincidence. Or perhaps they didn't actually happen at the same time at all; one of them began long before the other.

The author of a causal argument assumes, then, that (1) there is no alternate cause, (2) the causation is not reversed, and (3) the correlation is not coincidental. In the future, remind yourself of these overlooked objections by using the acronym **ARC**. And, because the author isn't considering them, we can give these flaws a nickname— we can say that the flaw in these arguments is that the author improperly assumes that there is "**No ARC.**" Try out an LSAT argument that includes a claim of causation based on evidence of a correlation and ask yourself which of these overlooked possibilities are most likely:

LSAT Argument	My Analysis
15. Of all the Arabic epic poems that have been popular at various times, only *Sirat Bani Hilal* is still publicly performed. Furthermore, while most other epics were only recited, *Sirat Bani Hilal* has usually been sung. The musical character of the performance, therefore, is the main reason for its longevity. *PrepTest56 Sec3 Q17*	

First, did you notice that the author's conclusion includes a claim of causation? Be on the lookout for such language in Assumption Family arguments. If you see that the author concludes that one thing is making another thing happen, you're dealing with a causal argument.

LSAT Argument	Analysis
15. Of all the Arabic epic poems that have been popular at various times, only *Sirat Bani Hilal* is still publicly performed. Furthermore, while most other epics were only recited, *Sirat Bani Hilal* has usually been sung. The musical character of the performance, therefore, is the main reason for its longevity. *PrepTest56 Sec3 Q17*	Conclusion: The fact that *Sirat Bani Hilal* has usually been sung is the main reason for its longevity.
$\longrightarrow$	Evidence: In contrast to other Arabic epic poems, *Sirat Bani Hilal* has usually been sung and is the only one still being performed.
	The author's evidence amounts to a correlation between a particular poem being sung and that same poem still being performed. The author's conclusion is a statement of causation: the fact that the poem has been sung is the reason for its longevity. The author assumes that there is no ARC: no alternative cause exists for the longevity, longevity isn't the reason for the musical nature of the play, and it doesn't just happen to be both enduring and musical.

497

Predictions: Assumptions about Circumstances

As you learned in Chapter 9, a conclusion stating that something is likely to happen in the future is called a "prediction." To illustrate the classic assumption underlying predictions, consider the following weather prediction:

> Due to the current prevailing northwesterly breeze, the weather in Flooville will remain clear and cold tomorrow.

The problem with this prediction is that if the northwesterly breeze unexpectedly shifts to, say, southeasterly, the weather in Flooville might not "remain clear and cold." The author assumes that the circumstances under which the prediction was made *will not change*.

Now consider this prediction:

> Despite the prevailing northwesterly breeze that is currently bringing clear and cold weather to Flooville, the weather in Flooville will shift tomorrow to overcast and warm.

This time, the author assumes that the northwesterly breeze will have changed direction by tomorrow—in other words, the assumption is that there *will be* a change in circumstances.

Anyone making a prediction is making an assumption about circumstances. Keep this in mind whenever you see that an argument's conclusion is a prediction. Now take a look at the following LSAT argument:

LSAT Argument	My Analysis
16. Carol Morris wants to own a majority of the shares of the city's largest newspaper, *The Daily*. The only obstacle to Morris's amassing a majority of these shares is that Azedcorp, which currently owns a majority, has steadfastly refused to sell. Industry analysts nevertheless predict that Morris will soon be the majority owner of *The Daily*. *PrepTest62 Sec2 Q4*	

Notice how this conclusion is phrased: a confident prediction that something will definitely happen soon. Take a look at how an LSAT expert evaluates this argument:

LSAT Argument	Analysis
16. Carol Morris wants to own a majority of the shares of the city's largest newspaper, *The Daily*. The only obstacle to Morris's amassing a majority of these shares is that Azedcorp, which currently owns a majority, has steadfastly refused to sell. Industry analysts nevertheless predict that Morris will soon be the majority owner of *The Daily*. *PrepTest62 Sec2 Q4* →	**Conclusion:** Morris will soon be the majority owner of *The Daily*. **Evidence:** The only obstacle to Morris owning a majority of *The Daily* is that Azedcorp has refused to sell. The author assumes that the current circumstances will change: something will happen to cause Azedcorp to change its mind. Perhaps the company will need money for something else, or it will lose interest in *The Daily*, or it will go out of business and have no choice but to sell.

As with Mismatched Concepts arguments, the better you can become at spotting these various Overlooked Possibilities argument patterns, the more efficient you will become at analyzing arguments. You'll be ahead of the game when you encounter Assumption, Strengthen, Weaken, and Flaw questions—which, taken together, constitute about one-fourth of the LSAT.

LSAT STRATEGY

Overlooked Possibilities tend to fit one of the following patterns:

· Fails to consider other explanations, reasons, or outcomes based on the evidence.
· Confuses sufficient and necessary terms.
· Does not consider potential advantages or disadvantages when making a recommendation.
· Assumes that something *will* occur just because it *could* occur.
· Author arrives at a claim of causation based on evidence that is only correlated.
· Prediction is based on an assumption that circumstances will or will not change.

Now it's time to put this knowledge into practice and analyze some arguments.

UNTANGLING AND ANALYZING LSAT ARGUMENTS

At this point, you should have more confidence in your ability to identify the assumption in LSAT arguments. If an argument contains a new concept in the conclusion that appears irrelevant or unrelated to the evidence, the author's assumption is that a logical relationship exists between mismatched concepts in the evidence and conclusion. On the other hand, if an argument uses relevant evidence to jump to a conclusion that overlooks unstated but relevant information, then the author's assumption is that there are no possible objections to the conclusion. Understanding the common ways an LSAT argument moves from its evidence to its conclusion will help you tackle Assumption Family questions. Use this new knowledge to analyze a few LSAT arguments.

Practice

In each of the arguments below, separate the evidence from the conclusion. Simplify each, and then compare them. Is the author assuming that two mismatched concepts are somehow related? Or is the author using relevant evidence to jump to an extreme conclusion without considering potential objections?

LSAT Argument	My Analysis
17. Researchers announced recently that over the past 25 years the incidence of skin cancer caused by exposure to harmful rays from the sun has continued to grow in spite of the increasingly widespread use of sunscreens. This shows that using sunscreen is unlikely to reduce a person's risk of developing skin cancer. *PrepTest62 Sec4 Q5*	
18. One should never sacrifice one's health in order to acquire money, for without health, happiness is not obtainable. *PrepTest62 Sec2 Q17*	
19. Commentator: Although the present freshwater supply is adequate for today's patterns of water use, the human population will increase substantially over the next few decades, drastically increasing the need for freshwater. Hence, restrictions on water use will be necessary to meet the freshwater needs of humankind in the not-too-distant future. *PrepTest58 Sec1 Q1*	
20. There are far fewer independent bookstores than there were 20 years ago, largely because chain bookstores prospered and multiplied during that time. Thus, chain bookstores' success has been to the detriment of book consumers, for the shortage of independent bookstores has prevented the variety of readily available books from growing as much as it otherwise would have. *PrepTest56 Sec3 Q9*	

Now, take a look at how an LSAT expert would untangle and evaluate the arguments you've just examined.

LSAT Argument	Analysis
17. Researchers announced recently that over the past 25 years the incidence of skin cancer caused by exposure to harmful rays from the sun has continued to grow in spite of the increasingly widespread use of sunscreens. This shows that using sunscreen is unlikely to reduce a person's risk of developing skin cancer. *PrepTest62 Sec4 Q5*	Conclusion: Using sunscreen is unlikely to reduce the risk of developing skin cancer. Evidence: Over the past 25 years, the incidence of skin cancer due to sun exposure has increased despite widespread use of sunscreens. → This author's conclusion isn't surprising given the evidence, so this is an Overlooked Possibilities argument as opposed to a Mismatched Concepts argument. The author does not consider the potential objections to the conclusion: any reason to suspect that sunscreen *is* helping. Perhaps the hole in the ozone layer is getting worse, or skin cancers that developed over the past 25 years were actually caused by sun exposure incurred *before* people started using sunscreen. The author assumes these, and other potential objections, do not exist.
18. One should never sacrifice one's health in order to acquire money, for without health, happiness is not obtainable. *PrepTest62 Sec2 Q17*	Conclusion: Don't give up health for money. Evidence: Without health, you can't be happy. → This is a classic Mismatched Concepts argument: the conclusion is about money, but the evidence is about happiness. (The term *health* shows up in both the evidence and the conclusion, so it can't be part of the mismatched concepts.) The author assumes these normally unrelated concepts have a relationship. Connect them to find the assumption: Don't give up something necessary to your happiness to pursue money.

LSAT Argument	Analysis
19. Commentator: Although the present freshwater supply is adequate for today's patterns of water use, the human population will increase substantially over the next few decades, drastically increasing the need for freshwater. Hence, restrictions on water use will be necessary to meet the freshwater needs of humankind in the not-too-distant future. *PrepTest58 Sec1 Q1*	Conclusion: Water use restrictions will be necessary to meet humanity's freshwater needs. Evidence: The present freshwater supply is adequate, but human populations are increasing, so demand for freshwater will rise. $\longrightarrow$ "Water use restrictions will be necessary" isn't very surprising given the evidence, but it does go too far, making this a problem of overlooked possibilities. The potential objections to this conclusion would be any information that suggests that water use restrictions *won't* be necessary. For example, the commentator overlooks the possibility that we might be able to increase the supply of freshwater to meet the growing demand between now and the future. The assumption is that this and any other potential objections to the conclusion don't exist.
20. There are far fewer independent bookstores than there were 20 years ago, largely because chain bookstores prospered and multiplied during that time. Thus, chain bookstores' success has been to the detriment of book consumers, for the shortage of independent bookstores has prevented the variety of readily available books from growing as much as it otherwise would have. *PrepTest56 Sec3 Q9*	Conclusion: Chain bookstores' success is bad for book consumers. Evidence: Shortage of independent bookstores means lack of variety. $\longrightarrow$ The conclusion of this argument is about what is a detriment to book consumers, but the evidence is actually about the lack of variety of books. This Mismatched Concepts argument needs these two normally unrelated concepts to have a relationship of equivalence: the author assumes a lack of variety of books is bad for consumers.

You've now had a lot of practice breaking down LSAT arguments and identifying the author's central assumption. But just evaluating and analyzing arguments alone won't get you to your target score; to do that, you'll have to correctly answer the Assumption Family questions you'll face on Test Day. The good news is that the fundamental understanding you now have of the common ways LSAT arguments move from their evidence to their conclusion puts you light-years ahead of your competition. You'll soon see that Assumption, Strengthen, Weaken, and Flaw questions—which taken together constitute about 25 percent of the LSAT—will seem much easier to analyze, evaluate, and correctly answer.

Let's take a look now at the first of these question types.

ASSUMPTION QUESTIONS

> ## LEARNING OBJECTIVES
>
> In this section, you'll learn to:
>
> · Identify Assumption questions.
> · Recognize Sufficient Assumption questions.
> · Recognize Necessary Assumption questions.
> · Phrase a prediction of the correct answer choice.

On Test Day, you will be asked to correctly answer roughly eight Assumption questions. Put plainly, these questions will ask you to determine an argument's assumption. This seems straightforward and easy enough; after all, you are now already in the habit of determining the unstated premise of each Assumption Family question argument you see. To identify an Assumption question, look for the words *assumption*, *assumes*, or *presupposes* in the question stem. The correct answer to these questions will always present a new piece of information that the author has not included in his argument. In fact, if an answer choice restates evidence that has already been explicitly stated in the argument, then it will never be correct in an Assumption question. The LSAT will phrase an Assumption question in one of two distinct ways. Take a look at these two LSAT question stems:

> The argument's conclusion follows logically if which one of the following is assumed?
>
> *PrepTest52 Sec1 Q20*

> The argument depends on the assumption that
>
> *PrepTest52 Sec3 Q13*

Although both question stems include references to the assumption—the terms *assumed* and *assumption*—they actually ask for two distinctly different things. Notice that the first question stem asks you to determine an assumption that, if true, would allow for the conclusion to be drawn. This means that the correct answer will be an assumption that, when added to the evidence, will *guarantee* the conclusion. We will refer to these as Sufficient Assumption questions.

Now take a look at the second question stem. Here, the testmaker asks you to determine an assumption that the argument requires, or depends on. For this question stem, a correct answer doesn't need to guarantee the conclusion; instead, the correct answer choice to such a Necessary Assumption question will be an assumption that is *necessary* for the conclusion to make logical sense.

To understand the basic difference between Sufficient and Necessary Assumption questions, let's revisit the argument about Dweezil:

> Dweezil is a zulzey alien. Therefore, Dweezil can perform the amazing *yeerchta* move.

Previously, we said that the assumption of this argument is that zulzey aliens are able to perform the amazing *yeerchta* move. So what if an answer choice to an Assumption question said something like this: "Every type of alien is capable of performing the *yeerchta* move." Would that be correct? Actually, we don't know—it all depends on whether or not the question we're evaluating is a Sufficient Assumption or Necessary Assumption question. First, let's look at this assumption in the context of a Sufficient Assumption question:

The argument's conclusion follows logically if which one of the following is assumed?

PrepTest52 Sec1 Q20

Here, "Every type of alien is capable of performing the *yeerchta* move" *would* be correct. Because we know that Dweezil is an alien (the type of alien doesn't really matter), we could add this assumption to the evidence and draw the conclusion that, yes, Dweezil can definitely perform the *yeerchta* move. But what about this next question? Will the assumption "Every type of alien is capable of performing the *yeerchta* move" be correct here, as well?

The argument depends on the assumption that

PrepTest52 Sec3 Q13

For this Necessary Assumption question, we don't need to find an assumption that guarantees the conclusion; instead, we need to find an assumption that is *necessary* or *required* for the conclusion to follow. The statement "Every type of alien is capable of performing the *yeerchta* move" doesn't satisfy this question because the author's argument doesn't *need* every alien to be able to do the *yeerchta* move, only zulzey aliens. So long as zulzey aliens are capable of doing it—and, particularly, so long as Dweezil herself is able to do it—the author's conclusion could still stand.

It is worth noting that a statement can be both necessary and sufficient to establish a conclusion. For example, in this fictional argument, the premise "Zuzley aliens named Dweezil can perform the amazing *yeertcha* move" is both necessary (the argument could not be completed if it were not true) and sufficient (it is enough to establish the conclusion beyond doubt on the basis of the evidence). Similarly, the premise "Nothing prevents a zuzley alien from performing the amazing *yeertcha* move" is necessary, but not sufficient, to establish the conclusion in that argument.

Though the two Assumption question sub-types are similar in some ways, you'll see that recognizing the distinction between the two will help you determine the right answer choice more efficiently and confidently.

Sufficient Assumption Questions

As you just saw, Sufficient Assumption questions will ask you to consider an assumption that, "if assumed," allows the conclusion to be drawn logically. In these questions, which make up about 40 percent of all Assumption questions, you are asked to find an assumption that would be *sufficient* to establish the conclusion from the evidence. In other words, when added to the evidence, the assumption will *guarantee* that the conclusion is true. The language of Sufficient Assumption question stems will include phrases like "if assumed," "conclusion follows logically," or "allows the conclusion to be drawn." You can also spot these questions by the words and terms they *don't* include; unlike Necessary Assumption questions, Sufficient Assumption questions won't use language like "needs," "requires," or "depends."

Take a look at some actual LSAT Sufficient Assumption question stems:

LSAT Question Stem		Analysis
The critic's conclusion follows logically if which one of the following is assumed? *PrepTest56 Sec2 Q10*	→	Sufficient Assumption question. Find an answer choice that, when connected to the evidence, would guarantee the conclusion.
Which one of the following, if assumed, allows the conclusion of the therapist's argument to be properly inferred? *PrepTest56 Sec3 Q16*	→	Sufficient Assumption question. Find an answer choice that, when combined with the evidence, will guarantee that the conclusion is true.

In Sufficient Assumption questions, the argument pattern is overwhelmingly Mismatched Concepts arguments that contain Formal Logic. Your goal for most of these questions, then, will be to find the mismatched terms between the evidence and the conclusion, connect those terms strongly, and eliminate any answer choices that bring in outside information. If you do come across the rare Sufficient Assumption question that uses an Overlooked Possibilities argument, be sure to find an answer choice that rules out *all* potential objections to the author's conclusion. Because the correct answer choice to a Sufficient Assumption question will, when added to the argument's evidence, definitely lead to the author's conclusion, it is acceptable for these assumptions to be broader than the argument itself.

LSAT STRATEGY

Some facts to remember about Sufficient Assumption Questions:

- Recognize these questions by the phrasing "if assumed" or "conclusion follows logically."
- The correct answer, when combined with the evidence, will guarantee the conclusion.
- Mismatched Concepts arguments with Formal Logic dominate Sufficient Assumption questions.

To demonstrate how Sufficient Assumption questions operate, let's revisit an argument you've seen before. This time, we've added the question stem. By identifying a stem as a Sufficient Assumption question, you gain a big advantage over the competition. Because nearly all of these questions use Mismatched Concepts arguments structured with Formal Logic, you can confidently jump into them with the goal of connecting mismatched concepts. First, reanalyze the argument.

LSAT Argument	My Analysis
Therapist: The ability to trust other people is essential to happiness, for without trust there can be no meaningful emotional connection to another human being, and without meaningful emotional connections to others we feel isolated. Which of the following, if assumed, allows the conclusion of the therapist's argument to be properly inferred? *PrepTest56 Sec3 Q16*	

After identifying this as a Sufficient Assumption question, move to Step 2 of the Kaplan Method: untangle the stimulus. The word *for* separates the conclusion from the evidence.

> Conclusion: The ability to trust others is essential to happiness.
>
> > In Formal Logic: If happy → trust
> >
> > Contrapositive: If no trust → no happiness
>
> Evidence: Without trust, there can be no meaningful emotional connection; without meaningful emotional connection, we feel isolated. Connect the terms and make a deduction: "without trust, we feel isolated."
>
> > In Formal Logic: If no trust → isolated

In Step 3, predict an answer choice for this specific question. The correct answer to a Sufficient Assumption question with mismatched concepts will connect those concepts strongly. Try to find the right answer now.

(A)	No one who is feeling isolated can feel happy.
(B)	Anyone who has a meaningful emotional connection to another human being can be happy.
(C)	To avoid feeling isolated, it is essential to trust other people.
(D)	At least some people who do not feel isolated are happy.
(E)	Anyone who is able to trust other people has a meaningful emotional connection to at least one other human being.

PrepTest56 Sec3 Q16

Did you notice that the correct answer, (A), not only includes the correct mismatched terms but also ties them together strongly? Isolation (in the evidence) and happiness (in the conclusion) are mutually exclusive mismatched concepts. An LSAT expert uses her prediction to quickly and confidently determine the right answer. Now, perhaps you saw and liked (A) but were tempted to take a peek at the other answer choices to see if there was an even better choice. On Test Day, evaluating every answer choice equally will cost you valuable time; as such, it's important that as you practice, you develop an ability to quickly and confidently find the answer that matches your prediction and move on. One way you can develop that ability is by understanding how the testmaker likes to create wrong answer choices.

In Sufficient Assumption questions, wrong answer choices often do one of four things: (1) they don't tie together mismatched concepts strongly enough, (2) they tie together the wrong mismatched concepts, (3) they bring in terms or concepts outside the scope of the argument, or (4) they confuse sufficient and necessary terms. Take another look at the answer choices above and see if you can identify the reasons *why* the wrong answers are wrong.

Answer choices (B), (C), and (E) all connect the wrong mismatched terms. Remember, we need to build a bridge between happiness and isolation. (B) and (E) both discuss meaningful emotional connection, which was the redundant term in the evidence. (C) also connects the wrong mismatched terms; specifically, this answer choice restates the evidence, albeit in contrapositive form. Answer choice (D) is out for two reasons: it doesn't connect the correct mismatched terms strongly enough, and it confuses necessary and sufficient terms. Our prediction was that happy people are not isolated, and that isolated people are not happy. As for people who are not isolated? We don't know whether they are happy or not.

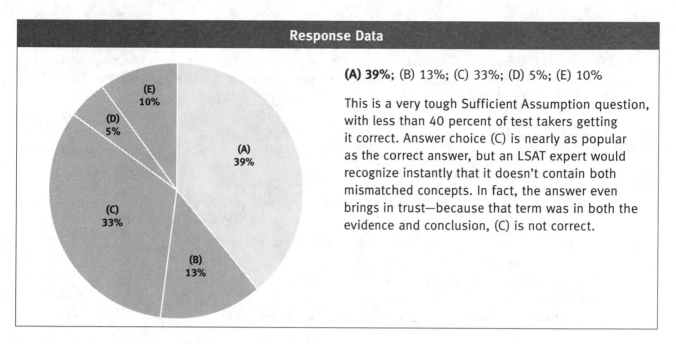

Response Data

(A) 39%; (B) 13%; (C) 33%; (D) 5%; (E) 10%

This is a very tough Sufficient Assumption question, with less than 40 percent of test takers getting it correct. Answer choice (C) is nearly as popular as the correct answer, but an LSAT expert would recognize instantly that it doesn't contain both mismatched concepts. In fact, the answer even brings in trust—because that term was in both the evidence and conclusion, (C) is not correct.

Later, in the Practice at the end of this section and in the Question Pool at the end of the chapter, you'll have an opportunity to work on even more Sufficient Assumption questions. Now, though, let's discuss Necessary Assumption questions.

Necessary Assumption Questions

Necessary Assumption questions are different from Sufficient Assumption questions in that they ask for an assumption that is *necessary* for the argument's conclusion to make sense. Necessary Assumption questions are a bit more common than Sufficient Assumption questions and tend to make up about 60 percent of all Assumption questions. You can identify these questions because they will use the terms *depends*, *require*, or *is necessary* in the question stems.

Take a look at some actual LSAT Necessary Assumption question stems:

LSAT Question Stem	Analysis
Which one of the following is an assumption required by the economist's argument? *PrepTest58 Sec1 Q19*	→ Necessary Assumption question. Find an assumption required for the conclusion to make logical sense.
Which one of the following is an assumption on which the argument depends? *PrepTest58 Sec1 Q22*	→ Necessary Assumption question. Find an assumption required for the conclusion to make logical sense.
The argument depends on the assumption that *PrepTest52 Sec3 Q13* →	Necessary Assumption question. Find an assumption required for the conclusion to make logical sense.

In Necessary Assumption questions, the argument pattern is as likely to be Mismatched Concepts as Overlooked Possibilities. If it's a Mismatched Concepts argument, look for an assumption that establishes some sort of relationship between the mismatched concepts. If it's an Overlooked Possibilities argument, look for an assumption that removes at least one possible objections to the conclusion that the author has not considered. In both argument types, look for an assumption that is required or essential to the argument. Additionally, because you are looking for an assumption that is necessary for the argument, you can test the validity of answer choices by "denying" them. We'll talk about that strategy more later. Now, though, let's discuss Mismatched Concepts arguments in Necessary Assumption questions.

LSAT STRATEGY

Some facts to remember about Necessary Assumption Questions:

- Recognize these questions by the phrasing "an assumption required by the argument" or "the argument depends on the assumption that."
- The correct answer doesn't have to be sufficient for the conclusion to be drawn, just necessary.
- Both Mismatched Concepts and Overlooked Possibilities arguments will be tested.
- Use the Denial Test to distinguish the correct answer.

Mismatched Concepts in Necessary Assumption Questions

To see the difference between necessary and sufficient assumptions in a Mismatched Concepts argument, evaluate the following test-like question and the two answer choices that follow:

Bill: A recent book reviewer called Mary's novel "boring and prosaic." But the reviewer is clearly wrong because not only is the entire first half of Mary's novel all about pirates, but part of the second half is, as well.

The argument depends on the assumption that

(A) any novel that mentions pirates cannot be boring and prosaic

(B) a novel that is mostly about pirates cannot be boring and prosaic

Start by untangling the argument. Bill's conclusion is that Mary's novel is not boring and prosaic. Why? Because more than half of Mary's novel is all about pirates. There is a disconnect here between the concepts "boring and prosaic" and "a novel mostly about pirates": Bill assumes that they are mutually exclusive. The correct answer will tie these two concepts together.

Both answer choices present assumptions formed from these mismatched concepts, and neither one brings in outside information. But are they both *necessary* assumptions? Answer choice (A) does give us a sufficient connection between the evidence and conclusion. After all, Mary's book mentions pirates, so if (A) is established, then it follows that her novel is not boring and prosaic. However, (A) is not a necessary assumption required for the conclusion to hold up. Bill's evidence is explicit: most of the novel is about pirates, and *that's* why it shouldn't be considered boring and prosaic. In fact, we have no idea what Bill thinks about novels that *only mention* pirates. It's possible that Bill would find a novel that discusses pirates once, in passing, to be boring and prosaic.

Now evaluate answer choice (B). Here, we see an assumption that *is* required by the argument. Bill's evidence directly states that a majority of Mary's novel is about pirates. It's not just because Mary's novel *mentions* pirates that Bill believes the reviewer to be wrong; it's because Mary's novel is *mostly* about pirates. To prove that this answer is correct, deny it and see what happens to the argument: "novels that are mostly about pirates *can* be boring and prosaic." If that's true, then Bill's entire argument falls apart, and his conclusion can no longer stand. We'll revisit this idea of "denying" the right answer choice to prove if it is correct later in the section.

Right now, though, let's work through an actual Necessary Assumption question with mismatched concepts. Take a look at this argument that you've seen earlier in the chapter. This time, we've added the question stem. As you analyze this argument again, work to make a specific prediction for this Necessary Assumption question.

LSAT Argument	My Analysis
The odds of winning any major lottery jackpot are extremely slight. However, the very few people who do win major jackpots receive a great deal of attention from the media. Thus, since most people come to have at least some awareness of events that receive extensive media coverage, it is likely that many people greatly overestimate the odds of their winning a major jackpot. Which one of the following is an assumption on which the argument depends? *PrepTest58 Sec4 Q21*	

Step 1 instructs us to identify the question type. In this Necessary Assumption question, we need to first untangle the stimulus—that's Step 2.

> Conclusion: It's likely that many people overestimate their chances of winning a major jackpot.

> Evidence: Most people have some awareness of major jackpot winners.

In Step 3, analyze the evidence and conclusion, try to determine the argument type, and phrase a prediction for the correct answer. In the evidence, the author talks about people becoming aware of lottery winners; in the conclusion, the author shifts to a discussion of people who will overestimate their chances of winning the lottery. While this argument uses more qualified language (*most, many, likely, some*) than the Sufficient Assumption question we saw earlier, the author still seems to be equating two different groups of people. The relevance of the relationship between the two groups is not apparent, so predict an assumption that connects them. Try that now, then evaluate the answer choices below.

(A)   Most people who overestimate the likelihood of winning a major jackpot do so at least in part because media coverage of other people who have won major jackpots downplays the odds against winning such a jackpot.

(B)   Very few people other than those who win major jackpots receive a great deal of attention from the media.

(C)   If it were not for media attention, most people who purchase lottery tickets would not overestimate their chances of winning a jackpot.

(D) Becoming aware of individuals who have won a major jackpot leads at least some people to incorrectly estimate their own chances of winning such a jackpot.

(E) At least some people who are heavily influenced by the media do not believe that the odds of their winning a major jackpot are significant.

PrepTest58 Sec4 Q21

You probably noticed that language in this argument is not nearly as strict as the language you saw in the Sufficient Assumption question dealing with isolation and happiness. Though the author here is assuming a relationship between mismatched terms, she is not doing so through the use of clear Formal Logic language. Instead, the author is assuming a somewhat tenuous connection between becoming aware of people winning the lottery and people overestimating their own lottery odds. The correct answer, (D), also reflects the qualified language of the argument. Becoming aware of others winning the lottery leads "at least some" people to overestimate their own chances of winning. This assumption is necessary for the argument's conclusion to be drawn. If you were to deny that answer choice—if you were to state that becoming aware of others winning the lottery *does not lead* some people to overestimate their own chances of winning—then the argument falls apart, and the conclusion can no longer stand.

You'll get more practice with Mismatched Concepts arguments in Necessary Assumption questions later in this section, as well as at the end of the chapter. Now, though, let's take a look at how Overlooked Possibilities arguments show up in Necessary Assumption questions.

Overlooked Possibilities in Necessary Assumption Questions

Not all Necessary Assumption questions contain mismatched concepts. In an Overlooked Possibilities argument that asks for a necessary assumption, your approach will change slightly. In these arguments, seek an answer choice that removes at least one possible objections to the author's conclusion. This is one of the reasons why learning to phrase the assumption of an Overlooked Possibilities argument in negative terms is so valuable.

To demonstrate, let's revisit this argument:

> Last night Maria parked her car in an area of town where lots of car thefts occur. This morning Maria woke up and discovered that her car was no longer in its parking spot. Therefore, Maria's car must have been stolen.

We said earlier that the possible objections to this argument include any other explanation for the vanishing car: Maria's friend Patty moving the car, her car being towed, that she moved the car to a different parking spot and forgot, etc. The author's *sufficient* assumption is that none of the potential objections happened. In other words, the answer to a Sufficient Assumption question would say something like this:

- There are no other ways Maria's car could have vanished aside from theft.
- Theft is the only possible reason for the disappearance of Maria's car.

Sufficient Assumption questions require you to rule out *all* other possible explanations to guarantee that the car was stolen. The correct answer to a Necessary Assumption question, on the other hand, only needs to rule out *one* possible objection. Consider the following answer choices:

- Maria's friend Patty didn't move the car.
- Maria's car was not towed.
- Maria didn't forget that she moved the car to a different parking spot in the middle of the night.

In a Necessary Assumption question, any one of the above answer choices would be correct because each one of them *needs* to be ruled out for this conclusion to be true. Unlike Mismatched Concepts arguments, the answers to Overlooked Possibilities arguments can and do routinely bring in new, but relevant, information. Because you can't always predict the exact objection that the answer choice will rule out, it's important to make a prediction that is broad enough that you can spot whichever one they choose.

The Denial Test

To test whether an answer choice in a Necessary Assumption question is actually necessary, you can use a strategy we call the "Denial Test." *Deny* in this context means to negate the assumption, or to say that it is not true. After all, if the assumption is *required* by the conclusion, then saying that the assumption is *not true* should directly undermine that conclusion. In the example above, let's deny the second answer choice and see what happens. As it is written, it reads, "Maria's car was not towed." Denied, that answer choice would say, "Maria's car *was* towed." If this newly denied assumption were true, then the author's conclusion could not stand. Therefore, it must be an assumption required by the argument and would be confirmed as the correct answer.

The Denial Test works only in Necessary Assumption questions and is not meant to be your initial approach to these questions. Tackling every Necessary Assumption question by denying each answer choice is ultimately a time-consuming and potentially confusing approach. Instead, use the Denial Test as a final strategy to "prove" the correct answer. If you are able to deny the assumption in an answer choice and still draw the conclusion, then that is not the right answer. Once you deny the assumption in the right answer, however, and add that newly denied assumption to the argument's evidence, you'll find that the argument crumbles and the conclusion no longer stands. Additionally, you can use the Denial Test on your prediction from Step 3 to determine whether you have predicted a valid Necessary Assumption.

Now, to see how Overlooked Possibilities arguments are tested in Necessary Assumption questions (and to get some practice with the Denial Test), let's revisit an argument you saw earlier in the chapter. This time, we'll add the question stem. Analyze the question stem and argument, identify the assumption, and phrase a prediction of the correct answer.

LSAT Argument	My Analysis
Commentator: Although the present freshwater supply is adequate for today's patterns of water use, the human population will increase substantially over the next few decades, drastically increasing the need for freshwater. Hence, restrictions on water use will be necessary to meet the freshwater needs of humankind in the not-too-distant future.	
Which one of the following is an assumption required by the argument?	
PrepTest58 Sec1 Q1	

Step 1 instructs us to evaluate the question stem. "[A]ssumption required by the argument" informs us that this is a Necessary Assumption question. Step 2, then, is to untangle the stimulus.

> Conclusion: Restrictions on water use are necessary to meet freshwater needs in the future.

> Evidence: Although present freshwater supply is currently adequate, demand for freshwater is set to drastically increase.

In Step 3, compare and analyze the evidence and conclusion, identify the argument structure and assumption, and predict a correct answer. Both the evidence and the conclusion discuss freshwater supply, but the conclusion jumps to an extreme prediction: that because demand is increasing, restrictions will be necessary in the future. This jump from evidence to conclusion in the argument is one of *degree*: the author assumes that because demand is going up, it will eventually go up *so much* that restrictions will be necessary. In this Overlooked Possibilities argument, phrase the author's assumption negatively: "It is not possible for the supply of freshwater to keep up with demand." Now take a look at the answer choices. Which one of the assumptions below is necessary for the conclusion to be drawn? If you think you've found the right answer and want to prove that it's correct, quickly try the Denial Test. Does the "denied" answer choice destroy the argument?

(A) Humans will adapt to restrictions on the use of water without resorting to wasteful use of other natural resources.

(B) The total supply of freshwater has not diminished in recent years.

(C) The freshwater supply will not increase sufficiently to meet the increased needs of humankind.

(D) No attempt to synthesize water will have an appreciable effect on the quantity of freshwater available.

(E) No water conservation measure previously attempted yielded an increase in the supply of freshwater available for human use.

PrepTest58 Sec1 Q1

You can see here that by identifying the structure of this argument as Overlooked Possibilities, an expert is able to form a prediction that helps to quickly and efficiently identify the correct answer choice. The assumption's negative phrasing here is key because it allows for seemingly unrelated answer choices to be correct. The author assumes any number of things: that scientists won't find a way to convert saltwater to freshwater, that there isn't an undiscovered supply of freshwater underneath the arctic ice caps, that humans won't fly to another planet and mine freshwater to bring back to Earth. Answer choice (C) matches this prediction by stating that freshwater supply won't increase to meet demand. Use the Denial Test to confirm that this answer is correct: "The freshwater supply *will* increase sufficiently to meet increased needs." If that were true, the argument would crumble.

The wrong answer choices in these types of questions typically take two forms: either they are irrelevant and beyond the scope of the argument, or they are relevant but do not affect the argument enough to be a required assumption. For example, the assumptions in both (D) and (E) seem relevant: they state that certain things are not increasing the supply of water. But they don't go far enough because ultimately it's not just whether or not the water supply can be increased: it's whether or not supply will increase enough to meet demand. Answer choice (A) is a classic Outside the Scope wrong answer because other natural resources are not relevant to the argument; choice (B) can be eliminated because the focus of the argument is about the amount of freshwater in the future, not the amount of freshwater now.

Good work. Now it's time to put into practice what you've learned about Sufficient and Necessary Assumption questions.

Practice

Try some Assumption questions on your own. Remember to attack each one of these with a plan and a process. In Step 1, identify the stem as a Sufficient or Necessary Assumption question. In Step 2, separate the evidence from the conclusion and paraphrase. In Step 3, compare evidence to conclusion: Does the author move from certain terms or concepts in the evidence to different terms or concepts in the conclusion? Or does the author use relevant evidence to draw a conclusion that is too strong? Find the argument's assumption and then match it to the correct answer. When you're finished, check the expert analyses on the following pages.

LSAT Question	My Analysis
21. Researcher: This fall I returned to a research site to recover the armadillos I had tagged there the previous spring. Since a large majority of the armadillos I recaptured were found within a few hundred yards of the location of their tagging last spring, I concluded that armadillos do not move rapidly into new territories.	**Step 2:**
Which one of the following is an assumption required by the researcher's argument?	**Step 1:**
	Step 3:
(A) Of the armadillos living in the area of the tagging site last spring, few were able to avoid being tagged by the researcher.	**Step 4:**
(B) Most of the armadillos tagged the previous spring were not recaptured during the subsequent fall.	
(C) Predators did not kill any of the armadillos that had been tagged the previous spring.	
(D) The tags identifying the armadillos cannot be removed by the armadillos, either by accident or deliberately.	
(E) A large majority of the recaptured armadillos did not move to a new territory in the intervening summer and then move back to the old territory by the fall.	

PrepTest58 Sec4 Q11

	LSAT Question	**My Analysis**
22.	Corporate businesses, like species, must adapt to survive. Businesses that are no longer efficient will become extinct. But sometimes a business cannot adapt without changing its core corporate philosophy. Hence, sometimes a business can survive only by becoming a different corporation.	**Step 2:**
	Which one of the following is an assumption required by the argument?	**Step 1:**
		Step 3:
(A)	No business can survive without changing its core corporate philosophy.	**Step 4:**
(B)	As a business becomes less efficient, it invariably surrenders its core corporate philosophy.	
(C)	Different corporations have different core corporate philosophies.	
(D)	If a business keeps its core corporate philosophy intact, it will continue to exist.	
(E)	A business cannot change its core corporate philosophy without becoming a different corporation.	

PrepTest58 Sec1 Q16

LSAT Question	My Analysis

23. The genuine creative genius is someone who is dissatisfied with merely habitual assent to widely held beliefs; thus these rare innovators tend to anger the majority. Those who are dissatisfied with merely habitual assent to widely held beliefs tend to seek out controversy, and controversy seekers enjoy demonstrating the falsehood of popular viewpoints.

Step 2:

The conclusion of the argument follows logically if which one of the following is assumed?

Step 1:

Step 3:

(A) People become angry when they are dissatisfied with merely habitual assent to widely held beliefs.

Step 4:

(B) People who enjoy demonstrating the falsehood of popular viewpoints anger the majority.

(C) People tend to get angry with individuals who hold beliefs not held by a majority of people.

(D) People who anger the majority enjoy demonstrating the falsehood of popular viewpoints.

(E) People who anger the majority are dissatisfied with merely habitual assent to widely held beliefs.

PrepTest58 Sec4 Q24

LSAT Question	My Analysis
24. Medications with an unpleasant taste are generally produced only in tablet, capsule, or soft-gel form. The active ingredient in medication M is a waxy substance that cannot tolerate the heat used to manufacture tablets because it has a low melting point. So, since the company developing M does not have soft-gel manufacturing technology and manufactures all its medications itself, M will most likely be produced in capsule form.	**Step 2:**
The conclusion is most strongly supported by the reasoning in the argument if which one of the following is assumed?	**Step 1:**
	Step 3:
(A) Medication M can be produced in liquid form.	**Step 4:**
(B) Medication M has an unpleasant taste.	
(C) No medication is produced in both capsule and soft-gel form.	
(D) Most medications with a low melting point are produced in soft-gel form.	
(E) Medications in capsule form taste less unpleasant than those in tablet or soft-gel form.	

PrepTest62 Sec2 Q3

LSAT Question	My Analysis
25. Chef: This mussel recipe's first step is to sprinkle the live mussels with cornmeal. The cornmeal is used to clean them out: they take the cornmeal in and eject the sand that they contain. But I can skip this step, because the mussels available at seafood markets are farm raised and therefore do not contain sand.	**Step 2:**
Which one of the following is an assumption required by the chef's argument?	**Step 1:**
	Step 3:
(A) Cornmeal is not used to clean out farm-raised mussels before they reach seafood markets.	**Step 4:**
(B) Mussels contain no contaminants other than sand.	
(C) Sprinkling the mussel with cornmeal does not affect their taste.	
(D) The chef's mussel recipe was written before farm-raised mussels became available.	
(E) The mussels the chef is using for the mussel recipe came from a seafood market.	

PrepTest56 Sec3 Q25

LSAT Question	My Analysis
26. The song of the yellow warbler signals to other yellow warblers that a particular area has been appropriated by the singer as its own feeding territory. Although the singing deters other yellow warblers from taking over the feeding territory of the singer, other yellow warblers may range for food within a portion of the singer's territory. However, a warbler sings a special song when it molts (sheds its feathers). Other yellow warblers will not enter the smaller core territory of a yellow warbler singing its molting song. Therefore yellow warblers, which can only fly short distances during molting, have no competition for the food supply within the range of their restricted flying.	**Step 2:**
The argument makes which one of the following assumptions?	**Step 1:**
	Step 3:
(A) The core areas contain just enough food to sustain one yellow warbler while it molts.	**Step 4:**
(B) Warblers are the only molting birds that lay claim to core areas of feeding territories by singing.	
(C) There are no birds other than yellow warblers that compete with yellow warblers for food.	
(D) Warblers often share their feeding areas with other kinds of birds, which often do not eat the same insects or seeds as warblers do.	
(E) The core areas of each feeding territory are the same size for each molting warbler.	

PrepTest56 Sec2 Q4

Take a look at how an LSAT expert evaluates these arguments.

LSAT Question	Analysis
21. Researcher: This fall I returned to a research site to recover the armadillos I had tagged there the previous spring. Since a large majority of the armadillos I recaptured were found within a few hundred yards of the location of their tagging last spring, I concluded that armadillos do not move rapidly into new territories. →	**Step 2:** Conclusion: Armadillos do not move rapidly into new territories. Evidence: A majority of the armadillos recaptured this fall were found near the location of their tagging the previous spring.
Which one of the following is an assumption required by the researcher's argument? →	**Step 1:** "[A]ssumption required"—a Necessary Assumption question. The correct answer is an unstated fact without which the author cannot reach his conclusion from the evidence.
	Step 3: This argument boils down to "I found the armadillos where I left them, so they must not have moved." It overlooks the possibility that the armadillos did move but then returned. As a Necessary Assumption question with an Overlooked Possibilities stimulus, the correct answer will rule out at least one potential objection that the author is not considering: anything suggesting the armadillos *do* move rapidly into new territories.
(A) Of the armadillos living in the area of the tagging site last spring, few were able to avoid being tagged by the researcher. →	**Step 4:** Irrelevant. What matters is what happened to the tagged armadillos, not how many were or were not tagged. Eliminate.
(B) Most of the armadillos tagged the previous spring were not recaptured during the subsequent fall. →	This choice may be interpreted in two ways: either as Irrelevant (the fact that most of the armadillos were not recaptured does not necessarily imply that they moved) or as a 180 (the majority of armadillos were not recaptured because they had moved to new territories). Regardless, this statement is not an assumption the author needs to add to the argument. Eliminate.
(C) Predators did not kill any of the armadillos that had been tagged the previous spring. →	Irrelevant. Armadillos eaten by predators will simply be absent from the site and not recaptured. What matters is only what happened to those tagged armadillos that were recaptured. Eliminate.

LSAT Question	Analysis
(D) The tags identifying the armadillos cannot be removed by the armadillos, either by accident or deliberately.	$\longrightarrow$ This just means that the tags stay on, which has no bearing on whether armadillos move around or not. Eliminate.
(E) A large majority of the recaptured armadillos did not move to a new territory in the intervening summer and then move back to the old territory by the fall. *PrepTest58 Sec4 Q11*	$\longrightarrow$ Correct. This rules out the possibility that the armadillos moved but came back. Use the Denial Test to prove: "A large majority of armadillos *did* move to a new territory, then moved back." If that were true, the argument would be destroyed.

LSAT Question	Analysis
22. Corporate businesses, like species, must adapt to survive. Businesses that are no longer efficient will become extinct. But sometimes a business cannot adapt without changing its core corporate philosophy. Hence, sometimes a business can survive only by becoming a different corporation.	$\longrightarrow$ **Step 2:** Conclusion: Sometimes a business can survive only by becoming a different corporation. Evidence: A business must adapt to survive; sometimes adapting requires changing its corporate philosophy.
Which one of the following is an assumption required by the argument?	$\longrightarrow$ **Step 1:** The phrase "assumption required" gives this question away as a Necessary Assumption question. The correct answer is an unstated fact without which the author cannot reach her conclusion from the evidence.
	Step 3: The evidence presents a link between the business adapting and changing its corporate philosophy. The missing link is between changing its corporate philosophy (in the evidence) and becoming a different corporation (in the conclusion). The author needs these two unrelated concepts to have a relationship of equivalence: that a business that changes its corporate philosophy becomes a different corporation. In a Necessary Assumption question with mismatched concepts, the answer must include both mismatched concepts and cannot bring in any outside concepts.

LSAT Question	Analysis
(A) No business can survive without changing its core corporate philosophy.	**Step 4:** Restatement of Evidence. The evidence, as an if-then, is "If survive → adapt → change." So changing its corporate philosophy is necessary to a business's survival. Eliminate.
(B) As a business becomes less efficient, it invariably surrenders its core corporate philosophy.	Outside the Scope. Becoming "less efficient" is not discussed. The language in the argument is one of polar opposites, not degrees: "survive" vs. "become extinct." Eliminate.
(C) Different corporations have different core corporate philosophies.	Outside the Scope. This argument is concerned with how one single business must change its philosophy to survive, not with whether different corporations have different or the same corporate philosophies. Eliminate.
(D) If a business keeps its core corporate philosophy intact, it will continue to exist.	Formal Logic error. The evidence says that if the corporate philosophy doesn't change, the company will *not* survive. Eliminate.
(E) A business cannot change its core corporate philosophy without becoming a different corporation.	Correct. This matches the missing link predicted in Step 3.

PrepTest58 Sec1 Q16

LSAT Question	Analysis
23. The genuine creative genius is someone who is dissatisfied with merely habitual assent to widely held beliefs; thus these rare innovators tend to anger the majority. Those who are dissatisfied with merely habitual assent to widely held beliefs tend to seek out controversy, and controversy seekers enjoy demonstrating the falsehood of popular viewpoints.	**Step 2:** Conclusion: "These" rare innovators tend to anger the majority. Replace the pronoun: creative geniuses tend to anger the majority. Evidence: The evidence includes a number of concepts. If possible, connect and remove redundant terms. Creative geniuses are dissatisfied with habitual assent; those dissatisfied with habitual assent seek out controversy; controversy seekers enjoy demonstrating the falsehood of popular viewpoints. Make a deduction: creative geniuses enjoy demonstrating the falsehood of popular viewpoints.

LSAT Question	Analysis
The conclusion of the argument follows logically if which one of the following is assumed? →	**Step 1:** The phrases "conclusion … follows logically" and "if … assumed" indicate that this is a Sufficient Assumption question. Suspect mismatched concepts with Formal Logic.
	Step 3: This argument boils down to the common "If A → B; therefore, If A → C" structure: "Creative geniuses *enjoy demonstrating the falsehood of popular viewpoints*; therefore, creative geniuses *tend to anger the majority*."
	Connect the mismatched concepts to form the assumption: "demonstrating the falsehood of popular viewpoints tends to anger the majority."
	In a Sufficient Assumption question with mismatched concepts, the correct answer must mention both mismatched concepts and cannot bring in new information.
(A) People become angry when they are dissatisfied with merely habitual assent to widely held beliefs. →	**Step 4:** Doesn't connect demonstrating the falsehood of popular viewpoints to angering the majority. Eliminate.
(B) People who enjoy demonstrating the falsehood of popular viewpoints anger the majority. →	Correct. This connects "demonstrating the falsehood of popular viewpoints" to "angering the majority."
(C) People tend to get angry with individuals who hold beliefs not held by a majority of people. →	Includes one of the mismatched terms but not the other. Eliminate.
(D) People who anger the majority enjoy demonstrating the falsehood of popular viewpoints. →	A classic example of an answer choice that includes the right mismatched terms but confuses what is sufficient and what is necessary. Eliminate.
(E) People who anger the majority are dissatisfied with merely habitual assent to widely held beliefs. *PrepTest58 Sec4 Q24* →	Again, doesn't connect demonstrating the falsehood of popular viewpoints to angering the majority. Eliminate.

Response Data

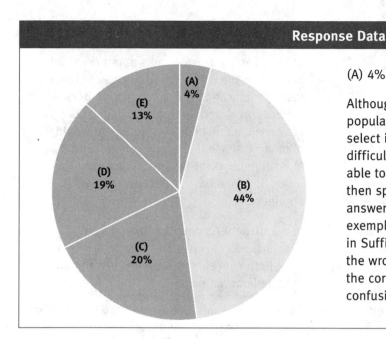

(A) 4%; **(B) 44%**; (C) 20%; (D) 19%; (E) 13%

Although the correct answer, (B), is the most popular response, less than half of respondents select it. Though this is a somewhat long and difficult question, well-trained LSAT experts are able to quickly connect terms in the evidence, then spot the mismatched concepts and predict an answer. The next two most popular answer choices exemplify a couple of classic wrong answer traps in Sufficient Assumption questions. (C) connects the wrong mismatched concepts while (D) connects the correct concepts but does so incorrectly by confusing sufficient and necessary terms.

LSAT Question		Analysis
24. Medications with an unpleasant taste are generally produced only in tablet, capsule, or soft-gel form. The active ingredient in medication M is a waxy substance that cannot tolerate the heat used to manufacture tablets because it has a low melting point. So, since the company developing M does not have soft-gel manufacturing technology and manufactures all its medications itself, M will most likely be produced in capsule form.	→	**Step 2:** Conclusion: Medication M will most likely be produced in capsule form.
		Evidence: Medications with an unpleasant taste are generally produced in one of three ways; medication M can't be produced in two of those ways (tablet or soft-gel), so it will probably be produced in the third way (capsule).
The conclusion is most strongly supported by the reasoning in the argument if which one of the following is assumed?	→	**Step 1:** The phrase "if which one of the following is assumed" indicates that this is a Sufficient Assumption question.

LSAT Question	Analysis
	Step 3: The conclusion talks about medication M only, while the evidence discusses unpleasant-tasting medications. The connection between medication M and unpleasant medications has not yet been established. This argument would make a lot more sense if it were explicit that medication M is an unpleasant-tasting medication. This is a classic Mismatched Concepts–Equivalence argument.
	In a Sufficient Assumption question with mismatched concepts, the correct answer must have both concepts and cannot bring in any outside information.
(A) Medication M can be produced in liquid form.	**Step 4:** This is missing the mismatched concept of "unpleasant taste." Eliminate.
(B) Medication M has an unpleasant taste.	Correct. Matches the prediction.
(C) No medication is produced in both capsule and soft-gel form.	This is missing both mismatched concepts. Eliminate.
(D) Most medications with a low melting point are produced in soft-gel form.	This is missing both mismatched concepts as well. Eliminate.
(E) Medications in capsule form taste less unpleasant than those in tablet or soft-gel form. *PrepTest62 Sec2 Q3*	This is missing the mismatched concept "medication M." Eliminate.

LSAT Question	Analysis
25. Chef: This mussel recipe's first step is to sprinkle the live mussels with cornmeal. The cornmeal is used to clean them out: they take the cornmeal in and eject the sand that they contain. But I can skip this step, because the mussels available at seafood markets are farm raised and therefore do not contain sand.	**Step 2:** Conclusion: I (the chef) can skip this step (sprinkling cornmeal into mussels as a way to clean out sand). Evidence: The mussels available at seafood markets do not contain sand.
Which one of the following is an assumption required by the chef's argument?	**Step 1:** The words "assumption" and "required" indicate that this is a Necessary Assumption question.

LSAT Question	Analysis
	Step 3: The conclusion is about the chef's mussels, but the evidence discusses mussels at the market. The author needs these two normally unrelated concepts to have a relationship of equivalence: The mussels are from the market.
	In a Necessary Assumption question with mismatched concepts, the correct answer must have both mismatched concepts and may not bring in outside information.
(A) Cornmeal is not used to clean out farm-raised mussels before they reach seafood markets.	→ **Step 4:** This doesn't mention the chef's mussels. Eliminate.
(B) Mussels contain no contaminants other than sand.	→ Outside the Scope. This doesn't have either mismatched concept. Eliminate.
(C) Sprinkling the mussels with cornmeal does not affect their taste.	→ Outside the Scope. This doesn't have either mismatched concept and brings up a new concept: taste. Eliminate.
(D) The chef's mussel recipe was written before farm-raised mussels became available.	→ Outside the Scope. This brings up when the recipe was written, which is a new concept. Eliminate.
(E) The mussels the chef is using for the mussel recipe came from a seafood market. *PrepTest56 Sec3 Q25*	→ Correct. Matches the prediction. Use the Denial Test to prove the right answer—if the chef is *not* using mussels from a seafood market, then the conclusion no longer stands.

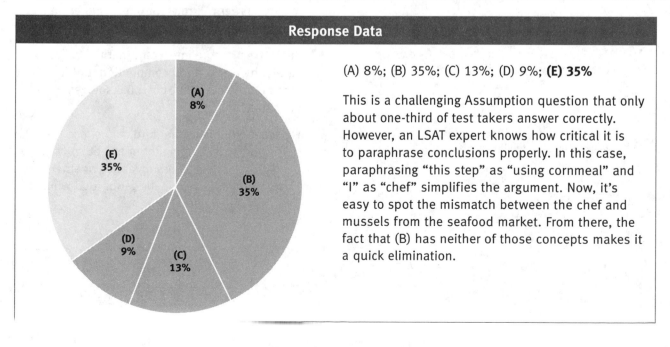

Response Data

(A) 8%; (B) 35%; (C) 13%; (D) 9%; **(E) 35%**

This is a challenging Assumption question that only about one-third of test takers answer correctly. However, an LSAT expert knows how critical it is to paraphrase conclusions properly. In this case, paraphrasing "this step" as "using cornmeal" and "I" as "chef" simplifies the argument. Now, it's easy to spot the mismatch between the chef and mussels from the seafood market. From there, the fact that (B) has neither of those concepts makes it a quick elimination.

LSAT Question	Analysis
26. The song of the yellow warbler signals to other yellow warblers that a particular area has been appropriated by the singer as its own feeding territory. Although the singing deters other yellow warblers from taking over the feeding territory of the singer, other yellow warblers may range for food within a portion of the singer's territory. However, a warbler sings a special song when it molts (sheds its feathers). Other yellow warblers will not enter the smaller core territory of a yellow warbler singing its molting song. Therefore yellow warblers, which can only fly short distances during molting, have no competition for the food supply within the range of their restricted flying.	**Step 2:** Conclusion: Yellow warblers have no competition for food in their limited range while molting. Evidence: Other yellow warblers stay away from the territory of a warbler singing its molting song.
The argument makes which one of the following assumptions?	**Step 1:** The wording in this question stem is rare, but it is asking for a Necessary Assumption. The correct answer will be *an* assumption the author makes.
	Step 3: The evidence relates to the conclusion, but the conclusion is extreme: a molting warbler will have *no* competition for food. This is a classic Overlooked Possibilities argument; the author is not considering possible objections to the conclusion like competition for food aside from other warblers. Perhaps the yellow warbler competes with other species of birds or animals. As always, the author assumes these possible objections don't exist. As a Necessary Assumption question, the correct answer will rule out one or more possible objections.
(A) The core areas contain just enough food to sustain one yellow warbler while it molts.	This makes it more important that the yellow warbler be free of food competition, but it does not rule out other potential sources of competition. Eliminate.
(B) Warblers are the only molting birds that lay claim to core areas of feeding territories by singing.	Irrelevant. Whether other birds announce their molting areas by singing (or in any other way, for that matter) says nothing about whether the yellow warbler has competition for food while it is molting. Eliminate.

LSAT Question	Analysis
(C) There are no birds other than yellow warblers that compete with yellow warblers for food.	Correct. Removes a big objection to the conclusion that the author has failed to consider: namely, any other type of bird that might also be a source of competition. Use the Denial Test to prove it's correct: "there *are* other birds that compete with yellow warblers for food." If true, the conclusion could no longer stand.
(D) Warblers often share their feeding areas with other kinds of birds, which often do not eat the same insects or seeds as warblers do.	Outside the Scope. The correct answer must rule out the possibility that the yellow warbler faces food competition from another species. The birds mentioned in this choice are *not* competing for the same food as the yellow warbler. Eliminate.
(E) The core areas of each feeding territory are the same size for each molting warbler. *PrepTest56 Sec2 Q4*	Whether territory size is uniform or variable has no bearing on the presence of competitors for food. Eliminate.

OTHER ASSUMPTION FAMILY QUESTION TYPES

By now, you should have a good grasp of the two main argument structures you'll see on the LSAT: Mismatched Concepts and Overlooked Possibilities. You've also seen the ways in which the testmaker can evaluate your understanding of these argument types by asking you to identify an argument's sufficient or necessary assumption. But the LSAT can test you on more than just your ability to discern an argument's assumption. From the same argument, the testmaker can ask you a number of different questions: you may be asked to identify the flaw in an author's reasoning, to strengthen or weaken an argument, or even to determine an underlying principle of the argument. One thing to keep in mind is that even though different question types may change the format of the answers, the argument itself and the assumption of the argument will not change. Each of the arguments you see on the LSAT will be constructed in a similar way: an author uses too little evidence to support a conclusion that is reached too quickly. As such, the way in which you approach these questions will be the same as the way in which you approach Assumption questions. The only difference is in Step 3; here, you will use your knowledge of the different question types to create an appropriate and question-specific prediction.

As an example, let's take a look at an argument we've seen before.

> Researcher: This fall I returned to a research site to recover the armadillos I had tagged there the previous spring. Since a large majority of the armadillos I recaptured were found within a few hundred yards of the location of their tagging last spring, I concluded that armadillos do not move rapidly into new territories.
>
> *PrepTest58 Sec4 Q11*

Previously, we saw this argument in the context of an Assumption question: "Which one of the following is an assumption required by the researcher's argument?" The correct answer was "A large majority of the recaptured armadillos did not move to a new territory in the intervening summer and then move back to the old territory by the fall."

But the testmaker could have easily asked a number of other questions based on this same argument. Look at these common LSAT question stems:

Question Stem		Analysis
The reasoning in the argument is most vulnerable to criticism on the grounds that the argument	$\longrightarrow$	The correct answer to this **Flaw** question will describe the way in which the author's reasoning is flawed. For the argument above, you might see an answer choice like "Overlooks the possibility that armadillos are capable of quickly moving to a new territory and then quickly moving back to the old territory."
Which of the following, if true, most seriously weakens the argument?	$\longrightarrow$	The correct answer to this **Weaken** question will present a new piece of information that, if true, will make the author's conclusion less likely. For the argument above, you might see an answer choice like "Some armadillos moved to a new territory during the summer, then returned to the old territory in the fall."

Question Stem	Analysis
Which of the following, if true, provides the most support for the reasoning above?	$\longrightarrow$ The correct answer to this **Strengthen** question will present a new piece of information that, if true, will make the author's conclusion more likely. For the argument above, you might see an answer choice like "When armadillos move to a new territory, they spend at least a year in the new territory before returning to the old territory."

In the next part of the chapter, we'll take a look at each one of these unique question types. By the end, you'll be able to (1) identify each question type based on the phrasing in the question stem and (2) turn any argument's assumption into a prediction that is appropriate for the specific question type.

FLAW QUESTIONS

LEARNING OBJECTIVES

In this section, you'll learn to:

- Identify Flaw questions.
- Recognize and characterize the most common flawed argument patterns.
- Recognize an abstractly worded but correct answer choice in a Flaw question.

One of the ways the LSAT can test your ability to analyze arguments is by asking you to determine the error in the author's reasoning. These Flaw questions, as we call them, might be thought of as *describe the flaw* questions because that's what you are being asked to do. On Test Day, you'll face roughly eight of these questions. With a few notable exceptions discussed later in this section, the arguments you'll find in Flaw questions are identical to the ones you see in other Assumption Family questions.

As always in the Logical Reasoning section, your first step is to identify the question type from the stem. To recognize a Flaw question, look for language that uses words or phrases like "point out a flaw," "identify the error in reasoning," or "vulnerable to criticism." Take a look below to see some common Flaw question stems:

LSAT Question Stem		Analysis
According to Lana, Chinh's argument is flawed in that it *PrepTest56 Sec2 Q5*	→	The correct answer to this Flaw question will describe the way in which the evidence fails to properly support the conclusion.
The reasoning in the argument is most vulnerable to criticism on the grounds that the argument *PrepTest56 Sec2 Q12*	→	The correct answer to this Flaw question will describe the way in which the evidence fails to properly support the conclusion.
The reasoning in the argument is most vulnerable to criticism on the grounds that the argument fails to consider the possibility that *PrepTest58 Sec1 Q9*	→	The first part of this stem is standard flaw fare, but an LSAT expert recognizes that the statement "fails to consider" indicates that this will be an overlooked possibilities argument.

Your approach to Flaw questions starts in the same way as your approach to other Assumption Family questions: untangle the stimulus into evidence and conclusion, then identify the author's assumption. The types of arguments you'll see in Flaw questions are generally the same as the ones discussed earlier in the chapter—either the author is using evidence that is not exactly related to the conclusion (Mismatched Concepts) or the author is using relevant evidence to draw an extreme conclusion (Overlooked Possibilities). The difference is that in Flaw questions, you're more likely to run into some of the more specific types of Mismatched Concepts and Overlooked Possibilities discussed earlier in the chapter. The good news is that the bulk of Flaw questions will ask you about just a handful of common argument types, which are listed below. Being able to anticipate the likelihood of certain argument patterns based on the question type will help you untangle arguments and form predictions more quickly and efficiently.

Common Flaw Types

> ### LSAT STRATEGY
>
> Flaw questions are dominated by these common argument types:
>
> · General Overlooked Possibilities: Failure to consider alternative explanations.
> · Overlooked Possibilities: A conclusion of causation based on evidence of correlation.
> · Overlooked Possibilities: Confusing necessary and sufficient terms.
> · Mismatched Concepts (including alike/equivalent, mutually exclusive, and representation).

For many test takers, finding the assumption or determining the pattern of an argument in a Flaw question is not hugely challenging. Instead, the difficult part of correctly answering a Flaw question is matching a prediction to the correct answer choice. This is because the LSAT words the correct answers to Flaw questions differently than it does the correct answers to other Assumption Family questions. Consider, for example, the following argument:

> Joe started feeling sick a short while after eating out at the restaurant around the corner. Clearly, he got food poisoning from the food he ate there!

This is a classic causal argument. The author takes two things that happened around the same time, eating at the restaurant and getting sick, and concludes that one of them must have caused the other. As you learned earlier in this chapter, the assumption of the argument is **No ARC**: there's no **alternative cause** for the illness, the illness isn't the reason why the author went out to eat (**reversal**), and the fact that the author went out to eat right before getting ill isn't just a **coincidence**. The correct answer to a Necessary Assumption question would rule out **A, R,** or **C.** Consider:

> Joe did not catch a stomach virus from his neighbor.

This rules out an **alternative cause**. But a Flaw question's answer might say something like . . .

> Overlooks the possibility that Joe caught a stomach virus from his neighbor.

or even . . .

> Mistakes a correlation between two events for one event causing the other.

The difference between the first two of these answer choices is not very great. The only distinction is that the Flaw answer choice is descriptive—it tells us that the author is overlooking something rather than ruling out a specific possibility. The difference between the Necessary Assumption answer and the second Flaw answer, however, is much bigger. The second Flaw answer is also describing the problem, but it is doing so in much more abstract terms. The key to being successful in Flaw questions is learning how to spot your prediction stated with different language.

For practice, let's revisit a Flaw question you saw in Chapter 8. Because it's a been a while, reanalyze this argument. Untangle the stimulus, identify the assumption, and, as much as possible, describe the *way* in which Beck's argument is flawed.

LSAT Argument	My Analysis
Beck: Our computer program estimates municipal automotive use based on weekly data. Some staff question the accuracy of the program's estimates. But because the figures it provides are remarkably consistent from week to week, we can be confident of its accuracy. The reasoning in Beck's argument is flawed in that it *PrepTest52 Sec1 Q6*	

Note that the word "flawed" indicates that this is a Flaw question. The correct answer will describe the error in Beck's reasoning. Step 2 of Kaplan Method instructs you to untangle the stimulus.

> Conclusion: We can be confident of the computer program's accuracy.

> Evidence: The computer program provides remarkably consistent estimates.

As you move to Step 3, use your pattern recognition skills to identify the problem in the argument. Begin by looking at the conclusion for any signs of mismatched concepts or a problem of overlooked possibilities. The fact that the conclusion brings up accuracy, which never shows up in the evidence, is a potential sign of a Mismatched Concepts argument. A quick glance at the evidence tells us that it is about consistency, which is never mentioned in the conclusion. The author is assuming that consistency and accuracy are somehow related. Specifically, we have a classic equivalence argument: the author is assuming that consistency makes the program accurate.

If this were a Necessary Assumption question, you would simply find an answer choice that says as much and move on. Because this is a Flaw question, however, you'll need to take a moment to consider how you might *describe* the problem with the argument. As you evaluate the answer choices to this question, ask, "Which one describes the flaw in the author's reasoning?"

(A) fails to establish that consistency is a more important consideration than accuracy

(B) fails to consider the program's accuracy in other tasks that it may perform

(C) takes for granted that the program's output would be consistent even if its estimates were inaccurate

(D) regards accuracy as the sole criterion for judging the program's value

(E) fails to consider that the program could produce consistent but inaccurate output

PrepTest52 Sec1 Q6

Remember that the author is assuming that being consistent means the program was accurate, but without additional information in the stimulus, it isn't certain that this is actually a true statement. The correct answer, choice (E), points out that fact. It is just a different way to say that the author is assuming that "consistent" is equivalent to "accurate." The heart of prediction in Assumption Family questions is learning how to say the same few things in a variety of different ways.

LSAT STRATEGY

Some facts to remember about Flaw questions:

- The correct answer will *describe* the error in the author's reasoning.
- You will be tested on your ability to identify flaws in both Mismatched Concepts arguments and Overlooked Possibilities arguments.
- Correct answer choices are often written in abstract language; form a prediction and match it to the closest answer choice.

Less Common Flaw Types

In addition to the common flaws previously listed (as well as the argument types you read about earlier in the chapter), the testmaker may ask you to identify a few rarer types of arguments. These are not included on the test often, but it's important to know them when you see them. Below are short descriptions of the most important ones:

Mismatched Concepts—Equivocation: On the LSAT, an error of equivocation means using the same word or phrase twice in an argument but with two different meanings. For example: "Jason says that when Alex is around, it drives him crazy; therefore I have decided to have him evaluated by a psychologist who specializes in crazy people." Notice that the argument uses the word *crazy* in the evidence to mean "annoyed," but it uses the word *crazy* in the conclusion to mean "mentally disturbed." This pattern is quite rare in LSAT stimuli. However, wrong answer choices in Flaw questions frequently refer to equivocation, so it's important to understand the flaw this term describes.

Mismatched Concepts—Parts to Whole: A parts-to-whole argument is very similar to a representation argument. The author of an argument looks at one piece of something—say a chapter in a book—and uses that to make a conclusion about the entirety of that thing—say the book itself. Or the author of an argument will look at many pieces individually and then make a deduction regarding the pieces together: "Each of these seven energy drinks is safe to drink, and so I'll be fine if I drink them all at once." This argument is rare, but when it shows up on the LSAT, it is almost always in a Flaw question.

Circular Reasoning: Circular reasoning describes an argument in which the author uses equivalent statements for both the evidence and the conclusion, for example, "Chris must be in debt, for if Chris says he is not in debt, he is surely lying." Much like equivocation, circular reasoning almost never shows up on the LSAT as the correct answer describing the author's flaw in the stimulus argument, but it is a common wrong answer choice in Flaw questions.

Evidence Contradicts Conclusion: There have been very few instances of this particular argument on the LSAT. Here is a simple example: "This book didn't sell well at all; nearly all copies printed were returned to the publisher. It follows that the publisher should print more copies as soon as possible." If the book didn't sell, the logical inference is that more copies should *not* be printed. Again, this pattern is rare; though the evidence in any Assumption Family question will never fully prove the conclusion, it almost never happens that the evidence actually contradicts the conclusion. Despite the fact that this pattern has shown up only a handful of times, it is a common wrong answer choice in Flaw questions. Be wary of choosing such an answer if you didn't initially predict it.

This list isn't an exhaustive one. Through the decades, LSAT Flaw questions have included rare instances of arguments that are unique or virtually unique.

LSAT STRATEGY

Some extremely rare flaw arguments you might see on the LSAT:

· Conflating numerical values with percent values

· Using evidence of belief to draw a conclusion of fact

· Attacking the person making the argument instead of the argument
  (ad hominem)

· Stating that absence of evidence is evidence of absence

· Making an inappropriate appeal to authority

· Failing to address the other speaker's point

Of course, the odds of running into any of the flaws listed above are extremely low. At the end of the day, if you know the common argument patterns discussed earlier in the chapter, you should be able to tackle everything you will see on Test Day.

Drill: Identifying Argument Types in Flaw Question Answer Choices

Understanding the different ways in which the LSAT can describe familiar argument patterns requires a careful study of the answer choices in Flaw questions. When you study, be sure to spend time looking at answer choices and asking yourself which argument patterns they are referencing. Doing so will help you quickly eliminate tempting choices on Test Day. Let's start that process now with a short exercise. Below is a list of sample answer choices. Your job is to match those answer choices to the flawed argument type they are describing.

Answer Choices	My Analysis
27. Overlooks the possibility that there are some red cars that do not take unleaded gas.	
28. Two events that merely occur together are taken as though one is the cause of the other.	
29. Bases a general claim on a few exceptional instances.	
30. Treats as similar two cases that may be different in a fundamental way.	
31. Allows a key term to shift in meaning during the course of the argument.	

Answer Choices	My Analysis
32. Presupposes what it seeks to establish.	
33. Mistakes something that is necessary to bring about a situation for something that merely can bring about that situation.	

Now take a look at the expert analysis to see how you did:

Answer Choices	Analysis
27. Overlooks the possibility that there are some red cars that do not take unleaded gas.	→ "Overlooks the possibility that" is a classic phrase that is most often a reference to Overlooked Possibilities arguments. In this case, it would mean the author assumes that all red cars take unleaded gas, overlooking the possibility that some do not.
28. Two events that merely occur together are taken as though one is the cause of the other.	→ Describes the flaw of confusing correlation for causation.
29. Bases a general claim on a few exceptional instances.	→ Making a general claim about a group using evidence about a smaller group is the definition of Mismatched Concepts—Representation.
30. Treats as similar two cases that may be different in a fundamental way.	→ This is just another way of describing Mismatched Concepts–Alike/Equivalent. The author assumes that two different things are the same.
31. Allows a key term to shift in meaning during the course of the argument.	→ Any answer choice that says that a term is given more than one meaning in an argument is a reference to equivocation (and is probably wrong).
32. Presupposes what it seeks to establish.	→ This is the definition of circular reasoning.
33. Mistakes something that is necessary to bring about a situation for something that merely can bring about that situation.	→ The word "necessary" indicates that this is an Overlooked Possibilities—Necessary versus Sufficient problem.

Putting It All Together

Now that you have a better understanding of how Flaw answer choices can and will be worded by the testmaker, try to apply that skill to the following Flaw question. First things first, though: untangle the stimulus and try to identify the specific argument pattern.

LSAT Argument	**My Analysis**
Recent studies indicate a correlation between damage to human chromosome number six and adult schizophrenia. We know, however, that there are people without damage to this chromosome who develop adult schizophrenia and that some people with damage to chromosome number six do not develop adult schizophrenia. So there is no causal connection between damage to human chromosome number six and adult schizophrenia.	
Which one of the following most accurately describes a reasoning flaw in the argument above?	
PrepTest58 Sec1 Q11	

The word "flaw" makes it clear this is a Flaw question. Step 2 instructs us to identify the conclusion and the evidence.

Conclusion: There is no causal connection between damage to human chromosome six and schizophrenia.

Evidence: Some people with damage to human chromosome six don't have schizophrenia, and some without damage do have schizophrenia.

Step 3 begins with pattern recognition, and the conclusion provides a great clue as to which argument type we have here: the word "causal." Causal arguments are common in Flaw questions, but this one has a bit of a twist. Instead of claiming that two things *are* causally linked, the author is claiming that they *aren't*. If the conclusion says that there isn't a causal link between these things, then unconsidered information suggesting that there *is* a causal link would act as an objection to the argument. As usual, the author assumes that these objections don't exist. Because this is a Flaw question, be on the lookout for an answer choice that describes the fact that the author overlooks these objections. Take a moment now and go through each of the answer choices one by one. Your job is not only to find the correct answer but also to try to figure out what kind of argument each of the wrong answers refers to.

(A) The argument ignores the possibility that some but not all types of damage to chromosome number six lead to schizophrenia.

(B) The argument presumes, without providing evidence, that schizophrenia is caused solely by chromosomal damage.

(C) The argument makes a generalization based on an unrepresentative sample population.

(D) The argument mistakes a cause for an effect.

(E) The argument presumes, without providing warrant, that correlation implies causation.

PrepTest58 Sec1 Q11

Answer choice (A) starts with the classic phrase "ignores the possibility that," which is often a reference to an Overlooked Possibilities argument. When an answer choice tells us that the author overlooks something, it is the same as saying that the author assumes that thing didn't happen. If it turns out that the overlooked possibility in the answer choice would make the author's conclusion invalid, then it is a legitimate objection, and that answer is correct. The answer tells us that the thing being overlooked is that some types of damage to the chromosome cause schizophrenia but not all types of damage will do so. If that's true, it would explain why some of the people mentioned in the evidence had damage to their chromosome but did not develop schizophrenia, and it would make the author's conclusion fall apart. This means that answer choice (A) is correct; the author definitely overlooks this possibility.

Remember, because the answer choices to Flaw questions can be difficult to decipher, it is just as important to study and identify the flaws in wrong answer choices as it is to study correct answers. Being able to quickly spot the flaw being described will help tremendously on Test Day. With that in mind, let's take a careful look at the remaining choices for this question.

Answer choice (B) starts with the generic phrase "presumes, without providing evidence." This is just another way of saying "the author assumes." It is an empty phrase that doesn't describe any particular argument type. The rest of the choice says that schizophrenia is only caused by chromosomal damage, but the author doesn't make that claim. The author attempts only to prove that damage to one particular chromosome doesn't lead to adult schizophrenia. She isn't interested in what *does* lead to schizophrenia.

Answer choice (C) is a very common way to phrase Mismatched Concepts—Representation. Look for phrasing like "generalization" or "unrepresentative" to indicate that an answer choice refers to a representation argument.

Answer choice (D) is a very straightforward reference to a causal argument. Though it may seem tempting, in this case the author wasn't trying to prove that two things were causally linked; rather, she was trying to prove that they weren't.

Answer choice (E) starts off with another empty phrase, "presumes, without providing warrant," which is just another way to say "assumes." The rest of this answer choice is another reference to a causal argument, and it is incorrect for the same reasons as choice (D).

Notice that some of the answer choices, like (A), were concrete, while others, like (C) and (D), were abstract and didn't use any language from the stimulus. Flaw answer choices tend to be a mixture of the two, and the more abstract answer choices can be very challenging. If an answer choice uses generic phrases like "treats something that is necessary as though it is sufficient" or "concludes that one thing caused another when the evidence given is consistent with the second thing having caused the first," don't treat them as vague! Match the generic language in the answer choices to the specifics in the stimulus. If you can't match them up, then the choice you are looking at is likely wrong. Taking a quick second or two to do this can help you deal with even the toughest answers.

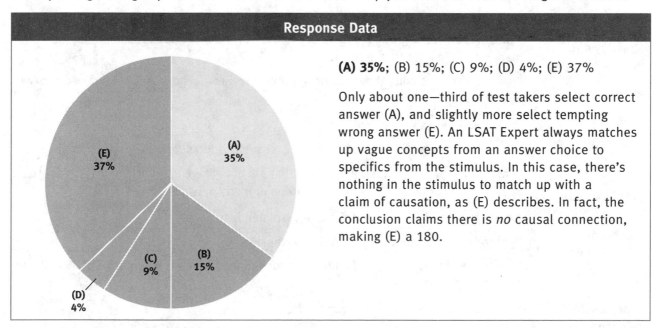

Response Data

(A) 35%; (B) 15%; (C) 9%; (D) 4%; (E) 37%

Only about one—third of test takers select correct answer (A), and slightly more select tempting wrong answer (E). An LSAT Expert always matches up vague concepts from an answer choice to specifics from the stimulus. In this case, there's nothing in the stimulus to match up with a claim of causation, as (E) describes. In fact, the conclusion claims there is *no* causal connection, making (E) a 180.

You should also be on the lookout for answer choices that are true but don't constitute a flaw. For example, imagine if we reworded answer choice (A) to say:

(A) Overlooks the possibility that some damage to chromosome seven leads to schizophrenia.

Technically this is a true statement; the author never once considered damage from chromosome seven. However, this answer doesn't accurately describe the argument's flaw. The author was only concerned with damage from chromosome six; any damage that chromosome seven might cause has no bearing on the argument. This answer choice might be tempting, but the fact that the author didn't mention something does not necessarily mean that she should have. After all, the author didn't mention the color of your shirt either, but that's not a problem she needs to correct!

Common Wording of Flaw Types in Answer Choices

Take a moment now to look over some of the most common argument patterns and answer types in Flaw questions in the "LSAT Strategy" box. Feel free to return to this list from time to time to hone your ability to get through Flaw answer choices quickly and efficiently.

LSAT STRATEGY

Common Flaw Question Answer Choices by Argument Pattern

Overlooked Possibilities— General	"overlooks the possibility that"/"ignores the possibility that"/"fails to consider"
	"assumes only one possibility when more exist"
	"treats one explanation of many as though it were the only one"
Overlooked Possibilities— Causation	"mistakes a correlation for causation"
	"presumes that because one event was followed by another, the first event caused the second"
	"ignores the possibility that two things that occur together may be only coincidentally related"
Overlooked Possibilities— Nec vs Suff	"confuses a result with a condition that is required to bring about that result"
	"mistakes something that is necessary for a particular outcome for something that is merely sufficient for that outcome"
	"ignores the possibility that a particular outcome may be sufficient but not necessary for another"
Mismatched Concepts— General	"relies on irrelevant evidence"
	"facts that are not directly related to the case are used to support a conclusion about it"
	"draws an analogy between two things that are not alike enough in the ways they would need to be in order for the conclusion to be properly drawn"
Mismatched Concepts— Representation	"draws a general conclusion from a few isolated instances"
	"generalizes from an unrepresentative sample"
	"treats the children living in County X as though they were representative of all children that age living in State Y"
Mismatched Concepts— Equivocation	"relies on an ambiguity in the term *plant*"
	"allows a key phrase to shift in meaning from one use to the next"
	"fails to provide a sufficient definition of a key term"

Circular Reasoning	"the conclusion is no more than a restatement of the evidence used to support it"
	"restates its conclusion without providing sufficient justification for accepting it"
	"presupposes the truth of what it seeks to establish"
Evidence Contradicts the Conclusion	"the evidence given actually undermines the argument's conclusion"
	"some of the evidence given is inconsistent with other evidence presented"
	"draws a recommendation that is inconsistent with the evidence given to support it"

Practice

Now that you've had a chance to learn the basics of Flaw questions, take some time to practice a few on your own. As always, follow the Kaplan Method and work to make a prediction in Step 3. After you've tried these on your own, check out the expert analyses on the following pages.

LSAT Question	My Analysis
34. Psychologist: A study of 436 university students found that those who took short naps throughout the day suffered from insomnia more frequently than those who did not. Moreover, people who work on commercial fishing vessels often have irregular sleep patterns that include frequent napping, and they also suffer from insomnia. So it is very likely that napping tends to cause insomnia.	**Step 2:**
The reasoning in the psychologist's argument is most vulnerable to criticism on the grounds that the argument	**Step 1:**
	Step 3:
(A) presumes, without providing justification, that university students suffer from insomnia more frequently than do members of the general population	**Step 4:**
(B) presumes that all instances of insomnia have the same cause	
(C) fails to provide a scientifically respectable definition for the term "napping"	

LSAT Question	My Analysis
(D) fails to consider the possibility that frequent daytime napping is an effect rather than a cause of insomnia	
(E) presumes, without providing justification, that there is such a thing as a regular sleep pattern for someone working on a commercial fishing vessel	

PrepTest52 Sec1 Q2

LSAT Question	My Analysis
35. No matter how conscientious they are, historians always have biases that affect their work. Hence, rather than trying to interpret historical events, historians should instead interpret what the people who participated in historical events thought about those events.	**Step 2:**
The reasoning in the argument is most vulnerable to criticism on the grounds that the argument fails to consider the possibility that	**Step 1:**
	Step 3:
(A) historians who have different biases often agree about many aspects of some historical events	**Step 4:**
(B) scholars in disciplines other than history also risk having their biases affect their work	
(C) many of the ways in which historians' biases affect their work have been identified	
(D) not all historians are aware of the effect that their particular biases have on their work	
(E) the proposed shift in focus is unlikely to eliminate the effect that historians' biases have on their work	

PrepTest52 Sec3 Q12

LSAT Question	My Analysis

36. Anna: Did you know that rainbows always occur opposite the sun, appearing high in the sky when the sun is low, and low in the sky when the sun is high? The Roman scholar Pliny the Elder claimed that this was so, in the first century A.D.

William: His claim cannot be correct. After all, Pliny the Elder wrote that there are tribes of of dog-headed people and beings with no heads or necks but with eyes on their shoulders, and said that smearing snails on your forehead cures headaches!

Step 2:

William's argument against Anna's claims about rainbows is most vulnerable to criticism because it

Step 1:

Step 3:

(A) inappropriately distorts Anna's conclusion, making it appear more extreme than it really is

Step 4:

(B) takes for granted that Pliny the Elder was in bad faith when he reported about unheard-of creatures

(C) illicitly infers that, because Pliny the Elder made some incorrect assertions, Pliny the Elder's assertions about rainbows are also incorrect

(D) accepts the assertions of an ancient scholar without presenting contemporary verification of that scholar's views

(E) implies that Pliny the Elder's writings are too outdated to be of any value

PrepTest56 Sec3 Q1

LSAT Question	My Analysis
37. The manufacturers of NoSmoke claim that their product reduces smokers' cravings for cigarettes. However, in a recent study, smokers given the main ingredient in NoSmoke reported no decrease in cravings for cigarettes. Thus, since NoSmoke has only two ingredients, if similar results are found for the second ingredient, we can conclude that NoSmoke does not reduce smokers' cravings.	**Step 2:**
The argument above is flawed in that it	**Step 1:**
	Step 3:
(A) illicitly presumes that a whole must lack a certain quality if all of its parts lack that quality	**Step 4:**
(B) confuses a mere correlation with a cause	
(C) relies on a sample that is likely to be unrepresentative	
(D) overlooks the possibility that NoSmoke helps people to quit smoking in ways other than by reducing smokers' cravings for cigarettes	
(E) illicitly presumes that a claim must be false because the people making the claim are biased	

PrepTest56 Sec3 Q4

LSAT Question	My Analysis
38. Travel agent: Although most low-fare airlines have had few, if any, accidents, very few such airlines have been in existence long enough for their safety records to be reliably established. Major airlines, on the other hand, usually have long-standing records reliably indicating their degree of safety. Hence, passengers are safer on a major airline than on one of the newer lowfare airlines.	**Step 2:**
Of the following, which one is the criticism to which the reasoning in the travel agent's argument is most vulnerable?	**Step 1:**
	Step 3:
(A) The argument fails to address adequately the possibility that the average major airline has had a total number of accidents as great as the average low-fare airline has had.	**Step 4:**
(B) The argument draws a general conclusion about how safe passengers are on different airlines on the basis of safety records that are each from too brief a period to adequately justify such a conclusion.	
(C) The argument fails to consider the possibility that long-standing and reliable records documenting an airline's degree of safety may indicate that the airline is unsafe.	
(D) The argument takes for granted that airlines that are the safest are also the most reliable in documenting their safety.	
(E) The argument fails to address adequately the possibility that even airlines with long-standing, reliable records indicating their degree of safety are still likely to have one or more accidents.	

PrepTest58 Sec1 Q18

Now that you've had a chance to do these on your own, check your reasoning against the expert analyses below.

LSAT Question	Analysis
34. Psychologist: A study of 436 university students found that those who took short naps throughout the day suffered from insomnia more frequently than those who did not. Moreover, people who work on commercial fishing vessels often have irregular sleep patterns that include frequent napping, and they also suffer from insomnia. So it is very likely that napping tends to cause insomnia.	**Step 2:** Conclusion: Napping probably causes insomnia. Evidence: People who nap are more likely to have insomnia than those who don't.
The reasoning in the psychologist's argument is most vulnerable to criticism on the grounds that the argument	**Step 1:** "[V]ulnerable to criticism" tells us this is a Flaw question.
	Step 3: "[T]ends to cause" in the conclusion signals a causal argument. In this case, however, the author does not assume napping is the only cause of insomnia, so there is no need to rule out alternate causes. He still must assume that causation is not reversed ("insomnia doesn't cause napping") and that the relationship is not merely coincidental. The correct answer will describe one of those flaws.
(A) presumes, without providing justification, that university students suffer from insomnia more frequently than do members of the general population	**Step 4:** Irrelevant Comparison. The study involves students and commercial fisherman, and seems to assume that they are representative of the general population, not that they are more likely to suffer from insomnia. Eliminate.
(B) presumes that all instances of insomnia have the same cause	The author's conclusion is simply that napping is likely *a cause* of insomnia—whether there are other causes doesn't affect that conclusion. Eliminate.
(C) fails to provide a scientifically respectable definition for the term "napping"	True, but not a flaw. There was no need to define napping scientifically in this argument—the author used the common definition of it. Eliminate.
(D) fails to consider the possibility that frequent daytime napping is an effect rather than a cause of insomnia	Correct. This choice states that the author assumes that causation wasn't reversed, which matches one of the predicted scenarios.
(E) presumes, without providing justification, that there is such a thing as a regular sleep pattern for someone working on a commercial fishing vessel	The author's argument is based on the irregular sleeping patterns of the commercial fishers. Any discussion of regular sleep patterns would be irrelevant to the conclusion. Eliminate.

PrepTest52 Sec1 Q2

LSAT Question	Analysis
35. No matter how conscientious they are, historians always have biases that affect their work. Hence, rather than trying to interpret historical events, historians should instead interpret what the people who participated in historical events thought about those events.	**Step 2:** Conclusion: Historians should focus on what the people participating in events thought. Evidence: Historians themselves always have bias.
The reasoning in the argument is most vulnerable to criticism on the grounds that the argument fails to consider the possibility that	**Step 1:** "[V]ulnerable to criticism" tells us this is a Flaw question, and the fact that we're already told the author "fails to consider" something indicates this is going to be an Overlooked Possibilities argument.
	Step 3: The question stem already indicates this is an Overlooked Possibilities argument, so determine possible objections to the conclusion that the author is not considering. The author only provides a reason why historians *should* adopt the plan, but makes no mention of the potential drawbacks. Imagine that every answer choice starts with "fails to consider the possibility that"—the correct one will provide a potential objection to the plan.
(A) historians who have different biases often agree about many aspects of some historical events	**Step 4:** Outside the Scope. Even if they agree, they are no less biased. This is not a reason to reject this plan. Eliminate.
(B) scholars in disciplines other than history also risk having their biases affect their work	The author's conclusion is about historians, so information about fields other than history doesn't affect whether or not historians should change their focus. Eliminate.
(C) many of the ways in which historians' biases affect their work have been identified	Even if this is true, that doesn't mean the bias doesn't exist, so this isn't a reason not to reject the proposed change in focus. Eliminate.
(D) not all historians are aware of the effect that their particular biases have on their work	The author's plan doesn't depend on whether or not historians are aware of biases, just that they have them. This is definitely not a reason to avoid the change in focus. Eliminate.
(E) the proposed shift in focus is unlikely to eliminate the effect that historians' biases have on their work *PrepTest52 Sec3 Q12*	Correct. This answer choice makes it clear that the proposed change in focus won't actually work, which is definitely a reason not to adopt it.

LSAT Question	Analysis
36. Anna: Did you know that rainbows always occur opposite the sun, appearing high in the sky when the sun is low, and low in the sky when the sun is high? The Roman scholar Pliny the Elder claimed that this was so, in the first century A.D. William: His claim cannot be correct. After all, Pliny the Elder wrote that there are tribes of of dog-headed people and beings with no heads or necks but with eyes on their shoulders, and said that smearing snails on your forehead cures headaches!	**Step 2:** Though the focus is on William, be sure not to ignore Anna's argument. Anna's argument: Rainbows always occur opposite the sun because Pliny said it was true. William's argument: Pliny is incorrect about rainbows because his claims about dog-headed people were incorrect.
William's argument against Anna's claims about rainbows is most vulnerable to criticism because it	**Step 1:** "[V]ulnerable to criticism" is classic flaw phrasing. The rest of the stem indicates that this is a dialogue stimulus but that the focus is on William's argument.
	Step 3: A quick look shows a conclusion about Pliny's opinion on rainbows with evidence about his views on the unrelated subject of dog-headed tribes, making this an issue of Mismatched Concepts. Specifically, it's an atypical representation argument: William assumes that Pliny is always wrong because of a few isolated instances. As a Flaw question, the answer will describe the fact that a few instances of being wrong don't represent everything Pliny has to say.
(A) inappropriately distorts Anna's conclusion, making it appear more extreme than it really is	**Step 4:** This looks nothing like the prediction and doesn't accurately describe Williams's argument.
(B) takes for granted that Pliny the Elder was in bad faith when he reported about unheard-of creatures	William's conclusion is about Pliny being wrong. Discussing *why* Pliny was wrong doesn't change that fact and thus doesn't affect the conclusion.
(C) illicitly infers that, because Pliny the Elder made some incorrect assertions, Pliny the Elder's assertions about rainbows are also incorrect	Correct. This points out the fact that it is inappropriate to assume that Pliny will always be wrong based on a few isolated instances.
(D) accepts the assertions of an ancient scholar without presenting contemporary verification of that scholar's views	180. William is arguing against Pliny, not for him. Eliminate.
(E) implies that Pliny the Elder's writings are too outdated to be of any value *PrepTest56 Sec3 Q1*	William's argument didn't hinge on Pliny being outdated, just on Pliny having been wrong about dog-headed tribespeople. Eliminate.

LSAT Question	**Analysis**
37. The manufacturers of NoSmoke claim that their product reduces smokers' cravings for cigarettes. However, in a recent study, smokers given the main ingredient in NoSmoke reported no decrease in cravings for cigarettes. Thus, since NoSmoke has only two ingredients, if similar results are found for the second ingredient, we can conclude that NoSmoke does not reduce smokers' cravings. →	**Step 2:** Conclusion: If the second ingredient of NoSmoke doesn't decrease craving, then NoSmoke doesn't decrease craving. Evidence: The main ingredient in NoSmoke doesn't decrease craving.
The argument above is flawed in that it →	**Step 1:** The word "flawed" explicitly indicates the question type.
	Step 3: The author makes a conclusion about NoSmoke as a whole but relies on evidence about individual ingredients of NoSmoke. In this Mismatched Concepts argument, the author assumes that what is true of the parts is true of the whole. It might be that, given together, the two ingredients reduce cravings. In a Flaw question, the answer will point out that what is true of the pieces may not be true of the whole.
(A) illicitly presumes that a whole must lack a certain quality if all of its parts lack that quality →	**Step 4:** Correct. This describes the argument type in generic terms. The author illicitly presumes that NoSmoke ("a whole") will not decrease cravings ("lack[s] a certain quality") because its only two ingredients ("all of its parts") don't individually decrease cravings ("lack that quality").
(B) confuses a mere correlation with a cause →	This is a reference to a causal argument, which doesn't match up with the prediction. Eliminate.
(C) relies on a sample that is likely to be unrepresentative →	Outside the Scope. There is no sample cited in the evidence. Eliminate.
(D) overlooks the possibility that NoSmoke helps people to quit smoking in ways other than by reducing smokers' cravings for cigarettes →	Outside the Scope. The argument is limited to the question of whether NoSmoke reduces cravings. Eliminate.
(E) illicitly presumes that a claim must be false because the people making the claim are biased *PrepTest56 Sec3 Q4* →	The author's evidence is about the main ingredient of NoSmoke not working. There is no biased group mentioned in the evidence, only in the background information. Eliminate.

LSAT Question	Analysis
38. Travel agent: Although most low-fare airlines have had few, if any, accidents, very few such airlines have been in existence long enough for their safety records to be reliably established. Major airlines, on the other hand, usually have long-standing records reliably indicating their degree of safety. Hence, passengers are safer on a major airline than on one of the newer low-fare airlines.	**Step 2:** Conclusion: Passengers are safer on major airlines than on newer ones. Evidence: Major airlines have long-standing records of their degree of safety that newer ones don't have.
Of the following, which one is the criticism to which the reasoning in the travel agent's argument is most vulnerable?	**Step 1:** The phrase "vulnerable to criticism" indicates a Flaw question.
	Step 3: The evidence mentions that major airlines have safety records, but does not say how safe those records say they are. Any information saying that major airlines *aren't* safer than newer ones damages the conclusion. The correct answer will point out that the author overlooks these possible objections.
(A) The argument fails to address adequately the possibility that the average major airline has had a total number of accidents as great as the average low-fare airline has had.	**Step 4:** The number of accidents is relevant only if we know the number of flights. Eliminate.
(B) The argument draws a general conclusion about how safe passengers are on different airlines on the basis of safety records that are each from too brief a period to adequately justify such a conclusion.	The author makes clear that the major airlines' safety records are "long-standing" and "reliabl[e]." The use of "each" in this choice does not match the stimulus, and thus, cannot describe the author's flaw. Eliminate.
(C) The argument fails to consider the possibility that long-standing and reliable records documenting an airline's degree of safety may indicate that the airline is unsafe.	Correct. The author was so concerned with the fact that major carriers had long-standing records that she forgot to consider what those records said. If those records show that major carriers are very unsafe, then the conclusion falls to pieces.
(D) The argument takes for granted that airlines that are the safest are also the most reliable in documenting their safety.	This choice misses the author's point. The concern in the argument is that low-fare airlines have documented their safety long enough. Eliminate.
(E) The argument fails to address adequately the possibility that even airlines with long-standing, reliable records indicating their degree of safety are still likely to have one or more accidents. *PrepTest58 Sec1 Q18*	The author argues that major carriers are *safer* than newer carriers, but that doesn't mean that major carriers are 100 percent safe. If major carriers have an accident or two, it doesn't damage the conclusion. Eliminate.

WEAKEN QUESTIONS

Another way in which the LSAT will test your ability to evaluate an argument is to ask you to identify a piece of information that, if true, would weaken the author's argument. Here, "weaken an argument" doesn't mean that you have to conclusively disprove the conclusion. All you need to do is find the answer choice containing a fact that makes the author's conclusion less likely to be true based on the evidence.

First, let's take a look at some typical Weaken question stems as they appear on the LSAT:

LSAT Question Stem		Analysis
Which of the following, if true, most weakens the argument? *PrepTest62 Sec4 Q5*	→	The correct answer will be a newly considered piece of information that will weaken the conclusion.
Which of the following, if true, most undermines the argument? *PrepTest58 Sec1 Q24*	→	"[U]ndermines" means weaken. Look for a choice that weakens the conclusion.
Which one of the following statements, if true, most weakens the reasoning above? *PrepTest56 Sec2 Q3*	→	The correct answer will weaken the author's reasoning.

Weaken questions tend to use the words *weaken*, *weakens*, or *undermines* in the question stem. Though most students are able to identify Weaken questions easily, some students occasionally confuse Weaken and Flaw questions. To keep the two question types straight, remember that in a Flaw question, the testmaker has already informed you that the argument's reasoning is flawed, and you are being asked to *describe* that argument's error in reasoning. In a Weaken question, the testmaker wants you to identify a *new piece of information* that, if true, will upend the author's assumption and thus weaken the conclusion. Accept the answer choices as true in a Weaken question and evaluate them by saying, "Okay, if this piece of information were true, would the author's conclusion be less likely to follow from her evidence?"

Your approach to Weaken questions begins in the same way as your approach to other Assumption Family questions: start by untangling the stimulus into evidence and conclusion; then find the author's central assumption. Only occasionally will you see a Mismatched Concepts argument in a Weaken question. Instead, the nature of Weaken questions is such that you will largely be asked to evaluate Overlooked Possibilities arguments. By now, you are already in the habit of phrasing the assumption of these types of arguments in negative terms: "the author is assuming that *no other* explanation or potential objections to this conclusion exists." To weaken an Overlooked Possibilities argument, then, identify one of these possible objections in the answer choices.

Give this a try by evaluating the following LSAT Weaken question. Work to untangle the stimulus, phrase the assumption, and then predict an answer choice containing the kind of fact that would weaken the argument.

LSAT Argument	**My Analysis**
Drug company manager: Our newest product is just not selling. One way to save it would be a new marketing campaign. This would not guarantee success, but it is one chance to save the product, so we should try it.	
Which one of the following, if true, most seriously weakens the manager's argument?	
PrepTest62 Sec2 Q22	

Note that the word *weakens* indicates that this is a Weaken question. The correct answer will weaken the argument's conclusion by making its assumption less likely. Step 2 of the Kaplan Method instructs you to untangle the stimulus.

> Conclusion: We should try the new marketing campaign.

> Evidence: The new marketing campaign provides a chance to save the product.

As you move to Step 3, focus on identifying the argument pattern and the assumption. Then use your knowledge of Weaken questions to predict the kinds of facts that will weaken the argument.

In this classic pro/con argument, the manager cites only one potential advantage of the new marketing campaign: it provides a chance to save the product. But the manager *fails to consider* any possible disadvantages that might outweigh this one potential advantage. The manager's assumption, then, is that no potential drawbacks to the new marketing campaign exist. Now, make a prediction that includes these overlooked objections: "to weaken this argument, I need a disadvantage to the marketing campaign that the author has overlooked." As you evaluate the answer choices to this question, which one best matches the prediction?

(A) The drug company has invested heavily in its newest product, and losses due to this product would be harmful to the company's profits.

(B) Many new products fail whether or not they are supported by marketing campaigns.

(C) The drug company should not undertake a new marketing campaign for its newest product if the campaign has no chance to succeed.

(D) Undertaking a new marketing campaign would endanger the drug company's overall position by necessitating cutbacks in existing marketing campaigns.

(E) Consumer demand for the drug company's other products has been strong in the time since the company's newest product was introduced.

PrepTest62 Sec2 Q22

Answer choice (D) matches the prediction. It presents a piece of information that, if true, casts significant doubt on the manager's conclusion. Indeed, if undertaking this marketing campaign requires cutbacks that would endanger the drug company's overall position, then the marketing campaign no longer seems reasonable to justify.

LSAT STRATEGY

Some facts to remember about Weaken questions:

- A correct answer doesn't have to disprove the conclusion, just weaken it.
- The most common argument type in Weaken questions is Overlooked Possibilities.
- Correct answer choices nearly always introduce a possible objection to the conclusion that the author has not considered.

If you find yourself getting lost or frustrated in a specific Weaken question, take a step back from the argument and focus solely on the argument's conclusion. While many Weaken questions require you to understand how the evidence relates to the conclusion, some Weaken questions do not. In these, simply understanding the conclusion will be enough to identify a correct answer choice.

To see how this works, take a look at an actual LSAT Weaken question. Untangle the argument and focus particularly on the conclusion.

LSAT Argument	**My Analysis**
Newspaper article: People who take vitamin C supplements tend to be healthier than average. This was shown by a study investigating the relationship between high doses of vitamin C and heart disease, which showed that people who regularly consume high doses of vitamin C supplements have a significantly lower than average risk of heart disease.	
Which one of the following, if true, would most weaken the argument in the newspaper article?	

PrepTest56 Sec3 Q20

As you worked through your analysis, you saw that the evidence presented a benefit of vitamin C consumption. From that, the author concluded that consuming vitamin C tends to make people healthier. Hopefully you were able to spot the assumption in this Overlooked Possibilities argument. But if not, that's okay. In this question, let's focus only on the argument's conclusion.

> Conclusion: People who take vitamin C supplements tend to be healthier than average.

What are the potential objections to this argument? Anything that shows consuming vitamin C supplements might not promote health or might even, in fact, *be harmful*. If that is established, then the author's conclusion will be severely weakened.

Take a look at these answer choices:

(A)   Vitamin C taken in the form of supplements has a different effect on the body than does vitamin C taken in food.

(B)   The reduction in risk of heart disease due to the consumption of vitamin C is no greater than the reduction due to certain other dietary changes.

(C)   Taking both vitamin C supplements and vitamin E supplements lowers one's risk of heart disease far more than does taking either one alone.

(D)   High doses of vitamin C supplements tend to reduce slightly one's resistance to certain common infectious diseases.

(E)   Taking vitamin C supplements has been found to lower one's risk of developing cancer.

PrepTest56 Sec3 Q20

Answer choice (D) fits our prediction. If consuming too many vitamin C supplements suppresses the immune system, then overall health might be harmed. This weakens the author's conclusion.

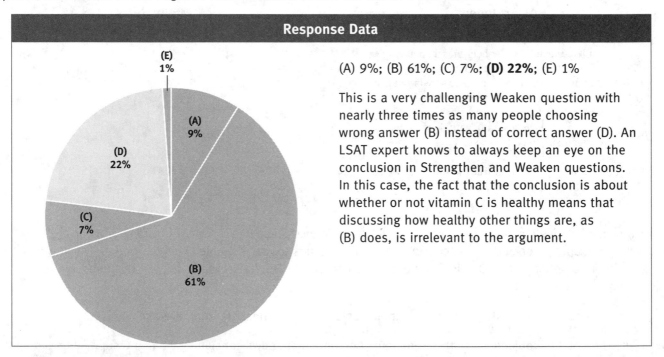

Response Data

(E) 1%

(A) 9%

(D) 22%

(C) 7%

(B) 61%

(A) 9%; (B) 61%; (C) 7%; **(D) 22%**; (E) 1%

This is a very challenging Weaken question with nearly three times as many people choosing wrong answer (B) instead of correct answer (D). An LSAT expert knows to always keep an eye on the conclusion in Strengthen and Weaken questions. In this case, the fact that the conclusion is about whether or not vitamin C is healthy means that discussing how healthy other things are, as (B) does, is irrelevant to the argument.

A quick reminder here about this strategy: While focusing on the conclusion can help you determine the possible objections to an Overlooked Possibilities argument, you must look at the relationship of the evidence to the conclusion to confirm the argument type before jumping to that approach. Many Weaken questions, even some with Overlooked Possibilities problems, *require* an understanding of how the evidence interacts with the conclusion. Weakening the conclusion without considering the evidence or the assumption should be a strategy of last resort.

Later, you'll get an opportunity to try some Weaken questions on your own and to compare your thinking to that of an LSAT expert. For now, though, take a look at a question type that is intimately related to Weaken questions: Strengthen questions.

STRENGTHEN QUESTIONS

LEARNING OBJECTIVES

In this section, you'll learn to:

- · Identify and answer Strengthen questions.
- · Turn assumptions into accurate predictions.
- · Recognize answer choices that strengthen the author's assumption.

At this point, you've learned how to evaluate an LSAT argument, find its assumption, describe its flaw, and identify an answer choice that would weaken the argument. Here's yet another task: identify a piece of information that, if true, would strengthen the argument. Strengthen, in this context, doesn't mean "prove" the argument or "confirm" the conclusion—that's too strong. Instead, Strengthen questions ask you to identify an answer choice that makes the conclusion more likely to be true. Combined, you will see about eight Strengthen and Weaken questions on Test Day.

First, let's take a look at some typical Strengthen question stems as they appear on the LSAT:

LSAT Question Stem		Analysis
Which of the following, if true, most supports the researchers' hypothesis? *PrepTest62 Sec4 Q22*	$\longrightarrow$	The fact that "the following, if true" (the answer choices) "most support" the argument indicates a Strengthen question.
Which one of the following, if true, lends the most support to the psychologist's conclusion? *PrepTest56 Sec2 Q14*	$\longrightarrow$	"[L]ends the most support" means that the correct choice strengthens the psychologist's conclusion.
Which one of the following statements, if true, most strengthens the argument? *PrepTest56 Sec2 Q24*	$\longrightarrow$	"[S]trengthens the argument" is a giveaway for a Strengthen question.

Your approach to Strengthen questions starts in the same way as your approach to other Assumption Family questions. Begin by untangling the author's argument into evidence and conclusion. Next, note the argument pattern and identify the assumption. Then predict an answer choice that would strengthen the argument's conclusion. For a Strengthen question that uses a Mismatched Concepts argument, that means looking for an answer choice that affirms the relationship the author assumes exists between mismatched terms. In a Strengthen question that uses an Overlooked Possibilities argument, seek an answer choice that removes a potential objection that the author is overlooking. And in both types of arguments, you may actually find that the correct answer choice simply provides information that directly strengthens the author's conclusion.

Take a look at the following Strengthen question. Use your knowledge of Assumption Family questions to untangle the argument, identify the assumption, and predict a correct answer.

LSAT Question Stem	**My Analysis**
Editorialist: In a large corporation, one of the functions of the corporation's president is to promote the key interests of the shareholders. Therefore, the president has a duty to keep the corporation's profits high.	
Which one of the following, if true, would most strengthen the editorialist's argument?	
PrepTest52 Sec1 Q4	

The phrasing "if true, would most strengthen" indicates that this is a Strengthen question. Step 2 of the Kaplan Method instructs you to find the argument's evidence and conclusion.

> Conclusion: The president has a duty to keep the corporation's profits high.

> Evidence: One of the president's functions is to promote the key interests of the shareholders.

As you move to Step 3, focus on identifying the argument pattern and finding the assumption. Then use your knowledge of Strengthen questions to phrase an appropriate prediction. Here, though the president of the corporation appears in both the evidence and the conclusion, the idea of keeping profits high is a seemingly new, unrelated concept that appears in the conclusion only, which should make you suspect a Mismatched Concepts argument. While the evidence discusses promoting the key interests of the shareholders, the conclusion moves to a discussion of the duty to keep the corporation's profits high. This is a standard argument of equivalence: one of the shareholders' key interests is keeping profits high.

Because this Strengthen question contains mismatched terms, predict an answer choice that affirms the assumption. Keep in mind, though, that the correct answer to a Strengthen question need not necessarily have both mismatched concepts so long as it would make their assumed relationship more likely. As you evaluate the answer choices, which one best matches the prediction?

(A) Shareholders sometimes will be satisfied even if dividends paid to them from company profits are not high.

(B) The president and the board of directors of a corporation are jointly responsible for advancing the key interests of the shareholders.

(C) Keeping a corporation's profit high is likely to advance the important interests of the corporation's shareholders.

(D) In considering where to invest, most potential shareholders are interested in more than just the profitability of a corporation.

(E) The president of a corporation has many functions besides advancing the important interests of the corporation's shareholders.

PrepTest52 Sec1 Q4

Here, answer choice (C) affirms the assumption by connecting the mismatched terms. If keeping a corporation's profit high advances the interests of the corporation's shareholders, then the editorialist's argument is strengthened.

Not all Strengthen questions contain Mismatched Concepts arguments, though. Most will ask you to strengthen an Overlooked Possibilities argument. In these arguments, predict an answer choice that removes a potential objection to the author's conclusion. In this LSAT question, evaluate the argument, find the assumption, and predict what a correct answer choice might look like.

LSAT Argument	My Analysis
39. Tissue biopsies taken on patients who have undergone throat surgery show that those who snored frequently were significantly more likely to have serious abnormalities in their throat muscles than those who snored rarely or not at all. This shows that snoring can damage the throat of the snorer. Which one of the following, if true, most strengthens the argument? *PrepTest62 Sec2 Q16*	

Did you notice the common argument structure here? The evidence presents a correlation between two conditions. From that evidence, the author of the argument moves to a conclusion in which one of the conditions causes the other. Causal arguments are common among Strengthen and Weaken questions—in fact, at least a quarter of the Strengthen and Weaken questions on most exams are based on causal arguments.

Here's how an LSAT expert would untangle and analyze this argument:

LSAT Argument	Analysis
39. Tissue biopsies taken on patients who have undergone throat surgery show that those who snored frequently were significantly more likely to have serious abnormalities in their throat muscles than those who snored rarely or not at all. This shows that snoring can damage the throat of the snorer. Which one of the following, if true, most strengthens the argument? *PrepTest62 Sec2 Q16*	Conclusion: Snoring can damage the throat of the snorer. Evidence: Biopsies have shown that people who snore frequently also tend to have more abnormalities in their throat muscles. → The author is concluding that a causal relationship exists when the evidence only shows correlation. The assumption here is that there is **No ARC**: there is not something other than snoring causing the damage (alternative cause); throat damage is not causing people to snore (reversed causality); and snoring and throat damage are not unrelated (mere coincidence).

You will revisit this argument when you try the full question in the Question Pool at the end of this chapter. Use this analysis to help find the correct answer choice.

LSAT STRATEGY

Some facts to remember about Strengthen Questions:

- The correct answer, when added to the evidence, doesn't have to prove the conclusion—just make it more likely.
- Both Mismatched Concepts and Overlooked Possibilities arguments show up in Strengthen questions, although overlooked possibilities are more common.
- In a Mismatched Concepts argument, look for an answer choice that either affirms the author's assumption or directly supports the conclusion.
- In an Overlooked Possibilities argument, look for an answer choice that removes a potential objection that the author is not considering.

As in some Weaken questions, it's possible in some Strengthen questions to find the right answer by focusing solely on an argument's conclusion. If you get lost or frustrated by a Strengthen question, return to the conclusion and try to find an answer choice that most strengthens that conclusion.

To see how this works, take a look at the following LSAT question. Untangle the argument and focus particularly on the conclusion.

LSAT Argument	My Analysis
Among people who live to the age of 100 or more, a large proportion have led "unhealthy" lives: smoking, consuming alcohol, eating fatty foods, and getting little exercise. Since such behavior often leads to shortened life spans, it is likely that exceptionally long-lived people are genetically disposed to having long lives.	
Which one of the following, if true, most strengthens the argument?	
PrepTest62 Sec2 Q2	

As you worked through your analysis, you saw that the argument presents evidence showing that a large proportion of people who engage in unhealthy behaviors actually end up living longer lives. From that, the author concludes that the explanation for these long lives is genetic. Hopefully, you were able to spot the assumption in this Overlooked Possibilities argument. But if not, there is another route to the right answer. Start by focusing only on the argument's conclusion:

Conclusion: It is likely that exceptionally long-lived people are genetically predisposed to having long lives.

What are the possible objections to this argument? In this case, it would be any other potential explanation for their longevity aside from genetics. Regardless of the evidence provided, what possible additional information could be presented to strengthen this conclusion? Look for a choice that presents support for the idea that centenarians are genetically predisposed to living long lives directly or that rules out an alternative explanation/objection.

(A)   There is some evidence that consuming a
       moderate amount of alcohol can counteract the
       effects of eating fatty foods.
(B)   Some of the exceptionally long-lived people
       who do not smoke or drink do eat fatty foods
       and get little exercise.
(C)   Some of the exceptionally long-lived people
       who exercise regularly and avoid fatty foods
       do smoke or consume alcohol.
(D)   Some people who do not live to the age of 100
       also lead unhealthy lives.
(E)   Nearly all people who live to 100 or more have
       siblings who are also long-lived.

PrepTest62 Sec2 Q2

Does one of those choices pop out at you? Answer choice (E) presents the type of information we are looking for. If it's true that long-lived people have siblings who are also long-lived, then a genetic cause is more likely.

Just as with Weaken questions, it is true here for Strengthen questions: focusing only on the conclusion is *not* meant to be your primary strategy in tackling Strengthen questions. As always, follow the Kaplan Method and work your way from Step 1 through Step 4. Only if you get confused or flustered by a stimulus should you attempt to find the right answer by zeroing in on the conclusion and finding the answer choice that strengthens that conclusion.

Later in this chapter, you'll get an opportunity to practice more Strengthen questions. Now, though, let's take a look at some rare types of Strengthen and Weaken questions.

Rare Strengthen and Weaken Questions

Weaken and Strengthen EXCEPT Questions

In addition to asking straightforward Weaken and Strengthen questions, the LSAT may ask you to identify an answer choice that *does not* weaken or *does not* strengthen the author's conclusion. Though these Strengthen/Weaken EXCEPT questions are rare (constituting fewer than 5 percent of all Strengthen/Weaken questions), it's important to know how to tackle them when you see them. The first thing you need to be able to do is identify these question types. Take a look at the following typical Strengthen/Weaken EXCEPT question stems:

Question Stem		Analysis
Each of the following, if true, weakens the argument EXCEPT	$\rightarrow$	The four wrong answer choices will weaken the conclusion. The right answer will strengthen the conclusion or have no impact.
Each of the following, if true, supports the claim above EXCEPT	$\rightarrow$	The four wrong answer choices will strengthen the conclusion. The right answer will weaken the conclusion or have no impact.

In these Weaken and Strengthen EXCEPT questions, understand that the correct answer does not need to strengthen or weaken an argument. In fact, the correct answer to these EXCEPT questions may have no impact on the argument at all. The only thing you can be sure of in these questions is that the four incorrect answer choices will *definitely* weaken the argument in a Weaken EXCEPT question and *definitely* strengthen the argument in a Strengthen EXCEPT question.

For this reason, you need to be able to characterize what the correct answer choice requires in Strengthen/Weaken EXCEPT questions. In a Weaken EXCEPT question, the correct answer will either strengthen the argument or have no impact. Similarly, the correct answer to a Strengthen EXCEPT question will either weaken the argument or have no impact.

LSAT STRATEGY

Some facts to remember about Strengthen and Weaken EXCEPT questions:

- Always slow down and characterize what the right and wrong answer choices will look like.
- The correct answer in a Strengthen EXCEPT question will either weaken the argument or have no impact.
- The correct answer in a Weaken EXCEPT question will either strengthen the argument or have no impact.

Evaluate Questions

Evaluate Questions are an even rarer subspecies of Strengthen and Weaken questions. In fact, it's likely you won't see one on the LSAT. On the last 21 released LSATs (seven years' worth), only 7 questions have fallen into this category. However, because they do show up on occasion, it's good to know about them and to have a plan, just in case. The first thing you need to be able to do is identify Evaluate questions. Take a look at the following typical Evaluate question stems:

Question Stem		Analysis
Which one of the following would be most useful to know in order to evaluate the legitimacy of the philosopher's argument?	$\longrightarrow$	The correct answer will provide a piece of information that, if true, would make the argument either stronger or weaker and, if false, would have the opposite effect. In other words, the correct answer is *relevant* to the argument's validity.
Information about which one of the following would be LEAST useful in evaluating the doctor's hypothesis?	$\longrightarrow$	Four of the answer choices will be useful in evaluating the hypothesis, while the correct answer choice won't be useful. That means it will be irrelevant or have no impact on the hypothesis.

As with other Assumption Family questions, start by breaking down an Evaluate argument into evidence and conclusion. Determine the assumption and use that information to identify an answer choice that will help you evaluate the argument. Answer choices in Evaluate questions are not straightforward strengtheners or weakeners—instead, they are typically phrased as questions, whose answers may or may not help you evaluate the validity of the argument. Select the answer choice that allows you to say that the argument is strong or weak. In an Evaluate EXCEPT or Evaluate LEAST question, your goal is to find the answer choice that has *no impact* on the argument.

> ## LSAT STRATEGY
>
> Some facts to remember about Evaluate questions:
>
> - These questions are similar to Strengthen and Weaken questions.
> - Untangle the stimulus; then find the assumption.
> - The correct answer will often present a question, whose answers have either a positive or negative impact on the argument.

Practice

Now it's time to try some Strengthen and Weaken questions on your own. Remember to tackle each question with a plan and an approach. First, identify the question and understand what task you are being asked to perform. Then, untangle the stimulus into evidence and conclusion. Next, use your knowledge of argument patterns to determine the author's assumption—in Weaken questions, the assumption is often that the author is overlooking potential objections to the conclusion, so be on the lookout for an answer choice that introduces one of these objections. In Strengthen questions, the correct answer affirms the assumption or removes a possible objection. And in both Strengthen and Weaken questions, you may see a correct answer choice that directly supports or weakens the conclusion. The expert analyses follow.

LSAT Question	My Analysis
40. A recent study of perfect pitch—the ability to identify the pitch of an isolated musical note—found that a high percentage of people who have perfect pitch are related to someone else who has it. Among those without perfect pitch, the percentage was much lower. This shows that having perfect pitch is a consequence of genetic factors.	**Step 2:**
Which one of the following, if true, most strengthens the argument?	**Step 1:**
	Step 3:
(A) People who have relatives with perfect pitch generally receive no more musical training than do others.	**Step 4:**
(B) All of the researchers conducting the study had perfect pitch.	
(C) People with perfect pitch are more likely than others to choose music as a career.	
(D) People with perfect pitch are more likely than others to make sure that their children receive musical training.	
(E) People who have some training in music are more likely to have perfect pitch than those with no such training.	

PrepTest62 Sec4 Q3

LSAT Question	My Analysis
41. Eight large craters run in a long straight line across a geographical region. Although some of the craters contain rocks that have undergone high-pressure shocks characteristic of meteorites slamming into Earth, these shocks could also have been caused by extreme volcanic events. Because of the linearity of the craters, it is very unlikely that some of them were caused by volcanoes and others were caused by meteorites. Thus, since the craters are all different ages, they were probably caused by volcanic events rather than meteorites.	**Step 2:**
Which one of the following statements, if true, would most strengthen the argument?	**Step 1:**
	Step 3:
(A) A similar but shorter line of craters that are all the same age is known to have been caused by volcanic activity.	**Step 4:**
(B) No known natural cause would likely account for eight meteorite craters of different ages forming a straight line.	
(C) There is no independent evidence of either meteorites or volcanic activity in the region where the craters are located.	
(D) There is no independent evidence of a volcanic event strong enough to have created the high-pressure shocks that are characteristic of meteorites slamming into Earth.	
(E) No known single meteor shower has created exactly eight impact craters that form a straight line.	

PrepTest58 Sec4 Q23

LSAT Question	**My Analysis**
42. This boulder is volcanic in origin and yet the rest of the rock in this area is sedimentary. Since this area was covered by southward-moving glaciers during the last ice age, this boulder was probably deposited here, hundreds of miles from its geological birthplace, by a glacier.	**Step 2:**
Which one of the following, if true, most seriously undermines the conclusion drawn in the argument above?	**Step 1:**
	Step 3:
(A) Most boulders that have been moved by glaciers have not been moved more than 100 miles.	**Step 4:**
(B) The closest geological source of volcanic rock is 50 miles south of this boulder.	
(C) The closest geological source of volcanic rock is 50 miles north of this boulder.	
(D) There are no geological sources of volcanic rock north of this boulder.	
(E) No other boulders of volcanic origin exist within 50 miles of this boulder.	

PrepTest56 Sec2 Q8

LSAT Question	My Analysis

43. The Kiffer Forest Preserve, in the northernmost part of the Abbimac Valley, is where most of the bears in the valley reside. During the eight years that the main road through the preserve has been closed the preserve's bear population has nearly doubled. Thus, the valley's bear population will increase if the road is kept closed.

Step 2:

Which one of the following, if true, most undermines the argument?

Step 1:

Step 3:

(A) Most of the increase in the preserve's bear population over the past eight years is due to migration.

Step 4:

(B) Only some of the increase in the preserve's bear population over the past eight years is due to migration of bears from other parts of the Abbimac Valley.

(C) Only some of the increase in the preserve's bear population over the past eight years is due to migration of bears from outside the Abbimac Valley.

(D) The bear population in areas of the Abbimac Valley outside the Kiffer Forest Preserve has decreased over the past eight years.

(E) The bear population in the Abbimac Valley has remained about the same over the past eight years.

PrepTest58 Sec1 Q24

LSAT Question	My Analysis
44. Doctor: While a few alternative medicines have dangerous side effects, some, such as many herbs, have been proven safe to consume. Thus, though there is little firm evidence of medicinal effect, advocates of these herbs as remedies for serious illnesses should always be allowed to prescribe them, since their patients will not be harmed, and might be helped, by the use of these products.	**Step 2:**
Which one of the following, if true, most seriously weakens the doctor's argument?	**Step 1:**
	Step 3:
(A) Many practitioners and patients neglect more effective conventional medicines in favor of herbal remedies.	**Step 4:**
(B) Many herbal remedies are marketed with claims of proven effectiveness when in fact their effectiveness is unproven.	
(C) Some patients may have allergic reactions to certain medicines that have been tolerated by other patients.	
(D) The vast majority of purveyors of alternative medicines are driven as much by the profit motive as by a regard for their patients' health.	
(E) Any pain relief or other benefits of many herbs have been proven to derive entirely from patients' belief in the remedy, rather than from its biochemical properties.	

PrepTest58 Sec1 Q5

LSAT Question	My Analysis
45. Tent caterpillars' routes between their nests and potential food sources are marked with chemical traces called pheromones that the caterpillars leave behind. Moreover, routes from food sources back to the nest are marked more heavily than are merely exploratory routes that have failed to turn up a food source. Thus, tent caterpillars are apparently among the insect species that engage in communal foraging, which consists in the conveying of information concerning the location of food to other members of the colony, nest, or hive.	**Step 2:**
Which one of the following, if true, adds the most support to the argument?	**Step 1:**
	Step 3:
(A) A hungry tent caterpillar is more likely to follow heavily marked routes than lightly marked routes.	**Step 4:**
(B) Tent caterpillars can detect the presence but not the concentration of pheromones.	
(C) Sometimes individual tent caterpillars will not return to the nest until a food source is located.	
(D) The pheromones left by tent caterpillars are different from the pheromones left by other animals.	
(E) The pheromones that tent caterpillars leave behind are detectable by certain other species of caterpillars.
PrepTest56 Sec3 Q13	

Now take a look at how an LSAT expert would approach and analyze these Strengthen and Weaken questions.

LSAT Question	Analysis
40. A recent study of perfect pitch—the ability to identify the pitch of an isolated musical note—found that a high percentage of people who have perfect pitch are related to someone else who has it. Among those without perfect pitch, the percentage was much lower. This shows that having perfect pitch is a consequence of genetic factors.	**Step 2:** Conclusion: Having perfect pitch is a consequence of genetic factors. Evidence: Study shows that a higher percentage of those with perfect than without it have a relative with perfect pitch.
Which one of the following, if true, most strengthens the argument?	**Step 1:** The word *strengthens* indicates a Strengthen question.
	Step 3: The argument moves from a statement of correlation in the evidence (perfect pitch is correlated with having a relative with perfect pitch) to a claim of causation (genetic factors cause perfect pitch). The argument assumes **No ARC**: there is no other possible cause for perfect pitch, such as musical training or listening to music at a critical period in auditory development; perfect pitch isn't responsible for the genetic factors; and the relationship isn't purely coincidental. To strengthen this argument, look for an answer choice that rules out one of these overlooked objections.
(A) People who have relatives with perfect pitch generally receive no more musical training than do others.	**Step 4:** Correct. This choice rules out another possible cause for perfect pitch (musical training). Ruling out one possible cause by no means proves that perfect pitch is caused by genetic factors, but doing so does make this conclusion more likely by eliminating a competing explanation.
(B) All of the researchers conducting the study had perfect pitch.	Outside the Scope. The musical abilities of the researchers don't affect whether perfect pitch is genetic. Eliminate.
(C) People with perfect pitch are more likely than others to choose music as a career.	Outside the Scope. The career choices of those with perfect pitch are irrelevant to whether or not perfect pitch is genetic. Eliminate.
(D) People with perfect pitch are more likely than others to make sure that their children receive musical training.	180. This choice is a weakener because it makes it more likely that perfect pitch is the result of musical training rather than genetic factors. Eliminate.
(E) People who have some training in music are more likely to have perfect pitch than those with no such training. *PrepTest62 Sec4 Q3*	Outside the Scope. This choice cites another correlation. A correlation is not proof of a causal relationship, so this by no means says that musical training causes perfect pitch. Eliminate.

LSAT Question	Analysis
41. Eight large craters run in a long straight line across a geographical region. Although some of the craters contain rocks that have undergone high-pressure shocks characteristic of meteorites slamming into Earth, these shocks could also have been caused by extreme volcanic events. Because of the linearity of the craters, it is very unlikely that some of them were caused by volcanoes and others were caused by meteorites. Thus, since the craters are all different ages, they were probably caused by volcanic events rather than meteorites.	**Step 2:** Conclusion: The craters were probably caused by volcanic events rather than by meteorites. Evidence: Because the craters run in a straight line and are different ages, it's unlikely that some were caused by volcanoes and others by meteorites.
Which one of the following statements, if true, would most strengthen the argument?	**Step 1:** The word "strengthen" indicates that this is a Strengthen question: the correct answer will support the argument's conclusion.
	Step 3: This argument presents two possible explanations for the craters—meteorites and volcanoes—and makes a claim for volcanoes as the more probable explanation. These "explaining a phenomenon" stimuli are classic Overlooked Possibilities setups, and the possible objections in this case would be any info that says meteors are the explanation. In this Strengthen question, the correct answer will either support volcanoes as the more likely explanation or discredit meteorites.
(A) A similar but shorter line of craters that are all the same age is known to have been caused by volcanic activity.	**Step 4:** Outside the Scope. The phrase "all the same age" is different from the argument, which concerns craters of *different* ages. Eliminate.
(B) No known natural cause would likely account for eight meteorite craters of different ages forming a straight line.	Correct. This choice discredits meteorites as a plausible explanation.
(C) There is no independent evidence of either meteorites or volcanic activity in the region where the craters are located.	If there is no evidence of either volcanoes or meteorites, the argument is not impacted either way, so this choice is irrelevant. Eliminate.
(D) There is no independent evidence of a volcanic event strong enough to have created the high-pressure shocks that are characteristic of meteorites slamming into Earth.	180. This choice contradicts the evidence that "these shocks could also have been caused by extreme volcanic events." Eliminate.
(E) No known single meteor shower has created exactly eight impact craters that form a straight line. *PrepTest58 Sec4 Q23*	Outside the Scope. A "single meteor shower" and its effects are irrelevant because a single meteor shower would give rise to impact craters that are all the same age. Eliminate.

Response Data

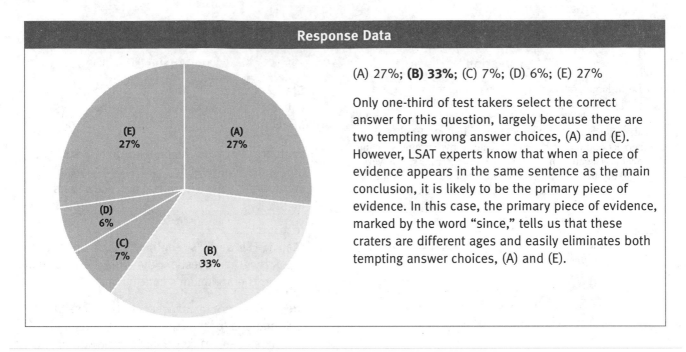

(A) 27%; **(B) 33%**; (C) 7%; (D) 6%; (E) 27%

Only one-third of test takers select the correct answer for this question, largely because there are two tempting wrong answer choices, (A) and (E). However, LSAT experts know that when a piece of evidence appears in the same sentence as the main conclusion, it is likely to be the primary piece of evidence. In this case, the primary piece of evidence, marked by the word "since," tells us that these craters are different ages and easily eliminates both tempting answer choices, (A) and (E).

LSAT Question	Analysis
42. This boulder is volcanic in origin and yet the rest of the rock in this area is sedimentary. Since this area was covered by southward-moving glaciers during the last ice age, this boulder was probably deposited here, hundreds of miles from its geological birthplace, by a glacier.	**Step 2:** Conclusion: Boulder was probably deposited at its current position by a glacier. → Evidence: Boulder is volcanic, while surrounding rock is sedimentary; area covered by southward-moving glaciers in last ice age.
Which one of the following, if true, most seriously undermines the conclusion drawn in the argument above?	**Step 1:** The word "undermines" indicates that this is a Weaken question. The correct answer will weaken the argument's conclusion by overturning the argument's assumption.

LSAT Question (cont.)	Analysis (cont.)
	Step 3: This is another "explain a phenomenon" Overlooked Possibilities argument. Because the glaciers cited in the evidence are southward moving, this argument concludes that the boulder came from a northern site "hundreds of miles" away from its current location. The possible objections to this argument would be any other explanation for how the boulder got to where it is.
	In a Weaken question, the correct answer will either make one of these possible objections/explanations more likely or rule out the explanation provided in the conclusion directly.
(A) Most boulders that have been moved by glaciers have not been moved more than 100 miles.	**Step 4:** This choice still allows for the possibility of a boulder being moved farther than 100 miles and thus does nothing to damage the argument's assumption that the boulder came from a northern location "hundreds of miles" from its current resting place. Eliminate.
(B) The closest geological source of volcanic rock is 50 miles south of this boulder.	Because the glacier cited by the author as evidence was southward moving, volcanic sources of rock *south* of the boulder are irrelevant. Eliminate.
(C) The closest geological source of volcanic rock is 50 miles north of this boulder.	The distance of the closest source of volcanic rock is irrelevant to the argument. The author has already told us that the boulder in question came hundreds of miles from its birthplace. Eliminate.
(D) There are no geological sources of volcanic rock north of this boulder.	Correct. This choice contradicts the argument's assumption that the boulder came from a source of volcanic rock to the north of the boulder's current location.
(E) No other boulders of volcanic origin exist within 50 miles of this boulder. *PrepTest56 Sec2 Q8*	This choice has no impact on the argument because the author concludes that the boulder probably came from "hundreds of miles" away from its current location. Eliminate.

LSAT Question	Analysis
43. The Kiffer Forest Preserve, in the northernmost part of the Abbimac Valley, is where most of the bears in the valley reside. During the eight years that the main road through the preserve has been closed the preserve's bear population has nearly doubled. Thus, the valley's bear population will increase if the road is kept closed.	**Step 2:** Conclusion: Valley's bear population will increase if road is kept closed. Evidence: Preserve is part of valley. While road through preserve was kept closed, preserve's bear population nearly doubled.
Which one of the following, if true, most undermines the argument?	**Step 1:** The word "undermines" indicates that this is a Weaken question. The correct answer will weaken the argument's conclusion by overturning the argument's assumption.
	Step 3: The author assumes that the new bears in the preserve did not migrate into the preserve from elsewhere in the valley. (To see this more readily, draw a map of the valley, with the preserve at its north end; include dots to represent bears and consider what happens if they move from the southern part of the valley into the preserve.)
(A) Most of the increase in the preserve's bear population over the past eight years is due to migration.	**Step 4:** This choice fails to stipulate from whence the bears are migrating. If they are migrating from outside the valley, then the conclusion is supported; if they are migrating from the southern part of the valley into the preserve, the conclusion is weakened. Eliminate.
(B) Only some of the increase in the preserve's bear population over the past eight years is due to migration of bears from other parts of the Abbimac Valley.	180. "Only some" means that other bears are migrating from outside the valley, which strengthens the conclusion rather than weakens it. Eliminate.
(C) Only some of the increase in the preserve's bear population over the past eight years is due to migration of bears from outside the Abbimac Valley.	180. Again, if even "some" bears migrated from outside the valley, the conclusion is strengthened, not weakened. Eliminate.

LSAT Question	Analysis
(D) The bear population in areas of the Abbimac Valley outside the Kiffer Forest Preserve has decreased over the past eight years.	$\longrightarrow$ Fails to stipulate by how much the bear population in other areas of the valley decreased. If the decrease in the rest of the valley equals the increase in the preserve, then the conclusion is weakened. But if the decrease in the rest of the valley is less than the increase in the preserve, the conclusion is strengthened. Eliminate.
(E) The bear population in the Abbimac Valley has remained about the same over the past eight years. *PrepTest58 Sec1 Q24* $\longrightarrow$	Correct. This choice suggests that if the bear population increased in the preserve, it must have decreased in the rest of the valley; in other words, the preserve's bear population increased because bears migrated into the preserve from elsewhere in the valley. This choice contradicts the argument's assumption.

Response Data

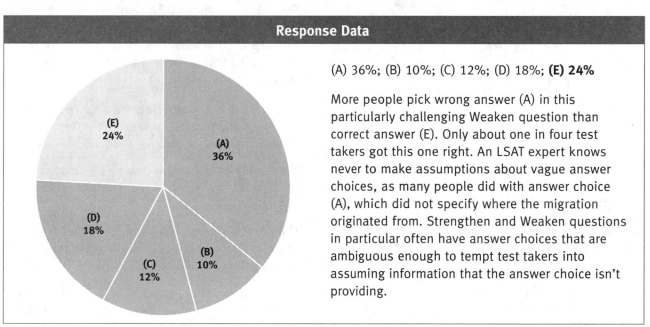

(A) 36%; (B) 10%; (C) 12%; (D) 18%; **(E) 24%**

More people pick wrong answer (A) in this particularly challenging Weaken question than correct answer (E). Only about one in four test takers got this one right. An LSAT expert knows never to make assumptions about vague answer choices, as many people did with answer choice (A), which did not specify where the migration originated from. Strengthen and Weaken questions in particular often have answer choices that are ambiguous enough to tempt test takers into assuming information that the answer choice isn't providing.

LSAT Question	Analysis
44. Doctor: While a few alternative medicines have dangerous side effects, some, such as many herbs, have been proven safe to consume. Thus, though there is little firm evidence of medicinal effect, advocates of these herbs as remedies for serious illnesses should always be allowed to prescribe them, since their patients will not be harmed, and might be helped, by the use of these products.	**Step 2:** Conclusion: Prescription of alternative medicines should always be allowed. → Evidence: Patients will not be harmed and might be helped by the use of alternative medicines.
Which one of the following, if true, most seriously weakens the doctor's argument?	**Step 1:** The word "weakens" gives this question → away as a Weaken question. The correct answer will weaken the argument's conclusion by overturning the argument's assumption.
	Step 3: When a conclusion recommends a course of action based on something's noted advantages or disadvantages, it is a pro/con Overlooked Possibilities argument. The author is not considering other possible advantages/disadvantages. Possible objections to this conclusion, then, would be anything that suggests that one should not prescribe herbal remedies. In a Weaken question, the correct answer will make one of these possible objections more likely to be true.
(A) Many practitioners and patients neglect more effective conventional medicines in favor of herbal remedies.	**Step 4:** Correct. This choice states a disadvantage → of using alternative medicines that outweighs their potential benefit.
(B) Many herbal remedies are marketed with claims of proven effectiveness when in fact their effectiveness is unproven.	Outside the Scope. How herbal remedies are → marketed doesn't affect whether or not they should be prescribed. Eliminate.
(C) Some patients may have allergic reactions to certain medicines that have been tolerated by other patients.	The author limits the conclusion to "these herbs," → that is, those that have "proven safe to consume." How different patients respond to herbs that have side effects is irrelevant. Eliminate.
(D) The vast majority of purveyors of alternative medicines are driven as much by the profit motive as by a regard for their patients' health.	Outside the Scope. The purveyors' motives don't → change whether or not it's a good idea to prescribe herbal remedies. Eliminate.
(E) Any pain relief or other benefits of many herbs have been proven to derive entirely from patients' belief in the remedy, rather than from its biochemical properties.	The source of herbal remedies' benefit is irrelevant → to whether or not prescribing them should be permitted. Eliminate.

PrepTest58 Sec1 Q5

LSAT Question	Analysis
45. Tent caterpillars' routes between their nests and potential food sources are marked with chemical traces called pheromones that the caterpillars leave behind. Moreover, routes from food sources back to the nest are marked more heavily than are merely exploratory routes that have failed to turn up a food source. Thus, tent caterpillars are apparently among the insect species that engage in communal foraging, which consists in the conveying of information concerning the location of food to other members of the colony, nest, or hive.	**Step 2:** Conclusion: Tent caterpillars convey information about food sources to each other. Evidence: The routes to food have more pheromones than the routes that don't go to food.
Which one of the following, if true, adds the most support to the argument?	**Step 1:** The phrase "adds the most support to the argument" signals a Strengthen question. The correct answer will support the argument's conclusion by affirming its assumption.
	Step 3: This argument amounts to "food trails are heavily marked, so tent caterpillars must be communicating." The author overlooks the possibility that there are other explanations for the trails being heavily marked. Because this is a Strengthen question, the correct answer may rule out alternative explanations or may support the conclusion directly.
(A) A hungry tent caterpillar is more likely to follow heavily marked routes than lightly marked routes.	**Step 4:** Correct. A caterpillar's privileging heavily marked trails over lightly marked ones would suggest that the caterpillar is "reading" the trail, which supports the notion of communication.
(B) Tent caterpillars can detect the presence but not the concentration of pheromones.	If caterpillars cannot detect the concentration of the chemical trails, there can be no communication of a food source via heavier trail marking. Eliminate.
(C) Sometimes individual tent caterpillars will not return to the nest until a food source is located.	This choice is irrelevant to the question of whether or not caterpillars leave trails for each other (or read trails left by others). Eliminate.
(D) The pheromones left by tent caterpillars are different from the pheromones left by other animals.	Outside the Scope. What other animals do has no bearing on what tent caterpillars do. Eliminate.
(E) The pheromones that tent caterpillars leave behind are detectable by certain other species of caterpillars.	Outside the Scope. Other species of caterpillars are irrelevant. Eliminate.

PrepTest56 Sec3 Q13

ARGUMENT-BASED PRINCIPLE QUESTIONS

> ## LEARNING OBJECTIVES
>
> In this section, you'll learn to:
>
> · Recognize Principle question stems.
> · Distinguish Identify the Principle questions from other Principle question types.
> · Use your knowledge of Assumption-based questions to attack Principle Assumption and Principle Strengthen questions.

Now that you've worked with several question types in the Assumption Family, let's turn our attention to Principle questions—a question type that often mimics Assumption Family questions. There has been an average of about five Principle questions per exam in recent years. Principle questions come in three main varieties: Identify the Principle, Apply the Principle, and Identify and Apply the Principle (aka Parallel Principle). In this section, you will learn to distinguish these three types, as well as how to attack argument-based Identify the Principle questions. You'll learn about Parallel Principle questions later in this chapter, and the remaining types of Principle questions will be covered in Chapter 11.

Recognizing Principle Question Stems

The common thread that appears throughout these three main Principle question types is the presence of a "principle." On the LSAT, a "principle" is a law-like general rule that can be applied not only to the particular situation in an argument but also to other, comparable situations. The question stem for a Principle question will often simply include the word *principle*. The words *proposition* or *policy*, as well as variations on the phrases "most closely conforms to" and "best illustrates," are all strong indicators of a Principle question. In general, any question that asks you to identify or apply a general rule is a Principle question.

Take a look at a few typical Principle question stems:

LSAT Question Stem	Analysis
Which one of the following principles, if valid, most helps to justify the consumer advocate's argumentation? *PrepTest62 Sec2 Q23*	"The following principles" indicates this is a Principle question stem.
Which one of the following principles is best illustrated by the study described above? *PrepTest62 Sec2 Q1*	Both the word "principles" and the phrase "best illustrated by" are clear indicators that this is a Principle question.
Which one of the following summer weather reports most closely conforms to the principles stated above? *PrepTest56 Sec3 Q23*	"[P]rinciples stated above" and "most closely conforms to" both indicate that this is a Principle question.
Which of the following arguments illustrates a principle most similar to the principle underlying the argument above? *PrepTest56 Sec2 Q18*	The words "principle" and "illustrates" signal a Principle question.

LSAT Question Stem	Analysis
The situation as Madden describes it best illustrates which one of the following propositions? *PrepTest58 Sec4 Q16*	→ The words "propositions" and "best illustrates" indicate that this is a Principle question.

Distinguishing Types of Principle Questions

Identify the Principle questions, a subset of which we will be examining in this chapter, present a specific argument or set of events in the stimulus, then ask you to identify an applicable, more generalized principle in the answer choices. Because Identify the Principle questions move from specific in the stimulus to general in the conclusion, using a ∧ can be a great shorthand note to yourself while tackling Step 1 in these questions.

Apply the Principle questions do just the opposite: they will present a general principle in the stimulus (often expressed as a Formal Logic statement), then ask you to identify a more specific, nonconflicting situation in the correct answer choice. Similarly to ID the Principle questions, using a ∨ is a great way to shorthand that you are moving from a general statement in your stimulus to a specific situation in your answer choices.

Identify and Apply the Principle questions combine the actions used in Identify and Apply the Principle questions. First, identify the underlying principle in the specific situation in the stimulus. Then, apply that general principle to a new specific situation located in one of the answer choices. These are also referred to as Parallel Principle questions. Your shorthand for this question type looks like this ◊ and represents moving from a specific stimulus to general and back to specific in the answer choices.

Take a look at the following question stems. Can you identify your specific task in each one?

LSAT Question Stem	My Analysis
46. Which one of the following principles, if valid, most helps to justify the consumer advocate's argumentation? *PrepTest62 Sec2 Q23*	
47. Which one of the following principles is best illustrated by the study described above? *PrepTest62 Sec2 Q1*	
48. Which one of the following summer weather reports most closely conforms to the principles stated above? *PrepTest56 Sec3 Q23*	
49. Which one of the following arguments illustrates a principle most similar to the principle underlying the argument above? *PrepTest56 Sec2 Q18*	
50. The situation as Madden describes it best illustrates which one of the following propositions? *PrepTest58 Sec4 Q16*	

Now take a look at how an LSAT Expert would break apart these questions stems.

LSAT Question Stem	Analysis
46. Which one of the following principles, if valid, most helps to justify the consumer advocate's argumentation? *PrepTest 62 Sec2 Q23* →	"Which of the following principles" indicates that the "following" answer choices are principles justifying the "consumer advocate's argumentation," a specific situation in the stimulus. This is an Identify the Principle question. ∧
47. Which one of the following principles is best illustrated by the study described above? *PrepTest62 Sec2 Q1* →	A "study" is "described above," which sounds pretty specific and is illustrating a "following principle" found below in the answer choices. This question moves from specific to general and is thus an Identify the Principle question. ∧
48. Which one of the following summer weather reports most closely conforms to the principles stated above? *PrepTest56 Sec3 Q23* →	"[T]he principles stated above" indicates there is a general statement in the stimulus to which one of the "following," more specific summer weather reports will conform. This question moves from general to specific, so it is an Apply the Principle question. ∨
49. Which one of the following arguments illustrates a principle most similar to the principle underlying the argument above? *PrepTest56 Sec2 Q18* →	Each of "the following arguments," or answer choices, is illustrating a principle, which means they are all specific. Additionally, the same principle being illustrated is "underlying" another specific "argument above," indicating we move from specific to general and back to specific in this Identify and Apply Principle question. ◇
50. The situation as Madden describes it best illustrates which one of the following propositions? *PrepTest58 Sec4 Q16* →	The "situation" as described by Madden, a specific person, is illustrating "one of the following propositions." *Propositions* is another way of saying *principles*. The word "following" indicates that the principle is located in the answer choices. This question moves from specific to general, so this is an Identify the Principle question. ∧

Principle Assumption and Principle Strengthen Questions

As we mentioned earlier, Identify the Principle questions often mimic familiar Assumption Family question types. Specifically, you are likely to see Identify the Principle questions that mimic Assumption and Strengthen questions. For example, consider the following question stem:

Which one of the following principles must be assumed
in order for the psychologist's conclusion to be properly
drawn?

PrepTest56 Sec2 Q20

This question stem states that the principle "must be assumed," indicating that the correct answer will be a necessary assumption and the stimulus should be attacked as you would attack an Assumption stimulus: find the conclusion and evidence and identify the disconnect. The only difference in approach will come in Step 3, when the scope of your prediction will be broadened. We'll discuss that difference in a moment. First, though, take a look at another example of a Principle question stem that mimics a different question type:

Which of the following principles, if valid, most
helps to justify the consumer advocate's argumentation?

PrepTest62 Sec2 Q23

The phrase "if valid, most helps to justify" sounds very much like phrasing from a Strengthen question stem. In this question, you can expect to see an argument with both a conclusion and evidence. Approach this question in the same way you would approach a Strengthen question, but expect the correct answer choice to be broader in scope and perhaps stronger in wording.

In fact, anticipating the broad wording of the correct answer is the only difference between tackling Assumption and Principle Assumption questions, and between tackling Strengthen and Principle Strengthen questions. Because Principle Assumption questions and Principle Strengthen questions move from specific situations in the stimulus to broadly worded answer choices (the choices describe principles, after all), once you have broken down the argument into evidence and conclusion and identified the assumption, take a moment to strip that assumption of words specific to the particular situation described in the stimulus. For example, if the stimulus in a Principle Strengthen question discusses "bank managers," expect the correct answer to be written in terms applicable to any manager, or even any person. Or if the stimulus discusses "fertilization methods of tulips," anticipate a correct answer that discusses the fertilization of all bulbous plants, or even all plants.

Practice

Now that we have covered the basics of Principle Assumption and Principle Strengthen questions, try your hand at a few examples. Remember to approach them exactly the same way you would approach ordinary Assumption and Strengthen questions in Steps 1 and 2, while broadening your scope in Step 3. The expert analyses follow.

LSAT Question	My Analysis
51. Consumer advocate: TMD, a pesticide used on peaches, shows no effects on human health when it is ingested in the amount present in the per capita peach consumption in this country. But while 80 percent of the population eat no peaches, others, including small children, consume much more than the national average, and thus ingest disproportionately large amounts of TMD. So even though the use of TMD on peaches poses minimal risk to most of the population, it has not been shown to be an acceptable practice.	**Step 2:**
Which one of the following principles, if valid, most helps to justify the consumer advocate's argumentation?	**Step 1:**
	Step 3:
(A) The possibility that more data about a pesticide's health effects might reveal previously unknown risks at low doses warrants caution in assessing that pesticide's overall risks.	**Step 4:**
(B) The consequences of using a pesticide are unlikely to be acceptable when a majority of the population is likely to ingest it.	
(C) Use of a pesticide is acceptable only if it is used for its intended purpose and the pesticide has been shown not to harm any portion of the population.	
(D) Society has a special obligation to protect small children from pesticides unless average doses received by the population are low and have not been shown to be harmful to children's health.	
(E) Measures taken to protect the population from a harm sometimes turn out to be the cause of a more serious harm to certain segments of the population.	

PrepTest62 Sec2 Q23

LSAT Question	My Analysis
52. In order to expand its mailing lists for e-mail advertising, the Outdoor Sports Company has been offering its customers financial incentives if they provide the e-mail addresses of their friends. However, offering such incentives is an unethical business practice, because it encourages people to exploit their personal relationships for profit, which risks damaging the integrity of those relationships.	**Step 2:**
Which one of the following principles, if valid, most helps to justify the reasoning in the argument?	**Step 1:**
	Step 3:
(A) It is unethical for people to exploit their personal relationships for profit if in doing so they risk damaging the integrity of those relationships.	**Step 4:**
(B) If it would be unethical to use information that was gathered in a particular way, then it is unethical to gather that information in the first place.	
(C) It is an unethical business practice for a company to deliberately damage the integrity of its customers' personal relationships in any way.	
(D) It is unethical to encourage people to engage in behavior that could damage the integrity of their personal relationships.	
(E) Providing a friend's personal information to a company in exchange for a financial reward will almost certainly damage the integrity of one's personal relationship with that friend.	

PrepTest56 Sec2 Q16

LSAT Question	My Analysis
53. Psychologist: Psychotherapists who attempt to provide psychotherapy on radio or television talk shows are expected to do so in ways that entertain a broad audience. However, satisfying this demand is nearly always incompatible with providing high-quality psychological help. For this reason, psychotherapists should never provide psychotherapy on talk shows.	**Step 2:**
Which one of the following principles must be assumed in order for the psychologist's conclusion to be properly drawn?	**Step 1:**
	Step 3:
(A) It is never appropriate for psychotherapists to attempt to entertain a broad audience.	**Step 4:**
(B) The context in which psychological help is presented has a greater impact on its quality than the nature of the advice that is given.	
(C) Psychotherapy should never be provided in a context in which there is any chance that the therapy might be of less than high quality.	
(D) Most members of radio and television talk show audiences are seeking entertainment rather than high-quality psychological help.	
(E) Psychotherapists should never attempt to provide psychological help in a manner that makes it unlikely to be of high quality.	

PrepTest56 Sec2 Q20

Now look at the approach an LSAT expert took.

LSAT Question	Analysis
51. Consumer advocate: TMD, a pesticide used on peaches, shows no effects on human health when it is ingested in the amount present in the per capita peach consumption in this country. But while 80 percent of the population eat no peaches, others, including small children, consume much more than the national average, and thus ingest disproportionately large amounts of TMD. So even though the use of TMD on peaches poses minimal risk to most of the population, it has not been shown to be an acceptable practice.	**Step 2:** Conclusion: Use of TMD on peaches is not an acceptable practice. Evidence: Certain people consume so many peaches that they ingest TMD in amounts greater than the amount known to be safe.
Which one of the following principles, if valid, most helps to justify the consumer advocate's argumentation?	**Step 1:** The words *principle* and *justify* signal a Principle Strengthen question. The correct answer will support the argument's conclusion in very broad, general terms.
	Step 3: The consumer advocate concludes that as long as TMD use is potentially unsafe for even some members of the population, its use is unacceptable. This is a classic Overlooked Possibilities argument: A recommendation argument with the author assuming that the cons outweigh any unmentioned pros. The correct answer will state a principle that justifies the argument that the particular con the author cited (a "minimal risk to most of the population") is enough to make the use of TMD a bad idea.
(A) The possibility that more data about a pesticide's health effects might reveal previously unknown risks at low doses warrants caution in assessing that pesticide's overall risks.	**Step 4:** This choice contradicts the consumer advocate's statement that "shows no effects on human health" at an average dose. Eliminate.
(B) The consequences of using a pesticide are unlikely to be acceptable when a majority of the population is likely to ingest it.	According to the consumer advocate, a majority of the population eats no peaches at all (and thus ingests no TMD). Eliminate.

LSAT Question	**Analysis**
(C) Use of a pesticide is acceptable only if it is used for its intended purpose and the pesticide has been shown not to harm any portion of the population.	Correct. If no pesticide should be used unless it is safe for everyone, then even minimal risk is enough to justify a recommendation against the use of TMD.
(D) Society has a special obligation to protect small children from pesticides unless average doses received by the population are low and have not been shown to be harmful to children's health.	The problem isn't that the "average dose" of TMD is harmful to children's health, but rather that some children ingest much more than the average dose. Eliminate.
(E) Measures taken to protect the population from a harm sometimes turn out to be the cause of a more serious harm to certain segments of the population. *PrepTest62 Sec2 Q23*	There is nothing in the consumer advocate's argument to indicate that TMD is a measure that has been taken to protect the population from harm. Eliminate.

LSAT Question	**Analysis**
52. In order to expand its mailing lists for e-mail advertising, the Outdoor Sports Company has been offering its customers financial incentives if they provide the e-mail addresses of their friends. However, offering such incentives is an unethical business practice, because it encourages people to exploit their personal relationships for profit, which risks damaging the integrity of those relationships.	**Step 2:** Conclusion: Offering financial incentives to customers who provide email addresses of their friends is unethical. Evidence: Offering such incentives encourages people to exploit their personal relationships for profit, which risks damaging the integrity of those relationships.
Which one of the following principles, if valid, most helps to justify the reasoning in the argument?	**Step 1:** The words *principles* and *justify* signal a Principle Strengthen question. The correct answer will support the argument's conclusion in very broad, general terms.
	Step 3: With a conclusion defining the incentives as unethical and evidence saying the incentives risk the integrity of personal relationships, this is a Mismatched Concepts—Equivalence argument. Combine the mismatched concepts to come up with the assumption: it is unethical to encourage people to do something that risks damaging the integrity of their personal relationships. The correct answer will support this assumption.
(A) It is unethical for people to exploit their personal relationships for profit if in doing so they risk damaging the integrity of those relationships.	**Step 4:** This choice is difficult because it includes the phrase "risk damaging the integrity of those relationships," which is one of the mismatched concepts. But the other half is wrong: the argument's assumption is that it is unethical to *ask* someone to risk damaging a relationship. The stimulus focuses on a business's unethical practice, not a person's unethical practice. Eliminate.

LSAT Question		Analysis
(B)	If it would be unethical to use information that was gathered in a particular way, then it is unethical to gather that information in the first place.	→ The stimulus is not concerned with the use of information, only with its source. Eliminate.
(C)	It is an unethical business practice for a company to deliberately damage the integrity of its customers' personal relationships in any way.	→ The company is not directly disrupting its customers' relationships, merely asking them to engage in behavior that might risk doing so. Eliminate.
(D)	It is unethical to encourage people to engage in behavior that could damage the integrity of their personal relationships.	→ Correct. This choice restates the assumption.
(E)	Providing a friend's personal information to a company in exchange for a financial reward will almost certainly damage the integrity of one's personal relationship with that friend. *PrepTest56 Sec2 Q16*	→ Extreme. The author merely says that there is a "risk" of damaging the relationship. Eliminate.

LSAT Question	Analysis
53. Psychologist: Psychotherapists who attempt to provide psychotherapy on radio or television talk shows are expected to do so in ways that entertain a broad audience. However, satisfying this demand is nearly always incompatible with providing high-quality psychological help. For this reason, psychotherapists should never provide psychotherapy on talk shows.	**Step 2:** Conclusion: Psychotherapists should never provide psychotherapy on talk shows. Evidence: Psychotherapists who provide psychotherapy on talk shows must entertain a broad audience, which nearly always precludes providing high-quality psychological help.
Which one of the following principles must be assumed in order for the psychologist's conclusion to be properly drawn?	**Step 1:** The words *principles* and *assumed* indicate that this is a Principle Assumption question. The word *must* indicates a Necessary Assumption.
	Step 3: The psychologist's problem is a classic Overlooked Possibilities pro/con issue. The author believes psychotherapists shouldn't be allowed to participate in these shows and cites a potential con as evidence. The possible objections are any reasons why it might be okay for a psychologist to be on one of these shows. The correct answer will eliminate any possible objection by making it clear that the con outweighs any pros.
(A) It is never appropriate for psychotherapists to attempt to entertain a broad audience.	**Step 4:** Extreme. Given what we know from the argument, perhaps it would be considered appropriate for psychotherapists to entertain a broad audience by tap dancing or doing magic tricks in their off hours. Eliminate.
(B) The context in which psychological help is presented has a greater impact on its quality than the nature of the advice that is given.	The argument's evidence states that the context in which the advice is provided affects its nature. This choice distorts that relationship. Eliminate.
(C) Psychotherapy should never be provided in a context in which there is any chance that the therapy might be of less than high quality.	Extreme. The psychologist's argument is about a situation in which there is a large chance therapy won't be high quality. This choice says psychotherapy shouldn't be provided if there is "any chance" the therapy might be less than high quality. Eliminate.
(D) Most members of radio and television talk show audiences are seeking entertainment rather than high-quality psychological help.	Outside the Scope. What audience members are "seeking" is irrelevant. Eliminate.
(E) Psychotherapists should never attempt to provide psychological help in a manner that makes it unlikely to be of high quality. *PrepTest56 Sec2 Q20*	Correct. If this is true, then it is assured that the con cited by the author outweighs any potential overlooked pros to providing their services on television or radio.

PARALLEL REASONING AND PARALLEL FLAW QUESTIONS

Another way in which you will be tested on your ability to recognize argument structures on the LSAT is to identify two different arguments that use the same pattern to reach a similar conclusion. Questions that ask you to spot two identically structured arguments are called Parallel Reasoning and Parallel Flaw questions.

LEARNING OBJECTIVES

In this section, you'll learn to:

- Rule out incorrect answer choices in Parallel Reasoning and Parallel Flaw questions based on conclusion type.
- Identify similar argument structures in Parallel Reasoning questions.
- In Parallel Flaw questions, find the answer choice whose flaw type matches the flaw type in the stimulus.

You won't see many Parallel Reasoning questions on Test Day. There have been an average of three to four per test over the past five years. For many students, however, their length and complexity can make these questions three or four of the most time-consuming questions they encounter. Parallel Reasoning and Parallel Flaw questions are, on average, the longest questions in the Logical Reasoning section. While the length of these questions is off-putting to many students, LSAT experts know that there is a way to tackle these questions quickly and efficiently. Because the correct answer choice in these questions will be an argument that is parallel to the argument in the stimulus, both arguments must have similar conclusions. More on that in a second. First, let's figure out how to identify Parallel Reasoning and Parallel Flaw question stems.

The question stem for Parallel Reasoning and Parallel Flaw questions will ask you to find the answer choice whose reasoning is "most parallel to," "most similar to," or "most like" the reasoning in the stimulus. The only difference between the two question types is that Parallel Flaw question stems also announce that the stimulus and correct answer both contain a "flaw" or an "error in reasoning."

First, let's take a look at some typical Parallel Reasoning question stems as they appear on the LSAT:

LSAT Question Stem		Analysis
The reasoning in which one of the following is most similar to the reasoning in the argument above? *PrepTest62 Sec4 Q25*	$\longrightarrow$	The phrase "reasoning . . . most similar to" identifies this as a Parallel Reasoning question.
The pattern of flawed reasoning in the argument most closely parallels that in which one of the following? *PrepTest58 Sec1 Q7*	$\longrightarrow$	The phrase "pattern of flawed reasoning . . . most closely parallels" indicates that this is a Parallel Flaw question.

Parallel Reasoning questions require you to find an answer choice that uses the same kind of evidence to reach the same kind of conclusion as in the stimulus. The *content* of the stimulus will likely be different from that in the correct answer; in fact, each answer choice will probably discuss material unrelated to the information in the stimulus. Additionally, the order in which the evidence and the conclusion are presented in the stimulus may be different from the order in which the evidence and conclusion appear in the correct answer. In other words, if the conclusion in the stimulus is the first sentence, the conclusion in the correct answer does not necessarily need to be the first sentence. In short, the correct answer will be similar in *structure* (though perhaps not in sequence of evidence and conclusion) to the stimulus—the only difference is that the answer will discuss different ideas and concepts.

The ability to correctly identify and characterize conclusions will help you tackle Parallel Reasoning questions. Remember the six different conclusion types discussed in Chapter 9: prediction, recommendation, comparison, assertion of fact, if/then, and value judgment. Because the correct answer must have the same type of evidence leading to the same type of conclusion, any answer choice that has a different type of conclusion than does the stimulus is automatically incorrect and can be eliminated. And because checking the conclusion in each answer choice is faster than reading (and characterizing the structure of) the entire stimulus and of each answer choice, your first line of attack when faced with a Parallel Reasoning or Parallel Flaw question should be to identify and characterize the conclusion in the stimulus, then eliminate any answer choices that do not contain the same conclusion type. This process will occasionally allow you to arrive at the correct answer even without breaking down the evidence. While other test takers spend minutes wading through six separate arguments (the stimulus and five answer choices), experts are able to quickly evaluate just the conclusions. Even if this strategy doesn't always lead directly to the right answer, it will at least eliminate a few wrong answer choices.

In addition to characterizing a conclusion's *type*, pay attention to two other things: whether the conclusion is positive or negative (does the author state that something is or will be true, or that something is not or won't become true) and the level of certainty that exists (whether the conclusion is forceful or uses qualified language). For example, a conclusion stating that something will definitely occur is very different from a conclusion stating that something might not occur. The former is a strong prediction that something will happen, while the latter is a qualified prediction that something might not happen.

To sharpen your ability to characterize conclusions, try out the following drill. You've seen these conclusions earlier in this chapter, so they may look familiar. Characterize each by type, level of certainty, positive or negative language, and any other unique qualities it may have. The more specific you can be in your description of the conclusion in a Parallel Reasoning stimulus, the more useful the conclusion-typing method will be when you attack the answer choices. Examine the conclusions in this drill closely, then turn the page and compare your thinking to the expert analysis that follows.

LSAT Conclusion	My Analysis
54. The ability to trust other people is essential to happiness. *PrepTest56 Sec3 Q16*	
55. [R]estrictions on water use will be necessary to meet the freshwater needs of humankind in the not-too-distant future. *PrepTest58 Sec1 Q1*	
56. [A]rmadillos do not move rapidly into new territories. *PrepTest58 Sec4 Q11*	

LSAT Conclusion	My Analysis
57. [I]t is likely that many people greatly overestimate the odds of their winning a major jackpot. *PrepTest58 Sec4 Q21*	
58. [S]ometimes a business can survive only by becoming a different corporation. *PrepTest58 Sec1 Q16*	
59. [F]ilm producers...tend to make films that theater managers consider attractive to younger audiences. *PrepTest58 Sec1 Q14*	
60. [Medication] M will most likely be produced in capsule form. *PrepTest62 Sec2 Q3*	
61. [Y]ellow warblers, which can only fly short distances during molting, have no competition for the food supply within the range of their restricted flying. *PrepTest56 Sec2 Q4*	
62. [I]f similar results are found for the second ingredient, we can conclude that NoSmoke does not reduce smokers' cravings. *PrepTest56 Sec 3 Q4*	
63. [I]t is very likely that napping tends to cause insomnia. *PrepTest52 Sec 1 Q2*	
64. [R]ather than trying to interpret historical events, historians should instead interpret what the people who participated in historical events thought about those events. *PrepTest52 Sec 3 Q12*	
65. [T]he president has a duty to keep the corporation's profits high. *PrepTest52 Sec1 Q4*	
66. [T]he use of TMD...has not been shown to be an acceptable practice. *PrepTest62 Sec2 Q23*	

Here's how an LSAT expert analyzed the conclusions you just characterized.

LSAT Conclusion		Analysis
54. The ability to trust other people is essential to happiness. *PrepTest56 Sec3 Q16*	→	The word "essential" means "necessary." This is a conditional conclusion and falls into the if-then category.
55. [R]estrictions on water use will be necessary to meet the freshwater needs of humankind in the not-too-distant future. *PrepTest58 Sec1 Q1*	→	The phrase "will be" indicates something the author believes will become true in the future. There is no qualifier, such as *possibly* or *perhaps*, so this is a strong positive prediction.
56. [A]rmadillos do not move rapidly into new territories. *PrepTest58 Sec4 Q11*	→	A fact the author definitely believes to be true: strong assertion of fact that something is not happening.
57. [I]t is likely that many people greatly overestimate the odds of their winning a major jackpot. *PrepTest58 Sec4 Q21*	→	Again a fact the author believes to be true, but this time there is a qualifier: "likely." This is a weak assertion of fact.
58. [S]ometimes a business can survive only by becoming a different corporation. *PrepTest58 Sec1 Q16*	→	The phrase "only by" indicates necessity, so this is an if-then. The word "sometimes" makes it a qualified if-then.
59. [F]ilm producers...tend to make films that theater managers consider attractive to younger audiences. *PrepTest58 Sec1 Q14*	→	Statement of a fact the author believes to be true; "tend to" serves to qualify. This is a weak assertion of fact.
60. [Medication] M will most likely be produced in capsule form. *PrepTest 62 Sec2 Q3*	→	The phrase "will most likely" signals a weak prediction that something will happen.
61. [Y]ellow warblers, which can only fly short distances during molting, have no competition for the food supply within the range of their restricted flying. *PrepTest56 Sec2 Q4*	→	Strong assertion of fact that something is not happening.
62. [I]f similar results are found for the second ingredient, we can conclude that NoSmoke does not reduce smokers' cravings. *PrepTest56 Sec3 Q4*	→	Strong if-then that if one thing does not happen, then another thing will not happen.
63. [I]t is very likely that napping tends to cause insomnia. *PrepTest52 Sec1Q2*	→	The phrase "very likely" and the word "tends" serve as qualifiers, so this is a weak assertion of fact. More specifically, it is a weak assertion that one thing may cause another.
64. [R]ather than trying to interpret historical events, historians should instead interpret what the people who participated in historical events thought about those events. *PrepTest52 Sec3 Q12*	→	The word "should" makes this conclusion a recommendation. The lack of a qualifier such as *perhaps* or *likely* makes it a strong recommendation. More specifically, it is a recommendation that someone should do one thing *rather than* another.

LSAT Conclusion		**Analysis**
65. [T]he president has a duty to keep the corporation's profits high. *PrepTest 52 Sec1 Q4*	$\longrightarrow$	Strong assertion of fact. More specifically, strong assertion of someone's "duty."
66. [T]he use of TMD...has not been shown to be an acceptable practice. *PrepTest 62 Sec2 Q23*	$\longrightarrow$	A statement that something is unacceptable is a value judgment. There is no qualifier such as *might*, so this is a strong value judgment.

LSAT STRATEGY

When approaching Parallel Reasoning questions

- · First characterize the conclusion in the stimulus.
- · Characterize the conclusion in the answer choices and then eliminate answer choices that have a different conclusion type than does the conclusion in the stimulus.
- · If more than one answer choice remains, analyze the evidence in the stimulus; find the answer choice that presents an argument structurally identical to the stimulus.

Now that we have covered the basics of Parallel Reasoning questions, try your hand at a couple of examples of this question type. Characterize the conclusion in the stimulus; then eliminate any choices that do not share the same conclusion type. Be sure to check each answer choice, as there may be more than one choice that has the same type of conclusion as the stimulus. If you are unable to rule out all incorrect choices based upon your characterization of the conclusion, then move back to the stimulus and examine the evidence. The correct answer will use the same type of evidence to support the same type of conclusion as the stimulus. If you need to, simplify the original argument by replacing the various terms and concepts with letters. Then match that same structure to one of the answer choices.

When you're finished, compare your analyses to those of an LSAT expert.

LSAT Question	My Analysis
67. Dana intentionally watered the plant every other day. But since the plant was a succulent, and needed dry soil, the frequent watering killed the plant. Therefore Dana intentionally killed the plant.	**Step 2:**
Which one of the following arguments exhibits a flawed pattern of reasoning most similar to the flawed pattern of reasoning exhibited in the argument above?	**Step 1:**
	Step 3:
(A) Jack stole $10 from Kelly and bet it on a race. The bet returned $100 to Jack. Therefore Jack really stole $100 from Kelly.	**Step 4:**
(B) Celeste knows that coffee is grown in the mountains in Peru and that Peru is in South America. Therefore Celeste should know that coffee is grown in South America.	
(C) The restaurant owner decided to take an item off her restaurant's menu. This decision disappointed Jerry because that item was his favorite dish. Therefore the restaurant owner decided to disappoint Jerry.	
(D) The heavy rain caused the dam to break, and the breaking of the dam caused the fields downstream to be flooded. Therefore the heavy rain caused the flooding of the fields.	
(E) The power plant raised the water temperature, and whatever raised the water temperature is responsible for the decrease in fish. Therefore the power plant is responsible for the decrease in fish.	
PrepTest56 Sec2 Q7	

LSAT Question	**My Analysis**
68. Cities with healthy economies typically have plenty of job openings. Cities with high-technology businesses also tend to have healthy economies, so those in search of jobs should move to a city with high-technology businesses.	**Step 2:**
The reasoning in which one of the following is most similar to the reasoning in the argument above?	**Step 1:**
	Step 3:

(A) Older antiques are usually the most valuable. Antique dealers generally authenticate the age of the antiques they sell, so those collectors who want the most valuable antiques should purchase their antiques from antique dealers.

Step 4:

(B) Antique dealers who authenticate the age of the antiques they sell typically have plenty of antiques for sale. Since the most valuable antiques are those that have had their ages authenticated, antique collectors in search of valuable antiques should purchase their antiques from antique dealers.

(C) Antiques that have had their ages authenticated tend to be valuable. Since antique dealers generally carry antiques that have had their ages authenticated, those collectors who want antiques that are valuable should purchase their antiques from antique dealers.

(D) Many antique collectors know that antique dealers can authenticate the age of the antiques they sell. Since antiques that have had their ages authenticated are always the most valuable, most antique collectors who want antiques that are valuable tend to purchase their antiques from antique dealers.

(E) Many antiques increase in value once they have had their ages authenticated by antique dealers. Since antique dealers tend to have plenty of valuable antiques, antique collectors who prefer to purchase the most valuable antiques should purchase antiques from antique dealers.

PrepTest62 Sec4 Q25

Here's how an LSAT expert worked through the questions you just completed.

LSAT Question	Analysis
67. Dana intentionally watered the plant every other day. But since the plant was a succulent, and needed dry soil, the frequent watering killed the plant. Therefore Dana intentionally killed the plant.	**Step 2:** Conclusion: A *strong assertion of fact* that Dana *intentionally* killed the plant. Evidence (if needed): Dana intentionally watered a succulent plant every day.
Which one of the following arguments exhibits a flawed pattern of reasoning most similar to the flawed pattern of reasoning exhibited in the argument above?	**Step 1:** Taken together, the phrase "most similar to" and the word "flawed" indicate a Parallel Flaw question.
	Step 3: Start by ruling out choices whose conclusion is not a statement of someone's intention. If there is more than one choice remaining, then go back and examine the evidence. If only one choice is an assertion of someone's intention, that choice will be the correct answer.
(A) Jack stole $10 from Kelly and bet it on a race. The bet returned $100 to Jack. Therefore Jack really stole $100 from Kelly.	**Step 4:** Assertion of fact, but not a statement of someone's intention. Eliminate.
(B) Celeste knows that coffee is grown in the mountains in Peru and that Peru is in South America. Therefore Celeste should know that coffee is grown in South America.	The word "should" may make this one look like a recommendation, but the author is not giving Celeste advice; rather, she is saying that Celeste ought to know something. This choice is an assertion of fact. Again, though, it's not an assertion of someone's intention. Eliminate.
(C) The restaurant owner decided to take an item off her restaurant's menu. This decision disappointed Jerry because that item was his favorite dish. Therefore the restaurant owner decided to disappoint Jerry.	Correct. "[D]ecided to disappoint" is a statement of someone's intention.
(D) The heavy rain caused the dam to break, and the breaking of the dam caused the fields downstream to be flooded. Therefore the heavy rain caused the flooding of the fields.	Assertion of fact, but not a statement of intention. Eliminate.
(E) The power plant raised the water temperature, and whatever raised the water temperature is responsible for the decrease in fish. Therefore the power plant is responsible for the decrease in fish.	Again an assertion of fact, but again, the fact that the power plant is "responsible" for the decrease in fish is not tantamount to saying that the power plant intended to produce that decrease. Eliminate.

PrepTest56 Sec2 Q7

Note that in the previous question, you could have arrived at the correct answer, choice (C), by eliminating the wrong choices based only on conclusion type.

LSAT Question	Analysis
68. Cities with healthy economies typically have plenty of job openings. Cities with high-technology businesses also tend to have healthy economies, so those in search of jobs should move to a city with high-technology businesses. $\rightarrow$	**Step 2:** Conclusion: A *strong positive recommendation* that those in search of a job should move to cities with high-tech businesses. Evidence (if needed): Cities with high-tech businesses tend to have healthy economies, and cities with healthy economies have lots of job openings.
The reasoning in which one of the following is most similar to the reasoning in the argument above? $\rightarrow$	**Step 1:** The phrase "reasoning . . . most similar to" identifies this as a Parallel Reasoning question.
	Step 3: In structural terms, the argument breaks down as follows: A (cities with high-tech businesses) tends to have B (healthy economies). B tends to have C (job openings). So, if you want C, do A.
(A) Older antiques are usually the most valuable. Antique dealers generally authenticate the age of the antiques they sell, so those collectors who want the most valuable antiques should purchase their antiques from antique dealers. $\rightarrow$	**Step 4:** Although its conclusion matches, choice (A) has four variables instead of three: old antiques, being valuable, antique dealers, and authenticated ages. Eliminate.
(B) Antique dealers who authenticate the age of the antiques they sell typically have plenty of antiques for sale. Since the most valuable antiques are those that have had their ages authenticated, antique collectors in search of valuable antiques should purchase their antiques from antique dealers. $\rightarrow$	Although the conclusion in (B) matches that in the stimulus, the evidence does not. The conclusion discusses antique dealers in general, but the evidence mentions only those antique dealers who authenticate the ages of their antiques. That's not the same term. Eliminate.
(C) Antiques that have had their ages authenticated tend to be valuable. Since antique dealers generally carry antiques that have had their ages authenticated, those collectors who want antiques that are valuable should purchase their antiques from antique dealers. $\rightarrow$	Correct. A (antique dealers) tend to have B (authenticated antiques). B tend to be C (valuable). So, if you want C, do A.
(D) Many antique collectors know that antique dealers can authenticate the age of the antiques they sell. Since antiques that have had their ages authenticated are always the most valuable, most antique collectors who want antiques that are valuable tend to purchase their antiques from antique dealers. $\rightarrow$	Conclusion here is *not* a recommendation. Eliminate.
(E) Many antiques increase in value once they have had their ages authenticated by antique dealers. Since antique dealers tend to have plenty of valuable antiques, antique collectors who prefer to purchase the most valuable antiques should purchase antiques from antique dealers. *PrepTest 62 Sec4 Q25*	The conclusion matches that in the stimulus, but the evidence has too few variables. The entire argument is the second sentence: A (antique dealers) have lots of B (valuable antiques), so people who want B should go to A. Eliminate.

This time, only one answer choice had a different conclusion type than did the stimulus, so it was necessary to take the evidence into account in order to arrive at the correct answer.

Note that the first of these two practice questions was actually a Parallel Flaw question, but that the conclusion-typing method allowed you to arrive at the answer without doing any further work. Indeed, Parallel Flaw questions are very similar to Parallel Reasoning questions in that the correct answer must also use the same kind of evidence as in the stimulus to reach the same kind of conclusion as in the stimulus. Parallel Flaw questions, however, require that the correct answer also share the same type of flaw that is present in the stimulus.

Parallel Flaw Questions

Your initial approach to Parallel Flaw questions should be the same as your approach to Parallel Reasoning questions: identify and characterize the conclusion in the stimulus and eliminate any answer choice that does not share that same conclusion type. If there is more than one remaining choice, break down the evidence and identify the central flaw in the argument. Find an answer choice that also contains the same flaw. Be aware that many Parallel Flaw questions will contain Formal Logic. When you see Formal Logic in a Parallel Flaw stimulus, jot the terms down in some sort of shorthand—you'll see in our explanations that we use letters to represent the various terms in Formal Logic statements. Doing this will help you identify more easily how the argument is flawed and find an answer choice that commits the same reasoning error in the same way.

For example, imagine a stimulus that says: "John plays catch whenever he goes to the beach. John said he played catch yesterday, so he must have been at the beach." This argument confuses necessary and sufficient terms. Let (A) replace "John plays catch" and let (B) replace "beach." The argument's structure is now revealed: whenever (B) →(A). Therefore, because (A) → (B). You would then seek an answer choice that messes up Formal Logic terms in the same way.

Now, take a look at a couple of Parallel Flaw questions. Work through them using the strategies above; then check the following pages to see how an LSAT expert would approach the same questions.

LSAT Question	**My Analysis**
69. A book tour will be successful if it is well publicized and the author is an established writer. Julia is an established writer, and her book tour was successful. So her book tour must have been well publicized.	**Step 2:**
Which of the following exhibits a pattern of flawed reasoning most closely parallel to the pattern of flawed reasoning exhibited by the argument above?	**Step 1:**
	Step 3:
(A) This recipe will turn out only if one follows it exactly and uses high-quality ingredients. Arthur followed the recipe exactly and it turned out. Thus, Arthur must have used high-quality ingredients.	**Step 4:**
(B) If a computer has the fastest microprocessor and the most memory available, it will meet Aletha's needs this year. This computer met Aletha's needs last year. So it must have had the fastest microprocessor and the most memory available last year.	
(C) If cacti are kept in the shade and watered more than twice weekly, they will die. This cactus was kept in the shade, and it is now dead. Therefore, it must have been watered more than twice weekly.	
(D) A house will suffer from dry rot and poor drainage only if it is built near a high water table. This house suffers from dry rot and has poor drainage. Thus, it must have been built near a high water table.	

LSAT Question	**My Analysis**

(E) If one wears a suit that has double vents and narrow lapels, one will be fashionably dressed. The suit that Joseph wore to dinner last night had double vents and narrow lapels, so Joseph must have been fashionably dressed.

PrepTest58 Sec4 Q22

LSAT Question	**My Analysis**

70. When the famous art collector Vidmar died, a public auction of her collection, the largest privately owned, was held. "I can't possibly afford any of those works because hers is among the most valuable collections ever assembled by a single person," declared art lover MacNeil.

Step 2:

The flawed pattern of reasoning in which one of the following is most closely parallel to that in MacNeil's argument?

Step 1:

Step 3:

(A) Each word in the book is in French. So the whole book is in French.

Step 4:

(B) The city council voted unanimously to adopt the plan. So councilperson Martinez voted to adopt the plan.

(C) This paragraph is long. So the sentences that comprise it are long.

(D) The members of the company are old. So the company itself is old.

(E) The atoms comprising this molecule are elements. So the molecule itself is an element.

PrepTest62 Sec2 Q7

Here's how an LSAT expert applied the Logical Reasoning Method to the questions you just tried.

LSAT Question	Analysis
69. A book tour will be successful if it is well publicized and the author is an established writer. Julia is an established writer, and her book tour was successful. So her book tour must have been well publicized. →	**Step 2:** Conclusion: Julia's book tour must have been well publicized. Evidence: If a book tour is well publicized and the author is well established, the book tour will be successful. Julia, an established writer, had a successful book tour.
Which of the following exhibits a pattern of flawed reasoning most closely parallel to the pattern of flawed reasoning exhibited by the argument above? →	**Step 1:** The phrase "pattern of flawed reasoning most closely parallel" identifies this as a Parallel Flaw question.
	Step 3: Use letters to simplify the structure of the Formal Logic. If A (well publicized) and B (established writer), then C (successful book tour). Julia has B and C, so she must have A. Find an answer choice that follows the same flawed logic: If A and B, then C. One has B and C, so one must have A.
(A) This recipe will turn out only if one follows it exactly and uses high-quality ingredients. Arthur followed the recipe exactly and it turned out. Thus, Arthur must have used high-quality ingredients. →	**Step 4:** If A (recipe turns out), then B (follows exactly) and C (high-quality ingredients). Arthur has A and B, so he has C. No flaw. Eliminate.
(B) If a computer has the fastest microprocessor and the most memory available, it will meet Aletha's needs this year. This computer met Aletha's needs last year. So it must have had the fastest microprocessor and the most memory available last year. →	If A (fastest microprocessor) and B (most memory), then C (meet needs). The computer has C, so it must have A and B. Different flaw. Eliminate.
(C) If cacti are kept in the shade and watered more than twice weekly, they will die. This cactus was kept in the shade, and it is now dead. Therefore, it must have been watered more than twice weekly. →	Correct. This displays the same conclusion as does the stimulus: If B (kept in shade) and A (watered more than twice weekly), then C (dead). The cactus has B and C, so it must have A.
(D) A house will suffer from dry rot and poor drainage only if it is built near a high water table. This house suffers from dry rot and has poor drainage. Thus, it must have been built near a high water table. →	If A (dry rot) and B (poor drainage), then C (built near high water table). The house has A and B, so it must have C. No flaw. Eliminate.
(E) If one wears a suit that has double vents and narrow lapels, one will be fashionably dressed. The suit that Joseph wore to dinner last night had double vents and narrow lapels, so Joseph must have been fashionably dressed. *PrepTest 58 Sec4 Q22* →	If A (double vents) and B (narrow lapels), then C (fashionably dressed). Joseph had A and B, so he was C. No flaw. Eliminate.

LSAT Question	Analysis
70. When the famous art collector Vidmar died, a public auction of her collection, the largest privately owned, was held. "I can't possibly afford any of those works because hers is among the most valuable collections ever assembled by a single person," declared art lover MacNeil. →	**Step 2:** Conclusion: MacNeil asserts that she cannot afford any of Vidmar's works. Evidence: The collection is one of the most valuable ever assembled.
The flawed pattern of reasoning in which one of the following is most closely parallel to that in MacNeil's argument? →	**Step 1:** The phrase "flawed pattern of reasoning . . . is most closely parallel to" identifies this as a Parallel Flaw question.
	Step 3: MacNeil incorrectly attributes a characteristic of the whole (Vidmar's collection is highly valuable) to each of its parts (each work must be highly valuable). Find an answer choice that also incorrectly attributes something about the whole to each of its parts.
(A) Each word in the book is in French. So the whole book is in French. →	**Step 4:** Instead of assuming that what is true of the whole must be true of its parts, this argument assumes that what is true of the parts (each word) must be true of the whole (the entire book). Eliminate.
(B) The city council voted unanimously to adopt the plan. So councilperson Martinez voted to adopt the plan. →	There is no flaw present. Eliminate.
(C) This paragraph is long. So the sentences that comprise it are long. →	Correct. This choice attributes a characteristic of the whole (the paragraph is long) to its individual parts (the sentences must be long).
(D) The members of the company are old. So the company itself is old. →	This argument, like the one in choice (A), assumes that a characteristic (being old) that is true of the parts (company members) must be true of the whole (the company). Eliminate.
(E) The atoms comprising this molecule are elements. So the molecule itself is an element. *PrepTest62 Sec2 Q7* →	This argument assumes that a characteristic (made up of elements) applicable to the parts (atoms) must be applicable to the whole (a molecule). Eliminate.

IDENTIFY AND APPLY THE PRINCIPLE QUESTIONS

The final question type we'll discuss in this chapter asks you to identify the principle underlying the argument in the stimulus and then apply the principle to a similar argument in the correct answer. These Identify and Apply Principle questions (also referred to as Parallel Principle questions) appear rarely on the LSAT. One has been included on only about half of all recently administered LSATs. Fortunately, Parallel Principle questions are very similar to Parallel Reasoning and Parallel Flaw questions, so if you feel comfortable with those other question types, you should feel comfortable with Parallel Principle questions as well.

In the same way that the stimulus and correct answer in Parallel Flaw questions both contain the same faulty pattern of reasoning, the stimulus and correct answer in Parallel Principle questions both follow the same principle. Parallel Principle questions are similar to Parallel Reasoning and Parallel Flaw questions in that the correct answer will likely discuss a different topic than the stimulus; the only requirement is that the correct answer must be founded on the same principle as the stimulus. To attack Identify and Apply Principle questions efficiently, identify the principle—the broad, general rule—at work in the stimulus and then go through the choices to find the one that applies the identical principle. Try out the following example:

LSAT Question	My Analysis
71. Psychologist: The best way to recall a certain word or name that one is having trouble remembering is to occupy one's mind with other things, since often the more we strive to remember a certain word or name that we can't think of, the less likely it becomes that the word will come to mind. $\longrightarrow$	**Step 2:**
The principle that underlies the psychologist's argument underlies which one of the following arguments? $\longrightarrow$	**Step 1:**
	Step 3:
(A) Often, the best way to achieve happiness is to pursue other things besides wealth and fame, for there are wealthy and famous people who are not particularly happy, which suggests that true happiness does not consist in wealth and fame. $\longrightarrow$	**Step 4:**
(B) The best way to succeed in writing a long document is not to think about how much is left to write but only about the current paragraph, since on many occasions thinking about what remains to be done will be so discouraging that the writer will be tempted to abandon the project.	

LSAT Question	My Analysis
(C) The best way to overcome a serious mistake is to continue on confidently as though all is well. After all, one can overcome a serious mistake by succeeding in new challenges, and dwelling on one's errors usually distracts one's mind from new challenges.	
(D) The best way to fall asleep quickly is to engage in some mental diversion like counting sheep, because frequently the more one concentrates on falling asleep the lower the chance of falling asleep quickly.	
(E) The best way to cope with sorrow or grief is to turn one's attention to those who are experiencing even greater hardship, for in many circumstances this will make our own troubles seem bearable by comparison.	

PrepTest58 Sec1 Q2

Here's how an LSAT expert applied the Logical Reasoning Method to the questions you just tried.

LSAT Question	Analysis
71. Psychologist: The best way to recall a certain word or name that one is having trouble remembering is to occupy one's mind with other things, since often the more we strive to remember a certain word or name that we can't think of, the less likely it becomes that the word will come to mind.	**Step 2:** Conclusion: The best way to recall a word you cannot remember is to occupy your mind with other things. Evidence: The more you strive to remember a word you cannot think of, the less likely it becomes that the word will come to mind.
The principle that underlies the psychologist's argument underlies which one of the following arguments?	**Step 1:** The word "principle" signals a Principle question. The fact that the principle "underlies" both the stimulus and the correct answer indicates that this is a Parallel Principle question. The correct answer will follow the same principle as the stimulus.
	Step 3: Generalize the situation in the stimulus. Find the choice that follows the same principle.
(A) Often, the best way to achieve happiness is to pursue other things besides wealth and fame, for there are wealthy and famous people who are not particularly happy, which suggests that true happiness does not consist in wealth and fame.	**Step 4:** The reason for not pursuing wealth and fame in this answer choice is not that pursuing wealth and fame will prevent its achievement but that some wealthy and famous people are not happy. Eliminate.
(B) The best way to succeed in writing a long document is not to think about how much is left to write but only about the current paragraph, since on many occasions thinking about what remains to be done will be so discouraging that the writer will be tempted to abandon the project.	This one might look tempting, but it distorts the principle at work in the psychologist's argument. This choice doesn't advise complete distraction from the document, just a shift in focus from the entire document to a single paragraph. Eliminate.
(C) The best way to overcome a serious mistake is to continue on confidently as though all is well. After all, one can overcome a serious mistake by succeeding in new challenges, and dwelling on one's errors usually distracts one's mind from new challenges.	Here, distraction sounds like a negative thing, not a positive thing. Eliminate.
(D) The best way to fall asleep quickly is to engage in some mental diversion like counting sheep, because frequently the more one concentrates on falling asleep the lower the chance of falling asleep quickly.	Correct. Focusing on the outcome of falling asleep prevents that outcome from occurring; distracting oneself is the way to go. This is a precise match for the principle in the stimulus.
(E) The best way to cope with sorrow or grief is to turn one's attention to those who are experiencing even greater hardship, for in many circumstances this will make our own troubles seem bearable by comparison.	There's nothing about turning one's attention elsewhere for the sake of "comparison" in the psychologist's principle. Eliminate.

PrepTest58 Sec1 Q2

IDENTIFYING QUESTION STEMS

You've seen how the LSAT can test your ability to analyze and evaluate argument-based questions in a number of different ways. On Test Day, it will be essential for you to be able to differentiate among question types. If you struggle to understand what a question is asking or how to get to the right answer, you'll lose valuable time and energy. Experts know that the path to success in the Logical Reasoning section is to become familiar with each question type and to know immediately how to attack each question.

Practice

For each of the question stems below, identify the question type and mentally characterize the correct answer. Then compare your thinking to the expert analysis that follows.

Question Stem	My Analysis
72. Which of the following, if added to the premises, allows the argument's conclusion to be properly drawn?	
73. Which of the following best characterizes the argument's error of reasoning?	
74. Each of the following, if true, casts doubt on the argument EXCEPT:	
75. In evaluating the argument's conclusion, it would be most valuable to know whether	
76. Which of the following is an assumption required by the argument?	
77. Which of the following, if true, would do most to justify the conclusion drawn above?	
78. Which of the following, if true, most calls into question the argument above?	
79. The reasoning in the argument above is questionable because	
80. Which of the following is an assumption upon which the argument depends?	
81. The argument is vulnerable to criticism on which of the following grounds?	
82. Which of the following lends most support to the argument above?	
83. The conclusion drawn above is unwarranted because	

Question Stem	My Analysis
84. Which of the following principles most helps to justify the reasoning above?	
85. The conclusion of the argument follows logically if which one of the following is presupposed?	
86. Which of the following, if true, most undermines the argument above?	
87. The author makes which one of the following assumptions?	
88. The flawed reasoning in which one of the following is most similar to that in the argument above?	

Here's how an LSAT expert characterized each question stem:

Question Stem		Analysis
72. Which of the following, if added to the premises, allows the argument's conclusion to be properly drawn?	→	Sufficient Assumption question. Correct answer will guarantee the conclusion.
73. Which of the following best characterizes the argument's error of reasoning?	→	Flaw question. Correct answer will describe the argument's flawed assumption.
74. Each of the following, if true, casts doubt on the argument EXCEPT:	→	Weaken EXCEPT question. Incorrect choices will each weaken the argument's conclusion. Correct answer will be a strengthener or will have no impact on the conclusion.
75. In evaluating the argument's conclusion, it would be most valuable to know whether	→	Evaluate question. The correct answer will provide information that, if true, will either strengthen or weaken the conclusion and, if false, will have the opposite effect. Incorrect choices will be irrelevant, having no effect on the conclusion's likelihood.
76. Which of the following is an assumption required by the argument?	→	Necessary Assumption question. Correct answer will state the assumption that is necessary for the conclusion to stand. Can check using the Denial Test: when correct answer is negated, the conclusion falls apart.
77. Which of the following, if true, would do most to justify the conclusion drawn above?	→	Strengthen question. Correct answer will strengthen conclusion by supporting the argument's assumption.
78. Which of the following, if true, most calls into question the argument above?	→	Weaken question. Correct answer will weaken conclusion by attacking the argument's assumption.
79. The reasoning in the argument above is questionable because	→	Flaw question. Correct answer will describe the argument's flawed assumption.
80. Which of the following is an assumption upon which the argument depends?	→	Necessary Assumption question. Correct answer will state the assumption that is necessary for the conclusion to stand. Can check using the Denial Test: when correct answer is negated, the conclusion falls apart.
81. The argument is vulnerable to criticism on which of the following grounds?	→	Flaw question. Correct answer will describe the argument's flawed assumption.
82. Which of the following lends most support to the argument above?	→	Strengthen question. Correct answer will strengthen conclusion by supporting the argument's assumption.
83. The conclusion drawn above is unwarranted because	→	Flaw question. Correct answer will describe the argument's flawed assumption.

Question Stem		Analysis
84. Which of the following principles most helps to justify the reasoning above?	$\longrightarrow$	Identify the Principle Strengthen question. Correct answer will strengthen the conclusion in broadly worded terms.
85. The conclusion of the argument follows logically if which one of the following is presupposed?	$\longrightarrow$	Sufficient Assumption question. Correct answer will guarantee the conclusion.
86. Which of the following, if true, most undermines the argument above?	$\longrightarrow$	Weaken question. Correct answer will weaken conclusion by attacking the argument's assumption.
87. The author makes which one of the following assumptions?	$\longrightarrow$	Necessary Assumption question. Correct answer will state the assumption that is necessary for the conclusion to stand. Can check using the Denial Test: when correct answer is negated, the conclusion falls apart.
88. The flawed reasoning in which one of the following is most similar to that in the argument above?	$\longrightarrow$	Parallel Flaw question. The correct answer will contain an argument that is flawed in the same way as the argument in the stimulus is flawed.

Reflection

You may find that as you work through more and more argument-based questions, you start to notice the weak points in the arguments that you confront in everyday life—in advertisements, on the news, in written articles, in conversations. That's a good thing! If you are noticing that a television news anchor has just made an assumption, or thinking about how an article in a popular science journal could strengthen its main point, or thinking about how you could knock down a friend's argument against going to see your favorite jazz band with you, or noticing that a subway advertisement leaps to a conclusion without considering alternate possibilities, then you are learning to think like a lawyer. The more you can engage with the arguments you encounter on a daily basis in a skeptical, thoughtful way, the better prepared you will be for the LSAT and for what lies ahead in law school.

QUESTION POOL

Assumption

Previously Seen Stimuli

Here are a few questions featuring stimuli covered in Chapters 9 and 10. This time they appear with answer choices. These questions are arranged in roughly increasing order of difficulty.

1. Reducing stress lessens a person's sensitivity to pain. This is the conclusion reached by researchers who played extended audiotapes to patients before they underwent surgery and afterward while they were recovering. One tape consisted of conversation; the other consisted of music. Those who listened only to the latter tape required less anesthesia during surgery and fewer painkillers afterward than those who listened only to the former tape.

Which one of the following is an assumption on which the researchers' reasoning depends?

(A) All of the patients in the study listened to the same tape before surgery as they listened to after surgery.

(B) Anticipating surgery is no less stressful than recovering from surgery.

(C) Listening to music reduces stress.

(D) The psychological effects of music are not changed by anesthesia or painkillers.

(E) Both anesthesia and painkillers tend to reduce stress.

PrepTest52 Sec3 Q9

2. Theater managers will not rent a film if they do not believe it will generate enough total revenue—including food-and-beverage concession revenue—to yield a profit. Therefore, since film producers want their films to be shown as widely as possible, they tend to make films that theater managers consider attractive to younger audiences.

Which one of the following is an assumption required by the argument?

(A) Adults consume less of the sort of foods and beverages sold at movie concession stands than do either children or adolescents.

(B) Movies of the kinds that appeal to younger audiences almost never also appeal to older audiences.

(C) Food-and-beverage concession stands in movie theaters are usually more profitable than the movies that are shown.

(D) Theater managers generally believe that a film that is attractive to younger audiences is more likely to be profitable than other films.

(E) Films that have an appeal to older audiences almost never generate a profit for theaters that show them.

PrepTest58 Sec1 Q14

3. A retrospective study is a scientific study that tries to determine the causes of subjects' present characteristics by looking for significant connections between the present characteristics of subjects and what happened to those subjects in the past, before the study began. Because retrospective studies of human subjects must use the subjects' reports about their own pasts, however, such studies cannot reliably determine the causes of human subjects' present characteristics.

Which one of the following, if assumed, enables the argument's conclusion to be properly drawn?

(A) Whether or not a study of human subjects can reliably determine the causes of those subjects' present characteristics may depend at least in part on the extent to which that study uses inaccurate reports about the subjects' pasts.

(B) A retrospective study cannot reliably determine the causes of human subjects' present characteristics unless there exist correlations between the present characteristics of the subjects and what happened to those subjects in the past.

(C) In studies of human subjects that attempt to find connections between subjects' present characteristics and what happened to those subjects in the past, the subjects' reports about their own pasts are highly susceptible to inaccuracy.

(D) If a study of human subjects uses only accurate reports about the subjects' pasts, then that study can reliably determine the causes of those subjects' present characteristics.

(E) Every scientific study in which researchers look for significant connections between the present characteristics of subjects and what happened to those subjects in the past must use the subjects' reports about their own pasts.

PrepTest 62 Sec2 Q9

4. Economist: Our economy's weakness is the direct result of consumers' continued reluctance to spend, which in turn is caused by factors such as high-priced goods and services. This reluctance is exacerbated by the fact that the average income is significantly lower than it was five years ago. Thus, even though it is not a perfect solution, if the government were to lower income taxes, the economy would improve.

Which one of the following is an assumption required by the economist's argument?

(A) Increasing consumer spending will cause prices for goods and services to decrease.

(B) If consumer spending increases, the average income will increase.

(C) If income taxes are not lowered, consumers' wages will decline even further.

(D) Consumers will be less reluctant to spend money if income taxes are lowered.

(E) Lowering income taxes will have no effect on government spending.

PrepTest58 Sec1 Q19

5. Critic: The idealized world portrayed in romance literature is diametrically opposed to the debased world portrayed in satirical literature. Nevertheless, the major characters in both types of works have moral qualities that reflect the worlds in which they are presented. Comedy and tragedy, meanwhile, require that the moral qualities of major characters change during the course of the action. Therefore, neither tragedy nor comedy can be classified as satirical literature or romance literature.

The critic's conclusion follows logically if which one of the following is assumed?

(A) Some characters in comedies and tragedies are neither debased nor idealized.

(B) The visions of the world portrayed in works of tragedy and works of comedy change during the course of the action.

(C) If a character in a tragedy is idealized at the beginning of the action depicted in the tragedy, he or she must be debased at the end.

(D) In romance literature and satirical literature, characters' moral qualities do not change during the course of the action.

(E) Both comedy and tragedy require that the moral qualities of minor characters change during the course of the action.

PrepTest56 Sec2 Q10

6. Anyone who believes in democracy has a high regard for the wisdom of the masses. Griley, however, is an elitist who believes that any artwork that is popular is unlikely to be good. Thus, Griley does not believe in democracy.

The conclusion follows logically if which one of the following is assumed?

(A) Anyone who believes that an artwork is unlikely to be good if it is popular is an elitist.

(B) Anyone who believes that if an artwork is popular it is unlikely to be good does not have a high regard for the wisdom of the masses.

(C) If Griley is not an elitist, then he has a high regard for the wisdom of the masses.

(D) Anyone who does not have a high regard for the wisdom of the masses is an elitist who believes that if an artwork is popular it is unlikely to be good.

(E) Unless Griley believes in democracy, Griley does not have a high regard for the wisdom of the masses.

PrepTest58 Sec4 Q19

7. Speaker: Like many contemporary critics, Smith argues that the true meaning of an author's statements can be understood only through insight into the author's social circumstances. But this same line of analysis can be applied to Smith's own words. Thus, if she is right we should be able, at least in part, to discern from Smith's social circumstances the "true meaning" of Smith's statements. This, in turn, suggests that Smith herself is not aware of the true meaning of her own words.

The speaker's main conclusion logically follows if which one of the following is assumed?

(A) Insight into the intended meaning of an author's work is not as important as insight into its true meaning.

(B) Smith lacks insight into her own social circumstances.

(C) There is just one meaning that Smith intends her work to have.

(D) Smith's theory about the relation of social circumstances to the understanding of meaning lacks insight.

(E) The intended meaning of an author's work is not always good evidence of its true meaning.

PrepTest62 Sec2 Q15

8. All etching tools are either pin-tipped or bladed. While some bladed etching tools are used for engraving, some are not. On the other hand, all pin-tipped etching tools are used for engraving. Thus, there are more etching tools that are used for engraving than there are etching tools that are not used for engraving.

The conclusion of the argument follows logically if which one of the following is assumed?

(A) All tools used for engraving are etching tools as well.
(B) There are as many pin-tipped etching tools as there are bladed etching tools.
(C) No etching tool is both pin-tipped and bladed.
(D) The majority of bladed etching tools are not used for engraving.
(E) All etching tools that are not used for engraving are bladed.

PrepTest62 Sec4 Q16

9. There are far fewer independent bookstores than there were 20 years ago, largely because chain bookstores prospered and multiplied during that time. Thus, chain bookstores' success has been to the detriment of book consumers, for the shortage of independent bookstores has prevented the variety of readily available books from growing as much as it otherwise would have.

Which one of the following is an assumption on which the argument relies?

(A) Book consumers would be better off if there were a greater variety of readily available books than there currently is.
(B) Independent bookstores typically do not sell the kinds of books that are available in chain bookstores.
(C) The average bookstore today is larger than the average bookstore of 20 years ago.
(D) The average bookstore today is smaller than the average bookstore of 20 years ago.
(E) Some book consumers value low prices more highly than wide selection.

PrepTest56 Sec3 Q9

10. Humanitarian considerations aside, sheer economics dictates that country X should institute, as country Y has done, a nationwide system of air and ground transportation for conveying seriously injured persons to specialized trauma centers. Timely access to the kind of medical care that only specialized centers can provide could save the lives of many people. The earnings of these people would result in a substantial increase in country X's gross national product, and the taxes paid on those earnings would substantially augment government revenues.

The argument depends on the assumption that

(A) lifetime per-capita income is roughly the same in country X as it is in country Y
(B) there are no specialized trauma centers in country X at present
(C) the treatment of seriously injured persons in trauma centers is not more costly than treatment elsewhere
(D) there would be a net increase in employment in country X if more persons survived serious injury
(E) most people seriously injured in automobile accidents in country X do not now receive treatment in specialized trauma centers

PrepTest52 Sec3 Q13

11. Neural connections carrying signals from the cortex (the brain region responsible for thought) down to the amygdala (a brain region crucial for emotions) are less well developed than connections carrying signals from the amygdala up to the cortex. Thus, the amygdala exerts a greater influence on the cortex than vice versa.

The argument's conclusion follows logically if which one of the following is assumed?

(A) The influence that the amygdala exerts on the rest of the brain is dependent on the influence that the cortex exerts on the rest of the brain.
(B) No other brain region exerts more influence on the cortex than does the amygdala.
(C) The region of the brain that has the most influence on the cortex is the one that has the most highly developed neural connections to the cortex.
(D) The amygdala is not itself controlled by one or more other regions of the brain.
(E) The degree of development of a set of neural connections is directly proportional to the influence transmitted across those connections.

PrepTest52 Sec1 Q20

12. Sociologist: Widespread acceptance of the idea that individuals are incapable of looking after their own welfare is injurious to a democracy. So legislators who value democracy should not propose any law prohibiting behavior that is not harmful to anyone besides the person engaging in it. After all, the assumptions that appear to guide legislators will often become widely accepted.

The sociologist's argument requires the assumption that

(A) democratically elected legislators invariably have favorable attitudes toward the preservation of democracy

(B) people tend to believe what is believed by those who are prominent and powerful

(C) legislators often seem to be guided by the assumption that individuals are incapable of looking after their own welfare, even though these legislators also seem to value democracy

(D) in most cases, behavior that is harmful to the person who engages in it is harmful to no one else

(E) a legislator proposing a law prohibiting an act that can harm only the person performing the act will seem to be assuming that individuals are incapable of looking after their own welfare

PrepTest52 Sec1 Q25

13. One should never sacrifice one's health in order to acquire money, for without health, happiness is not obtainable.

The conclusion of the argument follows logically if which one of the following is assumed?

(A) Money should be acquired only if its acquisition will not make happiness unobtainable.

(B) In order to be happy one must have either money or health.

(C) Health should be valued only as a precondition for happiness.

(D) Being wealthy is, under certain conditions, conducive to unhappiness.

(E) Health is more conducive to happiness than wealth is.

PrepTest62 Sec2 Q17

14. People want to be instantly and intuitively liked. Those persons who are perceived as forming opinions of others only after cautiously gathering and weighing the evidence are generally resented. Thus, it is imprudent to appear prudent.

Which one of the following, if assumed, enables the argument's conclusion to be properly drawn?

(A) People who act spontaneously are well liked.

(B) Imprudent people act instantly and intuitively.

(C) People resent those less prudent than themselves.

(D) People who are intuitive know instantly when they like someone.

(E) It is imprudent to cause people to resent you.

PrepTest52 Sec1 Q17

15. University president: Our pool of applicants has been shrinking over the past few years. One possible explanation of this unwelcome phenomenon is that we charge too little for tuition and fees. Prospective students and their parents conclude that the quality of education they would receive at this institution is not as high as that offered by institutions with higher tuition. So, if we want to increase the size of our applicant pool, we need to raise our tuition and fees.

The university president's argument requires the assumption that

(A) the proposed explanation for the decline in applications applies in this case

(B) the quality of a university education is dependent on the amount of tuition charged by the university

(C) an increase in tuition and fees at the university would guarantee a larger applicant pool

(D) there is no additional explanation for the university's shrinking applicant pool

(E) the amount charged by the university for tuition has not increased in recent years

PrepTest62 Sec2 Q25

New Questions

Practice on questions that have not yet appeared in the book. These questions are arranged in roughly increasing order of difficulty.

16. Paleontologist: Plesiosauromorphs were gigantic, long-necked marine reptiles that ruled the oceans during the age of the dinosaurs. Most experts believe that plesiosauromorphs lurked and quickly ambushed their prey. However, plesiosauromorphs probably hunted by chasing their prey over long distances. Plesiosauromorph fins were quite long and thin, like the wings of birds specialized for long-distance flight.

    Which one of the following is an assumption on which the paleontologist's argument depends?

    (A) Birds and reptiles share many physical features because they descend from common evolutionary ancestors.

    (B) During the age of dinosaurs, plesiosauromorphs were the only marine reptiles that had long, thin fins.

    (C) A gigantic marine animal would not be able to find enough food to meet the caloric requirements dictated by its body size if it did not hunt by chasing prey over long distances.

    (D) Most marine animals that chase prey over long distances are specialized for long-distance swimming.

    (E) The shape of a marine animal's fin affects the way the animal swims in the same way as the shape of a bird's wing affects the way the bird flies.

    PrepTest62 Sec2 Q12

17. Critic: Works of modern literature cannot be tragedies as those of ancient playwrights and storytellers were unless their protagonists are seen as possessing nobility, which endures through the calamities that befall one. In an age that no longer takes seriously the belief that human endeavors are governed by fate, it is therefore impossible for a contemporary work of literature to be a tragedy.

    Which one of the following is an assumption required by the critic's argument?

    (A) Whether or not a work of literature is a tragedy should not depend on characteristics of its audience.

    (B) The belief that human endeavors are governed by fate is false.

    (C) Most plays that were once classified as tragedies were misclassified.

    (D) Those whose endeavors are not regarded as governed by fate will not be seen as possessing nobility.

    (E) If an ignoble character in a work of literature endures through a series of misfortunes, that work of literature is not a tragedy.

    PrepTest58 Sec4 Q17

18. City councilperson: Many city residents oppose the city art commission's proposed purchase of an unusual stone edifice, on the grounds that art critics are divided over whether the edifice really qualifies as art. But I argue that the purpose of art is to cause experts to debate ideas, including ideas about what constitutes art itself. Since the edifice has caused experts to debate what constitutes art itself, it does qualify as art.

    Which one of the following, if assumed, enables the conclusion of the city councilperson's argument to be properly inferred?

    (A) Nothing qualifies as art unless it causes debate among experts.

    (B) If an object causes debate among experts, no expert can be certain whether that object qualifies as art.

    (C) The purchase of an object that fulfills the purpose of art should not be opposed.

    (D) Any object that fulfills the purpose of art qualifies as art.

    (E) The city art commission should purchase the edifice if it qualifies as art.

    PrepTest58 Sec1 Q12

19. Fund-raiser: A charitable organization rarely gives its
donors the right to vote on its policies. The
inability to directly influence how charities spend
contributions makes potential donors feel less of
an emotional connection to the charity. Thus,
most charities could probably increase the amount
of money they raise through donations by giving
donors the right to vote.

Which one of the following is an assumption that the
fund-raiser's argument depends on?

(A) The most effective way for a charity to give
potential donors the ability to directly
influence what that charity does is by giving
donors the right to vote on the charity's
policies.

(B) Most charities that have increased the amount
of money they raise through donations have
done so by making potential donors feel a
greater emotional connection to the charity.

(C) Every charity that has given donors the right to
vote on its policies has seen a marked increase
in the emotional connection donors have to
that charity.

(D) Most potential donors to a charity are unwilling
to give that charity any money if there is no
possible way for them to have any influence
on that charity's policies.

(E) The emotional connection potential donors feel
to a charity can affect the amount of money
that charity raises through donations.

PrepTest56 Sec3 Q18

20. If there are sentient beings on planets outside our solar
system, we will not be able to determine this anytime in
the near future unless some of these beings are at least
as intelligent as humans. We will not be able to send
spacecraft to planets outside our solar system anytime in
the near future, and any sentient being on another planet
capable of communicating with us anytime in the near
future would have to be at least as intelligent as we are.

The argument's conclusion can be properly inferred if
which one of the following is assumed?

(A) There are no sentient beings on planets in our
solar system other than those on Earth.

(B) Any beings that are at least as intelligent as
humans would want to communicate with
sentient beings outside their own solar systems.

(C) If there is a sentient being on another planet
that is as intelligent as humans are, we will not
be able to send spacecraft to the being's planet
anytime in the near future.

(D) If a sentient being on another planet cannot
communicate with us, then the only way to
detect its existence is by sending a spacecraft
to its planet.

(E) Any sentient beings on planets outside our solar
system that are at least as intelligent as humans
would be capable of communicating with us.

PrepTest62 Sec4 Q18

Flaw

Previously Seen Stimuli

Here are a few questions featuring stimuli covered in Chapters 9 and 10. This time they appear with answer choices. These questions are arranged in roughly increasing order of difficulty.

21. Area resident: Childhood lead poisoning has declined steadily since the 1970s, when leaded gasoline was phased out and lead paint was banned. But recent statistics indicate that 25 percent of this area's homes still contain lead paint that poses significant health hazards. Therefore, if we eliminate the lead paint in those homes, childhood lead poisoning in the area will finally be eradicated.

The area resident's argument is flawed in that it

(A) relies on statistical claims that are likely to be unreliable

(B) relies on an assumption that is tantamount to assuming that the conclusion is true

(C) fails to consider that there may be other significant sources of lead in the area's environment

(D) takes for granted that lead paint in homes can be eliminated economically

(E) takes for granted that children reside in all of the homes in the area that contain lead paint

PrepTest62 Sec2 Q5

22. Science journalist: Europa, a moon of Jupiter, is covered with ice. Data recently transmitted by a spacecraft strongly suggest that there are oceans of liquid water deep under the ice. Life as we know it could evolve only in the presence of liquid water. Hence, it is likely that at least primitive life has evolved on Europa.

The science journalist's argument is most vulnerable to criticism on the grounds that it

(A) takes for granted that if a condition would be necessary for the evolution of life as we know it, then such life could not have evolved anywhere that this condition does not hold

(B) fails to address adequately the possibility that there are conditions necessary for the evolution of life in addition to the presence of liquid water

(C) takes for granted that life is likely to be present on Europa if, but only if, life evolved on Europa

(D) overlooks the possibility that there could be unfamiliar forms of life that have evolved without the presence of liquid water

(E) takes for granted that no conditions on Europa other than the supposed presence of liquid water could have accounted for the data transmitted by the spacecraft

PrepTest62 Sec4 Q10

23. Chinh: Television producers should not pay attention to the preferences of the viewing public when making creative decisions. Great painters do not consider what the museum-going public wants to see.

Lana: But television is expressly for the viewing public. So a producer is more like a CEO than like an artist. Just as a company would be foolhardy not to consider consumers' tastes when developing products, the TV producer must consider viewers' preferences.

According to Lana, Chinh's argument is flawed in that it

(A) is circular

(B) relies on a sample of consumers that is unrepresentative of consumers in general

(C) infers from the effect produced by an action that the action is intended to produce that effect

(D) fails to consider the possibility that painters may in fact try to please the museum-going public

(E) offers a faulty analogy

PrepTest56 Sec2 Q5

24. Of all the Arabic epic poems that have been popular at various times, only *Sirat Bani Hilal* is still publicly performed. Furthermore, while most other epics were only recited, *Sirat Bani Hilal* has usually been sung. The musical character of the performance, therefore, is the main reason for its longevity.

The argument is most vulnerable to criticism on the grounds that it

(A) relies on evidence that is in principle impossible to corroborate

(B) relies on a source of evidence that may be biased

(C) takes for granted that a particular correlation is causal

(D) takes what may be mere popular opinion to be an established fact

(E) takes a sufficient condition to be a necessary condition

PrepTest56 Sec3 Q17

25. If Agnes's research proposal is approved, the fourth-floor lab must be cleaned out for her use. Immanuel's proposal, on the other hand, requires less space. So if his proposal is approved, he will continue to work in the second-floor lab. Only those proposals the director supports will be approved. So since the director will support both proposals, the fourth-floor lab must be cleaned out.

The argument's reasoning is flawed because the argument

(A) presumes, without providing justification, that the fourth-floor lab is bigger than the second-floor lab

(B) fails to consider the possibility that a proposal will be rejected even with the director's support

(C) presumes, without providing justification, that the director will support both proposals with equal enthusiasm

(D) fails to consider the possibility that Immanuel will want to move to a bigger lab once his proposal is approved

(E) presumes, without providing justification, that no lab other than the fourth-floor lab would be adequate for Agnes's research

PrepTest56 Sec2 Q15

26. The average length of stay for patients at Edgewater Hospital is four days, compared to six days at University Hospital. Since studies show that recovery rates at the two hospitals are similar for patients with similar illnesses, University Hospital could decrease its average length of stay without affecting quality of care.

The reasoning in the argument is most vulnerable to criticism on the grounds that the argument

(A) equates the quality of care at a hospital with patients' average length of stay

(B) treats a condition that will ensure the preservation of quality of care as a condition that is required to preserve quality of care

(C) fails to take into account the possibility that patients at Edgewater Hospital tend to be treated for different illnesses than patients at University Hospital

(D) presumes, without providing justification, that the length of time patients stay in the hospital is never relevant to the recovery rates of these patients

(E) fails to take into account the possibility that patients at University Hospital generally prefer longer hospital stays

PrepTest52 Sec3 Q16

The explanations to these questions begin on page 649.

New Questions

Practice on questions that have not yet appeared in the book. These questions are arranged in roughly increasing order of difficulty.

27. This region's swimmers generally swim during the day because they are too afraid of sharks to swim after dark but feel safe swimming during daylight hours. Yet all recent shark attacks on swimmers in the area have occurred during the day, indicating that, contrary to popular opinion, it is not more dangerous to swim here at night than during the day.

    The reasoning in the argument is most vulnerable to criticism on the grounds that it

    (A) overlooks the possibility that some sharks are primarily nocturnal hunters

    (B) bases its conclusion on evidence from an unreliable source

    (C) overlooks the possibility that swimmers might feel anxiety caused by not being able to see one's surroundings in the dark

    (D) presumes, without providing justification, that swimmers cannot be the most knowledgeable about which times of day are safest for swimming

    (E) fails to take into account the possibility that the number of shark attacks at night would increase dramatically if more people swam at night

    PrepTest56 Sec2 Q1

28. Panelist: Medical research articles cited in popular newspapers or magazines are more likely than other medical research articles to be cited in subsequent medical research. Thus, it appears that medical researchers' judgments of the importance of prior research are strongly influenced by the publicity received by that research and do not strongly correspond to the research's true importance.

    The panelist's argument is most vulnerable to criticism on the grounds that it

    (A) presents counterarguments to a view that is not actually held by any medical researcher

    (B) fails to consider the possibility that popular newspapers and magazines do a good job of identifying the most important medical research articles

    (C) takes for granted that coverage of medical research in the popular press is more concerned with the eminence of the scientists involved than with the content of their research

    (D) fails to consider the possibility that popular newspapers and magazines are able to review only a minuscule percentage of medical research articles

    (E) draws a conclusion that is logically equivalent to its premise

    PrepTest52 Sec3 Q4

29. Factory manager: One reason the automobile parts this factory produces are expensive is that our manufacturing equipment is outdated and inefficient. Our products would be more competitively priced if we were to refurbish the factory completely with new, more efficient equipment. Therefore, since to survive in today's market we have to make our products more competitively priced, we must completely refurbish the factory in order to survive.

    The reasoning in the factory manager's argument is flawed because this argument

    (A) fails to recognize that the price of a particular commodity can change over time

    (B) shifts without justification from treating something as one way of achieving a goal to treating it as the only way of achieving that goal

    (C) argues that one thing is the cause of another when the evidence given indicates that the second thing may in fact be the cause of the first

    (D) recommends a solution to a problem without first considering any possible causes of that problem

    (E) fails to make a definite recommendation and instead merely suggests that some possible course of action might be effective

    PrepTest58 Sec4 Q8

30. A good way to get over one's fear of an activity one finds terrifying is to do it repeatedly. For instance, over half of people who have parachuted only once report being extremely frightened by the experience, while less than 1 percent of those who have parachuted ten times or more report being frightened by it.

    The reasoning in the argument is most vulnerable to criticism on the grounds that the argument

    (A) takes for granted that the greater the number of dangerous activities one engages in the less one is frightened by any one of them

    (B) neglects to consider those people who have parachuted more than once but fewer than ten times

    (C) takes for granted that people do not know how frightening something is unless they have tried it

    (D) fails to take into account the possibility that people would be better off if they did not do things that terrify them

    (E) overlooks the possibility that most people who have parachuted many times did not find it frightening initially

    PrepTest52 Sec3 Q21

31. Editorial: A recent survey shows that 77 percent of
    people feel that crime is increasing and that
    87 percent feel the judicial system should be handing
    out tougher sentences. Therefore, the government
    must firmly address the rising crime rate.

    The reasoning in the editorial's argument is most
    vulnerable to criticism on the grounds that the argument

    (A) appeals to survey results that are inconsistent
        because they suggest that more people are
        concerned about the sentencing of criminals
        than are concerned about crime itself
    (B) presumes, without providing justification, that
        there is a correlation between criminal offenders
        being treated leniently and a high crime rate
    (C) fails to consider whether other surveys showing
        different results have been conducted over the
        years
    (D) fails to distinguish between the crime rate's
        actually rising and people's believing that the
        crime rate is rising
    (E) presumes, without providing justification, that
        tougher sentences are the most effective means
        of alleviating the crime problem

    PrepTest58 Sec4 Q14

32. Many symptoms of mental illnesses are affected by
    organic factors such as a deficiency in a compound in
    the brain. What is surprising, however, is the tremendous
    variation among different countries in the incidence of
    these symptoms in people with mental illnesses. This
    variation establishes that the organic factors that affect
    symptoms of mental illnesses are not distributed evenly
    around the globe.

    The reasoning above is most vulnerable to criticism on
    the grounds that it

    (A) does not say how many different mental
        illnesses are being discussed
    (B) neglects the possibility that nutritional factors
        that contribute to deficiencies in compounds in
        the brain vary from culture to culture
    (C) fails to consider the possibility that cultural
        factors significantly affect how mental illnesses
        manifest themselves in symptoms
    (D) presumes, without providing justification, that
        any change in brain chemistry manifests itself
        as a change in mental condition
    (E) presumes, without providing justification, that
        mental phenomena are only manifestations of
        physical phenomena

    PrepTest62 Sec4 Q13

33. Despite the efforts of a small minority of graduate
    students at one university to unionize, the majority of
    graduate students there remain unaware of the attempt.
    Most of those who are aware believe that a union would
    not represent their interests or that, if it did, it would not
    effectively pursue them. Thus, the graduate students at
    the university should not unionize, since the majority of
    them obviously disapprove of the attempt.

    The reasoning in the argument is most vulnerable to
    criticism on the grounds that the argument

    (A) tries to establish a conclusion simply on the
        premise that the conclusion agrees with a
        long-standing practice
    (B) fails to exclude alternative explanations for why
        some graduate students disapprove of unionizing
    (C) presumes that simply because a majority of a
        population is unaware of something, it must
        not be a good idea
    (D) ignores the possibility that although a union
        might not effectively pursue graduate student
        interests, there are other reasons for unionizing
    (E) blurs the distinction between active disapproval
        and mere lack of approval

    PrepTest58 Sec4 Q18

34. George: Throughout the 1980s and early 1990s, hardly
    anyone learned ballroom dancing. Why is it that a
    large number of people now take ballroom
    dancing lessons?

    Boris: It's because, beginning in 1995, many people
    learned the merengue and several related
    ballroom dances. Because these dances are so
    popular, other ballroom dances are now catching on.

    Boris's response to George is most vulnerable to
    criticism because it fails to

    (A) show that the people who learned the merengue
        are the same people who are now interested in
        other ballroom dances
    (B) explain why ballroom dancing was so unpopular
        before 1995
    (C) relate the merengue to the forms of dancing that
        were more prevalent before 1995
    (D) account for the beginning of the revival of
        interest in ballroom dancing
    (E) demonstrate that all types of ballroom dancing
        are currently popular

    PrepTest56 Sec3 Q21

Strengthen/Weaken

Previously Seen Stimuli

Here are a few questions featuring stimuli covered in Chapters 9 and 10. This time they appear with answer choices. These questions are arranged in roughly increasing order of difficulty.

35. To keep one's hands warm during the winter, one never needs gloves or mittens. One can always keep one's hands warm simply by putting on an extra layer of clothing, such as a thermal undershirt or a sweater. After all, keeping one's vital organs warm can keep one's hands warm as well.

Which one of the following, if true, most weakens the argument?

(A) Maintaining the temperature of your hands is far less important, physiologically, than maintaining the temperature of your torso.
(B) Several layers of light garments will keep one's vital organs warmer than will one or two heavy garments.
(C) Wearing an extra layer of clothing will not keep one's hands warm at temperatures low enough to cause frostbite.
(D) Keeping one's hands warm by putting on an extra layer of clothing is less effective than turning up the heat.
(E) The physical effort required to put on an extra layer of clothing does not stimulate circulation enough to warm your hands.

PrepTest58 Sec4 Q2

36. Carol Morris wants to own a majority of the shares of the city's largest newspaper, *The Daily*. The only obstacle to Morris's amassing a majority of these shares is that Azedcorp, which currently owns a majority, has steadfastly refused to sell. Industry analysts nevertheless predict that Morris will soon be the majority owner of *The Daily*.

Which one of the following, if true, provides the most support for the industry analysts' prediction?

(A) Azedcorp does not own shares of any newspaper other than *The Daily*.
(B) Morris has recently offered Azedcorp much more for its shares of *The Daily* than Azedcorp paid for them.
(C) No one other than Morris has expressed any interest in purchasing a majority of *The Daily*'s shares.
(D) Morris already owns more shares of *The Daily* than anyone except Azedcorp.
(E) Azedcorp is financially so weak that bankruptcy will probably soon force the sale of its newspaper holdings.

PrepTest62 Sec2 Q4

37. Robert: The school board is considering adopting a year-round academic schedule that eliminates the traditional three-month summer vacation. This schedule should be adopted, since teachers need to cover more new material during the school year than they do now.

Samantha: The proposed schedule will not permit teachers to cover more new material. Even though the schedule eliminates summer vacation, it adds six new two-week breaks, so the total number of school days will be about the same as before.

Which one of the following, if true, is a response Robert could make that would counter Samantha's argument?

(A) Teachers would be willing to accept elimination of the traditional three-month summer vacation as long as the total vacation time they are entitled to each year is not reduced.
(B) Most parents who work outside the home find it difficult to arrange adequate supervision for their school-age children over the traditional three-month summer vacation.
(C) In school districts that have adopted a year-round schedule that increases the number of school days per year, students show a deeper understanding and better retention of new material.
(D) Teachers spend no more than a day of class time reviewing old material when students have been away from school for only a few weeks, but have to spend up to a month of class time reviewing after a three-month summer vacation.
(E) Students prefer taking a long vacation from school during the summer to taking more frequent but shorter vacations spread throughout the year.

PrepTest52 Sec1 Q9

38. Researchers announced recently that over the past
25 years the incidence of skin cancer caused by
exposure to harmful rays from the sun has continued to
grow in spite of the increasingly widespread use of
sunscreens. This shows that using sunscreen is unlikely
to reduce a person's risk of developing such skin cancer.

Which one of the following, if true, most weakens the
argument?

(A) Most people who purchase a sunscreen product
will not purchase the most expensive brand
available.

(B) Skin cancer generally develops among the very
old as a result of sunburns experienced when
very young.

(C) The development of sunscreens by pharmaceutical
companies was based upon research conducted
by dermatologists.

(D) People who know that they are especially
susceptible to skin cancer are generally
disinclined to spend a large amount of time
in the sun.

(E) Those who use sunscreens most regularly are
people who believe themselves to be most
susceptible to skin cancer.

PrepTest62 Sec4 Q5

39. Perry: Worker-owned businesses require workers to
spend time on management decision-making and
investment strategy, tasks that are not directly
productive. Also, such businesses have less
extensive divisions of labor than do investor-
owned businesses. Such inefficiencies can lead to
low profitability, and thus increase the risk for
lenders. Therefore, lenders seeking to reduce their
risk should not make loans to worker-owned
businesses.

Which one of the following, if true, most seriously
weakens Perry's argument?

(A) Businesses with the most extensive divisions of
labor sometimes fail to make the fullest use of
their most versatile employees' potential.

(B) Lenders who specialize in high-risk loans are
the largest source of loans for worker-owned
businesses.

(C) Investor-owned businesses are more likely than
worker-owned businesses are to receive
start-up loans.

(D) Worker-owned businesses have traditionally
obtained loans from cooperative lending
institutions established by coalitions of
worker-owned businesses.

(E) In most worker-owned businesses, workers
compensate for inefficiencies by working
longer hours than do workers in investor-
owned businesses.

PrepTest52 Sec1 Q12

40. Tissue biopsies taken on patients who have undergone
throat surgery show that those who snored frequently
were significantly more likely to have serious
abnormalities in their throat muscles than those who
snored rarely or not at all. This shows that snoring can
damage the throat of the snorer.

Which one of the following, if true, most strengthens
the argument?

(A) The study relied on the subjects' self-reporting
to determine whether or not they snored
frequently.

(B) The patients' throat surgery was not undertaken
to treat abnormalities in their throat muscles.

(C) All of the test subjects were of similar age and
weight and in similar states of health.

(D) People who have undergone throat surgery are
no more likely to snore than people who have
not undergone throat surgery.

(E) The abnormalities in the throat muscles discovered
in the study do not cause snoring.

PrepTest62 Sec2 Q16

New Questions

Practice on questions that have not yet appeared in the book. These questions are arranged in roughly increasing order of difficulty.

41. Economist: During a recession, a company can cut personnel costs either by laying off some employees without reducing the wages of remaining employees or by reducing the wages of all employees without laying off anyone. Both damage morale, but layoffs damage it less, since the aggrieved have, after all, left. Thus, when companies must reduce personnel costs during recessions, they are likely to lay off employees.

    Which one of the following, if true, most strengthens the economist's reasoning?

    (A) Employee morale is usually the primary concern driving companies' decisions about whether to lay off employees or to reduce their wages.
    (B) In general, companies increase wages only when they are unable to find enough qualified employees.
    (C) Some companies will be unable to make a profit during recessions no matter how much they reduce personnel costs.
    (D) When companies cut personnel costs during recessions by reducing wages, some employees usually resign.
    (E) Some companies that have laid off employees during recessions have had difficulty finding enough qualified employees once economic growth resumed.

    PrepTest56 Sec3 Q8

42. Letter to the editor: The Planning Department budget increased from $100,000 in 2001 to $524,000 for this year. However, this does not justify your conclusion in yesterday's editorial that the department now spends five times as much money as it did in 2001 to perform the same duties.

    Which one of the following, if true, most helps to support the claim made in the letter regarding the justification of the editorial's conclusion?

    (A) Departments other than the Planning Department have had much larger budget increases since 2001.
    (B) Since 2001, the Planning Department has dramatically reduced its spending on overtime pay.
    (C) In some years between 2001 and this year, the Planning Department budget did not increase.
    (D) The budget figures used in the original editorial were adjusted for inflation.
    (E) A restructuring act, passed in 2003, broadened the duties of the Planning Department.

    PrepTest58 Sec1 Q3

43. One theory to explain the sudden extinction of all dinosaurs points to "drug overdoses" as the cause. Angiosperms, a certain class of plants, first appeared at the time that dinosaurs became extinct. These plants produce amino-acid-based alkaloids that are psychoactive agents. Most plant-eating mammals avoid these potentially lethal poisons because they taste bitter. Moreover, mammals have livers that help detoxify such drugs. However, dinosaurs could neither taste the bitterness nor detoxify the substance once it was ingested. This theory receives its strongest support from the fact that it helps explain why so many dinosaur fossils are found in unusual and contorted positions.

    Which one of the following, if true, would most undermine the theory presented above?

    (A) Many fossils of large mammals are found in contorted positions.
    (B) Angiosperms provide a great deal of nutrition.
    (C) Carnivorous dinosaurs mostly ate other, vegetarian, dinosaurs that fed on angiosperms.
    (D) Some poisonous plants do not produce amino-acid-based alkaloids.
    (E) Mammals sometimes die of drug overdoses from eating angiosperms.

    PrepTest 52 Sec3 Q19

44. Researchers have found that children in large families—particularly the younger siblings—generally have fewer allergies than children in small families do. They hypothesize that exposure to germs during infancy makes people less likely to develop allergies.

    Which one of the following, if true, most supports the researchers' hypothesis?

    (A) In countries where the average number of children per family has decreased over the last century, the incidence of allergies has increased.
    (B) Children in small families generally eat more kinds of very allergenic foods than children in large families do.
    (C) Some allergies are life threatening, while many diseases caused by germs produce only temporary discomfort.
    (D) Children whose parents have allergies have an above-average likelihood of developing allergies themselves.
    (E) Children from small families who entered day care before age one were less likely to develop allergies than children from small families who entered day care later.

    PrepTest62 Sec4 Q22

45. Politician: It has been proposed that the national parks
in our country be managed by private companies
rather than the government. A similar privatization
of the telecommunications industry has benefited
consumers by allowing competition among a
variety of telephone companies to improve
service and force down prices. Therefore, the
privatization of the national parks would probably
benefit park visitors as well.

Which one of the following, if true, most weakens the
politician's argument?

(A) It would not be politically expedient to privatize
the national parks even if doing so would, in
the long run, improve service and reduce the
fees charged to visitors.

(B) The privatization of the telecommunications
industry has been problematic in that it has led
to significantly increased unemployment and
economic instability in that industry.

(C) The vast majority of people visiting the national
parks are unaware of proposals to privatize the
management of those parks.

(D) Privatizing the national parks would benefit a
much smaller number of consumers to a much
smaller extent than did the privatization of the
telecommunications industry.

(E) The privatization of the national parks would
produce much less competition between
different companies than did the privatization
of the telecommunications industry.

PrepTest62 Sec4 Q14

The explanations to these questions begin on page 657.

Principle (Identify)

Previously Seen Stimuli

Here are a few questions featuring stimuli covered in Chapters 9 and 10. This time they appear with answer choices. These questions are arranged in roughly increasing order of difficulty.

46. Mariah: Joanna has argued that Adam should not judge the essay contest because several of his classmates have entered the contest. However, the essays are not identified by author to the judge and, moreover, none of Adam's friends are classmates of his. Still, Adam has no experience in critiquing essays. Therefore, I agree with Joanna that Adam should not judge the contest.

    Which one of the following principles, if valid, most helps to justify Mariah's argument?

    (A) A suspicion of bias is insufficient grounds on which to disqualify someone from judging a contest.
    (B) Expertise should be the primary prerequisite for serving as a contest judge.
    (C) The ability of a judge to make objective decisions is more important than that judge's content expertise.
    (D) In selecting a contest judge, fairness concerns should override concern for the appropriate expertise.
    (E) A contest judge, no matter how well qualified, cannot judge properly if the possibility of bias exists.

    PrepTest56 Sec3 Q3

47. Educator: It has been argued that our professional organization should make decisions about important issues—such as raising dues and taking political stands—by a direct vote of all members rather than by having members vote for officers who in turn make the decisions. This would not, however, be the right way to decide these matters, for the vote of any given individual is much more likely to determine organizational policy by influencing the election of an officer than by influencing the result of a direct vote on a single issue.

    Which one of the following principles would, if valid, most help to justify the educator's reasoning?

    (A) No procedure for making organizational decisions should allow one individual's vote to weigh more than that of another.
    (B) Outcomes of organizational elections should be evaluated according to their benefit to the organization as a whole, not according to the fairness of the methods by which they are produced.
    (C) Important issues facing organizations should be decided by people who can devote their full time to mastering the information relevant to the issues.
    (D) An officer of an organization should not make a particular decision on an issue unless a majority of the organization's members would approve of that decision.
    (E) An organization's procedures for making organizational decisions should maximize the power of each member of the organization to influence the decisions made.

    PrepTest52 Sec1 Q19

New Questions

Practice on questions that have not yet appeared in the book. These questions are arranged in roughly increasing order of difficulty.

48. Jewel collectors, fearing that their eyes will be deceived by a counterfeit, will not buy a diamond unless the dealer guarantees that it is genuine. But why should a counterfeit give any less aesthetic pleasure when the naked eye cannot distinguish it from a real diamond? Both jewels should be deemed of equal value.

    Which one of the following principles, if valid, most helps to justify the reasoning in the argument above?

    (A) Jewel collectors should collect only those jewels that provide the most aesthetic pleasure.
    (B) The value of a jewel should depend at least partly on market demand.
    (C) It should not be assumed that everyone who likes diamonds receives the same degree of aesthetic pleasure from them.
    (D) The value of a jewel should derive solely from the aesthetic pleasure it provides.
    (E) Jewel collectors should not buy counterfeit jewels unless they are unable to distinguish counterfeit jewels from real ones.

    PrepTest62 Sec4 Q15

49. Editorial: It has been suggested that private, for-profit companies should be hired to supply clean drinking water to areas of the world where it is unavailable now. But water should not be supplied by private companies. After all, clean water is essential for human health, and the purpose of a private company is to produce profit, not to promote health.

    Which one of the following principles, if valid, would most help to justify the reasoning in the editorial?

    (A) A private company should not be allowed to supply a commodity that is essential to human health unless that commodity is also supplied by a government agency.
    (B) If something is essential for human health and private companies are unwilling or unable to supply it, then it should be supplied by a government agency.
    (C) Drinking water should never be supplied by an organization that is not able to consistently supply clean, safe water.
    (D) The mere fact that something actually promotes human health is not sufficient to show that its purpose is to promote health.
    (E) If something is necessary for human health, then it should be provided by an organization whose primary purpose is the promotion of health.

    PrepTest62 Sec2 Q26

50. Journalist: To reconcile the need for profits sufficient to support new drug research with the moral imperative to provide medicines to those who most need them but cannot afford them, some pharmaceutical companies feel justified in selling a drug in rich nations at one price and in poor nations at a much lower price. But this practice is unjustified. A nation with a low average income may still have a substantial middle class better able to pay for new drugs than are many of the poorer citizens of an overall wealthier nation.

    Which one of the following principles, if valid, most helps to justify the journalist's reasoning?

    (A) People who are ill deserve more consideration than do healthy people, regardless of their relative socioeconomic positions.
    (B) Wealthy institutions have an obligation to expend at least some of their resources to assist those incapable of assisting themselves.
    (C) Whether one deserves special consideration depends on one's needs rather than on characteristics of the society to which one belongs.
    (D) The people in wealthy nations should not have better access to health care than do the people in poorer nations.
    (E) Unequal access to health care is more unfair than an unequal distribution of wealth.

    PrepTest52 Sec1 Q8

51. Many workers who handled substance T in factories became seriously ill years later. We now know T caused at least some of their illnesses. Earlier ignorance of this connection does not absolve T's manufacturer of all responsibility. For had it investigated the safety of T before allowing workers to be exposed to it, many of their illnesses would have been prevented.

Which one of the following principles most helps to justify the conclusion above?

(A) Employees who are harmed by substances they handle on the job should be compensated for medical costs they incur as a result.

(B) Manufacturers should be held responsible only for the preventable consequences of their actions.

(C) Manufacturers have an obligation to inform workers of health risks of which they are aware.

(D) Whether or not an action's consequences were preventable is irrelevant to whether a manufacturer should be held responsible for those consequences.

(E) Manufacturers should be held responsible for the consequences of any of their actions that harm innocent people if those consequences were preventable.

PrepTest62 Sec4 Q20

52. Claude: When I'm having lunch with job candidates, I watch to see if they salt their food without first tasting it. If they do, I count that against them, because they're making decisions based on inadequate information.

Larissa: That's silly. It's perfectly reasonable for me to wear a sweater whenever I go into a supermarket, because I already know supermarkets are always too cool inside to suit me. And I never open a credit card offer that comes in the mail, because I already know that no matter how low its interest rate may be, it will never be worthwhile for me.

The two analogies that Larissa offers can most reasonably be interpreted as invoking which one of the following principles to criticize Claude's policy?

(A) In matters involving personal preference, performing an action without first ascertaining whether it is appropriate in the specific circumstances should not be taken as good evidence of faulty decision making, because the action may be based on a reasoned policy relating to knowledge of a general fact about the circumstances.

(B) In professional decision-making contexts, those who have the responsibility of judging other people's suitability for a job should not use observations of job-related behavior as a basis for inferring general conclusions about those people's character.

(C) General conclusions regarding a job candidate's suitability for a position should not be based exclusively on observations of the candidate's behavior in situations that are neither directly job related nor likely to be indicative of a pattern of behavior that the candidate engages in.

(D) Individuals whose behavior in specific circumstances does not conform to generally expected norms should not automatically be considered unconcerned with meeting social expectations, because such individuals may be acting in accordance with reasoned policies that they believe should be generally adopted by people in similar circumstances.

(E) Evidence that a particular individual uses bad decision-making strategies in matters of personal taste should not be considered sufficient to warrant a negative assessment of his or her suitability for a job, because any good decision maker can have occasional lapses of rationality with regard to such matters.

PrepTest58 Sec4 Q25

53. Advice columnist: Several scientific studies have shown
that, when participating in competitive sports,
those people who have recently been experiencing
major stress in their lives are several times more
likely to suffer serious injuries than are other
participants in competitive sports. Since risking
serious injury is unwise, no sports activity should
be used as a method for coping with stress.

Which one of the following principles, if valid, most
helps to justify the reasoning in the advice columnist's
argument?

(A) If people recently under stress should avoid a
subset of activities of a certain type, they
should avoid all activities of that type.

(B) A method for coping with stress should be used
only if it has been subjected to scientific study.

(C) People who have not been experiencing major
stress in their lives should participate in
competitive sports.

(D) When people have been under considerable
stress, they should engage in competitive
activities in order to relieve the stress.

(E) People with a history of sports injuries should
not engage in sports activities if they have
recently been under stress.

PrepTest56 Sec3 Q12

Parallel Reasoning and Parallel Flaw

New Questions

Practice on questions that have not yet appeared. These questions are arranged in roughly increasing order
of difficulty.

54. Although many political candidates object to being made
the target of advertising designed to cast them in an
adverse light, such advertising actually benefits its targets
because most elections have been won by candidates
who were the targets of that kind of advertising.

The pattern of flawed reasoning in the argument most
closely parallels that in which one of the following?

(A) Although many people dislike physical exercise,
they should exercise because it is a good way
to improve their overall health.
(B) Although many actors dislike harsh reviews of
their work, such reviews actually help their
careers because most of the really prestigious
acting awards have gone to actors who have
had performances of theirs reviewed harshly.
(C) Although many students dislike studying, it
must be a good way to achieve academic
success because most students who study pass
their courses.
(D) Although many film critics dislike horror films,
such films are bound to be successful because
a large number of people are eager to attend them.
(E) Although many people dislike feeling sleepy as
a result of staying up late the previous night,
such sleepiness must be acceptable to those
who experience it because most people who
stay up late enjoy doing so.

PrepTest58 Sec1 Q7

55. If a mother's first child is born before its due date, it is
likely that her second child will be also. Jackie's second
child was not born before its due date, so it is likely that
Jackie's first child was not born before its due date either.

The questionable reasoning in the argument above is
most similar in its reasoning to which one of the
following?

(A) Artisans who finish their projects before the
craft fair will probably go to the craft fair.
Ben will not finish his project before the fair.
So he probably will not go to the craft fair.
(B) All responsible pet owners are likely to be good
with children. So anyone who is good with
children is probably a responsible pet owner.
(C) If a movie is a box-office hit, it is likely that its
sequel will be also. *Hawkman II*, the sequel to
Hawkman I, was not a box-office hit, so
Hawkman I was probably not a box-office hit.
(D) If a business is likely to fail, people will not
invest in it. Pallid Starr is likely to fail,
therefore no one is likely to invest in it.
(E) Tai will go sailing only if the weather is nice.
The weather will be nice, thus Tai will
probably go sailing.

PrepTest62 Sec4 Q9

56. Many movies starring top actors will do well at the box office because the actors are already well known and have a loyal following. Movies starring unknown actors are therefore unlikely to do well.

The flawed reasoning in the argument above is most similar to that in which one of the following?

(A) Many animals must devote most of their energy to locating food, or they will not get enough food to maintain optimal energy levels. Thus, if immediate survival requires such an animal to devote most of its energy to some other purpose, optimal energy levels generally will not be maintained.

(B) Often the presence of the flower bee balm in a garden will attract bumblebees that pollinate the plants and enable the garden to produce an abundant crop. So, gardens that lack bee balm usually do not produce abundant crops.

(C) A person's ability to keep confidences is a large part of being a friend, since frequently such an ability enables a high degree of openness in communication. Thus, a high degree of openness in communication is an essential feature of friendship.

(D) Visual aids can be very useful in effectively teaching math skills, because they generally allow vivid conceptualization of math principles. If such visual aids were never employed, therefore, teaching math skills might sometimes be more difficult.

(E) An understanding of the rules of perspective is necessary for achieving success as a painter, since it is the understanding of these most basic rules that allows the painter to paint realistically. Thus, painters with an understanding of the rules of perspective will achieve success.

PrepTest56 Sec3 Q14

57. Whenever Joe's car is vacuumed, the employees of K & L Auto vacuum it; they are the only people who ever vacuum Joe's car. If the employees of K & L Auto vacuumed Joe's car, then Joe took his car to K & L Auto to be fixed. Joe's car was recently vacuumed. Therefore, Joe took his car to K & L Auto to be fixed.

The pattern of reasoning exhibited by the argument above is most similar to that exhibited by which one of the following?

(A) Emily's water glass is wet and it would be wet only if she drank water from it this morning. Since the only time she drinks water in the morning is when she takes her medication, Emily took her medication this morning.

(B) Lisa went to the hair salon today since either she went to the hair salon today or she went to the bank this morning, but Lisa did not go to the bank this morning.

(C) There are no bills on John's kitchen table. Since John gets at least one bill per day and he always puts his bills on his kitchen table, someone else must have checked John's mail today.

(D) Linda is grumpy only if she does not have her coffee in the morning, and Linda does not have her coffee in the morning only if she runs out of coffee. Therefore, Linda runs out of coffee only on days that she is grumpy.

(E) Jeff had to choose either a grapefruit or cereal for breakfast this morning. Given that Jeff is allergic to grapefruit, Jeff must have had cereal for breakfast this morning.

PrepTest52 Sec1 Q3

58. Books that present a utopian future in which the inequities and sufferings of the present are replaced by more harmonious and rational social arrangements will always find enthusiastic buyers. Since gloomy books predicting that even more terrifying times await us are clearly not of this genre, they are unlikely to be very popular.

The questionable pattern of reasoning in which one of the following arguments is most similar to that in the argument above?

(A) Art that portrays people as happy and contented has a tranquilizing effect on the viewer, an effect that is appealing to those who are tense or anxious. Thus, people who dislike such art are neither tense nor anxious.

(B) People who enjoy participating in activities such as fishing or hiking may nevertheless enjoy watching such spectator sports as boxing or football. Thus, one cannot infer from someone's participating in vigorous contact sports that he or she is not also fond of less violent forms of recreation.

(C) Action movies that involve complicated and dangerous special-effects scenes are enormously expensive to produce. Hence, since traditional dramatic or comedic films contain no such scenes, it is probable that they are relatively inexpensive to produce.

(D) Adults usually feel a pleasant nostalgia when hearing the music they listened to as adolescents, but since adolescents often like music specifically because they think it annoys their parents, adults rarely appreciate the music that their children will later listen to with nostalgia.

(E) All self-employed businesspeople have salaries that fluctuate with the fortunes of the general economy, but government bureaucrats are not self-employed. Therefore, not everyone with an income that fluctuates with the fortunes of the general economy is a government bureaucrat.

PrepTest52 Sec3 Q24

59. The local radio station will not win the regional ratings race this year. In the past ten years the station has never finished better than fifth place in the ratings. The station's manager has not responded to its dismal ratings by changing its musical format or any key personnel, while the competition has often sought to respond to changing tastes in music and has aggressively recruited the region's top radio personalities.

The reasoning in which one of the following is most similar to that in the argument above?

(A) Every swan I have seen was white. Therefore all swans are probably white.

(B) A fair coin was fairly flipped six times and was heads every time. The next flip will probably be heads too.

(C) All lions are mammals. Therefore Leo, the local zoo's oldest lion, is a mammal too.

(D) Recently stock prices have always been lower on Mondays. Therefore they will be lower this coming Monday too.

(E) Only trained swimmers are lifeguards, so it follows that the next lifeguard at the local pool will be a trained swimmer.

PrepTest56 Sec3 Q24

60. Anyone who believes in extraterrestrials believes in UFOs. But the existence of UFOs has been conclusively refuted. Therefore a belief in extraterrestrials is false as well.

Which one of the following arguments contains flawed reasoning most similar to that in the argument above?

(A) Anyone who believes in unicorns believes in centaurs. But it has been demonstrated that there are no centaurs, so there are no unicorns either.

(B) Anyone who believes in unicorns believes in centaurs. But you do not believe in centaurs, so you do not believe in unicorns either.

(C) Anyone who believes in unicorns believes in centaurs. But you do not believe in unicorns, so you do not believe in centaurs either.

(D) Anyone who believes in unicorns believes in centaurs. But there is no good reason to believe in centaurs, so a belief in unicorns is unjustified as well.

(E) Anyone who believes in unicorns believes in centaurs. But it has been conclusively proven that there is no such thing as a unicorn, so a belief in centaurs is mistaken as well.

PrepTest52 Sec1 Q16

Principle (Parallel Principle)

New Questions

Practice on questions that have not yet appeared in the book. These questions are arranged in roughly increasing order of difficulty.

61. Linguist: Most people can tell whether a sequence of words in their own dialect is grammatical. Yet few people who can do so are able to specify the relevant grammatical rules.

   Which one of the following best illustrates the principle underlying the linguist's statements?

   (A) Some people are able to write cogent and accurate narrative descriptions of events. But these people are not necessarily also capable of composing emotionally moving and satisfying poems.

   (B) Engineers who apply the principles of physics to design buildings and bridges must know a great deal more than do the physicists who discover these principles.

   (C) Some people are able to tell whether any given piece of music is a waltz. But the majority of these people cannot state the defining characteristics of a waltz.

   (D) Those travelers who most enjoy their journeys are not always those most capable of vividly describing the details of those journeys to others.

   (E) Quite a few people know the rules of chess, but only a small number of them can play chess very well.

   PrepTest58 Sec4 Q4

62. Some credit card companies allow cardholders to skip payments for up to six months under certain circumstances, but it is almost never in a cardholder's interest to do so. Finance charges accumulate during the skipped-payment period, and the cost to the cardholder is much greater in the long run.

   Which one of the following arguments illustrates a principle most similar to the principle underlying the argument above?

   (A) Although insecticides are effective in ridding the environment of insect pests, they often kill beneficial insects at the same time. Since these beneficial insects are so important, we must find other ways to combat insect pests.

   (B) Increasing the base salary of new employees is good for a company. Although the company's payroll will increase, it will be easier for the company to recruit new employees.

   (C) It is unwise to use highway maintenance funds for construction of new roads. There is some immediate benefit from new roads, but if these funds are not used for maintenance, the total maintenance cost will be greater in the long run.

   (D) It is better to invest in a used piece of equipment than to purchase a new one. Although used equipment requires more repairs and is sometimes more costly in the long run, buying a new machine requires a far greater initial outlay of capital.

   (E) Sports cars are impractical for most drivers. While there is undoubtedly a certain thrill associated with driving these cars, their small size makes them incapable of transporting any but the smallest amounts of cargo.

   PrepTest56 Sec2 Q18

The explanations to these
questions begin on page 666.

63. Buying elaborate screensavers—programs that put moving images on a computer monitor to prevent damage—can cost a company far more in employee time than it saves in electricity and monitor protection. Employees cannot resist spending time playing with screensavers that flash interesting graphics across their screens.

Which one of the following most closely conforms to the principle illustrated above?

(A) A school that chooses textbooks based on student preference may not get the most economical package.

(B) An energy-efficient insulation system may cost more up front but will ultimately save money over the life of the house.

(C) The time that it takes to have a pizza delivered may be longer than it takes to cook a complete dinner.

(D) A complicated hotel security system may cost more in customer goodwill than it saves in losses by theft.

(E) An electronic keyboard may be cheaper to buy than a piano but more expensive to repair.

PrepTest62 Sec2 Q13

64. Some people mistakenly believe that since we do not have direct access to the distant past we cannot learn much about it. Contemporary historians and archaeologists find current geography, geology, and climate to be rich in clues about a given region's distant history. However, the more distant the period we are studying is, the less useful the study of the present becomes.

Of the following, which one most closely conforms to the principle that the passage illustrates?

(A) Astronomers often draw inferences about the earlier years of our solar system on the basis of recently collected data. Unfortunately, they have been able to infer comparatively little about the origin of our solar system.

(B) Much can be learned about the perpetrator of a crime by applying scientific methods of investigation to the crime scene. But the more the crime scene has been studied the less likely anything will be learned from further study.

(C) To understand a literary text one needs to understand the author's world view. However, the farther that world view gets from one's own the less one will be able to appreciate the text.

(D) We often extrapolate from ordinary sensory experience to things beyond such experience and form a rash judgment, such as the claim that the earth is the center of the universe because it appears that way to us.

(E) One crucial clue to the extent of the ancient Egyptians' mathematical knowledge came from studying the pyramids. The more we studied such structures, the more impressed we were by how much the Egyptians knew.

PrepTest52 Sec3 Q25

Mixed Assumption, Flaw, and Strengthen/Weaken

Try out some mixed practice on questions. You may have seen the stimulus for one or more of these questions earlier. These questions are NOT arranged in increasing order of difficulty.

65. Company president: For the management consultant position, we shall interview only those applicants who have worked for management consulting firms generally recognized as in the top 1 percent of firms worldwide. When we finally select somebody, then, we can be sure to have selected one of the best management consultants available.

The company president's reasoning is most vulnerable to criticism on the grounds that it

(A) takes for granted that only the best management consultants have worked for the top management consulting firms

(B) generalizes from too small a sample of management consulting firms worldwide

(C) takes for granted that if something is true of each member of a collection, then it is also true of the collection as a whole

(D) presumes, without providing warrant, that persons who have worked for the top companies will accept a job offer

(E) presumes, without providing justification, that highly competent management consultants are highly competent at every task

PrepTest58 Sec4 Q5

66. In order to reduce traffic congestion and raise revenue for the city, the mayor plans to implement a charge of $10 per day for driving in the downtown area. Payment of this charge will be enforced using a highly sophisticated system that employs digital cameras and computerized automobile registration. This system will not be ready until the end of next year. Without this system, however, mass evasion of the charge will result. Therefore, when the mayor's plan is first implemented, payment of the charge will not be effectively enforced.

Which one of the following is an assumption on which the argument depends for its conclusion to be properly drawn?

(A) The mayor's plan to charge for driving downtown will be implemented before the end of next year.

(B) The city will incur a budget deficit if it does not receive the revenue it expects to raise from the charge for driving downtown.

(C) The plan to charge for driving downtown should be implemented as soon as payment of the charge can be effectively enforced.

(D) Raising revenue is a more important consideration for the city than is reducing traffic congestion.

(E) A daily charge for driving downtown is the most effective way to reduce traffic congestion.

PrepTest52 Sec1 Q10

67. Psychologist: We asked 100 entrepreneurs and
    100 business managers to answer various questions
    and rate how confident they were that their
    responses were correct. While members of each
    group were overconfident, in general the
    entrepreneurs were much more so than the
    business managers. This indicates that people
    who are especially overconfident are more likely
    to attempt to start a business in spite of the
    enormous odds against success than people who
    are less confident.

    Which one of the following, if true, lends the most
    support to the psychologist's conclusion?

    (A) The questions asked of the entrepreneurs and
        business managers included personal, political,
        and business questions.
    (B) At least some of the entrepreneurs surveyed had
        accurately determined before attempting to
        start their businesses what the odds were
        against their attempts being successful.
    (C) Another survey showed that degree of
        confidence was highly correlated with success
        in business.
    (D) The business managers who were most
        overconfident were found to have attempted to
        start businesses in the past.
    (E) How confident each person surveyed was that
        his or her answers to the questions asked were
        correct corresponded closely to that person's
        confidence in his or her business acumen.

    PrepTest56 Sec2 Q14

68. When a society undergoes slow change, its younger
    members find great value in the advice of its older
    members. But when a society undergoes rapid change,
    young people think that little in the experience of their
    elders is relevant to them, and so do not value their
    advice. Thus, we may measure the rate at which a
    society is changing by measuring the amount of
    deference its younger members show to their elders.

    Which one of the following is an assumption on which
    the argument depends?

    (A) A society's younger members can often
        accurately discern whether that society is
        changing rapidly.
    (B) How much deference young people show to
        their elders depends on how much of the
        elders' experience is practically useful to them.
    (C) The deference young people show to their
        elders varies according to how much the young
        value their elders' advice.
    (D) The faster a society changes, the less relevant
        the experience of older members of the society
        is to younger members.
    (E) Young people value their elders' advice just
        insofar as the elders' experience is practically
        useful to them.

    PrepTest58 Sec1 Q22

69. Principle: It is healthy for children to engage in an
    activity that promotes their intellectual
    development only if engaging in that activity
    does not detract from their social development.

    Application: Although Megan's frequent reading
    stimulates her intellectually, it reduces the
    amount of time she spends interacting with other
    people. Therefore, it is not healthy for her to read
    as much as she does.

    The application of the principle is most vulnerable to
    criticism on which one of the following grounds?

    (A) It misinterprets the principle as a universal
        claim intended to hold in all cases without
        exception, rather than as a mere generalization.
    (B) It overlooks the possibility that the benefits of a
        given activity may sometimes be important
        enough to outweigh the adverse health effects.
    (C) It misinterprets the principle to be, at least in
        part, a claim about what is unhealthy, rather
        than solely a claim about what is healthy.
    (D) It takes for granted that any decrease in the
        amount of time a child spends interacting with
        others detracts from that child's social
        development.
    (E) It takes a necessary condition for an activity's
        being healthy as a sufficient condition for its
        being so.

    PrepTest52 Sec1 Q23

70. Dietitian: High consumption of sodium increases some people's chances of developing heart disease. To maintain cardiac health without lowering sodium consumption, therefore, these people should eat fresh, rather than canned or frozen, fruit and vegetables, since the potassium in plant foods helps to prevent sodium's malign effects.

Which one of the following is an assumption required by the dietitian's argument?

(A) Fresh fruits and vegetables contain more potassium than sodium.

(B) Food processing businesses often add sodium to foods being canned or frozen.

(C) Potassium is the only mineral that helps to prevent sodium's malign effects.

(D) Potassium in fruits and vegetables has few negative side effects.

(E) Fresh fruits and vegetables contain more potassium than do canned or frozen ones.

PrepTest56 Sec2 Q6

71. A leading critic of space exploration contends that it would be wrong, given current technology, to send a group of explorers to Mars, since the explorers would be unlikely to survive the trip. But that exaggerates the risk. There would be a well-engineered backup system at every stage of the long and complicated journey. A fatal catastrophe is quite unlikely at any given stage if such a backup system is in place.

The reasoning in the argument is flawed in that the argument

(A) infers that something is true of a whole merely from the fact that it is true of each of the parts

(B) infers that something cannot occur merely from the fact that it is unlikely to occur

(C) draws a conclusion about what must be the case based on evidence about what is probably the case

(D) infers that something will work merely because it could work

(E) rejects a view merely on the grounds that an inadequate argument has been made for it

PrepTest62 Sec2 Q8

72. The *Iliad* and the *Odyssey* were both attributed to Homer in ancient times. But these two poems differ greatly in tone and vocabulary and in certain details of the fictional world they depict. So they are almost certainly not the work of the same poet.

Which one of the following statements, if true, most weakens the reasoning above?

(A) Several hymns that were also attributed to Homer in ancient times differ more from the *Iliad* in the respects mentioned than does the *Odyssey*.

(B) Both the *Iliad* and the *Odyssey* have come down to us in manuscripts that have suffered from minor copying errors and other textual corruptions.

(C) Works known to have been written by the same modern writer are as different from each other in the respects mentioned as are the *Iliad* and the *Odyssey*.

(D) Neither the *Iliad* nor the *Odyssey* taken by itself is completely consistent in all of the respects mentioned.

(E) Both the *Iliad* and the *Odyssey* were the result of an extended process of oral composition in which many poets were involved.

PrepTest52 Sec1 Q21

The explanations to these
questions begin on page 671.

73. Scientist: To study the comparative effectiveness of two experimental medications for athlete's foot, a representative sample of people with athlete's foot were randomly assigned to one of two groups. One group received only medication M, and the other received only medication N. The only people whose athlete's foot was cured had been given medication M.

Reporter: This means, then, that if anyone in the study had athlete's foot that was not cured, that person did not receive medication M.

Which one of the following most accurately describes the reporter's error in reasoning?

(A) The reporter concludes from evidence showing only that M can cure athlete's foot that M always cures athlete's foot.

(B) The reporter illicitly draws a conclusion about the population as a whole on the basis of a study conducted only on a sample of the population.

(C) The reporter presumes, without providing justification, that medications M and N are available to people who have athlete's foot but did not participate in the study.

(D) The reporter fails to allow for the possibility that athlete's foot may be cured even if neither of the two medications studied is taken.

(E) The reporter presumes, without providing justification, that there is no sizeable subgroup of people whose athlete's foot will be cured only if they do not take medication M.

PrepTest62 Sec2 Q11

74. If a wig has any handmade components, it is more expensive than one with none. Similarly, a made-to-measure wig ranges from medium-priced to expensive. Handmade foundations are never found on wigs that do not use human hair. Furthermore, any wig that contains human hair should be dry-cleaned. So all made-to-measure wigs should be dry-cleaned.

The conclusion of the argument follows logically if which one of the following is assumed?

(A) Any wig whose price falls in the medium-priced to expensive range has a handmade foundation.

(B) If a wig's foundation is handmade, then it is more expensive than one whose foundation is not handmade.

(C) A wig that has any handmade components should be dry-cleaned.

(D) If a wig's foundation is handmade, then its price is at least in the medium range.

(E) Any wig that should be dry-cleaned has a foundation that is handmade.

PrepTest58 Sec1 Q25

75. Over 40,000 lead seals from the early Byzantine Empire remain today. Apart from the rare cases where the seal authenticated a document of special importance, most seals had served their purpose when the document was opened. Lead was not expensive, but it was not free: most lead seals would have been recast once they had served their purpose. Thus the number of early Byzantine documents sealed in such a fashion must have been many times the number of remaining lead seals.

Which one of the following statements, if true, most strengthens the argument?

(A) Most of the lead seals produced during the early Byzantine Empire were affixed to documents that were then opened during that period.

(B) Most of the lead seals produced during the early Byzantine Empire were affixed to documents that have since been destroyed.

(C) The amount of lead available for seals in the early Byzantine Empire was much greater than the amount of lead that remains in the seals today.

(D) During the time of the early Byzantine Empire there were at most 40,000 documents of enough importance to prevent the removing and recycling of the seal.

(E) During the time of the early Byzantine Empire there were fewer than 40,000 seals affixed to documents at any given time.

PrepTest56 Sec2 Q24

76. Throughout a certain nation, electricity has actually
become increasingly available to people in urban areas
while energy production has been subsidized to help
residents of rural areas gain access to electricity.
However, even with the subsidy, many of the most
isolated rural populations still have no access to
electricity. Thus, the energy subsidy has failed to
achieve its intended purpose.

The reasoning in the argument is most vulnerable to
criticism on the grounds that the argument

(A) takes for granted that the subsidy's intended
purpose could have been achieved if the
subsidy had not existed

(B) takes for granted that if a subsidy has any
benefit for those whom it was not intended to
benefit, then that subsidy has failed to achieve
its intended purpose

(C) presumes, without providing justification, that
the intended purpose of the subsidy was to
benefit not only rural populations in the nation
who have no electricity, but other people in the
nation as well

(D) overlooks the possibility that even many of the
people in the nation who live in urban areas
would have difficulty gaining access to
electricity without the subsidy

(E) fails to take into account that the subsidy could
have helped many of the rural residents in the
nation gain access to electricity even if many
other rural residents in the nation were not
helped in this way

PrepTest56 Sec2 Q12

77. Banking analyst: Banks often offer various services to
new customers at no charge. But this is not an
ideal business practice, since regular, long-term
customers, who make up the bulk of the business
for most banks, are excluded from these special
offers.

Which one of the following, if true, most strengthens
the banking analyst's argument?

(A) Most banks have similar charges for most
services and pay similar interest rates on
deposits.

(B) Banks do best when offering special privileges
only to their most loyal customers.

(C) Offering services at no charge to all of its
current customers would be prohibitively
expensive for a bank.

(D) Once they have chosen a bank, people tend to
remain loyal to that bank.

(E) Some banks that offer services at no charge to
new customers are very successful.

PrepTest52 Sec3 Q3

78. Gotera: Infants lack the motor ability required to
voluntarily produce particular sounds, but
produce various babbling sounds randomly. Most
children are several years old before they can
voluntarily produce most of the vowel and
consonant sounds of their language. We can
conclude that speech acquisition is entirely a
motor control process rather than a process that is
abstract or mental.

Which one of the following is an assumption required
by Gotera's argument?

(A) Speech acquisition is a function only of one's
ability to produce the sounds of spoken
language.

(B) During the entire initial babbling stage, infants
cannot intentionally move their tongues while
they are babbling.

(C) The initial babbling stage is completed during
infancy.

(D) The initial babbling stage is the first stage of the
speech acquisition process.

(E) Control of tongue and mouth movements
requires a sophisticated level of mental
development.

PrepTest52 Sec3 Q7

79. Concert promoter: Some critics claim that our concert
series lacks popular appeal. But our income from
the sales of t-shirts and other memorabilia at the
concerts is equal to or greater than that for similar
sales at comparable series. So those critics are
mistaken.

The concert promoter's argument is flawed in that it

(A) attacks the critics on the basis of emotional
considerations rather than factual ones

(B) takes for granted that income from sales of
memorabilia is the sole indicator of popular
appeal

(C) takes for granted that the comparable series
possess popular appeal

(D) draws a conclusion about the popularity of a
series based on a comparison with other,
dissimilar events

(E) fails to adequately distinguish the series as a
whole from individual concerts in it

PrepTest56 Sec3 Q10

The explanations to these questions begin on page 674.

80. Economist: A country's rapid emergence from an economic recession requires substantial new investment in that country's economy. Since people's confidence in the economic policies of their country is a precondition for any new investment, countries that put collective goals before individuals' goals cannot emerge quickly from an economic recession.

Which one of the following, if assumed, enables the economist's conclusion to be properly drawn?

(A) No new investment occurs in any country that does not emerge quickly from an economic recession.

(B) Recessions in countries that put collective goals before individuals' goals tend not to affect the country's people's support for their government's policies.

(C) If the people in a country that puts individuals' goals first are willing to make new investments in their country's economy, their country will emerge quickly from an economic recession.

(D) People in countries that put collective goals before individuals' goals lack confidence in the economic policies of their countries.

(E) A country's economic policies are the most significant factor determining whether that country's economy will experience a recession.

PrepTest52 Sec3 Q15

81. People who need to reduce their intake of fat and to consume fewer calories often turn to fat substitutes, especially those with zero calories such as N5. But studies indicate that N5 is of no use to such people. Subjects who ate foods prepared with N5 almost invariably reported feeling hungrier afterwards than after eating foods prepared with real fat and consequently they ate more, quickly making up for the calories initially saved by using N5.

The reasoning in the argument is most vulnerable to criticism on the grounds that the argument fails to consider the possibility that

(A) many foods cannot be prepared with N5

(B) N5 has mild but unpleasant side effects

(C) not everyone who eats foods prepared with N5 pays attention to caloric intake

(D) people who know N5 contains zero calories tend to eat more foods prepared with N5 than do people who are unaware that N5 is calorie-free

(E) the total fat intake of people who eat foods prepared with N5 tends to decrease even if their caloric intake does not

PrepTest58 Sec1 Q9

82. Nutritionists believe that a person's daily requirement for vitamins can readily be met by eating five servings of fruits and vegetables daily. However, most people eat far less than this. Thus, most people need to take vitamin pills.

Which one of the following statements, if true, most seriously weakens the argument?

(A) Even five servings of fruits and vegetables a day is insufficient unless the intake is varied to ensure that different vitamins are consumed.

(B) Certain commonly available fruits and vegetables contain considerably more nutrients than others.

(C) Nutritionists sometimes disagree on how much of a fruit or vegetable constitutes a complete serving.

(D) Many commonly consumed foods that are neither fruits nor vegetables are fortified by manufacturers with the vitamins found in fruits and vegetables.

(E) Fruits and vegetables are also important sources of fiber, in forms not found in vitamin pills.

PrepTest58 Sec4 Q10

83. Doctor: Medical researchers recently examined a large group of individuals who said that they had never experienced serious back pain. Half of the members of the group turned out to have bulging or slipped disks in their spines, conditions often blamed for serious back pain. Since these individuals with bulging or slipped disks evidently felt no pain from them, these conditions could not lead to serious back pain in people who do experience such pain.

The reasoning in the doctor's argument is most vulnerable to the criticism that it fails to consider which one of the following possibilities?

(A) A factor that need not be present in order for a certain effect to arise may nonetheless be sufficient to produce that effect.

(B) A factor that is not in itself sufficient to produce a certain effect may nonetheless be partly responsible for that effect in some instances.

(C) An effect that occurs in the absence of a particular phenomenon might not occur when that phenomenon is present.

(D) A characteristic found in half of a given sample of the population might not occur in half of the entire population.

(E) A factor that does not bring about a certain effect may nonetheless be more likely to be present when the effect occurs than when the effect does not occur.

PrepTest62 Sec4 Q19

84. Film preservation requires transferring old movies from
their original material—unstable, deteriorating nitrate
film—to stable acetate film. But this is a time-consuming,
expensive process, and there is no way to transfer all
currently deteriorating nitrate films to acetate before
they disintegrate. So some films from the earliest years
of Hollywood will not be preserved.

Which one of the following is an assumption on which
the argument depends?

(A)   No new technology for transferring old movies
from nitrate film to acetate film will ever be
developed.

(B)   Transferring films from nitrate to acetate is not
the least expensive way of preserving them.

(C)   Not many films from the earliest years of
Hollywood have already been transferred to
acetate.

(D)   Some films from the earliest years of Hollywood
currently exist solely in their original material.

(E)   The least popular films from the earliest years
of Hollywood are the ones most likely to be lost.

PrepTest62 Sec4 Q23

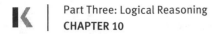

Part Three: Logical Reasoning
CHAPTER 10

These explanations refer to
questions that begin on page 606.

ANSWERS AND EXPLANATIONS

In the following explanations, we have tagged each Assumption, Strengthen, Weaken, and Flaw question by question type and argument type. Next to each question type designation, look for one of the following abbreviations indicating the pattern of argument found in the stimulus.

Argument Type Key:

OP (Overlooked Possibilities)

OP-C (Overlooked Possibilities: Causation)

OP-NvS (Overlooked Possibilities: Necessity vs Sufficiency)

OP-P (Overlooked Possibilities: Prediction)

OP-PvC (Overlooked Possibilities: Possibility vs Certainty)

OP-R (Overlooked Possibilities: Advantages/Disadvantages in Recommendations)

MC-E (Mismatched Concepts- Alike/Equivalent)

MC-ME (Mismatched Concepts: Mutually Exclusive)

MC-N (Mismatched Concepts: Need Evidence for Conclusion)

MC-R (Mismatched Concepts: Representation)

MC-BvF (Mismatched Concepts: Belief vs Fact)

MC-PvW (Mismatched Concepts: Parts vs Whole)

1. (C) Assumption (MC-E) ★☆☆☆

Step 1: Identify the Question Type

The question asks for the argument's assumption. Because the argument "depends" on the assumption, you're looking for a Necessary Assumption, and you can use the Denial Test to confirm or eliminate answers.

Step 2: Untangle the Stimulus

The conclusion comes in the first sentence: less stress = less pain sensitivity. The evidence is based on a study. People who listened to music before and after surgery seemed to have less pain than did those who listened to talking.

Step 3: Make a Prediction

The conclusion is about stress, but the evidence is about music. The assumption must connect these two different ideas. For the argument to make any sense, the author must be assuming that listening to the music tape diminished stress.

Step 4: Evaluate the Answer Choices

(C) directly matches the prediction by providing the crucial connection between music and stress.

(A) is a Distortion. It's possible that some patients listened to a mix of the two tapes, but the author is only concerned with those who listened to only music or only conversation.

(B) makes an Irrelevant Comparison between the stress of pre- and post-surgery. Meanwhile, the evidence is about the calming effects of music versus conversation.

(D) is Outside the Scope because the argument addresses stress only, not any psychological effects. Further, the argument is about how listening to music affects the need for anesthesia or painkillers, not about how drugs might change the effect listening to music has.

(E) is a Distortion. That anesthesia and painkillers reduce stress may be true, but it doesn't affect the researchers' argument that reducing stress reduces the need for the two in the first place.

2. (D) Assumption (MC-E) ★★☆☆

Step 1: Identify the Question Stem

This is most definitely an Assumption question, since it directs us to find the "assumption required by the argument."

Step 2: Untangle the Stimulus

The conclusion is that film producers make films that theater managers will find attractive to younger audiences. The evidence for this is that film producers want their film to be shown as widely as possible, and the managers of the theaters that show the films will show only those films that they believe will turn a profit.

Step 3: Make a Prediction

Finding the central assumption in mismatched concepts argument is, at its most basic, a matter of bridging together unmatched terms or concepts from evidence to conclusion. In the evidence, we learn that film producers only have a shot at getting their films shown at theaters if the managers are convinced that the films will turn a profit. In the conclusion, we learn that film producers will therefore make films that theater managers are convinced will appeal to younger audiences. We need to connect the idea of profitable films to films directed at younger audiences. Therefore, the author must be assuming that theater managers consider films that attract younger audiences to be more profitable on the whole than other films.

Step 4: Evaluate the Answers

(D) is a clear match for this prediction. It correctly bridges unmatched terms between the evidence and the conclusion.

(A) doesn't hold up to the Denial Test. Even if adults consume *more* of the foods and beverages sold at movie concession stands than do either children or adolescents, that doesn't necessarily mean that they'll be buying enough of those foods to yield a profit. Besides, food-and-beverage concession revenue is just a part of the profit and not the primary focus of this argument.

(B) need not be true in order for the argument to work. The theater managers are only concerned with whether the films they show appeal to younger audiences. The films don't have

These explanations refer to questions that begin on page 606.

Part Three: Logical Reasoning
Assumption Family Questions

to appeal *exclusively* to younger audiences, though; they could also appeal to older audiences, and the managers would surely just consider this icing on the cake.

(C) blows up a detail of the argument. Food-and-beverage concession revenue is mentioned as a part of the overall revenue, but for this argument to work, it doesn't need to be true that concession stands generate more revenue than ticket sales to the films themselves.

(E) is a distortion. Films that appeal to older audiences don't have to be flops for this argument to work; it need only be true that films geared toward younger audiences are generally more profitable than other films, in a relative sense.

3. (C) Assumption (MC-ME)   ★★☆☆

Step 1: Identify the Question Type

The question asks for an assumption that, if true, will support the conclusion (i.e., a sufficient assumption). Unlike a necessary assumption, a sufficient assumption doesn't have to be true, so the Denial Test may not be useful. But if the assumption is true, it acts as a strengthener to support the conclusion.

Step 2: Untangle the Stimulus

This stimulus is wordy, so use careful strategic reading to simplify it. The Keyword "however" signals the author's point, and the word "[b]ecause" provides the evidence leading up to that point. Paraphrasing, the conclusion is simply that the retrospective studies described cannot be reliable. The reason is that these studies depend upon the subjects' own reports about their pasts.

Step 3: Make a Prediction

Always be on the lookout for a mismatch between evidence and conclusion. The scope of the conclusion is the unreliability of these retrospective studies. The scope of the evidence is the nature of the information the studies rely upon. To draw a conclusion about reliability based upon the source of information, the author is assuming that the source is unreliable (i.e., the subjects won't provide reliable reports).

Step 4: Evaluate the Answer Choices

(C) is wordy, but it fits the prediction. Rather than say "in retrospective studies," it describes the study at length, and rather than say the subjects' reports are "unreliable," it says they are "highly susceptible to inaccuracy." Good paraphrasing skills really come in handy in selecting this correct answer choice.

(A) is Outside the Scope. The argument is not about what's needed to make a study reliable or not. The conclusion is that it cannot be reliable, and the evidence provides a factual reason why.

(B) is a Distortion. The word "unless" indicates that there is a condition under which the study could be made reliable. However, the conclusion of the argument is an unqualified assertion that the studies cannot be reliable.

(D) is Outside the Scope. The argument is not about what would make the study reliable.

(E) is a restatement of the evidence. Retrospective studies must use the subjects' own reports about their past. We are told this in the argument, so it is not the assumption.

4. (D) Assumption (OP-P)   ★★☆☆

Step 1: Identify the Question Stem

The stem asks for the "assumption required" by the argument, so this is an Assumption question.

Step 2: Untangle the Stimulus

The economist's conclusion (signaled by "[t]hus") is that the economy would improve if the government were to lower income taxes. The evidence is that the current weak state of the economy is caused by reluctance on the part of consumers to spend their money. That reluctance has been made worse by the fact that the average income has lowered significantly over the past five years.

Step 3: Make a Prediction

When an argument concludes with a prediction, we can often find the assumption if we ask ourselves, "What would have to happen in order for that prediction to come true?" For lowering income taxes to actually help the economy improve, it would have to be true that lower income taxes would alleviate the reluctance of consumers to spend their money. After all, it's that reluctance that's keeping the economy from improving. Apparently, the economist assumes that lowering the income tax will remove that impediment.

Step 4: Evaluate the Answers

(D) matches our prediction perfectly. If you're unsure, use the Denial Test. Let's say that, contrary to **(D)**, consumers wouldn't be less reluctant to spend money even if their income taxes were lowered. If that's true, then there's no reason to lower the income tax because the cause of the weak economy would still be there. So since we can't make the argument work without **(D)**, it must be the central assumption.

(A) isn't necessary to the argument because it has nothing to do with income taxes, which are what the economist says will affect the economy.

(B) gets it backward. The argument says that lower average income is part of what's keeping consumers from spending their money. Reversing that causal relationship isn't necessary to make the argument work. To establish the economist's conclusion, it needs to be true that lowering income taxes will

K

Part Three: Logical Reasoning
CHAPTER 10

These explanations refer to
questions that begin on page 607.

increase the average income enough to make consumers more willing to spend money and strengthen the economy.

(C) indicates that the problem of the weak economy may worsen if income taxes stay where they are, but this isn't the same as indicating that lowering income taxes is all the government needs to do to improve the economy (which is what the economist is arguing in the first place).

(E) discusses government spending, which doesn't figure in the argument at all. The economist is concerned with consumer spending.

5. (D) Assumption (MC-ME) ★★☆☆

Step 1: Identify the Question Type

The phrase "if which one of the following is assumed" indicates an Assumption question. Because the conclusion follows logically from the assumption, you are looking for a Sufficient Assumption. Identify the conclusion, paraphrase the relevant evidence, and pinpoint the gap between the two.

Step 2: Untangle the Stimulus

Search for Keywords that help unlock the author's argument. "Therefore," at the bottom of the stimulus, introduces the conclusion: tragedy isn't satire or romance, and comedy isn't satire or romance. In the sentences preceding the conclusion, the author lays out the main difference: major characters in comedy and tragedy go through moral changes, whereas major characters in satire and romance have morals that mirror their world.

Step 3: Make a Prediction

In the conclusion, the author states there's no overlap between two different sets of genres (tragedy and comedy versus satire and romance). For there to be absolutely no overlap between the two sets, it must be true that their distinguishing features are mutually exclusive. Thus, the author assumes major characters in satire and romance do not go through moral changes, and major characters in tragedy and comedy don't reflect their worlds. Either one of these could be the right answer.

Step 4: Evaluate the Answer Choices

(D) directly matches the prediction.

(A) goes Outside the Scope of the argument by mentioning "[s]ome" characters. The critic is concerned only with major characters. Additionally, this choice discusses only the characteristics of romance and satire and doesn't address tragedy and comedy (or their characteristics), which are included in the conclusion.

(B) goes Outside the Scope by focusing on changing visions of the world, rather than on changing moral qualities. Additionally, change is associated with tragedy and comedy

in the stimulus, so this answer doesn't show the link (or lack thereof) with satire and romance.

(C) is a Distortion. Idealized worlds (and thus characters) are an aspect of romance literature, while debased worlds (and characters) are an aspect of satire. According to the stimulus, characters in tragedies change, but that doesn't mean they have to run the gamut from idealized to debased. This choice jumbles up all the vocabulary in the stimulus but ignores the central assumption: satire and romance are different than tragedy and comedy.

(E) introduces minor characters, who are Outside the Scope. The argument revolves around major characters only. Additionally, even if this choice was about major characters, it would simply restate a piece of the evidence. The correct answer in an Assumption question will never simply restate evidence.

6. (B) Assumption (MC-ME) ★★☆☆

Step 1: Identify the Question Stem

The question stem tells us that one of the answer choices, if assumed, will make the conclusion follow from the evidence. That makes this an Assumption question.

Step 2: Untangle the Stimulus

The conclusion of the argument is signaled by "[t]hus." Griley does not believe in democracy. The evidence comes in two parts. Apparently, Griley believes that any popular artwork is probably not good. Also, the first sentence gives us a more general rule: anyone who believes in democracy has a high regard for the wisdom of the masses.

Step 3: Make a Prediction

We should rearrange the pieces of this argument so that we can clearly see the gap in the logic. The first sentence tells us something that's true of *anyone* who believes in democracy, so it can be translated into Formal Logic. "If one believes in democracy, then one has high regard for mass wisdom." Now, we see that the conclusion tells us that Griley does not believe in democracy. This is our cue to contrapose our Formal Logic statement. "If one doesn't have high regard for mass wisdom, then one doesn't believe in democracy." The only other thing we know about Griley from the evidence is his belief that popular artwork isn't likely to be good. So if we can tie that belief to a disregard for the wisdom of the masses, then our contrapositive will be triggered and Griley will indeed not believe in democracy, which is the argument's conclusion. So we can phrase our prediction as "If one believes that popular artwork is unlikely to be good, then one does not have high regard for the wisdom of the masses."

Step 4: Evaluate the Answers

(B) matches this prediction perfectly.

These explanations refer to
questions that begin on page 607.

Part Three: Logical Reasoning
Assumption Family Questions

(A) tells us that Griley's belief about popular artwork is enough to guarantee that he's an elitist, but that has no connection to the first statement about belief in democracy.

(C) gives us a conditional statement based on Griley's not being an elitist. But the evidence confirms that Griley is an elitist, and besides, we need an answer choice that will tell us that Griley does *not* have a high regard for the wisdom of the masses. That's the only way to guarantee the argument's conclusion that he doesn't believe in democracy.

(D) gets the terms backward. To guarantee that the conclusion follows from the evidence, we need an answer choice that says that the belief that popular artwork isn't good is *sufficient* for a disregard for the wisdom of the masses, not *necessary*.

(E) merely mixes up the sufficient and necessary conditions of the first sentence of the argument. The first sentence of the argument tells us that a high regard for the wisdom of the masses is necessary for belief in democracy. **(E)** tells us the opposite. Without a connection to Griley's elitism or his belief that popular artwork is substandard, **(E)** can't properly bridge together the terms of the argument.

7. (B) Assumption (MC-E)   ★★☆☆

Step 1: Identify the Question Type

The question asks for an assumption that, if true, will support the conclusion (i.e., a sufficient assumption). Unlike a necessary assumption, a sufficient assumption doesn't have to be true, so the Denial Test may not be useful. If the sufficient assumption is true, it acts like a strengthener to support the conclusion.

Step 2: Untangle the Stimulus

Complicated stimuli require careful strategic reading. Use the Keywords to follow the reasoning. "Smith argues" gives us somebody's theory. The word "[b]ut" signals the author's disagreement. The word "[t]hus" signals a conclusion. But this is followed by "This, in turn, suggests." The final conclusion then, is in this last sentence: "Smith herself is not aware of the true meaning of her own words." This is supported by a subsidiary conclusion (signaled by "[t]hus")—if Smith's theory is correct, we can use Smith's social circumstances to discover at least some of the meaning of her statements. Smith's theory, given in the first sentence, is that understanding the true meaning of an author's statements requires insight into the author's social circumstances.

Step 3: Make a Prediction

There is a mismatch between the scope of the evidence and the scope of the conclusion. The evidence states: to understand her own true meaning, Smith must have insight into her own social circumstance. The conclusion is this: Smith is unaware of the true meaning of her words. The conclusion is likely true if Smith lacks insight into her social circumstances.

Quick note on sufficient assumptions: The conclusion that Smith is unaware of her true meaning does not *require* that she lack awareness of her social circumstances. There could be other reasons why she is unaware. However, given her own theory, a lack of insight helps to conclude that she is unaware. This demonstrates the difference between a sufficient assumption and a necessary assumption.

Step 4: Evaluate the Answer Choices

(B) fits the prediction perfectly. By her own theory, if Smith lacked insight into her own social circumstances, it would follow that she could not understand her own meaning.

(A) is Outside the Scope. The argument does not address "intended meaning," and the relative importance of different kinds of meaning is not an issue.

(C) is Outside the Scope. The argument is not concerned with Smith's intended meaning, only with her awareness of her true meaning.

(D) is a Distortion. It is not Smith's theory that lacks insight. The theory is about the relationship of lack of insight to lack of understanding.

(E) is Outside the Scope. "[I]ntended meaning" plays no role in this argument.

8. (B) Assumption (OP)   ★★★☆

Step 1: Identify the Question Type

The phrase "is assumed" signals a sufficient Assumption question. Find the conclusion and evidence and then predict a missing premise that would plug the gap between them.

Step 2: Untangle the Stimulus

The Keyword "[t]hus" in the last sentence points out the author's conclusion: There are more engraving than non-engraving etching tools. The remainder of the stimulus is evidence. First, all engraving tools are either pin-tipped or bladed. Next, some bladed tools are used for engraving and some aren't, but all pin-tipped tools are used for engraving. It seems reasonable, then, to suppose that engraving tools are more common than etching tools.

Step 3: Make a Prediction

What the author has forgotten is that there might be a lot more bladed tools than pin-tipped ones. For example, if there are 1,000 bladed tools and only 10 pin-tipped ones, then there could well be a lot more nonengraving tools. Only one of those 1,000 bladed tools might be used for engraving, in which case you'd have 999 nonengraving tools and only 11 engraving ones.

The author must take for granted, then, either that there are at least as many pin-tipped tools as bladed tools or that the majority of bladed tools are used for etching. Either

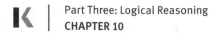

Part Three: Logical Reasoning
CHAPTER 10

These explanations refer to
questions that begin on page 608.

EXPLANATIONS

assumption is sufficient to prevent the prevalence of more bladed tools than pin-tipped ones.

Step 4: Evaluate the Answer Choices

(B) matches one of your predictions exactly, point for point.

(A) is a challenging Out of Scope attempt. Just because all engraving tools are also etching tools doesn't mean that nonengraving tools *aren't* etching tools. Thus, the counterexample scenario you found in Step 3 could still occur.

(C) is also Out of Scope. It removes the possibility that a tool would have both a blade and a pin-tip, but this possibility isn't what causes the argument as written to fail—it's the possibility that there are many more bladed tools than pin-tipped ones and that most of the bladed tools aren't used for engraving. This choice doesn't address that possibility.

(D) is a 180. If the majority of bladed tools are *not* used for engraving, then a minority of them *are*. But the author wants to prove that *more* tools are used for engraving, not fewer. Notice that if you removed the word "not" from this choice to make it read, "The majority of bladed etching tools are used for engraving," then it would be correct.

(E) restates the evidence. If all pin-tipped tools are used for engraving and bladed tools are the only other kind, then you can already deduce from the stimulus that all non-engraving tools must be bladed. It adds no new information, so it can't possibly be a missing piece of evidence.

9. (A) Assumption (MC-E)   ★★★☆

Step 1: Identify the Question Type

The word "assumption" identifies this as an Assumption question. Additionally, the word "relies" indicates you are looking for a Necessary Assumption, one without which the conclusion cannot be logically drawn from the evidence. You can use the Denial Test to check or eliminate answer choices.

Step 2: Untangle the Stimulus

The Keyword "[t]hus" identifies the author's conclusion: The success of chain bookstores is a detriment to book consumers. Why? The Keyword "for" identifies the author's main piece of evidence: this success has put a damper on the variety of available books.

Step 3: Make a Prediction

Bridging the mismatched terms in the evidence and conclusion can lead to solid predictions. Here, the author must assume that a lack of variety is a detriment to consumers.

Step 4: Evaluate the Answer Choices

(A) is correct and matches your prediction: consumers would be better off with more variety. If they were not better off with variety, then there would be no reason to claim that

the success of chain bookstores has been to the detriment of consumers.

(B) is a 180. This choice points out a benefit of chain stores, making their success seem more positive and less detrimental. The author wouldn't assume good things about chain bookstores and then conclude they are bad for consumers.

(C) is an Irrelevant Comparison. The size of the average bookstore (which would factor in both chain and independent stores) today versus the size 20 years ago is irrelevant to the author's conclusion. In addition, if bookstores are now larger, that could weaken the argument by showing how consumers now have more books from which to choose.

(D) is also an Irrelevant Comparison. The author is not concerned about comparing the physical sizes of the average bookstore over time. He is concerned with the total number of independent versus chain bookstores.

(E) is Outside the Scope. Without evidence stating chain stores are more expensive, this answer doesn't factor into the author's argument. This choice also weakens the author's argument by suggesting that the variety of books is not as important to consumers as price.

10. (D) Assumption (OP-R)   ★★★☆

Step 1: Identify the Question Type

The question asks for the argument's assumption. Since the argument "depends" on the Necessary Assumption, you can use the Denial Test to confirm or eliminate answers.

Step 2: Untangle the Stimulus

The conclusion is in the first sentence: country X should institute a nationwide system for transporting seriously injured people to specialized trauma centers. The evidence is that getting injured people to medical care faster could save lives, and the people saved would end up contributing a lot to the nation's economy.

Step 3: Make a Prediction

The author says saving lives would boost country X's gross national product. To complete his argument, the author must assume that the people whose lives are saved would actually get jobs and earn money.

Step 4: Evaluate the Answer Choices

(D) is the author's Necessary Assumption. Use the Denial Test to prove it. When choice **(D)** is denied, it says if more persons survived serious injury, there would be no change in total employment. If there were no change in total employment, then there would be no change in earnings. Without the change in earnings, there would be no increase in taxes paid to the government. Thus, denying **(D)** destroys the author's reasoning.

These explanations refer to
questions that begin on page 608.

Part Three: Logical Reasoning
Assumption Family Questions

(A) makes an Irrelevant Comparison. The author doesn't rely on any financial information from country Y in formulating his argument; he only mentions that the other country has implemented such a transportation system.

(B) goes Outside the Scope; the issue is transportation to trauma centers, not their existence.

(C) is another Irrelevant Comparison; you don't know (or care) anything about the cost anywhere else. The author isn't concerned with the cost of the treatment, just the future income of the patient. Even if the cost at trauma centers is more expensive than elsewhere, the author's argument may still be valid.

(E) is a Distortion. The author indicates improved transportation to specialized trauma centers makes long-term financial sense. Whether or not most people seriously injured in auto accidents currently use those facilities does not impact that financial question. Perhaps the improved transportation network would increase the use of the facilities in the future. Furthermore, the word "most" should always be a red flag in Necessary Assumption questions.

11. (E) Assumption (MC-E)   ★★★☆

Step 1: Identify the Question Type

The phrase "if which one of the following is assumed" indicates that this is a Sufficient Assumption question.

Step 2: Untangle the Stimulus

The author concludes that the amygdala has more influence over the cortex than the cortex has over the amygdala. The evidence is that the neural connections carrying signals from the amygdala to the cortex are better developed.

Step 3: Make a Prediction

This is a classic Mismatched Concepts argument. Because both the evidence and conclusion mention the amygdala and the cortex, these are not the mismatched terms. Looking past the amygdala and the cortex, the conclusion is about exerting influence. The evidence is about the development of neural connections. The assumption will connect these two ideas. The author must be assuming that the more development there is in a set of neural connections, the more influence it has.

Step 4: Evaluate the Answer Choices

(E) matches the prediction. "[D]irectly proportional" just means that as one thing goes up, so too does another. That would be Extreme if this was a Necessary Assumption question, but here it is acceptable because this is a Sufficient Assumption question.

(A) goes Outside the Scope by introducing the rest of the brain, rather than just the amygdala and cortex.

(B) also goes Outside the Scope. Other brain regions are irrelevant to whether the development of neural connections is an indication of influence.

(C) goes Outside the Scope by discussing the region "that has the most influence on the cortex." The stimulus is only about the amygdala and the cortex. **(C)** would strengthen the argument, but by itself, it is not sufficient to reach the conclusion that the amygdala exerts a greater influence on the cortex than vice versa.

(D) also goes Outside the Scope, much like **(A)** and **(B)**, by introducing areas of the brain besides the amygdala and the cortex.

12. (E) Assumption (MC-E)   ★★★★

Step 1: Identify the Question Type

Because the "argument requires the assumption," this is a Necessary Assumption question.

Step 2: Untangle the Stimulus

The conclusion is that legislators who value democracy shouldn't propose laws barring behavior that only hurts the person engaging in the behavior. The evidence is that general acceptance of the idea that individuals can't look out for themselves hurts society, and the assumptions imputed to our legislators tend to spread to the rest of society.

Step 3: Make a Prediction

Start by identifying the mismatched terms. Both the evidence and conclusion discuss protecting democracy, so that idea doesn't need to be in the assumption. The idea of widely spread ideas comes up in both pieces of the evidence, so that doesn't need to be in the assumption either. What's left over in the conclusion is laws barring self-destructive behaviors. What's left over in the evidence is individuals not being able to look out for themselves. The assumption will connect the ideas of laws barring self-destructive behaviors and of individuals not being able to look out for themselves.

Step 4: Evaluate the Answer Choices

(E) connects legislators banning self-destructive behaviors and individuals being seen as incapable of looking out for themselves.

(A) goes Outside the Scope by focusing on what legislators value, rather than on what they should not do. Additionally the word "invariably" is too Extreme to be needed by the argument.

(B) is a Faulty Use of Detail. It repeats an idea from the evidence in more general terms. The evidence states that people accept the assumptions of legislators, so it is irrelevant whether people accept the beliefs of other prominent and powerful people as well.

K | Part Three: Logical Reasoning
CHAPTER 10

These explanations refer to
questions that begin on page 609.

(C) goes Outside the Scope by discussing what legislators already do, rather than what they should do in the future. The author may believe that legislators may currently be undertaking an action injurious to democracy, despite valuing it.

(D) goes Outside the Scope by focusing just on the likelihood that behavior that is harmful to the person who does it is also harmful to others. The stimulus focuses on whether or not to propose legislation barring such behavior, not its frequency.

13. (A) Assumption (MC-N) ★★★★

Step 1: Identify the Question Type

The question asks for an assumption that, if true, will support the conclusion (i.e., a sufficient assumption). Unlike a necessary assumption, a sufficient assumption doesn't have to be true, so the Denial Test may not be useful. If the sufficient assumption is true, it acts like a strengthener to support the conclusion.

Step 2: Untangle the Stimulus

This is a short argument, but short doesn't necessarily mean simple! As always, think critically as you read. The Keyword "for" in the second clause identifies the evidence. So, the argument starts with the conclusion in the first clause: one should never sacrifice health to acquire money.

The reason is that you can't obtain happiness without health.

$$\text{If happiness} \rightarrow \text{health}$$
$$\text{If ~health} \rightarrow \text{~ happiness}$$

In other words, if acquiring money sacrifices your health, don't do it, because you need your health to obtain happiness.

Step 3: Make a Prediction

This argument relies on Formal Logic. The signal for this is the word "without," which establishes a necessary relationship between health and happiness. However, the complexity of the terms might make the use of Formal Logic confusing to start out. Instead, start by looking for the terms in the conclusion that must be tied with the terms of the evidence. Once the relevant terms are identified, Formal Logic might help.

The author recommends against the acquisition of money if it means sacrificing health in the conclusion, based upon evidence that sacrificing health makes happiness unobtainable. The assumption that ties this together would be that one should never acquire money if it makes happiness unobtainable. In Formal Logic:

$$\text{If makes happiness} \rightarrow \text{don't acquire money}$$
$$\text{unobtainable}$$

Step 4: Evaluate the Answer Choices

(A) fits the prediction. This answer is essentially a contrapositive form of the prediction made above. Translating the Formal Logic demonstrates:

$$\text{If acquire money} \rightarrow \text{doesn't make happiness}$$
$$\text{unobtainable}$$

(B) is a Distortion. Health and money are not alternative requirements for happiness; only health is needed. In this argument, money can only detract from happiness (if it sacrifices health), not create it.

(C) is Outside the Scope. The argument is not about the conditions under which health is to be valued. Rather, it is about the conditions under which one should or should not acquire money.

(D) is a Distortion. First, "[b]eing wealthy" is not necessarily synonymous with acquiring money. Even if it were, the argument does not assume that acquiring money makes one unhappy. The assumption, like the argument itself, is conditional—if it makes happiness unobtainable, then don't do it!

(E) is a Distortion, as well as an Irrelevant Comparison. The argument rests on the assertion that without health, happiness cannot be obtained. The fact that health is necessary for happiness does not mean it's conducive to happiness, nor does it have anything to do with the comparative benefits of health and money.

14. (E) Assumption (MC-E) ★★★★

Step 1: Identify the Question Type

The phrase "if assumed, enables the argument's conclusion to be properly drawn," indicates that this is a Sufficient Assumption question.

Step 2: Untangle the Stimulus

The author concludes that it is "imprudent to appear prudent." The reason is that people are generally resented when they wait for evidence in order to judge others.

Step 3: Make a Prediction

As in many arguments, the conclusion introduces an element that wasn't anywhere to be found in the evidence. Here that element is "imprudent." The element of prudence is in the evidence because prudence is doing things cautiously, like waiting for evidence to make a judgment about someone. The evidence also includes an element not found in the conclusion—here it is being resented by others. The correct answer will connect imprudence to inspiring resentment in others.

Step 4: Evaluate the Answer Choices

(E) strongly connects inspiring resentment to imprudence.

(A) fails to include anything about the mismatched term of imprudence.

(B) fails to include anything about the mismatched term of resentment.

These explanations refer to questions that begin on page 609.

Part Three: Logical Reasoning
Assumption Family Questions

K

(C) is a Distortion. People resent those who appear prudent, not people who appear less prudent.

(D) goes Outside the Scope by focusing on people who are intuitive, rather than on the connection between imprudence and resentment.

15. (A) Assumption (OP-PvC) ★★★★

Step 1: Identify the Question Type

The question asks for an assumption that the argument depends upon (i.e., a necessary assumption). When in doubt, the Denial Test might help.

Step 2: Untangle the Stimulus

The Keyword "[s]o" begins the president's conclusion: to increase the number of applicants, the university needs to raise tuition and fees. The support for this is given in the president's explanation for why the applicant pool has been shrinking: low tuition and fees could lead prospective students to the conclusion that the quality of the education at that institution is low.

Step 3: Make a Prediction

Notice that the conclusion is about what we *need* to do while the evidence is about a *possible* explanation. That is a classic Possibility vs. Certainty argument, a subtype of the Overlooked Possibilities pattern. The correct answer will make clear that the possible explanation is, in fact, the right one.

Step 4: Evaluate the Answer Choices

(A) fits the prediction. The president is assuming his explanation of why applications are low applies to this case, which leads to his conclusion that tuition needs to be raised.

If an answer choice is worded in a way that isn't immediately clear, the Denial Test will confirm the choice. Restate choice **(A)** in the negative: If the proposed explanation does not apply in this case (students don't equate low tuition with low quality), then the president's conclusion that they need to raise tuition is undermined.

(B) is a Distortion. The president speculates that students may believe this to be true, but the president himself doesn't necessarily assume it's true.

(C) is a Distortion, confusing a necessary condition for a sufficient one. The president states that if they wish to increase the applicant pool, they need to raise tuition and fees. By this reasoning, raising tuition would be necessary to achieve the goal, but he doesn't assume it will guarantee it.

(D) is Outside the Scope. The existence of an "additional" explanation adds nothing to the president's reasoning. His conclusion that tuition needs to be raised to attract applicants is based solely on his explanation.

If this answer choice had said "alternative explanation" rather than "additional explanation," then it would have

been another way of expressing the correct assumption given already in answer choice **(A)**. Careful reading avoids traps like this.

(E) is Outside the Scope. The argument is about what is needed to correct the problem of a shrinking applicant pool and speculates that low tuitions are the cause of the problem. Past failure to increase tuition may explain why tuitions are low, but the president's argument doesn't need an explanation for the low tuition in order to make his point.

16. (E) Assumption (MC-E) ★★★★

Step 1: Identify the Question Type

The question asks for an assumption that the argument depends upon (i.e., a necessary assumption). When in doubt, the Denial Test might help.

Step 2: Untangle the Stimulus

The conclusion is signaled by the word "[h]owever." Contrary to the experts' belief that the plesiosauromorph lurked and ambushed its prey, the author concludes that it hunted by chasing its prey over long distances. The support for this is the shape of the dinosaur's fins, which were similar to the wing shape of birds that specialize in flying long distances.

Step 3: Make a Prediction

The argument states that because the dinosaur's fin was shaped like the wings of birds that specialize in flying long distances, the dinosaur must have swum long distances. This equivalence argument only works if the shape of the dinosaur's fin relates to its behavior in water the same way the bird's wing shape relates to its behavior in the air.

Step 4: Evaluate the Answer Choices

(E) fits the prediction precisely. The Denial Test confirms: if the shape of the marine animal's fin did not affect its swimming in the same way the shape of the bird's wing affects its flying, the argument would fail to convince.

(A) is Outside the Scope of the argument. The argument draws a conclusion about how the plesiosauromorph behaved based upon the shape of its fin. Evolutionary ancestors are not the issue.

(B) is Outside the Scope. The argument draws a conclusion about plesiosauromorph behavior based on the shape of its fin. Whether or not its fins were unique is not the issue.

(C) is Outside the Scope of the argument. While this fact may give support to the conclusion that the plesiosauromorph chased its prey over long distances, it has nothing to do with the argument in the stimulus, which draws its conclusion from the shape of the dinosaur's fins. **(C)** is, therefore, not a necessary assumption for this argument.

(D) is Out of Scope. Even if most animals that chase their prey are specialized for long-distance swimming, as this choice

K Part Three: Logical Reasoning
CHAPTER 10

These explanations refer to
questions that begin on page 610.

says, some animals that are specialized for long-distance swimming might still lurk and ambush. This answer doesn't lead to the conclusion that this particular dinosaur chased prey over long distances. However, it should also be noted that the resemblance of the plesiosauromorph's fin to the wing of a bird that is specialized for long-distance flying does not necessarily mean that the dinosaur was specialized for long-distance swimming. Choice **(D)** makes the same assumption that the argument makes.

17. (D) Assumption (MC-N)

Step 1: Identify the Question Stem

The language in this stem ("assumption required by the . . . argument") is standard language for an Assumption question.

Step 2: Untangle the Stimulus

The critic concludes that it is impossible for contemporary literary works to be tragedies. There are two pieces of evidence: that modern works can't be tragedies in the classical sense unless their protagonists are seen as possessing nobility and that our current age is one in which no one believes that human endeavors are governed by fate.

Step 3: Make a Prediction

The words "cannot" and "unless" in the first sentence are a good indication that Formal Logic might be helpful. That sentence translates to "If the protagonist is not seen as possessing nobility, then modern works cannot be tragedies." However, the author concludes that modern works are certainly not tragedies without establishing the condition that the protagonists are not seen as noble. Instead, the author claims that people don't believe in endeavors governed by fate. For the argument to work, the author must assume a necessary relationship between the concept of endeavors not being governed by fate and the condition that protagonists are not seen as noble.

Step 4: Evaluate the Answers

(D) provides exactly the missing link we predicted.

(A) is a 180. Clearly the critic thinks that classification of a work as a tragedy should depend on characteristics of its audience, since the critic invokes audience beliefs to declare that modern works can't be tragedies.

(B) is Extreme. It needn't be true that the belief that human endeavors are governed by fate is false; the evidence merely says that no one takes the belief seriously anymore. Furthermore, **(B)** provides no link between the evidence and conclusion.

(C) isn't necessary to the argument either. Even if all plays that were once classified as tragedies meet the author's criteria for classification as tragedies, the argument can still be made,

since the critic is concerned with how to classify *contemporary* works of literature.

(E) is merely a contrapositive (and an impure one, at that) of the Formal Logic statement in the argument's first sentence. However, since the critic doesn't assert that all modern literature contains ignoble characters who persevere, **(E)** doesn't enable the critic to reach the conclusion from the evidence provided.

18. (D) Assumption (MC-E)

Step 1: Identify the Question Stem

The stem tells us that one of the choices, if assumed, will make the conclusion follow from the evidence. This means we're dealing with an Assumption question.

Step 2: Untangle the Stimulus

The councilperson's conclusion is that the edifice that the art commission wants to purchase qualifies as art. The evidence is that the edifice has caused experts to debate what constitutes art and that causing such a debate is the purpose of art.

Step 3: Make a Prediction

Notice the scope shift between the evidence and the conclusion of this argument. The evidence mentions that the edifice *fulfills the purpose* of art. But the conclusion suddenly asserts that the edifice *is actually* art. There's a difference here. The purpose of an umbrella is to shield me from the rain. A plastic sheet held over my head could fulfill that same purpose, but that doesn't automatically make a plastic sheet an umbrella. So the councilperson assumes here that anything that fulfills art's purpose qualifies as art.

Step 4: Evaluate the Answers

(D) is a clear match for our prediction.

(A) says that causing debate among experts is necessary for something to qualify as art. But to enable the conclusion to follow directly from the evidence, **(A)** would need to say that causing debate among experts is *sufficient* for something to qualify as art. Then the edifice would be art just by virtue of the debate it inspired and nothing else.

(B), if assumed, would mean that no expert would be certain that the edifice qualifies as art. So that would make it even more difficult to establish the councilperson's conclusion that the edifice does qualify as art.

(C) would enable the councilperson to conclude that no city resident should oppose the art commission's purchase of the edifice, since the edifice does actually fulfill the purpose of art. But the conclusion of the argument is that the edifice qualifies as art, and **(C)** alone doesn't establish that conclusion.

(E) doesn't help link the evidence to the conclusion because the conclusion itself is that the edifice qualifies as art.

These explanations refer to
questions that begin on page 611.

Part Three: Logical Reasoning
Assumption Family Questions

K

(E) doesn't help prove that because it's contingent upon the conclusion already being true.

19. (E) Assumption (MC-A) ★★★★

Step 1: Identify the Question Type

The word "assumption" identifies this as an Assumption question. Additionally, the word "depends" indicates you are looking for a Necessary Assumption, one without which the fund-raiser's conclusion cannot be logically drawn from the evidence. You can use the Denial Test to check or eliminate answer choices.

Step 2: Untangle the Stimulus

The fund-raiser states donors often don't have the right to vote on charities' policies. She argues this lack results in donors feeling less emotionally connected to their charity. The fund-raiser then argues that giving donors the right to vote will increase the amount of money donated.

Step 3: Make a Prediction

By saying the lack of a vote decreases donors' emotional connection to a charity, the fund-raiser suggests having the right to vote would result in donors having a greater emotional connection to a charity. However, she makes an unsupported jump to the conclusion. There is a distinction between having an emotional connection and giving money for which the fund-raiser does not account. The fund-raiser must therefore assume a greater emotional connection will lead to larger monetary donations.

Step 4: Evaluate the Answer Choices

(E) is correct and captures the essence of that assumption.

(A) is Extreme. There are many problems with this answer, the most important of which is that it offers no connection as to why the author feels that a right to vote will lead to increased donations. Furthermore, a right to vote does not have to be the *most* effective way for donors to influence the charity's decisions. As long as it's *a* way, donors will probably feel more emotionally connected.

(B) is a Distortion. This choice is tempting but problematic because it only tells you about charities that have increased their donations. What about all of the charities that *have not* increased donations? The fund-raiser is trying to show that increasing emotional connections leads to increased donations. This answer too conveniently ignores the possibility that a lot of charities may also have increased emotional connections but *failed* to increase donations. By reversing the cause and effect, this answer distorts the assumption and is therefore incorrect. This answer choice may strengthen the argument, but it is not a necessary assumption.

(C) is Extreme. It strengthens the evidence about increasing emotional connections but fails to connect that evidence to the concept of increased donations mentioned in the conclusion. **(C)** also would fail the Denial Test because even if it wasn't "every" charity that had this result, the conclusion that "most charities could probably increase the amount of money they raise" could still hold.

(D) is also Extreme. The fund-raiser may feel that reducing a donor's influence may lead to a decrease in donations. However, the fund-raiser never goes so far as to suggest that donors would stop giving *any* money to the charity. Furthermore, the right to vote is described as a direct influence on policies, but the fund-raiser never suggests what would happen if donors did not have "any influence" whatsoever. Lastly, the author would not need to assume that "[m]ost potential donors" would have this reaction. Even if it was less than half, it would not affect the force of the argument.

20. (D) Assumption (OP) ★★★★

Step 1: Identify the Question Type

The phrase "if . . . assumed" signifies a sufficient Assumption question. Find the gap between the evidence and conclusion and then predict a missing piece of information that affirms the conclusion.

Step 2: Untangle the Stimulus

The argument features no conclusion or evidence Keywords, so use the One-Sentence Test to find the author's opinion. It's the conditional statement in the first sentence: If aliens exist outside our solar system, we're not going to find them anytime soon unless they're at least as smart as we are. Translate the Formal Logic:

> *If find aliens soon* → *aliens as smart as us*
>
> *If ~ aliens smart as us* → *~ find aliens soon*

The remainder of the argument states why: Our spaceships can't reach planets beyond our solar system, and aliens below our intelligence level won't be able to communicate with us across space.

Step 3: Make a Prediction

Though the argument seems sensible, it overlooks some important possibilities: the conclusion talks about *finding* aliens, whereas the evidence talks about *communicating* with them. Just because we can't communicate with aliens doesn't mean we can't find them. The author rules out one alternative—landing a ship on an alien planet—but never states that it's the *only* alternative. Thus, the author takes for granted that the only way to find aliens is to communicate with them or send spacecraft to their planet. Look for some variation of this assumption in the choices.

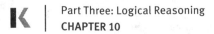
Part Three: Logical Reasoning
CHAPTER 10

These explanations refer to
questions that begin on page 612.

Step 4: Evaluate the Answer Choices

(D) rewards your hard work in Step 3. It says, in so many words, that talking with aliens and landing a ship on their planet are the only possible ways to find them.

(A) is Out of Scope. It talks about aliens within our solar system, whereas the argument is concerned with aliens outside our solar system.

(B) is also Out of Scope. It provides information about aliens who are as intelligent as we are, but it fails to explain why the aliens have to be as intelligent as we are in the first place.

(C) fails because it merely expands on a piece of evidence. The author already said that our ships can't reach planets outside our solar system, and this choice extends that restriction to planets within our solar system as well. However, the fact remains that we might not need ships to find aliens at all.

(E) shares the same flaw as choice (B). By stating what's true about equally intelligent aliens, it fails to address the author's assumption that the aliens need to be as intelligent as we are in the first place.

21. (C) Flaw (OP)   ★★★★

Step 1: Identify the Question Type

The question states that the argument in the stimulus is flawed. This means that the evidence does not support the conclusion. The answer choice will describe why.

Step 2: Untangle the Stimulus

The conclusion, indicated by the Keyword "[t]herefore," is that eliminating lead paint from homes will end the problem of childhood lead poisoning. The reason given is that cases of lead poisoning have decreased since the ban of lead paint and leaded gasoline; however, there are still homes that contain lead paint.

Step 3: Make a Prediction

To predict this flaw, notice the extreme language in the conclusion that lead poisoning will "finally be eradicated" (i.e., completely eliminated). Why? Because the lead paint will be gone. The author of this argument is making the assumption that there are no sources of hazardous lead other than the lead paint. This is the classic flaw of overlooked possibility.

Step 4: Evaluate the Answer Choices

(C) tells us that the argument "fails to consider" other potential sources of lead. This is exactly what was predicted.

(A) is a Distortion. The conclusion does not rely on the percentage of houses that have lead paint but rather on the fact that eliminating lead paint from any homes that have it will eradicate the poisoning hazard.

(B) is awkwardly worded in order to confuse. To paraphrase, (B) states that the argument assumes its conclusion (i.e., is circular). That is not the flaw here.

(D) is Outside the Scope. The argument is about eliminating lead poisoning by eliminating lead paint. The economic feasibility of doing so is not an issue.

(E) is Extreme and Outside the Scope. The argument does not rely on children living in the homes and certainly not in *all* of the homes.

22. (B) Flaw (OP-NvS)   ★★★★

Step 1: Identify the Question Type

The word "vulnerable" signals a Flaw question. Identify the conclusion, summarize the evidence, and then predict the flaw.

A quick scan of the answer choices tells you that the author has (1) taken something for granted, (2) failed to adequately address something, or (3) overlooked a possibility. Keep these potential flaws in mind as you read the stimulus.

Step 2: Untangle the Stimulus

This argument features the conclusion Keyword "[h]ence," which makes finding the conclusion a snap: It's likely that primitive life has evolved on Europa. Perhaps a shocking claim, but the author has evidence: there's liquid water on Europa, and you need liquid water for life to evolve.

Step 3: Make a Prediction

Anytime you see the word "only" in a Flaw question, check for the classic sufficiency/necessity mix-up. Doing so makes short work of this problem. The word "only" tells you that water is necessary for life, but the author acts as though water is sufficient for life: from the fact that there is water, she concludes that there must be life.

Using the potential flaws identified earlier, predict the answer. Perhaps the author is taking for granted that something necessary for life to evolve is sufficient for life to evolve. Or perhaps the author is failing to adequately address that other things might be necessary for life to evolve. Finally, perhaps the author is overlooking the possibility that other things are necessary for life to evolve. All three statements describe the same flaw, so be somewhat flexible in how the correct answer choice might be worded.

Step 4: Evaluate the Answer Choices

(B) says, in so many words, "Water might not be sufficient for life." Circle it and move on.

(A) accuses the author of taking something "for granted," but the thing being taken for granted in choice (A) is logically true. If a condition is necessary for the evolution of life, then life indeed could not evolve anywhere that condition isn't met. In any case, the argument talks about a

These explanations refer to questions that begin on page 612.

Part Three: Logical Reasoning
Assumption Family Questions

K

place that *does* have water, so places where "this condition does not hold"—that is, places that *don't* have water—are irrelevant.

(C) is tempting because the author does take for granted that life would have evolved "if, but only if" liquid water was present. But that's not what choice **(C)** says. It instead connects the presence of life to the evolution of life, and the author doesn't care about the presence of life, only its evolution.

(D) talks again about there not being water, which has no bearing on the argument because Europa *does* have water.

(E) is Extreme yet tempting, because it appears to cast doubt on the data submitted by the spacecraft. If there's no liquid water on Europa, then life couldn't have evolved there. However, the author doesn't take for granted that "no" conditions besides liquid water could have caused the data. She states that the data "strongly suggest" the presence of liquid water, implicitly acknowledging that the presence of water may be a mistaken interpretation. Furthermore, she qualifies her conclusion with the word "likely." Although unjustified certainty is a classic pattern of flawed reasoning on the LSAT, this author has carefully avoided that error.

23. (E) Flaw (MC-E) ★☆☆☆

Step 1: Identify the Question Type

The question stem asks for the flaw Lana points out in Chinh's argument, so this is a Flaw question. Use Lana's comments to direct your evaluation of Chinh's argument. Keep an eye out for common flaw types.

Step 2: Untangle the Stimulus

Start by summarizing each argument. Chinh's conclusion is that TV producers should disregard the preferences of the viewers when making creative decisions. Chinh's evidence is that great painters don't think about what the public wants to see. Lana contradicts Chinh by introducing a new point about TV: It is made for the public. From there, Lana suggests that TV producers are more like CEOs than artists. This supports her recommendation that TV producers should consider the preferences of viewers.

Step 3: Make a Prediction

Both speakers use an analogy for their evidence. Chinh thinks TV producers are like great painters, whereas Lana thinks TV producers are like CEOs. Whenever an author uses an analogy for evidence, the author assumes the two things in the analogy are sufficiently alike to be comparable. So, Chinh's assumption is TV producers are sufficiently similar to great painters. Lana's assumption is TV producers and CEOs are sufficiently alike. Lana's disagreement with Chinh's argument is the choice of analogy; she essentially says TV producers

and artists are not sufficiently alike for Chinh to use evidence about one to draw a conclusion about the other.

Step 4: Evaluate the Answer Choices

(E) is a short and sweet match to the prediction.

(A) describes a circular reasoning flaw, which is very rarely the correct answer to a Flaw question. Circular reasoning describes an argument that uses the same idea for both evidence and conclusion. Here, Lana doesn't argue Chinh's evidence is the same as Chinh's conclusion; instead she debates the relevance of the evidence.

(B) describes a representativeness flaw, which isn't occurring here. Both Lana and Chinh's arguments address the "viewing public" as a whole, which is a perfectly representative group of consumers. Lana doesn't critique Chinh's sample selection.

(C) says Chinh incorrectly infers that a causal relationship is intentional. However, Chinh's argument is a recommendation based on an analogy, not any sort of cause-and-effect relationship.

(D) may be a flaw that Chinh commits, but the question stem asks for how Lana addresses Chinh's argument. Lana suggests that Chinh is wrong about TV producers, not about painters. Lana doesn't think TV producers should be compared to painters at all, and therefore painters' objectives are irrelevant.

24. (C) Flaw (OP-C) ★★☆☆

Step 1: Identify the Question Type

The phrase "most vulnerable to criticism" identifies this as a Flaw question. Break down the author's argument, identifying his conclusion and evidence and determining his assumption. Then, evaluate how the author's reasoning goes wrong. Remember to keep an eye out for common flaw types.

Step 2: Untangle the Stimulus

The author presents you with two pieces of information: *Sirat Bani Hilal* is the only Arabic epic poem still performed today, and it is usually sung (unlike most other epics). It is an interesting correlation, but the author then makes the sudden leap that the singing factor is the primary reason for the epic's continued performance.

Step 3: Make a Prediction

This argument is a textbook example of an author implying causation based on a mere correlation. Just because two things occur together does not mean that one caused the other.

Step 4: Evaluate the Answer Choices

(C) is correct and points out this classic LSAT flaw.

(A) is Extreme. None of the evidence here seems impossible (or even that difficult) to corroborate.

Part Three: Logical Reasoning
CHAPTER 10

These explanations refer to
questions that begin on page 613.

(B) is Outside the Scope. The fact that the play is still performed and the fact that it is sung do not indicate biased information.

(D) is Outside the Scope. The only opinion offered in this argument is the author's. Without knowing what the popular opinion is, you cannot claim that the author is turning opinion into fact.

(E) is also Outside the Scope. The evidence is merely a collection of facts. There are no sufficient or necessary conditions for the author to confuse.

25. (B) Flaw (OP-NvS)   ★★★☆

Step 1: Identify the Question Type

The phrase "reasoning is flawed" indicates this is a Flaw question. Break down the argument into conclusion and evidence and find the gap between the two. Identify where the author's reasoning goes wrong, keeping common flaw types in mind.

Step 2: Untangle the Stimulus

The conclusion is that the fourth-floor lab must be cleaned out. The stimulus presents three Formal Logic statements, signaled by the words "if" and "only," as evidence:

If Agnes's proposal is approved	→	the fourth floor lab must be cleaned out.
If Immanuel's proposal is approved	→	he will work in the second floor lab.
If a proposal is approved	→	director supports it.

Additionally, the author says the director will support both Agnes's and Immanuel's proposals.

Step 3: Make a Prediction

In a Flaw question, the word *only* is a huge clue to use Formal Logic and to consider overlooked alternatives. You know that the director will support both proposals. But that is a necessary consequence, rather than a trigger; nothing follows from the director supporting a proposal. The author mistakenly assumes that just because the author supports Agnes's and Immanuel's proposals that both will be approved. The correct answer could be phrased as a necessary versus sufficient flaw or as an overlooked alternative: It may be that despite the director's support, one or the other or both will be denied.

Step 4: Evaluate the Answer Choices

(B) matches the prediction. The author overlooks the chance that the director could support a proposal that still gets rejected.

(A) goes Outside the Scope by focusing on lab size rather than the gap in logic between the director supporting a proposal and the proposal being approved. The author doesn't have to

justify that the fourth-floor lab is larger; accept the evidence, in Formal Logic form, as true.

(C) is an Irrelevant Comparison. The *level* of the director's support, or enthusiasm, is irrelevant. The stimulus introduces a yes/no situation: Does the director support a proposal or no? In addition, nothing in the stimulus indicates these proposals are in competition with each another.

(D) goes Outside the Scope by focusing on what Immanuel will want. Based on the Formal Logic, regardless of his desire, Immanuel will work on the second-floor lab. The author doesn't address his wants, but that isn't what is flawed with this argument.

(E), like **(A)** and **(D)**, also introduces something the author does not discuss in his evidence. But because the evidence on the LSAT is to be taken as true, the Formal Logic statements he presents are sufficient. The author doesn't need to prove that they are accurate or that there aren't other options. The correct answer choice needs to address the gap between the evidence and the conclusion, not attack the evidence itself.

26. (C) Flaw (OP)   ★★★★

Step 1: Identify the Question Type

The phrase "most vulnerable to criticism" is common language for a Flaw question. Look for the unwarranted assumption or the common LSAT flaw.

Step 2: Untangle the Stimulus

The author concludes that University Hospital could discharge people sooner without affecting quality of care. The evidence is that Edgewater Hospital has a shorter average stay, even though people treated for similar illnesses recover at similar rates in the two hospitals.

Step 3: Make a Prediction

The conclusion is about the average length of stay for all patients at University Hospital, but the evidence is about a particular subset of patients, those with similar illnesses in the two hospitals. What the author doesn't explicitly demonstrate is whether the patients with the illnesses described in the evidence are actually representative of all the patients at University. The author overlooks the fact that, in general, the patients at University might be much more seriously ill than those at Edgewater. It could be true, for example, that the patients with minor colds at both hospitals recover in the same amount of time. However, if minor colds account for a large proportion of the patients at Edgewater but only a small proportion of the patients at University, then the average length of stay at both hospitals should not, in fact, be equal.

Step 4: Evaluate the Answer Choices

(C) correctly exposes the overlooked possibility that the patient populations at each hospital could be different.

These explanations refer to
questions that begin on page 614.

Part Three: Logical Reasoning
Assumption Family Questions

(A) directly contradicts the conclusion, where the author suggests that the average length of stay could be decreased without affecting the quality of care.

(B) inappropriately suggests that the author has confused necessity and sufficiency in the argument. The argument, however, is not stated in terms of Formal Logic. For example, the author never states that length of stay is necessary to quality of care.

(D) is Extreme because the author never states that length of stay "never" affects recovery.

(E) goes Outside the Scope by focusing on patient preferences.

27. (E) Flaw (OP) ★★★★

Step 1: Identify the Question Type

The phrase "most vulnerable to criticism" is common language for a Flaw question. Look for the unwarranted assumption or the common LSAT flaw.

Step 2: Untangle the Stimulus

The author concludes swimming at night is not more dangerous than swimming during the day based on one piece of evidence: all recent regional shark attacks have occurred during the day, not at night. The author uses this to challenge the general preference—stated in the first sentence—of the region's swimmers to swim in the daytime.

Step 3: Make a Prediction

The problem here is the completeness of the author's evidence. More attacks may be occurring during the day, but that's simply because that's also the time most people are swimming. The author overlooks that an increase in night swimming could increase the likelihood of shark attacks at night. After all, if no one's currently in the water at night, the sharks have no one to attack. If the number of swimmers were equal at all times, then it's possible the number of attacks *would* show swimming at night is more dangerous.

Step 4: Evaluate the Answer Choices

(E) matches the prediction.

(A) might be true but is not a logical flaw in the argument. *Some* sharks may prefer to hunt at night, but that doesn't hurt the author's argument. *Most* sharks may prefer to hunt in the daytime. Therefore, the author's argument could still be correct.

(B) goes Outside the Scope because the source of the author's evidence is never identified.

(C) is Outside the Scope because the author is solely focused on the actual danger posed by shark attacks. People may feel more anxious because of the dark, but the author is not suggesting people should swim at night (if she was, this would be good reason why his recommendation is flawed); she's simply saying it's not more dangerous.

(D) also goes Outside the Scope by attacking the swimmers themselves, focusing on how knowledgeable they are. Granted, the author says popular opinion is wrong, but she is basing her conclusion on statistics, not the assumption that others are simply less knowledgeable and therefore incorrect. This stimulus does not include an ad hominem attack.

28. (B) Flaw (OP-C)

Step 1: Identify the Question Type

"[V]ulnerable to criticism" is classic language used to indicate that the argument is inherently flawed, making this a Flaw question.

Step 2: Untangle the Stimulus

The panelist concludes that publicity influences the judgment of medical researchers when they're determining the importance of prior research. His evidence is that research that has received a lot of mainstream press coverage is more likely to be cited in later medical research.

Step 3: Make a Prediction

This argument follows the classic causation pattern: the panelist assumes the mainstream press coverage causes the subsequent citations in medical research. The panelist overlooks the three alternatives to causation: Is it just a coincidence? Is causation reversed? Is there another factor that caused both? In this case, that last possibility seems most likely; maybe there's a reason everyone is citing the same medical research.

Step 4: Evaluate the Answer Choices

(B) gives a plausible reason why everyone is citing the same medical research: it actually is important, and the press is doing a good job covering it.

(A) goes Outside the Scope; the stimulus includes no "counterarguments."

(C) goes Outside the Scope by discussing how the "eminence of the scientists" affects the press, rather than how mainstream press coverage affects subsequent medical research. The panelist never mentions scientists' eminence.

(D) goes Outside the Scope because the panelist isn't concerned that the mainstream press isn't reviewing more medical research articles but simply with the fact that when they do, the same articles tend to pop up again later in medical research. In fact, if the media only covers a small amount, then that would make the panelist's worry even more valid because the likelihood of coincidental overlap would diminish.

(E) incorrectly suggests that the panelist uses circular reasoning. As seen in Step 2, though, the evidence and conclusion are not logical equivalents because the conclusion introduces a claim of causation.

EXPLANATIONS

K | Part Three: Logical Reasoning
CHAPTER 10

These explanations refer to
questions that begin on page 614.

29. (B) Flaw (OP-NvS)

Step 1: Identify the Question Stem

We're asked to find why the factory manager's argument is flawed, so this is definitely a Flaw question.

Step 2: Untangle the Stimulus

The factory manager concludes that in order to survive, the factory's products must be more competitively priced, and the only way to do this is to completely refurbish the factory. The evidence for this is that if the factory were to be refurbished with new equipment, then the factory's products would be more competitively priced.

Step 3: Make a Prediction

Always keep classic flaws in mind as you untangle arguments in Flaw questions. One of the most common flaws is confusing necessity and sufficiency. In the evidence of this argument, the factory manager says that refurbishing the factory would be sufficient to make the products more competitively priced. But all of a sudden, the conclusion seems to treat refurbishment as necessary to lower prices and stay afloat. This unwarranted shift from sufficiency to necessity is always a logical flaw—after all, couldn't there conceivably be other ways to make the products more competitively priced? The evidence allows for such alternative solutions, but the conclusion doesn't.

Step 4: Evaluate the Answers

(B) matches our predicted flaw. The manager improperly treats one solution to the price problem as the only solution.

(A) is not the flaw here. The factory manager actually does recognize that the price of auto parts can change over time; that's why the manager proposes a way to lower that price to make it more competitive.

(C) misrepresents the manager's argument. The manager does argue that outdated and inefficient equipment is one cause of the high price of the factory's auto parts, but it's not logical to reverse that cause and effect in this argument. Causal patterns do figure prominently in arguments throughout the LSAT; they just aren't the problem here.

(D) is untrue. The manager does consider causes of the problem; he explicitly states that one cause of the high price of the factory's auto parts is the factory's outdated, inefficient machinery.

(E) is also untrue; the manager does make a definite recommendation. He recommends completely refurbishing the factory as the only way to keep prices competitive.

30. (E) Flaw (OP)

Step 1: Identify the Question Type

The phrase "most vulnerable to criticism" is common language for a Flaw question. Look for the unwarranted assumption or the common LSAT flaw.

Step 2: Untangle the Stimulus

The author concludes that repeating an activity is a good way to get past fear of that activity. Her evidence is simply an example: people who have parachuted ten times or more are less fearful of parachuting than first-timers.

Step 3: Make a Prediction

The author assumes that the increased experience of the people in the evidence is the only reason they're less fearful. In classic flaw terms, she's overlooking alternative possible explanations. Maybe there is some other reason why the people who parachuted many times report being less fearful.

Step 4: Evaluate the Choices

(E) correctly suggests that the author overlooks the possibility that the people who parachuted many times were people who were not frightened of parachuting in the first place. This is a case of reverse causation. Instead of repeat parachuting resulting in less fear, less fear led to repeat parachuting.

(A) goes Outside the Scope by including the idea of participating in lots of different dangerous activities. The argument is only about repeating one particular dangerous activity that inspires fear.

(B) is true but has no effect on the argument—the author has simply compared two distinct groups. It is not a logical flaw for the author to not include a third group in the comparison.

(C) is Outside the Scope. The stimulus does not weigh in on whether people's fear of an activity is accurate before trying it, just that they should do it repeatedly to get over that fear.

(D) is also Outside the Scope. The argument isn't about what's good or bad for people to do but about whether a particular method is effective for reducing fear.

31. (D) Flaw (MC-BvF)

Step 1: Identify the Question Stem

Since we need to determine why the editorial's argument is "most vulnerable to criticism," this is a Flaw question.

Step 2: Untangle the Stimulus

The editorial concludes that the government must address the rising crime rate. The only support for this is a recent survey in which 77 percent of people feel the crime rate is increasing and 87 percent of people are in favor of tougher sentences for criminals.

Step 3: Make a Prediction

The conclusion is a recommendation that the government "firmly address the rising crime rate," but it hasn't even been established that the crime rate is on the rise. The only thing that's been established is that the majority of survey respondents *feel* that the crime rate is on the rise. But those people aren't necessarily correct. This editorial seems to place inappropriate reliance on people's perceptions of the crime

These explanations refer to questions that begin on page 615.

Part Three: Logical Reasoning
Assumption Family Questions

K

rate, and this is definitely a logical flaw, since feelings aren't the same as facts.

Step 4: Evaluate the Answers

(D) expresses our prediction in slightly different words, but it is nonetheless our correct answer.

(A). The survey results aren't necessarily inconsistent. It's possible to believe that criminals should receive harsher sentences without believing that the crime rate is increasing.

(B) describes something the argument isn't doing. If the argument had concluded that the government should punish criminals more severely to lower the crime rate, then it would be presuming a connection between punishment and the crime rate. But there's no such recommendation in the editorial, so **(B)** is not the flaw here.

(C) is irrelevant because the editorial is only addressing the current state of affairs. The results of similar surveys administered in past years wouldn't do anything to bolster or undermine the reliability of the survey cited by the editorial.

(E). While the argument does mention that the majority of survey respondents feel that crime is becoming more frequent and that criminals aren't being punished harshly enough, that's a far cry from presuming that tougher sentences are the most effective means of lowering the crime rate. The editorial merely presses the government to solve the crime problem; it doesn't tell the government how to solve the problem.

32. (C) Flaw (OP) ★★★☆

Step 1: Identify the Question Type

The phrase "vulnerable to criticism" foretells that there's already something wrong with the argument, heralding a Flaw question. Break down the argument into evidence and conclusion; then characterize the error in the author's reasoning.

Step 2: Untangle the Stimulus

The conclusion Keyword phrase "[t]his variation establishes" signals the author's main point. Note it is densely written and requires some unraveling. Symptoms of mental illness are affected by some organic factors, and these factors, the author concludes, aren't spread equally around the world. This sentence also gives the strategic reader a clue that the central piece of evidence is some kind of "variation." Catching such clues helps you confirm that you've identified the components of an argument correctly.

The opening sentence introduces the idea that mental illness symptoms are affected by organic factors. The emphasis Keyword "surprising" and the contrast Keyword "however" in the second sentence signal that something interesting is about to come up, and this is where the author introduces the "variation" that serves as the primary piece of evidence:

among people with mental illnesses, the incidence of symptoms is very different in different countries.

Step 3: Make a Prediction

To find the assumption (and corresponding flaw) in this argument, pay careful attention to the terms used in the evidence and conclusion. The evidence shows that there is variation in the *incidence* of symptoms, while the conclusion claims a variation in the *organic factors that affect* the symptoms. Organic factors do affect the symptoms, but the author never states that they're the *only* things that affect the symptoms. Something else besides organic factors could affect the incidence of symptoms, too. The author has overlooked that possibility, and that's your prediction.

Step 4: Evaluate the Answer Choices

(C) satisfies your prediction. It points out that cultural factors, which the author overlooked, affect the incidence of symptoms ("how mental illnesses manifest themselves").

(A) is Out of Scope. While the author indeed never specifies how many mental illnesses she's discussing, the number of mental illnesses doesn't matter. What matters is whether the symptoms of those illnesses, however many there are, can be affected by anything besides organic factors.

(B) is a clever Faulty Use of Detail and also a 180. Brain compounds, which are tagged by the illustration Keywords "such as" in the stimulus, are just one example of organic factors. Even if the author has neglected to consider something about brain compounds, there may be other organic factors that do what the author needs them to do. Furthermore, the possibility that organic factors vary from culture to culture actually strengthens the author's claim that organic factors are spread unevenly around the world.

(D) is Extreme and a Distortion. The author doesn't have to assume that something is true of "any" change in brain chemistry, since her evidence doesn't hinge on brain chemistry changes. For that matter, notice that the "change" mentioned in this choice is actually a distortion of the word "variation" in the stimulus. The "variation" in the stimulus refers to different places having different numbers of symptoms, not changes in the symptoms themselves.

(E) is Extreme. The author doesn't have to assume anything about *all* "mental phenomena" or *all* "physical phenomena," just mental illness symptoms and organic factors, respectively. Furthermore, it doesn't matter whether mental phenomena could or couldn't be "manifestations" of anything else.

33. (E) Flaw (OP) ★★★★

Step 1: Identify the Question Stem

Anytime we see "vulnerable to criticism," we know we're dealing with a Flaw question.

K | Part Three: Logical Reasoning
CHAPTER 10

These explanations refer to
questions that begin on page 615.

Step 2: Untangle the Stimulus

The conclusion of the argument dissuades the university's grad students from unionizing, and it supports that position by stating that most of the grad students disapprove of a recent attempt by a small minority of students to unionize. The argument admits that most grad students were unaware of the attempt, but most of those who were aware don't believe that a union would effectively represent or pursue their interests.

Step 3: Make a Prediction

There's a big discrepancy in the argument. The first sentence tells us that most graduate students at the university are unaware of the minority who attempted to unionize. How can most of the grad students disapprove of the attempt at unionization, as the argument concludes, if most of them don't even know it happened? This author appears to be mistaking an absence of approval for compelling evidence of disapproval, which isn't logically sound because there's no proof that students wouldn't approve of the unionization attempt if they found out about it.

Step 4: Evaluate the Answers

(E) puts this flaw in different words, but that makes **(E)** no less correct.

(A). No long-standing practice is discussed in the argument, so **(A)** isn't even relevant to the argument.

(B). The point of the argument isn't to give reasons why some grad students disapprove; the point is that students shouldn't unionize simply because there is disapproval in the first place.

(C). The argument doesn't conclude that the grad students shouldn't unionize because most of them were unaware of the previous attempt at unionization; it discourages unionization on the basis of the purported disapproval from the majority of grad students.

(D). There might well be other possible reasons for unionizing, but they don't need to be considered in order for this argument to work. For this argument to be logically sound, the author needs proof that there is the mass disapproval cited in the last sentence. That proof would make the conclusion follow from the evidence.

34. (D) Flaw (OP) ★★★★

Step 1: Identify the Question Type

The phrase "most vulnerable to criticism" clearly identifies this as a Flaw question. Break down Boris's argument, identifying his conclusion and evidence, and look for something that he fails to do in his response to George.

Step 2: Untangle the Stimulus

George wants to know why people are now so interested in learning ballroom dancing when it was not very popular in the 1980s and early 1990s. Boris responds by saying that people started learning certain ballroom dances in 1995, and the popularity of ballroom dancing caught on from there.

Step 3: Make a Prediction

Referring again to the additional direction in the question stem, take a moment to consider what Boris failed to do. Notice that Boris explained why dances other than merengue and related dances exploded in popularity, but he never actually answered the big question: Why is there interest in dancing in the first place? To answer that, he would have needed to explain *why* many people learned merengue and related dances starting in 1995.

Step 4: Evaluate the Answer Choices

(D) is correct and points out the flaw in Boris's argument. He accounts for the subsequent popularity expansion but not the initial revival.

(A) is Outside the Scope. There is no need for the people learning specific dances in 1995 to be the same people learning other dances now. If this were the case, it could weaken Boris's answer because it limits the dancing population to those who started in 1995, but it is not a flaw inherent in his argument.

(B) is Outside the Scope. George does not want to know why it was *un*popular before 1995; he wants to know why it *is* popular now.

(C) is Outside the Scope. There is no need to connect a specific type of ballroom dancing to any other form of dancing—prevalent or not. The fact is ballroom dancing is of interest now, and other types of dancing are irrelevant to the question.

(E) is Extreme. Because George never asked about all types of ballroom dancing, just ballroom dancing in general, there was no need for Boris to account for all types.

35. (C) Weaken (OP)

Step 1: Identify the Question Stem

This stem uses the word "weakens," so we can be confident that this is a Weaken question.

Step 2: Untangle the Stimulus

The argument concludes with a recommendation. To keep our hands warm during the winter, gloves are unnecessary; we simply need to put on an extra layer of clothing. The evidence for this is that our hands can be kept warm as long as our vital organs are warm under that extra undershirt or sweater.

These explanations refer to
questions that begin on page 616.

Part Three: Logical Reasoning
Assumption Family Questions

Step 3: Make a Prediction

Notice the author's extreme language in the argument: "one never needs gloves or mittens . . . . One can *always* keep one's hands warm . . . by putting on an extra layer." Anytime an author uses extreme language like that in an argument, jump on it. Here, to draw so strong a conclusion, the author assumes that the extra layer of clothing will always protect one's hands or that there will never be an extreme circumstance in which it will be dangerous to have one's hands exposed, no matter how many layers one wears. Therefore, to weaken the argument, let's seek out an answer choice that gives us such an extreme circumstance.

Step 4: Evaluate the Answers

(C) provides that extreme circumstance. If at any point during the winter, temperatures dip low enough to cause frostbite, and the extra layer fails to keep one's hands warm, then the author's argument is in serious trouble, and gloves would certainly be necessary in some circumstances.

(A) is Outside the Scope because the argument doesn't concern which body parts are more important to keep warm from a physiological standpoint. The author is merely recommending a surefire way to keep your hands warm during the winter, so the argument is unaffected whether or not **(A)** is true.

(B) makes a comparison between several layers of light garments and one or two heavy garments when it comes to keeping one's vital organs warm. But without a connection to keeping one's hands warm, that comparison is totally irrelevant.

(D) doesn't affect the argument since the author isn't trying to argue that putting on an extra layer of clothing is the *most* effective way to keep one's hands warm. As long as putting on an extra layer of clothing is effective at all, the author's argument is still sound.

(E) also goes too far. The author doesn't argue that putting on an extra layer of clothing warms one's hands by stimulating circulation through physical effort, so even if **(E)** is true, the author's argument remains untouched.

36. (E) Strengthen (OP-P)   ★★★★

Step 1: Identify the Question Type

The question asks us to find an answer choice that supports the "industry analysts' prediction." The information in the question stem not only tells you that you are finding a strengthener but also alerts you to what conclusion needs to be supported.

One quick note: This question could have been presented equally effectively as a Paradox question. This reminds us of how closely related the question types are and how they rely on the same kinds of reasoning.

Step 2: Untangle the Stimulus

The prediction is that Morris will soon own a majority of the shares of the newspaper. However, no support for the prediction is provided. The facts only state that Morris wants to own a majority, but the company that currently owns a majority refuses to sell its shares. Even so, analysts predict that Morris will soon get the shares.

Step 3: Make a Prediction

To make the prediction more likely to come true, some fact is needed to ensure that Azedcorp will abandon its "steadfast" refusal and sell its shares. Don't waste time speculating why Azedcorp won't sell—the correct answer will clearly give a reason to expect Azedcorp will sell its shares.

Step 4: Evaluate the Answer Choices

(E) gives a fairly certain reason to expect that Azedcorp will sell its shares. Choice **(E)** is therefore correct.

(A) is no help. Even if Azedcorp owns no other newspaper stock, no reason is given for it to sell its *Daily* shares. This could even provide a reason to hold the shares and perhaps weaken the prediction.

(B) doesn't help. The evidence states that Azedcorp has steadfastly refused to sell. There is no reason to believe that a "recent" offer of more money has changed or will change that refusal.

(C) doesn't help either. Even if Morris is the only interested buyer, no reason is provided for Azedcorp to sell to her if it doesn't want to sell.

(D) is Out of Scope. The prediction is about what Morris will own, not what she currently owns. This fact contributes nothing to the analysts' prediction.

37. (D) Weaken (OP)   ★★★★

Step 1: Identify the Question Type

The correct answer is something that would go against Samantha's argument, so this is a Weaken question. The stimulus is in dialogue format, so even though you'll read both parts, focus on Samantha's argument.

Step 2: Untangle the Stimulus

Samantha concludes that a year-round schedule won't allow teachers to cover more new material. Her evidence is that the number of school days will be roughly the same.

Step 3: Make a Prediction

Start by finding Samantha's assumption. Here, Samantha is assuming that if the number of school days is roughly the same, no other factor might give the teachers more opportunity to teach new material on the proposed schedule. So, look for the answer choice that weakens the argument by

K | Part Three: Logical Reasoning
CHAPTER 10

These explanations refer to
questions that begin on page 617.

pointing out some factor that could allow teachers to cover more material in the year-round schedule.

Step 4: Evaluate the Answer Choices

(D) matches the prediction, suggesting that the year-round schedule would cut back on review time, thus allowing teachers to cover more new material.

(A) goes Outside the Scope by focusing on what teachers would accept rather than on how much new material they would be able to cover.

(B) also goes Outside the Scope by focusing on child supervision. The supervision schedule does not affect whether or not more material can be covered by the teachers.

(C) goes Outside the Scope by discussing school districts where the year-round schedule increases the total number of school days. As Samantha's evidence points out, the proposed schedule does not increase the total number of school days.

(E) is another Outside the Scope wrong answer. Focusing on student preferences is immaterial to whether or not the proposed schedule will allow more material to be taught.

38. (B) Weaken (OP) ★★☆☆

Step 1: Identify the Question Type

The word "weakens" tells you that this is a Weaken question. Bracket the conclusion, find the evidence, and predict what kind of information would undermine the link between the two.

Step 2: Untangle the Stimulus

The conclusion Keyword phrase "[t]his shows that" in the final sentence signals the arrival of the author's voice: Sunscreen isn't likely to reduce your risk of getting skin cancer. The author's belief is based on the evidence that we've seen more and more skin cancer cases in the last 25 years, despite our increased use of sunscreen.

Step 3: Make a Prediction

The only evidence offered in this argument is a piece of research. The conclusion talks about getting skin cancer *in general*, whereas the research is limited to the past 25 years. To weaken the argument, look for a choice that shows how the 25-year limit makes the research insufficient to establish a general claim about the effect of sunscreen on skin cancer.

Step 4: Evaluate the Answer Choices

(B) matches the prediction perfectly. It undermines the argument by highlighting the limitation of the 25-year window. If skin cancer is the result of sunburns that occurred before the widespread use of sunscreen, then the effect of sunscreen on skin cancer is impossible to determine.

(A) is Out of Scope. For it to weaken the argument, you have to assume that the most expensive brands are effective at preventing cancer and any cheaper brands are not. Choices

that require additional information to strengthen or weaken a conclusion are never right answers to these types of questions on the LSAT.

(C) is Out of Scope because dermatologists are irrelevant to the argument. The use of their research can't hurt or help the study, because nothing is known about them.

(D) is also Out of Scope. The evidence clearly states that the overall skin cancer rate has gone up, so it is unimportant who is or isn't able to reduce their own risk of getting the disease.

(E) is an Irrelevant Comparison. It doesn't matter who uses sunscreen most regularly; what matters is whether those people, having used the sunscreen, are less likely to get skin cancer or not. Choice **(E)** doesn't provide this information.

39. (E) Weaken (OP-R)

Step 1: Identify the Question Type

Because the stem directly asks for the answer choice that "weakens" Perry's argument, this is a Weaken question.

Step 2: Untangle the Stimulus

Perry concludes that lenders who want to minimize risks shouldn't loan money to worker-owned businesses. His evidence is that inefficiencies in worker-owned businesses can lead to low profitability and increase the risk for lenders.

Step 3: Make a Prediction

Start by finding Perry's assumption. Perry's evidence cites just one factor against worker-owned businesses: operational inefficiency. On the basis of that one factor, Perry broadly concludes that worker-owned businesses are risky to lend money to. For this to be true, Perry must assume that there are no other relevant factors that might make worker-owned businesses a safe borrower. The correct answer will suggest some new factor about worker-owned businesses that makes them likely to be safe borrowers.

Step 4: Evaluate the Answer Choices

(E) weakens the argument because if workers at worker-owned businesses compensate for their inefficiencies, then worker-owned businesses are less likely to be a risky investment.

(A) goes Outside the Scope by focusing on "[b]usinesses with the most extensive divisions of labor," rather than on worker-owned businesses.

(B) goes Outside the Scope by focusing narrowly on "[l]enders who specialize in high-risk loans," while the stimulus is about whether lenders in general should loan to worker-owned businesses.

(C) makes an Irrelevant Comparison between investor-owned businesses and worker-owned businesses; the stimulus is just about worker-owned businesses.

These explanations refer to
questions that begin on page 617.

Part Three: Logical Reasoning
Assumption Family Questions

(D) goes Outside the Scope by discussing where the loans come from; the argument is just about how risky the loans would be, not where the loans have traditionally originated.

40. (E) Strengthen (OP-C)

Step 1: Identify the Question Type

"[M]ost strengthens" identifies a Strengthen question. The correct answer choice will contain a fact that will make the conclusion more likely to be true.

Step 2: Untangle the Stimulus

The words "[t]his shows that" take us right to the conclusion: "snoring can damage the throat." The evidence is that tissue biopsies show that people who snore frequently are more likely to have serious abnormalities in their throat muscles than people who snore infrequently or never.

Step 3: Make a Prediction

This is a classic cause-and-effect argument pattern. When the conclusion is that X (snoring) causes Y (throat damage), keep the classic assumptions in mind: (1) Y didn't cause X, (2) something else didn't cause Y, or (3) the correlation isn't coincidental. Since this is a Strengthen question, scan the answer choices for a fact that confirms that throat damage didn't cause the snoring or a fact that eliminates the likelihood of any other cause of the throat damage.

Step 4: Evaluate the Answer Choices

(E) fits the prediction with a clear statement that the throat abnormalities were not the cause of the snoring. This doesn't prove that the snoring caused the abnormalities, but it improves the likelihood, and that's all that's needed for an LSAT strengthener.

(A) is a possible 180. If true, this fact might cast doubt on the conclusion by questioning the reliability of the evidence. In any event, it's not a strengthener.

(B) is Outside the Scope. Why the patients were being treated has no bearing on the findings of the biopsies.

(C) is Outside the Scope. The argument is the causal relationship between frequent snoring and throat damage; other characteristics of the patients are not at issue.

(D) is an Irrelevant Comparison. The argument is about people who had throat surgery and snore. Whether these people were more or less likely to snore than anyone else is irrelevant.

41. (A) Strengthen (OP-R)

Step 1: Identify the Question Type

The phrase "most strengthens the economist's reasoning" identifies this as a Strengthen question. Break down the argument into conclusion and evidence, predict the central

assumption, and find an answer choice that validates the economist's assumption.

Step 2: Untangle the Stimulus

The economist states there are two solutions to cutting personnel costs: lay off some employees or reduce wages across the board. Both hurt morale, with laying off employees being less damaging. The economist then concludes that companies are likely to lay off employees when they need to reduce personnel costs.

Step 3: Make a Prediction

Notice that the economist concludes companies are likely to lay off employees for the sole reason that layoffs are less damaging to morale—as if morale was the most important consideration in making the decision. The economist focuses on only one factor in making a decision and ignores other potentially more important factors. To strengthen the economist's view, find an answer that verifies his assumption that companies make personnel moves based on their effect on morale.

Step 4: Evaluate the Answer Choices

(A) is correct and strengthens the economist's conclusion that layoffs are likely when companies must reduce personnel costs during recessions. If morale is the biggest deciding factor in such decisions, then layoffs make the most sense.

(B) is Outside the Scope. This choice talks about when companies would *increase* wages, whereas the argument only discusses when companies would decrease wages.

(C) is Outside the Scope. The argument is not about whether companies can make a profit but about how companies can reduce costs. That some companies can't make a profit doesn't help explain why the economist would think companies would choose laying off employees over reducing wages.

(D) is Outside the Scope. Although this choice may explain what would happen if companies chose to reduce wages, it does not strengthen the economist's point that layoffs are the likely route. Furthermore, if reduced wages *did* lead to resignations, one could argue (perhaps a little cynically) that companies would be more likely to choose this route instead, as it would lead to a potentially greater reduction in personnel costs. That would make this answer choice a 180.

(E) is a 180. This choice actually goes against the economist by providing a reason why companies would *not* want to lay off employees.

42. (E) Strengthen (OP)

Step 1: Identify the Question Stem

Since the stem asks us to "support the claim made," this is a Strengthen question.

K | Part Three: Logical Reasoning
CHAPTER 10

These explanations refer to
questions that begin on page 618.

Step 2: Untangle the Stimulus

The letter to the editor argues that the editorial is unjustified in its conclusion that the Planning department spends five times as much money now as it did in 2001 to perform the same duties. The editorial's conclusion was apparently based on evidence that the department's budget went from $100,000 in 2001 to $524,000 for this year.

Step 3: Make a Prediction

The only fact that we have is that the Planning Department's budget has indeed increased fivefold from 2001 to this year. However the editorial alleges that the department is performing the same duties as before; it's just spending more money to do it. The letter to the editor claims that that allegation is unjustified, and we need to strengthen the letter writer's claim, so we need an choice that will support the idea that the editorial's conclusion is illogical. Since the editorial doesn't seem to allow for the possibility that the Planning Department took on more duties between 2001 and this year, we can probably exploit this vulnerability to shore up the letter writer's position.

Step 4: Evaluate the Answers

(E) strengthens the letter writer's criticism of the editorial by stating that the Planning Department's duties have actually expanded since 2001.

(A) is irrelevant to the argument. No matter what we might learn about other departments, the editorial's conclusion about the Planning Department's budget could still be justified.

(B) also doesn't help. Even if certain areas of the Planning Department's budget have been reduced, the overall budget has still increased fivefold, so without any information about the department's duties, the editorial can still argue that the department is spending more money to perform the same duties.

(C) The editorial's argument hinges on a comparison between this year's budget and the budget in 2001. The fluctuations in the budget in the intervening years have no bearing on that comparison.

(D) doesn't provide enough information to help anyone's argument. We don't know how the adjustment for inflation affected the figures. Besides, the figures provided by the letter writer are in line with the editorial's conclusion, so even if the editorial adjusted for inflation, that didn't seem to have much impact on the editorial's conclusion.

43. (A) Weaken (OP) ★★★☆

Step 1: Identify the Question Type

The question asks for something that undermines the theory in the stimulus, so this is a Weaken question.

Step 2: Untangle the Stimulus

The theory is introduced in the first sentence: drug overdose caused the dinosaur extinction. Push past the scientific language in the middle of the stimulus and notice the Emphasis and Evidence Keywords, "strongest support," in the last sentence. So, the author's central evidence is that the theory explains why dinosaur fossils are found in contorted positions.

Step 3: Make a Prediction

The conclusion is that dinosaurs overdosed. The evidence is that overdoses would explain contorted fossil positions. That's a somewhat flimsy piece of evidence, and this argument is left with a gaping hole. The author's assumption will fill that hole. Thus, the author assumes that nothing besides overdoses would explain why dinosaur fossils are in contorted positions. The weakener will suggest some other explanation that could better explain why dinosaur fossils are in contorted positions.

Step 4: Evaluate the Answer Choices

(A) says mammals are also found in contorted positions, which would strengthen the argument if mammals are also overdosing and weaken it if they are not. If "large mammals" appear to be Outside the Scope, go back and research the science details in the middle of the stimulus. There, the author mentions that mammals both avoid the plants dinosaurs theoretically overdosed on and have livers that can detoxify the drugs. If mammals aren't overdosing and they're still contorted, then something besides overdoses must be the cause of the contortions. The extinction theory's main support is now no longer pertinent. This makes choice **(A)** correct.

(B) may be true but doesn't hurt the idea that the "drugs" caused the dinosaurs to die off.

(C) might appear to undermine the idea that all dinosaurs were overdosing, but if the carnivorous dinosaurs ate the dinosaurs who had consumed the angiosperms, they might still have suffered the effects. Or, if vegetarian dinosaurs died off, then carnivorous dinosaurs would have been left without a food source.

(D) goes Outside the Scope by talking about other plants. The argument is about only those plants that do produce amino acid–based alkaloids.

(E) is a 180. It actually strengthens the argument, confirming that angiosperms cause fatal drug overdoses in other animals.

44. (E) Strengthen (OP-C) ★★★☆

Step 1: Identify the Question Type

The Keyword "supports" marks this as a classic Strengthen stem. Find the evidence and conclusion and then predict what would make the conclusion more likely. The stem offers a bonus by telling you that you're supporting "the researchers' hypothesis," so you know what the conclusion will be.

These explanations refer to
questions that begin on page 619.

Part Three: Logical Reasoning
Assumption Family Questions

K

Step 2: Untangle the Stimulus

The researchers' hypothesis appears in the last sentence: children are less likely to develop allergies if they're exposed to germs as infants. The researchers base this hypothesis on the fact that allergies are less common among children from larger families.

Step 3: Make a Prediction

Like many Strengthen stimuli, this one features a couple of gaps between the evidence and the conclusion. The conclusion is about germs, but the evidence is about growing up in a large family. The author must take for granted that growing up in a large family exposes you to more germs.

This is a pretty reasonable assumption—being around lots of people does, presumably, expose one to more germs. So, consider what else the author takes for granted: She must believe that it's the increased exposure to germs—and not some other quality of children from larger families—that accounts for the lack of allergies. Consider both of the author's assumptions when you evaluate the choices.

Step 4: Evaluate the Answer Choices

(E) provides a match for your second assumption. Entering day care is like growing up in a larger family: children in day care are surrounded by more people and thus get exposed to more germs. Choice **(E)** compares children from small families who entered day care and those who did not and finds that those who did were less likely to get allergies. This corroborates the author's assumption that being exposed to more germs is the key distinguishing quality of children who don't get allergies.

(A) is a Distortion. If allergies increase when average family size decreases, then that would seem to support the author's argument. Notice, however, that this actually confirms the author's *evidence*, not her conclusion! To support the *link* between the evidence and the conclusion, you either need to show that being around more people exposes one to more germs or that the increased exposure to germs—and not some other difference between children from large families and children from small ones—is the cause of the difference in allergy incidence.

(B) is a perfect 180. It weakens the hypothesis by presenting a factor other than germ exposure that makes children from large families less likely to get allergies.

(C) is an Irrelevant Comparison. The author is concerned with the factors that make people more or less likely to develop allergies; the relative deadliness of allergies and germs is beside the point.

(D) is a 180 similar to choice **(B)**. It states that hereditary factors play an important role in determining allergy incidence among children, making it less likely that germ exposure makes any difference.

45. (E) Weaken (MC-E) ★★★☆

Step 1: Identify the Question Type

The word "weakens" tells you that this is a Weaken question. Analyze the argument and then predict what would make the conclusion less likely to be true.

Step 2: Untangle the Stimulus

The Keyword "[t]herefore" highlights the argument's conclusion. The author predicts that privatizing national parks will benefit park visitors. The evidence is that privatizing telecommunications benefited consumers by increasing competition among phone companies. Since privatization worked for the telecommunications industry, the author predicts it will work for national parks as well.

Step 3: Make a Prediction

This argument tests knowledge of classic LSAT patterns. The conclusion is a *prediction*, so think critically about under what circumstances the prediction would fail. Since the argument relies on an equivalence between the national park system and the phone industry, predict that the analogy doesn't hold up. If the national park system is sufficiently different from the phone industry, then a plan that worked for one wouldn't necessarily work for the other.

Step 4: Evaluate the Answer Choices

(E) rewards your excellent prediction. Privatization worked well for the phone industry because it increased competition; if privatizing parks will not produce as much competition, then the author's prediction is less likely to come true.

(A) is Out of Scope. It doesn't matter whether privatization is or isn't "politically expedient"; what matters is whether or not it benefits park visitors.

(B) is Out of Scope. Again, the question is whether or not privatization benefits consumers. Whether or not it causes other problems is irrelevant.

(C) is Out of Scope. Park visitors could benefit from a proposal with or without knowing what's going on behind the scenes.

(D) is an Irrelevant Comparison. While it may sound hostile to the author's argument that privatizing parks will benefit fewer people than privatizing telecommunications, this might just be because the number of people who go to parks is smaller than the number of people who use phones. In that case, privatization could still benefit the people who do use parks.

46. (B) Principle (Identify) ★☆☆☆

Step 1: Identify the Question Type

The word "principles" clearly identifies this as a Principle question. In addition, the phrase "most helps to justify" indicates a task identical to that in Strengthen questions. So, approach this question the same way you would a Strengthen

EXPLANATIONS

K | Part Three: Logical Reasoning
CHAPTER 10

These explanations refer to
questions that begin on page 620.

question: look for an answer that would make the conclusion more likely to follow from the evidence. The correct answer will be a principle that supports the argument's assumption. Also, when a question asks about one of two opinions in a stimulus, watch out for answers that validate the wrong opinion.

Step 2: Untangle the Stimulus

In this argument, Mariah concludes that Adam should not judge the essay contest. However, unlike Joanna (who suggests bias, which Mariah refutes due to the anonymity of the contestants), Mariah's reasoning is that Adam has no experience in critiquing essays.

Step 3: Make a Prediction

The principle, or broader rule, behind Mariah's argument is that a lack of experience constitutes a reason to be dismissed as a judge.

Step 4: Evaluate the Answer Choices

(B) is correct and matches your prediction. Mariah doesn't necessarily assume expertise has to be the "primary" prerequisite, but, if valid, this principle certainly would justify her argument.

(A) is a Distortion. This may be tempting because Mariah does reject Joanna's suggestion of bias. However, Mariah doesn't reject this reasoning because she feels that bias is insufficient grounds for dismissal. She rejects it because the essay authors are anonymous, which suggests that there wouldn't be bias in this case.

(C) is a 180. Mariah suggests expertise is the main factor for dismissing Adam as a judge, whereas Joanna would say objectivity is more important.

(D) is also a 180 and is almost identical to answer choice **(C)** Two such similar answers suggest both are wrong. Again, Mariah suggests that Adam should be dismissed for lack of expertise, not because of fairness concerns.

(E) is Outside the Scope. This might be a principle that Joanna would use, but Mariah's argument is about expertise, not bias. As Mariah says, the essays' authors aren't identified, so bias is irrelevant.

47. (E) Principle (Identify) ★★★★

Step 1: Identify the Question Type

The phrase "most help to justify the educator's reasoning" indicates that the correct answer will identify a principle that strengthens the educator's argument.

Step 2: Untangle the Stimulus

Attack the stimulus like a Strengthen question. The educator's conclusion is that the organization should not make decisions by direct vote but should continue to elect officers to make decisions. The evidence is that by electing officers, individual voters will likely have more influence on policy.

Step 3: Make a Prediction

Start by identifying the assumption. In the conclusion, the author recommends against organizations making decisions in a certain way. In the evidence, the author talks about giving individuals more influence on policy. Thus, the author assumes that the organization should do things that would give individuals more influence on policy. The correct answer will reinforce this assumption, likely in general terms.

Step 4: Evaluate the Answer Choices

(E) matches the prediction. The reason to choose one decision-making procedure over another is maximizing the influence of individuals.

(A) goes Outside the Scope by focusing on the weight of each individual's vote. It fails to address the educator's recommendation that decision making should be done by elected officials.

(B) goes Outside the Scope by including organizational "benefits" and "fairness," neither of which figure into the educator's argument.

(C) is Outside the Scope. It might match the educator's conclusion about having elected officials make decisions, but it completely neglects the educator's evidence and instead adds the element of mastering information.

(D) goes Outside the Scope by focusing on what individual officers should do. The stimulus is about whether or not officers should be the decision makers, not about how they should make particular decisions.

48. (D) Principle (Identify) ★★★★

Step 1: Identify the Question Type

The word "principles" signals a Principle question, but since Principle questions come in many flavors, don't stop there. This problem asks you to select the principle that would "justify the reasoning" in the stimulus, so treat it like a Strengthen question. Find the conclusion and evidence and then predict the principle that would plug the gap between them.

Step 2: Untangle the Stimulus

The Opinion Keyword "should" in the last line points out the author's conclusion: Fake jewels should have as much value as real ones. Unravel the rhetorical question in the preceding sentence to find the author's evidence: the two types of jewels deliver an equal amount of "aesthetic pleasure."

Step 3: Make a Prediction

This argument features a classic Mismatched Concepts pattern. The author shifts from "aesthetic pleasure" in the evidence to "value" in the conclusion. Thus, she takes for

These explanations refer to questions that begin on page 621.

Part Three: Logical Reasoning
Assumption Family Questions

K

granted that if two things provide equal aesthetic pleasure, then they're also equally valuable.

Step 4: Evaluate the Answer Choices

(D) paraphrases the prediction perfectly. It's the only choice that even tries to connect "value" to "aesthetic pleasure."

(A) is Out of Scope. What jewelers should or shouldn't collect has no effect on the author's claim that fake jewels are as valuable as real ones.

(B) is Out of Scope. "[M]arket demand" has no bearing on the argument.

(C) is Out of Scope but is perhaps more tempting because of the negative phrasing. It says, more simply, that fans of diamonds might get different amounts of aesthetic pleasure from them. However, it doesn't say which kind of diamond (real or fake) delivers more pleasure and so has no bearing on the argument.

(E) is an interesting Distortion. It offers a restriction on when jewelers should buy counterfeit jewels, which does nothing to justify the reasoning in the argument.

49. (E) Principle (Identify) ★★★★

Step 1: Identify the Question Type

This Principle question asks for a broad rule that helps "justify the reasoning" in the editorial. That makes this akin to a Strengthen question, which means using argument-based skills to untangle the stimulus.

Step 2: Untangle the Stimulus

First, a suggestion is presented. The Keyword "[b]ut" in the second sentence signals the editor's rebuttal of the suggestion and gives the conclusion: Water should not be supplied by private, for-profit companies. Support is given by the next sentence (beginning with the Keywords "[a]fter all ... "): clean water is essential to health, and promoting health is not the primary purpose of a private company.

Step 3: Make a Prediction

Connecting the evidence and conclusion, a general statement of the principle underlying this argument would be this: if a company's primary purpose is not to promote health, then it should not be hired to perform a service that is necessary to human health.

Step 4: Evaluate the Answer Choices

(E) restates the prediction in its contrapositive form.

(A) is Outside the Scope. The condition that a government agency be included plays no role in this argument.

(B) is Outside the Scope. Concluding that a private, for-profit company should not supply the water does not suggest that a government should. Also, the company's willingness or ability to supply the water is not under consideration.

(C) is a Distortion. The argument merely states that promoting health is not the company's primary purpose. The editor is not asserting that the private company *could* not consistently supply clean water. At most he's suggesting that maybe it won't if that's not its primary purpose.

(D) is a Distortion. In answer choices that rely on "something" or "a thing" or on vague pronouns, paraphrase by substituting in the appropriate noun to see if the answer makes sense. In this case, "clean water" is the noun. While the editor states that clean water is essential for human health, he then discusses the purpose of the private companies—not the purpose of clean water.

50. (C) Principle (Identify) ★★★★

Step 1: Identify the Question Type

The phrase "most helps to justify the ... reasoning" indicates that the correct answer will identify a principle that strengthens the argument.

Step 2: Untangle the Stimulus

The journalist's conclusion is that the practice of pricing drugs lower in poorer countries is unjustified. The evidence is that the overall wealth of a country doesn't necessarily reflect the ability of individual citizens to pay.

Step 3: Make a Prediction

As in a regular Strengthen question, start by finding the assumption. Here, the conclusion is about what should happen to entire countries, whereas the evidence is about the ability of some individual citizens to pay. Thus, the assumption is that companies should make their decisions about entire countries on the basis of some individual citizens of those countries. The correct answer will reinforce this assumption in general terms.

Step 4: Evaluate the Answer Choices

(C) matches the prediction in general terms. The characteristics of individuals are more important than the characteristics of the societies.

(A) makes an Irrelevant Comparison regarding ill people. The stimulus is about ability to pay, not how much somebody needs the drugs.

(B) is a Distortion of the stimulus. The pharmaceutical companies are already expending some resources to help the less fortunate by making the drugs available at a much lower price in poor nations. However, the journalist disagrees with the fairness of the effects of that practice, not the original intent of it.

(D) goes Outside the Scope. The author does not discuss a disparity in the quality of care available in wealthy or poor nations. The same drugs are available in both types of nations; the respective price points of those drugs in the two types of

K | Part Three: Logical Reasoning
CHAPTER 10

These explanations refer to
questions that begin on page 622.

countries is what the author thinks is currently unjustified. The author is concerned about giving middle class people in poor nations breaks on drug prices, when poor people in wealthy nations do not receive the same breaks.

(E) makes an Irrelevant Comparison by introducing distribution of wealth in comparison to access to health care.

are responsible for any health risk that could have been avoided, whether the manufacturer was aware of it or not.

(D) is a 180. Whether or not an outcome is preventable is far from irrelevant; in fact, the illnesses' preventability is the author's very basis for holding T's manufacturer responsible for them.

51. (E) Principle (Identify)

Step 1: Identify the Question Type

Don't stop after the word "principles" signals that you're working on a Principle question. Analyze the entire stem to determine which flavor of Principle question this is. Since you have to "justify the conclusion" of the stimulus, this Principle question is acting as a Strengthen question. Find the conclusion and evidence, then predict and bolster the assumption.

Step 2: Untangle the Stimulus

The Evidence Keyword "[f]or" in the last sentence suggests that the conclusion is in the previous line: T's manufacturer is partly to blame for the illnesses, even though it didn't know that T was unsafe. The author's reasoning, given in the last line, is that the manufacturer could have prevented the illnesses if it had investigated T before letting people handle it.

Step 3: Make a Prediction

On any Strengthen or Strengthen-like problem, expect a scope shift from the evidence to the conclusion. This argument certainly delivers: The evidence talks about being *able to prevent* something, whereas the conclusion talks about being *to blame for* something. To justify this reasoning, the author must believe that having the ability to affect an outcome makes one responsible for that outcome. Look for this principle in the choices.

Step 4: Evaluate the Answer Choices

(E) is a match. If the consequences of a manufacturer's actions are preventable, then the manufacturer has the ability to affect them. And the choice says the manufacturer is responsible for those consequences if that's the case, which is your prediction.

(A) is Out of Scope. Medical compensation is irrelevant to the argument.

(B) is Extreme. It's perfect except for the word "only." The author takes for granted that manufacturers *are* responsible for preventable consequences, not that they *aren't* responsible for any other kind.

(C) is a subtle Distortion. It holds manufacturers responsible for health risks "of which they are aware," but the author makes no such restriction: She thinks manufacturers

52. (A) Principle (Identify)

Step 1: Identify the Question Stem

This is a long stem, but if we read it closely, we see that we're being asked to find the principle underlying Larissa's critique of Claude's argument, so let's approach this as a Principle question.

Step 2: Untangle the Stimulus

Claude argues that candidates for a job who salt their food without first tasting it are less desirable because they are making a decision based on inadequate information. Larissa makes two analogies to criticize that policy. Even before setting foot into a supermarket, Larissa wears a sweater in anticipation of it being too cold inside. Also, before opening any credit card offer that comes in the mail, Larissa already knows it won't be worth her time.

Step 3: Make a Prediction

We need to find the principle underlying both of Larissa's analogies. The one thing they have in common is that in each case, Larissa has made a decision without having all the information, which would count against her in Claude's eyes. But Larissa's defense is that she already knows that supermarkets are invariably too cold for her and that credit card offers that arrive in the mail are invariably not worthwhile for her. Presumably, then, Larissa might argue that some of Claude's job candidates salt their food before tasting it not because they have poor judgment but because food is invariably too bland for them. So Larissa's principle, broadly stated, is that something that appears to be bad decision making may just be an application of what is generally true in a given set of circumstances.

Step 4: Evaluate the Answers

(A) is a bit long-winded, but it is a great match for our prediction.

(B) is not a valid principle to use in criticizing Claude's policy because Claude isn't using job-related behavior as a basis for his inferences—he's basing his inferences on whether job candidates salt their food.

(C) is Extreme, since Claude doesn't necessarily use his food-salting observations as exclusive indication of a candidate's job suitability. Besides, this principle has no relationship to either of the analogies Larissa uses in her rebuttal of Claude's reasoning.

These explanations refer to
questions that begin on page 623.

Part Three: Logical Reasoning
Assumption Family Questions

K

(D) goes Outside the Scope. There's no indication of the generally expected social norms when it comes to salting one's food, much less any indication that the job candidates' behavior doesn't conform to those norms.

(E) is off the mark because Larissa doesn't use her supermarket/credit card analogies as examples of occasional lapses of rationality in an otherwise reasonable pattern of decision making.

53. (A) Principle (Identify) ★★★☆

Step 1: Identify the Question Type

The word "principles" identifies this as a Principle question. In addition, the phrase "most helps to justify the reasoning" indicates a task identical to that in Strengthen questions. So, approach this question the same way you would a Strengthen question: Look for an answer that would make the conclusion more likely to follow from the evidence. The correct answer will be a principle that supports the argument's assumption.

Step 2: Untangle the Stimulus

The advice columnist presents data that show people suffering from major stress are more likely to be seriously injured playing competitive sports than people without stress. Because of this, the columnist goes one step further and suggests *no* sports activity should be used to combat stress.

Step 3: Make a Prediction

The columnist assumes that if people with stress should avoid one type of activity (in this case, competitive sports), then they should also avoid all types of activities in the same general category (in this case, sports in general). Find an answer choice that states this prediction in broad terms.

Step 4: Evaluate the Answer Choices

(A) is correct and matches your prediction perfectly.

(B) is Outside the Scope. The columnist's recommendation is about a method for coping with stress that *shouldn't* be used. The columnist says nothing about methods that *should* be used, and while the columnist uses some studies' results as evidence, the focus of this argument is not on the importance of scientific study.

(C) is Outside the Scope. Recommending one thing for a group of people does not mean recommending the opposite for the opposite group. So, just because the columnist recommends that stressed people avoid competitive sports does not mean the columnist thinks nonstressed people should compete in competitive sports. This answer choice is essentially an incorrect contrapositive of the columnist's argument.

(D) is a 180. If the columnist makes the jump from avoiding competitive sports to avoiding all sports, it would seem just as likely that the columnist would make the jump from avoiding

competitive sports to avoiding any competitive activity. This principle is contrary to the columnist's reasoning.

(E) is Outside the Scope. It may be a good idea to avoid sports activities in this case, but the choice focuses too narrowly on people with a history of sports injuries, whereas the columnist is concerned with anyone coping with stress—regardless of injury history.

54. (B) Parallel Flaw ★★★★

Step 1: Identify the Question Stem

Since we're looking for the reasoning in the choices that most closely parallels that in the stimulus, this is certainly a Parallel Reasoning question. More specifically, we know that both the stimulus and the right answer will have logical flaws, so we should seek those out as well.

Step 2: Untangle the Stimulus

According to the stimulus, negative ads, despite candidates' objections, actually benefit their targets. The evidence for this conclusion is that most elections have been won by candidates who were the targets of such ads.

Step 3: Make a Prediction

The main problem with this argument is that it confuses correlation with causation. In other words, it doesn't consider the very logical possibility that the candidates who win elections do so *despite* the negative ads aimed at them, not because of those ads. Now, we need to find the choice that argues that a perceived detriment is actually a benefit simply because most of those who have experienced the detriment went on to succeed.

Step 4: Evaluate the Answers

(B) is a perfect match because, like the stimulus, **(B)** argues that a perceived detriment (harsh reviews) is actually a benefit because most people who experienced that detriment went on to succeed. Also, like the stimulus, **(B)** doesn't consider the possibility that the actors won awards despite their harsh reviews and not because of them.

(A) argues that an activity that many people dislike should nonetheless be undertaken because of its benefits. However, unlike the original stimulus, the evidence doesn't illustrate a correlation between most people experiencing the detriment and the suggested benefit.

(C) doesn't attempt to turn a negative thing into something positive. Studying doesn't have the same similarity to negative campaign ads that harsh reviews do. Also, in **(C)** the studying is an action carried out by the students themselves in pursuit of a goal. In the stimulus, the politicians aren't running negative ads against themselves in pursuit of any goal.

K | Part Three: Logical Reasoning
CHAPTER 10

These explanations refer to
questions that begin on page 624.

(D) would be on the right track if it said that horror films are beneficial to film critics *despite* their dislike of such films. But saying that horror films are successful because other people enjoy them is another idea entirely.

(E) says that the sleepiness that many people dislike must be acceptable to those who experience it. But that's different from saying that the sleepiness actually benefits them.

55. (C) Parallel Flaw ★☆☆☆

Step 1: Identify the Question Type

The phrase "similar in its reasoning" indicates a Parallel question, and the fact that the original reasoning is "questionable" tells you that you're looking at a Parallel Flaw question. Find and characterize the flaw in the argument; then pick the choice that has the same flaw.

Step 2: Untangle the Stimulus

The little word "so" in the third line signals the conclusion: it's likely that Jackie's first child wasn't born early. When doing Parallel questions, don't forget to use the Kaplan shortcut: characterize the conclusion and then look at each choice's conclusion and eliminate the ones whose types don't match. In this problem, the Kaplan shortcut actually eliminates all of the incorrect answer choices.

This conclusion is a qualified ("likely") assertion of fact about something that happened in the past.

Note the ostensible conditional statement in the argument. If the first child is early, then the second child is likely to be as well. Take care to note that the first sentence is *not* a Formal Logic rule because of the qualifier "likely." Thus, a first child's being born early is not sufficient to guarantee anything, and a second child's being born early is not a requirement for anything.

The flaw, of course, is that the author treats this statement as valid Formal Logic, attempting to invoke the contrapositive. Also note that the author applies "likely" to the result in both statements; he doesn't carry it over when he flips the terms. So, he concludes that Jackie's first child was likely born before its due date on the basis of knowing that her second child was not born before its due date.

Step 3: Make a Prediction

This argument follows a common pattern of LSAT reasoning in which the evidence combines a rule and a fact to produce the conclusion. The flaw has to do with the fact that the rule isn't actually a rule, but you should still sketch out the author's reasoning in the abstract to make the parallel argument easier to spot:

> *IF A (Child 1 early)* → *B likely (Child 2 early)*
> *Fact: ~ (Child 2 early)*

Thus, IF ~ B (Child 2 early) → *~ A likely (Child 1 early)*

Apart from the fact that the Formal Logic rule isn't valid, this argument otherwise correctly forms the contrapositive. Thus, look for the choice that also tries to apply the contrapositive from a condition statement but doesn't recognize that the conditional statement is qualified. The conclusion should be in the form of a qualified assertion of fact.

Step 4: Evaluate the Answer Choices

Choice **(C)**'s argument matches your prediction to the letter. Using Kaplan's shortcut, choice **(C)** is the best place to start because it's the only choice whose conclusion is a qualified assertion of fact about the past. *Hawkman I* and *Hawkman II* are analogous to the first and second children, respectively, and the author concludes that the first *Hawkman* probably wasn't a hit because the second *Hawkman* wasn't. The quasi-rule is that if the first movie *is* a hit, then its sequel is likely to be as well. In the abstract, the arguments translates as

> *IF A (original a hit)* → *B likely (sequel a hit)*
> *Fact: ~B (Hawkman II a hit)*

Thus, IF ~B (sequel a hit) → *~A likely (original a hit)*

(A) is incorrect because its conclusion is a qualified prediction. Also, this choice makes a bad contrapositive: it negates the sufficient and necessary conditions without flipping them.

(B) is incorrect because its conclusion expresses a qualified necessary/sufficient relationship ("anyone … is probably …"). Furthermore, it contains a fake rule but doesn't have a fact to pair it with.

(D) also has a qualified prediction conclusion. Interestingly, this choice is actually a sound argument. By being likely to fail, Pallid Starr meets the sufficient condition for the given rule. Sound logic can never be the correct answer to a Parallel Flaw question.

(E)'s conclusion is yet another qualified prediction. Also, it uses a rule that's true Formal Logic, whereas the original stimulus contained information that was only likely rather than definite. The flaw with this choice is the classic error of confusing necessity with sufficiency: if Tai has gone sailing, then the weather must be nice; but if the weather is nice, then you don't know anything. Remember that "only" always signals the necessary piece of a Formal Logic relationship.

56. (B) Parallel Flaw ★★☆☆

Step 1: Identify the Question Type

The phrase "flawed reasoning . . . most similar to" identifies this as a Parallel Flaw question. Approach the argument as you would a standard Flaw question. Identify the evidence and conclusion and pinpoint the relevant gap between the two, keeping in mind common flaw types. The correct answer

These explanations refer to questions that begin on page 625.

Part Three: Logical Reasoning
Assumption Family Questions

choice will exhibit the same pattern of reasoning and the same flaw as the stimulus.

Step 2: Untangle the Stimulus

The argument makes a subsidiary conclusion that because top actors have a loyal following, movies with top actors tend to do well. It then concludes that movies with unknown actors likely will not do well.

Step 3: Make a Prediction

This argument is a classic example of treating a characteristic of a group as if the characteristic were unique to that group. It's like saying, "Dogs have four legs; therefore, animals that are not dogs cannot have four legs." Recognizing this flaw, find the one answer that has the exact same flaw in logic. In Formal Logic terms, the stimulus says, "If a movie has a top actor, then it's likely to do well." The conclusion negates this statement without reversing: "if a movie does not have a top actor, then it's unlikely to do well." You want an answer choice whose conclusion simply negates the evidence.

Step 4: Evaluate the Answer Choices

(B) is correct. Here, you are told that gardens with bee balm often have the eventual characteristic of abundant crops. Then the argument concludes that gardens *without* bee balm will likely *not* have abundant crops. That is the same flaw as the original argument, making this the correct answer.

(A) is incorrect because it contains no flaw. This argument says animals need to devote most of their energy to finding food to maintain optimal energy levels. It then concludes that devoting energy elsewhere will result in less than optimal energy levels. The logic of this argument is sound.

(C) is flawed, but in a different way than the original argument. This argument states that keeping confidences is important to friendship because keeping confidences allows for openness. The argument then goes a little too far in claiming that openness is therefore *essential* to friendship. The conclusion of the stimulus includes the qualifier "unlikely," and nothing similar is present in the conclusion of **(C)**. Additionally, in the original argument, the main conclusion negates the subsidiary conclusion. In this answer choice, however, the main conclusion discusses a "high degree of openness," which is part of the evidence *for* the subsidiary conclusion but not the subsidiary conclusion itself.

(D) is close but not quite right. Here, visual aids can help teach math skills. However, the conclusion doesn't say that *without* visual aids you likely *cannot* teach math skills. It just says that teaching math skills will be more difficult. This would be correct only if the original argument concluded that movies with unknown actors would have a harder time doing well.

(E) is incorrect because it contains a different flaw than does the original argument. This argument nicely illustrates the classic LSAT flaw of confusing necessity with sufficiency. The argument states that understanding rules of perspective is *necessary* for success but then concludes that understanding rules will lead to success. A necessary condition is not sufficient to guarantee a definite result.

57. (A) Parallel Reasoning ★★☆☆

Step 1: Identify the Question Type

The phrase "pattern of reasoning . . . most similar to" indicates that this is a Parallel Reasoning question. Analyze the argument into evidence and conclusion, as you would for any other argument-based question.

Step 2: Untangle the Stimulus

The conclusion, marked by "[t]herefore," is that Joe took his car to K & L to get it fixed.

The evidence describes a chain of Formal Logic: If Joe's car was vacuumed, K & L employees did it; if K & L employees did it, Joe took his car to K & L for service. Finally, the author also informs us that Joe's car was indeed vacuumed.

Step 3: Make a Prediction

The conclusion can be characterized as an assertion of fact: something definitely happened. Eliminate answers when possible by comparing the conclusions of each answer choice to the conclusion in the stimulus. The entire argument can be rewritten in Formal Logic algebra to help reveal its underlying structure: If A → B → C; A, therefore C. The conclusion type and overall argument structure of the stimulus and correct answer will be the same.

Step 4: Evaluate the Answer Choices

(A) matches both the type of conclusion and overall argument structure of the stimulus. Correct.

(B) fails on the conclusion test—its conclusion asserts that something did not happen rather than that something did happen. Incorrect.

(C) matches in terms of its conclusion, but its evidence is very different, as it lacks the chain of Formal Logic statements found in the stimulus. Incorrect.

(D) fails on the conclusion test because it adds a qualifier (i.e., only on certain days). Incorrect.

(E) matches in terms of its conclusion, but the evidence goes Outside the Scope by introducing an either/or choice rather than giving a chain of Formal Logic statements. Incorrect.

58. (C) Parallel Flaw ★★★☆

Step 1: Identify the Question Type

The phrase "questionable pattern of reasoning" coupled with "most similar to" indicates this is a Parallel Flaw question. Approach the argument as you would a Flaw question. As

K | Part Three: Logical Reasoning
CHAPTER 10

These explanations refer to
questions that begin on page 626.

you identify the conclusion and evidence and pinpoint the gap between the two, keep common flaw types in mind. The correct answer choice will exhibit the same pattern of reasoning and the same flaw as the stimulus.

Step 2: Untangle the Stimulus

The opening piece of evidence, the first sentence, suggests that if a book presents a utopian future, then it will be popular. The next statement, after "[s]ince," suggests that books that predict a gloomy future aren't utopian. Based on that, the author concludes that such gloomy books will not likely be popular.

Step 3: Make a Prediction

The author has made a classic LSAT flaw in this argument by incorrectly contraposing a Formal Logic statement. The first statement, "If utopian future, then popular," should be contraposed as "If not popular, then not utopian future." The author's conclusion is based on an incorrect contrapositive that negates both sides of the Formal Logic but fails to reverse them. Basically, the author's conclusion is "If not utopian, then not popular." The correct answer will make the same Formal Logic error—negating both sides of a statement without reversing them.

Step 4: Evaluate the Answer Choices

(C) makes the same mistake as the stimulus because it starts from this statement—"If complicated with special effects, then expensive"—and ends by incorrectly contraposing it as "If not complicated and no special effects, then not expensive."

(A) is different from the stimulus in two important ways. First, its opening statement has an extra piece in its Formal Logic chain: if art portrays people as happy, then it tranquilizes, and then it appeals to certain people. Second, the conclusion to **(A)** starts by negating the final result of the evidence rather than by negating the evidence's sufficient condition. In other words, **(A)** does not make the same contrapositive error that the stimulus does.

(B) fails to match the stimulus by not using Formal Logic statements. The first sentence of **(B)** is much more tempered and cautious than the evidence in the stimulus, suggesting only that something "may" happen, not that it "will always" happen.

(D) also fails to match the stimulus by not using Formal Logic statements. The first sentence of **(D)** describes what "usually" and "often" happens rather than what "will always" happen.

(E) has Formal Logic, but the structure doesn't match the stimulus. **(E)** starts with the Formal Logic statement "If self-employed, then fluctuating salaries." Then, it describes government bureaucrats as not self-employed. For **(E)** to be parallel with the stimulus, its conclusion would have to be that government bureaucrats do not have fluctuating salaries.

Instead, it concludes that not everyone with a fluctuating salary is a government bureaucrat.

59. (D) Parallel Reasoning ★★★☆

Step 1: Identify the Question Type

The phrase "reasoning . . . most similar to" identifies this as a Parallel Reasoning question. Characterize the conclusion in the argument and eliminate any answer choice with a different type of conclusion. Alternatively, analyze the argument and find an answer choice that matches the reasoning piece by piece.

Step 2: Untangle the Stimulus

Despite its length, the argument in the stimulus is pretty straightforward. The author concludes that the local radio station will not win first place this year in the regional ratings race. Why? The author claims that the radio station has never finished better than fifth place in the ratings and conditions haven't changed positively for the station.

Step 3: Make a Prediction

The author predicts something will not happen this year because it has not happened in the past. Find an answer choice that provides another argument that uses past performance to indicate a definite continuation of that trend in the next occurrence.

Step 4: Evaluate the Answer Choices

(D) is correct. Based on past performance (stock prices have always been lower on Mondays), the author predicts, with certainty, that the stock will be lower the next Monday. That perfectly matches the structure of the stimulus, even though the stimulus has a negative prediction: "will not win." That could also be viewed in the affirmative by saying that it will lose the ratings race. Likewise, **(D)** could be rewritten to say stock prices will not be the same or higher. So, positive/negative is not applicable here to determine whether the stimulus and **(D)** are parallel.

(A) Here, the past trend is that every swan the author has seen is white. To be parallel to the original argument, the author must claim that the next swan spotted will also be white. However, this argument concludes that *all* swans are therefore probably white. That is like saying the radio station in the original argument will probably *never* win the ratings race. That is not what the original argument says, so this is not exactly parallel. Additionally, the conclusion in the original argument is an unequivocal prediction, while this conclusion is an assertion of probable fact.

(B) is incorrect because of the level of certainty. The past trend here is the coin coming up heads. Like the original argument, the next toss is predicted to be heads. However, unlike in the original argument, the prediction is qualified: It says the next

These explanations refer to questions that begin on page 626.

Part Three: Logical Reasoning
Assumption Family Questions

K

toss will *probably* be heads. The original argument has no such qualification, making these arguments unparallel.

(C) fails to provide any past trend that supports a prediction. Instead, it simply provides an assertion of fact stating all lions are mammals.

(E) also fails to support a conclusion about the future based on past trends. Rather, this choice uses a Formal Logic statement ("[o]nly trained swimmers are lifeguards") to predict that the next lifeguard will be a trained swimmer as well.

60. (A) Parallel Flaw

Step 1: Identify the Question Type

The phrase "flawed reasoning most similar to" indicates that the right answer will have the same logical flaw as the stimulus. This is a Parallel Flaw question.

Step 2: Untangle the Stimulus

Because the stimulus is brief and includes some Formal Logic, starting with its first word, "[a]nyone," attack by taking its entire structure into account. The author's argument boils down to this:

If you believe in ETs, then you believe in UFOs.

There are no UFOs.

Therefore, there are no ETs.

Step 3: Make a Prediction

Whenever Formal Logic comes up in a Flaw or Parallel Flaw question, think carefully about contrapositives. Here, it looks like the second and third statements simply form the contrapositive of the first—but there's an element in the first sentence that doesn't reappear: belief. The initial statement in this argument isn't about whether or not ETs or UFOs exist—it's about believing in them. Thus, the true contrapositive of the first sentence would simply be this:

If you don't believe in UFOs, then you don't believe in ETs.

We have no information that ties the actual existence of ETs to the actual existence of UFOs. The correct answer will make the same error by starting from a Formal Logic statement about belief and improperly shifting to evidence and conclusion about existence. In other words, the correct answer needs to have this overall structure:

If believe in X, then believe in Y. No Y. Therefore, No X.

Step 4: Evaluate the Answer Choices

(A) has the exact same structure as the stimulus and thus contains the same flaw. Correct.

(B) is actually logical, not flawed. Here, the second statement is a valid contrapositive of the first.

(C) makes a contrapositive error but doesn't shift scopes like the stimulus. In **(C)**, both statements are about belief, rather than one being about belief and the other about existence.

(D) is much less definite than the stimulus. "[N]o good reason to believe" is much weaker than "conclusively refuted."

(E) switches the order of the elements. The sufficient term from the initial Formal Logic statement (unicorns) "has been conclusively proven" not to exist, rather than the necessary term (centaurs). In the stimulus, the necessary term (UFOs) from the initial Formal Logic statement is the one that was proven not to exist.

61. (C) Principle (Identify and Apply)

Step 1: Identify the Question Stem

The presence of "principle" in the stem is a likely clue that this is a Principle question, but pay close attention to the rest of the stem. There will be a broad principle underlying the linguist's narrow statements, and that same broad principle will be illustrated by another narrow set of statements in the answer choices.

Step 2: Untangle the Stimulus

The linguist points out that despite the ability of most people to identify whether a sequence of words in their own dialect is grammatical, many of those same people can't specify the exact grammatical rules that apply to that particular sequence of words.

Step 3: Make a Prediction

We can't predict the subject matter of the right answer, but we can certainly extract the principle from the stimulus before applying it to the choices. The linguist appears to invoke the principle that sometimes people can know whether or not a thing meets certain criteria without knowing exactly what the criteria are. In other words, people may not be able to define a thing, but they can still know it when they see it. The correct answer choice will be a successful application of the same principle to a different situation.

Step 4: Evaluate the Answers

(C) is a perfect match. Just as the linguist says that people can identify a grammatical sequence without knowing what makes a sequence grammatical, **(C)** says that people can identify a waltz without knowing what makes a piece of music a waltz. This is our correct answer.

(A) discusses how some people's writing ability doesn't translate from a journalistic style to a poetic style. But **(A)** is missing the key component of identification. No one in **(A)** is identifying whether a poem is emotionally moving or satisfying without knowing what makes a poem emotionally moving or satisfying, so it doesn't apply our principle.

(B), if it invokes a principle at all, invokes the principle that applying concepts to concrete tasks requires more knowledge that it does to discover the concepts in the first place. This doesn't match our principle.

K | Part Three: Logical Reasoning
CHAPTER 10

These explanations refer to
questions that begin on page 627.

(D) tells us that an experience can be enjoyable even if we're unable to describe it in vivid detail, which is a vastly different principle from the one in the stimulus. The linguist's statements have nothing to do with an experience or the description of that experience.

(E) would be correct if it said that people could identify a game as chess even without knowing the defining characteristics of chess, but **(E)** veers off track when it introduces the idea of playing ability.

62. (C) Principle (Identify and Apply)　★★★★

Step 1: Identify the Question Type

The word "principle" makes it clear that this is a Principle question. This particular Principle question mimics a Parallel Reasoning question, as evidenced by the phrase "most similar to." First, broaden the conclusion to identify the principle behind the argument in the stimulus. Then, search for the answer choice that follows the same reasoning and correctly applies that same principle.

Step 2: Untangle the Stimulus

The conclusion comes in the middle of the stimulus, marked by the word "but." The author concludes that even though skipping credit card payments is sometimes permitted, it's almost never good for the cardholder to do so. In other words, cardholders usually shouldn't skip payments. The evidence is that finance charges keep accumulating, and the cardholder ends up paying overall much more than she would have months earlier.

Step 3: Make a Prediction

The evidence is about how deferring payments leads to greater costs in the long run. The conclusion is about what is bad for the cardholder. Therefore, the author's assumption is that things that lead to greater costs in the long run are bad for cardholders. This assumption can be generalized to other situations besides cardholders. So, look for the answer choice that matches by showing a situation where greater costs in the long run are ultimately bad.

Step 4: Evaluate the Answer Choices

(C) matches the stimulus. Just like the offer in the stimulus above, which carries heavy finance charges later on, the immediate benefit of using funds for new roads will result in greater maintenance costs in the long run.

(A) goes Outside the Scope by introducing the idea of finding other ways to achieve the same benefit. The author in the stimulus never states that cardholders should find other ways to achieve the same benefit (retaining money in the short term). Additionally, this answer choice ignores the concept of short term versus long term.

(B) isn't parallel because it makes a positive recommendation whereas the stimulus makes a negative one. The stimulus says people should *not* do something that is good in the short term but bad in the long term. But that doesn't mean the stimulus would agree that people *should* do something that is bad in the short term (increased payroll) but good in the long run (greater hiring power). Additionally, increased payroll could arguably be bad for a company in both the short and long term, which confounds the time aspect of the stimulus.

(D) is a 180. It recommends a plan (buying used equipment) that is good in the short term but will actually cost more in the long run. The stimulus recommends *against* a plan with that pattern.

(E) goes Outside the Scope by focusing on practicality rather than the costs associated with time.

63. (D) Principle (Identify and Apply)　★★★★

Step 1: Identify the Question Type

This Principle question asks us to find a specific factual situation in an answer choice that follows the same principle that underlies the factual situation presented in the stimulus. We must first read to identify the principle and then apply it to the answer choices.

Step 2: Untangle the Stimulus

The facts state that buying screensavers to save money can backfire and actually end up costing more money than is saved. The reason is that the interesting graphics will cause users of the program to waste time. Generalize these facts to a broader rule of thumb that might apply to a different situation.

Step 3: Make a Prediction

Generalize the screensaver program to any technology used to save costs and generalize the employees who use the program to any human affected by the money-saving technology. Then, the underlying principle becomes this: there may be unanticipated human costs associated with using the money-saving technology.

Step 4: Evaluate the Answer Choices

(D) fits the prediction nicely. It states that a security system used to reduce losses by theft (money-saving technology) can cost more in customer goodwill (human costs) than it saves.

(A) is Outside the Scope. This choice states that money may not be saved if a product is chosen based on user preferences. In the principle, money *is* saved, but it may be offset by other unanticipated costs.

(B) is Outside the Scope. The principle is not about saving money in the long run.

(C) is Outside the Scope. This choice makes a comparison of the times it takes to perform two alternative activities. This

These explanations refer to questions that begin on page 628.

Part Three: Logical Reasoning
Assumption Family Questions

does not match the elements of the principle, which deal with the hidden costs of one alternative.

(E) is Outside the Scope. This choice compares the relative costs of choosing between two alternative products. The principle makes no such comparisons.

64. (A) Principle (Identify and Apply)

Step 1: Identify the Question Type

The word "principle" makes it clear that this is a Principle question. This particular Principle question mimics a Parallel Reasoning question, as evidenced by the phrase "most closely conforms ... illustrates." First, identify the principle behind the argument in the stimulus. Then, search for the answer choice that follows the same reasoning and correctly applies that same principle.

Step 2: Untangle the Stimulus

Historians can find clues about a region's distant history by studying the present, but the further distant the period is, the less useful study of the present becomes. In other words, the further removed we are from the period, the less we can learn about it by looking at the present.

Step 3: Make a Prediction

While the correct answer could introduce many different specific situations, it must still conform to the principle that the further in the past something is, the less one can learn about it by looking at current data.

Step 4: Evaluate the Choices

(A) conforms to the principle illustrated by the stimulus. While astronomers can make some inferences about the past of the solar system, they know less about the very earliest era of the solar system's history, its origin. Correct.

(B) goes Outside the Scope by suggesting the amount of studying makes learning new things harder. The stimulus suggests the passage of time makes it harder to learn about things.

(C) goes Outside the Scope. It introduces the element of "world view," rather than focusing on the passage of time.

(D) also goes Outside the Scope. It discusses things beyond ordinary sensory experience and fails to include anything about the passage of time.

(E) goes Outside the Scope by introducing the element of being impressed. Like **(C)** and **(D)**, it also fails to mention the passage of time as an obstacle to knowledge.

65. (A) Flaw (OP) ★☆☆☆

Step 1: Identify the Question Stem

Since we're asked to find why the company president's reasoning is "most vulnerable to criticism," this is a Flaw question.

Step 2: Untangle the Stimulus

The president declares that her company will interview applicants for the management consultant position only if those applicants have worked for firms from the top 1 percent of firms worldwide. She believes that this will ensure that the applicant selected for the job is one of the best consultants available.

Step 3: Make a Prediction

When we're analyzing an argument in a Flaw question, we should always ask ourselves, "Why isn't the conclusion established by the evidence?" In this case, we need to determine why the president's plan might not guarantee that her company will hire one of the best consultants. Of course, it's entirely possible that the company could hire someone who, despite working for a top firm, isn't one of the best consultants. Just because someone was employed by a top firm doesn't mean that he or she is automatically one of the best consultants. But this is something that the president erroneously assumes.

Step 4: Evaluate the Answers

(A) states this flaw in a different way. When predicting the answer to a Flaw question, be sure to scan the answer choices for the issue you predicted, not the precise language of your prediction.

(B) is irrelevant, since we have no idea of the size of the sample of management consulting firms worldwide. For all we know, the president could be taking into account every single management consulting firm existent across the globe.

(C) gets it backward. The president takes for granted that if a firm is recognized as being one of the top 1 percent of firms worldwide, then all of its individual employees will be among the best consultants.

(D) is Outside the Scope of the argument. The president's argument is concerned with selecting a top applicant. She hasn't predicted with any certainty that the applicant selected will accept the position once it is offered.

(E) isn't something the president presumes at all. The argument doesn't discuss whether the president believes the new hire will be competent at all tasks in the new job. The president is merely concerned with making sure her company hires one of the best consultants available.

EXPLANATIONS

K | Part Three: Logical Reasoning
CHAPTER 10

These explanations refer to
questions that begin on page 629.

66. (A) Assumption (OP) ★★★☆

Step 1: Identify the Question Type

Because the question stem directly asks for the assumption that the argument depends on, this is a Necessary Assumption question.

Step 2: Untangle the Stimulus

The conclusion, marked by "[t]herefore," is that, at first, the mayor won't be able to collect the money that he plans to charge drivers for being downtown. The evidence is that the mayor's plan requires the sophisticated camera system for enforcement, and that system will not be ready until the end of next year.

Step 3: Make a Prediction

If the mayor's plan won't work without the camera system, and the author's conclusion is that the mayor's plan won't work, then we know that the author is assuming that the mayor will implement his plan before the camera system is ready. That means that the mayor will implement his plan sometime before the end of next year, when the system will be ready.

Step 4: Evaluate the Answer Choices

(A) matches the prediction.

(B) goes Outside the Scope by introducing the idea of a budget deficit and neglecting the idea of whether or not the mayor's plan will be effectively enforced.

(C) contradicts the argument rather than providing its missing piece. The author is suggesting that at first the plan will not be effectively enforced. **(C)** goes against this, suggesting that the plan should not be implemented until it can be effectively enforced.

(D) makes an Irrelevant Comparison between the importance of raising revenue and reducing congestion.

(E) is both Outside the Scope and Extreme. It does not matter whether or not the mayor's plan is the most effective; it does matter whether or not the plan will be implemented before it can be fully enforced. Furthermore, referring to the plan as the "most effective way" is a red flag that the answer will fail the Denial Test.

67. (D) Strengthen (OP-C) ★★★☆

Step 1: Identify the Question Type

Because the stem indicates that the correct answer will support the psychologist's conclusion, this is a Strengthen question. Break the argument down into conclusion and evidence and find the psychologist's assumption. Look for an answer choice that makes that assumption more likely to be true.

Step 2: Untangle the Stimulus

The conclusion is that very, very overconfident people are more likely to start a business. The evidence comes from a survey taken of entrepreneurs and business managers. In the survey, the entrepreneurs showed much more confidence than the business managers.

Step 3: Make a Prediction

The conclusion can be restated as a causal argument. The psychologist is really arguing that being super overconfident causes people to start businesses. The evidence is a correlation—people who started businesses (entrepreneurs) are more confident. The psychologist must then be assuming three things. First, the causality is not reversed (starting a business raised confidence); second, an outside thing didn't cause both the overconfidence and the entrepreneurship; and third, the two are not merely coincidentally correlated. The correct answer will strengthen the link between overconfidence and starting businesses.

Step 4: Evaluate the Answer Choices

(D) reinforces the connection between confidence and starting a business by adding the fact that the most overconfident business managers also tried to start businesses at one time.

(A) is Outside the Scope because the *types* of questions asked in the survey are irrelevant; rather, the confidence of the participants' responses matter. The psychologist might be able to determine how overconfident the survey respondents were no matter what kind of question was asked. If anything, this could weaken the argument because it could be the psychologist asked the wrong type of questions for this group of people.

(B) goes Outside the Scope by focusing on some entrepreneurs' preparation. The psychologist is concerned solely with confidence and bases his conclusion on that. That some entrepreneurs knew the accurate odds (rather than just the fact that they are enormous) doesn't factor in to his argument.

(C) goes Outside the Scope by introducing the idea of success in business. The argument is just concerned with the likelihood of *starting* a business, regardless of whether it eventually fails or succeeds. Also, this wouldn't help the psychologist prove there is a connection between confidence and entrepreneurship: the business managers (as managers) could be incredibly successful too.

(E) goes Outside the Scope by introducing business acumen and failing to mention likelihood of starting a business.

These explanations refer to questions that begin on page 630.

Part Three: Logical Reasoning
Assumption Family Questions

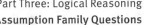

68. (C) Assumption (MC-E) ★★★★

Step 1: Identify the Question Stem

We're asked to find the assumption on which the argument depends, so this is definitely a Necessary Assumption question.

Step 2: Untangle the Stimulus

The conclusion is signaled by the word "[t]hus": the rate at which a society changes can be measured by monitoring the amount of deference that the young show to the old. The evidence tells us that the rate of change in a society is inversely proportional to the value that its younger members find in the advice of its older members.

Step 3: Make a Prediction

Whenever the conclusion of an argument introduces a brand-new term not mentioned in the evidence, look for the central assumption to use that term. Here, the new term is "deference." The evidence only discusses the value that young people find in the advice of older people. To make the argument work, the author must be assuming that there's some sort of connection between the two; in other words, the assumption is that the deference that young people show to their elders is a function of how much they value their elders' advice.

Step 4: Evaluate the Answers

(C) is the clearest match for our prediction and is quite necessary in order for the argument to be logically cohesive.

(A). The argument doesn't depend on the younger members of a society being conscious of the society's rate of change. Besides, **(A)** doesn't allow the author to reach a conclusion about deference.

(B) may be tempting, but it distorts the author's evidence. According the argument, young people don't value advice that they *think* is irrelevant to them. However, just because they think it's irrelevant doesn't mean that it actually is. The concept we need to connect to deference is the perceived value (or perceived usefulness), not the actual value (or actual usefulness).

(D) is all but stated in the evidence, so it isn't something the author really assumes implicitly. Also, **(D)** has nothing to do with deference, which is another reason to eliminate it.

(E), too, doesn't allow the author to reach a conclusion about deference, and it should be eliminated on that basis alone. The correct assumption has to be somehow connected to the new term or idea in the conclusion, even if that assumption doesn't use the term verbatim.

69. (D) Flaw (MC-ME) ★★★☆

Step 1: Identify the Question Type

The phrase "most vulnerable to criticism" indicates that this is a Flaw question. The correct answer will describe the flaw in the application of the principle.

Step 2: Untangle the Stimulus

Simply put, the Principle states that if an activity is healthy for a kid's intellectual development, then it does not take away from the child's social development. Contraposed, it states that if something does take away from a kid's social development, then it is not healthy for the kid. The Application seems to fit with the contrapositive. Because Megan's reading decreases the amount of time she spends with others, the author concludes that reading is unhealthy for her.

Step 3: Make a Prediction

Find the assumption that the Application makes. Because the Application concludes that Megan's reading is unhealthy, the author must assume that Megan's reading takes away from her social development. Note, the Application only suggests that it reduces the amount of time she spends with others, not that it actually takes away from her social development. The correct answer will suggest that the author assumes that just because something reduces the amount of social time, that it actually gets in the way of social development.

Step 4: Evaluate the Answer Choices

(D) matches the prediction by calling out the author's assumption.

(A) goes against the language of both the Principle and the Application. The language in the Principle is categorical, and the Application takes it that way.

(B) is a Distortion of the conclusion of the application. The Application is about whether or not the activity is healthy, not about whether or not some other benefit to the activity is more important than its healthiness.

(C) almost describes the Application accurately—the Application does interpret the Principle to be about what is unhealthy. This is perfectly logical, though, and not a misinterpretation. By contraposing the Principle's Formal Logic, we deduced a logical statement about one sufficient explanation for something to be unhealthy.

(E) suggests that the Application confuses sufficiency and necessity or, in other words, misforms the contrapositive. But, the Application gets the logical structure of the contrapositive correct. The problem with the Application is that it makes an unwarranted assumption about what would satisfy the sufficient condition of the contrapositive.

K | Part Three: Logical Reasoning
CHAPTER 10

These explanations refer to
questions that begin on page 631.

70. (E) Assumption (OP-R)

Step 1: Identify the Question Stem

Because the question asks for an assumption, this is an Assumption question. Additionally, because the assumption is "required," the answer will be a Necessary Assumption, one without which the conclusion could not follow. Break down the argument into conclusion and evidence and look for the gap between the two. You can use the Denial Test to check or confirm answer choices.

Step 2: Untangle the Stimulus

The dietitian concludes that individuals who are more susceptible to heart disease as a result of high sodium intake should eat fresh fruit and vegetables rather than canned or frozen fruit and vegetables. The dietician bases her conclusion on the single piece of evidence that potassium in plant foods—such as fruits and vegetables—helps prevent sodium's bad effects.

Step 3: Make a Prediction

Given that the dietitian recommends fresh produce over canned or frozen produce, there must be something preferable about fresh produce. In the evidence, the dietitian suggests potassium in plant foods is beneficial. The assumption will connect these ideas. So, the dietitian must be assuming fresh produce has more of the beneficial potassium than canned or frozen produce does.

Step 4: Evaluate the Answer Choices

(E) matches the prediction.

(A) is an Irrelevant Comparison. It wrongly compares the amount of potassium to sodium in all fruits and vegetables. Yet the argument in the stimulus compares just the amount of potassium in fresh versus canned or frozen vegetables.

(B) is Outside the Scope because it incorrectly focuses on sodium. The dietitian argues people should eat fresh produce as a way of maintaining heart health without *lowering* sodium consumption. Within the scope of this argument, she is unconcerned about *increasing* sodium consumption. Rather, her main evidence is about the intake of potassium. The dietitian is concerned about which type of produce has the most potassium, not the most sodium.

(C) is Extreme. The dietitian never says—or needs to say—potassium is the *only* way to protect against sodium, just that it is one way.

(D) is Outside the Scope and not required for the conclusion to follow. Even if the potassium in fruits and vegetables has zero or many negative side effects, the dietitian still may correctly argue eating fruits and vegetables would benefit people, if the positives outweigh the negatives. This argument is all about the good effects of potassium, not the bad.

71. (A) Flaw (MC-PvW)

Step 1: Identify the Question Type

"The reasoning in the argument is flawed ..." Characterize the flaw and look for the answer choice that describes it.

Step 2: Untangle the Stimulus

The first sentence gives us an argument made by a critic of space exploration. The word "[b]ut" at the start of the next sentence signals the author's disagreement. The conclusion is that the critic exaggerates the risk of sending explorers to Mars. The reason is that every stage of the long journey has a backup system, so any given stage of the journey has a low probability of failure resulting in death.

Step 3: Make a Prediction

The words "at any given stage" should alert you to watch for a scope problem. The conclusion is about the risk of the whole "long and complicated journey." The evidence is about the risk at any given stage of the trip. The author is assuming that because each stage by itself has a low risk of failure, the risk is correspondingly low over the entire duration of the trip.

Step 4: Evaluate the Answer Choices

(A) fits the prediction.

(B) is Outside the Scope. The author does not conclude that something cannot occur. He merely concludes the risk is exaggerated.

(C) is a Distortion. Get past the abstract language in this answer choice by asking what the argument concludes *must* be true. The conclusion is that the risk is exaggerated. The conclusion is not based on any evidence that the risk is *probably* exaggerated

(D) is Outside the Scope. The conclusion isn't about whether something will or won't work.

(E) is Outside the Scope. The author does not attack the adequacy of the critic's argument. He offers factual evidence to refute it.

72. (C) Weaken (OP)

Step 1: Identify the Question Type

Because the right answer is the one statement that "weakens the reasoning" in the stimulus, this is a Weaken question.

Step 2: Untangle the Stimulus

The author concludes that the *Iliad* and the *Odyssey* were almost certainly not the work of the same author. His evidence is that there are significant differences in tone, vocabulary, and details.

Step 3: Make a Prediction

Start by finding the assumption. Here, the author is assuming that significant differences between two works means that the two works must not have the same author. In other words,

These explanations refer to questions that begin on page 632.

Part Three: Logical Reasoning
Assumption Family Questions

K

he's overlooking the possibility that an author could change his tone and vocabulary between works. The correct answer will attack the author's assumption, perhaps by pointing out that an author could change his writing style significantly in two different works.

Step 4: Evaluate the Answer Choices

(C) matches the prediction by giving a modern example that shows an author can use different styles in different works.

(A) might indicate that the attributions of the hymns are also wrong, but because we have no evidence that these varied works were indeed created by the same author, it doesn't affect the likelihood that Homer wrote both the *Iliad* and *Odyssey*.

(B) might explain how two works by the same author came to differ, but the errors and corruptions described here are "minor" and don't account for the "great" discrepancies the author describes in Homer.

(D) goes Outside the Scope by focusing on internal consistency in a work rather than on the consistency between two different works. Similar to **(B)**, a book can fail to have "complete consistency" without having the kind of large differences discussed in the stimulus.

(E) is a 180 because it directly supports the author's conclusion. It gives another reason why the two works would not have had the same author.

73. (A) Flaw (OP-NvS) ★☆☆☆

Step 1: Identify the Question Type

"[E]rror in reasoning" identifies this as a Flaw question. In this dialogue stimulus, we are asked to identify the reasoning error in the Reporter's response to the Scientist.

Step 2: Untangle the Stimulus

The Scientist states that in a study testing two athlete's foot medications, M and N, only the people who were given M were cured. Because of the word "only," we can translate this into Formal Logic:

$$Cured \quad \rightarrow \quad M$$

Be careful with the confusing wording. The word "only" signals the necessary condition, but it can sometimes be tricky to determine which word "only" modifies, especially when the passive voice is used. In this case, the sense of the statement is that only those who were given medication M were cured. Taking M is the necessary condition.

The Reporter responds by stating that this means anyone who wasn't cured didn't get medication M. In other words:

$$\sim Cured \quad \rightarrow \quad \sim M$$

This improper contrapositive is the key to the reporter's error.

Step 3: Make a Prediction

This is a classic flaw of confusing sufficient and necessary conditions. The reporter misinterprets the scientist's statement to say that anyone who wasn't cured didn't take M. Using the logic of the contrapositive, anyone who took M was cured. In other words, *M always cured athlete's foot*. However, the scientist actually said that people who were cured took M. This doesn't preclude the possibility that some people who *weren't* cured took M as well!

Sufficient/Necessary flaws can be expressed in a number of ways: sufficient/necessary, can/must, overlooked possibility. Be flexible when reading answer choices.

Step 4: Evaluate the Answer Choices

(A) fits the prediction. The reporter mistakes the fact that M can cure athlete's foot to mean it must always cure athlete's foot.

(B) is Outside the Scope. The reporter draws no conclusions about the population as a whole. His conclusion is simply about the results of the study.

(C) is Outside the Scope. The availability of M outside of the study is not an issue.

(D) and **(E)** are Distortions. The reporter states a conclusion about people who were not cured, not about people who were cured.

74. (A) Assumption (MC-E) ★★★★

Step 1: Identify the Question Stem

The stem asks us to find the choice that, if assumed, would make the conclusion follow from the evidence, so this is a Sufficient Assumption question.

Step 2: Untangle the Stimulus

The ultimate conclusion of the argument is that all made-to-measure wigs should be dry-cleaned. There are four key pieces of evidence. Wigs with handmade components are more expensive than those with none; made-to-measure wigs range in price from medium-priced to expensive; wigs that don't use human hair don't have handmade foundations; and wigs that do contain human hair should be dry-cleaned.

Step 3: Make a Prediction

Words like "[i]f," "any," and "all" in the stimulus are clear signs that Formal Logic is present here. When you have many pieces of evidence with these Keywords, turn them into Formal Logic statements and try to string them together. This will help you see where the gap is.

Our four pieces of evidence as Formal Logic statements are:

K Part Three: Logical Reasoning
CHAPTER 10

These explanations refer to
questions that begin on page 632.

If handmade components	→	*more expensive than without*
If made-to-measure	→	*ranges from medium-priced to expensive*
If no human hair used	→	*no handmade foundation*
If human hair used	→	*should be dry-cleaned*

The conclusion can be translated to:

If made-to-measure	→	*should be dry-cleaned*

If we contrapose the third piece of evidence ("If handmade foundation → human hair used"), we can connect that to the fourth piece:

If handmade foundation	→	*human hair used*
	→	*should be dry-cleaned*

So our conclusion will have to follow from our evidence when we connect the necessary condition in the second piece of evidence to the sufficient condition in the chain above:

If made-to-measure	→	*ranges from medium-priced to expensive*
	→	*handmade foundation*
	→	*human hair used*
	→	*should be dry-cleaned*

Our assumption, therefore, is that all wigs ranging from medium-priced to expensive have handmade foundations. That, if true, will make it logically necessary for made-to-measure wigs to be dry-cleaned.

Step 4: Evaluate the Answers

(A) is a direct match for our prediction.

(B) provides no connection to made-to-measure wigs, so it can't help us establish the conclusion from the evidence.

(C) simply combines the Formal Logic of the evidence, but it still fails to connect made-to-measure wigs to the logic and therefore doesn't help us establish the conclusion.

(D) comes close, but the evidence tells us that made-to-measure wigs are priced at least in the medium range. Choice **(D)** would establish that wigs with handmade foundations are similarly priced, but this doesn't guarantee that made-to-measure wigs have handmade foundations. They could be two totally different types of wigs that just happen to be similarly priced.

(E) also doesn't properly establish a connection between made-to-measure wigs and handmade foundations the way that choice **(A)** does.

75. (A) Strengthen (OP)   ★★★★

Step 1: Identify the Question Type

The word "strengthens" indicates a Strengthen question. Break down the argument into conclusion and evidence, predict the central assumption, and find an answer choice that validates the author's assumption.

Step 2: Untangle the Stimulus

The conclusion is in the last sentence, marked by "[t]hus." The author says there must have been many more Byzantine documents sealed with lead than there are lead seals remaining. The evidence is that because lead was relatively valuable, people would recycle the lead seals after opening the document that the seal was on.

Step 3: Make a Prediction

The evidence says a lead seal is recast into something else after its document is opened. The conclusion says the number of total documents sealed in the empire greatly outnumbered the number of remaining seals. Therefore, the author assumes that a significant number of seals were destroyed and thus must have been on documents that got opened. The correct answer will support this assumption.

Step 4: Evaluate the Answer Choices

(A) fills in the author's missing link. If the *majority* of seals were on documents that got opened, then those seals likely were recycled. That would support the notion that the number of documents sealed was well over 40,000.

(B) goes Outside the Scope by introducing the destruction of the documents, which is not in the stimulus. Whether or not the documents were destroyed doesn't affect the total number of original documents and how it stacks up against the number of seals.

(C) makes an Irrelevant Comparison. The amount of lead in the seals today as compared to their original amount of lead doesn't address the number of documents issue.

(D) would help explain why 40,000 lead seals remain, but it doesn't discuss the total number of documents. It's possible that there were at most 40,000 important documents and then only 2 unimportant documents. If anything, **(D)** would weaken the author's argument that the number of documents many times over outnumbered the number of seals.

(E) goes Outside the Scope by including "at any given time." The argument is about how many documents and seals there were *throughout* a given period rather than at any specific point in that period.

These explanations refer to
questions that begin on page 633.

Part Three: Logical Reasoning
Assumption Family Questions |

EXPLANATIONS

76. (E) Flaw (OP)

Step 1: Identify the Question Type

The phrase "most vulnerable to criticism" is common language for a Flaw question. Look for the unwarranted assumption or the common LSAT flaw.

Step 2: Untangle the Stimulus

The author concludes the energy subsidy has not accomplished its goal. The evidence outlines what that goal is: to help rural residents gain access to electricity. The author thinks the subsidy has failed because many of the most isolated rural populations still have no electricity.

Step 3: Make a Prediction

The author incorrectly interprets the subsidy's goal to the extreme. According to the author himself, the subsidy was intended to *help* rural areas. That doesn't mean *all* rural areas would gain electricity. So it may be possible that even though the results of the subsidy (electricity access) haven't touched everyone (the most isolated rural populations), the subsidy has still helped residents of rural areas in general and has therefore arguably achieved its purpose. The author overlooks this possibility.

Step 4: Evaluate the Answer Choices

(E) raises the overlooked alternative by suggesting many people could have benefited from the subsidy, even if not everyone did.

(A) goes Outside the Scope by contemplating what might have happened without granting the subsidy. The author's argument is simply that the subsidy failed. The author doesn't go even further to say the subsidy's inexistence could have led to success.

(B) goes Outside the Scope by introducing a new criterion for failure. The author never suggests that the subsidy is a failure because it helps people besides those whom it was intended to help. Rather, the author suggests the subsidy is a failure because it didn't help all the intended people.

(C) goes Outside the Scope by introducing other people in the nation, when the author's argument is only about the subsidy directed toward the rural population.

(D) also goes Outside the Scope by discussing people who live in urban areas. While the author touches on urban populations earlier in the stimulus, he (correctly) doesn't include them in his discussion of the subsidy itself. This isn't a flaw in his argument.

77. (B) Strengthen (OP-R)

Step 1: Identify the Question Type

Because the question asks for something that will strengthen the banking analyst's argument, this is a Strengthen question.

Step 2: Untangle the Stimulus

The contrast Keyword "[b]ut" indicates the banking analyst's conclusion: It's "not an ideal business practice" to offer free services only to new customers. Her evidence, indicated by the Keyword "since," is that this practice excludes long-term customers, who make up most of a bank's business.

Step 3: Make a Prediction

The banking analyst argues against excluding long-term customers. Thus, the banking analyst assumes any undesirable or negative consequences that result from excluding long-term customers would outweigh any possible benefits. You want an answer choice that increases the likelihood that neglecting regular customers is detrimental to banks.

Step 4: Evaluate the Answer Choices

(B) suggests banks greatly benefit by giving special deals only to long-term customers. This supports the bank analyst's argument because it provides evidence why excluding long-time customers from special deals is a bad idea. While this answer choice doesn't completely prove the bank analyst's argument, it does make the argument more likely to be true, which is exactly what a strengthener needs to do.

(A) goes Outside the Scope because it only compares banks to each other. It doesn't address the main comparison at issue: the advantages of offering promotions to new versus long-term customers.

(C) is a 180. It weakens the banking analyst's argument by suggesting a reason why banks shouldn't extend special deals to their long-term customers.

(D) is another 180. It weakens the argument because it makes it unlikely that banks will lose their long-term customers by failing to offer them free services.

(E) is yet another 180. It weakens the argument by showing that at least one bank that doesn't follow the analyst's advice is very successful.

78. (A) Assumption (OP) ★★☆☆

Step 1: Identify the Question Type

The question asks for the argument's assumption. Because the assumption is "required," the question is looking for a Necessary Assumption, and you can, if need be, use the Denial Test to confirm or eliminate answers.

Step 2: Untangle the Stimulus

Gotera's conclusion, indicated by "[w]e can conclude," is categorical: Speech acquisition is entirely a motor control process and not an abstract or mental one. His evidence is that babies are physically unable to produce particular sounds but babble randomly, and that it takes years for

K Part Three: Logical Reasoning
CHAPTER 10

These explanations refer to
questions that begin on page 633.

children to develop the ability to produce all of the required
sounds for language.

Step 3: Make a Prediction

The categorical language in the conclusion is a tip-off that
Gotera is overlooking an alternative possibility, namely that
speech acquisition could be a function of more than one thing,
like motor control and something else (perhaps cognitive
ability). The correct answer will fill the hole in Gotera's
argument by ruling out anything besides motor control as a
factor in speech acquisition.

Step 4: Evaluate the Choices

(A) gets it exactly right by eliminating any other possible factor
in speech acquisition—it is only the ability to produce the
sounds that matters.

(B) is Outside the Scope. Gotera is concerned with whether
infants can intentionally produce particular sounds, which is
different from intentionally moving their tongues.

(C) is also Outside the Scope. It incorrectly focuses on the
babbling stage. Gotera isn't concerned with when the babbling
stage ends but about when the voluntary production of sounds
starts.

(D) is Outside the Scope. It's possible there is another stage
before babbling, but that doesn't affect Gotera's conclusion
that speech acquisition is a motor control process. Note that
the detail about babbling in the first sentence is mentioned in
three tempting wrong answers, but it is not an essential piece
of evidence for Gotera's conclusion.

(E) is a 180 because it actually contradicts Gotera's argument
by saying that speech acquisition has a mental aspect.

79. (C) Flaw (MC-E/OP) ★★★★

Step 1: Identify the Question Type

The word "flawed" clearly identifies this as a Flaw question.
Break down the concert promoter's argument, identifying his
conclusion and evidence and determining his assumption.
Then, evaluate how his reasoning goes wrong. If an argument
has more than one possible flaw, beware of answers that
distort one of those flaws or are too extreme.

Step 2: Untangle the Stimulus

The concert promoter suggests critics are mistaken and
a particular concert series *does* have popular appeal. His
evidence is merely that sales of memorabilia are equal to
those of comparable concert series.

Step 3: Make a Prediction

There are two issues with the concert promoter's argument.
First, he must assume that the sale of memorabilia indicates
popular appeal. Second, the promoter concludes that the one
series has popular appeal because of its similarity to other
series. However, he never explicitly states whether those other

series have popular appeal; instead, he assumes they do. If
those other series were unpopular, then having equivalent
sales would probably indicate a lack of popularity in the
promoter's series.

Step 4: Evaluate the Answer Choices

(C) is correct and matches your prediction. The promoter errs
by assuming the popularity of the comparable series.

(A) is Outside the Scope. The sale figures cited by the concert
promoter are facts, not emotional considerations.

(B) is Extreme. The promoter merely assumes that memorabilia
sales are one indicator, not necessarily the *only* indicator of
popular appeal. That word should have sent up a red flag.
Eliminate.

(D) is a 180. The promoter states the other events are
"comparable," not dissimilar.

(E) is Outside the Scope. The argument does not have a classic
parts-versus-the-whole flaw. Although the concert promoter
does not make a distinction between the series and the
individual concerts, this is not why his argument is flawed.
The argument is entirely concerned with the quality of the
series, not of the individual components of the series.

80. (D) Assumption (MC-ME) ★★★☆

Step 1: Identify the Question Type

The word "assumed" identifies this as an Assumption
question. Furthermore, the "if" indicates that you are looking
for a Sufficient Assumption. While there may be several
assumptions that would be sufficient to ensure that the
conclusion follows logically from the evidence, only one
answer choice will state such an assumption.

Step 2: Untangle the Stimulus

The economist concludes that countries that put collective
goals first can't emerge quickly from a recession. The
economist's evidence is that rapid emergence requires
investment, and investment only happens when citizens have
confidence. The Formal Logic would look like this:

Evidence:

Emerge from Recession → New Infrastructure → Confidence

Conclusion:

If Collective > Individual → ~ Emerge from Recession

Step 3: Make a Prediction

There's a big gap between evidence and conclusion—the
evidence is about confidence, and the conclusion is about
putting collective goals ahead of individuals' goals. The author
assumes a connection between putting collective goals first
and lack of confidence.

These explanations refer to
questions that begin on page 634.

Part Three: Logical Reasoning
Assumption Family Questions

Argument:

If Collective > Individual → ~ Confidence → ~ New
Infrastructure → ~ Emerge from Recession

Step 4: Evaluate the Answer Choices

(D) explicitly connects putting collective goals first and lack of confidence. In fact, it is the only answer choice of the five that mentions confidence.

(A) goes Outside the Scope by discussing countries that do not emerge quickly from recessions. The economist says if a country will rapidly emerge, then investment is needed. She presents no information about what happens investment-wise if a country does not quickly emerge from a recession. This answer goes backward on the Formal Logic.

(B) is a Distortion. The author never argues that recessions do or do not affect people's support for government policies. Rather, people's confidence in government policies affects their investment, which affects the quick emergence or lack thereof from the recession.

(C) goes Outside the Scope by discussing the wrong countries: those that put individuals first. The argument provides information only about countries that put collective goals first. This answer choice, like **(A)**, also goes backward on the Formal Logic.

(E) goes Outside the Scope by focusing on what would cause a country to experience, not get out of, a recession. The argument is about what kind of policies would keep a country in recession rather than how the country's recession started in the first place.

81. (E) Flaw (OP) ★★☆☆

Step 1: Identify the Question Stem

The words "vulnerable to criticism" indicate that this is a Flaw question, but if we read on, we see that we're given a clue to the flaw: the argument fails to consider some possibility. So let's keep this in mind as we untangle the argument and predict our answer.

Step 2: Untangle the Stimulus

Fat substitutes such as N5 are often used by people who need to reduce their fat intake. But the argument concludes that these fat substitutes are useless. In studies cited as evidence, subjects who ate foods prepared with N5 ended up hungrier afterward than after eating foods prepared with real fat and ate more to quell that hunger, consuming more calories than they saved by eating N5 in the first place.

Step 3: Make a Prediction

Remember that we need to predict a possibility that the argument fails to consider. The conclusion that N5 is useless is quite strong and not necessarily proven by the evidence. After all, N5 isn't supposed to be a *calorie* substitute, just

a *fat* substitute. So what if the subjects in the study, after eating food prepared with N5, moved on to eat other food that contained more calories but didn't contain any fat? Then N5 has done its job as a fat substitute, and it isn't useless, as the argument alleges.

Step 4: Evaluate the Answers

(E) is another way of phrasing the overlooked possibility we predicted. Even if people's total caloric intake doesn't decrease, N5 can still be useful, as long as people's fat intake decreases.

(A) is irrelevant to the argument. Even if only one or two foods can be prepared with N5, that has no bearing on whether or not it's useful as a fat substitute.

(B) introduces side effects, which are Outside the Scope of the argument. The author is only concerned with N5's effectiveness as a fat substitute.

(C) isn't a possibility that the author needs to consider. The argument here is that N5 doesn't actually reduce a person's fat intake because it could increase that person's overall caloric intake. Whether or not people who consume N5 pay attention to their caloric intake doesn't matter in the studies.

(D) might need to be considered if the author were trying to argue that people who want to reduce their fat intake should remain unaware that N5 is calorie-free. But for the purposes of this argument, whether or not they know that N5 contains no calories isn't relevant. The point is that people who consume N5 consume more calories later than they saved by eating the N5-prepared foods.

82. (D) Weaken (OP) ★★☆☆

Step 1: Identify the Question Stem

This stem uses the phrase "most seriously weakens," so this is clearly a Weaken question.

Step 2: Untangle the Stimulus

The argument concludes that most people need to take vitamin pills. The reason for this is that most people eat far fewer than the five servings of fruits and vegetables that nutritionists believe can meet a person's daily vitamin requirement.

Step 3: Make a Prediction

The most straightforward way to weaken an argument is to challenge its central assumption. The author sees vitamin pills as the only alternative to the five daily servings of fruits and vegetables that most people don't get. In reaching the conclusion, the author assumes that there's no other way to get those vitamins. So we should seek an answer choice that involves a source other than vitamin pills for the vitamins people aren't getting from fruits and vegetables.

EXPLANATIONS

Part Three: Logical Reasoning
CHAPTER 10

These explanations refer to
questions that begin on page 634.

Step 4: Evaluate the Answers

(D) provides that source. If manufacturers of foods that aren't fruits and vegetables fortify those foods with vitamins, then the people who don't eat enough fruits and vegetables can still get their vitamins without taking pills.

(A) suggests that even people who eat the recommended number of servings of fruits and vegetables may not get enough vitamins from those servings. But this doesn't undermine the idea that they need to get their vitamins from pills. If anything, it strengthens the idea that they'll need to get their vitamins from alternative sources.

(B) offers an Irrelevant Comparison. The strength or weakness of an argument urging people to take vitamin pills doesn't depend on whether or not certain fruits and vegetables contain more nutrients than others.

(C), if true, might make it difficult to agree on a universal amount of fruits and vegetables that will constitute five daily servings. But that does nothing to support or undermine the idea that people will need to turn to vitamin pills to make up for the vitamins they aren't getting from produce.

(E) introduces fiber, which is Outside the Scope of the argument. The author is only concerned with how people can get the vitamins in fruits and vegetables without eating five daily servings of them.

83. (B) Flaw (OP-NvS) ★★★★

Step 1: Identify the Question Type

The word "vulnerable" signals a Flaw question, and the stem also offers a hint as to the type of flaw: The author has overlooked a possibility. Find the author's conclusion and evidence; then predict what was overlooked.

Step 2: Untangle the Stimulus

The Keyword "[s]ince" in the last sentence signals evidence, and the structure of the sentence indicates that the last phrase of the stimulus is the conclusion: Bulging or slipped disks ("these conditions") can't possibly lead to serious back pain. The evidence is that a large number of people had such disks yet never experienced serious back pain.

Step 3: Make a Prediction

This problem rewards your solid grasp of the concepts of sufficiency and necessity. The evidence proves that bulging or slipped disks aren't sufficient by themselves to cause serious back pain. However, they might still *contribute* to serious back pain by acting in concert with something else. This is what the author has overlooked.

Step 4: Evaluate the Answer Choices

(B) is a perfect match to your prediction.

(A) is Out of Scope. It highlights a classic flaw, but not the one in this argument. It says, in so many words, that something can be sufficient without being necessary. However, bad disks are *not* sufficient to produce serious back pain.

(C) is a Distortion. It talks about an effect occurring in the absence of a phenomenon, whereas the argument talks about a phenomenon (bad disks) occurring in the absence of an effect (back pain).

(D), like choice **(A)**, pokes at the wrong classic flaw. It attacks the representativeness of the survey, but the author's flaw isn't that her conclusion makes a claim about a sample the evidence is unrepresentative of. The flaw is that she misapplies the study's results due to her misunderstanding of sufficiency.

(E) offers a Distortion similar to choice **(C)**. It discusses the likelihood of a factor occurring in the presence of an effect, whereas the argument talks about the likelihood of an effect (back pain) occurring in the presence of a factor (bad disks).

84. (D) Assumption (MC-E) ★★★☆

Step 1: Identify the Question Type

The Keyword "assumption" clearly marks this as an Assumption question. Bracket the conclusion, find the evidence, and then predict what the author left out.

Step 2: Untangle the Stimulus

The little but significant Keyword "[s]o" in the last sentence signifies the conclusion: some of Hollywood's earliest movies will perish. The evidence points out that transferring movies from unstable to stable material is laborious and expensive, and that there's no way we'll be able to save all the movies currently on unstable material before some of them disintegrate.

Step 3: Make a Prediction

Even the most difficult and reasonable-seeming arguments have a scope shift somewhere, and this argument is no exception. The conclusion brings up "films from the earliest years of Hollywood," which the evidence never mentions; instead, the evidence talks about preserving movies in general. Thus, the author must take for granted that Hollywood's earliest movies need preserving in the first place.

Step 4: Evaluate the Answer Choices

(D) fits the bill. The author must assume that "[s]ome" (at least one) of Hollywood's earliest movies still exist on unstable material. If none of them do, then none of them need saving, and the argument falls apart.

These explanations refer to
questions that begin on page 635.

Part Three: Logical Reasoning
Assumption Family Questions

K

(A) is Extreme and Out of Scope. The author doesn't have to
assume that our current technology for preserving movies will
never get an update, because the evidence already asserts
that we won't be able to finish preserving every movie before
some of them disintegrate. On Assumption questions, choices
that directly argue with the evidence are always wrong.

(B) is an Irrelevant Comparison that fails for a similar reason
as choice **(A)**. It doesn't matter if there are cheaper ways to
preserve movies because, again, the evidence already assures
you that some movies will be lost. Avoid choices that argue
with the evidence.

(C) is a Distortion. At first glance, it appears to match your
prediction by stating that not many of Hollywood's earliest
movies have already been moved to stable film. It would
seem, then, that a lot of films from the earliest years of
Hollywood still require preservation. This isn't actually true,
however, due to the fuzziness of the phrase "[n]ot many." On
the LSAT, *many* and *not many* mean exactly the same thing,
as the term *many* is subjective. One out of 100 infants getting
a life-threatening disease might be considered "many," for
example. Thus, if there are 100 early Hollywood movies that
need saving, then 99 of them could already have been saved
as far as "not many" is concerned.

For this choice to work, you have to assume that "[n]ot many"
represents a substantial majority of Hollywood's earliest
movies, and choices that require an assumption are never
right on the LSAT.

(E) is another Irrelevant Comparison. What matters is whether
or not any of Hollywood's earliest movies will be lost; the
relative popularity of the perished movies has no bearing on
the argument.

EXPLANATIONS

677

Non-Argument Questions

Not all questions in the Logical Reasoning section involve analyzing or evaluating arguments. A significant number of questions test your ability to make deductions; we will call these Inference questions, an inference—in LSAT terms—being a valid deduction from a set of statements or assertions. Inference questions give you a set of facts or assertions and ask for what must be true based on the facts or what follows logically from them. Other questions give you a general principle and ask for a specific case that correctly applies the principle, or they supply a case and ask you to infer the principle upon which it was decided. A small number of questions give you two paradoxical or seemingly inconsistent statements and ask for a fact that would help explain or reconcile the apparent inconsistency.

Let's break it down by the numbers. Inference questions account for just over 13 percent of the Logical Reasoning section, around six or seven questions per test. Add to that one or two Principle questions calling for inferences and typically three or four Paradox questions per test, and the material in this chapter constitutes a healthy chunk of the Logical Reasoning section.

None of these questions is based on an argument; there's no need for you to determine conclusion and evidence here or to try to figure out what an author is assuming. Rather, these questions all reward you for seeing the implications of facts and assertions. In non-argument questions, you're interested in what *follows from* the statements in the stimulus, not in what you could add to the stimulus to make it stronger, weaker, or more complete.

MAKING DEDUCTIONS AND INFERENCE QUESTIONS

Here's an example of a typical LSAT Inference question. Feel free to try it now or just read through it to get a sense of what these questions require. You'll see this question explained in detail a little later in the chapter. In this section, you will learn how to handle questions such as this one; you'll learn what the testmaker is asking for and how to untangle the stimulus effectively.

Everyone in Biba's neighborhood is permitted to swim at Barton Pool at some time during each day that it is open. No children under the age of 6 are permitted to swim at Barton Pool between noon and 5 P.M. From 5 P.M. until closing, Barton Pool is reserved for adults only.

If all the sentences above are true, then which one of the following must be true?

(A)   Few children under the age of 6 live in Biba's neighborhood.

(B)   If Biba's next-door neighbor has a child under the age of 6, then Barton Pool is open before noon.

(C)   If most children who swim in Barton Pool swim in the afternoon, then the pool is generally less crowded after 5 P.M.

(D)   On days when Barton Pool is open, at least some children swim there in the afternoon.

(E)   Any child swimming in Barton Pool before 5 P.M. must be breaking Barton Pool rules.

PrepTest52 Sec1 Q5

By asking for an answer that must be true based on the statements in the stimulus, the LSAT is asking you to make a valid deduction from those statements. Now, you make deductions every day. You might wake up to find the ground wet and water dripping from the trees and deduce that it rained during the night. You might find a piece of pie you left in the refrigerator gone, and given that the only person in the house was your roommate, deduce that she ate your pie. But many of the deductions we make in real life are based on partial information and hunches. In most cases, they're very likely, but they may or may not be true.

A deduction, as defined on the LSAT, applies logic more rigorously than most real-life deductions. To illustrate the difference between the kind of deduction rewarded by an LSAT question and the kind we make in everyday life, suppose a house guest told you, "I don't eat ice cream." Given this fact about your guest, you might speculate, "She must be on a diet," or "I wonder if she's lactose intolerant." Either is possible. However, neither of your reasonable speculations would be a valid deduction on the LSAT because neither *must be true* and neither follows unequivocally from the statement itself. On the LSAT, a valid inference, were it negated, would contradict the given information. So, if the LSAT asked you for an inference based on your guest's statement, the correct answer would be something like "If the only dessert I serve at dinner tonight is ice cream, she won't eat any dessert." This fact is conditional, a little convoluted, and may even seem obvious, but it must be true given that your guest does not eat ice cream.

While all of the questions covered in this chapter deal with what follows from the statements in the stimulus, let's begin with Inference questions. They're the most numerous of the questions covered here, and more importantly, they're the ones that most directly reward you for assessing statements and making valid deductions based on them.

LEARNING OBJECTIVES

In this section, you'll learn to:

· Make valid inferences from single statements of fact.
· Combine two or more statements to make valid inferences.
· Recognize and use Keywords to make valid inferences.
· Recognize and use Formal Logic to make valid inferences.
· Recognize and use uncertain statements to make valid inferences.
· Identify and answer Inference questions.

What Inference Question Stems Ask For

An "inference" on the LSAT is a deduction made from facts given in the question. For LSAT purposes, treat *inference* and *deduction* as synonyms. With a few exceptions, the stimulus of an Inference question serves the same role as the rules of a logic game. Like a deduction in a logic game, the correct answer to an Inference question is a fact that *must be true* given the statements that the testmaker provides.

The question stem in the previous sample question was very direct: If the stimulus is true, the right answer must be true also. Here are a few other representative Inference question stems along with the LSAT expert's analysis.

LSAT Question		Analysis
Which of the following statements follows logically from the statements above? *PrepTest56 Sec2 Q19*	→	The correct answer "follows logically from" the stimulus. So, the right choice is a valid deduction from the stimulus.
Of the following, which one most logically completes the argument? *PrepTest62 Sec4 Q24*	→	This stimulus will be like evidence (statements or assertions) without a conclusion. The correct answer is a valid conclusion (deduction) drawn from those statements.
Which of the following can be properly inferred from the ecologist's statements? *PrepTest56 Sec2 Q23*	→	The correct answer is a valid deduction ("properly inferred") from the statements in the stimulus.
The information above most strongly supports which one of the following conclusions about frogs in the Yucatán peninsula? *PrepTest58 Sec4 Q13*	→	The "information above" (statements in the stimulus) supports the correct answer (the valid inference).

All of these stems ask for essentially the same thing: the answer choice that *must be true* if the facts in the stimulus are true. (Note that from time to time, the test will ask for the choice that *must be false* or *could be true* based on the statements. We'll cover those relatively rare question stems before the end of the section.) A precise understanding of what the testmaker is asking for leads to a handful of important observations about Inference questions that make learning how to make deductions more meaningful.

LSAT STRATEGY

Some facts to remember about LSAT inferences:

- An inference follows only from the facts given. No outside knowledge is required.
- An inference need not be mind-blowing. Sometimes it will be simple, even obvious.
- An inference may come from a single fact, or it may require combining multiple facts. It may not be necessary to take into account all the facts given in the stimulus.

Every Inference question stem contains a strong reminder of these strategy points: the correct answer must be based entirely and exclusively on the statements in the stimulus. Thus, it makes a lot of sense to untangle the stimulus by looking for the strongest statements (those that lead to the strongest deductions) and by looking for statements that can be combined (those that share the same terms, for example).

Cataloging and Paraphrasing Statements in the Stimulus

Without an argument to analyze—that is, without an explicit conclusion and evidence to identify—untrained test takers may find themselves at a loss when approaching Inference stimuli. Add to this confusion the fact that Inference stimuli often use wordy, complicated, or confusing language. The LSAT expert, however, untangles the Inference stimulus efficiently by asking, "What do I *know* to be true?" Asking this question focuses the expert's attention on two criteria: (1) She notes statements that are the most concrete, and (2) she spots statements that can be combined. As always, the LSAT expert actively paraphrases convoluted statements to be sure she understands precisely what the statement does *and does not* assert.

Note the Most Concrete Statements

Think back for a moment to the example we used earlier, your guest's statement: "I don't eat ice cream." You were able to draw a valid inference from that statement because it was so strong. Had she said, "I don't know—maybe I'll have some ice cream," you could draw no conclusion about what she might have for dessert. When untangling an Inference stimulus, the LSAT expert is always on the lookout for the most concrete statements.

LSAT Question	Analysis
Shareholder: The company's current operations are time-proven successes. The move into food services may siphon off funds needed by these other operations. Also, the food service industry is volatile, with a higher inherent risk than with, for instance, pharmaceuticals, another area into which the company has considered expanding.	The strongest statement here is the comparison: food service is more volatile than pharmaceuticals. The other statements are provisional: "*may* siphon off funds" and "*considered* expanding."
PrepTest56 Sec3 Q2	

Identifying the strongest statements can have immediate benefits. Look at the full question from which the above stimulus came.

LSAT Question	Analysis
Shareholder: The company's current operations are time-proven successes. The move into food services may siphon off funds needed by these other operations. Also, the food service industry is volatile, with a higher inherent risk than with, for instance, pharmaceuticals, another area into which the company has considered expanding.	**Step 2:** The strongest statement here is the comparison: food service is more volatile than pharmaceuticals. The other statements are provisional: a move to food service "*may* siphon off funds," and pharmaceuticals is an area into which the company has "*considered* expanding."
If the shareholder's statements are true, which one of the following is most strongly supported by them?	**Step 1:** The stimulus supports the correct answer: an Inference question.
Step 3: The correct answer will follow from the statements.
(A) The company's present operations require increased funding.	**Step 4:** The company's current operations are a success. It's considering other ventures. Nothing suggests that the current operations need more funding. Eliminate.
(B) Investment into pharmaceuticals would not siphon off money from other operations.	A move to food service may siphon off funds. The stimulus doesn't say whether a move to pharmaceuticals would, too. Eliminate.
(C) The company will lose money as it expands into the food service industry.	Extreme. There's a greater risk that the company would lose money in food service, but that doesn't mean it absolutely will. Eliminate.
(D) Only if the company expands its operations into pharmaceuticals are increased profits possible.	Extreme. Pharmaceuticals is a less risky area than food service, but that doesn't exclude the possibility that the company could increase profits by going into food service or any number of other ventures. Eliminate.
(E) The company has a greater chance of losing money in food services than in pharmaceuticals.	Correct. This follows directly from the strong comparison in the stimulus.

PrepTest56 Sec3 Q2

In this case, the correct answer is a paraphrase of a single, strong statement in the stimulus. From time to time, the testmaker rewards you for making Inferences that are really this straightforward. Note, too, that answer choices (C) and (D) are wrong because they make statements too strong for the stimulus to support. Pay attention to what stimulus statements *fail to say* as well as what they do establish.

Practice

Catalog the statements in another Inference stimulus. Identify the strongest, most concrete assertions you find. As a hint, there is more than one concrete statement in this stimulus.

LSAT Question	My Analysis
1. Proofs relying crucially on computers provide less certainty than do proofs not requiring computers. Human cognition alone cannot verify computer-dependent proofs; such proofs can never provide the degree of certainty that attends our judgments concerning, for instance, simple arithmetical facts, which can be verified by human calculation. Of course, in these cases one often uses electronic calculators, but here the computer is a convenience rather than a supplement to human cognition. *PrepTest58 Sec4 Q15*	

Here's how an LSAT expert would catalog the statements in that stimulus.

LSAT Question	Analysis
1. Proofs relying crucially on computers provide less certainty than do proofs not requiring computers. Human cognition alone cannot verify computer-dependent proofs; such proofs can never provide the degree of certainty that attends our judgments concerning, for instance, simple arithmetical facts, which can be verified by human calculation. Of course, in these cases one often uses electronic calculators, but here the computer is a convenience rather than a supplement to human cognition. *PrepTest58 Sec4 Q15*	Three strong statements, but the third is the strongest, summing up the first two: (1) a comparison—proofs that rely crucially on computers are less certain than those that don't; (2) an assertion—proofs that rely crucially on computers can't be verified by human cognition alone; and (3) proofs that rely crucially on computers are *never* as certain as proofs that humans can verify.

Note the lack of provisional or conditional language here. The only place in which the author softens his tone is at the end with the little aside about using calculators as a convenience. Notice, too, that all three of the strong statements are about computer-dependent proofs, those relying *crucially* on computer verification. This suggests that the correct answer will draw a valid inference about that subject. Use that as a hint when you try this question in its entirety in the Question Pool at the end of the chapter.

Combine Statements to Make Valid Inferences

In most cases, you won't be able to get the correct answer to an Inference question by rephrasing a single statement; when this happens, you'll need to combine two or more statements (much as you combine the rules in logic games) in order to predict the correct answer. Even so, it is still crucial to pay attention to the strength or concreteness of the statements in the stimulus. Imagine you learn two facts: (1) All practicing attorneys are eligible for the state bar's insurance plan, and (2) Joe graduated from a law school in the state. From those statements, the best you can say is that Joe may be eligible for the bar's insurance plan. After all, he may or may not be a practicing attorney. But, make the second statement more concrete as it applies to the first statement—Joe is a practicing attorney in the state—and you can easily conclude that Joe is eligible for the plan.

Take a look at an example stimulus from a real LSAT Inference question.

LSAT Question	Analysis
The sun emits two types of ultraviolet radiation that damage skin: UV-A, which causes premature wrinkles, and UV-B, which causes sunburn. Until about ten years ago, sunscreens protected against UV-B radiation but not against UV-A radiation. *PrepTest56 Sec3 Q11*	**Step 2:** Statement (2): Until 10 years ago sunscreen protected against UV-B but not against UV-A. Why is that important? Statement (1): UV-B causes sunburn, and UV-A causes wrinkles. Combining the statements: more than 10 years ago, sunscreen stopped sunburn but did not stop wrinkles.

The final sentence in the stimulus can be combined with the first because the two sentences share certain terms. Again, this should feel very familiar if you've completed the chapters on logic games. There, rules sharing common entities (Duplications, we called them) could be combined to produce valid deductions. The principle is much the same with the statements in Inference questions. Take a look at the full question from which we drew that stimulus. You'll see that the correct answer directly rewards the logical combination of statements the expert noted.

LSAT Question	Analysis
The sun emits two types of ultraviolet radiation that damage skin: UV-A, which causes premature wrinkles, and UV-B, which causes sunburn. Until about ten years ago, sunscreens protected against UV-B radiation but not against UV-A radiation.	**Step 2:** Statement (2): Until 10 years ago sunscreen protected against UV-B but not against UV-A. Why is that important? Statement (1): UV-B causes sunburn, and UV-A causes wrinkles. Combining the statements: More than 10 years ago, sunscreen stopped sunburn but did not stop wrinkles.
Which one of the following is best supported by the information above?	**Step 1:** The right answer follows from the stimulus—an Inference question.
	Step 3: The right answer is likely to reward the logical combination of the stimulus statements: more than 10 years ago, sunscreen stopped sunburn but did not stop wrinkles.
(A) Since about ten years ago, the percentage of people who wear sunscreen every time they spend time in the sun has increased.	**Step 4:** Outside the Scope. No information about the percentage of people using sunscreen. Eliminate.
(B) Most people whose skin is prematurely wrinkled have spent a large amount of time in the sun without wearing sunscreen.	Outside the Scope. There may be other reasons for wrinkles. Who knows? Eliminate.
(C) The specific cause of premature skin wrinkling was not known until about ten years ago.	The stimulus is about sunscreen preventing wrinkles, not knowledge of what causes them. Eliminate.
(D) People who wear sunscreen now are less likely to become sunburned than were people who spent the same amount of time in the sun wearing sunscreen ten years ago.	180. Old sunscreen *did* protect against sunburn. Eliminate.
(E) Until about ten years ago, people who wore sunscreen were no less likely to have premature wrinkles than were people who spent the same amount of time in the sun without wearing sunscreen. *PrepTest56 Sec3 Q11*	Correct. This matches the prediction. Old sunscreen did not protect against UV-A, the cause of wrinkles.

Practice

Try another example. Catalog the statements in the following Inference stimulus and note how they can be combined.

LSAT Question	My Analysis
2. Inertia affects the flow of water pumped through a closed system of pipes. When the pump is first switched on, the water, which has mass, takes time to reach full speed. When the pump is switched off, inertia causes the decrease in the water flow to be gradual. The effects of inductance in electrical circuits are similar to the effects of inertia in water pipes. *PrepTest52 Sec1 Q7*	

Did you note that the final sentence draws an analogy between inertia (the subject of the first three sentences) and inductance? Always pay attention when an analogy surfaces in a piece of LSAT text. The testmaker is likely to reward you for applying it appropriately. Here's how the LSAT expert untangled that stimulus.

LSAT Question	Analysis
2. Inertia affects the flow of water pumped through a closed system of pipes. When the pump is first switched on, the water, which has mass, takes time to reach full speed. When the pump is switched off, inertia causes the decrease in the water flow to be gradual. The effects of inductance in electrical circuits are similar to the effects of inertia in water pipes. *PrepTest52 Sec1 Q7*	→ Catalog the statements: (1) inertia affects water flow, (2) and (3) inertia slows an increase or decrease in water flow, and (4) inductance does to electricity what inertia does to water. Combining the statements: inductance slows electricity.

Here, the expert used the analogy to combine all of the statements in the stimulus. You will try this full question in the question pool. Use our comments about the analogy as a clue to predicting the correct answer.

In the examples we just looked at, two or more statements shared common terms and thus combined to produce valid conclusions, affirmative assertions that must be true based on statements in the stimulus. Statements can be combined in a couple of other ways to yield inferences.

Using Keywords to Make Valid Inferences

You'll learn more about strategic reading in the Reading Comprehension section, but you've already been introduced to the concept of Keywords in Chapter 9, where you learned to analyze arguments. In Inference stimuli, pay attention to words that indicate how an author intends for statements to relate to one another. Conclusion Keywords may appear here, indicating that the author feels that one statement follows from another. Even more important are Contrast Keywords—words like *but*, *yet*, or *despite* or phrases such as *on the other hand*. These Keywords tell you that the author considers two terms or concepts to be at odds, and they allow you to connect statements that might not obviously share common terms. Take a look at the following LSAT Inference stimulus.

LSAT Question	Analysis
Legal commentator: The goal of a recently enacted law that bans smoking in workplaces is to protect employees from secondhand smoke. But the law is written in such a way that it cannot be interpreted as ever prohibiting people from smoking in their own homes. $\rightarrow$ *PrepTest62 Sec2 Q24*	"But" contrasts the fact that the law allows smoking in private homes with the law's purpose: to protect workers from secondhand smoke. Combining the statements, deduce: workers in private homes won't be protected.

The legal commentator never comes out and says, "the workplace smoking ban won't achieve its goal," but the Contrast Keyword makes clear that he considers the second sentence to be evidence for precisely that conclusion. In many Inference questions, the testmaker designs the stimulus as evidence in search of a conclusion. Look at the full question from which that stimulus came, and you'll see this pattern played out. Pay special attention to the question stem here; it calls for a claim that can be rejected on the basis of the stimulus. In other words, the correct answer is the one that *cannot* follow from the stimulus.

LSAT Question	Analysis
Legal commentator: The goal of a recently enacted law that bans smoking in workplaces is to protect employees from secondhand smoke. But the law is written in such a way that it cannot be interpreted as ever prohibiting people from smoking in their own homes. $\rightarrow$	**Step 2:** "But" contrasts the fact that the law allows smoking in private homes with the law's purpose: to protect workers from secondhand smoke. Combining the statements, deduce: workers in private homes won't be protected.
The statements above, if true, provide a basis for rejecting which one of the following claims? $\rightarrow$	**Step 1:** The correct answer will be false ("reject[ed]") based on the stimulus statements. That means the four wrong answers could be true.
	Step 3: The commentator implies that some workers (those in private homes) won't be protected from secondhand smoke. The correct answer must say that these workers will be protected.
(A) The law will be interpreted in a way that is inconsistent with the intentions of the legislators who supported it. $\rightarrow$	**Step 4:** Distortion. The commentator says nothing about how the law *will* be interpreted, only that it is written in a way that prevents one interpretation. Eliminate.
(B) Supporters of the law believe that it will have a significant impact on the health of many workers. $\rightarrow$	Outside the Scope. The stimulus does not address supporter's beliefs. Eliminate.
(C) The law offers no protection from secondhand smoke for people outside of their workplaces. $\rightarrow$	Who knows? Neither the law nor the commentary tries to address this issue. Eliminate.

LSAT Question	Analysis
(D) Most people believe that smokers have a fundamental right to smoke in their own homes.	→ Outside the Scope. The stimulus doesn't address rights or people's beliefs. Eliminate.
(E) The law will protect domestic workers such as housecleaners from secondhand smoke in their workplaces. *PrepTest62 Sec2 Q24*	→ Correct. This statement is directly opposed to the author's evidence. He contrasts the fact that people can still smoke at home with the goal of the law—protecting workers from secondhand smoke.

The author states the goal of the law and then prefaces a fact about the law with the word *but*. From this, the LSAT expert deduced that the author believes that the law will not accomplish its goal because of the fact in that second statement. The correct answer to this negated Inference question simply contradicted the author's implied conclusion.

Practice

Use Keywords to combine the statements in the following stimulus.

LSAT Question	My Analysis
3. Music historian: Some critics lament the fact that impoverished postwar recording studios forced early bebop musicians to record extremely short solos, thus leaving a misleading record of their music. But these musicians' beautifully concise playing makes the recordings superb artistic works instead of mere representations of their live solos. Furthermore, the conciseness characteristic of early bebop musicians' recordings fostered a compactness in their subsequent live playing, which the playing of the next generation lacks. *PrepTest58 Sec1 Q10*	

Here's how the LSAT expert would catalog and combine the statements in that stimulus.

LSAT Question	Analysis
3. Music historian: Some critics lament the fact that impoverished postwar recording studios forced early bebop musicians to record extremely short solos, thus leaving a misleading record of their music. But these musicians' beautifully concise playing makes the recordings superb artistic works instead of mere representations of their live solos. Furthermore, the conciseness characteristic of early bebop musicians' recordings fostered a compactness in their subsequent live playing, which the playing of the next generation lacks. *PrepTest58 Sec1 Q10*	→ "But" contrasts the music historian's statements about postwar bebop recordings with the opinion of some critics. The historian thinks the short solos were great on records and made musicians better live, too. The critics think the short solos, which resulted from technical limitations in the studios, were terrible. Combining the statements: the historian implies that the results of technical limitations in the studios weren't all bad.

The LSAT expert noted that the music historian takes direct issue with the critics' assessment of the quality of the postwar bebop recordings (she likes them; they don't). But there aren't any deductions to be drawn from such direct statements of opinion. The LSAT expert notes, however, that the critics go one step further by placing the blame for the recordings they dislike on the state of the studios at the time. From this, the LSAT expert can logically infer that the music historian doesn't think those studios were all bad and, in fact, thinks that there were some positive results from their limited recording capacity. You can try this complete question in the Question Pool at the end of the chapter.

There is one more important way in which statements in Inference stimuli can produce valid deductions: Formal Logic.

Using Formal Logic to Make Valid Inferences

Think back to the work you did on Formal Logic in Chapter 1 and again in the Logic Games part of this book, and it will be clear why the testmaker often uses Formal Logic in Inference stimuli. While challenging to read and interpret, conditional Formal Logic statements combine perfectly to allow for deductions they don't state explicitly. From "If A, then B," and "If B, then C," you can deduce "If A, then C," with absolute confidence. Sometimes, Logical Reasoning inferences are just that straightforward, although you can expect to encounter some pretty convoluted language in these stimuli. Your familiarity with Formal Logic will be an enormous benefit on many Inference questions. Once you recognize that a stimulus contains Formal Logic, its statements are easy to catalog and assess. You can, of course, even jot them down in Formal Logic shorthand in your test booklet.

With that in mind, take a look at how an LSAT expert would analyze the stimulus from the first Inference question you saw in this chapter.

LSAT Question	Analysis
Everyone in Biba's neighborhood is permitted to swim at Barton Pool at some time during each day that it is open. No children under the age of 6 are permitted to swim at Barton Pool between noon and 5 P.M. From 5 P.M. until closing, Barton Pool is reserved for adults only. *PrepTest52 Sec1 Q5* →	Three Formal Logic statements: (1) *If in Biba's neighborhood* → *can swim at BP each day* (2) *If < 6 y.o.* → *CANNOT swim at BP from noon to 5 P.M.* (3) *If NOT adult* → *CANNOT swim at BP from 5 P.M. to closing*

At this point, the LSAT expert realizes that these statements could be combined to lead to a number of valid inferences. Rather than try to run through all of the possible permutations, she focuses on where the statements overlap: everyone in Biba's neighborhood can swim at some time each day Barton Pool is open, but children are forbidden to swim at certain hours. Rather than try to predict all of the possible statements that must follow from these Formal Logic rules, the LSAT expert will test the answer choices against them.

LSAT Question	**Analysis**
Everyone in Biba's neighborhood is permitted to swim at Barton Pool at some time during each day that it is open. No children under the age of 6 are permitted to swim at Barton Pool between noon and 5 P.M. From 5 P.M. until closing, Barton Pool is reserved for adults only.	**Step 2:** Three Formal Logic statements:
	(1) *If in Biba's neighborhood* → *can swim at BP each day*
→	(2) *If < 6 y.o.* → *CANNOT swim at BP from noon to 5 P.M.*
	(3) *If NOT adult* → *CANNOT swim at BP from 5 P.M. to closing*
If all the sentences above are true, then which one of the following must be true? →	**Step 1:** The correct answer must be true based on the stimulus statements—an Inference question.
	Step 3: There are too many possible combinations to list them all. The correct answer must be true based on the statements; all four wrong answers could be false.
(A) Few children under the age of 6 live in Biba's neighborhood. →	**Step 4:** None of the rules allows us to determine the number of children, let alone children of a certain age group, in the neighborhood. Eliminate.
(B) If Biba's next-door neighbor has a child under the age of 6, then Barton Pool is open before noon.	Correct. Because everyone must be able to swim each day and because children under 6 could not swim from noon to 5 P.M. or from 5 P.M. until closing, if there is a child under 6 in Biba's neighborhood, Barton Pool must be open for some time before noon. This choice must be true.
(C) If most children who swim in Barton Pool swim in the afternoon, then the pool is generally less crowded after 5 P.M.	None of the statements address Barton Pool's capacity or how much it's used by adults or children. It may have mainly adult users, so this choice could be false. Eliminate.
(D) On days when Barton Pool is open, at least some children swim there in the afternoon.	The statements in the stimulus don't tell us whether any children use the pool. Even if children over the age of 6 are allowed to use the pool from noon to 5 P.M., we don't know whether they do. This choice could be false. Eliminate.
(E) Any child swimming in Barton Pool before 5 P.M. must be breaking Barton Pool rules. *PrepTest52 Sec1 Q5*	Children over the age of 6 may be allowed to swim between noon and 5 P.M., and we know nothing about the rules before noon. This choice could be false. Eliminate.

In that example, three Formal Logic statements overlapped one another. In other cases, the testmaker designs the stimulus to make it clear how two Formal Logic statements are intended to combine. Try cataloging and paraphrasing the statements in a stimulus of this type.

Practice

Untangle the following Inference stimulus. Translate any Formal Logic statements you find and determine whether and how they can be combined.

LSAT Question	My Analysis
4. Although some nutritional facts about soft drinks are listed on their labels, exact caffeine content is not. Listing exact caffeine content would make it easier to limit, but not eliminate, one's caffeine intake. If it became easier for people to limit, but not eliminate, their caffeine intake, many people would do so, which would improve their health. *PrepTest62 Sec2 Q6*	

The final sentence is marked as conditional Formal Logic by the word "[i]f" at the beginning, but did you notice that the second sentence in the stimulus also makes an assertion of necessity and sufficiency? Review the LSAT expert's analysis of the statements.

LSAT Question	Analysis
4. Although some nutritional facts about soft drinks are listed on their labels, exact caffeine content is not. Listing exact caffeine content would make it easier to limit, but not eliminate, one's caffeine intake. If it became easier for people to limit, but not eliminate, their caffeine intake, many people would do so, which would improve their health. *PrepTest62 Sec2 Q6*	The first statement is just a fact: caffeine content is not listed. The next two statements can be translated as Formal Logic: *If caffeine content listed* → *easier to limit intake* → *If easier to limit intake* › *many people's health would improve* Those two statements fit the pattern: If A → B and If B → C, so combining them, we deduce: *If caffeine content listed* → *many people's health would improve.*

You can try the full question that accompanies that stimulus in the Question Pool at the end of the chapter. For now, though, just notice how the LSAT expert used a familiarity with Formal Logic to paraphrase the stimulus statements and zero in on the connection the testmaker designed the question to reward.

On occasion, you may need to form the contrapositive of a Formal Logic statement to see clearly how it can be combined with another statement in the stimulus. Try analyzing the statements in the following stimulus to see this pattern.

Practice

Untangle the following stimulus. Catalog and paraphrase the statements, translating any conditional Formal Logic. Look for clues as to how the author considers the statements to relate to one another.

LSAT Question	My Analysis
5. Ecologist: Without the intervention of conservationists, squirrel monkeys will become extinct. But they will survive if large tracts of second-growth forest habitat are preserved for them. Squirrel monkeys flourish in second-growth forest because of the plentiful supply of their favorite insects and fruit. *PrepTest56 Sec2 Q23*	

Did you notice that the first statement provides a necessary condition for the squirrel monkey's survival, while the second provides a condition sufficient for its continued existence? Take a look at how the LSAT expert pieces all of that together to make a solid inference.

LSAT Question	Analysis
5. Ecologist: Without the intervention of conservationists, squirrel monkeys will become extinct. But they will survive if large tracts of second-growth forest habitat are preserved for them. Squirrel monkeys flourish in second-growth forest because of the plentiful supply of their favorite insects and fruit. *PrepTest56 Sec2 Q23* →	"Without" and "if" signal Formal Logic: *If conservationists → monkey extinct* * NOT intervene (NOT survive)* *If forest set aside → monkey survives* * (NOT extinct)* To combine, form the contrapositive of the second statement: *If Monkey extinct → forest NOT* * (NOT survive) set aside.* The "If" clause in the second statement's contrapositive matches the "Then" clause of the first statement, so they combine: *If conservationists → forest NOT* * NOT intervene set aside* or (the contrapositive): *If forest set aside → conservationists* * intervene.*

Once again, you can try the full question that accompanies this stimulus in the Question Pool at the end of the chapter. When you do, review the analysis you've just seen, and you'll be able to predict the correct answer. You won't always have to form contrapositives in order to combine statements in Inference questions, but always be prepared to do so. The testmaker finds multiple ways to test the same core skills over and over. It's no surprise to find that the LSAT will reward you in some Logical Reasoning questions for exactly the same critical reasoning skills it asks you to demonstrate in the Logic Games section.

Using Uncertain Statements to Make Valid Inferences

The process of making inferences from Formal Logic statements probably felt a lot like the deduction step in logic games. You used conditional assertions to assess the truth of other statements or combined If/then statements to reveal unstated certainties. For you, as a well-trained test taker, words like *any, all,* and *none* signal clear Formal Logic relationships of necessity and sufficiency. In many Inference questions, however, you will also have to deal with statements that are less absolute, statements that use words like *most, many, several,* and *some.*

The good news is that the LSAT follows reliable conventions that can help to create inferences out of statements containing these indeterminate terms. The word *most,* for example, means any amount greater than 50 percent. The word *some,* on the other hand, signifies one or more (i.e., *some* = not none). Note that both of these words—*most* and *some*—have the possibility of also meaning *all.* Although this runs counter to our normal usage and our instincts, it is important to understand how the LSAT uses these words because they can be used to create inferences in some predictable ways. Other indeterminate words—*several, many,* and *few*—should be treated in the same way as the word *some.* Don't try to give them any special meaning; they're inclusive of every possibility between *one* and *all.*

LSAT STRATEGY

Levels of Certainty

Here are the types of statements you'll encounter in Inference stimuli, arranged from most concrete to least:

- **Unqualified Assertions** (e.g., *Bob is an attorney* or *Monday will be a rainy day*)
- **Conditional Statements/Formal Logic** (e.g., *If the company hopes to meet its budget, then it must cut travel costs* or *McLaren will lose the election unless the county sees record voter turnout*)
- **Statements with "most"**—this means *more than half* but could include *all* (e.g., *Most of Company Y's employees are college graduates* or *A majority of the respondents preferred the new logo*)
- **Statements with "some" or "few"**—this means anywhere from one to all, just not zero (e.g., *Some architects are painters*)

It's rare for a stimulus to be comprised exclusively of uncertain statements. You might, on occasion, see something along the lines of "Most pizza restaurants in town are family-run businesses, and most pizza restaurants in town employ more than 10 people." Do you see what that allows you to infer? Right, at least one family-run business in town employs more than 10 people. Most of the time, however, the testmaker will include stronger statements—assertions of fact or conditional Formal Logic statements—along with statements containing less certain terms like *many* or *most.* Take a look at the following representative stimulus.

LSAT Question	Analysis
None of the students taking literature are taking physics, but several of the students taking physics are taking art. In addition, none of the students taking rhetoric are taking physics. *PrepTest56 Sec2 Q19*	Two statements with "none"; they translate into Formal Logic: *If physics → NOT literature* and → *If physics → NOT rhetoric* "[S]everal" is the same as "some": At least one student (maybe more) takes both physics and art. Combining the statements: The one or more students who take physics and art are NOT taking literature and NOT taking rhetoric.

Notice that the LSAT expert organizes the statements from most concrete to least. When combining statements to make valid inferences, it is almost always helpful to build from a foundation of the most certain facts and layer on the less certain possibilities as they apply. Take a look now at the full question from which that stimulus was taken, and you'll see how the LSAT expert's analysis of the stimulus leads directly to the correct answer.

LSAT Question	Analysis
None of the students taking literature are taking physics, but several of the students taking physics are taking art. In addition, none of the students taking rhetoric are taking physics.	**Step 2:** Two statements with "none"; they translate into Formal Logic: *If physics → NOT literature* and → *If physics → NOT rhetoric* "[S]everal" is the same as "some": at least one student (maybe more) takes both physics and art. Combining the statements: The one or more students who take physics and art are NOT taking literature and NOT taking rhetoric.
Which one of the following statements follows logically from the statements above?	→ **Step 1:** The correct answer "follows logically" from the stimulus—an Inference question.
	Step 3: The correct answer is likely to reward a logical connection between the less certain "several" statement and one of the two Formal Logic statements.

LSAT Question		Analysis
(A)	There are students who are taking art but not literature.	$\rightarrow$	**Step 4:** Correct. This must be true because there is at least one student taking physics and art and he cannot be taking literature.
(B)	None of the students taking literature are taking art.	$\rightarrow$	This could be false. There may be a student taking literature and art but not physics. Eliminate.
(C)	There are students who are taking rhetoric but not literature.	$\rightarrow$	This could be false. For all we know, every rhetoric student is taking literature, too. Eliminate.
(D)	None of the students taking rhetoric are taking literature.	$\rightarrow$	This could be false. There may well be one or more rhetoric students taking literature, too. Eliminate.
(E)	There are students who are taking both art and literature. *PrepTest56 Sec2 Q19*	$\rightarrow$	This could be false. Maybe none of the school's art students has a literature class at this time. Eliminate.

The LSAT expert in that question demonstrates two vital Inference question skills. First, he has learned to read the test strategically, determining what is known and what is not, what must be true and what is merely possible. Second, even though he is unable to predict the exact language of the correct answer, the LSAT expert uses Step 3 to prepare himself to evaluate the answer choices. He does so by characterizing the right and wrong answers. Based on the stimulus, the correct answer must be true, meaning that all four wrong answers could be false. Moreover, he has used his understanding of the certainty level of the various statements in the stimulus to anticipate the type of inference the testmaker is likely to reward with the correct answer.

To get used to reading in this way, try untangling a stimulus containing several statements with varying degrees of certainty among them.

Practice

Untangle the following stimulus. Look for statements of greater and lesser certainty. Catalog the statements from most certain to least and determine what can be logically inferred.

LSAT Question	My Analysis
6. In West Calverton, most pet stores sell exotic birds, and most of those that sell exotic birds also sell tropical fish. However, any pet store there that sells tropical fish but not exotic birds does sell gerbils; and no independently owned pet stores in West Calverton sell gerbils. *PrepTest62 Sec2 Q19*	_____ _____ _____ _____ _____

Which of the statements were more concrete? If you didn't distinguish among the statements in that way, go back to the stimulus for a moment and note which statements were introduced by the word *most*, which one by the word *any*, and which one by the word *no*. Ask, too, which statements can be combined to make valid inferences.

Here's how an LSAT expert would untangle that stimulus.

LSAT Question	Analysis
6. In West Calverton, most pet stores sell exotic birds, and most of those that sell exotic birds also sell tropical fish. However, any pet store there that sells tropical fish but not exotic birds does sell gerbils; and no independently owned pet stores in West Calverton sell gerbils. *PrepTest62 Sec2 Q19*	"[A]ny" and "no" signal Formal Logic: *If sell tropical fish but not exotic birds* → *sell gerbils* and *If sell gerbils* → *NOT independently owned* These statements combine: *If sell tropical fish but not exotic birds* → *NOT independently owned* or (contrapositive) *If independently owned* → *NOT [sell tropical fish but not exotic birds]* The first two statements in the stimulus contain "most": *More than half the stores in town sell exotic birds and, of those, more than half sell tropical fish.* So, more than a quarter of pet stores in town sell both tropical fish and exotic birds (but we can't be more certain than that). Because the Formal Logic statements involve stores that sell tropical fish but do NOT sell exotic birds, the "most" statements don't add much more to those.

Revisit that analysis when you try the full question associated with this stem in the Question Pool at the end of the chapter. Take note of how separating out the Formal Logic made the combination of those statements clear-cut. Keep in mind that the correct answer to the question need not take every statement into account. The testmaker could reward you simply for noticing how the two Formal Logic statements interact or how the two "most" statements work together. In any event, use this rather knotty stimulus as a reminder to evaluate the strength of statements: The more concrete the statement, the more likely it is to contribute to a valid inference.

Reflection

In day-to-day life, we make inferences all the time, but we are seldom as rigorous as the LSAT requires us to be. Over the coming days, pay attention to the unstated implications of statements you hear and read, anything from television news analysis to your friends' conversations. Try to assess what can be inferred or deduced from them. Are the inferences logical and supported by the statements themselves, or are you bringing in outside information? Are the deductions within the scope of the statements, or are they actually too extreme to be supported?

Inference Questions

You are just about ready to tackle some full Inference questions in practice, but first, do a quick review of what the question stems ask for. Throughout the previous examples, you saw the LSAT expert characterize the one right and four wrong answer choices before diving into his evaluation. While most LSAT Inference questions ask for a deduction that must be true, some questions create a twist by asking instead for a fact that could be true or must be false. Take a moment to drill on this important step with a handful of different Inference question stems.

Practice

Consider the following question stems and characterize the one correct and four incorrect answer choices for each. When you're done, turn the page and check your analysis against that of the LSAT expert.

LSAT Question	My Analysis
7. Which one of the following statements follows logically from the statements above? *PrepTest56 Sec2 Q19*	
8. Of the following, which one most logically completes the argument? *PrepTest62 Sec4 Q24*	
9. If the statements above are true, then each of the following could be true EXCEPT: *PrepTest56 Sec3 Q22*	
10. Which one of the following statements can be properly inferred from the statements above? *PrepTest58 Sec4 Q9*	
11. The statements above, if true, provide a basis for rejecting which one of the following claims? *PrepTest62 Sec2 Q24*	

Here's how an LSAT expert would characterize the answer choices for each of those question stems.

LSAT Question	Analysis
7. Which one of the following statements follows logically from the statements above? *PrepTest56 Sec2 Q19* ⟶	Correct answer choice: Must be true based on the stimulus. Wrong answer choices: Could be false based on the stimulus.
8. Of the following, which one most logically completes the argument? *PrepTest62 Sec4 Q24*	Correct answer choice: Must be true based on the stimulus. ⟶ Wrong answer choices: Could be false based on the stimulus. NOTE: Here, the stimulus will end with a blank representing a logical conclusion based on the evidence (statements) in the stimulus.
9. If the statements above are true, then each of the following could be true EXCEPT: *PrepTest56 Sec3 Q22* ⟶	Correct answer choice: Must be false based on the stimulus. Wrong answer choices: Could be true based on the stimulus.
10. Which one of the following statements can be properly inferred from the statements above? *PrepTest58 Sec4 Q9* ⟶	Correct answer choice: Must be true based on the stimulus. Wrong answer choices: Could be false based on the stimulus.
11. The statements above, if true, provide a basis for rejecting which one of the following claims? *PrepTest62 Sec2 Q24* ⟶	Correct answer choice: Must be false based on the stimulus (will contradict the author). Wrong answer choices: Could be true based on the stimulus (will not contradict the author).

In every section of the test, the LSAT expert makes a habit of characterizing right and wrong answers before evaluating the choices. With Inference questions, it's a good idea to do that even before untangling the stimulus, especially as a way to avoid confusion in EXCEPT questions. Many test takers find it helpful to jot down a shorthand note (such as "MBT" for *must be true*) in their test booklets to remind them of the correct answer's characteristic. Don't be overly concerned with the EXCEPT variations, though; over the past five years, they've represented just over 3 percent of the Inference questions in released exams.

Frequently (especially in high-difficulty questions), it is not immediately obvious that an answer choice must be true. In that case, testing whether each answer could be false helps to eliminate wrong choices. An answer choice that must be false can often be found by eliminating any answer choice that is possible in light of the facts.

Before you practice full questions, review two more questions accompanied by the LSAT expert's analysis. Read through them following the order of the Logical Reasoning Method. Pay special attention to what the expert has to say about the wrong answer choices. On many Inference questions, keeping in mind what you cannot deduce from the stimulus may be as important as seeing what you can deduce.

LSAT Question	Analysis
A person with a type B lipid profile is at much greater risk of heart disease than a person with a type A lipid profile. In an experiment, both type A volunteers and type B volunteers were put on a low-fat diet. The cholesterol levels of the type B volunteers soon dropped substantially, although their lipid profiles were unchanged. The type A volunteers, however, showed no benefit from the diet, and 40 percent of them actually shifted to type B profiles.	**Step 2:** First statement—a strong comparison: Type B means much greater risk of heart disease than type A. The rest describes an experiment: type B people improved with a low-fat diet. Type A people did not, and 40 percent actually went to a type B profile.
If the information above is true, which one of the following must also be true?	**Step 1:** Inference question—the correct answer must be true based on the stimulus; the four wrong answers could be false.
	Step 3: Low-fat diets don't help all people, and they can actually make type A people worse off (by turning them into higher-risk type B).
(A) In the experiment, most of the volunteers had their risk of heart disease reduced at least marginally as a result of having been put on the diet.	**Step 4:** We don't know that the two types were equally represented in the experiment. Even if they were, only type B people improved as far as we know. Could be false. Eliminate.
(B) People with type B lipid profiles have higher cholesterol levels, on average, than do people with type A lipid profiles.	The stimulus does not compare cholesterol levels of the two types. Could be false. Eliminate.
(C) Apart from adopting the low-fat diet, most of the volunteers did not substantially change any aspect of their lifestyle that would have affected their cholesterol levels or lipid profiles.	Outside the Scope. The stimulus doesn't go into what else the test subjects did or didn't do. Eliminate.
(D) The reduction in cholesterol levels in the volunteers is solely responsible for the change in their lipid profiles.	Extreme. "[S]olely responsible" is too strong to be supported by the stimulus. Something else about the low-fat diet may have affected the type A people who changed profiles. Eliminate.
(E) For at least some of the volunteers in the experiment, the risk of heart disease increased after having been put on the low-fat diet. *PrepTest58 Sec1 Q20*	Correct. This must be true. Of type A people, 40 percent changed to the higher-risk type B profile.

LSAT Question	Analysis
On the basis of relatively minor morphological differences, some scientists suggest that Neanderthals should be considered a species distinct from Cro-Magnons, the forerunners of modern humans. Yet the fact that the tools used by these two groups of hominids living in different environments were of exactly the same type indicates uncanny behavioral similarities, for only if they faced the same daily challenges and met them in the same way would they have used such similar tools. This suggests that they were members of the same species, and that the morphological differences are due merely to their having lived in different environments.	**Step 2:** "Yet" signals that the author is presenting evidence against some scientists. Some scientists: Neanderthals and Cro-Magnons are distinct species. Why? Minor differences in appearance (morphological). Author: Neanderthals and Cro-Magnons same species. Why? Different environments but same tools (and tools should be the same only if daily challenges were the same). Difference in appearance due to environment, but tools show real similarity.
If the statements above are true, then each of the following could be true EXCEPT:	**Step 1:** Inference EXCEPT—the correct answer must be false based on the stimulus; the four wrong answers could be true.
	Step 3: The correct answer will have to contradict the author—it will give some reason that the tools don't actually show that Neanderthals and Cro-Magnons were the same species.
(A) Morphological differences between the members of two populations do not guarantee that the two populations do not belong to the same species	**Step 4:** This could be true. The author thinks they're the same species despite their different appearances. Eliminate.
(B) The daily challenges with which an environment confronts its inhabitants are unique to that environment.	Correct. This must be false. The author believes the two groups are the same species because they had the same tools. In the author's view, that means they must have had the same daily challenges even though they lived in different environments. Therefore, these daily challenges could not have been unique to a given environment.
(C) There are greater morphological differences between Cro-Magnons and modern humans than there are between Cro-Magnons and Neanderthals.	Irrelevant Comparison. Neither group is compared to modern humans in the stimulus. This could be true. Eliminate.
(D) Use of similar tools is required if members of two distinct groups of tool-making hominids are to be considered members of the same species.	The author doesn't comment on this, but it could be true according to his statements. He thinks similarity in tools is sufficient to prove a common species; it doesn't contradict him to say that it's necessary, too. Eliminate.
(E) Through much of their coexistence, Cro-Magnons and Neanderthals were geographically isolated from one another. *PrepTest56 Sec3 Q22*	Outside the Scope. The author makes no claim that the two groups interacted or borrowed from one another. He just thinks they're the same species. Eliminate.

Practice

For each of the following, apply the Kaplan Method to a complete Logical Reasoning question. You can use the corresponding blanks to record your thinking for each step. After each question, compare your work to the thinking of an LSAT expert on the following pages.

LSAT Question	My Analysis
12. Storytelling appears to be a universal aspect of both past and present cultures. Comparative study of traditional narratives from widely separated epochs and diverse cultures reveals common themes such as creation, tribal origin, mystical beings and quasi-historical figures, and common story types such as fables and tales in which animals assume human personalities.	Step 2:
The evidence cited above from the study of traditional narratives most supports which one of the following statements?	Step 1:
	Step 3:
(A) Storytellers routinely borrow themes from other cultures.	Step 4:
(B) Storytellers have long understood that the narrative is a universal aspect of human culture.	
(C) Certain human concerns and interests arise in all of the world's cultures.	
(D) Storytelling was no less important in ancient cultures than it is in modern cultures.	
(E) The best way to understand a culture is to understand what motivates its storytellers.	

PrepTest62 Sec4 Q8

LSAT Question	My Analysis
13. A bacterial species will inevitably develop greater resistance within a few years to any antibiotics used against it, unless those antibiotics eliminate that species completely. However, no single antibiotic now on the market is powerful enough to eliminate bacterial species X completely.	**Step 2:**
Which one of the following is most strongly supported by the statements above?	**Step 1:**
	Step 3:
(A) It is unlikely that any antibiotic can be developed that will completely eliminate bacterial species X.	**Step 4:**
(B) If any antibiotic now on the market is used against bacterial species X, that species will develop greater resistance to it within a few years.	
(C) The only way of completely eliminating bacterial species X is by a combination of two or more antibiotics now on the market.	
(D) Bacterial species X will inevitably become more virulent in the course of time.	
(E) Bacterial species X is more resistant to at least some antibiotics that have been used against it than it was before those antibiotics were used against it.

PrepTest62 Sec4 Q11 | |

LSAT Question	My Analysis
14. Journalist: Recent studies have demonstrated that a regular smoker who has just smoked a cigarette will typically display significantly better short-term memory skills than a nonsmoker, whether or not the nonsmoker has also just smoked a cigarette for the purposes of the study. Moreover, the majority of those smokers who exhibit this superiority in short-term memory skills will do so for at least eight hours after having last smoked.	**Step 2:**
If the journalist's statements are true, then each of the following could be true EXCEPT:	**Step 1:**
	Step 3:

(A) The short-term memory skills exhibited by a nonsmoker who has just smoked a cigarette are usually substantially worse than the short-term memory skills exhibited by a nonsmoker who has not recently smoked a cigarette.

Step 4:

(B) The short-term memory skills exhibited by a nonsmoker who has just smoked a cigarette are typically superior to those exhibited by a regular smoker who has just smoked a cigarette

(C) The short-term memory skills exhibited by a nonsmoker who has just smoked a cigarette are typically superior to those exhibited by a regular smoker who has not smoked for more than eight hours.

(D) A regular smoker who, immediately after smoking a cigarette, exhibits short-term memory skills no better than those typically exhibited by a nonsmoker is nevertheless likely to exhibit superior short-term memory skills in the hours following a period of heavy smoking.

(E) The short-term memory skills exhibited by a regular smoker who last smoked a cigarette five hours ago are typically superior to those exhibited by a regular smoker who has just smoked a cigarette.

PrepTest52 Sec1 Q18

LSAT Question	My Analysis
15. University administrator: Any proposal for a new department will not be funded if there are fewer than 50 people per year available for hire in that field and the proposed department would duplicate more than 25 percent of the material covered in one of our existing departments. The proposed Area Studies Department will duplicate more than 25 percent of the material covered in our existing Anthropology Department. However, we will fund the new department.	**Step 2:**
Which one of the following statements follows logically from the university administrator's statements?	**Step 1:**
	Step 3:
(A) The field of Area Studies has at least 50 people per year available for hire.	**Step 4:**
(B) The proposed Area Studies Department would not duplicate more than 25 percent of the material covered in any existing department other than Anthropology.	
(C) If the proposed Area Studies Department did not duplicate more than 25 percent of the material covered in Anthropology, then the new department would not be funded.	
(D) The Anthropology Department duplicates more than 25 percent of the material covered in the proposed Area Studies Department.	
(E) The field of Area Studies has fewer than 50 people per year available for hire.	

PrepTest62 Sec4 Q6

LSAT Question	My Analysis
16. Adult frogs are vulnerable to dehydration because of their highly permeable skins. Unlike large adult frogs, small adult frogs have such a low ratio of body weight to skin surface area that they cannot survive in arid climates. The animals' moisture requirements constitute the most important factor determining where frogs can live in the Yucatán peninsula, which has an arid climate in the north and a wet climate in the south.	**Step 2:**
The information above most strongly supports which one of the following conclusions about frogs in the Yucatán peninsula?	**Step 1:**
	Step 3:
(A) Large adult frogs cannot coexist with small adult frogs in the wet areas.	**Step 4:**
(B) Frogs living in wet areas weigh more on average than frogs in the arid areas.	
(C) Large adult frogs can live in more of the area than small adult frogs can.	
(D) Fewer small adult frogs live in the south than do large adult frogs.	
(E) Small adult frogs in the south have less permeable skins than small adult frogs in the north.	

PrepTest58 Sec4 Q13

Here's how an LSAT expert looked at the questions you just tried.

LSAT Question	Analysis
12. Storytelling appears to be a universal aspect of both past and present cultures. Comparative study of traditional narratives from widely separated epochs and diverse cultures reveals common themes such as creation, tribal origin, mystical beings and quasi-historical figures, and common story types such as fables and tales in which animals assume human personalities. →	**Step 2:** The first sentence tells us the evidence seems to apply to all cultures: "appears to be . . . universal." The second is stronger: Traditional narratives have common themes and story types even when cultures are widely separated.
The evidence cited above from the study of traditional narratives most supports which one of the following statements? →	**Step 1:** The "evidence" in the stimulus supports the correct answer—an Inference question.
	Step 3: The correct answer will follow from the statements that some stories show up in every culture. The four wrong answer choices will not be supported by the stimulus.
(A) Storytellers routinely borrow themes from other cultures. →	**Step 4:** Outside the Scope. The evidence was from "widely separated" times and cultures. This does not support a claim of borrowing. Eliminate.
(B) Storytellers have long understood that the narrative is a universal aspect of human culture. →	Outside the Scope. The stimulus doesn't go into what storytellers know; they might not even be aware that they share themes and story types with others. Eliminate.
(C) Certain human concerns and interests arise in all of the world's cultures. →	Correct. This must be true for the evidence to appear "universal."
(D) Storytelling was no less important in ancient cultures than it is in modern cultures. →	The stimulus doesn't go into the relative importance of storytelling in different cultures. This might be false even if story types and themes are similar. Eliminate.
(E) The best way to understand a culture is to understand what motivates its storytellers. *PrepTest62 Sec4 Q8* →	Extreme. The author makes no claim that stories are "the best way" to understand cultures. Eliminate.

LSAT Question	Analysis
13. A bacterial species will inevitably develop greater resistance within a few years to any antibiotics used against it, unless those antibiotics eliminate that species completely. However, no single antibiotic now on the market is powerful enough to eliminate bacterial species X completely. →	**Step 2:** Two strong Formal Logic statements: (1) *If antibiotics do NOT eliminate a bacteria species* → *bacteria species will increase their resistance to antibiotics.* (2) *If antibiotic currently on the market* → *NOT strong enough to kill bacteria X.*
Which one of the following is most strongly supported by the statements above? →	**Step 1:** The correct answer is supported by the stimulus—an Inference question. The four wrong answers will not be supported by the stimulus.
	Step 3: The statements combine to make a strong deduction: if any current antibiotic is used against bacteria X → bacteria X will increase its resistance to that antibiotic.
(A) It is unlikely that any antibiotic can be developed that will completely eliminate bacterial species X. →	**Step 4:** The stimulus doesn't speculate about antibiotics that may be created in the future, so who knows? This could be false. Eliminate.
(B) If any antibiotic now on the market is used against bacterial species X, that species will develop greater resistance to it within a few years. →	Correct. This matches the prediction perfectly and must be true based on the stimulus.
(C) The only way of completely eliminating bacterial species X is by a combination of two or more antibiotics now on the market. →	It might be that there is no way to kill off bacteria X, or maybe something other than an antibiotic could do the trick. This could be false. Eliminate.
(D) Bacterial species X will inevitably become more virulent in the course of time. →	Again, this stimulus doesn't go into the future. This could be false. Eliminate.
(E) Bacterial species X is more resistant to at least some antibiotics that have been used against it than it was before those antibiotics were used against it. *PrepTest62 Sec4 Q11* →	The stimulus doesn't tell us that any antibiotic has ever been used against bacteria X. If a currently available one were, then bacteria X would get more resistant, but that's hypothetical, not empirical. This could be false. Eliminate.

LSAT Question	Analysis
14. Journalist: Recent studies have demonstrated that a regular smoker who has just smoked a cigarette will typically display significantly better short-term memory skills than a nonsmoker, whether or not the nonsmoker has also just smoked a cigarette for the purposes of the study. Moreover, the majority of those smokers who exhibit this superiority in short-term memory skills will do so for at least eight hours after having last smoked.	**Step 2:** Study results: A regular smoker who has just smoked a cigarette has a better short-term memory than a nonsmoker (whether the nonsmoker has a cigarette or not). "Moreover" signals another fact: the smoker continues to show better short-term memory for at least eight hours after her last cigarette.
If the journalist's statements are true, then each of the following could be true EXCEPT:	**Step 1:** Inference EXCEPT—the correct answer must contradict the journalist's statements; the four wrong answers will not contradict them.
	Step 3: There are two statements—the comparison and the additional fact about duration. The correct answer will contradict at least one of them.
(A) The short-term memory skills exhibited by a nonsmoker who has just smoked a cigarette are usually substantially worse than the short-term memory skills exhibited by a nonsmoker who has not recently smoked a cigarette.	**Step 4:** This compares nonsmokers to nonsmokers. Because the stimulus doesn't mention what happens to nonsmokers who don't smoke cigarettes, this might be true. Eliminate.
(B) The short-term memory skills exhibited by a nonsmoker who has just smoked a cigarette are typically superior to those exhibited by a regular smoker who has just smoked a cigarette.	Correct. This directly contradicts the first statement in the stimulus. A regular smoker who has just had a cigarette shows superior short-term memory over nonsmokers (whether they've just smoked or not).
(C) The short-term memory skills exhibited by a nonsmoker who has just smoked a cigarette are typically superior to those exhibited by a regular smoker who has not smoked for more than eight hours.	The stimulus doesn't say what happens to the smokers after eight hours. This could be true. Eliminate.
(D) A regular smoker who, immediately after smoking a cigarette, exhibits short-term memory skills no better than those typically exhibited by a nonsmoker is nevertheless likely to exhibit superior short-term memory skills in the hours following a period of heavy smoking.	The stimulus doesn't go into this scenario about heavy smoking. It might be true, but there's no way of knowing one way or the other from the journalist's statements. Eliminate.
(E) The short-term memory skills exhibited by a regular smoker who last smoked a cigarette five hours ago are typically superior to those exhibited by a regular smoker who has just smoked a cigarette. *PrepTest52 Sec1 Q18*	This compares smokers to smokers; the stimulus, however, draws no distinction between smokers who have just smoked and smokers who have not smoked for five hours. This doesn't contradict anything in the journalist's statements. Eliminate.

LSAT Question		**Analysis**
15. University administrator: Any proposal for a new department will not be funded if there are fewer than 50 people per year available for hire in that field and the proposed department would duplicate more than 25 percent of the material covered in one of our existing departments. The proposed Area Studies Department will duplicate more than 25 percent of the material covered in our existing Anthropology Department. However, we will fund the new department.	→	**Step 2:** Three statements: (1) A rule for funding new departments: *If <50 people/year for hire AND new department duplicates >25% of material from an existing department → NOT fund new department.* (2) A fact: The new Area Studies department duplicates >25% of Anthropology's material. (3) "However"—a seemingly contradictory fact: The school will fund the Area Studies department.
Which one of the following statements follows logically from the university administrator's statements?	→	**Step 1:** The correct answer "follows logically" from the stimulus—an Inference question.
		Step 3: There are two conditions that, if they both happen, would cause the school NOT to fund the new department. One of them has happened—Area Studies duplicates >25% of Anthropology's material. Because Area Studies is going to be funded, it is certain that the other condition has not occurred. The correct answer will say: There are 50+ people per year available for hire in the Area Studies field.
(A) The field of Area Studies has at least 50 people per year available for hire.	→	**Step 4:** Correct. This matches the prediction. It must be true because if it weren't, the school would have to decline funding for the Area Studies department.
(B) The proposed Area Studies Department would not duplicate more than 25 percent of the material covered in any existing department other than Anthropology.	→	Irrelevant. The rule doesn't go into how many different departments a new department might duplicate. Eliminate.
(C) If the proposed Area Studies Department did not duplicate more than 25 percent of the material covered in Anthropology, then the new department would not be funded.	→	180. Duplicating >25% of another department's material is a negative to funding, not a requirement for funding a new department. Eliminate.
(D) The Anthropology Department duplicates more than 25 percent of the material covered in the proposed Area Studies Department.	→	There's no way to know whether this is true. You can't say that because at least 25% of NBA players graduated from college, 25% of college graduates play in the NBA. Eliminate.
(E) The field of Area Studies has fewer than 50 people per year available for hire. *PrepTest62 Sec4 Q6*	→	180. If this were true, the school would have to decline funding for Area Studies, but the school is approving it. Eliminate.

LSAT Question	Analysis
16. Adult frogs are vulnerable to dehydration because of their highly permeable skins. Unlike large adult frogs, small adult frogs have such a low ratio of body weight to skin surface area that they cannot survive in arid climates. The animals' moisture requirements constitute the most important factor determining where frogs can live in the Yucatán peninsula, which has an arid climate in the north and a wet climate in the south.	**Step 2:** Two comparisons: (1) Large frogs can survive in arid climates; small frogs can't. (2) Northern Yucatán has an arid climate; southern Yucatán has wet climate.
The information above most strongly supports which one of the following conclusions about frogs in the Yucatán peninsula?	**Step 1:** Inference question—the correct answer will follow from the stimulus; the four wrong answers will not.
	Step 3: Combining the statements, deduce that large frogs can live in more of the Yucatán than small frogs can.
(A) Large adult frogs cannot coexist with small adult frogs in the wet areas.	**Step 4:** Nothing in the stimulus suggests that either size of frog has trouble in wet climates. Eliminate.
(B) Frogs living in wet areas weigh more on average than frogs in the arid areas.	180. If anything, the stimulus suggests the opposite because large frogs are better equipped for dry areas. Eliminate.
(C) Large adult frogs can live in more of the area than small adult frogs can.	Correct. Large frogs are likely able to survive in the north and south. Small frogs definitely can't survive in the arid north.
(D) Fewer small adult frogs live in the south than do large adult frogs.	Irrelevant Comparison. Either type seems able to live in the wet south, and the stimulus doesn't say anything about relative populations. Eliminate.
(E) Small adult frogs in the south have less permeable skins than small adult frogs in the north.	Irrelevant Comparison. According to the stimulus, all adult frogs have permeable skins. Eliminate.

PrepTest58 Sec4 Q13

Reflection

For some students, Inference questions are the most challenging question type on the LSAT. They find it very difficult to avoid bringing in outside information or to avoid choosing answers with extreme language. You can practice reading for Inference questions whenever you read things like editorials or news articles. Catalog the facts and paraphrase the author's statements. Ask whether the author has drawn valid deductions from the studies, reports, or evidence she cites. Did she exaggerate statements? Did she rely on her own assumptions and outside knowledge to make inferences not directly supported? No matter how strong your analytical skills are now, you'll become a much more rigorous and critical reader in law school. Think of Inference practice as getting a head start (while improving your LSAT score at the same time).

PRINCIPLE QUESTIONS ASKING FOR INFERENCES

In Chapter 10, you learned about Principle questions that contain an argument in the stimulus. Those rewarded largely the same skills tested in Assumption, Strengthen, Weaken, and Parallel Reasoning questions—the ability to identify the abstract principle that underlies and supports the reasoning of the argument. However, other Principle questions mimic Inference questions. The stimulus in these Principle questions may state a principle and ask you to identify the answer choice containing a specific case that applies the principle appropriately, or the stimulus may present a specific case and ask you to infer the principle that case follows. Either way, you'll be rewarded for approaching these questions with the same skills you just learned and practiced for standard Inference questions.

Most recent tests have featured one Apply the Principle—Inference question and one or two Identify the Principle—Inference questions.

Here's a typical question asking you to infer the principle illustrated by the specific case described in the stimulus. Try it now if you like. You'll see it solved by an LSAT expert later in the chapter.

In a recent study, a group of young children were taught the word "stairs" while walking up and down a flight of stairs. Later that day, when the children were shown a video of a person climbing a ladder, they all called the ladder stairs.

Which one of the following principles is best illustrated by the study described above?

(A) When young children repeatedly hear a word without seeing the object denoted by the word, they sometimes apply the word to objects not denoted by the word.

(B) Young children best learn words when they are shown how the object denoted by the word is used.

(C) The earlier in life a child encounters and uses an object, the easier it is for that child to learn how not to misuse the word denoting that object.

(D) Young children who learn a word by observing how the object denoted by that word is used sometimes apply that word to a different object that is similarly used.

(E) Young children best learn the names of objects when the objects are present at the time the children learn the words and when no other objects are simultaneously present.

PrepTest62 Sec2 Q1

Note that the question stem asks for an answer containing a principle *illustrated by* the scenario or case described in the stimulus. That tells you that the correct answer will represent a broad rule that has been applied in the stimulus. Apply the Principle questions take the same task and turn it around. They state a broad rule in the stimulus and ask you to identify the narrow case that correctly applies the principle. In both formats, you can think of your job as identifying the one answer choice that provides a perfect one-to-one matchup with the stimulus.

LEARNING OBJECTIVES

In this section, you'll learn to:

· Infer a principle (general rule) from a specific case that illustrates it.
· Identify a specific case that appropriately applies a principle (general rule).
· Identify and answer Identify the Principle—Inference questions.
· Identify and answer Apply the Principle questions.

Infer a Principle (General Rule) from a Specific Case That Illustrates It

The stimuli for Principle questions that ask you to identify the principle illustrated by a specific case tend to fall into two broad categories: (1) cases that describe a set of actions and outcomes, and (2) cases that make recommendations. Take a look at an example of each.

Cases That Describe Actions and Outcomes

If you look back at the first Principle question in this section, you'll see that it describes the way young children responded to being taught a word in a particular way. For the purposes of a Principle question asking you to infer a general rule, you would want to try to generalize that case into a rule covering other, similar cases. How might the teacher have taught the children the word *curtain* or *chair*, and how might they have confused those objects for other objects with similar uses? By generalizing, you can paraphrase that case into a general rule and use that rule as your prediction for the correct answer.

Take a look at an LSAT expert's thinking as it relates to another Principle question stimulus.

LSAT Question	Analysis
Madden: Industrialists address problems by simplifying them, but in farming that strategy usually leads to oversimplification. For example, industrialists see water retention and drainage as different and opposite functions— that good topsoil both drains and retains water is a fact alien to industrial logic. To facilitate water retention, they use a terrace or a dam; to facilitate drainage, they use drain tile, a ditch, or a subsoiler. More farming problems are created than solved when agriculture is the domain of the industrialist, not of the farmer. *PrepTest58 Sec4 Q16*	A generalization about industrialists' approach to farming problems: they oversimplify them. Examples of this tendency to oversimplify. $\longrightarrow$ Summary: Industrialists (because of their approach) cause more farming problems than they solve.

There's not much of an argument here, not in the LSAT sense of conclusion and evidence at any rate. But the scenario, illustrated with a long example, emphasizes the problems inherent in the industrialists' oversimplification strategy. If that's the problem, what must the author, Madden, believe is the best general rule (or principle) for solving farming problems? He would endorse an approach that embraces complexity. Keep this analysis in mind when we come back to the full question from which this stimulus was taken.

Cases That Make Recommendations

Sometimes, a Principle question may ask you to infer a general rule from a specific case in which the author advances a recommendation. Take a look at the following example.

LSAT Question	Analysis
Politician: We should impose a tariff on imported fruit to make it cost consumers more than domestic fruit. Otherwise, growers from other countries who can grow better fruit more cheaply will put domestic fruit growers out of business. This will result in farmland's being converted to more lucrative industrial uses and the consequent vanishing of a unique way of life. *PrepTest58 Sec1 Q23*	Conclusion: We *should* raise tariffs on fruit imports. Evidence: We'll lose business to better, cheaper foreign fruit, causing our farmland and unique, traditional way of life to be lost to industrial use.

Take note of the politician's main concern. The specific action he supports is less important in this kind of question than his reasons for recommending it. He is willing to sacrifice economic benefits (cheaper fruit and profitable manufacturing) to preserve a "unique way of life." By focusing on his motivation, you're able to zero in on his principle, the general rule that guides his position on the issues.

These "recommendation" stimuli are more like standard LSAT arguments. The recommendation is the author's conclusion and the examples or illustrations his evidence. But, unlike most questions featuring arguments in the stimulus, the Principle questions asking you to infer the general rule to which the case conforms are more interested in your ability to generalize from the specific case than they are with your ability to recognize the author's assumption. We'll see this stimulus in the context of its full question shortly, but first, take a look at the kinds of principles most often used in the stimuli for Apply the Principle questions.

Identify a Specific Case That Applies a Principle (General Rule)

Apply the Principle questions, more than most LSAT questions, mirror the kind of deductions a student makes on a law school exam. For example, as a first-year law student, you will learn the elements of the tort of battery: the intentional offensive touching of a person without consent. The exam question will present you with some facts. Your task will be to match the facts to the elements of battery to determine if the defendant described in the exam's fact pattern is liable for the offense. Was the victim touched? Was the touch intentional? Was the intentional touch offensive? Did the victim give consent to be touched? If you determine that the given facts correctly match each of the elements of the rule, you can conclude that the defendant is liable. But, if even one of those elements is missing, the defendant will prevail.

In the same way, Apply the Principle questions will present you with one or more rules, very often in the form of conditional, Formal Logic statements. Your task is to examine five cases (the five answer choices) and select the one that perfectly matches or applies the rule(s) articulated in the stimulus.

Take a look at how an LSAT expert would untangle the stimulus to an Apply the Principle question. Focus on how he identifies the principles or general rules found there.

LSAT Question	Analysis
Moralist: A statement is wholly truthful only if it is true and made without intended deception. A statement is a lie if it is intended to deceive or if its speaker, upon learning that the statement was misinterpreted, refrains from clarifying it. *PrepTest52 Sec1 Q22*	Two rules, stated as Formal Logic: *If truthful → true AND no intended deception* and → *If intended to deceive → Lie* *OR misunderstanding* *intentionally not clarified* The first rule gives two elements, both of which are necessary for something to be truthful. The second gives two elements, either of which is sufficient for something to be a lie.

This analysis puts the LSAT expert in a perfect position to evaluate the choices. The correct answer will describe a case that follows one of two patterns: (1) Someone has not told the truth because one or both of the necessary elements are missing, or (2) someone has told a lie because one or both of the elements is present. Likewise, the expert will be able to spot wrong answers, each of which is likely to mangle the application of the Formal Logic in one of the rules in some way. A wrong answer might, for example, state that one of the elements necessary for truthfulness is present and conclude that a person's statement is therefore truthful. Or, it might negate one of the elements sufficient for something to be a lie and conclude therefore that someone's statement is not a lie. There will be no way to predict the precise scenario the correct answer will illustrate, but an assessment like the one above, treating both statements as rules that can be tested, puts the expert in an ideal position to evaluate the choices. We'll come back to the full question associated with this stimulus shortly.

Now, try untangling an Apply the Principle stimulus. Identify the general rule(s) the stimulus articulates and anticipate the kinds of cases that could be described in the correct answer to this question.

LSAT Question	My Analysis
17. Columnist: Although there is and should be complete freedom of thought and expression, that does not mean that there is nothing wrong with exploiting depraved popular tastes for the sake of financial gain. *PrepTest58 Sec1 Q21*	

This stimulus sets forth only one rule, but it has two elements. Did you paraphrase both of them?

LSAT Question	Analysis
17. Columnist: Although there is and should be complete freedom of thought and expression, that does not mean that there is nothing wrong with exploiting depraved popular tastes for the sake of financial gain. *PrepTest58 Sec1 Q21* $\longrightarrow$	"Although" signals a contrast, so the author sees that the two parts of his rule appear to be at odds. First element: There should be no restrictions on thought and expression. Second element: Making money off of people's depraved tastes may still be wrong. The author can hold both parts because the first applies to the law and the second to morality.

With that analysis, you're ready to evaluate the answer choices, and by the way, you can find the full question associated with this stimulus in the Question Pool at the end of the chapter. The correct answer choice will describe a specific situation compatible with both of the elements in the columnist's principle. It might, for example, describe a movie hoping to profit by showing some distasteful scenes and conclude that although marketing the movie is immoral, we still cannot censor it under the law. Keep in mind that the scenario could just as easily involve books, websites, or even services, but it will definitely fit the pattern of being wrong but legal. The wrong answers, of course, will conclude that some kind of expression or thought can be outlawed or will mischaracterize the author's opinion on those taking advantage of human depravity.

Now that you've seen how to infer a general rule from a specific situation and how to determine the kind of case to which a principle was applied, it's time to work with some full LSAT questions that reward these skills.

Identify the Principle—Inference and Apply the Principle Questions

When an LSAT expert confronts a question stem identifying a Principle question calling for an inference, the first thing she's likely to note is whether the broad, general rule is in the stimulus or in the correct answer. Take a look at the thinking that helps a well-trained test taker distinguish between "Identify the Principle—Inference" questions and their "Apply the Principle" cousins.

LSAT Question	Analysis
The reasoning above conforms most closely to which of the following general propositions? *PrepTest62 Sec4 Q2*	The correct answer will be a broad rule that generalizes the specific case described in the stimulus. This is an Identify the Principle—Inference question.
Which one of the following judgments conforms most closely to the principle cited by the columnist? *PrepTest58 Sec1 Q21*	The correct answer will be a specific case that applies the principle (general rule) stated in the stimulus. This is an Apply the Principle question.

Practice identifying your task in the following question stems. For each, make sure you can accurately say whether the stimulus contains the broad principle and the answer choices contain specific cases, or vice versa.

LSAT Question	My Analysis
18. The situation as Madden describes it best illustrates which one of the following propositions? *PrepTest58 Sec4 Q16*	
19. Which one of the following judgments most closely conforms to the principles stated by the moralist? *PrepTest52 Sec1 Q22*	
20. Which one of the following principles is best illustrated by the study described above? *PrepTest62 Sec2 Q1*	
21. Each of the following assignments of computer programmers is consistent both with the principle expressed by Vanessa and with the principle expressed by Jo EXCEPT: *PrepTest62 Sec2 Q18*	

Here's how the LSAT expert would examine each of those question stems and what she would anticipate about the rest of the question.

LSAT Question		**Analysis**
18. The situation as Madden describes it best illustrates which one of the following propositions? *PrepTest58 Sec4 Q16*	→	The correct answer is a principle ("proposition") that can be generalized from the specific situation in the stimulus. This is an Identify the Principle—Inference question.
19. Which one of the following judgments most closely conforms to the principles stated by the moralist? *PrepTest52 Sec1 Q22*	→	The correct answer will be a decision ("judgment") about a specific case that matches the broad principles set forth in the stimulus. This is an Apply the Principle question.
20. Which one of the following principles is best illustrated by the study described above? *PrepTest62 Sec2 Q1*	→	The stimulus will describe a specific study. The correct answer will be a broad rule that can be generalized from the study's results. This is an Identify the Principle—Inference question.
21. Each of the following assignments of computer programmers is consistent both with the principle expressed by Vanessa and with the principle expressed by Jo EXCEPT: *PrepTest62 Sec2 Q18*	→	This is an Apply the Principle question variant. The stimulus will have two different people's principles. The four wrong answers will be fine according to the principles, but the correct answer will violate one or both of them.

Don't be too alarmed by that last question stem; it looks convoluted, but as you can see from the expert's analysis, the right answer is pretty easy to characterize. You'll see that question in the Question Pool at the end of the chapter. When you get to it, just understand and paraphrase the rules Vanessa and Jo would follow and look for the one answer that violates one of those rules.

Before practicing full Principle questions asking for inferences, take a look at the LSAT expert's analysis of the full questions associated with the stimuli you analyzed earlier in this section. Pay attention to how the expert uses her analysis of the stimulus material to evaluate the answer choices efficiently and confidently. We'll start first with the question you saw in full at the beginning of this section.

LSAT Question	Analysis
In a recent study, a group of young children were taught the word "stairs" while walking up and down a flight of stairs. Later that day, when the children were shown a video of a person climbing a ladder, they all called the ladder stairs.	**Step 2:** Study results: Children were taught the word "stairs" while climbing stairs. Later, they saw people climbing a ladder and called the ladder "stairs."
Which one of the following principles is best illustrated by the study described above?	**Step 1:** The stimulus will describe a specific study. The correct answer will be a broad rule that can be generalized from the study's results. This is an Identify the Principle—Inference question.
	Step 3: Generalize the study—when children learn a word while using the object the word describes, they may misname other things used in the same way.
(A) When young children repeatedly hear a word without seeing the object denoted by the word, they sometimes apply the word to objects not denoted by the word.	**Step 4:** "[W]ithout seeing the object" distorts the study. They were climbing stairs as they learned the word *stairs*. Eliminate.
(B) Young children best learn words when they are shown how the object denoted by the word is used.	"[B]est" is too Extreme to fit the study results. And this choice says nothing about misnaming similar objects. Eliminate.
(C) The earlier in life a child encounters and uses an object, the easier it is for that child to learn how not to misuse the word denoting that object.	This is a Distortion of the study. There's nothing in the stimulus about learning "earlier in life," and in the study, the children *did* misname another object. Eliminate.
(D) Young children who learn a word by observing how the object denoted by that word is used sometimes apply that word to a different object that is similarly used.	Correct. This matches the prediction and represents a general rule that would account for the study results in the stimulus.
(E) Young children best learn the names of objects when the objects are present at the time the children learn the words and when no other objects are simultaneously present.	This doesn't match the study described in the stimulus. There is nothing here about misnaming a similar object. Eliminate.

PrepTest62 Sec2 Q1

LSAT Question	Analysis
Madden: Industrialists address problems by simplifying them, but in farming that strategy usually leads to oversimplification. For example, industrialists see water retention and drainage as different and opposite functions—that good topsoil both drains and retains water is a fact alien to industrial logic. To facilitate water retention, they use a terrace or a dam; to facilitate drainage, they use drain tile, a ditch, or a subsoiler. More farming problems are created than solved when agriculture is the domain of the industrialist, not of the farmer.	**Step 2:** A generalization about industrialists' approach to farming problems: They oversimplify them. Examples of this tendency to oversimplify. Summary: Industrialists (because of their approach) cause more farming problems than they solve.
The situation as Madden describes it best illustrates which one of the following propositions?	**Step 1:** The correct answer is a principle ("proposition") that can be generalized from the specific situation in the stimulus. This is an Identify the Principle—Inference question.
	Step 3: The correct answer will state a principle that farming problems are best solved with a strategy that embraces complexity. After all, the problems caused by the industrialists are a result of oversimplification.
(A) The handling of water drainage and retention is the most important part of good farming.	**Step 4:** "[M]ost important" is too Extreme to fit Madden's critique. Moreover, this misses Madden's point about oversimplification. Eliminate.
(B) The problems of farming should be viewed in all their complexity.	Correct. This matches the prediction and accords well with Madden's criticism of industrialists for oversimplifying farming problems.
(C) Farmers are better than anyone else at solving farming problems.	"[B]etter than anyone else" is too Extreme to fit Madden's critique. All we know is that farmers avoid the industrialists' mistake of oversimplification. Eliminate.
(D) Industrial solutions for problems in farming should never be sought.	"[N]ever" is too Extreme to be Madden's principle. Moreover, this choice says nothing about oversimplification. Eliminate.
(E) The approach to problem solving typical of industrialists is fundamentally flawed. *PrepTest58 Sec4 Q16*	This choice is not limited to farming. The industrialists' strategy may work well in other domains. Eliminate.

LSAT Question	Analysis
Politician: We should impose a tariff on imported fruit to make it cost consumers more than domestic fruit. Otherwise, growers from other countries who can grow better fruit more cheaply will put domestic fruit growers out of business. This will result in farmland's being converted to more lucrative industrial uses and the consequent vanishing of a unique way of life.	**Step 2:** Conclusion: We *should* raise tariffs on fruit imports. Evidence: We'll lose business to better, cheaper foreign fruit, causing our farmland and unique, traditional way of life to be lost to industrial use.
The politician's recommendation most closely conforms to which one of the following principles?	**Step 1:** The correct answer will be a broad principle that fits the politician's recommendation. This is an Identify the Principle—Inference question.
	Step 3: The correct answer will generalize from the politician's reasoning: We should preserve unique ways of life even if there is economic cost.
(A) A country should put its own economic interest over that of other countries.	**Step 4:** This distorts the politician's position. He recommends tariffs even though they will harm his country's economy. Eliminate.
(B) The interests of producers should always take precedence over those of consumers.	Comparing the interests of producers to those of consumers is irrelevant to the politician's point. Eliminate.
(C) Social concerns should sometimes take precedence over economic efficiency.	Correct. This is a very broad principle, but it fits the politician's reasoning. The "[s]ocial concern" is the preservation of the country's unique way of life.
(D) A country should put the interests of its own citizens ahead of those of citizens of other countries.	Comparing the interests of the country's citizens to those of another country is irrelevant to the politician's point. Eliminate.
(E) Government intervention sometimes creates more economic efficiency than free markets. *PrepTest58 Sec1 Q23*	Focusing on "efficiency" distorts the politician's reasoning. Eliminate.

LSAT Question	Analysis
Moralist: A statement is wholly truthful only if it is true and made without intended deception. A statement is a lie if it is intended to deceive or if its speaker, upon learning that the statement was misinterpreted, refrains from clarifying it.	**Step 2:** Two rules, stated as Formal Logic: *If truthful → true AND no intended deception* and *If intended to deceive → Lie OR misunderstanding intentionally not clarified* The first rule gives two elements, both of which are necessary for something to be truthful. The second gives two elements, either of which is sufficient for something to be a lie.
Which one of the following judgments most closely conforms to the principles stated by the moralist? →	**Step 1:** The correct answer will be a decision ("judgment") about a specific case that matches the broad principles set forth in the stimulus. This is an Apply the Principle question.
	Step 3: The correct answer will apply one of the Formal Logic rules correctly. The wrong answers will distort the Formal Logic in some way.
(A) Ted's statement to the investigator that he had been abducted by extraterrestrial beings was wholly truthful even though no one has ever been abducted by extraterrestrial beings. After all, Ted was not trying to deceive the investigator. →	**Step 4:** The rule about truthfulness has two necessary conditions, one of which is that the statement is true. The event Ted claimed happened, didn't happen, so his claim can't be "wholly truthful." Eliminate.
(B) Tony was not lying when he told his granddaughter that he did not wear dentures, for even though Tony meant to deceive his granddaughter, she made it clear to Tony that she did not believe him. →	According to the second rule, an intention to deceive is sufficient to make a statement a lie. The rule says nothing about whether the speaker was successful in deceiving the listener. Eliminate.
(C) Siobhan did not tell a lie when she told her supervisor that she was ill and hence would not be able to come to work for an important presentation. However, even though her statement was true, it was not wholly truthful. →	Since Siobhan didn't lie, we know she had no intention of deceiving her supervisor. Since it was also true that she was ill, her claim has both elements necessary to be considered "wholly truthful." This choice gives no reason to conclude that her statement was not wholly truthful. Eliminate.
(D) Walter's claim to a potential employer that he had done volunteer work was a lie. Even though Walter had worked without pay in his father's factory, he used the phrase "volunteer work" in an attempt to deceive the interviewer into thinking he had worked for a socially beneficial cause. →	Correct. According to the rule, saying something with the intention of deceiving the listener is sufficient to make one's statement a lie. Because Walter intended to deceive the employer, he lied.

LSAT Question	Analysis
(E) The tour guide intended to deceive the tourists when he told them that the cabin they were looking at was centuries old. Still, his statement about the cabin's age was not a lie, for if he thought that this statement had been misinterpreted, he would have tried to clarify it. *PrepTest52 Sec1 Q22*	Knowing that the tour guide "intended to deceive" is sufficient to conclude that he told a lie. That he would have clarified is thus irrelevant. Eliminate.

Take a moment to notice that the incorrect answers are all, in one way or another, mismatched to the stimuli. Sometimes, they contradict the stimulus outright. In other cases, they distort the stimulus or simply offer a statement irrelevant to it. As you try the practice problems below, make sure you take the time to articulate why each wrong answer is wrong, even if you can correctly eliminate it based on a "gut" reaction. On Test Day, you may encounter a tough question in which you need to distinguish between two choices. If you are unable to say with certainty which answer is correct, you'll be glad you've practiced pinpointing where and how incorrect answers go wrong.

Practice

Apply the Kaplan Method to the following question. You can use the corresponding blanks to record your thinking for each step. After each, compare your work to the thinking of an LSAT expert on the following pages.

LSAT Question	My Analysis
22. Any museum that owns the rare stamp that features an airplane printed upside down should not display it. Ultraviolet light causes red ink to fade, and a substantial portion of the stamp is red. If the stamp is displayed, it will be damaged. It should be kept safely locked away, even though this will deny the public the chance to see it.	**Step 2:**
The reasoning above most closely conforms to which one of the following principles?	**Step 1:**
	Step 3:
(A) The public should judge the quality of a museum by the rarity of the objects in its collection.	**Step 4:**
(B) Museum display cases should protect their contents from damage caused by ultraviolet light.	
(C) Red ink should not be used on items that will not be exposed to ultraviolet light.	
(D) A museum piece that would be damaged by display should not be displayed.	
(E) The primary purpose of a museum is to educate the public.	

PrepTest52 Sec3 Q1

LSAT Question	My Analysis
23. A summer day is "pleasant" if there are intermittent periods of wind and the temperature stays below 84°F (29°C) all afternoon. A summer day with high humidity levels is "oppressive" either if the temperature stays above 84°F (29°C) all afternoon or if there is no wind.	**Step 2:**
Which one of the following summer weather reports most closely conforms to the principles stated above?	**Step 1:**
	Step 3:
(A) The temperature on Friday stayed below 82°F (28°C) all day, and there was no wind at all. It was a day of low humidity, and it was a pleasant day.	**Step 4:**
(B) On Monday, the temperature ranged from 85°F to 90°F (30°C to 32°C) from early morning until night. It was an oppressive day even though the humidity levels were low.	
(C) On Tuesday, the temperature neither rose above nor fell below 84°F (29°C) throughout late morning and all afternoon. It was a pleasant day because there were occasional periods of wind.	
(D) On Wednesday, a refreshing breeze in the early morning became intermittent by late morning, and the day's humidity levels were constantly high. It was an oppressive day, even though the temperature did not rise above 84°F (29°C) all day.	
(E) On Thursday morning, the air was very still, and it remained windless for the whole day. Humidity levels for the day were high, and even though the temperature fell below 84°F (29°C) between early and late afternoon, it was an oppressive day.	

PrepTest56 Sec3 Q23

LSAT Question	My Analysis
24. At mock trials in which jury instructions were given in technical legal jargon, jury verdicts tended to mirror the judge's own opinions. Jurors had become aware of the judge's nonverbal behavior: facial expressions, body movements, tone of voice. Jurors who viewed the same case but were given instruction in clear, nontechnical language, however, were comparatively more likely to return verdicts at odds with the judge's opinion.	**Step 2:**
Which one of the following is best illustrated by the example described above?	**Step 1:**
	Step 3:
(A) Technical language tends to be more precise than nontechnical language.	**Step 4:**
(B) A person's influence is proportional to that person's perceived status.	
(C) Nonverbal behavior is not an effective means of communication.	
(D) Real trials are better suited for experimentation than are mock trials.	
(E) The way in which a judge instructs a jury can influence the jury's verdict.	

PrepTest58 Sec1 Q4

Here's how an LSAT expert tackled the questions you just saw. Review her analysis step-by-step, following the Logical Reasoning Method. The more consistently you approach both your practice and review, the faster and more confident you'll be on Test Day.

LSAT Question	Analysis
22. Any museum that owns the rare stamp that features an airplane printed upside down should not display it. Ultraviolet light causes red ink to fade, and a substantial portion of the stamp is red. If the stamp is displayed, it will be damaged. It should be kept safely locked away, even though this will deny the public the chance to see it. →	**Step 2:** A recommendation: A museum with the rare stamp should lock it away and not display it, even though this means the public won't get to see it. The reason is that displaying the stamp could damage it.
The reasoning above most closely conforms to which one of the following principles? →	**Step 1:** The correct answer is a principle (general rule) that fits the specific case in the stimulus. This is an Identify the Principle—Inference question.
	Step 3: Generalize out from the specific "stamp" case—a museum should lock away rarities that could be damaged by display.
(A) The public should judge the quality of a museum by the rarity of the objects in its collection. →	**Step 4:** Outside the Scope. The author isn't giving guidelines about how to judge museum quality but rather a recommendation for how to treat a rare stamp. Eliminate.
(B) Museum display cases should protect their contents from damage caused by ultraviolet light. →	This choice suggests a possible solution to the problem raised by the author, but it isn't a principle that supports his recommendation to lock away the stamp. Eliminate.
(C) Red ink should not be used on items that will not be exposed to ultraviolet light. →	This is too narrow to cover the author's reasoning. It might be a good rule of thumb for printers to remember, but it says nothing about how museums should treat their treasures. Eliminate.
(D) A museum piece that would be damaged by display should not be displayed. →	Correct. This is a general rule that covers the author's recommendation about the stamp perfectly.
(E) The primary purpose of a museum is to educate the public. *PrepTest52 Sec3 Q1* →	If anything, this runs counter to the author's point, because he recommends preserving the stamp even if it means the public doesn't get to see it. Eliminate.

LSAT Question	Analysis
23. A summer day is "pleasant" if there are intermittent periods of wind and the temperature stays below 84°F (29°C) all afternoon. A summer day with high humidity levels is "oppressive" either if the temperature stays above 84°F (29°C) all afternoon or if there is no wind.	**Step 2:** Two rules, stated in Formal Logic terms: *If periods of wind AND <84° all day → pleasant* and *If humid AND (NO wind OR >84° all day) → oppressive* The first rule says what's sufficient for "pleasant" and the second what's sufficient for "oppressive."
Which one of the following summer weather reports most closely conforms to the principles stated above?	**Step 1:** The correct answer will follow from the principle(s) set forth in the stimulus. This is an Apply the Principle question. Expect to see Formal Logic.
	Step 3: The correct answer will apply one of the rules appropriately to conclude that a day was either "pleasant" or "oppressive." The wrong answers will mangle the Formal Logic in some way or will fall Outside the Scope.
(A) The temperature on Friday stayed below 82°F (28°C) all day, and there was no wind at all. It was a day of low humidity, and it was a pleasant day.	**Step 4:** The first rule says wind AND a temperature below 84° make a day "pleasant." Since there was no wind on Friday, we can't conclude that it was pleasant. Eliminate.
(B) On Monday, the temperature ranged from 85°F to 90°F (30°C to 32°C) from early morning until night. It was an oppressive day even though the humidity levels were low.	The second rule, about "oppressive" days, applies only to humid days. Because Monday wasn't humid, we can't conclude that it was oppressive. Eliminate.
(C) On Tuesday, the temperature neither rose above nor fell below 84°F (29°C) throughout late morning and all afternoon. It was a pleasant day because there were occasional periods of wind.	The first rule says wind AND a temperature *below* 84° make a day "pleasant." Because 84° on the dot is NOT *below* 84°, we can't conclude that Tuesday was pleasant. Eliminate.
(D) On Wednesday, a refreshing breeze in the early morning became intermittent by late morning, and the day's humidity levels were constantly high. It was an oppressive day, even though the temperature did not rise above 84°F (29°C) all day.	The second rule says that if a day is humid AND either windless OR has a temperature above 84°, then the day is "oppressive." Wednesday was humid, but it wasn't windless and it didn't have a temperature over 84°, so we can't conclude that it was oppressive. Eliminate.
(E) On Thursday morning, the air was very still, and it remained windless for the whole day. Humidity levels for the day were high, and even though the temperature fell below 84°F (29°C) between early and late afternoon, it was an oppressive day. *PrepTest56 Sec3 Q23*	Correct. The second rule says that if a day is humid AND either windless OR has a temperature above 84°, then the day is "oppressive." Thursday was humid AND windless. That's enough (sufficient) to make it oppressive and render the temperature irrelevant.

LSAT Question	Analysis
24. At mock trials in which jury instructions were given in technical legal jargon, jury verdicts tended to mirror the judge's own opinions. Jurors had become aware of the judge's nonverbal behavior: facial expressions, body movements, tone of voice. Jurors who viewed the same case but were given instruction in clear, nontechnical language, however, were comparatively more likely to return verdicts at odds with the judge's opinion. →	**Step 2:** Study results: (1) Mock jurors who heard technical legal jargon reached the same verdict as the judge. (Apparently, they watched the judge and followed his nonverbal cues.) (2) Mock jurors who heard clear, jargon-free language more often disagreed with the judge's verdict.
Which one of the following is best illustrated by the example described above? →	**Step 1:** The correct answer will be illustrated by the example in the stimulus. Because the example will be a specific case fitting the more general answer, this is an Identify the Principle—Inference question.
	Step 3: The correct answer will state a principle (general rule) that the manner in which a person in authority instructs a group of people can affect the decisions made by that group of people. →
(A) Technical language tends to be more precise than nontechnical language. →	**Step 4:** Precision of language is irrelevant to the author's example. Eliminate.
(B) A person's influence is proportional to that person's perceived status. →	A rule about influence being proportional to status is completely Outside the Scope of this example. Eliminate.
(C) Nonverbal behavior is not an effective means of communication. →	This doesn't account for the differences in jury behavior and, if anything, is a 180 because apparently, the "confused" jurors effectively followed the judge's nonverbal cues. Eliminate.
(D) Real trials are better suited for experimentation than are mock trials. →	Perhaps true, but irrelevant to the author's point in the example. Eliminate.
(E) The way in which a judge instructs a jury can influence the jury's verdict. →	Correct. Here is a simple, broad principle that accounts for the results in the jury study.

PrepTest58 Sec1 Q4

Reflection

Congratulations on acquiring another valuable LSAT (and law school) skill. In the coming days, pay attention to conversations you have in which people apply or infer principles from specific events and situations. Even simple statements can provide practice for these Principle/Inference question types. For example, if you hear a father tell a child, "You should clean up your room because I told you to," he's implying the principle that children should obey their parents. On the other hand, if you hear a mom say, "You need to clean up your room because everyone in this family has responsibilities," she's implying a different principle. What is it?

We generalize rules from specific cases all the time, and we often expect people to act in a certain way or have a particular response because of general rules we follow. As you encounter situations of this type, take the time to make the implied rules explicit to yourself and to note the principles upon which people are acting even when they haven't articulated those principles.

RESOLVING DISCREPANCIES AND PARADOX QUESTIONS

One more non-argument-based Logical Reasoning question type, the Paradox question, features a stimulus that contains two seemingly contradictory statements. That's the essence of a paradox, a situation that seems impossible, inconsistent, or contradictory but actually isn't. The correct answer to an LSAT Paradox question will always be a fact that, if true, will help explain how the apparent discrepancy can be resolved, that is, how the two problematic facts can be shown to be consistent. Over the past five years, most LSAT tests have included three or four Paradox questions.

Take a look at a typical LSAT Paradox question. Go ahead and try it now. You'll see this question explained in full a little later in the chapter.

A survey taken ten years ago of residents of area L showed that although living conditions were slightly below their country's average, most residents of L reported general satisfaction with their living conditions. However, this year the same survey found that while living conditions are now about the same as the national average, most residents of L report general dissatisfaction with their living conditions.

Which one of the following, if true, would most help to resolve the apparent conflict between the results of the surveys described above?

(A) Residents of area L typically value aspects of living conditions different from the aspects of living conditions that are valued by residents of adjacent areas.

(B) Between the times that the two surveys were conducted, the average living conditions in L's country had substantially declined.

(C) Optimal living conditions were established in the survey by taking into account governmental policies and public demands on three continents.

(D) Living conditions in an area generally improve only if residents perceive their situation as somehow in need of improvement.

(E) Ten years ago the residents of area L were not aware that their living conditions were below the national average.

PrepTest58 Sec1 Q17

Notice that the question stem asks you to resolve the apparent conflict in the stimulus. Two terms should really stand out: *resolve* and *apparent conflict*. Virtually every Paradox question will ask you to *explain*, *resolve*, or *reconcile* two statements. The fact that these statements merely *appear* contradictory or inconsistent tells you that they are actually compatible.

LEARNING OBJECTIVES

In this section, you'll learn to:

- · Identify and paraphrase an apparent contradiction.
- · Infer what must be true to resolve an apparent contradiction.
- · Identify and answer Paradox questions.
- · Identify and answer Paradox EXCEPT questions.

Identify and Paraphrase an Apparent Contradiction and Infer What Must Be True to Resolve It

Before you can spot the answer choice that will explain or resolve the paradox in the stimulus, you must be sure you've correctly understood the seeming discrepancy. To make sure you are clear on the scope and terms of the situation, always paraphrase the paradox in your own words. Once you've got a clear picture of the situation, you can predict the kind of fact that will help explain that the facts or statements are actually compatible. Practice spotting paradoxes and predicting facts that would resolve them.

Take a look at how an LSAT expert identifies and paraphrases the paradoxes found in a couple of Paradox question stimuli. You'll see that there is almost always a Contrast Keyword signaling the facts or assertions apparently in conflict. Let's start with the stimulus from the example at the beginning of this section.

LSAT Question	Analysis
A survey taken ten years ago of residents of area L showed that although living conditions were slightly below their country's average, most residents of L reported general satisfaction with their living conditions. However, this year the same survey found that while living conditions are now about the same as the national average, most residents of L report general dissatisfaction with their living conditions. *PrepTest58 Sec1 Q17*	Survey results with two statements separated by "[h]owever," indicating a perceived discrepancy: → Over the past 10 years, area L's conditions have improved from below national average to national average, *but* residents are less satisfied with their living conditions. Paradox: Residents are less satisfied even though the area has improved relative to the country.

Can you anticipate the kind of fact that might help resolve the apparent discrepancy? Notice how careful the LSAT expert was to stick close to the facts of the stimulus. She didn't paraphrase the stimulus by saying conditions are now better in area L; rather, she noted that they are better relative to the country as a whole. But, what if conditions in the country as a whole are worse? Think about the Great Depression in the United States. A person may have been better off in a below-average area during the Roaring '20s than he would at the national average after the stock market crash. Alternatively, what if the residents of area L are just more aware of poor conditions than they were in the past? For example, problems in area L may have been publicized to a greater extent over the past decade even though overall conditions are better than they were. The LSAT expert doesn't stray from the terms of the stimulus, so she can predict that the correct answer will be something along the lines of "The correct answer will explain why residents of area L report higher levels of dissatisfaction despite being closer to the national average than they were a decade ago."

Here's another example. Read the stimulus and review the expert's analysis of it.

LSAT Question	Analysis
For one academic year all the students at a high school were observed. The aim was to test the hypothesis that studying more increased a student's chances of earning a higher grade. It turned out that the students who spent the most time studying did not earn grades as high as did many students who studied less. Nonetheless, the researchers concluded that the results of the observation supported the initial hypothesis. *PrepTest52 Sec1 Q14*	"Nonetheless" signals facts the author thinks are at odds with one another: The researchers concluded that more study time led to higher grades *despite the fact* that many students who studied less got better grades than those who studied more. Paradox: The researchers' conclusion (more study time = better grades) seems in conflict with its evidence (many who studied less got better grades).

If you find yourself scratching your head after reading a Paradox stimulus, good for you. That means you've really spotted the apparent contradiction. But remember that there is *always* a way to reconcile or resolve the discrepancy in these LSAT questions. What fact might the researchers produce that could support their conclusion about study time? Again, you'll find the answer by sticking close to the terms of the stimulus. The hypothesis said study time "increased a student's chances of earning a higher grade": It makes students better than they otherwise would be. So, the evidence that some of the top students didn't study as much as some of the poorer ones is misleading; sure, some super smart kids may have gotten As without as much study time. The fact the researchers will need to produce is that students who studied more got better grades than they would had they not studied as much.

Now, try doing the same kind of analysis on your own.

Practice

Untangle the following stimuli. Identify the two facts that the author believes are in conflict. Paraphrase the paradox or apparent discrepancy the facts raise. Then, anticipate the kind of fact(s) that would explain, resolve, or reconcile the seeming contradiction.

LSAT Question	My Analysis
25. Automated flight technology can guide an aircraft very reliably, from navigation to landing. Yet this technology, even when functioning correctly, is not a perfect safeguard against human error. *PrepTest58 Sec4 Q1*	
26. There are two ways to manage an existing transportation infrastructure: continuous maintenance at adequate levels, and periodic radical reconstruction. Continuous maintenance dispenses with the need for radical reconstruction, and radical reconstruction is necessitated by failing to perform continuous maintenance. Over the long run, continuous maintenance is far less expensive; nevertheless, it almost never happens. *PrepTest52 Sec3 Q20*	
27. A 24-year study of 1,500 adults showed that those subjects with a high intake of foods rich in beta-carotene were much less likely to die from cancer or heart disease than were those with a low intake of such foods. On the other hand, taking beta-carotene supplements for 12 years had no positive or negative effect on the health of subjects in a separate study of 20,000 adults. *PrepTest62 Sec4 Q17*	

Did you take advantage of the Contrast Keywords in each example? If so, you likely spotted the apparent contradiction. Having done that, were you able to see how the paradox might be resolved? Compare your analysis to that of the LSAT expert on the next page.

Here's how an LSAT expert untangled the stimuli you just saw. Take note of the expert's paraphrasing of the paradox in each example and how she anticipates the apparent discrepancies may be resolved.

LSAT Question	Analysis
25. Automated flight technology can guide an aircraft very reliably, from navigation to landing. Yet this technology, even when functioning correctly, is not a perfect safeguard against human error. *PrepTest58 Sec4 Q1*	"Yet" signals a perceived discrepancy: Automated flight technology is reliable *but* doesn't, even when it's working correctly, safeguard against human error.
	$\longrightarrow$ This stimulus is succinct. The paradox is that *while* technology can guide an airplane in many situations, it doesn't prevent human error. A fact that resolves the paradox will explain how human error still affects the automated system.
26. There are two ways to manage an existing transportation infrastructure: continuous maintenance at adequate levels, and periodic radical reconstruction. Continuous maintenance dispenses with the need for radical reconstruction, and radical reconstruction is necessitated by failing to perform continuous maintenance. Over the long run, continuous maintenance is far less expensive; nevertheless, it almost never happens. *PrepTest52 Sec3 Q20*	"[N]evertheless" signals the statements the author believes are in conflict: Continuous maintenance is more economical *but* we almost never do it. (The rest of the stimulus is just a long definition of continuous maintenance versus periodic radical reconstruction.) Paradox: *Although* continuous maintenance saves money in the long run, it's rarely used. The paradox could be resolved with a fact explaining why people don't use the cost-saving approach.
27. A 24-year study of 1,500 adults showed that those subjects with a high intake of foods rich in beta-carotene were much less likely to die from cancer or heart disease than were those with a low intake of such foods. On the other hand, taking beta-carotene supplements for 12 years had no positive or negative effect on the health of subjects in a separate study of 20,000 adults. *PrepTest62 Sec4 Q17*	"On the other hand" signals the apparent discrepancy: A 24-year study correlated a high beta-carotene diet with reduced cancer risk, *but* a 12-year study showed no correlation between beta-carotene supplements and reduced cancer risk. (Both studies used a large number of subjects, so sample size is not an issue.)
	$\longrightarrow$ Paradox: Two large-scale studies gave different results with respect to the relationship between beta-carotene and cancer. One study was twice as long and used a high beta-carotene diet instead of supplements. The paradox could be explained by facts showing why the duration of the studies or the different methods of taking the beta-carotene gave different results.

You will see the complete questions accompanying the stimuli for questions 25 and 27 a little later in this section. You'll have a chance to practice the complete LSAT question from which number 26 was drawn in the Question Pool at the end of this chapter.

As you reflect on the stimuli you just untangled, take a moment to consider a key distinction. In an Inference question, the stimulus provides facts that are mutually consistent and can be combined to create a new deduction. By contrast, a Paradox question provides facts that appear to be incompatible but actually are not. Allow your paraphrase of the apparent discrepancy or paradox to guide your prediction of the correct answer. Ask what is in need of explanation. Indeed, you should be able to say, "The fact that *x* and *y* are both true is confusing." Then, when you select the correct answer, you can say, "Okay. This clears it up."

Paradox Questions and Paradox EXCEPT Questions

Paradox question stems overwhelmingly use one of three verbs: *resolve*, *reconcile*, or *explain*. Sometimes, there will be an extra word in the question stem indicating that it is a discrepancy, anomaly, or paradox. Other times, the content of the paradox will even be mentioned in the question stem. Rarely, the test will ask a Paradox EXCEPT question, asking for the only answer that doesn't help to reconcile the seeming contradiction. Take a look at how an LSAT expert analyzes Paradox question stems.

LSAT Question	Analysis
Which of the following, if true, most helps to resolve the apparent discrepancy in the statements above? *PrepTest56 Sec2 Q22*	→ The correct answer will be a fact that reconciles the apparent discrepancy—a Paradox question.
Each of the following, if true, contributes to an explanation of the differences in recovery rates EXCEPT: *PrepTest52 Sec1 Q11*	→ The four wrong answers will provide facts that help explain the apparent discrepancy in recovery rates. The correct answer will not (it may deepen the paradox or simply be Outside the Scope)—a Paradox EXCEPT question.

Practice Step 1 of the Logical Reasoning Method on a handful of Paradox question stems. Take note of the verbs signaling a Paradox question. Is there any additional guidance in the stem helping you see what to look for as you untangle the stimulus? How would you characterize the correct and incorrect answer choices?

LSAT Question	My Analysis
28. Which of the following, if true, would most help to resolve the apparent conflict between the results of the surveys described above? *PrepTest58 Sec1 Q17*	
29. Each of the following, if true, would help to resolve the apparent discrepancy between the results of the two studies EXCEPT: *PrepTest62 Sec4 Q17*	
30. Which of the following, if true, most helps to explain the situation described above? *PrepTest58 Sec4 Q1*	

Here's how the LSAT expert viewed each of those question stems.

LSAT Question	Analysis
28. Which of the following, if true, would most help to resolve the apparent conflict between the results of the surveys described above? *PrepTest58 Sec1 Q17*	The correct answer will be a fact that reconciles an apparent discrepancy between the results of two surveys—a Paradox question.
29. Each of the following, if true, would help to resolve the apparent discrepancy between the results of the two studies EXCEPT: *PrepTest62 Sec4 Q17*	The four wrong answers will provide facts that explain why apparently discrepant study results are actually consistent. The correct answer will not (it might deepen the paradox or simply be Outside the Scope)—a Paradox EXCEPT question.
30. Which of the following, if true, most helps to explain the situation described above? *PrepTest58 Sec4 Q1*	"[E]xplain" indicates that there will be a seeming contradiction in the situation referred to. The correct answer will resolve this seeming conflict—a Paradox question.

Notice that the LSAT expert used the question stem not only to identify the question type but also to anticipate how she would need to approach the stimulus. Paradox EXCEPT questions ask for an answer choice that does *not* resolve the contradiction. Wrong answer choices provide four possible explanations, and the correct answer will likely be Outside the Scope of the facts or will only talk about one of the facts.

LSAT STRATEGY

Remember this about Paradox questions:

- The statements in a Paradox question stimulus appear to be contradictory only because a fact is missing that explains how everything can be true.
- The correct answer to a Paradox question must account for all of the facts and not merely state that the situation described is common or that one of the facts in the paradox is easy to understand.

Paradox questions run the gamut of difficulty levels. Don't become complacent if you find that some of the Paradox questions you practice seem obvious or easy. That's true of all question types. The best test takers are rigorous and vigilant against sloppy reading or taking statements for granted. Taking time to understand the nature of the paradoxical facts in the stimulus is essential to recognizing what is needed to explain them.

Before you practice full Paradox questions, take a look at the LSAT expert's analysis of the questions associated with the stimuli you've seen in this section. Pay close attention to how the expert predicts the kind of fact she will find in the correct answer and to why she eliminated each of the wrong answers in these questions.

LSAT Question	**Analysis**
A survey taken ten years ago of residents of area L showed that although living conditions were slightly below their country's average, most residents of L reported general satisfaction with their living conditions. However, this year the same survey found that while living conditions are now about the same as the national average, most residents of L report general dissatisfaction with their living conditions. →	**Step 2:** Survey results with two statements separated by "[h]owever," indicating a perceived discrepancy: Over the past 10 years, area L's conditions have improved from below national average to national average, *but* residents are less satisfied with their living conditions. Paradox: Residents are less satisfied even though the area has improved relative to the country.
Which one of the following, if true, would most help to resolve the apparent conflict between the results of the surveys described above? →	**Step 1:** The correct answer will be a fact that reconciles an apparent discrepancy between two surveys' results—a Paradox question.
	Step 3: The correct answer will explain why area L residents are more dissatisfied with their living conditions even though they have improved relative to the nation as a whole. →
(A) Residents of area L typically value aspects of living conditions different from the aspects of living conditions that are valued by residents of adjacent areas.	**Step 4:** Irrelevant Comparison. The paradox involves the views of area L residents now and 10 years ago, not how they rate conditions differently than their neighbors do. Eliminate. →
(B) Between the times that the two surveys were conducted, the average living conditions in L's country had substantially declined.	Correct. If the whole country has declined dramatically, area L could be worse off than it was a decade ago, even though it's no longer below the national average. →
(C) Optimal living conditions were established in the survey by taking into account governmental policies and public demands on three continents.	If anything, this makes the paradox even more confusing because it helps establish the validity of the survey. This does nothing to explain why the residents are less happy now. Eliminate. →
(D) Living conditions in an area generally improve only if residents perceive their situation as somehow in need of improvement.	Outside the Scope. Knowing what motivates people to improve their lives doesn't explain why area L's residents are less happy now. Eliminate. →
(E) Ten years ago the residents of area L were not aware that their living conditions were below the national average. *PrepTest58 Sec1 Q17* →	First, we don't know if the residents are any more aware of their circumstances today. Second, if they are, wouldn't knowing that they're about as well off as the average citizens make them more happy rather than less? To make this choice relevant, we need to speculate too much about additional information. Eliminate.

LSAT Question	Analysis
For one academic year all the students at a high school were observed. The aim was to test the hypothesis that studying more increased a student's chances of earning a higher grade. It turned out that the students who spent the most time studying did not earn grades as high as did many students who studied less. Nonetheless, the researchers concluded that the results of the observation supported the initial hypothesis.	**Step 2:** "Nonetheless" signals facts the author thinks are at odds with one another: the researchers concluded that more study time led to higher grades *despite the fact* that many students who studied less got better grades than those who studied more. Paradox: The researchers' conclusion (more study time = better grades) seems in conflict with its evidence (many who studied less got better grades).
Which one of the following, if true, most helps to explain why the researchers drew the conclusion described above?	**Step 1:** Because the researchers' conclusion is in need of explanation, there must be some other fact that casts doubt upon it. The correct answer will help explain why the researchers' conclusion makes sense even in light of that fact—a Paradox question.
	Step 3: To understand the researchers' conclusion, we need to know how studying affected individual students—in other words, how the same student would perform with and without more study hours.
(A) The students who spent the most time studying earned higher grades than did some students who studied for less time than the average.	**Step 4:** This doesn't affect the paradox at all. The stimulus states that students who studied more did not earn higher grades than many students who studied less. This leaves open the possibility that some students who studied more may have earned higher grades than some students who studied less. This still doesn't explain why studying more improves grades. Eliminate.
(B) The students tended to get slightly lower grades as the academic year progressed.	Irrelevant. This could happen for any number of reasons (harder material, absences, etc.) other than number of study hours. Moreover, this choice doesn't distinguish between the two groups. Eliminate.
(C) In each course, the more a student studied, the better his or her grade was in that course.	Correct. This compares the same student with and without more study hours. Since the student performed better when studying, the researchers' conclusion is confirmed.
(D) The students who spent the least time studying tended to be students with no more than average involvement in extracurricular activities.	Outside the Scope. Without knowing at least something about how extracurricular activities affect grades, this can't explain the paradox.
(E) Students who spent more time studying understood the course material better than other students did.	Outside the Scope. Understanding course materials is not the same as getting better grades. Eliminate.

PrepTest52 Sec1 Q14

LSAT Question	Analysis
Automated flight technology can guide an aircraft very reliably, from navigation to landing. Yet this technology, even when functioning correctly, is not a perfect safeguard against human error.	**Step 2:** "Yet" signals a perceived discrepancy: Automated flight technology is reliable *but* doesn't, even when it's working correctly, safeguard against human error.
	This stimulus is succinct. The paradox is that *while* technology can guide an airplane in many situations, it doesn't prevent human error.
Which one of the following, if true, most helps to explain the situation described above?	**Step 1:** "[E]xplain" indicates a Paradox question; there will be a seeming contradiction in the situation referred to. The correct answer will resolve this seeming conflict—a Paradox question.
	Step 3: The correct answer will be a fact that explains how human error still affects the automated system.
(A) Automated flight technology does not always function correctly.	**Step 4:** Irrelevant. The stimulus says that "even when functioning correctly," the systems don't prevent human error. Eliminate.
(B) Smaller aircraft do not always have their automated flight technology updated regularly.	Nothing in the stimulus addresses a need for updates. Besides, human error can be a problem "even when [the technology is] functioning correctly." Eliminate.
(C) If a plane's automated flight technology malfunctions, crew members have to operate the plane manually.	Outside the Scope. The paradox is that the technology is problematic even when it doesn't malfunction. Eliminate.
(D) Some airplane crashes are due neither to human error nor to malfunction of automated flight technology.	Irrelevant. The paradox is between technology and human error, not something else (Natural disaster? Sabotage?). Eliminate.
(E) Automated flight technology invariably executes exactly the commands that humans give it. *PrepTest58 Sec4 Q1*	Correct. Because humans program the flight technology, it might reliably execute flawed commands. This explains the paradox.

LSAT Question	Analysis
A 24-year study of 1,500 adults showed that those subjects with a high intake of foods rich in beta-carotene were much less likely to die from cancer or heart disease than were those with a low intake of such foods. On the other hand, taking beta-carotene supplements for 12 years had no positive or negative effect on the health of subjects in a separate study of 20,000 adults.	**Step 2:** "On the other hand" signals the apparent discrepancy: A 24-year study correlated a high beta-carotene diet with reduced cancer risk, *but* a 12-year study showed no correlation between beta-carotene supplements and reduced cancer risk. (Both studies used a large number of subjects, so sample size is not an issue.)
	Paradox: Two large-scale studies gave different results with respect to the relationship between beta-carotene and cancer. One study was twice as long and used a high beta-carotene diet instead of supplements.
Each of the following, if true, would help to resolve the apparent discrepancy between the results of the two studies EXCEPT:	**Step 1:** The four wrong answers will provide facts that explain why apparently discrepant study results are actually consistent. The correct answer will not (it might deepen the paradox or simply be Outside the Scope)—a Paradox EXCEPT question.
	Step 3: The wrong answers will contain facts showing why the duration of the studies or the different methods of taking the beta-carotene gave different results. The correct answer will leave the paradox unresolved.
(A) The human body processes the beta-carotene present in foods much more efficiently than it does beta-carotene supplements.	**Step 4:** This would explain why the 24-year study (food) showed a decrease in cancer while the 12-year study (supplements) did not. Eliminate.
(B) Beta-carotene must be taken for longer than 12 years to have any cancer-preventive effects.	This explains why the 24-year study (food) showed a decrease in cancer while the 12-year study (supplements) did not. Eliminate.
(C) Foods rich in beta-carotene also tend to contain other nutrients that assist in the human body's absorption of beta-carotene.	This explains why the 24-year study (food) showed a decrease in cancer while the 12-year study (supplements) did not. Eliminate.
(D) In the 12-year study, half of the subjects were given beta-carotene supplements and half were given a placebo.	Correct. This doesn't clear up anything. Without knowing the methodology of the 24-year study, it's not even clear that this is different. At any rate, it does nothing to explain why the people who got real supplements didn't show a decrease in cancer.
(E) In the 24-year study, the percentage of the subjects who had a high intake of beta-carotene-rich foods who smoked cigarettes was much smaller than the percentage of the subjects with a low intake of beta-carotene-rich foods who smoked.	This adds a relevant distinction between the studies. Smoking could increase cancer risk in the 12-year group. If this choice were true, it would help resolve the paradox. Eliminate.

PrepTest62 Sec4 Q17

In the Paradox EXCEPT question, notice that three of the wrong answer choices—(A), (B), and (C)—seized upon differences between the studies mentioned in the stimulus and explained how they could account for a difference in cancer rates. The other wrong answer—(E)—added a new fact, but one that, if true, presents another relevant distinction between the two studies. Smoking is a new *term* here, but it is not Outside the Scope because it is relevant to the precise paradox troubling the author.

Now, try some full Paradox questions. As you untangle the stimulus, paraphrase the apparent discrepancy in your own words. While you may not be able to predict the exact fact that the correct answer will contain, make sure you're preparing yourself to evaluate the choices by predicting the kind of fact that the right answer needs to have.

Practice

For each of the following, apply the Logical Reasoning Method to a Paradox question. Use the corresponding blanks to record your thinking for each step. After each, compare your work to the thinking of an LSAT expert on the following pages.

LSAT Question	My Analysis
31. Conservation officers justified their decision to remove a pack of ten coyotes from a small island by claiming that the coyotes, which preyed on wild cats and plover, were decimating the plover population and would soon wipe it out. After the coyotes were removed, however, the plover population plummeted dramatically, and within two years plover could no longer be found on the island.	**Step 2:**
Which one of the following would, if true, most help explain the phenomenon described above?	**Step 1:**
	Step 3:
(A) Plover are ground-nesting birds, which makes them easy prey for coyotes.	**Step 4:**
(B) Wild cat and plover populations tend to fluctuate together.	
(C) Coyotes are not susceptible to any of the diseases that commonly infect plover or wild cats.	
(D) The wild cat population on the island was once significantly larger than it is currently.	
(E) The coyotes preyed mainly on wild cats, and wild cats prey on plover.	

PrepTest56 Sec3 Q7

LSAT Question	My Analysis
32. A recent study confirmed that salt intake tends to increase blood pressure and found that, as a result, people with high blood pressure who significantly cut their salt intake during the study had lower blood pressure by the end of the study. However, it was also found that some people who had very high salt intake both before and throughout the study maintained very low blood pressure.	**Step 2:**
Which one of the following, if true, contributes the most to an explanation of the results of the study?	**Step 1:**
	Step 3:
(A) Study participants with high blood pressure who cut their salt intake only slightly during the study did not have significantly lower blood pressure by the end of the study.	**Step 4:**
(B) Salt intake is only one of several dietary factors associated with high blood pressure.	
(C) For most people who have high blood pressure, reducing salt intake is not the most effective dietary change they can make to reduce their blood pressure.	
(D) At the beginning of the study, some people who had very low salt intake also had very high blood pressure.	
(E) Persons suffering from abnormally low blood pressure have heightened salt cravings, which ensure that their blood pressure does not drop too low.	

PrepTest58 Sec4 Q20

LSAT Question	**My Analysis**
33. A recent study revealed that the percentage of people treated at large, urban hospitals who recover from their illnesses is lower than the percentage for people treated at smaller, rural hospitals.	**Step 2:**
Each of the following, if true, contributes to an explanation of the difference in recovery rates EXCEPT:	**Step 1:**
	Step 3:
(A) Because there are fewer patients to feed, nutritionists at small hospitals are better able to tailor meals to the dietary needs of each patient.	**Step 4:**
(B) The less friendly, more impersonal atmosphere of large hospitals can be a source of stress for patients at those hospitals.	
(C) Although large hospitals tend to draw doctors trained at the more prestigious schools, no correlation has been found between the prestige of a doctor's school and patients' recovery rate.	
(D) Because space is relatively scarce in large hospitals, doctors are encouraged to minimize the length of time that patients are held for observation following a medical procedure.	
(E) Doctors at large hospitals tend to have a greater number of patients and consequently less time to explain to staff and to patients how medications are to be administered.	

PrepTest52 Sec1 Q11

LSAT Question	My Analysis
34. The writing styles in works of high literary quality are not well suited to the avoidance of misinterpretation. For this reason, the writing in judicial decisions, which are primarily intended as determinations of law, is rarely of high literary quality. However, it is not uncommon to find writing of high literary quality in dissenting opinions, which are sometimes included in written decisions in cases heard by a panel of judges.	**Step 2:**
Which one of the following, if true, most helps to resolve the apparent discrepancy in the statements above?	**Step 1:**
	Step 3:
(A) It is not uncommon for more than one judge to have an influence on the way a dissenting opinion is written.	**Step 4:**
(B) Unlike literary works, legal opinions rely heavily on the use of technical terminology.	
(C) The law is not to any great extent determined by dissenting opinions.	
(D) Judges spend much more time reading judicial decisions than reading works of high literary quality.	
(E) Judicial decisions issued by panels of judges are likely to be more widely read than are judicial decisions issued by a single judge who hears a case alone.	

PrepTest56 Sec2 Q22

Check your work by studying the LSAT expert's analysis of the questions you just practiced. Review the analysis by following the steps of the Logical Reasoning Method and pay attention to why the expert eliminated each wrong answer (even if you got the question correct).

LSAT Question	Analysis
31. Conservation officers justified their decision to remove a pack of ten coyotes from a small island by claiming that the coyotes, which preyed on wild cats and plover, were decimating the plover population and would soon wipe it out. After the coyotes were removed, however, the plover population plummeted dramatically, and within two years plover could no longer be found on the island.	**Step 2:** A narrative with an unexpected outcome: In hopes of saving endangered plover, conservationists removed coyotes (which eat cats and plover), but the result was that the plover died out. Paradox: Removing a predator of an endangered prey species resulted in the extinction of the prey species.
Which one of the following would, if true, most help explain the phenomenon described above?	**Step 1:** "[E]xplain" indicates a Paradox question. There will be a seeming conflict in the phenomenon described.
	Step 3: There must be some reason that the stimulus mentions wild cats. If they, too, are predators of the plover, removing the cats' natural predators (the coyotes) may have indirectly harmed the plover.
(A) Plover are ground-nesting birds, which makes them easy prey for coyotes.	**Step 4:** 180. If plover were easy prey for coyotes, it's even more confusing why removing the coyotes did not help the plover. Eliminate.
(B) Wild cat and plover populations tend to fluctuate together.	This is vague. Does it mean that plover populations go up when cat populations do? If so, that makes the paradox even more confusing. Eliminate.
(C) Coyotes are not susceptible to any of the diseases that commonly infect plover or wild cats.	Outside the Scope. This doesn't say that coyotes prevent diseases that kill plover. If they did, then removing them could have harmed the plover. But just knowing that they don't catch the same diseases as the plover or the cats doesn't explain anything. Eliminate.
(D) The wild cat population on the island was once significantly larger than it is currently.	To make this relevant, too much outside information is required. Did the cat population go up or down after the coyotes were removed? Is it low now because the cats ate all of the plover? Who knows? Eliminate.
(E) The coyotes preyed mainly on wild cats, and wild cats prey on plover. *PrepTest56 Sec3 Q7*	Correct. This matches the prediction and explains the paradoxical result of removing the coyotes.

LSAT Question	Analysis
32. A recent study confirmed that salt intake tends to increase blood pressure and found that, as a result, people with high blood pressure who significantly cut their salt intake during the study had lower blood pressure by the end of the study. However, it was also found that some people who had very high salt intake both before and throughout the study maintained very low blood pressure.	**Step 2:** "However" signals the apparent contradiction: One group in the study had high blood pressure, cut their salt intake, and lowered their blood pressure, but another group had very low blood pressure, continued their high salt intake, and kept their very low blood pressure. Paradox: High salt intake increased blood pressure in some subjects (and lowering salt intake decreased this group's blood pressure) *while* another group maintained low blood pressure despite high salt intake.
Which one of the following, if true, contributes the most to an explanation of the results of the study?	**Step 1:** "[C]ontributes to . . . an explanation" signals a Paradox question. There will be an apparent conflict in the study's findings. The correct answer will show that there's no real conflict.
	Step 3: The correct answer will have to explain the pattern in the second group (as the first group confirmed that high salt intake increases blood pressure). We need a fact explaining why the second group is consistent with the study.
(A) Study participants with high blood pressure who cut their salt intake only slightly during the study did not have significantly lower blood pressure by the end of the study.	**Step 4:** This is consistent with the study and doesn't do anything to account for the high-salt, low–blood pressure group that presents the paradox. Eliminate.
(B) Salt intake is only one of several dietary factors associated with high blood pressure.	Outside the Scope. Salt intake is the only factor in the study. Eliminate.
(C) For most people who have high blood pressure, reducing salt intake is not the most effective dietary change they can make to reduce their blood pressure.	This is interesting information, but it does nothing to explain the paradoxical high-salt, low–blood pressure group. Eliminate.
(D) At the beginning of the study, some people who had very low salt intake also had very high blood pressure.	This group is irrelevant to the paradoxical results. They must have high blood pressure for some other reason. Eliminate.
(E) Persons suffering from abnormally low blood pressure have heightened salt cravings, which ensure that their blood pressure does not drop too low.	Correct. This explains the group of people who had low blood pressure despite high salt intake.

PrepTest58 Sec4 Q20

LSAT Question	Analysis
33. A recent study revealed that the percentage of people treated at large, urban hospitals who recover from their illnesses is lower than the percentage for people treated at smaller, rural hospitals.	**Step 2:** Study results: Recovery rates are lower for patients at large, urban hospitals than for those at small, rural hospitals.
	Paradox: Why would size or location make a difference in recovery rates?
Each of the following, if true, contributes to an explanation of the difference in recovery rates EXCEPT:	**Step 1:** A Paradox EXCEPT question—four answers will help explain a seeming conflict in the recovery rates data, but the correct answer will not. It might make the paradox more confusing, or it might be Outside the Scope (and simply *not explain* the rates).
	Step 3: All four wrong answers will help to explain why small and/or rural hospitals are better for recovering patients than large and/or urban hospitals are. The correct answer will either make large, urban hospitals sound better or it will be Outside the Scope.
(A) Because there are fewer patients to feed, nutritionists at small hospitals are better able to tailor meals to the dietary needs of each patient.	**Step 4:** This gives a reason smaller hospitals are better for recovering patients. Eliminate.
(B) The less friendly, more impersonal atmosphere of large hospitals can be a source of stress for patients at those hospitals.	This gives a reason large hospitals are worse for recovering patients. Eliminate.
(C) Although large hospitals tend to draw doctors trained at the more prestigious schools, no correlation has been found between the prestige of a doctor's school and patients' recovery rate.	Correct. This gives a fact that makes large hospitals unique but then turns around and says that fact is irrelevant to recovery rates. Because the right answer does *not* explain the paradox, this choice is correct.
(D) Because space is relatively scarce in large hospitals, doctors are encouraged to minimize the length of time that patients are held for observation following a medical procedure.	This gives a reason large hospitals are worse for recovering patients. Eliminate.
(E) Doctors at large hospitals tend to have a greater number of patients and consequently less time to explain to staff and to patients how medications are to be administered.	This gives a reason large hospitals are worse for recovering patients. Eliminate.

PrepTest52 Sec1 Q11

LSAT Question	Analysis
34. The writing styles in works of high literary quality are not well suited to the avoidance of misinterpretation. For this reason, the writing in judicial decisions, which are primarily intended as determinations of law, is rarely of high literary quality. However, it is not uncommon to find writing of high literary quality in dissenting opinions, which are sometimes included in written decisions in cases heard by a panel of judges.	**Step 2:** "However" signals the paradox: Writing in "high literary" style is open to misinterpretation and thus, not used in judicial decisions (which settle the meaning of law), *but* the style is often found in dissenting opinions. Paradox: A style inappropriate to the determination of the law is found in dissenting judicial opinions.
Which one of the following, if true, most helps to resolve the apparent discrepancy in the statements above?	**Step 1:** A straightforward Paradox question stem— the correct answer will help resolve an apparent discrepancy.
	Step 3: The correct answer will present a fact about dissenting opinions that explains why it's okay for them to have "high literary" style even though it is open to misinterpretation.
(A) It is not uncommon for more than one judge to have an influence on the way a dissenting opinion is written.	**Step 4:** This is interesting, but it doesn't explain why dissenting opinions are in a writing style inappropriate to most judicial decisions. Eliminate.
(B) Unlike literary works, legal opinions rely heavily on the use of technical terminology.	This helps explain why judicial decisions aren't written like literature, but that just leaves the confusion over why dissenting opinions are written that way. Eliminate.
(C) The law is not to any great extent determined by dissenting opinions.	Correct. Because the dissenting opinions are not used to determine the meaning of law, the high literary style isn't problematic, as it is in majority judicial opinions.
(D) Judges spend much more time reading judicial decisions than reading works of high literary quality.	This might help us understand judicial writing style generally, but it doesn't clear up the odd fact that dissenting opinions are more often in the "high literary" style. Eliminate.
(E) Judicial decisions issued by panels of judges are likely to be more widely read than are judicial decisions issued by a single judge who hears a case alone.	Irrelevant Comparison. How widely read an opinion is doesn't help clear up the apparent discrepancy in writing styles. Eliminate.

PrepTest56 Sec2 Q22

That set of practice questions gives you a good idea of how the testmaker varies the difficulty of Paradox questions. The first question—about coyotes and plover—is answered correctly by over 80 percent of test takers. The last—on judicial opinions—is answered correctly by less than 40 percent of test takers. What accounts for that huge difference in performance? Some of the factors are simple—most test takers are probably more familiar with an ecological situation similar to that presented in the Coyotes and Plover question than they are with academic-sounding analyses of judicial writing style. Other factors may be subtler: for example, the prose is denser in the Judicial Writing Styles question, in both the stimulus and the answer choices. For you as a well-trained test taker, however, those two questions should seem more alike than different. In both, the author explains a situation and highlights what appears to be a surprising outcome. You can apply the Logical Reasoning Method and the strategies you learned (such as spotting the Contrast Keyword) to both examples. As you continue to practice with questions in the Question Pool, you'll find that not only can you handle the easiest Paradox questions with more confidence, but you'll also start to feel that even the harder examples are routine and follow the same patterns.

Reflection

Keep an eye out for apparent discrepancies, seeming contradictions, and paradoxes in your day-to-day life. The next time a friend sees something that puzzles him and asks you, "How can that be?" take the opportunity to practice your Paradox question skills. Find facts that show how the situation can be resolved, reconciled, or explained. You may be surprised to discover how often we fail to explain paradoxes but instead respond by saying things like, "Oh, that happens all the time; don't be surprised," or how often (just as do wrong answers on the LSAT) we explain only one side of the discrepancy and fail to clear up the paradox at all.

Summary

Congratulations. Over the last three chapters, you've learned how to answer all of the Logical Reasoning question types on the LSAT. Continue to improve your performance on non-argument-based questions with the items in the Question Pool following this section. When you're ready to move on, Chapter 12 covers Logical Reasoning section management; it will give you the best strategies for being efficient and effective with your time, not getting bogged down, and using the 35 minutes in each Logical Reasoning section to get the most points possible.

QUESTION POOL

Inference

Previously Seen Stimuli

Here are a few of the stimuli covered earlier in this chapter or elsewhere in the book. This time they appear with answer choices. These questions are arranged in order of increasing difficulty.

1. Although some nutritional facts about soft drinks are listed on their labels, exact caffeine content is not. Listing exact caffeine content would make it easier to limit, but not eliminate, one's caffeine intake. If it became easier for people to limit, but not eliminate, their caffeine intake, many people would do so, which would improve their health.

    If all the statements above are true, which one of the following must be true?

    (A) The health of at least some people would improve if exact caffeine content were listed on soft-drink labels.
    (B) Many people will be unable to limit their caffeine intake if exact caffeine content is not listed on soft-drink labels.
    (C) Many people will find it difficult to eliminate their caffeine intake if they have to guess exactly how much caffeine is in their soft drinks.
    (D) People who wish to eliminate, rather than simply limit, their caffeine intake would benefit if exact caffeine content were listed on soft-drink labels.
    (E) The health of at least some people would worsen if everyone knew exactly how much caffeine was in their soft drinks.

    PrepTest62 Sec2 Q6

2. Music historian: Some critics lament the fact that impoverished postwar recording studios forced early bebop musicians to record extremely short solos, thus leaving a misleading record of their music. But these musicians' beautifully concise playing makes the recordings superb artistic works instead of mere representations of their live solos. Furthermore, the conciseness characteristic of early bebop musicians' recordings fostered a compactness in their subsequent live playing, which the playing of the next generation lacks.

    The music historian's statements, if true, most strongly support which one of the following?

    (A) Representations of live solos generally are not valuable artistic works.
    (B) The difficult postwar recording conditions had some beneficial consequences for bebop.
    (C) Short bebop recordings are always superior to longer ones.
    (D) The music of the generation immediately following early bebop is of lower overall quality than early bebop.
    (E) Musicians will not record extremely short solos unless difficult recording conditions force them to do so.

    PrepTest58 Sec1 Q10

The explanations to these
questions begin on page 763.

3. Inertia affects the flow of water pumped through a closed system of pipes. When the pump is first switched on, the water, which has mass, takes time to reach full speed. When the pump is switched off, inertia causes the decrease in the water flow to be gradual. The effects of inductance in electrical circuits are similar to the effects of inertia in water pipes.

The information above provides the most support for which one of the following?

(A) The rate at which electrical current flows is affected by inductance.
(B) The flow of electrical current in a circuit requires inertia.
(C) Inertia in the flow of water pumped by an electrically powered pump is caused by inductance in the pump's circuits.
(D) Electrical engineers try to minimize the effects of inductance in electrical circuits.
(E) When a water pump is switched off it continues to pump water for a second or two.

PrepTest52 Sec1 Q7

4. In West Calverton, most pet stores sell exotic birds, and most of those that sell exotic birds also sell tropical fish. However, any pet store there that sells tropical fish but not exotic birds does sell gerbils; and no independently owned pet stores in West Calverton sell gerbils.

If the statements above are true, which one of the following must be true?

(A) Most pet stores in West Calverton that are not independently owned do not sell exotic birds.
(B) No pet stores in West Calverton that sell tropical fish and exotic birds sell gerbils.
(C) Some pet stores in West Calverton that sell gerbils also sell exotic birds.
(D) No independently owned pet store in West Calverton sells tropical fish but not exotic birds.
(E) Any independently owned pet store in West Calverton that does not sell tropical fish sells exotic birds.

PrepTest62 Sec2 Q19

5. Proofs relying crucially on computers provide less certainty than do proofs not requiring computers. Human cognition alone cannot verify computer-dependent proofs; such proofs can never provide the degree of certainty that attends our judgments concerning, for instance, simple arithmetical facts, which can be verified by human calculation. Of course, in these cases one often uses electronic calculators, but here the computer is a convenience rather than a supplement to human cognition.

The statements above, if true, most strongly support which one of the following?

(A) Only if a proof's result is arrived at without the help of a computer can one judge with any degree of certainty that the proof is correct.
(B) We can never be completely sure that proofs relying crucially on computers do not contain errors that humans do not detect.
(C) Whenever a computer replaces human calculation in a proof, the degree of certainty provided by the proof is reduced.
(D) If one can corroborate something by human calculation, one can be completely certain of it.
(E) It is impossible to supplement the cognitive abilities of humans by means of artificial devices such as computers.

PrepTest58 Sec4 Q15

6. Ecologist: Without the intervention of conservationists, squirrel monkeys will become extinct. But they will survive if large tracts of second-growth forest habitat are preserved for them. Squirrel monkeys flourish in second-growth forest because of the plentiful supply of their favorite insects and fruit.

   Which one of the following can be properly inferred from the ecologist's statements?

   (A) No habitat other than second-growth forest contains plentiful supplies of squirrel monkeys' favorite insects and fruit.

   (B) At least some of the conservationists who intervene to help the squirrel monkeys survive will do so by preserving second-growth forest habitat for the monkeys.

   (C) Without plentiful supplies of their favorite insects and fruit, squirrel monkeys will become extinct.

   (D) If conservationists intervene to help squirrel monkeys survive, then the squirrel monkeys will not become extinct.

   (E) Without the intervention of conservationists, large tracts of second-growth forest habitat will not be preserved for squirrel monkeys.

   PrepTest56 Sec2 Q23

New Questions

Try out some questions that have not yet appeared. These questions are arranged in order of increasing difficulty.

7. Early urban societies could not have been maintained without large-scale farming nearby. This is because other methods of food acquisition, such as foraging, cannot support populations as dense as urban ones. Large-scale farming requires irrigation, which remained unfeasible in areas far from rivers or lakes until more recent times.

Which one of the following is most strongly supported by the information above?

(A) Most peoples who lived in early times lived in areas near rivers or lakes.
(B) Only if farming is possible in the absence of irrigation can societies be maintained in areas far from rivers or lakes.
(C) In early times it was not possible to maintain urban societies in areas far from rivers or lakes.
(D) Urban societies with farms near rivers or lakes do not have to rely upon irrigation to meet their farming needs.
(E) Early rural societies relied more on foraging than on agriculture for food.

PrepTest52 Sec3 Q14

8. Some paleontologists believe that certain species of dinosaurs guarded their young in protective nests long after the young hatched. As evidence, they cite the discovery of fossilized hadrosaur babies and adolescents in carefully designed nests. But similar nests for hatchlings and adolescents are constructed by modern crocodiles, even though crocodiles guard their young only for a very brief time after they hatch. Hence _____.

Which one of the following most logically completes the argument?

(A) paleontologists who believe that hadrosaurs guarded their young long after the young hatched have no evidence to support this belief
(B) we will never be able to know the extent to which hadrosaurs guarded their young
(C) hadrosaurs guarded their young for at most very brief periods after hatching
(D) it is unclear whether what we learn about hadrosaurs from their fossilized remains tells us anything about other dinosaurs
(E) the construction of nests for hatchlings and adolescents is not strong evidence for the paleontologists' belief

PrepTest52 Sec1 Q13

9. Almost all advances in genetic research give rise to ethical dilemmas. Government is the exclusive source of funding for most genetic research; those projects not funded by government are funded solely by corporations. One or the other of these sources of funding is necessary for any genetic research.

If all the statements above are true, then which one of the following must be true?

(A) Most advances in genetic research occur in projects funded by government rather than by corporations.
(B) Most genetic research funded by government results in advances that give rise to ethical dilemmas.
(C) At least some advances in genetic research occur in projects funded by corporations.
(D) No ethical dilemmas resulting from advances in genetic research arise without government or corporate funding.
(E) As long as government continues to fund genetic research, that research will give rise to ethical dilemmas.

PrepTest58 Sec1 Q15

10. As part of a new trend in the writing of history, an emphasis on the details of historical events and motivations has replaced the previous emphasis on overarching historical trends and movements, with the result that the latter are often overlooked. In consequence, the ominous parallels that may exist between historical trends and current trends are also overlooked, which lessens our ability to learn from history.

The statements above, if true, most strongly support which one of the following?

(A) Studying the details of historical events and motivations lessens our ability to learn from history.
(B) Overarching historical trends and movements can be discerned only when details of historical events and motivations are not emphasized.
(C) Those who attend to overall trends and movements in history and not to details are the best able to learn from history.
(D) A change in emphasis in the interpretation of history has lessened our ability to learn from history.
(E) History should be interpreted in a way that gives equal emphasis to overarching historical trends and movements and to the details of historical events and motivations.

PrepTest56 Sec3 Q15

11. Researchers had three groups of professional cyclists cycle for one hour at different levels of intensity. Members of groups A, B, and C cycled at rates that sustained, for an hour, pulses of about 60 percent, 70 percent, and 85 percent, respectively, of the recommended maximum pulse rate for recreational cyclists. Most members of Group A reported being less depressed and angry afterward. Most members of Group B did not report these benefits. Most members of Group C reported feeling worse in these respects than before the exercise.

Which one of the following is most strongly supported by the information above?

(A) The higher the pulse rate attained in sustained exercise, the less psychological benefit the exercise tends to produce.

(B) The effect that a period of cycling has on the mood of professional cyclists tends to depend at least in part on how intense the cycling is.

(C) For professional cyclists, the best exercise from the point of view of improving mood is cycling that pushes the pulse no higher than 60 percent of the maximum pulse rate.

(D) Physical factors, including pulse rate, contribute as much to depression as do psychological factors.

(E) Moderate cycling tends to benefit professional cyclists physically as much or more than intense cycling.

PrepTest52 Sec1 Q15

12. Most large nurseries sell raspberry plants primarily to commercial raspberry growers and sell only plants that are guaranteed to be disease-free. However, the shipment of raspberry plants that Johnson received from Wally's Plants carried a virus that commonly afflicts raspberries.

Which one of the following is most strongly supported by the information above?

(A) If Johnson is a commercial raspberry grower and Wally's Plants is not a large nursery, then the shipment of raspberry plants that Johnson received was probably guaranteed to be disease-free.

(B) Johnson is probably not a commercial raspberry grower if the shipment of raspberry plants that Johnson received from Wally's Plants was not entirely as it was guaranteed to be.

(C) If Johnson is not a commercial raspberry grower, then Wally's Plants is probably not a large nursery.

(D) Wally's Plants is probably not a large, well-run nursery if it sells its raspberry plants primarily to commercial raspberry growers.

(E) If Wally's Plants is a large nursery, then the raspberry plants that Johnson received in the shipment were probably not entirely as they were guaranteed to be.

PrepTest62 Sec2 Q21

13. In a recent study of arthritis, researchers tried but failed to find any correlation between pain intensity and any of those features of the weather—humidity, temperature swings, barometric pressure—usually cited by arthritis sufferers as the cause of their increased pain. Those arthritis sufferers in the study who were convinced of the existence of such a correlation gave widely varying accounts of the time delay between the occurrence of what they believed to be the relevant feature of the weather and the increased intensity of the pain. Thus, this study _____.

Of the following, which one most logically completes the argument?

(A) indicates that the weather affects some arthritis sufferers more quickly than it does other arthritis sufferers

(B) indicates that arthritis sufferers' beliefs about the causes of the pain they feel may affect their assessment of the intensity of that pain

(C) suggests that arthritis sufferers are imagining the correlation they assert to exist

(D) suggests that some people are more susceptible to weather-induced arthritis pain than are others

(E) suggests that the scientific investigation of possible links between weather and arthritis pain is impossible

PrepTest62 Sec4 Q24

14. Two months ago a major shipment of pythons arrived from Africa, resulting in a great number of inexpensive pythons in pet stores. Anyone interested in buying a python, however, should beware: many pythons hatched in Africa are afflicted with a deadly liver disease. Although a few pythons recently hatched in North America have this disease, a much greater proportion of African-hatched pythons have it. The disease is difficult to detect in its early stages, and all pythons die within six months of contracting the disease.

Which one of the following statements can be properly inferred from the statements above?

(A) Some pythons hatched in North America may appear fine but will die within six months as a result of the liver disease.

(B) Pythons that hatch in Africa are more susceptible to the liver disease than are pythons that hatch in North America.

(C) Any python that has not died by the age of six months does not have the liver disease.

(D) The pythons are inexpensively priced because many of them suffer from the liver disease.

(E) Pythons hatched in neither Africa nor North America are not afflicted with the liver disease.

PrepTest58 Sec4 Q9

15. In response to several bacterial infections traced to its apple juice, McElligott now flash pasteurizes its apple juice by quickly heating and immediately rechilling it. Intensive pasteurization, in which juice is heated for an hour, eliminates bacteria more effectively than does any other method, but is likely to destroy the original flavor. However, because McElligott's citrus juices have not been linked to any bacterial infections, they remain unpasteurized.

The statements above, if true, provide the most support for which one of the following claims?

(A) McElligott's citrus juices contain fewer infectious bacteria than do citrus juices produced by other companies.
(B) McElligott's apple juice is less likely to contain infectious bacteria than are McElligott's citrus juices.
(C) McElligott's citrus juices retain more of the juices' original flavor than do any pasteurized citrus juices.
(D) The most effective method for eliminating bacteria from juice is also the method most likely to destroy flavor.
(E) Apple juice that undergoes intensive pasteurization is less likely than McElligott's apple juice is to contain bacteria.

PrepTest52 Sec1 Q24

16. Certain bacteria that produce hydrogen sulfide as a waste product would die if directly exposed to oxygen. The hydrogen sulfide reacts with oxygen, removing it and so preventing it from harming the bacteria. Furthermore, the hydrogen sulfide tends to kill other organisms in the area, thereby providing the bacteria with a source of food. As a result, a dense colony of these bacteria produces for itself an environment in which it can continue to thrive indefinitely.

Which one of the following is most strongly supported by the information above?

(A) A dense colony of the bacteria can indefinitely continue to produce enough hydrogen sulfide to kill other organisms in the area and to prevent oxygen from harming the bacteria.
(B) The hydrogen sulfide produced by the bacteria kills other organisms in the area by reacting with and removing oxygen.
(C) Most organisms, if killed by the hydrogen sulfide produced by the bacteria, can provide a source of food for the bacteria.
(D) The bacteria can continue to thrive indefinitely only in an environment in which the hydrogen sulfide they produce has removed all oxygen and killed other organisms in the area.
(E) If any colony of bacteria produces hydrogen sulfide as a waste product, it thereby ensures that it is both provided with a source of food and protected from harm by oxygen.

PrepTest52 Sec3 Q23

Principle

Previously Seen Stimuli

Here are a few of the stimuli covered earlier in this chapter or elsewhere in the book. This time they appear with answer choices. These questions are arranged in order of increasing difficulty.

17. Columnist: Although there is and should be complete freedom of thought and expression, that does not mean that there is nothing wrong with exploiting depraved popular tastes for the sake of financial gain.

    Which one of the following judgments conforms most closely to the principle cited by the columnist?

    (A) The government should grant artists the right to create whatever works of art they want to create so long as no one considers those works to be depraved.
    (B) People who produce depraved movies have the freedom to do so, but that means that they also have the freedom to refrain from doing so.
    (C) There should be no laws restricting what books are published, but publishing books that pander to people with depraved tastes is not thereby morally acceptable.
    (D) The public has the freedom to purchase whatever recordings are produced, but that does not mean that the government may not limit the production of recordings deemed to be depraved.
    (E) One who advocates complete freedom of speech should not criticize others for saying things that he or she believes to exhibit depraved tastes.

    PrepTest58 Sec1 Q21

18. Historian: In rebuttal of my claim that West influenced Stuart, some people point out that West's work is mentioned only once in Stuart's diaries. But Stuart's diaries mention several meetings with West, and Stuart's close friend, Abella, studied under West. Furthermore, Stuart's work often uses West's terminology which, though now commonplace, none of Stuart's contemporaries used.

    Which one of the following propositions is most supported by the historian's statements, if those statements are true?

    (A) Stuart's discussions with Abella were one of the means by which West influenced Stuart.
    (B) It is more likely that Stuart influenced West than that West influenced Stuart.
    (C) Stuart's contemporaries were not influenced by West.
    (D) Stuart's work was not entirely free from West's influence
    (E) Because of Stuart's influence on other people, West's terminology is now commonplace.

    PrepTest52 Sec3 Q18

New Questions

Try out some questions that have not yet appeared. These questions are arranged in order of increasing difficulty.

19. To discover what percentage of teenagers believe in telekinesis—the psychic ability to move objects without physically touching them—a recent survey asked a representative sample of teenagers whether they agreed with the following statement: "A person's thoughts can influence the movement of physical objects." But because this statement is particularly ambiguous and is amenable to a naturalistic, uncontroversial interpretation, the survey's responses are also ambiguous.

    The reasoning above conforms most closely to which one of the following general propositions?

    (A) Uncontroversial statements are useless in surveys.
    (B) Every statement is amenable to several interpretations.
    (C) Responses to surveys are always unambiguous if the survey's questions are well phrased.
    (D) Responses people give to poorly phrased questions are likely to be ambiguous.
    (E) Statements about psychic phenomena can always be given naturalistic interpretations.

    PrepTest62 Sec4 Q2

20. Spreading iron particles over the surface of the earth's oceans would lead to an increase in phytoplankton, decreasing the amount of carbon dioxide in the atmosphere and thereby counteracting the greenhouse effect. But while counteracting the greenhouse effect is important, the side effects of an iron-seeding strategy have yet to be studied. Since the oceans represent such an important resource, this response to the greenhouse effect should not be implemented immediately.

    The reasoning above most closely conforms to which one of the following principles?

    (A) A problem-solving strategy should be implemented if the side effects of the strategy are known.
    (B) Implementing a problem-solving strategy that alters an important resource is impermissible if the consequences are not adequately understood.
    (C) We should not implement a problem-solving strategy if the consequences of doing so are more serious than the problem itself.
    (D) We should not implement a problem-solving strategy if that strategy requires altering an important resource.
    (E) As long as there is a possibility that a strategy for solving a problem may instead exacerbate that problem, such a solution should not be adopted.

    PrepTest52 Sec3 Q11

21. Vanessa: All computer code must be written by a pair of programmers working at a single workstation. This is needed to prevent programmers from writing idiosyncratic code that can be understood only by the original programmer.

    Jo: Most programming projects are kept afloat by the best programmers on the team, who are typically at least 100 times more productive than the worst. Since they generally work best when they work alone, the most productive programmers must be allowed to work by themselves.

    Each of the following assignments of computer programmers is consistent both with the principle expressed by Vanessa and with the principle expressed by Jo EXCEPT:

    (A) Olga and Kensuke are both programmers of roughly average productivity who feel that they are more productive when working alone. They have been assigned to work together at a single workstation.
    (B) John is experienced but is not among the most productive programmers on the team. He has been assigned to mentor Tyrone, a new programmer who is not yet very productive. They are to work together at a single workstation.
    (C) Although not among the most productive programmers on the team, Chris is more productive than Jennifer. They have been assigned to work together at a single workstation.
    (D) Yolanda is the most productive programmer on the team. She has been assigned to work with Mike, who is also very productive. They are to work together at the same workstation.
    (E) Kevin and Amy both have a reputation for writing idiosyncratic code; neither is unusually productive. They have been assigned to work together at the same workstation.

    PrepTest62 Sec2 Q18

Paradox

Previously Seen Stimuli

Here is a stimulus covered earlier in the chapter. This time it appears with answer choices.

22. There are two ways to manage an existing transportation infrastructure: continuous maintenance at adequate levels, and periodic radical reconstruction. Continuous maintenance dispenses with the need for radical reconstruction, and radical reconstruction is necessitated by failing to perform continuous maintenance. Over the long run, continuous maintenance is far less expensive; nevertheless, it almost never happens.

    Which one of the following, if true, most contributes to an explanation of why the first alternative mentioned is almost never adopted?

    (A) Since different parts of the transportation infrastructure are the responsibility of different levels of government, radical reconstruction projects are very difficult to coordinate efficiently.

    (B) When funds for transportation infrastructure maintenance are scarce, they are typically distributed in proportion to the amount of traffic that is borne by different elements of the infrastructure.

    (C) If continuous maintenance is performed at less-than-adequate levels, the need for radical reconstruction will often arise later than if maintenance had been restricted to responding to emergencies.

    (D) Radical reconstruction projects are, in general, too costly to be paid for from current revenue.

    (E) For long periods, the task of regular maintenance lacks urgency, since the consequences of neglecting it are very slow to manifest themselves.

    PrepTest52 Sec3 Q20

New Questions

Try out some questions that have not yet appeared. These questions are arranged in order of increasing difficulty.

23. Researcher: Over the course of three decades, we kept records of the average beak size of two populations of the same species of bird, one wild population, the other captive. During this period, the average beak size of the captive birds did not change, while the average beak size of the wild birds decreased significantly.

    Which one of the following, if true, most helps to explain the researcher's findings?

    (A) The small-beaked wild birds were easier to capture and measure than the large-beaked wild birds.
    (B) The large-beaked wild birds were easier to capture and measure than the small-beaked wild birds.
    (C) Changes in the wild birds' food supply during the study period favored the survival of small-beaked birds over large-beaked birds.
    (D) The average body size of the captive birds remained the same over the study period.
    (E) The researcher measured the beaks of some of the wild birds on more than one occasion.

    PrepTest62 Sec4 Q7

24. Heart attacks are most likely to occur on Mondays. The accepted explanation is that because Monday is the first day of the workweek, people feel more stress on Mondays than on other days. However, research shows that even unemployed retired people are more likely to have heart attacks on Mondays than on other days.

    Which one of the following, if true, most helps to explain the increased likelihood that an unemployed retiree will have a heart attack on a Monday?

    (A) Because they associate Monday with work, retired people are more likely to begin large projects on Mondays.
    (B) Many retired people take up part-time jobs after they retire from their careers.
    (C) People seldom change their dietary and other health habits after retirement.
    (D) Stress is the major factor influencing the risk of heart attack.
    (E) Unemployed retired people are even more likely to have heart attacks than are people who have jobs.

    PrepTest56 Sec2 Q13

25. Working residents of Springfield live, on average, farther from their workplaces than do working residents of Rorchester. Thus, one would expect that the demand for public transportation would be greater in Springfield than in Rorchester. However, Springfield has only half as many bus routes as Rorchester.

    Each of the following, if true, contributes to a resolution of the apparent discrepancy described above EXCEPT:

    (A) Three-fourths of the Springfield workforce is employed at the same factory outside the city limits.
    (B) The average number of cars per household is higher in Springfield than in Rorchester.
    (C) Rorchester has fewer railway lines than Springfield.
    (D) Buses in Springfield run more frequently and on longer routes than in Rorchester.
    (E) Springfield has a larger population than Rorchester does.

    PrepTest58 Sec1 Q8

26. Astronomer: Earlier estimates of the distances of certain stars from Earth would mean that these stars are about 1 billion years older than the universe itself, an impossible scenario. My estimates of the distances indicate that these stars are much farther away than previously thought. And the farther away the stars are, the greater their intrinsic brightness must be, given their appearance to us on Earth. So the new estimates of these stars' distances from Earth help resolve the earlier conflict between the ages of these stars and the age of the universe.

    Which one of the following, if true, most helps to explain why the astronomer's estimates of the stars' distances from Earth help resolve the earlier conflict between the ages of these stars and the age of the universe?

    (A) The stars are the oldest objects yet discovered in the universe.
    (B) The younger the universe is, the more bright stars it is likely to have.
    (C) The brighter a star is, the younger it is.
    (D) How bright celestial objects appear to be depends on how far away from the observer they are.
    (E) New telescopes allow astronomers to see a greater number of distant stars.

    PrepTest62 Sec2 Q20

27. Sociologist: A recent study of 5,000 individuals found, on the basis of a physical exam, that more than 25 percent of people older than 65 were malnourished, though only 12 percent of the people in this age group fell below government poverty standards. In contrast, a greater percentage of the people 65 or younger fell below poverty standards than were found in the study to be malnourished.

Each of the following, if true, helps to explain the findings of the study cited by the sociologist EXCEPT:

(A) Doctors are less likely to correctly diagnose and treat malnutrition in their patients who are over 65 than in their younger patients.

(B) People over 65 are more likely to take medications that increase their need for certain nutrients than are people 65 or younger.

(C) People over 65 are more likely to suffer from loss of appetite due to medication than are people 65 or younger.

(D) People 65 or younger are no more likely to fall below government poverty standards than are people over 65.

(E) People 65 or younger are less likely to have medical conditions that interfere with their digestion than are people over 65.

PrepTest62 Sec4 Q26

28. Farmer: Because water content is what makes popcorn pop, the kernels must dry at just the right speed to trap the correct amount of water. The best way to achieve this effect is to have the sun dry the corn while the corn is still in the field, but I always dry the ears on a screen in a warm, dry room.

Which one of the following, if true, most helps to resolve the apparent discrepancy between the farmer's theory and practice?

(A) The region in which the farmer grows popcorn experiences a long, cloudy season that begins shortly before the popcorn in fields would begin to dry.

(B) Leaving popcorn to dry on its stalks in the field is the least expensive method of drying it.

(C) Drying popcorn on its stalks in the field is only one of several methods that allow the kernels' water content to reach acceptable levels.

(D) When popcorn does not dry sufficiently, it will still pop, but it will take several minutes to do so, even under optimal popping conditions.

(E) If popcorn is allowed to dry too much, it will not pop.

PrepTest58 Sec4 Q7

29. Most economists believe that reducing the price of any product generally stimulates demand for it. However, most wine merchants have found that reducing the price of domestic wines to make them more competitive with imported wines with which they were previously comparably priced is frequently followed by an increase in sales of those imported wines.

Which one of the following, if true, most helps to reconcile the belief of most economists with the consequences observed by most wine merchants?

(A) Economists' studies of the prices of grocery items and their rates of sales rarely cover alcoholic beverages.

(B) Few merchants of any kind have detailed knowledge of economic theories about the relationship between item prices and sales rates.

(C) Consumers are generally willing to forgo purchasing other items they desire in order to purchase a superior wine.

(D) Imported wines in all price ranges are comparable in quality to domestic wines that cost less.

(E) An increase in the demand for a consumer product is compatible with an increase in demand for a competing product.

PrepTest52 Sec3 Q22

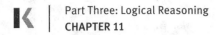

These explanations refer to
questions that begin on page 751.

ANSWERS AND EXPLANATIONS

Inference

1. (A) Inference

Step 1: Identify the Question Type

The question "[W]hich one of the following must be true?" asks us to draw an inference from the statements in the stimulus.

Step 2: Untangle the Stimulus

Read the stimulus for what is true: (1) soft drink labels do not contain exact caffeine content; (2) if exact caffeine content were listed, it would be easier to limit caffeine intake, but not eliminate it; (3) if it were easier to limit intake, many people would do so, and limiting intake would improve their health.

Step 3: Make a Prediction

When reading a sequence of likely consequences like this, look for the most definite statements of fact rather than struggling to make a prediction. The correct answer could be a number of things, so it's best to take stock of what you know.

The most definite statements are that (1) exact caffeine content is not provided on soft drinks, (2) caffeine intake wouldn't be eliminated by content labeling, and (3) many people would limit intake if caffeine content was labeled and this would improve their health.

Step 4: Evaluate the Answer Choices

(A) follows directly from the last statement. "At least some" on the LSAT means "at least one," and this is consistent with "many."

(B) is Outside the Scope. We know what content labeling enables people to do. We do not know what effect the absence of content labeling has. (Maybe people could limit their intake without the information or get the information another way.)

(C) is Outside the Scope. The facts provide us with no information about the difficulties of eliminating caffeine intake other than the fact that content labeling doesn't help.

(D) is a 180. The facts state that content labeling does not help eliminate caffeine intake.

(E) could be true, but not necessarily. Some people's health might not improve as a result of content labeling, but it doesn't follow that some people's health would worsen.

2. (B) Inference

Step 1: Identify the Question Stem

The stem tells us that the stimulus is a set of statements, not an argument, and that those statements will support our choice of the right answer. Those are both strong clues that this is an Inference question.

Step 2: Untangle the Stimulus

The music historian points out that some critics think that the poverty of postwar recording studios was bad for bebop because it forced them to record short solos. But the historian believes that the concise nature of these recordings makes them superb artistic works and contributed to a conciseness in the musicians' live playing as well.

Step 3: Make a Prediction

There's no Formal Logic in these statements, and not very many connections can be made between the statements. So we should proceed directly to the choices, keeping in mind that the correct answer is a statement that must be true if the music historian's statements are true.

Step 4: Evaluate the Answers

(A) is unsupported because the historian doesn't suggest that representations of live solos have no artistic value at all; he merely suggests that they are not comparable to the recorded solos.

(B), however, is directly supported because it accurately summarizes the historian's main points. If, as a result of the impoverished postwar recording conditions, bebop musicians recorded solos that survive as superb artistic works and that brought a worthwhile conciseness to their live solos, then the bad conditions seem to have had some beneficial consequences.

(C) is ruined by the word "always." The historian indicates that the conciseness of these recorded solos is of value, but this isn't to say that short recordings are invariably better than longer ones. That's too broad a statement to be supported by this stimulus.

(D) similarly uses the misleading word "overall." The live music of the generation immediately following bebop does lack the compactness of early bebop musicians' live music, but this is just one factor contributing to the overall quality of these musicians' work.

(E) says that difficult recording conditions are necessary for the recording of short solos, an idea that is completely unsupported by the stimulus. The difficult conditions contributed to the shortness of the solos, but perhaps other conditions could have just as easily caused early bebop musicians to record short solos.

These explanations refer to questions that begin on page 752.

Part Three: Logical Reasoning
Non-Argument Questions

K

3. (A) Inference ★★☆☆

Step 1: Identify the Question Type

Because the information in the stimulus "provides the most support" for the right answer, the right answer must be true based on the stimulus. This is an Inference question.

Step 2: Untangle the Stimulus

Don't get caught up in the scientific language. As with any other Inference question, take inventory of the information given in the stimulus. Inertia affects the flow of water. When the pump is switched on, it takes time to get the water up to speed; when the pump is switched off, it takes time for the water to slow down and stop. The last sentence introduces a new element, but all it does is tell us that inductance in electrical circuits works like water in pipes.

Step 3: Make a Prediction

If inductance in electrical circuits works like water in pipes, it must be true that electrical circuits take time to get up to speed and then again to taper off.

Step 4: Evaluate the Answer Choices

(A) is vaguer than the prediction but a solid match. For inductance to be like inertia, it must affect the rate of flow.

(B) is a Distortion of the stimulus. While the stimulus does indicate that inductance is similar to inertia, it does not support the statement that electrical circuits require inertia.

(C) is another Distortion of the connection between inertia and inductance. The stimulus says that they are similar, not that one causes the other.

(D) goes Outside the Scope by introducing electrical engineers.

(E) goes Outside the Scope by introducing very specific details about exactly how long it takes a water pump to taper off. (E) is possible, but it is not something that must be true based on the stimulus.

4. (D) Inference ★★★☆

Step 1: Identify the Question Type

The question "[W]hich one of the following must be true?" identifies this as an Inference question. Read the statements in the stimulus and determine what must be true based upon them.

Step 2: Untangle the Stimulus

Look for the statements in the stimulus that provide the most certain facts. The first two statements provide facts about "most" pet stores in the city. Most stores sell birds, and of those, most also sell fish. This may not be much help in determining what must be true, since "most" is an ambiguous word on the LSAT. However, the next sentence states two certain facts: any store that sells fish, but not birds, sells gerbils; and if a store is independently owned, it does not sell gerbils.

Step 3: Make a Prediction

The wording of the last two statements confirms that Formal Logic will be the key to connecting the statements in this stimulus and arriving at an inference:

> **If fish and ~ birds** → **gerbils**

and

> **If independently owned** → **~ gerbils**

To make an inference by joining these statements, make the contrapositive of the second statement:

> **If gerbils** → **~ independently owned**

Using "gerbils" as the common term, join the statements to reveal:

> **If fish and ~ birds** → **~ independently owned**

Therefore, we know that no independently owned pet store in the city sells tropical fish but not exotic birds.

When evaluating answer choices in Formal Logic Inference questions, remember: given a sufficient condition, the necessary condition can be inferred, but given a necessary condition, nothing can be inferred!

Step 4: Evaluate the Answer Choices

(D) is the exact prediction.

(A) is a Distortion. This answer reverses the sufficient and necessary terms of the proper inference.

> **If ~ independently owned** → **~ birds**

In the facts of the stimulus, "not independently owned" is a necessary condition following from the fact "the store sells gerbils." An inference cannot be drawn from a necessary condition.

(B) is Outside the Scope. No facts link stores that sell both fish and birds with stores that sell gerbils. The only connection with stores that sell gerbils given is with stores that sell fish but not birds. This statement may or may not be true.

(C) is Outside the Scope. The use of the word "[s]ome" to qualify stores that sell gerbils takes this answer choice beyond the facts given, since the only facts we are given about stores that sell gerbils pertain to all of them. This statement may or may not be true.

(E) is Outside the Scope. No facts allow any inference about independently owned stores that do not sell fish. The facts state that independently owned stores don't sell gerbils, and from this it follows that they don't sell "fish but not birds." But no inference can be drawn about those that do not sell fish.

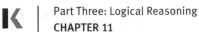
5. (B) Inference ★★★★

Step 1: Identify the Question Stem

The stem says that the statements in the stimulus will support one of the answer choices, so that makes this an Inference question.

Step 2: Untangle the Stimulus

Computer-dependent proofs are less certain than proofs that don't require computers. This is because human cognition, which would be used to provide certainty, can't verify computer-dependent proofs. More certainty can be achieved with proofs that don't rely on computers because human calculation can often verify such proofs.

Step 3: Make a Prediction

On Inference questions, it's often inefficient to attempt to predict answers. However, we must always keep in mind that we're seeking the answer choice that must be true if the stimulus is true. It's not good enough to find a choice that seems believable or reasonable; we need the answer that is indisputable based on the stimulus.

Step 4: Evaluate the Answers

(A) is Extreme. Computer-dependent proofs provide less certainty than those that don't depend on computers, but a computer-dependent proof could still provide *some* certainty. We don't have to completely remove the computer from the proof in order to achieve any degree of certainty.

(B) is supported by the part of the stimulus that says that "[h]uman cognition alone cannot verify computer-dependent proofs." If this is true, then a computer-dependent proof could contain errors that humans can't detect, and we would never know, because our cognition alone wouldn't be able to verify the proofs.

(C). The stimulus tells us that on the whole, proofs that *depend primarily* on computers are less certain than those that don't. But a computer could potentially replace human calculation in one single instance in a proof without the overall certainty of the proof being reduced.

(D) distorts the stimulus by turning an issue of relative certainty into one of absolute certainty. Human calculation helps provide a greater degree of certainty to proofs that aren't dependent on computers, but this is not to say that human calculation automatically lends complete certainty to anything.

(E) is Extreme. The stimulus merely says that when verifying simple arithmetic, electronic calculators are used for convenience rather than as a supplement to human cognition. This still leaves the door open for technology to provide artificial devices to supplement the cognitive abilities of humans in other instances. When dealing with an Inference question, beware answer choices that use extreme language; such choices are rarely correct.

6. (E) Inference ★★★★

Step 1: Identify the Question Type

This is an Inference question because the right answer is "properly inferred" from the stimulus. Accept each sentence in the stimulus as true and find an answer choice that must be true on the basis of one or more of those sentences. Stick to the information given and beware of making faulty assumptions.

Step 2: Untangle the Stimulus

In the first sentence, the ecologist makes a Formal Logic statement: without conservationists' intervention, squirrel monkeys will become extinct. In other words, the conservationists' intervention is required for the squirrel monkeys' survival. This statement yields the following translation:

If squirrel monkeys survive → conservationists intervene

Then the ecologist gives us a condition that will result in the squirrel monkeys' survival:

If large tracts of habitat preserved → squirrel monkeys survive

These two statements can be combined to form one chain:

If large tracts of habitat preserved → *squirrel monkeys survive* → *conservationists intervene*

The last sentence doesn't include any Formal Logic but simply provides a fact about squirrel monkeys: they do well in second-growth forests because of the food supply.

Step 3: Make a Prediction

Stay focused on how the first two statements can be connected through common terms. The term common to both Formal Logic statements is *squirrel monkeys*. The two statements can be combined to form one chain:

If large tracts of habitat preserved → *squirrel monkeys survive* → *conservationists intervene*

We can contrapose those connected statements like this:

If conservationists DON'T intervene → *squirrel monkeys DON'T survive (extinct)* → *large tracts of habitat NOT preserved.*

The right answer will follow from these connected statements.

Step 4: Evaluate the Answer Choices

(E) matches the prediction. Based on the contrapositive of the connected Formal Logic statements, it must be true that if no conservationists' intervention occurs, then no large tracts of habitat are preserved.

(A) goes Outside the Scope because the ecologist's statements are only about the second-growth forests, not other habitats.

These explanations refer to
questions that begin on page 754.

Part Three: Logical Reasoning
Non-Argument Questions | K

(B) goes Outside the Scope by suggesting that at least one conservationist will actually be doing the work of preserving second-growth forest. We know that if those forests are preserved that the conservationists did *something*, but we don't know exactly what they did. There could be ways of intervening that resulted in *others* preserving the forest.

(C) is Extreme. The ecologist never states that the squirrel monkeys would die off without this food supply, just that they flourish when it is there. Even if their favorites disappear, squirrel monkeys could arguably eat something else.

(D) wrongly contraposes the Formal Logic in the stimulus. According to the first sentence, if the squirrel monkeys survive, it is because the conservationists have intervened. The ecologist never states that intervention alone will guarantee their existence. This answer choice incorrectly negates the Formal Logic without reversing.

7. (C) Inference

Step 1: Identify the Question Type

In typical Inference question style, you're asked to identify the choice that is supported by the statements above. Accept each statement as true, seek out Formal Logic, and pay careful attention to the level of certainty exhibited by the language in the stimulus. The correct answer choice is the one that must be true based on the information in the stimulus.

Step 2: Untangle the Stimulus

Early urban societies needed to be close to big farming areas because large-scale farming is the only way to support the dense populations of urban societies. Until recently, big farming areas needed to be near rivers or lakes.

Step 3: Make a Prediction

Connect the chain of information given in the stimulus to predict the right answer. Early urban societies needed to be close to large-scale farming, which needed to be close to rivers or lakes. Therefore, it must be true that early urban societies were close to rivers or lakes.

Step 4: Evaluate the Answer Choices

(C) might look slightly different from the prediction, but it is the exact same idea, just in negative terms. If early urban societies had to be near rivers or lakes, then it must also be true that there were no urban societies far from rivers of lakes.

(A) is Extreme. The stimulus indicated urban societies needed to be close to rivers or lakes, but it did not indicate whether "[m]ost" people lived in those types of societies.

(B) is too broad by covering "societies" in general, rather than just "urban societies." It is a subtle difference, but one that affects whether the answer follows from the stimulus.

(D) is a 180. It contradicts the stimulus because according to the stimulus, "[l]arge-scale farming requires irrigation."

(E) goes Outside the Scope by focusing on rural societies rather than urban ones.

8. (E) Inference

Step 1: Identify the Question Type

Because the right answer "logically completes the argument," it is a statement that must be true on the basis of the stimulus. Thus, this is an Inference question.

Step 2: Untangle the Stimulus

Make an inventory of the statements. Some paleontologists thought that dinosaurs guarded their young for a long time after they hatched because of fossils discovered in special nests. However, crocodiles build special nests, too, but do not guard their young for long.

Step 3: Make a Prediction

Whenever a stimulus on the LSAT starts by telling you what "some [people] believe," look for a Contrast Keyword. Typically, authors discuss what "some [people] believe" in order to disagree with it. Here, that seems to be the case. Although the evidence about dinosaur fossils might seem to support the paleontologists' hypothesis, the evidence about crocodiles seems to go against it. Therefore, the author would logically conclude the stimulus by saying that the paleontologists haven't yet proved their case.

Step 4: Evaluate the Answer Choices

(E) matches the prediction.

(A) is a 180. It directly contradicts the stimulus because we know the paleontologists in question have some evidence; the author just happens to think that evidence is not convincing.

(B) is Extreme. The author only suggests that the one piece of evidence offered by paleontologists is insufficient. That does not mean they will "never" know.

(C) is also Extreme. Just because the evidence about crocodiles seems to go against the paleontologists' belief, it isn't enough prove what hadrosaurs did or didn't do. It could be true that hadrosaurs built similar nests to those of crocodiles but still watched their young for a long time.

(D) goes Outside the Scope by introducing other dinosaurs. The point is not whether the hadrosaur fossils are evidence for conclusions about other dinosaurs but whether or not the nests containing hadrosaur fossils are actually good evidence for a conclusion about hadrosaurs.

K | Part Three: Logical Reasoning
CHAPTER 11

These explanations refer to
questions that begin on page 754.

9. (D) Inference

Step 1: Identify the Question Stem

The stem asks us to accept all the statements in the stimulus as true and then determine the choice that must be true on the basis of them. That makes this an Inference question.

Step 2: Untangle the Stimulus

Genetic research funding only comes from two sources: government exclusively funds most research, and the rest is funded exclusively by corporations. Research can't proceed without funding from one of these two sources. Also, almost all advances in that research create ethical dilemmas.

Step 3: Make a Prediction

Instead of predicting the content of the correct answer, we should proceed directly to the choices, prepared to eliminate any choice that doesn't have to be true based on the stimulus.

Step 4: Evaluate the Answers

(D) may seem obvious, but that's a good sign. Since government or corporate funding is necessary for genetic research, then any advances in genetic research (and the ethical dilemmas that arise from them) are made possible only with the help of that funding.

(A) and **(C)**. We know from the stimulus that advances lead to ethical dilemmas, but no information is given indicating whether government or corporations fund the projects that achieve advances in genetic research.

(B) distorts the stimulus. Most genetic research is funded by the government, and most advances in genetic research give rise to ethical dilemmas, but that doesn't mean that most government-funded research leads to advances that give rise to ethical dilemmas.

(E) doesn't have to be true, since the stimulus doesn't say that government funding is what leads to the ethical dilemmas in genetic research.

10. (D) Inference

Step 1: Identify the Question Type

The phrase "statements above, if true, most strongly support" identifies this as an Inference question. Accept each sentence in the stimulus as true and find an answer choice that must be true on the basis of one or more of those sentences. Watch out for answers that use the exact words from the stimulus but distort the author's meaning.

Step 2: Untangle the Stimulus

This stimulus discusses a recent trend in history writing: an emphasis on historical trends is being replaced by an emphasis on details. As a result, the author states, historical trends are overlooked. As a further result, parallels between historic trends and current trends are also overlooked, and this lessens our ability to learn from the past.

Step 3: Make a Prediction

Combining all of this information shows the author is saying that the change from an emphasis on historical trends to an emphasis on details has resulted in a lessening of our ability to learn.

Step 4: Evaluate the Answer Choices

(D) is correct and matches your prediction.

(A) is a Distortion. *Studying* details is not the problem. The problem is emphasizing those details *in writing* such that historical trends become overlooked.

(B) is Extreme. The author says emphasis on details has replaced the emphasis on trends, with the latter being *often* overlooked. But that doesn't mean that the *only* time trends can be noticed is when details aren't emphasized. Nothing in the stimulus says the two can't occur together, just that they often haven't been.

(C) is Extreme. What lessens the ability to learn is overlooking the parallels between historical and current trends. Just looking at historical trends does not necessarily result in the "best" ability to learn. Also, this answer says people who look at historical trends and *not* details are "best" able to learn. Maybe the people who learn best are those who look at *both*. In short, because the statements just identify what lessens our ability to learn, you cannot truly infer what enhances our ability to learn the best.

(E) is Extreme because it is too specific. Studying trends and details does not have to be "equal." The author might go for this, but it is just as likely that the author would want a mixture of the two in something other than a 50/50 split. The author may even want a return to emphasizing only historical trends or mainly historical trends. The author never makes a clear indication, so this is not supported.

11. (B) Inference

Step 1: Identify the Question Type

Because the correct answer is "most strongly supported" by the stimulus, it is a statement that must be true based on the stimulus. This is an Inference question.

Step 2: Untangle the Stimulus

Make an inventory of the statements. Three groups of professional cyclists cycled for an hour, one at each of three levels of intensity. The lowest-intensity group reported the most benefits related to anger and depression, the middle group less, and the highest-intensity group reported some negative effects.

These explanations refer to questions that begin on page 755.

Part Three: Logical Reasoning
Non-Argument Questions | **K**

Step 3: Make a Prediction

Because the stimulus gives information about "[m]ost members" of each of the three groups, the right answer will need to be phrased cautiously. Comparing the three studies, it looks like the level of intensity could have some effect on the emotions of the cyclists.

Step 4: Evaluate the Answer Choices

(B) is cautious enough ("tends to depend at least in part") and is in scope, focusing on how intensity affected mood. It must be true.

(A) goes Outside the Scope by being too broad, referring to "sustained exercise" in general. The stimulus covered only a small range of pulse rates and one specific type of exercise. Additionally, be cautious of an answer indicating two things are indefinitely directly proportional. Perhaps the trend of the three studies would not hold at higher or lower intensities.

(C) is Extreme. Just because one form of exercise is better than two others for improving mood doesn't mean that it must be the absolute best form of exercise for improving mood.

(D) makes an Irrelevant Comparison between psychological factors and physical factors that contribute to depression. The stimulus does not support that those factors equally contribute to depression.

(E) goes Outside the Scope by focusing on physical benefits, rather than on benefits for mood. Further, the stimulus doesn't define "[m]oderate" or "intense" cycling, so it cannot support a comparison of those two things.

12. (E) Inference ★★★★

Step 1: Identify the Question Type

The words "[w]hich of the following ... supported by the information above" identify this as an Inference question. The facts in the stimulus will support one of the answer choices. Summarize the facts.

Step 2: Untangle the Stimulus

First, two facts about most large nurseries: They sell raspberries primarily to commercial growers, and all of their plants are guaranteed to be free of disease. "However" signals a contrasting fact: a shipment of raspberries from Wally's Plants had a common virus.

Step 3: Make a Prediction

We have no facts to indicate whether Wally's Plants is a large nursery. If it's not, no inferences are possible. If it is, then selling raspberries with a common virus might be a violation of its guarantee. However, the facts state only that "[m]ost" large nurseries have guarantees, which may or may not include Wally's. This stimulus has lots of wiggle room. Don't waste time trying to formulate a firm prediction. Instead, think critically about the scope of the facts and be alert to the qualifying language. Elimination will likely be the primary strategy in a question such as this.

Step 4: Evaluate the Answer Choices

(E) must be true. It starts with the condition that Wally's Plants is a large nursery. This condition is necessary to make any inference, since the only facts given are about large nurseries. If Wally's is a large nursery, and "[m]ost" large nurseries guarantee their plants, it's accurate to say that Wally's diseased raspberries "probably" weren't what they were guaranteed to be. (*Most* on the LSAT means more than half, and *probably* means more likely than not.)

(A) is a Distortion. This choice presents two hypothetical conditions, neither of which permits an inference to be drawn. Nothing can be inferred from the fact that Johnson is a commercial grower, and nothing can be inferred from the fact that Wally's is not a large nursery. Joining them with an "and" doesn't help.

(B) is a Distortion. Paraphrase to identify the sufficient and necessary terms: if the plants weren't as guaranteed (i.e., weren't disease-free), then Johnson is probably not a commercial grower. (Or the contrapositive: If Johnson is likely to be a commercial grower, then the plants are disease-free.)

Nothing in the stimulus makes "commercial grower" a necessary condition following from diseased plants. Nor does it make "disease-free" a necessary condition following from "commercial grower."

(C) is a Distortion. The facts state that most large nurseries sell primarily to commercial growers. The LSAT uses the word *most* to mean more than half and the word *probably* to mean more likely than not, so it can be properly inferred that Johnson is probably a commercial grower. However, the contrapositive doesn't work when using this kind of semiformal logic. It cannot be inferred that if Johnson is not a commercial grower, then Wally's is probably not a large nursery. Large nurseries sell to noncommercial growers as well, just not as many.

(D) is Outside the Scope. No facts suggest that Johnson is or is not a commercial grower, so no inference can be drawn from that. Also, the extra term "well-run" is not an element of the facts given.

13. (C) Inference ★★★★

Step 1: Identify the Question Type

Your task is to "logically complete" the stimulus, so this is an Inference question. Wrap your head around the given information and then find the choice that it logically supports.

K | Part Three: Logical Reasoning
CHAPTER 11

These explanations refer to
questions that begin on page 755.

Step 2: Untangle the Stimulus

This stimulus deals with the old wives' tale that weather affects arthritis. A study found no correlation between various features of the weather and arthritic flare-ups. The researchers also surveyed the people who believed in the myth and found that these people gave "widely varying" estimates of how long it takes for the pain to kick in after the supposed arthritis-inducing weather occurs.

Step 3: Make a Prediction

Since there's no correlation between weather and arthritis pain, and since the people who believe in a correlation can't seem to agree on when the pain starts after the weather changes, the study points to one thing: arthritis isn't actually affected by the weather. Look for some version of this conclusion in the choices.

Step 4: Evaluate the Answer Choices

(C) is your match. If the correlation is being imagined, then it's not real.

(A) is a Distortion. The fact that there were "widely varying accounts of the time delay" between weather changes and the arrival of bad pain is given as evidence that there was *no* connection between the weather and the pain, not that some people were more quickly affected by the weather than others. According to the stimulus, the weather doesn't affect arthritis at all.

(B) may be true, but it's Out of Scope. It offers no information about people's assessments of pain "intensity."

(D), like **(A)**, is a Distortion. It claims that weather in some way affects arthritis, which contradicts the entire point of the stimulus.

(E) is Extreme and also contradicts the stimulus. The author makes a claim about the links between weather and arthritis (there aren't any), so she surely doesn't believe that scientific investigation into the matter is "impossible."

14. (A) Inference ★★★★

Step 1: Identify the Question Stem

The words "properly inferred" are a clear indication that this is an Inference question.

Step 2: Untangle the Stimulus

Thanks to a major shipment from Africa, pythons have gotten much less expensive to own. But there's a catch. Many African pythons are afflicted with a liver disease that is difficult to detect early on but that is always fatal within six months of contraction. Some pythons hatched in North America also have the disease, but not nearly in the same proportion as those hatched in Africa.

Step 3: Make a Prediction

There's no Formal Logic present, and no immediate or obvious connections to make between the statements. Many different valid inferences can be made based on this information, so instead of trying to pre-phrase them all, let's instead go to the answer choices prepared to find the choice that must be true. Any choice that we wish to select as the correct answer must be directly supported by information from the stimulus.

Step 4: Evaluate the Answers

(A) must be true if we accept the stimulus as true. If some North American pythons have the liver disease, then according to the stimulus, the disease will be undetectable in its early stages but will prove fatal within six months. In other words, the pythons will appear to be healthy but will die within six months of contracting the disease. Don't be afraid of **(A)** simply because it seems obvious. If it must be true, it's a correct Inference.

(B) isn't a valid inference. Yes, the stimulus says that a higher proportion of African-hatched pythons has the liver disease, but that could simply be because there are far more pythons in Africa and therefore more of an opportunity for the disease to spread. There need not be a higher inherent susceptibility on the part of the African pythons.

(C) is Extreme. The disease does have a six-month incubation period, but what if a python catches the disease several months after hatching? In that case, it could live to be much older than six months despite ultimately contracting the disease.

(D) certainly doesn't have to be true. There could be a number of reasons why the pythons are inexpensive, one reason being the drop in demand due to the increase in the number of available pythons over the past two months.

(E) is Outside the Scope; we can't properly infer anything about pythons that were hatched in either Africa or North America. If a stimulus tells you that all the tall kids wear red, that doesn't mean that the short kids don't wear red.

15. (E) Inference ★★★★

Step 1: Identify the Question Type

The phrase "provide the most support for which one of the following claims" indicates that the right answer must be true based on the information in the stimulus. Thus, this is an Inference question.

Step 2: Untangle the Stimulus

Make an inventory of the information in the stimulus. McElligott flash pasteurizes its apple juice because of past bacterial infections traced to the juice. Intensive pasteurization would kill more bacteria, but it also kills the taste. Citrus juices seem to be safe, so they're not pasteurized.

These explanations refer to questions that begin on page 756.

Part Three: Logical Reasoning
Non-Argument Questions

K

Step 3: Make a Prediction

Because McElligott now does some pasteurizing of its apple juice, it is likely that its apple juice has fewer bacteria than it used to. At the same time, both its citrus and apple juices could still have some bacteria because the company isn't using the most effective method for eliminating bacteria in either of them.

Step 4: Evaluate the Answer Choices

(E) must be true based on the stimulus because intensive pasteurization does eliminate more bacteria than the flash process that McElligott's uses.

(A) goes Outside the Scope because the stimulus provides absolutely no information about other companies' citrus juices.

(B) could be true, but it need not be. There is no support for a comparison between McElligott's apple and citrus juices. Just because the citrus juice isn't pasteurized doesn't say anything about how much bacteria there is in it.

(C) goes Outside the Scope by comparing McElligott's citrus juices with pasteurized citrus juices in general. The stimulus doesn't tell us whether or not there are some pasteurization processes (perhaps even flash pasteurization) that do not affect flavor.

(D) is Extreme because it talks about "[t]he most effective method." The stimulus compared two specific methods, but there could be other methods out there that are more effective at eliminating bacteria but don't destroy flavor.

16. (A) Inference ★★★★

Step 1: Identify the Question Type

In typical Inference question style, you're asked to identify the choice that is supported by the statements in the stimulus. Accept each statement as true, seek out Formal Logic, and pay careful attention to the level of certainty exhibited by the language in the stimulus. The correct answer choice is the one that must be true based on the information in the stimulus.

Step 2: Untangle the Stimulus

Take inventory: certain bacteria produce hydrogen sulfide. Oxygen would kill these bacteria, but the hydrogen sulfide removes it. The hydrogen sulfide also kills other organisms, which the bacteria can use as a food source. So a dense colony of this bacteria can "continue to thrive indefinitely."

Step 3: Make a Prediction

If the dense colony is thriving indefinitely, then it must be able keep making enough hydrogen sulfide to take care of the potential oxygen problem and to kill the other organisms for food.

Step 4: Evaluate the Answer Choices

(A) explains that the colony is able to produce hydrogen sulfide indefinitely. That's exactly what it would take for the colony to thrive indefinitely.

(B) is a Distortion, blurring two concepts in the stimulus. The author says hydrogen sulfide both removes oxygen and kills other organisms. However, the author doesn't say that hydrogen sulfide kills other organisms by removing oxygen.

(C) is Extreme because of "[m]ost." The stimulus tells us that hydrogen sulfide kills other organisms, thus producing food, but it doesn't say how many of those organisms can function as a food source.

(D) is Extreme because of "only." The stimulus never says that this is the only way this bacterium can thrive, just that it's one way.

(E) is Extreme because it includes all types of bacteria that produce hydrogen sulfide. The stimulus tells us only about certain bacteria.

Principle

17. (C) Principle (Apply) ★★★☆

Step 1: Identify the Question Stem

The word "principle" in the stem indicates a Principle question, but let's read more closely to find our exact task. Here, the broad, law-like principle will be in the stimulus, and we'll need to find the narrow choice that is the correct application of the principle.

Step 2: Untangle the Stimulus

The columnist's principle, in a nutshell, is that the presence of total freedom of thought and expression is no excuse to profit from exploiting depraved popular tastes.

Step 3: Make a Prediction

It's impossible to say with any certainty what form the correct answer will take. We just know that it will be an instance of the principle being applied in a more specific context.

Step 4: Evaluate the Answers

(A) cites a condition under which freedom of expression should not be guaranteed. The stimulus advocates unfettered freedom of thought. Also, **(A)** contains no element of profit from exploiting depravity, so we should eliminate it.

(B) also doesn't contain an element of profit or attempted profit, so it's missing a crucial part of the principle in the stimulus. Eliminate.

(C), like the stimulus, is in favor of complete freedom of expression when it comes to publishing. Also, **(C)** says that this freedom does not give publishers carte blanche to attempt

K | Part Three: Logical Reasoning
CHAPTER 11

These explanations refer to
questions that begin on page 757.

to profit from pandering to depraved tastes, which is exactly the qualification provided in the stimulus.

(D) leaves the door open for the government to intervene in the freedom of production of certain recordings, which flies in the face of the unconditional freedom of expression advocated by the columnist.

(E) merely cautions against criticism of statements that exhibit depravity. The columnist doesn't touch this issue; the stimulus says that freedom of thought doesn't necessarily relieve people of their moral responsibility to refrain from profiting from depravity.

18. (D) Principle (Identify)

Step 1: Identify the Question Type

You're asked to identify the "proposition" that is supported by the statements in the stimulus. That makes this an Identify the Principle question. Accept each statement as true and seek out an answer choice that is broader than the stimulus. The correct answer must be true based on the information in the stimulus.

Step 2: Untangle the Stimulus

The historian starts by giving us the opinion of "some people." These people have disputed the historian's claim that West influenced Stuart. In other words, they think that West did not influence Stuart. Their evidence is that that Stuart's diaries seldom mention West's work. The Contrast Keyword "[b]ut" suggests that the historian disagrees with these people. After "[b]ut," he lists a series of facts connecting Stuart and West.

Step 3: Make a Prediction

The contrast Keyword "[b]ut" indicates the historian wants to counter those who think the single mention of West's work in Stuart's diaries prove West didn't influence Stuart. In response, the historian presents a list of connections between Stuart and West. He must be trying to prove West likely had some sort of influence on Stuart.

Step 4: Evaluate the Answer Choices

(D) cautiously suggests that Stuart's work was influenced, at least a little bit, by West. That must be true based on the historian's evidence of the connections between the two. Additionally, even the historian's opponents agree Stuart's diaries mention West's work once.

(A) could be true but also could be false. The historian cites Stuart's discussions with Abella as a possible way that West influenced Stuart, but that is not the only way provided. Thus, even if Stuart's discussions with Abella did nothing to spread West's influence to Stuart, it could still be true that West influenced Stuart at one of their several meetings.

(B) makes an Irrelevant Comparison. This could be true, but the stimulus gives us no information about Stuart influencing

West. Therefore, the stimulus provides no grounds for weighing that likelihood.

(C) is a Distortion. The only thing we know about Stuart's contemporaries is that they didn't use West's terminology. It's possible they were influenced by West in some other way.

(E) is another Distortion. While it is true West's terminology is now commonplace, the stimulus says nothing about how it got that way. It may or may not have been Stuart's influence on other people.

19. (D) Principle (Identify)

Step 1: Identify the Question Type

The word "propositions" signals that this is a Principle question, but since Principle questions come in many flavors, your work isn't done. Specifically, note that you need to identify the principle, or general idea, that the stimulus adheres or "conforms" to. Additionally, the stem mentions "reasoning," which tells you that the stimulus will contain an argument. Get ready to bracket the conclusion and look for evidence.

Step 2: Untangle the Stimulus

The Evidence Keyword "because" in the last sentence signals evidence, which means that the conclusion will soon follow; the author wants to convince you that the survey's responses are ambiguous. Her evidence is that the statement used in the survey was ambiguous.

The survey, introduced in the first sentence, evaluated how many teenagers believe in telekinesis. This is really just background information though, because the entire argument is contained in the last sentence. The contrast Keyword "[b]ut" suggests that the author isn't a fan of this survey statement, hinting at the negative conclusion.

Step 3: Make a Prediction

Notice that the evidence gives information about the statement teenagers were responding to, whereas the conclusion makes a claim about the responses themselves. Here we see a subtle shift in scope: the author takes for granted that responses to an ambiguous question are themselves ambiguous. This is the general idea ("proposition") to which the argument conforms, so look for a choice that paraphrases it.

Step 4: Evaluate the Answer Choices

(D) matches your prediction by providing the link between ambiguous ("poorly phrased") questions and ambiguous responses. Notice that the correct choice is the only one that doesn't use extreme language.

(A) is Extreme and Out of Scope. The author never mentions uncontroversial statements or their usefulness.

These explanations refer to
questions that begin on page 758.

Part Three: Logical Reasoning
Non-Argument Questions | K

(B) is also Extreme and Out of Scope. It doesn't matter whether every statement is ambiguous ("amenable to several interpretations"); what matters is whether responses to such statements are also ambiguous.

(C) is yet another Extreme, Out of Scope choice. The author doesn't care what makes things *un*ambiguous; she cares about what makes things *am*biguous.

(E) is *yet another* Extreme choice, with its use of the word "always." In addition, this choice is Out of Scope because it tells you nothing about ambiguity. Furthermore, whether statements can or can't always have naturalistic interpretations is irrelevant.

20. (B) Principle (Identify) ★★☆☆

Step 1: Identify the Question Type

The question stem asks for a Principle. The stimulus will provide a specific argument, and the correct answer will present the reasoning behind that argument in more general terms.

Step 2: Untangle the Stimulus

The author's conclusion is that we should not yet spread iron particles over the surface of the oceans. His evidence is that the side effects of iron seeding have not been tested and the oceans are very important.

Step 3: Make a Prediction

Start by finding the author's assumption. The conclusion is about avoiding a course of action for now. The evidence says the action has both a known benefit to the atmosphere and unknown side effects for the ocean, an important resource. So, the author assumes the possible negative side effects outweigh the known positives when an important resource is at stake. The assumption will lead us to the matching principle. Remember that the principle may be in more general terms than the assumption.

Step 4: Evaluate the Answer Choices

(B) is the match. The "problem-solving strategy" is iron seeding, and it should not be done because its side effects on the oceans are unknown.

(A) is Out of Scope. The stimulus only discusses a situation in which the side effects are unknown. The author doesn't give any direction as to what should happen were the side effects known.

(C) goes Out of the Scope by introducing an idea not in the stimulus—"consequences . . . more serious than the problem itself." The author's evidence is that the consequences are unknown. Granted, they might be more serious than the problem, but currently that's unclear.

(D) is more Extreme than the author. The author hasn't said the resource (oceans) shouldn't be altered, only that

first he recommends having a solid understanding of the consequences of such an action.

(E) is a Distortion of the stimulus by suggesting that the risk would be exacerbating the original problem. The author, however, was concerned with unknown side effects creating a new problem in the oceans, not that spreading the iron particles would "exacerbate" the greenhouse effect.

21. (D) Principle (Apply) ★★★☆

Step 1: Identify the Question Type

This is an unusual Principle question—two principles are presented in the Dialogue-Response stimulus. The task is to identify both Vanessa's and Jo's principles. Since this is also an EXCEPT question, the facts in four of the answer choices will be consistent with both of the principles. The correct answer choice will violate one or both.

Step 2: Untangle the Stimulus

Vanessa states that all computer code must be written by two programmers working together at the same workstation in order to avoid writing code only one programmer could understand. Jo states an exception to this rule: highly productive programmers should work alone because they work best alone.

Step 3: Make a Prediction

Four of the answer choices will be fact patterns that are consistent both with Vanessa's rule that programmers work in pairs and with Jo's exception that highly productive programmers work alone. The correct answer will most likely describe average or below-average programmers working alone or highly productive programmers working in pairs.

Step 4: Evaluate the Answer Choices

(D) is the correct answer because it violates Jo's principle. Yolanda and Mike are both very productive programmers who have been assigned to work together at the same workstation. By Jo's principle, they should work alone.

(A) is consistent with both principles. Eliminate. Olga and Kensuke both have average productivity, and therefore they should be, and are, assigned together. How they feel about it is not relevant.

(B) is consistent with both principles. Eliminate. John is not one of the most productive programmers even though he is experienced. Therefore, his assignment to work with Tyrone, an underproductive novice, is consistent with Vanessa's principle without violating Jo's exception.

(C) is consistent with both principles. Eliminate. Chris is not one of the most productive programmers. Since he is more productive than Jennifer, Jennifer is not among the most productive, either. Therefore, assigning them together is

K | Part Three: Logical Reasoning
CHAPTER 11

These explanations refer to
questions that begin on page 759.

consistent with Vanessa's principle without violating Jo's
exception.

(E) is consistent with both principles. Eliminate. Kevin and Amy
are both average, and they have been assigned together in
order to avoid having their idiosyncrasies appear
in the code.

Paradox

22. (E) Paradox

Step 1: Identify the Question Type

The phrase "contributes to an explanation" indicates that this
is a Paradox question. The paradox in question is why the first
alternative mentioned is almost never adopted.

Step 2: Untangle the Stimulus

Given that not adopting the first alternative, continuous
maintenance, is the paradox that needs to be explained, there
must be some important benefit of continuous maintenance.
The third sentence informs us that the benefit of continuous
maintenance is that it costs much less in the long run than
radical reconstruction.

Step 3: Make a Prediction

The prediction doesn't need to be specific because there could
be many different ways to resolve the paradox. Instead, predict
more generally. The correct answer will give some reason why
continuous maintenance is not done, even though it is more
cost-effective.

Step 4: Evaluate the Answer Choices

(E) shows that continuous maintenance is not done because
there's no urgency spurring people to do it. If problems show
up very gradually, people might very well put off fixing them
until it's too late and radical reconstruction is needed.

(A) is a 180 because it makes the paradox deeper by
suggesting that radical reconstruction has severe drawbacks.
Given that, we would expect continuous maintenance to be
used more frequently.

(B) goes Outside the Scope by introducing specifics about how
funds are distributed when money is tight. That information
has nothing to do with the method generally used to repair
transportation infrastructure.

(C) is another 180 because it gives another reason why
continuous maintenance is good, and thus it deepens the
paradox.

(D) also is a 180. It gives another reason why radical
reconstruction is bad, making continuous maintenance even
more attractive and thus deepening the paradox.

23. (C) Paradox

Step 1: Identify the Question Type

The word "explain" indicates a Paradox question. Figure
out what seems strange about the researcher's findings
and then come up with something that would explain that
inconsistency.

Step 2: Untangle the Stimulus

Begin by paraphrasing the argument. The researcher tracked
the beak size of two groups of birds. Both groups were the
same species, but one group was wild while the other was
captive. Whereas the captive birds' beak size didn't change,
the wild birds' beaks got smaller over time.

Step 3: Make a Prediction

The author's dilemma is that the beak size changed for
one group but not the other, even though they're the same
species. However, the familiar pattern of *representativeness*
pops up in this problem—perhaps as something the author
is overlooking here. Since the stimulus presents statistical
information about two groups, it's foreseeable that some
difference between the wild group and the captive group will
explain the different outcome. Perhaps something different
about the wild birds made their beaks *more* inclined to shrink,
or something different about the captive birds made their
beaks *less* inclined to shrink.

Step 4: Evaluate the Answer Choices

(C) is an excellent match that rewards a thorough analysis.
It presents a feature that explains why the wild birds' beaks
would have shrunk but not those of the captive birds.

(A) may be tempting. It appears to explain why the study
would have reported smaller beak sizes for the wild birds. But
the flaws with this choice are extremely illustrative.

First, the answer choice requires you to make an unwarranted
assumption. The stimulus doesn't say that the researchers
obtained the beak sizes by capturing and measuring the
birds, so the ease of doing either is irrelevant. Second, note
that the stimulus never compares the beak size of wild birds
to the beak size of captive birds. It compares the size of wild
beaks at the end of the study to the size of wild beaks at the
beginning of the study, and it does the same for the captive
beaks. So, even if the error in **(A)** did cause the researchers'
data to report the wild birds' beaks as smaller than they really
are, it still doesn't explain why the beak size *decreased* over
the course of the study. If it was easier to catch small-beaked
birds at the start of the study, this would also be true at the
end of the study.

(B) has the same flaws as **(A)**, and it's a 180. If anything, this
choice makes the stimulus even more puzzling, as the greater
ease of catching large-beaked wild birds (if you accept the

These explanations refer to
questions that begin on page 760.

Part Three: Logical Reasoning
Non-Argument Questions

flawed reasoning) should have made the beak size increase,
not shrink.

(D) doesn't explain the paradox. The birds' body sizes are
irrelevant to the apparent paradox.

(E) doesn't explain the paradox, either. The choice doesn't
tell you whether the repeated beaks were small or large, so it
doesn't explain the apparent findings without an additional
assumption. If anything, it points out a flaw in the data
collection: measuring the same beak more than once unfairly
skews the data toward that bird's beak size.

24. (A) Paradox ★☆☆☆

Step 1: Identify the Question Type

The phrase "most helps to explain" is common language for a
Paradox question. Additionally, the question stem reveals the
paradoxical situation—unemployed retirees are more likely to
have heart attacks on Mondays than on other days.

Step 2: Untangle the Stimulus

The question stem indicates the paradoxical fact—unemployed
retirees are more likely to have heart attacks on Mondays.
What makes this paradoxical is that *employed* people are more
likely to have heart attacks because Monday is the first day of
the workweek and therefore extra stressful. So, if unemployed
retirees aren't going to work on Mondays, why do they still
have more heart attacks on Mondays than on other days?

Step 3: Make a Prediction

The correct answer will suggest something about Mondays
and stress that would lead unemployed retirees to have more
attacks on that day.

Step 4: Evaluate the Answer Choices

(A) suggests that even though unemployed retirees don't go to
work on Mondays, they still treat that day as the beginning of
the "workweek" for their large projects. This could lead them
to experience the same kind of heart attack–inducing stress
on Mondays that employed people experience, thus resolving
the paradox.

(B) goes Outside the Scope by discussing retired people
who have part-time jobs. Having a part-time job may explain
why these specific retired people are more likely to have
heart attacks on Mondays, but the stimulus only mentions
unemployed retired people.

(C) doesn't solve the paradox because it eliminates a possible
explanation. Declining health habits might explain the
risk to unemployed retirees, but if they remain unchanged
from employment to retirement, then that possible reason
disappears. Additionally, this answer choice fails to provide
any new information as to why Mondays are special.

(D) may be true, but it doesn't explain why Mondays
specifically are more dangerous to unemployed retired people
than any other day.

(E) is a 180 because it strengthens the paradox. If *work-related*
stress causes increased heart attacks on Mondays, then the
fact that unemployed retired people are more at risk than
employed people seems even more bizarre.

25. (E) Paradox

Step 1: Identify the Question Stem

This is a Paradox question because it asks us to find answers
that resolve a discrepancy in the stimulus. However, we need
to eliminate such answers in this case because this is an
EXCEPT question. The right answer will be a fact that doesn't
help resolve the paradox.

Step 2: Untangle the Stimulus

Despite the fact that, on average, Springfield residents live
farther from their places of employment than Rorchester
residents do from theirs, the demand for public transportation
is not necessarily higher in Springfield, since Springfield has
only half as many bus routes as does Rorchester.

Step 3: Make a Prediction

As the stimulus suggests, we would expect Springfield to have
more bus lines. We need to find a reason why Springfield
would have fewer. Any answer that shows why Springfield
residents wouldn't need additional lines would do the trick.
Before checking out the choices, let's characterize the choices.
We know that there will be four choices that will help resolve
this discrepancy and one that will not. That odd man out will
be our correct answer.

Step 4: Evaluate the Answers

(A) resolves the paradox. If three-quarters of Springfield's
residents are commuting to the same workplace every day,
then they could all get to work on the same bus route, and
Springfield wouldn't need nearly as many bus routes to make
sure that everyone gets to work.

(B) resolves the paradox by suggesting that Springfield
residents don't need public transportation because they can
drive to work.

(C) resolves the paradox by suggesting that Springfield
residents rely more heavily on their railway system than their
bus system to get around town, thereby explaining the lower
demand for bus lines.

(D) resolves the paradox by suggesting that the few bus routes
that do exist in Springfield come more often and travel farther.
So Springfield's bus system could transport more people to
locations that are farther away despite not having as many bus
routes as Rorchester.

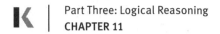

These explanations refer to questions that begin on page 760.

(E) does not help resolve the paradox. If Springfield's population were larger than Rorchester's, one would expect there to be higher demand for city services such as public transportation. So **(E)** deepens the mystery rather than resolving it.

26. (C) Paradox

Step 1: Identify the Question Type

The words "helps to explain" identify this as a Paradox question. The long question stem requires careful reading to establish what needs explaining. The astronomer has resolved a conflict between the ages of stars and the age of the universe by his estimates of star distances. The task is to explain why his estimates resolved the conflict.

Step 2: Untangle the Stimulus

First, the conflict is explained: earlier estimates of star distances meant that some stars were older than the universe, which is impossible. This astronomer estimates that the stars are actually farther away, which also means they are brighter. This, he claims, resolves the age conflict.

Step 3: Make a Prediction

In this stimulus, the astronomer transitions from the fact that stars are farther and brighter to the fact that they are not as old as previously thought (thereby avoiding the contradiction with the age of the universe). A farther and brighter star, therefore, must be an indication of a younger star to resolve the discrepancy. Look for a fact that links the brightness of a star with its age.

Step 4: Evaluate the Answer Choices

(C) is exactly the fact needed. The astronomer's estimates place the stars farther away, which makes them brighter. If brighter stars are younger stars, then this explains why the stars are no longer estimated to be older than the universe.

(A) is Outside the Scope. The age of the stars relative to everything else in the universe does nothing to explain why the astronomer now has a more realistic estimate of their age than before.

(B) is a 180. If more bright stars indicate a younger universe, this fact would make the conflict between the age of the stars and the age of the universe worse.

(D) is a valid inference that follows from the astronomer's statements about stellar brightness. However, it provides no information about the age of the stars, which is what is needed to explain how the astronomer resolved the conflict in the ages of the stars and the universe.

(E) is Outside the Scope. The number of stars that astronomers are able to see has no bearing on the distance and age estimates of the stars that are the subject of the astronomer's conflict.

27. (D) Paradox

Step 1: Identify the Question Type

The Keyword "explain" signals a Paradox question. Since the stem ends with "EXCEPT," look for the choice that *doesn't* resolve the seeming contradiction in the stimulus.

Step 2: Untangle the Stimulus

The stimulus presents the findings of a study that looked at poverty and malnourishment among old and young people. In the 66 and older group, more people were malnourished than impoverished; in the 65 and younger group, the opposite was true—more people were impoverished than malnourished. In other words, some people in the older group had enough money to buy food yet were malnourished, while some people in the younger group were very poor yet *weren't* malnourished. This is the paradox.

Step 3: Make a Prediction

On a Paradox EXCEPT question, the wrong choices are easier to predict than the correct one. Since the study looked at two different groups, predict that some difference between the two groups accounts for the study's results. Specifically, cross out any choice that explains either of the following:

1. How old people can be malnourished without being poor
2. How young people can be poor without being malnourished

Step 4: Evaluate the Answer Choices

(D) is the only choice that doesn't highlight a relevant difference between the two groups. It states that both groups are equally likely to be impoverished, but this doesn't explain how old people can be malnourished without being impoverished or how young people can be impoverished without being malnourished.

(A) explains the paradox in a roundabout way. If doctors incorrectly diagnose malnutrition among older patients, then many more old people are malnourished than was reported by the study.

(B) explains the paradox more directly. If older people take medications that increase their need for nutrients, then the medications might cause malnutrition regardless of the patient's wealth.

(C) explains the paradox in yet another way: If older people are more likely to lose their appetite, then they won't eat as much,

These explanations refer to questions that begin on page 761.

Part Three: Logical Reasoning
Non-Argument Questions

which may cause them to become malnourished even if they have the means to feed themselves.

(E) provides one more biological explanation for older people's malnutrition: interference with their digestion.

28. (A) Paradox

Step 1: Identify the Question Stem

Any question stem asking you to "resolve an apparent discrepancy" is a Paradox question.

Step 2: Untangle the Stimulus

The farmer admits that the best way to ensure that corn kernels dry at the right speed is to sun dry the corn while it is still in the field. However, the farmer doesn't follow this method. Instead, he dries the ears of corn on a screen in a warm, dry room.

Step 3: Make a Prediction

We don't need to know exactly why the farmer acts contrary to what he recognizes is the best method, but we do need to know how to recognize the right answer when we see it. Here, we need a reason why the farmer doesn't sun dry his corn.

Step 4: Evaluate the Answers

(A) tells us that circumstances prevent the farmer from being able to sun dry his corn. At the time of year when the corn would ordinarily be drying in the sun, the region where the farmer grows his corn experiences a long cloudy season. This is our correct answer since it explains why the farmer has to resort to drying the corn indoors.

(B) deals with expense, which is Outside the Scope of this stimulus. If anything, **(B)** deepens the mystery because it confirms that the farmer's method of drying the corn is less effective *and* less cost-efficient than the preferred method.

(C) tells us that the preferred method of drying isn't the only method, but that doesn't explain why the farmer chooses to follow a method that he knows isn't preferable to drying the corn in the field.

(D) and **(E)** discuss what happens to kernels that aren't sufficiently dry or that are too dry. Neither choice explains why the farmer has chosen his particular method of drying, so neither choice can be correct here.

29. (E) Paradox ★★★★

Step 1: Identify the Question Type

The phrase "most helps to reconcile" indicates that this is a Paradox question. Something about the beliefs of economists will not seem to fit with the consequences observed by most wine merchants. The correct answer will show how they do fit together.

Step 2: Untangle the Stimulus

The belief of most economists is in the first sentence—reducing price should result in increased demand. The Contrast Keyword, "[h]owever," introduces the other side of the paradox: when wine merchants reduce the price of domestic wine, sales of more expensive imported wine that costs more than the newly priced domestic wine increase.

Step 3: Make a Prediction

The economists' reasoning indicates that decreasing the price of domestic wine should lead to an increased demand for that wine. While the wine merchants report that sales of imported wine actually goes up, they say nothing about what happens to domestic wine. Perhaps demand for all wine, including the domestic wine, increases.

Step 4: Evaluate the Answer Choices

(E) puts together the observed increase in demand for imported wine with the economists' prediction that domestic sales should increase. According to **(E)**, when one goes up, they both should.

(A) provides a reason that the wine merchants' experience might deviate from the economists' theory, but it doesn't reconcile the two.

(B) is Outside the Scope. The economic phenomenon should occur whether or not the wine sellers understand or anticipate it.

(C) goes Outside the Scope by introducing the element of superiority. We have no information about one wine or the other being superior.

(D) is a 180. It deepens the paradox by suggesting another reason why imported wines should not sell more than domestic wines. Not only are the imported wines more expensive, they are also no better in quality.

CHAPTER 12

Logical Reasoning: Managing the Section

INTRODUCTION

As you've learned, every LSAT has two scored Logical Reasoning sections, typically containing 25 or 26 questions each. Those questions are spread out over eight pages, with anywhere from two to four questions on each page. That's a lot of content to get through in 35 minutes. In terms of word count, in fact, each Logical Reasoning section presents you with approximately as much reading as does a Reading Comprehension section.

This isn't by accident, of course. Getting through these sections in the time provided is *supposed* to be difficult. Although a handful of test takers in each test administration will confidently get through all of the questions in a section in 35 minutes, many more either will not be able to do so or will be forced to rush and cut corners. That's because the LSAT is not testing only how well you can complete a variety of tasks, but also your ability to manage time effectively and perform as well as possible within time constraints. Law schools are interested in this facet of the test. They realize that good lawyers (and law students) don't spend all of their resources fighting losing battles. Instead, effective lawyers successfully prioritize the most important elements of their cases.

LEARNING OBJECTIVES

In this chapter, you'll learn to:

- Move through individual Logical Reasoning questions efficiently.
- Recognize and approach strategically the difficult questions in the Logical Reasoning section.

LOGICAL REASONING SECTION MANAGEMENT—WHY IT MATTERS

When it comes to the Logical Reasoning section of the test, here's what LSAT experts know: successful time management is more than a matter of moving from the first question to the last, answering *x* number of questions in *y* amount of time. The distribution of questions in the Logical Reasoning section is patterned so that typically one or two difficult problems show up early in the section, while a handful of less difficult questions show up at the end of the section. In this way, the LSAT is able to evaluate test takers' time management ability: Do you sink your finite time and energy into a few objectively difficult questions, or do you move on with the knowledge that easier questions await? Take a look at the following graph:

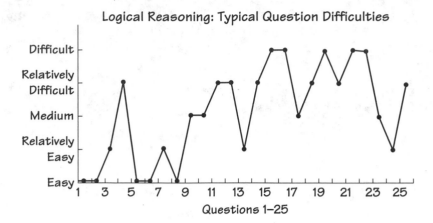

Notice that, in general, the difficulty level of questions in the Logical Reasoning section moves from relatively easy to relatively difficult. However, there are a few surprises along the way. The first speed bump comes in one of the first 10 questions—usually somewhere between questions 4 and 9. At this point in the section, a difficult question could rattle an insecure or unprepared test taker. But LSAT experts know not to get rattled. They know that a methodical approach will help them answer even the most difficult questions; additionally, they realize that if they face a particularly difficult or troublesome question on one of the first two pages, they can simply skip that question and move on to the easier questions among the following pages.

LSAT experts are also cognizant of the fact that the most difficult questions in the Logical Reasoning section are clustered together somewhere among questions 15 to 24. Because of the distribution of difficult questions in this part of the section, we call this area the "Danger Zone." Knowing about the "Danger Zone" is an important tool in the LSAT expert's toolbox: Not only is the LSAT expert mentally prepared for some difficult questions in this part of the section, but she also knows that one or two less difficult questions likely await her at the end of the section, if she can get to them.

Understanding how the Logical Reasoning section is structured helps LSAT experts move through this section effectively and confidently, but even this knowledge is not a cure-all for the challenge of getting to and correctly answering as many questions as possible. After all, even if you are skipping questions and coming back to them later, you may find that you are still unable to get to a significant number of questions in a section because you are spending too long on individual questions. So, how can good section management help you avoid this situation? How do you deal with the section's timing restriction in a way that allows you to both answer individual questions in an appropriate amount of time *and* answer the questions in such a way that you avoid the most difficult of the bunch until the end?

The answer has two parts. First, success in the Logical Reasoning section does not require you to evaluate and correctly answer every question. LSAT experts know that a test taker can miss four or five questions per section and still receive a 90th percentile score. Letting go of the need to read and evaluate every single question is a powerful way to take control of the test. If you decide to confront, evaluate, and answer only the questions that you believe are the easiest in a section, you will be light-years ahead of your competition.

But section management is not simply a matter of improving your ability to efficiently navigate each section as a whole by recognizing and avoiding difficult questions. The second, and arguably more important, way to improve your efficiency in this section is to improve your timing on individual problems by reading question stems and stimuli strategically, using that reading to predict the correct answer, and using that prediction to evaluate answer choices efficiently and purposefully. In short, use the Logical Reasoning Method to make you more efficient on individual questions and thus faster throughout the section as a whole.

To use those two strategies, you'll need a thorough understanding of the structure of the Logical Reasoning section as well as the construction of individual Logical Reasoning questions. And don't ignore your personal performance. Expert section management relies on the test taker knowing her individual strengths and weaknesses. As you read through this chapter, keep in mind that developing specific time management goals is an important step in conquering the LSAT—especially if you're one of those students who struggles to get through each section in 35 minutes. Don't make the mistake of just reading through this chapter passively. Find the strategies that work for you and put them into practice.

HONING YOUR APPROACH TO EACH QUESTION—GETTING FASTER BY GETTING BETTER

The first and best way to improve your timing efficiency in the Logical Reasoning section is simple: just get better and faster at tackling individual questions. Easily said, right? It would be great to snap your fingers and say, "Now go—be faster!"

If only it were that easy to do. If you struggle with timing in Logical Reasoning, then telling yourself to "read faster" isn't going to cut it on the LSAT. In fact, the mantra of "read faster" often makes a bad situation worse. Ask yourself if this has ever happened to you: after reading a question stem too quickly, you read the stimulus without a clear goal or objective; as a result, you're not sure what the argument is saying, so you reread it, this time even faster than before. Still lacking a full understanding of either the question or the statements in the stimulus (but now with a heightened concern that you need to speed up even more), you skip the prediction step and move directly to the answer choices. There, once again, you find yourself rereading as you search through answer choices without ever really knowing what you're looking for. Sound familiar? Reflect on that (perhaps familiar) scenario. Even if you actually did "read faster," the underlying dilemma remains unresolved. It's not a pacing issue—it's a comprehension issue. Ultimately, this negative feedback loop of confusion and frustration is a time killer. Though you may feel like you're moving through the test at a brisk pace, the constant re-evaluation of question stems, stimuli, and answer choices is actually slowing you down and preventing you from maximizing your performance. You aren't reading too slowly; you're reading the same sentences too many times. All of that unfocused reading and rereading leads to a predictable result: you end up spending longer on individual questions, which in turn leads to increased anxiety, which in turn leads to—you guessed it—an even greater perceived need to "read faster" on other problems.

If the above paragraph describes you, good news: while it's difficult to read *faster*, it's definitely possible to read *better*. Reading efficiently and effectively is a vital LSAT skill that you *can* improve. And that improvement will lead to points on Test Day because reading more strategically will allow you to work through problems in less time. LSAT experts know this, and they utilize four positive habits to keep them focused and engaged in the Logical Reasoning section. These can be distilled down to four words: *Plan*, *Pause*, *Paraphrase*, and *Predict*. By focusing on these steps, LSAT experts are able to move through individual questions in this section in a confident, controlled, and efficient manner. And while some of these skills have been discussed in previous chapters, it's good to see them again in a way that demonstrates how they tie into Logical Reasoning section management.

Plan: Knowing What to Do for Each Question

Your approach to questions in the Logical Reasoning section of the LSAT shouldn't be left to chance. Would you walk into court and present an argument without knowing whether you were working for the prosecution or the defense? Of course you wouldn't. Yet in the Logical Reasoning section of the test, many students try to tackle questions without knowing exactly what the question is asking or what the statements in the stimulus are saying. Without an understanding of the specific task required by each question, Logical Reasoning can be difficult and time-consuming.

In previous chapters, you've seen the various types of questions you'll face in the Logical Reasoning section and how each rewards you for untangling the stimulus differently. Knowing, for example, that an Assumption question is composed of evidence leading to a conclusion will help you attack that question type with maximum effectiveness. The LSAT expert has internalized the various Logical Reasoning question types and knows instantly how to approach each one. This is the first building block to Logical Reasoning mastery: for each question, you must have a plan.

Having a plan gives the LSAT expert confidence in the Logical Reasoning section, confidence that leads to speed and accuracy. If Step 1 of the Kaplan Method for Logical Reasoning is not yet second nature to you, you're squandering time and leaving points on the table. Ask yourself a question: Am I able to read and then *immediately* know how to attack each question type? Take a look at the following question stems and answer the questions that follow:

"The statements above, if true, most strongly support which of the following?"

"Which of the following, if true, most strongly supports the argument above?"

What question type is each of these? What will your task be as you evaluate each question's stimulus? In each question, how will the statements in the stimulus relate to each other?

Even though these question types may look similar (the first question stem includes the phrase "strongly support," while the second includes "strongly supports"), your task for each question differs significantly. The first stem is an Inference question that asks you to determine an answer choice that must be true based on the statements in the stimulus, while the second is a Strengthen question that asks you to bolster an argument that is composed of evidence and a conclusion (and therefore contains an assumption). Approaching one type of question as though it is the other will invariably lead to confusion and frustration.

Of course, all of this confusion and frustration comes at a cost. Students who misread question types are often unable to correctly deconstruct stimuli; in turn, they struggle to make accurate predictions. This fog of misunderstanding leads to a predictable result: as students feel themselves getting off track, they start over and attempt to do the question again. As they do so, the clock ticks away, and precious time is lost.

If you were able to immediately and confidently (and correctly) answer those question stems above, excellent work. If instead you struggled to type the questions, or if you were in any way a bit unsure how to attack those different question types, then you've just identified an opportunity to improve your timing and efficiency in this section.

SUGGESTED EXERCISE

Find a Logical Reasoning section that you've already completed (you can use one of the tests in the back of this book, for example). Next to each question stem, write the type of question it is (Flaw, Assumption, Inference, etc.) and the strategy that best fits that question type. Do this without looking at the stimuli or reworking the problems. Once you have identified the question types and written a strategy next to each question, go back through and evaluate your original performance. Compare your approach the first time you did the question to the approach you now have written down next to each stimulus. Then, check the explanations and make sure that you were identifying question types correctly and that the strategies and approaches you outlined for each question type matched up with those outlined in the explanations. Finally, ask yourself a few questions: Did you simply not have an approach the first time? Did you confuse Inference questions with Strengthen questions or Weaken questions with Flaw questions? Were there specific question types that consistently gave you trouble? Use this knowledge to help you quickly and correctly identify future Logical Reasoning question types.

Think back to the question stems you just categorized. Although confusing Inference questions with Strengthen questions is a common mistake, it's certainly not the only problem students have when it comes to recognizing and tackling question types. In addition to knowing how to type a question stem quickly, it's also important to know exactly how to tackle each corresponding question. Understanding that you're facing a Paradox question, for example, is only part of the battle. The next step requires you to analyze and evaluate the stimulus. The LSAT expert knows that in a Paradox question, her task is to immediately identify the two seemingly contradictory facts in the stimulus, then find an answer choice that explains the relationship between them.

Becoming more efficient and effective in the Logical Reasoning section requires a plan. First, immediately recognize and identify each question, then analyze the stimulus and break down its different parts in the way or ways appropriate to that question type. As you untangle the stimulus, though, remember to do two things: Pause and Paraphrase.

Pausing and Paraphrasing: Reading the Stimulus for Maximum Clarity

So you've mastered Step 1 of the Kaplan Method. But what about Step 2? What exactly does "untangle" the stimulus mean? For untrained test takers, their handling of the stimulus amounts to reading it through quickly and superficially. LSAT experts, on the other hand, "untangle" the stimulus by slowing down, seeking out key information, and putting the concepts expressed in the stimulus into their own words. We'll call this process "pausing and paraphrasing." Logical Reasoning questions are often wordy and indirect, so being able to whittle away excess verbiage in a stimulus and home in on just those parts of the stimulus that are useful for answering the question will increase your efficiency and proficiency. One of the problems with tackling an entire Logical Reasoning question without this strategy is that short-term memory allows us to hold only a certain amount of information in our heads at one time. By reducing the amount of text to remember and the number of concepts to evaluate, you are able to more easily pick out the statements in the stimulus relevant to answering the question.

Take a look at the following question:

Reducing stress lessens a person's sensitivity to pain. This is the conclusion reached by researchers who played extended audiotapes to patients before they underwent surgery and afterward while they were recovering. One tape consisted of conversation; the other consisted of music. Those who listened only to the latter tape required less anesthesia during surgery and fewer painkillers afterward than those who listened only to the former tape.

Which one of the following is an assumption on which the researchers' reasoning depends?

PrepTest52 Sec3 Q9

In Step 1, the LSAT expert recognizes this as an Assumption question. She then pauses to ask, "What am I looking for in the statements above?" This pause between Step 1 and Step 2 is important. Knowing that this is an Assumption question, the expert knows that her first task is to look for language that indicates the conclusion. Now, the expert's eye is drawn to the start of the second sentence: "This is the conclusion reached by . . . ." She has found the conclusion—it must be the first sentence.

The expert also knows it will be easier to digest this argument by putting that conclusion into her own words. Thus, she paraphrases: "So, researchers believe that less stress means less pain." With that clear paraphrase of the conclusion in hand, the expert next asks, "Why do the researchers think this is true?" This question helps the expert zero in on the author's primary piece of evidence. After all, the LSAT expert knows that not every single piece of the stimulus is equally important. Instead of taking note of each individual word, she is going to evaluate the evidence by pausing after each sentence and paraphrasing. This simple process clarifies the concepts present in the stimulus, which helps the expert better comprehend the argument being made.

Sentence 2 (evidence): Researchers played audiotapes for patients during and after surgery.

Sentence 3 (evidence): One tape was conversation; the other was music.

Sentence 4 (evidence): Patients who listened to music needed less anesthesia and fewer painkillers than those who listened to conversations.

The LSAT expert knows to combine these three statements, if possible. Concepts that are repeated, or redundant, within a stimulus often link two other ideas together. Here, the second sentence provides background for the argument but does not provide the evidence that the researchers use to draw their conclusion. The third sentence provides information regarding what is on each tape, important only in that it allows us to replace "former" and "latter" in the fourth sentence. Finally, the fourth sentence discusses patients who need "less anesthesia during surgery and fewer painkillers afterward," which is a long-winded way of saying those patients felt less pain. When all three sentences are combined, the expert is able to paraphrase the entirety of the evidence: "Listening to music instead of listening to conversations reduces the amount of pain a person feels."

With a clear plan, the LSAT expert was able to slow down, pause, and ultimately paraphrase the conclusion and evidence. One good habit that allows experts to understand how the evidence compares to the conclusion is to read the argument back using the following template: "Conclusion because evidence." Though this may take an additional few seconds, the clearer understanding of the argument's structure and logic it provides will save time by allowing the LSAT expert to quickly home in on the right answer. The argument now looks like this: "Reducing stress reduces the amount of pain a person feels; researchers believe this because listening to music instead of listening to conversations reduced the amount of pain a person feels."

Does this rewrite of the argument make more sense to you? It's the same argument as above; it's just been shortened and "demystified" by the process of pausing and paraphrasing. Here, we wrote out the entire thought process, but with practice, untangling a stimulus in this way takes only a few seconds. By the way, are you now easily able to determine the researchers' assumption? They assume that listening to music reduces stress. This approach will help you understand Logical Reasoning arguments more clearly, and that understanding will in turn help you answer questions more confidently and more quickly.

Predict by Looking for Patterns

Reading questions strategically and with purpose is a hugely important skill that LSAT experts utilize as they approach the Logical Reasoning section. But another significant tool in the LSAT expert's toolbox is the ability to recognize common argument patterns and to predict correct answer choices. This skill can be developed by recognizing that the LSAT, by virtue of the fact that it is a standardized test, asks the same types of questions over and over again.

So how do you improve your ability to recognize patterns in Logical Reasoning questions? It requires a two-step process. The first step is to use a resource (like this book, for example) to identify the patterns that the testmaker uses when constructing this test. In earlier chapters, you saw, for example, how the LSAT structures Assumption-family arguments in a number of recognizable, repeated configurations. You've also practiced questions with familiar Logical Reasoning flaws that show up on test after test. Know the patterns and then move on to the second step: practice, practice, practice. As you become more familiar with the material, you will begin to recognize more and more of the test's patterns.

SUGGESTED EXERCISE

If you're having trouble identifying patterns in Logical Reasoning questions, perform an exercise we call "Post-phrasing." Here's what you do: before you attempt the problems in a Logical Reasoning section, turn to the explanations and note the correct answer choice for each question in the section. Go through and mark the right answers before you ever read the questions. Now that you've done that, go through the question set and explain to yourself why each marked correct answer is correct. There is no guessing or searching for the right answer on your part here. Because you already know the correct answers, your goal instead is to link the right answer to the relevant part or parts of the stimulus. In an Assumption question, how does the correct answer link with the evidence to lead to the conclusion? In a Strengthen/Weaken question, how does the correct answer either negatively or positively affect the argument? In an Inference question, why is the right answer supported by the statements in the stimulus, and why are the wrong answer choices not supported? Continue in this manner for each question in the set.

APPROACHING THE SECTION EFFICIENTLY

LSAT experts Plan, Pause, Paraphrase, and Predict to efficiently and strategically tackle individual questions. But improving accuracy and timing on individual questions is only part of Logical Reasoning section management. Effective time management also involves knowing which questions to tackle and which to avoid.

Think of it this way. Imagine you're participating in a scavenger hunt at a friend's house and your goal is to find as many items as possible in, say, five minutes. The list contains some familiar items: keys, a remote control, a spoon, a pillow, a mug. But in addition, there are some odd items, like an old postcard and a pocket watch. You've been to your friend's house enough times to know where the keys, the remote, and the silverware can be found. But old postcards and pocket watches? Those might be anywhere—the attic, garage, or bedroom closet. Now, here's the real kicker: The list isn't in order of familiarity—"old postcard" might be dropped in among several more familiar items. Your friend yells, "Go!" and the hunt is on. What do you do? Do you immediately rush to a far corner of the house in search of the mysterious objects? Of course you don't, because the reward isn't worth the trouble. And you don't necessarily tackle the list in order, either. Instead, you're going to gather as many items as possible from the familiar landscape in front of you: the spoon and the mug from the kitchen, the pillow and remote control from the living room. Only *after* the easily accessible items are found and gathered will you think about possibly searching for the obscure items.

The type of person who starts the hunt by searching for the pocket watch and the postcard is an ineffective time manager. On the LSAT, this is the person who spends nearly all of her time on a few of the most difficult questions in each section. Now, it may be satisfying to be the only person to come up with the most unusual item on the scavenger hunt list, but the objective of the game was to get the *most* items. Likewise, while it feels good to get the most difficult Logical Reasoning questions right, the LSAT does not award bonus points or extra credit for harder questions. A test taker who manages time well and answers 20 questions correctly while missing the five most difficult questions will have performed—by the only measure that matters, the LSAT score—better than a test taker who answers the five most difficult questions but runs out of time and is not able to answer the section's final seven questions. Every right answer is worth exactly the same, so make it a priority to answer the easier and faster questions first.

Where Are the Difficult Questions?

It's easy enough to say that the ideal strategy is to avoid difficult questions when possible, tackling instead the problems that are easier and more comprehensible, but how do you know when a question is "hard"? For one thing, "hard" and "easy" are to some degree subjective—one student, for example, may be an ace at questions containing Formal Logic, while another finds them a consistent challenge. Beyond personal preference, there are also a few objective features that signal the more difficult questions.

As the question difficulty graph from earlier in the chapter showed, the difficulty level of questions in the Logical Reasoning section moves from relatively easy to relatively difficult. Question difficulty doesn't increase linearly, though. Most of the section's difficult questions are clustered in the "Danger Zone," stretching roughly from question 15 to question 24. Here, you'll find a high frequency of three- and four-star questions. A couple of things to note, though: First of all, not every question in this range is extremely difficult. Within the Danger Zone, there will be a couple of questions that most students find to be pretty manageable. That means it's not a good idea to completely skip this part of the section and leave those easy points behind. The other thing to be cognizant of is the difficulty level of questions *after* the Danger Zone. LSAT experts know that a couple of manageable questions typically wait at or near the end of the section.

Because the Logical Reasoning section is consistently structured in this way, many students find that an effective strategy for dealing with the Danger Zone is to work progressively from question 1 to question 15, then jump to the end of the section and work backward. This strategy effectively guarantees that the Danger Zone questions—those most likely to be harder, more time-consuming, and often the most frustrating—will be the last questions a test taker faces. This simple strategy, however, is often not enough to completely maximize time management in this section. Even though difficult questions may show up in predictable areas of the test, no one can predict exactly the questions in a section that are considered high difficulty. Thus, experts are able to recognize when a question is difficult, no matter where it appears in the section.

Recognizing Difficult Questions

Given that all test takers have individual strengths and weaknesses, questions can be difficult on a personal and subjective level. The difference between an average student and an LSAT expert is that the expert is self-aware enough to realize where she is strong and where she is weak. There is no substitute for self-evaluation.

But the best test takers know that the test will present questions that, at least at first, are hard to figure out. That's why it's good to give yourself the option of moving on from a question that you feel is difficult or confusing. Regardless of whether it is question 2 or question 22, your best strategy for a question on which you are making no progress is to move on and, if time allows, return to the question later. As a general rule, if after 30 seconds you're confused and frustrated by the stimulus, move on to the next question. If you're approaching the section and utilizing good time management techniques, then you know that you will most likely have an opportunity to return to this question later and see it again with fresh eyes. If it turns out that you don't have the chance to come back, you've strategically skipped a question you were unlikely to get right anyway.

In addition to subjective factors, difficult questions generally contain one or more of the following attributes:

It is difficult to know what the question is asking. Even though LSAT experts are able to read a question stem and quickly recognize the question type, a few question stems have the potential to be confusing and ambiguous. If you're not able to determine precisely what a question is asking, it's probably a good candidate to skip and return to later.

It is difficult to break the stimulus into its parts. As you are now aware, the ability to untangle the stimulus into its various parts is crucial. If you are having difficulty finding the evidence and conclusion in an argument-based question, for example, skip the question and return to it later.

The answer choices are difficult to evaluate. Rarely, a question and stimulus are straightforward enough, but the language in the answer choices is difficult to understand. You may have noticed this in some of the more difficult Flaw, Method of Argument, and Role of a Statement questions. The answer choices to these questions are often presented in abstract and convoluted terms. When dealing with these problems, your best strategy is to make a prediction and then work to match it as best you can to one of the answer choices. However, if you're simply too confused or frustrated by the wording in the answer choices, strike through those you are certain are incorrect, then move on and return when your mind is clearer.

The stimulus includes Formal Logic. Although some test takers naturally pick up the concepts of Formal Logic and master the art of piecing together sufficient and necessary statements, many students struggle with these concepts. Additionally, when the test maker uses Formal Logic, the answer choices often rearrange the sufficient and necessary terms. This leads to confusion among test takers who are not able to distinguish among answer choices containing the same terms but presenting different logical relationships. Tackling or skipping questions with Formal Logic is definitely a subjective measure. Know yourself—your strengths and weaknesses. If you determine that Formal Logic statements in Logical Reasoning questions give you trouble, then these are good questions to skip and return to later.

Every test taker is different. Evaluate your performance after every timed Logical Reasoning section to determine your strengths and weaknesses. Did you get bogged down by one of the difficult questions and spend an impractical amount of time on it? Did you get mired in the Danger Zone without finding time to evaluate the questions at the end of the section? Did you struggle with a particular question type? Did you find yourself making predictions and then second-guessing yourself once you started reading the answers?

Ultimately, your Test Day goal for the Logical Reasoning section is to be able to recognize when a question is difficult, to be comfortable skipping it and returning to it later, and to have a methodical approach and plan to tackle that question when you do eventually get to it.

Putting the Pencil to Paper

Now that you know that skipping questions and returning to them later is an important strategy for managing time in the Logical Reasoning section, you'll want to develop a written system that allows "present you" to make things as easy and straightforward as possible for "future you."

Marking your test booklet clearly and gridding answer choices strategically can have an immediate impact on your timing proficiency in the Logical Reasoning section. If you skip a question, how can you signal that to "future you"? A good strategy is to circle questions that you've skipped and to cross out or draw a line through questions that you've answered. Additionally, it's often helpful to "future you" to write down the letters when "present you" is between two choices. For example, if you're between answer choices (A) and (D), write "A/D" next to the stimulus and return later. Making clear and understandable marks in your test booklet will clarify the task that "present you" has assigned to "future you."

Another way to improve your efficiency in this section is to strategically grid in answer choices on the bubble sheet. This is especially important for test takers at a testing facility where the desks have small surface areas. Determining an answer choice in your test booklet and transferring that information to your answer grid can be a multistep process for these students. If you find that you're losing precious seconds every time you grab your answer grid, fill in a bubble, and then return to your test booklet, utilize this strategy: wait until you have finished answering questions on two facing pages, then grab your answer grid and bubble in the six to eight answer choices at that time (minus any questions you've skipped, of course).

SUGGESTED EXERCISE

In addition to bubbling in answer choices strategically, making specific notations in your test booklet is an excellent way to practice great test-taking habits. By tying a physical process (the movement of your pencil) to a psychological process, you'll be able to figure out not only where some of your issues are coming from, but also how to overcome them. Here are some notations you can start making today that will help you think like an expert. First, write down an "R" whenever you find yourself excessively rereading. These are questions on which it would be beneficial to slow down—remember the mantra of "pause and paraphrase." Another notation you can make is a "P" next to any question where you find yourself skipping the prediction stage. Additionally, when a question seems as if it will be especially time-consuming after 30 seconds of evaluation, put a star next to it. When you go back and review your performance, check to see how your markings lined up with your performance. How could you have performed better on the questions you marked with a "P" or "R"? For the questions you starred, did you end up skipping them and, if so, was that a wise move? Or did a question simply seem harder than it really was? Use your notations to continue to evaluate and hone your performance.

COMMON FRUSTRATIONS—DIAGNOSING YOUR ISSUE AND WAYS TO IMPROVE

Becoming an LSAT expert doesn't happen by accident. Great test takers recognize the areas in which they need improvement, then work to improve and hone their approach in those areas. Here, we've written descriptions of four archetypical LSAT students, each of whom is not reaching his or her maximum LSAT scores because of one or more bad habits. Now, chances are that none of these imaginary students describes you perfectly, but ask yourself if any of their issues describe any of your issues. If so, check out and implement the recommended exercises.

The Real World Applicator

Some students get so frustrated with the abstract nature of some LSAT questions that they lose sight of the fact that the LSAT exists as its own self-contained evaluative test. If you are always thinking about how scenarios relate to the real world, then you are unnecessarily making the test more difficult for yourself. For example, consider this simple, LSAT-like argument: "The basketball player who distributes the most assists should be considered the most valuable player in the league because in hockey, players who accumulate the most assists are often deemed to be the most valuable." What is the assumption that underlies this argument?

Maybe you were tempted to make a prediction like "We should give the most valuable player award to the basketball player with the most assists because she deserves it the most." Whether that is the right standard for evaluating basketball players (it might or might not be) in the real world is beside the point. More importantly for the LSAT test taker, that is not what the argument assumes. On the LSAT, all we care about is the argument presented to us and the ideas and concepts it contains. If you keep this in mind, the test should instantly become much easier for you. In this argument, the assumption must connect hockey and basketball and state that their players should be evaluated by similar standards. We don't even need to look to the answer choices to help us out. This is the power of predicting correct answer choices. The right answer must bridge the gap between the evidence and the conclusion. Though it may be reasonable (in the real world) to discuss whether or not a player deserves to win the most valuable player award, the concept of what is or is not "deserved" is not addressed in the argument, so it won't be a part of the right answer choice.

To overcome this tendency to be a "Real World Applicator," keep a few things in mind. First of all, go back to the basics and read with purpose (pausing and paraphrasing). By breaking an argument into pieces that can be compared (assumption family) or combined (inference), you keep yourself from bringing in ideas that are out of scope. If you focus on predicting the correct answer by using only the terms in the stimulus, then you will be less tempted by wrong answer choices involving concepts Outside the Scope of the argument, making Irrelevant Comparisons, or making Extreme claims.

SUGGESTED EXERCISE

Go through several Logical Reasoning questions, untimed, and write down the different pieces of the stimulus (using your paraphrasing skills). Without looking at any of the answer choices, use the pieces to predict, as clearly as possible, what the right answer will contain. In argument-based questions, rewrite each stimulus in this form: "Conclusion *because* evidence." In non-argument-based questions, jot down the paraphrased pieces of the stimulus with an eye toward spotting the most concrete claims and combining statements if possible. Once you have the pieces written down, check the explanations. Did your prediction match the correct answer choice as described by the explanation? If you didn't make a prediction, does the explanation describe how to connect the pieces of the stimulus to arrive at the right answer?

If you are a "Real World Applicator," it is incredibly important for you to slow down and focus on Steps 2 and 3 of the Logical Reasoning Method. This exercise will help you see the value of those two steps.

The Rusher

Some test takers simply don't have a clear understanding of question types and approaches. In fact, some test takers even forget to read the question stem first, rushing headlong into every problem as though tackling the LSAT with the appropriate level of enthusiasm will be sufficient to do well. But as we've seen before, attacking the Logical Reasoning section without a plan and a purpose can negatively affect both timing and accuracy.

Impatient test takers often get tripped up by the learning curve involved in mastering Logical Reasoning questions. That's understandable given all that must be learned at the outset—the Logical Reasoning Method, the many different question types, and a variety of reading and reasoning skills. In their rush to use newfound strategies and tactics, overeager test takers allow themselves to get sloppy, skipping steps in the Method, or failing to identify the question type before jumping into the stimulus paragraph. For anxious test takers, it can even feel as if the Logical Reasoning Method is slowing them down or making them miss questions. That is just because they haven't practiced enough to make the Method second nature. It's comparable to learning to drive a car with a stick shift and manual transmission. At the beginning, each step—depressing the clutch, engaging the gear, pressing the gas while releasing the clutch—seems awkward and frustrating. But you cannot skip one of those steps. So, you practice, maybe failing more often than you succeed at first. Then, one day it all comes together and you begin doing all of the steps automatically, without thinking. The Logical Reasoning Method will be much like that. Just keep at it, reminding yourself consciously of each step. Before you know it, you'll be using the Method effortlessly, and your timing and accuracy will both improve.

A person who is having difficulty categorizing questions will often struggle with timing in the Logical Reasoning section. After adequate practice, that tendency will turn around because identifying question types allows you to slow down, approach each question with a plan, and predict the correct answer before evaluating answer choices. And LSAT experts know that there is a direct, positive correlation between predicting the correct answer and time management.

SUGGESTED EXERCISE

Flip to a Logical Reasoning section and identify each question's type before actually tackling any questions. If you are really struggling, note the question type *and* jot down your strategy for it. After you do this, go back through the section and actually answer the questions. Note that this is an exercise, not a Test Day strategy. The point of this exercise is to show you that knowing the type of question, the pattern it will present, and the best strategy to use will allow for greater control and mastery, which ultimately leads to effective time management.

The Anxious One

Mastery of Steps 1–3 of the Logical Reasoning Method is an integral part of conquering the Logical Reasoning section. But correctly identifying question stem types and analyzing stimuli isn't enough for complete mastery. At the end of the day, you still have to find the correct answer choice.

Imagine this scenario: you've read a question stem, you've analyzed the question's stimulus, and you've predicted the correct answer. So far, so good. Then you look down and evaluate the answer choices and you notice that choice (A) seems somewhat convincing. It doesn't quite fit your prediction, but what if that's the right answer and you just overlooked something important in the stimulus? You keep reading, and you notice that (C) and (D) are also convincing. Did you possibly misread the question stem? You go back and reread, only to confirm that you identified the question type correctly. Now, you reread the stimulus and again find you analyzed it well. Your prediction also remains the same, and as you reread the answer choices, you see that answer choice (D) matches your prediction the best. Earlier, you had been thrown off by answer choices (A) and (C), but now you see that they introduce Extreme language that pushes them into wrong answer territory. You select (D) and move on.

Sound familiar? Notice that the Anxious One actually gets this question correct, but he does so by essentially doing the problem twice. The tendency to rework problems is a time killer on the LSAT. To improve your ability to get through the Logical Reasoning section in time, you need to be able to make good predictions, have the confidence to match those predictions to correct answer choices, and be comfortable moving on from answer choices that do not match your prediction.

SUGGESTED EXERCISE

If the Anxious One description fits you, then it's hard for you to believe, "I should be more confident in my initial reading of the question." So, to overcome the doubts that impair your performance, try this: In the next Logical Reasoning section you do, time yourself for each question. Start the timer when you start a question, then work through it as you normally would, making a prediction and matching it as best you can. Stop the timer when you've spotted the answer choice that most closely matches your answer. Write down that time on your page next to the question. Now, start the timer again and continue with the same problem, evaluating answer choices more thoroughly. Reread the question stem or the stimulus if you need more clarity. If you like, change your answer based on this second pass. Stop the timer once you're reasonably comfortable that you have the right answer. Now ask yourself a few questions. How much time did the second pass of the question cost you? Did you change your answer? If you did change your answer, did you change it to the *correct* answer? Look at this extra time in terms of a cost/benefit analysis: How many more points are you answering correctly because of this constant questioning versus how much time are you losing? If you notice that you are losing a lot of time and that you are not, actually, answering more questions correctly, then you will finally be able to convince yourself that an initial, thorough, strategic reading of the stimulus is the best strategy to manage time effectively in this section.

The Perfectionist

If you're taking the LSAT, then you're probably planning to go to law school, and if you're planning to attend law school, then chances are good that you're interested in being a lawyer. And boy, do lawyers enjoy being right. "Perfectionist" is a common personality type among budding lawyers, and while that trait has its positive aspects, it can also be a drawback on the LSAT. Students who get into a battle with the test by silently arguing with answer choices or by refusing to skip questions will invariably see their score suffer. The desire to confront and conquer every single question leads the Perfectionist to a familiar but unfortunate destination: the proctor announcing "time" before she is able to finish the section.

The first thing the Perfectionist needs to do is let go. Change your focus from *perfection* (achieving a perfect score, getting every difficult question correct, or hitting each timing benchmark to the second) to *ideal performance* (maximizing my results, remaining strategic, and managing time effectively). Remember, just like the scavenger hunter who is trying to collect as many items as possible, you don't care where you find your points; it only matters that you get as many of them as possible.

One thing the Perfectionist needs to determine as soon as possible is just how long, exactly, it takes to do a question. Ask yourself: Am I cognizant of how long it takes me to read a stimulus? To make a prediction? To evaluate answer choices? If you are a person who can easily get lost in a problem and has no idea how long it takes to do individual questions, then it would be instructive to time yourself on individual questions. Keep track of how and where you get bogged down—is it in the stimulus-reading stage (rereading), the prediction stage (trying too hard to come up with an exact prediction), the evaluating answer choices stage (thoroughly reading each answer choice), or all three?

SUGGESTED EXERCISE

To break the habit of reading straight through from beginning to end, set yourself the challenge of taking 15 minutes to answer as many questions correct out of the last 15 questions in a Logical Reasoning section. What will you do? You know there's no way you will be able to answer all 15 questions—that approach is immediately out the door. But your goal is to answer correctly as many as possible, so you start by tackling the easiest or shortest questions. This "game" is the same game the LSAT presents in a full section. To break the habit of reading every answer choice, evaluate how often your prediction is correct by drawing a line under the first answer choice you think is correct. If you changed your answer, was it correct? If you didn't change your answer, do you know how long it took you to evaluate the other answer choices?

Individual Problems Require Individual Solutions

In this chapter, we've discussed the good habits that LSAT experts utilize to get through the Logical Reasoning section in a timely manner. Planning for each question type, pausing and paraphrasing as you read, and predicting answer choices will help you manage each question effectively and efficiently. In addition, knowing where the difficult questions are can help you manage your time well by answering the easier questions first, then tackling difficult questions later.

The important thing to keep in mind is that if you're having difficulty getting through this section in time, it could be because of a number of different issues. Evaluate yourself and figure out what is preventing you from moving through the section efficiently. Ultimately, you will need to find the approach that allows you to answer as many questions correctly as possible.

CHAPTER 13

The Kaplan Reading Comprehension Method

Every administration of the LSAT features one scored Reading Comprehension section. There are always four passages, each around 450–500 words long and with typically a set of 6–8 questions, for a total of 26–28 questions in the section. For many first-time LSAT test takers, Reading Comprehension is the section that feels most familiar, so it should be no surprise if it is your strongest section initially. Reading Comprehension is the section most similar to other tests you've probably taken, such as the SAT or ACT. Given that the Reading Comprehension section tasks you with reading academic material and answering questions about it, the section may even remind you a bit of standard college class tests.

This superficial similarity to other kinds of testing, however, masks some very unique features of LSAT Reading Comprehension. Moreover, LSAT test takers' initial comfort with Reading Comprehension often leads them to ignore this section to the detriment of their overall LSAT score. From over 40 years of experience working with LSAT test takers, we at Kaplan know that Reading Comprehension is the section in which many test takers have the hardest time improving their performance. After all, having been good readers throughout their academic careers, LSAT test takers are reluctant to change the way in which they read to suit the types of questions the LSAT testmaker asks.

We also know, however, that LSAT Reading Comprehension tests reading and reasoning skills that can be learned and mastered. Mastering them requires that you understand what is being tested and adopt a strategic reading approach that will distinguish the text relevant to LSAT questions from the details and general background information the test questions will largely ignore. And once you understand what the test is asking for, learning to read and answer Reading Comprehension questions quickly and accurately will take practice—a lot of practice.

A STRATEGIC APPROACH TO LSAT READING COMPREHENSION

Notice that we referred to the kind of reading that the expert test taker does as *strategic*. This is an important concept for all that follows. Rather than *deep* or *critical* reading, the kind you might do for a difficult seminar course in college, your job on the LSAT is to get the big picture of a passage—the author's Purpose and Main Idea—and to zero in on how the author makes key points and illustrates ideas or concepts. You're not preparing to have an in-depth conversation about the passage; you're preparing to answer LSAT questions. Take a look at one, and we'll discuss what it reveals about this important LSAT section.

Based on the passage, the fact that the proposed reforms were introduced shortly after the French Revolution most clearly suggests that the proposals

(A)   were a reaction to the excesses of the new government

(B)   had their roots in a belief in the power of education

(C)   had vast popular support within French society

(D)   treated education for women as a prerequisite to the implementation of other reforms

(E)   were influenced by egalitarian ideals

PrepTest56 Sec4 Q26

In a moment, you'll see the passage from which this question came. For now, start your analysis by looking at the question stem. First off, it begins with "[b]ased on the passage." LSAT Reading Comprehension questions can always be answered from the text you're given; outside knowledge of the subject matter is neither expected nor rewarded. How many future law students are likely to have any expertise in the subject of post-Revolutionary French education, anyway? Even more important, the question references a fact stated in the passage and asks what this detail "suggests." The correct answer to this question doesn't contain information about the fact but rather will state the implications *the author* draws from the fact. *How* the author uses a detail or *why* she has included it is far more relevant to LSAT questions than what might be true about the detail.

Now, let's put that question into its context on the test. On the next two pages, you'll see the passage and the complete question set from which this example was drawn. Try it out on your own. Read the passage and take down whatever notes seem relevant and helpful. Try to answer the six questions that accompany it. Don't take too much time, though—no more than 8–10 minutes. We'll spend the rest of this chapter using this passage and its questions to illustrate how an LSAT expert reads and analyzes a Reading Comprehension passage and subsequently answers its questions efficiently and effectively. Along the way, you'll learn the 5-step Kaplan Reading Comprehension Method, the approach you'll use to tackle many more passages in the two chapters that follow this one.

During most of the nineteenth century, many French women continued to be educated according to models long established by custom and religious tradition. One recent observer has termed the failure
(5) to institute real and lasting educational reform at the end of the eighteenth century a "missed opportunity"—for in spite of the egalitarian and secular aims of the French Revolution in 1789, a truly nondiscriminatory education system for both
(10) women and men would not be established in the country until the 1880s. However, legislators had put forth many proposals for educational reform in the years just after the revolution; two in particular attempted to institute educational systems for women
(15) that were, to a great extent, egalitarian.

The first of these proposals endeavored to replace the predominantly religious education that women originally received in convents and at home with reformed curricula. More importantly, the proposal
(20) insisted that, because education was a common good that should be offered to both sexes, instruction should be available to everyone. By the same token, teachers would be drawn from both sexes. Thus the proposal held it essential that schools for both men
(25) and women be established promptly throughout the country and that these schools be public, a tangible sign of the state's interest in all of its citizens. One limitation of this proposal, however, was that girls, unlike boys, were to leave school at age eight in
(30) order to be educated at home in the skills necessary for domestic life and for the raising of families. The second proposal took a more comprehensive approach. It advocated equal education for women and men on the grounds that women and men enjoy
(35) the same rights, and it was the only proposal of the time that called for coeducational schools, which were presented as a bulwark against the traditional gender roles enforced by religious tradition. In other respects, however, this proposal also continued to
(40) define women in terms of their roles in the domestic sphere and as mothers.

That neither proposal was able to envision a system of education that was fully equal for women, and that neither was adopted into law even as such,
(45) bespeaks the immensity of the cultural and political obstacles to egalitarian education for women at the time. Nevertheless, the vision of egalitarian educational reform was not entirely lost. Nearly a century later, in the early 1880s, French legislators
(50) recalled the earlier proposals in their justification of new laws that founded public secondary schools for women, abolished fees for education, and established compulsory attendance for all students. In order to pass these reforms, the government needed to
(55) demonstrate that its new standards were rooted in a long philosophical, political, and pedagogical

tradition. Various of the resulting institutions also made claim to revolutionary origin, as doing so allowed them to appropriate the legitimacy conferred
(60) by tradition and historical continuity.

1. It can be inferred from the passage that the French legislators who passed new educational laws in the early 1880s were

    (A) committed to removing education in the skills necessary for domestic life from the public school curriculum

    (B) unaware of the difficulties that the earlier legislators faced when advocating similar legislation

    (C) concerned with improving educational equality across economic strata as well as between the sexes

    (D) more open to political compromise than were the legislators who introduced the previous proposals for reform

    (E) more inclined to give religious authorities a role in education than were the legislators who introduced the previous proposals for reform

2. Which one of the following most accurately describes the organization of the passage?

    (A) Education in France during one historical period is described; two proposals that attempted to reform the educational system are presented; inconsistencies within each proposal are identified and lamented.

    (B) The movement toward gender equality in France during one historical period is discussed; two proposals for educational reform are presented; the differences between the proposals and the educational system of that era are outlined.

    (C) The traditional nature of French education for women is described; proposed breaks with tradition are discussed, followed by a discussion of why eventual change required less of a break with tradition.

    (D) The egalitarian aims in France during one historical period are presented; proposals that foreshadowed eventual reform are described; the initial characterization of the aims is modified.

    (E) The nature of education for women in France during one historical period is described; proposals for educational reform are presented; the relationship between the proposals and eventual reform is indicated.

3. Suppose that two proposals were put forward by lawmakers concerning housing reform today. Which one of the following pairs of proposals is most closely analogous to the pair of proposals discussed in the second paragraph of the passage?

(A) "Housing should be made available to all" and "Real estate practices should be nondiscriminatory"

(B) "Housing should be made available to all" and "The quality of housing should be improved"

(C) "There should be housing for all who can pay" and "Housing should be of uniform quality"

(D) "The quality of housing should be improved" and "Real estate practices should be nondiscriminatory"

(E) "Low-cost housing should be constructed" and "Housing should be of uniform quality"

4. According to the passage, the second of the two proposals discussed was distinctive because it asserted that

(A) everyone should both learn and teach

(B) males and females should go to the same schools

(C) education should involve lifelong learning

(D) religious schools should be abolished

(E) education for girls should be both public and secular

5. Based on the passage, the fact that the proposed reforms were introduced shortly after the French Revolution most clearly suggests that the proposals

(A) were a reaction to the excesses of the new government

(B) had their roots in a belief in the power of education

(C) had vast popular support within French society

(D) treated education for women as a prerequisite to the implementation of other reforms

(E) were influenced by egalitarian ideals

6. The author would most likely describe the proposals mentioned in the passage with which one of the following statements?

(A) They espoused reforms that were very modest by the standards of the day.

(B) They were fundamentally unethical due to their incomplete view of equality.

(C) They were well-meaning attempts to do as much as was feasible at the time.

(D) They were reasonable, and it is difficult to understand why they failed.

(E) They were not adopted because their aims were not fully comprehensive.

PrepTest56 Sec4 Q22–27

Reflect a moment on your performance. How long did you spend reading the passage? Did you distinguish certain parts of the passage as more important or more likely to be asked about in the questions? When you turned to the questions, were you surprised by what they asked? Did you have a good idea where in the passage the relevant text could be found?

By the time you've learned and mastered the Reading Comprehension Method you'll see in this chapter, you'll find that even as you read the passage initially, you can create a Roadmap of circled Keywords within the passage and brief notes in the margins that will allow you to research the passage very quickly to find the portions of the text that provide the answers to the questions. In fact, if you learn to read as strategically as the best LSAT experts, you'll find that you can anticipate many, if not most, of the questions before you even read them.

Using the Roadmap to Answer Reading Comprehension Questions

To learn how to read Reading Comprehension passages strategically and to make good, useful Roadmaps of the passage, it's important to see how LSAT experts use Roadmaps to answer questions. Take a look at how an LSAT expert approached three of the questions from the passage you just tried. Don't worry if you're not sure why the expert circled certain words in the passage at this point. You'll learn to read and analyze as she did when we introduce the Reading Comprehension Method in full, and you'll practice it extensively in the next two chapters.

First up is the question you saw at the beginning of this chapter.

LSAT Question	Analysis
During most of the nineteenth century, many Frenchwomen continued to be educated according to models long established by custom and religious tradition. One recent observer has termed the failure (5) to institute real and lasting educational reform at the end of the eighteenth century a "missed opportunity"—for in spite of the egalitarian and secular aims of the French Revolution in 1789, a truly nondiscriminatory education system for both (10) women and men would not be established in the country until the 1880s. However, legislators had put forth many proposals for educational reform in the years just after the revolution; two in particular attempted to institute educational systems for women (15) that were, to a great extent, egalitarian.	Paragraph 1 tells of how women's education in 19th-century France remained traditional and religious despite proposed reforms, following the Revolution, to make women's education more egalitarian and secular.

Margin notes: Trad. ed. of Fr. women in 19th C. / Critic: needed reform / Au: 2 prop. Made

5. Based on the passage, the fact that the proposed reforms were introduced shortly after the French Revolution most clearly suggests that the proposals	This question refers to paragraph 1, which gives background about the reforms. Researching the paragraph shows that the proposed reforms were intended to give women more equality in education and to make their educations more secular (lines 7–8 and again at line 15). It's also clear that the reforms were not instituted until much later (lines 8–11). The correct answer will paraphrase one of these two points.
(A) were a reaction to the excesses of the new government	Distortion. The reforms appear to be in line with the goals of the Revolution. Eliminate.
(B) had their roots in a belief in the power of education	Outside the Scope. "[B]elief in the power of education" isn't mentioned here. Eliminate.
(C) had vast popular support within French society	180. The reforms failed, so they likely lacked support. Eliminate.
(D) treated education for women as a prerequisite to the implementation of other reforms	Outside the Scope. The passage focuses on educational reform for its own sake. Eliminate.
(E) were influenced by egalitarian ideals *PrepTest56 Sec4 Q26*	Correct. This is supported directly by lines 7–8 and the author's emphatic "to a great extent" at line 15.

Notice that the LSAT expert is interested only in a correct answer "[b]ased on the passage." While other answer choices here—especially (B) and (D)—seem reasonable enough, the expert easily eliminates them as being beyond the purview of the passage. In LSAT Reading Comprehension, you will never be asked to bring in any outside knowledge or to link up information in the passage to what might be reasonable in the "real world." The LSAT expert focused on the author's interest in the proposed reforms—their "aims" (line 8) and what "two in particular" (line 13) tried to achieve. Let the author be your guide as you read LSAT Reading Comprehension passages; when she tells you *why* a detail is included or when she emphasizes a particular example, take note (indeed, make a note in the text or the margin). These are the parts of the passage that LSAT questions will ask about.

Another question here was prefaced with "[a]ccording to the passage." That indicates to the LSAT expert that the correct answer will closely paraphrase a statement made explicitly in the passage. You'll practice several of these Detail questions in Chapter 14.

LSAT Question	Analysis
...The second proposal took a more comprehensive approach. It advocated equal education for women and men on the grounds that women and men enjoy (35) the same rights, and it was the only proposal of the time that called for coeducational schools, which were presented as a bulwark against the traditional gender roles enforced by religious tradition. In other respects, however, this proposal also continued to (40) define women in terms of their roles in the domestic sphere and as mothers. *Second prop:* *—coed* *—radical* *—Problem*	Paragraph 2 outlines the author's two highlighted proposals. The first was an attempt to create women's schools and to replace the primarily religious education they received. The second was more comprehensive and the *only one* to promote coeducational schools.
4. According to the passage, the second of the two proposals discussed was distinctive because it asserted that $\longrightarrow$	"According to the passage" signals that the correct answer will come directly from the passage. The second proposal was discussed in paragraph 2, lines 31–41. The author gives its goal—"equal education" based on equal rights (lines 33–35), and she emphasizes that it was the *only* proposal to advocate coed schools (lines 35–36). The correct answer will closely paraphrase one of those two points.
(A) everyone should both learn and teach $\longrightarrow$	Outside the Scope. The author says nothing about everyone teaching. Eliminate.
(B) males and females should go to the same schools $\longrightarrow$	Correct. This corresponds exactly to the author's Emphasis Keyword, "only."
(C) education should involve lifelong learning $\longrightarrow$	Outside the Scope. Lifelong learning is not associated with the second proposal in the passage. Eliminate.
(D) religious schools should be abolished $\longrightarrow$	Extreme and Outside the Scope. The author doesn't say that either proposal called for the abolition of religious schools. Eliminate.
(E) education for girls should be both public and secular *PrepTest56 Sec4 Q25* $\longrightarrow$	Faulty Use of Detail. The first proposal was explicitly associated with public education for women. Eliminate.

Did you notice that the correct answer again came straight from a point that the author had emphasized in the passage? This is not by chance. The LSAT rewards you for understanding the author's purposes and intentions, and the LSAT expert capitalized on this fact by circling "only" as he was reading. Thus, when researching the passage to predict the correct answer to this question, his eye was drawn to the relevant point. Likewise, he could largely ignore lines 39–41, in which the author signaled an unexceptional aspect of the second proposed reform with the Contrast Keyword "however."

Take a look at the LSAT expert's work on one more question. Note how he interprets the question stem.

LSAT Question	**Analysis**
That neither proposal was able to envision a system of education that was fully equal for women, and that neither was adopted into law even as such, (45) bespeaks the immensity of the cultural and political obstacles to egalitarian education for women at the time. Nevertheless, the vision of egalitarian educational reform was not entirely lost.... *Prop. failed b/c cult. & pol. obst.*	Paragraph 3 summarizes the reasons that the post-Revolutionary reforms failed to gain traction at the time. It goes on to tell how the reforms were eventually instituted in the 1880s.
6. The author would most likely describe the proposals mentioned in the passage with which one of the following statements?	This question calls for the author's characterization of the reforms. This points to paragraph 3 where the author summed up the reasons for their initial failure: there were just too many cultural and political obstacles (lines 44–46). It was not due to any inherent problems with the proposals themselves (as the later ratification of similar proposals makes clear).
(A) They espoused reforms that were very modest by the standards of the day.	180. Just the opposite—they were too radical for their time. Eliminate.
(B) They were fundamentally unethical due to their incomplete view of equality.	180. The author judges the proposals in a positive light. She wouldn't call them "unethical." Eliminate.
(C) They were well-meaning attempts to do as much as was feasible at the time.	Correct. The egalitarian intentions of the proposals are not in doubt, but they tried to do too much for their time.
(D) They were reasonable, and it is difficult to understand why they failed.	Half-Right/Half-Wrong. While the author considers the proposals "reasonable" in the long run, she is very clear In lines 44–46 about the reasons they failed. Eliminate.
(E) They were not adopted because their aims were not fully comprehensive. *PrepTest56 Sec4 Q27*	Distortion. The author discusses the second proposal as "more comprehensive" in paragraph 2. This is not linked to why the proposals failed as explained in paragraph 3, however. Eliminate.

Many LSAT Reading Comprehension questions ask what the author implies or suggests in the passage. The LSAT expert knew from his Roadmap that paragraph 3 contained the author's evaluation and summary of the proposals. From there, researching the relevant text was straightforward. Note how the correct answer to this question paraphrases the author's position. The author takes a positive view of the proposed reforms and concludes that they failed for cultural and political reasons, not on their merits.

The LSAT expert never considered the possibility that two or more answers were technically correct and then try to choose the one that was more correct. He stuck to the principle of "one right; four demonstrably wrong" in all cases. It may be hard to accept that the correct and incorrect answers are just as clear-cut in Reading Comprehension as they are in Logic Games and Logical Reasoning, but they are.

Now that you've seen how the LSAT expert uses the Roadmap to research the passage and predict the correct answer, let's examine the entire process from start to finish.

THE KAPLAN READING COMPREHENSION METHOD

To handle four passages in 35 minutes and to get as many right answers as possible from this section, you need to have an approach that you can use consistently. There are 5 steps to the Kaplan Reading Comprehension Method. The first is all about reading and Roadmapping the passage. The next four give the fastest and surest way to answer the questions.

THE KAPLAN READING COMPREHENSION METHOD

Step 1: Read the Passage Strategically—circle Keywords and jot down margin notes to summarize the portions of the passage relevant to LSAT questions; summarize the author's Topic/Scope/Purpose/Main Idea.

Step 2: Read the Question Stem—identify the question type, characterize the correct and incorrect answers, and look for clues to guide your research.

Step 3: Research the Relevant Text—based on the clues in the question stem, consult your Roadmap; for open-ended questions, refer to your Topic/ Scope/Purpose/Main Idea summaries.

Step 4: Predict the Correct Answer—based on research (or, for open-ended questions, your Topic/Scope/Purpose/Main Idea summaries) predict the meaning of the correct answer.

Step 5: Evaluate the Answer Choices—select the choice that matches your prediction of the correct answer or eliminate the four wrong answer choices.

As you practice, make it your goal to complete Step 1 in about 3–4 minutes, leaving 4–5 minutes for the question set. If you've completed the chapters on Logical Reasoning, Steps 2–5 of the Reading Comprehension Method should look pretty familiar. They're identical to the steps for handling a Logical Reasoning question with the exception of Step 3. In Reading Comprehension, you will already have read and Roadmapped the passage before you analyze the question stem. Discipline yourself to *research* targeted parts of the passage (that is, to consult the Roadmap you've already made) based on the clues in the stem. Test takers who *reread* the passage (or big chunks of it) for each question run out of time; it's clear that these test takers do not trust their original reading of the passage and aren't reading strategically from the start.

Step 1—Read the Passage Strategically

Reading strategically means reading not to memorize factual details but to get LSAT questions correct. As you've already seen, the LSAT is far more interested in *how* the author uses a detail than in *what* the facts about the detail are. Similarly, the LSAT is interested in your ability to discern *why* the author is writing the passage (or some portion of it)—his Purpose in writing, if you will. The first step of the Reading Comprehension Method targets the parts of the passage the test is likely to ask about and, when mastered, allows you to read the passage one time and be ready to research and answer every question.

There are two aspects to Strategic Reading, one physical and one mental.

The Physical Roadmap—Keywords and Margin Notes

As an LSAT expert reads a Reading Comprehension passage, she reads with pencil in hand. This allows her to circle or underline Keywords, words that indicate the structure of the passage. As you learn to identify Keywords, your reading will become much more strategic because Keywords prompt you to read actively, asking why the author is emphasizing a certain point or contrasting one idea with another. There are six categories of Keywords you should look for. You'll see them highlighted in every Roadmap you review in Chapter 14, in the Sample Roadmaps accompanying the explanations for the passages in Chapter 15, and in the online explanations for full-length tests at the end of the book.

LSAT STRATEGY

Strategic Reading Keywords

- **Emphasis/Opinion**—words that signal that the author finds a detail noteworthy or has a positive or negative opinion about it or, indeed, any subjective or evaluative language on the author's part (e.g., *especially*, *crucial*, *unfortunately*, *disappointing*)

- **Contrast**—words indicating that the author thinks two details or ideas are incompatible or illustrate conflicting points (e.g., *but*, *yet*, *despite*, *on the other hand*)

- **Logic**—words that indicate an argument, either the author's or someone else's (e.g., *thus*, *therefore*, *because*)

- **Illustration**—words indicating an example offered to clarify or support another point (e.g., *for example*, *this shows*, *to illustrate*)

- **Sequence/Chronology**—words showing an order to certain steps in a process or to developments over time (e.g., *traditionally*, *in the past*, *recently*, *today*, *first*, *second*, *finally*, *earlier*, *since*)

- **Continuation**—words indicating that a subsequent example or detail support the same point or illustrate the same idea (e.g., *moreover*, *in addition*, *and*, *also*, *further*)

As you review sample Roadmaps, you'll see that the LSAT experts seldom circle the sorts of factual information you would likely pinpoint in a conventional textbook for a subject-matter course in school. Instead, their focus on Keywords helps them discern the structure of the passage and thus the author's point of view and purpose in writing.

The other thing the LSAT expert does with her pencil is to jot down brief, abbreviated margin notes wherever she encounters an important point in the text. As you review the LSAT experts' Roadmaps, don't make too much of the specific wording in these margin notes. They may be as simple as "Ex" for an example or as thorough as a short description. Everyone will have slightly different notes next to a passage. The important thing is that your margin notes are simple, accurate, and legible and that they target the author's key points in the passage and are not just a list of facts that repeats the passage.

Some test takers wonder why they should take notes at all. The answer is simple: Your job in strategic reading is to distinguish between the relevant parts of the passage and the factual minutiae and background. If you leave a passage entirely blank, you haven't distinguished the parts you're likely to need when researching the questions. Likewise, if you have circled or underlined almost everything in the passage, you haven't distinguished what's relevant in that case either. During the 3–4 minutes a test taker has to read and Roadmap a passage, no one is likely to make a perfect Roadmap. Don't let your desire for perfection prevent you from creating a very helpful set of notes, however. The LSAT expert leaves the passage marked up in a way that is extremely helpful when it comes to answering the questions.

The Mental Roadmap—Summarizing Topic/Scope/Purpose/Main Idea

While the LSAT expert's pencil is occupied circling Keywords and jotting down margin notes, her mind is also keeping track of the author's "big picture" in the passage. The most helpful way to grasp the big picture is to build a summary as you read. Pay attention to the four concepts outlined below. You'll usually encounter them in the text in the order they're presented in the strategy box.

LSAT STRATEGY

Reading Comprehension—the "big picture"

· **Topic**—the overall subject of the passage

· **Scope**—the particular aspect of the Topic that the author is focusing on

· **Purpose**—the author's reason for writing the passage (express this as a verb—e.g., *to refute, to outline, to evaluate, to critique*)

· **Main Idea**—the author's conclusion or overall takeaway; if you combine the author's Purpose and Scope, you'll usually have a good sense of the Main Idea.

On Test Day, there is no need for you to write down your summaries. Just make sure you can clearly articulate the author's Purpose and Main Idea within the scope of the passage so that you can predict the correct answers to Global questions and Inference questions that ask you for the author's overall point of view or opinion. In practice, it is a good idea to jot down your summaries of the author's Purpose and Main Idea so that you can compare them to the summaries outlined in the explanations. You'll quickly start to see when and why your summaries were too broad or too narrow or missed the scope of the passage.

Take a look now at an LSAT expert's strategic reading and Roadmap for the passage on Women's Education in Post-Revolutionary France. We'll take Step 1 paragraph by paragraph. In the left-hand column you'll see the physical Roadmap of Keywords and margin notes. In the right-hand "Analysis" column, you get some idea of what the LSAT expert was thinking as he read the passage.

LSAT Passage	Analysis
(5) During most of the nineteenth century, many Frenchwomen continued to be educated according to models long established by custom and religious tradition. One recent observer has termed the failure to institute real and lasting educational reform at the (10) end of the eighteenth century a "missed opportunity"—for in spite of the egalitarian and secular aims of the French Revolution in 1789, a truly nondiscriminatory education system for both women and men would not be established in the (15) country until the 1880s. However, legislators had put forth many proposals for educational reform in the years just after the revolution; two in particular attempted to institute educational systems for women that were, to a great extent, egalitarian. *Trad. ed. of Fr. women in 19th C. Critic: needed reform Au: 2 prop. Made*	**Step 1:** This paragraph describes how the education of women in 19th-century France (the **Topic**) followed long-standing traditions. That's followed by a complaint by one observer that France missed an opportunity after the Revolution to make education less discriminatory. Once the author uses the word "[h]owever" in line 11, it's clear the author has a bone to pick with that particular observation (the **Scope**). The author points out that legislators did, in fact, try to reform education during that time, and the author mentions two proposals in particular.

Take note of how the LSAT expert zeros in on Keywords in order to ask what the author is trying to present and why. You'll usually, as the LSAT expert did here, find the Topic and Scope in the first paragraph. Don't force these summaries, however. If the Scope doesn't emerge until the second paragraph, that's okay.

The end of the first paragraph of this passage sets the strategic reader up perfectly for paragraph 2. By ending with a mention of two "particular" proposals, the author has signaled to the expert reader exactly what to expect. Indeed, expert strategic readers are always anticipating where the author will go. That's a great benefit of active reading.

LSAT Passage	Analysis
The first of these proposals endeavored to replace the predominantly religious education that women originally received in convents and at home with reformed curricula. More importantly, the proposal (20) insisted that, because education was a common good that should be offered to both sexes, instruction should be available to everyone. By the same token, teachers would be drawn from both sexes. Thus the proposal held it essential that schools for both men (25) and women be established promptly throughout the country and that these schools be public, a tangible sign of the state's interest in all of its citizens. One limitation of this proposal, however, was that girls, unlike boys, were to leave school at age eight in (30) order to be educated at home in the skills necessary for domestic life and for the raising of families. The second proposal took a more comprehensive approach. It advocated equal education for women and men on the grounds that women and men enjoy (35) the same rights, and it was the only proposal of the time that called for coeducational schools, which were presented as a bulwark against the traditional gender roles enforced by religious tradition. In other respects, however, this proposal also continued to (40) define women in terms of their roles in the domestic sphere and as mothers.	**Step 1 (cont.):** The proposals mentioned at the end of Paragraph 1 are outlined here. The first proposal suggested that women's curricula be revised to have less religious emphasis, that instruction be available to people (and taught by people) of both sexes, and that public schools be established for both men and women. Another "however" in line 28 indicates the problem with this first proposal: girls would be removed from this education at the young age of eight so that they could learn domestic skills at home. The second proposal was a little more radical and recommended coed schools where women and men had the same rights to education. Unfortunately, another "however" in line 39 details the problem with the second proposal: women were still defined as having domestic roles in society.

Notes in passage margin:
First prop:
—less religious emph.
—available to both sexes
—taught by both sexes
—Problem
Second prop:
—coed
—radical
—Problem

Notice that the LSAT expert is now really in the swing of things. He knew what was likely to be covered in this paragraph and focuses on the aspects of each proposal emphasized by the author. He uses Keywords to signal where the author contrasts positive and exceptional aspects of the proposals with their more problematic and conventional traits.

Leaving this paragraph, the LSAT expert expects a summary or evaluation in the passage's final paragraph, and naturally that's just what the author provides.

LSAT Passage	Analysis

(45) That neither proposal was able to envision a system of education that was fully equal for women, and that neither was adopted into law even as such, bespeaks the immensity of the cultural and political obstacles to egalitarian education for women at the time. Nevertheless, the vision of egalitarian
(50) educational reform was not entirely lost. Nearly a century later, in the early 1880s, French legislators recalled the earlier proposals in their justification of new laws that founded public secondary schools for women, abolished fees for education, and established
(55) compulsory attendance for all students. In order to pass these reforms, the government needed to demonstrate that its new standards were rooted in a long philosophical, political, and pedagogical tradition. Various of the resulting institutions also
(60) made claim to revolutionary origin, as doing so allowed them to appropriate the legitimacy conferred by tradition and historical continuity.

Prop. failed b/c cult. & pol. obst.

late 19th C—reform began to take shape

How obst. overcome

Step 1 (cont.): After comparing the two proposals (the first part of the passage's Purpose), Paragraph 3 suggests that their failure showed the immensity of the obstacles that needed to be overcome. However, those obstacles were eventually overcome ("[n]evertheless" in line 47). The rest of the paragraph explains how the two proposals were recalled and used as a foundation for later reforms because they were then considered legitimate examples of historical tradition. So the **Purpose** is not only to compare the two proposals but also to show how they eventually served as the foundation for later reform. The **Main Idea** is that legislators didn't necessarily miss an opportunity for reforming women's education after the Revolution. They had proposals to reform education; they just weren't successful due to obstacles they couldn't overcome until nearly a century later.

As you learn to emulate the LSAT expert's approach in Step 1, you'll find yourself summarizing the Purpose and Main Idea without even having to stop and remind yourself to do so.

You'll see more examples of LSAT experts' strategic reading and Roadmapping in the next chapter. But keep Step 1 in perspective. You don't get LSAT points directly from the Roadmap, and there's no such thing as an objectively right or wrong Roadmap as there are credited and incorrect answer choices. The Roadmap is a tool to help you answer questions correctly, quickly, and confidently. If, upon completing Step 1, you find yourself ready for the question set and able to move through it efficiently, you're Roadmapping well.

Steps 2–5—Answering Reading Comprehension Questions

Several standard question types accompany Reading Comprehension passages—Global, Inference, Detail, Logic Reasoning, and Logic Function. You'll learn the characteristics of each of these in the next chapter along with strategies specific to each.

Earlier in this chapter, you saw how the LSAT expert consulted his Roadmap to answer three of the questions associated with the passage on Women's Education in Post-Revolutionary France. Now, take a look at how the expert answered the other three questions with this passage. This time, though, we'll be explicit about the expert's thinking during each of the four steps of the Reading Comprehension Method focused on answering the questions. Whenever you need to refer to the passage, turn to the preceding pages and refresh your memory of the expert's Roadmap.

LSAT Question	Analysis
1. It can be inferred from the passage that the French legislators who passed new educational laws in the early 1880s were	**Step 2:** This question (asking about the legislators in the 1880s) points to Paragraph 3. The correct answer will follow from what the author says about these legislators' motives and actions.
	→ **Step 3:** Lines 47–53 give the relevant information. The legislators maintained egalitarian ideals. They made education public, free, and mandatory for all.
	Step 4: The correct answer will be true (inferred) from these details.
(A) committed to removing education in the skills necessary for domestic life from the public school curriculum	→ **Step 5:** Faulty Use of Detail. Balancing out the over-emphasis on domestic skills in women's education was a goal of the earlier reformers (¶2), but the passage doesn't say the legislators in the 1880s tried to remove teaching of domestic skills from public education generally. Eliminate.
(B) unaware of the difficulties that the earlier legislators faced when advocating similar legislation	→ 180. The passage goes on to say the legislators were well aware of the past struggles and revolutionary origins of these proposals. Eliminate.
(C) concerned with improving educational equality across economic strata as well as between the sexes	→ Correct. The legislators were motivated by egalitarian ideals and made education free for all.
(D) more open to political compromise than were the legislators who introduced the previous proposals for reform	→ Distortion. The author says that the earlier proposals encountered cultural and political resistance (lines 45–46), but doesn't imply that the earlier reformers were too intransigent to compromise. Eliminate.
(E) more inclined to give religious authorities a role in education than were the legislators who introduced the previous proposals for reform	→ Outside the Scope. The discussion of the 1880s legislators doesn't touch on their relationship to religious officials. Eliminate.

PrepTest56 Sec4 Q22

In this Inference question, the correct answer followed directly from the passage although it paraphrased a couple of statements made by the author. Importantly, the LSAT expert knew right where to look for the part of the passage relevant to answer this question. Taking a few seconds to locate the relevant text and catalogue the statements there allowed the expert to make a broad, but effective, prediction of the right answer. From there, he could either spot that choice (C) was the correct answer or eliminate the other four.

The next question associated with this passage is far broader in scope than any of the others you've seen so far. It's a Global question asking about the passage as a whole. Nonetheless, the expert's Roadmap will provide the answer. Take a look.

LSAT Question	Analysis
2. Which one of the following most accurately describes the organization of the passage?	**Step 2:** This Global question calls for an answer that summarizes the organization of the entire passage. **Step 3:** To research this question, check the margin notes beside each paragraph. → **Step 4:** Checking the Roadmap: The author started by discussing the status of women's education in the 19th century following the Revolution. After presenting a complaint about this status, the author provides two proposals that were presented to change that status. Next, the author outlines the two proposals. Then, she cites the obstacles to their passage at the time and concludes by showing the eventual reform and how it came about.
(A) Education in France during one historical period is described; two proposals that attempted to reform the educational system are presented; inconsistencies within each proposal are identified and lamented.	→ **Step 5:** Half-Right/Half-Wrong. This answer is fine up until "inconsistencies . . . are identified and lamented." The author doesn't lament inconsistencies. This choice also misses the eventual adoption of the proposals. Eliminate.
(B) The movement toward gender equality in France during one historical period is discussed; two proposals for educational reform are presented; the differences between the proposals and the educational system of that era are outlined.	→ Distortion. This answer misses the discussion of traditional women's education, the reasons the proposals initially failed, and the eventual adoption of similar proposals. Eliminate.
(C) The traditional nature of French education for women is described; proposed breaks with tradition are discussed, followed by a discussion of why eventual change required less of a break with tradition.	→ Distortion. The phrase "why the eventual change required less of a break with tradition" misses the mark. Eliminate.
(D) The egalitarian aims in France during one historical period are presented; proposals that foreshadowed eventual reform are described; the initial characterization of the aims is modified.	→ Distortion. This answer is missing the discussion of traditional women's education. Moreover, the phrase "initial characterization of the aims is modified" doesn't fit the author's point. Eliminate.
(E) The nature of education for women in France during one historical period is described; proposals for educational reform are presented; the relationship between the proposals and eventual reform is indicated. *PrepTest56 Sec4 Q23*	→ Correct. This concisely states the same structure indicated by the Roadmap and predicted in Step 4.

Here, the research step does not target one part of the passage but rather encompasses the passage as a whole. It is not surprising that all five answers match the passage in some aspects, but pay attention to how the LSAT expert is able to pinpoint specific phrases in the wrong answers that miss the meaning in the passage. The expert hasn't memorized the passage, but he has summarized the author's big-picture ideas and mapped the paragraphs in ways that allow him to evaluate the choices boldly.

The final question you'll look at may remind you of a Logical Reasoning question type from Chapter 10. Take a look at the expert's analysis and see how he puts his mastery of LSAT reasoning to work.

LSAT Question	Analysis
3. Suppose that two proposals were put forward by lawmakers concerning housing reform today. Which one of the following pairs of proposals is most closely analogous to the pair of proposals discussed in the second paragraph of the passage?	**Step 2:** "[M]ost closely analogous" makes this question like a Parallel Reasoning question from Logical Reasoning. The answer choices will present concepts from subject matter different from that in the passage, but the correct answer will model the same features the author pointed out with regard to the educational reform proposals.
	→ **Step 3:** The proposals were discussed in paragraph 2. The first proposal emphasized availability, providing education separately to everyone. The second proposal emphasized equality, even to the point of creating coeducational schools.
	Step 4: The answer choices all involve housing. The correct answer will say something along the lines of "housing available to all" and "housing equal for all."
(A) "Housing should be made available to all" and "Real estate practices should be nondiscriminatory"	→ **Step 5:** Correct. This matches the prediction, and thus the passage, perfectly.
(B) "Housing should be made available to all" and "The quality of housing should be improved"	→ Half-Right/Half-Wrong. The first part is accurate here, but the concept of improvement misses the second proposal's point. Eliminate.
(C) "There should be housing for all who can pay" and "Housing should be of uniform quality"	→ Distortion. The additional stipulation "for all who can pay" doesn't match anything in the passage. Moreover, "uniform" is probably too strong. Eliminate.
(D) "The quality of housing should be improved" and "Real estate practices should be nondiscriminatory"	→ Distortion. "[N]ondiscriminatory" may match the second proposal, but "should be improved" misses the points of both proposals. Eliminate.
(E) "Low-cost housing should be constructed" and "Housing should be of uniform quality" *PrepTest56 Sec4 Q24*	→ Outside the Scope. Neither "[l]ow-cost" nor "uniform *quality*" really correspond to either proposed education reform. Eliminate.

Although the answer choices bring in a new subject in a question like this one, the correct answer still corresponds to the passage. As you review and work on different passages and their questions in the next two chapters, make sure you are always asking, "Where is the support in the passage for this answer choice?" Both in practice and on Test Day, you will see tempting *but wrong* choices that allude to what you know from the real world, what sounds like the ethical or politically expedient thing to do, and even what you think the test "wants you to say." Steel yourself against all of those wrong answer types by taking Steps 2, 3, and 4 of the Reading Comprehension Method seriously.

The majority of Reading Comprehension questions start with something like "[a]ccording to the passage" or "[b]ased on the passage," and support for the correct answer is present in the text. Take your cue from the LSAT expert: note the clues in the stem, research the passage, and predict the correct answer. Never answer based on what you think you remember from the passage or what "sounds right" to you. Learn to make a helpful Roadmap and then use it to identify precisely what the correct answer must say.

As you were reviewing the LSAT expert's work on the Women's Education in Post-Revolutionary France passage, you may have noticed certain wrong answer types popping up over and over again. This is not by chance. Just as you saw in Logical Reasoning, the testmaker uses certain patterns of distracters test after test, question after question. Take a few minutes to learn about the wrong answers most common in Reading Comprehension before you move on to the next chapter.

Reading Comprehension Wrong Answer Types

Not every wrong answer you see will fit neatly into one of the types you see described here. After all, sometimes when a question asks for what the passage suggests, the wrong answer will just be something the author does *not* suggest, without clearly being a 180 or Extreme. Other wrong answers might fit more than one category. Still, it's worth your time to learn the wrong answer types in the list that follows. You'll see them referred to many times in the questions illustrated in the coming chapters.

LSAT STRATEGY

Reading Comprehension—Wrong Answer Types

- **Outside the Scope**—a choice containing a statement that is too broad, too narrow, or beyond the purview of the passage
- **Extreme**—a choice containing language too emphatic (*all, never, every, none*) to be supported by the passage
- **Distortion**—a choice that mentions details or ideas from the passage but mangles or misstates the relationship between them given or implied by the author
- **180**—a choice that directly contradicts what the correct answer must say
- **Faulty Use of Detail**—a choice that accurately states something from the stimulus but in a matter that incorrectly answers the question
- **Half-Right/Half-Wrong**—a choice in which one clause follows from the passage but has another clause that contradicts or distorts the passage

---

Along the way, you'll see a handful of wrong answers that appear to defy categorization. When that happens, we'll still explain clearly how the LSAT expert can recognize them as demonstrably incorrect. Whenever a wrong answer does fit clearly into one of the types outlined above, however, we'll note that too.

Now that you have the big picture of Reading Comprehension in order, we'll practice applying it to passages and question sets representative of what you're likely to encounter on Test Day. In the next chapter, we'll dive deeper into each step of the Reading Comprehension Method. Additionally, you'll see examples of passages that fit a handful of rhetorical or structural patterns the testmaker uses over and over. As you become more familiar with these passage structures, your strategic reading will become even more targeted. In some passages, for example, you will focus on the author's disagreement with a critic. In others, you'll see that the author has no personal opinion to express but rather is simply interested in explaining other experts' ideas on a subject. In any case, remember that the LSAT questions will focus on the author's Purpose and Main Idea and will reward you for paying attention to *why* the author has included a detail or *how* he's using it within the text. We'll outline the common Reading Comprehension question types in Chapter 14 as well.

Reading Comprehension: Passage Types and Question Types

In this chapter, you'll learn the specific skills involved in applying the Reading Comprehension Method to passages and their question sets. Along the way, you'll discover that the LSAT uses certain patterns over and over, both in the way passages are structured and in the types of questions the test asks.

If you have already worked in or completed the sections on Logic Games and Logical Reasoning, this chapter will feel different. That's because it's difficult to practice Reading Comprehension skills outside the context of full passages. We won't be able to atomize the skills as neatly in this chapter as we have in others. That makes it very important for you to study the Learning Objectives at the beginning of each section and keep them in mind as you're reviewing the expert analysis of the LSAT material. Don't hesitate to mark the pages where Learning Objectives are introduced and refer to them often to keep the goals of the lessons at the front of your mind.

Because LSAT Reading Comprehension passages are often densely written and because the questions shift their focus from the passage as a whole to details scattered throughout the text, it's easy to miss the forest for the trees in this section. To remain strategic and effective in Reading Comprehension, you must proactively engage the material. Don't sit back and read passively, waiting for the author's point to come to you. LSAT experts constantly question and challenge the author as they read. They anticipate where the passage will go and even the questions that the testmaker will ask. That's not easy, but it will make a huge difference in law school where you have to do a similar kind of targeted, interrogative, and skeptical reading. Start disciplining yourself as a strategic reader now, and you'll be well ahead of the game on Test Day and in your first year as a law student.

Job one in gaining this expertise is to internalize the Reading Comprehension Method. Use it unfailingly until it becomes second nature.

THE KAPLAN READING COMPREHENSION METHOD

Step 1: Read the Passage Strategically—circle Keywords and jot down margin notes to summarize the portions of the passage relevant to LSAT questions; summarize the author's Topic/Scope/Purpose/Main Idea.

Step 2: Read the Question Stem—identify the question type, characterize the correct and incorrect answers, and look for clues to guide your research.

Step 3: Research the Relevant Text—based on the clues in the question stem, consult your Roadmap; for open-ended questions, refer to your Topic/Scope/Purpose/Main Idea summaries.

Step 4: Predict the Correct Answer—based on research (or, for open-ended questions, your Topic/Scope/Purpose/Main Idea summaries) predict the meaning of the correct answer.

Step 5: Evaluate the Answer Choices—select the choice that matches your prediction of the correct answer or eliminate the four wrong answer choices.

The first big section of this chapter will concentrate on Step 1, on the active reading and note taking you'll need to do in order to answer all of the passage's questions efficiently. As you learn and practice Step 1, we'll also introduce common passage structures you'll see in LSAT passages.

The second section of the chapter will cover Steps 2–5. You'll learn and practice the most effective ways to answer Reading Comprehension questions. As you do so, you'll learn the characteristics of the question types the testmaker uses for this section.

At the end of the chapter, you'll have a chance to practice a complete passage and question set and compare your work to that of an LSAT expert step-by-step. Chapter 15 contains 11 more full passages, so you'll have ample opportunity to put all that you learn here to work.

STRATEGIC READING AND READING COMPREHENSION PASSAGE TYPES

With 4 passages in the 35-minute Reading Comprehension section, you have about 8½ minutes per passage. Of that, you'll spend between three and four minutes on Step 1 of the Reading Comprehension Method, reading the passage strategically and creating a Roadmap. In Chapter 13, you saw an example of how this targeted reading and note taking sets you up to answer the questions quickly and confidently. Let's quickly outline and explain the skills associated with Step 1.

Strategic Reading and Roadmapping Skills

If you ask most untrained test takers how they start out in Reading Comprehension, they would probably say something like, "I read the passage, I guess." That's accurate, as far as it goes. If you ask LSAT experts, however, their answer would be more nuanced: "I prepare myself to answer all of the passage's questions." Step 1 is not just reading; it's reading strategically, and that's a complex task. You'll be taking note of Keywords that reveal the author's opinion and the passage structure, you'll make margin notes to correspond with the most important points in the passage, and you'll summarize the author's Purpose and Main Idea. Here's the good news: Each of those tasks has a handful of manageable, learnable skills associated with it.

LEARNING OBJECTIVES

In this portion of the chapter, you'll learn to use:

Keywords

- Identify Keywords from six categories (Emphasis/Opinion, Contrast, Logic, Illustration, Sequence/Chronology, Continuation).
- Use Keywords to accurately paraphrase the text (author's purpose, method of argument, etc.).
- Use Keywords to accurately predict where the passage will go (scope and purpose of remaining paragraphs, for example).
- Use Keywords to predict points in the passage to which LSAT questions will refer.

Margin Notes

- Identify text that warrants a margin note.
- Capture key content in a brief, accurate margin note.

"Big-Picture" Summaries—Topic/Scope/Purpose/Main Idea

- Read a passage and identify the author's Topic and Scope.
- Read a passage and identify the author's Purpose.
- Read a passage and identify the author's Main Idea.

Let's briefly explain what each of these skill sets includes and why they're vital to the strategic reading of LSAT Reading Comprehension passages.

Why Use Keywords?

The short, but very compelling, answer is that Keywords indicate differences in opinion and structure, and knowing those is often the key to distinguishing between right and wrong answers on the test. Here's why. Take two simple statements:

Jessica earned an outstanding LSAT score. Jessica is going to attend Gilligan University Law School next fall.

If that was all you knew, you could not answer this typical LSAT question: "With which one of the following statements about Gilligan University Law School would the author most likely agree?" You know two facts about Jessica but nothing about the author's point of view towards her future alma mater. Add a Contrast Keyword, however, and the answer to the LSAT question is clear:

Jessica earned an outstanding LSAT score; despite this fact, she will attend Gilligan University Law School next fall.

Now, you know that the correct answer to the LSAT question would be something along the lines of "It's unexpected that someone with an outstanding LSAT score would choose Gilligan." On the other hand, what if the two facts were connected by a logic Keyword?

Because Jessica earned an outstanding LSAT score, she will attend Gilligan University Law School next fall.

This signals a profound difference in the author's point of view. The correct answer now would be something like, "Gilligan University Law School generally requires high LSAT scores for admission." Consider the implications of this example: In both cases, the facts were absolutely identical, yet the correct answers to the LSAT question were polar opposites. Keywords signal an author's purpose or position, they highlight what she wants to emphasize, and they reveal how she is making her argument. These are the aspects of the text that LSAT questions focus upon.

LSAT Reading Comprehension questions never ask for factual details that a test taker might just happen to know from the outside world. Take the following assertion, for example.

During the Civil War, President Lincoln deliberately sought out the advice of cabinet members whose opinions were at odds with his own.

The LSAT will not ask, "Which of the following is true of Lincoln's cabinet?" and expect you to report on the multiplicity of opinions. After all, you may be able to answer a question like that without reading the passage at all. Indeed, it would not even matter if you were a history major who could write an essay on the subject and challenge the statement about Lincoln with facts of your own. LSAT Reading Comprehension is not a test of expertise; like the rest of the LSAT, it's a test of skill.

Now, put the statement about Lincoln into the context of an LSAT passage.

Effective leaders allow for open dialogue. For example, during the Civil War, President Lincoln deliberately sought out the advice of cabinet members whose opinions were at odds with his own.

From this, the LSAT might draw a question such as "The author most likely refers to Lincoln and his cabinet in order to . . . ." The correct answer, you'll notice, must start with a verb. Because the sentence on Lincoln is prefaced with the Illustration Keywords "[f]or example," the correct answer here would say something like "to illustrate one characteristic of effective leaders." Regardless of how much (or how little) you know about leadership or the Lincoln administration, strategic reading will get you the LSAT point.

As you learned in Chapter 13, there are six types of Keywords you'll want identify and use as you are reading LSAT passages. In the chart that follows, the categories are listed roughly in order of importance.

LSAT STRATEGY

Strategic Reading Keywords

- **Emphasis/Opinion**—words that signal that the author finds a detail noteworthy or has a positive or negative opinion about it or, indeed, any subjective or evaluative language on the author's part (e.g., *especially, crucial, unfortunately, disappointing*)

- **Contrast**—words indicating that the author thinks two details or ideas are incompatible or illustrate conflicting points (e.g., *but, yet, despite, on the other hand*)

- **Logic**—words that indicate an argument, either the author's or someone else's (e.g., *thus, therefore, because*)

- **Illustration**—words indicating an example offered to clarify or support another point (e.g., *for example, this shows, to illustrate*)

- **Sequence/Chronology**—words showing an order to certain steps in a process or to developments over time (e.g., *traditionally, in the past, recently, today, first, second, finally, earlier, since*)

- **Continuation**—words indicating that a subsequent example or detail supports the same point or illustrates the same idea (e.g., *moreover, in addition, and, also, further*)

As you start to make the recognition of Keywords a part of your strategic reading approach, concentrate first on Emphasis/Opinion and Contrast signals. You'll see that they are most often associated directly with LSAT questions because they most directly reveal the author's point of view and purpose in including a detail in the passage. Once you're comfortable recognizing those categories, move on to Logic (these should be familiar to you from working with Logical Reasoning questions) and Illustration. Finally, add the Sequence/Chronology and Continuation signals to your repertoire. You'll find that you understand LSAT passages more quickly and are able to stay focused on the most important aspects of the passages as you read.

As you review the LSAT experts' analyses below, pay attention to where they noted Keywords and used them to understand the passages.

Why Take Margin Notes?

LSAT passages are around 450–500 words long, and while they stay focused on a single Topic and Scope, they abound in details and often reflect two or more points of view. Labeling the key points in the margin next to the passage makes it much easier for you to target your research for individual questions. Unlike some pre-college tests, the order of LSAT Reading Comprehension questions doesn't necessarily correspond to the order of the passage. Question 2 might take you to the third paragraph, question 3 might point back to the first paragraph, and question 4 might ask for an answer about the passage as a whole. Margin notes help you navigate the passage quickly to find the text relevant to a specific question.

No two test takers' margin notes will be identical. Even two high-scoring LSAT experts who routinely ace the Reading Comprehension section will not jot down exactly the same words or phrases. So, don't construct the unrealistic idea of a "perfect Roadmap" in your mind. The expert's notes will have some things in common, however.

Take a look at the work of one expert on the opening paragraph of a passage about a celebrated African writer.

With his first published works in the 1950s, Amos Tutuola became the first Nigerian writer to receive wide international recognition. Written in a mix of

(5) standard English, idiomatic Nigerian English, and literal translation of his native language, Yoruba, Tutuola's works were quick to be praised by many literary critics as fresh, inventive approaches to the form of the novel. Others, however, dismissed his

Fans praise inventive approach to novel

(10) works as simple retellings of local tales, full of unwelcome liberties taken with the details of the well-known story lines. However, to estimate properly Tutuola's rightful position in world literature, it is

Critics dismissive; rehashing & taking liberties

essential to be clear about the genre in which he

(15) wrote; literary critics have assumed too facilely that he wrote novels.

Au—T's works significant —can't class. as novel

PrepTest56 Sec4 Qs1–7

Notice that the expert has accounted for the three points of view present here: those of Tutuola's fans, of his critics, and of the author. LSAT experts are always cognizant of multiple voices within a passage, and they know that the testmaker will reward them for keeping those points of view distinct.

At times, you may have as little as one note per paragraph. Something like "Prof. Brown's hypothesis" or "steps in the process" may suffice if the scope of a paragraph is limited and its organization clear. When the author uses a single paragraph to portray two or more ideas, examples, or theories, however, multiple notes are in order. Take another look at how the LSAT expert Roadmapped the second paragraph of the passage on Women's Education in Post-Revolutionary France that you saw in Chapter 13:

The first of these proposals endeavored to replace the predominantly religious education that women originally received in convents and at home with reformed curricula. More importantly, the proposal

(20) insisted that, because education was a common good that should be offered to both sexes, instruction should be available to everyone. By the same token, teachers would be drawn from both sexes. Thus the proposal held it essential that schools for both men

(25) and women be established promptly throughout the country and that these schools be public, a tangible sign of the state's interest in all of its citizens. One limitation of this proposal, however, was that girls, unlike boys, were to leave school at age eight in

(30) order to be educated at home in the skills necessary for domestic life and for the raising of families. The second proposal took a more comprehensive approach. It advocated equal education for women and men on the grounds that women and men enjoy

(35) the same rights, and it was the only proposal of the time that called for coeducational schools, which were presented as a bulwark against the traditional gender roles enforced by religious tradition. In other respects, however, this proposal also continued to

(40) define women in terms of their roles in the domestic sphere and as mothers.

First prop:

—less religious emph.

—available to both sexes
—taught by both sexes

—Problem

Second prop:

—coed
—radical

—Problem

PrepTest56 Sec4 Qs22–27

That's a long paragraph outlining two related, but distinct proposals. After each, the author identifies a problematic aspect of the proposal. Another LSAT expert may not include the notes about the two proposals' individual features, but a glance at almost any expert's Roadmap would make clear where each proposal is described and where the author's evaluations could be pinpointed. As you examine more expert Roadmaps below, take the time to study their margin notes and reflect on why the test takers noted certain details.

Why Summarize the Author's Topic, Scope, Purpose, and Main Idea?

The answer here isn't much different than it has been for the other features of the Roadmap. We summarize the big picture of the passage because the LSAT asks questions that reward you for having these summaries in mind. Global questions ask for the Purpose or Main Idea directly:

Which one of the following most accurately states the main point of the passage?

PrepTest52 Sec4 Q1

The primary purpose of the passage is to

PrepTest52 Sec4 Q19

In fact, as you'll see when we discuss the Reading Comprehension question types below, we recommend that you answer a passage's Global questions first among any of the questions accompanying a passage. That way, the big picture of the passage is still fresh in your mind.

Global questions aren't the only ones that are made easier by having overall summaries in your mind, however. Open-ended Inference questions asking for a statement with which the author would agree and those asking about the author's attitude also benefit from having the passage succinctly summarized.

It can be inferred that the author would be most likely to agree that

PrepTest52 Sec4 Q25

The passages most strongly support which one of the following inferences regarding the authors' relationships to the professions they discuss?

PrepTest52 Sec4 Q8

Both of those are questions in which knowing the authors' overall Scope, Purpose, and Main Idea will help you to identify the correct answer, eliminate wrong answers, or both.

LSAT STRATEGY

Reading Comprehension—the "big picture"

- **Topic**—the overall subject of the passage
- **Scope**—the particular aspect of the Topic that the author is focusing on
- **Purpose**—the author's reason for writing the passage (express this as a verb—e.g., *to refute, to outline, to evaluate, to critique*)
- **Main Idea**—the author's conclusion or overall takeaway; if you combine the author's Purpose and Scope, you'll usually have a good sense of the Main Idea.

Whenever you see an LSAT expert's physical Roadmap (circled Keywords and margin notes) below, you'll also have a chance to consider his "mental Roadmap" (the big-picture summaries) as you review his analysis of the passage. Don't gloss over the way in which the LSAT expert paraphrases and condenses the author's points and perspective. Strong paraphrasing is perhaps the most important indicator of active, strategic reading.

Summary: Step 1—Read the Passage Strategically

Now, think back to the LSAT expert's answer to the question about how she starts out in Reading Comprehension: "I prepare myself to answer all of the passage's questions." Step 1 is a complex process, but each of its elements has a clear objective: highlight the parts of the passage that will help get correct answers. The Roadmap an expert produces (both on the test booklet page and in her mind) is a tool for answering the questions. Keep that as your primary objective, and you'll improve your strategic reading skills and your Reading Comprehension score.

LSAT Reading Comprehension Passage Types

Before turning to examples and practice with passages, take a few minutes to learn about the common passage structures you'll see in LSAT Reading Comprehension. There are two ways to categorize LSAT Reading Comprehension passages: by subject matter or by passage structure.

Subject Matter

Every LSAT Reading Comprehension section contains four passages, and it's true that nearly every section has one passage each in the areas of natural science, social science, humanities, and law. Most future law students come from undergraduate backgrounds in the social sciences or the humanities, so there may be a sort of instinctive preference for passages on topics from these areas and a concomitant distrust of one's ability in natural science passages dealing with physics, chemistry, or biology. However, empirical data show that there is little, if any, correlation between subject matter areas and difficulty levels. So, if you encounter a passage and have a subjective preference for the topic, that's fine, but don't make subject matter more important than it is. Learn to read all Reading Comprehension passages strategically, and you'll be at a decided advantage over much of your competition on the exam.

Passage Structures

For you as a test taker, organizing Reading Comprehension passages by their structures may be a much more meaningful taxonomy. The passage structure offers you a clue to the author's purpose in writing the passage, and that in turn gives you a start in creating a helpful Roadmap. There are four structures you should recognize, listed here from most common to least.

READING COMPREHENSION PASSAGE TYPES

- **Theory/Perspective**—The passage focuses on a thinker's theory or perspective on some part of the Topic; typically (though not always), the author disagrees and critiques the opponent's perspective or defends his own.

- **Event/Phenomenon**—The passage focuses on a event, a breakthrough development, or a problem that has arisen; when a solution to the problem is proposed, the author most often agrees with the solution (and that represents the passage's Main Idea).

- **Biography**—The passage discusses something about a notable person; the aspect of the person's life emphasized by the author reflects the Scope of the passage.

- **Debate**—The passage outlines two opposing positions (neither of which is the author's) on some aspect of the Topic; the author may side with one of the positions, may remain neutral, or may critique both. (This structure has been rare on recent LSATs.)

In this chapter, you'll see examples of each of the first three structures. The passages you work on in Chapter 15 and in the full-length tests offer additional examples. A few years ago, Debate passages were much more common than they have been on tests since 2008 or so. This may be because it was in 2007 that the testmaker introduced the paired Comparative Reading passages that now accompany one of the four question sets on LSAT exams. At any rate, if you use older materials and tests during your LSAT preparation, be aware that you may overestimate the likelihood of encountering this passage structure.

Step 1 in Action: Strategic Reading Examples and Practice

In this section, you'll see three Reading Comprehension passages. In each case, you'll have a chance to practice Step 1 of the Reading Comprehension Method; that is, you'll read the passage strategically and create a Roadmap. On the test, you'll take 3–4 minutes for this step, but don't worry if you take a little longer at this point. It's more important to practice the skills outlined above and get comfortable with this likely new and different way of approaching a piece of text. Along the way, we'll give you clues about how to approach passages with different structures. Additionally, you'll see a note about Comparative Reading when you have the opportunity to try out a set of paired passages (something you'll do just once in a full Reading Comprehension section).

Theory/Perspective Passages

Passages with this structure account for over half of all passages on recent LSATs, and that means they account for over half of the points you can get from the Reading Comprehension section. As previously noted, Theory/Perspective passages outline an opinion of someone other than the author on some aspect of the passage's Topic. Once you identify the presence of another opinion, pay attention to the author's response. Does he agree or disagree? Why? What arguments and evidence does the author or his opponent offer? Use margin notes to keep track of where you hear the differing opinions in the passage. Summarize the author's Purpose (most likely, to critique his opponents' position or defend his own) and Main Idea ("the opposing view is faulty because . . . " or "my view prevails because . . . ").

With that in mind, read and Roadmap the following passage. We've left space for you to add additional analysis or record your thoughts paragraph by paragraph, but make sure you are marking Keywords within the passage itself and recording margin notes that would fit into the limited space next to the passage in the test booklet. The LSAT expert's Roadmap and analysis begins on the following pages.

LSAT Passage	My Analysis
Proponents of the tangible-object theory of copyright argue that copyright and similar intellectual-property rights can be explained as logical extensions of the right to own concrete, tangible objects. This (5) view depends on the claim that every copyrightable work can be manifested in some physical form, such as a manuscript or a videotape. It also accepts the premise that ownership of an object confers a number of rights on the owner, who may essentially do whatever he or (10) she pleases with the object to the extent that this does not violate other people's rights. One may, for example, hide or display the object, copy it, or destroy it. One may also transfer ownership of it to another.	Step 1:
In creating a new and original object from (15) materials that one owns, one becomes the owner of that object and thereby acquires all of the rights that ownership entails. But if the owner transfers ownership of the object, the full complement of rights is not necessarily transferred to the new owner; instead, the (20) original owner may retain one or more of these rights. This notion of retained rights is common in many areas of law; for example, the seller of a piece of land may retain certain rights to the land in the form of easements or building restrictions. Applying the notion (25) of retained rights to the domain of intellectual property, theorists argue that copyrighting a work secures official recognition of one's intention to retain certain rights to that work. Among the rights typically retained by the original producer of an object such as a literary (30) manuscript or a musical score would be the right to copy the object for profit and the right to use it as a guide for the production of similar or analogous things—for example, a public performance of a musical score.	

LSAT Passage	**My Analysis**

(35)   According to proponents of the tangible-object theory, its chief advantage is that it justifies intellectual property rights without recourse to the widely accepted but problematic supposition that one can own abstract, intangible things such as ideas. But while this account

(40) seems plausible for copyrightable entities that do, in fact, have enduring tangible forms, it cannot accommodate the standard assumption that such evanescent things as live broadcasts of sporting events can be copyrighted. More importantly, it does not

(45) acknowledge that in many cases the work of conceiving ideas is more crucial and more valuable than that of putting them into tangible form. Suppose that a poet dictates a new poem to a friend, who writes it down on paper that the friend has supplied. The

(50) creator of the tangible object in this case is not the poet but the friend, and there would seem to be no ground for the poet's claiming copyright unless the poet can be said to already own the ideas expressed in the work.

PrepTest58 Sec2 Qs14–20

Now, compare your Roadmap to that of an LSAT expert. Look for places in which you missed an important Keyword or mischaracterized a point in the passage. Determine whether your big-picture summaries were similar to those of the LSAT expert as well.

LSAT Passage	Analysis

Proponents of the tangible-object theory of copyright argue that copyright and similar intellectual-property rights can be explained as logical extensions of the right to own concrete, tangible objects. This
(5) view depends on the claim that every copyrightable work can be manifested in some physical form, such as a manuscript or a videotape. It also accepts the premise that ownership of an object confers a number of rights on the owner, who may essentially do whatever he or
(10) she pleases with the object to the extent that this does not violate other people's rights. One may, for example, hide or display the object, copy it, or destroy it. One may also transfer ownership of it to another.

Margin notes:
© Tangible-prop. theory

You can "hold" it

Right to do whatever

Step 1: Paragraph 1 starts off with the proponents' view of the **Topic** of the passage, tangible-object theory of copyright. (Anticipate that the author will discuss the opponents' view or an alternative.) The proponents' basic tenet: "every copyrightable work can be manifested in some physical form," in other words, that it can be held. In addition, the owner has the right to do as she sees fit as long as those actions do not infringe upon another person's rights. Basically, the proponents feel that the owner has the right to do whatever she wants.

In creating a new and original object from
(15) materials that one owns, one becomes the owner of that object and thereby acquires all of the rights that ownership entails. But if the owner transfers ownership of the object, the full complement of rights is not necessarily transferred to the new owner; instead, the
(20) original owner may retain one or more of these rights. This notion of retained rights is common in many areas of law; for example, the seller of a piece of land may retain certain rights to the land in the form of easements or building restrictions. Applying the notion
(25) of retained rights to the domain of intellectual property, theorists argue that copyrighting a work secures official recognition of one's intention to retain certain rights to that work. Among the rights typically retained by the original producer of an object such as a literary
(30) manuscript or a musical score would be the right to copy the object for profit and the right to use it as a guide for the production of similar or analogous things—for example, a public performance of a musical score.

Margin notes:
Creator gets rights

Can retain some rights on transfer

Common rules

In IP, keep rights to copy perform.

Paragraph 2 begins with the rights of the owner as creator of the object. Although the owner can transfer property, the owner can still retain some rights after transfer—the notion of "retained rights." Retained rights are common—example: sale of land. But what about retained rights and intellectual property? In intellectual property, an owner who transfers ownership can still retain the right to copy the object for profit and to use it as a guide for the production of similar things, like a performance.

So far, it would seem the author is focusing on the proponents of tangible-object theory because she's just written a great analysis of their position.

LSAT Passage	Analysis

(35)   According to proponents of the tangible-object theory, its chief advantage is that it justifies intellectual property rights without recourse to the widely accepted but problematic supposition that one can own abstract, intangible things such as ideas. But while this account

(40)   seems plausible for copyrightable entities that do, in fact, have enduring tangible forms, it cannot accommodate the standard assumption that such evanescent things as live broadcasts of sporting events can be copyrighted. More importantly, it does not

(45)   acknowledge that in many cases the work of conceiving ideas is more crucial and more valuable than that of putting them into tangible form. Suppose that a poet dictates a new poem to a friend, who writes it down on paper that the friend has supplied. The

(50)   creator of the tangible object in this case is not the poet but the friend, and there would seem to be no ground for the poet's claiming copyright unless the poet can be said to already own the ideas expressed in the work.

PrepTest58 Sec2 Qs14–20

T.O. proponents: you can own idea

Author: Problem— tangible form isn't the imp't part

poet analogy

Paragraph 3 begins with the primary advantage proponents believe tangible-object theory has: you can own ideas. The author takes a turn immediately after, though, and begins detailing problems with the abstract, intangible nature associated with things such as ideas. The author's **Scope** is now confirmed: the tangible-object theory's proponents and its problems. In addition, the author's **Purpose** for writing the passage is to outline the position of those in favor of tangible-object theory and show problems with the logic of that view. The author concedes that their view is compatible with tangible objects. However, it's difficult to apply these same concepts to such "evanescent" things as ideas or broadcasts. The author ends with a poet analogy: a poet could dictate an entire poem to a friend, and if the friend writes it down, then the friend is the owner, unless the poet can show ownership of the ideas expressed in the poem. In sum, the **Main Idea** is that tangible-object theory's emphasis on ownership going to the creator of a tangible form is problematic.

Did you notice how focusing on the passage structure made the specific subject matter—here, an obscure legal theory— feel much less important and intimidating? It took a good while (39 lines, to be exact) for the author's response to the tangible-object theory's proponents to emerge. The LSAT expert, however, was anticipating the author's response from the moment the proponents' ideas were introduced in Paragraph 1. Moreover, that helped the expert not get too lost in the extended discussion of how tangible-object theory applies to intellectual property that took up all of Paragraph 2.

Up until line 39, the author is fairly expository—"[p]roponents . . . argue" or "[i]t [the theory] accepts"—with none of his own opinion on display. The most prominent Keywords in the first two paragraphs are Illustration signals, such as "for example" (at lines 11, 22, and 33). This, too, indicates that the author is explaining someone else's idea. Notice, though, how different the Keywords become once the author joins the argument. "*But while* this account *seems* plausible" (lines 39–40) indicates Contrast and Opinion. The LSAT expert is ready to note the author's point of view. "More importantly" (line 44) is another Emphasis/Opinion Keyword that raises the stakes even further. "Suppose" (line 47) indicates that the author will provide a hypothetical example in support of his position.

The next time you see a Theory/Perspective structure, the subject matter may be drawn from natural science or humanities rather than law, and the author's response to the theory or perspective may surface much earlier in the passage. That said, you'll encounter the same kind of shift in tone (and likely a similar shift in Keywords) that will help you stay focused on the two points of view and highlight the pieces of the passage that will be tested in the question set.

You'll see the questions associated with this passage a little later in the chapter. For now, continue to practice Roadmapping, this time on a passage with a different structure.

Event/Phenomenon Passages

On recent tests, the Event/Phenomenon structure has appeared in a little over 25 percent of the passages. While not as common as the Theory/Perspective structure, this is still significant. Here, the author will inform you about a recent or historical event, a change that has occurred over time, or a problem or dilemma. Always ask whether the author presents an interpretation of the event or change or presents a solution to the problem (identified as her own solution or someone else's proposal). These passages are often neutral and detail heavy—note names, dates, or places as you see them, but don't lose sight of the big picture by getting too caught up in the small stuff.

Before practicing the next passage (or more properly, passages), it's important that we take a moment to discuss Comparative Reading because that's the format you're about to see.

LSAT STRATEGY

A Note on Comparative Reading

One time per section, the LSAT presents a Comparative Reading selection. Instead of seeing a single 450- to 500-word passage, you'll see two shorter passages labeled Passage A and Passage B. The two passages always share a common Topic and sometimes a common Scope. The passages almost always differ, however, in terms of Purpose and Main Idea. That doesn't mean that the two authors must oppose each other. Indeed, it's often not clear that either passage was written in response to (or even with knowledge of) the other. It may be that Passage A presents an argument against a theory while Passage B presents a model for testing the validity of such theories. It could be that Passage A identifies a problem confronting biologists and Passage B offers a solution to the problem. Of course, a good, old-fashioned debate could take place as well, with Passage A arguing that a proposed law will be good for the country and Passage B contending that it will be bad.

Regardless of how the passages are related, your approach to Comparative Reading should differ little from your approach to Reading Comprehension passages in general. You'll still begin by reading strategically and Roadmapping the passages. The primary difference in preparing yourself to answer the questions comes right after you finish your Roadmaps but before you tackle the question set. Because almost all of the questions associated with these paired passages ask you to compare the passages in some way, you need to take a moment to briefly catalog the similarities and differences between Passage A and Passage B. Here are a handful of questions to ask and answer before diving into the questions:

- Are the passages different in Scope, Purpose, or Main Idea? The answer will generally be yes; make sure to characterize the differences.

- Do the passages share common details, examples, or evidence? The answer is often yes, but beware, the two authors may reach very different conclusions or make different recommendations based on the same underlying facts.

- If either author makes a contention or recommendation, how would the other author respond to it? The test is fond of Inference questions that ask whether one author would agree or disagree with something the other said.

- Do the two passages share a common principle? If yes, paraphrase the principle. If no, characterize how the authors approach the Topic differently.

Comparing and contrasting the two passages should only take a few seconds, but it will leave you much better prepared to research and answer the questions that follow.

With that in mind, read and Roadmap the following Comparative Reading passages. We've left space for you to add additional analysis or record your thoughts paragraph by paragraph, but make sure you are marking Keywords within the passage itself and recording margin notes that would fit into the limited space next to the passage in the test booklet. Here's a clue before you begin: only Passage A fits the Event/Phenomenon structure. As you read Passage B, see if you can identify its structure from what you've already learned in this chapter. After you finish reading and Roadmapping the passages individually, take a minute or two to record what you find similar and different about the two passages. Then check your work against the LSAT expert's analysis that follows.

LSAT Passage	My Analysis
Passage A	**Step 1:**

Passage A

There is no universally accepted definition within international law for the term "national minority." It is most commonly applied to (1) groups of persons—not necessarily citizens—under the jurisdiction of one
(5) country who have ethnic ties to another "homeland" country, or (2) groups of citizens of a country who have lasting ties to that country and have no such ties to any other country, but are distinguished from the majority of the population by ethnicity, religion, or
(10) language. The terms "people" and "nation" are also vaguely defined in international agreements. Documents that refer to a "nation" generally link the term to the concept of "nationalism," which is often associated with ties to land. It also connotes sovereignty, for
(15) which reason, perhaps, "people" is often used instead of "nation" for groups subject to a colonial power.

While the lack of definition of the terms "minority," "people," and "nation" presents difficulties to numerous minority groups, this lack is particularly problematic
(20) for the Roma (Gypsies). The Roma are not a colonized people, they do not have a homeland, and many do not bear ties to any currently existing country. Some Roma are not even citizens of any country, in part because of their nomadic way of life, which developed in response
(25) to centuries of fleeing persecution. Instead, they have ethnic and linguistic ties to other groups of Roma that reside in other countries.

Passage B

Capotorti's definition of a minority includes four empirical criteria—a group's being numerically smaller
(30) than the rest of the population of the state; their being nondominant; their having distinctive ethnic, linguistic, or religious characteristics; and their desiring to preserve their own culture—and one legal criterion, that they be citizens of the state in question. This last
(35) element can be problematic, given the previous nomadic character of the Roma, that they still cross borders between European states to avoid persecution, and that some states have denied them citizenship, and thus minority status. Because this element essentially
(40) grants the state the arbitrary right to decide if the Roma constitute a minority without reference to empirical characteristics, it seems patently unfair that it should be included in the definition.

LSAT Passage	**My Analysis**

However, the Roma easily fulfill the four
(45) objective elements of Capotorti's definition and
should, therefore, be considered a minority in all major
European states. Numerically, they are nowhere near a
majority, though they number in the hundreds of
thousands, even millions, in some states. Their
(50) nondominant position is evident—they are not even
acknowledged as a minority in some states. The Roma
have a number of distinctive linguistic, ethnic, and
religious characteristics. For example, most speak
Romani, an Indo-European language descended from
(55) Sanskrit. Roma groups also have their own distinctive
legal and court systems, which are group oriented
rather than individual-rights oriented. That they have
preserved their language, customs, and identity
through centuries of persecution is evidence enough
(60) of their desire to preserve their culture.

PrepTest56 Sec4 Qs16–21

Compare/Contrast the Passages

Now, compare your Roadmap to that of an LSAT expert. Look for places in which you missed an important Keyword or mischaracterized a point in the passage. Compare your big-picture summaries to those of the LSAT expert and review her notes on how these paired passages were similar and how they were different.

LSAT Passage	Analysis
Passage A	**Step 1:** The **Topic** of Passage A is presented

Passage A

There is no universally accepted definition within international law for the term "national minority." It is most commonly applied to (1) groups of persons—not necessarily citizens—under the jurisdiction of one
(5) country who have ethnic ties to another "homeland" country, or (2) groups of citizens of a country who have lasting ties to that country and have no such ties to any other country, but are distinguished from the majority of the population by ethnicity, religion, or
(10) language. The terms "people" and "nation" are also vaguely defined in international agreements. Documents that refer to a "nation" generally link the term to the concept of "nationalism," which is often associated with ties to land. It also connotes sovereignty, for
(15) which reason, perhaps, "people" is often used instead of "nation" for groups subject to a colonial power.

No univ. def for "nat'l min"

2 appl. of "nat'l min"

terms are vague

Step 1: The **Topic** of Passage A is presented immediately in the first sentence: national minority. Passage A's author notes a problem: there is no universally accepted definition for the term "national minority." This lack of definition constitutes the **Scope** of Passage A. The author offers two frequent applications of the term but further complains that other terms (e.g., "nation" and "people") used in defining national minority are similarly vague.

While the lack of definition of the terms "minority," "people," and "nation" presents difficulties to numerous minority groups, this lack is particularly problematic
(20) for the Roma (Gypsies). The Roma are not a colonized people, they do not have a homeland, and many do not bear ties to any currently existing country. Some Roma are not even citizens of any country, in part because of their nomadic way of life, which developed in response
(25) to centuries of fleeing persecution. Instead, they have ethnic and linguistic ties to other groups of Roma that reside in other countries.

Problem e.g. Roma

In the second paragraph, the author discusses how this lack of accepted definitions is potentially harmful, particularly to one group: the Roma. The author's **Purpose** is merely to describe this problem and how it affects the Roma in particular. Because the author offers no solution, the **Main Idea** of Passage A is simply that the lack of an agreed upon definition of "national minority" (as well as "nation" and "people") has negative consequences for certain groups, including the Roma.

Passage B

Capotorti's definition of a minority includes four empirical criteria—a group's being numerically smaller
(30) than the rest of the population of the state; their being nondominant; their having distinctive ethnic, linguistic, or religious characteristics; and their desiring to preserve their own culture—and one legal criterion, that they be citizens of the state in question. This last
(35) element can be problematic, given the previous nomadic character of the Roma, that they still cross borders between European states to avoid persecution, and that some states have denied them citizenship, and thus minority status. Because this element essentially
(40) grants the state the arbitrary right to decide if the Roma constitute a minority without reference to empirical characteristics, it seems patently unfair that it should be included in the definition.

Cap's def of min. 5 crit

Problem e.g. Roma meet 4 of 5 crit

As would be expected, the **Topic** of Passage B is also national minority. However, the author of Passage B isn't concerned about the lack of a definition. The **Scope** of Passage B is one specific definition of national minority: Capotorti's definition. Passage B starts off by laying out the five criteria for Capotorti's definition: four empirical ones and one legal. The author of Passage B then discusses a problem with the legal criterion, particularly in respect to the Roma. Similar to Passage A, one purpose of Passage B is to describe how a national minority definition is problematic for the Roma.

LSAT Passage	Analysis

However, the Roma **easily** fulfill the four
(45) objective elements of Capotorti's definition and
should, therefore, be considered a minority in all major
European states. Numerically, they are nowhere near a
majority, though they number in the hundreds of
thousands, even millions, in some states. Their
(50) nondominant position is evident—they are not even
acknowledged as a minority in some states. The Roma
have a number of distinctive linguistic, ethnic, and
religious characteristics. **For example,** most speak
Romani, an Indo-European language descended from
(55) Sanskrit. Roma groups also have their own distinctive
legal and court systems, which are group oriented
rather than individual-rights oriented. That they have
preserved their language, customs, and identity
through centuries of persecution is evidence enough
(60) of their desire to preserve their culture.

Au—Roma
meet def of
nat'l min

The second paragraph provides a more
refined **Purpose:** show how the Roma
should qualify as a national minority using
the remaining, more objective criteria. The
Main Idea of Passage B is that the legal
criterion of Capotorti's definition poses
a problem to the Roma by denying them
status as a national minority despite their
fulfillment of the remaining objective
criteria.

PrepTest56 Sec4 Qs16–21

Compare/Contrast the Passages

Before going to the questions, note the relationship between the two passages. Both are concerned with the definition of national minority—although one is concerned about the lack of an accepted definition and one is concerned about the criteria of one definition in particular. More notably, both passages are concerned with how these issues cause problems in the case of the Roma. The passages are different in that Passage A emphasizes the problematic nature of the Roma case for minority status while Passage B argues that Caportorti's definition of minority status fits the Roma well if the legal criterion is dropped.

Here, Passage A fits the Event/Phenomenon passage structure because it emphasizes—"particularly problematic" (line 19)—the unique difficulties of the Roma case. Passage B is different in tone and in structure. Passage B's author kicks off his second paragraph with the positive Opinion Keyword "easily." Passage B has a Theory/Perspective structure. The Scope focuses on Capotorti's perspective on minority status. Here, In Passage B, the author embraces Caportorti's definition generally but critiques its fifth criterion. Note the similarities between this passage and the earlier one in which the author set out to demonstrate the shortcomings of tangible-object theory.

You'll see the questions for these paired passages a little later in the chapter. Look forward to applying your analysis of the similarities and differences between the two short passages on several questions.

Now, let's return to a standard-length LSAT passage to look at the third and last of the passage structures we'll practice with.

Biography Passages

This passage structure is less common than the previous two, constituting somewhere around 10 percent of recent passages. You're unlikely to see more than one of these in a Reading Comprehension section, and on some tests, they may be absent altogether. Make sure to distinguish Biography passages from Theory/Perspective passages that may focus on the point of view of a particular individual. In Biography passages, the author sets out to explain the contribution of a person to a particular field of study or form of art. (Note that Biography passages focus on what someone has *done*, rather than what he or she has *said* or argued.) These passages are more likely to be narrative than argumentative in purpose, although they may involve showing that a person's work should be reevaluated in light of his or her biographical information. When you encounter a biography passage, always ask, "What does the author find to be significant about this person's life or work?" The answer will help define the Scope of the passage.

With that in mind, read and Roadmap the following passage. We've left space for you to add additional analysis or record your thoughts paragraph by paragraph, but make sure you are marking Keywords within the passage itself and recording margin notes that would fit into the limited space next to the passage in the test booklet. When you're finished, compare your work to that of the LSAT expert on the following pages.

LSAT Passage	My Analysis
	Step 1:

This passage was adapted from articles published in the 1990s.

The success that Nigerian-born computer scientist Philip Emeagwali (b. 1954) has had in designing computers that solve real-world problems has been fueled by his willingness to reach beyond established
(5) paradigms and draw inspiration for his designs from nature. In the 1980s, Emeagwali achieved breakthroughs in the design of parallel computer systems. Whereas single computers work sequentially, making one calculation at a time, computers
(10) connected in parallel can process calculations simultaneously. In 1989, Emeagwali pioneered the use of massively parallel computers that used a network of thousands of smaller computers to solve what is considered one of the most computationally difficult
(15) problems: predicting the flow of oil through the subterranean geologic formations that make up oil fields. Until that time, supercomputers had been used for oil field calculations, but because these supercomputers worked sequentially, they were too
(20) slow and inefficient to accurately predict such extremely complex movements.

To model oil field flow using a computer requires the simulation of the distribution of the oil at tens of thousands of locations throughout the field. At each
(25) location, hundreds of simultaneous calculations must be made at regular time intervals relating to such variables as temperature, direction of oil flow, viscosity, and pressure, as well as geologic properties of the basin holding the oil. In order to solve this
(30) problem, Emeagwali designed a massively parallel computer by using the Internet to connect to more than 65,000 smaller computers. One of the great difficulties of parallel computing is dividing up the tasks among the separate smaller computers so that
(35) they do not interfere with each other, and it was here that Emeagwali turned to natural processes for ideas, noting that tree species that survive today are those that, over the course of hundreds of millions of years, have developed branching patterns that have
(40) maximized the amount of sunlight gathered and the quantity of water and sap delivered. Emeagwali demonstrated that, for modeling certain phenomena such as subterranean oil flow, a network design based on the mathematical principle that underlies the
(45) branching structures of trees will enable a massively parallel computer to gather and broadcast the largest quantity of messages to its processing points in the shortest time.

LSAT Passage	My Analysis

In 1996 Emeagwali had another breakthrough
(50)   when he presented the design for a massively parallel
computer that he claims will be powerful enough to
predict global weather patterns a century in advance.
The computer's design is based on the geometry of
bees' honeycombs, which use an extremely efficient
(55)   three-dimensional spacing. Emeagwali believes that
computer scientists in the future will increasingly
look to nature for elegant solutions to complex
technical problems. This paradigm shift, he asserts,
will enable us to better understand the systems
(60)   evolved by nature and, thereby, to facilitate the
evolution of human technology.

PrepTest58 Sec2 Qs8–13

Now, compare your Roadmap to that of an LSAT expert. Look for places in which you missed an important Keyword or mischaracterized a point in the passage. Determine whether your big-picture summaries were similar to those of the LSAT expert as well.

LSAT Passage	Analysis
This passage was adapted from articles published in the 1990s.	**Step 1:** The first sentence in paragraph 1 introduces the **Topic**: Philip Emeagwali's computer innovations. Initially, the author discusses the reason for Emeagwali's success with designing computers to solve real-world problems, namely that his pursuit of innovation in design draws heavily upon nature. This may be a hint of the author's **Scope**. The author narrows her discussion to the 1980s, when Emeagwali had a breakthrough with successful parallel computer systems. After distinguishing parallel computer systems, the author gives an example of how the parallel computer systems were successful: oil flow prediction.

The success that Nigerian-born computer scientist Philip Emeagwali (b. 1954) has had in designing computers that solve real-world problems has been fueled by his willingness to reach beyond established
(5) paradigms and draw inspiration for his designs from nature. In the 1980s, Emeagwali achieved breakthroughs in the design of parallel computer systems. Whereas single computers work sequentially, making one calculation at a time, computers
(10) connected in parallel can process calculations simultaneously. In 1989, Emeagwali pioneered the use of massively parallel computers that used a network of thousands of smaller computers to solve what is considered one of the most computationally difficult
(15) problems, predicting the flow of oil through the subterranean geologic formations that make up oil fields. Until that time, supercomputers had been used for oil field calculations, but because these supercomputers worked sequentially, they were too
(20) slow and inefficient to accurately predict such extremely complex movements.

PE—designs comps to solve real-world problems

Breakthrough parallel comps on task

Ex. oil flow prediction 1989

To model oil field flow using a computer requires the simulation of the distribution of the oil at tens of thousands of locations throughout the field. At each
(25) location, hundreds of simultaneous calculations must be made at regular time intervals relating to such variables as temperature, direction of oil flow, viscosity, and pressure, as well as geologic properties of the basin holding the oil. In order to solve this
(30) problem, Emeagwali designed a massively parallel computer by using the Internet to connect to more than 65,000 smaller computers. One of the great difficulties of parallel computing is dividing up the tasks among the separate smaller computers so that
(35) they do not interfere with each other, and it was here that Emeagwali turned to natural processes for ideas, noting that tree species that survive today are those that, over the course of hundreds of millions of years, have developed branching patterns that have
(40) maximized the amount of sunlight gathered and the quantity of water and sap delivered. Emeagwali demonstrated that, for modeling certain phenomena such as subterranean oil flow, a network design based on the mathematical principle that underlies the
(45) branching structures of trees will enable a massively parallel computer to gather and broadcast the largest quantity of messages to its processing points in the shortest time.

Why oil flow hard to calculate

hard to break up tasks on parallel comps

PE—used tree analogy

In paragraph 2, the author continues discussing oil flow prediction and begins by explaining why oil field flow is so difficult to calculate. Mid-paragraph, the author confirms her **Scope**: natural processes showed Emeagwali how to design computers. Specifically, the author describes how Emeagwali referenced a tree-branching pattern as a model for how parallel computers could operate without interfering with the smaller separate computers' tasks. The paragraph ends by detailing Emeagwali's tree analogy. It is now clear that the author's **Purpose** for writing the passage is to explain how Emeagwali used natural processes to model parallel computer design.

LSAT Passage	Analysis

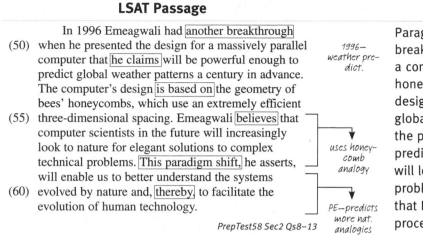

In 1996 Emeagwali had another breakthrough
(50) when he presented the design for a massively parallel
computer that he claims will be powerful enough to
predict global weather patterns a century in advance.
The computer's design is based on the geometry of
bees' honeycombs, which use an extremely efficient
(55) three-dimensional spacing. Emeagwali believes that
computer scientists in the future will increasingly
look to nature for elegant solutions to complex
technical problems. This paradigm shift, he asserts,
will enable us to better understand the systems
(60) evolved by nature and, thereby, to facilitate the
evolution of human technology.

PrepTest58 Sec2 Qs8–13

1996—weather predict.

uses honeycomb analogy

PE—predicts more nat. analogies

Analysis

Paragraph 3 focuses on another Emeagwali breakthrough. In 1996, Emeagwali designed a computer based on the geometry of honeybees' combs. This massively parallel design may allow the computer to predict global weather patterns. The author ends the passage by pointing out that Emeagwali predicts more and more computer scientists will look to nature for ways to solve complex problems. In sum, the author's **Main Idea** is that Emeagwali used analogies to natural processes to design massive parallel computer systems in order to solve real-world problems.

Instead of viewing this as a natural science passage (and thus focusing on how much he doesn't know about complex computer models and oil field flow), the LSAT expert identifies this as a classic Biography passage. Doing so demystifies the subject matter and makes it easier to understand the author's Purpose and the overall organization of the passage.

That passage has three fairly long paragraphs, but by staying focused on Keywords, the LSAT expert was able to read actively and create a helpful Roadmap. While a Biography passage like this one lacks an opposing voice or point of view, its author is not without a point of view. Here, the author signals his reason for writing about Emeagwali by using the word "breakthrough" twice (lines 7 and 49). A strong strategic reader will make sure she knows what those breakthroughs accomplished, how they were achieved, and why those breakthroughs were important—how did parallel computing provide solutions supercomputers could not? It also helps to keep her focused on what is relevant in the extended discussion of oil field flow in Paragraph 2. The author will use that example to reinforce his reason for finding Emeagwali's work to be groundbreaking and influential.

Keep the author's emphases and examples in mind when we turn to the questions associated with this passage, which we'll do in the next section of this chapter.

Reflection

In all three of the examples you just looked at, the LSAT expert:

- Used Keywords to discern the structure of the passage and note the author's purpose for offering certain details and examples.
- Took down brief, accurate margin notes highlighting the points in the passage most likely to surface in the questions.
- Summarized the author's Topic, Scope, Purpose, and Main Idea while reading the passage.

Keep those examples in mind as you practice additional Reading Comprehension passages. For all of the passages included in this book, you'll find sample Roadmaps and complete discussions of the passages in addition to explanations of individual questions. In practice, don't hesitate to spend 3–4 minutes reading and Roadmapping a passage and then compare your work in Step 1 to that of the LSAT expert reflected in the explanations. After you review the strategic reading step, you'll feel much more confident going into the question set.

It is possible to practice the kind of strategic reading you'll do on the LSAT with almost anything you read, at least anything academic or nonfiction. Next time you're perusing a newspaper editorial, a well-written commentary piece, or an article in a science magazine, roadmap it. Try to imagine, or even write, the kinds of questions the LSAT would ask about the piece you've just finished. Look for places in which the author has used Contrast, Illustration, or Opinion Keywords in ways that would allow for the testmaker to ask an Inference or Logic Function question. Learning to read in a new way will not happen overnight, but if you start to read this way consistently, by Test Day, you'll be far ahead of the average test taker.

READING COMPREHENSION QUESTION STRATEGIES

The universal characteristic of LSAT Reading Comprehension questions is this: *they reward you for having read and understood the passage.* That may sound almost tautological—Reading Comprehension questions are obviously about whether I comprehended the reading?! Well, yes. But that obvious truth masks a subtler, more important one: Reading Comprehension questions do *not* reward what you (or anyone else) knew before reading the passage. The questions are always worded such that they must be answered from the text. We'll keep coming back to that truth, and we'll build the strategies for answering the questions based on the text throughout this section.

Reading Comprehension Question Types

The LSAT testmaker uses five main types of questions in the Reading Comprehension section. You'll learn to recognize them shortly. Moreover, depending on the wording of the question stem, many of those question types may contain clues that will allow you to target your research to specific portions of the text.

LEARNING OBJECTIVES

In this portion of the chapter, you'll learn to:

· Recognize Global questions.
· Recognize Inference questions.
· Recognize Detail questions.
· Recognize Logic Function questions.
· Recognize Logic Reasoning questions.
· Determine whether the question stem contains research clues.

Let's define and see examples of each Reading Comprehension question type. As we go through the question types, pay attention to the analysis that the LSAT expert does for Step 2—read the question stem and look for clues—of the Reading Comprehension Method.

Global Questions

Global questions ask about the passage as a whole. They are designed to test your comprehension of the author's Main Idea or Purpose. These questions lack research clues, naturally, as they take the entire passage into account. To predict the correct answer, use your summary of the Purpose or Main Idea. Nearly all passages contain one Global question, and it is usually (but not always) the first question in the set. Occasionally, you'll encounter a passage with two Global questions. In such cases, one is likely to be the first question in the set and the other near or at the end of the question set. Very rarely, you'll find a passage with no Global question accompanying it.

LSAT Question Stem		Analysis
Which one of the following most accurately expresses the main point of the passage? *PrepTest58 Sec2 Q1*	→	**Step 2:** "[M]ain point"—a Global question. Use the Main Idea summary to predict the correct answer and evaluate the choices.
The primary purpose of the passage is to *PrepTest52 Sec4 Q19*	→	**Step 2:** "[P]rimary purpose—a Global question. Use the Purpose summary to predict the correct answer and evaluate the choices.

The language of Global question stems is fairly standardized. You may find small variations, but expect to see "main point" or "primary purpose" most often.

One rare variation on the Global question asks you to describe the organization of the passage. You actually saw an example of this type among the questions accompanying the Women's Education in Post-Revolutionary France passage in Chapter 13.

LSAT Question Stem	Analysis
Which one of the following most accurately describes the organization of the passage? *PrepTest56 Sec4 Q23*	**Step 2:** "[D]escribes the organization of the passage"—a Global question variant. Consult the Roadmap to outline the overall structure and use that to evaluate the choices.

This is the one type of Global question that benefits from research. Whereas the standard "main point" and "primary purpose" Global questions can be answered with your big-picture summaries, "organization" Global questions need you to match the correct answer to the flow of the passage. It's helpful with "organization" Global questions to consult the Roadmap before you evaluate the choices.

Inference Questions

Inference questions account for a little less than half of the points in Reading Comprehension. In a typical 27-question section, there will usually be anywhere from 10 to 12 Inference questions, although one recent test had 14. Inference questions are characterized by language in the stem telling you that the correct answer *is based on* or *follows from* the passage without necessarily being stated in the passage.

LSAT Question Stem	Analysis
Based on the passage, the author would be most likely to agree with which one of the following statements about evolutionary explanations of kin recognition? *PrepTest56 Sec4 Q10*	**Step 2:** "Based on the passage" and "most likely to agree"—an Inference question. "[E]volutionary explanations of kin recognition" is the research clue.
The passage suggests which one of the following about the behavior of *A. aperta* in conflict situations? *PrepTest52 Sec4 Q18*	**Step 2:** "The passage suggests"—an Inference question. "*A. aperta* in conflict situations" is the research clue.
Given the information in the passage, to which one of the following would lichenometry likely be most applicable? *PrepTest62 Sec1 Q8*	**Step 2:** "Given the information in the passage" and "likely be . . . applicable"*—an Inference question. The correct answer follows from the passage. "[L]ichenometry" is the research clue.

*When a question stem asks you to apply something from the passage, treat it as an Inference question. The correct answer still follows from the information in the passage; it's just applied to a new or hypothetical context in the correct answer.

In each of those cases, the expert noted research clues in the question stem. She will be able to quickly check her Roadmap at those points and use the text to predict the correct answer. Other Inference questions are open-ended, and a different approach to evaluating the choices is called for.

LSAT Question Stem	Analysis
It can be inferred that the author would be most likely to agree that *PrepTest52 Sec4 Q25* →	**Step 2:** "[I]nferred"—an Inference question. No research clues. Evaluate the choices using the Scope, Purpose, and Main Idea summaries *or* use the answer choices as research clues and check them against the text.
Which one of the following statements is most strongly supported by the passage? *PrepTest62 Sec1 Q4* →	**Step 2:** "[S]upported by the passage"—an Inference question. No research clues. Evaluate the choices using the Scope, Purpose, and Main Idea summaries *or* use the answer choices as research clues and check them against the text.

In those questions, no targeted research clue is present. When you see an Inference question of this type, quickly check the answer choices. If they all relate to the same portion of the passage, you can simply use them as research clues and test each one against the text. If they seem vague, broad, or scattered, start by checking the choices against your Scope, Purpose, and Main Idea summaries. Eliminate all those with which the author would not agree. That will either leave you with the one correct choice or will narrow down the number of choices you need to research.

One other variant on the Inference question is fairly common: the Author's Attitude question. A strong strategic reader, who has identified Emphasis/Opinion Keywords in the passage, can research these questions quickly.

LSAT Question Stem	Analysis
The author's attitude toward the testimony of medical experts in personal injury cases is most accurately described as *PrepTest62 Sec1 Q13* →	**Step 2:** "[A]uthor's attitude"—an Inference question about the author's attitude. "[T]estimony of medical experts in personal injury cases" is the research clue. Look for Opinion Keywords that indicate the author's view.
The author's stance regarding the theory of philosophical anarchism can most accurately be described as one of *PrepTest52 Sec4 Q22* →	**Step 2:** "[A]uthor's stance"—an Inference question about the author's attitude. "[P]hilosophical anarchism" is the research clue. Look for Opinion Keywords that indicate the author's view.

You may see other slight variations in the wording of Inference question stems, but don't let that throw you. The feature they all have in common is that the correct answer follows from the passage without being directly stated in it.

Detail Questions

Detail questions are less common than Inference questions. You'll typically see 4–5 per test, though not every passage will necessarily be accompanied by a Detail question. The identifying characteristic of the Detail question stem is that, in some way, it tells you that the correct answer will closely paraphrase something stated explicitly in the passage: "according to the passage" and "the passage states" are common phrasings of these questions.

LSAT Question Stem	Analysis
According to the passage, some critics have criticized Tutuola's work on the ground that *PrepTest56 Sec4 Q4*	**Step 2:** "According to the passage"—a Detail question. "[C]ritics have criticized Tutuola's work on the ground that" is the research clue.
The passage states that a role of medical experts in relation to custom-made medical illustrations in the courtroom is to *PrepTest62 Sec1 Q11*	**Step 2:** "The passage states"—a Detail question. "[M]edical experts in relation to custom-made medical illustrations in the courtroom" is the research clue.
The author identifies which one of the following as a commonly held belief? *PrepTest52 Sec4 Q21*	**Step 2:** "[I]dentifies which one"—a Detail question. "[C]ommonly held belief" is the research clue.

Almost all Detail questions contain research clues; after all, you're looking for a detail. Do not, however, think that questions containing line references are Detail questions. When the question stem points you to a particular line in the passage, it is usually asking for an Inference that can be drawn from what is said there, or it is a Logic Function question asking you *why* the author has included that particular detail.

Be ready to encounter 1–2 Detail EXCEPT questions. Not every test includes one of these, but if you should see one, treat it as the LSAT expert does in these examples.

LSAT Question Stem	Analysis
The passage does NOT provide evidence that Sembène exhibits which one of the following attitudes in one or more of his films? *PrepTest52 Sec4 Q6*	**Step 2:** "NOT provide evidence"—a Detail EXCEPT question. Use the answer choices as research clues and eliminate the four stated in the passage.
The author attributes each of the following to Tutuola EXCEPT: *PrepTest56 Sec4 Q5*	**Step 2:** "The author attributes each . . . EXCEPT"— a Detail EXCEPT question. Use the answer choices as research clues and eliminate the four stated in the passage.

Because all four wrong answers are included in the text, you can use the answer choices as research clues. Eliminate any answers that are stated. If, as you're checking the choices, you find a choice with which the author would clearly disagree or that falls completely outside the scope of the passage, you can choose it with confidence as the correct answer.

Logic Function Questions

Logic Function questions are less common than Detail questions. You'll usually see around three of these in a Reading Comprehension section. These questions will always include a research clue, and it's easy to see why. The question stem points you to a portion of the passage—a detail, a reference, or a paragraph—and asks you *why* the author included it or *how* it functions within the passage.

LSAT Question Stem	Analysis
The author of the passage mentions Galápagos tortoises in the first paragraph most likely in order to *PrepTest52 Sec4 Q14*	**Step 2:** "[I]n order to"—a Logic Function question. The correct answer states *why* the author mentions the Galápagos tortoise. "[F]irst paragraph" is the research clue.
The author's discussion of people's positive moral duty to care for one another (lines 44–49) functions primarily to *PrepTest52 Sec4 Q26*	**Step 2:** "[F]unctions primarily to"—a Logic Function question. The correct answer states why the author discusses people's positive moral duty. The line reference is the research clue.
Which one of the following best states the function of the third paragraph of the passage? *PrepTest52 Sec4 Q17*	**Step 2:** "[S]tates the function"—a Logic Function question. "[T]hird paragraph" is the research clue. This is almost like a mini Global question asking for the purpose of Paragraph 3 instead of the "primary purpose" of the entire passage.

Be careful, on Logic Function questions, of answer choices that accurately reflect what the passage said about the detail or reference but do not explain *why* the author included it.

Logic Reasoning Questions

These questions are slightly more common than Logic Function questions. You'll likely see 3–4 per section. It's very unlikely that every passage will have a Logic Reasoning question in its question set. The distinguishing characteristic of Logic Reasoning questions in Reading Comprehension is that they mirror the task of a question type typically found in the Logical Reasoning section. Take a look at the LSAT expert's analyses of a couple of questions to see this illustrated.

LSAT Question Stem	Analysis
Which one of the following would, if true, most strengthen the claim made by the author in the last sentence of the passage (lines 54–58)? *PrepTest52 Sec4 Q3*	**Step 2:** "[I]f true, most strengthen"—a Logic Reasoning question mirroring a Strengthen question from the LR section. Research the passage around the line reference.
Suppose that two proposals were put forward by lawmakers concerning housing reform today. Which one of the following pairs of proposals is most closely analogous to the pair of proposals discussed in the second paragraph of the passage? *PrepTest56 Sec4 Q24*	**Step 2:** "[M]ost closely analogous"—a Logic Reasoning question mirroring a Parallel Reasoning question from the LR section. "[T]he pair of proposals" is the research clue.

The most common Logical Reasoning question types mirrored by Reading Comprehension Logic Reasoning questions are Strengthen/Weaken, Parallel Reasoning, Method of Argument, and Principle (with the first two types in the list being far more common than the others). When you encounter one of these questions in the Reading Comprehension section, just use the same approach you would in the Logical Reasoning section, treating the referenced portion of the passage as the question's stimulus.

A note about research clues. In their analyses of the question stems above, you saw that the LSAT expert identified research clues whenever they were present. Knowing where to look in the passage for the text relevant to the correct answer will make you faster and more accurate throughout the question set. As you prepare to do more practice with Reading Comprehension question stems, learn to spot these five types of research clues.

LSAT STRATEGY

Reading Comprehension Research Clues

- **Line References**—research around the referenced detail; look for Keywords indicating why the referenced text has been included or how it's used.
- **Paragraph References**—consult your Roadmap to see the paragraph's scope and function.
- **Quoted Text** (often accompanied by a line reference)—check the context of the quoted term or phrase; ask what the author meant by it in the passage.
- **Proper Nouns**—check the context of the person, place, or thing; ask whether the author had a positive, negative, or neutral evaluation of it; ask why it was included in the passage.
- **Content Clues**—terms, concepts, or ideas highlighted in the passage, but not included as direct quotes in the question stem; these will almost always refer you to something the author emphasized or stated an opinion on.

You'll see those research clues in action when we turn to Steps 3 and 4 of the Reading Comprehension Method. For now, get a little practice with Step 2 using the questions that accompany the Tangible-Object Theory passage.

Practice

For each of the following, identify the question type and state whether the question stem includes a research clue. You can check your work against the expert analysis on the following pages.

LSAT Question Stem	My Analysis
1. Which one of the following most accurately expresses the main point of the passage?	**Step 2:**
2. According to the passage, the theory that copyright and other intellectual-property rights can be construed as logical extensions of the right to own concrete, tangible objects depends on the claim that	**Step 2:**
3. The passage most directly answers which one of the following questions?	**Step 2:**
4. Suppose an inventor describes an innovative idea for an invention to an engineer, who volunteers to draft specifications for a prototype and then produces the prototype using the engineer's own materials. Which one of the following statements would apply to this case under the tangible-object theory of intellectual property, as the author describes that theory?	**Step 2:**

LSAT Question Stem	My Analysis
5. Legal theorists supporting the tangible-object theory of intellectual property are most likely to believe which one of the following?	**Step 2:**
6. The passage provides the most support for inferring which one of the following statements?	**Step 2:**
7. It can be inferred that the author of the passage is most likely to believe which one of the following?	**Step 2:**

PrepTest58 Sec2 Qs14–20

Here's how an LSAT expert would analyze each of those question stems.

LSAT Question Stem	Analysis
1. Which one of the following most accurately expresses the main point of the passage?	**Step 2:** "[M]ain point"—a Global question. Use the Main Idea summary to predict the correct answer.
2. According to the passage, the theory that copyright and other intellectual-property rights can be construed as logical extensions of the right to own concrete, tangible objects depends on the claim that	**Step 2:** "According to the passage"—a Detail question. "[T]he theory that . . . depends on the claim" is the research clue. The correct answer is a claim *necessary* for tangible-object theory.
3. The passage most directly answers which one of the following questions?	**Step 2:** "[A]nswers which one of the following questions"—a Detail question variant. No research clue. Use the answer choices (which will be worded as questions) to check the text. The correct answer is a question for which an answer can be found in the passage.*
4. Suppose an inventor describes an innovative idea for an invention to an engineer, who volunteers to draft specifications for a prototype and then produces the prototype using the engineer's own materials. Which one of the following statements would apply to this case under the tangible-object theory of intellectual property, as the author describes that theory?	**Step 2:** "Which . . . would apply"—an Inference question variant. The correct answer is the correct application of tangible-object theory to the hypothetical example in the question stem. Use that example as the research clue and look for an analogous or applicable case in the passage.**
5. Legal theorists supporting the tangible-object theory of intellectual property are most likely to believe which one of the following?	**Step 2:** "[M]ost likely to believe"—an Inference question. The correct answer will agree with the tangible-object theory proponents (not with the author). Research the passage where the proponents' beliefs are stated.
6. The passage provides the most support for inferring which one of the following statements?	**Step 2:** "[I]nferring"—an Inference question. No research clue. Use the Scope, Purpose, and Main Idea summaries to evaluate the answers or check the answer choices against the text.
7. It can be inferred that the author of the passage is most likely to believe which one of the following? *PrepTest58 Sec2 Qs14–20*	**Step 2:** "[C]an be inferred"—an Inference question. No research clue. Use the Scope, Purpose, and Main Idea summaries to evaluate the answers or check the answer choices against the text.

*This is a fairly common variation on the Detail question (at least on recent tests) in which you need to use the answer choices as research clues. Nevertheless, the correct answer is the one for which an answer is stated directly in the passage.

**This question is similar to Apply the Principle questions in the Logical Reasoning section.

How did you do? You'll have more opportunities to perform Step 2, interpreting the question stems and looking for research clues, as you work with the questions from the passages on Roma as a National Minority and Philip Emeagwali below. For now, though, let's take the questions from the Tangible-Object Theory passage and work through the next two steps of the Reading Comprehension Method: Step 3—Research the Relevant Text and Step 4—Predict the Correct Answer.

Researching Reading Comprehension Questions and Predicting the Correct Answer

In Reading Comprehension, poorly trained test takers often lose a lot of points (and, just as importantly, a lot of time) because they essentially answer questions by re-reading the passage. They aren't sure quite where to find the correct answer and wind up looking all over the passage in response to each answer choice. You *should* answer the questions based on the passage, of course, but there is a big difference between researching the relevant text and simply re-reading the passage.

LEARNING OBJECTIVES

In this part of the chapter, you'll learn to:

- Identify and employ five kinds of research clues (line reference, paragraph reference, quoted text, proper names, and content clues) in question stems to research the relevant text in a passage.
- Research the relevant text and accurately predict the correct answer to Inference questions featuring referent reading clues.
- Use Topic, Scope, Purpose, and Main Idea summaries to predict the correct answer to Global questions.
- Use Topic, Scope, Purpose, and Main Idea summaries to predict broadly the correct answer to Inference questions lacking referent reading clues.

Step 3 is where you earn the payoff for the time you spend reading the passage strategically and creating a helpful Roadmap. Take a look at how an LSAT expert handles Steps 3 and 4 in the Tangible-Object Theory passage. For reference, we've reprinted the expert's Roadmap and Step 1 analysis. Consult it along with the expert to see how he's working through the Research and Prediction steps.

LSAT Passage	Analysis
Proponents of the tangible-object theory of copyright argue that copyright and similar intellectual-property rights can be explained as logical extensions of the right to own concrete, tangible objects. This (5) view depends on the claim that every copyrightable work can be manifested in some physical form, such as a manuscript or a videotape. It also accepts the premise that ownership of an object confers a number of rights on the owner, who may essentially do whatever he or (10) she pleases with the object to the extent that this does not violate other people's rights. One may, for example, hide or display the object, copy it, or destroy it. One may also transfer ownership of it to another. *© Tangible–prop. theory* *You can "hold" it* *Right to do whatever*	**Step 1:** Paragraph 1 starts off with the proponents' view of the **Topic** of the passage, tangible-object theory of copyright. (Anticipate that the author will discuss the opponents' view or an alternative.) The proponents' basic tenet: "every copyrightable work can be manifested in some physical form"—in other words, that it can be held. In addition, the owner has the right to do as she sees fit as long as those actions do not infringe upon another person's rights. Basically, the proponents feel that the owner has the right to do whatever she wants.

LSAT Passage		Analysis

| | *Creator get rights* | Paragraph 2 begins with the rights of the owner as creator of the object. Although the owner can transfer property, the owner can still retain some rights after transfer—the notion of "retained rights." Retained rights are common—example: sale of land. But, what about retained rights and intellectual property? In intellectual property, an owner who transfers ownership can still retain the right to copy the object for profit and to use it as a guide for the production of similar things, like a performance. |

(15) In creating a new and original object from materials that one owns, one becomes the owner of that object and thereby acquires all of the rights that ownership entails. But if the owner transfers ownership of the object, the full complement of rights is not necessarily transferred to the new owner; instead, the

(20) original owner may retain one or more of these rights. This notion of retained rights is common in many areas of law; for example, the seller of a piece of land may retain certain rights to the land in the form of easements or building restrictions. Applying the notion

(25) of retained rights to the domain of intellectual property, theorists argue that copyrighting a work secures official recognition of one's intention to retain certain rights to that work. Among the rights typically retained by the original producer of an object such as a literary

(30) manuscript or a musical score would be the right to copy the object for profit and the right to use it as a guide for the production of similar or analogous things—for example, a public performance of a musical score.

Creator get rights

Can retain some rights on transfer

Common rules

In IP, keep rights to copy perform.

So far, it would seem the author is focusing on the proponents of tangible-object theory because she's just written a great analysis of their position.

(35) According to proponents of the tangible-object theory, its chief advantage is that it justifies intellectual property rights without recourse to the widely accepted but problematic supposition that one can own abstract, intangible things such as ideas. But while this account

(40) seems plausible for copyrightable entities that do, in fact, have enduring tangible forms, it cannot accommodate the standard assumption that such evanescent things as live broadcasts of sporting events can be copyrighted. More importantly, it does not

(45) acknowledge that in many cases the work of conceiving ideas is more crucial and more valuable than that of putting them into tangible form. Suppose that a poet dictates a new poem to a friend, who writes it down on paper that the friend has supplied. The

(50) creator of the tangible object in this case is not the poet but the friend, and there would seem to be no ground for the poet's claiming copyright unless the poet can be said to already own the ideas expressed in the work.

T.O. proponents: you can own idea

Author: Problem— tangible form isn't the imp't part

↓

poet analogy

Paragraph 3 begins with the primary advantage proponents believe tangible-object theory has: you can own ideas. The author takes a turn immediately after, though, and begins detailing problems with the abstract, intangible nature associated with things such as ideas. The author's **Scope** is now confirmed: the tangible-object theory's proponents and its problems. In addition, the author's **Purpose** for writing the passage is to outline the position of those in favor of tangible-object theory and show problems with the logic of that view. The author concedes that their view is compatible with tangible objects. However, it's difficult to apply these same concepts to such "evanescent" things as ideas or broadcasts. The author ends with a poet analogy: a poet could dictate an entire poem to a friend, and if the friend writes it down, then the friend is the owner, unless the poet can show ownership of the ideas expressed in the poem. In sum, the **Main Idea** is that tangible-object theory's emphasis on ownership going to the creator of a tangible form is problematic.

PrepTest58 Sec2 Qs14–20

LSAT Question Stem	Analysis
Which one of the following most accurately expresses the main point of the passage? *PrepTest58 Sec2 Q14*	**Step 2:** "[M]ain point"—a Global question. Use the Main Idea summary to predict the correct answer. **Step 3:** The Main Idea reflects the author's voice at the end of the passage: tangible-object theory's views are problematic because they don't protect the creator of intellectual property. **Step 4:** The correct answer will discuss how the application of tangible-object theory to copyright and intellectual property is problematic.
According to the passage, the theory that copyright and other intellectual-property rights can be construed as logical extensions of the right to own concrete, tangible objects depends on the claim that *PrepTest58 Sec2 Q15*	**Step 2:** "According to the passage"—a Detail question. "[T]he theory that . . . depends on the claim" is the research clue. The correct answer is a claim *necessary* for tangible-object theory. **Step 3:** Reference in paragraph 1 where the author discussed the basis for tangible-object theory. Specifically, the author mentioned that it *"depends on the claim that every copyrightable work can be manifested in some physical form."* It can be extended to anything that you can hold a copy of in your hand. **Step 4:** The correct answer will need to state the basis of the idea that copyright and intellectual property are capable of being in physical form.
The passage most directly answers which one of the following questions? *PrepTest58 Sec2 Q16*	**Step 2:** "[A]nswers which of the following questions"—a Detail question variant. No research clue. Use the answer choices (which will be worded as questions) to check the text. The correct answer is a question for which an answer can be found in the passage. **Step 3:** Because there's no content clue or line reference in the question stem, go through each answer choice one by one. **Step 4:** Rather than make a prediction, characterize the answer choices: In the correct answer, the question posed can be answered from information in the passage. All four wrong answer choices will be Outside the Scope of the passage.

LSAT Question Stem	Analysis
Suppose an inventor describes an innovative idea for an invention to an engineer, who volunteers to draft specifications for a prototype and then produces the prototype using the engineer's own materials. Which one of the following statements would apply to this case under the tangible-object theory of intellectual property, as the author describes that theory? *PrepTest58 Sec2 Q17*	**Step 2:** "Which . . . would apply"—an Inference question variant. The correct answer is the correct application of tangible-object theory to the hypothetical example in the question stem. Use that example as the research clue and look for an analogous or applicable case in the passage. **Step 3:** In the question stem, the inventor describes an innovative idea to an engineer, who then drafts a prototype that the engineer then produces from his own materials. Reference the poet analogy at the end of paragraph 3 (lines 47–53). The author uses the poet example to show that tangible-object theory would grant ownership of the poem to the wrong person— that is, to the transcriber, rather than the poet—because the act of writing down the poem constitutes the creation of the physical object. In the example cited in the question stem, the application of tangible-object theory would be similarly problematic because the creator of the tangible object would be the engineer, not the inventor. **Step 4:** The correct answer will indicate that the engineer, and not the inventor, is entitled to claim ownership.

LSAT Question Stem	Analysis
Legal theorists supporting the tangible-object theory of intellectual property are most likely to believe which one of the following? *PrepTest58 Sec2 Q18*	**Step 2:** "[M]ost likely to believe"—an Inference question. The correct answer will agree with the tangible-object theory proponents (not with the author). Research the passage where the proponents' beliefs are stated. **Step 3:** Research all references to the legal theorists who are the proponents of the tangible-object theory. → In paragraph 1, the author explains that the legal theorists believe copyright and similar intellectual property rights can be explained as a logical extension of the right to own concrete tangible objects (those that can be manifested in physical form). In paragraph 3, the author states that the proponents see the primary advantage of tangible-object theory's application to intellectual property as a means to provide ownership to intangible/abstract things such as ideas. **Step 4:** The correct answer choice must be something that the proponents of tangible-object theory believe and will be consistent with both of the expressed viewpoints.
The passage provides the most support for inferring which one of the following statements? *PrepTest58 Sec2 Q19*	**Step 2:** "[I]nferring"—an Inference question. No research clue. Use the Scope, Purpose, and Main Idea summaries to evaluate the answers or check the answer choices against the text. → **Step 3:** Because there's no content clue or line reference in the question stem, go through each answer choice one by one or use the big-picture summaries to eliminate wrong answers. **Step 4:** Characterize the answer choices: The correct answer is supported by information in the passage. All four wrong answer choices will contradict the author, be Outside the Scope of the passage, or be Extreme.

LSAT Question Stem	Analysis
It can be inferred that the author of the passage is most likely to believe which one of the following? *PrepTest58 Sec2 Q20*	**Step 2:** "[C]an be inferred"—an Inference question. No research clue. Use the Scope, Purpose, and Main Idea summaries to evaluate the answers or check the answer choices against the text.
$\rightarrow$	**Step 3:** Because there's no content clue or line reference in the question stem, go through each answer choice one by one or use the big-picture summaries to eliminate wrong answers.
	Step 4: Characterize the answer choices: The correct answer is supported by information in the passage. All four wrong answer choices will contradict the author, be Outside the Scope of the passage, or be Extreme.

You'll see the answer choices for those questions shortly, when we discuss Step 5 of the Reading Comprehension Method. It is actually very good for you to practice predicting the correct answers without seeing the answer choices. As you work through additional passages in Chapter 15, you may find it very helpful to cover up the answer choices until you've predicted the correct answer, especially if you find it difficult to fully invest in Step 4 of the Method.

Step-by-step, you're building the Reading Comprehension skills. By the end of the chapter, you'll be able to tackle full passages, from reading and Roadmapping all the way through answering the questions.

Practice

Before moving on to the answer choices, try Steps 2–4 on the passages discussing Roma as a National Minority. For your convenience, we'll reprint the paired Comparative Reading passages and the expert's Roadmap and analysis. Review those briefly before you dive into the question stems. When you've completed Steps 2–4, check your work against that of the LSAT expert on the following pages.

LSAT Passage		Analysis
Passage A		**Step 1:** The **Topic** of Passage A is presented immediately in the first sentence: national minority. Passage A's author notes a problem: there is no universally accepted definition for the term "national minority." This lack of definition constitutes the **Scope** of Passage A. The author offers two frequent applications of the term but further complains that other terms (e.g., "nation" and "people") used in defining national minority are similarly vague.
There is no universally accepted definition within international law for the term "national minority." It is most commonly applied to (1) groups of persons—not necessarily citizens—under the jurisdiction of one	*No univ. def for "nat'l min"*	
(5) country who have ethnic ties to another "homeland" country, or (2) groups of citizens of a country who have lasting ties to that country and have no such ties to any other country, but are distinguished from the majority of the population by ethnicity, religion, or	*2 appl. of "nat'l min"*	
(10) language. The terms "people" and "nation" are also vaguely defined in international agreements. Documents that refer to a "nation" generally link the term to the concept of "nationalism," which is often associated with ties to land. It also connotes sovereignty, for	*terms are vague*	
(15) which reason, perhaps, "people" is often used instead of "nation" for groups subject to a colonial power.		

LSAT Passage		Analysis

While the lack of definition of the terms "minority," "people," and "nation" presents difficulties to numerous minority groups, this lack is particularly problematic

(20) for the Roma (Gypsies). The Roma are not a colonized people, they do not have a homeland, and many do not bear ties to any currently existing country. Some Roma are not even citizens of any country, in part because of their nomadic way of life, which developed in response

(25) to centuries of fleeing persecution. Instead, they have ethnic and linguistic ties to other groups of Roma that reside in other countries.

Problem e.g. Roma

In the second paragraph, the author discusses how this lack of accepted definitions is potentially harmful, particularly to one group: the Roma. The author's **Purpose** is merely to describe this problem and how it affects the Roma in particular. Because the author offers no solution, the **Main Idea** of Passage A is simply that the lack of an agreed upon definition of "national minority" (as well as "nation" and "people") has negative consequences for certain groups, including the Roma.

Passage B

Capotorti's definition of a minority includes four empirical criteria—a group's being numerically smaller

(30) than the rest of the population of the state; their being nondominant; their having distinctive ethnic, linguistic, or religious characteristics; and their desiring to preserve their own culture—and one legal criterion, that they be citizens of the state in question. This last

(35) element can be problematic, given the previous nomadic character of the Roma, that they still cross borders between European states to avoid persecution, and that some states have denied them citizenship, and thus minority status. Because this element essentially

(40) grants the state the arbitrary right to decide if the Roma constitute a minority without reference to empirical characteristics, it seems patently unfair that it should be included in the definition.

Cap's def of min. 5 crit

Problem e.g. Roma meet 4 of 5 crit

As would be expected, the **Topic** of Passage B is also national minority. However, the author of Passage B isn't concerned about the lack of a definition. The **Scope** of Passage B is one specific definition of national minority: Capotorti's definition. Passage B starts off by laying out the five criteria for Capotorti's definition: four empirical ones and one legal. The author of Passage B then discusses a problem with the legal criterion, particularly in respect to the Roma. Similar to Passage A, one purpose of Passage B is to describe how a national minority definition is problematic for the Roma.

However, the Roma easily fulfill the four

(45) objective elements of Capotorti's definition and should, therefore, be considered a minority in all major European states. Numerically, they are nowhere near a majority, though they number in the hundreds of thousands, even millions, in some states. Their

(50) nondominant position is evident—they are not even acknowledged as a minority in some states. The Roma have a number of distinctive linguistic, ethnic, and religious characteristics. For example, most speak Romani, an Indo-European language descended from

(55) Sanskrit. Roma groups also have their own distinctive legal and court systems, which are group oriented rather than individual-rights oriented. That they have preserved their language, customs, and identity through centuries of persecution is evidence enough

(60) of their desire to preserve their culture.

Au—Roma meet def of nat'l min

The second paragraph provides a more refined **Purpose**: Show how the Roma should qualify as a national minority using the remaining, more objective criteria. The **Main Idea** of Passage B is that the legal criterion of Capotorti's definition poses a problem to the Roma by denying them status as a national minority despite their fulfillment of the remaining objective criteria.

PrepTest56 Sec4 Qs16–21

| **LSAT Passage** | **Analysis** |

Compare/Contrast the Passages

Before going to the questions, note the relationship between the two passages. Both are concerned with the definition of national minority—although one is concerned about the lack of an accepted definition and one is concerned about the criteria of one definition in particular. More notably, both passages are concerned with how these issues cause problems in the case of the Roma. They are different in that Passage A emphasizes the problematic nature of the Roma case for minority status while Passage B argues that Caportorti's definition of minority status fits the Roma well if the legal criterion is dropped.

LSAT Question Stem	**My Analysis**
8. Which one of the following most accurately expresses the main point of passage A?	**Step 2:** **Step 3:** **Step 4:**
9. The term "problematic" has which one of the following meanings in both passage A (line 19) and passage B (line 35)?	**Step 2:** **Step 3:** **Step 4:**
10. Which one of the following claims about the Roma is NOT made in passage A?	**Step 2:** **Step 3:** **Step 4:**
11. The authors' views regarding the status of the Roma can most accurately be described in which one of the following ways?	**Step 2:** **Step 3:** **Step 4:**
12. The relationship between which one of the following pairs of documents is most analogous to the relationship between passage A and passage B?	**Step 2:** **Step 3:** **Step 4:**
13. Which one of the following is a principle that can be most reasonably considered to underlie the reasoning in both of the passages? *PrepTest56 Sec4 Qs16–21*	**Step 2:** **Step 3:** **Step 4:**

Here's how the LSAT expert analyzed each of those question stems. Compare your work to his. Did your identification of the question types match? Did you know where in the passage to find the relevant text for those questions containing research clues?

LSAT Question Stem	Analysis
8. Which one of the following most accurately expresses the main point of passage A? *PrepTest56 Sec4 Q16*	**Step 2:** Even though this question asks for the main point of only one passage, it's still a Global question because it focuses on that passage as a whole. → **Step 3:** Use the Roadmap and understanding of the big picture (Topic, Scope, Purpose, and Main Idea) to predict the correct answer. **Step 4:** The main point of Passage A is straightforward: the lack of definition for "national minority" (as well as "nation" and "people") has led to problems for certain groups, particularly the Roma.
9. The term "problematic" has which one of the following meanings in both passage A (line 19) and passage B (line 35)? *PrepTest56 Sec4 Q17*	**Step 2:** A question asking how the author defines a word in context is an Inference question. The correct answer follows from, but is not stated in, the text. → **Step 3:** The question stem references lines 19 and 35. To predict the answer, read the sentences containing "problematic" to derive context. **Step 4:** In both passages, the word *problematic* is used to describe how the Roma are affected by the definition (or lack of definition) of national minority. In Passage A, the vague definitions are too broad for the Roma, and in Passage B, the legal criterion of the definition is too narrow for the Roma. In both cases, "problematic" refers to causing difficulties.
10. Which one of the following claims about the Roma is NOT made in passage A? *PrepTest56 Sec4 Q18*	**Step 2:** Because this question focuses on claims stated (or, in this case, NOT stated) in the passage, it's a Detail question. Four of the answer choices to this question will be found in Passage A, and one will not. → **Step 3:** The only part of Passage A that discusses the Roma is paragraph 2. **Step 4:** It's always hard to predict what the outlier will be. Check each choice against lines 17–27. There's also a good chance that the right answer will appear in Passage B.

LSAT Question Stem	Analysis
11. The authors' views regarding the status of the Roma can most accurately be described in which one of the following ways? *PrepTest56 Sec4 Q19*	**Step 2:** This is an Inference question because it asks you to crystallize the authors' points of view as they're presented in the passages. → **Step 3:** Passage A discusses the Roma in paragraph 2 and Passage B in lines 34–60. **Step 4:** Both passages present the Roma as a specific group that experiences problems due to issues with the international definitions of national minority. The correct answer will convey that shared attitude.
12. The relationship between which one of the following pairs of documents is most analogous to the relationship between passage A and passage B? *PrepTest56 Sec4 Q20*	**Step 2:** Because this question stem asks for an answer choice containing the relationship "most analogous to" that between the passages, this is a Logic Reasoning question resembling a Parallel Reasoning question from the Logical Reasoning section. → **Step 3:** Instead of researching specific lines from the passage, use a broader assessment of the passages' relationship to predict the correct answer. **Step 4:** Both passages are concerned with how the Roma are affected by national minority definitions. However, while Passage A is primarily concerned with how vague definitions affect the Roma, Passage B is concerned with one particular definition and has the additional purpose of showing how the Roma mainly satisfy that definition. The right answer to this question should apply the same conceptual purposes to an entirely different situation.

LSAT Question Stem	Analysis
13. Which one of the following is a principle that can be most reasonably considered to underlie the reasoning in both of the passages? *PrepTest56 Sec4 Q21*	**Step 2:** This question wants a principle underlying both passages. This is a Logic Reasoning question—specifically, a Principle question, as it asks for a principle underlying both passages. **Step 3:** Examine the Roadmap for each passage; look for areas of overlap between the passages. → **Step 4:** Both passages are concerned with how the Roma are affected by issues concerning definitions of "national minority." In both cases, the Roma are negatively affected because they aren't technically covered by current definitions. The correct answer choice will get across the idea that not being definitively covered by the rules can cause problems for some groups.

With all of that work done, evaluating the answer choices will be much easier and much faster. That's what you'll do in the next part of this chapter.

Evaluating Reading Comprehension Answer Choices

This is what the entire Reading Comprehension Method is set up to do, answer the questions correctly. There's not a lot to add except to remind you to pay close attention to how the LSAT expert uses his prediction to make bold, accurate assessments of whether each choice is correct or incorrect.

LEARNING OBJECTIVES

In this portion of the chapter, you'll learn to:

· Use a prediction of the correct answer to evaluate the answer choices.

· Use the Topic, Scope, Purpose, and Main Idea summaries to evaluate the answer choices.

· Evaluate answer choices by efficiently checking them against the passage text.

It is not uncommon for test takers to get bogged down in the Reading Comprehension section, especially as they evaluate the answer choices. Do you find yourself reading through answer choices multiple times, unsure which of two or three tempting choices is correct? The way to overcome that hesitation, and thus to increase your speed and accuracy, is to practice the Reading Comprehension Method. The more comfortable you get researching the passage and making accurate, pointed predictions, the quicker you'll find, and the more confidently you'll select, the correct answer. As you review the LSAT expert's evaluations below, keep all of the work you've done through Steps 1–4 in mind.

Let's start by taking one more look at the Tangible-Object Theory passage. We'll reprint the passage, Roadmap, and Step 1 analysis for reference. Along with each question, we'll repeat the expert's Step 2–4 analyses as well. This time, though, we'll add the answer choices and show you how the expert zeros in on the correct choice.

LSAT Passage		Analysis

Proponents of the tangible-object theory of copyright argue that copyright and similar intellectual-property rights can be explained as logical extensions of the right to own concrete, tangible objects. This
(5) view depends on the claim that every copyrightable work can be manifested in some physical form, such as a manuscript or a videotape. It also accepts the premise that ownership of an object confers a number of rights on the owner, who may essentially do whatever he or
(10) she pleases with the object to the extent that this does not violate other people's rights. One may, for example, hide or display the object, copy it, or destroy it. One may also transfer ownership of it to another.

© Tangible-prop. theory

You can "hold" it

Right to do whatever

Step 1: Paragraph 1 starts off with the proponents' view of the **Topic** of the passage, tangible-object theory of copyright. (Anticipate that the author will discuss the opponents' view or an alternative.) The proponents' basic tenet: "every copyrightable work can be manifested in some physical form" or that it can be held. In addition, the owner has the right to do as she sees fit as long as those actions do not infringe upon another person's rights. Basically, the proponents feel that the owner has the right to do whatever she wants.

In creating a new and original object from
(15) materials that one owns, one becomes the owner of that object and thereby acquires all of the rights that ownership entails. But if the owner transfers ownership of the object, the full complement of rights is not necessarily transferred to the new owner; instead, the
(20) original owner may retain one or more of these rights. This notion of retained rights is common in many areas of law; for example, the seller of a piece of land may retain certain rights to the land in the form of easements or building restrictions. Applying the notion
(25) of retained rights to the domain of intellectual property, theorists argue that copyrighting a work secures official recognition of one's intention to retain certain rights to that work. Among the rights typically retained by the original producer of an object such as a literary
(30) manuscript or a musical score would be the right to copy the object for profit and the right to use it as a guide for the production of similar or analogous things—for example, a public performance of a musical score.

Creator get rights

Can retain some rights on transfer

Common rules

In IP, keep rights to copy perform.

Paragraph 2 begins with the rights of the owner as creator of the object. Although the owner can transfer property, the owner can still retain some rights after transfer—the notion of "retained rights." Retained rights are common—example: sale of land. But, what about retained rights and intellectual property? In intellectual property, an owner who transfers ownership can still retain the right to copy the object for profit and to use it as a guide for the production of similar things, like a performance.

So far, it would seem the author is focusing on the proponents of tangible-object theory because she's just written a great analysis of that position.

LSAT Passage	Analysis

(35)   According to proponents of the tangible-object theory, its chief advantage is that it justifies intellectual property rights without recourse to the widely accepted but problematic supposition that one can own abstract, intangible things such as ideas. But while this account

(40) seems plausible for copyrightable entities that do, in fact, have enduring tangible forms, it cannot accommodate the standard assumption that such evanescent things as live broadcasts of sporting events can be copyrighted. More importantly, it does not

(45) acknowledge that in many cases the work of conceiving ideas is more crucial and more valuable than that of putting them into tangible form. Suppose that a poet dictates a new poem to a friend, who writes it down on paper that the friend has supplied. The

(50) creator of the tangible object in this case is not the poet but the friend, and there would seem to be no ground for the poet's claiming copyright unless the poet can be said to already own the ideas expressed in the work.

PrepTest58 Sec2 Qs14–20

T.O. proponents: you can own idea

Author: Problem— tangible form isn't the imp't part

poet analogy

Paragraph 3 begins with the primary advantage proponents believe tangible-object theory has: you can own ideas. The author takes a turn immediately after, though, and begins detailing problems with the abstract, intangible nature associated with things such as ideas. The author's **Scope** is now confirmed: the tangible-object theory's proponents and its problems. In addition, the author's **Purpose** for writing the passage is to outline the position of those in favor of tangible-object theory and show problems with the logic of that view. The author concedes that their view is compatible with tangible objects. However, it's difficult to apply these same concepts to such "evanescent" things as ideas or broadcasts. The author ends with a poet analogy: a poet could dictate an entire poem to a friend, and if the friend writes it down, then the friend is the owner unless the poet can show ownership of the ideas expressed in the poem. In sum, the **Main Idea** is that tangible-object theory's emphasis on ownership going to the creator of a tangible form is problematic.

LSAT Question	Analysis
Which one of the following most accurately expresses the main point of the passage?	**Step 2:** "[M]ain point"—a Global question. Use the Main Idea summary to predict the correct answer.
	Step 3: The Main Idea reflects the author's voice at the end of the passage: Tangible-object theory's views are problematic because they don't protect the creator of intellectual property.
	Step 4: The correct answer will discuss how the application of tangible-object theory to copyright and intellectual property is problematic.
(A) Copyright and other intellectual-property rights can be explained as logical extensions of the right to own concrete objects.	**Step 5:** Although it is true that the notion of retained rights as applied to copyright and intellectual property can help clarify ownership, it is too neutral and does not characterize the author's critique. Eliminate.
(B) Attempts to explain copyright and similar intellectual-property rights purely in terms of rights to ownership of physical objects are ultimately misguided.	Correct. This encompasses the author's exact sentiments and matches the prediction.
(C) Copyrighting a work amounts to securing official recognition of one's intention to retain certain rights to that work.	While the author focuses heavily on retained rights, the author does not go so far as to say that retained rights is all there is to say about copyrighting. Eliminate.
(D) Explanations of copyright and other intellectual-property rights in terms of rights to ownership of tangible objects fail to consider the argument that ideas should be allowed to circulate freely.	The circulation of ideas, free or not, is never discussed in the passage. Eliminate.
(E) Under the tangible-object theory of intellectual property, rights of ownership are straightforwardly applicable to both ideas and physical objects. *PrepTest58 Sec2 Q14*	The author's critique in the third paragraph— especially the poet analogy—indicates that the application of tangible-object theory to ideas is not straightforward and is problematic at best. Eliminate.

LSAT Question	Analysis
According to the passage, the theory that copyright and other intellectual-property rights can be construed as logical extensions of the right to own concrete, tangible objects depends on the claim that	**Step 2:** "According to the passage"—a Detail question. "[T]he theory that . . . depends on the claim" is the research clue. The correct answer is a claim *necessary* for tangible-object theory.
	Step 3: Reference in paragraph 1 where the author discussed the basis for tangible-object theory. Specifically, the author mentioned that it "*depends on the claim that every copyrightable work can be manifested in some physical form.*" It can be extended to anything that you can hold a copy of in your hand.
	Step 4: The correct answer will need to state the basis of the idea that copyright and intellectual property are capable of being in physical form.
(A) any work entitled to intellectual-property protection can be expressed in physical form	**Step 5:** Correct. This is a close paraphrase of lines 5–7 and is a match to the prediction.
(B) only the original creator of an intellectual work can hold the copyright for that work	180. The proponents' of tangible-object theory acknowledge that the owner can transfer ownership and still retain some rights. In that instance, tangible-object theory would still be applicable. Eliminate.
(C) the work of putting ideas into tangible form is more crucial and more valuable than the work of conceiving those ideas	180. In paragraph 3, the author explicitly states that tangible-object theory's application to copyright and intellectual property is problematic because "the work of conceiving ideas is more crucial and more valuable than that of putting them into tangible form." Eliminate.
(D) in a few cases, it is necessary to recognize the right to own abstract, intangible things	Irrelevant. Recognizing the right to own abstract, intangible things is not the appropriate basis for applying tangible-object theory to copyright and intellectual property. Also, this application would extend to more than a few cases. Eliminate.
(E) the owner of an item of intellectual property may legally destroy it	Distortion. The owner's right to destroy an item of intellectual property does not necessarily indicate that the item is in tangible form. Eliminate.

PrepTest58 Sec2 Q15

LSAT Question	Analysis
The passage most directly answers which one of the following questions?	**Step 2:** "[A]nswers which of the following questions"—a Detail question variant. No research clue. Use the answer choices (which will be worded as questions) to check the text. The correct answer is a question for which an answer can be found in the passage.
	Step 3: Because there's no content clue or line reference in the question stem, go through each answer choice one by one.
	Step 4: Rather than make a prediction, characterize the answer choices: In the correct answer, the question posed can be answered from information in the passage. All four wrong answer choices will be Outside the Scope of the passage.
(A) Do proponents of the tangible-object theory of intellectual property advocate any changes in existing laws relating to copyright?	**Step 5:** Outside the Scope. Changes to existing laws related to copyright are never discussed in the passage. Eliminate.
(B) Do proponents of the tangible-object theory of intellectual property hold that ownership of anything besides real estate can involve retained rights?	Correct. In addition to the sale of land, the proponents of tangible-object theory also hold that ownership of copyright and intellectual property—specifically a literary manuscript or a musical score—can involve retained rights (lines 24–34).
(C) Has the tangible-object theory of intellectual property influenced the ways in which copyright cases or other cases involving issues of intellectual property are decided in the courts?	Outside the Scope. The effect of tangible-object theory on how cases involving intellectual property issues are decided is never discussed. Eliminate.
(D) Does existing copyright law provide protection against unauthorized copying of manuscripts and musical scores in cases in which their creators have not officially applied for copyright protection?	Outside the Scope. Whether existing copyright law provides protection against unauthorized copying of items in which the creator has not yet applied for protection is never discussed. Eliminate.
(E) Are there standard procedures governing the transfer of intellectual property that are common to most legal systems? *PrepTest58 Sec2 Q16*	Outside the Scope. The standard procedures concerning the transfer of intellectual property are never discussed, let alone what about them is common to most legal systems. Eliminate.

LSAT Question	Analysis
Suppose an inventor describes an innovative idea for an invention to an engineer, who volunteers to draft specifications for a prototype and then produces the prototype using the engineer's own materials. Which one of the following statements would apply to this case under the tangible-object theory of intellectual property, as the author describes that theory?	**Step 2:** "Which . . . would apply"—an Inference question variant. The correct answer is the correct application of tangible-object theory to the hypothetical example in the question stem. Use that example as the research clue and look for an analogous or applicable case in the passage.
	Step 3: In the question stem, the inventor describes an innovative idea to an engineer, who then drafts a prototype that the engineer then produces from his own materials. Reference the poet analogy at the end of paragraph 3 (lines 47–53). The author uses the poet example to show that tangible-object theory would grant ownership of the poem to the wrong person—that is, to the transcriber, rather than the poet—because the act of writing down the poem constitutes the creation of the physical object.
	In the example cited in the question stem, the application of tangible-object theory would be similarly problematic because the creator of the tangible object would be the engineer, not the inventor.
	Step 4: The correct answer will indicate that the engineer, and not the inventor, is entitled to claim ownership.
(A) Only the engineer is entitled to claim the invention as intellectual property.	**Step 5:** Correct. This choice properly indicates that only the engineer can claim ownership of the invention.
(B) Only the inventor is entitled to claim the invention as intellectual property.	180. The inventor is not entitled to claim ownership of the invention. Eliminate.
(C) The inventor and the engineer are equally entitled to claim the invention as intellectual property.	180. The engineer and the inventor are not equally entitled to claim ownership of the invention. Eliminate.
(D) The engineer is entitled to claim the invention as intellectual property, but only if the inventor retains the right to all profits generated by the invention.	Distortion. Tangible-object theory, as described in the passage, doesn't split rights on the basis of one party's retention of the rights to profit from intellectual property. Eliminate.
(E) The inventor is entitled to claim the invention as intellectual property, but only if the engineer retains the right to all profits generated by the invention.	180 and Distortion. The inventor cannot claim ownership of the invention regardless of who retains any rights. Eliminate.

PrepTest58 Sec2 Q17

LSAT Question	Analysis
Legal theorists supporting the tangible-object theory of intellectual property are most likely to believe which one of the following?	**Step 2:** "[M]ost likely to believe"—an Inference question. The correct answer will agree with the tangible-object theory proponents (not with the author). Research the passage where the proponents' beliefs are stated.
	Step 3: Research all references to the legal theorists who are the proponents of the tangible-object theory.
	→ In paragraph 1, the author explains that the legal theorists believe copyright and similar intellectual property rights can be explained as a logical extension of the right to own concrete tangible objects (those that can be manifested in physical form).
	In paragraph 3, the author states that the proponents see the primary advantage of tangible-object theory's application to intellectual property as a means to provide ownership to intangible/abstract things such as ideas.
	Step 4: The correct answer choice must be something that the proponents of tangible-object theory believe and will be consistent with both of the expressed viewpoints.
(A) A literary work cannot receive copyright protection unless it exists in an edition produced by an established publisher.	**Step 5:** Outside the Scope. The proponents' view → regarding what constitutes copyright protection of a literary work does not depend on the edition being produced by an established publisher. Eliminate.
(B) Most legal systems explicitly rely on the tangible-object theory of intellectual property in order to avoid asserting that one can own abstract things.	Outside the Scope. We don't know whether the proponents feel that legal systems rely on the → tangible-object theory of intellectual property to avoid asserting ownership of abstract ideas. Eliminate.
(C) Copyright protects the right to copy for profit, but not the right to copy for other reasons.	Distortion. In paragraph 2, the author states that under the notion of retained rights, the original producer does retain the right to copy the object for → profit. However, this is "[a]mong the rights typically retained by the original producer," not necessarily one of the only two rights the author mentions. Eliminate.

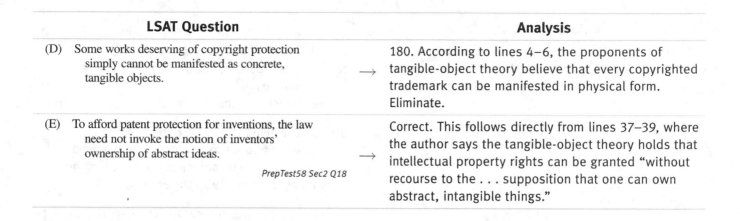

LSAT Question	Analysis
(D) Some works deserving of copyright protection simply cannot be manifested as concrete, tangible objects.	180. According to lines 4–6, the proponents of tangible-object theory believe that every copyrighted trademark can be manifested in physical form. Eliminate.
(E) To afford patent protection for inventions, the law need not invoke the notion of inventors' ownership of abstract ideas. *PrepTest58 Sec2 Q18*	Correct. This follows directly from lines 37–39, where the author says the tangible-object theory holds that intellectual property rights can be granted "without recourse to the . . . supposition that one can own abstract, intangible things."

Response Data

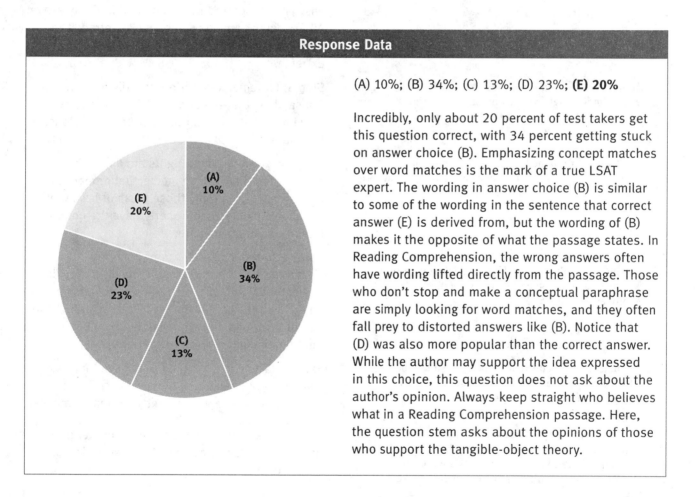

(A) 10%; (B) 34%; (C) 13%; (D) 23%; **(E) 20%**

Incredibly, only about 20 percent of test takers get this question correct, with 34 percent getting stuck on answer choice (B). Emphasizing concept matches over word matches is the mark of a true LSAT expert. The wording in answer choice (B) is similar to some of the wording in the sentence that correct answer (E) is derived from, but the wording of (B) makes it the opposite of what the passage states. In Reading Comprehension, the wrong answers often have wording lifted directly from the passage. Those who don't stop and make a conceptual paraphrase are simply looking for word matches, and they often fall prey to distorted answers like (B). Notice that (D) was also more popular than the correct answer. While the author may support the idea expressed in this choice, this question does not ask about the author's opinion. Always keep straight who believes what in a Reading Comprehension passage. Here, the question stem asks about the opinions of those who support the tangible-object theory.

LSAT Question	Analysis
The passage provides the most support for inferring which one of the following statements?	**Step 2:** "[I]nferring"—an Inference question. No research clue. Use the Scope, Purpose, and Main Idea summaries to evaluate the answers or check the answer choices against the text.
	Step 3: Because there's no content clue or line reference in the question stem, go through each answer choice one by one or use the big-picture summaries to eliminate wrong answers.
	Step 4: Characterize the answer choices: The correct answer is supported by information in the passage. All four wrong answer choices will contradict the author, be Outside the Scope of the passage, or be Extreme.
(A) In most transactions involving the transfer of non-intellectual property, at least some rights of ownership are retained by the seller.	**Step 5:** Extreme. It is not necessarily in most transactions that rights are retained. Rather, we only know that they can be in certain situations. Eliminate.
(B) The notion of retained rights of ownership is currently applied to only those areas of law that do not involve intellectual property.	Extreme. While retained rights are applicable to areas of law that involve intellectual property, it is not for sure that only those areas of laws that do involve intellectual property have the notion of retained rights. Eliminate.
(C) The idea that ownership of the right to copy an item for profit can be transferred is compatible with a tangible-object theory of intellectual property.	Correct. In the last sentence of Paragraph 1, where the author defines the tangible-object theory, he states that "[o]ne may also transfer ownership of [an object] to another." At the end of Paragraph 2, the author mentions that an owner of an object has the right to copy that object for profit.
(D) Ownership of intellectual property is sufficiently protected by the provisions that, under many legal systems, apply to ownership of material things such as land.	Extreme. There is no reason to believe that ownership of intellectual property is *sufficiently* protected as the law is currently written. Eliminate.
(E) Protection of computer programs under intellectual-property law is justifiable only if the programs are likely to be used as a guide for the production of similar or analogous programs.	Outside the Scope. Protection of computer programs under intellectual property law is never discussed. Eliminate.

PrepTest58 Sec2 Q19

LSAT Question	Analysis
It can be inferred that the author of the passage is most likely to believe which one of the following?	**Step 2:** "[C]an be inferred"—an Inference question. No research clue. Use the Scope, Purpose, and Main Idea summaries to evaluate the answers or check the answer choices against the text.
	$\longrightarrow$ **Step 3:** Because there's no content clue or line reference in the question stem, go through each answer choice one by one or use the big-picture summaries to eliminate wrong answers.
	Step 4: Characterize the answer choices: The correct answer is supported by information in the passage. All four wrong answer choices will contradict the author, be Outside the Scope of the passage, or be Extreme.
(A) Theorists who suggest that the notion of retained rights is applicable to intellectual property do not fully understand what it means to transfer ownership of property.	$\longrightarrow$ **Step 5:** Distortion. The author never attacks the notion of retained rights and why the proponents believe it applies to intellectual property. If anything, the author seems to go into great detail about why the proponents believe that retained rights applies to intellectual property. Eliminate.
(B) If a work does not exist in a concrete, tangible form, there is no valid theoretical basis for claiming that it should have copyright protection.	$\longrightarrow$ Distortion. The opinion expressed in this choice is that of the proponents of tangible-object theory, not that of the author. Eliminate.
(C) Under existing statutes, creators of original tangible works that have intellectual or artistic significance generally do not have the legal right to own the abstract ideas embodied in those works.	$\longrightarrow$ 180. The author would likely believe that creators of original tangible works do own those ideas upon which the work is based. Eliminate.
(D) An adequate theoretical justification of copyright would likely presuppose that a work's creator originally owns the ideas embodied in that work.	$\longrightarrow$ Correct—supported by the information in Paragraph 3. To have ownership under the existing law, the creator of the work would be assumed to own the ideas contained within those works. Otherwise, the producer could claim ownership.
(E) It is common, but incorrect, to assume that such evanescent things as live broadcasts of sporting events can be copyrighted. *PrepTest58 Sec2 Q20*	$\longrightarrow$ 180. In paragraph 3, the author states that the belief that evanescent things such as live broadcasts of sporting events can be copyrighted is a "standard assumption." Eliminate.

Notice that the expert never compares the answers to one another. She never thinks, "Which is more correct, choice (A) or choice (C)?" Knowing what the correct answer must contain, having predicted its meaning accurately, she can assess the choices with confidence. Naturally, she may confirm a choice by referring to the text. Likewise, she may do a quick research check to be certain that a wrong answer distorts or contradicts the passage. Never, though, will she engage in multiple re-reads as she makes her way through a set of questions.

Practice

Now, try Step 5 on your own. Use the work you've already done with the Comparative Reading passages on Roma as a National Minority. Take a few moments to refresh your memory of the passages, Roadmap, and strategic reading analysis. Then, turn to the questions one at a time. You've already completed Steps 2–4 here, so review the research you did and predictions you made. Use them to evaluate the answer choices. Avoid comparing answers to one another and keep in mind that the one correct answer will be justified by the passage, while all four wrong answers will not. When you're finished, check your answers and compare your analysis to that of an LSAT expert on the following pages.

LSAT Passage	Analysis
Passage A	**Step 1:** The **Topic** of Passage A is presented immediately in the first sentence: national minority. Passage A's author notes a problem: there is no universally accepted definition for the term "national minority." This lack of definition constitutes the **Scope** of Passage A. The author offers two frequent applications of the term but further complains that other terms (e.g., "nation" and "people") used in defining national minority are similarly vague.

Passage A

    There is no universally accepted definition within international law for the term "national minority." It is most commonly applied to (1) groups of persons—not necessarily citizens—under the jurisdiction of one
(5) country who have ethnic ties to another "homeland" country, or (2) groups of citizens of a country who have lasting ties to that country and have no such ties to any other country, but are distinguished from the majority of the population by ethnicity, religion, or
(10) language. The terms "people" and "nation" are also vaguely defined in international agreements. Documents that refer to a "nation" generally link the term to the concept of "nationalism," which is often associated with ties to land. It also connotes sovereignty, for
(15) which reason, perhaps, "people" is often used instead of "nation" for groups subject to a colonial power.

Margin notes: No univ. def for "nat'l min"; 2 appl. of "nat'l min"; terms are vague

    While the lack of definition of the terms "minority," "people," and "nation" presents difficulties to numerous minority groups, this lack is particularly problematic
(20) for the Roma (Gypsies). The Roma are not a colonized people, they do not have a homeland, and many do not bear ties to any currently existing country. Some Roma are not even citizens of any country, in part because of their nomadic way of life, which developed in response
(25) to centuries of fleeing persecution. Instead, they have ethnic and linguistic ties to other groups of Roma that reside in other countries.

Margin note: Problem e.g. Roma

In the second paragraph, the author discusses how this lack of accepted definitions is potentially harmful, particularly to one group: the Roma. The author's **Purpose** is merely to describe this problem and how it affects the Roma in particular. Because the author offers no solution, the **Main Idea** of Passage A is simply that the lack of an agreed upon definition of "national minority" (as well as "nation" and "people") has negative consequences for certain groups, including the Roma.

LSAT Passage	Analysis

Passage B

Capotorti's definition of a minority includes four empirical criteria—a group's being numerically smaller (30) than the rest of the population of the state; their being nondominant; their having distinctive ethnic, linguistic, or religious characteristics; and their desiring to preserve their own culture—and one legal criterion, that they be citizens of the state in question. This last (35) element can be problematic, given the previous nomadic character of the Roma, that they still cross borders between European states to avoid persecution, and that some states have denied them citizenship, and thus minority status. Because this element essentially (40) grants the state the arbitrary right to decide if the Roma constitute a minority without reference to empirical characteristics, it seems patently unfair that it should be included in the definition.

Cap's def of min. 5 crit

Problem e.g. Roma meet 4 of 5 crit

As would be expected, the **Topic** of Passage B is also national minority. However, the author of Passage B isn't concerned about the lack of a definition. The **Scope** of Passage B is one specific definition of national minority: Capotorti's definition. Passage B starts off by laying out the five criteria for Capotorti's definition: four empirical ones and one legal. The author of Passage B then discusses a problem with the legal criterion, particularly in respect to the Roma. Similar to Passage A, one purpose of Passage B is to describe how a national minority definition is problematic for the Roma.

However, the Roma easily fulfill the four (45) objective elements of Capotorti's definition and should, therefore, be considered a minority in all major European states. Numerically, they are nowhere near a majority, though they number in the hundreds of thousands, even millions, in some states. Their (50) nondominant position is evident—they are not even acknowledged as a minority in some states. The Roma have a number of distinctive linguistic, ethnic, and religious characteristics. For example, most speak Romani, an Indo-European language descended from (55) Sanskrit. Roma groups also have their own distinctive legal and court systems, which are group oriented rather than individual-rights oriented. That they have preserved their language, customs, and identity through centuries of persecution is evidence enough (60) of their desire to preserve their culture.

Au–Roma meet def of nat'l min

The second paragraph provides a more refined **Purpose**: show how the Roma should qualify as a national minority using the remaining, more objective criteria. The **Main Idea** of Passage B is that the legal criterion of Capotorti's definition poses a problem to the Roma by denying them status as a national minority despite their fulfillment of the remaining objective criteria.

PrepTest56 Sec4 Qs16–21

Compare/Contrast the Passages

Before going to the questions, note the relationship between the two passages. Both are concerned with the definition of national minority—although one is concerned about the lack of an accepted definition and one is concerned about the criteria of one definition in particular. More notably, both passages are concerned with how these issues cause problems in the case of the Roma. The passages are different in that Passage A emphasizes the problematic nature of the Roma case for minority status while Passage B argues that Caportorti's definition of minority status fits the Roma well if the legal criterion is dropped.

LSAT Question	**My Analysis**
14. Which one of the following most accurately expresses the main point of passage A?	**Step 2:** Even though this question asks for the main point of only one passage, it's still a Global question because it focuses on that passage as a whole.
	→ **Step 3:** Use the Roadmap and understanding of the big picture (Topic, Scope, Purpose, and Main Idea) to predict the correct answer.
	Step 4: The main point of Passage A is straightforward: The lack of definition for "national minority" (as well as "nation" and "people") has led to problems for certain groups, particularly the Roma.
(A) Different definitions of certain key terms in international law conflict with one another in their application to the Roma.	**Step 5:**
(B) In at least some countries in which they live, the Roma are not generally considered a minority group.	
(C) The lack of agreement regarding the definitions of such terms as "minority," "people," and "nation" is partly due to the unclear application of the terms to groups such as the Roma.	
(D) Any attempt to define such concepts as people, nation, or minority group will probably fail to apply to certain borderline cases such as the Roma.	
(E) The absence of a clear, generally agreed-upon understanding of what constitutes a people, nation, or minority group is a problem, especially in relation to the Roma.	

PrepTest56 Sec4 Q16

LSAT Question	My Analysis
15. The term "problematic" has which one of the following meanings in both passage A (line 19) and passage B (line 35)?	**Step 2:** A question asking how the author defines a word in context is an Inference question. The correct answer follows from, but is not stated in, the text. **Step 3:** The question stem references lines 19 and 35. To predict the answer, read the sentences containing "problematic" to derive context. → **Step 4:** In both passages, the word "problematic" is used to describe how the Roma are affected by the definition (or lack of definition) of national minority. In Passage A, the vague definitions are too broad for the Roma, and in Passage B, the legal criterion of the definition is too narrow for the Roma. In both cases, "problematic" refers to causing difficulties.
(A) giving rise to intense debate	**Step 5:**
(B) confusing and unclear	
(C) resulting in difficulties	
(D) difficult to solve	
(E) theoretically incoherent	

PrepTest56 Sec4 Q17

LSAT Question	My Analysis
16. Which one of the following claims about the Roma is NOT made in passage A?	**Step 2:** Because this question focuses on claims stated (or, in this case, NOT stated) in the passage, it's a Detail question. Four of the answers to this question will be found in Passage A, and one will not.
	→ **Step 3:** The only part of Passage A that discusses the Roma is paragraph 2.
	Step 4: It's always hard to predict what the outlier will be. Check each choice against lines 17–27. There's also a good chance that the right answer will appear in Passage B.
(A) Those living in one country have ethnic ties to Roma in other countries.	**Step 5:**
(B) Some of them practice a nomadic way of life.	
(C) They, as a people, have no recognizable homeland.	
(D) In some countries, their population exceeds one million.	
(E) The lack of a completely satisfactory definition of "minority" is a greater problem for them than for most.	

PrepTest56 Sec4 Q18

LSAT Question	My Analysis
17. The authors' views regarding the status of the Roma can most accurately be described in which one of the following ways?	**Step 2:** This is an Inference question because it asks you to crystallize the authors' points of view as they're presented in the passages.
	Step 3: Passage A discusses the Roma in paragraph 2 and Passage B in lines 34–60.
	Step 4: Both passages present the Roma as a specific group that experiences problems due to issues with the international definitions of national minority. The correct answer will convey that shared attitude.
(A) The author of passage A, but not the author of passage B, disapproves of the latitude that international law allows individual states in determining their relations to nomadic Roma populations.	**Step 5:**
(B) The author of passage B, but not the author of passage A, considers the problems of the Roma to be a noteworthy example of how international law can be ineffective.	
(C) The author of passage B, but not the author of passage A, considers the Roma to be a paradigmatic example of a people who do not constitute a nation.	
(D) Both authors would prefer that the political issues involving the Roma be resolved on a case-by-case basis within each individual country rather than through international law.	
(E) Both authors consider the problems that the Roma face in relation to international law to be anomalous and special.	

PrepTest56 Sec4 Q19

LSAT Question	My Analysis
18. The relationship between which one of the following pairs of documents is most analogous to the relationship between passage A and passage B?	**Step 2:** Because this question stem asks for an answer choice containing the relationship "most analogous to" that between the passages, this is a Logic Reasoning question resembling a Parallel Reasoning question from the Logical Reasoning section.
	Step 3: Instead of researching specific lines from the passage, use a broader assessment of the passages' relationship to predict the correct answer.
	Step 4: Both passages are concerned with how the Roma are affected by national minority definitions. However, while Passage A is primarily concerned with how vague definitions affect the Roma, Passage B is concerned with one particular definition and has the additional purpose of showing how the Roma mainly satisfy that definition. The right answer to this question should apply the same conceptual purposes to an entirely different situation.
(A) "The Lack of Clear-Cut Criteria for Classifying Jobs as Technical Causes Problems for Welders" and "A Point-by-Point Argument That Welding Fulfills the Union's Criteria for Classification of Jobs as 'Technical'"	**Step 5:**
(B) "Why the Current Criteria for Professional Competence in Welding Have Not Been Effectively Applied" and "A Review of the Essential Elements of Any Formal Statement of Professional Standards"	
(C) "The Need for a Revised Definition of the Concept of Welding in Relation to Other Technical Jobs" and "An Enumeration and Description of the Essential Job Duties Usually Carried Out by Union Welders"	
(D) "The Lack of Competent Welders in Our Company Can Be Attributed to a General Disregard for Professional and Technical Staff Recruitment" and "A Discussion of the Factors That Companies Should Consider in Recruiting Employees"	
(E) "The Conceptual Links Between Professionalism and Technical Expertise" and "A Refutation of the Union's Position Regarding Which Types of Jobs Should Be Classified as Neither Professional nor Technical"	

PrepTest56 Sec4 Q20

LSAT Question	My Analysis
19. Which one of the following is a principle that can be most reasonably considered to underlie the reasoning in both of the passages?	**Step 2:** This question wants a principle underlying both passages. This is a Logic Reasoning question—specifically, a Principle question, as it asks for a principle underlying both passages.

Step 3: Examine the Roadmap for each passage; look for areas of overlap between the passages.

→ **Step 4:** Both passages are concerned with how the Roma are affected by issues concerning definitions of "national minority." In both cases, the Roma are negatively affected because they aren't technically covered by current definitions. The correct answer choice will get across the idea that not being definitively covered by the rules can cause problems for some groups.

(A) A definition that is vaguely formulated cannot serve as the basis for the provisions contained in a document of international law.

Step 5:

(B) A minority group's not being officially recognized as such by the government that has jurisdiction over it can be detrimental to the group's interests.

(C) Provisions in international law that apply only to minority groups should not be considered valid.

(D) Governments should recognize the legal and court systems used by minority populations within their jurisdictions.

(E) A group that often moves back and forth across a boundary between two countries can be legitimately considered citizens of both countries.

PrepTest56 Sec4 Q21

Here's how an LSAT expert answered the questions from the Roma as a National Minority passage. Compare your analysis of the correct and incorrect answers to his.

LSAT Question	Analysis
14. Which one of the following most accurately expresses the main point of passage A?	**Step 2:** Even though this question asks for the main point of only one passage, it's still a Global question because it focuses on that passage as a whole.
	→ **Step 3:** Use the Roadmap and understanding of the big picture (Topic, Scope, Purpose, and Main Idea) to predict the correct answer.
	Step 4: The main point of Passage A is straightforward: the lack of definition for "national minority" (as well as "nation" and "people") has led to problems for certain groups, particularly the Roma.
(A) Different definitions of certain key terms in international law conflict with one another in their application to the Roma.	→ **Step 5:** Outside the Scope. The author doesn't mention a conflict of definitions. The problem for the Roma is caused by the lack of one universally accepted definition. Eliminate.
(B) In at least some countries in which they live, the Roma are not generally considered a minority group.	→ This choice ignores the entire reason *why* the Roma are not considered a minority. It leaves out the discussion of vague definitions that constituted the entire first paragraph. Additionally, this is actually a detail from lines 38–39 of Passage B. Eliminate.
(C) The lack of agreement regarding the definitions of such terms as "minority," "people," and "nation" is partly due to the unclear application of the terms to groups such as the Roma.	→ 180. This reverses the causality. It's the lack of an accepted definition that causes problems in applying terms to the Roma, not the other way around. Eliminate.
(D) Any attempt to define such concepts as people, nation, or minority group will probably fail to apply to certain borderline cases such as the Roma.	→ Extreme. The author complains that there's no universally accepted definition but never goes so far as to say any definition will fail, even if it is applied to a group like the Roma. Eliminate.
(E) The absence of a clear, generally agreed-upon understanding of what constitutes a people, nation, or minority group is a problem, especially in relation to the Roma.	→ Correct. This matches the prediction precisely.

PrepTest56 Sec4 Q16

LSAT Question	Analysis
15. The term "problematic" has which one of the following meanings in both passage A (line 19) and passage B (line 35)?	**Step 2:** A question asking how the author defines a word in context is an Inference question. The correct answer follows from, but is not stated in, the text.
	Step 3: The question stem references lines 19 and 35. To predict the answer, read the sentences containing "problematic" to derive context.
	Step 4: In both passages, the word "problematic" is used to describe how the Roma are affected by the definition (or lack of definition) of national minority. In Passage A, the vague definitions are too broad for the Roma, and in Passage B, the legal criterion of the definition is too narrow for the Roma. In both cases, "problematic" refers to causing difficulties.
(A) giving rise to intense debate	**Step 5:** Outside the Scope. Neither passage discusses an intense debate arising over the definition or lack thereof. Eliminate.
(B) confusing and unclear	Extreme. The lack of definition may be considered confusing and unclear to the author of Passage A, but the definition is crystal clear in Passage B—it just causes problems. Eliminate.
(C) resulting in difficulties	Correct. This matches the prediction and fits perfectly within the context of the passage.
(D) difficult to solve	Outside the Scope. Solving the problem isn't a primary concern in either passage. Additionally, given that the author of Passage B feels that the Roma satisfy all the criteria except for one, the problem doesn't seem all that difficult to solve. In fact, at the end of the first paragraph of Passage B, the author even implies the easy solution: exclude the legal criterion. Eliminate.
(E) theoretically incoherent *PrepTest56 Sec4 Q17*	Extreme. Again, there's nothing really incoherent about the definition provided in Passage B. It just causes problems in its inapplicability to the Roma.

LSAT Question	Analysis
16. Which one of the following claims about the Roma is NOT made in passage A?	**Step 2:** Because this question focuses on claims stated (or, in this case, NOT stated) in the passage, it's a Detail question. Four of the answers to this question will be found in Passage A, and one will not.
	→ **Step 3:** The only part of Passage A that discusses the Roma is paragraph 2.
	Step 4: It's always hard to predict what the outlier will be. Check each choice against lines 17–27. There's also a good chance that the right answer will appear in Passage B.
(A) Those living in one country have ethnic ties to Roma in other countries.	→ **Step 5:** Pretty much rewords the last sentence of Passage A. Eliminate.
(B) Some of them practice a nomadic way of life.	→ Directly mentioned in line 24 of Passage A. Eliminate.
(C) They, as a people, have no recognizable homeland.	→ Found in line 21, which tells you the Roma have no homeland. Eliminate.
(D) In some countries, their population exceeds one million.	→ Correct. This isn't mentioned in Passage A. In fact, this detail comes from lines 48–49 of Passage B.
(E) The lack of a completely satisfactory definition of "minority" is a greater problem for them than for most.	→ Matches the claim that the Roma are worse off than other groups, a claim from lines 19–20. Eliminate.

PrepTest56 Sec4 Q18

LSAT Question	Analysis
17. The authors' views regarding the status of the Roma can most accurately be described in which one of the following ways?	**Step 2:** This is an Inference question because it asks you to crystallize the authors' points of view as they're presented in the passages.
	Step 3: Passage A discusses the Roma in paragraph 2 and Passage B in lines 34–60.
	Step 4: Both passages present the Roma as a specific group that experiences problems due to issues with the international definitions of national minority. The correct answer will convey that shared attitude.
(A) The author of passage A, but not the author of passage B, disapproves of the latitude that international law allows individual states in determining their relations to nomadic Roma populations.	**Step 5:** 180. It's the author of Passage B who explicitly complains about the states' "arbitrary right to decide if the Roma constitute a minority" (lines 40–41). Eliminate.
(B) The author of passage B, but not the author of passage A, considers the problems of the Roma to be a noteworthy example of how international law can be ineffective.	180. The author of Passage A uses the Roma as a specific example of the difficulties caused by the lack of a universally accepted definition of "national minority" within international law. The author of Passage B also uses the Roma as a noteworthy example, but Capotorti's definition is simply that: one possible definition. It is not necessarily an international law. Eliminate.
(C) The author of passage B, but not the author of passage A, considers the Roma to be a paradigmatic example of a people who do not constitute a nation.	If anything, the author of Passage A seems more inclined to argue that the Roma are an example of a group that doesn't constitute a nation. Passage B doesn't discuss the idea of "nation"; therefore, while the author may agree, this answer choice is not supported by the content of the passage. Eliminate.
(D) Both authors would prefer that the political issues involving the Roma be resolved on a case-by-case basis within each individual country rather than through international law.	180. The author of Passage A is concerned with the lack of an internationally approved definition of minority, while the author of Passage B bemoans states' "arbitrary" right to decide whether the Roma are a minority or not. Neither one seems inclined to champion case-by-case decisions. Eliminate.
(E) Both authors consider the problems that the Roma face in relation to international law to be anomalous and special. *PrepTest56 Sec4 Q19*	Correct. It's a perfect match that accurately expresses both authors' shared idea that the Roma case illustrates unique problems with the definition of national minority.

LSAT Question	Analysis
18. The relationship between which one of the following pairs of documents is most analogous to the relationship between passage A and passage B?	**Step 2:** Because this question stem asks for an answer choice containing the relationship "most analogous to" that between the passages, this is a Logic Reasoning question resembling a Parallel Reasoning question from the Logical Reasoning section.
	Step 3: Instead of researching specific lines from the passage, use a broader assessment of the passages' relationship to predict the correct answer.
	Step 4: Both passages are concerned with how the Roma are affected by national minority definitions. However, while Passage A is primarily concerned with how vague definitions affect the Roma, Passage B is concerned with one particular definition and has the additional purpose of showing how the Roma mainly satisfy that definition. The right answer to this question should apply the same conceptual purposes to an entirely different situation.
(A) "The Lack of Clear-Cut Criteria for Classifying Jobs as Technical Causes Problems for Welders" and "A Point-by-Point Argument That Welding Fulfills the Union's Criteria for Classification of Jobs as 'Technical'"	**Step 5:** Correct. Here, instead of a group of nomadic people, you have welders. Like Passage A, the first article is concerned with a vague definition of a term (here, "[t]echnical") that affects the group. And, like Passage B, the second article argues that the group should satisfy the definition of that term under a particular set of criteria (here, the "[u]nion's [c]riteria").
(B) "Why the Current Criteria for Professional Competence in Welding Have Not Been Effectively Applied" and "A Review of the Essential Elements of Any Formal Statement of Professional Standards"	Distorts Passage A. The author of Passage A doesn't feel that there is an accepted definition of national minority. That doesn't match the first article's suggestion that there are accepted "[c]urrent [c]riteria." Additionally, the second document is too broad to match Passage B. Passage B is concerned with one particular standard (not "[a]ny") and, further, how one group fits it. Eliminate.
(C) "The Need for a Revised Definition of the Concept of Welding in Relation to Other Technical Jobs" and "An Enumeration and Description of the Essential Job Duties Usually Carried Out by Union Welders"	Distorts Passage B. Passage B is an argument that the Roma fit a certain definition as laid out earlier in the passage. The second article here focuses too much on the descriptive aspect only, without a further point. Additionally, the first article doesn't quite match Passage A. The author of Passage A doesn't want a "[r]evised [d]efinition"; instead the author shows the issues that arise from having *no* agreed upon definition. Eliminate.

LSAT Question	Analysis
(D) "The Lack of Competent Welders in Our Company Can Be Attributed to a General Disregard for Professional and Technical Staff Recruitment" and "A Discussion of the Factors That Companies Should Consider in Recruiting Employees"	→ Outside the Scope. The first article here attacks people who are responsible for maintaining a set of quality standards—not for a lack of standards or definitions. That doesn't match Passage A. Additionally, the second article discusses essentially how to create criteria, not how one group matches already existing criteria. Eliminate.
(E) "The Conceptual Links Between Professionalism and Technical Expertise" and "A Refutation of the Union's Position Regarding Which Types of Jobs Should Be Classified as Neither Professional nor Technical" *PrepTest56 Sec4 Q20*	→ Outside the Scope. These two articles express two differing opinions on the relationship between two terms: "[p]rofessionalism" and "[t]echnical [e]xpertise." The original two passages are both only concerned primarily with one term: "minority." Also, the second article has a negative slant ("Classified as *Neither*") that the author of Passage B doesn't include. Eliminate.

LSAT Question	Analysis
19. Which one of the following is a principle that can be most reasonably considered to underlie the reasoning in both of the passages?	**Step 2:** This question wants a principle underlying both passages. This is a Logic Reasoning question—specifically, a Principle question, as it asks for a principle underlying both passages. **Step 3:** Examine the Roadmap for each passage; look for areas of overlap between the passages. → **Step 4:** Both passages are concerned with how the Roma are affected by issues concerning definitions of "national minority." In both cases, the Roma are negatively affected because they aren't technically covered by current definitions. The correct answer choice will get across the idea that not being definitively covered by the rules can cause problems for some groups.
(A) A definition that is vaguely formulated cannot serve as the basis for the provisions contained in a document of international law.	→ **Step 5:** This works great for Passage A, but the author of Passage B doesn't have any concern about vague definitions. Eliminate.
(B) A minority group's not being officially recognized as such by the government that has jurisdiction over it can be detrimental to the group's interests.	→ Correct. This fits both passages very well. Specifically, in both passages, the Roma aren't officially recognized as a national minority in some countries, and that has a detrimental effect on their interests.

LSAT Question	Analysis
(C) Provisions in international law that apply only to minority groups should not be considered valid.	→ 180. Neither author would likely have problems with provisions that apply to minority groups. In fact, given both authors' concern for the Roma, they would both probably favor provisions that apply to minority groups. Eliminate.
(D) Governments should recognize the legal and court systems used by minority populations within their jurisdictions.	→ This doesn't apply to both authors. The author of Passage B mentions that the Roma have legal and court systems in their jurisdictions, but he introduces it to prove that the Roma try to preserve their culture, not to argue that other governments should recognize those court systems. Additionally, the author of Passage A doesn't mention this at all. Eliminate.
(E) A group that often moves back and forth across a boundary between two countries can be legitimately considered citizens of both countries. *PrepTest56 Sec4 Q21*	→ Distortion. Neither author seems to mind that the Roma aren't considered citizens, and they do not discuss whether the Roma should be allowed dual citizenship. The problem is that the Roma are denied status as a national minority. Eliminate.

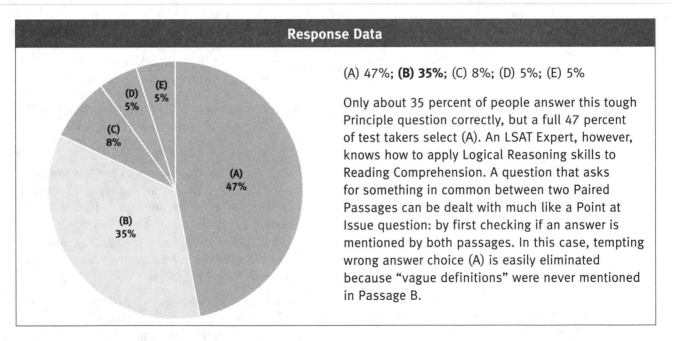

Response Data

(A) 47%; **(B) 35%**; (C) 8%; (D) 5%; (E) 5%

Only about 35 percent of people answer this tough Principle question correctly, but a full 47 percent of test takers select (A). An LSAT Expert, however, knows how to apply Logical Reasoning skills to Reading Comprehension. A question that asks for something in common between two Paired Passages can be dealt with much like a Point at Issue question: by first checking if an answer is mentioned by both passages. In this case, tempting wrong answer choice (A) is easily eliminated because "vague definitions" were never mentioned in Passage B.

It's good to build up your practice step-by-step as you're learning the Method. If you continue to practice these steps diligently, by Test Day you'll do them as if they were second nature.

Practice

Now you're ready to try Steps 2–5 on a question set. Next, you'll see the Biography passage on Philip Emeagwali, complete with the Roadmap and strategic reading analysis. This time, all of the questions associated with that passage are included. Take a few minutes to refresh your memory of the passage and then work through the entire question set. Don't time yourself. Record your analysis for each Step of the Reading Comprehension Method involved in handling the question set. When you're done, compare your work to the expert analysis that follows.

LSAT Passage	Analysis
This passage was adapted from articles published in the 1990s.	The first sentence in paragraph 1 introduces the **Topic**: Philip Emeagwali's computer innovations. Initially, the author discusses the reason for Emeagwali's success with designing computers to solve real-world problems, namely that his pursuit of innovation in design draws heavily upon nature. This may be a hint of the author's **Scope**. The author narrows her discussion to the 1980s, when Emeagwali had a breakthrough with successful parallel computer systems. After distinguishing parallel computer systems, the author gives an example of how the parallel computer systems were successful: oil flow prediction.

The success that Nigerian-born computer scientist Philip Emeagwali (b. 1954) has had in designing computers that solve real-world problems has been fueled by his willingness to reach beyond established
(5) paradigms and draw inspiration for his designs from nature. In the 1980s, Emeagwali achieved breakthroughs in the design of parallel computer systems. Whereas single computers work sequentially, making one calculation at a time, computers
(10) connected in parallel can process calculations simultaneously. In 1989, Emeagwali pioneered the use of massively parallel computers that used a network of thousands of smaller computers to solve what is considered one of the most computationally difficult
(15) problems: predicting the flow of oil through the subterranean geologic formations that make up oil fields. Until that time, supercomputers had been used for oil field calculations, but because these supercomputers worked sequentially, they were too
(20) slow and inefficient to accurately predict such extremely complex movements.

PE—designs comps to solve real-world problems

Breakthrough parallel comps on task

Ex. oil flow prediction 1989

To model oil field flow using a computer requires the simulation of the distribution of the oil at tens of thousands of locations throughout the field. At each
(25) location, hundreds of simultaneous calculations must be made at regular time intervals relating to such variables as temperature, direction of oil flow, viscosity, and pressure, as well as geologic properties of the basin holding the oil. In order to solve this
(30) problem, Emeagwali designed a massively parallel computer by using the Internet to connect to more than 65,000 smaller computers. One of the great difficulties of parallel computing is dividing up the tasks among the separate smaller computers so that
(35) they do not interfere with each other, and it was here that Emeagwali turned to natural processes for ideas, noting that tree species that survive today are those that, over the course of hundreds of millions of years, have developed branching patterns that have
(40) maximized the amount of sunlight gathered and the quantity of water and sap delivered. Emeagwali demonstrated that, for modeling certain phenomena such as subterranean oil flow, a network design based on the mathematical principle that underlies the
(45) branching structures of trees will enable a massively parallel computer to gather and broadcast the largest quantity of messages to its processing points in the shortest time.

Why oil flow hard to calculate

hard to break up tasks on parallel comps

PE—used tree analogy

In paragraph 2, the author continues discussing oil flow prediction and begins by explaining why oil field flow is so difficult to calculate. Mid-paragraph, the author confirms her **Scope**: natural processes showed Emeagwali how to design computers. Specifically, the author describes how Emeagwali referenced a tree-branching pattern as a model for how parallel computers could operate without interfering with the smaller separate computers' tasks. The paragraph ends by detailing Emeagwali's tree analogy. It is now clear that the author's **Purpose** for writing the passage is to explain how Emeagwali used natural processes to model parallel computer design.

LSAT Passage	Analysis

In 1996 Emeagwali had another breakthrough
(50) when he presented the design for a massively parallel
computer that he claims will be powerful enough to
predict global weather patterns a century in advance.
The computer's design is based on the geometry of
bees' honeycombs, which use an extremely efficient
(55) three-dimensional spacing. Emeagwali believes that
computer scientists in the future will increasingly
look to nature for elegant solutions to complex
technical problems. This paradigm shift, he asserts,
will enable us to better understand the systems
(60) evolved by nature and, thereby, to facilitate the
evolution of human technology.

*1996—
weather predict.*

*uses honeycomb
analogy*

*PE—predicts
more nat.
analogies*

PrepTest58 Sec2 Qs8–13

Analysis

Paragraph 3 focuses on another Emeagwali breakthrough. In 1996, Emeagwali designed a computer based on the geometry of honeybees' combs. This massively parallel design may allow the computer to predict global weather patterns. The author ends the passage by pointing out that Emeagwali predicts more and more computer scientists will look to nature for ways to solve complex problems. In sum, the author's **Main Idea** is that Emeagwali used analogies to natural processes to design massive parallel computer systems in order to solve real-world problems.

LSAT Question	My Analysis

20. Which one of the following most accurately expresses the main point of the passage?

Step 2:

Step 3:

Step 4:

(A) Emeagwali's establishment of new computational paradigms has enabled parallel computer systems to solve a wide array of real-world problems that supercomputers cannot solve.

Step 5:

(B) Emeagwali has shown that scientists' allegiance to established paradigms has until now prevented the solution of many real-world computational problems that could otherwise have been solved with little difficulty.

(C) Emeagwali's discovery of the basic mathematical principles underlying natural systems has led to a growing use of parallel computer systems to solve complex real-world computational problems.

(D) Emeagwali has designed parallel computer systems that are modeled on natural systems and that are aimed at solving real-world computational problems that would be difficult to solve with more traditional designs.

(E) The paradigm shift initiated by Emeagwali's computer designs has made it more likely that scientists will in the future look to systems evolved by nature to facilitate the evolution of human technology.

PrepTest58 Sec2 Q8

LSAT Question	My Analysis
21. According to the passage, which one of the following is true?	**Step 2:** **Step 3:** **Step 4:**
(A) Emeagwali's breakthroughs in computer design have begun to make computers that work sequentially obsolete.	**Step 5:**
(B) Emeagwali's first breakthrough in computer design came in response to a request by an oil company.	
(C) Emeagwali was the first to use a massively parallel computer to predict the flow of oil in oil fields.	
(D) Emeagwali was the first computer scientist to use nature as a model for human technology.	
(E) Emeagwali was the first to apply parallel processing to solving real-world problems.	

PrepTest58 Sec2 Q9

LSAT Question	My Analysis
22. The passage most strongly suggests that Emeagwali holds which one of the following views?	**Step 2:** **Step 3:** **Step 4:**
(A) Some natural systems have arrived at efficient solutions to problems that are analogous in significant ways to technical problems faced by computer scientists.	**Step 5:**
(B) Global weather is likely too complicated to be accurately predictable more than a few decades in advance.	
(C) Most computer designs will in the future be inspired by natural systems.	
(D) Massively parallel computers will eventually be practical enough to warrant their use even in relatively mundane computing tasks.	
(E) The mathematical structure of branching trees is useful primarily for designing computer systems to predict the flow of oil through oil fields.	

PrepTest58 Sec2 Q10

LSAT Question	My Analysis
23. Which one of the following most accurately describes the function of the first two sentences of the second paragraph?	Step 2: Step 3: Step 4:
(A) They provide an example of an established paradigm that Emeagwali's work has challenged.	Step 5:
(B) They help explain why supercomputers are unable to accurately predict the movements of oil through underground geologic formations.	
(C) They provide examples of a network design based on the mathematical principles underlying the branching structures of trees.	
(D) They describe a mathematical model that Emeagwali used in order to understand a natural system.	
(E) They provide specific examples of a paradigm shift that will help scientists understand certain systems evolved by nature. *PrepTest58 Sec2 Q11*	

LSAT Question	My Analysis
24. Which one of the following, if true, would provide the most support for Emeagwali's prediction mentioned in lines 55–58?	**Step 2:** **Step 3:** **Step 4:** **Step 5:**
(A) Until recently, computer scientists have had very limited awareness of many of the mathematical principles that have been shown to underlie a wide variety of natural processes.	
(B) Some of the variables affecting global weather patterns have yet to be discovered by scientists who study these patterns.	
(C) Computer designs for the prediction of natural phenomena tend to be more successful when those phenomena are not affected by human activities.	
(D) Some of the mathematical principles underlying Emeagwali's model of oil field flow also underlie his designs for other massively parallel computer systems.	
(E) Underlying the designs for many traditional technologies are mathematical principles of which the designers of those technologies were not explicitly aware.	

PrepTest58 Sec2 Q12

LSAT Question	My Analysis
25. It can be inferred from the passage that one of the reasons massively parallel computers had not been used to model oil field flow prior to 1989 is that	**Step 2:** **Step 3:** **Step 4:** **Step 5:**
(A) supercomputers are sufficiently powerful to handle most computational problems, including most problems arising from oil production	
(B) the possibility of using a network of smaller computers to solve computationally difficult problems had not yet been considered	
(C) the general public was not yet aware of the existence or vast capabilities of the Internet	
(D) oil companies had not yet perceived the need for modeling the flow of oil in subterranean fields	
(E) smaller computers can interfere with one another when they are connected together in parallel to solve a computationally difficult problem	

PrepTest58 Sec2 Q13

Here's how the LSAT expert performed Steps 2–5 on the passage about Philip Emeagwali. Compare your work to that of the expert. Don't check merely to see whether you got the correct answers. Ask questions that help you dig into your mastery of these important steps in the Reading Comprehension Method. Did you recognize each question type? Where there were research clues, did you use them to research the passage? Did you predict the correct answer whenever possible?

LSAT Question	Analysis
20. Which one of the following most accurately expresses the main point of the passage?	**Step 2:** "[M]ain point" signals a Global question. **Step 3:** Consult the Purpose and Main Idea Summaries. **Step 4:** Something along the lines of this: Emeagwali used analogies from natural processes to design parallel computer systems to solve real-world problems.
(A) Emeagwali's establishment of new computational paradigms has enabled parallel computer systems to solve a wide array of real-world problems that supercomputers cannot solve.	**Step 5:** Extreme. "[W]ide array of real-world problems" goes too far. Eliminate.
(B) Emeagwali has shown that scientists' allegiance to established paradigms has until now prevented the solution of many real-world computational problems that could otherwise have been solved with little difficulty.	Extreme. "[W]ith little difficulty" is not supported; also, this answer choice distorts the main idea by taking the focus off E's accomplishments and putting it on other scientists' shortcomings. Eliminate.
(C) Emeagwali's discovery of the basic mathematical principles underlying natural systems has led to a growing use of parallel computer systems to solve complex real-world computational problems.	Distortion. This puts emphasis on E's "discovery" of mathematical principles rather than on his pioneering of parallel computing. Eliminate.
(D) Emeagwali has designed parallel computer systems that are modeled on natural systems and that are aimed at solving real-world computational problems that would be difficult to solve with more traditional designs.	Correct. This matches the prediction.
(E) The paradigm shift initiated by Emeagwali's computer designs has made it more likely that scientists will in the future look to systems evolved by nature to facilitate the evolution of human technology.	Distortion. This places undue emphasis on E's prediction in the last paragraph. Eliminate.

PrepTest58 Sec2 Q8

LSAT Question	Analysis
21. According to the passage, which one of the following is true?	**Step 2:** "According to the passage" signals a Detail question.
	Step 3: Because there is no content clue or line reference in the question stem, go through each answer choice one by one. Find the answer choice that is directly stated in or supported by the passage.
	Step 4: Rather than make a prediction, characterize the answer choices: The correct answer will be directly stated in or supported by the passage. All four wrong answer choices will be Outside the Scope of the passage.
(A) Emeagwali's breakthroughs in computer design have begun to make computers that work sequentially obsolete.	**Step 5:** No indication in the passage that this is true. Eliminate.
(B) Emeagwali's first breakthrough in computer design came in response to a request by an oil company.	The passage says that E had computer breakthroughs in the 1980s while working on parallel computer systems and that in 1989 he found a way to predict oil flow. However, it never indicated that the 1989 discovery was his *first* breakthrough, nor did it state that his work was completed at the request of an oil company. Eliminate.
(C) Emeagwali was the first to use a massively parallel computer to predict the flow of oil in oil fields.	Correct. Expressly supported by lines 11–18: "Emeagwali pioneered the use of . . . parallel computers . . . predicting the flow of oil through the subterranean geologic formations that make up oil fields."
(D) Emeagwali was the first computer scientist to use nature as a model for human technology.	The passage states that E turned to natural processes for ideas, but nowhere in the passage does it say he was the first to do so. Eliminate.
(E) Emeagwali was the first to apply parallel processing to solving real-world problems. *PrepTest58 Sec2 Q9*	While the passage does state that E pioneered the use of parallel computing to predict oil flow, it doesn't mention anything about E being the first to apply parallel processing to other problems. Eliminate.

LSAT Question	Analysis
22. The passage most strongly suggests that Emeagwali holds which one of the following views?	**Step 2:** "[M]ost strongly suggests" indicates an Inference question.
	Step 3: Many possible inferences here; we'll have to research each answer choice to see if it's supported by the passage.
	→ **Step 4:** Since most of the passage is about E, and because there could be many inferences, it's difficult to form a precise prediction. Instead, characterize the answer choices: the correct answer will be directly supported by the passage, and it will be something that E believes. The four wrong answer choices will not be supported by the passage.
(A) Some natural systems have arrived at efficient solutions to problems that are analogous in significant ways to technical problems faced by computer scientists.	**Step 5:** Correct. Research E's views about natural systems in the passage: paragraph 3 tells us "Emeagwali believes that computer scientists in the future will increasingly look to nature for elegant solutions to complex technical problems." We can infer he believes those natural models are efficient.
(B) Global weather is likely too complicated to be accurately predictable more than a few decades in advance.	→ 180. Directly contradicted by the first sentence of paragraph 3. Eliminate.
(C) Most computer designs will in the future be inspired by natural systems.	→ Extreme. "[Most]" goes too far. Eliminate.
(D) Massively parallel computers will eventually be practical enough to warrant their use even in relatively mundane computing tasks.	→ Outside the scope. The passage discusses parallel computing as a way to solve complex problems. "[R]elatively mundane computing tasks" are not addressed. Eliminate.
(E) The mathematical structure of branching trees is useful primarily for designing computer systems to predict the flow of oil through oil fields.	→ Distortion. The word "primarily" is problematic—E doesn't downplay other possible uses of the mathematical structure of branching trees. Eliminate.

PrepTest58 Sec2 Q10

LSAT Question	Analysis
23. Which one of the following most accurately describes the function of the first two sentences of the second paragraph?	**Step 2:** "[D]escribes the function"—a Logic Function question
	Step 3: Research the first two sentences of the second paragraph in context.
	→ **Step 4:** The textual clue "In order to solve this problem, Emeagwali . . ." in the third sentence of Paragraph 2 defines the function of the first two sentences in the paragraph. Those sentences describe a problem that E solves later in the paragraph. Describe the problem: trying to model oil flow is so complex that supercomputers alone can't do it.
(A) They provide an example of an established paradigm that Emeagwali's work has challenged.	→ **Step 5:** Those two sentences don't describe an "established paradigm." Eliminate.
(B) They help explain why supercomputers are unable to accurately predict the movements of oil through underground geologic formations.	→ Correct. This matches the prediction nicely.
(C) They provide examples of a network design based on the mathematical principles underlying the branching structures of trees.	→ Distortion. The reference to branching trees is relevant to E's solution—not to the problem posed by supercomputers. Eliminate.
(D) They describe a mathematical model that Emeagwali used in order to understand a natural system.	→ The two sentences in question don't describe a mathematical model—they describe a problem that needed to be solved using a mathematical model. Eliminate.
(E) They provide specific examples of a paradigm shift that will help scientists understand certain systems evolved by nature.	→ The two sentences in question don't describe or exemplify a "paradigm shift." Eliminate.

PrepTest58 Sec2 Q11

LSAT Question	Analysis
24. Which one of the following, if true, would provide the most support for Emeagwali's prediction mentioned in lines 55–58?	**Step 2:** We're asked to take the answer choices as true and to find one that supports something in the passage, so it's a Strengthen question.
	Step 3: Re-read and understand the lines mentioned: E says that in the future, computer scientists will use natural models to solve complex problems.
	Step 4: Correct answer choice will be anything that makes it *more likely* that in the future, computer scientists will use natural models to solve complex problems.
(A) Until recently, computer scientists have had very limited awareness of many of the mathematical principles that have been shown to underlie a wide variety of natural processes.	**Step 5:** Correct. This makes it more likely that computer scientists will use these models more in the future by giving us a reason why they'll be increasingly able to. It doesn't make it inevitable that E's prediction will come true, but it does make it just slightly more likely, so it's a winner.
(B) Some of the variables affecting global weather patterns have yet to be discovered by scientists who study these patterns.	The fact that some variables affecting global weather patterns are unknown does not affect whether scientists will use natural models more or less in the future. Eliminate.
(C) Computer designs for the prediction of natural phenomena tend to be more successful when those phenomena are not affected by human activities.	Whether the natural phenomena are unaffected by humans is irrelevant. Eliminate.
(D) Some of the mathematical principles underlying Emeagwali's model of oil field flow also underlie his designs for other massively parallel computer systems.	Whether some principles underlie more than one of E's projects has no bearing on the work of other computer scientists in the future. Eliminate.
(E) Underlying the designs for many traditional technologies are mathematical principles of which the designers of those technologies were not explicitly aware.	What may or may not have underlain traditional technologies doesn't affect E's prediction. Eliminate.

PrepTest58 Sec2 Q12

LSAT Question	Analysis
25. It can be inferred from the passage that one of the reasons massively parallel computers had not been used to model oil field flow prior to 1989 is that	**Step 2:** "[I]nferred" = Inference question. **Step 3:** Research places in the passage that discuss prior strategies used to model oil flow, starting around line 11 and going through the second paragraph. We're looking for a reason why they didn't use parallel computers before E pioneered his strategy. Lines 32–35 give us "One of the great difficulties of parallel computing is dividing up the tasks among the separate smaller computers so that they do not interfere with each other." So that's why parallel computing didn't work until E found a solution. **Step 4:** Prediction will sound something like this: there hadn't previously been a solution to the problem of smaller computers interfering with each other.
(A) supercomputers are sufficiently powerful to handle most computational problems, including most problems arising from oil production	**Step 5:** 180. The passage tells us that supercomputers had trouble modeling oil flow, one aspect of oil production. Eliminate.
(B) the possibility of using a network of smaller computers to solve computationally difficult problems had not yet been considered	We don't know whether it had been considered or not—just that it hadn't been tried successfully with regard to oil flow. Eliminate.
(C) the general public was not yet aware of the existence or vast capabilities of the Internet	Outside the scope. This passage is about developments in advanced computer science, so discussion of "the general public" is irrelevant. Eliminate.
(D) oil companies had not yet perceived the need for modeling the flow of oil in subterranean fields	Based on the passage, it seems likely that oil companies wanted to model oil flow because scientists had been attempting to use supercomputers to do so. Eliminate.
(E) smaller computers can interfere with one another when they are connected together in parallel to solve a computationally difficult problem	Correct. This matches the prediction that "smaller computers interfere with each other."

PrepTest58 Sec2 Q13

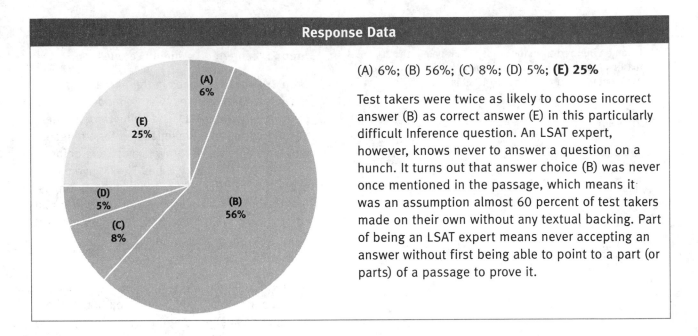

Response Data

(A) 6%; (B) 56%; (C) 8%; (D) 5%; **(E) 25%**

Test takers were twice as likely to choose incorrect answer (B) as correct answer (E) in this particularly difficult Inference question. An LSAT expert, however, knows never to answer a question on a hunch. It turns out that answer choice (B) was never once mentioned in the passage, which means it was an assumption almost 60 percent of test takers made on their own without any textual backing. Part of being an LSAT expert means never accepting an answer without first being able to point to a part (or parts) of a passage to prove it.

Reflection

Take a moment to reflect on how you built your skills to the point where you could more efficiently tackle that last question set. You're certainly not yet as fast and confident as you will be after more practice, but already, by concentrating on the steps of the Reading Comprehension Method, you're almost certainly taking a straighter, more effective line to the correct answer.

FULL PASSAGE PRACTICE

Congratulations on learning all of the skills associated with LSAT Reading Comprehension. Finish up this chapter by trying a complete passage and question set start to finish. At this point (and in the passages you'll practice in Chapter 15), we'll remove the boxes for you to record your analysis and lay out the passage and question set just as it would appear on Test Day. Even though there are no boxes to prompt you, continue to use the Reading Comprehension Method and to do the analyses just as you have been. Remember, the LSAT experts whose work you've been reviewing have done dozens, if not hundreds, of these passages and hundreds, if not thousands, of these questions. To reach their level of proficiency, you need to practice diligently with the Method. So, go to it!

Here's a clue for you as you tackle the following passage. The Topic is about the work of a fiction writer named Sarah Orne Jewett, but this is not a Biography passage. It fits the Theory/Perspective passage structure. Make sure you note why that's the case as you're reading and Roadmapping.

Recent criticism has sought to align Sarah Orne
Jewett, a notable writer of regional fiction in the
nineteenth-century United States, with the domestic
novelists of the previous generation. Her work does
(5) resemble the domestic novels of the 1850s in its focus
on women, their domestic occupations, and their social
interactions, with men relegated to the periphery. But
it also differs markedly from these antecedents. The
world depicted in the latter revolves around children.
(10) Young children play prominent roles in the domestic
novels and the work of child rearing—the struggle to
instill a mother's values in a child's character—is their
chief source of drama. By contrast, children and child
rearing are almost entirely absent from the world of
(15) Jewett's fiction. Even more strikingly, while the
literary world of the earlier domestic novelists is
insistently religious, grounded in the structures of
Protestant religious belief, to turn from these writers to
Jewett is to encounter an almost wholly secular world.

(20) To the extent that these differences do not merely
reflect the personal preferences of the authors, we
might attribute them to such historical transformations
as the migration of the rural young to cities or the
increasing secularization of society. But while such
(25) factors may help to explain the differences, it can be
argued that these differences ultimately reflect
different conceptions of the nature and purpose of
fiction. The domestic novel of the mid-nineteenth
century is based on a conception of fiction as part of
(30) a continuum that also included writings devoted to
piety and domestic instruction, bound together by a
common goal of promoting domestic morality and
religious belief. It was not uncommon for the same
multipurpose book to be indistinguishably a novel, a
(35) child-rearing manual, and a tract on Christian duty.
The more didactic aims are absent from Jewett's
writing, which rather embodies the late nineteenth-
century "high-cultural" conception of fiction as an
autonomous sphere with value in and of itself.

(40) This high-cultural aesthetic was one among
several conceptions of fiction operative in the United
States in the 1850s and 1860s, but it became the
dominant one later in the nineteenth century and
remained so for most of the twentieth. On this
(45) conception, fiction came to be seen as pure art: a work
was to be viewed in isolation and valued for the formal
arrangement of its elements rather than for its larger
social connections or the promotion of extraliterary
goods. Thus, unlike the domestic novelists, Jewett
(50) intended her works not as a means to an end but as an
end in themselves. This fundamental difference should
be given more weight in assessing their affinities than
any superficial similarity in subject matter.

26. The passage most helps to answer which one of the
following questions?

(A) Did any men write domestic novels in the
1850s?
(B) Were any widely read domestic novels written
after the 1860s?
(C) How did migration to urban areas affect the
development of domestic fiction in the 1850s?
(D) What is an effect that Jewett's conception of
literary art had on her fiction?
(E) With what region of the United States were at
least some of Jewett's writings concerned?

27. It can be inferred from the passage that the author
would be most likely to view the "recent criticism"
mentioned in line 1 as

(A) advocating a position that is essentially correct
even though some powerful arguments can be
made against it
(B) making a true claim about Jewett, but for the
wrong reasons
(C) making a claim that is based on some
reasonable evidence and is initially plausible
but ultimately mistaken
(D) questionable, because it relies on a currently
dominant literary aesthetic that takes too
narrow a view of the proper goals of fiction
(E) based on speculation for which there is no
reasonable support, and therefore worthy of
dismissal

28. In saying that domestic fiction was based on a
conception of fiction as part of a "continuum" (line 30),
the author most likely means which one of the following?

(A) Domestic fiction was part of an ongoing
tradition stretching back into the past.
(B) Fiction was not treated as clearly distinct from
other categories of writing.
(C) Domestic fiction was often published in serial
form.
(D) Fiction is constantly evolving.
(E) Domestic fiction promoted the cohesiveness and
hence the continuity of society.

GO ON TO THE NEXT PAGE.

29. Which one of the following most accurately states the primary function of the passage?

(A) It proposes and defends a radical redefinition of several historical categories of literary style.

(B) It proposes an evaluation of a particular style of writing, of which one writer's work is cited as a paradigmatic case.

(C) It argues for a reappraisal of a set of long-held assumptions about the historical connections among a group of writers.

(D) It weighs the merits of two opposing conceptions of the nature of fiction.

(E) It rejects a way of classifying a particular writer's work and defends an alternative view.

30. Which one of the following most accurately represents the structure of the second paragraph?

(A) The author considers and rejects a number of possible explanations for a phenomenon, concluding that any attempt at explanation does violence to the unity of the phenomenon.

(B) The author shows that two explanatory hypotheses are incompatible with each other and gives reasons for preferring one of them.

(C) The author describes several explanatory hypotheses and argues that they are not really distinct from one another.

(D) The author proposes two versions of a classificatory hypothesis, indicates the need for some such hypothesis, and then sets out a counterargument in preparation for rejecting that counterargument in the following paragraph.

(E) The author mentions a number of explanatory hypotheses, gives a mildly favorable comment on them, and then advocates and elaborates another explanation that the author considers to be more fundamental.

31. The differing conceptions of fiction held by Jewett and the domestic novelists can most reasonably be taken as providing an answer to which one of the following questions?

(A) Why was Jewett unwilling to feature children and religious themes as prominently in her works as the domestic novelists featured them in theirs?

(B) Why did both Jewett and the domestic novelists focus primarily on rural as opposed to urban concerns?

(C) Why was Jewett not constrained to feature children and religion as prominently in her works as domestic novelists were?

(D) Why did both Jewett and the domestic novelists focus predominantly on women and their concerns?

(E) Why was Jewett unable to feature children or religion as prominently in her works as the domestic novelists featured them in theirs?

PrepTest62 Sec1 Qs22–27

K | Part Four: Reading Comprehension
CHAPTER 14

These explanations refer to
questions that begin on page 888.

EXPLANATIONS

ANSWERS AND EXPLANATIONS

Sample Roadmap

Recent criticism has sought to align Sarah Orne Jewett, a notable writer of regional fiction in the nineteenth-century United States, with the domestic novelists of the previous generation. Her work does

(5) resemble the domestic novels of the 1850s in its focus on women, their domestic occupations, and their social interactions, with men relegated to the periphery. But it also differs markedly from these antecedents. The world depicted in the latter revolves around children.

(10) Young children play prominent roles in the domestic novels and the work of child rearing—the struggle to instill a mother's values in a child's character—is their chief source of drama. By contrast, children and child rearing are almost entirely absent from the world of

(15) Jewett's fiction. Even more strikingly, while the literary world of the earlier domestic novelists is insistently religious, grounded in the structures of Protestant religious belief, to turn from these writers to Jewett is to encounter an almost wholly secular world.

(20) To the extent that these differences do not merely reflect the personal preferences of the authors, we might attribute them to such historical transformations as the migration of the rural young to cities or the increasing secularization of society. But while such

(25) factors may help to explain the differences, it can be argued that these differences ultimately reflect different conceptions of the nature and purpose of fiction. The domestic novel of the mid-nineteenth century is based on a conception of fiction as part of

(30) a continuum that also included writings devoted to piety and domestic instruction, bound together by a common goal of promoting domestic morality and religious belief. It was not uncommon for the same multipurpose book to be indistinguishably a novel, a

(35) child-rearing manual, and a tract on Christian duty. The more didactic aims are absent from Jewett's writing, which rather embodies the late nineteenth-century "high-cultural" conception of fiction as an autonomous sphere with value in and of itself.

(40) This high-cultural aesthetic was one among several conceptions of fiction operative in the United States in the 1850s and 1860s, but it became the dominant one later in the nineteenth century and remained so for most of the twentieth. On this

(45) conception, fiction came to be seen as pure art: a work was to be viewed in isolation and valued for the formal arrangement of its elements rather than for its larger social connections or the promotion of extraliterary goods. Thus, unlike the domestic novelists, Jewett

(50) intended her works not as a means to an end but as an end in themselves. This fundamental difference should be given more weight in assessing their affinities than any superficial similarity in subject matter.

Margin notes: Recent crit– Jewett ≈ 19ᵗʰ c. dom. nov. / Au = but she's diff. / less about child care / Jewett not religious / Soc/cult changes part of diff. / Au = But big diff is Jewett has diff view of fiction / old dom nov was multi-purpose; not Jewett / late 19ᵗʰ c. novel as work of art / So, Jewett trying to make self-contained "art"

PrepTest62 Sec1 Qs22–27

Step 1: Read the Passage Strategically

The work of fiction writer Sarah Orne Jewett is the **Topic** of this passage. How to classify Jewett's writing is the **Scope**. The author begins by stating that critics have sought to align Jewett with domestic novelists of an earlier era, but he quickly reveals a contrary opinion by noting how Jewett's work differs "markedly" from that of the mid-nineteenth-century writers. The subsequent discussion and support for this alternative view serves as the author's **Purpose**. The rest of the first paragraph introduces two primary differences between Jewett's work and domestic novels: (1) the role of children, prominent in domestic novels and absent in Jewett's, and (2) religiosity, which is a strong part of domestic novels but hardly present in Jewett's work.

In the second paragraph, the author attempts to account for these differences, acknowledging that societal changes could be a factor but quickly turning to the central idea: that the nature and purpose of fiction writing itself had shifted by the end of the nineteenth century. Domestic novels, the passage states, had many functions, serving to provide instruction and promote beliefs. But by Jewett's time, literature had become more esoteric.

The third paragraph expounds on this notion further, tracing the changing conception of fiction and underscoring the author's **Main Idea:** that Jewett's works were not intended as "a means to an end but as an end in themselves" (lines 50–51) and that this "fundamental difference" should be a factor in classifying Jewett's novels differently from the domestic literature that had been written for different reasons.

26. (D) Detail

Step 2: Identify the Question Type

This question poses questions in the answer choices. The question stem asks which question the passage answers. It's a Detail question.

Step 3: Research the Relevant Text

The format of this question requires each answer choice to be researched for its merits. Work quickly, but be sure to justify the answer you choose on the basis of text written in the passage.

Step 4: Make a Prediction

The one correct answer will be something that is addressed within the text of the passage.

Step 5: Evaluate the Answer Choices

(D) finds its justification in the final lines of the passage: the conception of fiction as pure art is discussed at line 45, leading to the assertion that Jewett's intent was for her fiction to be read for its own sake. Correct.

These explanations refer to
questions that begin on page 888.

Part Four: Reading Comprehension
Reading Comprehension: Passage Types and Question Types

K

(A), (B), and (E) each raise topics (male writers, post-1860s domestic novels, and U.S. regions, respectively) that are Out of Scope for this passage.

(C)'s use of the effects of migration on fiction mentioned in the second paragraph is a Distortion/Faulty Use of a Detail. The passage's mention of migration to urban centers was relative to fiction of the later nineteenth century, not that of the 1850s. Moreover, the passage doesn't mention *how* it affected fiction, just that it did.

27. (C) Inference

Step 2: Identify the Question Type

"It can be inferred ..." is a dead giveaway for an Inference question.

Step 3: Research the Relevant Text

The question stem provides both a content clue and a line reference. Go right to the beginning of the passage to double-check: the recent criticism is an effort to categorize Jewett as a domestic fiction writer.

Step 4: Make a Prediction

Despite the specific references to the first words of the passage, the question demands understanding of an attitude that unfolds in the next couple of lines. The author initially admits that Jewett's works and domestic novels do resemble one another. However, the "[b]ut" that ends line 7 signals the author's ultimate opinion, supported throughout the passage: the literary critics who attempt to align Jewett with domestic fiction writers are wrong.

Step 5: Evaluate the Answer Choices

(C) is the only choice in line with the author's view that casting Jewett as a domestic novelist is a mistake.

(A) is a 180. The author clearly believes that the recent criticism is incorrect.

(B) is also a 180, with Distorted reasoning to support it.

(D) may be tempting, but casting the current criticism as reliant on a too-narrow view of the proper goals of fiction distorts the passage's commentary. Nothing states that the recent criticism about Jewett is necessarily "dominant," nor does the passage state what that criticism relies upon. The goals of fiction also aren't discussed pejoratively, so casting goals as "proper" is inappropriate as well.

(E) is incorrect. It is Extreme to state that there is "*no* reasonable support" for the critics' position. Indeed, the author acknowledges that Jewett's work "does resemble" the domestic fiction genre, right in the second sentence of the passage.

28. (B) Logic Function

Step 2: Identify the Question Type

A question asking why an author used a certain word is always a Logic Function question.

Step 3: Research the Relevant Text

The stem directs the research here: seek out the word "continuum" at line 30 and then search around it for context.

Step 4: Make a Prediction

The "continuum" in question is described as including various writings that share a common goal. Domestic fiction, and fiction in general, is seen as part of that group. Therefore, the correct answer will get across the idea that this continuum groups fiction with these other writings as a conglomerate.

Step 5: Evaluate the Answer Choices

(B) reflects fiction as part of a range of written works and is correct.

(A) reaches to a past unmentioned in the passage. It is Out of Scope.

(C) is Out of Scope because the format of domestic novel publication is never mentioned in this article.

(D) is tempting if the concept of "continuum" is taken out of context. However, it does not match the prediction, and it offers a broad platitude that distorts the one evolution in fiction discussed in the passage.

(E) confuses the word "continuum" with "continuity" and will not tempt test takers who follow the Kaplan Method by seeking a match to a strategically researched prediction.

29. (E) Global

Step 2: Identify the Question Type

Any question asking about the passage as a whole is a Global question. It's unusual for Global questions to be buried in the middle of the set, which provides a good reminder that an initial scan of all the questions is always wise. The strategic test taker will have tackled this problem first.

Step 3: Research the Relevant Text

A good Roadmap helps answer Global questions, which test understanding of the complete passage.

Step 4: Make a Prediction

The author exposes a trend in literary criticism toward categorizing the work of a particular author and then argues against this view.

Step 5: Evaluate the Answer Choices

(E) succinctly and accurately states the prediction.

(A) is Extreme with its language of "radical redefinition."

K Part Four: Reading Comprehension
CHAPTER 14

These explanations refer to
questions that begin on page 889.

(B) distorts the passage, which neither really proposes an evaluation of a particular style of writing nor finds Jewett's work as "paradigmatic" of anything.

(C) is Out of Scope because nothing is said in the passage about any "long-held assumptions" about any group of writers.

(D) is another Distortion, as there is no weighing of merits, nor are the two conceptions of fiction discussed by the passage necessarily "opposing," as suggested by the proposed answer.

30. (E) Logic Function

Step 2: Identify the Question Type

When a question asks about the structure of a paragraph, it's classified as a Logic Function problem.

Step 3: Research the Relevant Text

This question names the second paragraph, which contains a discussion attempting to explain the differences between mid-nineteenth-century domestic fiction and the work of author Jewett.

Step 4: Make a Prediction

The paragraph begins by suggesting a few possible reasons for the differences and acknowledges the plausibility of these factors, but then it proposes another explanation: the differing conceptions of fiction. The correct answer will trace this structure.

Step 5: Evaluate the Answer Choices

(E) accurately describes both the structure and the tone of paragraph 2.

(A) is Extreme: nothing is really rejected by the author, and there's certainly no suggestion of "violence" of any sort!

(B) is likewise Extreme and even a 180; while the passage does mention differing hypotheses to explain the difference between fictional works of two eras, the hypotheses are shown to overlap rather than be incompatible.

(C) is inaccurate and incomplete. Stick to your prediction to avoid such traps.

(D) takes quite a while to state something completely fanciful. Nothing in the paragraph follows what's described by the answer choice, which seems designed to tire the test taker with its convoluted language.

31. (C) Detail

Step 2: Identify the Question Type

This wordy question stem might be difficult to categorize quickly: the term "most reasonably" could be construed as the language of an Inference question. However, the question really wants you to identify something that was directly discussed in the passage, making it a Detail question.

Step 3: Research the Relevant Text

"[C]onceptions of fiction" are first discussed in the second paragraph. Start at line 24 to review the content and its context.

Step 4: Make a Prediction

The right answer will reflect the key phrase that the differences between Jewett's writing and that of earlier domestic novelists "ultimately reflect different conceptions of the nature and purpose of fiction." Those differences are described in the first paragraph, which should also be double-checked before any answer gets a commitment.

Step 5: Evaluate the Answer Choices

(C) reflects the key differences between the domestic novelists and Jewett's work, and it is a question that is answered by the author's hypothesis about differing conceptions of fiction's aims. It's a winner.

(A) Distorts the information about Jewett's writing: although the passage states that Jewett's work did not feature children and religious themes, it does not go so far as to say she was "unwilling" to include such themes.

(B) is a Faulty Use of Detail that hangs on the information presented in the early lines of paragraph 2, when migration from rural to urban communities is mentioned. However, it is not mentioned as a subject matter of Jewett or the domestic novelists, and its use in this answer choice is incorrect.

(D) poses a valid question but one that is Outside the Scope of this passage.

(E), like **(A)**, is similarly distorted: the passage does not say that Jewett was "unable" to write about religion and children, merely that she did not do so.

Reading Comprehension Practice

Now that you've mastered the steps in the Reading Comprehension Method, it's time to apply what you've learned to passages and question sets you haven't seen. In the pages that follow, you'll find 11 additional passages, all from recently released tests. Among these passages, you'll find both standard and Comparative Reading passages, you'll see further examples of the common structural patterns found on the LSAT, and you'll get more practice with all of the Reading Comprehension question types. This set of practice passages is representative of the various passage patterns and subject matter that has appeared on official LSATs over the past five years.

NOTES ON READING COMPREHENSION PRACTICE

The passages in this chapter are arranged by difficulty, meaning that we calculated the average difficulty of all questions from the passage's question set. That said, don't place undue emphasis on the difficulty assessment of entire passages. Even the easiest passages may have one or more very difficult questions, and the hardest may have a couple of "gimmes." As you review, check the difficulty level of each question and read the explanations to see what may have made it easier or harder for the majority of test takers. Because the passages are organized by difficulty, if you practice them straight through the chapter, you will encounter different patterns and subject matter at random, just as you will on the exam. That is a good reminder that subject matter alone does not determine the difficulty of Reading Comprehension questions and that different subject areas are easier or harder for different individuals. You need not do all of the passages in order. If you have limited time, you may decide to do some easy and some difficult passages to balance your practice.

As you tackle the Reading Comprehension passages and questions in this chapter, keep the following pointers in mind.

Use the Reading Comprehension Method consistently. Chapter 14 was organized around the 5-Step Reading Comprehension Method introduced in Chapter 13. That's because having a consistent, strategic approach is essential in this section of the test. Be conscious of each step as you practice. If you practice without instilling the Method and its associated strategies, you're likely to repeat your old patterns, and that means continuing to be frustrated by the same Reading Comprehension pitfalls over and over again.

For your convenience, here's the Reading Comprehension Method one more time.

THE KAPLAN READING COMPREHENSION METHOD

Step 1: Read the Passage Strategically—circle Keywords and jot down margin notes to summarize the portions of the passage relevant to LSAT questions; summarize the author's Topic/Scope/Purpose/Main Idea.

Step 2: Read the Question Stem—identify the question type, characterize the correct and incorrect answers, and look for clues to guide your research.

Step 3: Research the Relevant Text—based on the clues in the question stem, consult your Roadmap; for open-ended questions, refer to your Topic/Scope/Purpose/Main Idea summaries.

Step 4: Predict the Correct Answer—based on research (or, for open-ended questions, your Topic/Scope/Purpose/Main Idea summaries) predict the meaning of the correct answer.

Step 5: Evaluate the Answer Choices—select the choice that matches your prediction of the correct answer or eliminate the four wrong answer choices.

As you practice, pay special attention to your work in Step 1 of the Method. Many test takers underestimate the importance of strategic reading. If you find that you are encountering questions that surprise you or for which you have little idea of where in the passage the relevant information would be, it's likely that you needed a stronger Roadmap or better big-picture summaries back in Step 1.

Review your work thoroughly. Complete explanations for the passages and questions in this chapter follow right after the question pool. Take the time to study them even if you get all of a passage's questions correct. Review how expert test takers Roadmapped the passage, the Keywords they circled, the margin notes they jotted down, and how they summarized the author's overall Purpose and Main Idea. You may well discover that with more effective strategic reading, your work on the questions could have been both faster and more accurate. Of course, when you miss a question, determine whether the problem came from a misunderstanding or oversight in the question itself, or whether you misread or overlooked a key piece of the passage.

Another way in which you can effectively use the explanations is to first complete Step 1—create a Roadmap and summarize the author's Purpose and Main Idea. Then, review just that much of the explanations for the passage before you even try the questions. This will let you focus on how you're doing in Step 1, laying the crucial groundwork for effective management of the question set. After you're sure that you understand the passage, try the questions and review them as well. This approach is especially helpful when you find a particular passage frustrating and you feel that you're making little progress working through the questions.

Finally, each question's difficulty is ranked in the explanations—from ★★★★ for the toughest questions to ★ for the easiest. Consulting these rankings will tell you a lot about the passages and questions you're practicing. You might, for example, distinguish a very hard question in an otherwise easy passage. In that case, you'll focus your review on what made that question confusing for test takers while reassuring yourself that your overall approach was on target. Conversely, you may find a passage in which, say, four out of six questions rate ★★★ or ★★★★. In that case, you'll know the passage was tough for everyone, which means you should spend extra time reviewing the Roadmap and big-picture summaries to discover how the testmaker made a passage so challenging.

Practice and Timing. On Test Day, you'll have about 8½ minutes per passage. Naturally, that kind of time pressure can make even routine reading feel stressful. As you practice individual passages, work quickly, but make your focus the successful implementation of the Method. Practicing too quickly could introduce time pressure at a point where you should really be working on consistency and accuracy. Speed will come with familiarity, practice, and (believe it or not) patience. When you take full tests or try 35-minute Reading Comprehension sections, time yourself strictly. But don't be in such a rush to get faster that you fail to gain the efficiencies that come from practicing the methodical application of good Reading Comprehension strategy. Chapter 16 will address timing in depth and will introduce you to strategies to effectively manage the 35-minute Reading Comprehension section that you'll complete on Test Day. In the present chapter, practice *and review* passages one by one to perfect your approach.

QUESTION POOL

Many critics agree that the primary characteristic of Senegalese filmmaker Ousmane Sembène's work is its sociopolitical commitment. Sembène was trained in Moscow in the cinematic methods of socialist
(5) realism, and he asserts that his films are not meant to entertain his compatriots, but rather to raise their awareness of the past and present realities of their society. But his originality as a filmmaker lies most strikingly in his having successfully adapted film,
(10) originally a Western cultural medium, to the needs, pace, and structures of West African culture. In particular, Sembène has found within African oral culture techniques and strategies that enable him to express his views and to reach both literate and
(15) nonliterate Senegalese viewers.

A number of Sembène's characters and motifs can be traced to those found in traditional West African storytelling. The tree, for instance, which in countless West African tales symbolizes knowledge, life, death,
(20) and rebirth, is a salient motif in *Emitaï*. The trickster, usually a dishonest individual who personifies antisocial traits, appears in *Borom Sarret*, *Mandabi*, and *Xala* as a thief, a corrupted civil servant, and a member of the elite, respectively. In fact, most of
(25) Sembène's characters, like those of many oral West African narratives, are types embodying collective ideas or attitudes. And in the oral tradition, these types face archetypal predicaments, as is true, for example, of the protagonist of *Borom Sarret*, who has
(30) no name and is recognizable instead by his trade— he is a street merchant—and by the difficulties he encounters but is unable to overcome.

Moreover, many of Sembène's films derive their structure from West African dilemma tales, the
(35) outcomes of which are debated and decided by their audiences. The open-endedness of most of his plots reveals that Sembène similarly leaves it to his viewers to complete his narratives: in such films as *Borom Sarret*, *Mandabi*, and *Ceddo*, for example, he
(40) provides his spectators with several alternatives as the films end. The openness of his narratives is also evidenced by his frequent use of freeze-frames, which carry the suggestion of continued action.

Finally, like many West African oral tales,
(45) Sembène's narratives take the form of initiatory journeys that bring about a basic change in the worldview of the protagonist and ultimately, Sembène hopes, in that of the viewer. His films denounce social and political injustice. and his protagonists'
(50) social consciousness emerges from an acute self-consciousness brought about by the juxtaposition of opposites within the films' social context: good versus evil, powerlessness versus power, or poverty versus wealth. Such binary oppositions are used analogously
(55) in West African tales, and it seems likely that these

dialectical elements are related to African oral storytelling more than, as many critics have supposed, to the Marxist components of his ideology.

1. Which one of the following most accurately states the main point of the passage?

(A)   Sembène's originality as a filmmaker lies in his adaptation of traditional archetypal predicaments and open-ended plots, both of which are derived from West African oral tales.

(B)   Many of the characters in Sembène's films are variations on character types common to traditional West African storytelling.

(C)   Sembène's films derive their distinctive characteristics from oral narrative traditions that had not previously been considered suitable subject matter for films.

(D)   Sembène's films give vivid expression to the social and political beliefs held by most of the Senegalese people.

(E)   Sembène's films are notable in that they use elements derived from traditional West African storytelling to comment critically on contemporary social and political issues.

GO ON TO THE NEXT PAGE.

2. The author says that Sembène does which one of the following in at least some of his films?

(A) uses animals as symbols
(B) uses slow motion for artistic effect
(C) provides oral narration of the film's story
(D) juxtaposes West African images and Marxist symbols
(E) leaves part of the story to be filled in by audiences

3. Which one of the following would, if true, most strengthen the claim made by the author in the last sentence of the passage (lines 54–58)?

(A) Several African novelists who draw upon the oral traditions of West Africa use binary oppositions as fundamental structures in their narratives, even though they have not read Marxist theory.
(B) Folklorists who have analyzed oral storytelling traditions from across the world have found that the use of binary oppositions to structure narratives is common to many of these traditions.
(C) When he trained in Moscow, Sembène read extensively in Marxist political theory and worked to devise ways of synthesizing Marxist theory and the collective ideas expressed in West African storytelling.
(D) Very few filmmakers in Europe or North America make use of binary oppositions to structure their narratives.
(E) Binary oppositions do not play an essential structuring role in the narratives of some films produced by other filmmakers who subscribe to Marxist principles.

4. Which one of the following inferences about Sembène is most strongly supported by the passage?

(A) His films have become popular both in parts of Africa and elsewhere.
(B) He has not received support from government agencies for his film production.
(C) His films are widely misunderstood by critics in Senegal.
(D) His characters are drawn from a broad range of social strata.
(E) His work has been subjected to government censorship.

5. Which one of the following most closely expresses the author's intended meaning in using the word "initiatory" (line 45)?

(A) beginning a series
(B) experimental
(C) transformative
(D) unprecedented
(E) prefatory

6. The passage does NOT provide evidence that Sembène exhibits which one of the following attitudes in one or more of his films?

(A) disenchantment with attempts to reform Senegalese government
(B) confidence in the aptness of using traditional motifs to comment on contemporary issues
(C) concern with social justice
(D) interest in the vicissitudes of ordinary people's lives
(E) desire to educate his audience

PrepTest52 Sec4 Qs1–6

The explanations to these questions begin on page 922.

To study centuries-old earthquakes and the geologic faults that caused them, seismologists usually dig trenches along visible fault lines, looking for sediments that show evidence of having shifted. Using radiocarbon

(5) dating, they measure the quantity of the radioactive isotope carbon 14 present in wood or other organic material trapped in the sediments when they shifted. Since carbon 14 occurs naturally in organic materials and decays at a constant rate, the age of organic

(10) materials can be reconstructed from the amount of the isotope remaining in them. These data can show the location and frequency of past earthquakes and provide hints about the likelihood and location of future earthquakes.

(15) Geologists William Bull and Mark Brandon have recently developed a new method, called lichenometry, for detecting and dating past earthquakes. Bull and Brandon developed the method based on the fact that large earthquakes generate numerous simultaneous

(20) rockfalls in mountain ranges that are sensitive to seismic shaking. Instead of dating fault-line sediments, lichenometry involves measuring the size of lichens growing on the rocks exposed by these rockfalls. Lichens—symbiotic organisms consisting of a fungus

(25) and an alga—quickly colonize newly exposed rock surfaces in the wake of rockfalls, and once established they grow radially, flat against the rocks, at a slow but constant rate for as long as 1,000 years if left undisturbed. One species of North American lichen, for example,

(30) spreads outward by about 9.5 millimeters each century. Hence, the diameter of the largest lichen on a boulder provides direct evidence of when the boulder was dislodged and repositioned. If many rockfalls over a large geographic area occurred simultaneously, that

(35) pattern would imply that there had been a strong earthquake. The location of the earthquake's epicenter can then be determined by mapping these rockfalls, since they decrease in abundance as the distance from the epicenter increases.

(40) Lichenometry has distinct advantages over radiocarbon dating. Radiocarbon dating is accurate only to within plus or minus 40 years, because the amount of the carbon 14 isotope varies naturally in the environment depending on the intensity of the radiation

(45) striking Earth's upper atmosphere. Additionally, this intensity has fluctuated greatly during the past 300 years, causing many radiocarbon datings of events during this period to be of little value. Lichenometry, Bull and Brandon claim, can accurately date an

(50) earthquake to within ten years. They note, however, that using lichenometry requires careful site selection and accurate calibration of lichen growth rates, adding that the method is best used for earthquakes that occurred within the last 500 years. Sites must be

(55) selected to minimize the influence of snow avalanches and other disturbances that would affect normal lichen growth, and conditions like shade and wind that promote faster lichen growth must be factored in.

7. Which one of the following most accurately expresses the main idea of the passage?

(A) Lichenometry is a new method for dating past earthquakes that has advantages over radiocarbon dating.

(B) Despite its limitations, lichenometry has been proven to be more accurate than any other method of discerning the dates of past earthquakes.

(C) Most seismologists today have rejected radiocarbon dating and are embracing lichenometry as the most reliable method for studying past earthquakes.

(D) Two geologists have revolutionized the study of past earthquakes by developing lichenometry, an easily applied method of earthquake detection and dating.

(E) Radiocarbon dating, an unreliable test used in dating past earthquakes, can finally be abandoned now that lichenometry has been developed.

8. The passage provides information that most helps to answer which one of the following questions?

(A) How do scientists measure lichen growth rates under the varying conditions that lichens may encounter?

(B) How do scientists determine the intensity of the radiation striking Earth's upper atmosphere?

(C) What are some of the conditions that encourage lichens to grow at a more rapid rate than usual?

(D) What is the approximate date of the earliest earthquake that lichenometry has been used to identify?

(E) What are some applications of the techniques involved in radiocarbon dating other than their use in studying past earthquakes?

GO ON TO THE NEXT PAGE.

9. What is the author's primary purpose in referring to the rate of growth of a North American lichen species (lines 29–30)?

(A) to emphasize the rapidity with which lichen colonies can establish themselves on newly exposed rock surfaces

(B) to offer an example of a lichen species with one of the slowest known rates of growth

(C) to present additional evidence supporting the claim that environmental conditions can alter lichens' rate of growth

(D) to explain why lichenometry works best for dating earthquakes that occurred in the last 500 years

(E) to provide a sense of the sort of timescale on which lichen growth occurs

10. Which one of the following statements is most strongly supported by the passage?

(A) Lichenometry is less accurate than radiocarbon dating in predicting the likelihood and location of future earthquakes.

(B) Radiocarbon dating is unlikely to be helpful in dating past earthquakes that have no identifiable fault lines associated with them.

(C) Radiocarbon dating and lichenometry are currently the only viable methods of detecting and dating past earthquakes.

(D) Radiocarbon dating is more accurate than lichenometry in dating earthquakes that occurred approximately 400 years ago.

(E) The usefulness of lichenometry for dating earthquakes is limited to geographic regions where factors that disturb or accelerate lichen growth generally do not occur.

11. The primary purpose of the first paragraph in relation to the rest of the passage is to describe

(A) a well-known procedure that will then be examined on a step-by-step basis

(B) an established procedure to which a new procedure will then be compared

(C) an outdated procedure that will then be shown to be nonetheless useful in some situations

(D) a traditional procedure that will then be contrasted with other traditional procedures

(E) a popular procedure that will then be shown to have resulted in erroneous conclusions about a phenomenon

12. It can be inferred that the statements made by Bull and Brandon and reported in lines 50–58 rely on which one of the following assumptions?

(A) While lichenometry is less accurate when it is used to date earthquakes that occurred more than 500 years ago, it is still more accurate than other methods for dating such earthquakes.

(B) There is no reliable method for determining the intensity of the radiation now hitting Earth's upper atmosphere.

(C) Lichens are able to grow only on the types of rocks that are common in mountainous regions.

(D) The mountain ranges that produce the kinds of rockfalls studied in lichenometry are also subject to more frequent snowfalls and avalanches than other mountain ranges are.

(E) The extent to which conditions like shade and wind have affected the growth of existing lichen colonies can be determined.

13. The passage indicates that using radiocarbon dating to date past earthquakes may be unreliable due to

(A) the multiplicity of the types of organic matter that require analysis

(B) the variable amount of organic materials caught in shifted sediments

(C) the fact that fault lines related to past earthquakes are not always visible

(D) the fluctuations in the amount of the carbon 14 isotope in the environment over time

(E) the possibility that radiation has not always struck the upper atmosphere

14. Given the information in the passage, to which one of the following would lichenometry likely be most applicable?

(A) identifying the number of times a particular river has flooded in the past 1,000 years

(B) identifying the age of a fossilized skeleton of a mammal that lived many thousands of years ago

(C) identifying the age of an ancient beach now underwater approximately 30 kilometers off the present shore

(D) identifying the rate, in kilometers per century, at which a glacier has been receding up a mountain valley

(E) identifying local trends in annual rainfall rates in a particular valley over the past five centuries

PrepTest62 Sec1 Qs1–8

The explanations to these
questions begin on page 927.

With his first published works in the 1950s, Amos Tutuola became the first Nigerian writer to receive wide international recognition. Written in a mix of standard English, idiomatic Nigerian English, and
(5) literal translation of his native language, Yoruba, Tutuola's works were quick to be praised by many literary critics as fresh, inventive approaches to the form of the novel. Others, however, dismissed his works as simple retellings of local tales, full of
(10) unwelcome liberties taken with the details of the well-known story lines. However, to estimate properly Tutuola's rightful position in world literature, it is essential to be clear about the genre in which he wrote; literary critics have assumed too facilely that
(15) he wrote novels.

No matter how flexible a definition of the novel one uses, establishing a set of criteria that enable Tutuola's works to be described as such applies to his works a body of assumptions the works are not
(20) designed to satisfy. Tutuola is not a novelist but a teller of folktales. Many of his critics are right to suggest that Tutuola's subjects are not strikingly original, but it is important to bear in mind that whereas realism and originality are expected of the
(25) novel, the teller of folktales is expected to derive subjects and frameworks from the corpus of traditional lore. The most useful approach to Tutuola's works, then, is one that regards him as working within the African oral tradition.

(30) Within this tradition, a folktale is common property, an expression of a people's culture and social circumstances. The teller of folktales knows that the basic story is already known to most listeners and, equally, that the teller's reputation depends on
(35) the inventiveness with which the tale is modified and embellished, for what the audience anticipates is not an accurate retelling of the story but effective improvisation and delivery. Thus, within the framework of the basic story, the teller is allowed
(40) considerable room to maneuver—in fact, the most brilliant tellers of folktales transform them into unique works.

Tutuola's adherence to this tradition is clear: specific episodes, for example, are often repeated for
(45) emphasis, and he embellishes familiar tales with personal interpretations or by transferring them to modern settings. The blend of English with local idiom and Yoruba grammatical constructs, in which adjectives and verbs are often interchangeable,
(50) re-creates the folktales in singular ways. And, perhaps most revealingly, in the majority of Tutuola's works, the traditional accents and techniques of the teller of folktales are clearly discernible, for example in the adoption of an omniscient, summarizing voice at the
(55) end of his narratives, a device that is generally recognized as being employed to conclude most folktales.

15. Which one of the following most accurately expresses the main point of the passage?

(A) Amos Tutuola is an internationally acclaimed writer of folktales whose unique writing style blends together aspects of Yoruba, Nigerian English, and standard English.

(B) Amos Tutuola's literary works should be evaluated not as novels but as unique and inventively crafted retellings of folktales.

(C) Amos Tutuola is an important author because he is able to incorporate the traditions of an oral art form into his novels.

(D) Critics are divided as to whether Amos Tutuola's literary works should be regarded as novels or folktales.

(E) The folktale is a valuable African literary genre that finds singular expression in the works of Amos Tutuola.

16. Tutuola's approach to writing folktales would be most clearly exemplified by a modern-day Irish author who

(A) applied conventions of the modern novel to the retelling of Irish folktales

(B) re-created important elements of the Irish literary style within a purely oral art form

(C) combined characters from English and Irish folktales to tell a story of modern life

(D) transplanted traditional Irish folktales from their original setting to contemporary Irish life

(E) utilized an omniscient narrator in telling original stories about contemporary Irish life

GO ON TO THE NEXT PAGE.

17. Which one of the following most accurately characterizes the author's attitude toward Tutuola's position in world literature?

   (A) convinced that Tutuola's works should be viewed within the context of the African oral tradition
   (B) certain that Tutuola's works will generate a renewed interest in the study of oral traditions
   (C) pleased at the reception that Tutuola's works have received from literary critics
   (D) confident that the original integrity of Tutuola's works will be preserved despite numerous translations
   (E) optimistic that Tutuola's works reflect what will become a growing new trend in literature

18. According to the passage, some critics have criticized Tutuola's work on the ground that

   (A) his literary works do not exhibit enough similarities to the African oral tradition from which they are drawn
   (B) his mixture of languages is not entirely effective as a vehicle for either traditional folktales or contemporary novels
   (C) his attempt to fuse elements of traditional storytelling style with the format of the novel is detrimental to his artistic purposes
   (D) his writing borrows substantially from well-known story lines and at the same time alters their details
   (E) his unique works are not actually novels, even though he characterizes them as such

19. The author attributes each of the following to Tutuola EXCEPT:

   (A) repetition of elements in his stories for emphasis
   (B) relocation of traditional stories to modern settings
   (C) attainment of international recognition
   (D) use of an omniscient narrator in his works
   (E) transformation of Yoruba folktales into modern novels

20. The author refers to the "corpus of traditional lore" (lines 26–27) as part of an attempt to

   (A) distinguish expectations that apply to one literary genre from those that apply to another literary genre
   (B) argue that two sharply differing literary genres are both equally valuable
   (C) challenge critics who ascribe little merit to innovative ways of blending two distinct literary genres
   (D) elucidate those characteristics of one literary genre that have direct counterparts in another, largely dissimilar genre
   (E) argue for a new, more precise analysis of two literary genres whose distinguishing characteristics are poorly understood

21. The primary purpose of the passage is to

   (A) illustrate the wide range of Tutuola's body of work
   (B) explain the significance of the literary genre of the folktale and to defend it as a valid art form
   (C) provide an account of Tutuola's body of work in order to help establish appropriate criteria for its evaluation
   (D) distinguish accurately between the genre of the novel and that of the folktale
   (E) summarize the disagreement among critics regarding Tutuola's place in world literature

PrepTest56 Sec4 Qs1–7

The explanations to these questions begin on page 932.

Traditional sources of evidence about ancient history are archaeological remains and surviving texts. Those investigating the crafts practiced by women in ancient times, however, often derive little information

(5) from these sources, and the archaeological record is particularly unavailing for the study of ancient textile production, as researchers are thwarted by the perishable nature of cloth. What shreds persisted through millennia were, until recently, often discarded

(10) by excavators as useless, as were loom weights, which appeared to be nothing more than blobs of clay. Ancient texts, meanwhile, rarely mention the creation of textiles; moreover, those references that do exist use archaic, unrevealing terminology. Yet despite these

(15) obstacles, researchers have learned a great deal about ancient textiles and those who made them, and also about how to piece together a whole picture from many disparate sources of evidence.

Technological advances in the analysis of

(20) archaeological remains provide much more information than was previously available, especially about minute remains. Successful modern methods include radiocarbon dating, infrared photography for seeing through dirt without removing it, isotope

(25) "fingerprinting" for tracing sources of raw materials, and thin-layer chromatography for analyzing dyes. As if in preparation for such advances, the field of archaeology has also undergone an important philosophical revolution in the past century. Once little

(30) more than a self-serving quest for artifacts to stock museums and private collections, the field has transformed itself into a scientific pursuit of knowledge about past cultures. As part of this process, archaeologists adopted the fundamental precept of

(35) preserving all objects, even those that have no immediately discernible value. Thus in the 1970s two researchers found the oldest known complete garment, a 5,000-year-old linen shirt, among a tumbled heap of dirty linens that had been preserved as part of the well-

(40) known Petrie collection decades before anyone began to study the history of textiles.

The history of textiles and of the craftswomen who produced them has also advanced on a different front: recreating the actual production of cloth.

(45) Reconstructing and implementing ancient production methods provides a valuable way of generating and checking hypotheses. For example, these techniques made it possible to confirm that the excavated pieces of clay once considered useless in fact functioned as loom

(50) weights. Similarly, scholars have until recently been obliged to speculate as to which one of two statues of Athena, one large and one small, was adorned with a dress created by a group of Athenian women for a festival, as described in surviving texts. Because

(55) records show that it took nine months to produce the dress, scholars assumed it must have adorned the large statue. But by investigating the methods of production

and the size of the looms used, researchers have ascertained that in fact a dress for the small statue

(60) would have taken nine months to produce.

22. Which one of the following most accurately expresses the main point of the passage?

(A) Archaeology is an expanding discipline that has transformed itself in response both to scientific advances and to changing cultural demands such as a recently increasing interest in women's history.

(B) A diversity of new approaches to the study of ancient textiles has enabled researchers to infer much about the history of textiles and their creators in the ancient world from the scant evidence that remains.

(C) Despite many obstacles, research into the textile production methods used by women in the ancient world has advanced over the past century to the point that archaeologists can now replicate ancient equipment and production techniques.

(D) Research into the history of textiles has spurred sweeping changes in the field of archaeology, from the application of advanced technology to the revaluation of ancient artifacts that were once deemed useless.

(E) Though researchers have verified certain theories about the history of textiles by using technological developments such as radiocarbon dating, most significant findings in this field have grown out of the reconstruction of ancient production techniques.

GO ON TO THE NEXT PAGE.

23. The author's attitude concerning the history of ancient textile production can most accurately be described as

   (A) skeptical regarding the validity of some of the new hypotheses proposed by researchers
   (B) doubtful that any additional useful knowledge can be generated given the nature of the evidence available
   (C) impatient about the pace of research in light of the resources available
   (D) optimistic that recent scholarly advances will attract increasing numbers of researchers
   (E) satisfied that considerable progress is being made in this field

24. The passage indicates that the re-creation of ancient techniques was used in which one of the following?

   (A) investigating the meanings of certain previously unintelligible technical terms in ancient texts
   (B) tracing the sources of raw materials used in the production of certain fabrics
   (C) constructing certain public museum displays concerning cloth-making
   (D) verifying that a particular 5,000-year-old cloth was indeed a shirt
   (E) exploring the issue of which of two statues of Athena was clothed with a particular garment

25. The author intends the term "traditional sources" (line 1) to exclude which one of the following?

   (A) ancient clay objects that cannot be identified as pieces of pottery by the researchers who unearth them
   (B) historically significant pieces of cloth discovered in the course of an excavation
   (C) the oldest known complete garment, which was found among other pieces of cloth in a collection
   (D) re-creations of looms from which inferences about ancient weaving techniques can be made
   (E) ancient accounts of the adornment of a statue of Athena with a dress made by Athenian women

26. The passage as a whole functions primarily as

   (A) a defense of the controversial methods adopted by certain researchers in a particular discipline
   (B) a set of recommendations to guide future activities in a particular field of inquiry
   (C) an account of how a particular branch of research has successfully coped with certain difficulties
   (D) a rejection of some commonly held views about the methodologies of a certain discipline
   (E) a summary of the hypotheses advanced by researchers who have used innovative methods of investigation

27. According to the passage, which one of the following was an element in the transformation of archaeology in the past century?

   (A) an increased interest in the crafts practiced in the ancient world
   (B) some archaeologists' adoption of textile conservation experts' preservation techniques
   (C) innovative methods of restoring damaged artifacts
   (D) the discovery of the oldest known complete garment
   (E) archaeologists' policy of not discarding ancient objects that have no readily identifiable value

28. Which one of the following most accurately describes the function of the first paragraph in relation to the rest of the passage?

   (A) A particularly difficult archaeological problem is described in order to underscore the significance of new methods used to resolve that problem, which are described in the following paragraphs.
   (B) A previously neglected body of archaeological evidence is described in order to cast doubt on received views regarding ancient cultures developed from conventional sources of evidence, as described in the following paragraphs.
   (C) The fruitfulness of new technologically based methods of analysis is described in order to support the subsequent argument that apparently insignificant archaeological remains ought to be preserved for possible future research.
   (D) The findings of recent archaeological research are outlined as the foundation for a claim advanced in the following paragraphs that the role of women in ancient cultures has been underestimated by archaeologists.
   (E) A recently developed branch of archaeological research is described as evidence for the subsequent argument that other, more established branches of archaeology should take advantage of new technologies in their research.

PrepTest58 Sec2 Qs1–7

The explanations to these questions begin on page 936.

Passage A

Readers, like writers, need to search for answers. Part of the joy of reading is in being surprised, but academic historians leave little to the imagination. The perniciousness of the historiographic approach became
(5) fully evident to me when I started teaching. Historians require undergraduates to read scholarly monographs that sap the vitality of history; they visit on students what was visited on them in graduate school. They assign books with formulaic arguments that transform
(10) history into an abstract debate that would have been unfathomable to those who lived in the past. Aimed so squarely at the head, such books cannot stimulate students who yearn to connect to history emotionally as well as intellectually.
(15) In an effort to address this problem, some historians have begun to rediscover stories. It has even become something of a fad within the profession. This year, the American Historical Association chose as the theme for its annual conference some putative connection to
(20) storytelling: "Practices of Historical Narrative." Predictably, historians responded by adding the word "narrative" to their titles and presenting papers at sessions on "Oral History and the Narrative of Class Identity," and "Meaning and Time: The Problem of
(25) Historical Narrative." But it was still historiography. intended only for other academics. At meetings of historians, we still encounter very few historians telling stories or moving audiences to smiles, chills, or tears.

Passage B

Writing is at the heart of the lawyer's craft, and so,
(30) like it or not, we who teach the law inevitably teach aspiring lawyers how lawyers write. We do this in a few stand-alone courses and, to a greater extent, through the constraints that we impose on their writing throughout the curriculum. Legal writing, because of the purposes
(35) it serves, is necessarily ruled by linear logic, creating a path without diversions, surprises, or reversals. Conformity is a virtue, creativity suspect, humor forbidden, and voice mute.

Lawyers write as they see other lawyers write, and,
(40) influenced by education, profession, economic constraints, and perceived self-interest, they too often write badly. Perhaps the currently fashionable call for attention to narrative in legal education could have an effect on this. It is not yet exactly clear what role
(45) narrative should play in the law, but it is nonetheless true that every case has at its heart a story—of real events and people, of concerns, misfortunes, conflicts, feelings. But because legal analysis strips the human narrative content from the abstract, canonical legal
(50) form of the case, law students learn to act as if there is no such story.

It may well turn out that some of the terminology and public rhetoric of this potentially subversive movement toward attention to narrative will find its
(55) way into the law curriculum, but without producing corresponding changes in how legal writing is actually taught or in how our future colleagues will write. Still, even mere awareness of the value of narrative could perhaps serve as an important corrective.

29. Which one of the following does each of the passages display?

(A) a concern with the question of what teaching methods are most effective in developing writing skills

(B) a concern with how a particular discipline tends to represent points of view it does not typically deal with

(C) a conviction that writing in specialized professional disciplines cannot be creatively crafted

(D) a belief that the writing in a particular profession could benefit from more attention to storytelling

(E) a desire to see writing in a particular field purged of elements from other disciplines

30. The passages most strongly support which one of the following inferences regarding the authors' relationships to the professions they discuss?

(A) Neither author is an active member of the profession that he or she discusses.

(B) Each author is an active member of the profession he or she discusses.

(C) The author of passage A is a member of the profession discussed in that passage, but the author of passage B is not a member of either of the professions discussed in the passages.

(D) Both authors are active members of the profession discussed in passage B.

(E) The author of passage B, but not the author of passage A, is an active member of both of the professions discussed in the passages.

GO ON TO THE NEXT PAGE.

31. Which one of the following does each passage indicate is typical of writing in the respective professions discussed in the passages?

    (A) abstraction
    (B) hyperbole
    (C) subversion
    (D) narrative
    (E) imagination

32. In which one of the following ways are the passages NOT parallel?

    (A) Passage A presents and rejects arguments for an opposing position, whereas passage B does not.
    (B) Passage A makes evaluative claims, whereas passage B does not.
    (C) Passage A describes specific examples of a phenomenon it criticizes, whereas passage B does not.
    (D) Passage B offers criticism, whereas passage A does not.
    (E) Passage B outlines a theory, whereas passage A does not.

33. The phrase "scholarly monographs that sap the vitality of history" in passage A (lines 6–7) plays a role in that passage's overall argument that is most analogous to the role played in passage B by which one of the following phrases?

    (A) "Writing is at the heart of the lawyer's craft" (line 29)
    (B) "Conformity is a virtue, creativity suspect, humor forbidden, and voice mute" (lines 37–38)
    (C) "Lawyers write as they see other lawyers write" (line 39)
    (D) "every case has at its heart a story" (line 46)
    (E) "Still, even mere awareness of the value of narrative could perhaps serve as an important corrective" (lines 57–59)

34. Suppose that a lawyer is writing a legal document describing the facts that are at issue in a case. The author of passage B would be most likely to expect which one of the following to be true of the document?

    (A) It will be poorly written because the lawyer who is writing it was not given explicit advice by law professors on how lawyers should write.
    (B) It will be crafted to function like a piece of fiction in its description of the characters and motivations of the people involved in the case.
    (C) It will be a concise, well-crafted piece of writing that summarizes most, if not all, of the facts that are important in the case.
    (D) It will not genuinely convey the human dimension of the case, regardless of how accurate the document may be in its details.
    (E) It will neglect to make appropriate connections between the details of the case and relevant legal doctrines.

PrepTest52 Sec4 Qs7–12

While courts have long allowed custom-made medical illustrations depicting personal injury to be presented as evidence in legal cases, the issue of whether they have a legitimate place in the courtroom
(5) is surrounded by ongoing debate and misinformation. Some opponents of their general use argue that while illustrations are sometimes invaluable in presenting the physical details of a personal injury, in all cases except those involving the most unusual injuries, illustrations
(10) from medical textbooks can be adequate. Most injuries, such as fractures and whiplash, they say, are rather generic in nature—certain commonly encountered forces act on particular areas of the body in standard ways—so they can be represented by
(15) generic illustrations.

Another line of complaint stems from the belief that custom-made illustrations often misrepresent the facts in order to comply with the partisan interests of litigants. Even some lawyers appear to share a version
(20) of this view, believing that such illustrations can be used to bolster a weak case. Illustrators are sometimes approached by lawyers who, unable to find medical experts to support their clients' claims, think that they can replace expert testimony with such deceptive
(25) professional illustrations. But this is mistaken. Even if an unscrupulous illustrator could be found, such illustrations would be inadmissible as evidence in the courtroom unless a medical expert were present to testify to their accuracy.

(30) It has also been maintained that custom-made illustrations may subtly distort the issues through the use of emphasis, coloration, and other means, even if they are technically accurate. But professional medical illustrators strive for objective accuracy and avoid
(35) devices that have inflammatory potential, sometimes even eschewing the use of color. Unlike illustrations in medical textbooks, which are designed to include the extensive detail required by medical students, custom-made medical illustrations are designed to
(40) include only the information that is relevant for those deciding a case. The end user is typically a jury or a judge, for whose benefit the depiction is reduced to the details that are crucial to determining the legally relevant facts. The more complex details often found
(45) in textbooks can be deleted so as not to confuse the issue. For example, illustrations of such things as veins and arteries would only get in the way when an illustration is supposed to be used to explain the nature of a bone fracture.

(50) Custom-made medical illustrations, which are based on a plaintiff's X rays, computerized tomography scans, and medical records and reports, are especially valuable in that they provide visual representations of data whose verbal description would
(55) be very complex. Expert testimony by medical professionals often relies heavily on the use of technical terminology, which those who are not

specially trained in the field find difficult to translate mentally into visual imagery. Since, for most people,
(60) adequate understanding of physical data depends on thinking at least partly in visual terms, the clearly presented visual stimulation provided by custom-made illustrations can be quite instructive.

35. Which one of the following is most analogous to the role that, according to the author, custom-made medical illustrations play in personal injury cases?

(A) schematic drawings accompanying an engineer's oral presentation
(B) road maps used by people unfamiliar with an area so that they will not have to get verbal instructions from strangers
(C) children's drawings that psychologists use to detect wishes and anxieties not apparent in the children's behavior
(D) a reproduction of a famous painting in an art history textbook
(E) an artist's preliminary sketches for a painting

36. Based on the passage, which one of the following is the author most likely to believe about illustrations in medical textbooks?

(A) They tend to rely less on the use of color than do custom-made medical illustrations.
(B) They are inadmissible in a courtroom unless a medical expert is present to testify to their accuracy.
(C) They are in many cases drawn by the same individuals who draw custom-made medical illustrations for courtroom use.
(D) They are believed by most lawyers to be less prone than custom-made medical illustrations to misrepresent the nature of a personal injury.
(E) In many cases they are more apt to confuse jurors than are custom-made medical illustrations.

37. The passage states that a role of medical experts in relation to custom-made medical illustrations in the courtroom is to

(A) decide which custom-made medical illustrations should be admissible
(B) temper the impact of the illustrations on judges and jurors who are not medical professionals
(C) make medical illustrations understandable to judges and jurors
(D) provide opinions to attorneys as to which illustrations, if any, would be useful
(E) provide their opinions as to the accuracy of the illustrations

GO ON TO THE NEXT PAGE.

38. According to the passage, one of the ways that medical textbook illustrations differ from custom-made medical illustrations is that

   (A) custom-made medical illustrations accurately represent human anatomy, whereas medical textbook illustrations do not
   (B) medical textbook illustrations employ color freely, whereas custom-made medical illustrations must avoid color
   (C) medical textbook illustrations are objective, while custom-made medical illustrations are subjective
   (D) medical textbook illustrations are very detailed, whereas custom-made medical illustrations include only details that are relevant to the case
   (E) medical textbook illustrations are readily comprehended by nonmedical audiences, whereas custom-made medical illustrations are not

39. The author's attitude toward the testimony of medical experts in personal injury cases is most accurately described as

   (A) appreciation of the difficulty involved in explaining medical data to judges and jurors together with skepticism concerning the effectiveness of such testimony
   (B) admiration for the experts' technical knowledge coupled with disdain for the communications skills of medical professionals
   (C) acceptance of the accuracy of such testimony accompanied with awareness of the limitations of a presentation that is entirely verbal
   (D) respect for the medical profession tempered by apprehension concerning the tendency of medical professionals to try to overwhelm judges and jurors with technical details
   (E) respect for expert witnesses combined with intolerance of the use of technical terminology

40. The author's primary purpose in the third paragraph is to

   (A) argue for a greater use of custom-made medical illustrations in court cases involving personal injury
   (B) reply to a variant of the objection to custom-made medical illustrations raised in the second paragraph
   (C) argue against the position that illustrations from medical textbooks are well suited for use in the courtroom
   (D) discuss in greater detail why custom-made medical illustrations are controversial
   (E) describe the differences between custom-made medical illustrations and illustrations from medical textbooks

PrepTest62 Sec1 Qs9–14

Passage A

In music, a certain complexity of sounds can be
expected to have a positive effect on the listener. A
single, pure tone is not that interesting to explore; a
measure of intricacy is required to excite human
(5) curiosity. Sounds that are too complex or disorganized,
however, tend to be overwhelming. We prefer some
sort of coherence, a principle that connects the various
sounds and makes them comprehensible.

In this respect, music is like human language.
(10) Single sounds are in most cases not sufficient to
convey meaning in speech, whereas when put together
in a sequence they form words and sentences.
Likewise, if the tones in music are not perceived to be
tied together sequentially or rhythmically—for
(15) example, in what is commonly called melody—
listeners are less likely to feel any emotional
connection or to show appreciation.

Certain music can also have a relaxing effect. The
fact that such music tends to be continuous and
(20) rhythmical suggests a possible explanation for this
effect. In a natural environment, danger tends to be
accompanied by sudden, unexpected sounds. Thus, a
background of constant noise suggests peaceful
conditions; discontinuous sounds demand more
(25) attention. Even soft discontinuous sounds that we
consciously realize do not signal danger can be
disturbing—for example, the erratic dripping of a
leaky tap. A continuous sound, particularly one that is
judged to be safe, relaxes the brain.

Passage B

(30) There are certain elements within music, such
as a change of melodic line or rhythm, that create
expectations about the future development of the
music. The expectation the listener has about the
further course of musical events is a key determinant
(35) for the experience of "musical emotions." Music
creates expectations that, if not immediately satisfied,
create tension. Emotion is experienced in relation to
the buildup and release of tension. The more elaborate
the buildup of tension, the more intense the emotions
(40) that will be experienced. When resolution occurs,
relaxation follows.

The interruption of the expected musical course,
depending on one's personal involvement, causes the
search for an explanation. This results from a
(45) "mismatch" between one's musical expectation and the
actual course of the music. Negative emotions will be
the result of an extreme mismatch between
expectations and experience. Positive emotions result
if the converse happens.

(50) When we listen to music, we take into account
factors such as the complexity and novelty of the
music. The degree to which the music sounds familiar
determines whether the music is experienced as
pleasurable or uncomfortable. The pleasure
(55) experienced is minimal when the music is entirely new

to the listener, increases with increasing familiarity,
and decreases again when the music is totally known.
Musical preference is based on one's desire to
maintain a constant level of certain preferable
(60) emotions. As such, a trained listener will have a
greater preference for complex melodies than will a
naive listener, as the threshold for experiencing
emotion is higher.

41. Which one of the following concepts is linked to
positive musical experiences in both passages?

(A) continuous sound
(B) tension
(C) language
(D) improvisation
(E) complexity

42. The passages most strongly suggest that both are
targeting an audience that is interested in which one of
the following?

(A) the theoretical underpinnings of how music is
composed
(B) the nature of the conceptual difference between
music and discontinuous sound
(C) the impact music can have on human emotional
states
(D) the most effective techniques for teaching
novices to appreciate complex music
(E) the influence music has had on the development
of spoken language

43. Which one of the following describes a preference that
is most analogous to the preference mentioned in the
first paragraph of passage A?

(A) the preference of some people for falling asleep
to white noise, such as the sound of an electric fan
(B) the preference of many moviegoers for movies
with plots that are clear and easy to follow
(C) the preference of many diners for restaurants
that serve large portions
(D) the preference of many young listeners for fast
music over slower music
(E) the preference of most children for sweet foods
over bitter foods

GO ON TO THE NEXT PAGE.

44. Which one of the following most accurately expresses the main point of passage B?

   (A) The type of musical emotion experienced by a listener is determined by the level to which the listener's expectations are satisfied.
   (B) Trained listeners are more able to consciously manipulate their own emotional experiences of complex music than are naive listeners.
   (C) If the development of a piece of music is greatly at odds with the listener's musical expectations, then the listener will experience negative emotions.
   (D) Listeners can learn to appreciate changes in melodic line and other musical complexities.
   (E) Music that is experienced by listeners as relaxing usually produces a buildup and release of tension in those listeners.

45. Which one of the following most undermines the explanation provided in passage A for the relaxing effect that some music has on listeners?

   (A) The musical traditions of different cultures vary greatly in terms of the complexity of the rhythms they employ.
   (B) The rhythmic structure of a language is determined in part by the pattern of stressed syllables in the words and sentences of the language.
   (C) Many people find the steady and rhythmic sound of a rocking chair to be very unnerving.
   (D) The sudden interruption of the expected development of a melody tends to interfere with listeners' perception of the melody as coherent.
   (E) Some of the most admired contemporary composers write music that is notably simpler than is most of the music written in previous centuries.

46. Which one of the following would be most appropriate as a title for each of the passages?

   (A) "The Biological Underpinnings of Musical Emotions"
   (B) "The Psychology of Listener Response to Music"
   (C) "How Music Differs from Other Art Forms"
   (D) "Cultural Patterns in Listeners' Responses to Music"
   (E) "How Composers Convey Meaning Through Music"

47. It can be inferred that both authors would be likely to agree with which one of the following statements?

   (A) The more complex a piece of music, the more it is likely to be enjoyed by most listeners.
   (B) More knowledgeable listeners tend to prefer music that is discontinuous and unpredictable.
   (C) The capacity of music to elicit strong emotional responses from listeners is the central determinant of its artistic value.
   (D) Music that lacks a predictable course is unlikely to cause a listener to feel relaxed.
   (E) Music that changes from soft to loud is perceived as disturbing and unpleasant by most listeners.

PrepTest58 Sec2 Qs21–27

The explanations to these
questions begin on page 948.

Most people acknowledge that not all
governments have a moral right to govern and that
there are sometimes morally legitimate reasons for
disobeying the law, as when a particular law
(5) prescribes behavior that is clearly immoral. It is also
commonly supposed that such cases are special
exceptions and that, in general, the fact that
something is against the law counts as a moral, as
well as legal, ground for not doing it; i.e., we
(10) generally have a moral duty to obey a law simply
because it is the law. But the theory known as
philosophical anarchism denies this view, arguing
instead that people who live under the jurisdiction of
governments have no moral duty to those
(15) governments to obey their laws. Some commentators
have rejected this position because of what they take
to be its highly counterintuitive implications: (1) that
no existing government is morally better than any
other (since all are, in a sense, equally illegitimate),
(20) and (2) that, lacking any moral obligation to obey any
laws, people may do as they please without scruple.
In fact, however, philosophical anarchism does not
entail these claims.

First, the conclusion that no government is
(25) morally better than any other does not follow from
the claim that nobody owes moral obedience to any
government. Even if one denies that there is a moral
obligation to follow the laws of any government, one
can still evaluate the morality of the policies and
(30) actions of various governments. Some governments
do more good than harm, and others more harm than
good, to their subjects. Some violate the moral rights
of individuals more regularly, systematically, and
seriously than others. In short, it is perfectly
(35) consistent with philosophical anarchism to hold that
governments vary widely in their moral stature.

Second, philosophical anarchists maintain that all
individuals have basic, nonlegal moral duties to one
another—duties not to harm others in their lives,
(40) liberty, health, or goods. Even if governmental laws
have no moral force, individuals still have duties to
refrain from those actions that constitute crimes in the
majority of legal systems (such as murder, assault,
theft, and fraud). Moreover, philosophical anarchists
(45) hold that people have a positive moral obligation to
care for one another, a moral obligation that they
might even choose to discharge by supporting
cooperative efforts by governments to help those in
need. And where others are abiding by established
(50) laws, even those laws derived from mere conventions,
individuals are morally bound not to violate those
laws when doing so would endanger others. Thus, if
others obey the law and drive their vehicles on the
right, one must not endanger them by driving on the
(55) left, for, even though driving on the left is not
inherently immoral, it is morally wrong to
deliberately harm the innocent.

48. Which one of the following most accurately expresses
the main point of the passage?

(A) Some views that certain commentators consider
to be implications of philosophical anarchism
are highly counterintuitive.

(B) Contrary to what philosophical anarchists
claim, some governments are morally superior
to others, and citizens under legitimate
governments have moral obligations to one
another.

(C) It does not follow logically from philosophical
anarchism that no government is morally
better than any other or that people have no
moral duties toward one another.

(D) Even if, as certain philosophical anarchists
claim, governmental laws lack moral force,
people still have a moral obligation to refrain
from harming one another.

(E) Contrary to what some of its opponents have
claimed, philosophical anarchism does not
conflict with the ordinary view that one should
obey the law because it is the law.

49. The author identifies which one of the following as a
commonly held belief?

(A) In most cases we are morally obligated to obey
the law simply because it is the law.

(B) All governments are in essence morally equal.

(C) We are morally bound to obey only those laws
we participate in establishing.

(D) Most crimes are morally neutral, even though
they are illegal.

(E) The majority of existing laws are intended to
protect others from harm.

50. The author's stance regarding the theory of
philosophical anarchism can most accurately be
described as one of

(A) ardent approval of most aspects of the theory

(B) apparent acceptance of some of the basic
positions of the theory

(C) concerned pessimism about the theory's ability
to avoid certain extreme views

(D) hesitant rejection of some of the central features
of the theory

(E) resolute antipathy toward both the theory and
certain of its logical consequences

GO ON TO THE NEXT PAGE.

51. By attributing to commentators the view that
philosophical anarchism has implications that are
"counterintuitive" (line 17), the author most likely
means that the commentators believe that

(A) the implications conflict with some commonly
held beliefs
(B) there is little empirical evidence that the
implications are actually true
(C) common sense indicates that philosophical
anarchism does not have such implications
(D) the implications appear to be incompatible with
each other
(E) each of the implications contains an internal
logical inconsistency

52. Which one of the following scenarios most completely
conforms to the views attributed to philosophical
anarchists in lines 37–44?

(A) A member of a political party that is illegal in a
particular country divulges the names of other
members because he fears legal penalties.
(B) A corporate executive chooses to discontinue
her company's practice of dumping chemicals
illegally when she learns that the chemicals are
contaminating the water supply.
(C) A person who knows that a coworker has stolen
funds from their employer decides to do
nothing because the coworker is widely admired.
(D) A person neglects to pay her taxes, even though
it is likely that she will suffer severe legal
penalties as a consequence, because she wants
to use the money to finance a new business.
(E) A driver determines that it is safe to exceed the
posted speed limit, in spite of poor visibility,
because there are apparently no other vehicles
on the road.

53. It can be inferred that the author would be most likely
to agree that

(A) people are subject to more moral obligations
than is generally held to be the case
(B) governments that are morally superior recognize
that their citizens are not morally bound to
obey their laws
(C) one may have good reason to support the efforts
of one's government even if one has no moral
duty to obey its laws
(D) there are some sound arguments for claiming
that most governments have a moral right to
require obedience to their laws
(E) the theory of philosophical anarchism entails
certain fundamental principles regarding how
laws should be enacted and enforced

54. The author's discussion of people's positive moral duty
to care for one another (lines 44–49) functions primarily to

(A) demonstrate that governmental efforts to help
those in need are superfluous
(B) suggest that philosophical anarchists maintain
that laws that foster the common good are
extremely rare
(C) imply that the theoretical underpinnings of
philosophical anarchism are inconsistent with
certain widely held moral truths
(D) indicate that philosophical anarchists recognize
that people are subject to substantial moral
obligations
(E) illustrate that people are morally obligated to
refrain from those actions that arc crimes in
most legal systems

55. In the passage, the author seeks primarily to

(A) describe the development and theoretical
underpinnings of a particular theory
(B) establish that a particular theory conforms to the
dictates of common sense
(C) argue that two necessary implications of a
particular theory are morally acceptable
(D) defend a particular theory against its critics by
showing that their arguments are mistaken
(E) demonstrate that proponents of a particular
theory are aware of the theory's defects

PrepTest52 Sec4 Qs20–27

The explanations to these questions begin on page 953.

Passage A

Because dental caries (decay) is strongly linked to consumption of the sticky, carbohydrate-rich staples of agricultural diets, prehistoric human teeth can provide clues about when a population made the transition
(5) from a hunter-gatherer diet to an agricultural one. Caries formation is influenced by several factors, including tooth structure, bacteria in the mouth, and diet. In particular, caries formation is affected by carbohydrates' texture and composition, since
(10) carbohydrates more readily stick to teeth.

Many researchers have demonstrated the link between carbohydrate consumption and caries. In North America, Leigh studied caries in archaeologically derived teeth, noting that caries rates differed between
(15) indigenous populations that primarily consumed meat (a Sioux sample showed almost no caries) and those heavily dependent on cultivated maize (a Zuni sample had 75 percent carious teeth). Leigh's findings have been frequently confirmed by other researchers, who
(20) have shown that, in general, the greater a population's dependence on agriculture is, the higher its rate of caries formation will be.

Under some circumstances, however, nonagricultural populations may exhibit relatively
(25) high caries rates. For example, early nonagricultural populations in western North America who consumed large amounts of highly processed stone-ground flour made from gathered acorns show relatively high caries frequencies. And wild plants collected by the Hopi
(30) included several species with high cariogenic potential, notably pinyon nuts and wild tubers.

Passage B

Archaeologists recovered human skeletal remains interred over a 2,000-year period in prehistoric Ban Chiang, Thailand. The site's early inhabitants,
(35) appear to have had a hunter-gatherer-cultivator economy. Evidence indicates that, over time, the population became increasingly dependent on agriculture.

Research suggests that agricultural intensification
(40) results in declining human health, including dental health. Studies show that dental caries is uncommon in pre-agricultural populations. Increased caries frequency may result from increased consumption of starchy-sticky foodstuffs or from alterations in tooth wear. The
(45) wearing down of tooth crown surfaces reduces caries formation by removing fissures that can trap food particles. A reduction of fiber or grit in a diet may diminish tooth wear, thus increasing caries frequency. However, severe wear that exposes a tooth's pulp
(50) cavity may also result in caries.

The diet of Ban Chiang's inhabitants included some cultivated rice and yams from the beginning of the period represented by the recovered remains. These were part of a varied diet that also included
(55) wild plant and animal foods. Since both rice and yams

are carbohydrates, increased reliance on either or both should theoretically result in increased caries frequency.

Yet comparisons of caries frequency in the Early and Late Ban Chiang Groups indicate that overall
(60) caries frequency is slightly greater in the Early Group. Tooth wear patterns do not indicate tooth wear changes between Early and Late Groups that would explain this unexpected finding. It is more likely that, although dependence on agriculture increased, the diet
(65) in the Late period remained varied enough that no single food dominated. Furthermore, there may have been a shift from sweeter carbohydrates (yams) toward rice, a less cariogenic carbohydrate.

56. Both passages are primarily concerned with examining which one of the following topics?

(A) evidence of the development of agriculture in the archaeological record

(B) the impact of agriculture on the overall health of human populations

(C) the effects of carbohydrate-rich foods on caries formation in strictly agricultural societies

(D) the archaeological evidence regarding when the first agricultural society arose

(E) the extent to which pre-agricultural populations were able to obtain carbohydrate-rich foods

57. Which one of the following distinguishes the Ban Chiang populations discussed in passage B from the populations discussed in the last paragraph of passage A?

(A) While the Ban Chiang populations consumed several highly cariogenic foods, the populations discussed in the last paragraph of passage A did not.

(B) While the Ban Chiang populations ate cultivated foods, the populations discussed in the last paragraph of passage A did not.

(C) While the Ban Chiang populations consumed a diet consisting primarily of carbohydrates, the populations discussed in the last paragraph of passage A did not.

(D) While the Ban Chiang populations exhibited very high levels of tooth wear, the populations discussed in the last paragraph of passage A did not.

(E) While the Ban Chiang populations ate certain highly processed foods, the populations discussed in the last paragraph of passage A did not.

GO ON TO THE NEXT PAGE.

58. Passage B most strongly supports which one of the
following statements about fiber and grit in a diet?

  (A) They can either limit or promote caries formation,
depending on their prevalence in the diet.

  (B) They are typically consumed in greater quantities
as a population adopts agriculture.

  (C) They have a negative effect on overall health
since they have no nutritional value.

  (D) They contribute to the formation of fissures in
tooth surfaces.

  (E) They increase the stickiness of carbohydrate-
rich foods.

59. Which one of the following is mentioned in both
passages as evidence tending to support the prevailing
view regarding the relationship between dental caries
and carbohydrate consumption?

  (A) the effect of consuming highly processed foods
on caries formation

  (B) the relatively low incidence of caries among
nonagricultural people

  (C) the effect of fiber and grit in the diet on caries
formation

  (D) the effect of the consumption of wild foods on
tooth wear

  (E) the effect of agricultural intensification on
overall human health

60. It is most likely that both authors would agree with
which one of the following statements about dental caries?

  (A) The incidence of dental caries increases
predictably in populations over time.

  (B) Dental caries is often difficult to detect in teeth
recovered from archaeological sites.

  (C) Dental caries tends to be more prevalent in
populations with a hunter-gatherer diet than in
populations with an agricultural diet.

  (D) The frequency of dental caries in a population
does not necessarily correspond directly to
the population's degree of dependence on
agriculture.

  (E) The formation of dental caries tends to be more
strongly linked to tooth wear than to the
consumption of a particular kind of food.

61. Each passage suggests which one of the following about
carbohydrate-rich foods?

  (A) Varieties that are cultivated have a greater
tendency to cause caries than varieties that
grow wild.

  (B) Those that require substantial processing do not
play a role in hunter-gatherer diets.

  (C) Some of them naturally have a greater tendency
than others to cause caries.

  (D) Some of them reduce caries formation because
their relatively high fiber content increases
tooth wear.

  (E) The cariogenic potential of a given variety
increases if it is cultivated rather than gathered
in the wild.

62. The evidence from Ban Chiang discussed in passage B
relates to the generalization reported in the second
paragraph of passage A (lines 20–22) in which one of
the following ways?

  (A) The evidence confirms the generalization.

  (B) The evidence tends to support the generalization.

  (C) The evidence is irrelevant to the generalization.

  (D) The evidence does not conform to the
generalization.

  (E) The evidence disproves the generalization.

PrepTest62 Sec1 Qs15–21

The explanations to these
questions begin on page 957.

Mechanisms for recognizing kin are found throughout the plant and animal kingdoms, regardless of an organism's social or mental complexity. Improvements in the general understanding of these
(5) mechanisms have turned some biologists' attention to the question of why kin recognition occurs at all. One response to this question is offered by the inclusive fitness theory, which was developed in the 1960s. The theory is based on the realization that an organism
(10) transmits its genetic attributes to succeeding generations not solely through its offspring, but more generally through all of its close relatives. Whereas the traditional view of evolution held that natural selection favors the continued genetic representation
(15) of individuals within a species that produce the greatest number of offspring, the inclusive fitness theory posits that natural selection similarly favors organisms that help their relatives, because doing so also increases their own total genetic representation.
(20) The theory has helped to explain previously mysterious phenomena, including the evolution of social insect species like the honeybee, most of whose members do not produce offspring and exist only to nurture relatives.

(25) Inclusive fitness theory has also been applied usefully to new findings concerning cannibalism within animal species. Based on the theory, cannibals should have evolved to avoid eating their own kin because of the obvious genetic costs of such a
(30) practice. Spadefoot toad tadpoles provide an illustration. Biologists have found that all tadpoles of that species begin life as omnivores, feeding mainly on organic debris in their soon-to-be-dry pool in the desert, but that occasionally one tadpole eats another
(35) or eats a freshwater shrimp. This event can trigger changes in the tadpole's physiology and dietary preference, causing the tadpole to become larger and exclusively carnivorous, feasting on other animals including members of its own species. Yet the
(40) cannibals have a procedure of discrimination whereby they nip at other tadpoles, eating nonsiblings but releasing siblings unharmed. This suggests that the inclusive fitness theory offers at least a partial answer to why kin recognition develops. Interestingly, a
(45) cannibal tadpole is less likely to avoid eating kin when it becomes very hungry, apparently putting its own unique genetic makeup ahead of its siblings'.

But there may be other reasons why organisms recognize kin. For example, it has recently been
(50) found that tiger salamander larvae, also either omnivorous or cannibalistic, are plagued in nature by a deadly bacterium. Furthermore, it was determined that cannibal larvae are especially likely to be infected by eating diseased species members. The fact
(55) that this bacterium is more deadly when it comes from a close relative with a similar immune system suggests that natural selection may favor cannibals that avoid such pathogens by not eating kin. For tiger salamanders then, kin recognition can be explained
(60) simply as a means by which an organism preserves its own life, not as a means to aid in relatives' survival.

63. Which one of the following most accurately expresses the main point of the passage?

(A) Some findings support the hypothesis that kin recognition emerged through natural selection because it increased organisms' total genetic representation, but this hypothesis may not explain all instances of kin recognition.

(B) Current research supports the view that the mechanisms enabling the members of a species to recognize close relatives are as various as the purposes served by that ability.

(C) Recent research involving tiger salamanders undermines the hypothesis concerning the purpose of kin recognition that is espoused by traditional evolutionary theorists.

(D) New research involving tiger salamanders indicates that the traditional theory of natural selection is more strongly supported by the evidence than is thought by those who consider only the case of the spadefoot toad tadpole.

(E) While traditional evolutionary theory was unable to account for the phenomenon of kin recognition, this phenomenon is fully explained by the inclusive fitness theory.

64. The passage states which one of the following about some spadefoot toad tadpoles?

(A) They develop the ability to recognize fellow carnivores.
(B) They feed only upon omnivorous tadpoles.
(C) They change in body size when they become carnivores.
(D) Their carnivorousness constitutes an important piece of evidence that calls into question the inclusive fitness theory.
(E) Their carnivorousness would not occur unless it contributed in some way to the evolutionary success of the spadefoot toad species.

GO ON TO THE NEXT PAGE.

65. Based on the passage, the author would be most likely to agree with which one of the following statements about evolutionary explanations of kin recognition?

(A) It is impossible to understand the mechanisms underlying kin recognition until an evolutionary explanation of such recognition has been attained.

(B) Such explanations require no modifications to traditional evolutionary theory.

(C) For any such explanation to be fully adequate it should ignore the differences of social or mental complexity of the organisms whose abilities it is intended to explain.

(D) Kin recognition may have different evolutionary explanations in different species.

(E) No other evolutionary explanation can account for the wide diversity of unusual phenomena with the same success as the inclusive fitness theory.

66. Which one of the following most accurately describes the function of the last sentence of the second paragraph?

(A) to draw attention to behavior that further complicates the set of facts to be explained by any theory of natural selection that accounts for kin recognition

(B) to explain why cannibals in most species eat their kin less often than do cannibal spadefoot toad tadpoles

(C) to describe behavior that lends support to the account of kin recognition presented in the second paragraph

(D) to offer evidence that the behavior of cannibal spadefoot toad tadpoles is unexplainable

(E) to imply that the described behavior is more relevant to the issue at hand than is the immediately preceding material

67. The passage most strongly supports which one of the following statements about the mechanism by which cannibal spadefoot toad tadpoles recognize their kin?

(A) It is not dependent solely on the use of visual cues.

(B) It is neither utilized nor possessed by those tadpoles that do not become cannibalistic.

(C) It does not always allow a tadpole to distinguish its siblings from tadpoles that are not siblings.

(D) It is rendered unnecessary by physiological changes accompanying the dietary shift from omnivorousness to carnivorousness.

(E) It could not have developed in a species in which all members are omnivorous.

68. The passage states which one of the following about the mechanisms that enable organisms to recognize their close genetic relatives?

(A) The mechanisms are most easily explained if we assume that they have a similar purpose in all species regardless of the species' social or mental complexities.

(B) The mechanisms have become more clearly understood, prompting interest in the purpose they serve.

(C) The mechanisms have become the focus of theoretical attention only since the 1960s.

(D) The detailed workings of these mechanisms must be better understood before their purpose can be fully explained.

(E) The mechanisms operate differently in different species even when they serve exactly the same function.

69. The information in the passage most strongly suggests that the fact that most honeybees exist only to nurture relatives

(A) was not known to be true before the 1960s

(B) can be explained only if we assume that these members are in turn nurtured by the relatives they nurture

(C) is what led most biologists to reject the traditional view of evolution

(D) calls into question the view that evolution proceeds by natural selection

(E) is difficult to explain without at least supplementing the traditional view of evolution with further explanatory hypotheses

70. Which one of the following would, if true, most help to undermine the author's evaluation in the last sentence of the passage?

(A) Many tiger salamander larvae infected by the deadly bacterium are not cannibalistic.

(B) The factor that determines which tiger salamander larvae are carnivorous and which are omnivorous is not contained in the genetic makeup of the larvae.

(C) Kin recognition helps tiger salamanders avoid inbreeding that may be life-threatening to their offspring.

(D) Noncannibalistic tiger salamanders tend to produce fewer offspring than cannibalistic tiger salamanders.

(E) Cannibalistic tiger salamanders are immune to certain diseases to which noncannibalistic salamanders are not.

PrepTest56 Sec4 Qs8–15

Traditional theories of animal behavior assert that animal conflict within a species is highly ritualized and does not vary from contest to contest. This species-specific model assumes that repetitive use of
(5) the same visual and vocal displays and an absence of escalated fighting evolved to prevent injury. The contestant that exhibits the "best" display wins the contested resource. Galápagos tortoises, for instance, settle contests on the basis of height: the ritualized
(10) display consists of two tortoises facing one another and stretching their necks skyward; the tortoise perceived as being "taller" wins.

In populations of the spider *Agelenopsis aperta*, however, fighting behavior varies greatly from contest
(15) to contest. In addition, fighting is not limited to displays: biting and shoving are common. Susan Riechert argues that a recently developed model, evolutionary game theory, provides a closer fit to *A. aperta* territorial disputes than does the species-
(20) specific model, because it explains variations in conflict behavior that may result from varying conditions, such as differences in size, age, and experience of combatants. Evolutionary game theory was adapted from the classical game theory that was
(25) developed by von Neumann and Morganstern to explain human behavior in conflict situations. In both classical and evolutionary game theory, strategies are weighed in terms of maximizing the average payoff against contestants employing both the same and
(30) different strategies. For example, a spider may engage in escalated fighting during a dispute only if the disputed resource is valuable enough to warrant the risk of physical injury. There are, however, two major differences between the classical and evolutionary
(35) theories. First, whereas in classical game theory it is assumed that rational thought is used to determine which action to take, evolutionary game theory assumes that instinct and long-term species advantage ultimately determine the strategies that are exhibited.
(40) The other difference is in the payoffs: in classical game theory, the payoffs are determined by an individual's personal judgment of what constitutes winning; in evolutionary game theory, the payoffs are defined in terms of reproductive success.
(45) In studying populations of *A. aperta* in a grassland habitat and a riparian habitat, Riechert predicts that such factors as the size of the opponents, the potential rate of predation in a habitat, and the probability of winning a subsequent site if the dispute
(50) is lost will all affect the behavior of spiders in territorial disputes. In addition, she predicts that the markedly different levels of competition for web sites in the two habitats will affect the spiders' willingness to engage in escalated fighting. In the grassland,
(55) where 12 percent of the habitat is available for occupation by *A. aperta*, Riechert predicts that spiders will be more willing to engage in escalated fighting than in the riparian habitat, where 90 percent of the habitat is suitable for occupation.

71. Which one of the following best states the main idea of the passage?

(A) Evolutionary game theory and classical game theory can be used to analyze the process of decision-making used by humans and animals in settling disputes.

(B) *A. aperta* in grassland habitats and riparian habitats exhibit an unusually wide variety of fighting behaviors in territorial disputes.

(C) Evolutionary game theory may be useful in explaining the behavior of certain spiders during territorial disputes.

(D) The traditional theory of animal behavior in conflict situations cannot be used to explain the fighting behavior of most species.

(E) Evolutionary game theory, adapted from classical game theory, is currently used by scientists to predict the behavior of spiders in site selection.

72. The author of the passage mentions Galápagos tortoises in the first paragraph most likely in order to

(A) describe a kind of fighting behavior that is used by only a few species

(B) suggest that repetitive use of the same visual and vocal displays is a kind of fighting behavior used by some but not all species

(C) provide evidence to support the claim that fighting behavior does not vary greatly from contest to contest for most species

(D) provide an example of a fighting behavior that is unique to a particular species

(E) provide an example of a ritualized fighting behavior of the kind that traditional theorists assume is the norm for most species

GO ON TO THE NEXT PAGE.

73. Which one of the following, if true, is LEAST consistent with Riechert's theory about fighting behavior in spiders?

   (A) Spiders in the grassland habitat engage in escalated fighting when a disputed site is highly desirable.

   (B) Spiders in the riparian habitat are not willing to engage in escalated fighting for less-than-suitable sites.

   (C) Spiders in the riparian habitat confine their fighting to displays more regularly than do spiders in the grassland habitat.

   (D) Spiders in the riparian habitat are as willing to engage in escalated fighting as are spiders in the grassland habitat.

   (E) Spiders in the riparian habitat are more likely to withdraw when faced with a larger opponent in territorial disputes than are spiders in the grassland habitat.

74. Which one of the following best states the function of the third paragraph of the passage?

   (A) It develops a comparison of the two theories that were introduced in the preceding paragraph.

   (B) It continues a discussion of a controversial theory described in the first two paragraphs of the passage.

   (C) It describes an experiment that provides support for the theory described in the preceding paragraph.

   (D) It describes a rare phenomenon that cannot be accounted for by the theory described in the first paragraph.

   (E) It describes predictions that can be used to test the validity of a theory described in a preceding paragraph.

75. The passage suggests which one of the following about the behavior of *A. aperta* in conflict situations?

   (A) They exhibit variations in fighting behavior from contest to contest primarily because of the different levels of competition for suitable sites in different habitats.

   (B) They may confine their fighting behavior to displays if the value of a disputed resource is too low and the risk of physical injury is too great.

   (C) They exhibit variations in fighting behavior that are similar to those exhibited by members of most other species of animals.

   (D) They are more likely to engage in escalated fighting during disputes than to limit their fighting behavior to visual and vocal displays.

   (E) They are more willing to engage in escalated fighting during conflict situations than are members of most other species of animals.

76. The primary purpose of the passage is to

   (A) present an alternative to a traditional approach
   (B) describe a phenomenon and provide specific examples
   (C) evaluate evidence used to support an argument
   (D) present data that refutes a controversial theory
   (E) suggest that a new theory may be based on inadequate research

PrepTest52 Sec4 Qs13–14 and 16–19

These explanations refer to
questions that begin on page 896.

ANSWERS AND EXPLANATIONS

Ousmane Sembène's Films

Step 1: Read the Passage Strategically

Sample Roadmap

Many critics agree that the primary characteristic of Senegalese filmmaker Ousmane Sembène's work is its sociopolitical commitment. Sembène was trained in Moscow in the cinematic methods of socialist
(5) realism, and he asserts that his films are not meant to entertain his compatriots, but rather to raise their awareness of the past and present realities of their society. But his originality as a filmmaker lies most strikingly in his having successfully adapted film,
(10) originally a Western cultural medium, to the needs, pace, and structures of West African culture. In particular, Sembène has found within African oral culture techniques and strategies that enable him to express his views and to reach both literate and
(15) nonliterate Senegalese viewers.

Critics – focus on Semb is sociopol

Semb – raise awareness

Auth – originality is using film in W Afr culture

A number of Sembène's characters and motifs can be traced to those found in traditional West African storytelling. The tree, for instance, which in countless West African tales symbolizes knowledge, life, death,
(20) and rebirth, is a salient motif in *Emitaï*. The trickster, usually a dishonest individual who personifies antisocial traits, appears in *Borom Sarret*, *Mandabi*, and *Xala* as a thief, a corrupted civil servant, and a member of the elite, respectively. In fact, most of
(25) Sembène's characters, like those of many oral West African narratives, are types embodying collective ideas or attitudes. And in the oral tradition, these types face archetypal predicaments, as is for example, of the protagonist of *Borom Sarret*, who has
(30) no name and is recognizable instead by his trade—he is a street merchant—and by the difficulties he encounters but is unable to overcome.

Semb – draws from W Afr storytelling

Moreover, many of Sembène's films derive their structure from West African dilemma tales, the
(35) outcomes of which are debated and decided by their audiences. The open-endedness of most of his plots reveals that Sembène similarly leaves it to his viewers to complete his narratives: in such films as *Borom Sarret*, *Mandabi*, and *Ceddo*, for example, he
(40) provides his spectators with several alternatives as the films end. The openness of his narratives is also evidenced by his frequent use of freeze-frames, which carry the suggestion of continued action.

Semb – uses dilemma tales with open endings

Finally, like many West African oral tales,
(45) Sembène's narratives take the form of initiatory journeys that bring about a basic change in the worldview of the protagonist and ultimately, Sembène hopes, in that of the viewer. His films denounce social and political injustice. and his protagonists'

Semb – type of narrative

(50) social consciousness emerges from an acute self-consciousness brought about by the juxtaposition of opposites within the films' social context: good versus evil, powerlessness versus power, or poverty versus wealth. Such binary oppositions are used analogously
(55) in West African tales, and it seems likely that these dialectical elements are related to African oral storytelling more than, as many critics have supposed, to the Marxist components of his ideology.

Auth: W Afr infl > Marxist infl

PrepTest52 Sec4 Qs1–6

These explanations refer to questions that begin on page 896.

Part Four: Reading Comprehension
Reading Comprehension Practice | K

Discussion

Paragraph 1 starts off with something "many critics" agree about: the sociopolitical commitment by filmmaker Ousmane Sembène. But that's not all, according to the author. What really makes Sembène's films stand out ("strikingly," line 9) is how Sembène used West African oral culture techniques in order to convey his sociopolitical messages to Senegalese audiences. In fact, by the end of the last sentence, this first paragraph has given you everything you're looking for: the **Topic** is Sembène's films, and the **Scope** is their use of African oral culture techniques. The **Purpose** of the passage is to discuss Sembène's use of African techniques in his films, and the author's **Main Idea** is a paraphrase of the last sentence: what makes Sembène's films so notable is that they use West African oral culture techniques to express Sembène's sociopolitical messages.

From there, the rest of the passage goes into detail about the specific techniques Sembène uses in his films. You don't have to memorize the multiple examples, but you should be aware that the answer to a Detail question will likely come from here. Paragraph 2 discusses the use of symbolic characters with multiple examples: tree, trickster, street merchant. "Moreover," (line 33) paragraph 3 discusses another connection to West African storytelling: the open-ended plot structure, which comes from the West African tradition of letting the audiences decide stories' endings. "Finally," (lines 44) paragraph 4 continues the list of links between Sembène's films and West African oral tales by showing how Sembène uses traditional "journey" narratives to make his sociopolitical commentary and to bring about change in the viewer (lines 46–48). The author goes even further, arguing that the binary oppositions found in Sembène's films stem not from his Marxist ideology but rather from techniques of African oral storytelling (lines 55–58).

1. (E) Global ★★☆☆

Step 2: Identify the Question Type

The phrase "main point" indicates that this is a Global question.

Step 3: Research the Relevant Text

For a Global question, Step 3 is less about finding specific information in the passage and more about consulting the Topic, Scope, Purpose, and Main Idea you determined during Step 1.

Step 4: Make a Prediction

Reviewing what you learned from paragraph 1, the author's main point was that Sembène's films are notable for their use of West African oral storytelling techniques to convey sociopolitical messages.

Step 5: Evaluate the Answer Choices

(E) says exactly the same as the prediction did.

(A) is too narrow because it focuses too much on the details of paragraphs 2 and 3 without mentioning paragraph 4 and how these techniques are used to convey sociopolitical messages.

(B) is even narrower than choice **(A)**, only discussing information from paragraph 2.

(C) is a Distortion. Nowhere does the author suggest that these techniques were previously considered unsuitable for film.

(D), in addition to leaving out the entire discussion about traditional techniques, also attributes Sembène's sociopolitical beliefs to "most of the Senegalese people," which is an Extreme suggestion at best.

2. (E) Detail ★☆☆☆

Step 2: Identify the Question Type

Any question that directly asks about what "[t]he author says" is a Detail question.

Step 3: Research the Relevant Text

Here, the question stem doesn't give you a lot of help finding a specific place to research because every single paragraph contains info about what Sembène does in his films.

Step 4: Make a Prediction

However, your Roadmap definitely comes in handy. A quick glance tells you that paragraph 2 talks about symbolic characters, paragraph 3 talks about open-ended plots, and paragraph 4 talks about characters experiencing journeys.

Step 5: Evaluate the Answer Choices

(E) sounds like the "open-ended plots" of paragraph 3. Sure enough, lines 36–38 say that, by using such plots, Sembène "leaves it to his viewers to complete his narratives." That's a perfect match, so choice **(E)** is correct.

(A)'s mention of symbols would take you to paragraph 2. However, the symbols mentioned there are a tree, a trickster, and a street merchant. No animals.

(B) doesn't look familiar. Paragraph 3 discusses freeze-frames but not slow motion. Plus, the passage is concerned with Sembène's use of traditional West African techniques, not his artistic ones, so choice **(B)** is Outside the Scope.

(C) uses the term "oral," which pops up several times within the passage. However, Sembène uses traditional West African oral techniques, not oral narration—a film technique as Outside the Scope as the "slow motion" of answer choice **(B)**.

(D) is another answer that takes a term from the passage ("juxtaposition" in paragraph 4) and distorts it. The paragraph says this juxtaposition is more a feature of African oral storytelling than it is of Marxist ideology. Plus, choice **(D)** talks about Marxist symbols, which the author never discusses.

EXPLANATIONS

K | Part Four: Reading Comprehension
CHAPTER 15

These explanations refer to
questions that begin on page 897.

3. (A) Logic Reasoning (Strengthen)

Step 2: Identify the Question Type

This question asks you to strengthen a claim made by the author in the passage. This resembles a Strengthen question in the Logical Reasoning section.

Step 3: Research the Relevant Text

The question stem directs you to lines 54–58, in which the author claims that the binary oppositions used by Sembène are more closely related to African storytelling than Marxist ideology.

Step 4: Make a Prediction

As with any other Strengthen question, examine the evidence given to support a claim and determine any relevant assumptions. The author provides evidence that Sembène's binary oppositions are also used in West African tales. The author assumes that this correlation is probably causal and more likely a reason than is Marxism for Sembène's use of binaries. You need an answer that strengthens this assumption.

Step 5: Evaluate the Answer Choices

(A) does that nicely, claiming several African novelists who are known to draw upon oral traditions and use binary oppositions, yet have never read Marxist theory. That indicates binary oppositions are a common component of West African oral traditions, which increases the likelihood that Sembène is pulling from there.

(B) is irrelevant. That binary oppositions are—or are not—found elsewhere in the world doesn't affect the author's claim: that binary oppositions specifically found in West African oral traditions have influenced Sembène's films. If anything, choice **(B)** is a weakener because if binary oppositions are common to narratives across the world, then the possible influences on Sembène's work are multiplied.

(C) would actually weaken the author's claim since it suggests Marxist theory actually has more of a role in Sembène's films than the author claims.

(D), like choice **(B),** is irrelevant. Just because few European or North American filmmakers use binary oppositions does not make it more likely that Sembène was influenced by African oral storytelling.

(E) is tempting but not good enough. While the filmmakers mentioned in this answer may subscribe to Marxist principles, that doesn't necessarily mean their films represent these principles. Furthermore, though binary oppositions don't play an "essential" role in those films, they might play a secondary role. If so, that would undermine the author's suggestion that Marxist ideology isn't the influence behind the binary oppositions found in Sembène's films.

4. (D) Inference

Step 2: Identify the Question Type

In addition to the word "inferences" in the question stem, you also have the phrase "most strongly supported by the passage," which also indicates an Inference question.

Step 3: Research the Relevant Text

As in the second question from the set, the stem doesn't give you anything to help you research because the entire passage is about Sembène.

Step 4: Make a Prediction

Because your research isn't limited to a specific part of the passage, the answer is tough to predict. You'll have to go into the answer choices prepared to select the one choice that *must* be true.

Step 5: Evaluate the Answer Choices

(D) must be true. Your Roadmap tells you that the author discusses characters in paragraph 2. Starting on line 20, the author mentions the example of "the trickster," who appears in various films as a thief, a civil servant, and a member of the elite. That's certainly a broad range of social strata. Choice **(D)** is therefore the correct answer.

(A) is Outside the Scope. You only know that Sembène is trying to reach African viewers with his message. Whether his films are popular (in Africa or elsewhere) isn't mentioned.

(B) mentions government support, which is definitely Outside the Scope. The passage discusses the techniques of Sembène's films, not their production.

(C) is a Distortion. The critics mentioned at the very beginning do not misunderstand Sembène's films. Their only mistake, according to the author, is not recognizing the primary importance of Sembène's use of West African oral tradition in his work. Additionally, the critics mentioned are not necessarily in Senegal, as this answer choice states.

(E) introduces government censorship, which is Outside the Scope. The author never discusses government responses to Sembène's films.

5. (C) Inference

Step 2: Identify the Question Type

The question stem asks you about the meaning of a specific word used by the author in context. This type of vocabulary question is classified as an Inference question, but you could also view it as a Logic Function question focused on *how* the author uses the word.

These explanations refer to questions that begin on page 897.

Part Four: Reading Comprehension
Reading Comprehension Practice

Step 3: Research the Relevant Text

The line reference takes you back to the beginning of paragraph 4. Since this question tests the meaning of vocabulary in context, read the entire sentence from lines 44 to 48.

Step 4: Make a Prediction

The "initiatory" journey is described as one that brings about a change in a person's worldview. You want an answer that suggests the idea of change.

Step 5: Evaluate the Answer Choices

(C) fits the bill perfectly.

(A) is tempting if you try to answer the question without going back to the passage. This is a good basic definition of the word *initiatory*, but it's not how the author uses it. This is the most common wrong answer trap for these kinds of questions. Always go back to the passage for context.

(B) is off because there's nothing experimental about the journey—it actually happens.

(D) may also be tempting because of a possible connection between "initial" and "unprecedented." But again, this is not correct in context.

(E) has the prefix "pre," which suggests the beginning or "initial" position, but given the definition of prefatory ("located at the beginning") and the context of "initiatory" in the passage, the two terms don't match up.

6. (A) Detail EXCEPT ★★★★

Step 2: Identify the Question Type

Because this question stem asks you to identify the answer choice NOT supported or mentioned by the passage, this is a Detail EXCEPT question. You'll have to do some careful research to eliminate the wrong answers.

Step 3: Research the Relevant Text

In a Detail EXCEPT question, your research will be guided by the answer choices themselves.

Step 4: Make a Prediction

You won't be able to predict the answer because there's a whole universe of things the passage *doesn't* mention. Instead, be prepared to find lines in the passage to justify any answer choice you want to eliminate.

Step 5: Evaluate the Answer Choices

(A) turns out to be correct. You know Sembène has a message to convey, but the passage never talks about his feelings toward other reformation attempts.

(B) appears in lines 12–15. Sembène uses the traditional techniques and strategies of West African oral culture to express his thoughts and reach contemporary viewers. In paragraph 2, the author further elaborates on those motifs.

(C) is mentioned in lines 48–49, which clearly states Sembène's films denounce social injustice.

(D) is discussed in lines 27–32. The beleaguered street merchant of *Borom Sarret* illustrates Sembène's interest in ordinary people's problems.

(E) can be found in lines 5–7, which claim Sembène is not trying to entertain his audience but rather to raise awareness.

K

Part Four: Reading Comprehension
CHAPTER 15

These explanations refer to
questions that begin on page 898.

EXPLANATIONS

Earthquake-Dating Techniques

Step 1: Read the Passage Strategically

Sample Roadmap

To study centuries-old earthquakes and the geologic
faults that caused them, seismologists usually dig
trenches along visible fault lines, looking for sediments
(5) that show evidence of having shifted. Using radiocarbon
dating, they measure the quantity of the radioactive   *Seismologists*
isotope carbon 14 present in wood or other organic   *use RC dating to*
material trapped in the sediments when they shifted.   *study ancient*
Since carbon 14 occurs naturally in organic materials   *earthquakes*
(10) and decays at a constant rate, <the age of organic
materials can be reconstructed from the amount of the
isotope remaining in them.> These data can show
the location and frequency of past earthquakes and
provide hints about the likelihood and location of
(15) future earthquakes.

Geologists William Bull and Mark Brandon have
recently developed a new method, called lichenometry,
for detecting and dating past earthquakes. Bull and   *Bell / Brandon*
Brandon developed the method based on the fact that   *invent*
(20) large earthquakes generate numerous simultaneous   *lichenometry*
rockfalls in mountain ranges that are sensitive to
seismic shaking. Instead of dating fault-line sediments,
lichenometry involves measuring the size of lichens
growing on the rocks exposed by these rockfalls.
(25) Lichens—symbiotic organisms consisting of a fungus   *Def.*
and an alga—quickly colonize newly exposed rock
surfaces in the wake of rockfalls, and once established
they grow radially, flat against the rocks, at a slow but
constant rate for as long as 1,000 years if left undisturbed.
(30) One species of North American lichen, for example,
spreads outward by about 9.5 millimeters each century.
Hence, the diameter of the largest lichen on a boulder
provides direct evidence of when the boulder was   *How*
dislodged and repositioned. If many rockfalls over a   *it works*
(35) large geographic area occurred simultaneously, that
pattern would imply that there had been a strong
earthquake. <The location of the earthquake's epicenter
can then be determined by mapping these rockfalls,>
since they decrease in abundance as the distance from
(40) the epicenter increases.

Lichenometry has distinct advantages over
radiocarbon dating. Radiocarbon dating is accurate   *Lichenometry*
only to within plus or minus 40 years, because the   *advantages*
amount of the carbon 14 isotope varies naturally in the
(45) environment depending on the intensity of the radiation
striking Earth's upper atmosphere. Additionally, this
intensity has fluctuated greatly during the past 300   *More acc.*
years, causing many radiocarbon datings of events   *dates*

during this period to be of little value. Lichenometry,
(50) Bull and Brandon claim, can accurately date an
earthquake to within ten years. They note, however,
that using lichenometry requires careful site selection
and accurate calibration of lichen growth rates, adding
that the method is best used for earthquakes that   *but sites have*
(55) occurred within the last 500 years. Sites must be   *to be just*
selected to minimize the influence of snow avalanches   *right*
and other disturbances that would affect normal lichen
growth, and conditions like shade and wind that
promote faster lichen growth must be factored in.

PrepTest62 Sec1 Qs1–8

These explanations refer to questions that begin on page 898.

Part Four: Reading Comprehension
Reading Comprehension Practice

Discussion

The general **Topic**—the study of earthquakes that occurred long ago—presents itself immediately, and the author wastes no time in telling us what seismologists "usually" do when researching past quakes. A detailed description of the traditional method of radiocarbon dating is presented, fleshing out paragraph 1. Even though it isn't fully clear by the end of the first paragraph, you can expect the **Scope** of the passage to involve alternative earthquake-dating methods.

Why? A discussion of how something is *usually* done is often followed by how it can be done differently. Furthermore, having so much specific information about a scientific method right in the first paragraph signals a classic LSAT RC pattern. It is common for a passage to describe one theory or method, present an alternative, and close with the author's assessment. The savvy reader will recognize this typical structure quickly. Even if the details about the scientific methods are conceptually difficult, focusing on the passage structure helps ensure a strategic initial read-through.

Sure enough, paragraph 2 introduces lichenometry, an alternative method of dating earthquakes, recently developed by geologists Bull and Brandon. The Keyword "[i]nstead" contrasts this new method to the old carbon dating technique: the old method requires analyzing fault-line sediments, but this new method measures lichens growing on rocks that became exposed during an earthquake. The remainder of the paragraph explains in detail what lichens are and how their constant growth rate provides useful evidence of when rockfalls caused by seismic activity have occurred.

All of this information has been presented in a neutral manner, so the author's opinion and Purpose have yet to be revealed. Predictably, this changes at the outset of paragraph 3: the author states that the new method, lichenometry, has "distinct advantages" over the old method of radiocarbon dating. Why? Because the old method is less precise, "accurate only to within plus or minus 40 years," due to the amounts by which the carbon 14 isotope naturally varies, especially over the past 300 years. In contrast, lichenometry can accurately date an earthquake within ten years, but there are caveats. Note the author's caution, stating this accuracy rate as Bull and Brandon's "claim" and outlining the specific requirements of sites amenable to lichenometry. Even though the author opened the paragraph with a strong endorsement of the new method, there is no hint of anything extreme or any suggestion that the old method does not still have its uses. Indeed, the passage closes with information about lichenometry's limitations. It's now clear that the **Purpose** of the passage was to introduce and evaluate the new method, with the **Main Idea** being that lichenometry is an alternative method for dating earthquakes that is advantageous under certain circumstances.

7. (A) Global ★☆☆☆

Step 2: Identify the Question Type

A Global question couldn't be any more straightforward to identify than this. A strategic reading of the passage should conclude with a summation of the Main Idea.

Step 3: Research the Relevant Text

The entire passage must be taken into account.

Step 4: Make a Prediction

The correct answer will express that the new dating method of lichenometry is useful and has certain advantages over the old method of radiocarbon dating, but it won't be Extreme.

Step 5: Evaluate the Answer Choices

(A) is accurate in content and tone.

(B) is a Distortion. Although the passage discusses lichenometry's limitations, the author was careful to note that accuracy rates were "claimed"—not "proven"—by Bull and Brandon.

(C) is wrong in many ways. It is Extreme, as lichenometry is never named the "most reliable" method in the passage. Whether this method is being embraced by "most" seismologists studying past earthquakes is never mentioned, making the answer choice Out of Scope. And the only mention of which method is usually used is made in the first paragraph, where radiocarbon dating, not lichenometry, wins.

(D) is a Distortion. With its specific site requirements, lichenometry is not "easily" applied. Also, whether or not the new method has revolutionized the study of earthquakes is never stated nor implied, and it certainly is not the focus of the passage.

(E) is a classic Extreme trap. Although the passage discusses some limitations of radiocarbon dating, it never calls the method "unreliable," nor does the passage call for it to be abandoned.

8. (C) Detail ★★★☆

Step 2: Identify the Question Type

The phrase "[t]he passage provides information" indicates a Detail question.

Step 3: Research the Relevant Text

The question does not offer any content clues, line references, or other hints. Each answer choice must be assessed, one by one, for justification based on the passage contents. This is potentially a time-consuming task, so although it's often wise to tackle Detail questions early in the set, this may be one to save for later.

Step 4: Make a Prediction

With nothing to go on, it really isn't possible to make a prediction without evaluating each answer choice.

EXPLANATIONS

K | Part Four: Reading Comprehension
CHAPTER 15

These explanations refer to
questions that begin on page 899.

Step 5: Evaluate the Answer Choices

(C) is correct. These answer choices are presented *Jeopardy!* style: as questions. But the Kaplan mantra "1 Right/4 Wrong" still applies: only one question is answered by the passage contents. **(C)** finds its support at the very end of the passage. Lines 57–58 state that shade and wind "promote faster lichen growth." This clearly tells us some of the conditions that encourage lichens to grow at a more rapid rate than usual.

(A) poses a question tangential to the lichen growth rates discussed in paragraph 2 and the need for their accurate calibration mentioned in paragraph 3, but the passage never explains how scientists measure these rates. The choice is Out of Scope.

(B) is likewise Out of Scope, glancing off the issue of variable intensities of radiation striking the upper atmosphere, indeed mentioned in lines 44–45. However, the passage never delves into how scientists determine the intensity.

(D) is a Distortion. Although the passage mentions near the end that lichenometry is *best* used to measure earthquakes less than 500 years old, this choice does not pose a question that the passage answers. This passage does not mention the date of any particular earthquake empirically identified through the use of lichenometry.

(E) offers a question that is completely Out of Scope, asking about other uses for radiocarbon dating.

9. (E) Logic Function ★★☆☆

Step 2: Identify the Question Type

"[T]he author's primary purpose" might initially suggest another Global question, but this stem doesn't ask about the entire passage. Instead, it's focused on why the author used one particular piece of information, which makes it a Logic Function question.

Step 3: Research the Relevant Text

This stem provides the starting point: lines 29–30. However, remember that context is key. The surrounding lines will help clarify the purpose.

Step 4: Make a Prediction

The information at lines 29–30 serves as an example supporting the previous assertion that lichens grow at a slow and steady rate over long periods of time. The example of just 9.5 millimeters of growth per 100 years most definitely conveys remarkably slow growth over many years' time.

Step 5: Evaluate the Answer Choices

(E) is correct. This is the only choice that addresses the relationship between time and lichen growth.

(A) is a Faulty Use of Detail, attaching the example cited in the question stem to an earlier comment. But the growth

rate of a species doesn't say anything about how quickly it establishes itself on newly exposed rock surfaces in the first place.

(B) may seem right: it's hard to imagine anything slower than 9.5 mm per century. But this, too, is a Faulty Use of Detail trap. How that specific variety of lichen's growth rate compares to those of other species is never mentioned, and it's not safe to assume that there aren't even slower varieties.

(C) is a Faulty Use of Detail wrong answer. The discussion about how environmental conditions can alter lichens' growth rates happens at the end of the passage, well after the phrase in question.

(D), likewise, refers to a later portion of the passage, irrelevant to the part cited in the question stem.

10. (B) Inference ★★★★

Step 2: Identify the Question Type

The "strongly supported" language is that of a classic Inference question.

Step 3: Research the Relevant Text

The open-ended wording of the question stem offers nothing to work with. A strategic test taker will often save such a labor-intensive question for last.

Step 4: Make a Prediction

Every answer choice must be reviewed. Although a specific prediction is impossible to form, remember that the correct answer *must be true* based on the contents of the passage. If the answer is a maybe, it's wrong.

Step 5: Evaluate the Answer Choices

(B) must be true as it draws on information in the very first sentence of the passage: seismologists dig along visible fault lines to find evidence of past shifts and use radiocarbon dating to estimate when those shifts occurred. If no fault lines are evident, then it must be true that this process would be hampered.

(A) relies on a Faulty Use of Detail to lure test takers. Predicting the likelihood and location of future earthquakes is mentioned as a usage of radiocarbon dating at the end of paragraph 1, but the predictive value of lichenometry is not discussed.

(C) is Outside the Scope. The scope of the passage is limited to discussion of just these two methods of dating earthquakes, not all possible methods, so answer choice **(C)** has no basis in the passage and cannot be taken as true.

(D) is a Distortion of the figures mentioned in paragraph 3.

(E) is Extreme, though it might have held some appeal, based on the information at the end of the passage. But note the contrast between the author's qualified statement

These explanations refer to questions that begin on page 899.

Part Four: Reading Comprehension
Reading Comprehension Practice

K

("minimize the influence") and the unconditional tone of the answer choice ("[t]he usefulness *is* limited"). The answer goes too far in delimiting the usefulness of lichenometry and therefore must be rejected.

11. (B) Logic Function   ★☆☆☆

Step 2: Identify the Question Type

This is another question seeking the author's primary purpose in placing a specific portion of the passage—here, the first paragraph, in context of the entire passage. That gives this Logic Function question something of a Global slant.

Step 3: Research the Relevant Text

A good Roadmap will note that the first paragraph introduced the first of two methods discussed by the passage: radiocarbon dating, the usual method employed by researchers to determine when past earthquakes occurred.

Step 4: Make a Prediction

The first paragraph introduces a conventional method, against which a recently developed technique will be compared. The correct answer will state this.

Step 5: Evaluate the Answer Choices

(B) accurately matches the prediction.

(A) is a Distortion. Radiocarbon dating is not examined on a step-by-step basis in the rest of the passage.

(C) is a Distortion. The passage never calls radiocarbon dating outdated.

(D) is Outside the Scope. It fails because lichenometry is not a traditional procedure and it is the only one other than radiocarbon dating that is discussed in the passage. "[O]ther traditional procedures" are never mentioned in the passage.

(E) is another Distortion. Don't be tempted by the known limitations of radiocarbon dating accuracy mentioned at the beginning of paragraph 3. Stick to the prediction.

12. (E) Logic Reasoning (Assumption)   ★★☆☆

Step 2: Identify the Question Type

A relatively rare Assumption RC question is signaled by the final words of the question stem.

Step 3: Research the Relevant Text

The stem points to lines 50–58, the discussion of lichenometry's inherent limitations.

Step 4: Make a Prediction

As with any LR Assumption question, the task here is to identify the conclusion and evidence and then determine the gap between them. The conclusion is complex: "[s]ites must be selected to minimize the influence of snow avalanches and other disturbances that would affect normal lichen growth,

and conditions like shade and wind that promote faster lichen growth must be factored in." Why? Because "using lichenometry requires ... accurate calibration of lichen growth rates." Can such conditions be accurately factored in? Bull and Brandon seem to assume so.

Step 5: Evaluate the Answer Choices

(E) nicely articulates Bull and Brandon's assumption and can be double-checked with Kaplan's Denial Test. After all, if the extent to which conditions like shade and wind affected the growth of lichen could *not* be determined, then Bull and Brandon's assertion that these conditions *must be* factored in would create an impossibility.

(A) is Outside the Scope and has no such effect. In fact, its subject matter—the accuracy of lichenometry relative to other methods used to date earthquakes more than 500 years old—is also irrelevant to Bull and Brandon's statements about site selection.

(B) is also Outside the Scope, as the mention of radiation intensity hitting Earth's upper atmosphere in paragraph 3 does not include any information about how it is measured, nor is it particularly salient to the information in lines 50–58.

(C) is Extreme and Out of Scope. There is no information in the passage about what types of rocks are or are not able to host lichens, and whether or not they are limited only to mountainous rock formations has no bearing on the considerations Bull and Brandon suggest for lichenometry site selection.

(D) can be dismissed by using the Denial Test. Whether or not its claim is true may *seem* pertinent to site selection, but it is not really a factor upon which Bull and Brandon's insistence that site selection be conducted rigorously relies. If rockfalls studied in lichenometry do tend to be subject to more frequent snowfalls and avalanches, then the care in site selection demanded by Bull and Brandon is warranted. If not, care is still required. While perhaps not totally irrelevant, the issue is not *central* to the geologists' point and thus not the assumption underlying their argument.

13. (D) Detail   ★☆☆☆

Step 2: Identify the Question Type

This Detail question is heralded by the words "[t]he passage indicates ..."

Step 3: Research the Relevant Text

Use the content clues to focus your research. The reliability of radiocarbon dating is discussed in paragraph 3.

K | Part Four: Reading Comprehension
CHAPTER 15

These explanations refer to
questions that begin on page 899.

Step 4: Make a Prediction

Lines 41–48 explain that the precision of radiocarbon dating is
hampered by naturally occurring inconsistencies in the amount
of carbon 14, depending on the varying intensity of radiation
striking Earth's upper atmosphere.

Step 5: Evaluate the Answer Choices

(D) paraphrases the prediction succinctly.

(A) and **(B)** mention factors not discussed in the passage and
are Out of Scope.

(C) might play on your memory of question 4, but it is Outside
the Scope. Invisible fault lines are not discussed within the
actual passage. Researching the relevant text in the passage,
and forming a strong prediction, make this answer choice
easily dismissible.

(E) brings up radiation striking the upper atmosphere, which
the passage does state is a factor in the carbon 14 variation.
However, there's no direct indication or even a suggestion that
the striking of the upper atmosphere hasn't always happened.

14. (D) Inference

Step 2: Identify the Question Type

Though the question is wordy, the phrases "[g]iven the
information in the passage" and "likely be most applicable"
are harbingers of an Inference question.

Step 3: Research the Relevant Text

The only clue in the question stem is that lichenometry might
be applicable to something other than earthquake dating.
Review paragraph 2 for the principles underlying lichenometry.

Step 4: Make a Prediction

Although a very specific prediction is neither easy to form nor
advisable, characterize the answer as something that must be
true based on what the passage states about lichenometry:
it requires measuring the size of lichens growing on rocks
exposed by a natural event in order to determine the date at
which that event occurred.

Step 5: Evaluate the Answer Choices

(D) is the only answer choice that offers a scenario that
provides conditions amenable to new lichen colonization and
subsequent growth.

(A) and **(C)** are both Out of Scope because lichenometry
involves analyzing lichens on *exposed* rock surfaces.

(B) fails the "must be true" standard. The potential for lichen
growth on a fossilized skeleton—while plausible—is not
guaranteed by anything in the passage.

(E) is eliminated because nothing in the passage provides
evidence that exposed rock could host steadily growing lichen
in a rainy valley.

These explanations refer to
questions that begin on page 900.

Part Four: Reading Comprehension
Reading Comprehension Practice

K

Literary Works of Amos Tutuola

Step 1: Read the Passage Strategically

Sample Roadmap

With his first published works in the 1950s, Amos
Tutuola became the first Nigerian writer to receive
wide international recognition. Written in a mix of
standard English, idiomatic Nigerian English, and
(5) literal translation of his native language, Yoruba,
Tutuola's works were quick to be praised by many
literary critics as fresh, inventive approaches to the
form of the novel. Others, however, dismissed his
works as simple retellings of local tales, full of
(10) unwelcome liberties taken with the details of the
well-known story lines. However, to estimate properly
Tutuola's rightful position in world literature, it is
essential to be clear about the genre in which he
wrote; literary critics have assumed too facilely that
(15) he wrote novels.

No matter how flexible a definition of the novel
one uses, establishing a set of criteria that enable
Tutuola's works to be described as such applies to his
works a body of assumptions the works are not
(20) designed to satisfy. Tutuola is not a novelist but a
teller of folktales. Many of his critics are right to
suggest that Tutuola's subjects are not strikingly
original, but it is important to bear in mind that
whereas realism and originality are expected of the
(25) novel, the teller of folktales is expected to derive
subjects and frameworks from the corpus of
traditional lore. <The most useful approach to
Tutuola's works, then, is one that regards him as
working within the African oral tradition.>

(30) Within this tradition, a folktale is common
property, an expression of a people's culture and
social circumstances. The teller of folktales knows
that the basic story is already known to most listeners
and, equally, that the teller's reputation depends on
(35) the inventiveness with which the tale is modified and
embellished, for what the audience anticipates is not
an accurate retelling of the story but effective
improvisation and delivery. Thus, within the
frame work of the basic story, the teller is allowed
(40) considerable room to maneuver— in fact, the most
brilliant tellers of folktales transform them into
unique works.

Tutuola's adherence to this tradition is clear:
specific episodes, for example, are often repeated for
(45) emphasis, and he embellishes familiar tales with
personal interpretations or by transferring them to
modern settings. The blend of English with local
idiom and Yoruba grammatical constructs, in which
adjectives and verbs are often interchangeable,
(50) re-creates the folktales in singular ways. And, perhaps
most revealingly, in the majority of Tutuola's works,
the traditional accents and techniques of the teller of

folktales are clearly discernible, for example in the
adoption of an omniscient, summarizing voice at the
(55) end of his narratives, a device that is generally
recognized as being employed to conclude most
folktales.

PrepTest56 Sec4 Qs1–7

*Fans praise
inventive
approach to
novel
Critics dismissive;
rehashing & taking
liberties*

*Au–T's works
significant
–can't class.
as novel*

*Au–T
is not
a true
novelist*

*–T is
teller of
folktales*

*Characteristics
of folk tale
teller in African
oral trad.*

*How T uses the
characteristics*

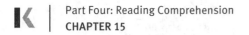

These explanations refer to
questions that begin on page 900.

EXPLANATIONS

Discussion

Paragraph 1 introduces you to the **Topic** of this passage, Amos Tutuola. Immediately, two contrasting opinions are provided about Tutuola's works: some critics praise his inventive approach to the novel, while others dismiss him for simply rehashing and taking liberties with well-known stories. The author's opinion appears with the contrast Keyword "[h]owever." The author doesn't obviously side with either group of literary critics, instead calling both groups out for assuming "too facilely" that Tutuola wrote novels. The author points out that true understanding of Tutuola's contribution to literature requires clearly defining the genre of Tutuola's works. The author thereby sets the stage for a discussion of the proper classification of Tutuola's works—and it probably won't be novels. This discussion of genre will serve as the **Scope** of the passage. In addition, the **Purpose** also seems pretty evident: illustrate how Tutuola's works can be better understood by classifying them under the proper genre. Notice how the author steers the discussion away from the conflict between groups of literary critics—whether Tutuola is a good writer or not is an idea the author introduces but is not the main focus. Additionally, the author remains quiet on his own view of the worth of Tutuola's works, focusing solely on the classification of them.

The first sentence of paragraph 2 finds the author claiming Tutuola's works won't satisfy the definition of "novel," no matter how loose the definition is. Therefore, Tutuola can't be a novelist. Instead, the author offers an alternative classification in a sentence that clearly lays out the **Main Idea** of the passage: "Tutuola is not a novelist but a teller of folktales." While agreeing with some of Tutuola's critics who say Tutuola isn't original, the author makes their criticism irrelevant by arguing they are using the wrong set of standards. Tutuola's not supposed to be original (like a novelist would be). Instead, Tutuola should be regarded as working in the African oral tradition of storytelling.

Paragraph 3 defines the characteristics of a folktale teller in this tradition. The stories are already known and shared by the community. The teller is praised not for the story itself but for the delivery and embellishments made to the tale for the sake of good storytelling. In fact, improvisation and modifications to the stories are expected and even valued.

Paragraph 4 shows how Tutuola utilizes these characteristics in his own works, thus solidifying the author's Main Point. The author provides multiple examples of Tutuola's adherence to the oral storytelling tradition (e.g., resetting stories in modern times, blending linguistic styles, and incorporating traditional folktale-telling techniques) as further evidence that Tutuola's works should be evaluated not as novels but as the literary equivalent of oral folktales.

15. (B) Global

Step 2: Identify the Question Type

Any question that asks you to determine the "main point" of the passage is a Global question.

Step 3: Research the Relevant Text

In most cases, the "relevant text" for a Global question is your own estimation of the Topic, Scope, Purpose, and Main Idea that you made during Step 1. But in this case, the author's unequivocal point of view appears in lines 20–21: "Tutuola is not a novelist but a teller of folktales."

Step 4: Make a Prediction

The claim from lines 20–21 serves as an efficient, concise paraphrase of the main point. Tutuola shouldn't be held to the novelist's standard of originality.

Step 5: Evaluate the Answer Choices

(B) accurately echoes this sentiment.

(A) is a Faulty Use of Detail. It contains nothing inaccurate. However, it merely regurgitates some minor facts from the first paragraph without touching on the overall theme of classifying Tutuola's works.

(C) sounds tempting but makes the mistake of suggesting Tutuola writes novels. That goes against everything the author says in the first sentence of paragraph 2.

(D) distorts the debate mentioned in the opening paragraph. The author does introduce two groups of critics, but their division is over the worth of Tutuola's works, not the classification of them. As the author implies, both groups of critics regard Tutuola's works as novels. Only the author suggests that Tutuola's works should be seen as folktales.

(E) makes folktales the center of attention, but that's not the focus of this passage. Amos Tutuola is not used in this passage as merely an example of the folktale genre, as this answer suggests. Instead, the folktale is introduced as the most applicable classification of Tutuola's works.

16. (D) Inference

Step 2: Identify the Question Type

This question asks you to apply Tutuola to a hypothetical modern-day Irish author. It resembles an Inference question because it looks for something that must be true about Tutuola applied to something not directly in the text. This could also potentially be construed as a Logical Reasoning (Parallel) question.

Step 3: Research the Relevant Text

You're looking to match Tutuola's writing approach to that of another author. Tutuola's approach was outlined by a few examples in the fourth paragraph: he embellishes familiar

These explanations refer to questions that begin on page 901.

Part Four: Reading Comprehension
Reading Comprehension Practice

K

tales with personal interpretations or by transferring them to modern settings.

Step 4: Make a Prediction

The best strategy here is to compare the answers to the examples in the fourth paragraph of the passage to find the match.

Step 5: Evaluate the Answer Choices

(D) sounds exactly like the passage. In lines 46–47, Tutuola is described as transferring traditional tales to modern settings. That sounds exactly like a modern Irish author transplanting traditional Irish tales into contemporary settings. This is consistent and thus the correct answer.

(A) is a 180. Tutuola applied folktale conventions to his modern works, not the other way around. Tutuola was criticized specifically for *not* following the conventions of the modern novel.

(B) also is a 180. Tutuola took an oral form of storytelling and turned it into a literary style. This answer choice has the Irish author taking a literary style and turning it into an oral form.

(C) is a Distortion of the passage. Tutuola may have blended languages and linguistic constructs, but nothing in the passage suggests that he combined *characters* from different cultures in his storytelling.

(E) is Half-Right, Half-Wrong. It mentions the omniscient narrator that, according to lines 53–55, Tutuola used. However, that narrative voice is described as one that summarizes the story at the end. More importantly, though, this answer discusses original stories. Tutuola didn't tell original stories; he told well-known stories in an inventive manner.

17. (A) Inference (Author's Attitude) ★☆☆☆

Step 2: Identify the Question Type

The question stem asks you to characterize the author's attitude toward something discussed in the passage. Thus, it belongs to a specific subset of Inference question.

Step 3: Research the Relevant Text

The author first mentions Tutuola's position in world literature in lines 10–15. The author wants to make sure Tutuola's genre is correctly classified, but you have to continue reading through paragraph 2 to find that classification. In lines 20–21, the author asserts Tutuola is a teller of folktales, not a novelist. The author goes on to say in lines 27–29 that classifying Tutuola's works as folktales in the African oral tradition is the "most useful approach."

Step 4: Make a Prediction

From this text, you can conclude the author feels Tutuola's place in world literature is defined by his being a teller of folktales.

Step 5: Evaluate the Answer Choices

(A) describes that feeling perfectly.

(B) is Outside the Scope. The author never discusses any renewed interest in the study of oral traditions.

(C) is a 180. The "[h]owever" in line 11, the "too facilely" in line 14, and the "but" in line 23 indicate the author is actually rather displeased by the literary critics' assumptions and oversights.

(D) suggests that some people feel translations are ruining the integrity of Tutuola's works. There's no suggestion in the passage that translations pose any problems (or that they even exist). Therefore, the author never expresses any attitude about this.

(E) is Outside the Scope. This passage is entirely devoted to Tutuola's works and does not discuss or suggest any future trends. You could have stopped reading at "optimistic." The author isn't "optimistic" about anything; he simply wants Tutuola's works to be properly characterized.

18. (D) Detail ★☆☆☆

Step 2: Identify the Question Type

The phrase "[a]ccording to the passage" is a sure sign of a Detail question.

Step 3: Research the Relevant Text

The question stem directs you to find the criticism of Tutuola's works. This criticism is described in lines 8–11.

Step 4: Make a Prediction

Basically, the criticism is that Tutuola retells well-known stories and takes unwelcome liberties with the details.

Step 5: Evaluate the Answer Choices

(D) says exactly that.

(A) is a 180. The author is the one who claims Tutuola's works are based on African oral tradition, not the critics. According to lines 8–9, the critics dislike that Tutuola's stories are "simple retellings of local tales." They wouldn't want even *more* adherence to the oral folk-telling tradition.

(B) is also a 180. The passage says Tutuola mixes languages, but this is not cited as a source of complaint. In fact, the author mentions it in the same sentence that he introduces the critics who *praise* Tutuola's works.

(C) is Outside the Scope. The author suggests critics incorrectly classify Tutuola's works as novels, not as folktales, but the critics themselves don't weigh in on the fusion of styles. They don't seem to be aware such a fusion is happening.

(E) is yet another 180. Again, the author suggests that critics *do* actually see Tutuola's works as novels. Furthermore, there's nothing in the passage to imply that Tutuola himself characterizes his stories as novels. If anything, the first half

K | Part Four: Reading Comprehension
CHAPTER 15

These explanations refer to
questions that begin on page 901.

of this answer choice is more along the lines of the author's
point of view.

19. (E) Detail EXCEPT ★★☆☆

Step 2: Identify the Question Type

The question stem asks what the author attributes (or, rather,
doesn't attribute) to Tutuola. That makes this a Detail EXCEPT
question. You need to find the one answer not mentioned in
the passage.

Step 3: Research the Relevant Text

Because the author discusses Tutuola throughout the passage,
one might expect this question to take a little more time than
others. You may need to use your global understanding of
the passage, coupled with some careful fact-checking of the
answer choices, to get through this one. If you want to knock
out wrong answers, however, a good place to start looking for
attributes of Tutuola's works is in the fourth paragraph.

Step 4: Make a Prediction

There's a whole universe of details not mentioned in the
passage, so predicting the outlier might be tough. However,
you do know from the passage's Main Idea what the author
wouldn't attribute to Tutuola, and that's anything having to do
with being a novelist.

Step 5: Evaluate the Answer Choices

(E) discusses turning folktales into novels. Given the author's
insistence that Tutuola didn't write novels, this seems like
something the author would never have claimed. As it turns
out, this is the exception and is therefore the correct answer.

(A), with the repetition of ideas for emphasis, is found in
lines 43–45.

(B), with the relocation to modern settings, is found in
lines 46–47.

(C) which mentions international recognition, can be found in
the first sentence of the passage.

(D) with the omniscient narrator, can be found in lines 54–55.

20. (A) Logic Function ★★☆☆

Step 2: Identify the Question Type

Because this question asks you to find what the author was
attempting to do with a particular reference, it's a Logic
Function question.

Step 3: Research the Relevant Text

Logic Function questions always have relevant text that goes
beyond the lines referenced in the question stem. In this case,
because the text in question is evidence, it's important to look
back up to what the author is trying to prove. Here, start back
at line 21. That's when the author talks about the critics who
complain Tutuola's stories aren't original. After the "but" in

line 23, the author makes the claim that original stories are
characteristics of novels, whereas pulling from traditional lore
is expected of folktales.

Step 4: Make a Prediction

The "corpus of traditional lore" is the collection of non-original
material that characterizes folktales. This characterization is
what the author uses to differentiate folktales from novels,
which require originality and realism.

Step 5: Evaluate the Answer Choices

(A) matches your prediction nearly exactly.

(B) is Outside the Scope. While the author is discussing two
literary genres here, he's doing it to explain differences in
characterization, not to argue for their equal worth. The author
isn't concerned with the value of the two genres. If anything,
the author is more concerned with the value of Tutuola's works
as folktales, not as novels.

(C) is a 180. The author here is trying to sharply differentiate
between the two genres, not explain why they should be
mixed. Additionally, the critics aren't against blending genres.
In fact, according to the author, they don't even see Tutuola's
works as a combination of genres—they see the works only as
novels.

(D) is a Distortion. This section of text describes the
characteristics of two dissimilar genres but does so in order
to point out the difference, not to illuminate any direct
counterparts between the two. The author's point is that
novels and folktales are essentially mutually exclusive (novels
require originality while folktales draw on traditions).

(E) is also a Distortion. The author might agree that the
distinguishing characteristics of novels and folktales are
poorly understood, but he doesn't want critics to analyze two
genres. Instead, he wants them to analyze Tutuola's works
within the confines of just one of the two.

21. (C) Global ★☆☆☆

Step 2: Identify the Question Type

Any question asking for the "primary purpose" of an entire
passage is a Global question.

Step 3: Research the Relevant Text

The Purpose of the passage comes across pretty clearly in the
author's use of the words "essential" in line 13 and "most
useful approach" in line 27. Additionally, think back to the
Topic, Scope, Purpose, and Main Idea that you outlined in
Step 1.

Step 4: Make a Prediction

The author recommends reclassifying Tutuola's works in order
to better understand them. The examples of Tutuola's works
in the last paragraph help provide specific evidence to back

These explanations refer to
questions that begin on page 901.

Part Four: Reading Comprehension
Reading Comprehension Practice   K

up that recommendation. So, a good prediction of the author's
Purpose would be "to use examples of Tutuola's works to
show how those works should be alternatively classified as
folktales for more proper evaluation."

Step 5: Evaluate the Answer Choices

(C) says basically that.

(A) is a Distortion. This passage predominantly narrows
Tutuola's works to the realm of folktales and doesn't ascribe
any further range.

(B) is too broad. This answer mischaracterizes the passage's
focus, which isn't on the literary genre of folktales in general
but on how Tutuola's works in particular fit that genre.
Additionally, the passage doesn't present a challenge to
folktales' validity, nor does it defend the genre. The author
simply *defines* the genre.

(D) is also too broad. While the author does distinguish
between the two genres, he has a purpose beyond just that.
He differentiates the two in order to prove that Tutuola's works
belong in the folktale category. Answers **(B)** and **(D)** misapply
the focus of the passage as being on the genres of literature
when the passage is really concerned about the works
of Tutuola.

(E) is a Distortion. The author covers the critics' disagreement
in the first paragraph, but there are two problems. First,
the critics' disagreement isn't over Tutuola's place in world
literature (the author introduces that idea), and second, their
disagreement isn't anything more than a starting place for the
author's main purpose: to prove Tutuola's works belong in the
folktale category.

EXPLANATIONS

K

Part Four: Reading Comprehension
CHAPTER 15

These explanations refer to
questions that begin on page 902.

Archaeology of Textiles

Step 1: Read the Passage Strategically

Sample Roadmap

Traditional sources of evidence about ancient *Trad. arch.*
history are archaeological remains and surviving texts. *sources*
Those investigating the crafts practiced by women in *remains/text*
ancient times, however, often derive little information
(5) from these sources, and the archaeological record is
particularly unavailing for the study of ancient textile
production, as researchers are thwarted by the *not useful for*
perishable nature of cloth. What shreds persisted *textile research*
through millennia were, until recently, often discarded
by excavators as useless, as were loom weights, which *Why*
(10) appeared to be nothing more than blobs of clay.
Ancient texts, meanwhile, rarely mention the creation
of textiles; moreover, those references that do exist use
archaic, unrevealing terminology. Yet despite these
obstacles, researchers have learned a great deal about *Still—res.*
(15) ancient textiles and those who made them, and also *learned a lot*
about how to piece together a whole picture from many
disparate sources of evidence.

Technological advances in the analysis of
archaeological remains provide much more information *Tech. advances*
(20) than was previously available, especially about minute *helped*
remains. Successful modern methods include
radiocarbon dating, infrared photography for seeing
through dirt without removing it, isotope
"fingerprinting" for tracing sources of raw materials,
(25) and thin-layer chromatography for analyzing dyes. As
if in preparation for such advances, the field of
archaeology has also undergone an important *Arch. changed*
philosophical revolution in the past century. Once little *as a sci.*
more than a self-serving quest for artifacts to stock
(30) museums and private collections, the field has
transformed itself into a scientific pursuit of knowledge
about past cultures. As part of this process,
archaeologists adopted the fundamental precept of
preserving all objects, even those that have no *Keep everything*
(35) immediately discernible value. Thus in the 1970s two *Results*
researchers found the oldest known complete garment,
a 5,000-year-old linen shirt, among a tumbled heap of
dirty linens that had been preserved as part of the well-
known Petrie collection decades before anyone began
(40) to study the history of textiles.

The history of textiles and of the craftswomen who
produced them has also advanced on a different front:
recreating the actual production of cloth. *Also learn*
Reconstructing and implementing ancient production *about prod.*
(45) methods provides a valuable way of generating and
checking hypotheses. For example, these techniques
made it possible to confirm that the excavated pieces of
clay once considered useless in fact functioned as loom
weights. Similarly, scholars have until recently been
(50)

obliged to speculate as to which one of two statues of *Ex. Statue*
Athena, one large and one small, was adorned with a *of Athena*
dress created by a group of Athenian women for a
festival, as described in surviving texts. Because
(55) records show that it took nine months to produce the
dress, scholars assumed it must have adorned the large
statue. But by investigating the methods of production
and the size of the looms used, researchers have
ascertained that in fact a dress for the small statue would
(60) have taken nine months to produce.

PrepTest58 Sec2 Qs1–7

These explanations refer to
questions that begin on page 902.

Part Four: Reading Comprehension
Reading Comprehension Practice

K

Discussion

Paragraph 1 introduces the **Topic** of the passage, the archaeology of textiles. Initially, the author discusses the "traditional" archaeological sources—remains and texts—which provide limited information for researchers. The remains are quite troubling for ancient textile production researchers due to the perishable nature of cloth. Now, the author starts to set up a current problem: these sources are not particularly useful for textile research, though researchers have been able to learn a lot about ancient textile production. At this point, a good strategic reader will anticipate that the author is going to address this problem in more depth or elaborate on the potential solution indicated by the Contrast Keywords "[Y]et despite…"

Sure enough, the first sentence of Paragraph 2 confirms the author's **Scope**: recent advances in the analysis of remains have yielded a great deal more information than researchers had before. Next, the author lists several modern methods of analysis that have proven successful. The author asserts that the field of archaeology has philosophically become more focused on itself as a science, even going so far as to preserve all objects regardless of noticeable value. The author finishes off the paragraph with an example of how researchers were able to find the oldest known complete garment from a heap of dirty linens preserved well before anyone began the study of ancient textile production. At this point, the author's **Purpose** should be clearer: to explain and illustrate how much archaeology now knows about ancient textile production.

Paragraph 3 continues with another example of how the study of ancient textile production has been aided by these recent research developments, but in a different way. Researchers can now re-create the processes of ancient textile production as a valuable way to test hypotheses. The two examples at the end of the paragraph—proper ID of looming weights that had long been disregarded and proper ID of production time for the Athena statue dress—serve to further reinforce the author's **Main Idea**—technological and philosophical changes in archaeology have made big gains in knowledge of ancient textile production.

22. (B) Global ★★★★

Step 2: Identify the Question Type

The phrase "main point" identifies this question as a Global question. A quick review of the Roadmap and brief paraphrase of the author's main points is all that is needed to confidently ascertain the correct answer choice.

Step 3: Research the Relevant Text

Since Global questions do not point you to one part of the passage in particular, you'll need to call upon your Roadmap for a review of the passage in its entirety.

Step 4: Make a Prediction

Take a brief moment to take stock of what you just read: There is little evidence for archaeologists studying ancient textile production. However, by studying a variety of new advances, researchers have been able to gain much more knowledge about ancient textiles and how they were produced.

Step 5: Evaluate the Answer Choices

(B) echoes that sentiment.

(A) and **(D)** are Extreme. The author never goes so far as to credit the entire discipline of archaeology with advance. Rather, the author stays focused on the advance in research concerning the archaeology of textiles.

(C) is a Faulty Use of Detail. Although it's a great summary of the author's points in paragraph 3, this question calls for a statement that encompasses the entire passage, not just one paragraph.

(E) In addition to focusing too closely on one detail in the passage, choice **(E)** also goes too far in attributing "most significant findings" to the advancements in reconstruction techniques.

23. (E) Inference ★★★★

Step 2: Identify the Question Type

In this Inference question, you'll need to glean the author's tone toward the history of ancient textile production from context within the passage.

Step 3: Research the Relevant Text

A brief review of the end of paragraph 1, along with the first sentences in paragraphs 2 and 3, clearly shows that the author believes advances are being made in this field. Pay attention to the Opinion/Emphasis Keywords the author uses: "researchers have learned a **great deal** about ancient textiles and those who made them" (lines 15–16); "[t]echnological advances in the analysis of archaeological remains provide **much more information than** was previously available" (lines 19–21); and "[t]he history of textiles and of the craftswoman who produced them has **also advanced on a different front**" (lines 43–44).

EXPLANATIONS

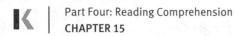

Part Four: Reading Comprehension
CHAPTER 15

These explanations refer to
questions that begin on page 903.

Step 4: Make a Prediction

The use of these Keywords indicates that the author feels that a great amount of progress is being made concerning the history of ancient textile production

Step 5: Evaluate the Answer Choices

(E) is correct. You can test this by eliminating incorrect answers.

A brief scan of the first word in each answer choice helps eliminate choices **(A)**, **(B)**, and **(C)** because the tone is negative ("skeptical," "doubtful," and "impatient"). Regardless of what else they say, you should be confident that each of these misses the mark.

(D) It is not known to what extent the author thinks the advances will attract more researchers. Rather, the author focuses heavily on how the advances already made are aiding existing researchers in new discoveries.

(E) must be the correct answer. Sure enough, it matches the prediction that the author believes that a number of advances are being made concerning the history of ancient textile production.

24. (E) Detail ★☆☆☆

Step 2: Identify the Question Type

In this Detail question, "[t]he passage indicates" tells you that the correct answer will be a close paraphrase, if not a direct quotation, from the passage.

Step 3: Research the Relevant Text

Pay close attention to the content clues in the question stem to guide your research. The question is directing you to the portion of the author's passage that discusses the "re-creation of ancient techniques." From your Roadmap, recall that the author discussed this information in paragraph 3. Specifically, the author discusses the re-creation of the actual production of cloth in lines 45–50 and then how that re-creation aided the determination of which two statues of Athena was adorned with a particular dress.

Step 4: Make a Prediction

The correct answer will likely focus on the statues of Athena as a specific example of how the researchers used the re-creation techniques to determine which statue wore the garment.

Step 5: Evaluate the Answer Choices

(E) mentions Athena and matches the prediction quite closely. None of the examples in choices **(A)**, **(B)**, **(C)**, and **(D)** are mentioned in paragraph 3 as examples of how the researchers used the re-creation techniques.

25. (D) Inference ★★★☆

Step 2: Identify the Question Type

This Inference question requires you to ascertain how narrowly defined the author means the term "traditional sources" to be.

Step 3: Research the Relevant Text

The line reference in the question stem (line 1) tells you to focus on the beginning of the passage and use context as your guide when making your prediction. The term "traditional sources" is defined in the very first line as "archaeological remains and surviving texts." The next sentence provides great Keywords to help you zero in on how narrowly the author means "traditional resources" to apply. "[H]owever" indicates that the author is switching gears and focusing on how little information these traditional sources of evidence provide to researchers. Also, the Opinion/Emphasis Keywords "particularly unavailing" further emphasize the lack of utility these traditional sources of evidence provide to researchers in aiding their discovery process in ancient textile production. More specifically, the author goes on to say that the perishable nature of cloth, along with the apparent uselessness of loom weights and the lack of reference to the creation of textiles, makes these researchers' job quite difficult.

Step 4: Make a Prediction

Based on this brief read of paragraph 1, you can be sure that the author intends for the term "traditional sources" to be quite narrow in its application and contrasted with newer re-creation and analysis techniques.

Step 5: Evaluate the Answer Choices

As you evaluate the answer choices, keep in mind that four of the answer choices will be considered "traditional sources" or not be mentioned in the passage. The correct answer will go beyond the scope of traditional sources of evidence as the author presents them in the passage.

(D) "[R]e-creations of looms" is something created by modern scholars as the author discusses in paragraph 3. Most certainly this goes beyond the scope of "traditional sources" of evidence according to the author. Thus, choice **(D)** is the correct answer. For the record:

(A) "[A]ncient clay objects" would be considered within the traditional sources of evidence, particularly coupled with the distinction that researchers cannot identify their utility under the traditional sources of evidence.

(B) and **(C)** can both be eliminated because each would be considered traditional sources of evidence according to the author's discussion at the end of paragraph 2.

EXPLANATIONS

These explanations refer to
questions that begin on page 903.

Part Four: Reading Comprehension
Reading Comprehension Practice

K

(E) The accounts of the adornment of the Athena statue have been available under the traditional sources of evidence. Rather, it's the re-creation techniques that allowed researchers to determine which statue was adorned with a particular dress that would be considered part of the new advances in research.

26. (C) Global

Step 2: Identify the Question Type

This Global question asks for the author's Purpose in writing the passage.

Step 3: Research the Relevant Text

Recall your Roadmap as well as the Topic, Scope, Purpose, and Main Idea. The author's Purpose is to explain and illustrate how much researchers within the field of archaeology now know about the history of ancient textile production in light of technological and philosophical advance made by researchers. Also, worth noting is how these advances have enabled researchers to cope with the scant "traditional sources" of evidence available to them.

Step 4: Make a Prediction

A brief review of your Roadmap gives you a great prediction: the author has written this passage to show how advances have enabled researchers to deal with the traditional lack of evidence available in the study of ancient textile production.

Step 5: Evaluate the Answer Choices

(C) is a match. The author gives an account of how researchers studying ancient textile production have been able to make discoveries using advances in technology in spite of the lack of evidence available. For the record:

(A) and **(D)** are out because the author never debates the methods used by researchers within this discipline.

(B) The author never makes any recommendations for future researchers based on the information presented in the passage.

(E) The author alludes to how these advances can help researchers test and confirm their hypotheses. However, the author never mentions what those hypotheses are, let alone focuses on them throughout the passage.

27. (E) Detail

Step 2: Identify the Question Type

In this Detail question, the phrase "[a]ccording to the passage" tells us that the answer will be a close paraphrase, if not a direct quotation, of the text.

Step 3: Research the Relevant Text

Pay close attention to the content clues in the question stem. "[A]n element in the transformation of archaeology in the past century" leads you to paragraph 2, specifically lines 31–33, which read "the field has transformed itself into a scientific pursuit of knowledge about past cultures." The next sentence starts, "[a]s part of this process," which is a clear indication of an element in the transformation—exactly what the question is asking for.

Step 4: Make a Prediction

The concept described in lines 33–36 ("preserving all objects, even those that have no discernible value") is a perfect prediction of the correct answer.

Step 5: Evaluate the Answer Choices

(E) is a great match for your prediction. For the record:

None of the theories mentioned in **(A)**, **(B)**, **(C)**, and **(D)** were mentioned in paragraph 2. Neither the methods nor the discovery of certain items is considered part of the philosophical transformation of archaeology during the past century.

28. (A) Logic Function

Step 2: Identify the Question Type

In this Logic Function question, the correct answer will properly encompass the author's purpose for including the information discussed in paragraph 1.

Step 3: Research the Relevant Text

Review your Roadmap, paying close attention to your margin notes and Keywords. The author uses paragraph 1 to set the stage for the remainder of the passage. Specifically, the author describes how the traditional sources of evidence available to researchers studying ancient textile production proved problematic. However, in response to these obstacles, the advances made in this field have been that much more important.

Step 4: Make a Prediction

The correct answer must show that the author presents the obstacles in order to emphasize how important the advances were to researchers studying ancient textile production.

Step 5: Evaluate the Answer Choices

(A) is a solid match to your prediction. For the record:

(B) is the exact opposite of why the author introduces the lack of evidence in paragraph 1.

(C), **(D)**, and **(E)** all miss the mark by focusing on "recent" findings and "new" technology-based methods of analysis. All that information comes after the first paragraph and is Out of Scope for this question.

These explanations refer to
questions that begin on page 904.

Professional Writing and Narrative

Step 1: Read the Passage Strategically

Sample Roadmap

Passage A

Readers, like writers, need to search for answers. Part of the joy of reading is in being surprised, but academic historians leave little to the imagination. The perniciousness of the historiographic approach became

(5) fully evident to me when I started teaching. Historians require undergraduates to read scholarly monographs that sap the vitality of history; they visit on students what was visited on them in graduate school. They assign books with formulaic arguments that transform

(10) history into an abstract debate that would have been unfathomable to those who lived in the past. Aimed so squarely at the head, such books cannot stimulate students who yearn to connect to history emotionally as well as intellectually.

Historical academic writing too abstract

(15) In an effort to address this problem, some historians have begun to rediscover stories. It has even become something of a fad within the profession. This year, the American Historical Association chose as the theme for its annual conference some putative connection to

(20) storytelling: "Practices of Historical Narrative." Predictably, historians responded by adding the word "narrative" to their titles and presenting papers at sessions on "Oral History and the Narrative of Class Identity," and "Meaning and Time: The Problem of

(25) Historical Narrative." But it was still historiography. intended only for other academics. At meetings of historians, we still encounter very few historians telling stories or moving audiences to smiles, chills, or tears.

Despite fad of 'narrative' still not enough stories stirring emotion

Passage B

(30) Writing is at the heart of the lawyer's craft, and so, like it or not, we who teach the law inevitably teach aspiring lawyers how lawyers write. We do this in a few stand-alone courses and, to a greater extent, through the constraints that we impose on their writing throughout

(35) the curriculum. Legal writing, because of the purposes it serves, is necessarily ruled by linear logic, creating a path without diversions, surprises, or reversals. Conformity is a virtue, creativity suspect, humor forbidden, and voice mute.

Legal writing + conformity - creativity, humor, voice

(40) Lawyers write as they see other lawyers write, and, influenced by education, profession, economic constraints, and perceived self-interest, they too often write badly. Perhaps the currently fashionable call for attention to narrative in legal education could have an

(45) effect on this. It is not yet exactly clear what role narrative should play in the law, but it is nonetheless true that every case has at its heart a story—of real events and people, of concerns, misfortunes, conflicts, feelings. But because legal analysis strips the human

(50) narrative content from the abstract, canonical legal

Narrative?

Legal analysis strips narrative of its story

form of the case, law students learn to act as if there is no such story.

It may well turn out that some of the terminology

(55) and public rhetoric of this potentially subversive movement toward attention to narrative will find its way into the law curriculum, but without producing corresponding changes in how legal writing is actually taught or in how our future colleagues will write. Still, even mere awareness of the value of narrative could perhaps serve as an important corrective.

Narrative could have + or - effects

PrepTest52 Sec4 Qs7–12

EXPLANATIONS

These explanations refer to questions that begin on page 904.

Part Four: Reading Comprehension
Reading Comprehension Practice

Discussion

The author of **Passage A** is unhappy. The author claims reading should both surprise and engage the imagination "but" (line 2) finds that the academic writings of historians are formulaic and unimaginative. As a teacher, the author is upset because the "perniciousness of the historiographic approach" prevents students from connecting to history emotionally. There seems to be a glimmer of hope in the second paragraph, when the author suggests that historians have started to discover the art of storytelling. However, a history conference supposedly devoted to "narratives" finds those stodgy historians adding "Narrative" to their titles but resorting to their usual dry, scholarly papers, interesting only to other historians. The **Topic** of this passage is academic historian writing; the **Scope** is its major shortcoming. The author's **Purpose** is to state dissatisfaction with the lack of interesting writing in the field of history. The **Main Idea** is that history writing is bland and uninspiring and, with a lack of narrative, it keeps students from connecting to history emotionally or intellectually.

Like the author of Passage A, the author of **Passage B** is also unhappy. And again, it's because of bad writing. In this passage, the author is concerned with legal writing. The first paragraph introduces the first concern: legal writing is too linear; there are no surprises and voice is constrained. But in the second paragraph, the author goes a step further by suggesting that legal writing has become just plain bad. Like the author of Passage A, this author sees a glimmer of hope in the current movement for attention to narrative in legal education. But that hope has a lot to overcome; current practice in legal analysis is to remove the story, or the human narrative content, from the abstract, legal aspect of the case. In the final paragraph, the author acknowledges that it's possible the current fashion might infiltrate education without changing how legal writing is taught—or written—but argues that even awareness of narrative could be an important adjustment. Here the **Topic** is legal writing, and the **Scope** is its major shortcoming. Again, that shortcoming is the lack of narrative. This author's **Purpose** is also to show concern about the lack of interesting writing, only this time in the field of legal writing. However, the last line offers a somewhat more optimistic outlook. The **Main Idea** is that legal writing is generally uninteresting and poorly written, but incorporating narrative could correct some of this.

Before going to the questions, you should always consider the relationship between the two passages. Both have writings in their respective profession as a **Topic**, and the **Scope** of both passages is the lack of quality of that writing. They both feel that their professions' writings are uninteresting, and they both feel that the use of narrative (or storytelling) could potentially add value to the writings.

29. (D) Global ★★☆☆

Step 2: Identify the Question Type

This question stem is vaguely worded, but the beginnings of each answer choice discuss a broad view of both authors. Most questions that ask about the broad views of an author are Global questions. If you had perceived this as an Inference question about the author's attitude though, that would have led you to the same line of thinking for Steps 3 and 4.

Step 3: Research the Relevant Text

There's no specific place in either passage to consult for your answer, so you may have to let your knowledge of the shared Topic and Scope, as well as the answer choices, guide your research.

Step 4: Make a Prediction

Simply knowing the relationship between the passages can save time. Reexamining the relationship between the two, you know both passages talk disparagingly about the lack of narrative in their respective profession's writings.

Step 5: Evaluate the Answer Choices

(D) turns that prediction into a positive. If the authors are upset by the lack of narrative, it's likely they would find more storytelling a welcome addition.

(A) is a Distortion. While both authors are teachers, neither discusses effective methodology.

(B) is Outside the Scope. Both passages are concerned with points of view well within the normal realm of their respective disciplines.

(C) is Extreme. While both authors believe writing in their disciplines is not currently creative, neither states that such a goal is impossible. In the last sentence of Passage B, the author sees some potential for the future of legal writing.

(E) is Outside the Scope. Neither author is happy with the current state of writing in their field, but they don't discuss eliminating elements from other fields. Instead, they do discuss bringing in new elements of narrative.

30. (B) Inference ★★☆☆

Step 2: Identify the Question Type

Both the word "inferences" and the phrase "passages most strongly support" indicate an Inference question. Instead of asking about how Passage A relates to Passage B, this question wants to know how the author of Passage A relates to the profession mentioned in Passage A, and the same for the author of Passage B.

Step 3: Research the Relevant Text

Look for clues in each passage that point to the identities of the authors—personal pronouns such as "I" or "we." Line 5 suggests the author of Passage A is a history teacher. "[W]e

K | Part Four: Reading Comprehension
CHAPTER 15

These explanations refer to
questions that begin on page 905.

EXPLANATIONS

who teach the law" in line 30 indicates the author of Passage B is a law professor.

Step 4: Make a Prediction

Passage A's history teacher discusses academic history writing, while Passage B's law professor critiques legal writing. Both appear to be professionals within the worlds they are scrutinizing.

Step 5: Evaluate the Answer Choices

(B) is the only answer that says that both authors are members of the discussed professions.

(A) is a 180. Both authors are definitively involved in the discussed professions.

(C) mischaracterizes Passage B, whose author is definitively involved in the law profession.

(D) is a Distortion. Both authors are active members, but of their respectively discussed professions. They're not both in the field of law.

(E) is also off because the author of passage B is not an active member of the history field.

31. (A) Detail ★★★☆

Step 2: Identify the Question Type

The question stem asks not about what the passage implies but what it indicates. That makes this a Detail question.

Step 3: Research the Relevant Text

The word "typical" in the question stem tells you to look for what each author identifies as the status quo in his or her respective field's writing. This leads you to paragraph 1 in Passage A and paragraphs 1 and 2 in Passage B.

Step 4: Make a Prediction

A scan of these lines yields several adjectives that are consistent with these authors' viewpoints: "sap the vitality" (line 7); "formulaic" (line 9); "abstract" (line 10); and "aimed . . . at the head" (lines 11–12) from Passage A are in line with "ruled by linear logic" (line 35); "without diversions, surprises, or reversals" (line 36); and "abstract" (line 49) from Passage B. The correct answer will agree with these words and phrases.

Step 5: Evaluate the Answer Choices

(A) is a great match. The impersonal implication of "abstraction" fits both authors' criticism that current historical or legal writing turns human situations into intellectual situations. Plus, Passage A uses the word "abstract" in line 10, and Passage B uses it in line 49. Choice **(A)** is therefore correct.

(B) goes against both passages because the authors describe the writings as "formulaic" (line 9) or "without diversions" (line 36). Hyperbole (or exaggeration) is out of the question.

(C) is not used to describe typical legal writing; Passage B uses the word "subversive" to describe the recent movement toward using narrative (line 53). And subversion isn't mentioned by Passage A at all.

(D) should be eliminated because while both authors discuss "narrative," each time it is in the context of discussing recent, possibly corrective trends. Neither uses "narrative" to describe typical, or status quo, writing.

(E) is a 180. Passage A says that historiography "leave[s] little to the imagination" (line 3), and Passage B says that in legal writing, "creativity [is] suspect" (line 37).

32. (C) Logic Reasoning (Method of Argument) ★★★☆

Step 2: Identify the Question Type

The question stem is vague, and again it helps to glance at the answer choices. All of them discuss how the authors present their arguments. That makes this a LR–Method of Argument question.

Step 3: Research the Relevant Text

The words "not parallel" mean that you'll have to determine what Passage A does that's different from what Passage B does. There's no specific text to research, so consult your global understanding of the passages' differences from Step 1 of the Kaplan Method.

Step 4: Make a Prediction

You might have found this answer tough to predict. When two passages are as similar as these two, you'll often have to go through the answer choices to find out what they don't have in common.

Step 5: Evaluate the Answer Choices

(C) is the correct answer. Passage A mentions the American Historical Association conference—a particular example—while Passage B has no such specificity. So this choice is correct.

(A) is out because Passage A presents an argument for the author's own position but never for the opposition. Plus, the passage doesn't reject any arguments.

(B) is Half-Right, Half-Wrong because Passage A certainly makes evaluative claims (calling the historiographic approach "pernicious" in line 4), but so does B (saying in lines 41–42 that lawyers too often write badly).

(D) is also Half-Right Half-Wrong because Passage B certainly offers criticism, but so does Passage A (lines 6–7 say that some scholarly monographs "sap the vitality of history").

(E) is wrong because neither passage discusses any theories.

These explanations refer to questions that begin on page 905.

Part Four: Reading Comprehension
Reading Comprehension Practice | K

33. (B) Logic Function

Step 2: Identify the Question Type

Some questions will require you to combine multiple LR skills. In this case, "the phrase . . . plays a role in" and "most analogous to the role played" sound like two LR question types: Role of a Statement and Parallel Reasoning. You will need to find the role or function of the statement from Passage A and then find another statement that has the same function in Passage B. So, this is a Logic Function question, although it could be classified other ways as well.

Step 3: Research the Relevant Text

As with any question containing a line reference, it's not just the lines themselves that you need to read. You also need to read the surrounding lines for context.

Step 4: Make a Prediction

First, you need to figure out what role the phrase from Passage A serves. Reading back for context, that phrase is part of the discussion about how unimaginative historical writing is. By saying that it "saps the vitality of history," the author emphasizes the writing's lack of appeal. Knowing that, you need to find a phrase in Passage B that does the same thing.

Step 5: Evaluate the Answer Choices

(B) highlights what the author sees as an attack on imagination within legal writing. This is certainly the correct answer.

(A) explains writing is important to law but doesn't critique that writing for being unimaginative.

(C) explains *why* the writing is so bad, but it doesn't emphasize what's bad about it.

(D) tells you why narrative should be used but doesn't explain that the lack of narrative is what makes current writing so unappealing.

(E) suggests that the author has hope for the future of legal writing but doesn't criticize the lifelessness of its current state.

34. (D) Inference

Step 2: Identify the Question Type

The phrase "the author . . . would be most likely to expect" indicates an Inference question. You'll have to combine the question stem's hypothetical with the information from Passage B to determine what *must* be true.

Step 3: Research the Relevant Text

To determine what Passage B's author would expect from a legal document describing the facts of a case, go back to your Roadmap. The author assesses the state of legal writing in paragraphs 1 and 2 of Passage B.

Step 4: Make a Prediction

According to lines 35–38, the author would expect a legal document to be linear, unsurprising, and without creative voice. Furthermore, at line 42, the author argues current legal writing is often bad. Finally, at lines 48–49, the author says that legal analysis strips away the case's human narrative content. So, the correct answer will be consistent with those ideas.

Step 5: Evaluate the Answer Choices

(D) is entirely consistent with lines 48–49, making it the correct answer.

(A) starts off well—the author would expect it to be poorly written, according to line 42. However, if you re-read that section of the passage, you see legal writing is bad primarily because lawyers mimic other lawyers, not because they missed out on advice from law professors. In fact, this answer choice is actually a 180. The author says poor writers are "influenced by education," which means law professors' advice is likely detrimental to legal writing's quality.

(B) is a 180. The author says at lines 48–49 that legal analysis strips away the personal narrative, meaning that it will not be "crafted to function like a piece of fiction."

(C) also conflicts with the author's characterization of legal writing. In lines 41–42, the passage says lawyers "too often write badly." As a result, the author certainly wouldn't expect the document to be "a well-crafted piece of writing."

(E) falls Outside the Scope. The author thinks legal writers neglect emotional details (e.g., concerns, conflicts, and feelings). However, the author never says those writers neglect to reference relevant legal doctrines.

K

Part Four: Reading Comprehension
CHAPTER 15

These explanations refer to
questions that begin on page 906.

Custom-Made Medical Illustrations as Evidence

Step 1: Read the Passage Strategically

Sample Roadmap

While courts have long allowed custom-made
medical illustrations depicting personal injury to be
presented as evidence in legal cases, the issue of
whether they have a legitimate place in the courtroom

(5) is surrounded by ongoing debate and misinformation.
Some opponents of their general use argue that while
illustrations are sometimes invaluable in presenting the
physical details of a personal injury, in all cases except
those involving the most unusual injuries, illustrations

(10) from medical textbooks can be adequate. Most
injuries, such as fractures and whiplash, they say, are
rather generic in nature—certain commonly
encountered forces act on particular areas of the body
in standard ways—so <they can be represented by

(15) generic illustrations.>
　　　Another line of complaint stems from the belief
that custom-made illustrations often misrepresent the
facts in order to comply with the partisan interests of
litigants. Even some lawyers appear to share a version

(20) of this view, believing that such illustrations can be
used to bolster a weak case. Illustrators are sometimes
approached by lawyers who, unable to find medical
experts to support their clients' claims, think that they
can replace expert testimony with such deceptive

(25) professional illustrations. But this is mistaken. Even if
an unscrupulous illustrator could be found, <such
illustrations would be inadmissible as evidence in the
courtroom unless a medical expert were present to
testify to their accuracy.>

(30) 　　　It has also been maintained that custom-made
illustrations may subtly distort the issues through the
use of emphasis, coloration, and other means, even if
they are technically accurate. But professional medical
illustrators strive for objective accuracy and avoid

(35) devices that have inflammatory potential, sometimes
even eschewing the use of color. Unlike illustrations
in medical textbooks, which are designed to include
the extensive detail required by medical students,
custom-made medical illustrations are designed to

(40) include only the information that is relevant for those
deciding a case. The end user is typically a jury or a
judge, for whose benefit the depiction is reduced to the
details that are crucial to determining the legally
relevant facts. The more complex details often found

(45) in textbooks can be deleted so as not to confuse the
issue. For example, illustrations of such things as
veins and arteries would only get in the way when an
illustration is supposed to be used to explain the nature
of a bone fracture.

(50) 　　　Custom-made medical illustrations, which are
based on a plaintiff's X rays, computerized

tomography scans, and medical records and reports,
are especially valuable in that they provide visual
representations of data whose verbal description would

(55) be very complex. Expert testimony by medical
professionals often relies heavily on the use of
technical terminology, which those who are not
specially trained in the field find difficult to translate
mentally into visual imagery. Since, for most people,

(60) adequate understanding of physical data depends on
thinking at least partly in visual terms, <the clearly
presented visual stimulation provided by custom-made
illustrations can be quite instructive.>

PrepTest62 Sec1 Qs9–14

*Custom
med. illust.
in court?*

debate–

*Con 1: med
textbook
pictures
adequate*

*Con 2: custom
pictures
misrepresent*

*Au = but
pictures must
be vetted by
experts*

*Con 3: custom
illust. distort
issue*

*Au = but prof.
illustrators
strive for
simple, accurate;*

*too complex
is bad*

*Au =
custom illust.
valuable;*

*informs
expert
test'y*

*Most users
not experts,
so pictures
useful*

EXPLANATIONS

These explanations refer to questions that begin on page 906.

Part Four: Reading Comprehension
Reading Comprehension Practice   K

Discussion

Custom-made medical illustrations make for a rather discrete **Topic**, with the **Scope** of the passage focusing on "whether they have a legitimate place in the courtroom." The author readily presents a point of view by referring to some of the rhetoric as "misinformation" and goes on to begin listing some of the points made by opponents of customized drawings. Paragraph 1 concludes with the first of these points: in most cases, generic illustrations from medical textbooks can be adequate.

Paragraph 2 introduces a second complaint about using custom-made medical drawings as evidence that "stems from the belief" (more language that hints at the author's disagreement) that such illustrations present a biased picture. The author rebuts this viewpoint, arguing that such illustrations would not be admitted as evidence without testimony from a medical expert to verify their accuracy.

A third objection to customized illustrations is presented in paragraph 3: these drawings might distort issues with various illustrative techniques. Again the author provides a rebuttal, noting that professional medical illustrators strive for accuracy. The author goes on to point out that custom-made drawings can provide more clarity for jurors and judges by omitting irrelevant anatomical details that would be a part of generic illustrations. By now it is quite clear that the author's **Purpose** is to defend the use of custom-made medical illustrations as evidence in legal cases.

The final paragraph reinforces the author's contention that custom-made medical illustrations are valuable, providing visual explanations for very complex data. In the end, the reader has no doubt of the author's **Main Idea**: contrary to criticism, custom-made medical illustrations are a useful tool for litigators trying to explain complicated medical terminology.

35. (A) Logic Reasoning (Parallel Reasoning)   ★★★☆

Step 2: Identify the Question Type

We may expect to see a Global question as the first problem of the set, but not so here, which is a reminder that nothing is guaranteed on the LSAT. Indeed, there's not a single Global question about this passage. Here we are faced with a Parallel Reasoning question, indicated by the phrase "[w]hich one of the following is most analogous . . . ."

Step 3: Research the Relevant Text

The question stem demands an analogy to the role "custom-made medical illustrations play in personal injury cases." The author describes this role in several places; the Roadmap should guide you to the discussions in the second half of the passage, especially at lines 53–55. There, the author states that these illustrations "provide visual representations of data whose verbal description would be very complex."

Step 4: Make a Prediction

The correct answer will refer to another item that would provide a clear visual explanation for something that requires a complex verbal description.

Step 5: Evaluate the Answer Choices

(A) describes illustrations that accompany a technical oral presentation. Perfect!

(B) suggests a visual tool to avoid, not accompany, verbal descriptions. That's off the mark.

(C) discusses drawings used as analytical tools for psychologists that are not related to the illustrative drawings used to clarify testimony.

(D) describes a graphic that doesn't offer any value as a visual explanation for a verbal presentation.

(E) is off because preliminary sketches don't provide any clarification of complex information.

36. (E) Inference   ★★☆☆

Step 2: Identify the Question Type

Inference questions are commonly "[b]ased on the passage" and often ask about what is "most likely."

Step 3: Research the Relevant Text

The question stem's only content clue is about medical textbook illustrations. These are discussed twice in the passage; the brief mention at line 10, however, does not really provide insight into the author's opinion of textbook drawing. The useful portion of the passage for this question is found at the end of paragraph 3: lines 36–49.

Step 4: Make a Prediction

The answer must be true based on the passage and should reflect the author's contention that medical textbook illustrations may be too detailed and complex compared to custom-made illustrations, which provide only relevant information.

Step 5: Evaluate the Answer Choices

(E) is correct. This choice relates to the prediction nicely, and it is supported by lines 44–46, which state that deleting complex details from textbooks can eliminate confusion.

(A) is a 180. Color use is discussed in the third paragraph, but custom-made illustrations are said to sometimes even avoid using color, which is another way of saying they, and not medical textbooks, are the ones that rely less on color use.

(B) is a Faulty Use of Detail, twisting the comment at the end of the second paragraph, which refers to custom-made drawings, not to medical textbooks.

(C) is Out of Scope, for the passage does not say anything about who creates the illustrations for either medical textbooks or custom-made drawings.

K | Part Four: Reading Comprehension
CHAPTER 15

These explanations refer to
questions that begin on page 906.

(D) distorts the information presented around lines 19–21. However, those lines only suggest that *some* lawyers may believe that, not *most*, making this answer Extreme. And the answer here really is a Distortion of that information and incorrect.

37. (E) Detail

Step 2: Identify the Question Type

This Detail question is identified by the phrase "[t]he passage states."

Step 3: Research the Relevant Text

Don't rely on your memory: check the passage (at lines 27–29) to verify what it says about medical experts in relation to custom-made medical illustrations.

Step 4: Make a Prediction

The passage says that custom-made illustrations are "inadmissible as evidence . . . unless a medical expert" is present to testify to their accuracy. The correct answer will paraphrase this.

Step 5: Evaluate the Answer Choices

(E) contains the expected paraphrase.

(A) is a Distortion. Medical experts confirm the accuracy of an illustration but wouldn't necessarily have any say about admissibility.

(B) is another Distortion: "temper the impact" implies a level of influence the passage does not ascribe to medical experts.

(C) is a 180. According to the passage, illustrations clarify the words of experts, not the other way around.

(D) is Out of Scope, as experts' advice to attorneys is never discussed in the passage.

38. (D) Detail ★☆☆☆

Step 2: Identify the Question Type

"According to the passage" is a hallmark Detail question phrase.

Step 3: Research the Relevant Text

The question stem offers a content clue: we need to check the passage for any discussion about the differences between medical textbook and custom-made illustrations. This can be found in the third paragraph.

Step 4: Make a Prediction

The information at lines 36–41 provides the most specific comparison between the illustrations in medical textbooks and those that are custom-made: the former are highly detailed, whereas the latter can be designed to include only pertinent information related to the lawsuit.

Step 5: Evaluate the Answer Choices

(D) correctly restates the prediction.

(A) makes an incorrect assertion (that medical textbook illustrations do not accurately represent human anatomy) and is also Out of Scope, as the accuracy of textbook drawings is never discussed.

(B) is a Distortion of the discussion of color at the beginning of the third paragraph. It is also Extreme: while the passage says custom illustrators sometimes eschew the use of color, it does not say that they "must" avoid it.

(C) is Out of Scope. The objectivity or subjectivity of drawings is never discussed.

(E) is a 180, since the whole point of custom-made illustrations is to make complex concepts easier to understand for nonmedical people in the court.

39. (C) Inference ★★☆☆

Step 2: Identify the Question Type

Asking about the "author's attitude" is an Inference question variant.

Step 3: Research the Relevant Text

The content clue in this question points to the final paragraph, where expert testimony is discussed (lines 55–63).

Step 4: Make a Prediction

The passage says, without reservation or other commentary, that expert medical testimony is often very technical and might be difficult for people without medical training to visualize. The correct answer will be true based on this information, and it will reflect an author attitude that is neither critical nor laudatory toward medical experts.

Step 5: Evaluate the Answer Choices

(C), with its neutral tone along with its mention of the limitations of a strictly verbal presentation, makes it the correct answer.

(A) questions the effectiveness of testimony and mentions the difficulty of explaining medical data, which is a Distortion of the author's assertion that illustrations can be instructive by supplementing complex testimony that might be difficult to translate mentally into visual imagery.

(B) is wrong because the author shows no "disdain" toward the experts.

(D) implies an accusation, never stated by the author, that experts are *trying* to overwhelm judges and jurors.

(E) is Extreme based on the word "intolerance."

These explanations refer to
questions that begin on page 907.

Part Four: Reading Comprehension
Reading Comprehension Practice |

40. (B) Logic Function ★★★★

Step 2: Identify the Question Type

Two types of questions ask about authorial purpose: Global
questions pertain to the overall passage, but this question
homes in on just one paragraph, making it a Logic Function
question.

Step 3: Research the Relevant Text

The third paragraph is the subject of this question. Remember
to consider it in context: the preceding paragraph discussed
the suggestion that customized drawings are biased—the
second of three critical points discussed by the passage. The
third paragraph goes on to list the third and final objection
to custom-made medical illustrations: that they might distort
issues. The author then argues against this criticism and
praises custom-made illustrations as useful for their ability
to include only those aspects of physiology relevant to the
case. This paves the way for the final paragraph, which
further advocates the use of customized illustrations in the
courtroom.

Step 4: Make a Prediction

The correct answer will focus on structure and context and
reflect this paragraph's treatment of a point of contention
against customized illustrations.

Step 5: Evaluate the Answer Choices

(B) is correct as it properly identifies the author's reply to
another objection. Note how this answer compares the
objection discussed in the third paragraph to the objection in
the previous paragraph—they're both variations on distorting
information. This underscores the importance of researching
the context of a content clue.

(A) calls for an argument that isn't actually made in the third
paragraph. Because this idea is somewhat in line with the
passage's overall purpose, it might tempt a test taker who
failed to follow Steps 3 and 4.

(C) overemphasizes the reference to medical textbook
illustrations, making this wrong answer a Distortion.

(D) is too vague. While the paragraph does add some detail
about the controversy, that's not its primary purpose.

(E), likewise, is too narrow, focusing only on the discussion
contained in the latter portion of the paragraph.

K

Part Four: Reading Comprehension
CHAPTER 15

These explanations refer to
questions that begin on page 908.

Music's Effects and Emotions

Step 1: Read the Passage Strategically

Sample Roadmap

Passage A

*Music
too simple—
uninteresting*

In music, a certain complexity of sounds can be
expected to have a positive effect on the listener. A
single, pure tone is not that interesting to explore; a
measure of intricacy is required to excite human
(5) curiosity. Sounds that are too complex or disorganized,
however, tend to be overwhelming. We prefer some
sort of coherence, a principle that connects the various
sounds and makes them comprehensible.

*too
complex—
overwhelming*

In this respect, music is like human language.
(10) Single sounds are in most cases not sufficient to
convey meaning in speech, whereas when put together
in a sequence they form words and sentences.
Likewise, if the tones in music are not perceived to be
tied together sequentially or rhythmically—for
(15) example, in what is commonly called melody—
listeners are less likely to feel any emotional
connection or to show appreciation.

*like
language—
sequence
needed*

Certain music can also have a relaxing effect. The
fact that such music tends to be continuous and
(20) rhythmical suggests a possible explanation for this
effect. In a natural environment, danger tends to be
accompanied by sudden, unexpected sounds. Thus, a
background of constant noise suggests peaceful
conditions; discontinuous sounds demand more
(25) attention. Even soft discontinuous sounds that we
consciously realize do not signal danger can be
disturbing—for example, the erratic dripping of a
leaky tap. A continuous sound, particularly one that is
judged to be safe, relaxes the brain.

*continuous/
rhythmic =
relaxing*

*Not like
danger
sounds*

Passage B

*Musical
emotion:
expectation*

(30) There are certain elements within music, such
as a change of melodic line or rhythm, that create
expectations about the future development of the
music. The expectation the listener has about the
further course of musical events is a key determinant
(35) for the experience of "musical emotions." Music
creates expectations that, if not immediately satisfied,
create tension. Emotion is experienced in relation to
the buildup and release of tension. The more elaborate
the buildup of tension, the more intense the emotions
(40) that will be experienced. When resolution occurs,
relaxation follows.

tension

satisfaction

The interruption of the expected musical course,
depending on one's personal involvement, causes the
search for an explanation. This results from a
(45) "mismatch" between one's musical expectation and the
actual course of the music. Negative emotions will be
the result of an extreme mismatch between
expectations and experience. Positive emotions result
if the converse happens.

*Course—
expectation
mismatch =
neg. emotion*

(50) When we listen to music, we take into account
factors such as the complexity and novelty of the
music. The degree to which the music sounds familiar
determines whether the music is experienced as
pleasurable or uncomfortable. The pleasure
(55) experienced is minimal when the music is entirely new
to the listener, increases with increasing familiarity,
and decreases again when the music is totally known.
Musical preference is based on one's desire to
maintain a constant level of certain preferable
(60) emotions. As such, a trained listener will have a
greater preference for complex melodies than will a
naive listener, as the threshold for experiencing
emotion is higher.

*Factors:
complexity
familiarity*

*too new = bad
↑ing famil. = good*

too old = bad

*trained listeners =
more complex*

PrepTest58 Sec2 Qs21–27

These explanations refer to
questions that begin on page 908.

Part Four: Reading Comprehension
Reading Comprehension Practice

Discussion

The **Topic** of Passage A is presented immediately in the first sentence: music's effects. According to the author of Passage A, if a sound is too simple or too complex, then we find it uninteresting and overwhelming. Rather, like language, the sounds need coherence to connect the individual sounds and make them easier to understand. The **Scope** of Passage A appears to be what's interesting and soothing about the effects of music. The author compares music to the human language in that a sequence is needed. The author also notes that a lack of sequence is not particularly moving for us and does not provide an opportunity for appreciation. Finally, the author discusses what's relaxing about music: its continuity and rhythm. Continuous noise indicates peace and a lack of disturbance. The author's **Purpose** is to delineate what makes music interesting and soothing as well as overwhelming. The **Main Idea** of Passage A is that music can be interesting and overwhelming depending on complexity, while it can also be soothing because of its rhythmic quality.

As would be expected, the **Topic** of Passage B also concerns music: specifically, the emotional aspect of music. The author of Passage B isn't concerned with what gives us pleasure when we listen to music but rather how these reactions are brought about. The author describes three certain elements that create expectations: expectation of the future course of the music, the buildup of tension, and the relaxation that follows the resolution of that tension. The **Scope** of Passage B is how the expectations and familiarity determine the satisfaction when listening to music. The author of Passage B then discusses how when expectations are mismatched, negative emotions result. Positive emotions result when expectations match the actual course of music. Similar to Passage A, one purpose of Passage B is to describe how complexity and familiarity determine satisfaction when listening to music. When music is too new or too old, we don't enjoy it. As familiarity with new music increases, though, we are more inclined to enjoy the music. A trained listener prefers more complex melodies. The **Purpose** of Passage B is to examine the relationship between expectations of music and satisfaction. The **Main Idea** of Passage B is that the degree of familiarity influences expectations of music and the emotions experienced.

Before going to the questions, it's important to note the relationship between the two passages. Both are concerned with the effect music has on the listener—although one is concerned with how the listener reacts and one is concerned with what brings about those reactions. More notably, both passages support the view that complexity and familiarity play a role in whether the listener enjoys the music.

41. (E) Detail ★★★☆

Step 2: Identify the Question Type

The correct answer to this Detail question will be a concept that both passages identified as a positive musical experience.

Step 3: Research the Relevant Text

In Passage A, the author states that "a certain complexity of sounds can be expected to have a positive effect on the listener," (lines 1–2). In Passage B, the author states that "a trained listener will have a greater preference for complex melodies" (lines 61–62).

Step 4: Make a Prediction

Thus, both passages reference "complexity" as a concept that influences a positive musical experience.

Step 5: Evaluate the Answer Choices

(E) is the correct answer choice because it lists the concept of complexity. For the record:

(A) The concept of continuous sound is only linked in Passage A to a positive musical experience (lines 20–30).

(B) The concept of tension is only referenced in Passage B as an element that can lead to a positive listening experience (lines 37–41).

(C) The concept of language is only referenced in Passage A as an analogous example of when sequence is needed to provide a positive listening experience (lines 10–17).

(D) The concept of improvisation is not discussed in either passage.

42. (C) Inference ★☆☆☆

Step 2: Identify the Question Type

The correct answer to this Inference question will correctly characterize something in common between the two passages that draws the attention of the reader.

Step 3: Research the Relevant Text

To determine what the passages have in common, go back to the Roadmap. Both passages discuss the emotional aspect behind music and what effect music has on the listener.

Step 4: Make a Prediction

The correct answer must reference the emotional aspect of music and how that affects the listener.

Step 5: Evaluate the Answer Choices

(C) is the correct answer because it references the impact music has on the emotions of the listener. For the record:

(A) is Outside the Scope. The theory behind how music is composed is never discussed in either passage.

(B) references a concept discussed only in Passage A.

K | Part Four: Reading Comprehension
CHAPTER 15

These explanations refer to questions that begin on page 908.

(D) is Outside the Scope. The most effective techniques for teaching novices to appreciate complex music are never discussed in either passage.

(E) is Outside the Scope. While music is analogized to human language, the effect music has had on the development of spoken language is not discussed.

43. (B) Logic Reasoning (Parallel Reasoning) ★★★☆

Step 2: Identify the Question Type

The correct answer to this Parallel Reasoning question will have the same preference mentioned in the first paragraph of Passage A.

Step 3: Research the Relevant Text

In the first paragraph of Passage A, the author believes the listener prefers "some sort of coherence" that connects the various sounds and makes them comprehensible.

Step 4: Make a Prediction

The correct answer will need to show a preference for continuity within a work or a sense of coherence that drives the listener's enjoyment.

Step 5: Evaluate the Answer Choices

(B) is the correct answer. The simplicity of the plot and coherence makes it easy to follow, resulting in a positive viewing experience, which is analogous to the preference for coherence among music listeners.

(A) is a Faulty Use of Detail from Passage A. Continuous sound is not discussed until the third paragraph.

(C) is Outside the Scope. The length (or amount) of music is never discussed in either passage.

(D) is Outside the Scope of the first paragraph in Passage A. While melody is important, the speed or tempo of the music is never discussed in either passage.

(E) is Outside the Scope. The preference of sweet to bitter is never discussed in either passage.

44. (A) Global ★★☆☆

Step 2: Identify the Question Type

The correct answer for this Global question will encompass the entirety of Passage B.

Step 3: Research the Relevant Text

A quick review of your Roadmap related to Passage B indicates that the author of Passage B wants the reader to come away knowing that the expectations of a listener determine what emotional experiences the listener experiences.

Step 4: Make a Prediction

The correct answer will need to discuss the satisfaction of emotions as a relevant concept concerning a positive listening experience.

Step 5: Evaluate the Answer Choices

(A) correctly contains the author of Passage B's sentiments because it characterizes the author's main point, which is that the type of emotion experienced is determined by whether the listener's expectations are satisfied. For the record:

(B) and **(D)** are both too narrow and unsupported. While the ability for trained listeners to appreciate more complex music is discussed, how they do so is not the primary focus of the author of Passage B.

(C) is too narrow to be the correct answer for a Global question. While the author of Passage B does discuss the negative emotions associated with the mismatch of the listener's expectations with the actual course of the music, that concept is not the primary focus of Passage B.

(E) is a Distortion. While relaxation eventually follows the buildup and release of tension, the author of Passage B never addresses the likelihood that relaxing music usually produces this effect.

45. (C) Logic Reasoning (Weaken) ★★☆☆

Step 2: Identify the Question Type

The correct answer choice will weaken the explanation provided in Passage A for why some music has a relaxing effect on listeners.

Step 3: Research the Relevant Text

The first two sentences in the third paragraph of Passage A warrant attention. The author of Passage A explains that the continuous and rhythmic nature of music produces a relaxing effect.

Step 4: Make a Prediction

The correct answer choice will present a fact that makes it less likely or believable that the continuous and rhythmic nature of music produces a relaxing effect.

Step 5: Evaluate the Answer Choices

(C) is the correct answer. If people find the steady and rhythmic nature of a rocking chair to be stressful, then surely we could question whether the continuous sounds of music have a relaxing effect. For the record:

(A) is Outside the Scope. The complexity of music is not offered in Passage A as an explanation for why music has a relaxing effect.

(B) is Irrelevant. How the rhythmic sound is produced has no effect on whether the rhythm itself is still a valid reason for why the listener finds the music relaxing.

These explanations refer to questions that begin on page 909.

Part Four: Reading Comprehension
Reading Comprehension Practice   K

(D) is Outside the Scope. The effect of expectations on the listener's satisfaction and relaxation is a concept discussed in Passage B.

(E) is Irrelevant. Although Passage A discusses the effect of simplicity on the listener, the amount of music that is written to be simpler now versus in the past is irrelevant to whether the listener experiences relaxation.

46. (B) Global   ★★☆☆

Step 2: Identify the Question Type

The correct answer to this Global question will target both passages' commonality.

Step 3: Research the Relevant Text

A quick review of your Roadmap indicates that both authors are focusing on the emotions experienced by the listeners as a result of various concepts related to how music is created and eventually heard.

Step 4: Make a Prediction

The correct answer's title must focus on the emotions associated with listening to music.

Step 5: Evaluate the Answer Choices

(B) is the correct answer because the title "The Psychology of Listener Response to Music" applies appropriately to the soothing and overwhelming listener experience described in Passage A as well as the satisfaction of emotional expectations described in Passage B. For the record:

(A) The biology behind the emotions associated with listening to music are never discussed. Both authors focus purely on the psychological response.

(C) The differences between music and other art forms is never discussed in either passage.

(D) The cultural patterns associated with listeners' responses to music is never discussed in either passage.

(E) How the conductor conveys meaning to the listener is never discussed in either passage.

47. (D) Inference   ★★★☆

Step 2: Identify the Question Type

The correct answer to this Inference question will indicate a point of agreement between both authors.

Step 3: Research the Relevant Text

The author of Passage A indicates that having a continuous sound makes music enjoyable to the listener. It makes the music safer and more predictable. Likewise, the author of Passage B indicates that having the music match the listener's expectations, along with the buildup and release of tension, causes music to have a relaxing effect.

Step 4: Make a Prediction

The correct answer will note this area of agreement between the authors, namely that the listener should know where the music is going or be able to predict its eventual course.

Step 5: Evaluate the Answer Choices

(D) is the correct answer because it must be true based on information in the passage. Since both authors agree that predictability of music's course is highly important to a satisfying listening experience, then it must be true that without it the listener is less likely to feel relaxed. For the record:

(A) The author of Passage B does not feel that most listeners appreciate more complex music. Rather, Passage B's author feels that "trained listeners" have a greater preference for complex melodies than naïve listeners.

(B) Neither author would agree that more knowledgeable listeners tend to prefer music that is discontinuous and unpredictable. Rather, Passage A's author highly values continuous sound to induce a positive listening experience, and Passage B's author believes that the listener should be able to match expectations to the actual course of music.

(C) The artistic value of music is never discussed by either author. Rather, the passages focus on how and why those strong emotional responses from listeners are elicited.

(E) The volume of music—softness versus loudness—is never discussed in either passage.

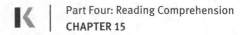

These explanations refer to
questions that begin on page 910.

Philosophical Anarchism

Step 1: Read the Passage Strategically

Sample Roadmap

Most people acknowledge that not all
governments have a moral right to govern and that
there are sometimes morally legitimate reasons for
disobeying the law, as when a particular law
(5) prescribes behavior that is clearly immoral. It is also
commonly supposed that such cases are special
exceptions and that, in general, the fact that
something is against the law counts as a moral, as
well as legal, ground for not doing it; i.e., we
(10) generally have a moral duty to obey a law simply
because it is the law. But the theory known as
philosophical anarchism denies this view, arguing
instead that people who live under the jurisdiction
of governments have no moral duty to those
(15) governments to obey their laws. Some commentators
have rejected this position because of what they take
to be its highly counterintuitive implications: (1) that
no existing government is morally better than any
other (since all are, in a sense, equally illegitimate),
(20) and (2) that, lacking any moral obligation to obey any
laws, people may do as they please without scruple.
In fact, however, philosophical anarchism does not
entail these claims.

First, the conclusion that no government is
(25) morally better than any other does not follow from
the claim that nobody owes moral obedience to any
government. Even if one denies that there is a moral
obligation to follow the laws of any government, one
can still evaluate the morality of the policies and
(30) actions of various governments. Some governments
do more good than harm, and others more harm than
good, to their subjects. Some violate the moral rights
of individuals more regularly, systematically, and
seriously than others. In short, it is perfectly
(35) consistent with philosophical anarchism to hold that
governments vary widely in their moral stature.

Second, philosophical anarchists maintain that all
individuals have basic, nonlegal moral duties to one
another—duties not to harm others in their lives,
(40) liberty, health, or goods. Even if governmental laws
have no moral force, individuals still have duties to
refrain from those actions that constitute crimes in the
majority of legal systems (such as murder, assault,
theft, and fraud). Moreover, philosophical anarchists
(45) hold that people have a positive moral obligation to
care for one another, a moral obligation that they
might even choose to discharge by supporting
cooperative efforts by governments to help those in
need. And where others are abiding by established
(50) laws, even those laws derived from mere conventions,
individuals are morally bound not to violate those
laws when doing so would endanger others. Thus, if

others obey the law and drive their vehicles on the
right, one must not endanger them by driving on the
(55) left, for, even though driving on the left is not
inherently immoral, it is morally wrong to
deliberately harm the innocent.

PrepTest52 Sec4 Qs20–27

Margin notes:

Common beliefs

Phil Anarchism disagrees – no moral duty to obey laws

Some reject due to 2 implications

Author disagrees with rejectors

Author rejects reason #1 – can still evaluate morality

Author rejects reason #2 – still moral duties even without laws

These explanations refer to
questions that begin on page 910.

Part Four: Reading Comprehension
Reading Comprehension Practice

Discussion

Paragraph 1 starts out with what "[m]ost people" acknowledge: while it may be morally legitimate to disobey the law in exceptional cases, people generally are morally bound to follow the law. Then, with the "[b]ut" in line 11, the author introduces the **Topic:** the theory of philosophical anarchism. According to this theory, society has no moral duty to obey government laws.

This is immediately followed by the opinion of commentators, who feel philosophical anarchism has two counterintuitive implications. The implications serve as the **Scope** of the passage. According to commentators, the first implication of philosophical anarchism is that because all governments are equally illegitimate, they are then all morally equal. The second is that people can do whatever they please. With the contrast Keyword "however" at line 22, the author's point of view appears. The author defends philosophical anarchism, saying these implications are not justified by the theory's tenets. You now know the **Purpose** of this passage, which is to defend philosophical anarchism against critics.

You can expect the author to back up his viewpoint, and he does. Paragraph 2 explains why the first implication doesn't logically follow from philosophical anarchism. Even if people are not morally bound to follow government laws, governments can still be evaluated on a moral scale. Some governments can have better moral policies and actions than others. Paragraph 3 lays out why the second implication doesn't hold water. According to philosophical anarchism, even without laws, people have a moral obligation to not only refrain from harming others but also to actively help others.

While the author argues that philosophical anarchism is unfairly criticized, he never actually gives full-fledged support for the theory. That means the **Main Idea** will be more neutral than an endorsement of philosophical anarchism. The author believes philosophical anarchism, though under fire, doesn't imply all governments are morally equal, and neither does it imply people can just do whatever they want.

48. (C) Global

Step 2: Identify the Question Type

Because this question asks for the "main point" of the entire passage, it's a Global question.

Step 3: Research the Relevant Text

Instead of researching a specific part of the passage, use your broader understanding of Topic, Scope, Purpose, and Main Idea to make your prediction.

Step 4: Make a Prediction

In a passage with multiple opinions, it's important to keep those opinions separate—especially the author's. According to the Main Idea from Step 1, the passage isn't necessarily

saying philosophical anarchism is the way to go, just that the philosophy doesn't imply what critics suggest.

Step 5: Evaluate the Answer Choices

(C) is consistent with the prediction. The author introduces commentators' two common (incorrect) conclusions in paragraph 1 and then dismisses each in paragraphs 2 and 3.

(A) distorts the point of view. While commentators believe the implications of philosophical anarchism are highly counterintuitive, the author does not call those commentators' beliefs "highly counterintuitive." Instead, he just says philosophical anarchism "does not entail these claims."

(B) distorts points of view again. As the author points out, neither of these two points is actually contrary to what philosophical anarchists claim. Commentators simply think they are.

(D) is too narrow because it focuses entirely on the author's rebuttal of the second assumed implication but completely ignores the rebuttal of the first.

(E) is a classic Half-Right, Half-Wrong answer. It starts off perfectly (as a contrast to the commentators). However, philosophical anarchism *does* conflict with the ordinary view of obeying the law because it is the law. This is not the point the author contests.

49. (A) Detail

Step 2: Identify the Question Type

This is a Detail question because it asks you to find what the author states or, in this case, "identifies."

Step 3: Research the Relevant Text

The phrase "commonly held belief" directs you to the first paragraph, where the author details what "[m]ost people acknowledge" (line 1) and what's "commonly supposed" (line 6).

Step 4: Make a Prediction

Lines 9–11 summarize the commonly held view perfectly: "we generally have a moral duty to obey a law simply because it is the law." Look for the answer choice that states or paraphrases this idea.

Step 5: Evaluate the Answer Choices

(A) is practically identical to the author's statement in the passage.

(B) is a Faulty Use of Detail. This is what commentators feel philosophical anarchism implies.

(C) falls Outside the Scope. The generally held opinion does not differentiate between laws you participate in establishing and other laws.

(D) is a 180. The general opinion is that you are morally obligated to follow the law, so breaking the law would generally be considered immoral, not morally neutral.

K | Part Four: Reading Comprehension
CHAPTER 15

These explanations refer to
questions that begin on page 910.

(E) misuses a detail from the passage. In paragraph 3, the author states that philosophical anarchists believe people have a moral duty to not harm others, but that's not necessarily a commonly held belief. Moreover, it's unknown how many existing laws do protect others from harm, so it is extreme to say a "majority" do.

50. (B) Inference (Author's Attitude)

Step 2: Identify the Question Type

The question stem asks you to characterize the author's "stance," which makes this a specific type of Inference question: one focusing on the author's attitude.

Step 3: Research the Relevant Text

There isn't one specific area where the author boldly declares his viewpoint. However, based on the Purpose and Main Idea, you can put together a prediction.

Step 4: Make a Prediction

Always begin predicting an author's attitude by first broadly determining whether it's positive, negative, or neutral. Because the author spends the majority of the passage defending philosophical anarchism, you're definitely looking for something positive. However, you should also note that the author doesn't necessarily endorse the theory; the author just says commentators' objections are invalid.

Step 5: Evaluate the Answer Choices

(B) is just moderate enough to be the right answer.

(A) is Extreme. The author finds two of the commentators' implications unjustified, but that doesn't mean he strongly approves of *most* of philosophical anarchism's ideas.

(C) is a 180. It is in line with the commentators' two assumed implications, which the author flatly denies.

(D) is also a 180. The author is defending the theory, not rejecting it, so choice **(D)** is out.

(E) is another 180. The author shows no displeasure with the theory or its logical consequences, so that eliminates choice **(E)**.

51. (A) Inference

Step 2: Identify the Question Type

When a question stem asks you what an author "most likely means" with a certain quote or reference, you're being asked to make an Inference.

Step 3: Research the Relevant Text

Going back to paragraph 1, you'll recall that the two implications are that all governments are morally equal or equally illegitimate and that people may do whatever they please.

Step 4: Make a Prediction

These implications seem to be completely against the majority opinion presented earlier in the paragraph. This would be what the commentators mean by "counterintuitive."

Step 5: Evaluate the Answer Choices

(A) is a perfect match.

(B) is a 180, as it is in line with the author's opinion, not the commentators'. Be careful of wrong answers that conflate the points of view in the passage.

(C) is a Distortion. The commentators *do* believe that philosophical anarchism has these implications. The implications just conflict with common sense. Meanwhile, the author says that logic indicates philosophical anarchism doesn't have such implications. Like choice **(B)**, this answer mixes opinions in the passage.

(D) also distorts the commentators' view. The implications are actually unrelated to one another. They just both are incompatible with common beliefs according to the commentators.

(E) is tempting, but the implications are not *internally* inconsistent, just inconsistent with common sense. At best, the author may feel this way, not the commentators themselves.

52. (B) Logic Reasoning (Principle)

Step 2: Identify the Question Type

This is an LR-Principle question because the stem asks you to take information in the passage—in this case, the broad views of the anarchists—and select the answer choice that has a specific similar scenario consistent with it. This question mimics an Apply the Principle Logical Reasoning question because the referenced lines present a "view," or principle, and the correct answer will be a specific situation that conforms to that principle.

Step 3: Research the Relevant Text

In the referenced lines, philosophical anarchists say that all people have moral duties to one another—duties not to harm others. In addition, people have a moral responsibility to avoid actions most governments consider illegal, such as murder and theft.

Step 4: Make a Prediction

You don't know exactly what the correct answer will say. However, you want to find a situation that illustrates a situation in which someone makes a moral choice to prevent causing others harm without committing widely forbidden crimes.

These explanations refer to
questions that begin on page 911.

Part Four: Reading Comprehension
Reading Comprehension Practice

Step 5: Evaluate the Answer Choices

(B) is an exact match. The executive chooses to stop dumping because doing so contaminates the water supply, something that would invariably cause harm to others. Choice **(B)** is correct.

(A) isn't a match. In this scenario, the party member is acting for her own benefit, not to prevent the harm of others. In fact, exposing other party members would likely cause them harm.

(C) doesn't match. While the person may be protecting his coworker from the harm that would result from being fired, he's still allowing the coworker to steal funds, a no-no according to philosophical anarchists.

(D) references yet another person acting in her own self-interest.

(E) is Outside the Scope of lines 37–44. While philosophical anarchists may be okay with this, this has nothing to do with the views in question, which deal with acting morally with respect to others' well-being. This answer actually relates to the discussion about conventional laws in lines 49–57.

53. (C) Inference ★★★☆

Step 2: Identify the Question Type

Even without the word "inferred," this would still be an Inference question because it asks you to find the answer choice with which "the author would be most likely to agree."

Step 3: Research the Relevant Text

The only clue from the question stem is the mention of the author. You'll need to stick closely to where the author's point of view is most clearly outlined. This probably means the last sentence of paragraph 1, or paragraphs 2 and 3 will provide support for the correct answer.

Step 4: Make a Prediction

With a vaguely worded Inference question, the best you can do is to compare the answer choices to what you know of the overall Scope, Purpose, and Main Idea. Fortunately, this author has a clear point of view throughout the passage, so you can quickly eliminate answer choices inconsistent with that view. Here, the author argues philosophical anarchism does not imply what some commentators believe; in fact, the theory says governments may be unequal morally, and people have a moral duty to not harm others.

Step 5: Evaluate the Answer Choices

(C) has evidence that can be found in lines 46–49, which says people may decide to support governmental efforts because of their moral duty to care for one another. That makes choice **(C)** the correct answer.

(A) is unsupported. You know that obeying the law is generally held to be moral, but you're not told know how much else

is generally considered moral, so you can't say whether the author thinks philosophical anarchism subjects one to more or less obligations than do commonly held beliefs.

(B) is likewise unsupported. Paragraph 2 talks about governments with different levels of morality, but the author never suggests that morally superior governments recognize that citizens can disobey the laws. Essentially, that would be saying morally superior governments are those that recognize philosophical anarchism, and while the author defends the theory, he never actually endorses it.

(D) isn't a valid inference. It's generally believed that people have a moral duty to obey the law because it is the law, but the author doesn't discuss or evaluate the arguments supporting that view. Moreover, the number of governments that have that moral right is unspecified, so "most" is Extreme.

(E) introduces the issue of enforcement. Philosophical anarchism wouldn't have any principles regarding the creation and enforcement of laws because the theory argues no one has a moral duty to obey such laws anyway.

54. (D) Logic Function ★★☆☆

Step 2: Identify the Question Type

The words at the end of the question stem ("functions primarily to") mean that you're being asked to determine what the author does with these lines, not what the author means. That makes this a Logic Function question.

Step 3: Research the Relevant Text

The text in question refers to the philosophical anarchists' belief that people have a moral duty to care for one another. The Keyword "[m]oreover" at the beginning of the sentence suggests the author is continuing a previous thought. Reading back, you can see this is all part of the author's defense against what commentators' believe is philosophical anarchism's second implication: that people can do whatever they want.

Step 4: Make a Prediction

The text in question is part of the author's defense, which says that while philosophical anarchists believe people are not morally obligated to follow the law, they still have basic, as well as positive, moral obligations to one another.

Step 5: Evaluate the Answer Choices

(D) is a great match. Not only are people required to not harm others, they actually have a moral obligation to help.

(A) is a 180. The passage says philosophical anarchists would support such efforts.

(B) falls Outside the Scope. The author implies such laws exist but doesn't mention what philosophical anarchists think about their rarity or frequency.

These explanations refer to
questions that begin on page 911.

(C) is a Distortion. The text in question suggests philosophical anarchism actually has a solid moral foundation, which isn't inconsistent with widely held beliefs. Choice **(C)** reflects what the commentators believe: that the theory is inconsistent with generally held beliefs. That opinion appears much earlier in the first paragraph. The text in question is used to support the author's defense of the theory, which appears in paragraphs 2 and 3.

(E) is the right idea with the wrong reference. This answer refers to the previous sentence (lines 40–44). And even though the two ideas are related, the text in question is not an example of an obligation to refrain from common crimes. Looking at Keywords could help you here. "Moreover" indicates the text introduces an additional idea; it doesn't illustrate the idea just presented.

55. (D) Global

Step 2: Identify the Question Type

The word "primarily" indicates a Global question. Specifically, you're asked to identify the author's primary purpose.

Step 3: Research the Relevant Text

For a Global question, there isn't a specific place in the passage to research. Instead, you'll consult your broader understanding of Topic, Scope, Purpose, and Main Idea.

Step 4: Make a Prediction

By the end of the first paragraph (lines 22–23, specifically), you can recognize that the author's Purpose is to defend political anarchism against the criticisms made by the commentators mentioned in line 15.

Step 5: Evaluate the Answer Choices

(D) comes straight from the prediction.

(A) is wrong because the author is defending the theory, not describing its origins.

(B) is a Distortion. The author defends the theory by showing how it doesn't go against common sense in the ways critics think. However, the idea of not having a moral obligation to follow the law is still against the grain. So the author doesn't quite establish all-around conformity.

(C) is a 180. The author argues the implications are fallacious, not "necessary."

(E) misses the mark because the author doesn't admit to the alleged defects of philosophical anarchism. The commentators do, but the author defends the theory against those criticisms.

These explanations refer to questions that begin on page 912.

Part Four: Reading Comprehension
Reading Comprehension Practice | K

Dental Caries and Archaeology

Step 1: Read the Passage Strategically

Sample Roadmap

Passage A

Because dental caries (decay) is strongly linked to consumption of the sticky, carbohydrate-rich staples of agricultural diets, prehistoric human teeth can provide clues about when a population made the transition
(5) from a hunter-gatherer diet to an agricultural one. Caries formation is influenced by several factors, including tooth structure, bacteria in the mouth, and diet. In particular, caries formation is affected by carbohydrates' texture and composition, since carbohydrates more readily stick to teeth.

Cavities linked to carbs—

clue of agri. development

(10) Many researchers have demonstrated the link between carbohydrate consumption and caries. In North America, Leigh studied caries in archaeologically derived teeth, noting that caries rates differed between indigenous populations that primarily consumed meat
(15) (a Sioux sample showed almost no caries) and those heavily dependent on cultivated maize (a Zuni sample had 75 percent carious teeth). Leigh's findings have been frequently confirmed by other researchers, who have shown that, in general, the greater a population's
(20) dependence on agriculture is, the higher its rate of caries formation will be.

North Am. ex.

More agri = more cavities

Under some circumstances, however, nonagricultural populations may exhibit relatively high caries rates. For example, early nonagricultural
(25) populations in western North America who consumed large amounts of highly processed stone-ground flour made from gathered acorns show relatively high caries frequencies. And wild plants collected by the Hopi included several species with high cariogenic
(30) potential, notably pinyon nuts and wild tubers.

Exception: gatherers who ate acorns & cavity-causing plants

Passage B

Archaeologists recovered human skeletal remains interred over a 2,000-year period in prehistoric Ban Chiang, Thailand. The site's early inhabitants appear to have had a hunter-gatherer-cultivator economy. Evidence indicates that, over time, the
(35) population became increasingly dependent on agriculture.

Thai Ex.

Group went from H/G to Agri

Research suggests that agricultural intensification results in declining human health, including dental
(40) health. Studies show that dental caries is uncommon in pre-agricultural populations. Increased caries frequency may result from increased consumption of starchy-sticky foodstuffs or from alterations in tooth wear. The wearing down of tooth crown surfaces reduces caries
(45) formation by removing fissures that can trap food particles. A reduction of fiber or grit in a diet may

Agri = ↓ health

Cavities more freq—why

diminish tooth wear, thus increasing caries frequency. However, severe wear that exposes a tooth's pulp
(50) cavity may also result in caries.

The diet of Ban Chiang's inhabitants included some cultivated rice and yams from the beginning of the period represented by the recovered remains. These were part of a varied diet that also included
(55) wild plant and animal foods. Since both rice and yams are carbohydrates, <increased reliance on either or both should theoretically result in increased caries frequency.>

Thai group ate grains/ rice

should show cavities

Yet comparisons of caries frequency in the Early and Late Ban Chiang Groups indicate that overall
(60) caries frequency is slightly greater in the Early Group. Tooth wear patterns do not indicate tooth wear changes between Early and Late Groups that would explain this unexpected finding. It is more likely that, although dependence on agriculture increased, the diet
(65) in the Late period remained varied enough that no single food dominated. Furthermore, there may have been a shift from sweeter carbohydrates (yams) toward rice, a less cariogenic carbohydrate.

But cavities ↓

Prob b/c diet was varied; yams < rice

PrepTest62 Sec1 Qs15–21

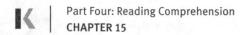
Discussion

Comparative Reading will test the similarities and differences between the two passages, so it's wise to be on the lookout for them from the outset. Each passage will be similar in terms of Topic and Scope, but the authors' Purposes and Main Ideas will likely vary.

Passage A introduces the link between dental caries (tooth decay) and carbohydrate-rich agricultural diets. This **Topic,** it turns out, is useful to researchers trying to determine when a population transitioned from relying on hunting and gathering to farming, especially because of the way carbohydrates stick to teeth, as the first paragraph mentions.

In the second paragraph, the connection between caries and carbohydrates is demonstrated with an example of work done by Leigh, who studied teeth (found through archaeology) for decay. The use of dental decay evidence to assess carbohydrate consumption by various populations is the passage's **Scope.** The second paragraph concludes with the author's **Main Idea**: generally, the more a population depends on agriculture, the higher its rate of caries formation will be.

The third paragraph of Passage A presents two exceptions to this general rule, attributing the high caries rate to particular foods prevalent in the gathered diets of these nonagricultural populations.

Passage B introduces Ban Chiang, an archaeological site in Thailand, and asserts in the first paragraph that the population interred there over a span of two millennia shifted from hunting, gathering, and cultivating to an increasingly agriculture-dependent lifestyle. Note the relation of this information to that in Passage A, which said that the link between caries and agricultural diets provides clues about such a transition.

The beginning of Passage B's second paragraph echoes this, and then this paragraph explains in greater detail how starchy foods or changes in tooth wear affect the development of caries.

Returning to Ban Chiang, the third paragraph instructs that its population ate carbohydrates as part of a varied diet all along. In line with the theory presented in Passage A as well as in Passage B's second paragraph, increased reliance on foods like yams and rice should result in more caries.

The final paragraph reveals the **Main Idea**: the Ban Chiang remains defy expectations by demonstrating somewhat decreased caries. To conclude, the author offers a theory about the surprising data, suggesting that the Ban Chiang population ate a continually varied diet, even with increased use of agriculture, and perhaps in later years consumed fewer yams (the sweeter and more damaging carbohydrate) in favor of more rice.

Both passages focus on the use of dental evidence as a tool for understanding historical populations' diets and lifestyles and, more specifically, how dental caries is linked to increased reliance on agriculture.

56. (A) Global

Step 2: Identify the Question Type

Global questions in Comparative Reading passages can address just one or, as here, both of the passages.

Step 3: Research the Relevant Text

No specific text should be reviewed for a Global question: consider the passages in their entireties and, because the question stem asks it, focus on what is true of both.

Step 4: Make a Prediction

Both passages study past populations, exploring the link between dental caries and reliance on agriculture. The correct answer will reflect this.

Step 5: Evaluate the Answer Choices

(A) matches the prediction, dental evidence being the "archaeological record."

(B) touches on something mentioned early in Passage B (line 40), but Passage A never mentions overall health.

(C) is too narrow, focusing only on one type of society. The passages do discuss the effects of carbohydrate-rich foods on caries formation but not just in strictly agricultural societies.

(D) is Out of Scope. No such thing as the "first agricultural society" is mentioned in either passage.

(E) is Out of Scope because the concept of to what extent carbohydrates could be obtained is never discussed.

57. (B) Detail

Step 2: Identify the Question Type

When a question mentions specific things "discussed" in a passage, that's a Detail question.

Step 3: Research the Relevant Text

Comparative Detail questions require checking both passages for the relevant information. This question stem points out the last paragraph of Passage A, but the first, third, and last paragraphs of Passage B should also be consulted.

Step 4: Make a Prediction

The right answer will reflect the contrast between the two populations. Those discussed at the end of Passage A were nonagricultural societies that ate gathered foods, but the Ban Chiang people were increasingly reliant on agriculture and always ate some cultivated foods.

Step 5: Evaluate the Answer Choices

These explanations refer to questions that begin on page 913.

Part Four: Reading Comprehension
Reading Comprehension Practice

(B) does the job.

(A) and **(C)** are 180s. The populations in the last paragraphs of Passage A did in fact eat cariogenic foods, including plenty of carbohydrates.

(C) is also Extreme because the Ban Chiang's diet was "varied," not *primarily* carbohydrates.

(D) is Out of Scope, as tooth wear is not discussed in Passage A.

(E) is a Distortion and a 180. Although Ban Chiang peoples were agriculturally dependent, food processing is not mentioned anywhere in Passage B. Furthermore, the first group mentioned in Passage A did consume "highly processed stone-ground flour."

58. (A) Inference

Step 2: Identify the Question Type

The phrase "strongly supports" is a typical Inference question marker.

Step 3: Research the Relevant Text

Comparative Reading question sets rarely include a question like this one, focusing on only one passage. Passage B mentions fiber and grit at line 47, but, for context, start a bit earlier, around line 42.

Step 4: Make a Prediction

The answer must be true based on the information given. The passage states that reducing fiber and grit would diminish tooth wear, suggesting that fiber and grit actually contribute to tooth wear. While some tooth wear helps prevent caries by eliminating surface food traps, too much wear exposes dental pulp, which could promote caries.

Step 5: Evaluate the Answer Choices

(A) is correct.

(B) and **(C)** are Out of Scope. Neither the typical consumption nor the nutritional value of fiber and grit is mentioned.

(D) mentions "fissures" which presents a combined Faulty Use of Detail/180 trap. It's suggested that fiber and grit actually remove fissures, not form them.

(E) is another Faulty Use of Detail, attempting to trigger memory about sticky carbohydrates mentioned elsewhere in the passage.

59. (B) Detail

Step 2: Identify the Question Type

The question asks about something "mentioned" in both passages. This is a Detail question that requires careful research.

Step 3: Research the Relevant Text

The question asks for stated evidence that supports the prevailing view regarding the effect of carbohydrates on caries. Research evidence for this view is provided in the second paragraph of both passages.

Step 4: Make a Prediction

The evidence used in Passage A is Leigh's study, which found little caries in primarily meat-eating populations and much caries in agricultural ones. The studies mentioned in Passage B as evidence (lines 41–42) indicate the uncommonness of caries in pre-agricultural societies. So, both passages provide evidence of populations that don't rely primarily on agriculture and display low levels of caries.

Step 5: Evaluate the Answer Choices

(B) matches the prediction perfectly.

(A) mentions highly processed foods, a topic never discussed in Passage B.

(C), (D), and **(E)** mention subject matter (fiber and grit, tooth wear, and overall health, respectively) discussed only in Passage B.

60. (D) Inference

Step 2: Identify the Question Type

"[M]ost likely" signals an Inference question.

Step 3: Research the Relevant Text

There is little in this question stem to guide specific research: both passages say a lot about dental caries throughout.

Step 4: Make a Prediction

Because of the lack of a strong content clue, this question requires the time-consuming task of checking each answer choice against the passages. The answer must be true for both passages!

Step 5: Evaluate the Answer Choices

(D) is supported in the final paragraphs of both Passage A and Passage B. In each case, anomalies in the usual correlation between agricultural dependence and dental caries are described.

(A) is a very broad statement that distorts both passages' central idea about dental caries incidence—especially given the exceptional cases provided that defy expected predictions.

(B) is Out of Scope. Difficulties with dental caries detection is not mentioned in either passage.

(C) serves up a 180, getting the story backwards.

(E) could not be an idea with which both authors agree because only Passage B discusses tooth wear.

K Part Four: Reading Comprehension
CHAPTER 15

These explanations refer to
questions that begin on page 913.

61. (C) Inference

Step 2: Identify the Question Type

The "passage suggests" language means this is an Inference question.

Step 3: Research the Relevant Text

The question stem offers one clue: "carbohydrate-rich foods." These are mentioned in Passage A's first and third paragraphs and in Passage B in the final two paragraphs.

Step 4: Make a Prediction

As with the previous question, there is a lot of information about carbohydrate-rich foods in both passages. Instead of trying to predict the one piece of information the correct answer will use, go through the answers and check them against both passages. The correct answer will be true according to both passages.

Step 5: Evaluate the Answer Choices

(C) reflects the varying cariogenic potential of different carbohydrates, as provided at lines 28–31 in Passage A and lines 67–68 of Passage B.

(A) and **(E)** are Out of Scope. Neither passage compares wild carbohydrates to cultivated ones in terms of cariogenic potential.

(B) is wrong because substantial processing is never mentioned in Passage B.

(D) is wrong because the issue of tooth wear is not discussed in Passage A.

62. (D) Logic Reasoning (Method of Argument)

Step 2: Identify the Question Type

The question asks to relate evidence from one passage to a generalization stated in the other. Kaplan treats such Comparative Reading problems similarly to Method of Argument problems found in Logical Reasoning.

Step 3: Research the Relevant Text

The stem provides one specific reference to lines 20–22: this is the assertion that a population more dependent on agriculture is more likely to demonstrate a higher rate of caries formation. The Ban Chiang population's caries formation is revealed in the final paragraph of Passage B.

Step 4: Make a Prediction

The Ban Chiang population defied expectations by demonstrating decreased caries frequency when it was more agriculturally reliant, contrary to the claim from Passage A in question.

Step 5: Evaluate the Answer Choices

(D) is the accurate summation.

(A) and **(B)** are 180s, with varying degrees of certainty.

(C) fails because it ignores the clear connection between the generalization and the "unexpected finding" in Passage B.

(E) is Extreme. While the Ban Chiang result is an exception to the generalization, it doesn't necessarily disprove it.

These explanations refer to
questions that begin on page 914.

Part Four: Reading Comprehension
Reading Comprehension Practice | **K**

Inclusive Fitness Theory of Kin Recognition

Step 1: Read the Passage Strategically

Sample Roadmap

Mechanisms for recognizing kin are found throughout the plant and animal kingdoms, regardless of an organism's social or mental complexity. Improvements in the general understanding of these
(5) mechanisms have turned some biologists' attention to the question of why kin recognition occurs at all. One response to this question is offered by the inclusive fitness theory, which was developed in the 1960s. The theory is based on the realization that an organism
(10) transmits its genetic attributes to succeeding generations not solely through its offspring, but more generally through all of its close relatives. Whereas the traditional view of evolution held that natural selection favors the continued genetic representation
(15) of individuals within a species that produce the greatest number of offspring, the inclusive fitness theory posits that natural selection similarly favors organisms that help their relatives, because doing so also increases their own total genetic representation.
(20) The theory has helped to explain previously mysterious phenomena, including the evolution of social insect species like the honeybee, most of whose members do not produce offspring and exist only to nurture relatives.
(25) Inclusive fitness theory has also been applied usefully to new findings concerning cannibalism within animal species. Based on the theory, cannibals should have evolved to avoid eating their own kin because of the obvious genetic costs of such a
(30) practice. Spadefoot toad tadpoles provide an illustration. Biologists have found that all tadpoles of that species begin life as omnivores, feeding mainly on organic debris in their soon-to-be-dry pool in the desert, but that occasionally one tadpole eats another
(35) or eats a freshwater shrimp. This event can trigger changes in the tadpole's physiology and dietary preference, causing the tadpole to become larger and exclusively carnivorous, feasting on other animals including members of its own species. Yet the
(40) cannibals have a procedure of discrimination whereby they nip at other tadpoles, eating nonsiblings but releasing siblings unharmed. This suggests that the inclusive fitness theory offers at least a partial answer to why kin recognition develops. Interestingly, a
(45) cannibal tadpole is less likely to avoid eating kin when it becomes very hungry, apparently putting its own unique genetic makeup ahead of its siblings'.
But there may be other reasons why organisms recognize kin. For example, it has recently been
(50) found that tiger salamander larvae, also either omnivorous or cannibalistic, are plagued in nature by

a deadly bacterium. Furthermore, it was determined that cannibal larvae are especially likely to be infected by eating diseased species members. The fact
(55) that this bacterium is more deadly when it comes from a close relative with a similar immune system suggests that natural selection may favor cannibals that avoid such pathogens by not eating kin. For tiger salamanders then, kin recognition can be explained
(60) simply as a means by which an organism preserves its own life, not as a means to aid in relatives' survival.

PrepTest56 Sec4 Qs8–15

Side notes:

Ways of Kin Recog. are common

Bio: Why? exist
Reason: IFT

goes beyond Nat. Sel. – not just offspring; all relatives

explains honeybee evol.

IFT --> may explain cannibalism

Ex. spadefoot toad tadpoles

ensure relatives' survival

They eat w/in species, but not own kin

except when starving

Other reasons

Ex: Tiger salamander larvae

avoid eating each other

b/c it can kill them

save own life

These explanations refer to
questions that begin on page 914.

Discussion

This passage starts off with a typical LSAT contrast. Scientific understanding of how an event occurs is improving, but there's still a big question about why that event occurs. In this passage, the event is kin recognition (the **Topic** of the passage). And, as in most Natural Sciences passages, you are introduced to one explanation. In this case, the offered explanation is the inclusive fitness theory (the **Scope** of the passage). The bulk of the first paragraph gives background information on the theory: Unlike traditional theories in which natural selection favors individuals with the most offspring, the inclusive fitness theory states that animals recognize family because natural selection favors organisms that nurture their relatives. The reason is that doing so aids the success of the total genetic makeup of an organism's family. The paragraph ends by showing how this theory has already been applied to help explain honeybees that don't reproduce but exist merely to nurture relatives.

Paragraph 2 offers another application of the inclusive fitness theory, this time to species that practice cannibalism. The theory again explains why animals would want to recognize their own kin. Eating kin would be detrimental to the success of one's genetic lineage. To illustrate this, the author provides an example of spadefoot toad tadpoles. In some cases, one tadpole will accidentally eat another (or something similar), which can trigger physical changes that lead the tadpole to feast frequently on fellow tadpoles. Inclusive fitness theory holds that it's adaptive for these cannibalistic tadpoles to recognize kin so as to avoid eating relatives, which would impair their families' genetic survival. While the theory seems to apply pretty well in general, an interesting note pops up at the end of the paragraph suggesting that in extreme circumstances (when tadpoles get very hungry), tadpoles may eat siblings in order to save themselves.

The "[b]ut" at the beginning of Paragraph 3 suggests exceptions to inclusive fitness theory's ability to account for cannibalism. Sure enough, the author provides the example of tiger salamander larvae. These larvae can also become cannibalistic. However, they are also plagued by a deadly bacterium. As it turns out, it's more deadly if the larvae get it from eating family than if they get it from another source. So, unlike the tadpoles, the salamander larvae don't avoid eating kin because of the desire to maintain genetic lineage; they avoid eating kin for personal reasons—they don't want to die.

There's a lot of scientific jargon, but the key to success here is to break things down into simple language. The **Purpose** of the passage is to discuss the inclusive fitness theory and show examples of when it explains kin recognition and when it can't. With no strong author opinion, the **Main Idea** is just that the inclusive theory suggests that kin recognition improves the overall survival of an animal's genetic makeup, and while the theory explains some instances of kin recognition, other cases suggest that other explanations for kin recognition may be needed.

63. (A) Global

Step 2: Identify the Question Type

This is a typical Global question stem. The correct answer will state the author's overall "main point."

Step 3: Research the Relevant Text

There's no reason to reread the text for Global questions. You've summarized the author's Purpose and Main Idea as part of your strategic reading. Structural Keywords often provide a pretty accurate basis for answering Main Idea questions in passages like this one without a strong authorial opinion. The passage begins with an introduction of a theory that "posits" (line 17) that kin recognition developed to aid an organism's total genetic representation. The theory is then applied to honeybees (lines 20–24) and tadpoles (Paragraph 2). The "[b]ut" in line 48 really drives home the final point—the inclusive theory can't explain everything (particularly not the salamander larvae).

Step 4: Make a Prediction

The correct answer will match your Main Idea summary: inclusive fitness (the theory that adaptive behavior improves the survival of an organism's gene pool, not just itself) can explain the adaptive value of some, but not all, examples of kin recognition in the animal kingdom.

Step 5: Evaluate the Answer Choices

(A) is a perfect fit. This answer accurately describes the inclusive fitness theory, mentions the supporting examples, and (most importantly) mentions the fact that it doesn't necessarily explain everything.

(B) is Extreme and Outside the Scope. The passage isn't focused on the mechanisms used to recognize kin but rather on the reasons that kin recognition may be adaptive. Moreover, the passage doesn't suggest that there are as many mechanisms as there are purposes.

(C) is a 180. The salamander example more likely supports traditional evolutionary theory (as described in lines 13–16), which argues that natural selection favors the survival of individual organisms. Remember, by recognizing kin, the salamanders are looking out for themselves. The salamander research runs contrast to the inclusive fitness theory, which posits that natural section favors an organism's total genetic representation (including family).

(D) is a Faulty Use of Detail. This may be accurate, but it focuses too much on the salamander research and the traditional theory of natural selection. It completely ignores the inclusive fitness theory, which is the primary focus of the entire passage.

These explanations refer to
questions that begin on page 914.

Part Four: Reading Comprehension
Reading Comprehension Practice | **K**

(E) is Extreme. The author concludes that inclusive fitness theory explains some, *but not all,* instances of kin recognition.

64. (C) Detail

Step 2: Identify the Question Type

The categorical nature of the phrase "[t]he passage states" indicates a Detail question.

Step 3: Research the Relevant Text

Spadefoot tadpoles are described throughout the second paragraph.

Step 4: Make a Prediction

There's a lot of information, so predicting the answer may not be feasible. Instead, let's go through the answers and research only the likely candidates. In heavily detailed passages, do not answer questions based on memory because wrong answers will usually include misapplied details.

Step 5: Evaluate the Answer Choices

(C) is mentioned in lines 35–39. The eating of another tadpole can change a tadpole's dietary habits (turning it carnivorous), which causes the tadpole to become larger. That detail about a change in body size makes this answer correct.

(A) is Outside the Scope. Lines 39–42 suggest that the tadpoles can differentiate between siblings and non-siblings, but there's nothing stated about recognizing other carnivores.

(B) is a Distortion and Extreme. Lines 37–39 describe how tadpoles can grow to become exclusively carnivorous, but there's nothing about the tadpoles being selective about what kind of animals they eat.

(D) is a 180. The behavior of the tadpoles is mentioned as direct support for the inclusive fitness theory.

(E) is a Distortion. The passage does not state that the carnivorousness develops to protect the evolutionary success of the species. The passage discusses the ability to recognize kin that develops to protect the species.

65. (D) Inference

Step 2: Identify the Question Type

Contrast the directness of the wording in the stem of the previous question with the looseness of the language here. You're asked to determine what the author "would be most likely to agree with" concerning something discussed in the passage. That makes this an Inference question.

Step 3: Research the Relevant Text

Look for where "evolutionary explanations of kin recognition" are discussed. According to the author, the inclusive fitness theory "has helped to explain" (line 20) and can be "applied usefully to" (lines 25–26) some instances of kin recognition.

"But" (line 48) there may be other explanations for kin recognition.

Step 4: Make a Prediction

You may not be able to predict verbatim what the correct answer will say, but look for the answer choice that must be true based on the information you gathered during Step 3.

Step 5: Evaluate the Answer Choices

(D) essentially paraphrases the passage.

(A) is a 180. According to the first paragraph, understanding of mechanisms has increased despite a lack of explanation for why kin recognition occurs.

(B) is yet another 180. Lines 12–19 directly show how the inclusive fitness theory runs in contrast to the traditional evolutionary theory.

(C) is Outside the Scope. There is no suggestion on the author's part that theories need to ignore any characteristics of any organisms.

(E) is Outside the Scope and a tad Extreme. The author doesn't mention any current theories outside of the inclusive fitness theory. However, by virtue of the last paragraph conflicting with the inclusive fitness theory, it's evident that the author does not find that theory to be entirely successful.

66. (A) Logic Function

Step 2: Identify the Question Type

This question stem asks for the function of a particular part of the passage, so it's a Logic Function question. Focus on what the author's *doing* as opposed to *saying*.

Step 3: Research the Relevant Text

To understand the function of the last sentence of the second paragraph, you need to remember the function of everything that came before it. The bulk of the second paragraph was about the tadpoles that avoided eating siblings in order to improve the survival of their genetic lineage. This example was provided in support of the inclusive fitness theory.

Step 4: Make a Prediction

However, the last sentence begins with "[i]nterestingly," suggesting that not all is as it seems. Sure enough, just as you're being led to believe that tadpoles would spare family members to protect the genes, you learn that some tadpoles will eat their siblings after all—so as not to die from hunger. So, the author uses this sentence to provide an instance that goes contrary to the other evidence, making the inclusive fitness theory seem inapplicable in certain cases.

Step 5: Evaluate the Answer Choices

(A) is a perfect match. Just as you were being lulled into believing that the inclusive fitness theory was a winner, along comes this fact that throws a monkey wrench into the system.

Part Four: Reading Comprehension
CHAPTER 15

These explanations refer to questions that begin on page 915.

(B) is Outside the Scope. The fact in the last sentence is referring only to the spadefoot toad tadpoles and makes no comparison to other species.

(C) is a 180. The Keyword "[i]nterestingly" means that the last sentence will probably run contrary to everything that came before it.

(D) is Extreme. While the sentence in question may undermine the validity of the inclusive fitness theory, it doesn't necessarily make the tadpoles' behavior unexplainable. In fact, it is explained—they're very hungry and are more interested in saving themselves.

(E) is another 180. The information that precedes the last sentence is not less relevant. It's plenty relevant as support for why the inclusive fitness theory is plausible.

67. (A) Inference ★★★★

Step 2: Identify the Question Type

Any question stem asking you to find what the passage "most strongly supports" is an Inference question.

Step 3: Research the Relevant Text

The mechanism of a tadpole for recognizing kin is described in lines 39–42. It involves nipping at other tadpoles to determine whether they are siblings or not.

Step 4: Make a Prediction

From this information, it's possible to determine several statements that must be true. However, only one such statement will be in the answer choices. Keep that in mind as you evaluate them.

Step 5: Evaluate the Answer Choices

(A) is definitely supported by the information in the passage. Nipping on other tadpoles is not a visual act, so the mechanism seems to be at least partially based on taste or touch.

(B) is Outside the Scope. You know this is the behavior of cannibalistic tadpoles, but you don't know what non-cannibalistic tadpoles do. For all you know, they may nip at other tadpoles, too. In fact, according to the passage, tadpoles can become cannibalistic after first accidentally eating another tadpole. So, it doesn't seem much of a stretch to consider that some non-carnivorous tadpoles might also nip other tadpoles.

(C) is also Outside the Scope. Based on the last sentence, you know that tadpoles will still eat siblings in extreme circumstances. However, that's not because the mechanism doesn't work—it's because of hunger. There's no support for this.

(D) is a 180. The tadpoles utilize this mechanism after changing physiologically and becoming carnivorous.

(E) is another 180. Lines 31–32 states that all of these tadpoles start life as omnivores. Furthermore, you don't have any information about other species beyond the tadpoles, so you can't infer this.

68. (B) Detail ★★★★

Step 2: Identify the Question Type

The phrase "[t]he passage states" indicates a Detail question.

Step 3: Research the Relevant Text

The question stem gives you another phrase ("the mechanisms that enable organisms to recognize . . . relatives"). "[M]echanisms" are mostly discussed early in the first paragraph.

Step 4: Make a Prediction

In fact, the answer to this question is clearly presented in lines 4–6: Improvements in understanding these mechanisms have led to questions about why they occur. Look for the correct answer to paraphrase this idea.

Step 5: Evaluate the Answer Choices

(B) is a clear match.

(A) is Outside the Scope and Extreme. The first sentence says that mechanisms exist throughout the animal kingdom, regardless of complexity. However, that doesn't mean that you should assume they have a similar purpose in *all* species. In fact, by the two examples in the second and third paragraph, you get the sense that mechanisms can serve multiple purposes.

(C) is a Distortion. Some people might be tempted by this because it uses "1960s" from the passage. However, the 1960s is only when the inclusive fitness theory was developed. For all you know, there were many other theories developed long before the 1960s.

(D) is Outside the Scope. While the passage may suggest that there is not a full explanation of their purpose, the author never states that this is because there is not more understanding of the mechanisms.

(E) is also Outside the Scope. While the passage may discuss different purposes for the mechanisms, there's no description of how similarly or differently the mechanisms operate.

69. (E) Inference ★★★★

Step 2: Identify the Question Type

Because this question asks about what the passage suggests rather than what it directly states, it's an Inference question.

Step 3: Research the Relevant Text

The honeybees were mentioned at the end of the first paragraph.

Step 4: Make a Prediction

According to the paragraph, the honeybees' behavior of nurturing relatives was "previously mysterious," but the inclusive fitness theory helped explain it. You want an answer choice that's consistent with this prediction.

These explanations refer to
questions that begin on page 915.

Part Four: Reading Comprehension
Reading Comprehension Practice

Step 5: Evaluate the Answer Choices

(E) is the correct answer. The honeybees' behavior was mysterious under traditional theories, so some supplement (in this case, the inclusive fitness theory) was needed to dispel some of the mystery.

(A) is a Distortion. The behavior was known, it was just unexplained.

(B) is Outside the Scope. There's no discussion of this kind of reciprocal nurturing.

(C) is Extreme. While the new theory helps to explain this behavior, the behavior was simply described as previously mysterious. This suggests the behavior was merely an enigma and not necessarily a catalyst for fully rejecting the traditional theory.

(D) is a Distortion. The inclusive fitness theory (which helps explain the honeybees' behavior) still states that evolution proceeds by natural selection—just in a different way from what traditional theories state.

70. (C) Logic Reasoning (Weaken) ★★★☆

Step 2: Identify the Question Type

The language of this question stem is almost identical to that of a Weaken question in the Logical Reasoning section. The correct answer will be a fact that makes the author's conclusion less likely to follow from the evidence presented. The research clue here is clear: Your task is to weaken the author's final statement.

Step 3: Research the Relevant Text

Classic ways of weakening arguments in Logical Reasoning will work equally effectively in Reading Comprehension Logic Reasoning questions. In the last sentence, the author concludes that kin recognition in tiger salamanders can be explained as a means for preserving their own lives and not as a means for aiding their relatives' survival. While the evidence regarding the deadly bacterium definitely supports kin recognition being used to preserve the individual, there is no evidence to say that kin recognition is not used to aid relatives' survival. The author overlooks the possibility that kin recognition may serve to protect oneself *and* one's relatives.

Step 4: Make a Prediction

To weaken the claim, the correct answer choice will show a way in which the tiger salamander's use of kin recognition protects an individual with which the predator salamander shares genetic material.

Step 5: Evaluate the Answer Choices

(C) gives a fact that would weaken the author's claim. If this were true, then kin recognition would provide a way for salamanders to protect their offspring, making kin recognition valuable beyond survival of the individual. By protecting

potential family, this weakens the author's claim that this case of kin recognition is exclusively self-serving. It's good to note for this question that the correct answer is the only one that focuses on kin recognition, the topic of the argument the question asks us to weaken.

(A) is Outside the Scope. What's relevant is not whether the disease affects cannibalistic or non-cannibalistic salamanders but whether or not it affects kin and kin recognition.

(B) is also Outside the Scope. It discusses what makes salamanders carnivorous or omnivorous, but it has no bearing on why salamanders recognize kin.

(D) is a Distortion. It misapplies some information from the first paragraph about the number of offspring (part of the traditional evolutionary view). However, once again, the number of offspring a salamander has is not directly relevant to the reason for being able to recognize kin.

(E) Is Outside the Scope. Even if this were true, according to the passage, the salamanders are still immune to the one deadly bacterium that's mentioned. The author uses this evidence because that particular bacterium is more deadly to the individual when consumed through kin. Greater immunity to *other* diseases isn't relevant to kin recognition.

These explanations refer to questions that begin on page 916.

Animal Conflict Behavior

Step 1: Read the Passage Strategically

Sample Roadmap

Traditional theories of animal behavior assert that
animal conflict within a species is highly ritualized
and does not vary from contest to contest. This
species-specific model assumes that repetitive use of

(5) the same visual and vocal displays and an absence of
escalated fighting evolved to prevent injury. The
contestant that exhibits the "best" display wins the
contested resource. Galápagos tortoises, for instance,
settle contests on the basis of height: the ritualized

(10) display consists of two tortoises facing one another
and stretching their necks skyward; the tortoise
perceived as being "taller" wins.

Trad. animal conflict theory – ritualized; no variation – prevents injury

Ex – Gal. tortoise

In populations of the spider *Agelenopsis aperta*,
however, fighting behavior varies greatly from contest

(15) to contest. In addition, fighting is not limited to
displays: biting and shoving are common. Susan
Riechert argues that a recently developed model,
evolutionary game theory, provides a closer fit to
A. aperta territorial disputes than does the species-

(20) specific model, because it explains variations in
conflict behavior that may result from varying
conditions, such as differences in size, age, and
experience of combatants. Evolutionary game theory
was adapted from the classical game theory that was

(25) developed by von Neumann and Morganstern to
explain human behavior in conflict situations. In both
classical and evolutionary game theory, strategies are
weighed in terms of maximizing the average payoff
against contestants employing both the same and

(30) different strategies. For example, a spider may engage
in escalated fighting during a dispute only if the
disputed resource is valuable enough to warrant the
risk of physical injury. There are, however, two major
differences between the classical and evolutionary

(35) theories. First, whereas in classical game theory it is
assumed that rational thought is used to determine
which action to take, evolutionary game theory
assumes that instinct and long-term species advantage
ultimately determine the strategies that are exhibited.

(40) The other difference is in the payoffs: in classical
game theory, the payoffs are determined by an
individual's personal judgment of what constitutes
winning; in evolutionary game theory, the payoffs are
defined in terms of reproductive success.

(45) In studying populations of *A. aperta* in a
grassland habitat and a riparian habitat, Riechert
predicts that such factors as the size of the opponents,
the potential rate of predation in a habitat, and the
probability of winning a subsequent site if the dispute

(50) is lost will all affect the behavior of spiders in
territorial disputes. In addition, she predicts that the
markedly different levels of competition for web sites

Spider exception

Riechert – evolutionary game theory better exp.

Similarities with classic game theory

2 differences

Instinct over rational thought

Payoffs – reproductive success

Richert predictions

in the two habitats will affect the spiders' willingness
to engage in escalated fighting. In the grassland,

(55) where 12 percent of the habitat is available for
occupation by *A. aperta*, Riechert predicts that
spiders will be more willing to engage in escalated
fighting than in the riparian habitat, where 90 percent
of the habitat is suitable for occupation.

More willing to fight when good habitat scarce

PrepTest52 Sec4 Qs13–19

These explanations refer to questions that begin on page 916.

Part Four: Reading Comprehension
Reading Comprehension Practice

Discussion

Paragraph 1 introduces the "[t]raditional theories" of animal conflicts within species—visual and vocal displays evolved to reduce injuries during contests. The Galápagos tortoises are provided as an example. So you have the **Topic**: conflict behavior in animals. Of course, rarely does an LSAT passage provide a "traditional" theory without contrasting it with a newfangled theory.

As anticipated, paragraph 2 introduces a counterexample of the spider *A. aperta*, which is sometimes willing to violently fight. Susan Riechert believes this behavior can be explained by evolutionary game theory, which states that animals' fighting may escalate if the prize is sufficiently important. This gives you your **Scope**: differing theories for animal conflict. The second half of paragraph 2 discusses the two differences between evolutionary game theory (for animals) and its predecessor, classical game theory (for humans). First, in classical theory, the level of fighting is decided based on rational thought, while in evolutionary theory the decision is based on instinct. Second, classical theory says the value of the payoff is based on personal judgment, but evolutionary theory says it's based on what's better for reproduction.

The author's opinion on this theory still hasn't appeared, and paragraph 3 doesn't introduce one. Instead, the paragraph discusses how Riechert uses the new theory to predict how *A. aperta* spiders would behave in two different habitats: grassland and riparian. In fact, paragraph 3 has three sentences and the verb in each of them is "predict." [So, when you come across the inevitable question about Paragraph 3, you can already bet that its predictions will be involved in the answers.] Based on the evolutionary game theory, Riechert believes spiders will be more willing to engage in escalated fighting in the grassland because a smaller percentage of land is suitable for occupation and thus territory is more valuable.

Without an author's opinion, the **Purpose** of this passage is purely to introduce the new theory, and the **Main Idea** is that the new theory may explain the fighting behavior of certain animals, notably the *A. aperta*.

71. (C) Global ★★★★

Step 2: Identify the Question Type

Any question seeking the "main idea" of the passage is definitely a Global question.

Step 3: Research the Relevant Text

Instead of looking for lines to re-read in the passage, go back to your assessment of the big picture: Topic, Scope, Purpose, and Main Idea.

Step 4: Make a Prediction

As stated before, the Main Idea is that there's a new theory (evolutionary game theory) that may better explain some animals' conflict behavior (namely, that of the spider *A.* *aperta*) than the traditional species-specific theory.

Step 5: Evaluate the Answer Choices

(C) matches well, even though it doesn't specifically mention *A. aperta*. Notice the tentative language: "may be useful." While this passage discusses Susan Riechert's theory, it never says evolutionary game theory is a proven model.

(A) is a Distortion. While these theories are both mentioned in the passage, classical game theory is included simply to explain the origins of evolutionary game theory; it's not part of the main point. Furthermore, this answer ignores the passage's spider example.

(B) is too narrow. It leaves out evolutionary game theory and instead focuses solely on details from paragraph 3.

(D) is Extreme. The traditional theory doesn't quite fit the behavior of *A. aperta*, but that's hardly enough to say it can't explain behavior of *most* species.

(E) is a Distortion. Evolutionary game theory doesn't explain *how* spiders choose web sites, just how they will act in conflict situations (which can be triggered by territorial disputes). Additionally, though Riechert believes evolutionary game theory can be used, the rest of the scientific community is not necessarily on board.

72. (E) Logic Function ★★★☆

Step 2: Identify the Question Type

The phrase "most likely in order to" indicates a Logic Function question. The focus is not on what the author says about the Galápagos tortoises but *why* the author introduces them in the first place.

Step 3: Research the Relevant Text

Examples usually come *after* the point they support, so be sure to check your Roadmap above the example for context.

Step 4: Make a Prediction

Paragraph 1 introduces the traditional theory of animal conflict: animals' fighting behavior has evolved so that conflicts don't result in injury. The Galápagos tortoise is an example of an animal whose behavior fits this theory.

Step 5: Evaluate the Answer Choices

(E) is exactly like the prediction. The Galápagos tortoise acts as evidentiary support of the statements that immediately precede it: that animals use displays to settle disputes.

(A) is a Distortion. According to the traditional species-specific theory, this kind of behavior is the norm for all animals. Even if the new theory is valid, you still don't know how many species may still fit the old theory—it could be a lot more than "only a few."

(B) is also a Distortion. The author does not mention the tortoise as an exceptional example of "some but not all" species. The author includes the tortoise as an excellent example of a species whose conflict behavior fits the classical model.

K Part Four: Reading Comprehension
CHAPTER 15

These explanations refer to
questions that begin on page 917.

(C) is another Distortion. The description of the tortoise extending its neck illustrates a *type* of contest and what it takes to win, not the consistency of that contest. Also, the traditional theory is just that: a theory. The example of one animal does not support that theory's application to "most species."

(D) is unsupported by the passage. The tortoise provides one example of a nonaggressive fighting style, but nothing suggests this display style is unique.

73. (D) Inference (EXCEPT)

Step 2: Identify the Question Type

The question stem asks you to find the answer choice that *doesn't* agree with a theory in the passage. Always characterize the answer choices so you don't accidentally choose a wrong answer.

Step 3: Research the Relevant Text

Riechert is introduced in paragraph 2, but a quick glance at the answers tells you that you want to check out her paragraph 3 predictions regarding grassland versus riparian habitats. Lines 51–59 say Riechert predicts spiders are more willing to engage in escalated fighting in the grassland (where only 12 percent of land can be occupied) than in the riparian habitat (where 90 percent of land can be occupied).

Step 4: Make a Prediction

It's impossible to know what the *least* consistent answer will say. However, you do know that four answers will fit this theory and one will not.

Step 5: Evaluate the Answer Choices

(D) sticks out as inconsistent right away. Riechert doesn't predict spiders in both habitats are equally prone to escalated fighting. **(D)** is the correct answer.

(A) fits the passage. Escalated fighting for desirable territory in the grassland agrees with Riechert.

(B) also fits. No escalated fighting for imperfect territory in the riparian habitat? Riechert would give that the thumbs-up.

(C) is consistent. Because territory in riparian areas is more plentiful, riparian spiders would be less prone to escalated fighting (i.e., more prone to displays) than grassland spiders.

(E) is consistent because it follows that if riparian spiders are less willing to engage in escalated fighting, they would be more willing to withdraw.

74. (E) Logic Function

Step 2: Identify the Question Type

Any question asking you to determine the function of a detail, quote, reference, or entire paragraph is a Logic Function question. Focus on the "why" or the "how," not the "what."

Step 3: Research the Relevant Text

The entirety of paragraph 3 has to be assessed. It could take a long time to re-read the entire paragraph, so this is where your Roadmap—especially any margin notes—will come in handy.

Step 4: Make a Prediction

Looking at your Roadmap should tell you paragraph 3 is all about Riechert's predictions—based on the recently introduced evolutionary game theory—for *A. aperta* in riparian and grassland habitats.

Step 5: Evaluate the Answer Choices

(E) is the only answer to mention these predictions and is therefore correct.

(A) is a Distortion. While evolutionary game theory was introduced in the preceding paragraph, the species-specific theory was introduced in paragraph 1. Additionally, paragraph 3 doesn't compare the two theories; it describes behavior that could be expected if the new theory is true.

(B) is Extreme. The author never states that evolutionary game theory (which, incidentally, was only described in paragraph 2, not the first two paragraphs) is controversial.

(C) is a Distortion. Paragraph 3 describes predictions, not an actual experiment.

(D) makes the same mistake. Paragraph 3 does not describe actual observed behavior. It's all predictions. Granted, paragraph 2 actually presents behavior that the theory in paragraph 1 can't account for, but this question is concerned with paragraph 3.

75. (B) Inference

Step 2: Identify the Question Type

Because this question asks for what the passage "suggests" rather than what it states, this is an Inference question.

Step 3: Research the Relevant Text

Be sure not to confuse anticipated results with actual observations. Remember that paragraph 3 refers to what Riechert *predicts* these spiders would do. That doesn't tell you what the passage suggests about their actual behavior. For that, you have to check paragraph 2—specifically, lines 13–23 and lines 30–33.

Step 4: Make a Prediction

Lines 13–23 say *A. aperta* spiders' fighting behavior is violent and varies from contest to contest, possibly because of differences in size, age, and experience. Lines 30–33 explain spiders may escalate their fighting only when the prize in dispute is sufficiently valuable. The correct answer choice will be consistent with this information.

EXPLANATIONS

These explanations refer to
questions that begin on page 917.

Part Four: Reading Comprehension
Reading Comprehension Practice | K

Step 5: Evaluate the Answer Choices

(B) matches. If *A. aperta* fights will escalate only if a resource is valuable, then you can infer the contrapositive: if a resource isn't valuable, fights won't escalate.

(A) is Extreme and a Distortion. Riechert *predicts* that site availability factors into spiders' fights, but the passage doesn't give any evidence to show it is an actual factor, let alone the primary one.

(C) is Extreme. While the *A. aperta* spider exhibits variations in fighting behavior, traditional theories assert that conflict within a species does *not* vary from contest to contest. The spiders, then, are not necessarily similar to "most" other species.

(D) is a Distortion. The passage says that the level of fighting varies from contest to contest, but nothing in the passage suggests which is more frequent: aggressive or nonaggressive.

(E) is too Extreme. You don't know which species, or how many species, are similar or dissimilar to *A. aperta*. So, saying *A. aperta* is more willing to fight than "most" other species is too extreme.

76. (A) Global ★★☆☆

Step 2: Identify the Question Type

The words "primary purpose" indicate this is a Global question.

Step 3: Research the Relevant Text

You can't research a specific part of the passage for a Global question. Instead, revisit the Topic, Scope, Purpose, and Main Idea to form the basis of your prediction. Keep an eye on the author's tone.

Step 4: Make a Prediction

This author introduced the new theory but never really had a strong opinion one way or the other.

Step 5: Evaluate the Answer Choices

(A) is an exact match. The verb "present" is consistent with the author's neutral tone.

(B) is a Distortion. While examples of a phenomenon are provided, this is not the author's Purpose. Those examples are provided to illustrate the new theory.

(C) mischaracterizes the author's tone. The author does no evaluation. This is simply a descriptive passage.

(D) is Extreme. While the *A.aperta* doesn't quite fit the traditional theory, the passage never suggests that the traditional theory is entirely refuted or is "controversial."

(E) is also a Distortion. The author doesn't suggest that the new theory may be inadequately supported. No critique is evident.

CHAPTER 16

Reading Comprehension: Managing the Section

INTRODUCTION

The layout of the Reading Comprehension section is very similar to the layout of the Logic Games section. In Reading Comprehension, there are four passages and the test taker has 35 minutes to complete the section. Superficially, the only difference is that while the Logic Games section has 22–24 questions, with 5–7 per game, the Reading Comprehension section has 26–28 questions and 5–8 questions per passage. This means that the test taker is required to do even more work in the same amount of time, which is no small feat. The time crunch leaves most test takers feeling out of control, as though the test is in charge and they are along for the ride.

This is why the highest scorers on the LSAT are not simply the folks who understand the content the best. Generally the difference between a good score and a great one is the difference between a good test taker and a great test taker. A great test taker understands how to look at a section both as a collection of individual questions and as a whole section of 26–28 questions. You may or may not have historically been a great test taker. Up until now, odds are no one has had any particular interest in making you great at it. Usually the people who talk to you about tests are the ones who wrote them, and your high school social studies teacher was not about to give you tips on which questions she wrote that were worth answering and which ones you should skip. Things have changed now, however, because you're learning the methods and strategies in this book. Today, you are on your way to being the test taker that everyone wishes they could be. To control the Reading Comprehension section, you need to understand how it's constructed.

LEARNING OBJECTIVES

In this chapter, you'll learn to:

- · Prioritize passages and questions to maximize the number of questions you get right.
- · Allocate your time efficiently to reading the passage and reading and researching each question.
- · Recognize when you should spend more time on a passage or question, as well as when you should skip a question altogether.

MASTERING READING COMPREHENSION

First, it is worth noting that the difficulty levels of Reading Comprehension passages are fairly consistent across tests. Each section will tend to have one easier passage, one challenging passage, and two passages that are somewhere in between. What changes, test to test, is the order in which these passages are presented. Test takers more often than not find that the easiest of the passages will be one of the first two and that the most challenging passage will be one of the last two. Beyond that, however, the specific ordering of the passages varies from test to test. Muddying the waters further is the fact that the individual questions themselves do not line up neatly with the difficulty of the passage. Much as they do in the Logic Games section, the testmaker distributes easy and challenging questions among each of the passages, which means that no one passage can be counted on as a slam dunk, and no one passage should be entirely written off.

Scoring in Reading Comprehension is the same as on the rest of the exam: Each question is worth one point, and there is no penalty for guessing. Do not be fooled by the simplicity of that statement, however. When it comes to the scoring on the LSAT, keep in mind that you can miss a question for one of two reasons: content or management. Most students understand the content side of things: if you don't know how to answer a particular question type or how to recognize a common wrong answer pattern, then you are likely to miss questions. Great test takers, however, also understand that the way you manage a question can affect not only that question but also those later in the section.

> ## SUGGESTED EXERCISE
>
> Whenever you review a timed RC exercise, make a list with two columns. The first column is for the "silly mistakes"—the questions you feel you missed for reasons other than content—like rushing, misreading, etc. The second column is for the questions you missed because there was something you just didn't know at the time—that is, for content reasons like failing to spot something as Out of Scope or not being certain of the Method. For each question you missed, put it into one of the columns. This is a great way to get an idea how many of the questions you missed are due to content issues and how many are management related. If there are a lot in the first column, then you need a heavy focus on section management. If they are mostly in the second column, then you have some content work to do first!

Managing the Questions

When dealing with an individual question, you can either get it right or wrong, and you can do so quickly or slowly. You understand intuitively that the best possible outcome for a question is to get it right quickly and the worst possible outcome is to get it wrong slowly. But what about getting a question right slowly or wrong quickly? Which one do you think is better? The correct answer is that, generally, it is better to get a question wrong quickly than it is to get it right slowly.

If this surprises you, imagine that you are working on question 10 in a section and you take so long doing it that it keeps you from getting to question 24, which you would have answered correctly. *If* you answer question 10 correctly, you will get that point, but you will lose the point from question 24. At the end of the day, it is a wash: you sacrificed a later point for an earlier one. Your score would have been the same either way.

But now imagine that you answer question 10 incorrectly. There is no penalty for answering a question incorrectly, so you simply do not get a point. But remember that you spent so much time on question 10 that you will not grab the point from question 24. You have traded in a question you would have answered correctly for a question you answered incorrectly. By spending so much time on question 10, you have effectively *lowered* your LSAT score. Now imagine you spend so much time on question 10 that it keeps you from getting to *two* later questions you would have answered correctly: you just lost two points! This only has to happen a few times in a section to put a serious dent in your score.

If that same test taker instead recognizes that question 10 is going to take him longer than it should and decides to skip out of it quickly, he will have plenty of time to pick up the points from those later questions. Even though he is probably going to get question 10 wrong (but never forget that, statistically, 20 percent of even completely random guesses turn out to be right), he has lost nothing and may very well gain more points because of it. Making these smart decisions over the course of a section can make a dramatic difference in your score.

A great test taker understands that the risk-versus-reward ratio for an individual question is highly skewed on the LSAT. No one question on the LSAT is ever worth more than one point, but a single question on the LSAT can cost you several points. So, while no one question can ever make your LSAT score, it can definitely break it.

For this reason, the fundamental rule of all section management is simple: never prioritize a harder, more time-consuming question over an easier, faster one. There are enough easy- to medium-level questions to get you into the high 150s–low 160s on any given exam. The reason why the majority of test takers will never achieve these scores, let alone score above them, is that they get so bogged down in harder questions that they never get to the easier ones, or they rush through the easiest ones and make careless mistakes just so they can get to harder questions they end up missing. Everything you read in the rest of this chapter, as well as the other section management chapters, is ultimately based on this one, simple philosophy.

Triaging the Passages and the One-Minute Rule

In the Reading Comprehension section, making these smart decisions about time investment begins with putting the order of the section in your control. As mentioned previously, you have only 35 minutes to tackle 4 passages of variable difficulty. Because the passages are not always printed in order of difficulty, however, harder passages may come before easier passages. Tackling the passages in an order based purely on where they fall in the section is potentially risky. If you do not end up getting to all of your passages, the one you skip might have yielded more points than one of the passages you did get to. Likewise, starting off with a passage that you find particularly challenging can trigger anxiety that can be hard to recover from. Being in control means doing things in the order that is best for *you,* not the order predetermined by the testmaker.

Learning to *triage* your passages will help you avoid these problems. In its most basic form, triaging a passage means quickly determining whether the passage is likely to be easier or harder. The quick and dirty way of figuring this out is to *very* briefly skim the introductory paragraph of a passage and then to glance at the first sentences of the other paragraphs. If you have some sense of what the passage is about and how it is organized, then it is probably a good passage to do up front. If you have only a vague sense of what is going on in the passage, then it is probably worth skipping the passage for now to see if any of the later passages in the section feel more manageable. This tactic works best when the passage has at least three paragraphs.

When you scan the passage, you are assessing three things:

· Language
· Structure
· Opinions

If the language of the passage is dense and abstract, then you will more than likely struggle with the passage. On the flip side, if the language is clear and concrete, then you will likely get through the passage efficiently. The number of paragraphs and obvious Keywords are another indication as to the difficulty of the passage. Because paragraphs make it visually clear when an author has started and finished a point, passages with more paragraphs tend to be easier to follow than passages with fewer paragraphs. The same goes for Keywords. Passages with more structural Keywords are easier to follow, and those with fewer of those words are harder to summarize accurately. Finally, because the LSAT tests opinions more heavily than anything else, it will be easier to predict where the questions will come from when reading a passage with clearly marked opinions than when reading a neutral passage with few or no opinions.

In general, don't focus on the number of questions attached to a passage. Most passages have six to eight questions. On any two passages—even one with five questions and another with eight—your goal is to get as many correct answers as possible. Keep in mind that a very difficult passage with eight questions might produce no more points (and could take much more of your time) than a very easy passage with only five or six questions in its set.

There are a few ways to triage the passages in a section. The simplest method is to do the passages roughly in order but to scan each passage as you get to it to figure out whether it is to be done now or later. Another method is to do the first passage first—assuming a quick scan confirms that it does not appear too challenging—and then upon completing it to scan each of the remaining three passages to figure out the best order to do them in. This often works well because the first passage *tends* to be one of the easier ones and the last passage *tends* to be one of the harder ones. Finally, some students prefer to spend the first minute of each section looking over each of the four passages briefly and ordering them up front. There are pros and cons to each of these strategies. Practice each of these methods a few times and use the one that is most effective for you. Note, however, that triaging the section should never take longer than one minute. Spending more time than that defeats the purpose of the exercise by taking up more time than you are saving.

It is also important to keep in mind that you are not psychic, and nobody expects you to be. Even those most adept at triage are sometimes wrong. As a fail-safe, if you are a minute into a passage and you are struggling, *get out*! Tackle another passage and come back to the one you're struggling with when you've finished the rest. Triage is your best guess at the difficulty level of the passages, but it is not set in stone. Your job on the LSAT is to keep moving. If one passage is harder than you thought it would be, there is a chance that another is easier than you expected. Go find it.

SUGGESTED EXERCISE

Whenever you triage a Reading Comprehension section, make sure you record the order in which you do the passages somewhere in the section. While you review the section, spend some time considering your triage order. If you could do it all again, would you have stuck to the same order? If not, what order would you have done the passages in, and using the checklist from above, how could you have known that was the best order up front?

The 8- to 9-Minute Rule

While you will generally have an easier time answering questions from easier passages than you will those from harder ones, remember that each of the passages is accompanied by a mix of easier questions and harder questions. It is to most test takers' advantage to get to those easier questions on each of the four passages, which means learning not to spend so much time on one passage that you are unable to get to another.

Here's why the 8- to 9-Minute Rule was invented. Subtracting approximately a minute for passage triage, you have about 34 minutes left to tackle your four passages. Divided evenly, this means you have approximately 8–9 minutes for each of those passages. The 8- to 9-Minute Rule is simple: *never spend more than eight or nine minutes on a passage if there are still passages you have not yet started.* Following the 8- to 9-Minute Rule ensures that you have an adequate amount of time to tackle the lion's share of questions in any given passage without sacrificing your ability to get the easier points from the other passages. Just as spending too much time on any one question can cost you more points down the line, spending too much time on any one passage can cost you. Your harder passages should generally be allotted more time than your easier passages. Start by giving yourself eight minutes for your two easier/earlier passages and nine minutes for your two later/harder passages. As you get better at managing your section, you may find that you need less time for the easier passages and can then spend more time on the later passages. Many test takers, however, find the 8/8/9/9 division to be their sweet spot. At first, following the 8- to 9-Minute Rule is likely to be challenging. But rest assured, mastering it is vital to your success on Test Day, and setting these time limits in advance will help you to become more efficient both in Roadmapping and answering questions.

Prioritizing Questions Over the Passage

To make the most of the 8- to 9-Minute Rule, it is crucial to keep in mind that the Reading Comprehension section requires a delicate balancing act between time spent reading a passage and time spent answering questions. The first instinct of most test takers is to spend as much time as they feel they need on the passage and then, with whatever time remains, to dive into the questions. As you have learned from previous chapters, you should spend about three to four minutes reading and Roadmapping a passage, leaving at least four minutes to tackle the question set. Unfortunately, many students spend significantly more time reading the passage, which means they are spending significantly less time answering the questions. In short, many test takers are prioritizing the *passage* over the *questions*. Years of reading for high school and college classes makes it feel as though this type of reading will make answering the questions easier, but this strategy tends to backfire for two reasons.

First, the human brain can only hold so much information at once in short-term memory. Picture your memory as an empty glass. What happens when someone pours more water into it than it can hold? Either the excess water has to spill over out of the glass, or the glass has to be emptied to make room for the new water. The same thing happens with your brain as you read. Reading a passage too carefully means filling your memory up quickly. This is why many students who spend too long reading only remember the first half of the passage: they fill up so fast that they cannot absorb the new information in the second half. Alternately, others can only remember the second half because they were forced to dump what they learned in the first half to make room for the rest of the passage. Either way, that student is in trouble when it comes to answering the questions.

The second reason is that the LSAT does not award points for memorizing the passage. The LSAT awards you points for answering the questions correctly. Even if you were able to read the passage carefully and retain all of the information, being the person who understands the passage best does not make you the person who scores best. The LSAT does not actually test the majority of the passage. In fact, on average, the LSAT only tests a few sentences. Most test takers read each sentence as though it has a good chance of being tested, but the opposite is true. Reading the whole passage carefully up front not only makes it harder to understand and remember what you are reading, but it also means less time to turn your reading into points. Additionally, by not trying to retain all of the information in a passage up front, you will be less likely to trick yourself into thinking you know the answer to a question without researching it.

SUGGESTED EXERCISE

If you are struggling to differentiate between trash and treasure, try out this RC post-phrasing exercise: Take a passage you haven't tried before, consult the explanations, and circle the correct answer to every non-Global question. Do a quick Roadmap as you normally would and tackle the Global questions. Then, one by one, read the answer to the remaining questions and go search backward in the passage and find out where that answer comes from. When you find it, read the explanation to be sure you are correct and then ask yourself why that piece of the passage was tested. The most common reasons are that the tested portion is someone's opinion, that it's part of a contrast, or that it's an important detail. Look for any clues, such as Keywords, that would have told you this was important enough to be tested, and write a Roadmap note that would have been helpful for you. When you are finished, put a big star next to each piece of the passage for each question that it yielded just to get a strong visual of which pieces of the passage mattered and which ones did not. Do this on occasion to help you build a sense of what matters and what doesn't.

For most test takers, the 8- to 9-Minute Rule's first benefit is helping them to realize that they are spending too much time reading the passage and not enough time earning points in the questions. Do not be alarmed if the first few times you follow the 8- to 9-Minute Rule, you end up feeling like the section is even harder: That's part of the point. Never confuse being *uncomfortable* with being *incapable*. You will not start learning to read and Roadmap more efficiently or to manage your questions better until you force yourself to deal with the timing constraints of the exam. By holding fast to the 8- to 9-Minute Rule, you will be building the foundation necessary to put you in control of your section.

Building Time Awareness

Most test takers have a hard time finishing their section, yet very few of them track their time carefully enough to figure out why. This lack of time awareness is responsible for many of the section management mistakes students make, as well as the anxiety that many students feel at the mere thought of being timed. Worse still, it is also what keeps many of these students from improving.

The simplest and most effective way to build time awareness is to incorporate timing notation into your timed Reading Comprehension work. Regardless of whether you are working on one passage or a section of four, you should always record your time at the following intervals:

· Start of Roadmap
· End of Roadmap
· When you leave the question set

This will allow you to track how much time you are spending reading the passage versus answering the actual questions. You should also check your time after two or three questions to figure out how much of your eight or nine minutes you have left before you have to move on.

Following the 8- to 9-Minute Rule makes this kind of time awareness a necessity. After all, you won't know when it's time to move on until you know how much time has passed. But these notations also give you the ability to review a section afterward to get a complete picture of why you are scoring what you are scoring. Remember that you can miss questions for content or section management reasons. Looking back over a section to see where you spent your time can help you determine which section management issues are affecting your overall score. Are you spending so much time reading that you do not have enough time to answer more than one or two questions? Are you reading the passage in a reasonable amount of time but getting so bogged down in one or two questions that you cannot get to the rest? Recording your timing intervals will take the guesswork out of determining your individual section management hurdles.

SUGGESTED EXERCISE

If you are spending too much time reading, time yourself reading a passage under normal conditions. Subtract 15–30 seconds from that time to come up with your Goal Time. Using a new passage, divide your Goal Time up among the paragraphs, giving longer paragraphs more time and shorter ones less time. Now, read and Roadmap the passage one paragraph at a time using a timer to let you know when the time is up for that paragraph. After time is up for each paragraph and before you read the next one, review the paragraph without time constraints and make a note of which parts of the passage you wish you had spent less time on and which parts you wish you had spent more time on. Repeat for every paragraph, trying to meet the timing goal you set for that paragraph. Repeat this regularly with new passages until you are able to hit your Goal Time comfortably. As soon as you can hit that Goal Time, reduce it by another 15–30 seconds and create a new Goal Time. Keep doing this from now until Test Day to slowly but surely reduce the time it takes you to Roadmap a passage.

Keep in mind the passages in this book that you can use for practice. There is the set of passages in Chapter 15, and there are the full-length tests at the back of the book as well.

QUESTIONS ARE CHOICES

Imagine that you have four minutes to answer four questions. Question 1 will take two minutes to answer, question 2 will take four minutes, and questions 3 and 4 will each take one minute.

If you add that up, answering all four questions would take eight minutes, which is far more time than you actually have. So no matter how you tackle this question set, you are not going to be able to get to every question. But the order in which you do the questions will have a huge impact on your score. Say, for example, that you ended up doing the questions in the order in which they are printed. Answering question 1 and question 2 will take a total of five minutes—one more than you have—so you will be forced to stop before you have finished answering the second question. This would leave you with only one point to show for your four minutes.

But, say you recognize that question 2 is going to be more time-consuming and decide to skip over it and answer question 3 instead. That will give you two points with a minute to spare. If you go to question 4 next, then you will answer it and get a total of three points. So the same person tackling the same question set with the same amount of time to do it suddenly gets a very different score.

You read earlier that one of the primary differences between good test takers and great test takers is the ability to see a full section and not just individual questions. Up to this point, you have been learning how to adopt a big-picture approach to your RC section. Now it is time to use that perspective to delve deeper into managing your individual questions effectively, and that begins by understanding that every question is a choice.

Earlier in the chapter, you learned that one question is never worth more than another, but it can definitely cost you more than another. Because of this, there are two choices you must always make for each question set: Which of the questions will you attempt, and in what order will you attempt them? The test taker who does the questions in the order they are printed is assuming that these decisions have already been made for her. This test taker is not in control. Great test takers, on the other hand, know that these decisions are theirs to make. In the next section, you will learn how to make those decisions.

SUGGESTED EXERCISE

If you are getting bogged down in individual questions, try adding the following to your timing notations: place a star next to a question number if, within 30 seconds, you feel the question is going to be time-consuming. This will help train you to constantly ask yourself whether or not a question feels worth your time. Also, circle a question the second you realize you are bogged down. This will help train you to skip out of questions more quickly. You can also use these notations when you review the section to help you figure out the characteristics of questions that tend to bog you down and those of questions that don't.

Question Triage

Learning to quickly spot low-hanging fruit and likely time sinks is a vital skill for determining the order in which you tackle a section, but how you go about it depends on the section. In Reading Comprehension, your first priority should always be Global questions. This is the reason why you should read passages primarily for the Big Picture: you are reading to predict the answers to these questions. Everything else in the passage can be researched, and during your initial read, you'll be highlighting the details likely to be tested as you note Keywords along the way.

Afterward, your job is to assess the remaining question stems to find the easier points. The single most important factor here is ease of research. Take for example, the following two question stems:

The author and the critics would most likely disagree over
which of the following statements?

Which of the following can be properly inferred from the passage?

Take a look at the first question stem. It has three very clear clues as to where in the passage the answer will come from. First, it mentions two speakers: the critics and the author. But it also mentions disagreeing. Ideally that should narrow things down enough for you to quickly research the passage and predict the answer to the question. This likewise means being able to spot the right answer quickly while evaluating the answer choices. Contrast that with the second stem. There are no clues in that stem to indicate where in the passage the answer will come from. You cannot do any research up front or make more than a basic prediction about the Big Picture, which means you will likely spend a significant amount of time in the answer choices reading them and comparing them against the passage. If there is a question you are not going to get to, you should hedge your bets and skip the second one in favor of the first.

Beyond that, you may also find it easier to answer the second question after having researched first. Remember that the LSAT only tests a handful of the sentences in a passage, but it uses five to eight questions to test them. That means that the LSAT routinely assigns multiple questions to the same part of a passage. After you have answered all of the more easily researched questions, you have a good chance of having already researched the area of the passage to which the second question stem refers.

Ease of research is the most important factor in deciding whether or not to do a question, but it is definitely not the only one. Other factors to consider are question type (if some are easier for you than others) and length of answer choices. Question order, however, only goes so far if you are not dealing with the questions properly.

Rushing Never Helps

Earlier in the chapter, you learned that you can miss a question for either content reasons or management reasons. In many cases, however, the root of content errors is actually poor section management. When a test taker mismanages the section, anxiety begins to kick in. And when anxiety kicks in, the rushing begins. If you have ever had the feeling that you weren't taking the test so much as the test was taking you, you were probably in the middle of just such a cycle. Consider the following common scenario:

You spent a lot of time reading the passage for the question set, and unfortunately, you now have less time than you had hoped to tackle the questions. After getting bogged down in a question, you finally guess and move on to the next one. You quickly glance at the question stem in front of you and notice that it mentions a speaker you remember from the passage. To save time, you skip researching and predicting and dive right into the answer choices because you hate the idea of skipping a question entirely. Because you don't have a strong prediction, you end up reading all of the answer choices just to be certain. Unfortunately, a few of the answer choices look good—you definitely remember seeing some of the phrases used in the choices. You stare at the answer choices for a minute or two, trying to figure out which of them is more correct than the others. The longer you stare at them, though, the better they all look. Panicking, you suddenly realize you have spent far too long on this question, and you finally pick an answer and move to the next question feeling even more stressed out and behind on time as the cycle continues.

Sound familiar? This is a classic example of cutting all the wrong corners to save time and losing time instead. At the end of the day, the order you do your questions in doesn't matter if you are not going to do them well. When timing-related anxiety takes over, it becomes very hard to stick to the Method, but sticking to the Method is the only way to stay in control. Rushing *never* helps. Invariably, upon reviewing a section you have rushed through, you will find that many of the questions you struggled with are actually quite manageable. It's a very frustrating experience to look back at a question and wonder, *Why on earth did I choose this answer*? Having such reactions when you review questions is the classic red flag that you are rushing and that it is hurting your score. When it comes to answering questions on the LSAT, you have to slow down to speed up.

The first mistake in the scenario above was taking too much time to read the passage. For many test takers, this is the beginning of the cycle in Reading Comprehension. Starting a question set stressed about timing is a recipe for disaster. From there, the mistakes predictably followed one after another.

Now, perceiving that time was short, the test taker failed to read the question stem carefully. It may sound basic, but it is shocking how often test takers rush through question stems and try to answer a question they don't understand. When the anxiety/rushing cycle starts, it is easy to focus on a question stem's reference to something you vaguely remember from the passage but to ignore the specific task the stem is setting for you. Always paraphrase the question stem *before* you research the passage. If you find yourself reading question stems simply to look for a name or a line reference, then you are needlessly costing yourself time and points. If you don't understand what the question is asking, it is impossible to research efficiently, and inefficient research costs you time in the long run.

From there, it is just as easy to make the mistake of skipping research entirely. Even if the answer to the question comes from the part of the passage you think it does, and even if you remember that part well, you probably don't understand it in the way the question needs you to. While you can predict which pieces of a passage will be tested, you cannot predict how the LSAT will test them. If the LSAT tests you on a specific example in a passage, it could ask you a Detail question that merely expects you to spot a paraphrase of the text, but it could instead ask you about someone's opinion on that detail. Alternately, it could ask you for the role that example played, or it might expect you to find a parallel argument to the one that the example is used in. Each of these questions requires a different prediction for the correct answer. This is why it is important to research the relevant pieces of the passage *after* reading the question. Understanding the need for research also allows you to Roadmap a passage more quickly up front: you know you will be able to come back to any piece you actually need.

Without proper research, it is impossible to make a good prediction. Even when you understand the question stem, foregoing research makes any prediction barely better than a guess. A poor prediction will have you jumping into the answer choices with no reliable way to assess them. At that point, the best anyone can do is to look for word matches between the answer choices and the passage. The problem is that there are usually several answer choices with phrasing from the passage; furthermore, the correct answers in the Reading Comprehension section are more likely to paraphrase the text than to repeat it directly, which makes looking for word matches counterproductive. There is a good chance that none of the answers that someone in this situation is choosing among are actually correct. And even if one of them is, there is no way to separate it from the others without going back to the passage. This is what leads to the inevitable "sit and stare" approach before finally doing what should have been done a long time ago: guess and move on. Unfortunately, a test taker caught in this cycle is probably going to feel even more anxious at this point and is likely on the way to doing it all over again on the next question. So how do you prevent this cycle from starting? How do you stop it once it starts? The answer is simple: skipping questions.

Proactive Skipping

On the LSAT, *strategically* skipping some questions can enhance your score. Though many test takers struggle initially with the idea of skipping questions, the choice between skipping and not skipping is clear. Take the four questions in four minutes example from earlier. If the test taker had been reluctant to skip and stuck with question 2, then he would have ended up skipping questions 3 and 4. But if that same person decided to strategically skip question 2, then he would actually end up getting to more questions. If your refusal to skip questions means spending so much time on a handful of them that you are not able to get to even more at the end, then you are already skipping. You're just not skipping strategically. As you probably guessed, for most test takers, the 8- to 9-Minute Rule will not leave enough time to correctly answer every question in the passage. Proactive skipping means strategically cutting out questions from the outset to buy you enough time to invest in the questions that are more likely to pay off quickly. If the idea of skipping questions outright makes you anxious, take a look at the following calculations and then read the explanation below:

LSAT STRATEGY

Skipping Strategically

Questions/Passage × 4 Passages + "Skip Points" = Total Score (out of 27)

3×4 passages $+ 3 = 15$

4×4 passages $+ 2 = 18$

5×4 passages $+ (1 \text{ or } 2) = 21 \text{ or } 22$

6×4 passages $+ (0 \text{ or } 1) = 24 \text{ or } 25$

Imagine that you only did three questions per passage in a 27-question Reading Comprehension section. The 8- to 9-Minute Rule gives you 8–9 minutes to Roadmap the passage and tackle those questions. Now imagine that you pick the three easiest questions for you—the ones you feel the most certain you can answer quickly and correctly. You have plenty of time to research the answer to the question, to make a strong prediction, and to read and analyze the answer choices against your prediction. Any question you see that seems time-consuming or that begins to bog you down, you skip out of quickly and confidently, knowing you have plenty of time to find another question that seems more likely to reward you. Then you guess on the remaining 16 questions in the section. For most test takers, this is a terrifying prospect that feels like a worst-case scenario. After all, guessing on 16 questions means guessing on over half of the section.

But take a moment and do the math. Assuming you selected the easiest questions and got them correct, that would give you 12 points total. And given that guessing on a question has a 1-in-5 chance of yielding a point, skipping 15 questions should give you 3 more points. The total score would be around a 15. For many test takers, this would be a solid improvement in score—or at least not much of a change from what they are getting now. If you bump that up to 4 questions per passage, you would still be skipping a total of 12 questions, but you would be getting around 18 correct answers—a correct response rate better than the majority of test takers will achieve on the test as a whole. And that scenario has you skipping from two to four questions per passage!

There are two main benefits to this kind of proactive skipping. First, it frees you from getting bogged down on time-consuming questions and allows you to instead focus on the questions that are more likely to pay off. If done well, it forces you to consistently ask yourself whether or not a question is worth your time. After all, if you are only getting to four, you have to be choosy about which four you get to. Secondly, it buys you enough time to do your questions well. On the LSAT, it is nearly always better to do a few questions well than to do more questions poorly. Your approach doesn't need to be as regimented as that in the chart, but you should look for a way to incorporate the basic idea into your management goals.

If you find yourself getting bogged down on individual questions, not getting to entire passages, or making a lot of "careless" mistakes, then you can use the sample calculations shown to help you set goals. If you are currently scoring around a 19, for example, then try doing only 5 questions per passage to improve your score. As you get more comfortable doing a certain number of questions per passage, you can set new goals to gradually improve.

SUGGESTED EXERCISE

If you are having a hard time convincing yourself to skip questions proactively, try doing a full Reading Comprehension section under timed conditions, but use a digital timer to time yourself on how long each individual question takes you. When you are finished, find the four questions you spent the longest on and add up the total time you spent on them and how many points they yielded. It's not uncommon to find you are spending 7–11 minutes on four questions for only 1 or 2 points. What would your score have been like if you had used the time you spent on the more time-consuming questions to slow down on some of the other questions you did or to get to questions you couldn't get to at the end?

Reactive Skipping

No matter how careful you are about question selection, research, and prediction, sometimes a question doesn't go your way. For each question you try, quickly decide whether or not the question is worth your time. If you are unsure of what the question is asking, if you are not sure where in the passage to research, or if you are struggling to make a prediction, then odds are the question is not going to turn into a point. Even if it does, it is likely it will cost you more time than it is worth. Keep moving and find yourself a question that is more likely to reward you quickly. This sort of reactive skipping is the bread and butter of any great test taker.

Sometimes, though, you will not realize that you are in trouble until you get to the answer choices. In an ideal situation, you will have a strong enough prediction that you can spot the correct answer easily, stop reading, and move on to the next question. Other times you may find yourself stuck between choices. Unfortunately, the longer you look at the right answer, the more you tend to poke holes in it. The longer you look at the wrong answers, the more you talk yourself into them. Avoid the "stare and compare" approach at all costs and instead keep in mind that the correct answer isn't perfect, it's flawless. If you are implicitly looking for the "best" answer, you are in for a world of trouble. All of the answers may have good things in them, and a wrong answer may seem to have more of what you are looking for in it than the right one does. The one thing that separates the right answer from the wrong ones, however, is that the right answer has nothing *wrong* with it. There is nothing to argue with in the correct answer. When stuck between answer choices, stop looking for what is right and start looking for what is wrong!

If looking for what is wrong does not immediately give you a clear answer, *get out*! Your best bet is to circle the answer your first instinct said is correct and to move on to another question. From there you have two options: you can return to the question or simply leave it alone. If you get out fast enough and have some time to spare, then you can come back to the question after you have done another question or two with a fresh perspective. You have probably had the experience of reviewing an answer choice after doing a section and realizing you grossly misread it. It is easy to rush your reading during timed sections and to make reading mistakes. Unfortunately, when you reread something you have just read, your brain has a tendency to read from memory and not from the page. This is why it can be so hard to spot a mistake in the moment. After you have moved on to another question or two, however, your brain replaces the information in your short-term memory with the new questions. When you return to the original question, you are forced to read from the page again, which gives you a better chance of catching your mistake.

Alternately, you can opt to let the question go. Never get into an ego battle with the test. If you feel that coming back to the question isn't likely to change anything, then don't bother. You will be far better off for the rest of the section if you avoid sinking time into a question you end up getting wrong. It is worth pointing out that you should always put an answer down for every question—even the ones you guess on. We recommend gridding by visiting your answer sheet between each of the passages and bubbling in your answers as a group. If there are any questions you have guessed on, you can either bubble in a guess letter for them now (and change the answer later if you end up coming back to the question) or leave them blank and return at the end of the section to fill them in. Practice both approaches to find out what works best for you. This means you are only going to the answer sheet four times during the section, and gridding the questions in groups makes it easier to avoid accidentally skipping a line.

> ## SUGGESTED EXERCISE
>
> Whenever you are doing timing work and get to an answer that you feel is correct, draw a line under it. Note to yourself whether you kept reading or moved on. When you are reviewing the section, ask yourself how often you continued to read and actually changed your answer. Many students spend a lot of time reading answer choices when it is clear they have already found the right answer. Others may struggle with impulsively selecting wrong answers and moving on before they have analyzed the answer carefully enough. Get an idea of how much time you are investing in your answers. Is continuing to read helping you or hurting you?

COMMON FRUSTRATIONS—DIAGNOSING YOUR ISSUE AND WAYS TO IMPROVE

Up to this point, you have been learning about how the Reading Comprehension section is structured. Great test takers, however, not only understand their sections, but they also understand themselves. Though everyone is unique, a few common archetypal student experiences are worth discussing: the anxious one, the rusher, and the perfectionist. You may relate exceedingly well to one of these, or you may relate in small part to more than one. Take a look at each to help you figure out what you need to work on specifically and, more importantly, how to address your challenges. No matter what those challenges are, the first step is to recognize that there is *always* a solution!

The Anxious One

Test taking and anxiety go hand in hand for most. For some test takers, though, it is the biggest mountain to climb. Test anxiety is a very real phenomenon that has potentially serious consequences. Fortunately, like all problems, it can be dealt with. When you are first learning the Reading Comprehension Method, don't put time pressure on yourself. Practice methodically and internalize the steps you need to take. As those steps become second nature, integrate timing practice into your regimen. If you find yourself repeatedly thinking, "I'm not ready for timing. I'll deal with it when I have my method completely down," then you are probably in an anxiety/avoidance cycle. While it is important to begin with mastery work in order to learn the Reading Comprehension Method, it is equally important to remember that with Reading Comprehension in particular, following the Method involves being able to go through the process in a certain amount of time. You don't need to make everything timed, but aside from the early stages of prep, you should never leave timing out entirely.

The good news is that once you begin timing, you don't need to jump right into full 35-minute sections or full-length tests. In fact, it's to your benefit to start with micro timing exercises. Begin your timed work with one passage and question set to help ease you into the process and to minimize your anxiety. If the mere thought of being timed sends you into an anxiety spiral, then give yourself a chance to adjust to having a timing device around while you work. Don't be prohibitive about your time at this point—you don't have to stop yourself for taking a long time. Just get used to the idea of having a timer around. As you become more comfortable, you can start setting time limits on yourself for reading and answering questions. Start off with a generous amount of time and consistently reduce the time by small amounts—challenge yourself just a little bit. Eventually, you can start adding more passages to your timed work until you are ready for a full section of four.

Finally, the more you suffer from anxiety, the more crucial the section management strategies mentioned in this chapter will become. Nothing kicks anxiety into gear like a lack of control. Pay special attention to the exercises that deal with time awareness and notation. Making these a regular part of what you do will help to keep you in control and keep your anxiety in check.

The Rusher

Rushing is a perennial problem on the LSAT, and it is very often related to anxiety. If your problem is rushing, be sure to read about the Anxious One above to make sure that's not your core issue. Looking at the problem of rushing itself, it is important to start by getting an idea of where the rushing begins. Everyone is different in this regard. Some people start by racing through reading their question stems. Others tend to forsake research and prediction but spend a lot of time on the answer choices, thinking over them carefully. Often, rushing starts with one step and then spreads to others as a consequence. As previously discussed, rushing through reading the question stem, for example, can lead to a series of "downstream" mistakes in research and prediction. If you don't understand the question stem well enough, then you can't efficiently research. If that happens, often enough you will find yourself increasingly eager to skip research entirely in order to save time, which will cost you time as you try to evaluate the answer choices. Ultimately, the steps you rush through and the ones you don't tell you a lot about how to tame this bad habit.

To figure out what triggers your rushing instinct, try a passage and its question set under timed conditions and make sure you record how long you spend reading. This will tell you if your rushing is a product of anxiety that comes from spending too much time in the passage. Then, as you tackle the questions, every time you find yourself racing through a question stem, make a note next to that stem. Every time you decide not to research a question that could have been researched, put a big "R" next to the question. If you end up jumping into the answer choices without making a prediction, put a big "P" next to the question. If you find yourself stuck between answer choices, put a big "A/B" (or whichever choices you were caught between) next to the question. Finally, if you get bogged down, circle the question the moment you realize you're spending too much time in it. When you are finished, figure out what your triggers are for rushing. If you are rushing through a series of steps, try to find the earliest step you are rushing through; in many cases, that is the important point.

Next retrain yourself to stop rushing through these steps. While doing another passage/question set under timed conditions, stop the timer at the beginning of each of the steps you identified in the previous exercise. Now record your step on another sheet of paper. If you are rushing through the stem, then write down your paraphrase of it; if you are skipping research, write down where you are going to go research. When you finish, start the timer again and continue. The key here is consistency. You are always either ingraining good habits or bad ones. The only way to ensure you don't rush through the Kaplan Method in the future is to force yourself to do each step properly every single time. By tying that to a physical process—writing it down on another sheet of paper—you will achieve that consistency.

When dealing with full sections, you should also use the goal-setting exercise mentioned in the last paragraph of the "Proactive Skipping" section of this chapter to buy yourself enough time to relax. As you become more comfortable, you can slowly increase the number of questions you do per passage.

The Perfectionist
The Perfectionist is someone who generally has a hard time letting go. Perfectionism is typically a product of anxiety, and it often leads to rushing to make up for lost time (see both the profiles above). Having said that, there are two particular areas that perfectionists tend to struggle with in Reading Comprehension.

The first area is the initial read of the passage. Perfectionists often have a difficult time coming to terms with having a limited understanding of the passage when jumping into the question set. The best defense against this is to face your fears head-on. Take a passage you have never done before and get out your timer. Give yourself two minutes to read the introductory paragraph and the first sentence of every paragraph after that, making a brief Roadmap as you go. Now, take a moment to go through each of the question stems for all of the non-Global questions. How many of these could you research at this point? Of those you couldn't quickly and easily research, is it because the question stem is too vague or because you genuinely don't recall the reference? What you will likely find is that the vast majority of the questions can be easily researched even when you haven't read a majority of the text. You will also likely find that most of the questions you can't easily research are hard to research because the stem is devoid of research clues, *not* because you didn't read carefully enough. On Test Day, you will read the entire passage, of course, but this exercise will stand as a strong reminder to read *strategically* and Roadmap the passage rather than to concentrate on comprehending every nuance and detail of the subject matter.

The other area that perfectionists tend to struggle with is question skipping. Once again, facing your fears is the solution. Go do the exercise in the gray box in the "Proactive Skipping" part of the chapter. If you want to simplify it, you can always use an individual passage instead of a full section. Perfectionists often struggle with the concept of leaving a question behind that they could have answered correctly when the real emphasis should be on how much time it will take to answer it correctly. When you have finished the exercise, ask yourself which questions you could have skipped to maximize the number of questions you could have answered. How long did it take you to realize that the questions that took you the longest weren't worth your time? Now, try another section under timed conditions. This time, whenever you feel you are getting bogged down, circle the question and move on immediately. When you finish the section, compare it to the original section. Which one went better? Which one felt more controlled?

You Are On Your Way

Clearly, a lot goes into becoming a great test taker, but hopefully at this point you have a good idea of how to start the process. The easiest way to grab points quickly and to keep your score consistent is to build these skills carefully from now until Test Day. There is no single skill on the LSAT that is worth more points than section management, so be sure to incorporate it as a regular part of your prep. Every time you sit down to do timed work, you should always have one or more section management goals in mind. Are you going to work on building time awareness? Do you need to work on spending less time reading the passage? Maybe this time you are going to work on proactively skipping questions or triaging questions. Remember that a good goal drives your process, as opposed to targeting a given result. A goal to make regular timing notations is a good one, but a goal to get a certain number of questions correct is not.

Acknowledgments

Acknowledgment is made to the following sources from which material has been adapted for use in this book:

Elizabeth Wayland Barber, *Women's Work: The First 20,000 Years: Women, Cloth, and Society in Early Times.* © 1994 by Elizabeth Wayland Barber.

Richard H. Brodhead, *Cultures of Letters: Scenes of Reading and Writing in Nineteenth-Century America.* © 1993 by the University of Chicago.

James P. Draper, ed., *Black Literature Criticism.* © 1992 by Gale Research Inc.

Geneviève Fraisse and Michelle Perrot, eds., *A History of Women in the West.* © 1993 by the President and Fellows of Harvard College.

Jonathan Glater and Alan Finder, "In Tuition Game, Popularity Rises with Price." © December 12, 2006 by The New York Times.

Josie Glausiusz, "Seismologists Go Green." © 1999 by the Walt Disney Company.

Dinha Kaplan, "When Less Is More." © 1997 by Sussex Publishers, Inc.

Françoise Pfaff, "The Uniqueness of Ousmane Sembène's Cinema." © 1993 by Five Colleges, Inc.

A. John Simmons, *On the Edge of Anarchy: Locke, Consent, and the Limits of Society.* © 1993 by Princeton University Press.

David W. Pfennig and Paul W. Sherman, "Kin Recognition." © 1995 by Scientific American, Inc.

Michael Pietrusewsky and Michele Toomay Douglas, "Intensification of Agriculture at Ban Chiang: Is There Evidence from the Skeletons?" © 2001 by University of Hawaii Press.

Karen Gust Schollmeyer and Christy G. Turner II, "Dental Caries, Prehistoric Diet, and the Pithouse-to-Pueblo Transition in Southwestern Colorado." © 2004 by Society for American Archaeology.

"Why Wages Do Not Fall in Recessions." © February 26, 2000 by The Economist Newspaper Limited.

CHAPTER 17

Test Day

Is it starting to feel like your whole life is a buildup to the LSAT? You've known about it for years, worried about it for months, and now spent weeks in solid preparation for it. As the test gets closer, you may find your anxiety is on the rise. You shouldn't worry. After the preparation you've done, you're in good shape for the test. To calm any pre-test jitters you may have, though, here are a few strategies for the days before the test.

THE WEEK BEFORE THE TEST

Your goal during the week before the LSAT is to set yourself up for success on Test Day. Up until this point, you have been working to build your LSAT potential, but Test Day is about achievement. That process begins with taking care of your basic needs: food, sleep, and exercise. It's easy to get caught up in the stress of balancing your life with your studying, but if taking an extra hour to study every night leaves you sleep deprived and exhausted on Test Day, it's hurting you more than helping. Figure out what time you need to go to sleep the night before the exam and make sure you're in bed at that time every night the week before the exam. This is particularly important if you're a night owl who tends to get a second wind later in the evening. If at all possible, start doing some LSAT work—even if it's only a few problems— each morning at the same time as the test. Finally, if you are someone who regularly goes to the gym or engages in other physical activity, this is *not* the week to stop. Physical activity helps lower stress and increases production of dopamine and norepinephrine, two neurotransmitters that play a crucial role in memory, attention, and mood!

You should also take at least one trip to your test center sometime before the actual exam to figure out the logistics: how long it takes to get there, where to park, how to get to your room, and where the bathrooms and drinking fountains are. The last thing you want to end up doing the morning of the test is running into unexpected construction on your route or not being able to find your room when you arrive! If the test center is a classroom or public building, try to take a practice test or timed section in the room to get a feel for it. Pay close attention to things like noise levels and temperature while you're there.

Early in the week, make sure to print out your admissions ticket from the LSAC website and check it against your government-issued ID. Be sure that the names match and that the ID isn't expired! If the names don't match, contact LSAC *immediately* so you can remedy the situation. If that isn't fixed by Test Day, you will be denied admission to the exam. You will also need a passport photo taken within the last six months to affix to your admissions ticket. LSAC is extremely strict about the photo requirements, so Kaplan recommends that you have your photos taken professionally at a place that specializes in passport photos, such as the post office, a chain drug store, or a photocopy shop.

For a complete list of the LSAC photo requirements, visit the LSAC's website, www.lsac.org.

The kind of practice that you do the week before the exam is important. Resist the temptation to focus on your weaknesses and instead focus primarily on shoring up your strengths. It's all fine and good to grab two more points in games, for example, but if you start losing points in the other sections from neglect, you may very well end up worse off than you started. The reality is that you are more likely to grab a few points in your strengths at the last minute than you are in the areas you struggle with the most. Of course, be sure to work on all three areas during this time: no one section should be fully ignored. Also keep in mind that the actual LSAT is a test of timing and endurance. A majority of your work should be under timed conditions, and you should try to fit in a test or two if you have the time in your schedule. Having said that, do not fall into the trap of doing nothing but tests right before the LSAT. As always, there is a balancing act between test taking and review: taking a test every day can make it difficult to find time to review them, which means you aren't learning from them. You also need to watch your stress levels carefully: taking too many exams can lead to a stress spiral that is hard to climb out of.

Finally, the week before the exam is the time to decide whether or not you are ready to take your test. As of the time of writing, LSAC's policy allows you to withdraw your registration all the way up until 11:59 P.M. EST the night before the exam without it showing up on your record. There is no right or wrong answer to the question of whether or not you are ready to take your exam, but if you are having any doubts, ask yourself a few questions:

- What is the lowest score I would be okay with an admissions officer seeing?
- Am I scoring at least that high now?

You can choose your goals in life, but you can't always choose your timelines. If the answer to the second question was a resounding no, then it may be in your best interest to change your test date. Though there is a modest benefit to applying early, submitting a score that is well below a school's median early is more likely to result in a faster rejection than a surprise admission. Don't expect any miracles on Test Day: It's possible that your score will suddenly jump up to an all-time high on the day of the exam, but it isn't likely. More importantly, it's risky. This is especially important if you already have one score or cancellation within the last five years on your record: admissions officers can be understanding about one blemish on your record, but two starts to become a pattern.

LSAT STRATEGY

In the last week before the test:

- · Print out your admission ticket.
- · Get your body on schedule for the time of your test (either 8:30 A.M. or 12:30 P.M.).
- · Visit the testing center.
- · Don't take any practice tests within 48 hours of the test.
- · Decide whether or not you want to take the test or withdraw.

THE DAY BEFORE THE TEST

The day before the test is as important as the six days before it. The first instinct of most test takers is to cram as much as possible in hopes of grabbing a few last-second points. But the LSAT isn't an AP exam or your history final: you cannot "cram" for the LSAT. You should think of Test Day as Game Day. An athlete doesn't try to run 10 miles the day before a big race: she rests up and makes sure that she can hit her potential when it counts. Though this advice is hard to follow, trust Kaplan's decades of experience with tens of thousands of students. You should make the day before the test a wonderful, relaxing day. There's a good chance that during the last few weeks or months, the stress of balancing prep with the rest of your life has meant you've had less time to yourself or with your family and loved ones. Spend a day with your significant other or kids. Go to the spa or spend the day in a movie marathon. Whatever you do, make sure that today is as restful and relaxing as possible. Put your LSAT materials away and leave them there because, while you aren't going to cram your way to a good score, you may cram your way into a bad one. Think of how you normally feel when you get a score on something that is less than you hoped for. Now imagine how it would feel the day before the exam and what that kind of anxiety could do to you on Test Day. The benefits to studying the day before are almost nonexistent, but the risks are sky-high.

Don't forget to cap off the day with a full meal for dinner and a good night of sleep. It's not going to be easy to fall asleep the night before the test, so make sure you are in bed on time. Resist the urge to stare at a television or computer screen: they tend to make it even harder to sleep. For what it's worth, however, the most important night of sleep isn't the night before the test; it's two nights before the test. For various reasons, the effects of sleep deprivation tend to skip a day, so getting a great night of sleep two nights before the exam will help make sure that you are well rested the day of the test!

LSAT STRATEGY

On the day before the test:

- Relax! Read a book, watch a movie, go shopping, etc.
- Get all of your materials together—your admission ticket, passport photo, watch, snack, plastic bag, etc.
- Eat a full meal for dinner and get plenty of sleep.

You also want to make sure that everything you need for tomorrow is packed up and ready. Don't put yourself in the position of fumbling around the next morning trying to find everything you need. Everything you bring into the test center **must** be in a clear, one-gallon zip-top bag.

LSAT FACTS

The following items are required for admission on Test Day:

- Admissions ticket
- Government-issued ID
- A passport photo affixed to your admissions ticket
- Regular No. 2 pencils (no mechanical pencils)

In addition to those required items, there are a few other things you should bring with you as well:

> ## LSAT STRATEGY
>
> Kaplan recommends you bring the following items with you on Test Day:
>
> · A snack for the break (things like granola bars are best; avoid sugary snacks that might make you crash)
> · Bottled water or juice box
> · Erasers
> · Tylenol
> · Tissues (even if they end up being for someone else in the room with the sniffles)
> · A nondigital timing device (i.e., an analog watch!)
> · A positive, upbeat attitude

On occasion, the LSAC will change its admissions requirements. Because of this, it's important that you consult its website (www.lsac.org) to get updated information on what is and is not acceptable to bring on Test Day!

THE MORNING OF THE TEST

On the morning of the exam, you should obviously get up early to give yourself some time to wake up and to leave for the test center early. A relaxed morning is a much better start than a frantic, stressful one. After you wake up, make sure you have a great breakfast that is both high in protein and high in carbohydrates. You'll need the energy later! Also, make sure you pack an appropriate snack. While it's important to have a protein-rich breakfast, you want to avoid a protein-rich snack. You will have a chance to eat your snack during the 15-minute break after the third section, and you'll want the energy it provides as quickly as possible. Because carbohydrates digest much faster than protein, foods like fruit and granola are much more practical than peanut butter and jelly sandwiches. Try to avoid any processed sugars or caffeine (a notorious diuretic), as they lead to a crash. Finally, you are allowed a drink, but it must either be a juice box or in a bottle of no more than 20 ounces. Avoid energy drinks (as they are mostly sugar and caffeine) and instead opt for water or 100 percent juice.

When choosing what to wear, go for layers. It's hard to tell what the temperature will be in the room, and heating and cooling systems tend to kick in erratically. You want to be sure you can adjust your clothing as needed to stay as comfortable as possible. It's important to note, however, that you may not wear hats or hoods during the exam unless LSAC has given you a religious exemption.

Before you head to the test center, be sure to read LSAC's website one more time to see a complete and official list of what is and is not allowed into the room beforehand.

LSAT FACTS

The following items are prohibited:

- Cell phones (Leave it at home or in the car.)
- Electronic devices of any kind, including tablets, MP3 players, or digital watches
- Ear plugs
- Backpacks or purses
- Mechanical pencils
- Papers or books
- Hats and hooded sweatshirts

This is not a complete list, so be sure to check the LSAC website to get the most updated information. But do know that once you check in, you may not have any of these items on your person. If you bring any of them into the actual test room, you risk having your score immediately cancelled and a misconduct letter placed in your file. So, as hard as it may be for you to part with it, leave the cell phone in the car—it's not worth the risk.

LSAT STRATEGY

On the morning of the test:

- Get up early and plan accordingly for traffic and parking.
- Eat an appropriate breakfast.
- Dress in layers (but do not wear a hooded sweatshirt).
- Gather your allowable items into a one-gallon plastic bag.

AT THE LSAC FACILITY AND DURING THE TEST

Aim to arrive at your testing facility at least 30 minutes before the test is scheduled to begin. Traffic, parking, and other unforeseen circumstances may delay you, so don't risk arriving late to the facility. The LSAC is strict about when the test begins—if you are even a minute late, the proctors have the right to deny you entry. Arriving early also allows you to familiarize yourself with your surroundings and to scope out where the bathrooms and drinking fountains are (though, as mentioned before, this is something you were hopefully able to do in the week leading up to the test).

There are also a number of things you'll want to do once you arrive at the testing facility. After all, if the only point of arriving 30 minutes early is to sit around and twiddle your thumbs, any anxiety you might feel would get worse, not better. That's why it's so important to have a game plan for what to do at the testing facility on Test Day. First of all, make sure you get a drink of water and go to the bathroom. Though that advice might seem like common sense, you'd be surprised by how many students get so nervous that they actually skip this important step. But going to the bathroom before the test is really important. After all, having to leave the testing room during Section 3 to go to the bathroom will cost you 10 minutes and, in the process, undo the months of effort and practice you put into this test.

The other thing you'll want to do at the testing facility in the minutes before the test begins is get your brain in "LSAT mode." Bring with you a quick warm-up exercise to do while you wait to check in. Find a game, passage, or set of Logical Reasoning questions that you've done before and that you know well. Reviewing LSAT material and walking through the various steps you took to get to the right answer will get your brain prepared for the test to come. Many students find that if they don't do this, they start the test "cold." Don't wait until the second section to get your brain "warmed up"; use the time before the test to get your brain in "LSAT mode." A word of caution: Be sure that your warm-up exercise is something you've already done. There's enough stress on Test Day without adding the anxiety of getting stumped by one of your warm-up questions right before the exam!

Because paper materials are not allowed in the testing room, do your warm-up exercise in a hallway or other room at the testing facility in the minutes leading up to the test start. While other students rush into the testing room 30 minutes before the test starts, take your time and review your material outside the testing room. Then, when there are 5–7 minutes to go, get in line and officially check in. Once you enter the testing room, you'll have little to do besides sit with your thoughts and wait for the proctors to begin the test.

Checking in on Test Day will involve showing your identification and having the proctors examine the materials you're bringing into the facility. Don't get flustered when they check your identification and belongings as you enter the testing room—this is standard operating procedure. The test administrators do this because (1) they want to make sure that everyone is who they say they are and (2) the materials used by each test taker should never distract others. That's one of the reasons why items like mechanical pencils (which can click) and cell phones (which can ring) are prohibited. To avoid any uncertainty or stress over what to bring, again, check out the LSAC website for a list of acceptable and prohibited items. Additionally, make sure to follow the most up-to-date requirements for identification, lest all of your preparation be squandered when you are not allowed into the facility.

Once you enter the testing room and find your seat, you'll have to wait for the proctors to let everyone else in the room, pass out the test booklets, and recite a long list of rules. For some students, this time before the test can be nerve-racking. What thoughts will go through your head when this moment comes? Some students, no doubt, will think, "Gee, I hope I do well," or "I better not bomb this, or my life is over!" This time before the test begins is an opportunity for you to take control of your thoughts for the next four hours. Visualize yourself doing well. Walk through a logic game in your head. Identify the assumption from an old Strengthen question you've done. Tell yourself you will be successful. "I am going to do really well on this test. I'm well prepared and have seen thousands of LSAT problems. I know exactly how to tackle every question they throw at me. If they give me an Inference question, I'm going to read the stimulus and make deductions . . . ." While the heads of the test takers around you fill with nervous thoughts, game-plan for the test and build your mental confidence.

After the test booklets have been handed out and once you've filled out the required information, the test will begin. Your proctor may or may not write the starting and ending time of each section in the front of the room, but the proctor should *always* announce a "five minutes remaining" warning. Even though this is one of the proctors' duties, don't rely solely on them for timing cues. Your watch is there to accurately measure time, so the only thing you need to hear from the proctor is "you may begin."

During the break, be sure to eat your snack, drink your beverage, and go to the bathroom. Stretch and move around a bit. Use the time during the break to recharge for the second half of the test. One thing you'll probably notice during the break is that people will talk—they'll talk about a section that was particularly hard, or particularly easy, or they may even talk about a section that you haven't even taken yet! That's because LSAT sections are organized differently in different test booklets. Your booklet may go LR, LG, LR in the first three sections, while the person next to you may have a booklet that goes RC, LR, LG. Additionally, you are never sure which section will end up being the experimental section until after the test is over. That's why the LSAC and the proctors will expressly prohibit discussion of the test during the break. Moral of the story? Don't worry about what people are talking about during the break; in fact, actively avoid anyone who seems to be discussing the test because it can lead to a misconduct letter or expulsion from the test. Focus only on yourself and your own progress. Forget about what happened during the first part of the test and turn your attention to the next three sections.

After the fifth section of the test, take a moment to relax and breathe. Congratulations. You have finished the scored sections of the LSAT. The only section that now remains is the Writing Sample. Though this section is not unimportant, it's nowhere near as important as the previous sections. Between the fifth and sixth sections, feel free to decompress before gathering yourself and moving forward to the Writing Sample.

LSAT STRATEGY

At the testing facility on Test Day

- Arrive 30 minutes early.
- Find and use the drinking fountains and bathroom.
- Get into "LSAT mode" by reviewing previous work.
- Enter the testing room a few minutes before the test is set to begin.
- Use the time before the test begins to mentally prepare yourself for the test.
- Look forward, not backward—always keep moving through the test and focus on the section you're currently in, not sections you've already done or will do in the future.

AFTER THE TEST

If it turns out that Test Day doesn't go *exactly* as planned, that's alright—it rarely, if ever, does, and the LSAT does not require perfection! All of your fellow test takers will likely experience some level of self-doubt as well; that's fairly typical.

If it turns out you feel like you did well on Test Day, then skip this section and head to the Post-LSAT Festivities section later in this chapter. If, however, you end up having a particularly unusual Test Day, you may think about canceling your score. Canceling your score means that neither you nor the law schools will have access to whatever your score would have been. But here's the rub: law schools will still know that you took the test at that administration, and it will count against your limit of three tests in a two-year period. For many law schools, a cancellation can raise a red flag. If you do cancel, you may want to consider attaching an addendum to your application explaining why you canceled.

You have two opportunities to cancel your score. The first opportunity is immediately after you finish the test on Test Day. In fact, there is a part of the scoring grid where you can indicate your wish to cancel. The second, less impetuous way, is to send in a written cancellation request to the LSAC within six calendar days after the exam. If you're considering canceling, check the LSAC's website to verify the most recent means and deadlines for canceling your score.

Should You Cancel Your Score?

If you're wondering whether canceling is the right decision, the information below should be helpful. If you feel confident in your Test Day abilities and are not considering canceling your score, feel free to skip this section entirely.

First, let's examine the *benefits* of not canceling your LSAT score.

No matter how you "feel" about how things went, you *don't know for sure*. You may have actually done much better than you think. According to LSAC, many test takers who cancel their score and then retest would've been better off sticking with the first score. (While the examinee never finds out the cancelled score, the LSAC still computes it internally and can compare the cancelled and subsequent results.)

Additionally, if you cancel your score, you will never have access to the answers you selected during Test Day. If you keep your score, you will receive an official score report and a PDF copy of the test you took (except for February administrations, for which the exam is not released). This information can be extremely helpful if you do choose to take the test again, as you will be able to review and evaluate the decisions you made during an official LSAT, when everything was on the line. Allowing your score to stay in place gives you access not only to the right answers but also to the answers *you* picked. Even weeks later, you'll be amazed as you go question by question through the sections of the exam and say, "Hmmm, now why did I find wrong answer (A) so alluring?" or "Shoot, I should've stuck with my first answer there!" By canceling your score, you forfeit access to this information.

Another reason why it may not be in your best interest to cancel a score is that in recent years, more and more law schools are *not* averaging scores. In fact, law schools have been given careful guidelines from LSAC *against* averaging. That doesn't mean that every school follows this policy, though, and our recommendation from above still stands: the most preferable scenario is to take the test once and ace it. However, if your decision is between canceling and taking it again and *not* canceling and taking it again, it's likely that the latter option will be preferable. (Again, schools can see when you cancel.) Even a so-so score followed by a much better score won't hurt you as it might have in the past, when averaging was the common practice. As a rule, law schools want to assess you fairly, and most agree that the fairest thing is to take the better of two scores, irrespective of the order in which tests were taken. So, even if you decide you want to retest at the next administration, there will be less pressure next time if you don't cancel *this time*. By having a score already on record, you won't have the anxiety of thinking that you absolutely must use the retest score.

So, based on the above benefits of not canceling, the following situations **would NOT warrant a score cancellation:**

- There were some minor distractions in the testing facility. Yes, it's hard to define exactly what counts as "minor" versus "major." Pencil tapping, coughing, and the humming of an air conditioner may all have been distractions, but that's also part of the test environment, and you'd likely experience the same things next time. It's highly unlikely you'll ever have a perfectly distraction-free atmosphere!

- You didn't get to finish or forgot to bubble in the last few questions of a section (or two), even though you usually finish those sections when you practice. Although these time-management issues are not ideal, they do not warrant a cancellation. Yes, a few questions here or there can affect your overall score, but the material at the end of a section can be of a higher level of difficulty, so even if you had completed those questions, there is no guarantee they would have markedly affected your score. Also, there is always the possibility that a section you struggled with was the Experimental section.

Now, let's talk about **when you should cancel your LSAT score:**

- If you have already taken the real test two or three (or more) times, you probably have a much better "feel" for whether or not a particular exam has truly gone well. Also, with two or three scores already on the record, one more cancellation isn't going to significantly damage your profile. However, remember that you can't take the LSAT more than three times in any two-year period. Those three times include any times you've opted to cancel your score.

- If you had been consistently scoring in a certain range but became physically ill with flu or nausea on Test Day, or had some other serious difficulty during the test that prevented you from staying focused to the point that you were unable to complete large sections of the exam, then you should consider cancellation. This may have been due to test anxiety, lack of sleep the night before, personal stress not related to the

LSAT, severe illness, etc. To be clear, the situations described above would have affected *every* section; they wouldn't cause just a moment of panic during a single section.

- If you realized that you made significant gridding mistakes for entire sections, thereby putting many questions in jeopardy of being incorrect, you should consider cancellation (e.g., #8 was gridded in spot #7, #9 in spot #8, etc.).

- Large-scale time issues, such as a proctor who mistakenly shorted time in a section (without having it immediately brought to his or her attention), can significantly change test performance. Minor issues related to the location of clocks, times written on the board, or the exact precision of a five-minute warning are all things that can be prevented by using one's own watch and only relying on the proctor for the words, "You may begin." So, a significant loss of time covering multiple sections could warrant a cancellation, but small, single-section timing issues will usually not.

Post-LSAT Festivities

So, you've just taken the LSAT. After months of preparation and hard work, it's finally over. What to do now? First, give yourself a great big pat on the back. You've just completed (and hopefully rocked) the most important factor in law school admissions. Go celebrate and enjoy the moment—but of course, don't celebrate *too* hard. Law schools are in the business of recruiting future lawyers, which means they're typically not interested in applicants with criminal records. Don't be the person who destroys the LSAT in the morning, then acts inappropriately in the evening.

Instead, take a moment to reach out to anyone who has helped you prepare for the test—teachers, tutors, study buddies, friends, and family members who have invested in your decision to go to law school and become a lawyer. Let them know how you did and share your success with them.

After you've celebrated, and after you've taken a couple of days off from thinking about the LSAT and law school, it's time to once again start thinking about putting together the other pieces of your application. Be sure to get a good head start on your letters of recommendation, personal statement, and transcripts.

Congratulations on your journey!

Full-Length Tests

One of the most difficult aspects of the LSAT is its length—a full 3.5 hours of testing time (and much more when you count breaks and delays). Building your test-taking stamina is critical to performing well on Test Day.

As you prepare for the LSAT, taking full-length exams is the best way to build your endurance. Four full-length exams are provided in this book:

> PrepTest 60 plus one section from PrepTest 46
> PrepTest 54 plus one section from PrepTest 46
> PrepTest 50 plus one section from PrepTest 46
> PrepTest 48 plus one section from PrepTest 46

When the LSAC releases a previously administered LSAT test, it does not include the Experimental section. In order to make your practice as test-like as possible, a full section from an earlier exam has been added to each test to function as an Experimental section. This extra section will not count toward your score. Just like on Test Day, the Experimental section will be indistinguishable from the other sections and can occur at any location within the five sections (although, to date, it has never been confirmed as the fifth section). You will find out which section was Experimental when you score your test, but you should still review that section's right and wrong answers just as you do with the other sections.

Once you're ready for Endurance practice, complete all five sections under timed conditions. If you do not have live proctoring opportunities available, we recommend downloading our proctoring app, "LSAT Proctor Anywhere."

We'd also recommend including the Writing Sample as the sixth timed section if you have the opportunity. Although the Writing Sample is unscored and it is the least important part of the LSAT, schools do use it to help them choose between students with very similar records.

TIMING

The timing for the exam should be as follows:

- First Section: 35 minutes
- Second Section: 35 minutes
- Third Section: 35 minutes
- Break: 10–15 minutes
- Fourth Section: 35 minutes
- Fifth Section: 35 minutes
- Writing Sample: 35 minutes

We recommend starting with the most recent tests, which are listed first; these are more likely to reflect what will be on your LSAT.

There are several answer grids approximating what you will see on Test Day in the back of this book. If you need additional grids, you'll find a PDF of the grid online that can be printed out. Mark you answer choices on the grid as you complete the exam.

After you've completed the test, enter your answers from the grid in your Online Center to see your test score, compare your scores from test to test, and see detailed analysis of your performance on specific question and game types.

Practice Test 1

PrepTest 60 with Additional Section from PrepTest 46

SECTION I
Time—35 minutes
22 Questions

Directions: Each group of questions in this section is based on a set of conditions. In answering some of the questions, it may be useful to draw a rough diagram. Choose the response that most accurately and completely answers each question and blacken the corresponding space on your answer sheet.

Questions 1–6

Exactly six guideposts, numbered 1 through 6, mark a mountain trail. Each guidepost pictures a different one of six animals—fox, grizzly, hare, lynx, moose, or porcupine. The following conditions must apply:

The grizzly is pictured on either guidepost 3 or guidepost 4.
The moose guidepost is numbered lower than the hare guidepost.
The lynx guidepost is numbered lower than the moose guidepost but higher than the fox guidepost.

1. Which one of the following could be an accurate list of the animals pictured on the guideposts, listed in order from guidepost 1 through guidepost 6?

   (A) fox, lynx, grizzly, porcupine, moose, hare
   (B) fox, lynx, moose, hare, grizzly, porcupine
   (C) fox, moose, grizzly, lynx, hare, porcupine
   (D) lynx, fox, moose, grizzly, hare, porcupine
   (E) porcupine, fox, hare, grizzly, lynx, moose

2. Which one of the following animals CANNOT be the one pictured on guidepost 3?

   (A) fox
   (B) grizzly
   (C) lynx
   (D) moose
   (E) porcupine

3. If the moose is pictured on guidepost 3, then which one of the following is the lowest numbered guidepost that could picture the porcupine?

   (A) guidepost 1
   (B) guidepost 2
   (C) guidepost 4
   (D) guidepost 5
   (E) guidepost 6

4. If guidepost 5 does not picture the moose, then which one of the following must be true?

   (A) The lynx is pictured on guidepost 2.
   (B) The moose is pictured on guidepost 3.
   (C) The grizzly is pictured on guidepost 4.
   (D) The porcupine is pictured on guidepost 5.
   (E) The hare is pictured on guidepost 6.

5. Which one of the following animals could be pictured on any one of the six guideposts?

   (A) fox
   (B) hare
   (C) lynx
   (D) moose
   (E) porcupine

6. If the moose guidepost is numbered exactly one higher than the lynx guidepost, then which one of the following could be true?

   (A) Guidepost 5 pictures the hare.
   (B) Guidepost 4 pictures the moose.
   (C) Guidepost 4 pictures the porcupine.
   (D) Guidepost 3 pictures the lynx.
   (E) Guidepost 3 pictures the porcupine.

GO ON TO THE NEXT PAGE.

Questions 7–11

Each side of four cassette tapes—Tapes 1 through 4—contains exactly one of the following four genres: folk, hip-hop, jazz, and rock. The following conditions must apply:

Each genre is found on exactly two of the eight sides.
Tape 1 has jazz on at least one side, but neither hip-hop nor rock.
Tape 2 has no jazz.
Folk is not on any tape numbered exactly one higher than a tape that has any rock on it.

7. Which one of the following could be an accurate matching of tapes with the musical genres found on them?

(A) Tape 1: folk and jazz; Tape 2: folk and jazz; Tape 3: hip-hop and rock; Tape 4: hip-hop and rock

(B) Tape 1: folk and jazz; Tape 2: folk and rock; Tape 3: hip-hop and jazz; Tape 4: hip-hop and rock

(C) Tape 1: folk and jazz; Tape 2: folk and rock; Tape 3: two sides of jazz; Tape 4: two sides of hip-hop

(D) Tape 1: hip-hop and jazz; Tape 2: folk and hip-hop; Tape 3: folk and jazz; Tape 4: two sides of rock

(E) Tape 1: two sides of jazz; Tape 2: folk and rock; Tape 3: hip-hop and rock; Tape 4: folk and hip-hop

8. Which one of the following must be true?

(A) If Tape 1 has two sides of jazz, Tape 4 has at least one side of rock.

(B) If Tape 2 has two sides of folk, Tape 3 has at least one side of hip-hop.

(C) If Tape 2 has two sides of rock, Tape 4 has at least one side of folk.

(D) If Tape 3 has two sides of folk, Tape 2 has at least one side of jazz.

(E) If Tape 4 has two sides of hip-hop, Tape 3 has at least one side of folk.

9. Which one of the following could be true?

(A) Tape 1 has jazz on both sides while Tape 4 has folk and hip-hop.

(B) Tape 2 has hip-hop on one side while Tape 3 has hip-hop and jazz.

(C) Tape 3 has folk on both sides while Tape 4 has jazz and rock.

(D) Tape 3 has jazz on one side while Tape 4 has folk on both sides.

(E) Tapes 2 and 3 each have jazz on one side.

10. Which one of the following could be true?

(A) Tape 1 has two sides of folk.
(B) Tape 2 has both hip-hop and jazz.
(C) Tape 4 has both folk and rock.
(D) Tapes 1 and 4 each have a side of hip-hop.
(E) Tapes 3 and 4 each have a side of folk.

11. Which one of the following CANNOT be true?

(A) Tape 2 has rock on both sides while Tape 3 has hip-hop on both sides.

(B) Tape 3 has rock on both sides while Tape 2 has hip-hop on both sides.

(C) Tape 3 has rock on both sides while Tape 4 has hip-hop on both sides.

(D) Tape 4 has rock on both sides while Tape 2 has hip-hop on both sides.

(E) Tape 4 has rock on both sides while Tape 3 has hip-hop on both sides.

GO ON TO THE NEXT PAGE.

Questions 12–16

One afternoon, a single thunderstorm passes over exactly five towns—Jackson, Lofton, Nordique, Oceana, and Plattesville—dropping some form of precipitation on each. The storm is the only source of precipitation in the towns that afternoon. On some towns, it drops both hail and rain; on the remaining towns, it drops only rain. It passes over each town exactly once and does not pass over any two towns at the same time. The following must obtain:

The third town the storm passes over is Plattesville.
The storm drops hail and rain on the second town it passes over.
The storm drops only rain on both Lofton and Oceana.
The storm passes over Jackson at some time after it passes over Lofton and at some time after it passes over Nordique.

12. Which one of the following could be the order, from first to fifth, in which the storm passes over the towns?

(A) Lofton, Nordique, Plattesville, Oceana, Jackson
(B) Lofton, Oceana, Plattesville, Nordique, Jackson
(C) Nordique, Jackson, Plattesville, Oceana, Lofton
(D) Nordique, Lofton, Plattesville, Jackson, Oceana
(E) Nordique, Plattesville, Lofton, Oceana, Jackson

13. If the storm passes over Oceana at some time before it passes over Jackson, then each of the following could be true EXCEPT:

(A) The first town the storm passes over is Oceana.
(B) The fourth town the storm passes over is Lofton.
(C) The fourth town the storm passes over receives hail and rain.
(D) The fifth town the storm passes over is Jackson.
(E) The fifth town the storm passes over receives only rain.

14. If the storm drops only rain on each town it passes over after passing over Lofton, then which one of the following could be false?

(A) The first town the storm passes over is Oceana.
(B) The fourth town the storm passes over receives only rain.
(C) The fifth town the storm passes over is Jackson.
(D) Jackson receives only rain.
(E) Plattesville receives only rain.

15. If the storm passes over Jackson at some time before it passes over Oceana, then which one of the following could be false?

(A) The storm passes over Lofton at some time before it passes over Jackson.
(B) The storm passes over Lofton at some time before it passes over Oceana.
(C) The storm passes over Nordique at some time before it passes over Oceana.
(D) The fourth town the storm passes over receives only rain.
(E) The fifth town the storm passes over receives only rain.

16. If the storm passes over Oceana at some time before it passes over Lofton, then which one of the following must be true?

(A) The third town the storm passes over receives only rain.
(B) The fourth town the storm passes over receives only rain.
(C) The fourth town the storm passes over receives hail and rain.
(D) The fifth town the storm passes over receives only rain.
(E) The fifth town the storm passes over receives hail and rain.

GO ON TO THE NEXT PAGE.

Questions 17–22

A reporter is trying to uncover the workings of a secret committee. The committee has six members—French, Ghauri, Hsia, Irving, Magnus, and Pinsky—each of whom serves on at least one subcommittee. There are three subcommittees, each having three members, about which the following is known:

> One of the committee members serves on all three subcommittees.
> French does not serve on any subcommittee with Ghauri.
> Hsia does not serve on any subcommittee with Irving.

17. If French does not serve on any subcommittee with Magnus, which one of the following must be true?

    (A) French serves on a subcommittee with Hsia.
    (B) French serves on a subcommittee with Irving.
    (C) Irving serves on a subcommittee with Pinsky.
    (D) Magnus serves on a subcommittee with Ghauri.
    (E) Magnus serves on a subcommittee with Irving.

18. If Pinsky serves on every subcommittee on which French serves and every subcommittee on which Ghauri serves, then which one of the following could be true?

    (A) Magnus serves on every subcommittee on which French serves and every subcommittee on which Ghauri serves.
    (B) Magnus serves on every subcommittee on which Hsia serves and every subcommittee on which Irving serves.
    (C) Hsia serves on every subcommittee on which French serves and every subcommittee on which Ghauri serves.
    (D) French serves on every subcommittee on which Pinsky serves.
    (E) Hsia serves on every subcommittee on which Pinsky serves.

19. If Irving serves on every subcommittee on which Magnus serves, which one of the following could be true?

    (A) Magnus serves on all of the subcommittees.
    (B) Irving serves on more than one subcommittee.
    (C) Irving serves on every subcommittee on which Pinsky serves.
    (D) French serves on a subcommittee with Magnus.
    (E) Ghauri serves on a subcommittee with Magnus.

20. Which one of the following could be true?

    (A) French serves on all three subcommittees.
    (B) Hsia serves on all three subcommittees.
    (C) Ghauri serves on every subcommittee on which Magnus serves and every subcommittee on which Pinsky serves.
    (D) Pinsky serves on every subcommittee on which Irving serves and every subcommittee on which Magnus serves.
    (E) Magnus serves on every subcommittee on which Pinsky serves, and Pinsky serves on every subcommittee on which Magnus serves.

21. Which one of the following must be true?

    (A) Ghauri serves on at least two subcommittees.
    (B) Irving serves on only one subcommittee.
    (C) French serves on a subcommittee with Hsia.
    (D) Ghauri serves on a subcommittee with Irving.
    (E) Magnus serves on a subcommittee with Pinsky.

22. Which one of the following must be true?

    (A) Every subcommittee has either French or Ghauri as a member.
    (B) Every subcommittee has either Hsia or Irving as a member.
    (C) No subcommittee consists of French, Magnus, and Pinsky.
    (D) Some committee member serves on exactly two subcommittees.
    (E) Either Magnus or Pinsky serves on only one subcommittee.

S T O P

IF YOU FINISH BEFORE TIME IS CALLED, YOU MAY CHECK YOUR WORK ON THIS SECTION ONLY.
DO NOT WORK ON ANY OTHER SECTION IN THE TEST.

SECTION II
Time—35 minutes
25 Questions

Directions: The questions in this section are based on the reasoning contained in brief statements or passages. For some questions, more than one of the choices could conceivably answer the question. However, you are to choose the best answer; that is, the response that most accurately and completely answers the question. You should not make assumptions that are by commonsense standards implausible, superfluous, or incompatible with the passage. After you have chosen the best answer, blacken the corresponding space on your answer sheet.

1. Jim's teacher asked him to determine whether a sample of a substance contained iron. Jim knew that magnets attract iron, so he placed a magnet near the substance. Jim concluded that the substance did contain iron, because the substance became attached to the magnet.

Jim's reasoning is questionable in that it fails to consider the possibility that

(A) iron sometimes fails to be attracted to magnets
(B) iron is attracted to other objects besides magnets
(C) the magnet needed to be oriented in a certain way
(D) magnets attract substances other than iron
(E) some magnets attract iron more strongly than others

2. All the books in the library have their proper shelf locations recorded in the catalog. The book Horatio wants is missing from its place on the library shelves, and no one in the library is using it. Since it is not checked out to a borrower nor awaiting shelving nor part of a special display, it must have been either misplaced or stolen.

Which one of the following most accurately describes the method of reasoning used in the argument?

(A) An observation about one object is used as a basis for a general conclusion regarding the status of similar objects.
(B) A deficiency in a system is isolated by arguing that the system failed to control one of the objects that it was intended to control.
(C) A conclusion about a particular object is rebutted by observing that a generalization that applies to most such objects does not apply to the object in question.
(D) A generalization is rejected by showing that it fails to hold in one particular instance.
(E) The conclusion is supported by ruling out other possible explanations of an observed fact.

3. The level of sulfur dioxide in the atmosphere is slightly higher than it was ten years ago. This increase is troubling because ten years ago the Interior Ministry imposed new, stricter regulations on emissions from coal-burning power plants. If these regulations had been followed, then the level of sulfur dioxide in the atmosphere would have decreased.

Which one of the following can be properly inferred from the statements above?

(A) If current regulations on emissions from coal-burning power plants are not followed from now on, then the level of sulfur dioxide in the atmosphere will continue to increase.
(B) There have been violations of the regulations on emissions from coal-burning power plants that were imposed ten years ago.
(C) If the regulations on emissions from coal-burning power plants are made even stronger, the level of sulfur dioxide in the atmosphere still will not decrease.
(D) Emissions from coal-burning power plants are one of the main sources of air pollution.
(E) Government regulations will never reduce the level of sulfur dioxide in the atmosphere.

GO ON TO THE NEXT PAGE.

4. Ecologist: Landfills are generally designed to hold ten years' worth of waste. Some people maintain that as the number of active landfills consequently dwindles over the coming decade, there will inevitably be a crisis in landfill availability. However, their prediction obviously relies on the unlikely assumption that no new landfills will open as currently active ones close and is therefore unsound.

The claim that there will be a crisis in landfill availability plays which one of the following roles in the ecologist's argument?

(A) It follows from the claim stated in the argument's first sentence.
(B) It is the main conclusion of the argument.
(C) It establishes the truth of the argument's conclusion.
(D) It is a claim on which the argument as a whole is designed to cast doubt.
(E) It is an intermediate conclusion of the argument.

5. Recent epidemiological studies report that Country X has the lowest incidence of disease P of any country. Nevertheless, residents of Country X who are reported to have contracted disease P are much more likely to die from it than are residents of any other country.

Which one of the following, if true, most helps to resolve the apparent discrepancy described above?

(A) There are several forms of disease P, some of which are more contagious than others.
(B) Most of the fatal cases of disease P found in Country X involve people who do not reside in Country X.
(C) In Country X, diagnosis of disease P seldom occurs except in the most severe cases of the disease.
(D) The number of cases of disease P that occur in any country fluctuates widely from year to year.
(E) Because of its climate, more potentially fatal illnesses occur in Country X than in many other countries.

6. After an oil spill, rehabilitation centers were set up to save sea otters by removing oil from them. The effort was not worthwhile, however, since 357 affected live otters and 900 that had died were counted, but only 222 affected otters, or 18 percent of those counted, were successfully rehabilitated and survived. Further, the percentage of all those affected that were successfully rehabilitated was much lower still, because only a fifth of the otters that died immediately were ever found.

Which one of the following, as potential challenges, most seriously calls into question evidence offered in support of the conclusion above?

(A) Do sea otters of species other than those represented among the otters counted exist in areas that were not affected by the oil spill?
(B) How is it possible to estimate, of the sea otters that died, how many were not found?
(C) Did the process of capturing sea otters unavoidably involve trapping and releasing some otters that were not affected by the spill?
(D) Were other species of wildlife besides sea otters negatively affected by the oil spill?
(E) What was the eventual cost, per otter rehabilitated, of the rehabilitation operation?

7. Psychologist: Research has shown that a weakened immune system increases vulnerability to cancer. So, cancer-patient support groups, though derided by those who believe that disease is a purely biochemical phenomenon, may indeed have genuine therapeutic value, as it is clear that participation in such groups reduces participants' stress levels.

Which one of the following is an assumption required by the psychologist's argument?

(A) Cancer patients can learn to function well under extreme stress.
(B) Disease is not a biochemical phenomenon at all.
(C) Stress can weaken the immune system.
(D) Discussing one's condition eliminates the stress of being in that condition.
(E) Stress is a symptom of a weakened immune system.

GO ON TO THE NEXT PAGE.

8. Adobe is an ideal material for building in desert environments. It conducts heat very slowly. As a result, a house built of adobe retains the warmth of the desert sun during the cool evenings and then remains cool during the heat of the day, thereby helping to maintain a pleasant temperature. In contrast, houses built of other commonly used building materials, which conduct heat more rapidly, grow hot during the day and cold at night.

Which one of the following most accurately expresses the main conclusion drawn in the argument above?

(A) Adobe is a suitable substitute for other building materials where the heat-conduction properties of the structure are especially important.

(B) In the desert, adobe buildings remain cool during the heat of the day but retain the warmth of the sun during the cool evenings.

(C) Because adobe conducts heat very slowly, adobe houses maintain a pleasant, constant temperature.

(D) Ideally, a material used for building houses in desert environments should enable those houses to maintain a pleasant, constant temperature.

(E) Adobe is an especially suitable material to use for building houses in desert environments.

9. In one study of a particular plant species, 70 percent of the plants studied were reported as having patterned stems. In a second study, which covered approximately the same geographical area, only 40 percent of the plants of that species were reported as having patterned stems.

Which one of the following, if true, most helps to resolve the apparent discrepancy described above?

(A) The first study was carried out at the time of year when plants of the species are at their most populous.

(B) The first study, but not the second study, also collected information about patterned stems in other plant species.

(C) The second study included approximately 15 percent more individual plants than the first study did.

(D) The first study used a broader definition of "patterned."

(E) The focus of the second study was patterned stems, while the first study collected information about patterned stems only as a secondary goal.

10. Letter to the editor: Sites are needed for disposal of contaminated dredge spoils from the local harbor. However, the approach you propose would damage commercial fishing operations. One indication of this is that over 20,000 people have signed petitions opposing your approach and favoring instead the use of sand-capped pits in another area.

Which one of the following most accurately describes a reasoning flaw in the letter's argument?

(A) The argument distorts the editor's view in a manner that makes that view seem more vulnerable to criticism.

(B) The argument fails to establish that the alternative approach referred to is a viable one.

(C) The argument attempts to establish a particular conclusion because doing so is in the letter writer's self-interest rather than because of any genuine concern for the truth of the matter.

(D) The argument's conclusion is based on the testimony of people who have not been shown to have appropriate expertise.

(E) The argument takes for granted that no third option is available that will satisfy all the interested parties.

GO ON TO THE NEXT PAGE.

11. Most universities today offer students a more in-depth and cosmopolitan education than ever before. Until recently, for example, most university history courses required only the reading of textbooks that hardly mentioned the history of Africa or Asia after the ancient periods, or the history of the Americas' indigenous cultures. The history courses at most universities no longer display such limitations.

Which one of the following, if true, most strengthens the argument above?

(A) The history courses that university students find most interesting are comprehensive in their coverage of various periods and cultures.

(B) Many students at universities whose history courses require the reading of books covering all periods and world cultures participate in innovative study-abroad programs.

(C) The extent to which the textbooks of university history courses are culturally inclusive is a strong indication of the extent to which students at those universities get an in-depth and cosmopolitan education.

(D) Universities at which the history courses are quite culturally inclusive do not always have courses in other subject areas that show the same inclusiveness.

(E) University students who in their history courses are required only to read textbooks covering the history of a single culture will not get an in-depth and cosmopolitan education from these courses alone.

12. The government has recently adopted a policy of publishing airline statistics, including statistics about each airline's number of near collisions and its fines for safety violations. However, such disclosure actually undermines the government's goal of making the public more informed about airline safety, because airlines will be much less likely to give complete reports if such information will be made available to the public.

The reasoning in the argument is most vulnerable to criticism on the grounds that it

(A) fails to consider that, even if the reports are incomplete, they may nevertheless provide the public with important information about airline safety

(B) presumes, without providing justification, that the public has a right to all information about matters of public safety

(C) presumes, without providing justification, that information about airline safety is impossible to find in the absence of government disclosures

(D) presumes, without providing justification, that airlines, rather than the government, should be held responsible for accurate reporting of safety information

(E) fails to consider whether the publication of airline safety statistics will have an effect on the revenues of airlines

13. Many economists claim that financial rewards provide the strongest incentive for people to choose one job over another. But in many surveys, most people do not name high salary as the most desirable feature of a job. This shows that these economists overestimate the degree to which people are motivated by money in their job choices.

Which one of the following, if true, most weakens the argument?

(A) Even high wages do not enable people to obtain all the goods they desire.

(B) In many surveys, people say that they would prefer a high-wage job to an otherwise identical job with lower wages.

(C) Jobs that pay the same salary often vary considerably in their other financial benefits.

(D) Many people enjoy the challenge of a difficult job, as long as they feel that their efforts are appreciated.

(E) Some people are not aware that jobs with high salaries typically leave very little time for recreation.

14. Editorial: A proposed new law would limit elementary school class sizes to a maximum of 20 students. Most parents support this measure and argue that making classes smaller allows teachers to devote more time to each student, with the result that students become more engaged in the learning process. However, researchers who conducted a recent study conclude from their results that this reasoning is questionable. The researchers studied schools that had undergone recent reductions in class size, and found that despite an increase in the amount of time teachers spent individually with students, the students' average grades were unchanged.

Which one of the following is an assumption required by the researchers' argument?

(A) The only schools appropriate for study are large elementary schools.

(B) Teachers generally devote the same amount of individualized attention to each student in a class.

(C) Reductions in class size would also involve a decrease in the number of teachers.

(D) Degree of student engagement in the learning process correlates well with students' average grades.

(E) Parental support for the proposed law rests solely on expectations of increased student engagement in the learning process.

GO ON TO THE NEXT PAGE.

15. Camille: Manufacturers of water-saving faucets exaggerate the amount of money such faucets can save. Because the faucets handle such a low volume of water, people using them often let the water run longer than they would otherwise.

Rebecca: It is true that showering now takes longer. Nevertheless, I have had lower water bills since I installed a water-saving faucet. Thus, it is not true that the manufacturers' claims are exaggerated.

The reasoning in Rebecca's argument is questionable in that she takes for granted that

(A) the cost of installing her water-saving faucet was less than her overall savings on her water bill
(B) she saved as much on her water bills as the manufacturers' claims suggested she would
(C) the manufacturers' claims about the savings expected from the installation of water-saving faucets are consistent with one another
(D) people who use water-saving faucets are satisfied with the low volume of water handled by such faucets
(E) installing more water-saving faucets in her house would increase her savings

16. Company spokesperson: In lieu of redesigning our plants, our company recently launched an environmental protection campaign to buy and dispose of old cars, which are generally highly pollutive. Our plants account for just 4 percent of the local air pollution, while automobiles that predate 1980 account for 30 percent. Clearly, we will reduce air pollution more by buying old cars than we would by redesigning our plants.

Which one of the following, if true, most seriously weakens the company spokesperson's argument?

(A) Only 1 percent of the automobiles driven in the local area predate 1980.
(B) It would cost the company over $3 million to reduce its plants' toxic emissions, while its car-buying campaign will save the company money by providing it with reusable scrap metal.
(C) Because the company pays only scrap metal prices for used cars, almost none of the cars sold to the company still run.
(D) Automobiles made after 1980 account for over 30 percent of local air pollution.
(E) Since the company launched its car-buying campaign, the number of citizen groups filing complaints about pollution from the company's plants has decreased.

17. Humankind would not have survived, as it clearly has, if our ancestors had not been motivated by the desire to sacrifice themselves when doing so would ensure the survival of their children or other close relatives. But since even this kind of sacrifice is a form of altruism, it follows that our ancestors were at least partially altruistic.

Which one of the following arguments is most similar in its reasoning to the argument above?

(A) Students do not raise their grades if they do not increase the amount of time they spend studying. Increased study time requires good time management. However, some students do raise their grades. So some students manage their time well.
(B) Organisms are capable of manufacturing their own carbohydrate supply if they do not consume other organisms to obtain it. So plants that consume insects must be incapable of photosynthesis, the means by which most plants produce their carbohydrate supplies.
(C) If fragile ecosystems are not protected by government action their endemic species will perish, for endemic species are by definition those that exist nowhere else but in those ecosystems.
(D) The natural resources used by human beings will be depleted if they are not replaced by alternative materials. But since such replacement generally requires more power, the resources used to create that power will become depleted.
(E) Public buildings do not harmonize with their surroundings if they are not well designed. But any well-designed building is expensive to construct. Thus, either public buildings are expensive to construct or else they do not harmonize with their surroundings.

GO ON TO THE NEXT PAGE.

18. Bus driver: Had the garbage truck not been exceeding the speed limit, it would not have collided with the bus I was driving. I, on the other hand, was abiding by all traffic regulations—as the police report confirms. Therefore, although I might have been able to avoid the collision had I reacted more quickly, the bus company should not reprimand me for the accident.

Which one of the following principles, if valid, most helps to justify the reasoning in the bus driver's argument?

(A) If a vehicle whose driver is violating a traffic regulation collides with a vehicle whose driver is not, the driver of the first vehicle is solely responsible for the accident.

(B) A bus company should not reprimand one of its drivers whose bus is involved in a collision if a police report confirms that the collision was completely the fault of the driver of another vehicle.

(C) Whenever a bus driver causes a collision to occur by violating a traffic regulation, the bus company should reprimand that driver.

(D) A company that employs bus drivers should reprimand those drivers only when they become involved in collisions that they reasonably could have been expected to avoid.

(E) When a bus is involved in a collision, the bus driver should not be reprimanded by the bus company if the collision did not result from the bus driver's violating a traffic regulation.

19. Item Removed From Scoring.

20. Historian: Radio drama requires its listeners to think about what they hear, picturing for themselves such dramatic elements as characters' physical appearances and spatial relationships. Hence, while earlier generations, for whom radio drama was the dominant form of popular entertainment, regularly exercised their imaginations, today's generation of television viewers do so less frequently.

Which one of the following is an assumption required by the historian's argument?

(A) People spend as much time watching television today as people spent listening to radio in radio's heyday.

(B) The more familiar a form of popular entertainment becomes, the less likely its consumers are to exercise their imaginations.

(C) Because it inhibits the development of creativity, television is a particularly undesirable form of popular entertainment.

(D) For today's generation of television viewers, nothing fills the gap left by radio as a medium for exercising the imagination.

(E) Television drama does not require its viewers to think about what they see.

GO ON TO THE NEXT PAGE.

21. Each of the candidates in this year's mayoral election is a small-business owner. Most small-business owners are competent managers. Moreover, no competent manager lacks the skills necessary to be a good mayor. So, most of the candidates in this year's mayoral election have the skills necessary to be a good mayor.

The pattern of flawed reasoning in which one of the following is most similar to that in the argument above?

(A) Anyone who has worked in sales at this company has done so for at least a year. Most of this company's management has worked in its sales department. So, since no one who has worked in the sales department for more than a year fails to understand marketing, most of this company's upper management understands marketing.

(B) Everything on the menu at Maddy's Shake Shop is fat-free. Most fat-free foods and drinks are sugar-free. And all sugar-free foods and drinks are low in calories. Hence, most items on the menu at Maddy's are low in calories.

(C) All the books in Ed's apartment are hardcover books. Most hardcover books are more than 100 pages long. Ed has never read a book longer than 100 pages in its entirety in less than 3 hours. So, Ed has never read any of his books in its entirety in less than 3 hours.

(D) Each of the avant-garde films at this year's film festival is less than an hour long. Most films less than an hour long do not become commercially successful. So, since no movie less than an hour long has an intermission, it follows that most of the movies at this year's film festival do not have an intermission.

(E) All of the bicycle helmets sold in this store have some plastic in them. Most of the bicycle helmets sold in this store have some rubber in them. So, since no helmets that have rubber in them do not also have plastic in them, it follows that most of the helmets in this store that have plastic in them have rubber in them.

22. One of the most useful social conventions is money, whose universality across societies is matched only by language. Unlike language, which is rooted in an innate ability, money is an artificial, human invention. Hence, it seems probable that the invention of money occurred independently in more than one society.

The argument's conclusion is properly drawn if which one of the following is assumed?

(A) Some societies have been geographically isolated enough not to have been influenced by any other society.

(B) Language emerged independently in different societies at different times in human history.

(C) Universal features of human society that are not inventions are rooted in innate abilities.

(D) If money were not useful, it would not be so widespread.

(E) No human society that adopted the convention of money has since abandoned it.

23. Libel is defined as damaging the reputation of someone by making false statements. Ironically, strong laws against libel can make it impossible for anyone in the public eye to have a good reputation. For the result of strong libel laws is that, for fear of lawsuits, no one will say anything bad about public figures.

Which one of the following principles, if valid, most helps to justify the reasoning in the argument?

(A) The absence of laws against libel makes it possible for everyone in the public eye to have a good reputation.

(B) Even if laws against libel are extremely strong and rigorously enforced, some public figures will acquire bad reputations.

(C) If one makes statements that one sincerely believes, then those statements should not be considered libelous even if they are in fact false and damaging to the reputation of a public figure.

(D) In countries with strong libel laws, people make negative statements about public figures only when such statements can be proved.

(E) Public figures can have good reputations only if there are other public figures who have bad reputations.

GO ON TO THE NEXT PAGE.

24. Mammals cannot digest cellulose and therefore cannot directly obtain glucose from wood. Mushrooms can, however; and some mushrooms use cellulose to make highly branched polymers, the branches of which are a form of glucose called beta-glucans. Beta-glucan extracts from various types of mushrooms slow, reverse, or prevent the growth of cancerous tumors in mammals, and the antitumor activity of beta-glucans increases as the degree of branching increases. These extracts prevent tumor growth not by killing cancer cells directly but by increasing immune-cell activity.

Which one of the following is most strongly supported by the information above?

(A) Mammals obtain no beneficial health effects from eating cellulose.

(B) If extracts from a type of mushroom slow, reverse, or prevent the growth of cancerous tumors in mammals, then the mushroom is capable of using cellulose to make beta-glucans.

(C) The greater the degree of branching of beta-glucans, the greater the degree of immune-cell activity it triggers in mammals.

(D) Immune-cell activity in mammals does not prevent tumor growth by killing cancer cells.

(E) Any organism capable of obtaining glucose from wood can use cellulose to make beta-glucans.

25. A law is successful primarily because the behavior it prescribes has attained the status of custom. Just as manners are observed not because of sanctions attached to them but because, through repetition, contrary behavior becomes unthinkable, so societal laws are obeyed not because the behavior is ethically required or because penalties await those who act otherwise, but because to act otherwise would be uncustomary.

Which one of the following comparisons is utilized by the argument?

(A) As with manners and other customs, laws vary from society to society.

(B) As with manners, the primary basis for a society to consider when adopting a law is custom.

(C) As with manners, the main factor accounting for compliance with laws is custom.

(D) As with manners, most laws do not prescribe behavior that is ethically required.

(E) As with manners, most laws do not have strict penalties awaiting those who transgress them.

S T O P

IF YOU FINISH BEFORE TIME IS CALLED, YOU MAY CHECK YOUR WORK ON THIS SECTION ONLY.
DO NOT WORK ON ANY OTHER SECTION IN THE TEST.

SECTION III
Time—35 minutes
23 Questions

<u>Directions:</u> Each group of questions in this section is based on a set of conditions. In answering some of the questions, it may be useful to draw a rough diagram. Choose the response that most accurately and completely answers each question and blacken the corresponding space on your answer sheet.

<u>Questions 1–6</u>

A community center will host six arts-and-crafts workshops—Jewelry, Kite-making, Needlepoint, Quilting, Rug-making, and Scrapbooking. The workshops will be given on three consecutive days: Wednesday, Thursday, and Friday. Each workshop will be given once, and exactly two workshops will be given per day, one in the morning and one in the afternoon. The schedule for the workshops is subject to the following constraints:

> Jewelry must be given in the morning, on the same day as either Kite-making or Quilting.
> Rug-making must be given in the afternoon, on the same day as either Needlepoint or Scrapbooking.
> Quilting must be given on an earlier day than both Kite-making and Needlepoint.

1. Which one of the following is an acceptable schedule for the workshops, with each day's workshops listed in the order in which they are to be given?

   (A) Wednesday: Jewelry, Kite-making
   Thursday: Quilting, Scrapbooking
   Friday: Needlepoint, Rug-making
   (B) Wednesday: Jewelry, Quilting
   Thursday: Kite-making, Needlepoint
   Friday: Scrapbooking, Rug-making
   (C) Wednesday: Quilting, Needlepoint
   Thursday: Scrapbooking, Rug-making
   Friday: Jewelry, Kite-making
   (D) Wednesday: Quilting, Scrapbooking
   Thursday: Jewelry, Kite-making
   Friday: Rug-making, Needlepoint
   (E) Wednesday: Scrapbooking, Rug-making
   Thursday: Quilting, Jewelry
   Friday: Kite-making, Needlepoint

2. Which one of the following workshops CANNOT be given on Thursday morning?

   (A) Jewelry
   (B) Kite-making
   (C) Needlepoint
   (D) Quilting
   (E) Scrapbooking

3. Which one of the following pairs of workshops CANNOT be the ones given on Wednesday morning and Wednesday afternoon, respectively?

   (A) Jewelry, Kite-making
   (B) Jewelry, Quilting
   (C) Quilting, Scrapbooking
   (D) Scrapbooking, Quilting
   (E) Scrapbooking, Rug-making

4. If Kite-making is given on Friday morning, then which one of the following could be true?

   (A) Jewelry is given on Thursday morning.
   (B) Needlepoint is given on Thursday afternoon.
   (C) Quilting is given on Wednesday morning.
   (D) Rug-making is given on Friday afternoon.
   (E) Scrapbooking is given on Wednesday afternoon.

5. If Quilting is given in the morning, then which one of the following workshops CANNOT be given on Thursday?

   (A) Jewelry
   (B) Kite-making
   (C) Needlepoint
   (D) Rug-making
   (E) Scrapbooking

6. How many of the workshops are there that could be the one given on Wednesday morning?

   (A) one
   (B) two
   (C) three
   (D) four
   (E) five

GO ON TO THE NEXT PAGE.

Questions 7–12

Exactly six actors—Geyer, Henson, Jhalani, Lin, Mitchell, and Paredes—will appear one after another in the opening credits of a television program. Their contracts contain certain restrictions that affect the order in which they can appear. Given these restrictions, the order in which the actors appear, from first to sixth, must conform to the following:

    Both Lin and Mitchell appear earlier than Henson.
    Both Lin and Paredes appear earlier than Jhalani.
    If Mitchell appears earlier than Paredes, then Henson
      appears earlier than Geyer.
    Geyer does not appear last.

7. Which one of the following could be the order, from first to last, in which the actors appear?

  (A) Geyer, Lin, Jhalani, Paredes, Mitchell, Henson
  (B) Geyer, Mitchell, Paredes, Lin, Henson, Jhalani
  (C) Henson, Lin, Paredes, Jhalani, Geyer, Mitchell
  (D) Lin, Paredes, Mitchell, Henson, Jhalani, Geyer
  (E) Paredes, Mitchell, Lin, Jhalani, Geyer, Henson

8. Which one of the following CANNOT be true?

  (A) Henson appears earlier than Geyer.
  (B) Henson appears sixth.
  (C) Lin appears fifth.
  (D) Paredes appears earlier than Mitchell.
  (E) Paredes appears second.

9. Exactly how many of the actors are there any one of whom could appear sixth?

  (A) 5
  (B) 4
  (C) 3
  (D) 2
  (E) 1

10. If Jhalani appears earlier than Mitchell, then which one of the following could be the order in which the other four actors appear, from earliest to latest?

  (A) Geyer, Lin, Paredes, Henson
  (B) Geyer, Paredes, Henson, Lin
  (C) Lin, Henson, Geyer, Paredes
  (D) Lin, Paredes, Henson, Geyer
  (E) Paredes, Lin, Henson, Geyer

11. If Lin appears immediately before Geyer, then which one of the following must be true?

  (A) Geyer appears no later than third.
  (B) Henson appears last.
  (C) Lin appears no later than third.
  (D) Mitchell appears earlier than Geyer.
  (E) Paredes appears first.

12. If Mitchell appears first, then which one of the following must be true?

  (A) Geyer appears fifth.
  (B) Henson appears third.
  (C) Jhalani appears sixth.
  (D) Lin appears second.
  (E) Paredes appears fourth.

GO ON TO THE NEXT PAGE.

Questions 13–17

Over the course of one day, a landscaper will use a truck to haul exactly seven loads—three loads of mulch and four loads of stone. The truck's cargo bed will be cleaned in between carrying any two loads of different materials. To meet the landscaper's needs as efficiently as possible, the following constraints apply:

The cargo bed cannot be cleaned more than three times.
The fifth load must be mulch.

13. Which one of the following is a pair of loads that can both be mulch?

   (A) the first and the third
   (B) the second and the third
   (C) the second and the sixth
   (D) the third and the sixth
   (E) the fourth and the sixth

14. Which one of the following must be true?

   (A) The second load is stone.
   (B) The first and second loads are the same material.
   (C) The second and third loads are different materials.
   (D) At least two loads of mulch are hauled consecutively.
   (E) At least three loads of stone are hauled consecutively.

15. If the third load is mulch, which one of the following must be true?

   (A) The sixth load is a different material than the seventh load.
   (B) The first load is a different material than the second load.
   (C) The seventh load is mulch.
   (D) The sixth load is mulch.
   (E) The first load is stone.

16. If the cargo bed is cleaned exactly twice, which one of the following must be true?

   (A) The second load is stone.
   (B) The third load is mulch.
   (C) The third load is stone.
   (D) The sixth load is mulch.
   (E) The seventh load is mulch.

17. If no more than two loads of the same material are hauled consecutively, then which one of the following could be true?

   (A) The first load is stone.
   (B) The fourth load is stone.
   (C) The third load is mulch.
   (D) The sixth load is mulch.
   (E) The seventh load is mulch.

GO ON TO THE NEXT PAGE.

Questions 18–23

A travel magazine has hired six interns—Farber, Gombarick, Hall, Jackson, Kanze, and Lha—to assist in covering three stories—Romania, Spain, and Tuscany. Each intern will be trained either as a photographer's assistant or as a writer's assistant. Each story is assigned a team of two interns—one photographer's assistant and one writer's assistant—in accordance with the following conditions:

    Gombarick and Lha will be trained in the same field.
    Farber and Kanze will be trained in different fields.
    Hall will be trained as a photographer's assistant.
    Jackson is assigned to Tuscany.
    Kanze is not assigned to Spain.

18. Which one of the following could be an acceptable assignment of photographer's assistants to stories?

    (A)   Romania: Farber
           Spain: Hall
           Tuscany: Jackson
    (B)   Romania: Gombarick
           Spain: Hall
           Tuscany: Farber
    (C)   Romania: Gombarick
           Spain: Hall
           Tuscany: Lha
    (D)   Romania: Gombarick
           Spain: Lha
           Tuscany: Kanze
    (E)   Romania: Hall
           Spain: Kanze
           Tuscany: Jackson

19. If Farber is assigned to Romania, then which one of the following must be true?

    (A)   Gombarick is assigned to Spain.
    (B)   Hall is assigned to Spain.
    (C)   Kanze is assigned to Tuscany.
    (D)   Lha is assigned to Spain.
    (E)   Lha is assigned to Tuscany.

20. If Farber and Hall are assigned to the same story as each other, then which one of the following could be true?

    (A)   Farber is assigned to Tuscany.
    (B)   Gombarick is assigned to Romania.
    (C)   Hall is assigned to Romania.
    (D)   Kanze is assigned to Tuscany.
    (E)   Lha is assigned to Spain.

21. If Farber is a writer's assistant, then which one of the following pairs could be the team of interns assigned to Romania?

    (A)   Farber and Gombarick
    (B)   Gombarick and Hall
    (C)   Hall and Kanze
    (D)   Kanze and Lha
    (E)   Lha and Hall

22. If Gombarick and Kanze are assigned to the same story as each other, then which one of the following could be true?

    (A)   Farber is assigned to Romania.
    (B)   Gombarick is assigned to Spain.
    (C)   Hall is assigned to Romania.
    (D)   Kanze is assigned to Tuscany.
    (E)   Lha is assigned to Spain.

23. Which one of the following interns CANNOT be assigned to Tuscany?

    (A)   Farber
    (B)   Gombarick
    (C)   Hall
    (D)   Kanze
    (E)   Lha

S T O P

IF YOU FINISH BEFORE TIME IS CALLED, YOU MAY CHECK YOUR WORK ON THIS SECTION ONLY.
DO NOT WORK ON ANY OTHER SECTION IN THE TEST.

SECTION IV
Time—35 minutes
25 Questions

Directions: The questions in this section are based on the reasoning contained in brief statements or passages. For some questions, more than one of the choices could conceivably answer the question. However, you are to choose the best answer; that is, the response that most accurately and completely answers the question. You should not make assumptions that are by commonsense standards implausible, superfluous, or incompatible with the passage. After you have chosen the best answer, blacken the corresponding space on your answer sheet.

1. A research study revealed that, in most cases, once existing highways near urban areas are widened and extended in an attempt to reduce traffic congestion and resulting delays for motorists, these problems actually increase rather than decrease.

    Which one of the following, if true, most helps to explain the discrepancy between the intended results of the highway improvements and the results revealed in the study?

    (A) Widened and extended roads tend to attract many more motorists than used them before their improvement.
    (B) Typically, road widening or extension projects are undertaken only after the population near the road in question has increased and then leveled off, leaving a higher average population level.
    (C) As a general rule, the greater the number of lanes on a given length of highway, the lower the rate of accidents per 100,000 vehicles traveling on it.
    (D) Rural, as compared to urban, traffic usually includes a larger proportion of trucks and vehicles used by farmers.
    (E) Urban traffic generally moves at a slower pace and involves more congestion and delays than rural and suburban traffic.

2. A study found that consumers reaching supermarket checkout lines within 40 minutes after the airing of an advertisement for a given product over the store's audio system were significantly more likely to purchase the product advertised than were consumers who checked out prior to the airing. Apparently, these advertisements are effective.

    Which one of the following, if true, most strengthens the argument?

    (A) During the study, for most of the advertisements more people went through the checkout lines after they were aired than before they were aired.
    (B) A large proportion of the consumers who bought a product shortly after the airing of an advertisement for it reported that they had not gone to the store intending to buy that product.
    (C) Many of the consumers reported that they typically bought at least one of the advertised products every time they shopped at the store.
    (D) Many of the consumers who bought an advertised product and who reached the checkout line within 40 minutes of the advertisement's airing reported that they could not remember hearing the advertisement.
    (E) Many of the consumers who bought an advertised product reported that they buy that product only occasionally.

GO ON TO THE NEXT PAGE.

3. Unless the building permit is obtained by February 1 of this year or some of the other activities necessary for construction of the new library can be completed in less time than originally planned, the new library will not be completed on schedule. It is now clear that the building permit cannot be obtained by February 1, so the new library will not be completed on schedule.

The conclusion drawn follows logically from the premises if which one of the following is assumed?

(A) All of the other activities necessary for construction of the library will take at least as much time as originally planned.

(B) The officials in charge of construction of the new library have admitted that it probably will not be completed on schedule.

(C) The application for a building permit was submitted on January 2 of this year, and processing building permits always takes at least two months.

(D) The application for a building permit was rejected the first time it was submitted, and it had to be resubmitted with a revised building plan.

(E) It is not possible to convince authorities to allow construction of the library to begin before the building permit is obtained.

4. In a study of patients who enrolled at a sleep clinic because of insomnia, those who inhaled the scent of peppermint before going to bed were more likely to have difficulty falling asleep than were patients who inhaled the scent of bitter orange. Since it is known that inhaling bitter orange does not help people fall asleep more easily, this study shows that inhaling the scent of peppermint makes insomnia worse.

Which one of the following, if true, most seriously weakens the argument above?

(A) Several studies have shown that inhaling the scent of peppermint tends to have a relaxing effect on people who do not suffer from insomnia.

(B) The patients who inhaled the scent of bitter orange were, on average, suffering from milder cases of insomnia than were the patients who inhaled the scent of peppermint.

(C) Because the scents of peppermint and bitter orange are each very distinctive, it was not possible to prevent the patients from knowing that they were undergoing some sort of study of the effects of inhaling various scents.

(D) Some of the patients who enrolled in the sleep clinic also had difficulty staying asleep once they fell asleep.

(E) Several studies have revealed that in many cases inhaling certain pleasant scents can dramatically affect the degree to which a patient suffers from insomnia.

5. Dogs learn best when they are trained using both voice commands and hand signals. After all, a recent study shows that dogs who were trained using both voice commands and hand signals were twice as likely to obey as were dogs who were trained using only voice commands.

The claim that dogs learn best when they are trained using both voice commands and hand signals figures in the argument in which one of the following ways?

(A) It is an explicit premise of the argument.

(B) It is an implicit assumption of the argument.

(C) It is a statement of background information offered to help facilitate understanding the issue in the argument.

(D) It is a statement that the argument claims is supported by the study.

(E) It is an intermediate conclusion that is offered as direct support for the argument's main conclusion.

6. Of the many test pilots who have flown the new plane, none has found it difficult to operate. So it is unlikely that the test pilot flying the plane tomorrow will find it difficult to operate.

The reasoning in which one of the following arguments is most similar to the reasoning in the argument above?

(A) All of the many book reviewers who read Rachel Nguyen's new novel thought that it was particularly well written. So it is likely that the average reader will enjoy the book.

(B) Many of the book reviewers who read Wim Jashka's new novel before it was published found it very entertaining. So it is unlikely that most people who buy the book will find it boring.

(C) Neither of the two reviewers who enjoyed Sharlene Lo's new novel hoped that Lo would write a sequel. So it is unlikely that the review of the book in next Sunday's newspaper will express hope that Lo will write a sequel.

(D) Many reviewers have read Kip Landau's new novel, but none of them enjoyed it. So it is unlikely that the reviewer for the local newspaper will enjoy the book when she reads it.

(E) None of the reviewers who have read Gray Ornsby's new novel were offended by it. So it is unlikely that the book will offend anyone in the general public who reads it.

GO ON TO THE NEXT PAGE.

7. Scientist: Any theory that is to be taken seriously must affect our perception of the world. Of course, this is not, in itself, enough for a theory to be taken seriously. To see this, one need only consider astrology.

The point of the scientist's mentioning astrology in the argument is to present

(A) an example of a theory that should not be taken seriously because it does not affect our perception of the world

(B) an example of something that should not be considered a theory

(C) an example of a theory that should not be taken seriously despite its affecting our perception of the world

(D) an example of a theory that affects our perception of the world, and thus should be taken seriously

(E) an example of a theory that should be taken seriously, even though it does not affect our perception of the world

8. Clark: Our local community theater often produces plays by critically acclaimed playwrights. In fact, the production director says that critical acclaim is one of the main factors considered in the selection of plays to perform. So, since my neighbor Michaela's new play will be performed by the theater this season, she must be a critically acclaimed playwright.

The reasoning in Clark's argument is most vulnerable to criticism on the grounds that the argument

(A) takes a condition necessary for a playwright's being critically acclaimed to be a condition sufficient for a playwright's being critically acclaimed

(B) fails to consider that several different effects may be produced by a single cause

(C) treats one main factor considered in the selection of plays to perform as though it were a condition that must be met in order for a play to be selected

(D) uses as evidence a source that there is reason to believe is unreliable

(E) provides no evidence that a playwright's being critically acclaimed is the result rather than the cause of his or her plays being selected for production

9. Legal theorist: Governments should not be allowed to use the personal diaries of an individual who is the subject of a criminal prosecution as evidence against that individual. A diary is a silent conversation with oneself and there is no relevant difference between speaking to oneself, writing one's thoughts down, and keeping one's thoughts to oneself.

Which one of the following principles, if valid, provides the most support for the legal theorist's argument?

(A) Governments should not be allowed to compel corporate officials to surrender interoffice memos to government investigators.

(B) When crime is a serious problem, governments should be given increased power to investigate and prosecute suspected wrongdoers, and some restrictions on admissible evidence should be relaxed.

(C) Governments should not be allowed to use an individual's remarks to prosecute the individual for criminal activity unless the remarks were intended for other people.

(D) Governments should not have the power to confiscate an individual's personal correspondence to use as evidence against the individual in a criminal trial.

(E) Governments should do everything in their power to investigate and prosecute suspected wrongdoers.

10. A ring of gas emitting X-rays flickering 450 times per second has been observed in a stable orbit around a black hole. In light of certain widely accepted physical theories, that rate of flickering can best be explained if the ring of gas has a radius of 49 kilometers. But the gas ring could not maintain an orbit so close to a black hole unless the black hole was spinning.

The statements above, if true, most strongly support which one of the following, assuming that the widely accepted physical theories referred to above are correct?

(A) Black holes that have orbiting rings of gas with radii greater than 49 kilometers are usually stationary.

(B) Only rings of gas that are in stable orbits around black holes emit flickering X-rays.

(C) The black hole that is within the ring of gas observed by the astronomers is spinning.

(D) X-rays emitted by rings of gas orbiting black holes cause those black holes to spin.

(E) A black hole is stationary only if it is orbited by a ring of gas with a radius of more than 49 kilometers.

GO ON TO THE NEXT PAGE.

11. A mass of "black water" containing noxious organic material swept through Laurel Bay last year. Some scientists believe that this event was a naturally occurring but infrequent phenomenon. The black water completely wiped out five species of coral in the bay, including mounds of coral that were more than two centuries old. Therefore, even if this black water phenomenon has struck the bay before, it did not reach last year's intensity at any time in the past two centuries.

Which one of the following is an assumption required by the argument?

(A) Masses of black water such as that observed last summer come into the bay more frequently than just once every two centuries.

(B) Every species of coral in the bay was seriously harmed by the mass of black water that swept in last year.

(C) The mass of black water that swept through the bay last year did not decimate any plant or animal species that makes use of coral.

(D) The mounds of centuries-old coral that were destroyed were not in especially fragile condition just before the black water swept in last year.

(E) Older specimens of coral in the bay were more vulnerable to damage from the influx of black water than were young specimens.

12. Many nurseries sell fruit trees that they label "miniature." Not all nurseries, however, use this term in the same way. While some nurseries label any nectarine trees of the Stark Sweet Melody variety as "miniature," for example, others do not. One thing that is clear is that if a variety of fruit tree is not suitable for growing in a tub or a pot, no tree of that variety can be correctly labeled "miniature."

Which one of the following can be properly inferred from the information above?

(A) Most nurseries mislabel at least some of their fruit trees.

(B) Some of the nurseries have correctly labeled nectarine trees of the Stark Sweet Melody variety only if the variety is unsuitable for growing in a tub or a pot.

(C) Any nectarine tree of the Stark Sweet Melody variety that a nursery labels "miniature" is labeled incorrectly.

(D) Some nectarine trees that are not labeled "miniature" are labeled incorrectly.

(E) Unless the Stark Sweet Melody variety of nectarine tree is suitable for growing in a tub or a pot, some nurseries mislabel this variety of tree.

13. Psychologist: Identical twins are virtually the same genetically. Moreover, according to some studies, identical twins separated at birth and brought up in vastly different environments show a strong tendency to report similar ethical beliefs, dress in the same way, and have similar careers. Thus, many of our inclinations must be genetic in origin, and not subject to environmental influences.

Which one of the following, if true, would most weaken the psychologist's argument?

(A) Many people, including identical twins, undergo radical changes in their lifestyles at some point in their lives.

(B) While some studies of identical twins separated at birth reveal a high percentage of similar personality traits, they also show a few differences.

(C) Scientists are far from being able to link any specific genes to specific inclinations.

(D) Identical twins who grow up together tend to develop different beliefs, tastes, and careers in order to differentiate themselves from each other.

(E) Twins who are not identical tend to develop different beliefs, tastes, and careers.

14. Human beings can live happily only in a society where love and friendship are the primary motives for actions. Yet economic needs can be satisfied in the absence of this condition, as, for example, in a merchant society where only economic utility motivates action. It is obvious then that human beings _____.

Which one of the following most logically completes the argument?

(A) can live happily only when economic utility is not a motivator in their society

(B) cannot achieve happiness unless their economic needs have already been satisfied

(C) cannot satisfy economic needs by means of interactions with family members and close friends

(D) can satisfy their basic economic needs without obtaining happiness

(E) cannot really be said to have satisfied their economic needs unless they are happy

GO ON TO THE NEXT PAGE.

15. Technologically, it is already possible to produce nonpolluting cars that burn hydrogen rather than gasoline. But the national system of fuel stations that would be needed to provide the hydrogen fuel for such cars does not yet exist. However, this infrastructure is likely to appear and grow rapidly. A century ago no fuel-distribution infrastructure existed for gasoline-powered vehicles, yet it quickly developed in response to consumer demand.

Which one of the following most accurately expresses the conclusion drawn in the argument?

(A) It is already technologically possible to produce nonpolluting cars that burn hydrogen rather than gasoline.

(B) The fuel-distribution infrastructure for hydrogen-powered cars still needs to be created.

(C) If a new kind of technology is developed, the infrastructure needed to support that technology is likely to quickly develop in response to consumer demands.

(D) The fuel-distribution infrastructure for hydrogen-powered cars is likely to appear and grow rapidly.

(E) Hydrogen-powered vehicles will be similar to gasoline-powered vehicles with regard to the amount of consumer demand for their fuel-distribution infrastructure.

16. Wildlife management experts should not interfere with the natural habitats of creatures in the wild, because manipulating the environment to make it easier for an endangered species to survive in a habitat invariably makes it harder for nonendangered species to survive in that habitat.

The argument is most vulnerable to criticism on the grounds that it

(A) fails to consider that wildlife management experts probably know best how to facilitate the survival of an endangered species in a habitat

(B) fails to recognize that a nonendangered species can easily become an endangered species

(C) overlooks the possibility that saving an endangered species in a habitat is incompatible with preserving the overall diversity of species in that habitat

(D) presumes, without providing justification, that the survival of each endangered species is equally important to the health of the environment

(E) takes for granted that preserving a currently endangered species in a habitat does not have higher priority than preserving species in that habitat that are not endangered

17. Any food that is not sterilized and sealed can contain disease-causing bacteria. Once sterilized and properly sealed, however, it contains no bacteria. There are many different acceptable food-preservation techniques; each involves either sterilizing and sealing food or else at least slowing the growth of disease-causing bacteria. Some of the techniques may also destroy natural food enzymes that cause food to spoil or discolor quickly.

If the statements above are true, which one of the following must be true?

(A) All food preserved by an acceptable method is free of disease-causing bacteria.

(B) Preservation methods that destroy enzymes that cause food to spoil do not sterilize the food.

(C) Food preserved by a sterilization method is less likely to discolor quickly than food preserved with other methods.

(D) Any nonsterilized food preserved by an acceptable method can contain disease-causing bacteria.

(E) If a food contains no bacteria, then it has been preserved by an acceptable method.

GO ON TO THE NEXT PAGE.

18. Activities that pose risks to life are acceptable if and only if each person who bears the risks either gains some net benefit that cannot be had without such risks, or bears the risks voluntarily.

Which one of the following judgments most closely conforms to the principle above?

(A) A door-to-door salesperson declines to replace his older car with a new model with more safety features; this is acceptable because the decision not to replace the car is voluntary.

(B) A smoker subjects people to secondhand smoke at an outdoor public meeting; the resulting risks are acceptable because the danger from secondhand smoke is minimal outdoors, where smoke dissipates quickly.

(C) A motorcyclist rides without a helmet; the risk of fatal injury to the motorcyclist thus incurred is acceptable because the motorcyclist incurs this risk willingly.

(D) Motor vehicles are allowed to emit certain low levels of pollution; the resulting health risks are acceptable because all users of motor vehicles share the resulting benefit of inexpensive, convenient travel.

(E) A nation requires all citizens to spend two years in national service; since such service involves no risk to life, the policy is acceptable.

19. Ecologist: One theory attributes the ability of sea butterflies to avoid predation to their appearance, while another attributes this ability to various chemical compounds they produce. Recently we added each of the compounds to food pellets, one compound per pellet. Predators ate the pellets no matter which one of the compounds was present. Thus the compounds the sea butterflies produce are not responsible for their ability to avoid predation.

The reasoning in the ecologist's argument is flawed in that the argument

(A) presumes, without providing justification, that the two theories are incompatible with each other

(B) draws a conclusion about a cause on the basis of nothing more than a statistical correlation

(C) treats a condition sufficient for sea butterflies' ability to avoid predators as a condition required for this ability

(D) infers, from the claim that no individual member of a set has a certain effect, that the set as a whole does not have that effect

(E) draws a conclusion that merely restates material present in one or more of its premises

20. Principle: One should criticize the works or actions of another person only if the criticism will not seriously harm the person criticized and one does so in the hope or expectation of benefiting someone other than oneself.

Application: Jarrett should not have criticized Ostertag's essay in front of the class, since the defects in it were so obvious that pointing them out benefited no one.

Which one of the following, if true, justifies the above application of the principle?

(A) Jarrett knew that the defects in the essay were so obvious that pointing them out would benefit no one.

(B) Jarrett's criticism of the essay would have been to Ostertag's benefit only if Ostertag had been unaware of the defects in the essay at the time.

(C) Jarrett knew that the criticism might antagonize Ostertag.

(D) Jarrett hoped to gain prestige by criticizing Ostertag.

(E) Jarrett did not expect the criticism to be to Ostertag's benefit.

21. Safety consultant: Judged by the number of injuries per licensed vehicle, minivans are the safest vehicles on the road. However, in carefully designed crash tests, minivans show no greater ability to protect their occupants than other vehicles of similar size do. Thus, the reason minivans have such a good safety record is probably not that they are inherently safer than other vehicles, but rather that they are driven primarily by low-risk drivers.

Which one of the following, if true, most strengthens the safety consultant's argument?

(A) When choosing what kind of vehicle to drive, low-risk drivers often select a kind that they know to perform particularly well in crash tests.

(B) Judged by the number of accidents per licensed vehicle, minivans are no safer than most other kinds of vehicles are.

(C) Minivans tend to carry more passengers at any given time than do most other vehicles.

(D) In general, the larger a vehicle is, the greater its ability to protect its occupants.

(E) Minivans generally have worse braking and emergency handling capabilities than other vehicles of similar size.

GO ON TO THE NEXT PAGE.

22. Consumer advocate: There is no doubt that the government is responsible for the increased cost of gasoline, because the government's policies have significantly increased consumer demand for fuel, and as a result of increasing demand, the price of gasoline has risen steadily.

Which one of the following is an assumption required by the consumer advocate's argument?

(A) The government can bear responsibility for that which it indirectly causes.

(B) The government is responsible for some unforeseen consequences of its policies.

(C) Consumer demand for gasoline cannot increase without causing gasoline prices to increase.

(D) The government has an obligation to ensure that demand for fuel does not increase excessively.

(E) If the government pursues policies that do not increase the demand for fuel, gasoline prices tend to remain stable.

23. A species in which mutations frequently occur will develop new evolutionary adaptations in each generation. Since species survive dramatic environmental changes only if they develop new evolutionary adaptations in each generation, a species in which mutations frequently occur will survive dramatic environmental changes.

The flawed pattern of reasoning in which one of the following is most closely parallel to that in the argument above?

(A) In a stone wall that is properly built, every stone supports another stone. Since a wall's being sturdy depends upon its being properly built, only walls that are composed entirely of stones supporting other stones are sturdy.

(B) A play that is performed before a different audience every time will never get the same reaction from any two audiences. Since no plays are performed before the same audience every time, no play ever gets the same reaction from any two audiences.

(C) A person who is perfectly honest will tell the truth in every situation. Since in order to be a morally upright person one must tell the truth at all times, a perfectly honest person will also be a morally upright person.

(D) An herb garden is productive only if the soil that it is planted in is well drained. Since soil that is well drained is good soil, an herb garden is not productive unless it is planted in good soil.

(E) A diet that is healthful is well balanced. Since a well-balanced diet includes fruits and vegetables, one will not be healthy unless one eats fruits and vegetables.

GO ON TO THE NEXT PAGE.

24. Music critic: How well an underground rock group's recordings sell is no mark of that group's success as an underground group. After all, if a recording sells well, it may be because some of the music on the recording is too trendy to be authentically underground; accordingly, many underground musicians consider it desirable for a recording not to sell well. But weak sales may simply be the result of the group's incompetence.

Which one of the following principles, if valid, most helps to justify the music critic's argument?

(A) If an underground rock group is successful as an underground group, its recordings will sell neither especially well nor especially poorly.

(B) An underground rock group is unsuccessful as an underground group if it is incompetent or if any of its music is too trendy to be authentically underground, or both.

(C) Whether an underground group's recordings meet criteria that many underground musicians consider desirable is not a mark of that group's success.

(D) An underground rock group is successful as an underground group if the group is competent but its recordings nonetheless do not sell well.

(E) For an underground rock group, competence and the creation of authentically underground music are not in themselves marks of success.

25. Graham: The defeat of the world's chess champion by a computer shows that any type of human intellectual activity governed by fixed principles can be mastered by machines and thus that a truly intelligent machine will inevitably be devised.

Adelaide: But you are overlooking the fact that the computer in the case you cite was simply an extension of the people who programmed it. It was their successful distillation of the principles of chess that enabled them to defeat a chess champion using a computer.

The statements above provide the most support for holding that Graham and Adelaide disagree about whether

(A) chess is the best example of a human intellectual activity that is governed by fixed principles

(B) chess is a typical example of the sorts of intellectual activities in which human beings characteristically engage

(C) a computer's defeat of a human chess player is an accomplishment that should be attributed to the computer

(D) intelligence can be demonstrated by the performance of an activity in accord with fixed principles

(E) tools can be designed to aid in any human activity that is governed by fixed principles

S T O P

IF YOU FINISH BEFORE TIME IS CALLED, YOU MAY CHECK YOUR WORK ON THIS SECTION ONLY.
DO NOT WORK ON ANY OTHER SECTION IN THE TEST.

Section V
Time—35 minutes
27 Questions

Directions: Each set of questions in this section is based on a single passage or a pair of passages. The questions are to be answered on the basis of what is <u>stated</u> or <u>implied</u> in the passage or pair of passages. For some of the questions, more than one of the choices could conceivably answer the question. However, you are to choose the <u>best</u> answer; that is, the response that most accurately and completely answers the question, and blacken the corresponding space on your answer sheet.

Over the past 50 years, expansive, low-density communities have proliferated at the edges of many cities in the United States and Canada, creating a phenomenon known as suburban sprawl. Andres
(5) Duany, Elizabeth Plater-Zyberk, and Jeff Speck, a group of prominent town planners belonging to a movement called New Urbanism, contend that suburban sprawl contributes to the decline of civic life and civility. For reasons involving the flow of
(10) automobile traffic, they note, zoning laws usually dictate that suburban homes, stores, businesses, and schools be built in separate areas, and this separation robs people of communal space where they can interact and get to know one another. It is as difficult
(15) to imagine the concept of community without a town square or local pub, these town planners contend, as it is to imagine the concept of family independent of the home.
Suburban housing subdivisions, Duany and his
(20) colleagues add, usually contain homes identical not only in appearance but also in price, resulting in a de facto economic segregation of residential neighborhoods. Children growing up in these neighborhoods, whatever their economic
(25) circumstances, are certain to be ill prepared for life in a diverse society. Moreover, because the widely separated suburban homes and businesses are connected only by "collector roads," residents are forced to drive, often in heavy traffic, in order to
(30) perform many daily tasks. Time that would in a town center involve social interaction within a physical public realm is now spent inside the automobile, where people cease to be community members and instead become motorists, competing for road space,
(35) often acting antisocially. Pedestrians rarely act in this manner toward each other. Duany and his colleagues advocate development based on early-twentieth-century urban neighborhoods that mix housing of different prices and offer residents a "gratifying
(40) public realm" that includes narrow, tree-lined streets, parks, corner grocery stores, cafes, small neighborhood schools, all within walking distance. This, they believe, would give people of diverse backgrounds and lifestyles an opportunity to interact
(45) and thus develop mutual respect.
Opponents of New Urbanism claim that migration to sprawling suburbs is an expression of people's legitimate desire to secure the enjoyment and personal mobility provided by the automobile and the
(50) lifestyle that it makes possible. However, the New Urbanists do not question people's right to their own values; instead, they suggest that we should take a more critical view of these values and of the sprawl-

conducive zoning and subdivision policies that reflect
(55) them. New Urbanists are fundamentally concerned with the long-term social costs of the now-prevailing attitude that individual mobility, consumption, and wealth should be valued absolutely, regardless of their impact on community life.

1. Which one of the following most accurately expresses the main point of the passage?

(A) In their critique of policies that promote suburban sprawl, the New Urbanists neglect to consider the interests and values of those who prefer suburban lifestyles.

(B) The New Urbanists hold that suburban sprawl inhibits social interaction among people of diverse economic circumstances, and they advocate specific reforms of zoning laws as a solution to this problem.

(C) The New Urbanists argue that most people find that life in small urban neighborhoods is generally more gratifying than life in a suburban environment.

(D) The New Urbanists hold that suburban sprawl has a corrosive effect on community life, and as an alternative they advocate development modeled on small urban neighborhoods.

(E) The New Urbanists analyze suburban sprawl as a phenomenon that results from short-sighted traffic policies and advocate changes to these traffic policies as a means of reducing the negative effects of sprawl.

2. According to the passage, the New Urbanists cite which one of the following as a detrimental result of the need for people to travel extensively every day by automobile?

(A) It imposes an extra financial burden on the residents of sprawling suburbs, thus detracting from the advantages of suburban life.

(B) It detracts from the amount of time that people could otherwise devote to productive employment.

(C) It increases the amount of time people spend in situations in which antisocial behavior occurs.

(D) It produces significant amounts of air pollution and thus tends to harm the quality of people's lives.

(E) It decreases the amount of time that parents spend in enjoyable interactions with their children.

GO ON TO THE NEXT PAGE.

3. The passage most strongly suggests that the New Urbanists would agree with which one of the following statements?

    (A) The primary factor affecting a neighborhood's conduciveness to the maintenance of civility is the amount of time required to get from one place to another.

    (B) Private citizens in suburbs have little opportunity to influence the long-term effects of zoning policies enacted by public officials.

    (C) People who live in suburban neighborhoods usually have little difficulty finding easily accessible jobs that do not require commuting to urban centers.

    (D) The spatial configuration of suburban neighborhoods both influences and is influenced by the attitudes of those who live in them.

    (E) Although people have a right to their own values, personal values should not affect the ways in which neighborhoods are designed.

4. Which one of the following most accurately describes the author's use of the word "communities" in line 2 and "community" in line 15?

    (A) They are intended to be understood in almost identical ways, the only significant difference being that one is plural and the other is singular.

    (B) The former is intended to refer to dwellings— and their inhabitants—that happen to be clustered together in particular areas; in the latter, the author means that a group of people have a sense of belonging together.

    (C) In the former, the author means that the groups referred to are to be defined in terms of the interests of their members; the latter is intended to refer generically to a group of people who have something else in common.

    (D) The former is intended to refer to groups of people whose members have professional or political ties to one another; the latter is intended to refer to a geographical area in which people live in close proximity to one another.

    (E) In the former, the author means that there are informal personal ties among members of a group of people; the latter is intended to indicate that a group of people have similar backgrounds and lifestyles.

5. Which one of the following, if true, would most weaken the position that the passage attributes to critics of the New Urbanists?

    (A) Most people who spend more time than they would like getting from one daily task to another live in central areas of large cities.

    (B) Most people who often drive long distances for shopping and entertainment live in small towns rather than in suburban areas surrounding large cities.

    (C) Most people who have easy access to shopping and entertainment do not live in suburban areas.

    (D) Most people who choose to live in sprawling suburbs do so because comparable housing in neighborhoods that do not require extensive automobile travel is more expensive.

    (E) Most people who vote in municipal elections do not cast their votes on the basis of candidates' positions on zoning policies.

6. The passage most strongly suggests that which one of the following would occur if new housing subdivisions in suburban communities were built in accordance with the recommendations of Duany and his colleagues?

    (A) The need for zoning laws to help regulate traffic flow would eventually be eliminated.

    (B) There would be a decrease in the percentage of suburban buildings that contain two or more apartments.

    (C) The amount of time that residents of suburbs spend traveling to the central business districts of cities for work and shopping would increase.

    (D) The need for coordination of zoning policies between large-city governments and governments of nearby suburban communities would be eliminated.

    (E) There would be an increase in the per capita number of grocery stores and schools in those suburban communities.

7. The second paragraph most strongly supports the inference that the New Urbanists make which one of the following assumptions?

    (A) Most of those who buy houses in sprawling suburbs do not pay drastically less than they can afford.

    (B) Zoning regulations often cause economically uniform suburbs to become economically diverse.

    (C) City dwellers who do not frequently travel in automobiles often have feelings of hostility toward motorists.

    (D) Few residents of suburbs are aware of the potential health benefits of walking, instead of driving, to carry out daily tasks.

    (E) People generally prefer to live in houses that look very similar to most of the other houses around them.

GO ON TO THE NEXT PAGE.

Passage A

In ancient Greece, Aristotle documented the ability of foraging honeybees to recruit nestmates to a good food source. He did not speculate on how the communication occurred, but he and naturalists since
(5) then have observed that a bee that finds a new food source returns to the nest and "dances" for its nestmates. In the 1940s, von Frisch and colleagues discovered a pattern in the dance. They observed a foraging honeybee's dance, deciphered it, and thereby
(10) deduced the location of the food source the bee had discovered. Yet questions still remained regarding the precise mechanism used to transmit that information.

In the 1960s, Wenner and Esch each discovered independently that dancing honeybees emit low-
(15) frequency sounds, which we now know to come from wing vibrations. Both researchers reasoned that this might explain the bees' ability to communicate effectively even in completely dark nests. But at that time many scientists mistakenly believed that
(20) honeybees lack hearing, so the issue remained unresolved. Wenner subsequently proposed that smell rather than hearing was the key to honeybee communication. He hypothesized that honeybees derive information not from sound, but from odors the
(25) forager conveys from the food source.

Yet Gould has shown that foragers can dispatch bees to sites they had not actually visited, something that would not be possible if odor were in fact necessary to bees' communication. Finally, using a
(30) honeybee robot to simulate the forager's dance, Kirchner and Michelsen showed that sounds emitted during the forager's dance do indeed play an essential role in conveying information about the food's location.

Passage B

(35) All animals communicate in some sense. Bees dance, ants leave trails, some fish emit high-voltage signals. But some species—bees, birds, and primates, for example—communicate symbolically. In an experiment with vervet monkeys in the wild,
(40) Seyfarth, Cheney, and Marler found that prerecorded vervet alarm calls from a loudspeaker elicited the same response as did naturally produced vervet calls alerting the group to the presence of a predator of a particular type. Vervets looked upward upon hearing
(45) an eagle alarm call, and they scanned the ground below in response to a snake alarm call. These responses suggest that each alarm call represents, for vervets, a specific type of predator.

Karl von Frisch was first to crack the code of the
(50) honeybee's dance, which he described as "language." The dance symbolically represents the distance, direction, and quality of newly discovered food. Adrian Wenner and others believed that bees rely on olfactory cues, as well as the dance, to find a food
(55) source, but this has turned out not to be so.

While it is true that bees have a simple nervous system, they do not automatically follow just any information. Biologist James Gould trained foraging bees to find food in a boat placed in the middle of a
(60) lake and then allowed them to return to the hive to indicate this new location. He found that hive members ignored the foragers' instructions, presumably because no pollinating flowers grow in such a place.

8. The passages have which one of the following aims in common?

(A) arguing that certain nonhuman animals possess human-like intelligence
(B) illustrating the sophistication with which certain primates communicate
(C) describing certain scientific studies concerned with animal communication
(D) airing a scientific controversy over the function of the honeybee's dance
(E) analyzing the conditions a symbolic system must meet in order to be considered a language

9. Which one of the following statements most accurately characterizes a difference between the two passages?

(A) Passage A is concerned solely with honeybee communication, whereas passage B is concerned with other forms of animal communication as well.
(B) Passage A discusses evidence adduced by scientists in support of certain claims, whereas passage B merely presents some of those claims without discussing the support that has been adduced for them.
(C) Passage B is entirely about recent theories of honeybee communication, whereas passage A outlines the historic development of theories of honeybee communication.
(D) Passage B is concerned with explaining the distinction between symbolic and nonsymbolic communication, whereas passage A, though making use of the distinction, does not explain it.
(E) Passage B is concerned with gaining insight into human communication by considering certain types of nonhuman communication, whereas passage A is concerned with these types of nonhuman communication in their own right.

GO ON TO THE NEXT PAGE.

10. Which one of the following statements is most strongly supported by Gould's research, as reported in the two passages?

(A) When a forager honeybee does not communicate olfactory information to its nestmates, they will often disregard the forager's directions and go to sites of their own choosing.

(B) Forager honeybees instinctively know where pollinating flowers usually grow and will not dispatch their nestmates to any other places.

(C) Only experienced forager honeybees are able to locate the best food sources.

(D) A forager's dances can draw other honeybees to sites that the forager has not visited and can fail to draw other honeybees to sites that the forager has visited.

(E) Forager honeybees can communicate with their nestmates about a newly discovered food source by leaving a trail from the food source to the honeybee nest.

11. It can be inferred from the passages that the author of passage A and the author of passage B would accept which one of the following statements?

(A) Honeybees will ignore the instructions conveyed in the forager's dance if they are unable to detect odors from the food source.

(B) Wenner and Esch established that both sound and odor play a vital role in most honeybee communication.

(C) Most animal species can communicate symbolically in some form or other.

(D) The work of von Frisch was instrumental in answering fundamental questions about how honeybees communicate.

(E) Inexperienced forager honeybees that dance to communicate with other bees in their nest learn the intricacies of the dance from more experienced foragers.

12. Which one of the following most accurately describes a relationship between the two passages?

(A) Passage A discusses and rejects a position that is put forth in passage B.

(B) Passage A gives several examples of a phenomenon for which passage B gives only one example.

(C) Passage A is concerned in its entirety with a phenomenon that passage B discusses in support of a more general thesis.

(D) Passage A proposes a scientific explanation for a phenomenon that passage B argues cannot be plausibly explained.

(E) Passage A provides a historical account of the origins of a phenomenon that is the primary concern of passage B.

GO ON TO THE NEXT PAGE.

Most scholars of Mexican American history mark César Chávez's unionizing efforts among Mexican and Mexican American farm laborers in California as the beginning of Chicano political activism in the
(5) 1960s. By 1965, Chávez's United Farm Workers Union gained international recognition by initiating a worldwide boycott of grapes in an effort to get growers in California to sign union contracts. The year 1965 also marks the birth of contemporary
(10) Chicano theater, for that is the year Luis Valdez approached Chávez about using theater to organize farm workers. Valdez and the members of the resulting Teatro Campesino are generally credited by scholars as having initiated the Chicano theater
(15) movement, a movement that would reach its apex in the 1970s.

In the fall of 1965, Valdez gathered a group of striking farm workers and asked them to talk about their working conditions. A former farm worker
(20) himself, Valdez was no stranger to the players in the daily drama that was fieldwork. He asked people to illustrate what happened on the picket lines, and the less timid in the audience delighted in acting out their ridicule of the strikebreakers. Using the farm
(25) workers' basic improvisations, Valdez guided the group toward the creation of what he termed "*actos*," skits or sketches whose roots scholars have traced to various sources that had influenced Valdez as a student and as a member of the San Francisco Mime
(30) Troupe. Expanding beyond the initial setting of flatbed-truck stages at the fields' edges, the *acto* became the quintessential form of Chicano theater in the 1960s. According to Valdez, the *acto* should suggest a solution to the problems exposed in the
(35) brief comic statement, and, as with any good political theater, it should satirize the opposition and inspire the audience to social action. Because *actos* were based on participants' personal experiences, they had palpable immediacy.
(40) In her book *El Teatro Campesino*, Yolanda Broyles-González rightly criticizes theater historians for having tended to credit Valdez individually with inventing *actos* as a genre, as if the striking farm workers' improvisational talent had depended entirely
(45) on his vision and expertise for the form it took. She traces especially the *actos*' connections to a similar genre of informal, often satirical shows known as *carpas* that were performed in tents to mainly working-class audiences. *Carpas* had flourished
(50) earlier in the twentieth century in the border area of Mexico and the United States. Many participants in the formation of the Teatro no doubt had substantial cultural links to this tradition and likely adapted it to their improvisations. The early development of the
(55) Teatro Campesino was, in fact, a collective accomplishment; still, Valdez's artistic contribution was a crucial one, for the resulting *actos* were neither *carpas* nor theater in the European tradition of Valdez's academic training, but a distinctive genre
(60) with connections to both.

13. Which one of the following most accurately expresses the main point of the passage?

(A) Some theater historians have begun to challenge the once widely accepted view that in creating the Teatro Campesino, Luis Valdez was largely uninfluenced by earlier historical forms.

(B) In crediting Luis Valdez with founding the Chicano theater movement, theater historians have neglected the role of César Chávez in its early development.

(C) Although the creation of the early material of the Teatro Campesino was a collective accomplishment, Luis Valdez's efforts and expertise were essential factors in determining the form it took.

(D) The success of the early Teatro Campesino depended on the special insights and talents of the amateur performers who were recruited by Luis Valdez to participate in creating *actos*.

(E) Although, as Yolanda Broyles-González has pointed out, the Teatro Campesino was a collective endeavor, Luis Valdez's political and academic connections helped bring it recognition.

14. The author uses the word "immediacy" (line 39) most likely in order to express

(A) how little physical distance there was between the performers in the late 1960s *actos* and their audiences

(B) the sense of intimacy created by the performers' technique of addressing many of their lines directly to the audience

(C) the ease with which the Teatro Campesino members were able to develop *actos* based on their own experiences

(D) how closely the director and performers of the Teatro Campesino worked together to build a repertoire of *actos*

(E) how vividly the *actos* conveyed the performers' experiences to their audiences

GO ON TO THE NEXT PAGE.

15. The second sentence of the passage functions primarily in which one of the following ways?

(A) It helps explain both a motivation of those who developed the first *actos* and an important aspect of their subject matter.

(B) It introduces a major obstacle that Valdez had to overcome in gaining public acceptance of the work of the Teatro Campesino.

(C) It anticipates and counters a possible objection to the author's view that the *actos* developed by Teatro Campesino were effective as political theater.

(D) It provides an example of the type of topic on which scholars of Mexican American history have typically focused to the exclusion of theater history.

(E) It helps explain why theater historians, in their discussions of Valdez, have often treated him as though he were individually responsible for inventing *actos* as a genre.

16. The passage indicates that the early *actos* of the Teatro Campesino and the *carpas* were similar in that

(A) both had roots in theater in the European tradition

(B) both were studied by the San Francisco Mime Troupe

(C) both were initially performed on farms

(D) both often involved satire

(E) both were part of union organizing drives

17. It can be inferred from the passage that Valdez most likely held which one of the following views?

(A) As a theatrical model, the *carpas* of the early twentieth century were ill-suited to the type of theater that he and the Teatro Campesino were trying to create.

(B) César Chávez should have done more to support the efforts of the Teatro Campesino to use theater to organize striking farm workers.

(C) Avant-garde theater in the European tradition is largely irrelevant to the theatrical expression of the concerns of a mainly working-class audience.

(D) Actors do not require formal training in order to achieve effective and artistically successful theatrical performances.

(E) The aesthetic aspects of a theatrical work should be evaluated independently of its political ramifications.

18. Based on the passage, it can be concluded that the author and Broyles-González hold essentially the same attitude toward

(A) the influences that shaped *carpas* as a dramatic genre

(B) the motives of theater historians in exaggerating the originality of Valdez

(C) the significance of *carpas* for the development of the genre of the *acto*

(D) the extent of Valdez's acquaintance with *carpas* as a dramatic form

(E) the role of the European tradition in shaping Valdez's contribution to the development of *actos*

19. The information in the passage most strongly supports which one of the following statements regarding the Teatro Campesino?

(A) Its efforts to organize farm workers eventually won the acceptance of a few farm owners in California.

(B) It included among its members a number of individuals who, like Valdez, had previously belonged to the San Francisco Mime Troupe.

(C) It did not play a major role in the earliest efforts of the United Farm Workers Union to achieve international recognition.

(D) Although its first performances were entirely in Spanish, it eventually gave some performances partially in English, for the benefit of non-Spanish-speaking audiences.

(E) Its work drew praise not only from critics in the United States but from critics in Mexico as well.

20. The passage most strongly supports which one of the following?

(A) The *carpas* tradition has been widely discussed and analyzed by both U.S. and Mexican theater historians concerned with theatrical performance styles and methods.

(B) Comedy was a prominent feature of Chicano theater in the 1960s.

(C) In directing the *actos* of the Teatro Campesino, Valdez went to great lengths to simulate or recreate certain aspects of what audiences had experienced in the *carpas*.

(D) Many of the earliest *actos* were based on scripts composed by Valdez, which the farm-worker actors modified to suit their own diverse aesthetic and pragmatic interests.

(E) By the early 1970s, Valdez was using *actos* as the basis for other theatrical endeavors and was no longer directly associated with the Teatro Campesino.

GO ON TO THE NEXT PAGE.

In October 1999, the Law Reform Commission of Western Australia (LRCWA) issued its report, "Review of the Civil and Criminal Justice System." Buried within its 400 pages are several important

(5) recommendations for introducing contingency fees for lawyers' services into the state of Western Australia. Contingency-fee agreements call for payment only if the lawyer is successful in the case. Because of the lawyer's risk of financial loss, such charges generally

(10) exceed regular fees.

Although there are various types of contingency-fee arrangements, the LRCWA has recommended that only one type be introduced: "uplift" fee arrangements, which in the case of a successful

(15) outcome require the client to pay the lawyer's normal fee plus an agreed-upon additional percentage of that fee. This restriction is intended to prevent lawyers from gaining disproportionately from awards of damages and thus to ensure that just compensation to

(20) plaintiffs is not eroded. A further measure toward this end is found in the recommendation that contingency-fee agreements should be permitted only in cases where two conditions are satisfied: first, the contingency-fee arrangement must be used only as a

(25) last resort when all means of avoiding such an arrangement have been exhausted; and second, the lawyer must be satisfied that the client is financially unable to pay the fee in the event that sufficient damages are not awarded.

(30) Unfortunately, under this recommendation, lawyers wishing to enter into an uplift fee arrangement would be forced to investigate not only the legal issues affecting any proposed litigation, but also the financial circumstances of the potential client

(35) and the probable cost of the litigation. This process would likely be onerous for a number of reasons, not least of which is the fact that the final cost of litigation depends in large part on factors that may change as the case unfolds, such as strategies adopted

(40) by the opposing side.

In addition to being burdensome for lawyers, the proposal to make contingency-fee agreements available only to the least well-off clients would be unfair to other clients. This restriction would unjustly

(45) limit freedom of contract and would, in effect, make certain types of litigation inaccessible to middle-income people or even wealthy people who might not be able to liquidate assets to pay the costs of a trial. More importantly, the primary reasons for entering

(50) into contingency-fee agreements hold for all clients. First, they provide financing for the costs of pursuing a legal action. Second, they shift the risk of not recovering those costs, and of not obtaining a damages award that will pay their lawyer's fees, from

(55) the client to the lawyer. Finally, given the convergence of the lawyer's interest and the client's interest under a contingency-fee arrangement, it is reasonable to assume that such arrangements increase lawyers' diligence and commitment to their cases.

21. As described in the passage, the uplift fee agreements that the LRCWA's report recommends are most closely analogous to which one of the following arrangements?

(A) People who join together to share the costs of purchasing lottery tickets on a regular basis agree to share any eventual proceeds from a lottery drawing in proportion to the amounts they contributed to tickets purchased for that drawing.

(B) A consulting firm reviews a company's operations. The consulting firm will receive payment only if it can substantially reduce the company's operating expenses, in which case it will be paid double its usual fee.

(C) The returns that accrue from the assumption of a large financial risk by members of a business partnership formed to develop and market a new invention are divided among them in proportion to the amount of financial risk each assumed.

(D) The cost of an insurance policy is determined by reference to the likelihood and magnitude of an eventual loss covered by the insurance policy and the administrative and marketing costs involved in marketing and servicing the insurance policy.

(E) A person purchasing a property receives a loan for the purchase from the seller. In order to reduce risk, the seller requires the buyer to pay for an insurance policy that will pay off the loan if the buyer is unable to do so.

22. The passage states which one of the following?

(A) Contingency-fee agreements serve the purpose of transferring the risk of pursuing a legal action from the client to the lawyer.

(B) Contingency-fee agreements of the kind the LRCWA's report recommends would normally not result in lawyers being paid larger fees than they deserve.

(C) At least some of the recommendations in the LRCWA's report are likely to be incorporated into the legal system in the state of Western Australia.

(D) Allowing contingency-fee agreements of the sort recommended in the LRCWA's report would not affect lawyers' diligence and commitment to their cases.

(E) Usually contingency-fee agreements involve an agreement that the fee the lawyer receives will be an agreed-upon percentage of the client's damages.

GO ON TO THE NEXT PAGE.

23. The author's main purpose in the passage is to

(A) defend a proposed reform against criticism
(B) identify the current shortcomings of a legal system and suggest how these should be remedied
(C) support the view that a recommended change would actually worsen the situation it was intended to improve
(D) show that a legal system would not be significantly changed if certain proposed reforms were enacted
(E) explain a suggested reform and critically evaluate it

24. Which one of the following is given by the passage as a reason for the difficulty a lawyer would have in determining whether—according to the LRCWA's recommendations—a prospective client was qualified to enter into an uplift agreement?

(A) The length of time that a trial may last is difficult to predict in advance.
(B) Not all prospective clients would wish to reveal detailed information about their financial circumstances.
(C) Some factors that may affect the cost of litigation can change after the litigation begins.
(D) Uplift agreements should only be used as a last resort.
(E) Investigating whether a client is qualified to enter into an uplift agreement would take time away from investigating the legal issues of the case.

25. The phrase "gaining disproportionately from awards of damages" (lines 18–19) is most likely intended by the author to mean

(A) receiving a payment that is of greater monetary value than the legal services rendered by the lawyer
(B) receiving a higher portion of the total amount awarded in damages than is reasonable compensation for the professional services rendered and the amount of risk assumed
(C) receiving a higher proportion of the damages awarded to the client than the client considers fair
(D) receiving a payment that is higher than the lawyer would have received had the client's case been unsuccessful
(E) receiving a higher proportion of the damages awarded to the client than the judge or the jury that awarded the damages intended the lawyer to receive

26. According to the passage, the LRCWA's report recommended that contingency-fee agreements

(A) be used only when it is reasonable to think that such arrangements will increase lawyers' diligence and commitment to their cases
(B) be used only in cases in which clients are unlikely to be awarded enormous damages
(C) be used if the lawyer is not certain that the client seeking to file a lawsuit could pay the lawyer's regular fee if the suit were to be unsuccessful
(D) not be used in cases in which another type of arrangement is practicable
(E) not be used except in cases where the lawyer is reasonably sure that the client will win damages sufficiently large to cover the lawyer's fees

27. Which one of the following, if true, most seriously undermines the author's criticism of the LRCWA's recommendations concerning contingency-fee agreements?

(A) The proportion of lawsuits filed by the least well-off litigants tends to be higher in areas where uplift fee arrangements have been widely used than in areas in which uplift agreements have not been used.
(B) Before the LRCWA's recommendations, lawyers in Western Australia generally made a careful evaluation of prospective clients' financial circumstances before accepting cases that might involve complex or protracted litigation.
(C) There is strong opposition in Western Australia to any legal reform perceived as favoring lawyers, so it is highly unlikely that the LRCWA's recommendations concerning contingency-fee agreements will be implemented.
(D) The total fees charged by lawyers who successfully litigate cases under uplift fee arrangements are, on average, only marginally higher than the total fees charged by lawyers who litigate cases without contingency agreements.
(E) In most jurisdictions in which contingency-fee agreements are allowed, those of the uplift variety are used much less often than are other types of contingency-fee agreements.

S T O P

IF YOU FINISH BEFORE TIME IS CALLED, YOU MAY CHECK YOUR WORK ON THIS SECTION ONLY.
DO NOT WORK ON ANY OTHER SECTION IN THE TEST.

Wait for the supervisor's instructions before you open the page to the topic.
Please print and sign your name and write the date in the designated spaces below.

Time: 35 Minutes

General Directions

You will have 35 minutes in which to plan and write an essay on the topic inside. Read the topic and the accompanying directions carefully. You will probably find it best to spend a few minutes considering the topic and organizing your thoughts before you begin writing. In your essay, be sure to develop your ideas fully, leaving time, if possible, to review what you have written. **Do not write on a topic other than the one specified. Writing on a topic of your own choice is not acceptable.**

No special knowledge is required or expected for this writing exercise. Law schools are interested in the reasoning, clarity, organization, language usage, and writing mechanics displayed in your essay. How well you write is more important than how much you write.

Confine your essay to the blocked, lined area on the front and back of the separate Writing Sample Response Sheet. Only that area will be reproduced for law schools. Be sure that your writing is legible.

Both this topic sheet and your response sheet must be turned over to the testing staff before you leave the room.

Topic Code	Print Your Full Name Here		
_____	Last	First	M.I.

Date	Sign Your Name Here
/ /	

Scratch Paper
Do not write your essay in this space.

LSAT Writing Sample Topic

In a total solar eclipse, the moon completely covers the sun and casts a rolling shadow along a track on the Earth's surface a few hundred kilometers wide. The eclipse lasts for a few minutes at any location within this track. The Ortegas are planning a trip to observe an upcoming eclipse during their family vacation. They have narrowed the possibilities down to two countries. Using the facts below, write an essay in which you argue in favor of one country over the other based on the following two criteria:

• The Ortegas want to minimize the chance that cloudiness will obscure the eclipse for them.
• The Ortegas want the trip to be worthwhile even if the eclipse is obscured by clouds.

For the first country, climatic data indicate that the probability of cloudiness in the area of the eclipse track is about 75 percent. The family would fly to the capital, which is a cultural center of almost unparalleled richness. Some members of the family have visited the capital before. On some days, they would drive their rental car to other cultural locations in the country. Having a rental car allows some adjustment of eclipse-viewing location according to weather forecasts.

The second country is about twice as far from the family's home as the first country, with correspondingly greater travel expense and inconvenience. No family member has been in the country before. Climatic data indicate that the probability of cloudiness in the area of the eclipse track in the country is about 25 percent. Because the country has some political instability, the family would travel on an eclipse tour organized by a respected company. Visits to several cultural sites are included.

Scratch Paper
Do not write your essay in this space.

LAST NAME (Print)

MI

FIRST NAME (Print)

SIGNATURE

Writing Sample Response Sheet

DO NOT WRITE
IN THIS SPACE

Begin your essay in the lined area below.
Continue on the back if you need more space.

This test can be scored automatically with your Online Center. The following Answer Key and Scoring Table are provided if you wish to score it offline.

Directions:

1. Use the Answer Key on the next page to check your answers.

2. Use the Scoring Worksheet below to compute your raw score.

3. Use the Score Conversion Chart to convert your raw score into the 120–180 scale.

Scoring Worksheet

1. Enter the number of questions you answered correctly in each section

	Number Correct
SECTION I	EXP
SECTION II	_____
SECTION III	_____
SECTION IV	_____
SECTION V	_____

2. Enter the sum here: _____

   This is your Raw Score.

Conversion Chart

For Converting Raw Score to the 120–180 LSAT Scaled Score LSAT PrepTest 60

Reported Score	Lowest Raw Score	Highest Raw Score
180	97	99
179	96	96
178	—*	—*
177	95	95
176	94	94
175	93	93
174	92	92
173	91	91
172	90	90
171	89	89
170	87	88
169	86	86
168	85	85
167	83	84
166	82	82
165	80	81
164	79	79
163	77	78
162	75	76
161	74	74
160	72	73
159	70	71
158	68	69
157	67	67
156	65	66
155	63	64
154	62	62
153	60	61
152	58	59
151	56	57
150	55	55
149	53	54
148	51	52
147	50	50
146	48	49
145	47	47
144	45	46
143	43	44
142	42	42
141	40	41
140	39	39
139	37	38
138	36	36
137	35	35
136	33	34
135	32	32
134	31	31
133	29	30
132	28	28
131	27	27
130	26	26
129	25	25
128	24	24
127	23	23
126	22	22
125	21	21
124	20	20
123	19	19
122	18	18
121	17	17
120	0	16

*There is no raw score that will produce this scaled score for this test.

SECTION I

1.	A	8.	C	15.	D	22.	D
2.	A	9.	B	16.	B		
3.	D	10.	C	17.	C		
4.	A	11.	B	18.	C		
5.	E	12.	A	19.	B		
6.	A	13.	C	20.	D		
7.	B	14.	E	21.	E		

SECTION II

1.	D	8.	E	15.	B	22.	A
2.	E	9.	D	16.	C	23.	E
3.	B	10.	D	17.	A	24.	C
4.	D	11.	C	18.	E	25.	C
5.	C	12.	A	19.	*		
6.	B	13.	C	20.	D		
7.	C	14.	D	21.	B		

SECTION III

1.	B	8.	C	15.	E	22.	E
2.	D	9.	D	16.	A	23.	C
3.	A	10.	A	17.	B		
4.	A	11.	C	18.	A		
5.	E	12.	C	19.	B		
6.	C	13.	E	20.	B		
7.	E	14.	D	21.	D		

SECTION IV

1.	A	8.	C	15.	D	22.	A
2.	B	9.	C	16.	E	23.	C
3.	A	10.	C	17.	D	24.	B
4.	B	11.	D	18.	C	25.	C
5.	D	12.	E	19.	D		
6.	D	13.	D	20.	A		
7.	C	14.	D	21.	E		

SECTION V

1.	D	8.	C	15.	A	22.	A
2.	C	9.	A	16.	D	23.	E
3.	D	10.	D	17.	D	24.	C
4.	B	11.	D	18.	C	25.	B
5.	D	12.	C	19.	C	26.	D
6.	E	13.	C	20.	B	27.	B
7.	A	14.	E	21.	B		

*Item removed from scoring.

Practice Test 2

PrepTest 54 with Additional Section from PrepTest 46

SECTION I

Time—35 minutes

27 Questions

<u>Directions:</u> Each set of questions in this section is based on a single passage or a pair of passages. The questions are to be answered on the basis of what is <u>stated</u> or <u>implied</u> in the passage or pair of passages. For some of the questions, more than one of the choices could conceivably answer the question. However, you are to choose the <u>best</u> answer; that is, the response that most accurately and completely answers the question, and blacken the corresponding space on your answer sheet.

This passage was adapted from an article published in 1996.

The Internet is a system of computer networks that allows individuals and organizations to communicate freely with other Internet users throughout the world. As a result, an astonishing
(5) variety of information is able to flow unimpeded across national and other political borders, presenting serious difficulties for traditional approaches to legislation and law enforcement, to which such borders are crucial.
(10)   Control over physical space and the objects located in it is a defining attribute of sovereignty. Lawmaking presupposes some mechanism for enforcement, i.e., the ability to control violations. But jurisdictions cannot control the information and
(15) transactions flowing across their borders via the Internet. For example, a government might seek to intercept transmissions that propagate the kinds of consumer fraud that it regulates within its jurisdiction. But the volume of electronic communications
(20) crossing its territorial boundaries is too great to allow for effective control over individual transmissions. In order to deny its citizens access to specific materials, a government would thus have to prevent them from using the Internet altogether. Such a draconian
(25) measure would almost certainly be extremely unpopular, since most affected citizens would probably feel that the benefits of using the Internet decidedly outweigh the risks.
     One legal domain that is especially sensitive to
(30) geographical considerations is that governing trademarks. There is no global registration of trademarks; international protection requires registration in each country. Moreover, within a country, the same name can sometimes be used
(35) proprietarily by businesses of different kinds in the same locality, or by businesses of the same kind in different localities, on the grounds that use of the trademark by one such business does not affect the others. But with the advent of the Internet, a business
(40) name can be displayed in such a way as to be accessible from any computer connected to the Internet anywhere in the world. Should such a display advertising a restaurant in Norway be deemed to infringe a trademark in Brazil just because it can be
(45) accessed freely from Brazil? It is not clear that any particular country's trademark authorities possess, or should possess, jurisdiction over such displays. Otherwise, any use of a trademark on the Internet

could be subject to the jurisdiction of every country
(50) simultaneously.
     The Internet also gives rise to situations in which regulation is needed but cannot be provided within the existing framework. For example, electronic communications, which may pass through many
(55) different territorial jurisdictions, pose perplexing new questions about the nature and adequacy of privacy protections. Should French officials have lawful access to messages traveling via the Internet from Canada to Japan? This is just one among many
(60) questions that collectively challenge the notion that the Internet can be effectively controlled by the existing system of territorial jurisdictions.

1. Which one of the following most accurately expresses the main point of the passage?

(A) The high-volume, global nature of activity on the Internet undermines the feasibility of controlling it through legal frameworks that presuppose geographic boundaries.

(B) The system of Internet communications simultaneously promotes and weakens the power of national governments to control their citizens' speech and financial transactions.

(C) People value the benefits of their participation on the Internet so highly that they would strongly oppose any government efforts to regulate their Internet activity.

(D) Internet communications are responsible for a substantial increase in the volume and severity of global crime.

(E) Current Internet usage and its future expansion pose a clear threat to the internal political stability of many nations.

GO ON TO THE NEXT PAGE.

2. The author mentions French officials in connection with messages traveling between Canada and Japan (lines 57–59) primarily to

(A) emphasize that the Internet allows data to be made available to users worldwide

(B) illustrate the range of languages that might be used on the Internet

(C) provide an example of a regulatory problem arising when an electronic communication intended for a particular destination passes through intermediate jurisdictions

(D) show why any use of a trademark on the Internet could be subject to the jurisdiction of every country simultaneously

(E) highlight the kind of international cooperation that made the Internet possible

3. According to the passage, which one of the following is an essential property of political sovereignty?

(A) control over business enterprises operating across territorial boundaries

(B) authority over communicative exchanges occurring within a specified jurisdiction

(C) power to regulate trademarks throughout a circumscribed geographic region

(D) control over the entities included within a designated physical space

(E) authority over all commercial transactions involving any of its citizens

4. Which one of the following words employed by the author in the second paragraph is most indicative of the author's attitude toward any hypothetical measure a government might enact to deny its citizens access to the Internet?

(A) benefits
(B) decidedly
(C) unpopular
(D) draconian
(E) risks

5. What is the main purpose of the fourth paragraph?

(A) to call into question the relevance of the argument provided in the second paragraph

(B) to provide a practical illustration that questions the general claim made in the first paragraph

(C) to summarize the arguments provided in the second and third paragraphs

(D) to continue the argument that begins in the third paragraph

(E) to provide an additional argument in support of the general claim made in the first paragraph

GO ON TO THE NEXT PAGE.

Passage A

Drilling fluids, including the various mixtures known as drilling muds, play essential roles in oil-well drilling. As they are circulated down through the drill pipe and back up the well itself, they lubricate the
(5) drill bit, bearings, and drill pipe; clean and cool the drill bit as it cuts into the rock; lift rock chips (cuttings) to the surface; provide information about what is happening downhole, allowing the drillers to monitor the behavior, flow rate, pressure, and
(10) composition of the drilling fluid; and maintain well pressure to control cave-ins.

Drilling muds are made of bentonite and other clays and polymers, mixed with a fluid to the desired viscosity. By far the largest ingredient of drilling
(15) muds, by weight, is barite, a very heavy mineral of density 4.3 to 4.6. It is also used as an inert filler in some foods and is more familiar in its medical use as the "barium meal" administered before X-raying the digestive tract.
(20) Over the years individual drilling companies and their expert drillers have devised proprietary formulations, or mud "recipes," to deal with specific types of drilling jobs. One problem in studying the effects of drilling waste discharges is that the drilling
(25) fluids are made from a range of over 1,000, sometimes toxic, ingredients—many of them known, confusingly, by different trade names, generic descriptions, chemical formulae, and regional or industry slang words, and many of them kept secret by companies or individual
(30) formulators.

Passage B

Drilling mud, cuttings, and associated chemicals are normally released only during the drilling phase of a well's existence. These discharges are the main environmental concern in offshore oil production, and
(35) their use is tightly regulated. The discharges are closely monitored by the offshore operator, and releases are controlled as a condition of the operating permit.

One type of mud—water-based mud (WBM)—is a mixture of water, bentonite clay, and chemical
(40) additives, and is used to drill shallow parts of wells. It is not particularly toxic to marine organisms and disperses readily. Under current regulations, it can be dumped directly overboard. Companies typically recycle WBMs until their properties are no longer
(45) suitable and then, over a period of hours, dump the entire batch into the sea.

For drilling deeper wells, oil-based mud (OBM) is normally used. The typical difference from WBM is the high content of mineral oil (typically 30 percent).
(50) OBMs also contain greater concentrations of barite, a powdered heavy mineral, and a number of additives. OBMs have a greater potential for negative environmental impact, partly because they do not disperse as readily. Barite may impact some
(55) organisms, particularly scallops, and the mineral oil may have toxic effects. Currently only the residues of OBMs adhering to cuttings that remain after the cuttings are sieved from the drilling fluids may be discharged overboard, and then only mixtures up to a
(60) specified maximum oil content.

6. A primary purpose of each of the passages is to

    (A) provide causal explanations for a type of environmental pollution
    (B) describe the general composition and properties of drilling muds
    (C) point out possible environmental impacts associated with oil drilling
    (D) explain why oil-well drilling requires the use of drilling muds
    (E) identify difficulties inherent in the regulation of oil-well drilling operations

7. Which one of the following is a characteristic of barite that is mentioned in both of the passages?

    (A) It does not disperse readily in seawater.
    (B) It is not found in drilling muds containing bentonite.
    (C) Its use in drilling muds is tightly regulated.
    (D) It is the most commonly used ingredient in drilling muds.
    (E) It is a heavy mineral.

8. Each of the following is supported by one or both of the passages EXCEPT:

    (A) Clay is an important constituent of many, if not all, drilling muds.
    (B) At least one type of drilling mud is not significantly toxic to marine life.
    (C) There has been some study of the environmental effects of drilling-mud discharges.
    (D) Government regulations allow drilling muds to contain 30 percent mineral oil.
    (E) During the drilling of an oil well, drilling mud is continuously discharged into the sea.

GO ON TO THE NEXT PAGE.

9. Which one of the following can be most reasonably inferred from the two passages taken together, but not from either one individually?

   (A) Barite is the largest ingredient of drilling muds, by weight, and also the most environmentally damaging.

   (B) Although barite can be harmful to marine organisms, it can be consumed safely by humans.

   (C) Offshore drilling is more damaging to the environment than is land-based drilling.

   (D) The use of drilling muds needs to be more tightly controlled by government.

   (E) If offshore drilling did not generate cuttings, it would be less harmful to the environment.

10. Each of the following is supported by one or both of the passages EXCEPT:

    (A) Drillers monitor the suitability of the mud they are using.

    (B) The government requires drilling companies to disclose all ingredients used in their drilling muds.

    (C) In certain quantities, barite is not toxic to humans.

    (D) Oil reserves can be found within or beneath layers of rock.

    (E) Drilling deep oil wells requires the use of different mud recipes than does drilling shallow oil wells.

11. Based on information in the passages, which one of the following, if true, provides the strongest support for a prediction that the proportion of oil-well drilling using OBMs will increase in the future?

    (A) The cost of certain ingredients in WBMs is expected to increase steadily over the next several decades.

    (B) The deeper an offshore oil well, the greater the concentration of barite that must be used in the drilling mud.

    (C) Oil reserves at shallow depths have mostly been tapped, leaving primarily much deeper reserves for future drilling.

    (D) It is unlikely that oil drillers will develop more efficient ways of removing OBM residues from cuttings that remain after being sieved from drilling fluids.

    (E) Barite is a common mineral, the availability of which is virtually limitless.

12. According to passage B, one reason OBMs are potentially more environmentally damaging than WBMs is that OBMs

    (A) are slower to disperse
    (B) contain greater concentrations of bentonite
    (C) contain a greater number of additives
    (D) are used for drilling deeper wells
    (E) cannot be recycled

GO ON TO THE NEXT PAGE.

Aida Overton Walker (1880–1914), one of the most widely acclaimed African American performers of the early twentieth century, was known largely for popularizing a dance form known as the cakewalk
(5) through her choreographing, performance, and teaching of the dance. The cakewalk was originally developed prior to the United States Civil War by African Americans, for whom dance was a means of maintaining cultural links within a slave society. It
(10) was based on traditional West African ceremonial dances, and like many other African American dances, it retained features characteristic of African dance forms, such as gliding steps and an emphasis on improvisation.

(15) To this African-derived foundation, the cakewalk added certain elements from European dances: where African dances feature flexible body postures, large groups and separate-sex dancing, the cakewalk developed into a high-kicking walk performed by a
(20) procession of couples. Ironically, while these modifications later enabled the cakewalk to appeal to European Americans and become one of the first cultural forms to cross the racial divide in North America, they were originally introduced with satiric
(25) intent. Slaves performed the grandiloquent walks in order to parody the processional dances performed at slave owners' balls and, in general, the self-important manners of slave owners. To add a further irony, by the end of the nineteenth century, the cakewalk was
(30) itself being parodied by European American stage performers, and these parodies in turn helped shape subsequent versions of the cakewalk.

While this complex evolution meant that the cakewalk was not a simple cultural phenomenon—
(35) one scholar has characterized this layering of parody upon parody with the phrase "mimetic vertigo"—it is in fact what enabled the dance to attract its wide audience. In the cultural and socioeconomic flux of the turn-of-the-century United States, where
(40) industrialization, urbanization, mass immigration, and rapid social mobility all reshaped the cultural landscape, an art form had to be capable of being many things to many people in order to appeal to a large audience.

(45) Walker's remarkable success at popularizing the cakewalk across otherwise relatively rigid racial boundaries rested on her ability to address within her interpretation of it the varying and sometimes conflicting demands placed on the dance. Middle-
(50) class African Americans, for example, often denounced the cakewalk as disreputable, a complaint reinforced by the parodies circulating at the time. Walker won over this audience by refining the cakewalk and emphasizing its fundamental grace.
(55) Meanwhile, because middle- and upper-class European Americans often felt threatened by the tremendous cultural flux around them, they prized what they regarded as authentic art forms as bastions of stability; much of Walker's success with this

(60) audience derived from her distillation of what was widely acclaimed as the most authentic cakewalk. Finally, Walker was able to gain the admiration of many newly rich industrialists and financiers, who found in the grand flourishes of her version of the
(65) cakewalk a fitting vehicle for celebrating their newfound social rank.

13. Which one of the following most accurately expresses the main point of the passage?

(A) Walker, who was especially well known for her success in choreographing, performing, and teaching the cakewalk, was one of the most widely recognized African American performers of the early twentieth century.

(B) In spite of the disparate influences that shaped the cakewalk, Walker was able to give the dance broad appeal because she distilled what was regarded as the most authentic version in an era that valued authenticity highly.

(C) Walker popularized the cakewalk by capitalizing on the complex cultural mix that had developed from the dance's original blend of satire and cultural preservation, together with the effects of later parodies.

(D) Whereas other versions of the cakewalk circulating at the beginning of the twentieth century were primarily parodic in nature, the version popularized by Walker combined both satire and cultural preservation.

(E) Because Walker was able to recognize and preserve the characteristics of the cakewalk as African Americans originally performed it, it became the first popular art form to cross the racial divide in the United States.

14. The author describes the socioeconomic flux of the turn-of-the-century United States in the third paragraph primarily in order to

(A) argue that the cakewalk could have become popular only in such complex social circumstances

(B) detail the social context that prompted performers of the cakewalk to fuse African and European dance forms

(C) identify the target of the overlapping parodic layers that characterized the cakewalk

(D) indicate why a particular cultural environment was especially favorable for the success of the cakewalk

(E) explain why European American parodies of the cakewalk were able to reach wide audiences

GO ON TO THE NEXT PAGE.

15. Which one of the following is most analogous to the author's account in the second paragraph of how the cakewalk came to appeal to European Americans?

(A) Satirical versions of popular music songs are frequently more popular than the songs they parody.

(B) A style of popular music grows in popularity among young listeners because it parodies the musical styles admired by older listeners.

(C) A style of music becomes admired among popular music's audience in part because of elements that were introduced in order to parody popular music.

(D) A once popular style of music wins back its audience by incorporating elements of the style of music that is currently most popular.

(E) After popular music begins to appropriate elements of a traditional style of music, interest in that traditional music increases.

16. The passage asserts which one of the following about the cakewalk?

(A) It was largely unknown outside African American culture until Walker popularized it.

(B) It was mainly a folk dance, and Walker became one of only a handful of people to perform it professionally.

(C) Its performance as parody became uncommon as a result of Walker's popularization of its authentic form.

(D) Its West African origins became commonly known as a result of Walker's work.

(E) It was one of the first cultural forms to cross racial lines in the United States.

17. It can be inferred from the passage that the author would be most likely to agree with which one of the following statements?

(A) Because of the broad appeal of humor, satiric art forms are often among the first to cross racial or cultural divisions.

(B) The interactions between African American and European American cultural forms often result in what is appropriately characterized as "mimetic vertigo."

(C) Middle-class European Americans who valued the cakewalk's authenticity subsequently came to admire other African American dances for the same reason.

(D) Because of the influence of African dance forms, some popular dances that later emerged in the United States featured separate-sex dancing.

(E) Some of Walker's admirers were attracted to her version of the cakewalk as a means for bolstering their social identities.

18. The passage most strongly suggests that the author would be likely to agree with which one of the following statements about Walker's significance in the history of the cakewalk?

(A) Walker broadened the cakewalk's appeal by highlighting elements that were already present in the dance.

(B) Walker's version of the cakewalk appealed to larger audiences than previous versions did because she accentuated its satiric dimension.

(C) Walker popularized the cakewalk by choreographing various alternative interpretations of it, each tailored to the interests of a different cultural group.

(D) Walker added a "mimetic vertigo" to the cakewalk by inserting imitations of other performers' cakewalking into her dance routines.

(E) Walker revitalized the cakewalk by disentangling its complex admixture of African and European elements.

19. The passage provides sufficient information to answer which one of the following questions?

(A) What were some of the attributes of African dance forms that were preserved in the cakewalk?

(B) Who was the first performer to dance the cakewalk professionally?

(C) What is an aspect of the cakewalk that was preserved in other North American dance forms?

(D) What features were added to the original cakewalk by the stage parodies circulating at the end of the nineteenth century?

(E) For about how many years into the twentieth century did the cakewalk remain widely popular?

GO ON TO THE NEXT PAGE.

In principle, a cohesive group—one whose members generally agree with one another and support one another's judgments—can do a much better job at decision making than it could if it were

(5) noncohesive. When cohesiveness is low or lacking entirely, compliance out of fear of recrimination is likely to be strongest. To overcome this fear, participants in the group's deliberations need to be confident that they are members in good standing and

(10) that the others will continue to value their role in the group, whether or not they agree about a particular issue under discussion. As members of a group feel more accepted by the others, they acquire greater freedom to say what they really think, becoming less

(15) likely to use deceitful arguments or to play it safe by dancing around the issues with vapid or conventional comments. Typically, then, the more cohesive a group becomes, the less its members will deliberately censor what they say out of fear of being punished socially

(20) for antagonizing their fellow members.

But group cohesiveness can have pitfalls as well: while the members of a highly cohesive group can feel much freer to deviate from the majority, their desire for genuine concurrence on every important

(25) issue often inclines them not to use this freedom. In a highly cohesive group of decision makers, the danger is not that individuals will conceal objections they harbor regarding a proposal favored by the majority, but that they will think the proposal is a good one

(30) without attempting to carry out a critical scrutiny that could reveal grounds for strong objections. Members may then decide that any misgivings they feel are not worth pursuing—that the benefit of any doubt should be given to the group consensus. In this way, they

(35) may fall victim to a syndrome known as "groupthink," which one psychologist concerned with collective decision making has defined as "a deterioration of mental efficiency, reality testing, and moral judgment that results from in-group pressures."

(40) Based on analyses of major fiascoes of international diplomacy and military decision making, researchers have identified groupthink behavior as a recurring pattern that involves several factors: overestimation of the group's power and morality,

(45) manifested, for example, in an illusion of invulnerability, which creates excessive optimism; closed-mindedness to warnings of problems and to alternative viewpoints; and unwarranted pressures toward uniformity, including self-censorship with

(50) respect to doubts about the group's reasoning and a concomitant shared illusion of unanimity concerning group decisions. Cohesiveness of the decision-making group is an essential antecedent condition for this syndrome but not a sufficient one, so it is important

(55) to work toward identifying the additional factors that determine whether group cohesiveness will deteriorate into groupthink or allow for effective decision making.

20. Which one of the following most accurately expresses the main point of the passage?

(A) Despite its value in encouraging frank discussion, high cohesion can lead to a debilitating type of group decision making called groupthink.

(B) Group members can guard against groupthink if they have a good understanding of the critical role played by cohesion.

(C) Groupthink is a dysfunctional collective decision-making pattern that can occur in diplomacy and military affairs.

(D) Low cohesion in groups is sometimes desirable when higher cohesion involves a risk of groupthink behavior.

(E) Future efforts to guard against groupthink will depend on the results of ongoing research into the psychology of collective decision making.

21. A group of closely associated colleagues has made a disastrous diplomatic decision after a series of meetings marked by disagreement over conflicting alternatives. It can be inferred from the passage that the author would be most likely to say that this scenario

(A) provides evidence of chronic indecision, thus indicating a weak level of cohesion in general

(B) indicates that the group's cohesiveness was coupled with some other factor to produce a groupthink fiasco

(C) provides no evidence that groupthink played a role in the group's decision

(D) provides evidence that groupthink can develop even in some groups that do not demonstrate an "illusion of unanimity"

(E) indicates that the group probably could have made its decision-making procedure more efficient by studying the information more thoroughly

GO ON TO THE NEXT PAGE.

22. Which one of the following, if true, would most support the author's contentions concerning the conditions under which groupthink takes place?

(A) A study of several groups, each made up of members of various professions, found that most fell victim to groupthink.

(B) There is strong evidence that respectful dissent is more likely to occur in cohesive groups than in groups in which there is little internal support.

(C) Extensive analyses of decisions made by a large number of groups found no cases of groupthink in groups whose members generally distrust one another's judgments.

(D) There is substantial evidence that groupthink is especially likely to take place when members of a group develop factions whose intransigence prolongs the group's deliberations.

(E) Ample research demonstrates that voluntary deference to group opinion is not a necessary factor for the formation of groupthink behavior.

23. The passage mentions which one of the following as a component of groupthink?

(A) unjustified suspicions among group members regarding an adversary's intentions

(B) strong belief that the group's decisions are right

(C) group members working under unusually high stress, leading to illusions of invulnerability

(D) the deliberate use of vapid, clichéd arguments

(E) careful consideration of objections to majority positions

24. It can be inferred from the passage that both the author of the passage and the researchers mentioned in the passage would be most likely to agree with which one of the following statements about groupthink?

(A) Groupthink occurs in all strongly cohesive groups, but its contribution to collective decision making is not fully understood.

(B) The causal factors that transform group cohesion into groupthink are unique to each case.

(C) The continued study of cohesiveness of groups is probably fruitless for determining what factors elicit groupthink.

(D) Outside information cannot influence group decisions once they have become determined by groupthink.

(E) On balance, groupthink cannot be expected to have a beneficial effect in a group's decision making.

25. In the passage, the author says which one of the following about conformity in decision-making groups?

(A) Enforced conformity may be appropriate in some group decision situations.

(B) A high degree of conformity is often expected of military decision-making group members.

(C) Inappropriate group conformity can result from inadequate information.

(D) Voluntary conformity occurs much less frequently than enforced conformity.

(E) Members of noncohesive groups may experience psychological pressure to conform.

26. In line 5, the author mentions low group cohesiveness primarily in order to

(A) contribute to a claim that cohesiveness can be conducive to a freer exchange of views in groups

(B) establish a comparison between groupthink symptoms and the attributes of low-cohesion groups

(C) suggest that there may be ways to make both cohesive and noncohesive groups more open to dissent

(D) indicate that both cohesive and noncohesive groups may be susceptible to groupthink dynamics

(E) lay the groundwork for a subsequent proposal for overcoming the debilitating effects of low cohesion

27. Based on the passage, it can be inferred that the author would be most likely to agree with which one of the following?

(A) Highly cohesive groups are more likely to engage in confrontational negotiating styles with adversaries than are those with low cohesion.

(B) It is difficult for a group to examine all relevant options critically in reaching decisions unless it has a fairly high degree of cohesiveness.

(C) A group with varied viewpoints on a given issue is less likely to reach a sound decision regarding that issue than is a group whose members are unified in their outlook.

(D) Intense stress and high expectations are the key factors in the formation of groupthink.

(E) Noncohesive groups can, under certain circumstances, develop all of the symptoms of groupthink.

S T O P

IF YOU FINISH BEFORE TIME IS CALLED, YOU MAY CHECK YOUR WORK ON THIS SECTION ONLY.
DO NOT WORK ON ANY OTHER SECTION IN THE TEST.

SECTION II

Time—35 minutes

26 Questions

<u>Directions:</u>   The questions in this section are based on the reasoning contained in brief statements or passages. For some questions, more than one of the choices could conceivably answer the question. However, you are to choose the <u>best</u> answer; that is, the response that most accurately and completely answers the question. You should not make assumptions that are by commonsense standards implausible, superfluous, or incompatible with the passage. After you have chosen the best answer, blacken the corresponding space on your answer sheet.

1. Sambar deer are physically incapable of digesting meat. Yet sambar deer have been reported feeding on box turtles after killing them.

    Which one of the following, if true, best resolves the discrepancy above?

    (A)   Sambar deer eat only the bony shells of box turtles.
    (B)   Sambar deer often kill box turtles by accident.
    (C)   Sambar deer kill box turtles only occasionally.
    (D)   Box turtles sometimes compete with sambar deer for food.
    (E)   Box turtles are much slower and clumsier than are sambar deer.

2. Benson: In order to maintain the quality of life in our city, we need to restrict growth. That is why I support the new zoning regulations.

    Willett: I had heard such arguments ten years ago, and again five years ago. Each time the city council was justified in deciding not to restrict growth. Since there is nothing new in this idea of restricting growth, I oppose the regulations.

    Which one of the following most accurately describes a way in which Willett's reasoning is questionable?

    (A)   It presumes that growth is necessarily good without offering support for that position.
    (B)   It is based on attacking Benson personally rather than responding to Benson's reasoning.
    (C)   It ignores the possibility that new reasons for restricting growth have arisen in the past five years.
    (D)   It fails to take into account the variety of factors that contribute to the quality of life in a city.
    (E)   It overlooks the possibility that the city council of ten years ago was poorly qualified to decide on zoning regulations.

3. A recent study involved feeding a high-salt diet to a rat colony. A few months after the experiment began, standard tests of the rats' blood pressure revealed that about 25 percent of the colony had normal, healthy blood pressure, about 70 percent of the colony had high blood pressure, and 5 percent of the colony had extremely high blood pressure. The conclusion from these results is that high-salt diets are linked to high blood pressure in rats.

    The answer to which one of the following questions is most relevant to evaluating the conclusion drawn above?

    (A)   How much more salt than is contained in a rat's normal diet was there in the high-salt diet?
    (B)   Did the high blood pressure have any adverse health effects on those rats that developed it?
    (C)   What percentage of naturally occurring rat colonies feed on high-salt diets?
    (D)   How many rats in the colony studied had abnormally high blood pressure before the study began?
    (E)   Have other species of rodents been used in experiments of the same kind?

4. Detective: Bill has been accused of committing the burglary at the warehouse last night. But no one saw Bill in the vicinity of the warehouse. So we must conclude that Bill did not commit the burglary.

    The reasoning in the detective's argument is most vulnerable to criticism on the grounds that the argument

    (A)   treats evidence that is irrelevant to the burglar's identity as if it were relevant
    (B)   merely attacks the character of Bill's accusers
    (C)   fails to provide independent evidence for the theory that Bill committed the burglary
    (D)   treats a lack of evidence against Bill as if it exonerated Bill
    (E)   fails to establish the true identity of the burglar

GO ON TO THE NEXT PAGE.

5. Psychologist: Because of a perceived social stigma against psychotherapy, and because of age discrimination on the part of some professionals, some elderly people feel discouraged about trying psychotherapy. They should not be, however, for many younger people have greatly benefited from it, and people in later life have certain advantages over the young—such as breadth of knowledge, emotional maturity, and interpersonal skills—that contribute to the likelihood of a positive outcome.

Which one of the following most accurately expresses the main conclusion of the psychologist's argument?

(A)   Certain psychotherapists practice age discrimination.
(B)   Elderly people are better able to benefit from psychotherapy than are younger people.
(C)   Elderly people should not be reluctant to undergo psychotherapy.
(D)   Characteristics associated with maturity are important factors in psychotherapy's success.
(E)   Elderly people are less inclined to try psychotherapy than are younger people.

6. Heavy salting of Albritten's roads to melt winter ice and snow began about 20 years ago. The area's groundwater now contains approximately 100 milligrams of dissolved salt per liter. Groundwater in a nearby, less highly urbanized area, where little salt is used and where traffic patterns resemble those of Albritten 20 years ago, contains only about 10 milligrams of dissolved salt per liter. Since water that contains 250 or more milligrams of dissolved salt per liter tastes unacceptably salty, continuing the salting of Albritten's roads at its present rate will render Albritten's groundwater unpalatable within the next few decades.

Which one of the following, if true, most seriously weakens the argument?

(A)   Even water that contains up to 5,000 milligrams of dissolved salt per liter is safe to drink.
(B)   The concentration of dissolved salt in Albritten's groundwater is expected to reach 400 milligrams per liter within a few decades.
(C)   Salting icy roads is the simplest way to prevent accidents on those roads.
(D)   Albritten's groundwater contained roughly 90 milligrams of dissolved salt per liter 20 years ago.
(E)   Salting of Albritten's roads is likely to decrease over the next few decades.

7. Numerous books describe the rules of etiquette. Usually the authors of such books merely codify standards of behavior by classifying various behaviors as polite or rude. However, this suggests that there is a single, objective standard of politeness. Clearly, standards of politeness vary from culture to culture, so it is absurd to label any one set of behaviors as correct and others as incorrect.

The reasoning in the argument is most vulnerable to criticism on the grounds that the argument

(A)   reaches a conclusion about how people actually behave on the basis of assertions regarding how they ought to behave
(B)   bases a generalization about all books of etiquette on the actions of a few authors
(C)   fails to justify its presumption regarding the influence of rules of etiquette on individual behavior
(D)   overlooks the possibility that authors of etiquette books are purporting to state what is correct behavior for one particular culture only
(E)   attempts to lend itself credence by unfairly labeling the position of the authors of etiquette books "absurd"

8. In jazz history, there have been gifted pianists who, because they had no striking musical ideas, led no memorable recording sessions. But precisely because they lacked such ideas, they were able to respond quickly to the ideas of imaginative and difficult leaders. Thus, these pianists are often heard adding masterful touches to some of the greatest jazz recordings.

Which one of the following principles is best illustrated by the information above?

(A)   The success of a group enterprise depends on the ability of the leader to recognize the weaknesses of others in the group.
(B)   The production of any great work requires contributions from those who are unimaginative but technically skilled.
(C)   People without forceful personalities cannot become great leaders in a field.
(D)   A trait that is a weakness in some settings can contribute to greatness in other settings.
(E)   No one can achieve great success without the help of others who are able to bring one's ideas to fruition.

GO ON TO THE NEXT PAGE.

9. Editorial: When legislators discover that some public service is not being adequately provided, their most common response is to boost the funding for that public service. Because of this, the least efficiently run government bureaucracies are the ones that most commonly receive an increase in funds.

The statements in the editorial, if true, most strongly support which one of the following?

(A) The least efficiently run government bureaucracies are the bureaucracies that legislators most commonly discover to be failing to provide some public service adequately.

(B) When legislators discover that a public service is not being adequately provided, they never respond to the problem by reducing the funding of the government bureaucracy providing that service.

(C) Throughout the time a government bureaucracy is run inefficiently, legislators repeatedly boost the funding for the public service that this bureaucracy provides.

(D) If legislators boost funding for a public service, the government bureaucracy providing that service will commonly become less efficient as a result.

(E) The most inefficiently run government bureaucracy receives the most funding of any government bureaucracy.

10. Fred argued that, since Kathleen is a successful film director, she has probably worked with famous actors. But, while Fred is right in supposing that most successful film directors work with famous actors, his conclusion is not warranted. For, as he knows, Kathleen works only on documentary films, and directors of documentaries rarely work with famous actors.

Which one of the following strategies is used above to criticize Fred's reasoning?

(A) maintaining that too little is known about Kathleen to justify any conclusion

(B) showing that Kathleen must not have worked with famous actors

(C) claiming that Fred has failed to take relevant information into account

(D) showing that Fred has mistakenly assumed that all successful film directors work with famous actors

(E) demonstrating that Fred has failed to show that most successful film directors work with famous actors

11. In early 1990, Queenston instituted a tax increase that gave its school system a larger operating budget. The school system used the larger budget to increase the total number of teachers in the system by 30 percent between 1990 and 1993. Nevertheless, there was no change in the average number of students per teacher between 1990 and 1993.

If the statements above are true, then on the basis of them which one of the following must also be true?

(A) No classes in Queenston's school system experienced an increase in enrollment between 1990 and 1993.

(B) The total number of students enrolled in Queenston's school system increased between 1990 and 1993.

(C) The operating budget of Queenston's school system increased by exactly 30 percent between 1990 and 1993.

(D) Most teachers who worked for Queenston's school system in 1990 were still working for the system in 1993.

(E) The quality of education in Queenston's school system improved between 1990 and 1993.

12. Our computer experts are asked from time to time to allocate funds for new hardware and software for our company. Unfortunately, these experts favor cutting-edge technologies, because that is what excites them, despite the fact that such experimental technologies are highly expensive, full of undiscovered "bugs," and thus are not the most profitable investments.

Of the following, which one conforms most closely to the principle illustrated by the situation described above?

(A) When senior executives choose to promote junior executives, they tend to favor those who share their professional interests, not those who have had the most education.

(B) When supermarkets choose foods, they choose the kinds that can be sold for the most profit, not the kinds of foods that are the most healthful for consumers.

(C) When librarians choose books for the library, they choose the kinds that they enjoy reading, not the kinds of books that serve the interests of the community.

(D) When students choose courses, they choose those that require the least amount of work, not those in which they might learn the most.

(E) When television executives choose programs to air, they choose the ones with the most sex and violence because that is what viewers want, not the shows with the highest artistic merit.

GO ON TO THE NEXT PAGE.

13. It is characteristic of great artists generally, and of great writers in particular, to have a discerning view of the basic social and political arrangements of the society in which they live. Therefore, the greater a writer one is, the more astute one will be in perceiving the basic social and political arrangements of one's society.

Which one of the following most accurately describes a flaw in the reasoning above?

(A) It assumes, without providing justification, that members of a group that is part of a larger group possess all of the characteristics possessed by members of the larger group.

(B) It assumes, without providing justification, that because something is sometimes the case it must always be the case.

(C) It assumes, without providing justification, that those artists with political insight do not have insight into matters outside of politics.

(D) It assumes, without providing justification, that only great individuals can make discerning criticisms of their societies.

(E) It assumes, without providing justification, that because people who have one quality tend to have a second quality, those who have more of the first quality will have more of the second.

14. Political scientist: The economies of a number of European countries are currently in severe difficulty. Germany is the only neighboring country that has the resources to resuscitate these economies. Therefore, Germany should begin aiding these economically troubled countries.

Which one of the following principles most helps to justify the political scientist's reasoning?

(A) Any nation that alone has an obligation to economically resuscitate neighboring countries ought to be the only nation to provide any economic aid.

(B) Any nation that alone has the capacity to economically resuscitate neighboring countries should exercise that capacity.

(C) Any nation that can afford to give economic aid to just a few other nations ought to aid just those few.

(D) Only nations that alone have the capacity to economically resuscitate neighboring countries should exercise that capacity.

(E) Only nations that can afford to give economic aid to just a few other nations ought to aid just those few.

15. Critic: Works of literature often present protagonists who scorn allegiance to their society and who advocate detachment rather than civic-mindedness. However, modern literature is distinguished from the literature of earlier eras in part because it more frequently treats such protagonists sympathetically. Sympathetic treatment of such characters suggests to readers that one should be unconcerned about contributing to societal good. Thus, modern literature can damage individuals who appropriate this attitude, as well as damage society at large.

Which one of the following is an assumption on which the critic's argument relies?

(A) Some individuals in earlier eras were more concerned about contributing to societal good than is any modern individual.

(B) It is to the advantage of some individuals that they be concerned with contributing to societal good.

(C) Some individuals must believe that their society is better than most before they can become concerned with benefiting it.

(D) The aesthetic merit of some literary works cannot be judged in complete independence of their moral effects.

(E) Modern literature is generally not as conducive to societal good as was the literature of earlier eras.

16. Psychologist: Some people contend that children should never be reprimanded. Any criticism, let alone punishment, they say, harms children's self-esteem. This view is laudable in its challenge to the belief that children should be punished whenever they misbehave, yet it gives a dangerous answer to the question of how often punishment should be inflicted. When parents never reprimand their children, they are in effect rewarding them for unacceptable behavior, and rewarded behavior tends to recur.

The view that children should never be reprimanded functions in the psychologist's argument as a statement of a position that the psychologist's argument

(A) is designed to discredit entirely

(B) is designed to establish as true

(C) is designed to establish as well intentioned

(D) claims has a serious flaw though is not without value

(E) claims is less reasonable than any other view mentioned

GO ON TO THE NEXT PAGE.

17. Traditionally, students at Kelly University have evaluated professors on the last day of class. But some professors at Kelly either do not distribute the paper evaluation forms or do so selectively, and many students cannot attend the last day of class. Soon, students will be able to use school computers to evaluate their professors at any time during the semester. Therefore, evaluations under the new system will accurately reflect the distribution of student opinion about teaching performance.

Which one of the following is an assumption required by the argument?

(A) Professors who distribute the paper evaluation forms selectively distribute them only to students they personally like.

(B) Students can wisely and insightfully assess a professor's performance before the end of the semester.

(C) The traditional system for evaluating teaching performance should not be used at any university.

(D) Nearly all professors who fail to distribute the paper evaluation forms do so because they believe the students will evaluate them unfavorably.

(E) Dissatisfied students are in general not more likely than satisfied students to submit a computerized evaluation.

18. A seriously maladaptive trait is unlikely to persist in a given animal population for long, since there is enough genetic variation in populations that some members will lack the trait. Those lacking the trait will compete more successfully for the available resources. Hence these members of the population survive and reproduce at a higher rate, crowding out those with the maladaptive trait.

The proposition that those lacking a maladaptive trait will compete more successfully for the available resources figures in the argument in which one of the following ways?

(A) It expresses a view that the argument as a whole is designed to discredit.

(B) It is the argument's main conclusion.

(C) It is a premise of the argument.

(D) It presents evidence that the argument attempts to undermine.

(E) It is an intermediate conclusion of the argument.

19. Tanya would refrain from littering if everyone else refrained from littering. None of her friends litter, and therefore she does not litter either.

Which one of the following uses flawed reasoning most similar to the flawed reasoning in the argument above?

(A) All residents of the same neighborhood have some goals in common. One group of neighborhood residents wants improvements made to a local park, so some other residents of that neighborhood must share this goal.

(B) If a talented artist is willing to starve for her career, then her friends should take her choice of profession seriously. Donna's friends take her choice of profession seriously, and she is willing to starve for her career, so she must be a talented artist.

(C) Herbert will stop selling office supplies in his store if none of his regular customers complains. Some of his regular customers never knew that Herbert sold office supplies, so those customers will not complain.

(D) If all whales need to surface for air, then whales must be easy to observe. Blue whales are easily observed, so they must surface for air.

(E) If all of a restaurant's customers like its food, it must be an exceptional restaurant. Everyone whom Sherryl consulted liked the food at Chez Louis, so it must be an exceptional restaurant.

GO ON TO THE NEXT PAGE.

20. Scientist: Genetic engineering has aided new
developments in many different fields. But
because these techniques require the manipulation
of the genetic codes of organisms, they are said
to be unethical. What the critics fail to realize is
that this kind of manipulation has been going on
for millennia; virtually every farm animal is the
result of selective breeding for desired traits.
Since selective breeding is genetic engineering of
a crude sort, genetic engineering is not unethical.

Which one of the following is an assumption on which
the scientist's argument depends?

(A) The manipulation of the genetic code of
organisms is never unethical.

(B) Anything that is accomplished by nature is not
unethical to accomplish with science.

(C) The manipulation of the genetic code through
selective breeding for desired traits is not
unethical.

(D) The manipulation of the genetic code through
selective breeding for desired traits is important
for human survival.

(E) Science can accomplish only what is already in
some sense natural, and nothing natural is
unethical.

21. Baumgartner's comparison of the environmental
hazards of gasoline-powered cars with those of electric
cars is misleading. He examines only production of the
cars, whereas it is the product's total life
cycle—production, use, and recycling—that matters in
determining its environmental impact. A typical
gasoline-powered car consumes 3 times more resources
and produces 15 to 20 times more air pollution than a
typical electric car.

Which one of the following most accurately expresses
the conclusion of the argument?

(A) Baumgartner makes a deceptive comparison
between the environmental hazards of gasoline-
powered and electric cars.

(B) The use of a typical gasoline-powered car
results in much greater resource depletion than
does the use of a typical electric car.

(C) Baumgartner uses inaccurate data in his
comparison of the environmental hazards of
gasoline-powered and electric cars.

(D) The total life cycle of a product is what matters
in assessing its environmental impact.

(E) The production of gasoline-powered cars creates
more environmental hazards than does that of
electric cars.

GO ON TO THE NEXT PAGE.

22. Over the last 10 years, there has been a dramatic increase in the number of people over the age of 65 living in this region. This is evident from the fact that during this time the average age of people living in this region has increased from approximately 52 to 57 years.

Which one of the following, if true, would most strengthen the argument?

(A) The number of people in the region under the age of 18 has increased over the last 10 years.

(B) The birth rate for the region decreased significantly over the last 10 years.

(C) The total number of people living in the region has decreased over the last 10 years.

(D) The number of people who moved into the region over the last 10 years is greater than the number of those who moved out.

(E) The average age for people in the region is higher than that for people in surrounding regions.

23. Editorial: A recently passed law limits freedom of speech in order to silence dissenters. It has been said that those who are ignorant of history will repeat its patterns. If this is true, then those responsible for passing the law must be ignorant of a great deal of history. Historically, silencing dissenters has tended to promote undemocratic policies and the establishment of authoritarian regimes.

The editorialist's reasoning is flawed in that it fails to take into account that

(A) the law may have other purposes in addition to silencing dissenters

(B) certain freedoms might sometimes need to be limited in order to ensure the protection of certain other freedoms

(C) some historical accounts report that legal restrictions on freedom of speech have occasionally undermined the establishment of authoritarian regimes

(D) many good laws have been passed by people who are largely ignorant of history

(E) even those who are not ignorant of history may repeat its patterns

24. Editorialist: Despite the importance it seems to have in our lives, money does not really exist. This is evident from the fact that all that would be needed to make money disappear would be a universal loss of belief in it. We witness this phenomenon on a small scale daily in the rises and falls of financial markets, whose fluctuations are often entirely independent of concrete causes and are the results of mere beliefs of investors.

The conclusion of the editorialist's argument can be properly drawn if which one of the following is assumed?

(A) Anything that exists would continue to exist even if everyone were to stop believing in it.

(B) Only if one can have mistaken beliefs about a thing does that thing exist, strictly speaking.

(C) In order to exist, an entity must have practical consequences for those who believe in it.

(D) If everyone believes in something, then that thing exists.

(E) Whatever is true of money is true of financial markets generally.

GO ON TO THE NEXT PAGE.

25. False chicory's taproot is always one half as long as the plant is tall. Furthermore, the more rain false chicory receives, the taller it tends to grow. In fact, false chicory plants that receive greater than twice the average rainfall of the species' usual habitat always reach above-average heights for false chicory.

If the statements above are true, then which one of the following must also be true?

(A) If two false chicory plants differ in height, then it is likely that the one with the shorter taproot has received less than twice the average rainfall of the species' usual habitat.

(B) If a false chicory plant has a longer-than-average taproot, then it is likely to have received more than twice the average rainfall of the species' usual habitat.

(C) It is not possible for a false chicory plant to receive only the average amount of rainfall of the species' usual habitat and be of above-average height.

(D) If the plants in one group of false chicory are not taller than those in another group of false chicory, then the two groups must have received the same amount of rainfall.

(E) If a false chicory plant receives greater than twice the average rainfall of the species' usual habitat, then it will have a longer taproot than that of an average-sized false chicory plant.

26. Fossilized teeth of an extinct species of herbivorous great ape have on them phytoliths, which are microscopic petrified remains of plants. Since only phytoliths from certain species of plants are found on the teeth, the apes' diet must have consisted only of those plants.

The argument assumes which one of the following?

(A) None of the plant species that left phytoliths on the apes' teeth has since become extinct.

(B) Plants of every type eaten by the apes left phytoliths on their teeth.

(C) Each of the teeth examined had phytoliths of the same plant species on it as all the other teeth.

(D) Phytoliths have also been found on the fossilized teeth of apes of other extinct species.

(E) Most species of great ape alive today have diets that consist of a fairly narrow range of plants.

S T O P

IF YOU FINISH BEFORE TIME IS CALLED, YOU MAY CHECK YOUR WORK ON THIS SECTION ONLY.
DO NOT WORK ON ANY OTHER SECTION IN THE TEST.

SECTION III

Time—35 minutes

26 Questions

<u>Directions:</u> The questions in this section are based on the reasoning contained in brief statements or passages. For some questions, more than one of the choices could conceivably answer the question. However, you are to choose the <u>best</u> answer; that is, the response that most accurately and completely answers the question. You should not make assumptions that are by commonsense standards implausible, superfluous, or incompatible with the passage. After you have chosen the best answer, blacken the corresponding space on your answer sheet.

1. Executive: Our company is proud of its long history of good relations with its employees. In fact, a recent survey of our retirees proves that we treat our employees fairly, since 95 percent of the respondents reported that they had always been treated fairly during the course of their careers with us.

The executive's argument is flawed in that it

(A) presents as its sole premise a claim that one would accept as true only if one already accepted the truth of the conclusion

(B) relies on evidence that cannot be verified

(C) equivocates on the word "fairly"

(D) bases a generalization on a sample that may not be representative

(E) presumes, without providing justification, that older methods of managing employees are superior to newer ones

2. Many of those who are most opposed to cruelty to animals in the laboratory, in the slaughterhouse, or on the farm are people who truly love animals and who keep pets. The vast majority of domestic pets, however, are dogs and cats, and both of these species are usually fed meat. Therefore, many of those who are most opposed to cruelty to animals do, in fact, contribute to such cruelty.

Which one of the following is an assumption made by the argument?

(A) Loving pets requires loving all forms of animal life.

(B) Many of those who are opposed to keeping dogs and cats as pets are also opposed to cruelty to animals.

(C) Some people who work in laboratories, in slaughterhouses, or on farms are opposed to cruelty to animals.

(D) Many popular pets are not usually fed meat.

(E) Feeding meat to pets contributes to cruelty to animals.

3. Statistics from the National Booksellers Association indicate that during the last five years most bookstores have started to experience declining revenues from the sale of fiction, despite national campaigns to encourage people to read more fiction. Therefore, these reading campaigns have been largely unsuccessful.

Which one of the following statements, if true, most seriously weakens the argument?

(A) Mail order book clubs have enjoyed substantial growth in fiction sales throughout the last five years.

(B) During the last five years the most profitable items in bookstores have been newspapers and periodicals rather than novels.

(C) Fierce competition has forced booksellers to make drastic markdowns on the cover price of best-selling biographies.

(D) Due to the poor economic conditions that have prevailed during the last five years, most libraries report substantial increases in the number of patrons seeking books on changing careers and starting new businesses.

(E) The National Booksellers Association statistics do not include profits from selling novels by mail to overseas customers.

4. People who consume a lot of honey tend to have fewer cavities than others have. Yet, honey is high in sugar, and sugar is one of the leading causes of tooth decay.

Which one of the following, if true, most helps to resolve the apparent paradox described above?

(A) People who eat a lot of honey tend to consume very little sugar from other sources.

(B) Many people who consume a lot of honey consume much of it dissolved in drinks.

(C) People's dental hygiene habits vary greatly.

(D) Refined sugars have been linked to more health problems than have unrefined sugars.

(E) Honey contains bacteria that inhibit the growth of the bacteria that cause tooth decay.

GO ON TO THE NEXT PAGE.

5. Byrne: One of our club's bylaws specifies that any officer who fails to appear on time for any one of the quarterly board meetings, or who misses two of our monthly general meetings, must be suspended. Thibodeaux, an officer, was recently suspended. But Thibodeaux has never missed a monthly general meeting. Therefore, Thibodeaux must have failed to appear on time for a quarterly board meeting.

The reasoning in Byrne's argument is flawed in that the argument

(A) fails to consider the possibility that Thibodeaux has arrived late for two or more monthly general meetings

(B) presumes, without providing justification, that if certain events each produce a particular result, then no other event is sufficient to produce that result

(C) takes for granted that an assumption required to establish the argument's conclusion is sufficient to establish that conclusion

(D) fails to specify at what point someone arriving at a club meeting is officially deemed late

(E) does not specify how long Thibodeaux has been an officer

6. Manufacturers of writing paper need to add mineral "filler" to paper pulp if the paper made from the pulp is to look white. Without such filler, paper products look grayish. To make writing paper that looks white from recycled paper requires more filler than is required to make such paper from other sources. Therefore, barring the more efficient use of fillers in paper manufacturing or the development of paper-whitening technologies that do not require mineral fillers, if writing paper made from recycled paper comes to replace other types of writing paper, paper manufacturers will have to use more filler than they now use.

Which one of the following is an assumption on which the argument depends?

(A) Certain kinds of paper cannot be manufactured from recycled paper.

(B) The fillers that are used to make paper white are harmful to the environment.

(C) Grayish writing paper will not be a universally acceptable alternative to white writing paper.

(D) Beyond a certain limit, increasing the amount of filler added to paper pulp does not increase the whiteness of the paper made from the pulp.

(E) The total amount of writing paper manufactured worldwide will increase significantly in the future.

7. Environmentalist: The excessive atmospheric buildup of carbon dioxide, which threatens the welfare of everyone in the world, can be stopped only by reducing the burning of fossil fuels. Any country imposing the strict emission standards on the industrial burning of such fuels that this reduction requires, however, would thereby reduce its gross national product. No nation will be willing to bear singlehandedly the costs of an action that will benefit everyone. It is obvious, then, that the catastrophic consequences of excessive atmospheric carbon dioxide are unavoidable unless _____.

Which one of the following most logically completes the argument?

(A) all nations become less concerned with pollution than with the economic burdens of preventing it

(B) multinational corporations agree to voluntary strict emission standards

(C) international agreements produce industrial emission standards

(D) distrust among nations is eliminated

(E) a world government is established

8. A clear advantage of digital technology over traditional printing is that digital documents, being patterns of electronic signals rather than patterns of ink on paper, do not generate waste in the course of their production and use. However, because patterns of electronic signals are necessarily ephemeral, a digital document can easily be destroyed and lost forever.

The statements above best illustrate which one of the following generalizations?

(A) A property of a technology may constitute an advantage in one set of circumstances and a disadvantage in others.

(B) What at first appears to be an advantage of a technology may create more problems than it solves.

(C) It is more important to be able to preserve information than it is for information to be easily accessible.

(D) Innovations in document storage technologies sometimes decrease, but never eliminate, the risk of destroying documents.

(E) Advances in technology can lead to increases in both convenience and environmental soundness.

GO ON TO THE NEXT PAGE.

9. Museum visitor: The national government has mandated a 5 percent increase in the minimum wage paid to all workers. This mandate will adversely affect the museum-going public. The museum's revenue does not currently exceed its expenses, and since the mandate will significantly increase the museum's operating expenses, the museum will be forced either to raise admission fees or to decrease services.

Which one of the following is an assumption required by the museum visitor's argument?

(A) Some of the museum's employees are not paid significantly more than the minimum wage.

(B) The museum's revenue from admission fees has remained constant over the past five years.

(C) Some of the museum's employees are paid more than the current minimum wage.

(D) The annual number of visitors to the museum has increased steadily.

(E) Not all visitors to the museum are required to pay an admission fee.

10. Helen: Reading a book is the intellectual equivalent of investing money: you're investing time, thereby foregoing other ways of spending that time, in the hope that what you learn will later afford you more opportunities than you'd get by spending the time doing something other than reading that book.

Randi: But that applies only to vocational books. Reading fiction is like watching a sitcom: it's just wasted time.

Which one of the following most accurately describes the technique Randi uses in responding to Helen's claims?

(A) questioning how the evidence Helen uses for a claim was gathered

(B) disputing the scope of Helen's analogy by presenting another analogy

(C) arguing that Helen's reasoning ultimately leads to an absurd conclusion

(D) drawing an analogy to an example presented by Helen

(E) denying the relevance of an example presented by Helen

11. Contrary to recent speculations, no hardware store will be opening in the shopping plaza. If somebody were going to open a store there, they would already have started publicizing it. But there has been no such publicity.

Which one of the following most accurately expresses the conclusion drawn in the argument?

(A) Some people have surmised that a hardware store will be opening in the shopping plaza.

(B) A hardware store will not be opening in the shopping plaza.

(C) If somebody were going to open a hardware store in the shopping plaza, that person would already have started publicizing it.

(D) It would be unwise to open a hardware store in the shopping plaza.

(E) There has been no publicity concerning the opening of a hardware store in the shopping plaza.

12. Ethicist: Although science is frequently said to be morally neutral, it has a traditional value system of its own. For example, scientists sometimes foresee that a line of theoretical research they are pursuing will yield applications that could seriously harm people, animals, or the environment. Yet, according to science's traditional value system, such consequences do not have to be considered in deciding whether to pursue that research. Ordinary morality, in contrast, requires that we take the foreseeable consequences of our actions into account whenever we are deciding what to do.

The ethicist's statements, if true, most strongly support which one of the following?

(A) Scientists should not be held responsible for the consequences of their research.

(B) According to the dictates of ordinary morality, scientists doing research that ultimately turns out to yield harmful applications are acting immorally.

(C) Science is morally neutral because it assigns no value to the consequences of theoretical research.

(D) It is possible for scientists to both adhere to the traditional values of their field and violate a principle of ordinary morality.

(E) The uses and effects of scientifically acquired knowledge can never be adequately foreseen.

GO ON TO THE NEXT PAGE.

13. Consumers seek to purchase the highest quality at the lowest prices. Companies that do not offer products that attract consumers eventually go bankrupt. Therefore, companies that offer neither the best quality nor the lowest price will eventually go bankrupt.

The conclusion above follows logically if which one of the following is assumed?

(A) No company succeeds in producing a product that is both highest in quality and lowest in price.

(B) Products that are neither highest in quality nor lowest in price do not attract consumers.

(C) Any company that offers either the highest quality or the lowest price will avoid bankruptcy.

(D) Some consumers will not continue to patronize a company purely out of brand loyalty.

(E) No company is driven from the market for reasons other than failing to meet consumer demands.

14. The number of serious traffic accidents (accidents resulting in hospitalization or death) that occurred on Park Road from 1986 to 1990 was 35 percent lower than the number of serious accidents from 1981 to 1985. The speed limit on Park Road was lowered in 1986. Hence, the reduction of the speed limit led to the decrease in serious accidents.

Which one of the following statements, if true, most weakens the argument?

(A) The number of speeding tickets issued annually on Park Road remained roughly constant from 1981 to 1990.

(B) Beginning in 1986, police patrolled Park Road much less frequently than in 1985 and previous years.

(C) The annual number of vehicles using Park Road decreased significantly and steadily from 1981 to 1990.

(D) The annual number of accidents on Park Road that did not result in hospitalization remained roughly constant from 1981 to 1990.

(E) Until 1986 accidents were classified as "serious" only if they resulted in an extended hospital stay.

15. Humans are supposedly rational: in other words, they have a capacity for well-considered thinking and behavior. This is supposedly the difference that makes them superior to other animals. But humans knowingly pollute the world's precious air and water and, through bad farming practices, deplete the soil that feeds them. Thus, humans are not rational after all, so it is absurd to regard them as superior to other animals.

The reasoning above is flawed in that it

(A) relies crucially on an internally contradictory definition of rationality

(B) takes for granted that humans are aware that their acts are irrational

(C) neglects to show that the irrational acts perpetrated by humans are not also perpetrated by other animals

(D) presumes, without offering justification, that humans are no worse than other animals

(E) fails to recognize that humans may possess a capacity without displaying it in a given activity

16. "Good hunter" and "bad hunter" are standard terms in the study of cats. Good hunters can kill prey that weigh up to half their body weight. All good hunters have a high muscle-to-fat ratio. Most wild cats are good hunters, but some domestic cats are good hunters as well.

If the statements above are true, which one of the following must also be true?

(A) Some cats that have a high muscle-to-fat ratio are not good hunters.

(B) A smaller number of domestic cats than wild cats have a high muscle-to-fat ratio.

(C) All cats that are bad hunters have a low muscle-to-fat ratio.

(D) Some cats that have a high muscle-to-fat ratio are domestic.

(E) All cats that have a high muscle-to-fat ratio can kill prey that weigh up to half their body weight.

GO ON TO THE NEXT PAGE.

17. Ethicist: The penalties for drunk driving are far more severe when the drunk driver accidentally injures people than when no one is injured. Moral responsibility for an action depends solely on the intentions underlying the action and not on the action's results. Therefore, legal responsibility, depending as it does in at least some cases on factors other than the agent's intentions, is different than moral responsibility.

The claim that the penalties for drunk driving are far more severe when the drunk driver accidentally injures people than when no one is injured plays which one of the following roles in the ethicist's argument?

(A) It is a premise offered in support of the claim that legal responsibility for an action is based solely upon features of the action that are generally unintended by the agent.

(B) It is offered as an illustration of the claim that the criteria of legal responsibility for an action include but are not the same as those for moral responsibility.

(C) It is offered as an illustration of the claim that people may be held morally responsible for an action for which they are not legally responsible.

(D) It is a premise offered in support of the claim that legal responsibility depends in at least some cases on factors other than the agent's intentions.

(E) It is a premise offered in support of the claim that moral responsibility depends solely on the intentions underlying the action and not on the action's result.

18. Columnist: Taking a strong position on an issue makes one likely to misinterpret or ignore additional evidence that conflicts with one's stand. But in order to understand an issue fully, it is essential to consider such evidence impartially. Thus, it is best not to take a strong position on an issue unless one has already considered all important evidence conflicting with that position.

The columnist's reasoning most closely conforms to which one of the following principles?

(A) It is reasonable to take a strong position on an issue if one fully understands the issue and has considered the evidence regarding that issue impartially.

(B) To ensure that one has impartially considered the evidence regarding an issue on which one has taken a strong position, one should avoid misinterpreting or ignoring evidence regarding that issue.

(C) Anyone who does not understand an issue fully should avoid taking a strong position on it.

(D) One should try to understand an issue fully if doing so will help one to avoid misinterpreting or ignoring evidence regarding that issue.

(E) It is reasonable to take a strong position on an issue only if there is important evidence conflicting with that position.

GO ON TO THE NEXT PAGE.

19. The coach of the Eagles used a computer analysis to determine the best combinations of players for games. The analysis revealed that the team has lost only when Jennifer was not playing. Although no computer was needed to discover this information, this sort of information is valuable, and in this case it confirms that Jennifer's presence in the game will ensure that the Eagles will win.

The argument above is most vulnerable to criticism on the grounds that it

(A) infers from the fact that a certain factor is sufficient for a result that the absence of that factor is necessary for the opposite result

(B) presumes, without providing justification, that a player's contribution to a team's win or loss can be reliably quantified and analyzed by computer

(C) draws conclusions about applications of computer analyses to sports from the evidence of a single case

(D) presumes, without providing justification, that occurrences that have coincided in the past must continue to coincide

(E) draws a conclusion about the value of computer analyses from a case in which computer analysis provided no facts beyond what was already known

20. Of the various food containers made of recycled Styrofoam, egg cartons are among the easiest to make. Because egg shells keep the actual food to be consumed from touching the Styrofoam, used Styrofoam need not be as thoroughly cleaned when made into egg cartons as when made into other food containers.

Which one of the following is most strongly supported by the information above?

(A) No food containers other than egg cartons can safely be made of recycled Styrofoam that has not been thoroughly cleaned.

(B) There are some foods that cannot be packaged in recycled Styrofoam no matter how the Styrofoam is recycled.

(C) The main reason Styrofoam must be thoroughly cleaned when recycled is to remove any residual food that has come into contact with the Styrofoam.

(D) Because they are among the easiest food containers to make from recycled Styrofoam, most egg cartons are made from recycled Styrofoam.

(E) Not every type of food container made of recycled Styrofoam is effectively prevented from coming into contact with the food it contains.

GO ON TO THE NEXT PAGE.

21. Most people who become migraine sufferers as adults were prone to bouts of depression as children. Hence it stands to reason that a child who is prone to bouts of depression is likely to suffer migraines during adulthood.

The flawed pattern of reasoning in the argument above is most parallel to that in which one of the following?

(A) Most good-tempered dogs were vaccinated against rabies as puppies. Therefore, a puppy that is vaccinated against rabies is likely to become a good-tempered dog.

(B) Most vicious dogs were ill-treated when young. Hence it can be concluded that a pet owner whose dog is vicious is likely to have treated the dog badly when it was young.

(C) Most well-behaved dogs have undergone obedience training. Thus, if a dog has not undergone obedience training, it will not be well behaved.

(D) Most of the pets taken to veterinarians are dogs. Therefore, it stands to reason that dogs are more prone to illness or accident than are other pets.

(E) Most puppies are taken from their mothers at the age of eight weeks. Thus, a puppy that is older than eight weeks is likely to have been taken from its mother.

22. Student: The publications of Professor Vallejo on the origins of glassblowing have reopened the debate among historians over whether glassblowing originated in Egypt or elsewhere. If Professor Vallejo is correct, there is insufficient evidence for claiming, as most historians have done for many years, that glassblowing began in Egypt. So, despite the fact that the traditional view is still maintained by the majority of historians, if Professor Vallejo is correct, we must conclude that glassblowing originated elsewhere.

Which one of the following is an error in the student's reasoning?

(A) It draws a conclusion that conflicts with the majority opinion of experts.

(B) It presupposes the truth of Professor Vallejo's claims.

(C) It fails to provide criteria for determining adequate historical evidence.

(D) It mistakes the majority view for the traditional view.

(E) It confuses inadequate evidence for truth with evidence for falsity.

23. At Southgate Mall, mattresses are sold only at Mattress Madness. Every mattress at Mattress Madness is on sale at a 20 percent discount. So every mattress for sale at Southgate Mall is on sale at a 20 percent discount.

Which one of the following arguments is most similar in its reasoning to the argument above?

(A) The only food in Diane's apartment is in her refrigerator. All the food she purchased within the past week is in her refrigerator. Therefore, she purchased all the food in her apartment within the past week.

(B) Diane's refrigerator, and all the food in it, is in her apartment. Diane purchased all the food in her refrigerator within the past week. Therefore, she purchased all the food in her apartment within the past week.

(C) All the food in Diane's apartment is in her refrigerator. Diane purchased all the food in her refrigerator within the past week. Therefore, she purchased all the food in her apartment within the past week.

(D) The only food in Diane's apartment is in her refrigerator. Diane purchased all the food in her refrigerator within the past week. Therefore, all the food she purchased within the past week is in her apartment.

(E) The only food that Diane has purchased within the past week is in her refrigerator. All the food that she has purchased within the past week is in her apartment. Therefore, all the food in her apartment is in her refrigerator.

GO ON TO THE NEXT PAGE.

24. There are 1.3 billion cows worldwide, and this population is growing to keep pace with the demand for meat and milk. These cows produce trillions of liters of methane gas yearly, and this methane contributes to global warming. The majority of the world's cows are given relatively low-quality diets even though cows produce less methane when they receive better-quality diets. Therefore, methane production from cows could be kept in check if cows were given better-quality diets.

Which one of the following, if true, adds the most support for the conclusion of the argument?

(A) Cows given good-quality diets produce much more meat and milk than they would produce otherwise.

(B) Carbon and hydrogen, the elements that make up methane, are found in abundance in the components of all types of cow feed.

(C) Most farmers would be willing to give their cows high-quality feed if the cost of that feed were lower.

(D) Worldwide, more methane is produced by cows raised for meat production than by those raised for milk production.

(E) Per liter, methane contributes more to global warming than does carbon dioxide, a gas that is thought to be the most significant contributor to global warming.

25. To face danger solely because doing so affords one a certain pleasure does not constitute courage. Real courage is manifested only when a person, in acting to attain a goal, perseveres in the face of fear prompted by one or more dangers involved.

Which one of the following statements can be properly inferred from the statements above?

(A) A person who must face danger in order to avoid future pain cannot properly be called courageous for doing so.

(B) A person who experiences fear of some aspects of a dangerous situation cannot be said to act courageously in that situation.

(C) A person who happens to derive pleasure from some dangerous activities is not a courageous person.

(D) A person who faces danger in order to benefit others is acting courageously only if the person is afraid of the danger.

(E) A person who has no fear of the situations that everyone else would fear cannot be said to be courageous in any situation.

26. The government will purchase and install new severe weather sirens for this area next year if replacement parts for the old sirens are difficult to obtain. The newspaper claims that public safety in the event of severe weather would be enhanced if new sirens were to be installed. The local company from which replacement parts were purchased last year has since gone out of business. So, if the newspaper is correct, the public will be safer during severe weather in the future.

The argument's conclusion follows logically from its premises if which one of the following is assumed?

(A) If public safety in the event of severe weather is enhanced next year, it will be because new sirens have been purchased.

(B) The newspaper was correct in claiming that public safety in the event of severe weather would be enhanced if new sirens were purchased.

(C) The local company from which replacement parts for the old sirens were purchased last year was the only company in the area that sold them.

(D) Replacement parts for the old sirens will be difficult to obtain if the government cannot obtain them from the company it purchased them from last year.

(E) Because the local company from which replacement parts had been purchased went out of business, the only available parts are of such inferior quality that use of them would make the sirens less reliable.

S T O P

IF YOU FINISH BEFORE TIME IS CALLED, YOU MAY CHECK YOUR WORK ON THIS SECTION ONLY.
DO NOT WORK ON ANY OTHER SECTION IN THE TEST.

SECTION IV

Time—35 minutes

23 Questions

Directions: Each group of questions in this section is based on a set of conditions. In answering some of the questions, it may be useful to draw a rough diagram. Choose the response that most accurately and completely answers each question and blacken the corresponding space on your answer sheet.

Questions 1–5

A dance is being choreographed for six dancers: three men—Felipe, Grant, and Hassan—and three women—Jaclyn, Keiko, and Lorena. At no time during the dance will anyone other than the dancers be on stage. Who is on stage and who is off stage at any particular time in the dance is determined by the following constraints:

    If Jaclyn is on stage, Lorena is off stage.
    If Lorena is off stage, Jaclyn is on stage.
    If Felipe is off stage, Jaclyn is also off stage.
    If any of the women are on stage, Grant is also on stage.

1. Which one of the following is a list of all of the dancers who could be on stage at a particular time?

    (A) Grant
    (B) Keiko, Lorena
    (C) Grant, Hassan, Lorena
    (D) Grant, Hassan, Jaclyn
    (E) Felipe, Grant, Jaclyn, Lorena

2. Which one of the following CANNOT be true at any time during the dance?

    (A) Felipe and Grant are the only men on stage.
    (B) Grant and Hassan are the only men on stage.
    (C) Jaclyn is the only woman on stage.
    (D) Keiko is the only woman on stage.
    (E) Jaclyn and Keiko are the only women on stage.

3. Which one of the following is a complete and accurate list of the dancers any one of whom could be off stage when Jaclyn is on stage?

    (A) Lorena
    (B) Felipe, Lorena
    (C) Hassan, Lorena
    (D) Hassan, Keiko
    (E) Hassan, Keiko, Lorena

4. If there are more women than men on stage, then exactly how many dancers must be on stage?

    (A) five
    (B) four
    (C) three
    (D) two
    (E) one

5. What is the minimum number of dancers that must be on stage at any given time?

    (A) zero
    (B) one
    (C) two
    (D) three
    (E) four

GO ON TO THE NEXT PAGE.

Questions 6–12

A critic has prepared a review of exactly six music CDs—
Headstrong, In Flight, Nice, Quasi, Reunion, and *Sounds Good.* Each CD received a rating of either one, two, three, or four stars, with each CD receiving exactly one rating. Although the ratings were meant to be kept secret until the review was published, the following facts have been leaked to the public:

> For each of the ratings, at least one but no more than two of the CDs received that rating.
>
> *Headstrong* received exactly one more star than *Nice* did.
> Either *Headstrong* or *Reunion* received the same number of stars as *In Flight* did.
> At most one CD received more stars than *Quasi* did.

6. Which one of the following could be an accurate matching of ratings to the CDs that received those ratings?

    (A)   one star: *In Flight, Reunion*; two stars: *Nice*; three stars: *Headstrong*; four stars: *Quasi, Sounds Good*

    (B)   one star: *In Flight, Reunion*; two stars: *Quasi, Sounds Good*; three stars: *Nice*; four stars: *Headstrong*

    (C)   one star: *Nice*; two stars: *Headstrong*; three stars: *In Flight, Sounds Good*; four stars: *Quasi, Reunion*

    (D)   one star: Nice, Sounds Good; two stars: *In Flight, Reunion;* three stars: *Quasi;* four stars: *Headstrong*

    (E)   one star: *Sounds Good*; two stars: *Reunion*; three stars: *Nice, Quasi*; four stars: *Headstrong, In Flight*

7. If Headstrong is the only CD that received a rating of two stars, then which one of the following must be true?

    (A)   *In Flight* received a rating of three stars.
    (B)   *Nice* received a rating of three stars.
    (C)   *Quasi* received a rating of three stars.
    (D)   *Reunion* received a rating of one star.
    (E)   *Sounds Good* received a rating of one star.

8. If *Reunion* received the same rating as *Sounds Good,* then which one of the following must be true?

    (A)   *Headstrong* received a rating of two stars.
    (B)   *In Flight* received a rating of three stars.
    (C)   *Nice* received a rating of two stars.
    (D)   *Quasi* received a rating of four stars.
    (E)   *Sounds Good* received a rating of one star.

9. If *Nice* and *Reunion* each received a rating of one star, then which one of the following could be true?

    (A)   *Headstrong* received a rating of three stars.
    (B)   *Headstrong* received a rating of four stars.
    (C)   *In Flight* received a rating of three stars.
    (D)   *Sounds Good* received a rating of two stars.
    (E)   *Sounds Good* received a rating of three stars.

10. Which one of the following CANNOT be true?

    (A)   *Quasi* is the only CD that received a rating of three stars.
    (B)   *Quasi* is the only CD that received a rating of four stars.
    (C)   *Reunion* is the only CD that received a rating of one star.
    (D)   *Reunion* is the only CD that received a rating of two stars.
    (E)   *Reunion* is the only CD that received a rating of three stars.

11. If Reunion is the only CD that received a rating of one star, then which one of the following could be true?

    (A)   *Headstrong* received a rating of four stars.
    (B)   *In Flight* received a rating of two stars.
    (C)   *Nice* received a rating of three stars.
    (D)   *Quasi* received a rating of three stars.
    (E)   *Sounds Good* received a rating of two stars.

12. Which one of the following CANNOT have received a rating of four stars?

    (A)   *Headstrong*
    (B)   *In Flight*
    (C)   *Quasi*
    (D)   *Reunion*
    (E)   *Sounds Good*

GO ON TO THE NEXT PAGE.

Questions 13–17

A cake has exactly six layers—lemon, marzipan, orange, raspberry, strawberry, and vanilla. There is exactly one bottom layer (the first layer), and each succeeding layer (from second through sixth) completely covers the layer beneath it. The following conditions must apply:

> The raspberry layer is neither immediately above nor immediately below the strawberry layer.
> The marzipan layer is immediately above the lemon layer.
> The orange layer is above the marzipan layer but below the strawberry layer.

13. Which one of the following could be an accurate list of the layers of the cake, from bottom to top?

   (A) lemon, marzipan, orange, strawberry, vanilla, raspberry
   (B) lemon, marzipan, orange, strawberry, raspberry, vanilla
   (C) marzipan, lemon, raspberry, vanilla, orange, strawberry
   (D) raspberry, lemon, marzipan, vanilla, strawberry, orange
   (E) raspberry, orange, lemon, marzipan, strawberry, vanilla

14. If the strawberry layer is not immediately above the orange layer, then which one of the following could be true?

   (A) The raspberry layer is immediately above the vanilla layer.
   (B) The raspberry layer is immediately above the orange layer.
   (C) The raspberry layer is immediately below the marzipan layer.
   (D) The raspberry layer is the second layer.
   (E) The raspberry layer is the top layer.

15. If the strawberry layer is not the top layer, then which one of the following is a complete and accurate list of the layers that could be the vanilla layer?

   (A) the first, the second, the third, the fourth, the fifth, the sixth
   (B) the second, the third, the fourth, the fifth, the sixth
   (C) the third, the fourth, the fifth, the sixth
   (D) the fourth, the fifth, the sixth
   (E) the fifth, the sixth

16. If the lemon layer is third, then which one of the following could be true?

   (A) The vanilla layer is fifth.
   (B) The vanilla layer is immediately above the raspberry layer.
   (C) The orange layer is not immediately above the marzipan layer.
   (D) The raspberry layer is above the marzipan layer.
   (E) The strawberry layer is not the top layer.

17. Which one of the following could be an accurate list of the two lowest layers of the cake, listed in order from the bottom up?

   (A) lemon, raspberry
   (B) vanilla, raspberry
   (C) marzipan, raspberry
   (D) raspberry, marzipan
   (E) raspberry, strawberry

GO ON TO THE NEXT PAGE.

Questions 18–23

A panel reviews six contract bids—H, J, K, R, S, and T. No two bids have the same cost. Exactly one of the bids is accepted. The following conditions must hold:

The accepted bid is either K or R and is either the second or the third lowest in cost.

H is lower in cost than each of J and K.

If J is the fourth lowest in cost, then J is lower in cost than each of S and T.

If J is not the fourth lowest in cost, then J is higher in cost than each of S and T.

Either R or S is the fifth lowest in cost.

18. Which one of the following could be an accurate list of the bids in order from lowest to highest in cost?

(A) T, K, H, S, J, R
(B) H, T, K, S, R, J
(C) H, S, T, K, R, J
(D) H, K, S, J, R, T
(E) H, J, K, R, S, T

19. Which one of the following bids CANNOT be the fourth lowest in cost?

(A) H
(B) J
(C) K
(D) R
(E) T

20. Which one of the following bids CANNOT be the second lowest in cost?

(A) H
(B) J
(C) K
(D) R
(E) T

21. If R is the accepted bid, then which one of the following must be true?

(A) T is the lowest in cost.
(B) K is the second lowest in cost.
(C) R is the third lowest in cost.
(D) S is the fifth lowest in cost.
(E) J is the highest in cost.

22. Which one of the following must be true?

(A) H is lower in cost than S.
(B) H is lower in cost than T.
(C) K is lower in cost than J.
(D) S is lower in cost than J.
(E) S is lower in cost than K.

23. If R is the lowest in cost, then which one of the following could be false?

(A) J is the highest in cost.
(B) S is the fifth lowest in cost.
(C) K is the third lowest in cost.
(D) H is the second lowest in cost.
(E) K is the accepted bid.

S T O P

IF YOU FINISH BEFORE TIME IS CALLED, YOU MAY CHECK YOUR WORK ON THIS SECTION ONLY.
DO NOT WORK ON ANY OTHER SECTION IN THE TEST.

SECTION V

Time—35 minutes

25 Questions

<u>Directions:</u> The questions in this section are based on the reasoning contained in brief statements or passages. For some questions, more than one of the choices could conceivably answer the question. However, you are to choose the <u>best</u> answer; that is, the response that most accurately and completely answers the question. You should not make assumptions that are by commonsense standards implausible, superfluous, or incompatible with the passage. After you have chosen the best answer, blacken the corresponding space on your answer sheet.

1. Editorialist: Advertisers devote millions of dollars to the attempt to instill attitudes and desires that lead people to purchase particular products, and advertisers' techniques have been adopted by political strategists in democratic countries, who are paid to manipulate public opinion in every political campaign. Thus, the results of elections in democratic countries cannot be viewed as representing the unadulterated preferences of the people.

Which one of the following, if true, most strengthens the editorialist's argument?

(A) Public opinion can be manipulated more easily by officials of nondemocratic governments than by those of democratic governments.

(B) Advertisers' techniques are often apparent to the people to whom the advertisements are directed.

(C) Many democratic countries have laws limiting the amount that may be spent on political advertisements in any given election.

(D) People who neither watch television nor read any print media are more likely to vote than people who do one or both of these activities.

(E) Unlike advertisements for consumer products, most of which only reinforce existing beliefs, political advertisements often change voters' beliefs.

2. Kris: Years ago, the chemical industry claimed that technological progress cannot occur without pollution. Today, in the name of technological progress, the cellular phone industry manufactures and promotes a product that causes environmental pollution in the form of ringing phones and loud conversations in public places. Clearly, the cellular industry must be regulated, just as the chemical industry is now regulated.

Terry: That's absurd. Chemical pollution can cause physical harm, but the worst harm that cellular phones can cause is annoyance.

Terry responds to Kris's argument by doing which one of the following?

(A) questioning the reliability of the source of crucial information in Kris's argument

(B) attacking the accuracy of the evidence about the chemical industry that Kris puts forward

(C) arguing that an alleged cause of a problem is actually an effect of that problem

(D) questioning the strength of the analogy on which Kris's argument is based

(E) rejecting Kris's interpretation of the term "technological progress"

GO ON TO THE NEXT PAGE.

3. Researcher: Any country can determine which type of public school system will work best for it by investigating the public school systems of other countries. Nationwide tests could be given in each country and other countries could adopt the system of the country that has the best scores on these tests.

Which one of the following is an assumption required by the researcher's argument?

(A) A type of school system that works well in one country will work well in any other country.
(B) A number of children in each country in the research sample are educated in private schools.
(C) If two countries performed differently on these nationwide tests, further testing could determine what features of the school systems account for the differences.
(D) Most countries in the research sample already administer nationwide tests to their public school students.
(E) The nationwide testing in the research sample will target as closely as possible grade levels that are comparable in the different countries in the research sample.

4. Ray: Cynthia claims that her car's trunk popped open because the car hit a pothole. Yet, she also acknowledged that the trunk in that car had popped open on several other occasions, and that on none of those other occasions had the car hit a pothole. Therefore, Cynthia mistakenly attributed the trunk's popping open to the car's having hit a pothole.

The reasoning in Ray's argument is most vulnerable to criticism in that the argument

(A) fails to consider the possibility that the trunks of other cars may pop open when those cars hit potholes
(B) fails to consider the possibility that potholes can have negative effects on a car's engine
(C) presumes, without providing justification, that if one event causes another, it cannot also cause a third event
(D) fails to consider the possibility that one type of event can be caused in many different ways
(E) presumes the truth of the claim that it is trying to establish

5. Journalists agree universally that lying is absolutely taboo. Yet, while many reporters claim that spoken words ought to be quoted verbatim, many others believe that tightening a quote from a person who is interviewed is legitimate on grounds that the speaker's remarks would have been more concise if the speaker had written them instead. Also, many reporters believe that, to expose wrongdoing, failing to identify oneself as a reporter is permissible, while others condemn such behavior as a type of lying.

Which one of the following is most supported by the information above?

(A) Reporters make little effort to behave ethically.
(B) There is no correct answer to the question of whether lying in a given situation is right or wrong.
(C) Omission of the truth is the same thing as lying.
(D) Since lying is permissible in some situations, reporters are mistaken to think that it is absolutely taboo.
(E) Reporters disagree on what sort of behavior qualifies as lying.

6. Wood-frame houses withstand earthquakes far better than masonry houses do, because wooden frames have some flexibility; their walls can better handle lateral forces. In a recent earthquake, however, a wood-frame house was destroyed, while the masonry house next door was undamaged.

Which one of the following, if true, most helps to explain the results of the earthquake described above?

(A) In earthquake-prone areas, there are many more wood-frame houses than masonry houses.
(B) In earthquake-prone areas, there are many more masonry houses than wood-frame houses.
(C) The walls of the wood-frame house had once been damaged in a flood.
(D) The masonry house was far more expensive than the wood-frame house.
(E) No structure is completely impervious to the destructive lateral forces exerted by earthquakes.

GO ON TO THE NEXT PAGE.

7. In an experiment, biologists repeatedly shone a bright light into a tank containing a sea snail and simultaneously shook the tank. The snail invariably responded by tensing its muscular "foot," a typical reaction in sea snails to ocean turbulence. After several repetitions of this procedure, the snail tensed its "foot" whenever the biologists shone the light into its tank, even when the tank was not simultaneously shaken. Therefore, the snail must have learned to associate the shining of the bright light with the shaking of the tank.

Which one of the following is an assumption required by the argument?

(A) All sea snails react to ocean turbulence in the same way as the sea snail in the experiment did.

(B) Sea snails are not ordinarily exposed to bright lights such as the one used in the biologists' experiment.

(C) The sea snail used in the experiment did not differ significantly from other members of its species in its reaction to external stimuli.

(D) The appearance of a bright light alone would ordinarily not result in the sea snail's tensing its "foot."

(E) Tensing of the muscular "foot" in sea snails is an instinctual rather than a learned response to ocean turbulence.

8. The university's purchasing department is highly efficient overall. We must conclude that each of its twelve staff members is highly efficient.

Which one of the following arguments exhibits flawed reasoning most similar to that exhibited by the argument above?

(A) The employees at this fast-food restaurant are the youngest and most inexperienced of any fast-food workers in the city. Given this, it seems obvious that customers will have to wait longer for their food at this restaurant than at others.

(B) The outside audit of our public relations department has exposed serious deficiencies in the competence of each member of that department. We must conclude that the department is inadequate for our needs.

(C) This supercomputer is the most sophisticated—and the most expensive—ever built. It must be that each of its components is the most sophisticated and expensive available.

(D) Literature critics have lavished praise on every chapter of this book. In light of their reviews, one must conclude that the book is excellent.

(E) Passing a driving test is a condition of employment at the city's transportation department. It follows that each of the department's employees has passed the test.

9. The Jacksons regularly receive wrong-number calls for Sara, whose phone number was misprinted in a directory. Sara contacted the Jacksons, informing them of the misprint and her correct number. The Jacksons did not lead Sara to believe that they would pass along the correct number, but it would be helpful to Sara and of no difficulty for them to do so. Thus, although it would not be wrong for the Jacksons to tell callers trying to reach Sara merely that they have dialed the wrong number, it would be laudable if the Jacksons passed along Sara's correct number.

Which one of the following principles, if valid, most helps to justify the reasoning in the argument?

(A) It is always laudable to do something helpful to someone, but not doing so would be wrong only if one has led that person to believe one would do it.

(B) Being helpful to someone is laudable whenever it is not wrong to do so.

(C) If one can do something that would be helpful to someone else and it would be easy to do, then it is laudable and not wrong to do so.

(D) Doing something for someone is laudable only if it is difficult for one to do so and it is wrong for one not to do so.

(E) The only actions that are laudable are those that it would not be wrong to refrain from doing, whether or not it is difficult to do so.

GO ON TO THE NEXT PAGE.

10. Albert: The government has proposed new automobile emissions regulations designed to decrease the amount of polycyclic aromatic hydrocarbons (PAHs) released into the atmosphere by automobile exhaust. I don't see the need for such regulations; although PAHs are suspected of causing cancer, a causal link has never been proven.

Erin: Scientists also blame PAHs for 10,000 premature deaths in this country each year from lung and heart disease. So the proposed regulations would save thousands of lives.

Which one of the following, if true, is the logically strongest counter that Albert can make to Erin's argument?

(A) Most automobile manufacturers are strongly opposed to additional automobile emissions regulations.

(B) It is not known whether PAHs are a causal factor in any diseases other than heart and lung disease and cancer.

(C) Even if no new automobile emissions regulations are enacted, the amount of PAHs released into the atmosphere will decrease if automobile usage declines.

(D) Most of the PAHs released into the atmosphere are the result of wear and tear on automobile tires.

(E) PAHs are one of several components of automobile exhaust that scientists suspect of causing cancer.

11. Australia has considerably fewer species of carnivorous mammals than any other continent does but about as many carnivorous reptile species as other continents do. This is probably a consequence of the unusual sparseness of Australia's ecosystems. To survive, carnivorous mammals must eat much more than carnivorous reptiles need to; thus carnivorous mammals are at a disadvantage in ecosystems in which there is relatively little food.

Which one of the following most accurately expresses the main conclusion of the argument?

(A) Australia has considerably fewer species of carnivorous mammals than any other continent does but about as many carnivorous reptile species as other continents do.

(B) In ecosystems in which there is relatively little food carnivorous mammals are at a disadvantage relative to carnivorous reptiles.

(C) The unusual sparseness of Australia's ecosystems is probably the reason Australia has considerably fewer carnivorous mammal species than other continents do but about as many carnivorous reptile species.

(D) The reason that carnivorous mammals are at a disadvantage in ecosystems in which there is relatively little food is that they must eat much more in order to survive than carnivorous reptiles need to.

(E) Because Australia's ecosystems are unusually sparse, carnivorous mammals there are at a disadvantage relative to carnivorous reptiles.

12. Linguist: The Sapir-Whorf hypothesis states that a society's world view is influenced by the language or languages its members speak. But this hypothesis does not have the verifiability of hypotheses of physical science, since it is not clear that the hypothesis could be tested.

If the linguist's statements are accurate, which one of the following is most supported by them?

(A) The Sapir-Whorf hypothesis is probably false.
(B) Only the hypotheses of physical science are verifiable.
(C) Only verifiable hypotheses should be seriously considered.
(D) We do not know whether the Sapir-Whorf hypothesis is true or false.
(E) Only the hypotheses of physical science should be taken seriously.

GO ON TO THE NEXT PAGE.

13. The highest mountain ranges are formed by geological forces that raise the earth's crust: two continent-bearing tectonic plates of comparable density collide and crumple upward, causing a thickening of the crust. The erosive forces of wind and precipitation inexorably wear these mountains down. Yet the highest mountain ranges tend to be found in places where these erosive forces are most prevalent.

Which one of the following, if true, most helps to reconcile the apparent conflict described above?

(A) Patterns of extreme wind and precipitation often result from the dramatic differences in elevation commonly found in the highest mountain ranges.

(B) The highest mountain ranges have less erosion-reducing vegetation near their peaks than do other mountain ranges.

(C) Some lower mountain ranges are formed by a different collision process, whereby one tectonic plate simply slides beneath another of lesser density.

(D) The amount of precipitation that a given region of the earth receives may vary considerably over the lifetime of an average mountain range.

(E) The thickening of the earth's crust associated with the formation of the highest mountain ranges tends to cause the thickened portion of the crust to sink over time.

14. Expert: A group of researchers claims to have shown that for an antenna to work equally well at all frequencies, it must be symmetrical in shape and have what is known as a fractal structure. Yet the new antenna developed by these researchers, which satisfies both of these criteria, in fact works better at frequencies below 250 megahertz than at frequencies above 250 megahertz. Hence, their claim is incorrect.

The reasoning in the expert's argument is flawed because the argument

(A) fails to provide a definition of the technical term "fractal"

(B) contradicts itself by denying in its conclusion the claim of scientific authorities that it relies on in its premises

(C) concludes that a claim is false merely on the grounds that there is insufficient evidence that it is true

(D) interprets an assertion that certain conditions are necessary as asserting that those conditions are sufficient

(E) takes for granted that there are only two possible alternatives, either below or above 250 megahertz

15. Singletary: We of Citizens for Cycling Freedom object to the city's new ordinance requiring bicyclists to wear helmets. If the city wanted to become a safer place for cyclists, it would not require helmets. Instead, it would construct more bicycle lanes and educate drivers about bicycle safety. Thus, passage of the ordinance reveals that the city is more concerned with the appearance of safety than with bicyclists' actual safety.

Which one of the following most accurately describes the role played in Singletary's argument by the statement that mentions driver education?

(A) It is cited as evidence for the claim that the city misunderstands the steps necessary for ensuring bicyclists' safety.

(B) It is used as partial support for a claim about the motivation of the city.

(C) It is offered as evidence of the total ineffectiveness of the helmet ordinance.

(D) It is offered as an example of further measures the city will take to ensure bicyclists' safety.

(E) It is presented as an illustration of the city's overriding interest in its public image.

16. Max: Although doing so would be very costly, humans already possess the technology to build colonies on the Moon. As the human population increases and the amount of unoccupied space available for constructing housing on Earth diminishes, there will be a growing economic incentive to construct such colonies to house some of the population. Thus, such colonies will almost certainly be built and severe overcrowding on Earth relieved.

Max's argument is most vulnerable to criticism on which one of the following grounds?

(A) It takes for granted that the economic incentive to construct colonies on the Moon will grow sufficiently to cause such a costly project to be undertaken.

(B) It takes for granted that the only way of relieving severe overcrowding on Earth is the construction of colonies on the Moon.

(C) It overlooks the possibility that colonies will be built on the Moon regardless of any economic incentive to construct such colonies to house some of the population.

(D) It overlooks the possibility that colonies on the Moon might themselves quickly become overcrowded.

(E) It takes for granted that none of the human population would prefer to live on the Moon unless Earth were seriously overcrowded.

GO ON TO THE NEXT PAGE.

17. Ethicist: An action is wrong if it violates a rule of the society in which the action is performed and that rule promotes the general welfare of people in the society. An action is right if it is required by a rule of the society in which the action is performed and the rule promotes the general welfare of the people in that society.

Which one of the following judgments most closely conforms to the principle cited by the ethicist?

(A) Amelia's society has a rule against lying. However, she lies anyway in order to protect an innocent person from being harmed. While the rule against lying promotes the general welfare of people in the society, Amelia's lie is not wrong because she is preventing harm.

(B) Jordan lives in a society that requires its members to eat certain ceremonial foods during festivals. Jordan disobeys this rule. Because the rule is not detrimental to the general welfare of people in her society, Jordan's disobedience is wrong.

(C) Elgin obeys a certain rule of his society. Because Elgin knows that this particular rule is detrimental to the general welfare of the people in his society, his obedience is wrong.

(D) Dahlia always has a cup of coffee before getting dressed in the morning. Dahlia's action is right because it does not violate any rule of the society in which she lives.

(E) Edward's society requires children to take care of their aged parents. Edward's taking care of his aged parents is the right thing for him to do because the rule requiring this action promotes the general welfare of people in the society.

18. Teresa: If their goal is to maximize profits, film studios should concentrate on producing big-budget films rather than small-budget ones. For, unlike big-budget films, small-budget films never attract mass audiences. While small-budget films are less expensive to produce and, hence, involve less risk of unprofitability than big-budget films, low production costs do not guarantee the highest possible profits.

Which one of the following is an assumption required by Teresa's argument?

(A) Each big-budget film is guaranteed to attract a mass audience.

(B) A film studio cannot make both big-budget films and small-budget films.

(C) A film studio will not maximize its profits unless at least some of its films attract mass audiences.

(D) It is impossible to produce a big-budget film in a financially efficient manner.

(E) A film studio's primary goal should be to maximize profits.

19. Cyclists in the Tour de France are extremely physically fit: all of the winners of this race have had abnormal physiological constitutions. Typical of the abnormal physiology of these athletes are exceptional lung capacity and exceptionally powerful hearts. Tests conducted on last year's winner did not reveal an exceptionally powerful heart. That cyclist must, therefore, have exceptional lung capacity.

The reasoning in the argument is most vulnerable to criticism on the grounds that it overlooks the possibility that

(A) having exceptional lung capacity and an exceptionally powerful heart is an advantage in cycling

(B) some winners of the Tour de France have neither exceptional lung capacity nor exceptionally powerful hearts

(C) cyclists with normal lung capacity rarely have exceptionally powerful hearts

(D) the exceptional lung capacity and exceptionally powerful hearts of Tour de France winners are due to training

(E) the notions of exceptional lung capacity and exceptional heart function are relative to the physiology of most cyclists

20. TV meteorologist: Our station's weather forecasts are more useful and reliable than those of the most popular news station in the area. After all, the most important question for viewers in this area is whether it will rain, and on most of the occasions when we have forecast rain for the next day, we have been right. The same cannot be said for either of our competitors.

Which one of the following, if true, most strengthens the meteorologist's argument?

(A) The meteorologist's station forecast rain more often than did the most popular news station in the area.

(B) The less popular of the competing stations does not employ any full-time meteorologists.

(C) The most popular news station in the area is popular because of its investigative news reports.

(D) The meteorologist's station has a policy of not making weather forecasts more than three days in advance.

(E) On most of the occasions when the meteorologist's station forecast that it would not rain, at least one of its competitors also forecast that it would not rain.

GO ON TO THE NEXT PAGE.

21. In an experiment, volunteers witnessed a simulated crime. After they witnessed the simulation the volunteers were first questioned by a lawyer whose goal was to get them to testify inaccurately about the event. They were then cross-examined by another lawyer whose goal was to cause them to correct the inaccuracies in their testimony. The witnesses who gave testimony containing fewer inaccurate details than most of the other witnesses during the first lawyer's questioning also gave testimony containing a greater number of inaccurate details than most of the other witnesses during cross-examination.

Which one of the following, if true, most helps to resolve the apparent conflict in the results concerning the witnesses who gave testimony containing fewer inaccurate details during the first lawyer's questioning?

(A) These witnesses were more observant about details than were most of the other witnesses.
(B) These witnesses had better memories than did most of the other witnesses.
(C) These witnesses were less inclined than most of the other witnesses to be influenced in their testimony by the nature of the questioning.
(D) These witnesses were unclear about the details at first but then began to remember more accurately as they answered questions.
(E) These witnesses tended to give testimony containing more details than most of the other witnesses.

22. The short-term and long-term interests of a business often conflict; when they do, the morally preferable act is usually the one that serves the long-term interest. Because of this, businesses often have compelling reasons to execute the morally preferable act.

Which one of the following, if assumed, enables the conclusion of the argument to be properly drawn?

(A) A business's moral interests do not always provide compelling reasons for executing an act.
(B) A business's long-term interests often provide compelling reasons for executing an act.
(C) The morally preferable act for a business to execute and the long-term interests of the business seldom conflict.
(D) The morally preferable act for a business to execute and the short-term interests of the business usually conflict.
(E) When a business's short-term and long-term interests conflict, morality alone is rarely the overriding consideration.

23. Politician: The current crisis in mathematics education must be overcome if we are to remain competitive in the global economy. Alleviating this crisis requires the employment of successful teaching methods. No method of teaching a subject can succeed that does not get students to spend a significant amount of time outside of class studying that subject.

Which one of the following statements follows logically from the statements above?

(A) If students spend a significant amount of time outside of class studying mathematics, the current crisis in mathematics education will be overcome.
(B) The current crisis in mathematics education will not be overcome unless students spend a significant amount of time outside of class studying mathematics.
(C) Few subjects are as important as mathematics to the effort to remain competitive in the global economy.
(D) Only if we succeed in remaining competitive in the global economy will students spend a significant amount of time outside of class studying mathematics.
(E) Students' spending a significant amount of time outside of class studying mathematics would help us to remain competitive in the global economy.

GO ON TO THE NEXT PAGE.

24. Downtown Petropolis boasted over 100 large buildings 5 years ago. Since then, 60 of those buildings have been demolished. Since the number of large buildings in a downtown is an indicator of the economic health of that downtown, it is clear that downtown Petropolis is in a serious state of economic decline.

Which one of the following is an assumption required by the argument?

(A) The demolitions that have taken place during the past 5 years have been evenly spread over that period.

(B) There have never been significantly more than 100 large buildings in downtown Petropolis.

(C) Most of the buildings demolished during the past 5 years were torn down because they were structurally unsound.

(D) The large buildings demolished over the past 5 years have been replaced with small buildings built on the same sites.

(E) Significantly fewer than 60 new large buildings have been built in downtown Petropolis during the past 5 years.

25. To get the free dessert, one must order an entree and a salad. But anyone who orders either an entree or a salad can receive a free soft drink. Thus, anyone who is not eligible for a free soft drink is not eligible for a free dessert.

The reasoning in the argument above is most similar to the reasoning in which one of the following arguments?

(A) To get an executive position at Teltech, one needs a university diploma and sales experience. But anyone who has worked at Teltech for more than six months who does not have sales experience has a university diploma. Thus, one cannot get an executive position at Teltech unless one has worked there for six months.

(B) To be elected class president, one must be well liked and well known. Anyone who is well liked or well known has something better to do than run for class president. Therefore, no one who has something better to do will be elected class president.

(C) To grow good azaleas, one needs soil that is both rich in humus and low in acidity. Anyone who has soil that is rich in humus or low in acidity can grow blueberries. So, anyone who cannot grow blueberries cannot grow good azaleas.

(D) To drive to Weller, one must take the highway or take Old Mill Road. Anyone who drives to Weller on the highway will miss the beautiful scenery. Thus, one cannot see the beautiful scenery without taking Old Mill Road to Weller.

(E) To get a discount on ice cream, one must buy frozen raspberries and ice cream together. Anyone who buys ice cream or raspberries will get a coupon for a later purchase. So, anyone who does not get the discount on ice cream will not get a coupon for a later purchase.

S T O P

IF YOU FINISH BEFORE TIME IS CALLED, YOU MAY CHECK YOUR WORK ON THIS SECTION ONLY.
DO NOT WORK ON ANY OTHER SECTION IN THE TEST.

Wait for the supervisor's instructions before you open the page to the topic.
Please print and sign your name and write the date in the designated spaces below.

Time: 35 Minutes

General Directions

You will have 35 minutes in which to plan and write an essay on the topic inside. Read the topic and the accompanying directions carefully. You will probably find it best to spend a few minutes considering the topic and organizing your thoughts before you begin writing. In your essay, be sure to develop your ideas fully, leaving time, if possible, to review what you have written. **Do not write on a topic other than the one specified. Writing on a topic of your own choice is not acceptable.**

No special knowledge is required or expected for this writing exercise. Law schools are interested in the reasoning, clarity, organization, language usage, and writing mechanics displayed in your essay. How well you write is more important than how much you write.

Confine your essay to the blocked, lined area on the front and back of the separate Writing Sample Response Sheet. Only that area will be reproduced for law schools. Be sure that your writing is legible.

Both this topic sheet and your response sheet must be turned over to the testing staff before you leave the room.

Topic Code	Print Your Full Name Here		
_____	Last	First	M.I.

Date	Sign Your Name Here
/ /	

Scratch Paper
Do not write your essay in this space.

LSAT WRITING SAMPLE TOPIC

<u>Directions</u>: The scenario presented below describes two choices, either one of which can be supported on the basis of the information given. Your essay should consider both choices and argue for one over the other, based on the two specified criteria and the facts provided. There is no "right" or "wrong" choice: a reasonable argument can be made for either.

Carol Hudson, the concert coordinator for Jordan Arena, a very large entertainment venue, must schedule one of two musical groups to perform on an open date in the arena's schedule. Using the facts below, write an essay in which you argue for one group over the other based on the following two criteria:

- Carol wants to continue Jordan Arena's long-standing record of sold-out concerts.
- Carol wants to attract an audience at least a third of whom are aged 14 to 24.

The first group, The Mustangs, plays cutting-edge music of a sort popular with the 14- to 24-year-old demographic. The Mustangs, gradually growing in popularity, have filled steadily larger venues. The group recently sold out in record time its largest venue ever, the Midvale Arena, located in a large metropolitan area. Jorden Arena, which is located in a different large metropolitan area, has twice the seating capacity of Midvale Arena. The Mustangs' video of the cover song for their debut album is scheduled for release a few weeks before the Jordan Arena concert date. If the music video is a success, as many expect, The Mustangs' popularity will rapidly soar.

The second group, Radar Love, is an aging but well-established hard rock band, which has consistently appealed to a wide-ranging audience. It has sold out all appearances for the past 20 years, including venues considerably larger than Jordan Arena. A song on the group's latest album quickly became a runaway hit among the 14- to 24-year-old demographic, the first time the group has appealed to this extent to this audience. Twenty percent of the audience at the group's most recent concert, which featured songs from the group's latest album, constituted 14- to 24-year-olds, a significant increase from prior concerts.

Scratch Paper
Do not write your essay in this space.

LAST NAME (Print)   MI   FIRST NAME (Print)

SIGNATURE

Writing Sample Response Sheet

DO NOT WRITE
IN THIS SPACE

**Begin your essay in the lined area below.
Continue on the back if you need more space.**

This test can be scored automatically with your Online Center. The following Answer Key and Scoring Table are provided if you wish to score it offline.

Directions:

1. Use the Answer Key on the next page to check your answers.

2. Use the Scoring Worksheet below to compute your raw score.

3. Use the Score Conversion Chart to convert your raw score into the 120–180 scale.

Scoring Worksheet

1. Enter the number of questions you answered correctly in each section

	Number Correct
SECTION I	_____
SECTION II	EXP
SECTION III	_____
SECTION IV	_____
SECTION V	_____

2. Enter the sum here: _____

This is your Raw Score.

Conversion Chart

For Converting Raw Score to the 120–180 LSAT Scaled Score LSAT PrepTest 54

Reported Score	Lowest Raw Score	Highest Raw Score
180	99	101
179	98	98
178	—*	—*
177	97	97
176	96	96
175	95	95
174	—*	—*
173	94	94
172	93	93
171	92	92
170	91	91
169	90	90
168	89	89
167	88	88
166	87	87
165	85	86
164	84	84
163	83	83
162	81	82
161	80	80
160	78	79
159	76	77
158	75	75
157	73	74
156	71	72
155	69	70
154	67	68
153	66	66
152	64	65
151	62	63
150	60	61
149	58	59
148	56	57
147	54	55
146	52	53
145	50	51
144	49	49
143	47	48
142	45	46
141	43	44
140	42	42
139	40	41
138	38	39
137	37	37
136	35	36
135	33	34
134	32	32
133	30	31
132	29	29
131	28	28
130	26	27
129	25	25
128	24	24
127	23	23
126	21	22
125	20	20
124	19	19
123	18	18
122	16	17
121	—*	—*
120	0	15

*There is no raw score that will produce this scaled score for this test.

SECTION I

1.	A	8.	E	15.	C	22.	C
2.	C	9.	B	16.	E	23.	B
3.	D	10.	B	17.	E	24.	E
4.	D	11.	C	18.	A	25.	E
5.	E	12.	A	19.	A	26.	A
6.	B	13.	C	20.	A	27	B
7.	E	14.	D	21.	C		

SECTION II

1.	A	8.	D	15.	B	22.	A
2.	C	9.	A	16.	D	23.	E
3.	D	10.	C	17.	E	24.	A
4.	D	11.	B	18.	C	25.	E
5.	C	12.	C	19.	E	26.	B
6.	D	13.	E	20.	C		
7.	D	14.	B	21.	A		

SECTION III

1.	D	8.	A	15.	E	22.	E
2.	E	9.	A	16.	D	23.	C
3.	A	10.	B	17.	D	24.	A
4.	E	11.	B	18.	C	25.	D
5.	B	12.	D	19.	D	26.	D
6.	C	13.	B	20.	E		
7.	C	14.	C	21.	A		

SECTION IV

1.	C	8.	D	15.	E	22.	C
2.	D	9.	E	16.	B	23.	A
3.	E	10.	D	17.	B		
4.	C	11.	E	18.	B		
5.	C	12.	B	19.	A		
6.	A	13.	A	20.	B		
7.	A	14.	B	21.	D		

SECTION V

1.	E	8.	C	15.	B	22.	B
2.	D	9.	A	16.	A	23.	B
3.	A	10.	D	17.	E	24.	E
4.	D	11.	C	18.	C	25.	C
5.	E	12.	D	19.	B		
6.	C	13.	A	20.	A		
7.	D	14.	D	21.	C		

Practice Test 3

PrepTest 50 with Additional Section from PrepTest 46

SECTION I

Time—35 minutes

28 Questions

Directions: Each passage in this section is followed by a group of questions to be answered on the basis of what is <u>stated</u> or <u>implied</u> in the passage. For some of the questions, more than one of the choices could conceivably answer the question. However, you are to choose the <u>best</u> answer; that is, the response that most accurately and completely answers the question, and blacken the corresponding space on your answer sheet.

One of the most prominent characteristics of the literature by United States citizens of Mexican descent is that it is frequently written in a combination of English and Spanish. By not limiting (5) itself to one language, such writing resonates with its authors' bicultural experiences. Their work is largely Mexican in its sensibility, its traditions, and its myths, but its immediate geographical setting is the United States. And though Mexican American literature is (10) solidly grounded in Mexican culture, it distinguishes itself from Mexican literature in its content and concerns.

Many Mexican Americans are only a generation away from the mostly agrarian culture of their (15) ancestors, and the work of most Mexican American writers shows evidence of heavy influence from this culture. Their novels are often simple in structure, and some of the common themes in these novels include the struggle to overcome the agricultural (20) adversity that caused their families to emigrate, and a feeling of being distanced from the traditions of rural Mexico and yet striving to hold on to them. These themes coexist with ever-present images of the land, which symbolizes the values of the characters' (25) culture, such as the spiritual and religious benefits of working the land.

Much of Mexican writing, on the other hand, has been criticized for being dominated by the prominent literary establishment concentrated in Mexico City. (30) Literary reputation and success in Mexico—including the attainment of publicly sponsored positions in the arts—are often bestowed or denied by this literary establishment. Moreover, the work of Mexican writers is often longer in form and marked by greater (35) cosmopolitanism and interest in theoretical ideas and arguments than is Mexican American writing. Not surprisingly, the Mexican literary community views Mexican American literature as a variety of "regional" writing. But the apparent simplicity of (40) what this community sees as parochial concerns belies the thematic richness of Mexican American writing.

The work of Mexican American writers can be richly textured in its complex mixture of concerns; (45) among other things, their work is distinguished by an overarching concern with the complexities of cultural transition. Many Mexican American writers assert that rather than working to be absorbed into U.S. society, they are engaged in the process of creating a new (50) identity. Physically distanced from Mexico and yet convinced of its importance, these writers depict a new reality by creating "in-between" characters. These characters inhabit a social and cultural milieu which is neither that of Mexico nor that of the U.S. (55) And while this new setting reflects the contemporary social realities of both Mexico and the U.S., it also derives a great deal of emotional power from an evocation of a romanticized memory of Mexico. What results is an intermediate cultural borderland in (60) which nostalgia and reality are combined in the service of forging a new identity.

1. Which one of the following most accurately states the main point of the passage?

(A) Mexican American literature is characterized by a strong sense of transition, which is due to its writers' physical distance from Mexico and their clear vision of the future of Mexican culture.

(B) Unlike Mexican writing, which is largely tied to an urban literary establishment, Mexican American writing is a movement that attempts through its works to develop a literary voice for agrarian workers.

(C) The work of Mexican American writers reflects Mexican Americans' bicultural experiences, both in its close links with the culture of rural Mexico and in its striving to develop a new identity out of elements of Mexican culture and U.S. culture.

(D) Mexican American literature, although unique in its content and concerns as well as in its stylistic innovations, has not yet achieved the prominence and reputation of Mexican literature.

(E) Many Mexican Americans are only a generation away from the culture of their ancestors and because of this, Mexican American literature is distinguished by the presence of powerful spiritual images, which are an organic part of the Mexican American agrarian culture.

GO ON TO THE NEXT PAGE.

2. It can most reasonably be inferred from the passage that the author would agree with which one of the following statements?

(A) While Mexican American writers are in the process of shaping their body of literature, one of their goals is to create a literary establishment in the U.S. essentially like the one concentrated in Mexico City.

(B) The use of a mixture of both Spanish and English in current Mexican American literature is evidence of a brief transitional period.

(C) The use of a romanticized Mexico in Mexican American literature is offensive to writers of the literary establishment of Mexico City, who find the images to be caricatures of their culture.

(D) Mexican American literature is noteworthy more for its thematic content than for its narrative structure.

(E) Mexican American writers are concerned that the importance of Mexico, currently central to their culture, will be diminished, and that Mexican American literature will be impoverished as a result.

3. It can most reasonably be inferred from the passage that many Mexican American writers tend to value which one of the following?

(A) stylistic innovations that distinguish their work from that of Mexican writers

(B) recognition from a U.S. literary establishment that is significantly different from that of Mexico

(C) an identity that resists absorption by U.S. culture

(D) critical acceptance of bilingual forms of literary expression

(E) the ability to express in their literature a more complex fabric of concerns than is found in most U.S. literature

4. To which one of the following questions does the passage most clearly provide an answer?

(A) What is an example of a specific literary work by a Mexican American writer?

(B) For what reason are many Mexican American writings concerned with agrarian themes or topics?

(C) What is the prevailing view of Mexican American literature among critics in the United States?

(D) How has the literature of the United States influenced Mexican American writers?

(E) Are the works of Mexican American writers written more in Spanish or in English?

5. It can most reasonably be inferred from the passage that the author holds which one of the following views?

(A) Mexican American literature advocates an agrarian way of life as a remedy for the alienation of modern culture.

(B) The Mexican American "in-between" character is an instance of a type found in the literature of immigrant groups in general.

(C) A predominant strength of Mexican American writers is that they are not tied to a major literary establishment and so are free to experiment in a way many Mexican writers are not.

(D) Writers of "regional" literature find it more difficult to attain reputation and success in Mexico than writers whose work is concerned with more urban themes.

(E) History has an importance in Mexican American culture that it does not have in Mexican culture because Mexican Americans have attached greater importance to their ancestry.

GO ON TO THE NEXT PAGE.

In many Western societies, modern bankruptcy laws have undergone a shift away from a focus on punishment and toward a focus on bankruptcy as a remedy for individuals and corporations in financial
(5) trouble—and, perhaps unexpectedly, for their creditors. This shift has coincided with an ever-increasing reliance on declarations of bankruptcy by individuals and corporations with excessive debt, a trend that has drawn widespread criticism. However,
(10) any measure seeking to make bankruptcy protection less available would run the risk of preventing continued economic activity of financially troubled individuals and institutions. It is for this reason that the temptation to return to a focus on punishment of
(15) individuals or corporations that become insolvent must be resisted. Modern bankruptcy laws, in serving the needs of an interdependent society, serve the varied interests of the greatest number of citizens.

The harsh punishment for insolvency in centuries
(20) past included imprisonment of individuals and dissolution of enterprises, and reflected societies' beliefs that the accumulation of excessive debt resulted either from debtors' unwillingness to meet obligations or from their negligence. Insolvent debtors
(25) were thought to be breaking sacrosanct social contracts; placing debtors in prison was considered necessary in order to remove from society those who would violate such contracts and thereby defraud creditors. But creditors derive little benefit from
(30) imprisoned debtors unable to repay even a portion of their debt. And if the entity to be punished is a large enterprise, for example, an auto manufacturer, its dissolution would cause significant unemployment and the disruption of much-needed services.
(35) Modern bankruptcy law has attempted to address the shortcomings of the punitive approach. Two beliefs underlie this shift: that the public good ought to be paramount in considering the financial insolvency of individuals and corporations; and that
(40) the public good is better served by allowing debt-heavy corporations to continue to operate, and indebted individuals to continue to earn wages, than by disabling insolvent economic entities. The mechanism for executing these goals is usually a
(45) court-directed reorganization of debtors' obligations to creditors. Such reorganizations typically comprise debt relief and plans for court-directed transfers of certain assets from debtor to creditor. Certain strictures connected to bankruptcy—such as the fact
(50) that bankruptcies become matters of public record and are reported to credit bureaus for a number of years—may still serve a punitive function, but not by denying absolution of debts or financial reorganization. Through these mechanisms, today's
(55) bankruptcy laws are designed primarily to assure continued engagement in productive economic activity, with the ultimate goal of restoring businesses and individuals to a degree of economic health and providing creditors with the best hope of collecting.

6. Which one of the following most accurately expresses the main point of the passage?

(A) The modern trend in bankruptcy law away from punishment and toward the maintenance of economic activity serves the best interests of society and should not be abandoned.

(B) Bankruptcy laws have evolved in order to meet the needs of creditors, who depend on the continued productive activity of private citizens and profit-making enterprises.

(C) Modern bankruptcy laws are justified on humanitarian grounds, even though the earlier punitive approach was more economically efficient.

(D) Punishment for debt no longer holds deterrent value for debtors and is therefore a concept that has been largely abandoned as ineffective.

(E) Greater economic interdependence has triggered the formation of bankruptcy laws that reflect a convergence of the interests of debtors and creditors.

7. In stating that bankruptcy laws have evolved "perhaps unexpectedly" (line 5) as a remedy for creditors, the author implies that creditors

(A) are often surprised to receive compensation in bankruptcy courts

(B) have unintentionally become the chief beneficiaries of bankruptcy laws

(C) were a consideration, though not a primary one, in the formulation of bankruptcy laws

(D) are better served than is immediately apparent by laws designed in the first instance to provide a remedy for debtors

(E) were themselves active in the formulation of modern bankruptcy laws

8. The author's attitude toward the evolution of bankruptcy law can most accurately be described as

(A) approval of changes that have been made to inefficient laws

(B) confidence that further changes to today's laws will be unnecessary

(C) neutrality toward laws that, while helpful to many, remain open to abuse

(D) skepticism regarding the possibility of solutions to the problem of insolvency

(E) concern that inefficient laws may have been replaced by legislation too lenient to debtors

GO ON TO THE NEXT PAGE.

9. The primary purpose of the passage is to

(A) offer a critique of both past and present approaches to insolvency

(B) compare the practices of bankruptcy courts of the past with those of bankruptcy courts of the present

(C) criticize those who would change the bankruptcy laws of today

(D) reexamine today's bankruptcy laws in an effort to point to further improvements

(E) explain and defend contemporary bankruptcy laws

10. Which one of the following claims would a defender of the punitive theory of bankruptcy legislation be most likely to have made?

(A) Debt that has become so great that repayment is impossible is ultimately a moral failing and thus a matter for which the law should provide punitive sanctions.

(B) Because insolvency ultimately harms the entire economy, the law should provide a punitive deterrent to insolvency.

(C) The insolvency of companies or individuals is tolerable if the debt is the result of risk-taking, profit-seeking ventures that might create considerable economic growth in the long run.

(D) The dissolution of a large enterprise is costly to the economy as a whole and should not be allowed, even when that enterprise's insolvency is the result of its own fiscal irresponsibility.

(E) The employees of a large bankrupt enterprise should be considered just as negligent as the owner of a bankrupt sole proprietorship.

11. Which one of the following sentences could most logically be appended to the end of the last paragraph of the passage?

(A) Only when today's bankruptcy laws are ultimately seen as inadequate on a large scale will bankruptcy legislation return to its original intent.

(B) Punishment is no longer the primary goal of bankruptcy law, even if some of its side effects still function punitively.

(C) Since leniency serves the public interest in bankruptcy law, it is likely to do so in criminal law as well.

(D) Future bankruptcy legislation could include punitive measures, but only if such measures ultimately benefit creditors.

(E) Today's bankruptcy laws place the burden of insolvency squarely on the shoulders of creditors, in marked contrast to the antiquated laws that weighed heavily on debtors.

12. The information in the passage most strongly suggests which one of the following about changes in bankruptcy laws?

(A) Bankruptcy laws always result from gradual changes in philosophy followed by sudden shifts in policy.

(B) Changes in bankruptcy law were initiated by the courts and only grudgingly adopted by legislators.

(C) The adjustment of bankruptcy laws away from a punitive focus was at first bitterly opposed by creditors.

(D) Bankruptcy laws underwent change because the traditional approach proved inadequate and contrary to the needs of society.

(E) The shift away from a punitive approach to insolvency was part of a more general trend in society toward rehabilitation and away from retribution.

13. Which one of the following, if true, would most weaken the author's argument against harsh punishment for debtors?

(A) Extensive study of the economic and legal history of many countries has shown that most individuals who served prison time for bankruptcy subsequently exhibited greater economic responsibility.

(B) The bankruptcy of a certain large company has had a significant negative impact on the local economy even though virtually all of the affected employees were able to obtain similar jobs within the community.

(C) Once imprisonment was no longer a consequence of insolvency, bankruptcy filings increased dramatically, then leveled off before increasing again during the 1930s.

(D) The court-ordered liquidation of a large and insolvent company's assets threw hundreds of people out of work, but the local economy nevertheless demonstrated robust growth in the immediate aftermath.

(E) Countries that continue to imprison debtors enjoy greater economic health than do comparable countries that have ceased to do so.

GO ON TO THE NEXT PAGE.

As the twentieth century draws to a close, we are learning to see the extent to which accounts and definitions of cultures are influenced by human biases and purposes, benevolent in what they include,
(5) incorporate, and validate, less so in what they exclude and demote. A number of recent studies have argued that the anxieties and agendas of the present exert an extraordinary influence on the national identities we construct from the cultural past. For example, Greek
(10) civilization was known originally to have had roots in Egyptian and various other African and Eastern cultures, but some current scholars charge that its identity was revised during the course of the nineteenth century to support an image of European
(15) cultural dominance—its African and other cultural influences either actively purged or hidden from view by European scholars. Because ancient Greek writers themselves openly acknowledged their culture's hybrid past, nineteenth-century European
(20) commentators habitually passed over these acknowledgments without comment.

Another example is the use of "tradition" to determine national identity. Images of European authority over other cultures were shaped and
(25) reinforced during the nineteenth century, through the manufacture and reinterpretation of rituals, ceremonies, and traditions. At a time when many of the institutions that had helped maintain imperial societies were beginning to recede in influence, and
(30) when the pressures of administering numerous overseas territories and large new domestic constituencies mounted, the ruling elites of Europe felt the clear need to project their power backward in time, giving it a legitimacy that only longevity could
(35) impart. Thus in 1876, Queen Victoria of England was declared empress of India and was celebrated in numerous "traditional" jamborees, as if her rule were not mainly a matter of recent edict but of age-old custom.
(40) Similar constructions have also been made by native cultures about their precolonial past, as in the case of Algeria during its war of independence from France, when decolonization encouraged Algerians to create idealized images of what they believed their
(45) culture to have been prior to French occupation. This strategy is at work in what many revolutionary poets say and write during wars of independence elsewhere, giving their adherents something to revive and admire.
(50) Though for the most part colonized societies have won their independence, in many cultures the imperial attitudes of uniqueness and superiority underlying colonial conquest remain. There is in all nationally defined cultures an aspiration to
(55) sovereignty and dominance that expresses itself in definitions of cultural identity. At the same time, paradoxically, we have never been as aware as we are now of the fact that historical and cultural experiences partake of many social and cultural
(60) domains and even cross national boundaries,

despite the claims to the contrary made by purveyors of nationalist dogma. Far from being unitary, monolithic, or autonomous, cultures actually include more "foreign" elements than
(65) they consciously exclude.

14. Which one of the following statements most accurately expresses the main point of the passage?

(A) Either by ignoring a native culture's own self-understanding or by substituting fabricated traditions and rituals, imperial societies often obscure the heterogeneous cultures of the peoples they colonize.

(B) Attempts to reconstruct a native, precolonial culture by members of decolonized societies are essentially no different from European colonial creation of traditions and rituals to validate their authority.

(C) In attempting to impose a monolithic culture on the peoples they colonize, imperial societies adopt artifices very similar to the tactics employed by revisionist historians of ancient Greek culture.

(D) While most colonized societies have regained their independence, they retain trappings of imperial culture that will need to be discarded if they are to regain the traditions of their past.

(E) Despite nationalistic creation of images of cultures as unified and monolithic, we now more clearly understand the extent to which cultures are in fact made up of heterogeneous elements.

15. The passage provides information to answer all of the following questions EXCEPT:

(A) What kinds of influences affect the national identities people construct from their past?

(B) Why did nineteenth-century European commentators ignore some discussion of Greek culture by ancient Greek writers?

(C) In what ways did African cultural influence affect the culture of ancient Greece?

(D) Why was Queen Victoria of England declared empress of India in 1876?

(E) What is one reason why revolutionary poets speak and write as they do?

GO ON TO THE NEXT PAGE.

16. The author's attitude toward the studies mentioned in line 6 is most likely

    (A) overall agreement with their conclusion about influences on cultural identity
    (B) reservation over their preoccupation with colonialism
    (C) skepticism toward the relevance of the examples they cite
    (D) concern that they fail to explain ancient Greek culture
    (E) unqualified disagreement with their insistence that cultures are monolithic

17. The author's use of the word "traditional" in line 37 is intended to indicate that the jamborees

    (A) had been revived after centuries of neglect
    (B) were legitimized by their historic use in the native culture
    (C) exemplified the dominance of the imperial culture
    (D) conferred spurious historical legitimacy upon colonial authority
    (E) combined historic elements of imperial and native cultures

18. The "purveyors of nationalist dogma" mentioned in line 62 would be most likely to agree with which one of the following?

    (A) Colonized nations should not attempt to regain their historical cultures.
    (B) Imperial cultures should incorporate the traditions of their colonies.
    (C) The cultural traditions of a nation should remain untainted by outside influences.
    (D) A country's cultural identity partakes of many social and cultural domains.
    (E) National histories are created to further aspirations to sovereignty and dominance.

19. Which one of the following would most likely be an example of one of the "rituals, ceremonies, and traditions" mentioned in lines 26–27?

    (A) an annual ceremony held by an institution of the colonizing culture to honor the literary and theatrical achievements of members of the native culture
    (B) a religious service of the colonizing culture that has been adapted to include elements of the native culture in order to gain converts
    (C) a traditional play that is part of a colonized nation's original culture, but is highly popular among the leaders of the imperial culture
    (D) a ritual dance, traditionally used to commemorate the union of two native deities, that is modified to depict the friendship between the colonial and native cultures
    (E) a traditional village oratory competition in which members of the native culture endeavor to outdo one another in allegorical criticisms of the colonizing culture

20. In the context of the passage, the examples in the second and third paragraphs best exemplify which one of the following generalizations?

    (A) Apparent traditions may be products of artifice.
    (B) National identity generally requires cultural uniformity.
    (C) Most colonial cultures are by nature artificial and contrived.
    (D) Historical and cultural experiences may cross national boundaries.
    (E) Revolutionary cultures are often more authentic than imperial cultures.

21. The primary purpose of the passage is to

    (A) argue for the creation of a global culture made up of elements from many national cultures
    (B) explain how the desire for cultural uniformity supports imperialist attitudes
    (C) stress the importance of objectivity in studying the actual sources of cultural identity
    (D) advance the claim that present concerns motivate the shaping of cultural identities
    (E) reveal the imperialist motivations of some nineteenth-century scholarship

GO ON TO THE NEXT PAGE.

One of the foundations of scientific research is that an experimental result is credible only if it can be replicated—only if performing the experiment a second time leads to the same result. But physicists
(5) John Sommerer and Edward Ott have conceived of a physical system in which even the least change in the starting conditions—no matter how small, inadvertent, or undetectable—can alter results radically. The system is represented by a computer model of a
(10) mathematical equation describing the motion of a particle placed in a particular type of force field.

Sommerer and Ott based their system on an analogy with the phenomena known as riddled basins of attraction. If two bodies of water bound a large
(15) landmass and water is spilled somewhere on the land, the water will eventually make its way to one or the other body of water, its destination depending on such factors as where the water is spilled and the geographic features that shape the water's path and
(20) velocity. The basin of attraction for a body of water is the area of land that, whenever water is spilled on it, always directs the spilled water to that body.

In some geographical formations it is sometimes impossible to predict, not only the exact destination
(25) of the spilled water, but even which body of water it will end up in. This is because the boundary between one basin of attraction and another is riddled with fractal properties; in other words, the boundary is permeated by an extraordinarily high number of
(30) physical irregularities such as notches or zigzags. Along such a boundary, the only way to determine where spilled water will flow at any given point is actually to spill it and observe its motion; spilling the water at any immediately adjacent point could give
(35) the water an entirely different path, velocity, or destination.

In the system posited by the two physicists, this boundary expands to include the whole system: i.e., the entire force field is riddled with fractal properties,
(40) and it is impossible to predict even the general destination of the particle given its starting point. Sommerer and Ott make a distinction between this type of uncertainty and that known as "chaos"; under chaos, a particle's general destination would be
(45) predictable but its path and exact destination would not.

There are presumably other such systems because the equation the physicists used to construct the computer model was literally the first one they
(50) attempted, and the likelihood that they chose the only equation that would lead to an unstable system is small. If other such systems do exist, metaphorical examples of riddled basins of attraction may abound in the failed attempts of scientists to replicate
(55) previous experimental results—in which case, scientists would be forced to question one of the basic principles that guide their work.

22. Which one of the following most accurately expresses the main point of the passage?

(A) Sommerer and Ott's model suggests that many of the fundamental experimental results of science are unreliable because they are contaminated by riddled basins of attraction.

(B) Sommerer and Ott's model suggests that scientists who fail to replicate experimental results might be working within physical systems that make replication virtually impossible.

(C) Sommerer and Ott's model suggests that experimental results can never be truly replicated because the starting conditions of an experiment can never be re-created exactly.

(D) Sommerer and Ott's model suggests that most of the physical systems studied by scientists are in fact metaphorical examples of riddled basins of attraction.

(E) Sommerer and Ott's model suggests that an experimental result should not be treated as credible unless that result can be replicated.

23. The discussion of the chaos of physical systems is intended to perform which one of the following functions in the passage?

(A) emphasize the extraordinarily large number of physical irregularities in a riddled basin of attraction

(B) emphasize the unusual types of physical irregularities found in Sommerer and Ott's model

(C) emphasize the large percentage of a riddled basin of attraction that exhibits unpredictability

(D) emphasize the degree of unpredictability in Sommerer and Ott's model

(E) emphasize the number of fractal properties in a riddled basin of attraction

24. Given the information in the passage, Sommerer and Ott are most likely to agree with which one of the following?

(A) It is sometimes impossible to determine whether a particular region exhibits fractal properties.

(B) It is sometimes impossible to predict even the general destination of a particle placed in a chaotic system.

(C) It is sometimes impossible to re-create exactly the starting conditions of an experiment.

(D) It is usually possible to predict the exact path water will travel if it is spilled at a point not on the boundary between two basins of attraction.

(E) It is usually possible to determine the path by which a particle traveled given information about where it was placed and its eventual destination.

GO ON TO THE NEXT PAGE.

25. Which one of the following most accurately describes the author's attitude toward the work of Sommerer and Ott?

(A) skeptical of the possibility that numerous unstable systems exist but confident that the existence of numerous unstable systems would call into question one of the foundations of science

(B) convinced of the existence of numerous unstable systems and unsure if the existence of numerous unstable systems calls into question one of the foundations of science

(C) convinced of the existence of numerous unstable systems and confident that the existence of numerous unstable systems calls into question one of the foundations of science

(D) persuaded of the possibility that numerous unstable systems exist and unsure if the existence of numerous unstable systems would call into question one of the foundations of science

(E) persuaded of the possibility that numerous unstable systems exist and confident that the existence of numerous unstable systems would call into question one of the foundations of science

26. According to the passage, Sommerer and Ott's model differs from a riddled basin of attraction in which one of the following ways?

(A) In the model, the behavior of a particle placed at any point in the system is chaotic; in a riddled basin of attraction, only water spilled at some of the points behaves chaotically.

(B) In a riddled basin of attraction, the behavior of water spilled at any point is chaotic; in the model, only particles placed at some of the points in the system behave chaotically.

(C) In the model, it is impossible to predict the destination of a particle placed at any point in the system; in a riddled basin of attraction, only some points are such that it is impossible to predict the destination of water spilled at each of those points.

(D) In a riddled basin of attraction, water spilled at two adjacent points always makes its way to the same destination; in the model, it is possible for particles placed at two adjacent points to travel to different destinations.

(E) In the model, two particles placed successively at a given point always travel to the same destination; in a riddled basin of attraction, water spilled at the same point on different occasions may make its way to different destinations.

27. Which one of the following best defines the term "basin of attraction," as that term is used in the passage?

(A) the set of all points on an area of land for which it is possible to predict the destination, but not the path, of water spilled at that point

(B) the set of all points on an area of land for which it is possible to predict both the destination and the path of water spilled at that point

(C) the set of all points on an area of land that are free from physical irregularities such as notches and zigzags

(D) the set of all points on an area of land for which water spilled at each point will travel to a particular body of water

(E) the set of all points on an area of land for which water spilled at each point will travel to the same exact destination

28. Which one of the following is most clearly one of the "metaphorical examples of riddled basins of attraction" mentioned in lines 52–53?

(A) A scientist is unable to determine if mixing certain chemicals will result in a particular chemical reaction because the reaction cannot be consistently reproduced since sometimes the reaction occurs and other times it does not despite starting conditions that are in fact exactly the same in each experiment.

(B) A scientist is unable to determine if mixing certain chemicals will result in a particular chemical reaction because the reaction cannot be consistently reproduced since it is impossible to bring about starting conditions that are in fact exactly the same in each experiment.

(C) A scientist is unable to determine if mixing certain chemicals will result in a particular chemical reaction because the reaction cannot be consistently reproduced since it is impossible to produce starting conditions that are even approximately the same from one experiment to the next.

(D) A scientist is able to determine that mixing certain chemicals results in a particular chemical reaction because it is possible to consistently reproduce the reaction even though the starting conditions vary significantly from one experiment to the next.

(E) A scientist is able to determine that mixing certain chemicals results in a particular chemical reaction because it is possible to consistently reproduce the reaction despite the fact that the amount of time it takes for the reaction to occur varies significantly depending on the starting conditions of the experiment.

S T O P

IF YOU FINISH BEFORE TIME IS CALLED, YOU MAY CHECK YOUR WORK ON THIS SECTION ONLY.
DO NOT WORK ON ANY OTHER SECTION IN THE TEST

SECTION II

Time—35 minutes

25 Questions

<u>Directions:</u> The questions in this section are based on the reasoning contained in brief statements or passages. For some questions, more than one of the choices could conceivably answer the question. However, you are to choose the <u>best</u> answer; that is, the response that most accurately and completely answers the question. You should not make assumptions that are by commonsense standards implausible, superfluous, or incompatible with the passage. After you have chosen the best answer, blacken the corresponding space on your answer sheet.

1. Extract from lease: The tenant should record all preexisting damage on the preexisting damage list, because the tenant need not pay for preexisting damage recorded there. The tenant must pay for damage that was not recorded on the preexisting damage list, except for any damage caused by a circumstance beyond the tenant's control.

In which one of the following instances does the extract from the lease most strongly support the view that the tenant is not required to pay for the damage?

(A) a hole in the wall that was not recorded on the preexisting damage list and that was the result of an event within the tenant's control

(B) a crack in a window caused by a factor beyond the tenant's control and not recorded on the preexisting damage list

(C) a tear in the linoleum that was not preexisting but that was caused by one of the tenant's children

(D) a missing light fixture that was present when the tenant moved in but was later removed by the tenant

(E) paint splatters on the carpet that should have been recorded on the preexisting damage list but were not

2. Randy: After Mega Cable Television Company refused to carry the competing Azco News Service alongside its own news channels, the mayor used her influence to get Azco time on a community channel, demonstrating her concern for keeping a diversity of news programming in the city.

Marion: The mayor's action is fully explained by cruder motives: she's rewarding Azco's owner, a political supporter of hers.

Of the following, which one, if true, is the logically strongest counter Randy can make to Marion's objection?

(A) The owner of Azco supported the mayor simply because he liked her political agenda, and not for any expected reward.

(B) The mayor also used her influence to get time on a community channel for another news service, whose owner supported the mayor's opponent in the last election.

(C) Azco's news coverage of the mayor has never been judged to be biased by an impartial, independent organization.

(D) The many people whose jobs depend on Azco's continued presence on a community channel are a potential source of political support for the mayor.

(E) The number of people who watch Mega Cable Television Company's programming has decreased during the mayor's term.

GO ON TO THE NEXT PAGE.

3. On the first day of trout season a team of biologists went with local trout anglers to the Macawber River. Each angler who caught at least 2 trout chose exactly 2 of these trout for the biologists to weigh. A total of 90 fish were weighed. The measurements show that at the beginning of this season the average trout in the Macawber River weighed approximately 1.6 kilograms.

The reasoning above is most vulnerable to criticism on the grounds that it

(A) makes a generalization from a sample that is unlikely to be representative
(B) relies on evidence that is anecdotal rather than scientific
(C) ignores the variations in weight that are likely to occur over the whole season
(D) fails to take into account measurements from the same time in previous seasons
(E) does not consider whether any fish other than trout were caught

4. A strong correlation exists between what people value and the way they act. For example, those who value wealth tend to choose higher-paying jobs in undesirable locations over lower-paying jobs in desirable locations. Thus, knowing what people value can help one predict their actions.

Which one of the following most accurately expresses the conclusion of the argument?

(A) Knowing how people behave allows one to infer what they value.
(B) People's claims concerning what they value are symptomatic of their actions.
(C) No two people who value different things act the same way in identical circumstances.
(D) People who value wealth tend to allow their desire for it to outweigh other concerns.
(E) What people value can be a reliable indicator of how they will act.

5. An analysis of the number and severity of health problems among the population of a certain community showed that elderly people who were born in the community and resided there all their lives had significantly worse health than elderly people who had moved there within the past five years.

Each of the following, if true, contributes to an explanation of the difference in health between these two groups EXCEPT:

(A) People who have the means to relocate tend to be in better-than-average health.
(B) Although most people who have moved into the community are young, most people who have lived in the community all their lives are elderly.
(C) The quality of health care available to the community is lower than that for the rest of the country.
(D) Changes in one's environment tend to have a beneficial effect on one's health.
(E) People in good health are more likely to move to new communities than are people in poor health.

6. Classical Roman architecture is beautiful, primarily because of its use of rounded arches and its symmetry. Postmodern architecture is dramatic, primarily because of its creative use both of materials and of the surrounding environment. An architectural style that combines elements of both classical Roman and postmodern architecture would therefore be both beautiful and dramatic.

The reasoning in the argument is flawed in that it

(A) presumes, without providing justification, that for an architectural style to have certain qualities, its components must have those qualities
(B) fails to justify its presumption that because postmodern architecture is dramatic, that is its most salient feature
(C) neglects to consider that an architectural style combining elements of two other architectural styles may lack certain qualities of one or both of those styles
(D) neglects to specify how the drama of an architectural style contributes to its beauty
(E) ignores the possibility that there are other architectural styles whose defining qualities include both drama and beauty

GO ON TO THE NEXT PAGE.

7. After being subjected to clinical tests like those used to evaluate the effectiveness of prescription drugs, a popular nonprescription herbal remedy was found to be as effective in treating painful joints as is a certain prescription drug that has been used successfully to treat this condition. The manufacturer of the herbal remedy cited the test results as proof that chemical agents are unnecessary for the successful treatment of painful joints.

The test results would provide the proof that the manufacturer claims they do if which one of the following is assumed?

(A) People are likely to switch from using prescription drugs to using herbal remedies if the herbal remedies are found to be as effective as the prescription drugs.

(B) The herbal remedy contains no chemical agents that are effective in treating painful joints.

(C) None of the people who participated in the test of the prescription drug had ever tried using an herbal remedy to treat painful joints.

(D) The researchers who analyzed the results of the clinical testing of the herbal remedy had also analyzed the results of the clinical testing of the prescription drug.

(E) The prescription drug treats the discomfort associated with painful joints without eliminating the cause of that condition.

8. When companies' profits would otherwise be reduced by an increase in the minimum wage (a wage rate set by the government as the lowest that companies are allowed to pay), the companies often reduce the number of workers they employ. Yet a recent increase in the minimum wage did not result in job cutbacks in the fast-food industry, where most workers are paid the minimum wage.

Which one of the following, if true, most helps to explain why the increase in the minimum wage did not affect the number of jobs in the fast-food industry?

(A) After the recent increase in the minimum wage, decreased job turnover in the fast-food industry allowed employers of fast-food workers to save enough on recruiting costs to cover the cost of the wage increase.

(B) If, in any industry, an increase in the minimum wage leads to the elimination of many jobs that pay the minimum wage, then higher-paying supervisory positions will also be eliminated in that industry.

(C) With respect to its response to increases in the minimum wage, the fast-food industry does not differ significantly from other industries that employ many workers at the minimum wage.

(D) A few employees in the fast-food industry were already earning more than the new, higher minimum wage before the new minimum wage was established.

(E) Sales of fast food to workers who are paid the minimum wage did not increase following the recent change in the minimum wage.

9. One should always capitalize the main words and the first and last words of a title. But one should never capitalize articles, or prepositions and conjunctions with fewer than five letters, when they occur in the middle of a title.

Which one of the following can be properly inferred from the statements above?

(A) If a word that is a preposition or conjunction should be capitalized, then it is the first or last word of the title.

(B) If a word in the middle of a title should be capitalized, then that word is neither an article nor a conjunction shorter than five letters.

(C) All prepositions and conjunctions with fewer than five letters should be uncapitalized in titles.

(D) If a word is neither a main word nor a first or last word of a title, then it should not be capitalized.

(E) Prepositions and conjunctions with five or more letters should be capitalized in any text.

10. Letter to the editor: Recently, the city council passed an ordinance that prohibits loitering at the local shopping mall. The council's declared goal was to eliminate overcrowding and alleviate pedestrian congestion, thereby improving the mall's business and restoring its family-oriented image. But despite these claims, reducing overcrowding and congestion cannot be the actual goals of this measure, because even when fully implemented, the ordinance would not accomplish them.

Which one of the following most accurately describes a flaw in the argument's reasoning?

(A) The argument ignores the possibility that an action may achieve its secondary goals even if it does not achieve its primary goals.

(B) The argument takes for granted that something cannot be the goal of an action performed unless the action will in fact achieve that goal.

(C) The argument dismisses a claim because of its source rather than because of its content.

(D) The argument takes for granted that an action that does not accomplish its stated goals will not have any beneficial effects.

(E) The argument treats a condition that is necessary for achieving an action's stated goals as if this condition were sufficient for achieving these goals.

GO ON TO THE NEXT PAGE.

11. Cynthia: Corporations amply fund research that generates marketable new technologies. But the fundamental goal of science is to achieve a comprehensive knowledge of the workings of the universe. The government should help fund those basic scientific research projects that seek to further our theoretical knowledge of nature.

Luis: The basic goal of government support of scientific research is to generate technological advances that will benefit society as a whole. So only research that is expected to yield practical applications in fields such as agriculture and medicine ought to be funded.

Cynthia's and Luis's statements provide the most support for the contention that they would disagree with each other about the truth of which one of the following statements?

(A)   The government should help fund pure theoretical research because such research might have unforeseen practical applications in fields such as agriculture and medicine.

(B)   A proposed study of the effects of chemical fertilizers on crops, for the purpose of developing more-resistant and higher-yielding breeds, should not receive government funding.

(C)   Although some research projects in theoretical science yield practical benefits, most do not, and so no research projects in theoretical science should be funded by the government.

(D)   Research for the sole purpose of developing new technologies ought to be financed exclusively by corporations.

(E)   Knowledge gained through basic scientific research need not be expected to lead to new and useful technologies in order for the research to merit government funding.

12. One can never tell whether another person is acting from an ulterior motive; therefore, it is impossible to tell whether someone's action is moral, and so one should evaluate the consequences of an action rather than its morality.

Which one of the following principles, if valid, most helps to justify the reasoning above?

(A)   The intention of an action is indispensable for an evaluation of its morality.

(B)   The assigning of praise and blame is what is most important in the assessment of the value of human actions.

(C)   One can sometimes know one's own motives for a particular action.

(D)   There can be good actions that are not performed by a good person.

(E)   One cannot know whether someone acted morally in a particular situation unless one knows what consequences that person's actions had.

13. Fossil-fuel producers say that it would be prohibitively expensive to reduce levels of carbon dioxide emitted by the use of fossil fuels enough to halt global warming. This claim is probably false. Several years ago, the chemical industry said that finding an economical alternative to the chlorofluorocarbons (CFCs) destroying the ozone layer would be impossible. Yet once the industry was forced, by international agreements, to find substitutes for CFCs, it managed to phase them out completely well before the mandated deadline, in many cases at a profit.

Which one of the following, if true, most strengthens the argument?

(A)   In the time since the chemical industry phased out CFCs, the destruction of the ozone layer by CFCs has virtually halted, but the levels of carbon dioxide emitted by the use of fossil fuels have continued to increase.

(B)   In some countries, the amount of carbon dioxide emitted by the use of fossil fuels has already been reduced without prohibitive expense, but at some cost in convenience to the users of such fuels.

(C)   The use of CFCs never contributed as greatly to the destruction of the ozone layer as the carbon dioxide emitted by the use of fossil fuels currently contributes to global warming.

(D)   There are ways of reducing carbon dioxide emissions that could halt global warming without hurting profits of fossil-fuel producers significantly more than phasing out CFCs hurt those of the chemical industry.

(E)   If international agreements forced fossil-fuel producers to find ways to reduce carbon dioxide emissions enough to halt global warming, the fossil-fuel producers could find substitutes for fossil fuels.

GO ON TO THE NEXT PAGE.

14. If legislators are to enact laws that benefit constituents, they must be sure to consider what the consequences of enacting a proposed law will actually be. Contemporary legislatures fail to enact laws that benefit constituents. Concerned primarily with advancing their own political careers, legislators present legislation in polemical terms; this arouses in their colleagues either repugnance or enthusiasm for the legislation.

Which one of the following is an assumption on which the argument depends?

(A) Legislation will not benefit constituents unless legislators become less concerned with their own careers.

(B) Legislatures that enact laws that benefit constituents are successful legislatures.

(C) The passage of laws cannot benefit constituents unless constituents generally adhere to those laws.

(D) Legislators considering a proposed law for which they have repugnance or enthusiasm do not consider the consequences that it will actually have.

(E) The inability of legislators to consider the actual consequences of enacting a proposed law is due to their strong feelings about that law.

15. Anderson maintains that travel writing has diminished in quality over the last few decades. Although travel writing has changed in this time, Anderson is too harsh on contemporary travel writers. Today, when the general public is better traveled than in the past, travel writers face a challenge far greater than that of their predecessors: they must not only show their readers a place but also make them see it anew. That the genre has not only survived but also flourished shows the talent of today's practitioners.

Which one of the following most accurately describes the role played in the argument by the statement that the general public is better traveled today than in the past?

(A) It is claimed to be a result of good travel writing.

(B) It is cited as evidence that contemporary travel writing is intended for a wider readership.

(C) It is part of a purported explanation of why readers are disappointed with today's travel writers.

(D) It is cited as a reason that travel writing flourishes more today than it has in the past.

(E) It is cited as a condition that has transformed the task of the travel writer.

16. Among multiparty democracies, those with the fewest parties will have the most-productive legislatures. The fewer the number of parties in a democracy, the more issues each must take a stand on. A political party that must take stands on a wide variety of issues has to prioritize those issues; this promotes a tendency to compromise.

Which one of the following is an assumption required by the argument?

(A) The more political parties a nation has, the more likely it is that there will be disagreements within parties.

(B) The fewer the number of a nation's political parties, the more important it is that those parties can compromise with each other.

(C) The tendency to compromise makes the legislative process more productive.

(D) The legislatures of nondemocracies are less productive than are those of democracies.

(E) Legislators in a multiparty democracy never all agree on important issues.

GO ON TO THE NEXT PAGE.

17. Warm air tends to be humid, and as humidity of air increases, the amount of rainfall also increases. So, the fact that rainfall totals for most continents have been increasing over the past five years is strong evidence that the air temperature is increasing as well.

Which one of the following has a flawed pattern of reasoning most similar to the flawed pattern of reasoning in the argument above?

(A) Food that is fresh tends to be nutritious, and the more nutritious one's diet the healthier one is. People today are generally healthier than people were a century ago. So it is likely that people today eat food that is fresher than the food people ate a century ago.

(B) Your refusal to make public your personal finances indicates some sort of financial impropriety on your part, for people who do not reveal their personal finances generally are hiding some sort of financial impropriety.

(C) People tend not to want to travel on mass transit when they are carrying bags and packages, and the more bags and packages one carries, the more awkward travel on mass transit becomes. Therefore, people who carry bags and packages tend to use automobiles rather than mass transit.

(D) Statistics show that people are generally living longer and healthier lives than ever before. However, more people are overweight and fewer people exercise than ever before. Therefore, being lean and physically fit is essential neither to long life nor to good health.

(E) People tend to watch only those television programs that they enjoy and appreciate. Since there are more television viewers today than there were ten years ago, it must be the case that viewers today are satisfied with at least some of the programs shown on television.

18. Asked by researchers to sort objects by shape, most toddlers in a large study had no trouble doing so. When subsequently told to sort by color, the toddlers seemed to have difficulty following the new rule and almost invariably persisted with their first approach. The researchers suggest such failures to adapt to new rules often result from insufficient development of the prefrontal cortex in toddlers. The cortex is essential for functions like adapting to new rules, yet is slow to mature, continuing to develop right into adolescence.

Which one of the following is most supported by the information above?

(A) Toddlers unable to sort objects by color tend to have a less developed prefrontal cortex than other children of the same age.

(B) Only adolescents and adults can solve problems that require adapting to new rules.

(C) Certain kinds of behavior on the part of toddlers may not be willfully disobedient.

(D) The maturing of the prefrontal cortex is more important than upbringing in causing the development of adaptive behavior.

(E) Skill at adapting to new situations is roughly proportional to the level of development of the prefrontal cortex.

19. Dietitian: It is true that nutrients are most effective when provided by natural foods rather than artificial supplements. While it is also true that fat in one's diet is generally unhealthy, eating raw carrots (which are rich in beta carotene) by themselves is nonetheless not an effective means of obtaining vitamin A, since the body cannot transform beta carotene into vitamin A unless it is consumed with at least some fat.

The statement that fat in one's diet is generally unhealthy plays which one of the following roles in the dietitian's argument?

(A) It is mentioned as a reason for adopting a dietary practice that the dietitian provides a reason for not carrying to the extreme.

(B) It is mentioned as the reason that is least often cited by those who recommend a dietary practice the dietitian disfavors.

(C) It is mentioned as a generally accepted hypothesis that the dietitian attempts to undermine completely.

(D) It is attacked as inadequate evidence for the claim that nutrients are most effective when provided by natural foods rather than artificial supplements.

(E) It is cited as a bad reason for adopting a dietary habit that the dietitian recommends.

GO ON TO THE NEXT PAGE.

20. Industrial engineer: Some people have suggested that the problem of global warming should be addressed by pumping some of the carbon dioxide produced by the burning of fossil fuels into the deep ocean. Many environmentalists worry that this strategy would simply exchange one form of pollution for an equally destructive form. This worry is unfounded, however; much of the carbon dioxide now released into the atmosphere eventually ends up in the ocean anyway, where it does not cause environmental disturbances as destructive as global warming.

Which one of the following most accurately expresses the conclusion of the industrial engineer's argument as a whole?

(A) Global warming from the emission of carbon dioxide into the atmosphere could be reduced by pumping some of that carbon dioxide into the deep ocean.

(B) Environmentalists worry that the strategy of pumping carbon dioxide into the deep ocean to reduce global warming would simply exchange one form of pollution for another, equally destructive one.

(C) Worrying that pumping carbon dioxide into the deep ocean to reduce global warming would simply exchange one form of pollution for another, equally destructive, form is unfounded.

(D) Much of the carbon dioxide now released into the atmosphere ends up in the ocean where it does not cause environmental disturbances as destructive as global warming.

(E) To reduce global warming, the strategy of pumping into the deep ocean at least some of the carbon dioxide now released into the atmosphere should be considered.

21. Several people came down with an illness caused by a type of bacteria in seafood. Health officials traced the history of each person who became ill to the same restaurant and date. Careful testing showed that most people who ate seafood at the restaurant on that date had not come in contact with the bacteria in question. Despite this finding, health officials remained confident that contaminated seafood from this restaurant caused the cases of illness.

Which one of the following, if true, most helps to resolve the apparent discrepancy indicated above?

(A) Most people are immune to the effects of the bacteria in question.

(B) Those made ill by the bacteria had all been served by a waiter who subsequently became ill.

(C) All and only those who ate contaminated seafood at the restaurant on that date were allergic to the monosodium glutamate in a sauce that they used.

(D) The restaurant in question had recently been given a warning about violations of health regulations.

(E) All and only those who ate a particular seafood dish at the restaurant contracted the illness.

22. Economist: Real wages in this country will increase significantly only if productivity increases notably. Thus, it is unlikely that real wages will increase significantly in the near future, since this country's businesses are currently investing very little in new technology and this pattern is likely to continue for at least several more years.

Which one of the following, if assumed about the economist's country, allows the economist's conclusion to be properly drawn?

(A) Neither real wages nor productivity have increased in the last several years.

(B) Real wages will increase notably if a significant number of workers acquire the skills necessary to use new technology.

(C) Sooner or later real wages will increase significantly.

(D) Productivity will not increase if businesses do not make a substantial investment in new technology.

(E) The new technology in which businesses are currently investing is not contributing to an increase in productivity.

GO ON TO THE NEXT PAGE.

23. In scientific journals, authors and reviewers have praised companies in which they have substantial investments. These scientists, with their potential conflict of interest, call into question the integrity of scientific inquiry, so there should be full public disclosure of scientific authors' commercial holdings.

Which one of the following conforms most closely to the principle illustrated by the argument above?

(A) Managers within any corporation should not make investments in the companies for which they work.
(B) Claims about the effectiveness of pharmaceuticals should be based on scientific studies.
(C) People with access to otherwise private information regarding the value of stocks should not be allowed to sell or purchase those stocks.
(D) Magazine publishers should not be allowed to invest in the companies that advertise in their magazines.
(E) Financial advisers should inform their clients about any incentives the advisers receive for promoting investments in particular companies.

24. Columnist: The amount of acidic pollutants released into the air has decreased throughout the world over the last several decades. We can expect, then, an overall decrease in the negative environmental effects of acid rain, which is caused by these acidic pollutants.

Each of the following, if true, would weaken the columnist's argument EXCEPT:

(A) Some ecosystems have developed sophisticated mechanisms that reduce the negative effects of increased levels of acids in the environment.
(B) The amount of acid-neutralizing buffers released into the air has decreased in recent years.
(C) The current decrease in acidic pollutants is expected to end soon, as more countries turn to coal for the generation of electricity.
(D) The effects of acid rain are cumulative and largely independent of current acid rain levels.
(E) The soils of many ecosystems exposed to acid rain have been exhausted of minerals that help protect them from acid rain's harmful effects.

25. Columnist: It is sometimes claimed that the only factors relevant to determining moral guilt or innocence are the intentions of the person performing an action. However, external circumstances often play a crucial role in our moral judgment of an action. For example, a cook at a restaurant who absentmindedly put an ingredient in the stew that is not usually in the stew would ordinarily be regarded as forgetful, not immoral. If, however, someone eating at the restaurant happens to be severely allergic to that ingredient, eats the stew, and dies, many people would judge the cook to be guilty of serious moral negligence.

Which one of the following propositions is best illustrated by the columnist's statements?

(A) It is sometimes fair to judge the morality of others' actions even without considering all of the circumstances under which those actions were performed.
(B) We sometimes judge unfairly the morality of other people's actions.
(C) We should judge all negligent people to be equally morally blameworthy, regardless of the outcomes of their actions.
(D) People are sometimes held morally blameworthy as a result of circumstances some of which were outside their intentional control.
(E) The intentions of the person performing an action are rarely a decisive factor in making moral judgments about that action.

S T O P

IF YOU FINISH BEFORE TIME IS CALLED, YOU MAY CHECK YOUR WORK ON THIS SECTION ONLY.
DO NOT WORK ON ANY OTHER SECTION IN THE TEST.

SECTION III

Time—35 minutes

22 Questions

Directions: Each group of questions in this section is based on a set of conditions. In answering some of the questions, it may be useful to draw a rough diagram. Choose the response that most accurately and completely answers each question and blacken the corresponding space on your answer sheet.

Questions 1–5

At each of six consecutive stops—1, 2, 3, 4, 5, and 6—that a traveler must make in that order as part of a trip, she can choose one from among exactly four airlines—L, M, N, and O—on which to continue. Her choices must conform to the following constraints:

Whichever airline she chooses at a stop, she chooses one of the other airlines at the next stop.

She chooses the same airline at stop 1 as she does at stop 6.

She chooses the same airline at stop 2 as she does at stop 4.

Whenever she chooses either L or M at a stop, she does not choose N at the next stop.

At stop 5, she chooses N or O.

1. Which one of the following could be an accurate list of the airlines the traveler chooses at each stop, in order from 1 through 6?

(A) L, M, M, L, O, L
(B) M, L, O, M, O, M
(C) M, N, O, N, O, M
(D) M, O, N, O, N, M
(E) O, M, L, M, O, N

2. If the traveler chooses N at stop 5, which one of the following could be an accurate list of the airlines she chooses at stops 1, 2, and 3, respectively?

(A) L, M, N
(B) L, O, N
(C) M, L, N
(D) M, L, O
(E) N, O, N

3. If the only airlines the traveler chooses for the trip are M, N, and O, and she chooses O at stop 5, then the airlines she chooses at stops 1, 2, and 3, must be, respectively,

(A) M, O, and N
(B) M, N, and O
(C) N, M, and O
(D) N, O, and M
(E) O, M, and N

4. Which one of the following CANNOT be an accurate list of the airlines the traveler chooses at stops 1 and 2, respectively?

(A) L, M
(B) L, O
(C) M, L
(D) M, O
(E) O, N

5. If the traveler chooses O at stop 2, which one of the following could be an accurate list of the airlines she chooses at stops 5 and 6, respectively?

(A) M, N
(B) N, L
(C) N, O
(D) O, L
(E) O, N

GO ON TO THE NEXT PAGE.

Questions 6–11

The members of a five-person committee will be selected from among three parents—F, G, and H—three students—K, L, and M—and four teachers—U, W, X, and Z. The selection of committee members will meet the following conditions:

> The committee must include exactly one student.
> F and H cannot both be selected.
> M and Z cannot both be selected.
> U and W cannot both be selected.
> F cannot be selected unless Z is also selected.
> W cannot be selected unless H is also selected.

6. Which one of the following is an acceptable selection of committee members?

   (A) F, G, K, L, Z
   (B) F, G, K, U, X
   (C) G, K, W, X, Z
   (D) H, K, U, W, X
   (E) H, L, W, X, Z

7. If W and Z are selected, which one of the following is a pair of people who could also be selected?

   (A) U and X
   (B) K and L
   (C) G and M
   (D) G and K
   (E) F and G

8. Which one of the following is a pair of people who CANNOT both be selected?

   (A) F and G
   (B) F and M
   (C) G and K
   (D) H and L
   (E) M and U

9. If W is selected, then any one of the following could also be selected EXCEPT:

   (A) F
   (B) G
   (C) L
   (D) M
   (E) Z

10. If the committee is to include exactly one parent, which one of the following is a person who must also be selected?

    (A) K
    (B) L
    (C) M
    (D) U
    (E) X

11. If M is selected, then the committee must also include both

    (A) F and G
    (B) G and H
    (C) H and K
    (D) K and U
    (E) U and X

GO ON TO THE NEXT PAGE.

Questions 12–17

Within a five-year period from 1991 to 1995, each of three friends—Ramon, Sue, and Taylor—graduated. In that period, each bought his or her first car. The graduations and car purchases must be consistent with the following:

Ramon graduated in some year before the year in which Taylor graduated.

Taylor graduated in some year before the year in which he bought his first car.

Sue bought her first car in some year before the year in which she graduated.

Ramon and Sue graduated in the same year as each other.

At least one of the friends graduated in 1993.

12. Which one of the following could be an accurate matching of each friend and the year in which she or he graduated?

   (A) Ramon: 1991; Sue: 1991; Taylor: 1993
   (B) Ramon: 1992; Sue: 1992; Taylor: 1993
   (C) Ramon: 1992; Sue: 1993; Taylor: 1994
   (D) Ramon: 1993; Sue: 1993; Taylor: 1992
   (E) Ramon: 1993; Sue: 1993; Taylor: 1995

13. Which one of the following could have taken place in 1995?

   (A) Ramon graduated.
   (B) Ramon bought his first car.
   (C) Sue graduated.
   (D) Sue bought her first car.
   (E) Taylor graduated.

14. Which one of the following must be false?

   (A) Two of the friends each bought his or her first car in 1991.
   (B) Two of the friends each bought his or her first car in 1992.
   (C) Two of the friends each bought his or her first car in 1993.
   (D) Two of the friends each bought his or her first car in 1994.
   (E) Two of the friends each bought his or her first car in 1995.

15. Which one of the following must be true?

   (A) None of the three friends graduated in 1991.
   (B) None of the three friends graduated in 1992.
   (C) None of the three friends bought his or her first car in 1993.
   (D) None of the three friends graduated in 1994.
   (E) None of the three friends bought his or her first car in 1995.

16. If Taylor graduated in the same year that Ramon bought his first car, then each of the following could be true EXCEPT:

   (A) Sue bought her first car in 1991.
   (B) Ramon graduated in 1992.
   (C) Taylor graduated in 1993.
   (D) Taylor bought his first car in 1994.
   (E) Ramon bought his first car in 1995.

17. If Sue graduated in 1993, then which one of the following must be true?

   (A) Sue bought her first car in 1991.
   (B) Ramon bought his first car in 1992.
   (C) Ramon bought his first car in 1993.
   (D) Taylor bought his first car in 1994.
   (E) Taylor bought his first car in 1995.

GO ON TO THE NEXT PAGE.

Questions 18–22

A child eating alphabet soup notices that the only letters left in her bowl are one each of these six letters: T, U, W, X, Y, and Z. She plays a game with the remaining letters, eating them in the next three spoonfuls in accord with certain rules. Each of the six letters must be in exactly one of the next three spoonfuls, and each of the spoonfuls must have at least one and at most three of the letters. In addition, she obeys the following restrictions:

> The U is in a later spoonful than the T.
> The U is not in a later spoonful than the X.
> The Y is in a later spoonful than the W.
> The U is in the same spoonful as either the Y or the Z, but not both.

18. Which one of the following could be an accurate list of the spoonfuls and the letters in each of them?

   (A)   first: Y
         second: T, W
         third: U, X, Z
   (B)   first: T, W
         second: U, X, Y
         third: Z
   (C)   first: T
         second: U, Z
         third: W, X, Y
   (D)   first: T, U, Z
         second: W
         third: X, Y
   (E)   first: W
         second: T, X, Z
         third: U, Y

19. If the Y is the only letter in one of the spoonfuls, then which one of the following could be true?

   (A)   The Y is in the first spoonful.
   (B)   The Z is in the first spoonful.
   (C)   The T is in the second spoonful.
   (D)   The X is in the second spoonful.
   (E)   The W is in the third spoonful.

20. If the Z is in the first spoonful, then which one of the following must be true?

   (A)   The T is in the second spoonful.
   (B)   The U is in the third spoonful.
   (C)   The W is in the first spoonful.
   (D)   The W is in the second spoonful.
   (E)   The X is in the third spoonful.

21. Which one of the following is a complete list of letters, any one of which could be the only letter in the first spoonful?

   (A)   T
   (B)   T, W
   (C)   T, X
   (D)   T, W, Z
   (E)   T, X, W, Z

22. If the T is in the second spoonful, then which one of the following could be true?

   (A)   Exactly two letters are in the first spoonful.
   (B)   Exactly three letters are in the first spoonful.
   (C)   Exactly three letters are in the second spoonful.
   (D)   Exactly one letter is in the third spoonful.
   (E)   Exactly two letters are in the third spoonful.

S T O P

IF YOU FINISH BEFORE TIME IS CALLED, YOU MAY CHECK YOUR WORK ON THIS SECTION ONLY.
DO NOT WORK ON ANY OTHER SECTION IN THE TEST.

SECTION IV

Time—35 minutes

25 Questions

Directions: The questions in this section are based on the reasoning contained in brief statements or passages. For some questions, more than one of the choices could conceivably answer the question. However, you are to choose the best answer; that is, the response that most accurately and completely answers the question. You should not make assumptions that are by commonsense standards implausible, superfluous, or incompatible with the passage. After you have chosen the best answer, blacken the corresponding space on your answer sheet.

1. Cox: The consumer council did not provide sufficient justification for its action when it required that Derma-35 be recalled from the market.

    Crockett: I disagree. Derma-35 in fact causes inflammation, but in citing only the side effect of blemishes as the justification for its decision, the council rightly acknowledged that blemishes are a legitimate health concern.

    Cox and Crockett disagree over whether

    (A) Derma-35 should remain on the market
    (B) blemishes are sometimes caused by inflammation
    (C) the council based its decision on the threat of inflammation or on the threat of blemishes
    (D) the council gave an adequate reason for its decision to recall Derma-35
    (E) inflammation is a serious health threat

2. Literary historian: William Shakespeare, a humble actor, could have written the love poetry attributed to him. But the dramas attributed to him evince such insight into the minds of powerful rulers that they could only have been written by one who had spent much time among them; Francis Bacon associated with rulers, but Shakespeare did not.

    Which one of the following logically follows from the literary historian's claims?

    (A) Bacon wrote the dramas attributed to Shakespeare, but could not have written the love poetry.
    (B) Bacon wrote both the love poetry and the dramas attributed to Shakespeare.
    (C) Shakespeare wrote neither the love poetry nor the dramas attributed to him.
    (D) One person could not have written both the love poetry and the dramas attributed to Shakespeare.
    (E) Shakespeare may have written the love poetry but did not write the dramas attributed to him.

3. Philosopher: Effective tests have recently been developed to predict fatal diseases having a largely genetic basis. Now, for the first time, a person can be warned well in advance of the possibility of such life-threatening conditions. However, medicine is not yet able to prevent most such conditions. Simply being informed that one will get a disease that is both fatal and incurable can itself be quite harmful to some people. This raises the question of whether such "early warning" tests should be made available at all.

    Which one of the following statements is best illustrated by the state of affairs described by the philosopher?

    (A) The advance of medicine fails to provide solutions to every problem.
    (B) The advance of medicine creates new contexts in which ethical dilemmas can arise.
    (C) Medical technologies continue to advance, increasing our knowledge and understanding of disease.
    (D) The more we come to learn, the more we realize how little we know.
    (E) The advance of technology is of questionable value.

GO ON TO THE NEXT PAGE.

4. Chapin: Commentators have noted with concern the recent electoral success by extremist parties in several democratic countries. But these successes pose no threat to democracy in those countries. The extremists have won pluralities, not majorities. Furthermore, they have won only when the moderate parties were preoccupied with arguing among themselves.

Which one of the following, if assumed, enables Chapin's conclusion to be properly drawn?

(A) Parties that win pluralities but not majorities never directly or indirectly effect changes in their country's political arrangements.

(B) Multiparty political systems are always more democratic than two-party political systems are.

(C) Countries in which extremist parties win pluralities sometimes have democratic governments as strong as those in countries that lack extremist parties.

(D) Members of moderate parties who consider extremist parties to be a serious threat to democracy will sometimes put aside their differences with each other to oppose them.

(E) People are not always supporting a move toward an extremist government when they vote for extremist parties in democratic elections.

5. Futurist: Artists in the next century will be supported largely by private patrons. Because these patrons will almost invariably be supporters of the social order—whatever it happens to be at the time—art in the next century will rarely express social and political doctrines that are perceived to be subversive of that social order.

Which one of the following principles, if valid, provides the most support for the futurist's inference?

(A) Art patrons tend not to support artists whose art expresses social and political views that are in opposition to their own.

(B) Art patrons tend to be more interested in formal artistic problems than in the social and political issues of their time.

(C) Artists are as prone to attack the contemporary social and political order in their work as they are to defend it.

(D) Artists tend to become more critical of contemporary social and political arrangements after they are freed of their dependency on private patrons.

(E) Art patrons tend to oppose all social change except that initiated by artists.

6. University budget committee: Athletes experience fewer injuries on artificial-turf athletic fields than on natural-grass fields. Additionally, natural-grass fields are more expensive to maintain than fields made of artificial turf. Nevertheless, this committee recommends replacing the university's current artificial-turf field with a natural-grass field.

Which one of the following, if true, most helps to resolve the apparent discrepancy in the committee's position?

(A) The university's current artificial-turf athletic field has required extensive maintenance since its original installation.

(B) Most injuries sustained on artificial-turf fields take longer to heal and require more expensive physical therapy than do injuries sustained on natural-grass fields.

(C) It is difficult for spectators at athletic events to determine whether an athletic field is artificial turf or natural grass.

(D) Maintaining artificial-turf fields involves the occasional replacement of damaged sections of turf, whereas natural-grass fields require daily watering and periodic fertilization.

(E) Athletes who have spent most of their playing time on natural-grass fields generally prefer not to play on artificial-turf fields.

7. Although instinct enables organisms to make complex responses to stimuli, instinctual behavior involves no reasoning and requires far fewer nerve cells than does noninstinctual (also called flexible) behavior. A brain mechanism capable of flexible behavior must have a large number of neurons, and no insect brain has yet reached a size capable of providing a sufficiently large number of neurons.

Which one of the following can be properly inferred from the statements above?

(A) The behavior of organisms with elaborate brain mechanisms is usually not instinctual.

(B) Insect behavior is exclusively instinctual.

(C) All organisms with brains larger than insects' brains are capable of some measure of flexible behavior.

(D) All organisms with large brains are biologically equipped for flexible behavior.

(E) Only organisms with brains of insect size or smaller engage in purely instinctual behavior.

GO ON TO THE NEXT PAGE.

8. The laboratory experiment, the most effective method for teaching science, is disappearing from most secondary school curricula, and students are now simulating experiments with computers. This trend should be stopped. It results in many students' completing secondary school and going on to a university without knowing how to work with laboratory equipment.

Which one of the following, if true, most weakens the argument?

(A) Scientific knowledge is changing so rapidly it is difficult for secondary schools to keep up without using computers.

(B) In some secondary schools, teachers conduct laboratory experiments while students observe.

(C) Computers have proven to be a valuable tool for teaching secondary school students scientific terminology.

(D) Secondary schools and universities across the nation have put a great deal of money into purchasing computers.

(E) University students can learn science effectively without having had experience in working with laboratory equipment.

9. Alice: In democracies, politicians garner support by emphasizing the differences between their opponents and themselves. Because they must rule in accord with their rhetoric, policies in democracies fluctuate wildly as one party succeeds another.

Elwell: But despite election rhetoric, to put together majority coalitions in democracies, politicians usually end up softening their stands on individual issues once they are elected.

The statements above provide the most support for the claim that Alice and Elwell disagree about whether

(A) politicians heighten the differences between themselves and their opponents during elections

(B) basic policies change drastically when one party succeeds another in a democracy

(C) in a democracy the best way of ensuring continuity in policies is to form a coalition government

(D) most voters stay loyal to a particular political party even as it changes its stand on particular issues

(E) the desire of parties to build majority coalitions tends to support democratic systems

10. Air traffic controllers and nuclear power plant operators are not allowed to work exceptionally long hours, because to do so would jeopardize lives. Yet physicians in residency training are typically required to work 80-hour weeks. The aforementioned restrictions on working exceptionally long hours should also be applied to resident physicians, since they too are engaged in work of a life-or-death nature.

Which one of the following is an assumption the argument depends on?

(A) There is no indispensable aspect of residency training that requires resident physicians to work exceptionally long hours.

(B) Resident physicians have a more direct effect on the lives of others than do air traffic controllers and nuclear power plant operators.

(C) The more hours one works in a week, the less satisfactorily one performs one's work.

(D) Those who are not engaged in work that has life-or-death consequences should only sometimes be allowed to work exceptionally long hours.

(E) Some resident physicians would like to complete their residency training without working exceptionally long hours.

11. Career consultant: The most popular career advice suggests emphasizing one's strengths to employers and downplaying one's weaknesses. Research shows this advice to be incorrect. A study of 314 managers shows that those who use self-deprecating humor in front of their employees are more likely to be seen by them as even-handed, thoughtful, and concerned than are those who do not.

The career consultant's reasoning is most vulnerable to criticism on the grounds that it

(A) bases a conclusion about how one group will respond to self-deprecation on information about how a different group responds to it

(B) ignores the possibility that what was viewed positively in the managers' self-deprecating humor was the self-deprecation and not its humor

(C) ignores the possibility that non-self-deprecating humor might have been viewed even more positively than self-deprecating humor

(D) infers from the fact that self-deprecating humor was viewed positively that nonhumorous self-deprecation would not be viewed positively

(E) bases a conclusion about certain popular career advice on a critique of only one part of that advice

12. Researcher: We studied two groups of subjects over a period of six months. Over this period, one of the groups had a daily routine of afternoon exercise. The other group, the control group, engaged in little or no exercise during the study. It was found that those in the exercise group got 33 percent more deep-sleep at night than did the control group. Exercising in the afternoon tends to raise body temperature slightly until after bedtime, and this extra heat induces deeper sleep.

The researcher's statements, if true, most strongly support which one of the following?

(A) Regular afternoon exercise is one of the things required for adequate deep-sleep.
(B) Exercise in the morning is almost as likely to have as many beneficial effects on sleep as is exercise in the afternoon.
(C) The best way to get increased deep-sleep is to induce a slight increase in body temperature just before bedtime.
(D) No one in the control group experienced a rise in body temperature just before bedtime.
(E) Raising body temperature slightly by taking a warm bath just before bedtime will likely result in increased deep-sleep.

13. Companies wishing to boost sales of merchandise should use in-store displays to catch customers' attention. According to a marketing study, today's busy shoppers have less time for coupon-clipping and pay little attention to direct-mail advertising; instead, they make two-thirds of their buying decisions on the spot at the store.

Which one of the following is an assumption that the argument requires?

(A) Companies are increasingly using in-store displays to catch customers' attention.
(B) Coupons and direct-mail advertising were at one time more effective means of boosting sales of merchandise than they are now.
(C) In-store displays are more likely to influence buying decisions made on the spot at the store than to influence other buying decisions.
(D) In-store displays that catch customers' attention increase the likelihood that customers will decide on the spot to buy the company's merchandise.
(E) Many of today's shoppers are too busy to pay careful attention to in-store displays.

14. Roger Bacon, the thirteenth-century scientist, is said to have made important discoveries in optics. He was an early advocate of hands-on experimentation, and as a teacher warned his students against relying uncritically on the opinions of authorities. Nevertheless, this did not stop Bacon himself from appealing to authority when it was expedient for his own argumentation. Thus, Bacon's work on optics should be generally disregarded, in view of the contradiction between his statements and his own behavior.

The reasoning in the argument is flawed because the argument

(A) presumes, without providing justification, that authority opinion is often incorrect
(B) attacks Bacon's uncritical reliance on authority opinion
(C) uses Bacon's remarks to his students as evidence of his opinions
(D) ignores the fact that thirteenth-century science may not hold up well today
(E) criticizes Bacon's character in order to question his scientific findings

15. One's palate is to a great extent socially determined: that is, if we notice that a lot of people enjoy consuming a certain type of food, we will eventually come to like the food as well, once we have become accustomed to the food.

Which one of the following most closely conforms to the principle above?

(A) Maxine spoke to her neighbor about the many different ways he prepared pasta, and after trying some of his recipes found out that she loves to eat pasta.
(B) Mike dislikes lima beans, due to his having parents who dislike them and few family members who enjoy them.
(C) All of George's Ukrainian relatives love to eat pierogis, and by staying with them for several summers, George has become very fond of pierogis as well.
(D) Yolanda dislikes pickles because she has observed that many of her relatives wince when eating pickles.
(E) Sally found jalapeño peppers to be too hot when she first tried them, but now she can eat them without discomfort, because her family members use them frequently in their cooking.

GO ON TO THE NEXT PAGE.

16. The ability to access information via computer is a tremendous resource for visually impaired people. Only a limited amount of printed information is accessible in braille, large type, or audiotape. But a person with the right hardware and software can access a large quantity of information from libraries and museums around the world, and can have the computer read the information aloud, display it in large type, or produce a braille version. Thus, visually impaired people can now access information from computers more easily than they can from most traditional sources.

Which one of the following, if true, most strengthens the argument?

(A) A computerized speech synthesizer is often less expensive than a complete library of audiotapes.

(B) Relatively easy-to-use computer systems that can read information aloud, display it in large type, or produce a braille version of it are widely available.

(C) Many visually impaired people prefer traditional sources of information to computers that can read information aloud, display it in large type, or produce a braille version of it.

(D) Most visually impaired people who have access to information via computer also have access to this same information via more traditional sources.

(E) The rate at which printed information is converted into formats easily accessible to visually impaired people will increase.

17. Legislator: The recently released crime statistics clearly show that the new laws requiring stiffer punishments for violators have reduced the crime rate. In the areas covered by those laws, the incidence of crime has decreased by one-fourth over the four years since the legislation was enacted.

Analyst: The statistics are welcome news, but they do not provide strong evidence that the new laws caused the drop in crime. Many comparable areas that lack such legislation have reported a similar drop in the crime rate during the same period.

Which one of the following most accurately describes the strategy used by the analyst to call into question the legislator's argument?

(A) pointing out that the legislator has provided no evidence of the reliability of the statistics on which the legislator's conclusion is based

(B) arguing that the legislator has unreasonably concluded that one event has caused another without ruling out the possibility that both events are effects of a common cause

(C) objecting that the statistics on which the legislator is basing his conclusion are drawn from a time period that is too short to yield a meaningful data sample

(D) claiming that the legislator has attempted to establish a particular conclusion because doing so is in the legislator's self-interest rather than because of any genuine concern for the truth of the matter

(E) implying that the legislator has drawn a conclusion about cause and effect without considering how often the alleged effect has occurred in the absence of the alleged cause

GO ON TO THE NEXT PAGE.

18. Many physicists claim that quantum mechanics may ultimately be able to explain all fundamental phenomena, and that, therefore, physical theory will soon be complete. However, every theory in the history of physics that was thought to be final eventually had to be rejected for failure to explain some new observation. For this reason, we can expect that quantum mechanics will not be the final theory.

Which one of the following arguments is most similar in its reasoning to the argument above?

(A) Only a few species of plants now grow in very dry climates; therefore, few species of animals can live in those climates.

(B) Four companies have marketed a new food processing product; therefore, a fifth company will not be able to market a similar product.

(C) Your sister is a very good chess player but she has never won a chess tournament; therefore, she will not win this chess tournament.

(D) A rare virus infected a group of people a decade ago; therefore, it will not reinfect the same population now.

(E) Each team member has failed to live up to people's expectations; therefore, the team will not live up to people's expectations.

19. In an experiment, researchers played a series of musical intervals—two-note sequences—to a large, diverse group of six-month-old babies. They found that the babies paid significantly more attention when the intervals were perfect octaves, fifths, or fourths than otherwise. These intervals are prevalent in the musical systems of most cultures around the world. Thus, humans probably have a biological predisposition to pay more attention to those intervals than to others.

Which one of the following, if true, most strengthens the argument?

(A) Several similar experiments using older children and adults found that these subjects, too, had a general tendency to pay more attention to octaves, fifths, and fourths than to other musical intervals.

(B) None of the babies in the experiment had previous exposure to music from any culture.

(C) All of the babies in the experiment had been exposed to music drawn equally from a wide variety of cultures around the world.

(D) In a second experiment, these same babies showed no clear tendency to notice primary colors more than other colors.

(E) Octaves, fifths, and fourths were played more frequently during the experiment than other musical intervals were.

20. Professor Donnelly's exams are always more difficult than Professor Curtis's exams. The question about dinosaurs was on Professor Donnelly's last exam. Therefore, the question must be difficult.

Which one of the following exhibits both of the logical flaws exhibited in the argument above?

(A) Lewis is a better baker than Stockman. Lewis made this cake. Therefore, it must be better than most of Stockman's cakes.

(B) Porter's new book of poetry is better than any of her other books of poetry. This poem is from Porter's new book, so it must be good.

(C) Professor Whitburn is teaching English this year and always assigns a lot of reading. Therefore, this year's English class will have to do more reading than last year's class.

(D) Shield's first novel has a more complicated plot than any other that she has written. Hence, that plot must be very complex.

(E) Mathematics is more difficult than history. Therefore, my calculus test will be more difficult than my history test.

GO ON TO THE NEXT PAGE.

21. Ethicist: As a function of one's job and societal role, one has various duties. There are situations where acting in accord with one of these duties has disastrous consequences, and thus the duties are not absolute. However, it is a principle of morality that if one does not have overwhelming evidence that fulfilling such a duty will have disastrous consequences, one ought to fulfill it.

Which one of the following most closely conforms to the principle of morality cited by the ethicist?

(A) A teacher thinks that a certain student has received the course grade merited by the quality of his work. The teacher should fulfill her duty not to raise the student's grade, even though the lower grade might harm the student's chance of obtaining an internship.

(B) A person should not fulfill his duty to tell his friend the truth about the friend's new haircut, because lying will make the friend happier than the truth would.

(C) A police investigator discovers that a contractor has slightly overcharged wealthy customers in order to lower rates for a charity. The investigator should not fulfill his duty to report the contractor provided that the contractor stops the practice.

(D) A psychiatrist's patient tells her about his recurring nightmares of having committed a terrible crime. The psychiatrist should fulfill her duty to report this to the authorities because the patient may have broken the law, even though the psychiatrist also has a duty of confidentiality to her patients.

(E) A journalist thinks there is a slight chance that a story about a developing crisis will endanger innocent lives. Therefore, the journalist should await further developments before fulfilling his duty to file the story.

22. Detective: Laser-printer drums are easily damaged, and any nick in a drum will produce a blemish of similar dimensions on each page produced by that printer. So in matching a blemish on a page with a nick on a drum, we can reliably trace a suspicious laser-printed document to the precise printer on which it was produced.

Which one of the following, if true, most weakens the detective's argument?

(A) Criminals are unlikely to use their own laser printers to produce suspicious documents.

(B) Drum nicks are usually so small that it requires skill to accurately determine their size and shape.

(C) The manufacturing process often produces the same nick on several drums.

(D) Blemishes on documents are sometimes totally concealed by characters that are printed over them.

(E) Most suspicious documents are not produced on laser printers.

23. Whoever is kind is loved by somebody or other, and whoever loves anyone is happy. It follows that whoever is kind is happy.

The conclusion follows logically if which one of the following is assumed?

(A) Whoever loves someone loves everyone.
(B) Whoever loves everyone loves someone.
(C) Whoever is happy loves everyone.
(D) Whoever loves no one is loved by no one.
(E) Whoever loves everyone is kind.

GO ON TO THE NEXT PAGE.

24. It is now clear that the ancient Egyptians were the first society to produce alcoholic beverages. It had been thought that the ancient Babylonians were the first; they had mastered the process of fermentation for making wine as early as 1500 B.C. However, archaeologists have discovered an Egyptian cup dating from 2000 B.C. whose sides depict what appears to be an Egyptian brewery, and whose chemical residue reveals that it contained a form of alcoholic beer.

The reasoning above is most vulnerable to criticism on which one of the following grounds?

(A) It makes a generalization about Egyptian society based on a sample so small that it is likely to be unrepresentative.

(B) It uses the term "alcoholic beverage" in a different sense in the premises than in the conclusion.

(C) It presumes, without providing justification, that because one society developed a technology before another, the development in the latter was dependent on the development in the former.

(D) It ignores the possibility that the first known instance of a kind is not the first instance of that kind.

(E) It provides no evidence for the claim that the Babylonians produced wine as early as 1500 B.C.

25. Studies have shown that specialty sports foods contain exactly the same nutrients in the same quantities as do common foods from the grocery store. Moreover, sports foods cost from two to three times more than regular foods. So very few athletes would buy sports foods were it not for expensive advertising campaigns.

Which one of the following, if true, most weakens the argument?

(A) Sports foods are occasionally used by world-famous athletes.

(B) Many grocery stores carry sports foods alongside traditional inventories.

(C) Sports foods are easier than regular foods to carry and consume during training and competition.

(D) Regular foods contain vitamins and minerals that are essential to developing strength and endurance.

(E) Sports foods can nutritionally substitute for regular meals.

S T O P

IF YOU FINISH BEFORE TIME IS CALLED, YOU MAY CHECK YOUR WORK ON THIS SECTION ONLY.
DO NOT WORK ON ANY OTHER SECTION IN THE TEST.

SECTION V

Time—35 minutes

25 Questions

<u>Directions:</u> The questions in this section are based on the reasoning contained in brief statements or passages. For some questions, more than one of the choices could conceivably answer the question. However, you are to choose the <u>best</u> answer; that is, the response that most accurately and completely answers the question. You should not make assumptions that are by commonsense standards implausible, superfluous, or incompatible with the passage. After you have chosen the best answer, blacken the corresponding space on your answer sheet.

1. Students in a first-year undergraduate course were divided into two groups. All the students in both groups were given newspaper articles identical in every respect, except for the headline, which was different for each group. When the students were later asked questions about the contents of the article, the answers given by the two groups were markedly different, though within each group the answers were similar.

   Which one of the following is most strongly supported by the information above?

   (A) Readers base their impressions of what is in a newspaper on headlines alone.
   (B) Newspaper headlines hamper a reader's ability to comprehend the corresponding articles.
   (C) Careless reading is more common among first-year undergraduates than among more senior students.
   (D) Newspaper headlines tend to be highly misleading.
   (E) Newspaper headlines influence a reader's interpretation of the corresponding articles.

2. All works of art are beautiful and have something to teach us. Thus, since the natural world as a whole is both beautiful and instructive, it is a work of art.

   The reasoning in the argument is flawed because the argument

   (A) uses the inherently vague term "beautiful" without providing an explicit definition of that term
   (B) attempts to establish an evaluative conclusion solely on the basis of claims about factual matters
   (C) concludes, simply because an object possesses two qualities that are each common to all works of art, that the object is a work of art
   (D) presumes, without providing justification, that only objects that are beautiful are instructive
   (E) fails to consider the possibility that there are many things that are both beautiful and instructive but are not part of the natural world

3. When Copernicus changed the way we think about the solar system, he did so not by discovering new information, but by looking differently at information already available. Edward Jenner's discovery of a smallpox vaccine occurred when he shifted his focus to disease prevention from the then more common emphasis on cure. History is replete with breakthroughs of this sort.

   The examples provided above illustrate which one of the following?

   (A) Many valuable intellectual accomplishments occur by chance.
   (B) Shifting from earlier modes of thought can result in important advances.
   (C) The ability to look at information from a different point of view is rare.
   (D) Understanding is advanced less often by better organization of available information than it is by the accumulation of new information.
   (E) Dramatic intellectual breakthroughs are more easily accomplished in fields in which the amount of information available is relatively small.

4. Politician: Suppose censorship is wrong in itself, as modern liberals tend to believe. Then an actor's refusing a part in a film because the film glamorizes a point of view abhorrent to the actor would be morally wrong. But this conclusion is absurd. It follows that censorship is not, after all, wrong in itself.

   The reasoning in the politician's argument is most vulnerable to criticism on the grounds that this argument

   (A) presumes, without providing justification, that actors would subscribe to any tenet of modern liberalism
   (B) uses the term "liberal" in order to discredit opponents' point of view
   (C) takes for granted that there is a moral obligation to practice one's profession
   (D) draws a conclusion that is inconsistent with a premise it accepts
   (E) presumes, without providing justification, that declining a film role constitutes censorship in the relevant sense

GO ON TO THE NEXT PAGE.

5. Motor oil serves to lubricate engines and thus retard engine wear. A study was conducted to assess the effectiveness of various brands of motor oil by using them in taxicabs over a 6,000-mile test period. All the oils did equally well in retarding wear on pistons and cylinders, the relevant parts of the engine. Hence, cheaper brands of oil are the best buys.

Which one of the following, if true, most weakens the argument?

(A) Cheaper brands of motor oil are often used by knowledgeable automobile mechanics for their own cars.

(B) Tests other than of the ability to reduce engine wear also can reliably gauge the quality of motor oil.

(C) The lubricating properties of all motor oils deteriorate over time, and the rate of deterioration is accelerated by heat.

(D) The engines of some individual cars that have had their oil changed every 3,000 miles, using only a certain brand of oil, have lasted an extraordinarily long time.

(E) Ability to retard engine wear is not the only property of motor oil important to the running of an engine.

6. Elena: The best form of government is one that fosters the belief among its citizens that they have a say in how the government is run. Thus, democracy is the best form of government.

Marsha: But there are many forms of government under which citizens can be manipulated into believing they have a say when they don't.

Marsha's claim that it is possible for governments to manipulate people into thinking that they have a say when they do not is used to

(A) concur with Elena's claim that democracy is the best form of government

(B) support Marsha's unstated conclusion that the best form of government is one that appears to be democratic but really is not

(C) suggest that the premise Elena uses to support her conclusion could be used to support a conflicting conclusion

(D) support Marsha's unstated conclusion that most people seek only the appearance of democracy rather than democracy itself

(E) reject Elena's conclusion that the best form of government is democracy

7. Researcher: The use of the newest drug in treating this disease should be discontinued. The treatment usually wreaks havoc with the normal functioning of the human body, causing severe side effects such as total loss of hair, debilitating nausea, and intense pain in the joints.

The argument's reasoning is flawed because the argument

(A) fails to specify what is meant by "normal functioning of the human body"

(B) fails to consider the consequences of not administering the treatment

(C) presumes that every patient with the disease is treated with the drug

(D) does not consider the length of time needed for the treatment to begin taking effect

(E) does not acknowledge that the effects of the treatment may not be of the same severity in all cases

8. Otis: Aristotle's principle of justice says that we should treat relevantly similar cases similarly. Therefore, it is wrong for a dentist to schedule an after-hours appointment to suit a family friend but refuse to do it for anyone else.

Tyra: I accept Aristotle's principle of justice, but it's human nature to want to do special favors for friends. Indeed, that's what friends are—those for whom you would do special favors. It's not unjust for dentists to do that.

It can be inferred on the basis of their statements that Otis and Tyra disagree about whether

(A) Aristotle's principle of justice is widely applicable

(B) situations involving friends and situations involving others should be considered relevantly similar cases

(C) human nature makes it impossible to treat relevantly similar cases similarly

(D) dentists should be willing to schedule an after-hours appointment for anyone who asks

(E) Aristotle recognizes that friendship sometimes morally outweighs justice

GO ON TO THE NEXT PAGE.

9. Typically, people who have diets high in saturated fat have an increased risk of heart disease. Those who replace saturated fat in their diets with unsaturated fat decrease their risk of heart disease. Therefore, people who eat a lot of saturated fat can lower their risk of heart disease by increasing their intake of unsaturated fat.

Which one of the following, if assumed, most helps to justify the reasoning above?

(A) People who add unsaturated fat to their diets will eat less food that is high in saturated fat.

(B) Adding unsaturated fat to a diet brings health benefits other than a reduced risk of heart disease.

(C) Diet is the most important factor in a person's risk of heart disease.

(D) Taking steps to prevent heart disease is one of the most effective ways of increasing life expectancy.

(E) It is difficult to move from a diet that is high in saturated fat to a diet that includes very little fat.

10. Only people who are willing to compromise should undergo mediation to resolve their conflicts. Actual litigation should be pursued only when one is sure that one's position is correct. People whose conflicts are based on ideology are unwilling to compromise.

If the statements above are true, then which one of the following must be true?

(A) People who do not undergo mediation to resolve their conflicts should be sure that their positions are correct.

(B) People whose conflicts are not based on ideology should attempt to resolve their conflicts by means of litigation.

(C) People whose conflicts are based on ideology are not always sure that their positions are correct.

(D) People who are sure of the correctness of their positions are not people who should undergo mediation to resolve their conflicts.

(E) People whose conflicts are based on ideology are not people who should undergo mediation to resolve their conflicts.

11. Scientists have long thought that omega-3 fatty acids in fish oil tend to lower blood cholesterol and strongly suspected that a diet that includes a modest amount of fish would provide substantial health benefits. Now these views have acquired strong support from a recent study showing that middle-aged people who eat fish twice a week are nearly 30 percent less likely to develop heart disease than are those who do not eat fish.

Which one of the following is an assumption required by the argument?

(A) The test subjects in the recent study who did not eat fish were not vegetarians.

(B) The test subjects in the recent study who ate fish twice a week did not have a diet that was otherwise conducive to the development of heart disease.

(C) The test subjects in the recent study who did not eat fish were significantly more likely to eat red meat several times per week than were those who did eat fish.

(D) The test subjects in the recent study who ate fish twice a week were not significantly more likely than those who did not to engage regularly in activities known to augment cardiorespiratory health.

(E) The test subjects in the recent study who ate fish twice a week were no more likely than those who did not to have sedentary occupations.

GO ON TO THE NEXT PAGE.

12. Researcher: A number of studies have suggested that, on average, clients in short-term psychotherapy show similar levels of improvement regardless of the kind of psychotherapy they receive. So any client improvement in short-term psychotherapy must be the result of some aspect or aspects of therapy that are common to all psychotherapies— for example, the presence of someone who listens and gives attention to the client.

Which one of the following, if true, would most weaken the researcher's argument?

(A) The methods by which the studies measured whether clients improved primarily concerned immediate symptom relief and failed to address other important kinds of improvement.

(B) On average, clients improve more dramatically when they receive long-term psychotherapy, a year or longer in duration, than when clients receive short-term psychotherapy.

(C) The studies found that psychotherapy by a trained counselor does not result in any greater improvement, on average, among clients than does simple counseling by an untrained layperson.

(D) The specific techniques and interventions used by therapists practicing different kinds of psychotherapy differ dramatically.

(E) More-experienced therapists tend to use a wider range of techniques and interventions in psychotherapy than do inexperienced therapists.

13. Journalists sometimes use historical photographs to illustrate articles about current events. But this recycling of old photographs overstates the similarities between past and present, and thereby denies the individual significance of those current events. Hence, the use of historical photographs in this manner by journalists distorts public understanding of the present by presenting current events as mere repetitions of historical incidents.

Which one of the following, if assumed, enables the conclusion of the argument to be properly inferred?

(A) Any practice by which journalists present current events as mere repetitions of historical incidents overstates the similarities between past and present.

(B) If the work of a journalist overstates the similarities between past and present, then it distorts public understanding of the present by presenting current events as mere repetitions of historical incidents.

(C) If a journalistic practice distorts public understanding of the present by overstating the similarities between past and present, then it denies the individual significance of any articles about current events.

(D) No article about a current event treats that event as merely a repetition of historical incidents unless it uses historical photographs to illustrate that article.

(E) If journalists believe current events to be mere repetitions of historical incidents, then public understanding of the present will be distorted.

GO ON TO THE NEXT PAGE.

14. If Juan went to the party, it is highly unlikely that Maria would have enjoyed the party. But in fact it turned out that Maria did enjoy the party; therefore, it is highly unlikely that Juan was at the party.

The pattern of reasoning in the argument above is most similar to that in which one of the following?

(A) According to the newspaper, all eight teams in the soccer tournament have an equal chance of winning it. If so, then we will probably lose our goalie, since if we do lose our goalie we will probably not win the tournament.

(B) Kapinski, our new neighbor, is probably friendly, for Kapinski sells insurance and most people who sell insurance are friendly.

(C) If the lottery were fair, the person who won the lottery would not have been likely to win it. Thus, since this person would have been likely to win the lottery if it were unfair, the lottery was probably unfair.

(D) If Clarissa missed the bus today, it is quite unlikely that she would have gotten to work on time. So, it is quite unlikely that Clarissa missed the bus, since she actually was at work on time today.

(E) This year's election will probably be fair. But Popov probably will not win unless the election is unfair. So, Popov will not win the election.

15. Sonya: Anyone who lives without constant awareness of the fragility and precariousness of human life has a mind clouded by illusion. Yet those people who are perpetually cognizant of the fragility and precariousness of human life surely taint their emotional outlook on existence.

Sonya's statements, if true, most strongly support which one of the following?

(A) Anyone who places a higher priority on maintaining a positive emotional outlook than on dispelling illusion will be completely unaware of the fragility and precariousness of human life.

(B) Either no one has a tainted emotional outlook on existence, or no one has a mind clouded by illusion.

(C) It is impossible for anyone to live without some degree of self-deception.

(D) Everyone whose emotional outlook on existence is untainted has a mind clouded by illusion.

(E) It is better to be aware of the fragility and precariousness of human life than to have an untainted emotional outlook on existence.

16. In a study, shoppers who shopped in a grocery store without a shopping list and bought only items that were on sale for half price or less spent far more money on a comparable number of items than did shoppers in the same store who used a list and bought no sale items.

Which one of the following, if true, most helps to explain the apparent paradox in the study's results?

(A) Only the shoppers who used a list used a shopping cart.

(B) The shoppers who did not use lists bought many unnecessary items.

(C) Usually, only the most expensive items go on sale in grocery stores.

(D) The grocery store in the study carries many expensive items that few other grocery stores carry.

(E) The grocery store in the study places relatively few items on sale.

17. A group of mountain climbers was studied to determine how they were affected by diminished oxygen in the air at high altitudes. As they climbed past 6,100 meters above sea level, the climbers slurred words, took longer to understand simple sentences, and demonstrated poor judgment. This combination of worsened performances disproves the theory that the area of the brain controlling speech is distinct from that controlling other functions.

The argument is most vulnerable to criticism on the grounds that it overlooks the possibility that

(A) the climbers' performance in speech, comprehension, and reasoning was impaired because oxygen deprivation affected their entire brains

(B) the climbers' performance in speech, comprehension, and reasoning was better than average before they were studied

(C) the climbers showed different levels of impairment in their performance in speech, comprehension, and reasoning

(D) some of the effects described were apparent just before the climbers reached 6,100 meters

(E) many of the climbers had engaged in special training before the climb because they wanted to improve the efficiency with which their bodies use oxygen

GO ON TO THE NEXT PAGE.

18. It was once thought that pesticide TSX-400 was extremely harmful to the environment but that pesticides Envirochem and Zanar were environmentally harmless. TSX-400 was banned; Envirochem and Zanar were not. However, according to recent studies, Envirochem and Zanar each cause greater environmental harm than does TSX-400. If these studies are accurate, then either Envirochem and Zanar should be banned or TSX-400 should be legalized.

Which one of the following principles, if valid, most helps to justify the argumentation?

(A) Two pesticides should not both be legal if one is measurably more harmful to the environment than the other is.

(B) Two pesticides should both be legal only if neither is harmful to the environment.

(C) Two pesticides should both be illegal only if both are harmful to the environment.

(D) One pesticide should be legal and another illegal only if the former is less harmful to the environment than is the latter.

(E) One pesticide should be legal and another illegal if the former is harmless to the environment and the latter is harmful to it.

19. Recent studies have demonstrated that smokers are more likely than nonsmokers to develop heart disease. Other studies have established that smokers are more likely than others to drink caffeinated beverages. Therefore, even though drinking caffeinated beverages is not thought to be a cause of heart disease, there is a positive correlation between drinking caffeinated beverages and the development of heart disease.

The argument's reasoning is most vulnerable to criticism on the grounds that the argument fails to take into account the possibility that

(A) smokers who drink caffeinated beverages are less likely to develop heart disease than are smokers who do not drink caffeinated beverages

(B) something else, such as dietary fat intake, may be a more important factor in the development of heart disease than are the factors cited in the argument

(C) drinking caffeinated beverages is more strongly correlated with the development of heart disease than is smoking

(D) it is only among people who have a hereditary predisposition to heart disease that caffeine consumption is positively correlated with the development of heart disease

(E) there is a common cause of both the development of heart disease and behaviors such as drinking caffeinated beverages and smoking

20. The layouts of supermarkets are not accidental: they are part of a plan designed to make customers walk all the way to the back of the store just to pick up a loaf of bread, passing tempting displays the whole way. But supermarkets can alienate customers by placing popular items in the rear; surveys list inconvenience as shoppers' top reason for disliking supermarkets.

Which one of the following propositions does the passage most precisely illustrate?

(A) Supermarkets should focus on customers who want to purchase many items in a single trip.

(B) Alienation of customers is not good for business.

(C) Even well-thought-out plans can fail.

(D) Distracting customers is not good for business.

(E) Manipulation of people can have unwelcome consequences.

21. Doctor: Medication to reduce blood pressure often has unhealthy side effects. However, lifestyle changes such as exercising more and avoiding fatty foods reduce blood pressure just as effectively as taking medication does. Therefore, it is healthier to rely on these lifestyle changes than on medication to reduce blood pressure.

Which one of the following is an assumption that the doctor's argument requires?

(A) Other than medication, the only way to reduce blood pressure is by making lifestyle changes such as exercising more and avoiding fatty foods.

(B) If it is healthier to rely on a lifestyle change than on medication to reduce blood pressure, then that lifestyle change reduces blood pressure at least as effectively as medication does.

(C) The side effects, if any, of exercising more and avoiding fatty foods in order to reduce blood pressure are less unhealthy than those of taking medication to reduce blood pressure.

(D) If an alternative to medication relieves a medical condition just as effectively as medication does, then it is always healthier to rely on that alternative than on medication to relieve that medical condition.

(E) If two different methods of treating a medical condition have similar side effects, then it is healthier to rely on the more effective method.

GO ON TO THE NEXT PAGE.

22. Columnist: Several recent studies show, and insurance statistics confirm, that more pedestrians are killed every year in North American cities when crossing with the light than when crossing against it. Crossing against the light in North American cities is therefore less dangerous than crossing with the light.

The columnist's reasoning is most vulnerable to criticism on the grounds that it

(A) relies on sources that are likely to be biased in their reporting
(B) presumes, without providing justification, that because two things are correlated there must be a causal relationship between them
(C) does not adequately consider the possibility that a correlation between two events may be explained by a common cause
(D) ignores the possibility that the effects of the types of actions considered might be quite different in environments other than the ones studied
(E) ignores possible differences in the frequency of the two actions whose risk is being assessed

23. Many scientific studies have suggested that taking melatonin tablets can induce sleep. But this does not mean that melatonin is helpful in treating insomnia. Most of the studies examined only people without insomnia, and in many of the studies, only a few of the subjects given melatonin appeared to be significantly affected by it.

Which one of the following, if true, most strengthens the argument?

(A) A weaker correlation between taking melatonin and the inducement of sleep was found in the studies that included people with insomnia than in the studies that did not.
(B) None of the studies that suggested that taking melatonin tablets can induce sleep examined a fully representative sample of the human population.
(C) In the studies that included subjects with insomnia, only subjects without insomnia were significantly affected by doses of melatonin.
(D) Several people who were in control groups and only given placebos claimed that the tablets induced sleep.
(E) If melatonin were helpful in treating insomnia, then every person with insomnia who took doses of melatonin would appear to be significantly affected by it.

GO ON TO THE NEXT PAGE.

24. The asteroid that hit the Yucatán Peninsula 65 million years ago caused both long-term climatic change and a tremendous firestorm that swept across North America. We cannot show that it was this fire that caused the extinction of the triceratops, a North American dinosaur in existence at the time of the impact of the asteroid. Nor can we show that the triceratops became extinct due to the climatic changes resulting from the asteroid's impact. Hence, we cannot attribute the triceratops's extinction to the asteroid's impact.

Which one of the following has flawed reasoning most similar to the flawed reasoning in the argument above?

(A) I know that one cannot move this piano unless one can lift at least 150 kilograms. I doubt that either Leon or Pam can lift 150 kilograms alone. So I doubt that either Leon or Pam can move this piano alone. Thus, I doubt that Leon and Pam can move this piano together.

(B) Since we are quite sure that Cheng and Lin are the only candidates in the mayoral election, we can be quite sure that either Cheng or Lin will win the election. Therefore, either we know that Cheng will win or we know that Lin will win.

(C) It has not been conclusively proven that the accident was caused by John's driving at excessive speeds. Nor has it been conclusively proven that the accident was the result of John's weaving out of his lane. Hence, it has been conclusively proven that the cause of the accident was neither John's driving at excessive speeds nor John's weaving out of his lane.

(D) The flooding in the basement caused damage to the furnace and also caused a short in the electrical system. Fire investigators could not show that the damage to the furnace caused the fire that resulted shortly after the flooding, nor could they show that the fire was caused by the short in the electrical system. Therefore, we cannot claim that the flooding in the basement caused the fire.

(E) We have good reason to believe that the cause of the flooding along the coast was the unusually high tides. We also have good reason to believe that the cause of the unusually high tides was either the sun or the moon. So it is reasonable to maintain that the cause of the flooding was either the sun or the moon.

25. Economist: Although obviously cuts in personal income tax rates for the upper income brackets disproportionately benefit the wealthy, across-the-board cuts for all brackets tend to have a similar effect. Personal income tax rates are progressive (i.e., graduated), and if total revenue remains constant, then across-the-board cuts in these taxes require increasing the amount of revenue generated through nonprogressive taxes, thereby favoring the wealthy. Yet if nonprogressive taxes are not increased to compensate for the cuts, then the budget deficit will increase, requiring more government borrowing and driving up interest rates. This favors those who have money to lend, once again benefiting primarily the wealthy.

Which one of the following statements most accurately expresses the main conclusion of the economist's argument?

(A) Cuts in personal income tax rates for upper income brackets benefit the wealthy more than they benefit others.

(B) Across-the-board cuts in personal income tax rates do not generate enough additional economic activity to prevent a net loss of revenue.

(C) It is the wealthy who are favored by generating a high amount of revenue through nonprogressive taxes.

(D) It is primarily the wealthy who benefit from increases in the budget deficit, which drive up interest rates.

(E) Across-the-board personal income tax rate cuts generally benefit the wealthy more than they benefit others.

S T O P

IF YOU FINISH BEFORE TIME IS CALLED, YOU MAY CHECK YOUR WORK ON THIS SECTION ONLY.
DO NOT WORK ON ANY OTHER SECTION IN THE TEST.

Acknowledgment is made to the following sources from which material has been adapted for use in this test booklet:

Elise Hancock, "Unpredictable Outcomes Could Be 'Poison' to Science." ©1994 by The Johns Hopkins University.

"Motor Oil: What's Best for Your Car?" ©1996 by Consumer Reports.

Angela Pirist, "Why Tots Can't Play by the Rules." © 1996 by Sussex Publishers Inc.

Martha Robles, "An Historical Adventure: Notes on Chicano Literature." © 1992 by TriQuarterly.

Edward W. Said, *Culture and Imperialism.* © 1993 by Edward W. Said.

James Shreeve, "Music of the Hemispheres" © October 1996 by Discover.

Wait for the supervisor's instructions before you open the page to the topic.
Please print and sign your name and write the date in the designated spaces below.

Time: 35 Minutes

General Directions

You will have 35 minutes in which to plan and write an essay on the topic inside. Read the topic and the accompanying directions carefully. You will probably find it best to spend a few minutes considering the topic and organizing your thoughts before you begin writing. In your essay, be sure to develop your ideas fully, leaving time, if possible, to review what you have written. **Do not write on a topic other than the one specified. Writing on a topic of your own choice is not acceptable.**

No special knowledge is required or expected for this writing exercise. Law schools are interested in the reasoning, clarity, organization, language usage, and writing mechanics displayed in your essay. How well you write is more important than how much you write.

Confine your essay to the blocked, lined area on the front and back of the separate Writing Sample Response Sheet. Only that area will be reproduced for law schools. Be sure that your writing is legible.

Both this topic sheet and your response sheet must be turned over to the testing staff before you leave the room.

Topic Code	Print Your Full Name Here		
_____	Last	First	M.I.

Date	Sign Your Name Here
/ /	

Scratch Paper
Do not write your essay in this space.

LSAT WRITING SAMPLE TOPIC

Calvin, the hiring manager for Ocean Blue Cruise Line, is seeking a permanent chef for a cruise ship. In the meantime, he has found someone who can commit to a three-month contract and someone else who can commit to a six-month contact. Calvin has decided that Ocean Blue should enter into one of the limited-term contracts. Write an essay in which you argue for choosing one chef over the other, keeping in mind the following two criteria:

- Ocean Blue would like to hire a chef who can take over management of the large galley staff.
- Ocean Blue would like to hire a permanent chef as soon as possible.

Marie, who has served as executive chef in a large resort kitchen for the past three years, is available for a three-month contract, with no possibility of her staying on permanently. She has earned a strong reputation for competence in kitchen organization and management. Her objective, should she be offered the contract, is to reorganize and streamline the galley operations to sustain a degree of efficiency and productivity even after she leaves. Because Marie is also affiliated with a cooking school, Calvin would have the opportunity to establish contacts that might lead to the permanent hire he desires to make.

Jared is available to take on a six-month contract. Early in his career, he served as an assistant pastry chef on a cruise ship in a nonmanagement role. He has since had a very successful fourteen-year career managing a small catering company, in which he was responsible for staffing, food planning, and quality control, but he has never managed a staff as large as the ship's galley staff and would have to learn on his feet. While the contract with Jared offers Ocean Blue a greater period of stability and security than the shorter three-month contract does, it takes the cruise line off the market for hiring a permanent employee for twice as long. However, Jared has indicated that he would probably be willing to accept the permanent position at the end of the contract.

Scratch Paper
Do not write your essay in this space.

LAST NAME (Print)   MI   FIRST NAME (Print)

SIGNATURE

Writing Sample Response Sheet

DO NOT WRITE
IN THIS SPACE

**Begin your essay in the lined area below.
Continue on the back if you need more space.**

This test can be scored automatically with your Online Center. The following Answer Key and Scoring Table are provided if you wish to score it offline.

Directions:

1. Use the Answer Key on the next page to check your answers.

2. Use the Scoring Worksheet below to compute your raw score.

3. Use the Score Conversion Chart to convert your raw score into the 120–180 scale.

Scoring Worksheet

1. Enter the number of questions you answered correctly in each section

   Number Correct

   SECTION I . . . . _____

   SECTION II . . . . _____

   SECTION III . . . . . . _____

   SECTION IV . . . . . . <u>EXP</u>

   SECTION V . . . . _____

2. Enter the sum here: _____

   This is your Raw Score.

Conversion Chart

For Converting Raw Score to the 120–180 LSAT Scaled Score LSAT Prep Test 50

Reported Score	Lowest Raw Score	Highest Raw Score
180	98	100
179	97	97
178	—*	—*
177	96	96
176	95	95
175	94	94
174	—*	—*
173	93	93
172	92	92
171	91	91
170	90	90
169	89	89
168	88	88
167	86	87
166	85	85
165	84	84
164	83	83
163	81	82
162	80	80
161	78	79
160	77	77
159	75	76
158	73	74
157	72	72
156	70	71
155	68	69
154	66	67
153	64	65
152	63	63
151	61	62
150	59	60
149	57	58
148	55	56
147	53	54
146	52	52
145	50	51
144	48	49
143	46	47
142	45	45
141	43	44
140	41	42
139	40	40
138	38	39
137	36	37
136	35	35
135	33	34
134	32	32
133	30	31
132	29	29
131	27	28
130	26	26
129	25	25
128	23	24
127	22	22
126	21	21
125	20	20
124	18	19
123	17	17
122	16	16
121	15	15
120	0	14

*There is no raw score that will produce this scaled score for this test.

SECTION I

1.	C	8.	A	15.	C	22.	B
2.	D	9.	E	16.	A	23.	D
3.	C	10.	A	17.	D	24.	C
4.	B	11.	B	18.	C	25.	E
5.	D	12.	D	19.	D	26.	C
6.	A	13.	E	20.	A	27.	D
7.	D	14.	E	21.	D	28.	B

SECTION II

1.	B	8.	A	15.	E	22.	D
2.	B	9.	B	16.	C	23.	E
3.	A	10.	B	17.	A	24.	A
4.	E	11.	E	18.	C	25.	D
5.	B	12.	A	19.	A		
6.	C	13.	D	20.	C		
7.	B	14.	D	21.	E		

SECTION III

1.	D	8.	B	15.	A	22.	A
2.	B	9.	A	16.	E		
3.	C	10.	E	17.	E		
4.	E	11.	B	18.	B		
5.	B	12.	B	19.	D		
6.	E	13.	B	20.	E		
7.	D	14.	C	21.	D		

SECTION IV

1.	D	8.	E	15.	C	22.	C
2.	E	9.	B	16.	B	23.	D
3.	B	10.	A	17.	E	24.	D
4.	A	11.	A	18.	C	25.	C
5.	A	12.	E	19.	B		
6.	B	13.	D	20.	B		
7.	B	14.	E	21.	A		

SECTION V

1.	E	8.	B	15.	D	22.	E
2.	C	9.	A	16.	C	23.	C
3.	B	10.	E	17.	A	24.	D
4.	E	11.	D	18.	D	25.	E
5.	E	12.	A	19.	A		
6.	C	13.	B	20.	E		
7.	B	14.	D	21.	C		

Practice Test 4

PrepTest 48 with Additional Section from PrepTest 46

SECTION I

Time—35 minutes

26 Questions

Directions: The questions in this section are based on the reasoning contained in brief statements or passages. For some questions, more than one of the choices could conceivably answer the question. However, you are to choose the best answer; that is, the response that most accurately and completely answers the question. You should not make assumptions that are by commonsense standards implausible, superfluous, or incompatible with the passage. After you have chosen the best answer, blacken the corresponding space on your answer sheet.

1. The effort involved in lying produces measurable physiological reactions such as a speedup of the heartbeat. Since lying is accompanied by physiological reactions, lie-detector tests that can detect these reactions are a sure way of determining when someone is lying.

Which one of the following statements, if true, most seriously weakens the argument?

(A) Lie-detector tests can measure only some of the physiological reactions that occur when someone is lying.

(B) People are often unaware that they are having physiological reactions of the sort measured by lie-detector tests.

(C) Lying about past criminal behavior does not necessarily produce stronger physiological reactions than does lying about other things.

(D) For people who are not lying, the tension of taking a lie-detector test can produce physiological reactions identical to the ones that accompany the act of lying.

(E) When employers use lie-detector tests as part of their preemployment screening, some candidates tested are highly motivated to lie.

2. Publishing executive: Our company must sell at least 100,000 books to make a profit this year. However, it is unlikely that we will sell that many, since of the twelve titles we will sell, the one with the best sales prospects, a novel, is unlikely to sell as many as 100,000 copies.

The publishing executive's argument is most vulnerable to criticism because it overlooks the possibility that

(A) the publishing company will sell considerably fewer than 100,000 copies of the novel

(B) the publishing company will not make a profit even if it sells more than 100,000 books

(C) what is true of the overall profitability of a publishing company is not true of its profitability in a particular year

(D) what is true of the sales prospects of the publishing company's individual titles is not true of the sales prospects of the group of titles as a whole

(E) the publishing company will sell even fewer books if it does not advertise its books efficiently

3. A recent study proves that at least some people possess an independent "sixth sense" that allows them to detect whether someone is watching them. In the study, subjects were seated one at a time in the center of a room facing away from a large window. On average, subjects decided correctly 60 percent of the time whether or not they were being watched through the window.

Which one of the following, if true, most supports the conclusion drawn from the study mentioned above?

(A) Most of the time, subjects said they were being watched.

(B) The person recording the experimental results was careful not to interact with the subjects after the experiment ended.

(C) A similar result was found when the subjects were watched from another room on a video monitor.

(D) The room in which the subjects were seated was not soundproof.

(E) The subjects were mostly graduate students in psychology from a nearby university.

GO ON TO THE NEXT PAGE.

4. Philosopher: We should not disapprove of the unearthing of truths that we would rather not acknowledge or that, by their dissemination, might influence society in pernicious ways.

Which one of the following conforms most closely to the principle stated by the philosopher?

(A) A law enforcement officer should not act upon illegally obtained information, even though such action might, in some cases, result in a benefit to society.

(B) Scientific research should not be restricted even if it could lead to harmful applications, such as the manufacture of sophisticated weapons.

(C) A physician should never withhold the truth from a patient, except in cases where depression induced by bad news might significantly affect the patient's recuperation.

(D) Investigative journalists who employ illegal means of obtaining information should not be subjected to moral disapproval, if the revelation of that information does more good for society than does its suppression.

(E) A poem need not adhere too strictly to the truth. Art is exempt from such requirements—it matters only that the poem provoke a response in the reader.

5. Compact discs (CDs) offer an improvement in artistic freedom over vinyl records. As the record needle moves in toward a vinyl record's center, it must fight centrifugal force. Wide, shallow, or jagged grooves will cause the needle to jump; consequently, the song nearest the center—the last song on the side—cannot have especially loud, high-pitched, or low-pitched passages. The CD suffers no such limitations, leaving artists free to end recordings with any song.

Which one of the following most accurately expresses the main conclusion of the argument?

(A) CDs provide greater artistic latitude than do vinyl records.

(B) On vinyl records, the song farthest from the center can have loud, high-pitched, or low-pitched passages.

(C) As the record needle moves in toward the vinyl record's center, the centrifugal force on the needle becomes stronger.

(D) CDs represent a considerable technological advance over vinyl records.

(E) CDs can have louder passages, as well as both higher- and lower-pitched passages, than can vinyl records.

6. The public interest comprises many interests and the broadcast media must serve all of them. Perhaps most television viewers would prefer an action show to an opera. But a constant stream of action shows on all channels is not in the public interest. Thus, _____.

Which one of the following most logically completes the argument?

(A) broadcasters' obligations are not satisfied if they look only to popularity to decide their programming schedules

(B) television networks should broadcast more artistic and cultural shows and fewer action shows

(C) the public interest should be considered whenever television producers develop a new program

(D) the popularity of a television program is a poor indicator of its artistic quality

(E) broadcast media could be rightly accused of neglecting the public interest only if all channels carried mostly action shows

7. Enthusiasm for the use of calculators in the learning of mathematics is misplaced. Teachers rightly observe that in some cases calculators enable students to focus on general principles rather than the tedious, largely rote calculations that constitute the application of these principles. But principles are more likely to be remembered when knowledge of them is grounded in habits ingrained by painstaking applications of those principles. The very fact that calculators make calculation easier, therefore, makes it reasonable to restrict their use.

Which one of the following, if true, most strengthens the argument?

(A) Some students who know how to use calculators also thoroughly understand the mathematical principles that calculators obey.

(B) Slide rules, which are less technologically sophisticated analogues of calculators, were widely used in the learning of mathematics several decades ago.

(C) It is much more important that students retain the knowledge of general principles than that this knowledge be easily acquired.

(D) Habits that are acquired by laborious and sometimes tedious practice are not as valuable as those that are painlessly mastered.

(E) Teachers' enthusiasm for new educational aids is often not proportional to the pedagogical effectiveness of those devices.

GO ON TO THE NEXT PAGE.

8. Commentator: Most journalists describe their individual political orientations as liberal, and it is often concluded that there is therefore a liberal bias in current journalism. This is not the case, however, because newspapers, magazines, radio, and television are all in the business of selling news and advertising, and therefore face market pressures that tend to keep them impartial, since in order to maximize profits they must target the broadest customer base possible.

Which one of the following most accurately expresses the main conclusion drawn by the commentator's argument?

(A) The individual political orientations of journalists do not constitute acceptable evidence regarding media bias.
(B) Major media face significant market pressures.
(C) Current journalism does not have a liberal political bias.
(D) Major media must target the broadest customer base possible in order to maximize profits.
(E) It is often maintained that current journalism has a liberal bias.

9. Theories generated by scientific research were used to develop several products that, although useful, damage the environment severely. The scientists who conducted the research, however, should not be held responsible for that damage, since they merely generated the theories and could neither foresee nor restrict the kinds of products that might be designed using those theories.

Which one of the following principles, if established, justifies the conclusion above?

(A) Individuals who develop something that has desirable characteristics should not be held responsible for any undesirable characteristics that the thing has if improperly used.
(B) Individuals are justified in performing an activity that has both desirable and undesirable foreseeable consequences only if they alone bear its undesirable consequences.
(C) Individuals should receive credit for the foreseeable desirable consequences of the activities they perform only if those individuals are to be held responsible for any unforeseeable undesirable consequences those activities might have.
(D) Individuals who perform an activity should not be held responsible for any unforeseen undesirable consequences that arise from the use to which others put the results of that activity.
(E) Individuals should be held responsible for the foreseeable undesirable consequences of the activities that they perform and receive credit for the foreseeable desirable consequences of those activities.

10. The administration at a certain university has explained this year's tuition increase by citing increased spending on faculty salaries and on need-based aid to students. However, this year's budget indicated that faculty salaries constitute a small part of the university's expenditure, and the only significant increases in scholarship aid have gone to academic scholarships awarded regardless of need. The administration's explanation is not believable.

Which one of the following, if true, most strengthens the argument that the administration's explanation is not believable?

(A) With this year's budget, the university has increased its total spending on scholarship aid by 5 percent.
(B) With this year's budget, the university increased the allotment for faculty salaries by 5 percent while tuition was increased by 6 percent.
(C) Faculty salaries at the university have increased in line with the national average, and substantial cuts in government student-loan programs have caused financial difficulties for many students at the university.
(D) Of the substantial items in the budget, the greatest increase was in administrative costs, facilities maintenance costs, and costs associated with the provision of athletic facilities.
(E) Because enrollment projections at the university are very unreliable, it is difficult to accurately estimate the amount of money the university will collect from tuition fees ahead of time.

11. Students asked by a psychologist to tell a lie before discussion groups vastly overestimated how many people in the discussion groups could tell they were lying. Other research has found that when volleyball players perform unusually poorly on the court, teammates notice this far less often than the players expect. Finally, in one research experiment a student wearing a funny T-shirt entered a room full of people. Questioning revealed that only a small fraction of the people in the room noticed the shirt, contrary to the student's expectations.

Which one of the following is best illustrated by the statements above?

(A) People tend to be far less aware of their own appearance and behavior than are other people.
(B) People tend not to notice the appearance or behavior of others.
(C) We are actually less observant of the appearance and behavior of others than we think ourselves to be.
(D) People will notice the appearance or behavior of others only if it is specifically highlighted in some way.
(E) People tend to believe their appearance and behavior are noticed by others more often than is actually the case.

GO ON TO THE NEXT PAGE.

12. Extinction is inevitable for all biological species. In fact, the vast majority of all species that have ever lived are now extinct. Since all species die out eventually, there is no justification for trying to protect species that are presently endangered, even those that can be saved from extinction now.

The reasoning in the argument above is most closely paralleled by the argument that there is no reason to

(A) look for a book in the library because it is sometimes checked out
(B) spend money on preventive maintenance of a car because no car can last indefinitely
(C) reinforce bridges against earthquakes in earthquake-prone areas because earthquakes occur only very infrequently
(D) take a route that will avoid the normal traffic jams because traffic jams can occur along any route
(E) plant a flower garden in soil that is not beneficial to plants because the plants are likely to die in such soil

13. Psychology professor: Applied statistics should be taught only by the various social science departments. These departments can best teach their respective students which statistical methodologies are most useful for their discipline, and how best to interpret collected data and the results of experiments.

Mathematics professor: I disagree. My applied statistics course covers much of the same material taught in the applied statistics courses in social science departments. In fact, my course uses exactly the same textbook as those courses!

Which one of the following most accurately describes a questionable aspect of the reasoning in the mathematics professor's response to the psychology professor?

(A) The response gives no evidence for its presumption that students willing to take a course in one department would choose a similar course in another.
(B) The response gives no evidence for its presumption that social science students should have the same competence in statistics as mathematics students.
(C) The response does not effectively address a key reason given in support of the psychology professor's position.
(D) The response depends for its plausibility on a personal attack made against the psychology professor.
(E) The response takes for granted that unless the course textbook is the same the course content will not be the same.

14. Among a sample of diverse coins from an unfamiliar country, each face of any coin portrays one of four things: a judge's head, an explorer's head, a building, or a tree. By examining the coins, a collector determines that none of them have heads on both sides and that all coins in the sample with a judge's head on one side have a tree on the other.

If the statements above are true, which one of the following must be true of the coins in the sample?

(A) All those with an explorer's head on one side have a building on the other.
(B) All those with a tree on one side have a judge's head on the other.
(C) None of those with a tree on one side have an explorer's head on the other.
(D) None of those with a building on one side have a judge's head on the other.
(E) None of those with an explorer's head on one side have a building on the other.

15. There are two supposedly conflicting hypotheses as to what makes for great national leaders: one is that such leaders successfully shape public opinion, and the other is that they are adept at reacting to it. However, treating these hypotheses as mutually exclusive is evidently a mistake. All leaders who have had success getting their programs passed by their country's legislature have been adroit both in shaping and reacting to public opinion.

Which one of the following is an assumption on which the argument depends?

(A) Having success getting programs passed by the legislature is indicative of being a great national leader.
(B) It is impossible to successfully shape public opinion without in some way reacting to it.
(C) To lead, one must either successfully shape public opinion or be adept at reacting to it, or both.
(D) Having a good rapport with the members of the legislature allows a leader to shape public opinion.
(E) To be a great leader one must not be swayed by public opinion.

GO ON TO THE NEXT PAGE.

16. Most business ethics courses and textbooks confine themselves to considering specific cases and principles. For example, students are often given lists of ethical rules for in-class discussion and role-playing. This approach fails to provide a framework for understanding specific principles and should thus be changed to include abstract ethical theory.

Which one of the following, if valid, most helps to justify the reasoning above?

(A) A moralizing approach that fails to recognize the diversity of the ethical rules in use is unacceptable.
(B) Courses that concentrate mainly on role-playing are undesirable because students must adopt alien personae.
(C) People have no obligation to always behave ethically unless they are acquainted with abstract ethical theory.
(D) Abstract ethical theory is the most appropriate of any context for understanding specific principles.
(E) An ethics course should acquaint students with a wide range of specific principles and appropriate applications.

17. Some classes of animal are so successful that they spread into virtually every ecosystem, whereas others gradually recede until they inhabit only small niches in geographically isolated areas and thereby become threatened. Insects are definitely of the former sort and ants are the most successful of these, ranging from the Arctic Circle to Tierra del Fuego. Hence, no species of ant is a threatened species.

The argument is flawed because it takes for granted that

(A) the Arctic Circle and Tierra del Fuego do not constitute geographically isolated areas
(B) because ants do not inhabit only a small niche in a geographically isolated area, they are unlike most other insects
(C) the only way a class of animal can avoid being threatened is to spread into virtually every ecosystem
(D) what is true of the constituent elements of a whole is also true of the whole
(E) what is true of a whole is also true of its constituent elements

18. Advocate: You claim that it is wrong to own gasoline-powered cars because they pollute too much; you have an electric car, which pollutes far less. But the company that made your car also makes millions of gasoline-powered vehicles, so your patronage benefits a producer of products to which you object. Thus, if you are right about gasoline-powered cars, you should not have your electric car either.

Which one of the following principles, if valid, would most help to justify the advocate's reasoning?

(A) An action can be wrong even if it has fewer negative consequences than another action.
(B) One should purchase a product only if it pollutes less than any competing product.
(C) One should purchase every product whose use has no negative consequences.
(D) One should not support an organization that does anything one believes to be wrong.
(E) One should not purchase products from companies that make no environmentally sound products.

19. Analyst: A recent survey showed that although professors of biology who teach but do not pursue research made up one twentieth of all science professors, they were appointed to fewer than one twentieth of all the scientific administrative positions in universities. We can conclude from this survey that failing to pursue research tends to bias university administrators against appointing these professors to scientific administrative positions.

Which one of the following, if true, most seriously weakens the support for the analyst's conclusion?

(A) In universities there are fewer scientific administrative positions than there are nonscientific administrative positions.
(B) Biologists who do research fill a disproportionately low number of scientific administrative positions in universities.
(C) Biology professors get more than one twentieth of all the science grant money available.
(D) Conducting biological research tends to take significantly more time than does teaching biology.
(E) Biologists who hold scientific administrative positions in the university tend to hold those positions for a shorter time than do other science professors.

GO ON TO THE NEXT PAGE.

20. Researcher: We have found that some cases of high blood pressure can be treated effectively with medicine. Since it is generally accepted that any illness caused by stress is treatable only by the reduction of stress, some cases of high blood pressure must not be caused by stress.

Which one of the following is an assumption required by the researcher's argument?

(A) The correlation between stress and all cases of high blood pressure is merely coincidental.
(B) The reduction of stress in a person's life can at times lower that person's blood pressure.
(C) Reduced stress does not reduce a person's responsiveness to medicine used to treat high blood pressure.
(D) Some conditions that are treated effectively by medicines are not also treatable through the reduction of stress.
(E) Medicine used to treat high blood pressure does not itself reduce stress.

21. Catmull: Although historians consider themselves to be social scientists, different historians never arrive at the same conclusions about specific events of the past. Thus historians never determine what actually happened; like novelists, they merely create interesting fictional stories about the many different problems that people have faced.

The reasoning in Catmull's argument is flawed because the argument

(A) draws a conclusion that simply restates a claim presented in support of that conclusion
(B) concludes, solely on the basis of the claim that different people have reached different conclusions about a topic, that none of these conclusions is true
(C) presumes, without providing justification, that unless historians' conclusions are objectively true, they have no value whatsoever
(D) bases its conclusion on premises that contradict each other
(E) mistakes a necessary condition for the objective truth of historians' conclusions for a sufficient condition for the objective truth of those conclusions

22. In a poll conducted by interviewing eligible voters in their homes just before the recent election, incumbent candidate Kenner was significantly ahead of candidate Muratori. Nonetheless, Muratori won the recent election.

Which one of the following, if true, most helps to resolve the apparent discrepancy described by the statements above?

(A) The positions taken by Muratori and Kenner on many election issues were not very similar to each other.
(B) Kenner had held elected office for many years before the recent election.
(C) In the year leading up to the election, Kenner was implicated in a series of political scandals.
(D) Six months before the recent election, the voting age was lowered by three years.
(E) In the poll, supporters of Muratori were more likely than others to describe the election as important.

GO ON TO THE NEXT PAGE.

23. Statistical analysis is a common tool for explanation in the physical sciences. It can only be used, however, to explain events that can be replicated to the last detail. Since human mental events never precisely recur, statistical analysis cannot be employed to explain these events. Therefore, they cannot be explained by the physical sciences.

Which one of the following arguments is most similar in its flawed reasoning to the argument above?

(A) Computer modeling is used to try to explain the way in which wind resistance affects the movement of bicycles. To use computer modeling, the phenomenon being modeled must be predictable. But wind resistance is not predictable. Therefore, the way in which wind resistance affects the movement of bicycles cannot be explained by computer modeling.

(B) The only way to explain how music affects the emotional state of a person is to appeal to the psychology of emotion. The psychology of emotion can be applied only to cases involving human beings. But not all music is created by human beings; some music is computer generated. Therefore, the way in which music affects the emotional state of a person cannot be explained.

(C) The best way to explain why an object has a particular color is in terms of the interaction of light and matter. It is sometimes impossible to find out what kind of matter constitutes an object. Therefore, the color of such objects has nothing to do with the interaction of light and matter.

(D) To determine which explanation of the origin of the universe is correct, we would need to know about the first moments of the existence of the universe. Due to the immense time that has passed since the universe began, it is impossible to get such information. Therefore, none of the explanations of the origin of the universe is likely to be correct.

(E) A good way to explain historical events is to construct a coherent narrative about those events. In order to construct such a narrative, a great many details about the events must be known. Virtually no details can be known of certain very ancient historical events. Therefore, no historical explanation can be given for these events.

24. Journalist: Although a recent poll found that more than half of all eligible voters support the idea of a political party whose primary concern is education, only 26 percent would like to join it, and only 16 percent would be prepared to donate money to it. Furthermore, there is overwhelming historical evidence that only a party that has at least 30 percent of eligible voters prepared to support it by either joining it or donating money to it is viable in the long run. Therefore, it is unlikely that an education party is viable in the long run.

The reasoning in the journalist's argument is most vulnerable to criticism on the grounds that the argument fails to consider that

(A) some of those who said they were willing to donate money to an education party might not actually do so if such a party were formed

(B) an education party could possibly be viable with a smaller base than is customarily needed

(C) the 16 percent of eligible voters prepared to donate money to an education party might donate almost as much money as a party would ordinarily expect to get if 30 percent of eligible voters contributed

(D) a party needs the appropriate support of at least 30 percent of eligible voters in order to be viable and more than half of all eligible voters support the idea of an education party

(E) some of the eligible voters who would donate money to an education party might not be prepared to join such a party

GO ON TO THE NEXT PAGE.

25. Almost all microbe species live together in dense, interdependent communities, supporting the environment for each other, and regulating the population balances for their different species through a complex system of chemical signals. For this reason, it is currently impossible to cultivate any one such species in isolation. Thus, microbiologists lack complete knowledge of most microbe species.

Which one of the following, if assumed, enables the argument's conclusion to be properly drawn?

(A)   It is currently impossible for microbiologists to reproduce the complex systems of chemical signals with which microbe communities regulate the population balances for their different species.

(B)   If it is currently impossible to reproduce the environmental supports and chemical signals in dense, interdependent communities of microbe species, then it is also impossible to cultivate any microbe species from such a community in isolation.

(C)   No microbiologist can have complete knowledge of any species of organism unless that microbiologist can cultivate that species in isolation.

(D)   At least some microbiologists lack complete knowledge of any microbe species that live together in dense, interdependent communities.

(E)   No microbe species that normally lives together with other microbe species in dense, interdependent communities can survive outside such a community.

26. Reza: Language requires the use of verbal signs for objects as well as for feelings. Many animals can vocally express hunger, but only humans can ask for an egg or an apple by naming it. And using verbal signs for objects requires the ability to distinguish these objects from other objects, which in turn requires conceptual thought.

If all of Reza's statements are true, then which one of the following must also be true?

(A)   Conceptual thought is required for language.

(B)   Conceptual thought requires the use of verbal signs for objects.

(C)   It is not possible to think conceptually about feelings.

(D)   All humans are capable of conceptual thought.

(E)   The vocal expressions of animals other than humans do not require conceptual thought.

S T O P

IF YOU FINISH BEFORE TIME IS CALLED, YOU MAY CHECK YOUR WORK ON THIS SECTION ONLY.
DO NOT WORK ON ANY OTHER SECTION IN THE TEST.

SECTION II

Time—35 minutes

22 Questions

<u>Directions:</u> Each group of questions in this section is based on a set of conditions. In answering some of the questions, it may be useful to draw a rough diagram. Choose the response that most accurately and completely answers each question and blacken the corresponding space on your answer sheet.

<u>Questions 1–6</u>

Henri has exactly five electrical appliances in his dormitory room: a hairdryer, a microwave oven, a razor, a television, and a vacuum. As a consequence of fire department regulations, Henri can use these appliances only in accordance with the following conditions:

Henri cannot use both the hairdryer and the razor simultaneously.

Henri cannot use both the hairdryer and the television simultaneously.

When Henri uses the vacuum, he cannot at the same time use any of the following: the hairdryer, the razor, and the television.

1. Which one of the following is a pair of appliances Henri could be using simultaneously?

   (A) the hairdryer and the razor
   (B) the hairdryer and the television
   (C) the razor and the television
   (D) the razor and the vacuum
   (E) the television and the vacuum

2. Assume that Henri is using exactly two appliances and is not using the microwave oven. Which one of the following is a list of all the appliances, other than the microwave oven, that Henri CANNOT be using?

   (A) hairdryer
   (B) razor
   (C) vacuum
   (D) hairdryer, razor
   (E) hairdryer, vacuum

3. Which one of the following CANNOT be true?

   (A) Henri uses the hairdryer while using the microwave oven.
   (B) Henri uses the microwave oven while using the razor.
   (C) Henri uses the microwave oven while using two other appliances.
   (D) Henri uses the television while using two other appliances.
   (E) Henri uses the vacuum while using two other appliances.

4. If Henri were to use exactly three appliances, then what is the total number of different groups of three appliances any one of which could be the group of appliances he is using?

   (A) one
   (B) two
   (C) three
   (D) four
   (E) five

5. Which one of the following statements, if true, guarantees that Henri is using no more than one of the following: the hairdryer, the razor, the television?

   (A) Henri is using the hairdryer.
   (B) Henri is using the television.
   (C) Henri is not using the hairdryer.
   (D) Henri is not using the microwave oven.
   (E) Henri is not using the vacuum.

6. Which one of the following must be true?

   (A) Henri uses at most three appliances simultaneously.
   (B) Henri uses at most four appliances simultaneously.
   (C) Henri uses at most one other appliance while using the microwave oven.
   (D) Henri uses at most one other appliance while using the razor.
   (E) Henri uses at least two other appliances while using the hairdryer.

GO ON TO THE NEXT PAGE.

Questions 7–12

A farmer harvests eight separate fields—G, H, J, K, L, M, P, and T. Each field is harvested exactly once, and no two fields are harvested simultaneously. Once the harvesting of a field begins, no other fields are harvested until the harvesting of that field is complete. The farmer harvests the fields in an order consistent with the following conditions:

Both P and G are harvested at some time before K.
Both H and L are harvested at some time before J.
K is harvested at some time before M but after L.
T is harvested at some time before M.

7. Which one of the following could be true?

   (A) J is the first field harvested.
   (B) K is the second field harvested.
   (C) M is the sixth field harvested.
   (D) G is the seventh field harvested.
   (E) T is the eighth field harvested.

8. If M is the seventh field harvested, then any one of the following could be the fifth field harvested EXCEPT:

   (A) H
   (B) J
   (C) K
   (D) L
   (E) P

9. Which one of the following CANNOT be the field that is harvested fifth?

   (A) G
   (B) J
   (C) M
   (D) P
   (E) T

10. If J is the third field harvested, then which one of the following must be true?

   (A) L is the first field harvested.
   (B) H is the second field harvested.
   (C) T is the fourth field harvested.
   (D) K is the seventh field harvested.
   (E) M is the eighth field harvested.

11. If H is the sixth field harvested, then which one of the following must be true?

   (A) G is harvested at some time before T.
   (B) H is harvested at some time before K.
   (C) J is harvested at some time before M.
   (D) K is harvested at some time before J.
   (E) T is harvested at some time before K.

12. If L is the fifth field harvested, then which one of the following could be true?

   (A) J is harvested at some time before G.
   (B) J is harvested at some time before T.
   (C) K is harvested at some time before T.
   (D) M is harvested at some time before H.
   (E) M is harvested at some time before J.

GO ON TO THE NEXT PAGE.

Questions 13–17

In a repair facility there are exactly six technicians: Stacy, Urma, Wim, Xena, Yolanda, and Zane. Each technician repairs machines of at least one of the following three types—radios, televisions, and VCRs—and no other types. The following conditions apply:

Xena and exactly three other technicians repair radios.
Yolanda repairs both televisions and VCRs.
Stacy does not repair any type of machine that Yolanda repairs.
Zane repairs more types of machines than Yolanda repairs.
Wim does not repair any type of machine that Stacy repairs.
Urma repairs exactly two types of machines.

13. For exactly how many of the six technicians is it possible to determine exactly which of the three types of machines each repairs?

(A) one
(B) two
(C) three
(D) four
(E) five

14. Which one of the following must be true?

(A) Of the types of machines repaired by Stacy there is exactly one type that Urma also repairs.
(B) Of the types of machines repaired by Yolanda there is exactly one type that Xena also repairs.
(C) Of the types of machines repaired by Wim there is exactly one type that Xena also repairs.
(D) There is more than one type of machine that both Wim and Yolanda repair.
(E) There is more than one type of machine that both Urma and Wim repair.

15. Which one of the following must be false?

(A) Exactly one of the six technicians repairs exactly one type of machine.
(B) Exactly two of the six technicians repair exactly one type of machine each.
(C) Exactly three of the six technicians repair exactly one type of machine each.
(D) Exactly one of the six technicians repairs exactly two types of machines.
(E) Exactly three of the six technicians repair exactly two types of machines each.

16. Which one of the following pairs of technicians could repair all and only the same types of machines as each other?

(A) Stacy and Urma
(B) Urma and Yolanda
(C) Urma and Xena
(D) Wim and Xena
(E) Xena and Yolanda

17. Which one of the following must be true?

(A) There is exactly one type of machine that both Urma and Wim repair.
(B) There is exactly one type of machine that both Urma and Xena repair.
(C) There is exactly one type of machine that both Urma and Yolanda repair.
(D) There is exactly one type of machine that both Wim and Yolanda repair.
(E) There is exactly one type of machine that both Xena and Yolanda repair.

GO ON TO THE NEXT PAGE.

Questions 18–22

Three folk groups—Glenside, Hilltopper, Levon—and three rock groups—Peasant, Query, Tinhead—each perform on one of two stages, north or south. Each stage has three two-hour performances: north at 6, 8, and 10; south at 8, 10, and 12. Each group performs individually and exactly once, consistent with the following conditions:

Peasant performs at 6 or 12.
Glenside performs at some time before Hilltopper.
If any rock group performs at 10, no folk group does.
Levon and Tinhead perform on different stages.
Query performs immediately after a folk group, though not necessarily on the same stage.

18. Which one of the following could be a complete and accurate ordering of performances on the north stage, from first to last?

(A) Glenside, Levon, Query
(B) Glenside, Query, Hilltopper
(C) Hilltopper, Query, Peasant
(D) Peasant, Levon, Tinhead
(E) Peasant, Query, Levon

19. Which one of the following groups must perform earlier than 10?

(A) Glenside
(B) Hilltopper
(C) Levon
(D) Peasant
(E) Tinhead

20. Which one of the following groups could perform at 6?

(A) Glenside
(B) Hilltopper
(C) Levon
(D) Query
(E) Tinhead

21. If Query performs at 12, then which one of the following could be an accurate ordering of the performances on the north stage, from first to last?

(A) Glenside, Levon, Query
(B) Peasant, Hilltopper, Tinhead
(C) Peasant, Tinhead, Glenside
(D) Peasant, Tinhead, Hilltopper
(E) Peasant, Tinhead, Levon

22. If a rock group performs at 10, then which one of the following must be true?

(A) A folk group performs at 6.
(B) A folk group performs at 8.
(C) A folk group performs at 12.
(D) A rock group performs at 8.
(E) A rock group performs at 12.

S T O P

IF YOU FINISH BEFORE TIME IS CALLED, YOU MAY CHECK YOUR WORK ON THIS SECTION ONLY.
DO NOT WORK ON ANY OTHER SECTION IN THE TEST.

SECTION III
Time—35 minutes
27 Questions

<u>Directions:</u> Each passage in this section is followed by a group of questions to be answered on the basis of what is <u>stated</u> or <u>implied</u> in the passage. For some of the questions, more than one of the choices could conceivably answer the question. However, you are to choose the <u>best</u> answer; that is, the response that most accurately and completely answers the question, and blacken the corresponding space on your answer sheet.

Economists have long defined prosperity in terms of monetary value, gauging a given nation's prosperity solely on the basis of the total monetary value of the goods and services produced annually.

(5) However, critics point out that defining prosperity solely as a function of monetary value is questionable since it fails to recognize other kinds of values, such as quality of life or environmental health, that contribute directly to prosperity in a broader sense.

(10) For example, as the earth's ozone layer weakens and loses its ability to protect people from ultraviolet radiation, sales of hats, sunglasses, and sunscreens are likely to skyrocket, all adding to the nation's total expenditures. In this way, troubling reductions in

(15) environmental health and quality of life may in fact initiate economic activity that, by the economists' measure, bolsters prosperity.

It can also happen that communities seeking to increase their prosperity as measured strictly in

(20) monetary terms may damage their quality of life and their environment. The situation of one rural community illustrates this point: residents of the community value the local timber industry as a primary source of income, and they vocally protested

(25) proposed limitations on timber harvests as a threat to their prosperity. Implicitly adopting the economists' point of view, the residents argued that the harvest limitations would lower their wages or even cause the loss of jobs.

(30) But critics of the economists' view argue that this view of the situation overlooks a crucial consideration. Without the harvest limitations, they say, the land on which the community depends would be seriously damaged. Moreover, they point out that the residents

(35) themselves cite the abundance of natural beauty as one of the features that make their community a highly desirable place to live. But it is also extremely poor, and the critics point out that the residents could double their incomes by moving only 150 kilometers

(40) away. From their decision not to do so, the critics conclude that their location has substantial monetary value to them. The community will thus lose much more—even understood in monetary terms—if the proposed harvest limits are not implemented.

(45) Economists respond by arguing that to be a useful concept, prosperity must be defined in easily quantifiable terms, and that prosperity thus should not include difficult-to-measure values such as happiness or environmental health. But this position dodges the

(50) issue—emphasizing ease of calculation causes one to

disregard substantive issues that directly influence real prosperity. The economists' stance is rather like that of a literary critic who takes total sales to be the best measure of a book's value—true, the number of

(55) copies sold is a convenient and quantifiable measure, but it is a poor substitute for an accurate appraisal of literary merit.

1. Which one of the following most accurately states the main point of the passage?

(A) According to critics, communities that seek to increase their prosperity recognize the need to gauge the value and ensure the long-term health of their local environment.

(B) Economists' definition of prosperity strictly in terms of monetary value is too narrow to truly capture our ordinary conception of this notion.

(C) If economists were to alter and expand their definition of prosperity, it is likely that the economic and environmental health of most communities would appear worse under the new definition than under the old definition.

(D) In contrast with the views of economists, some critics believe that prosperity can be neither scientifically measured nor accurately defined, and as a concept is therefore of little use for economists.

(E) While they are generally an accurate and practical measure of current economic prosperity, figures for the total expenditures of a nation do not aid in providing an indication of that nation's future economic prospects.

GO ON TO THE NEXT PAGE.

2. The example in the passage of the timber industry and its effect on a poor rural community suggests that the critics would most likely agree with which one of the following statements?

(A) Harvest limitations have little relationship to lower wages or fewer jobs in the community.

(B) Harvest limitations should be imposed only when the limitations have wide public support in the community.

(C) The advantages to the community that would be created by harvest limitations are likely to outweigh the disadvantages.

(D) Communities protest harvest limitations primarily because they do not understand the long-term monetary impact of such regulation.

(E) It is the arguments of economists that often cause residents of rural communities to view harvest limitations more negatively.

3. Based on the information in the passage, the author would be most likely to agree with which one of the following statements regarding the weakening of the earth's ozone layer?

(A) Paradoxically, the weakening of the ozone layer actually contributes to environmental health and quality of life.

(B) The environmental effects of this problem are likely to occur more gradually than the economic effects.

(C) The appearance of prosperity that results from this problem has directed attention away from solving it.

(D) This problem should be regarded primarily as threatening rather than contributing to true prosperity.

(E) This problem has resulted in part from the failure of economists to recognize it in its formative stages.

4. According to the passage, economists defend their concept of prosperity in which one of the following ways?

(A) by claiming that alternative definitions of the concept would not be easily quantifiable

(B) by asserting that environmental preservation can cause the loss of jobs

(C) by citing the relevance of nonmonetary values such as environmental health

(D) by showing that the value of natural beauty can be understood in quantifiable terms

(E) by detailing the historical development of their definition of the concept

5. The author compares the economists' position to that of a literary critic (lines 52–57) primarily to

(A) introduce the idea that the assessment of worth is basically subjective

(B) advocate an innovative method of measuring literary merit

(C) suggest that quality of life is mainly an aesthetic issue

(D) provide additional evidence that prosperity cannot be quantified

(E) illustrate the limitations of the economists' position

6. In the passage, the author cites which one of the following claims?

(A) that hats, sunglasses, and sunscreens provide an adequate substitute for the ozone layer

(B) that environmental protection measures are unpopular and often rejected by communities

(C) that the value of a locale's environment can be gauged by the incomes of its residents

(D) that timber harvest limits are needed to save one area from environmental damage

(E) that most nations measure their own prosperity in terms broader than monetary value

7. The primary purpose of the passage is to

(A) argue that there is an inherent and potentially detrimental conflict between two schools of thought concerning a certain concept

(B) summarize and illustrate the main points of the conflict between two schools of thought over the definition of a certain concept

(C) question one school of thought's definition of a certain concept and suggest several possible alternative definitions

(D) criticize one school of thought's definition of a certain concept by providing examples that illustrate the implications of adhering to this definition

(E) bring one school of thought's perspective to bear on a concept traditionally considered to be the exclusive territory of another school of thought

GO ON TO THE NEXT PAGE.

Joy Kogawa's *Obasan* is an account of a Japanese-Canadian family's experiences during World War II. The events are seen from the viewpoint of a young girl who watches her family disintegrate as it
(5) undergoes the relocation that occurred in both Canada and the United States. Although the experience depicted in *Obasan* is mainly one of dislocation, Kogawa employs subtle techniques that serve to emphasize her major character's heroism and to
(10) critique the majority culture. The former end is achieved through the novel's form and the latter through the symbols it employs.

The form of the novel parallels the three-stage structure noted by anthropologists in their studies of
(15) rites of passage. According to these anthropologists, a rite of passage begins with separation from a position of security in a highly structured society; proceeds to alienation in a deathlike state where one is stripped of status, property, and rank; and concludes with
(20) reintegration into society accompanied by a heightened status gained as a result of the second stage. The process thus has the effect of transforming a society's victim into a hero. The first eleven chapters of *Obasan* situate the young protagonist
(25) Naomi Nakane in a close-knit, securely placed family within Vancouver society. Chapters 12–32 chronicle the fall into alienation, when Naomi's family is dislodged from its structured social niche and removed from the city into work camps or exile.
(30) Separated from her parents, Naomi follows her aunt Aya Obasan to the ghost town of Slocan, where Naomi joins the surrogate family of her uncle and aunt. In chapters 33–39 this surrogate family nurtures Naomi as she develops toward a final integration with
(35) the larger society and with herself: as an adult, when she receives a bundle of family documents and letters from her aunt, Naomi breaks through the personal and cultural screens of silence and secretiveness that have enshrouded her past, and reconciles herself with
(40) her history.

Kogawa's use of motifs drawn from Christian rituals and symbols forms a subtle critique of the professed ethics of the majority culture that has shunned Naomi. In one example of such symbolism,
(45) Naomi's reacquaintance with her past is compared with the biblical story of turning stone into bread. The bundle of documents—which Kogawa refers to as "stone-hard facts"—brings Naomi to the recognition of her country's abuse of her people. But
(50) implicit in these hard facts, Kogawa suggests, is also the "bread" of a spiritual sustenance that will allow Naomi to affirm the durability of her people and herself. Through the careful deployment of structure and symbol, Kogawa thus manages to turn Naomi's
(55) experience—and by extension the wartime experiences of many Japanese Canadians—into a journey of heroic transformation and a critique of the majority culture.

8. Which one of the following most accurately states the main idea of the passage?

(A) While telling a story of familial disruption, *Obasan* uses structure and symbolism to valorize its protagonist and critique the majority culture.

(B) By means of its structure and symbolism, *Obasan* mounts a harsh critique of a society that disrupts its citizens' lives.

(C) Although intended primarily as social criticism, given its structure *Obasan* can also be read as a tale of heroic transformation.

(D) With its three-part structure that parallels rites of passage, *Obasan* manages to valorize its protagonist in spite of her traumatic experiences.

(E) Although intended primarily as a story of heroic transformation, *Obasan* can also be read as a work of social criticism.

9. Item removed from scoring.

GO ON TO THE NEXT PAGE.

10. Which one of the following most accurately describes the organization of the passage?

    (A) Two points are made about a novel, the first supported with a brief example, the second reasserted without support.

    (B) Two points are made about a novel, the first supported with an extended analogy, the second reasserted without support.

    (C) Two points are made about a novel, the first reasserted without support, the second supported with an extended analogy.

    (D) Two points are made about a novel, the first supported with a brief example, the second supported with an extended analogy.

    (E) Two points are made about a novel, the first supported with an extended analogy, the second supported with a brief example.

11. It can be inferred that the heroism Naomi gains in the course of *Obasan* is manifested in her

    (A) reconciliation with her past
    (B) careful deployment of structure and symbol
    (C) relationship with her surrogate family
    (D) renewal of her religious beliefs
    (E) denunciation of the majority culture

12. According to the anthropologists cited by the author, rites of passage are best described by which one of the following sequences of stages?

    (A) alienation, dislocation, integration
    (B) separation, alienation, reintegration
    (C) integration, alienation, disintegration
    (D) dislocation, reconciliation, reintegration
    (E) disintegration, transformation, reintegration

13. According to the passage, the agent of Naomi's reconciliation with her past is

    (A) her reunion with her parents
    (B) the exile of her parents
    (C) her critique of the majority society
    (D) her separation from her aunt and uncle
    (E) her receipt of documents and letters

14. The passage suggests that Joy Kogawa believes which one of the following about the society that shuns Naomi?

    (A) It discouraged its citizens from seeking out their heritage.
    (B) It endeavored to thwart its citizens' attempts at heroic transformation.
    (C) It violated its own supposed religious ethics by doing so.
    (D) It prohibited its citizens from participating in rites of passage.
    (E) It demanded that loyalty to the government replace loyalty to the family.

15. Based on the passage, which one of the following aspects of Kogawa's work does the author of the passage appear to value most highly?

    (A) her willingness to make political statements
    (B) her imaginative development of characters
    (C) her subtle use of literary techniques
    (D) her knowledge of Christian rituals and symbols
    (E) her objectivity in describing Naomi's tragic life

GO ON TO THE NEXT PAGE.

The pronghorn, an antelope-like mammal that lives on the western plains of North America, is the continent's fastest land animal, capable of running 90 kilometers per hour and of doing so for several
(5) kilometers. Because no North American predator is nearly fast enough to chase it down, biologists have had difficulty explaining why the pronghorn developed its running prowess. One biologist, however, has recently claimed that pronghorns run as
(10) fast as they do because of adaptation to predators known from fossil records to have been extinct for 10,000 years, such as American cheetahs and long-legged hyenas, either of which, it is believed, were fast enough to run down the pronghorn.
(15) Like all explanations that posit what is called a relict behavior—a behavior that persists though its only evolutionary impetus comes from long-extinct environmental conditions—this one is likely to meet with skepticism. Most biologists distrust explanations positing relict
(20) behaviors, in part because testing these hypotheses is so difficult due to the extinction of a principal component. They typically consider such historical explanations only when a lack of alternatives forces them to do so. But present-day observations sometimes yield
(25) evidence that supports relict behavior hypotheses.
In the case of the pronghorn, researchers have identified much supporting evidence, as several aspects of pronghorn behavior appear to have been shaped by enemies that no longer exist. For example,
(30) pronghorns—like many grazing animals—roam in herds, which allows more eyes to watch for predators and diminishes the chances of any particular animal being attacked but can also result in overcrowding and increased competition for food. But, since
(35) pronghorns have nothing to fear from present-day carnivores and thus have nothing to gain from herding, their herding behavior appears to be another adaptation to extinct threats. Similarly, if speed and endurance were once essential to survival, researchers would
(40) expect pronghorns to choose mates based on these athletic abilities, which they do—with female pronghorns, for example, choosing the victor after male pronghorns challenge each other in sprints and chases.
Relict behaviors appear to occur in other animals
(45) as well, increasing the general plausibility of such a theory. For example, one study reports relict behavior in stickleback fish belonging to populations that have long been free of a dangerous predator, the sculpin. In the study, when presented with sculpin, these
(50) stickleback fish immediately engaged in stereotypical antisculpin behavior, avoiding its mouth and swimming behind to bite it. Another study found that ground squirrels from populations that have been free from snakes for 70,000 to 300,000 years still clearly recognize
(55) rattlesnakes, displaying stereotypical antirattlesnake behavior in the presence of the snake. Such fear, however, apparently does not persist interminably. Arctic ground squirrels, free of snakes for about 3 million years, appear to be unable to recognize the
(60) threat of a rattlesnake, exhibiting only disorganized caution even after being bitten repeatedly.

16. Which one of the following most accurately states the main point of the passage?

(A) Evidence from present-day animal behaviors, together with the fossil record, supports the hypothesis that the pronghorn's ability to far outrun any predator currently on the North American continent is an adaptation to predators long extinct.

(B) Although some biologists believe that certain animal characteristics, such as the speed of the pronghorn, are explained by environmental conditions that have not existed for many years, recent data concerning arctic ground squirrels make this hypothesis doubtful.

(C) Research into animal behavior, particularly into that of the pronghorn, provides strong evidence that most present-day characteristics of animals are explained by environmental conditions that have not existed for many years.

(D) Even in those cases in which an animal species displays characteristics clearly explained by long-vanished environmental conditions, evidence concerning arctic ground squirrels suggests that those characteristics will eventually disappear.

(E) Although biologists are suspicious of hypotheses that are difficult to test, there is now widespread agreement among biologists that many types of animal characteristics are best explained as adaptations to long-extinct predators.

17. Based on the passage, the term "principal component" (line 21) most clearly refers to which one of the following?

(A) behavior that persists even though the conditions that provided its evolutionary impetus are extinct

(B) the original organism whose descendants' behavior is being investigated as relict behavior

(C) the pronghorn's ability to run 90 kilometers per hour over long distances

(D) the environmental conditions in response to which relict behaviors are thought to have developed

(E) an original behavior of an animal of which certain present-day behaviors are thought to be modifications

GO ON TO THE NEXT PAGE.

18. The last paragraph most strongly supports which one of the following statements?

    (A) An absence of predators in an animal's environment can constitute just as much of a threat to the well-being of that animal as the presence of predators.

    (B) Relict behaviors are found in most wild animals living today.

    (C) If a behavior is an adaptation to environmental conditions, it may eventually disappear in the absence of those or similar conditions.

    (D) Behavior patterns that originated as a way of protecting an organism against predators will persist interminably if they are periodically reinforced.

    (E) Behavior patterns invariably take longer to develop than they do to disappear.

19. Which one of the following describes a benefit mentioned in the passage that grazing animals derive from roaming in herds?

    (A) The greater density of animals tends to intimidate potential predators.

    (B) The larger number of adults in a herd makes protection of the younger animals from predators much easier.

    (C) With many animals searching it is easier for the herd to find food and water.

    (D) The likelihood that any given individual will be attacked by a predator decreases.

    (E) The most defenseless animals can achieve greater safety by remaining in the center of the herd.

20. The passage mentions each of the following as support for the explanation of the pronghorn's speed proposed by the biologist referred to in line 8 EXCEPT:

    (A) fossils of extinct animals believed to have been able to run down a pronghorn

    (B) the absence of carnivores in the pronghorn's present-day environment

    (C) the present-day preference of pronghorns for athletic mates

    (D) the apparent need for a similar explanation to account for the herding behavior pronghorns now display

    (E) the occurrence of relict behavior in other species

21. The third paragraph of the passage provides the most support for which one of the following inferences?

    (A) Predators do not attack grazing animals that are assembled into herds.

    (B) Pronghorns tend to graze in herds only when they sense a threat from predators close by.

    (C) If animals do not graze for their food, they do not roam in herds.

    (D) Female pronghorns mate only with the fastest male pronghorn in the herd.

    (E) If pronghorns did not herd, they would not face significantly greater danger from present-day carnivores.

GO ON TO THE NEXT PAGE.

Many legal theorists have argued that the only morally legitimate goal in imposing criminal penalties against certain behaviors is to prevent people from harming others. Clearly, such theorists would oppose
(5) laws that force people to act purely for their own good or to refrain from certain harmless acts purely to ensure conformity to some social norm. But the goal of preventing harm to others would also justify legal sanctions against some forms of nonconforming
(10) behavior to which this goal might at first seem not to apply.

In many situations it is in the interest of each member of a group to agree to behave in a certain way on the condition that the others similarly agree.
(15) In the simplest cases, a mere coordination of activities is itself the good that results. For example, it is in no one's interest to lack a convention about which side of the road to drive on, and each person can agree to drive on one side assuming the others do
(20) too. Any fair rule, then, would be better than no rule at all. On the assumption that all people would voluntarily agree to be subject to a coordination rule backed by criminal sanctions, if people could be assured that others would also agree, it is argued to
(25) be legitimate for a legislature to impose such a rule. This is because prevention of harm underlies the rationale for the rule, though it applies to the problem of coordination less directly than to other problems, for the act that is forbidden (driving on the other side
(30) of the road) is not inherently harm-producing, as are burglary and assault; instead, it is the lack of a coordinating rule that would be harmful.

In some other situations involving a need for legally enforced coordination, the harm to be averted
(35) goes beyond the simple lack of coordination itself. This can be illustrated by an example of a coordination rule—instituted by a private athletic organization—which has analogies in criminal law. At issue is whether the use of anabolic steroids, which
(40) build muscular strength but have serious negative side effects, should be prohibited. Each athlete has at stake both an interest in having a fair opportunity to win and an interest in good health. If some competitors use steroids, others have the option of either
(45) endangering their health or losing their fair opportunity to win. Thus they would be harmed either way. A compulsory rule could prevent that harm and thus would be in the interest of all competitors. If they understand its function and trust the techniques
(50) for its enforcement, they will gladly consent to it. So while it might appear that such a rule merely forces people to act for their own good, the deeper rationale for coercion here—as in the above example—is a somewhat complex appeal to the legitimacy of
(55) enforcing a rule with the goal of preventing harm.

22. Which one of the following most accurately states the main point of the passage?

(A) In order to be morally justifiable, laws prohibiting activities that are not inherently harm-producing must apply equitably to everyone.

(B) It is justifiable to require social conformity where noncompliance would be harmful to either the nonconforming individual or the larger group.

(C) Achieving coordination can be argued to be a morally legitimate justification for rules that prevent directly harmful actions and others that prevent indirectly harmful actions.

(D) It is reasonable to hold that restricting individual liberty is always justified on the basis of mutually agreed-upon community standards.

(E) The principle of preventing harm to others can be used to justify laws that do not at first glance appear to be designed to prevent such harm.

23. It can be most reasonably inferred from the passage that the author considers which one of the following factors to be generally necessary for the justification of rules compelling coordination of people's activities?

(A) evidence that such rules do not force individuals to act for their own good

(B) enactment of such rules by a duly elected or appointed government lawmaking organization

(C) the assurance that criminal penalties are provided as a means of securing compliance with such rules

(D) some form of consent on the part of rational people who are subject to such rules

(E) a sense of community and cultural uniformity among those who are required to abide by such rules

GO ON TO THE NEXT PAGE.

24. It can be most reasonably inferred from the passage that the author would agree with which one of the following statements?

    (A) In all situations in which compulsory rules are needed for the coordination of human activities, any uniformly enforced rule is as acceptable as any other.

    (B) No private organizational rules designed to coordinate the activities of members have as complex a relation to the goal of preventing harm as have some criminal statutes.

    (C) Every fair rule that could be effectively used to prescribe which side of the road to drive on is a rule whose implementation would likely cause less harm than it would prevent.

    (D) There would be little need for formal regulation and enforcement of conventional driving patterns if all drivers understood and accepted the rationale behind such regulation and enforcement.

    (E) Unlike rules forbidding such acts as burglary and assault, those that are designed primarily to prevent the inconvenience and chaos of uncoordinated activities should not involve criminal penalties.

25. The author distinguishes between two examples of coordinating rules on the basis of whether or not such rules

    (A) prevent some harm beyond that which consists simply in a lack of coordination

    (B) are intended to ensure conformity to a set of agreed-upon standards

    (C) are voluntarily agreed upon by all those affected by such rules

    (D) could be considered justifiable by the legal theorists discussed in the passage

    (E) apply less directly to the problem of preventing harm than do rules against burglary and assault

26. Which one of the following is a rule that primarily addresses a problem of coordination most similar to that discussed in the second paragraph?

    (A) a rule requiring that those who wish to dig for ancient artifacts secure the permission of relevant authorities and the owners of the proposed site before proceeding with their activities

    (B) a rule requiring that pharmacists dispense certain kinds of medications only when directed to do so by physicians' prescriptions, rather than simply selling medicines at the customers' request

    (C) a rule requiring that advertisers be able to substantiate the claims they make in advertisements, rather than simply saying whatever they think will help to attract customers

    (D) a rule requiring that employees of a certain restaurant all wear identical uniforms during their hours of employment, rather than wearing whatever clothes they choose

    (E) a rule requiring different aircraft to fly at different altitudes rather than flying at any altitude their pilots wish

27. In line 54, the author uses the expression "somewhat complex" primarily to describe reasoning that

    (A) involves two layers of law, one governing the private sector and the other governing the public sector

    (B) requires that those affected by the rule understand the motivation behind its imposition

    (C) involves a case in which a harm to be prevented is indirectly related to the kind of act that is to be prohibited

    (D) can convince athletes that their health is as important as their competitive success

    (E) illustrates how appeals to the need for coordination can be used to justify many rules that do not involve coordination

S T O P

IF YOU FINISH BEFORE TIME IS CALLED, YOU MAY CHECK YOUR WORK ON THIS SECTION ONLY.
DO NOT WORK ON ANY OTHER SECTION IN THE TEST.

SECTION IV

Time—35 minutes

27 Questions

<u>Directions:</u> Each passage in this section is followed by a group of questions to be answered on the basis of what is <u>stated</u> or <u>implied</u> in the passage. For some of the questions, more than one of the choices could conceivably answer the question. However, you are to choose the <u>best</u> answer; that is, the response that most accurately and completely answers the question, and blacken the corresponding space on your answer sheet.

One of the intriguing questions considered by anthropologists concerns the purpose our early ancestors had in first creating images of the world around them. Among these images are 25,000-year-
(5) old cave paintings made by the Aurignacians, a people who supplanted the Neanderthals in Europe and who produced the earliest known examples of representational art. Some anthropologists see these paintings as evidence that the Aurignacians had a
(10) more secure life than the Neanderthals. No one under constant threat of starvation, the reasoning goes, could afford time for luxuries such as art; moreover, the art is, in its latter stages at least, so astonishingly well-executed by almost any standard of excellence
(15) that it is highly unlikely it was produced by people who had not spent a great deal of time perfecting their skills. In other words, the high level of quality suggests that Aurignacian art was created by a distinct group of artists, who would likely have spent
(20) most of their time practicing and passing on their skills while being supported by other members of their community.

Curiously, however, the paintings were usually placed in areas accessible only with extreme effort
(25) and completely unilluminated by natural light. This makes it unlikely that these representational cave paintings arose simply out of a love of beauty or pride in artistry—had aesthetic enjoyment been the sole purpose of the paintings, they would presumably
(30) have been located where they could have been easily seen and appreciated.

Given that the Aurignacians were hunter-gatherers and had to cope with the practical problems of extracting a living from a difficult environment, many
(35) anthropologists hypothesize that the paintings were also intended to provide a means of ensuring a steady supply of food. Since it was common among pretechnological societies to believe that one can gain power over an animal by making an image of it,
(40) these anthropologists maintain that the Aurignacian paintings were meant to grant magical power over the Aurignacians' prey—typically large, dangerous animals such as mammoths and bison. The images were probably intended to make these animals
(45) vulnerable to the weapons of the hunters, an explanation supported by the fact that many of the pictures show animals with their hearts outlined in red, or with bright, arrow-shaped lines tracing paths to vital organs. Other paintings clearly show some
(50) animals as pregnant, perhaps in an effort to assure

plentiful hunting grounds. There is also evidence that ceremonies of some sort were performed before these images. Well-worn footprints of dancers can still be discerned in the clay floors of some caves, and
(55) pictures of what appear to be shamans, or religious leaders, garbed in fantastic costumes, are found among the painted animals.

1. Which one of the following most accurately describes the author's position regarding the claims attributed to anthropologists in the third paragraph?

    (A)   implicit acceptance
    (B)   hesitant agreement
    (C)   noncommittal curiosity
    (D)   detached skepticism
    (E)   broad disagreement

2. The passage provides information that answers which one of the following questions?

    (A)   For how long a period did the Neanderthals occupy Europe?
    (B)   How long did it take for the Aurignacians to supplant the Neanderthals?
    (C)   Did the Aurignacians make their homes in caves?
    (D)   What are some of the animals represented in Aurignacian cave paintings?
    (E)   What other prehistoric groups aside from the Aurignacians produced representational art?

GO ON TO THE NEXT PAGE.

3. The author would be most likely to agree with which one of the following statements?

   (A) The cave paintings indicate that the Aurignacians lived a relatively secure life compared to most other hunter-gatherer cultures.

   (B) Skill in art was essential to becoming an Aurignacian shaman.

   (C) Prehistoric hunter-gatherers did not create any art solely for aesthetic purposes.

   (D) All art created by the Aurignacians was intended to grant magical power over other beings.

   (E) The Aurignacians sought to gain magical power over their prey by means of ceremonial acts in addition to painted images.

4. The author mentions the relative inaccessibility of the Aurignacian cave paintings primarily to

   (A) stress the importance of the cave paintings to the lives of the artists who painted them by indicating the difficulties they had to overcome to do so

   (B) lay the groundwork for a fuller explanation of the paintings' function

   (C) suggest that only a select portion of the Aurignacian community was permitted to view the paintings

   (D) help explain why the paintings are still well preserved

   (E) support the argument that Aurignacian artists were a distinct and highly skilled group

5. The passage suggests that the author would be most likely to agree with which one of the following claims about the Aurignacians?

   (A) They were technologically no more advanced than the Neanderthals they supplanted.

   (B) They were the first humans known to have worn costumes for ceremonial purposes.

   (C) They had established some highly specialized social roles.

   (D) They occupied a less hostile environment than the Neanderthals did.

   (E) They carved images of their intended prey on their weapons to increase the weapons' efficacy.

GO ON TO THE NEXT PAGE.

The poet Louise Glück has said that she feels comfortable writing within a tradition often characterized as belonging only to male poets. About her own experience reading poetry, Glück notes that
(5) her gender did not keep her from appreciating the poems of Shakespeare, Blake, Keats, and other male poets. Rather she believed this was the tradition of her language and that it was for this reason her poetic inheritance. She thus views the canon of poets in
(10) English as a literary family to which she clearly belongs. Whereas many contemporary women poets have rejected this tradition as historically exclusionary and rhetorically inadequate for women, Glück embraces it with respect and admiration.
(15) Glück's formative encounters with poetry also provided her with the theoretical underpinnings of her respect for this tradition; she notes that in her youth she could sense many of the great themes and subjects of poetry even before experiencing them in
(20) her own life. These subjects—loss, the passage of time, desire—are timeless, available to readers of any age, gender, or social background. Glück makes no distinction between these subjects as belonging to female or male poets alone, calling them "the great
(25) human subjects." If the aim of a poem is to explore the issue of human mortality, for example, then issues of gender distinction fade behind the presence of this universal reality.
Some of Glück's critics claim that this idea of the
(30) universal is suspect and that the idea that gender issues are transcended by addressing certain subjects may attribute to poetry an innocence that it does not have. They maintain that a female poet writing within a historically male-dominated tradition will on some
(35) level be unable to avoid accepting certain presuppositions, which, in the critics' view, are determined by a long-standing history of denigration and exclusion of female artists. Furthermore, they feel that this long-standing history cannot be confronted
(40) using tools—in Glück's case, poetic forms—forged by the traditions of this history. Instead critics insist that women poets should strive to create a uniquely female poetry by using new forms to develop a new voice.
(45) Glück, however, observes that this ambition, with its insistence on an essentially female perspective, is as limiting as her critics believe the historically male-dominated tradition to be. She holds that to the extent that there are some gender differences that have been
(50) shaped by history, they will emerge in the differing ways that women and men write about the world—indeed, these differences will be revealed with more authority in the absence of conscious intention. She points out that the universal subjects of literature do
(55) not make literature itself timeless and unchanging. Literature, she maintains, is inescapably historical, and every work, both in what it includes and in what it omits, inevitably speaks of its social and historical context.

6. Which one of the following most accurately expresses the main point of the passage?

(A) In response to her critics, Glück argues that the attempt to develop a uniquely female voice is as restrictive as they believe the male tradition in poetry to be.

(B) Although critics have taken Glück to task for writing poetry that is generic in subject rather than specifically aimed at addressing women's concerns, she believes that poetry must instead concern itself with certain universal themes.

(C) In spite of critics who attempt to limit art to expressing the unique perspectives of the artist's gender, Glück believes that art in fact represents a perspective on its subject matter that is equally male and female.

(D) In opposition to some critics, Glück writes on universal themes rather than striving for a uniquely female voice, believing that whatever gender differences are present will emerge unconsciously in any case.

(E) Aside from the power and accomplishment of her writing, Glück has yet to offer a completely satisfying response to the critics' demand that her work reflect the conflict between male and female perspectives on poetic subject matter.

7. Based on the passage, with which one of the following statements regarding the poetic tradition in English would Glück be most likely to agree?

(A) This tradition is somewhat diminished for its lack of recognized female poets.

(B) This tradition transcends its social and historical context.

(C) The male-dominated aspect of this tradition can be overcome only by developing a uniquely female voice in poetry.

(D) The view of this tradition as an inheritance is necessary for a poet to be successful.

(E) This tradition, though male dominated, addresses universal subjects.

GO ON TO THE NEXT PAGE.

8. As it is used in the passage, "inheritance" (line 9) refers most specifically to

    (A) the burden that a historically male-dominated poetic canon places on a contemporary woman poet
    (B) the set of poetic forms and techniques considered acceptable within a linguistic culture
    (C) the poetry written in a particular language, whose achievement serves as a model for other poets writing in that language
    (D) the presumption that contemporary poets can write only on subjects already explored by the poets in that language who are considered to be the most celebrated
    (E) the imposition on a poet, based on the poetry of preceding generations in that language, of a particular writing style

9. Based on the description in the passage, a poem that reveals gender differences in the absence of any specific intention by the poet to do so is most like

    (A) a bird's flight that exposes unseen air currents
    (B) a ship's prow that indicates how strong a wave it is designed to withstand
    (C) a building's facade that superficially embellishes an ordinary structure
    (D) a railroad track, without which travel by train is impossible
    (E) a novel that deliberately conceals the motives of its main character

10. According to the passage, Glück believes that art reveals gender differences with more authority when which one of the following is true?

    (A) The artist refuses to accept certain presuppositions about gender.
    (B) The artist uses the tools of that art's tradition.
    (C) The artist does not consciously intend to reveal such differences.
    (D) The artist comments on gender issues through the use of other subject matter.
    (E) The artist embraces that art's tradition with respect.

11. Which one of the following statements about Glück is made in the passage?

    (A) She objects to the use of traditional poetic forms to confront the history of the poetic tradition.
    (B) She recognizes that the idea of the universal in poetry is questionable.
    (C) She claims to accept only male poets as her literary family.
    (D) She claims to write from a gender-neutral perspective.
    (E) She claims to have sensed the great themes and subjects of poetry while in her youth.

12. Based on the passage, which one of the following most accurately characterizes the author's attitude toward Glück's view of poetry?

    (A) respectful dismissal
    (B) grudging acceptance
    (C) detached indifference
    (D) tacit endorsement
    (E) enthusiastic acclaim

GO ON TO THE NEXT PAGE.

Although the rights of native peoples of Canada have yet to be comprehensively defined in Canadian law, most native Canadians assert that their rights include the right not only to govern themselves and
(5) their land, but also to exercise ownership rights over movable cultural property—artifacts ranging from domestic implements to ceremonial costumes. Assignment of such rights to native communities has been difficult to achieve, but while traditional
(10) Canadian statute and common law has placed ownership of movable property with current custodians such as museums, recent litigation by native Canadians has called such ownership into question.
(15) Canadian courts usually base decisions about ownership on a concept of private property, under which all forms of property are capable of being owned by individuals or by groups functioning legally as individuals. This system is based on a
(20) philosophy that encourages the right of owners to use their property as they see fit without outside interference. But litigation by native Canadians challenges courts to recognize a concept of property ownership that clashes with the private property
(25) concept. Although some tribes now recognize the notion of private property in their legal systems, they have traditionally employed a concept of collective ownership—and in all cases in which native Canadians have made legal claim to movable
(30) property they have done so by invoking this latter concept, which is based on the philosophy that each member should have an equal say regarding the use of the community's resources. Under this collective ideology, access to and use of resources is determined
(35) by the collective interests of the community. Furthermore, collective ownership casts an individual in the role of guardian or caretaker of property rather than as a titleholder; while every tribe member is an owner of the property, individual members cannot sell
(40) this right, nor does it pass to their heirs when they die. Nevertheless, their children will enjoy the same rights, not as heirs but as communal owners.
Because the concept of collective property assigns ownership to individuals simply because they are
(45) members of the community, native Canadians rarely possess the legal documents that the concept of private property requires to demonstrate ownership. Museums, which are likely to possess bills of sale or proof of prior possession to substantiate their claims
(50) of ownership, are thus likely to be recognized as legally entitled to the property they hold, even when such property originated with native Canadian communities. But as their awareness of the inappropriateness of applying the private property
(55) concept to all cultural groups grows, Canadian courts will gradually recognize that native Canadians, while they cannot demonstrate ownership as prescribed by the notion of private property, can clearly claim ownership as prescribed by the notion of collective
(60) property, and that their claims to movable cultural property should be honored.

13. Which one of the following most accurately expresses the main idea of the passage?

(A) Litigation by native Canadians to regain control of their movable cultural property illustrates how the concept of private ownership has become increasingly obsolete and demonstrates that this concept should be replaced by the more modern concept of collective ownership.

(B) Litigation by native Canadians to regain control of their movable cultural property is likely to succeed more frequently as courts begin to acknowledge that the concept of collective ownership is more appropriate than the concept of private ownership in such cases.

(C) The conflict between the concepts of collective and private ownership that has led to litigation by native Canadians to regain control of their movable cultural property is in reality a debate over whether individuals should act as titleholders or merely as caretakers with respect to their property.

(D) The conflict between the concepts of collective and private ownership that has led to litigation by native Canadians to regain control of their movable cultural property cannot be resolved until the rights of native Canadians have been comprehensively defined in Canadian law.

(E) The conflict between the concepts of collective and private ownership that has led to litigation by native Canadians to regain control of their movable cultural property illustrates the need to expand the concept of private property to include cases of joint ownership by a collection of individuals.

14. According to the concept of private property as presented in the passage, which one of the following most completely describes the meaning of the term "property owner"?

(A) one who possesses a bill of sale to substantiate his or her claims to property ownership

(B) one who possesses proof of prior possession to substantiate his or her claims to property ownership ·

(C) one who is allowed to make use of his or her property in whatever manner he or she wishes

(D) one who is allowed to transfer ownership rights to his or her children as heirs

(E) one who is allowed to exercise property rights because of his or her membership in a community

GO ON TO THE NEXT PAGE.

15. The author's attitude toward the possibility of courts increasingly assigning ownership rights to native communities is best described as which one of the following?

    (A)   certain that it will never be realized and concerned that it should

    (B)   concerned that it will never be realized but hopeful that it will

    (C)   uncertain whether it will be realized but hopeful that it will

    (D)   uncertain whether it will be realized but confident that it should

    (E)   convinced that it will be realized and pleased that it will

16. The primary function of the first paragraph of the passage is to

    (A)   identify some of the specific types of property at issue in litigation by native Canadians to regain control of their movable cultural property from museums

    (B)   describe the role of the concept of property ownership in litigation by native Canadians to regain control of their movable cultural property from museums

    (C)   summarize the difficulties that have been experienced in attempting to develop a comprehensive definition of the rights of native Canadians under the law

    (D)   provide the context within which litigation by native Canadians to regain control of their movable cultural property is occurring

    (E)   discuss the difficulty of deciding legal cases that rest on a clash between two cultures' differing definitions of a legal concept

17. Given the information in the passage, Canadian courts hearing a dispute over movable cultural property between a museum and a group of native Canadians will be increasingly unlikely to treat which one of the following as a compelling reason for deciding the case in the museum's favor?

    (A)   The museum is able to produce evidence that the property did not originate in the native community.

    (B)   The museum cannot produce written documentation of its claims to ownership of the property.

    (C)   The group of native Canadians produces evidence that the property originated in their community.

    (D)   The group of native Canadians cannot produce written documentation of their claims to ownership of the property.

    (E)   The group of native Canadians do not belong to a tribe that employs a legal system that has adopted the concept of private property.

18. The passage suggests that the concepts of collective and private ownership differ in each of the following ways EXCEPT:

    (A)   The collective concept allows groups of individuals to own property; the private concept does not.

    (B)   The collective concept requires consideration of community interests; the private concept does not.

    (C)   The collective concept assigns ownership on the basis of membership in a community; the private concept does not.

    (D)   The private concept allows owners to function as titleholders to their property; the collective concept does not.

    (E)   The private concept permits individuals to sell property; the collective concept does not.

19. The passage most supports which one of the following statements about the tribal legal systems mentioned in the second paragraph of the passage?

    (A)   All tribes whose legal system employs the concept of collective property have engaged in litigation over control of movable cultural property.

    (B)   Only tribes that have engaged in litigation over control of movable property have a legal system that employs the concept of collective property.

    (C)   All tribes that have engaged in litigation over control of movable cultural property have a legal system that employs the concept of collective property.

    (D)   All tribes whose legal system recognizes the concept of private property can expect to succeed in litigation over control of movable cultural property.

    (E)   Only those tribes whose legal system recognizes the concept of private property can expect to succeed in litigation over control of movable cultural property.

GO ON TO THE NEXT PAGE.

The first thing any embryo must do before it can develop into an organism is establish early polarity— that is, it must set up a way to distinguish its top from its bottom and its back from its front. The
(5) mechanisms that establish the earliest spatial configurations in an embryo are far less similar across life forms than those relied on for later development, as in the formation of limbs or a nervous system: for example, the signals that the developing fruit fly uses
(10) to know its front end from its back end turn out to be radically different from those that the nematode, a type of worm, relies on, and both appear to be quite different from the polarity signals in the development of humans and other mammals.
(15) In the fruit fly, polarity is established by signals inscribed in the yolklike cytoplasm of the egg before fertilization, so that when the sperm contributes its genetic material, everything is already set to go. Given all the positional information that must be
(20) distributed throughout the cell, it takes a fruit fly a week to make an egg, but once that well-appointed egg is fertilized, it is transformed from a single cell into a crawling larva in a day. By contrast, in the embryonic development of certain nematodes, the
(25) point where the sperm enters the egg appears to provide crucial positional information. Once that information is present, little bundles of proteins called p-granules, initially distributed uniformly throughout the cytoplasm, begin to congregate at one end of the
(30) yolk; when the fertilized egg divides, one of the resulting cells gets all the p-granules. The presence or absence of these granules in cells appears to help determine whether their subsequent divisions will lead to the formation of the worm's front or back
(35) half. A similar sperm-driven mechanism is also thought to establish body orientation in some comparatively simple vertebrates such as frogs, though apparently not in more complex vertebrates such as mammals. Research indicates that in human
(40) and other mammalian embryos, polarity develops much later, as many stages of cell division occur with no apparent asymmetries among cells. Yet how polarity is established in mammals is currently a tempting mystery to researchers.
(45) Once an embryo establishes polarity, it relies on sets of essential genes that are remarkably similar among all life forms for elaboration of its parts. There is an astonishing conservation of mechanism in this process: the genes that help make eyes in flies
(50) are similar to the genes that make eyes in mice or humans. So a seeming paradox arises: when embryos of different species are at the one- or few-cell stage and still appear almost identical, the mechanisms of development they use are vastly different; yet when
(55) they start growing brains or extremities and become identifiable as distinct species, the developmental mechanisms they use are remarkably similar.

20. Which one of the following most accurately expresses the main point of the passage?

(A) Species differ more in the mechanisms that determine the spatial orientation in an embryo than they do in their overall genetic makeup.

(B) Embryos determine their front from their back and top from bottom by different methods, depending on whether the organism is simple or more complex.

(C) While very similar genes help determine the later embryonic development of all organisms, the genetic mechanisms by which embryos establish early polarity vary dramatically from one organism to the next.

(D) The mechanisms by which embryos establish early polarity differ depending on whether the signals by which polarity is achieved are inscribed in the cytoplasm of the egg or the p-granules of the sperm.

(E) Despite their apparent dissimilarity from species to species, the means by which organisms establish polarity rely on essentially the same genetic mechanisms.

21. The passage suggests that the author would be most likely to agree with which one of the following statements?

(A) The simpler the organism, the greater the speed at which it develops from fertilized egg to embryo.

(B) Scientists have determined how polarity is established in most simple vertebrates.

(C) Scientists will try to determine how polarity is established in humans.

(D) Very few observations of embryonic development after polarity is established are generalizable to more than a single species.

(E) Simpler organisms take longer to establish polarity than do more complex organisms.

GO ON TO THE NEXT PAGE.

22. The passage provides information to suggest that which one of the following relationships exists between the development of humans and the development of fruit flies?

    (A) Since humans and fruit flies use similar genetic material in their development, analogies from fruit fly behavior can be useful in explaining human behavior.
    (B) For the elaboration of parts, human development relies on genetic material quite different in nature, though not in quantity, from that of a fruit fly.
    (C) Positional information for establishing polarity in a human embryo, as in that of the fruit fly, is distributed throughout the egg prior to fertilization.
    (D) A study of the development of the fruit fly's visual system would more likely be applicable to questions of human development than would a study of the mechanisms that establish the fruit fly's polarity.
    (E) While the fruit fly egg becomes a larva in a single day, a human embryo takes significantly longer to develop because humans cannot develop limbs until they have established a nervous system.

23. According to the passage, polarity is established in a human embryo

    (A) after more stages of cell division than in frogs
    (B) before the sperm enters the egg
    (C) after positional information is provided by the massing of p-granules
    (D) by the same sperm-driven mechanism as in the nematode
    (E) in the same way as in simpler vertebrates

24. By "conservation of mechanism" (line 48) the author is probably referring to

    (A) how the same mechanism can be used to form different parts of the same organism
    (B) the fact that no genetic material is wasted in development
    (C) how few genes a given organism requires in order to elaborate its parts
    (D) a highly complex organism's requiring no more genetic material than a simpler one
    (E) the fact that analogous structures in different species are brought about by similar genetic means

25. Which one of the following most accurately states the main purpose of the second paragraph?

    (A) to illustrate the diversity of processes by which organisms establish early polarity
    (B) to elaborate on the differences between embryonic formation in the fruit fly and in the nematode
    (C) to suggest why the process of establishing early polarity in humans is not yet understood
    (D) to demonstrate the significance and necessity for genetic development of establishing polarity
    (E) to demonstrate that there are two main types of mechanism by which early polarity is established

26. According to the passage, which one of the following is a major difference between the establishment of polarity in the fruit fly and in the nematode?

    (A) The fruit fly embryo takes longer to establish polarity than does the nematode embryo.
    (B) The mechanisms that establish polarity are more easily identifiable in the nematode than in the fruit fly.
    (C) Polarity signals for the fruit fly embryo are inscribed entirely in the egg and these signals for the nematode embryo are inscribed entirely in the sperm.
    (D) Polarity in the fruit fly takes more stages of cell division to become established than in the nematode.
    (E) Polarity is established for the fruit fly before fertilization and for the nematode through fertilization.

27. The author's primary purpose in the passage is to

    (A) articulate a theory of how early polarity is established and support the theory by an analysis of data
    (B) describe a phase in the development of organisms in which the genetic mechanisms used are disparate and discuss why this disparity is surprising
    (C) provide a classification of the mechanisms by which different life forms establish early polarity
    (D) argue that a certain genetic process must occur in all life forms, regardless of their apparent dissimilarity
    (E) explain why an embryo must establish early polarity before it can develop into an organism

S T O P

IF YOU FINISH BEFORE TIME IS CALLED, YOU MAY CHECK YOUR WORK ON THIS SECTION ONLY.
DO NOT WORK ON ANY OTHER SECTION IN THE TEST.

SECTION V

Time—35 minutes

26 Questions

Directions: The questions in this section are based on the reasoning contained in brief statements or passages. For some questions, more than one of the choices could conceivably answer the question. However, you are to choose the best answer; that is, the response that most accurately and completely answers the question. You should not make assumptions that are by commonsense standards implausible, superfluous, or incompatible with the passage. After you have chosen the best answer, blacken the corresponding space on your answer sheet.

1. While 65 percent of the eligible voters who were recently polled favor Perkins over Samuels in the coming election, the results of that poll are dubious because it was not based on a representative sample. Given that Perkins predominantly advocates the interests of the upper-middle class and that the survey was conducted at high-priced shopping malls, it is quite probable that Perkins's supporters were overrepresented.

Which one of the following statements most accurately expresses the main conclusion of the argument?

(A) The poll was intentionally designed to favor Perkins over Samuels.

(B) Samuels's supporters believe that they were probably not adequately represented in the poll.

(C) The poll's results probably do not accurately represent the opinions of the voters in the coming election.

(D) Samuels is quite likely to have a good chance of winning the coming election.

(E) Those who designed the poll should have considered more carefully where to conduct the survey.

2. Sleep research has demonstrated that sleep is characterized by periods of different levels of brain activity. People experience dreams during only one of these periods, known as REM (rapid eye movement) sleep. Test subjects who are chronically deprived of REM sleep become irritable during waking life. This shows that REM sleep relieves the stresses of waking life.

Which one of the following, if true, most strengthens the argument?

(A) Test subjects who are chronically deprived of non-REM sleep also become irritable during waking life.

(B) Chronically having bad dreams can cause stress, but so can chronically having pleasant but exciting dreams.

(C) During times of increased stress, one's REM sleep is disturbed in a way that prevents one from dreaming.

(D) Only some people awakened during REM sleep can report the dreams they were having just before being awakened.

(E) Other factors being equal, people who normally have shorter periods of REM sleep tend to experience more stress.

GO ON TO THE NEXT PAGE.

3. Since 1989 the importation of ivory from African elephants into the United States and Canada has been illegal, but the importation of ivory from the excavated tusks of ancient mammoths remains legal in both countries. Following the ban, there was a sharp increase in the importation of ivory that importers identified as mammoth ivory. In 1989 customs officials lacked a technique for distinguishing elephant ivory from that of mammoths. Just after such a technique was invented and its use by customs officials became widely known, there was a dramatic decrease in the amount of ivory presented for importation into the U.S. and Canada that was identified by importers as mammoth ivory.

Which one of the following is most strongly supported by the information above?

(A) Customs officials still cannot reliably distinguish elephant ivory from mammoth ivory.

(B) Most of the ivory currently imported into the U.S. and Canada comes from neither African elephants nor mammoths.

(C) In the period since the technique for distinguishing elephant ivory from mammoth ivory was implemented, the population of African elephants has declined.

(D) Much of the ivory imported as mammoth ivory just after the ban on ivory from African elephants went into effect was actually elephant ivory.

(E) Shortly after the importation of ivory from African elephants was outlawed, there was a sharp increase in the total amount of all ivory presented for importation into the U.S. and Canada.

4. My suspicion that there is some truth to astrology has been confirmed. Most physicians I have talked to believe in it.

The flawed pattern of reasoning in the argument above is most similar to that in which one of the following?

(A) Professor Smith was convicted of tax evasion last year. So I certainly wouldn't give any credence to Smith's economic theories.

(B) I have come to the conclusion that several governmental social programs are wasteful. This is because most of the biology professors I have discussed this with think that this is true.

(C) Quantum mechanics seems to be emerging as the best physical theory we have today. Most prominent physicists subscribe to it.

(D) Most mechanical engineers I have talked to say that it is healthier to refrain from eating meat. So most mechanical engineers are vegetarians.

(E) For many years now, many people, some famous, have reported that they have seen or come in contact with unidentified flying objects. So there are probably extraterrestrial societies trying to contact us.

5. The best explanation for Mozart's death involves the recently detected fracture in his skull. The crack, most likely the result of an accident, could have easily torn veins in his brain, allowing blood to leak into his brain. When such bleeding occurs in the brain and the blood dries, many of the brain's faculties become damaged, commonly, though not immediately, leading to death. This explanation of Mozart's death is bolstered by the fact that the fracture shows signs of partial healing.

The claim that the fracture shows signs of partial healing figures in the argument in which one of the following ways?

(A) It shows that Mozart's death could have been avoided.

(B) It shows that the fracture did not occur after Mozart's death.

(C) It shows that the dried blood impaired Mozart's brain's faculties.

(D) It shows that Mozart's death occurred suddenly.

(E) It suggests that Mozart's death was accidental.

6. In the first phase of the Industrial Revolution, machines were invented whose main advantage was that they worked faster than human workers. This technology became widely used because it was economically attractive; many unskilled workers could be replaced by just a few skilled workers. Today managers are looking for technology that will allow them to replace highly paid skilled workers with a smaller number of less-skilled workers.

The examples presented above best illustrate which one of the following propositions?

(A) Employers utilize new technology because it allows them to reduce labor costs.

(B) Workers will need to acquire more education and skills to remain competitive in the labor market.

(C) In seeking employment, highly skilled workers no longer have an advantage over less-skilled workers.

(D) Technology eliminates many jobs but also creates just as many jobs.

(E) Whereas technological innovations were once concentrated in heavy industry, they now affect all industries.

GO ON TO THE NEXT PAGE.

7. For many types of crops, hybrid strains have been developed that have been found in test plantings to produce significantly higher yields than were produced by traditional nonhybrid strains of those crops planted alongside them. However, in many parts of the world where farmers have abandoned traditional nonhybrid strains in favor of the hybrid strains, crop yields have not increased.

Which one of the following, if true, most helps to resolve the apparent discrepancy?

(A) Most farmers who plant the hybrid strains of their crops have larger farms than do farmers who continue to plant traditional nonhybrid strains of the same crops.

(B) Hybrid strains of crops produced higher yields in some areas than did nonhybrid strains in those areas.

(C) The hybrid strains were tested under significantly better farming conditions than are found in most areas where farmers grow those strains.

(D) Many traditional nonhybrid strains of plants produce crops that taste better and thus sell better than the hybrid strains of those crops.

(E) Many governments subsidize farmers who plant only hybrid strains of staple crops.

8. This stamp is probably highly valuable, since it exhibits a printing error. The most important factors in determining a stamp's value, assuming it is in good condition, are its rarity and age. This is clearly a fine specimen, and it is quite old as well.

The conclusion is properly inferred if which one of the following is assumed?

(A) The older a stamp is, the more valuable it is.

(B) Printing errors are always confined to a few individual stamps.

(C) Most stamps with printing errors are already in the hands of collectors.

(D) Rarity and age are of equal importance to a stamp's value.

(E) Even old and rare stamps are usually not valuable if they are in poor condition.

9. A recent study of several hundred female physicians showed that their tendency to develop coronary disease was inversely proportional to their dietary intake of two vitamins, folate and B6. The researchers concluded that folate and B6 inhibit the development of heart disease in women.

Which one of the following would, if true, most weaken the researchers' conclusion?

(A) The foods that contain significant amounts of the vitamins folate and B6 also contain significant amounts of nonvitamin nutrients that inhibit heart disease.

(B) It is very unlikely that a chemical compound would inhibit coronary disease in women but not in men.

(C) Physicians are more likely than nonphysicians to know a great deal about the link between diet and health.

(D) The physicians in the study had not been screened in advance to ensure that none had preexisting heart conditions.

(E) The vitamins folate and B6 are present only in very small amounts in most foods.

10. The proposed coal-burning electric plant should be approved, since no good arguments have been offered against it. After all, all the arguments against it have been presented by competing electricity producers.

Which one of the following is an assumption on which the reasoning above depends?

(A) The competing electricity producers would stand to lose large amounts of revenue from the building of the coal-burning electric plant.

(B) If a person's arguments against a proposal are defective, then that person has a vested interest in seeing that the proposal is not implemented.

(C) Approval of the coal-burning electric plant would please coal suppliers more than disapproval would please suppliers of fuel to the competing electricity producers.

(D) If good arguments are presented for a proposal, then that proposal should be approved.

(E) Arguments made by those who have a vested interest in the outcome of a proposal are not good arguments.

GO ON TO THE NEXT PAGE.

11. Psychiatrist: While the first appearance of a phobia is usually preceded by a traumatizing event, not everyone who is traumatized by an event develops a phobia. Furthermore, many people with phobias have never been traumatized. These two considerations show that traumatizing events do not contribute to the occurrence of phobias.

The reasoning in the psychiatrist's argument is most vulnerable to criticism on the grounds that the argument

(A) treats the cause of the occurrence of a type of phenomenon as an effect of phenomena of that type

(B) presumes, without providing justification, that some psychological events have no causes that can be established by scientific investigation

(C) builds the conclusion drawn into the support cited for that conclusion

(D) takes for granted that a type of phenomenon contributes to the occurrence of another type of phenomenon only if phenomena of these two types are invariably associated

(E) derives a causal connection from mere association when there is no independent evidence of causal connection

12. Some species are called "indicator species" because the loss of a population of such a species serves as an early warning of problems arising from pollution. Environmentalists tracking the effects of pollution have increasingly paid heed to indicator species; yet environmentalists would be misguided if they attributed the loss of a population to pollution in all cases. Though declines in population often do signal environmental degradation, they are just as often a result of the natural evolution of an ecosystem. We must remember that, in nature, change is the status quo.

Which one of the following most accurately expresses the argument's conclusion?

(A) Environmentalists sometimes overreact to the loss of a specific population.

(B) The loss of a specific population should not always be interpreted as a sign of environmental degradation.

(C) Environmentalists' use of indicator species in tracking the effects of pollution is often problematic.

(D) The loss of a specific population is often the result of natural changes in an ecosystem and in such cases should not be resisted.

(E) The loss of a specific population as a result of pollution is simply part of nature's status quo.

13. Columnist: Tagowa's testimony in the Pemberton trial was not heard outside the courtroom, so we cannot be sure what she said. Afterward, however, she publicly affirmed her belief in Pemberton's guilt. Hence, since the jury found Pemberton not guilty, we can conclude that not all of the jury members believed Tagowa's testimony.

Which one of the following describes a flaw in the columnist's reasoning?

(A) It overlooks that a witness may think that a defendant is guilty even though that witness's testimony in no way implicates the defendant.

(B) It confuses facts about what certain people believe with facts about what ought to be the case.

(C) It presumes, without providing warrant, that juries find defendants guilty only if those defendants committed the crimes with which they are charged.

(D) It presumes, without providing warrant, that a jury's finding a defendant not guilty is evidence of dishonesty on the part of someone who testified against the defendant.

(E) It fails to consider that jury members sometimes disagree with each other about the significance of a particular person's testimony.

14. A new tax law aimed at encouraging the reforestation of cleared land in order to increase the amount of forested land in a particular region offers lumber companies tax incentives for each unit of cleared land they reforest. One lumber company has accordingly reduced its tax liability by purchasing a large tract of cleared land in the region and reforesting it. The company paid for the purchase by clearing a larger tract of land in the region, a tract that it had planned to hold in long-term reserve.

If the statements above are true, which one of the following must be true about the new tax law?

(A) It is a failure in encouraging the reforestation of cleared land in the region.

(B) It will have no immediate effect on the amount of forested land in the region.

(C) It will ultimately cause lumber companies to plant trees on approximately as much land as they harvest in the region.

(D) It can provide a motivation for companies to act in a manner contrary to the purpose of the law while taking advantage of the tax incentives.

(E) It will provide lumber companies with a tax incentive that will ultimately be responsible for a massive decrease in the number of mature forests in the region.

GO ON TO THE NEXT PAGE.

15. Trustee: The recent exhibit at the art museum was extensively covered by the local media, and this coverage seems to have contributed to the record-breaking attendance it drew. If the attendance at the exhibit had been low, the museum would have gone bankrupt and closed permanently, so the museum could not have remained open had it not been for the coverage from the local media.

The reasoning in the trustee's argument is most vulnerable to criticism on the grounds that the argument

(A) confuses a necessary condition for the museum's remaining open with a sufficient condition for the museum's remaining open

(B) takes for granted that no previous exhibit at the museum had received such extensive media coverage

(C) takes for granted that most people who read articles about the exhibit also attended the exhibit

(D) fails to address the possibility that the exhibit would have drawn enough visitors to prevent bankruptcy even without media coverage

(E) presupposes the very conclusion that it is trying to prove

16. Economist: A tax is effective if it raises revenue and burdens all and only those persons targeted by the tax. A tax is ineffective, however, if it does not raise revenue and it costs a significant amount of money to enforce.

Which one of the following inferences is most strongly supported by the principles stated by the economist?

(A) The tax on cigarettes burdens most, but not all, of the people targeted by it. Thus, if it raises revenue, the tax is effective.

(B) The tax on alcohol raises a modest amount of revenue, but it costs a significant amount of money to enforce. Thus, the tax is ineffective.

(C) The tax on gasoline costs a significant amount of money to enforce. Thus, if it does not raise revenue, the tax is ineffective.

(D) The tax on coal burdens all of the people targeted by it, and this tax does not burden anyone who is not targeted by it. Thus, the tax is effective.

(E) The tax on steel does not cost a significant amount of money to enforce, but it does not raise revenue either. Thus, the tax is ineffective.

17. A large amount of rainfall in April and May typically leads to an increase in the mosquito population and thus to an increased threat of encephalitis. People cannot change the weather. Thus people cannot decrease the threat of encephalitis.

The reasoning in the argument above is flawed in that the argument

(A) takes for granted that because one event precedes another the former must be the cause of the latter

(B) presumes, without providing justification, that a certain outcome would be desirable

(C) ignores the possibility that a certain type of outcome is dependent on more than one factor

(D) takes for granted that a threat that is aggravated by certain factors could not occur in the absence of those factors

(E) draws a conclusion about what is possible from a premise about what is actually the case

18. Leadership depends as much on making one's followers aware of their own importance as it does on conveying a vivid image of a collective goal. Only if they are convinced both that their efforts are necessary for the accomplishment of this goal, and that these efforts, if expended, will actually achieve it, will people follow a leader.

If all of the statements above are true, then which one of the following CANNOT be true?

(A) Some leaders who convince their followers of the necessity of their efforts in achieving a goal fail, nevertheless, to lead them to the attainment of that goal.

(B) One who succeeds in conveying to one's followers the relationship between their efforts and the attainment of a collective goal succeeds in leading these people to this goal.

(C) Only if one is a leader must one convince people of the necessity of their efforts for the attainment of a collective goal.

(D) Sometimes people succeed in achieving a collective goal without ever having been convinced that by trying to do so they would succeed.

(E) Sometimes people who remain unsure of whether their efforts are needed for the attainment of a collective goal nevertheless follow a leader.

GO ON TO THE NEXT PAGE.

19. Fifty chronic insomniacs participated in a one-month study conducted at an institute for sleep disorders. Half were given a dose of a new drug and the other half were given a placebo every night before going to bed at the institute. Approximately 80 percent of the participants in each group reported significant relief from insomnia during the first two weeks of the study. But in each group, approximately 90 percent of those who had reported relief claimed that their insomnia had returned during the third week of the study.

Which one of the following, if true, most helps to explain all the data from the study?

(A) Because it is easy to build up a tolerance to the new drug, most people will no longer experience its effects after taking it every night for two weeks.

(B) The psychological comfort afforded by the belief that one has taken a sleep-promoting drug is enough to prevent most episodes of insomnia.

(C) The new drug is very similar in chemical composition to another drug, large doses of which have turned out to be less effective than expected.

(D) Most insomniacs sleep better in a new environment, and the new drug has no effect on an insomniac's ability to sleep.

(E) Some insomniacs cannot reliably determine how much sleep they have had or how well they have slept.

20. Advertisement: The Country Classic is the only kind of car in its class that offers an antilock braking system that includes TrackAid. An antilock braking system keeps your wheels from locking up during hard braking, and TrackAid keeps your rear wheels from spinning on slippery surfaces. So if you are a safety-conscious person in the market for a car in this class, the Country Classic is the only car for you.

The advertisement is misleading if which one of the following is true?

(A) All of the cars that are in the same class as the Country Classic offer some kind of antilock braking system.

(B) Most kinds of cars that are in the same class as the Country Classic are manufactured by the same company that manufactures the Country Classic.

(C) Without an antilock braking system, the wheels of the Country Classic and other cars in its class are more likely to lock up during hard braking than they are to spin on slippery surfaces.

(D) Other cars in the same class as the Country Classic offer an antilock braking system that uses a method other than TrackAid to prevent rear wheels from spinning on slippery surfaces.

(E) The Country Classic is more expensive than any other car in its class.

21. Sociologist: Traditional norms in our society prevent sincerity by requiring one to ignore unpleasant realities and tell small lies. But a community whose members do not trust one another cannot succeed. So, if a community is to succeed, its members must be willing to face unpleasant realities and speak about them honestly.

The sociologist's conclusion follows logically if which one of the following is assumed?

(A) Sincerity is required if community members are to trust each other.

(B) The more sincere and open community members are, the more likely that community is to succeed.

(C) A community sometimes can succeed even if its members subscribe to traditional norms.

(D) Unless a community's members are willing to face unpleasant realities, they cannot be sincere.

(E) A community's failure is often caused by its members' unwillingness to face unpleasant realities and to discuss them honestly.

GO ON TO THE NEXT PAGE.

22. If there is an election, you can either vote or not. If you vote, you have the satisfaction of knowing you influenced the results of the election; if you do not vote, you have no right to complain about the results. So, following an election, either you will have the satisfaction of knowing you influenced its results or you will have no right to complain.

The reasoning in which one of the following most closely resembles that in the argument above?

(A) When you rent a car, you can either take out insurance or not. If you take out insurance you are covered, but if you are uninsured, you are personally liable for any costs incurred from an accident. So in case of an accident, you will be better off if you are insured.

(B) If you go for a walk, when you are finished either you will feel relaxed or you will not. If you feel relaxed, then your muscles will likely not be sore the next day, though your muscles will more likely become conditioned faster if they do feel sore. Therefore, either your muscles will feel sore, or they will become better conditioned.

(C) If you attend school, you will find the courses stimulating or you will not. If your teachers are motivated, you will find the courses stimulating. If your teachers are not motivated, you will not. So either your teachers are motivated, or their courses are not stimulating.

(D) If you use a computer, its messages are either easily readable or not. If the messages are easily readable, they are merely password protected. If they are not easily readable, they are electronically encrypted. So any message on the computer you use is either password protected or electronically encrypted.

(E) When manufacturers use a natural resource, they are either efficient or inefficient. If they are inefficient, the resource will be depleted quickly. If they are efficient, the resource will last much longer. So either manufacturers are efficient or they should be fined.

23. Company president: Our consultants report that, in general, the most efficient managers have excellent time management skills. Thus, to improve productivity I recommend that we make available to our middle-level managers a seminar to train them in techniques of time management.

Each of the following, if true, would weaken the support for the company president's recommendation EXCEPT:

(A) The consultants use the same criteria to evaluate managers' efficiency as they do to evaluate their time management skills.

(B) Successful time management is more dependent on motivation than on good technique.

(C) Most managers at other companies who have attended time management seminars are still unproductive.

(D) Most managers who are already efficient do not need to improve their productivity.

(E) Most managers who are efficient have never attended a time management seminar.

24. Many Seychelles warblers of breeding age forgo breeding, remaining instead with their parents and helping to raise their own siblings. This behavior, called cooperative breeding, results from the scarcity of nesting territory for the birds on the tiny island that, until recently, was home to the world's population of Seychelles warblers. Yet when healthy warblers were transplanted to a much larger neighboring island as part of an experiment, most of those warblers maintained a pattern of cooperative breeding.

Which one of the following, if true, most helps to explain the result of the experiment?

(A) Many of the Seychelles warblers that were transplanted to the neighboring island had not yet reached breeding age.

(B) The climate of the island to which Seychelles warblers were transplanted was the same as that of the warblers' native island.

(C) Most of the terrain on the neighboring island was not of the type in which Seychelles warblers generally build their nests.

(D) Cooperative breeding in species other than the Seychelles warbler often results when the environment cannot sustain a rise in the population.

(E) The Seychelles warblers had fewer competitors for nesting territory on the island to which they were transplanted than on their native island.

GO ON TO THE NEXT PAGE.

25. Therapist: In a recent study, researchers measured how quickly 60 different psychological problems waned as a large, diverse sample of people underwent weekly behavioral therapy sessions. About 75 percent of the 60 problems consistently cleared up within 50 weeks of therapy. This shows that 50 weekly behavioral therapy sessions are all that most people need.

The therapist's argument is logically most vulnerable to criticism on the grounds that it

(A) takes for granted that there are no psychological problems that usually take significantly longer to clear up than the 60 psychological problems studied

(B) fails to address the possibility that any given one of the 60 psychological problems studied might afflict most people

(C) takes for granted that no one suffers from more than one of the 60 psychological problems studied

(D) fails to address the possibility that some forms of therapy have never been proven to be effective as treatments for psychological problems

(E) takes for granted that the sample of people studied did not have significantly more psychological problems, on average, than the population as a whole

26. Researcher: It is commonly believed that species belonging to the same biological order, such as rodents, descended from a single common ancestor. However, I compared the genetic pattern in 3 rodent species—guinea pigs, rats, and mice—as well as in 13 nonrodent mammals, and found that while rats and mice are genetically quite similar, the genetic differences between guinea pigs and mice are as great as those between mice and some nonrodent species. Thus, despite their similar physical form, guinea pigs stem from a separate ancestor.

Which one of the following, if true, most seriously undermines the researcher's reasoning?

(A) The researcher examined the genetic material of only 3 of over 2,000 species of rodents.

(B) Some pairs of species not having a common ancestor are genetically more similar to each other than are some pairs that do have a common ancestor.

(C) The researcher selected nonrodent species that have the specific cell structures she wanted to analyze genetically, though many nonrodent mammals lack these cell structures.

(D) For some genuine biological orders, the most recent common ancestor dates from later epochs than does the most recent common ancestor of other biological orders.

(E) Peculiarities of body structure, such as distinctive teeth and olfactory structures, are shared by all rodents, including guinea pigs.

S T O P

IF YOU FINISH BEFORE TIME IS CALLED, YOU MAY CHECK YOUR WORK ON THIS SECTION ONLY.
DO NOT WORK ON ANY OTHER SECTION IN THE TEST.

Wait for the supervisor's instructions before you open the page to the topic.
Please print and sign your name and write the date in the designated spaces below.

Time: 35 Minutes

General Directions

You will have 35 minutes in which to plan and write an essay on the topic inside. Read the topic and the accompanying directions carefully. You will probably find it best to spend a few minutes considering the topic and organizing your thoughts before you begin writing. In your essay, be sure to develop your ideas fully, leaving time, if possible, to review what you have written. **Do not write on a topic other than the one specified. Writing on a topic of your own choice is not acceptable.**

No special knowledge is required or expected for this writing exercise. Law schools are interested in the reasoning, clarity, organization, language usage, and writing mechanics displayed in your essay. How well you write is more important than how much you write.

Confine your essay to the blocked, lined area on the front and back of the separate Writing Sample Response Sheet. Only that area will be reproduced for law schools. Be sure that your writing is legible.

Both this topic sheet and your response sheet must be turned over to the testing staff before you leave the room.

Topic Code	Print Your Full Name Here		
_____	Last	First	M.I.

Date	Sign Your Name Here
/ /	

Scratch Paper
Do not write your essay in this space.

LSAT WRITING SAMPLE TOPIC

The owner of Avanti Pizza, which currently makes pizzas for pickup or delivery only, is considering expanding his business. He can either purchase a brick pizza oven or he can add a small dining room to his restaurant. Write an essay in which you argue for one option over the other, keeping in mind the following two criteria:

• Avanti's owner wants to increase profits by offering customers something of value that Avanti does not currently provide.
• Avanti's owner wants to distinguish his restaurant from local competitors.

Brick-oven pizza has become extremely popular, and Avanti's owner estimates that including it on the menu would substantially increase takeout and delivery business. The profit margin on such pizzas is higher than on conventional pizzas. In addition, Avanti's pizza chef could use the opportunity to introduce a selection of gourmet pizzas with creative toppings. Avanti's competitors consist of a well-established Italian restaurant, La Stella, and a franchisee of the large pizza delivery chain Pronto. Neither has a brick oven, although La Stella is rumored to be considering the option. The new oven could be up and running two weeks after the start of construction.

Avanti does not currently have space for a dining room, but the adjacent storefront property has recently become available on good lease terms. Obtaining permits and remodeling would take six months to a year, during which time the rest of the business could continue to operate. Avanti's chef would like to expand the menu to include dishes other than pizza, and with an eat-in option for customers she could easily do so. La Stella already offers sit-down dining, but in a relatively formal setting. Avanti could be more relaxed and family-friendly. In addition, Avanti could allow patrons to bring their own wine or beer, which would attract economy-minded customers. La Stella, which has a liquor license and a full bar, charges a substantial markup on all alcoholic beverages it serves.

Scratch Paper
Do not write your essay in this space.

LAST NAME (Print) MI FIRST NAME (Print)

SIGNATURE

Writing Sample Response Sheet

DO NOT WRITE
IN THIS SPACE

Begin your essay in the lined area below.
Continue on the back if you need more space.

This test can be scored automatically with your Online Center. The following Answer Key and Scoring Table are provided if you wish to score it offline.

Directions:

1. Use the Answer Key on the next page to check your answers.

2. Use the Scoring Worksheet below to compute your raw score.

3. Use the Score Conversion Chart to convert your raw score into the 120–180 scale.

Scoring Worksheet

1. Enter the number of questions you answered correctly in each section

	Number Correct
SECTION I	_____
SECTION II	_____
SECTION III	__EXP__
SECTION IV	_____
SECTION V	_____

2. Enter the sum here: _____

    This is your Raw Score.

Conversion Chart

For Converting Raw Score to the 120–180 LSAT Scaled Score LSAT PrepTest 48

Reported Score	Lowest Raw Score	Highest Raw Score
180	100	101
179	—*	—*
178	99	99
177	98	98
176	—*	—*
175	97	97
174	96	96
173	—*	—*
172	95	95
171	94	94
170	93	93
169	92	92
168	90	91
167	89	89
166	88	88
165	86	87
164	85	85
163	83	84
162	81	82
161	80	80
160	78	79
159	76	77
158	74	75
157	72	73
156	70	71
155	68	69
154	66	67
153	64	65
152	62	63
151	60	61
150	58	59
149	56	57
148	54	55
147	52	53
146	50	51
145	49	49
144	47	48
143	45	46
142	43	44
141	41	42
140	39	40
139	38	38
138	36	37
137	34	35
136	33	33
135	31	32
134	30	30
133	29	29
132	27	28
131	26	26
130	25	25
129	23	24
128	22	22
127	21	21
126	20	20
125	19	19
124	18	18
123	17	17
122	16	16
121	15	15
120	0	14

*There is no raw score that will produce this scaled score for this test.

Answer Key

SECTION I

1.	D	8.	C	15.	A	22.	E
2.	D	9.	D	16.	D	23.	E
3.	C	10.	D	17.	E	24.	E
4.	B	11.	E	18.	D	25.	C
5.	A	12.	B	19.	B	26.	A
6.	A	13.	C	20.	E		
7.	C	14.	D	21.	B		

SECTION II

1.	C	8.	B	15.	D	22.	B
2.	E	9.	C	16.	C		
3.	E	10.	E	17.	C		
4.	A	11.	D	18.	A		
5.	A	12.	E	19.	A		
6.	A	13.	C	20.	A		
7.	C	14.	A	21.	D		

SECTION III

1.	B	8.	A	15.	C	22.	E
2.	C	9.	*	16.	A	23.	D
3.	D	10.	E	17.	D	24.	C
4.	A	11.	A	18.	C	25.	A
5.	E	12.	B	19.	D	26.	E
6.	D	13.	E	20.	B	27.	C
7.	D	14.	C	21.	E		

SECTION IV

1.	A	8.	C	15.	E	22.	D
2.	D	9.	A	16.	D	23.	A
3.	E	10.	C	17.	D	24.	E
4.	B	11.	E	18.	A	25.	A
5.	C	12.	D	19.	C	26.	E
6.	D	13.	B	20.	C	27.	B
7.	E	14.	C	21.	C		

SECTION V

1.	C	8.	B	15.	D	22.	D
2.	E	9.	A	16.	C	23.	D
3.	D	10.	E	17.	C	24.	C
4.	B	11.	D	18.	E	25.	B
5.	B	12.	B	19.	D	26.	B
6.	A	13.	A	20.	D		
7.	C	14.	D	21.	A		

*Item removed from scoring.

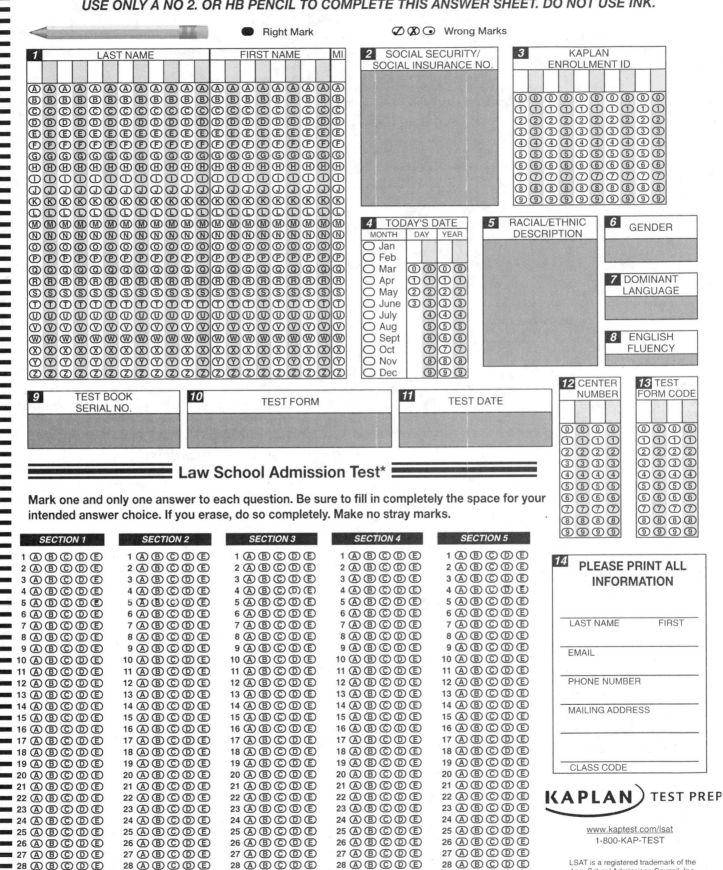

General Directions for the LSAT* Answer Sheet

The actual testing time for this portion of the test will be 2 hours 55 minutes. There are five sections, each with a time limit of 35 minutes. The supervisor will tell you when to begin and end each section. If you finish a section before time is called, you may check your work on that section <u>only</u>; do not turn to any other section of the test book and do not work on any other section either in the test book or on the answer sheet.

There are several different types of questions on the test, and each question type has its own directions. <u>Be sure you understand the directions for each question type before attempting to answer any questions in that section.</u>

Not everyone will finish all the questions in the time allowed. Do not hurry, but work steadily and as quickly as you can without sacrificing accuracy. You are advised to use your time effectively. If a question seems too difficult, go on to the next one and return to the difficult question after completing the section. MARK THE BEST ANSWER YOU CAN FOR EVERY QUESTION. NO DEDUCTIONS WILL BE MADE FOR WRONG ANSWERS. YOUR SCORE WILL BE BASED ONLY ON THE NUMBER OF QUESTIONS YOU ANSWER CORRECTLY.

ALL YOUR ANSWERS MUST BE MARKED ON THE ANSWER SHEET. Answer spaces for each question are lettered to correspond with the letters of the potential answers to each question in the test book. After you have decided which of the answers is correct, blacken the corresponding space on the answer sheet. BE SURE THAT EACH MARK IS BLACK AND COMPLETELY FILLS THE ANSWER SPACE. Give only one answer to each question. If you change an answer, be sure that all previous marks are <u>erased completely</u>. Since the answer sheet is machine scored, incomplete erasures may be interpreted as intended answers. ANSWERS RECORDED IN THE TEST BOOK WILL NOT BE SCORED.

There may be more questions noted on this answer sheet than there are questions in a section. Do not be concerned but be certain that the section and number of the question you are answering matches the answer sheet section and question number. Additional answer spaces in any answer sheet section should be left blank. Begin your next section in the number one answer space for that section.

Kaplan takes various steps to ensure that answer sheets are returned from test centers in a timely manner for processing. In the unlikely event that an answer sheet(s) is not received, Kaplan will permit the examinee to either retest at no additional fee or to receive a refund of his or her test fee. THESE REMEDIES ARE THE EXCLUSIVE REMEDIES AVAILABLE IN THE UNLIKELY EVENT THAT AN ANSWER SHEET IS NOT RECEIVED BY KAPLAN.

Score Cancellation

Complete this section only if you are absolutely certain you want to cancel your score. A CANCELLATION REQUEST CANNOT BE RESCINDED. IF YOU ARE AT ALL UNCERTAIN, YOU SHOULD <u>NOT</u> COMPLETE THIS SECTION.

To cancel your score from this administration, you **must**:

A. fill in both ovals here..... ○ ○

B. read the following statement. Then sign your name and enter the date. **YOUR SIGNATURE ALONE IS NOT SUFFICIENT FOR SCORE CANCELLATION. BOTH OVALS MUST BE FILLED IN FOR SCANNING EQUIPMENT TO RECOGNIZE YOUR REQUEST FOR SCORE CANCELLATION.**

I certify that I wish to cancel my test score from this administration. I understand that my request is irreversible and that my score will not be sent to me or to the law schools to which I apply.

Sign your name in full

Date

HOW DID YOU PREPARE FOR THE LSAT*?
(Select all that apply.)

Responses to this item are voluntary and will be used for statistical research purposes only.

- ○ By attending a Kaplan LSAT* prep course or tutoring program
- ○ By attending a non-Kaplan prep course or tutoring program (Please specify:_____)
- ○ By using a Kaplan LSAT* prep book
- ○ By using a non-Kaplan prep book (Please specify: _____)
- ○ By working through the sample questions and free sample tests provided by the LSAC
- ○ By working through official LSAT* PrepTests and/or other LSAC test prep products
- ○ Other preparation (Please specify: _____)
- ○ No preparation

CERTIFYING STATEMENT

Please write (DO NOT PRINT) the following statement. Sign and date.

I certify that I am the examinee whose name appears on this answer sheet and that I am here to take the LSAT for the sole purpose of being considered for application to law school. I further certify that I will neither assist nor receive assistance from any other candidate, and I agree not to copy or retain examination questions or to transmit them to or discuss them with any other person in any form.

_____

_____

_____

_____

_____

_____

_____

_____

_____

_____

SIGNATURE: _____ TODAY'S DATE: _____/_____/_____
                                                          MONTH   DAY   YEAR

*LSAT is a registered trademark of the Law School Admissions Council, Inc.

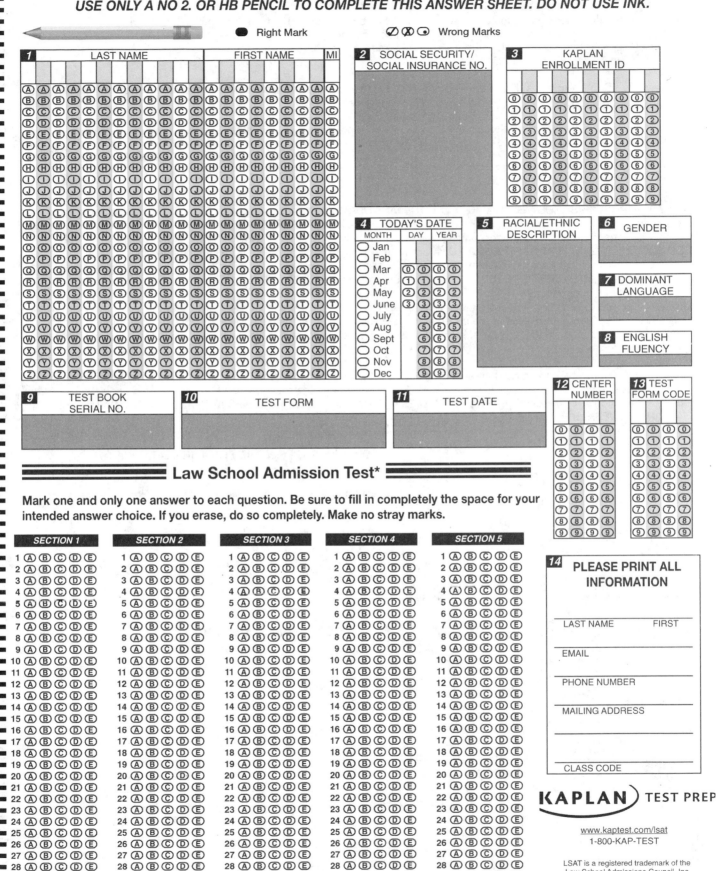

General Directions for the LSAT* Answer Sheet

The actual testing time for this portion of the test will be 2 hours 55 minutes. There are five sections, each with a time limit of 35 minutes. The supervisor will tell you when to begin and end each section. If you finish a section before time is called, you may check your work on that section <u>only</u>; do not turn to any other section of the test book and do not work on any other section either in the test book or on the answer sheet.

There are several different types of questions on the test, and each question type has its own directions. <u>Be sure you understand the directions for each question type before attempting to answer any questions in that section.</u>

Not everyone will finish all the questions in the time allowed. Do not hurry, but work steadily and as quickly as you can without sacrificing accuracy. You are advised to use your time effectively. If a question seems too difficult, go on to the next one and return to the difficult question after completing the section. MARK THE BEST ANSWER YOU CAN FOR EVERY QUESTION. NO DEDUCTIONS WILL BE MADE FOR WRONG ANSWERS. YOUR SCORE WILL BE BASED ONLY ON THE NUMBER OF QUESTIONS YOU ANSWER CORRECTLY.

ALL YOUR ANSWERS MUST BE MARKED ON THE ANSWER SHEET. Answer spaces for each question are lettered to correspond with the letters of the potential answers to each question in the test book. After you have decided which of the answers is correct, blacken the corresponding space on the answer sheet. BE SURE THAT EACH MARK IS BLACK AND COMPLETELY FILLS THE ANSWER SPACE. Give only one answer to each question. If you change an answer, be sure that all previous marks are <u>erased completely</u>. Since the answer sheet is machine scored, incomplete erasures may be interpreted as intended answers. ANSWERS RECORDED IN THE TEST BOOK WILL NOT BE SCORED.

There may be more questions noted on this answer sheet than there are questions in a section. Do not be concerned but be certain that the section and number of the question you are answering matches the answer sheet section and question number. Additional answer spaces in any answer sheet section should be left blank. Begin your next section in the number one answer space for that section.

Kaplan takes various steps to ensure that answer sheets are returned from test centers in a timely manner for processing. In the unlikely event that an answer sheet(s) is not received, Kaplan will permit the examinee to either retest at no additional fee or to receive a refund of his or her test fee. THESE REMEDIES ARE THE EXCLUSIVE REMEDIES AVAILABLE IN THE UNLIKELY EVENT THAT AN ANSWER SHEET IS NOT RECEIVED BY KAPLAN.

Score Cancellation

Complete this section only if you are absolutely certain you want to cancel your score. A CANCELLATION REQUEST CANNOT BE RESCINDED. IF YOU ARE AT ALL UNCERTAIN, YOU SHOULD <u>NOT</u> COMPLETE THIS SECTION.

To cancel your score from this administration, you **must**:

A. fill in both ovals here..... ◯ ◯

B. read the following statement. Then sign your name and enter the date. **YOUR SIGNATURE ALONE IS NOT SUFFICIENT FOR SCORE CANCELLATION. BOTH OVALS MUST BE FILLED IN FOR SCANNING EQUIPMENT TO RECOGNIZE YOUR REQUEST FOR SCORE CANCELLATION.**

I certify that I wish to cancel my test score from this administration. I understand that my request is irreversible and that my score will not be sent to me or to the law schools to which I apply.

_____
Sign your name in full

_____
Date

HOW DID YOU PREPARE FOR THE LSAT*?
(Select all that apply.)

Responses to this item are voluntary and will be used for statistical research purposes only.

- ◯ By attending a Kaplan LSAT* prep course or tutoring program
- ◯ By attending a non-Kaplan prep course or tutoring program (Please specify:_____)
- ◯ By using a Kaplan LSAT* prep book
- ◯ By using a non-Kaplan prep book (Please specify: _____)
- ◯ By working through the sample questions and free sample tests provided by the LSAC
- ◯ By working through official LSAT* PrepTests and/or other LSAC test prep products
- ◯ Other preparation (Please specify: _____)
- ◯ No preparation

CERTIFYING STATEMENT

Please write (DO NOT PRINT) the following statement. Sign and date.

I certify that I am the examinee whose name appears on this answer sheet and that I am here to take the LSAT for the sole purpose of being considered for application to law school. I further certify that I will neither assist nor receive assistance from any other candidate, and I agree not to copy or retain examination questions or to transmit them to or discuss them with any other person in any form.

_____
_____
_____
_____
_____
_____
_____
_____
_____
_____

SIGNATURE:_____   TODAY'S DATE: _____/_____/_____
                                                                                                MONTH   DAY   YEAR

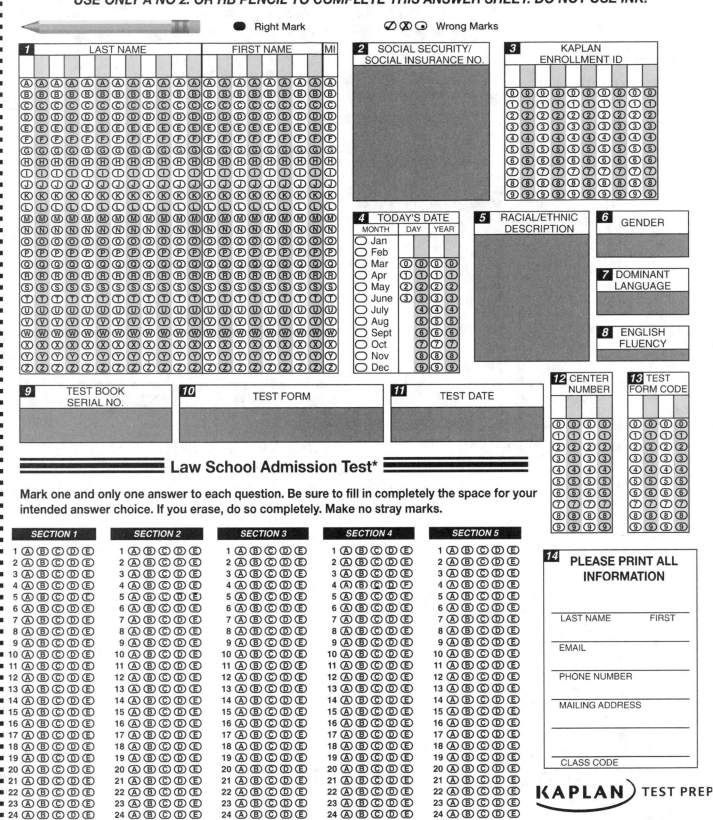

General Directions for the LSAT* Answer Sheet

The actual testing time for this portion of the test will be 2 hours 55 minutes. There are five sections, each with a time limit of 35 minutes. The supervisor will tell you when to begin and end each section. If you finish a section before time is called, you may check your work on that section <u>only</u>; do not turn to any other section of the test book and do not work on any other section either in the test book or on the answer sheet.

There are several different types of questions on the test, and each question type has its own directions. <u>Be sure you understand the directions for each question type before attempting to answer any questions in that section.</u>

Not everyone will finish all the questions in the time allowed. Do not hurry, but work steadily and as quickly as you can without sacrificing accuracy. You are advised to use your time effectively. If a question seems too difficult, go on to the next one and return to the difficult question after completing the section. MARK THE BEST ANSWER YOU CAN FOR EVERY QUESTION. NO DEDUCTIONS WILL BE MADE FOR WRONG ANSWERS. YOUR SCORE WILL BE BASED ONLY ON THE NUMBER OF QUESTIONS YOU ANSWER CORRECTLY.

ALL YOUR ANSWERS MUST BE MARKED ON THE ANSWER SHEET. Answer spaces for each question are lettered to correspond with the letters of the potential answers to each question in the test book. After you have decided which of the answers is correct, blacken the corresponding space on the answer sheet. BE SURE THAT EACH MARK IS BLACK AND COMPLETELY FILLS THE ANSWER SPACE. Give only one answer to each question. If you change an answer, be sure that all previous marks are <u>erased completely</u>. Since the answer sheet is machine scored, incomplete erasures may be interpreted as intended answers. ANSWERS RECORDED IN THE TEST BOOK WILL NOT BE SCORED.

There may be more questions noted on this answer sheet than there are questions in a section. Do not be concerned but be certain that the section and number of the question you are answering matches the answer sheet section and question number. Additional answer spaces in any answer sheet section should be left blank. Begin your next section in the number one answer space for that section.

Kaplan takes various steps to ensure that answer sheets are returned from test centers in a timely manner for processing. In the unlikely event that an answer sheet(s) is not received, Kaplan will permit the examinee to either retest at no additional fee or to receive a refund of his or her test fee. THESE REMEDIES ARE THE EXCLUSIVE REMEDIES AVAILABLE IN THE UNLIKELY EVENT THAT AN ANSWER SHEET IS NOT RECEIVED BY KAPLAN.

Score Cancellation

Complete this section only if you are absolutely certain you want to cancel your score. A CANCELLATION REQUEST CANNOT BE RESCINDED. IF YOU ARE AT ALL UNCERTAIN, YOU SHOULD <u>NOT</u> COMPLETE THIS SECTION.

To cancel your score from this administration, you **must**:

A. fill in both ovals here..... ◯ ◯

B. read the following statement. Then sign your name and enter the date. **YOUR SIGNATURE ALONE IS NOT SUFFICIENT FOR SCORE CANCELLATION. BOTH OVALS MUST BE FILLED IN FOR SCANNING EQUIPMENT TO RECOGNIZE YOUR REQUEST FOR SCORE CANCELLATION.**

I certify that I wish to cancel my test score from this administration. I understand that my request is irreversible and that my score will not be sent to me or to the law schools to which I apply.

_____
Sign your name in full

_____
Date

HOW DID YOU PREPARE FOR THE LSAT*?
(Select all that apply.)

Responses to this item are voluntary and will be used for statistical research purposes only.

- ◯ By attending a Kaplan LSAT* prep course or tutoring program
- ◯ By attending a non-Kaplan prep course or tutoring program (Please specify:_____)
- ◯ By using a Kaplan LSAT* prep book
- ◯ By using a non-Kaplan prep book (Please specify: _____)
- ◯ By working through the sample questions and free sample tests provided by the LSAC
- ◯ By working through official LSAT* PrepTests and/or other LSAC test prep products
- ◯ Other preparation (Please specify: _____)
- ◯ No preparation

CERTIFYING STATEMENT

Please write (DO NOT PRINT) the following statement. Sign and date.

I certify that I am the examinee whose name appears on this answer sheet and that I am here to take the LSAT for the sole purpose of being considered for application to law school. I further certify that I will neither assist nor receive assistance from any other candidate, and I agree not to copy or retain examination questions or to transmit them to or discuss them with any other person in any form.

_____

_____

_____

_____

_____

_____

_____

_____

_____

_____

SIGNATURE:_____ TODAY'S DATE: _____/_____/_____
　　　　　　　　　　　　　　　　　　　　　　　　　　　MONTH　DAY　YEAR

*LSAT is a registered trademark of the Law School Admissions Council, Inc.

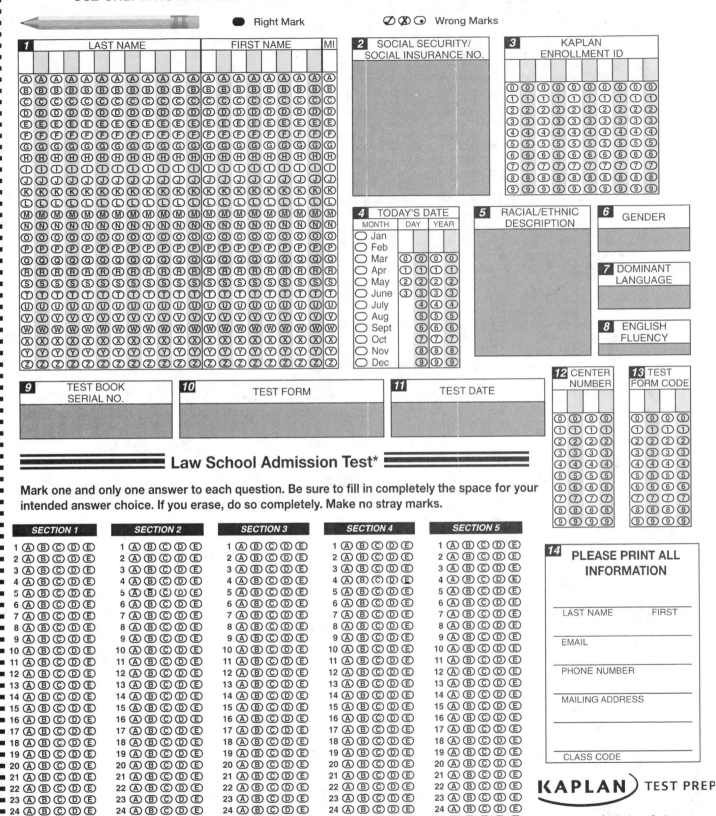

USE ONLY A NO 2. OR HB PENCIL TO COMPLETE THIS ANSWER SHEET. DO NOT USE INK.

● Right Mark   ⊘ ⊗ ⊙ Wrong Marks

1 LAST NAME   FIRST NAME   MI

2 SOCIAL SECURITY/ SOCIAL INSURANCE NO.

3 KAPLAN ENROLLMENT ID

4 TODAY'S DATE
MONTH | DAY | YEAR
○ Jan
○ Feb
○ Mar
○ Apr
○ May
○ June
○ July
○ Aug
○ Sept
○ Oct
○ Nov
○ Dec

5 RACIAL/ETHNIC DESCRIPTION

6 GENDER

7 DOMINANT LANGUAGE

8 ENGLISH FLUENCY

9 TEST BOOK SERIAL NO.

10 TEST FORM

11 TEST DATE

12 CENTER NUMBER

13 TEST FORM CODE

=== **Law School Admission Test*** ===

Mark one and only one answer to each question. Be sure to fill in completely the space for your intended answer choice. If you erase, do so completely. Make no stray marks.

SECTION 1

1 Ⓐ Ⓑ Ⓒ Ⓓ Ⓔ
2 Ⓐ Ⓑ Ⓒ Ⓓ Ⓔ
3 Ⓐ Ⓑ Ⓒ Ⓓ Ⓔ
4 Ⓐ Ⓑ Ⓒ Ⓓ Ⓔ
5 Ⓐ Ⓑ Ⓒ Ⓓ Ⓔ
6 Ⓐ Ⓑ Ⓒ Ⓓ Ⓔ
7 Ⓐ Ⓑ Ⓒ Ⓓ Ⓔ
8 Ⓐ Ⓑ Ⓒ Ⓓ Ⓔ
9 Ⓐ Ⓑ Ⓒ Ⓓ Ⓔ
10 Ⓐ Ⓑ Ⓒ Ⓓ Ⓔ
11 Ⓐ Ⓑ Ⓒ Ⓓ Ⓔ
12 Ⓐ Ⓑ Ⓒ Ⓓ Ⓔ
13 Ⓐ Ⓑ Ⓒ Ⓓ Ⓔ
14 Ⓐ Ⓑ Ⓒ Ⓓ Ⓔ
15 Ⓐ Ⓑ Ⓒ Ⓓ Ⓔ
16 Ⓐ Ⓑ Ⓒ Ⓓ Ⓔ
17 Ⓐ Ⓑ Ⓒ Ⓓ Ⓔ
18 Ⓐ Ⓑ Ⓒ Ⓓ Ⓔ
19 Ⓐ Ⓑ Ⓒ Ⓓ Ⓔ
20 Ⓐ Ⓑ Ⓒ Ⓓ Ⓔ
21 Ⓐ Ⓑ Ⓒ Ⓓ Ⓔ
22 Ⓐ Ⓑ Ⓒ Ⓓ Ⓔ
23 Ⓐ Ⓑ Ⓒ Ⓓ Ⓔ
24 Ⓐ Ⓑ Ⓒ Ⓓ Ⓔ
25 Ⓐ Ⓑ Ⓒ Ⓓ Ⓔ
26 Ⓐ Ⓑ Ⓒ Ⓓ Ⓔ
27 Ⓐ Ⓑ Ⓒ Ⓓ Ⓔ
28 Ⓐ Ⓑ Ⓒ Ⓓ Ⓔ
29 Ⓐ Ⓑ Ⓒ Ⓓ Ⓔ
30 Ⓐ Ⓑ Ⓒ Ⓓ Ⓔ

SECTION 2

1 Ⓐ Ⓑ Ⓒ Ⓓ Ⓔ
2 Ⓐ Ⓑ Ⓒ Ⓓ Ⓔ
3 Ⓐ Ⓑ Ⓒ Ⓓ Ⓔ
4 Ⓐ Ⓑ Ⓒ Ⓓ Ⓔ
5 Ⓐ Ⓑ Ⓒ Ⓓ Ⓔ
6 Ⓐ Ⓑ Ⓒ Ⓓ Ⓔ
7 Ⓐ Ⓑ Ⓒ Ⓓ Ⓔ
8 Ⓐ Ⓑ Ⓒ Ⓓ Ⓔ
9 Ⓐ Ⓑ Ⓒ Ⓓ Ⓔ
10 Ⓐ Ⓑ Ⓒ Ⓓ Ⓔ
11 Ⓐ Ⓑ Ⓒ Ⓓ Ⓔ
12 Ⓐ Ⓑ Ⓒ Ⓓ Ⓔ
13 Ⓐ Ⓑ Ⓒ Ⓓ Ⓔ
14 Ⓐ Ⓑ Ⓒ Ⓓ Ⓔ
15 Ⓐ Ⓑ Ⓒ Ⓓ Ⓔ
16 Ⓐ Ⓑ Ⓒ Ⓓ Ⓔ
17 Ⓐ Ⓑ Ⓒ Ⓓ Ⓔ
18 Ⓐ Ⓑ Ⓒ Ⓓ Ⓔ
19 Ⓐ Ⓑ Ⓒ Ⓓ Ⓔ
20 Ⓐ Ⓑ Ⓒ Ⓓ Ⓔ
21 Ⓐ Ⓑ Ⓒ Ⓓ Ⓔ
22 Ⓐ Ⓑ Ⓒ Ⓓ Ⓔ
23 Ⓐ Ⓑ Ⓒ Ⓓ Ⓔ
24 Ⓐ Ⓑ Ⓒ Ⓓ Ⓔ
25 Ⓐ Ⓑ Ⓒ Ⓓ Ⓔ
26 Ⓐ Ⓑ Ⓒ Ⓓ Ⓔ
27 Ⓐ Ⓑ Ⓒ Ⓓ Ⓔ
28 Ⓐ Ⓑ Ⓒ Ⓓ Ⓔ
29 Ⓐ Ⓑ Ⓒ Ⓓ Ⓔ
30 Ⓐ Ⓑ Ⓒ Ⓓ Ⓔ

SECTION 3

1 Ⓐ Ⓑ Ⓒ Ⓓ Ⓔ
2 Ⓐ Ⓑ Ⓒ Ⓓ Ⓔ
3 Ⓐ Ⓑ Ⓒ Ⓓ Ⓔ
4 Ⓐ Ⓑ Ⓒ Ⓓ Ⓔ
5 Ⓐ Ⓑ Ⓒ Ⓓ Ⓔ
6 Ⓐ Ⓑ Ⓒ Ⓓ Ⓔ
7 Ⓐ Ⓑ Ⓒ Ⓓ Ⓔ
8 Ⓐ Ⓑ Ⓒ Ⓓ Ⓔ
9 Ⓐ Ⓑ Ⓒ Ⓓ Ⓔ
10 Ⓐ Ⓑ Ⓒ Ⓓ Ⓔ
11 Ⓐ Ⓑ Ⓒ Ⓓ Ⓔ
12 Ⓐ Ⓑ Ⓒ Ⓓ Ⓔ
13 Ⓐ Ⓑ Ⓒ Ⓓ Ⓔ
14 Ⓐ Ⓑ Ⓒ Ⓓ Ⓔ
15 Ⓐ Ⓑ Ⓒ Ⓓ Ⓔ
16 Ⓐ Ⓑ Ⓒ Ⓓ Ⓔ
17 Ⓐ Ⓑ Ⓒ Ⓓ Ⓔ
18 Ⓐ Ⓑ Ⓒ Ⓓ Ⓔ
19 Ⓐ Ⓑ Ⓒ Ⓓ Ⓔ
20 Ⓐ Ⓑ Ⓒ Ⓓ Ⓔ
21 Ⓐ Ⓑ Ⓒ Ⓓ Ⓔ
22 Ⓐ Ⓑ Ⓒ Ⓓ Ⓔ
23 Ⓐ Ⓑ Ⓒ Ⓓ Ⓔ
24 Ⓐ Ⓑ Ⓒ Ⓓ Ⓔ
25 Ⓐ Ⓑ Ⓒ Ⓓ Ⓔ
26 Ⓐ Ⓑ Ⓒ Ⓓ Ⓔ
27 Ⓐ Ⓑ Ⓒ Ⓓ Ⓔ
28 Ⓐ Ⓑ Ⓒ Ⓓ Ⓔ
29 Ⓐ Ⓑ Ⓒ Ⓓ Ⓔ
30 Ⓐ Ⓑ Ⓒ Ⓓ Ⓔ

SECTION 4

1 Ⓐ Ⓑ Ⓒ Ⓓ Ⓔ
2 Ⓐ Ⓑ Ⓒ Ⓓ Ⓔ
3 Ⓐ Ⓑ Ⓒ Ⓓ Ⓔ
4 Ⓐ Ⓑ Ⓒ Ⓓ Ⓔ
5 Ⓐ Ⓑ Ⓒ Ⓓ Ⓔ
6 Ⓐ Ⓑ Ⓒ Ⓓ Ⓔ
7 Ⓐ Ⓑ Ⓒ Ⓓ Ⓔ
8 Ⓐ Ⓑ Ⓒ Ⓓ Ⓔ
9 Ⓐ Ⓑ Ⓒ Ⓓ Ⓔ
10 Ⓐ Ⓑ Ⓒ Ⓓ Ⓔ
11 Ⓐ Ⓑ Ⓒ Ⓓ Ⓔ
12 Ⓐ Ⓑ Ⓒ Ⓓ Ⓔ
13 Ⓐ Ⓑ Ⓒ Ⓓ Ⓔ
14 Ⓐ Ⓑ Ⓒ Ⓓ Ⓔ
15 Ⓐ Ⓑ Ⓒ Ⓓ Ⓔ
16 Ⓐ Ⓑ Ⓒ Ⓓ Ⓔ
17 Ⓐ Ⓑ Ⓒ Ⓓ Ⓔ
18 Ⓐ Ⓑ Ⓒ Ⓓ Ⓔ
19 Ⓐ Ⓑ Ⓒ Ⓓ Ⓔ
20 Ⓐ Ⓑ Ⓒ Ⓓ Ⓔ
21 Ⓐ Ⓑ Ⓒ Ⓓ Ⓔ
22 Ⓐ Ⓑ Ⓒ Ⓓ Ⓔ
23 Ⓐ Ⓑ Ⓒ Ⓓ Ⓔ
24 Ⓐ Ⓑ Ⓒ Ⓓ Ⓔ
25 Ⓐ Ⓑ Ⓒ Ⓓ Ⓔ
26 Ⓐ Ⓑ Ⓒ Ⓓ Ⓔ
27 Ⓐ Ⓑ Ⓒ Ⓓ Ⓔ
28 Ⓐ Ⓑ Ⓒ Ⓓ Ⓔ
29 Ⓐ Ⓑ Ⓒ Ⓓ Ⓔ
30 Ⓐ Ⓑ Ⓒ Ⓓ Ⓔ

SECTION 5

1 Ⓐ Ⓑ Ⓒ Ⓓ Ⓔ
2 Ⓐ Ⓑ Ⓒ Ⓓ Ⓔ
3 Ⓐ Ⓑ Ⓒ Ⓓ Ⓔ
4 Ⓐ Ⓑ Ⓒ Ⓓ Ⓔ
5 Ⓐ Ⓑ Ⓒ Ⓓ Ⓔ
6 Ⓐ Ⓑ Ⓒ Ⓓ Ⓔ
7 Ⓐ Ⓑ Ⓒ Ⓓ Ⓔ
8 Ⓐ Ⓑ Ⓒ Ⓓ Ⓔ
9 Ⓐ Ⓑ Ⓒ Ⓓ Ⓔ
10 Ⓐ Ⓑ Ⓒ Ⓓ Ⓔ
11 Ⓐ Ⓑ Ⓒ Ⓓ Ⓔ
12 Ⓐ Ⓑ Ⓒ Ⓓ Ⓔ
13 Ⓐ Ⓑ Ⓒ Ⓓ Ⓔ
14 Ⓐ Ⓑ Ⓒ Ⓓ Ⓔ
15 Ⓐ Ⓑ Ⓒ Ⓓ Ⓔ
16 Ⓐ Ⓑ Ⓒ Ⓓ Ⓔ
17 Ⓐ Ⓑ Ⓒ Ⓓ Ⓔ
18 Ⓐ Ⓑ Ⓒ Ⓓ Ⓔ
19 Ⓐ Ⓑ Ⓒ Ⓓ Ⓔ
20 Ⓐ Ⓑ Ⓒ Ⓓ Ⓔ
21 Ⓐ Ⓑ Ⓒ Ⓓ Ⓔ
22 Ⓐ Ⓑ Ⓒ Ⓓ Ⓔ
23 Ⓐ Ⓑ Ⓒ Ⓓ Ⓔ
24 Ⓐ Ⓑ Ⓒ Ⓓ Ⓔ
25 Ⓐ Ⓑ Ⓒ Ⓓ Ⓔ
26 Ⓐ Ⓑ Ⓒ Ⓓ Ⓔ
27 Ⓐ Ⓑ Ⓒ Ⓓ Ⓔ
28 Ⓐ Ⓑ Ⓒ Ⓓ Ⓔ
29 Ⓐ Ⓑ Ⓒ Ⓓ Ⓔ
30 Ⓐ Ⓑ Ⓒ Ⓓ Ⓔ

14 PLEASE PRINT ALL INFORMATION

LAST NAME   FIRST

EMAIL

PHONE NUMBER

MAILING ADDRESS

CLASS CODE

KAPLAN TEST PREP

www.kaptest.com/lsat
1-800-KAP-TEST

LSAT is a registered trademark of the Law School Admissions Council, Inc.

SCANTRON® Mark Reflex® EM-284925-2:654321   LL3225A

General Directions for the LSAT* Answer Sheet

The actual testing time for this portion of the test will be 2 hours 55 minutes. There are five sections, each with a time limit of 35 minutes. The supervisor will tell you when to begin and end each section. If you finish a section before time is called, you may check your work on that section <u>only</u>; do not turn to any other section of the test book and do not work on any other section either in the test book or on the answer sheet.

There are several different types of questions on the test, and each question type has its own directions. <u>Be sure you understand the directions for each question type before attempting to answer any questions in that section.</u>

Not everyone will finish all the questions in the time allowed. Do not hurry, but work steadily and as quickly as you can without sacrificing accuracy. You are advised to use your time effectively. If a question seems too difficult, go on to the next one and return to the difficult question after completing the section. MARK THE BEST ANSWER YOU CAN FOR EVERY QUESTION. NO DEDUCTIONS WILL BE MADE FOR WRONG ANSWERS. YOUR SCORE WILL BE BASED ONLY ON THE NUMBER OF QUESTIONS YOU ANSWER CORRECTLY.

ALL YOUR ANSWERS MUST BE MARKED ON THE ANSWER SHEET. Answer spaces for each question are lettered to correspond with the letters of the potential answers to each question in the test book. After you have decided which of the answers is correct, blacken the corresponding space on the answer sheet. BE SURE THAT EACH MARK IS BLACK AND COMPLETELY FILLS THE ANSWER SPACE. Give only one answer to each question. If you change an answer, be sure that all previous marks are <u>erased completely</u>. Since the answer sheet is machine scored, incomplete erasures may be interpreted as intended answers. ANSWERS RECORDED IN THE TEST BOOK WILL NOT BE SCORED.

There may be more questions noted on this answer sheet than there are questions in a section. Do not be concerned but be certain that the section and number of the question you are answering matches the answer sheet section and question number. Additional answer spaces in any answer sheet section should be left blank. Begin your next section in the number one answer space for that section.

Kaplan takes various steps to ensure that answer sheets are returned from test centers in a timely manner for processing. In the unlikely event that an answer sheet(s) is not received, Kaplan will permit the examinee to either retest at no additional fee or to receive a refund of his or her test fee. THESE REMEDIES ARE THE EXCLUSIVE REMEDIES AVAILABLE IN THE UNLIKELY EVENT THAT AN ANSWER SHEET IS NOT RECEIVED BY KAPLAN.

Score Cancellation

Complete this section only if you are absolutely certain you want to cancel your score.   A CANCELLATION REQUEST CANNOT BE RESCINDED. IF YOU ARE AT ALL UNCERTAIN, YOU SHOULD <u>NOT</u> COMPLETE THIS SECTION.

To cancel your score from this administration, you **must**:

A. fill in both ovals here..... ◯ ◯

B. read the following statement. Then sign your name and enter the date. **YOUR SIGNATURE ALONE IS NOT SUFFICIENT FOR SCORE CANCELLATION. BOTH OVALS MUST BE FILLED IN FOR SCANNING EQUIPMENT TO RECOGNIZE YOUR REQUEST FOR SCORE CANCELLATION.**

I certify that I wish to cancel my test score from this administration. I understand that my request is irreversible and that my score will not be sent to me or to the law schools to which I apply.

_____
Sign your name in full

_____
Date

HOW DID YOU PREPARE FOR THE LSAT*?
(Select all that apply.)

Responses to this item are voluntary and will be used for statistical research purposes only.

◯ By attending a Kaplan LSAT* prep course or tutoring program
◯ By attending a non-Kaplan prep course or tutoring program (Please specify:_____)
◯ By using a Kaplan LSAT* prep book
◯ By using a non-Kaplan prep book (Please specify: _____)
◯ By working through the sample questions and free sample tests provided by the LSAC
◯ By working through official LSAT* PrepTests and/or other LSAC test prep products
◯ Other preparation (Please specify: _____)
◯ No preparation

CERTIFYING STATEMENT

Please write (DO NOT PRINT) the following statement. Sign and date.

I certify that I am the examinee whose name appears on this answer sheet and that I am here to take the LSAT for the sole purpose of being considered for application to law school. I further certify that I will neither assist nor receive assistance from any other candidate, and I agree not to copy or retain examination questions or to transmit them to or discuss them with any other person in any form.

_____
_____
_____
_____
_____
_____
_____
_____
_____
_____

SIGNATURE:_____   TODAY'S DATE: _____/_____/_____
                                                                                            MONTH   DAY   YEAR

*LSAT is a registered trademark of the Law School Admissions Council, Inc.